Encyclopedia of
African~American
Culture and History

Editorial Board

second edition

THE BLACK EXPERIENCE
IN THE AMERICAS

ENCYCLOPEDIA *of*
AFRICAN~AMERICAN
CULTURE *and* HISTORY

published in association with
THE SCHOMBURG CENTER FOR RESEARCH IN BLACK CULTURE

COLIN A. PALMER
Editor in Chief

2 *C-F*
VOLUME

MACMILLAN REFERENCE USA
An imprint of Thomson Gale, a part of The Thomson Corporation

THOMSON
GALE

Detroit • New York • San Francisco • San Diego • New Haven, Conn. • Waterville, Maine • London • Munich

THOMSON

GALE

Encyclopedia of African-American Culture and History, Second Edition

Colin A. Palmer, Editor in Chief

© 2006 Thomson Gale, a part of The Thomson Corporation.

Thomson, Star Logo and Macmillan Reference USA are trademarks and Gale is a registered trademark used herein under license.

For more information, contact
Macmillan Reference USA
An imprint of Thomson Gale
27500 Drake Rd.
Farmington, Hills, MI 48331-3535
Or you can visit our Internet site at
http://www.gale.com

For permission to use material from this product, submit your request via Web at http://www.gale-edit.com/permissions, or you may download our Permissions Request form and submit your request by fax or mail to:

Permissions
Thomson Gale
27500 Drake Rd.
Farmington Hills, MI 48331-3535
Permissions Hotline:
248-699-8006 or 800-877-4253 ext. 8006
Fax: 248-699-8074 or 800-762-4058

Since this page cannot legibly accommodate all copyright notices, the acknowledgments constitute an extension of the copyright notice.

While every effort has been made to ensure the reliability of the information presented in this publication, Thomson Gale does not guarantee the accuracy of the data contained herein. Thomson Gale accepts no payment for listing; and inclusion in the publication of any organization, agency, institution, publication, service, or individual does not imply endorsement of the editors or publisher. Errors brought to the attention of the publisher and verified to the satisfaction of the publisher will be corrected in future editions.

LIBRARY OF CONGRESS CATALOGING-IN-PUBLICATION DATA

Encyclopedia of African-American culture and history : the Black experience in the Americas / Colin A. Palmer, editor in chief.— 2nd ed.
 p. cm.
  Includes bibliographical references and index.
  ISBN 0-02-865816-7 (set hardcover : alk. paper) —
  ISBN 0-02-865817-5 (v. 1) — ISBN 0-02-865818-3 (v. 2) —
  ISBN 0-02-865819-1 (v. 3) — ISBN 0-02-865820-5 (v. 4) —
  ISBN 0-02-865821-3 (v. 5) — ISBN 0-02-865822-1 (v. 6)
  1. African Americans—Encyclopedias. 2. African Americans—History—Encyclopedias. 3. Blacks—America—Encyclopedias. 4. Blacks—America—History—Encyclopedias. I. Palmer, Colin A., 1942-

E185.E54 2005
973'.0496073'003—dc22   2005013029

This title is also available as an e-book.
ISBN 0-02-866071-4

Contact your Thomson Gale representative for ordering information.

Printed in the United States of America
10 9 8 7 6 5 4 3 2 1

Editorial and Production Staff

Contents

CAESAR, SHIRLEY

OCTOBER 13, 1938

Born in Durham, North Carolina, gospel singer Shirley Caesar began singing as a child, inspired by her father, "Big Jim" Caesar, a singer in the Just Come Four gospel quartet. Nicknamed "Baby Shirley," she made her first recording, "I'd Rather Have Jesus," in 1951, and sang throughout the South during her teenage years. In 1958 she began to gain national recognition as a soloist with the Caravan Singers, which included Albertina Walker and Inez Andrews. Although at the time a Baptist, Caesar adopted the "sanctified" style of gospel singing, characterized by fast tempos and extensive improvisation. Recordings from this period include "I've Been Running for Jesus a Long Time, and I'm Not Tired Yet" (1958), "Hallelujah, It's Done" (1961), and "I Won't Be Back" (1962). In 1966 she left the Caravan Singers and formed the Caesar Singers. She continued to perform and record, but her style became less energetic and ornamental. Instead, she favored the "song and sermonette" approach then popular with gospel singers, performing songs such as "Don't Drive Your Mama Away" (1969), "No Charge" (1978), and "Faded Roses" (1980).

Caesar continued to enjoy success in the 1990s, earning five Grammy Awards during this period. In 1997 she released an album titled *A Miracle in Harlem* that was recorded live at the First Corinthian Baptist Church in Harlem. That same year she published her autobiography, *Shirley Caesar: The Lady, the Melody, the Word.* In 2000 she released *You Can Make It,* a compilation album. In 2002 she released *Hymns.*

In addition to performing and recording, Caesar, the winner of numerous Grammy Awards and seventeen Dove Awards, the Gospel Music Association's highest tribute, has had several other careers. She received a B.S. in business education from Shaw University in Raleigh, North Carolina, and went on to serve from 1987 to 1991 on the Durham City Council. She then became pastor of the Mt. Calvary Word of Faith Church in Raleigh, as well as president of Shirley Caesar Outreach Ministries, an emergency social services organization. Her husband, Harold T. Williams, is bishop of the Mt. Calvary Holy Churches of America, a small African-American holiness denomination.

See also Gospel Music

■ ■ *Bibliography*

"The First Lady of Gospel." *Ebony* (September 1977): 98–102.

Heilbut, Tony. *The Gospel Sound: Good News and Bad Times.* New York: Simon and Schuster, 1975.

"Putting the Gospel Truth into Politics." *Ebony* (December 1988): 66–70.

"Shirley Caesar." In *Contemporary Musicians.* Vol. 40. Detroit, Mich.: Gale, 2002.

"Shirley Caesar, the Queen of Gospel." *American Gospel* (March-April 1992): 18–27.

KATHY WHITE BULLOCK (1996)
Updated by publisher 2005

CAIN, RICHARD HARVEY

APRIL 12, 1825
JANUARY 18, 1887

▮▮▮ ─────────

The clergyman and politician Richard Cain was born free in Greenbriar County, Virginia (now West Virginia), and moved with his African-born father and Cherokee mother to Gallipolis, Ohio, in 1831. While still a young boy he worked on the steamboat service on the Ohio River. In 1841 he converted to the Methodist Episcopal Church, and four years later became licensed to preach in Hannibal, Missouri. He returned to Ohio soon thereafter and joined the African Methodist Episcopal (AME) Church in Cincinnati, where he was ordained as a deacon in 1859. The following year he studied at Wilberforce University in Xenia, Ohio, before transferring to Brooklyn, New York, where he served as a minister for four years.

In 1865, at the end of the Civil War, the AME Church Council assigned Cain to Charleston, South Carolina, to minister to recently freed slaves. In 1866 he became editor of the *Missionary Record,* a black newspaper, a position he held until 1872. During that time he launched a political career wherein he became known as a fiery and eloquent campaigner for the Republican Party, a land reformer, and a vigorous civil rights advocate. In 1868 he was sent as a delegate to the South Carolina Constitutional Convention, where he advocated for Congress to appropriate funds to purchase land for freed blacks. In July of that year, Cain was elected to the state senate, where he served for one term. Soon thereafter he became involved in an ambitious plan to buy three thousand acres of land to sell in small plots to freedmen. The project went bankrupt, however, and Cain was indicted on charges of fraud, though the case was never brought to trial. In 1872 Cain was elected to the

U.S. House of Representatives, where he spent much of his time lobbying on behalf of a civil rights bill. He did not run for re-election in 1874, but he ran in 1876 and was again elected. In that session he campaigned for women's suffrage and for more funding for education. But by that time Cain's outlook on the possibilities for political advancement by blacks in the United States had diminished, and he supported the renewed Liberia emigration movement and put more of his energies into his ministry.

In 1880 Cain was elected the fourteenth bishop of the AME Church and assigned to Louisiana and Texas. He helped found Paul Quinn College in Waco, Texas, and served as the college's second president. He returned to his post as bishop in 1880 and presided over the New York, New Jersey, New England, and Philadelphia districts. He died in Washington, D.C., in 1887.

See also African Methodist Episcopal Church; Politics in the United States

■ ■ *Bibliography*

Foner, Eric. *Freedom's Lawmakers: A Directory of Black Officeholders During Reconstruction.* New York: Oxford University Press, 1993.

Logan, Rayford W., and Michael R. Winston, eds. *Dictionary of American Negro Biography.* New York: Norton, 1982.

Ragsdale, Bruce A. and Joel D. Treese. *Black Americans in Congress, 1870–1989.* Washington, D.C.: U.S. Government Printing Office, 1990.

LYDIA MCNEILL (1996)
JOSEPH W. LOWNDES (1996)

CALLOWAY, CAB

DECEMBER 25, 1907
NOVEMBER 18, 1994

▮▮▮ ─────────

Born in Rochester, New York, jazz singer and bandleader Cabell "Cab" Calloway was raised in Baltimore, Maryland. In high school he sang with a local vocal group called the Baltimore Melody Boys. The Calloway family, including Cab's sister, singer Blanche Calloway, then moved to Chicago, where Cab attended Crane College. Calloway began his career as a singer, drummer, and master of ceremonies at nightclubs in Chicago and other midwestern cities. In the late 1920s in Chicago Calloway worked with the Missourians, a big band; in the male vocal quartet in *Plantation Days;* and as leader of the Alabamians. In 1929 he took the Alabamians to Harlem's Savoy Ballroom and that same year was featured in Fats Waller and Andy Razaf's Hot Chocolates revue.

In 1929 Calloway began to lead the Missourians under his own name. In 1931 they replaced Duke Ellington as the Cotton Club's house band. During the 1930s Calloway became a household name, the country's prototypical "hipster," renowned for his infectious vocal histrionics, his frenzied dashing up and down the stage in a white satin zoot suit, and leading audience sing-alongs, particularly on his biggest hit, "Minnie the Moocher" (1931). That song, with its "Hi-de-ho" chorus, was a million-copy seller and earned him the nickname "Hi-de-ho Man."

Calloway's talents were not limited to comic entertainment. During the swing era Calloway's band was one of the most popular in the country, known for such songs as "At the Clambake Carnival" (1938), "Jumpin' Jive" (1939), and "Pickin' the Cabbage" (1940), and he nurtured some of the best instrumentalists of the day, including saxophonists Ben Webster and Chuck Berry, trumpeters Jonah Jones and Dizzy Gillespie, bassist Milt Hinton, and drummer Cozy Cole. The orchestra held its own in competitions throughout the 1930s with the bands of Count Basie, Duke Ellington, Chick Webb, and Jimmy Lunceford. Calloway's orchestra left the Cotton Club in 1934 for a European tour. In addition to its success in nightclubs and on the concert stage, the Calloway orchestra also appeared in movies, including *The Big Broadcast* (1932), *The Singing Kid* (1936), *St. Louis Blues* (1939), and *Stormy Weather* (1943). Calloway disbanded the orchestra in 1948 and worked with a sextet before touring England as a soloist.

Calloway returned to his roots in musical theater in 1952 for a two-year run in the role of Sportin' Life in a touring version of George Gershwin's *Porgy and Bess*. Throughout the 1950s and 1960s he continued to perform both as a solo act and as the leader of big bands. In the mid-1960s he toured with the Harlem Globetrotters comic basketball team. In 1974 he appeared in an all-black version of *Hello, Dolly!*, and two years later he published his autobiography, *Of Minnie the Moocher and Me*. Calloway appeared on Broadway in *Bubbling Brown Sugar* in 1975, and his cameo in *The Blues Brothers* (1980) brought a revival of interest in him. In 1984 he sang with his vocalist daughter, Chris, in an engagement at New York's Blue Note nightclub. In 1987 he again appeared with Chris Calloway, this time in *His Royal Highness of Hi-De-Ho* in New York.

See also Basie, William James "Count"; Cotton Club; Ellington, Edward Kennedy "Duke"; Gillespie, Dizzy

Cab Calloway (1907–1994). *One of the most popular performers of the 1930s and 1940s, jazz musician Calloway was known for his dramatic vocals and white satin zoot suit, and for the "Hi-de-ho" chorus in his hit song "Minnie the Moocher" (1931).* © BETTMANN/CORBIS

■ ■ *Bibliography*

Popa, James. *Cab Calloway and His Orchestra 1925–1958*, rev. ed. Zephyrhills, Fla.: Norbert Ruecker, 1987.

Simon, George. T. *The Big Bands*. New York: Macmillan, 1981.

MICHAEL D. SCOTT (1996)

CALLOWAY, NATHANIEL

OCTOBER 10, 1907
DECEMBER 3, 1979

The chemist and physician Nathaniel Oglesby Calloway was born in Tuskegee, Alabama, the son of James and Marietta (Oglesby) Calloway. He graduated from Iowa State College in 1930. In 1933, when he earned a Ph.D. in organic chemistry (also at Iowa State), Calloway became the first African American to receive an academic doctorate from an institution west of the Mississippi. He taught chemistry until 1940 at Tuskegee Institute and then at Fisk University. In 1935, he prepared the first English-language review of the so-called Friedel-Crafts reaction (1877), a phenomenon in organic chemistry with important applications in the plastics, perfume, textile, and petroleum industries. Calloway's work was widely cited.

Calloway enrolled in medical school at the University of Illinois, graduating with an M.D. in 1943. During World War II, he directed a government-sponsored study of convalescence practices. He became a staunch advocate of early ambulation, the theory (now generally accepted) that post-operative patients improve more rapidly when not confined to their beds. After 1947 his research focused on topics in gerontology and geriatrics. He proposed a "general theory of senescence" (or aging) in 1964. Over the next ten years, he published twenty-six articles in the *Journal of the American Geriatrics Society*.

Calloway served as medical director of Provident Hospital in Chicago until 1949, when he founded Medical Associates of Chicago, a black group-practice in the inner city. After fourteen years as president of Medical Associates, he became chief of medical services for the Veterans Administration Hospital in Tomah, Wisconsin. A civil rights activist, he was president of the Chicago Urban League from 1955 to 1960 and of the Madison, Wisconsin, branch of the NAACP in 1969.

See also Science

■ ■ *Bibliography*

Calloway, N. O. "The Friedel-Crafts Syntheses." *Chemical Reviews* 17 (1935): 327–392.

PHILIP N. ALEXANDER (1996)

CALYPSO

Born in post-emancipation Trinidad, calypso possesses a unique and lasting quality that has carried it far beyond the Caribbean. The distinctive music that became its hallmark in the latter half of the twentieth century was a major change from early calypso, which evolved out of simple efforts at communication among the largely African underclass. Singers, first called *chantwells*, extemporized songs in which they flattered friends, attacked adversaries, or poked good-natured fun at one another. This mock warfare led them to adopt sobriquets that complemented the

battles (e.g., Hubert Raphael Charles was known as Roaring Lion, or Neville Marcano as Growling Tiger), and the tradition of singing under an assumed name has persisted, although the newer versions (e.g., Slinger Francisco as Mighty Sparrow, or Hollis Liverpool as Chalkdust) are far less warlike, and many contemporary singers simply use their real names (e.g., David Rudder).

Calypso was already being sung when the British came to Trinidad, but it was known by other names, among them *kaiso*, apparently derived from a West African (Hausa) term meaning "bravo." The word *calypso* was an attempt to anglicize that appellation, and both terms have survived to the present, with *kaiso* being used for a more authentic version of the song, or as a term of praise and encouragement when a calypso is felt to be particularly well rendered.

As the chantwell evolved into the calypsonian, calypso's role as the people's newspaper or purveyor of social commentary began to take shape. Calypsonians sang about nearly every aspect of life in Trinidad and the world beyond, providing a healthy and often humorous dose of down-to-earth philosophizing. By the 1940s a large body of these songs was already on record, contributing in no small way to calypso's international appeal. The Andrews Sisters, with "Rum and Coca Cola" in 1944, and Harry Belafonte, with his pioneering LP *Calypso* in 1956, are only two of the bigger recording acts who helped popularize calypso.

In its most elementary form, a calypso consists of three or four stanzas with a chorus after each one. The early melodies were fairly simple and frequently recycled among singers. As a result, listeners paid close attention to what the singers were saying. This type of calypso is still the favorite of many aficionados, who go to hear the newly composed songs as they are presented—at venues called *tents*—before each year's carnival.

Any consideration of calypso must take into account its close link with Trinidad carnival and its post-emancipation development. Calypsos would provide nearly all the music accompanying the revelers who took to the streets in the annual masquerade. Gradually, a dual expectation arose: infectious music for street revelers to dance to, as well as traditional lyrics to entertain and even educate the listeners. Ideally, the perfect calypso combines both. Increasingly, though, with the advent in the mid-1970s of a popular new strain of calypso called *soca*—allegedly derived from a combination of soul and calypso—the music and its commercial potential are overshadowing the importance of the lyric.

In 1956, Mighty Sparrow won the coveted annual competition to select the king (now monarch) of calypso.

The lyrics of his winning "Yankees Gone" were hard hitting; his melody was unforgettable; the combination was perfect. That calypso was not the first to comment on the devastating increase in prostitution as a result of the American presence in Trinidad after World War II, but it is, deservedly, the best known. Sparrow boasted in his chorus, easily learned by carnival revelers as they paraded in the streets the very morning following Sparrow's victory:

Well, is Jean and Dinah
Rosita and Clementina
Round the corner posing
Bet your life is something they selling
But if you catch them broken
You can get it all for nutten
Don't make a row
Yankees gone, Sparrow take over now.

Sparrow revolutionized the art form. After him, calypso melody would no longer be of secondary importance—an encouraging development for soca two decades later. But he did not overlook the powerful lyric, and his political and social commentaries were so forceful and on target that he could openly boast later on that "if Sparrow say so, is so."

Calypso, ably assisted by its cultural twin, carnival, has spread throughout the Caribbean, and to the major metropolitan cities where Caribbean communities have established themselves. At home, calypso's duality has been entrenched with the growing popularity of soca, and the composition of songs whose lyrics have very little of substance—the so-called party songs, in which the public is encouraged to "put your hands in the air" or to "get something and wave." However, the prestigious annual calypso monarch competition is dominated by calypsos of social or political commentary, to the point where government officials attending the performance have at times felt under attack. It is all good natured, however, and there is no official censorship of these songs, despite spasmodic outcries from the various groups being pilloried. Calypsonians and their craft have gained acceptance in Trinidad and Tobago society and beyond. No longer are they seen as the undesirables, for, as Sparrow sang in his calypso "Outcast," "Calypsonians really catch hell for a long time / To associate yourself with them was a big crime." It is inconceivable that such a state of affairs could ever arise again, given the local and international recognition earned by this truly indigenous art form.

See also Carnival in Brazil and the Caribbean; Nationalism and Race in the Caribbean; Reggae

▪ ▪ *Bibliography*

Regis, Louis. *The Political Calypso: True Opposition in Trinidad and Tobago, 1962–1987.* Gainesville: University Press of Florida, 1999.

Rohlehr, Gordon. *Calypso and Society in Pre-Independence Trinidad.* Trinidad: Gordon Rohlehr, 1990.

Warner, Keith Q. *Kaiso! The Trinidad Calypso: A Study of the Calypso as Oral Literature,* 2d ed. Pueblo, Colo.: Passeggiata, 1999.

KEITH Q. WARNER (2005)

CAMBRIDGE, GODFREY MACARTHUR

FEBRUARY 26, 1933
NOVEMBER 29, 1976

▪ ▪ ▪

Actor Godfrey Cambridge was born in New York City in 1933 and grew up in Harlem with his parents, Sarah and Alexander Cambridge. He attended Flushing High School, where he excelled as both a student and a leader of extracurricular activities. Cambridge won a scholarship to Hofstra College (now University) on Long Island, where he majored in English and had his first acting experience, appearing in a school production of *Macbeth*. After racial threats forced him to leave Hofstra during his junior year, Cambridge attended City College in New York City. Upon graduating, he worked at a number of jobs including stints as an airplane wing cleaner, a judo instructor, a cab driver, and a clerk for the New York City Housing Authority.

In 1956 Cambridge landed his first professional role, as a bartender in an Off-Broadway revival of Louis Peterson's *Take a Giant Step*. The play ran for nine months and led to television appearances in shows such as *The United States Steel Hour, Naked City,* and *You'll Never Get Rich* (with Phil Silvers as Sergeant Bilko). In 1961 Cambridge appeared in Jean Genet's *The Blacks,* a savage drama about racial hatred, and for his efforts he received the *Village Voice*'s Obie Award for best performer of 1961. The following year he appeared in Ossie Davis's *Purlie Victorious,* for which he earned a Tony nomination. Cambridge went on to perform in other plays, including *A Funny Thing Happened on the Way to the Forum* (1962), *The Living Promise* (1963), and *How to Be a Jewish Mother* (1967), in which he played every part but the title role.

After a successful appearance on *The Jack Paar Program* in 1964, Cambridge was able to choose his roles and began turning down film parts that stereotyped him. Instead he played a wide variety of movie characters, including a reprise of his role in the film version of *Purlie Victorious,* titled *Gone Are the Days* (1963); an Irishman in *The Troublemaker* (1964); a Jewish cab driver in *Bye, Bye, Braverman* (1968); and a concert violinist in *The Biggest Bundle of Them All* (1968). Cambridge is probably best known for his leading roles in the popular films *Watermelon Man* (1970) and *Cotton Comes to Harlem* (1970).

In addition to his film appearances, Cambridge was a successful stand-up comedian. His sense of humor, while not alienating to white audiences, did not lack bite. Essentially a social satirist, his comedy often dealt with ordinary people, black and white, struggling with the problems of everyday life.

During the civil rights movement Cambridge performed at rallies and organized support for the employment of more African Americans in the entertainment industry. A compulsive eater who at times weighed as much as three hundred pounds, in 1976 Cambridge collapsed and died on the set of the TV movie *Victory at Entebbe,* in which he played the Ugandan dictator Idi Amin.

See also Civil Rights Movement, U.S.

■ ■ *Bibliography*

Bogle, Donald. *Blacks in American Films and Television.* New York: Garland, 1988.

New York Times Biographical Services. November 30, 1976, p. 1521.

THADDEUS RUSSELL (1996)

CAMPBELL, CLIFFORD CLARENCE

JUNE 28, 1892

1991

▬▬▬

Sir Clifford Clarence Campbell, the first native governor general of Jamaica, was born in Petersfield, in Westmoreland Parish, to James Campbell, a civil servant, and his wife Blance, née Ruddock. Clifford Campbell was educated at Petersfield Elementary School from 1901 to 1912 and at Mico Training College, a teachers college, in Kingston from 1913 to 1915. After graduating from Mico, he began his teaching career as headmaster at Fullersfield Government School in 1916, where he served until 1918, when he moved to Friendship Elementary School. He served as headmaster of this school for ten years, then as headmaster

of the Grange Hill Government School from 1928 to 1944. On August 1, 1920, Campbell married Alice Estephene, with whom he had four children.

Apart from teaching and politics, Campbell took a keen interest in music, painting, community, and professional services. He was a member of the Manchester Committee of the Westend Federation of Teachers, the board of visitors to Savalamar Public Hospital, the Advisory Committee of the Knockalva Practical Training Center, the Board of Education from 1944 to 1945, the Westmoreland School Board, the Issa Scholarship Awards Committee in 1945, the Westmoreland Rice Growers Association, and the Committee on Training of Government Officers in 1945. Campbell became the first vice president of the Association of Westmoreland Branches of the Jamaica Agricultural Society, and he served in 1945 as a member of a delegation sent to investigate the conditions of Jamaican farmworkers in the United States.

The constitution of Jamaica provides that "There shall be a Parliament of Jamaica which shall consist of Her Majesty, the Senate, and a House of Representatives." The governor general is by the same constitution declared to be the representative of the queen in Jamaica. The Jamaican Parliament therefore consists of three branches: the House of Representatives; the Senate; and in the context of Jamaica, the governor general. Campbell had the great distinction of being not only the first native governor general of Jamaica, but also the first Jamaican to have served the country in all three branches of government.

Campbell inaugurated his career in politics in 1944 when, as a member of the Jamaica Labour Party, he won a seat (Westmoreland Western) to the House of Representatives in the first elections under universal adult suffrage. Campbell was chairman of the House Committee on Education from 1945 to 1949 and was first vice president of the Elected Members Association from 1945 to 1954. In 1950 he became speaker of the House of Representatives, and in 1962 he was appointed president of the Senate.

When Jamaica became independent in 1962, Campbell was appointed by Queen Elizabeth as governor general of Jamaica. He greeted the news of his appointment with these words: "I shall maintain that humility in which state I came into the world, in which state I have lived among the human element and in which state I hope to die—with a spirit of humility and respect for my fellow men." Over the intervening years he did not in any way deviate from his avowed intent.

In 1989 Campbell was awarded the Order of the Nation, the second highest honor in Jamaica after the Order of National Hero. Queen Elizabeth also awarded him with the honor of Knight Grand Cross of Saint Michael and

Saint George and later with the Knight Grand Cross of the Royal Victorian Order.

Jamaican Prime Minister Michael Manley's tribute to Campbell emphasizes the role he played in nation building. According to Manley: "As the first Jamaican-born Governor, he had the very special constitutional responsibility of guiding the country through a new unchartered journey in which we were no longer dependent on outside authority to shape our destiny. He had to instill in us his own personal faith and conviction in our ability as a people to travel along this new road. He well understood that we would have to help each other move the obstacles in our path. He knew he had to inspire us to become architects and builders of our nation."

See also Jamaica Labour Party

LEO GUNTER (2005)

CANADA, BLACKS IN

People of African descent first came to what is currently called Canada in the seventeenth century, serving as explorers, translators, trappers, servants, and farmers. Though still a young man when he made his passage across the Atlantic, Mathieu Da Costa became the first recorded African to reach the burgeoning French colony of New France when he arrived around 1603. According to early reports, Da Costa's linguistic and commercial skills proved most valuable to Portuguese and French merchants, for whom he interpreted. In 1608, Da Costa also bore witness to the founding of Québec City, a monumental event signaling France's determination to remain in North America. Da Costa's ultimate fate is not known, though for a time he is said to have worked as servant in Acadia, a settlement in what is now Nova Scotia.

Within two decades of Da Costa's arrival in New France, conditions had dramatically changed for Africans. The institution of slavery, already well entrenched in the American colonies to the south, had been haphazardly established by missionaries and a handful of the wealthiest colonists. Though only six years old at the time of his enslavement in Madagascar, Olivier Le Jeune earned the dubious distinction of being the first enslaved African brought to New France (he arrived between 1629 and 1632). Le Jeune eventually became the property of Jesuit priests in Québec City, where he worked as a domestic until he died in 1654.

Slavery received full royal sanction in 1689, when Louis XIV endorsed the sale of slaves in New France. Even if slavery never thrived in New France, for those Africans and Panis (Native Canadians) robbed of their freedom, that distinction rarely mattered. Panis slaves were typically used for fur trading and exploration, while enslaved Africans worked as domestics and artisans. They were even paraded as curios among the rich. Throughout the eighteenth century, the number of slaves grew steadily, namely in Québec, Trois-Rivières, Montréal, and Detroit, thanks to colonists and slave traders who ferried slaves up from the American South and the Caribbean. It is estimated that more than 4,000 Panis and Africans were enslaved in present-day Canada between 1632 and 1820.

Even if the daily rigors of enslavement in Canada paled in comparison to those in the colonies to the south, slaves employed a host of strategies when challenging their bondage. For example, in 1734, Marie-Joseph Angélique, a Portuguese-born slave woman of a prominent Montréal family, plotted her escape with her white lover, Claude Thibault. Fearing that their plot would be foiled, Angélique set fire to her mistress's house as a diversion, inadvertently burning down half of Montréal in the process. Her trial, subsequent torture, and death by hanging called attention to the desperation experienced by slaves. In fact, by 1784, a southbound Underground Railroad had developed. This network of early abolitionists facilitated the escape of enslaved Africans from New France into New England and the Northwest Territories, where slavery had by then been outlawed.

If most blacks in Canada lived in New France before 1750, by the end of the century, the Maritime provinces (Nova Scotia and New Brunswick) became home to the largest number of black migrants. The outbreak of the American Revolution in 1776 forced the immigration of United Empire Loyalists into present-day Ontario, Québec, and the Maritimes. From the outset of the conflict, Britain encouraged rebellion among African Americans, promising freedom, goods, and land to those who fought on their side. As many as 5,000 Black Loyalists—both freedmen and rebels—came to Canada between 1781 and 1784, with more than fifty percent of them settling in Nova Scotia alone. For the most part, these black migrants eked out a difficult existence in the Maritimes because, more often than not, British officials failed to deliver on their promises of land and supplies. Moreover, white Loyalists who headed to the Maritimes, often with chattel in tow, had not made the decision to relocate north because of a distaste for slavery. In fact, they most often resented efforts to give blacks land and waged work, and black émigrés found themselves increasingly forced onto the poorest and most remote lots of land.

Even so, Black Loyalists and other black migrants who poured into the Maritimes at the end of the eighteenth century created communities that in many cases still exist today. Historian Bridglal Pachai posits that Birchtown, one such township populated by 2,700 blacks in 1784, may well have been one of the largest free black urban centers outside of Africa at the time. The port city of Halifax, certainly the largest urban center in the Maritimes, also became home to many people of African descent during this period, with most finding work in the seafaring industry.

After trying their hand at British "freedom" for more than a decade, some Black Loyalists had reached a point of saturation with British land mismanagement and the failed promise of citizenship. By the end of the eighteenth century, a utopian back-to-Africa movement developed among blacks in Canada, supported in no small measure by British officials happy to see disgruntled migrants relocated off shore. In 1792 approximately 1,200 Black Loyalists elected to abandon North America for resettlement to Africa, driven by both missionary zeal and the prospect of greater independence once away from white bureaucrats.

However much whites in the Maritimes might have begrudged their black neighbors, the Africa-bound exodus aggravated the need for labor in the region, which likely explains, at least in part, the British decision to import some 600 Jamaican Maroons in 1796. Their arrival, originally welcomed by local whites, quickly turned to frustration as these new migrants fought off attempts at subjugating them as either indentured workers or slaves. To complicate matters, Maroons had already earned a reputation back in Jamaica for their resistance to British rule, making it far less likely that they could be easy quelled once in Canada. Though they joined forces with other blacks in the Maritimes, most of the Maroon migrants never established permanent lives in Canada, choosing instead to follow those who had set off for Sierra Leone just a few years earlier. By 1800, only ten percent of Maroons still remained in Canada.

A third wave of Southern black migrants arrived in Canada during the War of 1812. Once again, British forces lured African-American soldiers and their families to their cause by promising safe passage to Canada and freedom to any who joined their army. Just as they had in 1776, countless African Americans risked imprisonment or death by helping the British battle the Americans. If many died earning their freedom, some 2,000 refugees eventually traveled to Canada, becoming much needed workers and small-scale farmers once there.

Events at the turn of the eighteenth century combined to bring an end to slavery in Canada. As early as the 1790s, judges and governors in Upper Canada (present-day Ontario) and Lower Canada (Québec) increasingly sided with slaves petitioning for their manumission. The Emancipa-

A group of refugee settlers, Windsor, Ontario. Twenty thousand people arrived in Canada between 1820 and 1860 via the Underground Railroad. Windsor, once known as Sandwich, Ontario, became a popular place for fugitive slaves to settle because they could keep in touch with their families in the United States while living free from fear of capture. PHOTOGRAPHS AND PRINTS DIVISION, SCHOMBURG CENTER FOR RESEARCH IN BLACK CULTURE, THE NEW YORK PUBLIC LIBRARY, ASTOR, LENOX AND TILDEN FOUNDATIONS.

tion Act of 1833 abolished slavery in the British Empire, but for the majority of blacks in Canada, the de facto end of slavery had come nearly a generation before. By 1833 the number of enslaved Africans was at best negligible. It is interesting to note that the tradition of hosting family reunions and carnival in Canada in early August actually dates back to the celebration of emancipation, officially declared on August 1, 1834.

If blacks in Canada breathed a sigh of relief once slavery ended, they remained keenly aware that in the United States most African Americans still lived in bondage. As of the 1830s, an increasing number of African Americans sought sanctuary in Canada, especially those from Southern border states. They braved harsh weather and slave catchers in the hope of a free life on British soil. Frustrated by runaway slaves and stories of Canada as Canaan, slave owners intensified their hunt for both escaped bondsmen and those helping them northward along what came to be known as the Underground Railroad. It was hoped that passage of Fugitive Slave Laws in the 1850s would deter fugitives and abolitionists, but in the end the laws aggravated tensions between those Americans intent on protecting their right to slaves and Canadian abolitionists determined to end what they saw as an inhumane practice.

The arrival of Freedom Seekers, as these runaway slaves are often called in Canadian historiography, represented the largest single influx of blacks in Canada until the late twentieth century, when West Indians and Africans arrived in record numbers. Not all African Americans coming to Canada between 1830 and 1865 were enslaved; a growing number of African Americans chose to relocate to Canada during that same era due to concerns that slavery could engulf even those states that had abandoned it. In addition, many feared being apprehended by slave catchers poaching in Ohio and Michigan, who were out to claim the often large rewards offered by disgruntled Southern slavers.

Estimates vary widely on the actual number of African Americans who settled in present-day Ontario and Québec, but perhaps as many as 40,000 successfully reached Canadian shores before the outbreak of the U.S. Civil War. These political asylum seekers established all-black townships along Lake Ontario, crafting the types of utopian models of freedom and agency that would also arise in the American South during Reconstruction. For example, in Chatham, blacks ran their own local government, produced a well-circulated black newspaper, set up Freemasonry temples, and operated their own schools. Even if such settlements were short lived due to limited resources and internal tensions, their mere existence proved inspiring for African Americans trapped south of the Mason-Dixon line. In fact, during Reconstruction, it is reported that a large number of black migrants in Canada returned to the United States to help with rebuilding efforts and to reunite with their families. For some, like Mary Ann Shadd Cary (1823–1893), chief editor of the *Provincial Freeman,* the rest of their lives would be spent shuttling between Canada and the United States, demonstrating the extent to which many blacks led a life that defied national borders.

Black immigration to Canada was not limited to the East. A steady stream of African Americans living in the West and in California also moved into Canada, hoping to secure homesteads and set up early businesses in Western cities like Calgary, Vancouver, and Victoria. By the 1860s, black Californians represented the largest single migrant group on Vancouver Island. They were the advance vanguard of black entrepreneurs and merchants who, fearing that white supremacists would take over the California

government, sold their land and businesses and headed north. Their arrival in western Canada was auspiciously timed, as these early migrants were perfectly poised once the gold rush started in the region.

By the 1880s, black migrants who came to Canada did so to set up farms. Their arrival coincided with the closing of the American frontier and worsening conditions in the Oklahoma, Kansas, and Arkansas basin. Already well acquainted with prairie farming, these black migrants saw Canada's offer of free land to would-be farmers as a godsend. For example, whole black counties in Oklahoma were evacuated, sometimes seemingly overnight, by immigrants determined to live outside of Jim Crow's reach. They came to Canada citing its abolitionist tradition and its generous land policies as their chief reasons for migrating. At this time, black Oklahomans were often quite prosperous, as evidenced by Tulsa's vibrant black business district. Canadian Immigration Department records indicate that Southern African Americans who emigrated to Canada between 1870 and 1911 frequently arrived with enough cash and supplies to succeed at farming.

African-American and West Indian immigrants were also headed to Canadian cities by the 1890s, where they often found work in the transportation industry, either as mariners or sleeping car porters. By World War I, the Canadian Pacific Railway had become the largest employer of black men in Canada. In fact, the Canadian Pacific Railway seemingly could not meet its insatiable demand for black railroaders, opting instead to import Southern African Americans and West Indians for their service. As a result of this employment, African Canadians were a highly urbanized population at the dawn of the twentieth century. By 1921, over sixty percent of blacks in Canada lived in urban centers, with Québec (80%) and Manitoba (88%) home to the most cosmopolitan black populations. What Canada then experienced was a dramatic increase in its urban black population: Montréal, Toronto, and Winnipeg, respectively, experienced a 49 percent, 21 percent, and 96 percent growth in their black citizenry in the first two decades of the twentieth century.

Not all Canadians welcomed this rapid change in the make-up of their cities. Many white Canadians, especially those living in the West, pointed to the arrival of blacks from the United States and the Caribbean as endangering the fabric of Canadian society. They reasoned, in the press and to their elected officials, that Canada should be kept "for the white race only" and petitioned for a more exacting defense of its borders from "undesirables." They also insisted that black migrants could not withstand Canada's harsh winters, making them "climactically unsuitable" for citizenship. Some even clamored for the Canadian government to adopt race-based exclusion laws and barring that, they at least expected that their government would levy head taxes on black immigrants. In the end, the Canadian government opted for a complete ban on black immigration in 1911. While the official law was short-lived, its exercise by border guards remained well into the 1950s, making it virtually impossible for all but the most determined black migrants to lawfully enter the country.

Many white Canadians insisted that their distaste for black migrants was born out of a desire "not to inherit Uncle Sam's problem." They pointed to alcohol, crime, changing sexual mores, and—worse still—jazz as problems produced by the mere presence of black migrants, ignoring the fact that the majority of blacks living in Canadian urban centers were industrial workers, small-scale business owners, university students, or children. In fact, in the first half of the twentieth century, Canada's black population was overwhelmingly young. In 1931, for example, more than half of blacks in Canada were under the age of twenty-five, with black children under the age of five accounting for the bulk of blacks living in urban centers. With so young a population, any rise in criminality and lasciviousness in Canada's urban centers could hardly be the singular work of blacks.

Even so, as of World War I, white Canadians called for a greater division of the races. Whereas segregation had been rare and haphazardly applied before, white Canadians adopted Jim Crow in just about every aspect of public life in Canada by the 1920s. To be sure, Canada did not enact Jim Crow laws, as was done in the Southern United States. Instead, just as in the American North, Canadians practiced de facto segregation, barring blacks from schools, pools, hotels, theatres, orphanages, restaurants, and even cemeteries used by whites. For instance, blacks who wanted to see an opera in Montréal in the 1920s were marooned in the "monkey cages," the upper balcony sectioned off for black patrons.

Black Canadians, especially Great War veterans and their families, did not sit idly by as "white only" signs spread across the country. For African-American émigrés from the American South, these new practices were far too reminiscent of the lives they had left behind in the United States. Blacks in Canada galvanized in defense of their civil rights, their families, and their communities. With the assistance of various self-help and racial uplift organizations, such as Marcus Garvey's Universal Negro Improvement Association (UNIA) and A. Philip Randolph's Brotherhood of Sleeping Car Porters (BSCP), black Canadians challenged segregation using a host of protest methods.

African Canadian women played a critical role as defenders of their communities. Ignoring social conventions requiring that women confine their work to the home, black Canadian women organized consumer boycotts of stores that would not employ people of African descent. When a theatre in Winnipeg aired around-the-clock showings of *The Klansman*, black women picketed the theater, calling attention to the film's racist and pernicious content and eventually causing the theater to shut down the movie before the end of its scheduled two-week run. Black club and church women also pressured local hospitals to admit young women to their nursing programs, increasing the earning potential of black women who could secure professional training. Where schools failed to provide their children with a good education, black women supplemented the curriculum with arts, music, and literature programs.

In effect, blacks in Canada were able to respond to violations of their civil rights because they had already established strong communities of their own. In many cases, the black church provided black communities with both a firm anchor and a site for organizing their legal, social, and political campaigns. When, in 1936, Jamaican-born Fred Christie decided to sue Montréal's York Tavern for refusing him service, citing their white-only policy, black Montréalers mapped out their legal plan at the Union United Church, the largest and most influential black church in Canada. Although the court ultimately rejected his petition, *Christie v. York* became the first civil rights case brought before Canada's Supreme Court.

Life for blacks in Canada during the interwar period mirrored that of other Canadians: they focused on navigating the Great Depression's troubled waters and protecting their loved ones when war broke out. Black communities across Canada rallied together and pooled their resources in order to survive an era made all the more taxing given the climate of "negrophobia," as Canadians liked to call it, tainting relations between whites and people of African descent. And just as they had during the World War I, blacks joined the Canadian military forces, serving in Europe alongside other British forces. Back in Canada, many others gained a foothold in war industries, bringing the destitution they had experienced during the 1930s to an end. The interwar period also witnessed the creation of a broad range of black organizations dedicated to civil rights work, most importantly the Canadian Association for the Advancement of Colored People, loosely modeled after its American counterpart.

With the return to peace, it seemed that Canadians now envisaged a very different society for themselves, incrementally abandoning longstanding attachments to discriminatory practices. The historian James Walker contends that after World War II, Canadians became increasingly invested in humanitarian efforts, especially within the context of United Nations programs. Accordingly, under the banner of various interracial human rights organizations, legal challenges to restrictive housing covenants, school segregation, unfair labor laws, and exclusionary immigration statutes slowly dismantled century-old practices. In their stead, Canadian legislators enacted the *Bill of Rights of 1960,* and by 1967 new immigration law opened the country's borders to people from Asia, the Caribbean, and Africa, finally admitting them on the basis of merit rather than excluding them on the basis of race. To be sure, the success of these laws was made possible by white and black Canadians committed to casting off the yoke of Jim Crow.

The result of Canada's new stand on immigration and civil rights could be felt immediately. For example, in 1931, 85 percent of blacks in Canada were born there, but by 1981, Canadian-born blacks accounted for only 15 percent of the black population. West Indians, especially Jamaicans, quickly became the largest black ethnic group in Canada, as evidenced by their dramatic increase within a twenty-year period: in 1961 the census reported that approximately 12,000 West Indians permanently resided in Canada, while two decades later their numbers swelled to over 200,000. An estimated 50,000 African migrants added to the diversity among black people in Canada. Whereas many of these migrants arrived in Canada with professional degrees from their countries of origin, many more emigrated to attend Canadian universities under programs designed to assist newly decolonized nations. The influx of this ostensibly highly educated and professional black migration created a Canadian black middle class that, more often then not, prospered and remained deeply committed to protecting their rights and privileges.

Regardless of ethnic background or nationality, blacks in Canada banded together, exposing discriminatory practices and breaking down barriers to their advancement. If that first generation of West Indian and African migrants thrived, their children did not, and by the end of the twentieth century there was a disparity in education that endangered black Canadians' middle-class foothold. By the close of the twentieth century, younger black Canadians pointed to discrimination in employment and housing as their greatest impediment, though dissatisfaction with educational options and racial skirmishes were also listed among their grievances. Particularly troubling was the rising rate of high school attrition among Canadian-born blacks, certainly singling them out for an even more insecure economic future in the twenty-first century.

The black experience in Canada has always been defined by a quest for full citizenship set against a background of laws and practices overwhelmingly designed to keep people of African descent confined to marginalized spaces, first as slaves, then as political asylum seekers, and finally as undesirable immigrants. Black migrants to Canada envisioned a very different plan for themselves and fought off attempts to keep them out of the country all together or to deny them meaningful citizenship. In the end, they successfully forged lives for themselves in every part of Canada, making clear that no barrier to their success proved too great.

See also African Diaspora; Canadian Writers; Migration

■ ■ *Bibliography*

Brand, Dionne. *No Burden to Carry: Narratives of Black Working Women in Ontario, 1920s to 1950s.* Toronto: Women's Press, 1991.

Bristow, Peggy, et. al. *'We're Rooted Here and They Can't Pull Us Up': Essays in African Canadian Women's History.* Toronto: University of Toronto Press, 1994.

Gilmore, John. *Swinging in Paradise: The Story of Jazz in Montreal.* Montreal: Véhicule Press, 1989.

Henry, Keith S. *Black Politics in Toronto since World War I.* Toronto: Multicultural History Society of Ontario, 1981.

Hill, Daniel G. *The Freedom Seekers: Blacks in Early Canada.* Agincourt, Ontario: The Book Society of Canada Limited, 1981.

Killian, Crawford. *Go Do Some Great Thing: The Black Pioneers of British Columbia.* Vancouver: Douglas & McIntyre, 1978.

Shepard, R. Bruce. *Deemed Unsuitable: Blacks from Oklahoma Move to the Canadian Prairies.* Toronto: Umbrella Press, 1997.

Walker, James W. *The West Indians in Canada.* Ottawa: Canadian Historical Association, 1984.

Walker, James W. *Racial Discrimination in Canada: The Black Experience.* Ottawa: Canadian Historical Association, 1985.

Walker, James W. *'Race,' Rights and the Law in the Supreme Court of Canada.* Waterloo, Ontario: Osgoode Society for Canadian Legal History and Wilfrid Laurier University Press, 1997.

Williams, Dorothy W. *The Road to Now: A History of Blacks in Montreal.* Montreal: Véhicule Press, 1997.

Winks, Robin. *The Blacks in Canada: A History.* 2d ed. Montreal & Kingston: McGill-Queen's University Press, 1997.

SARAH-JANE (SAJE) MATHIEU (2005)

CANADIAN WRITERS

This entry consists of two distinct articles with differing linguistic domains.

CANADIAN WRITERS IN ENGLISH
George Elliott Clarke

CANADIAN WRITERS IN FRENCH
Max Dorsinville

CANADIAN WRITERS IN ENGLISH

African-Canadian literature in English begins in the same ruptures that gave birth to African-American literature. Its arrival was later, however, both chronologically and culturally, and it has become a product of the general African diaspora. Both facts render it superficially similar to its American counterpart, yet also radically *other*. If the first is characterized by DuBoisian "double-consciousness," the latter may be said to possess a "polyphonous consciousness."

While African-American letters locates its effective genesis in the American Revolutionary poet Phillis Wheatley, African-Canadian writing originates in British Loyalist—and evangelical—pamphleteers such as David George, Boston King, and John Marrant, all Americans who sided with Britain during the War of Independence, and, losing, later took refuge in the northern Royalist colonies. Naturally, George, King, and Marrant may be claimed as "Canadian" only with an asterisk, for Canada proper did not exist when they spoke (or wrote) their testaments about slavery and redemption, with George's appearing in 1793, King's in 1798, and Marrant's native-captivity narrative in 1785. Indeed, the latter's *Narrative of the Lord's Wonderful Dealings with John Marrant, a Black (Now Going to Preach the Gospel in Nova-Scotia)*, the fount of African-Canadian literature, received at least twenty-one printings.

Most of the 3,400 so-called black Loyalists who flooded into Nova Scotia and New Brunswick in 1783 were illiterate, so their archival documents consist of letters inked (or dictated) after 1,200 of these black pilgrims abandoned frigid, inclement "Acadia" for Sierra Leone in 1792. Among this party, an ex-Virginian, Susannah Smith, directed a letter, dated May 12, 1792, to colonial authorities, requesting "sope" for her family. This missive inaugurates the "womanist" side of African-Canadian literature.

Between 1783 and the mid-nineteenth-century, African-Canadian publications were few. For one thing, British North America remained legally an oppressive, slave-holding territory until 1834 (although slavery died a de facto death by the beginning of the nineteenth century). Though another two thousand black refugees (that is, African-American slaves liberated by British troops during the War of 1812) entered Nova Scotia and New Brunswick between 1812 and 1815, these émigrés, again illiterate, could not enter the nascent canon. However, with the arrival to Upper Canada (Ontario) and Lower Canada (Quebec), between the 1830s and the 1860s, of up to forty thousand African Americans—voting with their feet against Southern slavery—several of them became nominally "African-Canadian" writers. Most prominent in this category is Martin Robinson Delany, whose *Blake, or the Huts of America* (1859, 1861–1862), written in Chatham, Ontario, from 1856 to 1859, is the third African-American novel but the *first* African-Canadian one. Other expatriate African-American writers now counted as "Canadian" include Mary Ann Shadd, whose *A Plea for Emigration, or, Notes of Canada West* (Ontario) was issued in 1853; Henry Bibb, whose *Narrative* was published in 1849; and Samuel Ringgold Ward, whose *Autobiography of a Fugitive Negro* saw publication in 1855. Also notable here is Josiah Henson, whose ghost-written narrative, released in 1849, served supposedly as a source for Harriet Beecher Stowe's *Uncle Tom's Cabin* (1852). Slave narratives were penned by one-time Americans Moses Roper (1838), Lewis and Milton Clarke (1845–1846), Thomas Smallwood (1851), Theophilus Steward (1856), Jermain Loguen (1859), and John William Robertson (1854), whose unique text fuses autobiography and sanguinary theology.

A set of diaries (1840–1865) kept by the Guyanese-born "octoroon" governor of British Columbia, Sir James Douglas, constitutes the earliest literary expression by a Caribbean-Canadian writer. (The diaries were partly published in 1965.)

With the conclusion of the American Civil War, many African Canadians, both long-settled and recent arrivals, removed to the United States, thus stranding the bulk of the black community in Nova Scotia, with pockets surviving in New Brunswick, Prince Edward Island, Canada (Québec and Ontario), and British Columbia. These colonies began to coalesce into the new Dominion of Canada in 1867.

From the mid-nineteenth century to the mid-twentieth century, then, African-Canadian literature consists of church documents sponsored by the African (United) Baptist Association of Nova Scotia and the British Methodist Episcopal Church in Ontario, plus other, smaller churches elsewhere; occasional sociological essays; two major church histories (*History of the Colored Baptists of Nova Scotia*, by Antigua native Peter E. McKerrow in 1895, and *History of the Colored Baptists of Nova Scotia, 1782–1953*, by Pearleen Oliver in 1954); various collections of hymns and songs, culminating in R. Nathaniel Dett's *Religious Folk-Songs of the Negro* in 1927; and a major folklore study (*Folk-Lore of Nova Scotia* in 1931 by Arthur Huff Fauset, an African-American anthropologist). Three novelists born in Canada in the mid-nineteenth century published their works at the century's end, all in the United States: See Amelia E. Johnson (1890, 1894, 1901), Lucretia Coleman (1890–1891), and William Haslip Stowers, or "Sanda" (1894). The Canadian-born Dett (1911) and Theodore Henry Shackelford (1916, 1918) issued the first poetry collections. The first important African-Canadian woman poet, Anna Minerva Henderson, released her single chapbook in 1967 when she was eighty years old and Canada was a hundred years old. For his part, John Hearne, born in Canada in 1926, became a top Jamaican novelist in the mid-twentieth century.

As the foregoing chronicle indicates, early African-Canadian literature possesses a skimpy corpus. Its bibliography expanded only with the onset of immigration from the Caribbean in the mid-1950s, then Africa in the 1970s. Thus, new energy came to its poetry in 1973, with the publication of *Dead Roots,* a posthumous work by South African exile and Canadian immigrant Arthur Nortje. Ex-Trinidadian Lennox Brown published the first African-Canadian play in English (*The Captive* in 1965), while Barbados native Austin Clarke produced the first "contemporary" novel (*The Survivors of the Crossing* in 1964).

Since 1964 for fiction, 1965 for drama, and 1973 for poetry, the majority of the writers contributing to a self-conscious African-Canadian *literary* canon are first-generation immigrants, primarily from the Caribbean. The major writers are such Trinidad and Tobago natives as Andre Alexis (1957–), Dionne Brand (1953–), Lennox Brown (1934–), Claire Harris (1937–), M. NourbeSe Phillip (1947–), and David Woods (1957–); ex-Jamaicans such as Lillian Allen (1951–), Hopeton Anderson (1950–), Louise Bennett (1919–), Afua Cooper (1957–), Ahdri Mandiela (1955?–), Pamela Mordecai (1942–), and Olive Senior (1941–); ex-"Bajans" such as Austin Clarke (1934–), Lorris Elliott (1932–1999), and Cecil Foster (1957–); former Antiguans such as Clifton Joseph (1957–) and Althea Prince (1945–); ex-Guyanese such as Jan Carew (1920–) and Nalo Hopkinson (1965?–); as well as native Grenadian Richardo Keens-Douglas (1955?–) and St. Vincentian H. Nigel Thomas (1947–). Vital African-born writers include former South Africans such as Archie Crail (1948–), Harold Head (1936–), Rozena Maart (1962–), and Arthur Nortje (1942–1970); Kenyans David Odhiambo (1965–) and Jan Tapsubei Creider (1950?–); as well as Malawian Paul Tiyambe Zeleza (1955–), Nigerian Ken Wiwa (1968–), Tanzania's Tololwa M. Mollel (1955?–), Ugandan George Seremba (1958–), and Ethiopian Nega Mezlekia (1958–).

African-American principals also continue to "infiltrate" the black Canuck canon. Note Rubin "Hurricane" Carter (1937–), Christopher Paul Curtis (1953–), Charles R. Saunders (1946–), and Frederick Ward (1937–). Crucial British-born authors are Djanet Sears (1955?–) and Rachel Manley (1947–), who is also of Caribbean heritage. Major native-born authors include George Boyd (1952–), Wendy Braithwaite (1970?–), George Elliott Clarke (1960–), Wayde Compton (1972–), Lorena Gale (1958–), Lawrence Hill (1957–), Sonnet L'Abbé (1970?–), Suzette Mayr (1967–), Andrew Moodie (1967–), Robert Sandiford (1968–), and Maxine Tynes (1949–). Given that second-generation immigrant youth constitute the largest portion of the African-Canadian community, "indigenous" authors will multiply.

The multicultural origins of African-Canadian literature give it a protean diversity. Its authors stress their "Canadian" identity (e.g., Alexis and Moodie), immigrant experience (e.g., NourbeSe Phillip and Mandiela), their homeland (e.g., Creider and Mezlekia), or the historical reality of "African Canada" (e.g., Compton and Tynes). The cosmopolitan, kaleidoscopic "fact" of the literature— its status as a callaloo of accents and a gumbo of perspectives—renders it a jazzy hubbub of voices, sans concord on "black identity," "Afrocentrism," "Canadian identity," or any topic of African diasporic concern. Assuredly, the "black community" in Canada is really a "community of communities" (to borrow a well-known Canadian political phrase), and the literature reflects this internal (in)consistency. Add the reality of regional difference (the West and Atlantic Canada versus the center, Québec versus the rest of Canada, the "ethnic" cities versus the homogeneous countryside), as well as the divisions among immigrant generations and those between immigrant and "indigenous" blacks, not to mention the distinctions between Anglophones and Francophones, and one ends up with a literature that, unlike its African-American and Afro-Caribbean cousins, can *never* pretend to certainty about its identity. Because no one definition of "blackness" rules in Canada, everyone is free to be "black" as he or she chooses.

Ultimately, African-Canadian literature is the literary laboratory of the African diaspora, for in this unique space, one created by transients—exiles, refugees, fugitives—as well as scattered, but hardy, "settlers," there is room for divergence, for a "blackness" that is a spectrum of skin tones and ideologies, for a multiplicity of discourse that can never be grounded in any one constricted (or constricting) faith or belief, for debates that can never be resolved for anyone's totalitarian satisfaction. "African Canada" is a homeland where no one need pledge allegiance, where "blackness" is defined as persistent, bitter, exhilarating, Sisyphean questioning.

See also Canadian Writers in French

▪ ▪ Bibliography

Bristow, Peggy. *"We're Rooted Here and They Can't Pull Us Up": Essays in African-Canadian Women's History.* Toronto: University of Toronto Press, 1994.

Clarke, George Elliott. *Eyeing the North Star: Directions in African-Canadian Literature.* Toronto: McClelland & Stewart, 1997.

Clarke, George Elliott. *Odysseys Home: Mapping African-Canadian Literature.* Toronto: University of Toronto Press, 2002.

Dalhousie Review 77, no. 2 (Summer 1997). Special "Africadian" issue.

Essays on Canadian Writing 75 (Winter 2002). Special issue on "Race."

Foster, Cecil. *A Place Called Heaven: The Meaning of Being Black in Canada.* Toronto: HarperCollins, 1996.

Sears, Djanet, ed. *Testifyin': Contemporary African-Canadian Drama,* vol. 1. Toronto: Playwrights Union of Canada, 2000.

GEORGE ELLIOTT CLARKE (2005)

CANADIAN WRITERS IN FRENCH

Black Canadian writers who write in French are of Haitian descent. Exiled by the chaos of the dictatorial rule in Haiti of François "Papa Doc" Duvalier (ruled 1957–1971) and his son Jean-Claude Duvalier (ruled 1971–1986), they are among the thousands of Haitians who fled their country in search of asylum in Canada. The novels, short stories, and poetry they have written in Canada, however, are not thematically different from the mainstream of modernist and postcolonial writing worldwide. Expatriation and the quest for reinvention are recurrent features in the works of Ezra Pound, T. S. Eliot, and Ernest Hemingway (among modernist writers), and those of Salman Rushdie, Derek Walcott, and Michael Ondaatje (among postcolonial writers).

Initially, Haitian writers in Canada had no alternative but to confront expatriation. Their works succeeded when they were inscribed in a literary continuum in which the commonplace theme of exile was accompanied by a reinvention in form. They failed, however, when they did not respond to the demands placed on art by both the modernists and the postcolonials.

For the icons of modernism and postcolonialism, the idea of "home" means the reinvention of place, but most Haitian writers in Canada are at first locked in the idea and the concreteness of a realistically represented "home," void of redefinition. Thus, the foremost concerns of the first generation of Haitian-Canadian writers are the nostalgic evocation of their lost homeland and, relatedly, the denunciation of the political regime responsible for that loss. The works of Gérard Etienne (*Le Nègre crucifié*), Émile Ollivier (*Mère-Solitude; La Discorde aux cent voix; Les Urnes scellées*), Anthony Phelps (*Mémoire en colinmaillard; Moins l'infini*), and Liliane Dévieux Dehoux (*L'Amour, oui, la mort, non*) are linked in this respect, being closely related to the writers' personal experiences of the Duvalier regime that led to their expatriation. They portray Haiti as a dichotomy of victims and victimizers, and the prevalent picture is one of relentless degradation unrelieved by the light of survival. Canada is not present in these works, except as an implicit "clean and well-lighted place" that allows for the act of writing as catharsis.

On the other hand, the works of a second generation of writers (e.g., Dany Laferrière, Stanley Péan, Joël des Rosiers, Marie-Célie Agnant, and Georges Anglade) are characterized by eclecticism in their formal and thematic reinvention beyond conventional realism.

In his first novel, *Comment faire l'amour avec un nègre sans se fatiguer* (1988), Dany Laferrière, the best-known writer of the group, builds on Ollivier's early symbolic use of a Canadian setting in *Paysage de l'aveugle* (1977). But, like Ollivier, his characters are not Canadians. While Ollivier's vision of the Duvalier years is at times leavened by satirical humor, Laferrière largely ignores this period, and while he also relies on humor, he does so to undermine interracial taboos. Laferrière's later work is set in Haiti and is mainly steeped in images of childhood filtered by an elliptical style of writing.

Laferrière paved the way for the writings of Péan, des Rosiers, and Agnant that intermingle different strategies distinct from the conventional representation of Haiti. However, nostalgia for the lost homeland is not altogether absent from Péan's *La Plage des songes* (1988), Agnant's *La Dot de Sara* (1995), and des Rosiers' *Vétiver* (1999). Nor is the horror of the Duvalier years ignored in des Rosiers' first book, *Métropolis Opéra* (1987)—whose dedication reads: "These verses are not dedicated to you who moans in the Tropics"—and Péan's *Zombie Blues* (1996), which echoes Etienne's early novels through the repulsive figure of a Duvalierist bogeyman let loose in Montreal. By contrast, Agnant's *La Dot de Sara* and, especially, *Le Livre d'Emma* (2001) proffer a modern feminist point of view on traditional gender imbalance in Haiti.

Georges Anglade, the most original writer of the group, adapts the Haitian oral narrative form of *lodyans* (a rough translation is "storytelling") in three collections of short stories (*Les Blancs de mémoire* [1999]; *Leurs jupons dépassent* [2000]; and *Ce pays qui m'habite* [2002]). His is a notable attempt at formal and thematic renewal in a series of interlocking stories set in Canada and Haiti using the village (Nedgé and Quina, respectively) as a unifying metaphor. These humorous stories are told by a first-person narrator who lives in Montreal and speaks from a more comprehensive temporal perspective than the restricted spatial perspective of most of his predecessors. The narrator's manipulation of language is undoubtedly reminiscent of Jacques Roumain's use of the language of the elite (French), yet it resounds with the tonality of the people's vernacular Creole. A conscious attempt is made to reconcile the polarities between classes, between expatriates and natives, and between Creole and French speakers in Haiti and in Canada.

Neither the first nor the second generation of Haitian-Canadian writers feels rooted in Canada to the extent of creating fully developed Canadian characters. There are no French-speaking Canadian characters in the novels and short stories of Ollivier, Laferrière, and Phelps. When they appear in other works, they are cardboard figures—victims of the bogeyman in the works of Péan and Etienne, and helpful allies of helpless Haitians in Etienne's *Un Ambassadeur macoute à Montréal* (1979) and *Une Femme muette* (1983). And, except for Laferrière's use of an African character in his first novel, none of the writers turns to Africa for a broadening of the representation of the Haitian condition. In *Passages* (1991), Ollivier traces the plight of Haitian boat people in Florida, and in *La Chair du maître* (1997), Laferrière caricatures the sex drive of American tourists.

There are a few English-Canadian coeds and do-gooders in Laferrière's first novel and in Etienne's *Une Femme muette*—they purportedly represent the bilingual nature of Canada. Ideology of a nationalist or racialist nature is identified with the excesses of *Négritude* personified by "Papa Doc" Duvalier, which the second generation chooses to exorcise in the process of reinvention.

Finally, there are the novels of Alix Renaud and Stanley Norris, whose characters are solely French-Canadians. Both writers follow the example of the early Haitian novelist Démesvar Delorme, who set his *Francesca* (1872) in sixteenth-century Italy (when Haiti did not exist as a nation). Delorme was also an expatriate writer. It is a measure of the relative achievements of his compatriots in Canada that they, as a whole, chose to create or reinvent their Haitianness.

See also Canadian Writers in English; Caribbean/North American Writers (Contemporary)

■ ■ *Bibliography*

Agnant, Marie-Célie. *La Dot de Sara*. Montreal: Editions du Remue-Ménage, 1995.

Agnant, Marie-Célie. *Le Livre d'Emma*. Montreal: Editions du Remue-Ménage, 2001.

Anglade, Georges. *Les Blancs de mémoire*. Montreal: Boréal, 1999.

Anglade, Georges. *Leurs jupons dépassent*. Montreal: Bibliothéque Haïtienne, 2000.

Anglade, Georges. *Ce pays qui m'habite*. Outremont, Quebec: Lanctôt, 2002.

Delorme, Démesvar. *Francesca: les jeux du sort*. Paris: E. Dentu, 1873.

des Rosiers, Joël. *Métropolis Opéra*. Montreal: Tryptique, 1987.

des Rosiers, Joël. *Vétiver*. Montreal: Tryptique, 1999.

Dévieux Dehoux, Liliane. *L'Amour, oui, la mort, non*. Sherbrooke, Quebec: Naaman, 1976.

Etienne, Gérard. *Le Nègre crucifié*. Montreal: Editions Nouvelle Optique. 1974.

Etienne, Gérard. *Un Ambassadeur macoute à Montréal*. Montreal: Editions Nouvelle Optique, 1979.

Etienne, Gérard. *Une Femme muette*. Montreal: Editions Nouvelle Optique, 1983.

Jonassaint, Jean. *Le Pouvoir des mots, les maux du pouvoir: Des romanciers Haïtiens de l'exil*. Paris, Arcantère; Montreal: Presses de l'Université de Montréal, 1986.

Laferrière, Dany. *Comment faire l'amour avec un nègre sans se fatiguer*. Montreal: VLB, 1985.

Laferrière, Dany. *L'odeur de café*. Montreal: VLB, 1991.

Laferrière, Dany. *Le Goût des jeunes filles*. Montreal: VLB, 1992.

Laferrière, Dany. *La Chair du maître*. Outremont: Lanctôt, 1997.

Laferrière, Dany. *Le Charme des après-midi sans fin*. Outremont: Lanctôt, 1997.

Norris, Stanley Lloyd. *L'Interdit*. Montreal: Libre Expression, 1991.

Norris, Stanley Lloyd. *La Pucelle*. Montreal: Libre Expression, 1993.

Norris, Stanley Lloyd. *L'Homme qui décrocha la lune*. Chicoutimi, Quebec: JCL, 1993.

Ollivier, Émile. *Paysage de l'aveugle*. Montreal: Editions Pierre Tisseyre, 1977.

Ollivier, Émile. *Mère-Solitude*. Paris: Albin Michel, 1983.

Ollivier, Émile. *La Discorde aux cent voix*. Paris: Albin Michel, 1986.

Ollivier, Émile. *Passages*. Montreal: L'Hexagone, 1991.

Ollivier, Émile. *Les Urnes scellées*. Paris: Albin Michel, 1995.

Péan, Stanley. *La Plage des songes*. Montreal: CIDIHCA, 1988.

Péan, Stanley. *Zombie Blues*. Montreal: Editions La Courte Echelle, 1996.

Phelps, Anthony. *Moins l'infini*. Paris: Les Editeurs Français Réunis, 1973.

Phelps, Anthony. *Mémoire en colin-maillard*. Montreal: Editions Nouvelle Optique, 1976.

Renaud, Alix. *A Corps joie*. Montreal: Editions Nouvelle Optique, 1985.

Roumain, Jacques. *Gouverneurs de la rosée.* Port-au-Prince, Haiti: Imprimerie de l'état, 1944.

MAX DORSINVILLE (2005)

CANDOMBLÉ

▗▗▗

Candomblé is one of the oldest and most popular Afro-Brazilian spiritual traditions. Created by enslaved Africans and their descendants, the religion emerged in late-eighteenth and nineteenth-century northeastern Brazil, particularly around the port city of Salvador, Bahia. Candomblé combines cosmologies and ritual practices from West and Central African sources with elements developed in the New World matrix of slavery, interactions with Native Americans and Europeans, and reconstructed meanings of identity and lineage. Much of the religion's historic and contemporary meaning can be attributed to its role as an instrument of resistance and transformation in the lives of black women and men who draw upon its resources to sustain the deepest sources of their humanity in the midst of great personal and collective trauma.

Fundamentally, Candomblé is a religion of balance and reciprocity that emphasizes the interconnectedness of all forms of life. Humans are recognized as part of a larger community of being that includes ancestors, the unborn, the entire natural world, and the world of the spirits. Most collective and personal rites within the tradition are related to addressing imbalances and nurturing the *axé* (life force or spiritual force) that enables healthy interactions among all elements of the created universe.

Candomblé is a hierarchical, initiatory religion with little moral dichotomy of good versus evil but with a strong ethical sense based in African values of reciprocity and ancestral obligation. There are six major divisions within the tradition, organized as ethno-liturgical "nations": Ketu, Ijexá, Jêje, Angola, Congo, and Caboclo. In their initial manifestations in the nineteenth century, the African nations of Candomblé represented the Yoruba (Ketu and Ijexá), Dahomean/Ewe (Jêje), and Bantu (Congo and Angola) ethnic identities of many of the individuals associated with ritual communities. Over the course of the development of the religion, as larger numbers of Brazilian-born participants entered the ceremonies, the identity of Candomblé nations became a liturgical designation and not a genetic or clan-based one. The Caboclo Candomblé is an additional division that specifically and extensively cultivates Amerindian ancestral spirits in addition to those of African origin. It is a more recent development, dating from the early twentieth century and prominently incorporating Brazilian national symbols such as the country's flag, its green and yellow colors, and the use of Portuguese as the language of ceremony.

Because of the strength and prestige of Yoruba-based candomblés, the Yoruba term *orixá* (*orisha*) has become the most common descriptor of the phenomenon of spiritual forces or divinities cultivated in the religion. Nonetheless, in the contexts of their own rituals, the Ewe and Bantu nations of Candomblé call the spirits by other names—voduns (among the Jêje) and *nkisis* (among the Congo and Angola communities).

In Brazil, the most commonly cultivated *orixás* of the Yoruba pantheon are: *Exú*, *orixá* of the crossroads who controls communication between human beings and the world of the spirits; *Ogun*, warrior god of metals and the forest who is the path-breaker; and *Oxôssi*, ancient head of the Kêtu kingdom, a hunter *orixá* characterized by mental acuity. *Omolû* or *Obaluaiye* is *orixá* of the earth and of both illness and healing. *Ossâin* is guardian of herbs and herbal wisdom, and *Oxumarê* is the serpent deity associated with life cycles of renewal. Another warrior energy, *Logun-Ede*, is son of Oxôssi and Oxum and shares their qualities. *Xangô*, the much beloved ancient king of Oyo, is *orixá* of fire, justice, storm, and friendship. *Oxum* is the *orixá* of sweet waters, creativity, beauty, and abundance. The energetic female warrior *orixá Oyá*, or *Iansã*, is associated with storm, transformation, and the spirits of the dead. *Iemanjá*, patroness of salt water, is an *orixá* of maternal strength and protection. *Obá* is another river deity, also a fierce female warrior energy; and *Euá*, a river nymph *orixá*, is associated with youthful grace and a fighting spirit. An ancient female energy, *Nana Burukû*, is *orixá* of still, muddy waters. *Oxalá*, father of the other *orixás*, is the principle of peace and protection. Like the Hindu deities of India, *orixás* in Afro-Brazilian Candomblé are recognized as having several different avatars, or manifestations, often of different ages, and each representing a slightly different variation on the general theme.

While each human being is believed to have been born under the guidance of a specific grouping of *orixás*, most are not required to do anything special to cultivate or develop their connection to these spiritual forces. An occasional offering of flowers, food, or even simple prayers is often sufficient to acknowledge and sustain the innate relationship between a person and his or her patron deities. For others, however, the responsibility is much greater. These are the *adoxu*, the devotees who have been "called" by the *orixá* to be their embodied human presence in the world, their priestesses and priests, their servants. These women and men are understood to have a ritual obligation to devote significant portions of their lives to the

A Candomblé religious ceremony in Salvador, Bahia, Brazil. Female dancers serving as spirit mediums enter into trances during a ceremony dedicated to some of their orishas, or gods. Men are in attendance to assist, and to aid the women if they fall while in a state of trance. Bahia maintains Brazil's earliest form of Candomblé worship, which is among the oldest and most popular of Afro-Brazilian religious traditions. © STEPHANIE MAZE/CORBIS

spiritual work of the *orixás,* incorporating the spirits' energies into their bodies, being the "voice" or the "presence" of the *orixá* in the human community, and carrying out the work of healing, reconciliation, blessing, and the balancing of personal, social, and environmental inequalities and instabilities. This responsibility, for which devotees are specially prepared through an extensive, years-long initiation process, is often seen as an inheritance from ancestors who also shared their connection to a particular *orixá.*

Candomblé ritual communities, or *terreiros,* exist in a variety of forms. In older or more well-off sites, there are often a series of buildings that include "houses" for the deities; living and cooking space for members of the community; a large hall, or *barracão,* for conducting ceremonies; and both garden and uncultivated spaces outdoors for essential plant resources. Newer and more urban *terreiros,* and those with fewer material means, are often incorporated into the homes of religious leaders where the living

room may be used as the *barracão* and bedrooms may be combined with altar spaces.

The Brazilian national census of 2000 indicates that devotees of Afro-Brazilian religions constitute three percent of the country's total population. Scholars of the religions, however, have calculated the figure at closer to eight percent. Most Candomblé ritual communities involve a small number of participants, generally no more than fifty, except in the case of the oldest "mother houses" of Bahia from which descend many *terreiros* around the country. Ceremonies open to the public may attract several times the number of actual members, and nonmembers may frequent the *terreiro* for spiritual advice and ritual assistance on a wide range of matters, including physical health, psychological stability, personal relationships, financial difficulties, and employment issues. Extensive traditions of ritual and medicinal pharmacopoeia support *trabalhos* (spiritual healing works), and many new adepts, as well as clients, are attracted to the religion by the reputation of priestesses and priests for successful intervention in problematic cases.

When a priest or priestess is approached, the first step is often a *consulta,* a private divinatory session, in which the religious leader will consult the *orixás* by means of the *jogo de búzios,* an oracle of cowrie shells. Reading and interpreting the shells, the *mãe* or *pai de santo* diagnoses the problem and, determining if it is within the purview of the religion's resources to be addressed, prescribes a remedy. This may be as simple as an herb bath and an offering of flowers or food at the seashore or as complex as the eventual need for a full initiation into the priesthood.

Most *terreiros* follow a fairly strict organization of ritual responsibilities according to gender and length of initiation. At the pinnacle of the *terreiro* leadership is the *mãe* or *pai de santo*—the head priestess or priest—whose authority is unchallenged in the context of the ritual community. Other titles for these individuals depend on the specific ritual language and tradition of each house: *iyalorixá* and *babalorixá* (mother and father of the *orixás*) are terms used in the Yoruba-based candomblés; *nenguankisi* and *tatankisi* (mother and father of the *nkisi*) are used in the Congo and Angola candomblés; and *doné* and *doté* (chief priestess and chief priest of the voduns) in Jêje candomblés. Initiated members of the communities are *filhos* and *filhas de santo* (children of the saint).

The majority of Candomblé devotees are women, and some *terreiros* have a longstanding tradition of exclusively consecrating women as supreme leaders of the community. Indeed, the place of women as utmost ritual authorities in many *terreiros* is a distinguishing characteristic of the religion. Candomblé communities have often been recognized as "privileged" women's spaces in Brazilian society.

The central rites of Candomblé are a series of initiations, periodic reinforcements of the spiritual energies of both devotees and *orixás,* and a cycle of annual ceremonies in honor of the *orixás.* Among the first rituals a new initiate experiences are the *banho de folhas* (ritual cleansing bath with herbs), *limpeza* (ritual cleansing with song, prayers, and a variety of animal and vegetable elements passed lightly over the body), *lavagem de contas* (consecration of beaded necklaces in herb mixtures sacred to the *orixás*), and *obí com agua,* an offering of kola nut and water to the *orixá* who most closely accompanies each devotee. Other rituals related more directly to the process of initiation, *fazer santo* (literally, "to make the saint"), are designed to reinforce the spiritual link between devotee and *orixá* as well as to prepare the new initiate to properly receive and care for the *orixá* that enters her body in ceremony. The rites associated with initiation, *obrigações,* are renewed in one-, three-, and seven-year cycles.

Each *terreiro* conducts a sequence of annual celebrations for the patron *orixás* of the house. These *festas* are the major public ceremonies of the religion. Initiated members who receive the *orixá* circle the *barracão* in festive ritual dress: lace and embroidered blouses, panes of cloth with stripes or lace designs wrapped around their chests, wide skirts of lush and beautiful fabrics—their fullness accentuated by starched underskirts—and the *contas,* beaded necklaces in colors and patterns associated with the various divinities. They dance barefoot, in a counterclockwise ring, varying their steps and gestures in accordance with the rhythms played on sacred drums, *atabaques:* a different rhythm for each *orixá.* The drums are accompanied by a metal bell, *agogô,* and songs calling the *orixás* to join their devotees in the circle of dancers.

After a while, the spirits begin to descend, temporarily occupying the bodies of their adepts. In the moments of transition, some devotees are in noticeable discomfort, clearly demonstrating that the process of sharing their physical being and consciousness with another entity is an immensely taxing effort. Others seem to make the shift almost imperceptibly; under all but the closest observation, the moment of change passes unnoticed. As the *orixás* arrive, they are ushered out of the *barracão* and into back rooms where they are dressed in their own ritual clothes, in colors, textures, and designs that clearly identify each—red and white for Xangô; light blue for Iemanjá; raffia palm and burlap for Omolú; white for Oxalá. They reemerge wearing beaded crowns that cover their eyes. They carry the implements associated with their dramatic and interwoven mythologies—Oxum's mirror and fan; Oyá's horsehair whisk; Ogun's sword and shield. They dance into the small hours of the morning, pausing to receive ritual greetings and to offer hugs and parental caresses (and sometimes a concise word of advice) to members of the community and guests.

In Candomblé, as in most Afro-Brazilian religions, ritual knowledge is primarily transmitted in oral and gestural forms. A popular saying in the religion is "Quem pergunte no Candomblé não aprende." (She who asks questions in Candomblé does not learn.) Knowledge passes as much from hand to hand in the conduct of daily tasks as from mouth to ear. The appropriate comportment in the ceremonial as well as quotidian contexts is one of manifest, corporeal respect for elders and for the *orixás.* This means that devotees with fewer years of initiation should defer to those who have more. Candomblé ceremony involves an elaborate etiquette of greeting and respect for elders that, even outside of the explicitly ritual context, requires initiates to acknowledge and ask the blessing of their elders and give special prostrated reverence to the chief priestess or priest.

Outside of the hierarchy of individual *terreiros,* there is no external organizing structure that dictates standards of ritual activity for Candomblé communities. The absence of a larger governing organization means that each ritual community is essentially autonomous. In some states there are licensing bodies to ensure "authenticity" and affirm the training of *pais* and *mães do santo,* but these do not set policy. Correspondingly, there is little institutional support for the religions beyond informal (but important) networks of friendship, mutual respect, and the rumors, reports, and inter-*terreiro* conversations that serve significantly as a kind of standardizing influence, especially among communities of the same "nation."

Most devotees of Afro-Brazilian religion are members of the Brazilian working classes. And although blacks have historically been in the majority as participants and leaders in the religions, beginning in the 1950s, people who claim no African ancestry have increasingly joined the ranks of adepts. In some parts of southeastern Brazil there are ritual communities in which more than half of the members are white. There are also Asians, Europeans, other Latin Americans, and blacks from the United States and the Caribbean who are attracted to Afro-Brazilian religion and who have been integrated into its communities. Candomblé and its sister-traditions continue to provide devotees an alternative space for the cultivation of connection to ancestral sources of strength, healing, and mystic/ritual approaches to the resolution of quotidian problems of modern life. Candomblé also offers access to deeper, more multifaceted, and more respected personal identities, an important resource for individuals who are severely marginalized by the political, racial, and economic structures of a profoundly unequal society.

See also Central African Religions and Culture in the Americas; Orisha; Religion; Santería; Spirituality; Yoruba Religion and Culture in the Americas

■ ■ *Bibliography*

Bastide, Roger. *The African Religions of Brazil: Toward a Sociology of the Interpenetration of Civilizations.* Baltimore, Md.: Johns Hopkins University Press, 1978.

Carybé. *Os deuses africanos no candomblé da Bahia (African Gods in the Candomblé of Bahia).* 2d ed. Salvador: Bigraf, 1993.

Dantas, Beatriz Góiz. "Repensando a pureza nagô." *Religião e Sociedade* 8 (1982): 15–20.

Harding, Rachel E. *A Refuge in Thunder: Candomblé and Alternative Spaces of Blackness.* Bloomington: Indiana University Press, 2000.

Johnson, Paul. *Secrets, Gossip and Gods: The Transformation of Brazilian Candomblé.* New York: Oxford University Press, 2002.

Landes, Ruth. *The City of Women.* New York: Macmillan, 1947. Reprint, Albuquerque: University of New Mexico Press, 1994.

Lima, Vivaldo da Costa. *A Familia de Santo nos Candomblés Jêje-Nagôs da Bahia.* 1977. Reprint, Salvador: Corrúpio Edições, 2003.

Nascimento, Abdias do. *Orixás: Os Deuses Vivos da Africa (Orishas: The Living Gods of Africa in Brazil).* Philadelphia: Temple University Press, 1997.

Prandi, Reginaldo. "African Gods in Contemporary Brazil: A Sociological Introduction to Candomblé Today." *International Journal of Sociology* 15, no. 4 (2000): 641–664.

Santos, Juana Elbein dos. *Os Nagô e a Morte: Pade, Asese e o Culto Egun na Bahia.* Petropolis, Brazil: Editora Vozes, 1975.

Sodré, Muniz. *O terreiro e a cidade: a forma social negro-brasileira.* Petrópolis, Brazil: Editora Vozes, 1988.

Verger, Pierre. *Dieux D'Afrique: Culte des Orishas et Vodouns a L'Ancienne Cote des Esclaves en Afrique et a Bahia.* Paris: Editions Revue Noire, 1995.

Voeks, Robert. *Sacred Leaves of Candomblé: African Magic, Medicine and Religion in Brazil.* Austin: University of Texas Press, 1997.

Walker, Sheila. "'The Feast of the Good Death': An Afro-Catholic Emancipation Celebration in Brazil." *SAGE: A Scholarly Journal on Black Women* 3, no. 2 (1986): 27–31.

Wimberly, Fayette. "The Expansion of Afro-Bahian Religious Practices in Nineteenth-Century Cachoeira." In *Afro-Brazilian Culture and Politics: Bahia, 1790s to 1990s,* edited by Hendrik Kraay. Armonk, N.Y.: ME Sharpe, 1998.

RACHEL E. HARDING (2005)

CAPOEIRA

Capoeira is a martial art of African origins that was once used by enslaved Africans in Brazil as a form of physical and social resistance. Despite years of persecution, the art has recently experienced a boom in popularity and spread throughout the world. This graceful art is practiced to music and combines a dynamic assortment of head butts, dodging movements, foot sweeps, and dynamic kicks. The origin of the word *capoeira* is uncertain, although a number of unproven etymological hypotheses link it to the Portuguese term *capoeira* for "basket" used to carry chickens, a Central African term for the fighting style of chickens, or Native American terms for a secondary-growth brushland. This unique martial art tradition itself, however, can be traced back to Central Africa, particularly the highland and Cabinda regions of Angola.

In the Angolan highlands the art evolved under the name *engolo* before the tenth century as part of a wider militarization of culture by pastoral peoples seeking to effectively protect their herds from cattle raids and engage

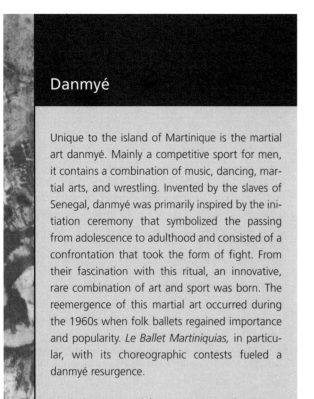

Danmyé

Unique to the island of Martinique is the martial art danmyé. Mainly a competitive sport for men, it contains a combination of music, dancing, martial arts, and wrestling. Invented by the slaves of Senegal, danmyé was primarily inspired by the initiation ceremony that symbolized the passing from adolescence to adulthood and consisted of a confrontation that took the form of fight. From their fascination with this ritual, an innovative, rare combination of art and sport was born. The reemergence of this martial art occurred during the 1960s when folk ballets regained importance and popularity. *Le Ballet Martiniquias,* in particular, with its choreographic contests fueled a danmyé resurgence.

Music is an essential component to danmyé as drummers follow the contestants closely, timing their drumrolls and crescendos to the fighters' blows. The wrestler has to hit and move in harmony with the drum rhythm as well. If this condition is not respected, the fight is stopped and the guilty wrestler is disqualified. While danmyé drumming has, for the most part, a specific basic rhythm pattern, there is room for very frequent and elaborate improvisations. Singing, too, sometimes provokes the wrestler. Lyrical phrasing often centers around the wrestlers themselves and can be provocative, critical, or used to stimulate the wrestler into performing at a higher level.

During the rise of the drum the opponent tries to do damage to his opponent, or outdo the other in terms of strength or agility. Danmyé, for the most part, is a nonviolent activity. The strokes must be restrained and given without intending to hit. In fact, they must be shown rather than given unless it is necessary to drive an opponent back to refuse a hand-to-hand fight. Victory assessment is dependent on two things, harmony with the sound and decisive blows that might have lead to a knockout had they really been carried out.

in lucrative raids of their own in times of famine. The three major techniques of the art were head butts in imitation of the fighting style of their prized cattle, acrobatic dodging ability, and sweeps and kicks. The latter were unique from other martial arts in that they were often executed from an inverted position in imitation of ancestors who were believed to live in an inverted state from our own. These skills were developed during practice rituals in which adepts would form a circle and enliven the exercise with percussion and song. Two adepts would enter the circle and practice trading attacks, evasions, and counterattacks in a graceful exchange. This ritual practice took place during rites of passage, healing rituals, and community festivals. It was also understood as a form of military training as it developed in young warriors the crucial ability to defend themselves with agility rather than shields, which were not utilized in the Angolan highlands.

More enslaved Africans were taken from Central Africa than any other region in Africa. Central African warriors took their martial art tradition everywhere they settled in the Americas. In North America the Angolan martial art of head butting and kicking became known as knocking (head butting) and kicking, which became the primary combat style of enslaved peoples in North America. It continued to play a role in covert religious rituals, community dances, initiation societies, and self-defense. Similarly the Central African martial art tradition was extended to Martinique, where it became known as *danmyé* and was also associated with secret societies during slavery.

The Central African martial art tradition also appeared in Brazil under the name of *capoeiragem* in the late eighteenth century. *Capoeiragem* appears to have been primarily located in such major urban centers as Salvador and particularly Rio de Janeiro, which was the epicenter of slavery and African culture in the late eighteenth century. The art was most associated with enslaved Africans who worked *de ganho,* as wage laborers who paid their masters much of their earnings but otherwise lived relatively autonomous lives. The martial art continued to be practiced in a number of contexts, including entertainment at dances *(batuques),* popular festivals, as well as bloody conflicts. However, by the early nineteenth century the primary context for the art was urban initiation societies called *maltas*. These societies were dedicated to the protection of the enslaved population of a given parish and often held ceremonies in the bell towers of the church. The *maltas* taught the martial art to youth, who would continue to advance in the art as they moved up the various levels of initiation in the society. A fully initiated member, called a *capoeira,* was expected to fight for the *malta* in administering punishments to those who failed

Two young men practice capoeira *in Bahia, Brazil.* An energetic hybrid form of martial arts and dance, capoeira originated in central Africa and was practiced by enslaved Africans in Brazil as a means of physical and social resistance. The art has experienced a twenty-first century resurgence, and is gaining popularity in many parts of the world. © THE COVER STORY/CORBIS

to respect their code or in clashes with other *maltas* or police. In the teeming streets of Rio de Janeiro, *capoeiras* were set apart by their characteristic clothes, style of walk, and often their drums, which were used to accompany the ritual practice of the art, the *jogo de capoeira*. Their visibility and the threat they posed to the slave system made them constant targets for police repression, which the *capoeiras* resisted in ongoing bloody battles with the police. Although the art was highly persecuted, it continued to spread through the urban African population in the first half of the nineteenth century.

In the second half of the nineteenth century, with the gradual elimination of the Atlantic slave trade, the African-born population dwindled, and the *maltas* began initiating Brazilian-born blacks and *pardos* (people of mixed heritage). As the art spread from enslaved Africans to other Brazilians, it also developed a sort of symbiosis with various Brazilian police and military institutions. *Capoeiras* were forcibly conscripted or voluntarily joined the ranks of these organizations, which afforded them some protection from persecution. During the War of

Paraguay beginning in 1865, many of the highest-ranking *capoeiras* were sent off as soldiers to the front lines. In their absence a large number of European immigrants filled the reduced ranks of the *maltas* as a means of survival on the harsh streets of Rio de Janeiro. At the war's end in 1870, however, the conscripted *capoeiras* returned as conquering heroes widely acknowledged for their bravery in the war. They reestablished control over the *maltas* and streets of Rio and, despite the continued prohibition against *capoeiragem*, many of these *malta* chiefs became immersed in Rio's political system. The *maltas* were loosely organized into two rival umbrella organizations, the *Nagoas* and *Guayamus*, each allied with different political parties. The *maltas* received patronage and political protection from elites in exchange for violently breaking up the political rallies of their opponents and stuffing ballot boxes during elections. Although often in conflict with one another, *capoeiras* tended to unify against the Republican Party, who were seen by many as proslavery.

The twentieth century was marked by alterations in the practice of this martial art. Throughout Brazilian urban centers the *maltas* were effectively disbanded, although *capoeiragem* continued to be perpetuated by independent experts called *bambas* or *valentões*. A number of musical transformations also took place in the region of Salvador, Bahia. Sometime around the first decade, the drum, formerly the main instrument used to accompany the *jogo de capoeira*, was replaced by a musical bow of Central African provenance. This musical bow, originally called *urucungo* in Brazil but later popularized as *berimbau*, was a more mobile instrument and doubled as a weapon. In the 1930s and 1940s new instruments were sporadically joined to the growing ad hoc orchestra, often including the tambourine *(pandeiro)*, double cow bell *(agogo)*, wooden scrapers *(reco-reco)*, or a new drum *(atabaque)*.

In Rio a *capoeiragem* expert, Mestre Macaco (Ciríaco Francisco da Silva), defeated a visiting jujitsu expert in a public challenge match in 1908. The national pride in his victory was an important watershed in the movement to end the ban on the art. A number of intellectuals and adepts of the art in Rio began publishing literature calling for the adoption of the art as a national sport. Despite this early drive for legitimacy in Rio, the successful transformation of the martial art into a national sport took place in Salvador, Bahia, in the 1930s and 1940s. This occurred in a larger political context in which a populist policy led by President Getúlio Vargas attempted to create a Brazilian identity by transforming African Brazilian cultural forms such as *candomble, samba, umbanda,* and *capoeiragem* into national symbols. In 1927 Mestre Bimba (Manuel dos Reis Machado) catalyzed this transformation by opening the first formal academy dedicated to promoting his new variant of *capoeiragem* termed *a luta regional Baiana,* or more popularly *capoeira regional*. The efforts of Mestre Bimba and the policies of Vargas together led to a legalization of a controlled *capoeira* separate from the art's earlier associations with Africa, violence, and the underclass. In 1935 Mestre Pastinha (Vicente Ferreira Pastinha) followed suit by opening the first academy for the purportedly unaltered style of the art, called *capoeira Angola*. Both masters promoted the art under the term *capoeira* ("regional" or Angola) to distinguish their styles and possibly to separate the art from the violence associated with the term *capoeiragem*. By teaching the art in structured school settings, these two masters proliferated their formalized teachings of the art and eclipsed the lineages of other *bambas*.

Capoeira regional in particular was adopted by the police and promoted by sporting federations. Students of Mestre Bimba spread this new variant throughout Brazil and more recently the world. Although not nearly as wide-spread as *capoeira regional, capoeira Angola* has also begun to spread worldwide during the last two decades. *Capoeira* is now recognized as a Brazilian national sport and is one of the fastest growing martial arts of the twenty-first century.

See also Candomblé; Samba

■ ■ Bibliography

Almeida, Bira. *Capoeira, a Brazilian Art Form: History, Philosophy, and Practice.* Berkeley, Calif.: North Atlantic Books, 1986.

Dawson, C. Daniel. "Capoeira: An Exercise of the Soul." *Icarus* 13 (1994): 13–28.

Desch-Obi, T. J. "Combat and the Crossing of the Kalunga." In *Central Africans and Cultural Transformations in the American Diaspora,* edited by Linda Heywood. Cambridge, UK: Cambridge University Press, 2000.

Dossar, Kenneth. "Dancing Between Two Worlds: An Aesthetic Analysis of *Capoeira Angola*." Ph.D. diss., Temple University, Philadelphia, 1994.

Thompson, Robert Farris, and C. Daniel Dawson. *Dancing Between Two Worlds: Kongo-Angola Culture and the Americas.* New York: Caribbean Cultural Center, 1991.

T. J. DESCH-OBI (2005)

CARDOZO, FRANCIS L.

FEBRUARY 1, 1837
JULY 22, 1903

Minister, educator, and politician Francis Louis Cardozo was born in Charleston, South Carolina, in 1837. His father, Isaac N. Cardozo, a prominent Jewish businessman and economist, was married to a free black woman. Cardozo's parents' wealth enabled him to be educated at a free Negro school in Charleston until he was twelve. His mother and father subsequently apprenticed him to a carpenter, and after completing his apprenticeship, Cardozo pursued this vocation for several years. When he was twenty-one, he went to Great Britain, where he studied for the ministry, and upon returning to the United States in 1864, he became a Congregational minister. Like a number of black churchmen, Cardozo went south after the Civil War. The conclusion of hostilities between North and South opened a vast missionary field for black ministers who wanted to work with freedmen.

Returning to Charleston as a missionary of the American Missionary Association, Cardozo became principal of the Saxton School, replacing his younger brother, Thomas, who had been forced to resign after a sexual indiscretion at his previous post was revealed. Cardozo did not remain long at this position; in 1866 he helped establish the Avery Normal Institute in Charleston and became its first superintendent. Avery was founded to train black teachers, and in the post–Civil War South the school played a prominent role in the education of blacks.

Serving as both educator and minister, Cardozo was drawn into the web of Reconstruction politics. He began his career as a politician inauspiciously as a delegate to the 1868 South Carolina state constitutional convention. He then served as South Carolina's secretary of state from 1868 to 1872, the first black in South Carolina's history to hold government office. He was state treasurer from 1872 to 1877. Compared with other black preacher-politicians during Reconstruction, Cardozo was fairly moderate. He did not alienate his white Republican peers in the ways that R. H. Cain, Tunis G. Campbell, and Henry McNeal Turner did. For example, Cardozo did not urge freedmen to seize their former masters' land, as Campbell did in Georgia. When the Reconstruction government of South Carolina was overthrown in 1877, Cardozo moved to Washington, D.C., where he became a member of the city's black elite. He died there in 1903.

See also Cain, Richard Harvey

■ ■ *Bibliography*

Drago, Edmund L. *Initiative, Paternalism, and Race Relations: Charleston's Avery Normal Institute.* Athens: University of Georgia Press, 1990, pp. 49–56.

Foner, Eric. *Freedom's Lawmakers: A Directory of Black Office-holders during Reconstruction.* New York: Oxford University Press, 1993, p. 39.

CLARENCE E. WALKER (1996)

CAREW, JAN
DECEMBER 24, 1920

Jan Rynveld Carew personifies Berbice, the Guyanese county of his birth. One might also trace his eclectic career to educational opportunities that mirrored what Eusi Kwayana described as Carew's "ideological self reliance." Perhaps these influences explain his oeuvre's continuing relevance.

Born in Agricola-Rome, Berbice County, when Guyana was still British Guiana, Carew benefited from the region's fertile climate. He has said that Berbice, known as "the ancient county," was underdeveloped but "had a remarkable texture, ambience, and quality for the arts" (Dance, 1992, p. 33). There is more to this statement than the pride of a native son, for along with Carew, Berbice fashioned Martin Carter, Edgar Mittelholzer, and Wilson Harris. Apparently channeling this rich atmosphere, Carew began to paint and write poetry. His brother-in-law, Wilson Harris, added another geographical aspect to Carew's intellectual development by making it "possible for [him] to enter into [Guyana's] rain forest" and bask in "the stimulating business" of being around Harris (Dance, 1992, p. 37). These particular consequences of Guyanese geographies shaped the author's educational career.

Though a serious childhood illness affected Carew's early academic success, it proved fortuitous because it enabled him to attend Berbice High School. Considered a distant second to the country's renowned Queen's College, the high school had an environment that suited the intellectually curious and creatively imaginative. Featuring what some might call lax attendance and curriculum policies, the high school attracted a progressive teaching staff. As a student who could "simply . . . gallop along and do whatever one wanted to do," Carew studied "Latin, French, math, geography, literature, art, and general science" (Dance, 1992, p. 33). High school master J. A. Rodway punctuated the perspicacious student's loosely guided romp through the classics by nurturing his creative writing (Ramchand, 2002, p. 60). Universities in countries as diverse as the United States (Howard and Western Reserve Universities), Czechoslovakia (Charles University), and France (the Sorbonne) allowed Carew to pursue the kind of "unstructured" learning he had begun in Guyana.

The socio-political climates of these countries also contributed to Carew's political consciousness and extended his personal experiences. The racism he faced in Washington, D.C., and being part of a vibrant, poor African-American community in Chicago solidified his "instinctive" connection to the United States' black community (Dance, 1992, pp. 34–35). Finally, his mother's response to U.S. racism (see Cooke) as well as both grandfathers' desire that their children learned trades (Dance, 1992, p. 34) confirmed what would come to be the activist's defining interests.

Jan Carew is respected for his contributions to the "freedom for the oppressed and downtrodden—teaching, writing, broadcasting, [and] engaging" all manner of people, including Claudia Jones, Cheddi Jagan, and Kwame Nkrumah (Sivanandan, 2002, p. 1). In fact, he parlayed his work with Nkrumah into a commitment to Pan-African

Studies as a discipline (Brutus, 2002, p. 72). His lasting influence might be due to his investment in shaping "the cultural revolution against colonialism and racism [through] poetry, painting, polemic, and play" (Sivanandan, 2002, p. 1). In fact, Carew's work is counted among Caribbean fiction "that informed the intellectual and cultural self-confidence of a generation" (Ramchand, 2002, p. 57).

Carew has written in several genres: adult and children's short and long prose, poetry, drama, and history/criticism. Suitably, each piece in his body of work reflects a holistic approach to intellectual/political explorations. One can find this mix in his most influential works: *Black Midas* (1958), in which the author uses an acquaintance's life to explore relationships between Indian and African Guyanese peoples; *The Wild Coast* (1958), in which Carew's study of New World African religions reflects semi-autobiographical experiences; *Moscow is Not My Mecca* (1964), which offers a critique of race and communism via the fictionalized experiences of Carew's distant cousin; *The Third Gift* (1975), a children's book using Amerindian myths; and the oft cited *Ghosts in Our Blood* (1994), in which the author explores the experiences of blacks in the diaspora through conversations with Malcolm X.

Despite advancing age, Jan Carew continues to be a voice for progressive change, not only through his commitment to oppressed peoples but also through his willingness to break genre and intellectual boundaries.

See also Literature of Guyane

■ ■ *Bibliography*

"Bibliography of Publications by Jan Carew." *Race and Class* 43, no. 3 (2002): 85–91.

Brutus, Dennis. "Jan Carew—Comrade in Struggle." *Race and Class* 43, no. 3 (2002): 72–73.

Carew, Joy Gleason. "Explorations into the 'Feminism' of Jan Carew." *Race and Class* 43, no. 3 (2002): 27–38.

Cooke, Mel. "Jan Carew Reads His Early Years." Available from <http://www.jamaica-gleaner.com/gleaner/20020606/ent/ent2.html>.

Dance, Daryl Cumber. "Jan Carew." *New World Adams: Conversations with Contemporary West Indian Writers.* Leeds, UK: Peepal Tree Press, 1992.

"Jan Carew: A Biographical Odyssey." *Race and Class* 43, no. 3 (2002): 81–84.

Kwayana, Eusi. "Jan Carew: Mission within the Mission." *ChickenBones: A Journal for Literary and Artistic African-American Themes.* Available from <http://www.nathanielturner.com/jancarew/htm>.

Ramchand, Ken. "Accessing the Light of Prophecy." *Race and Class* 43, no. 3 (2002): 57–63.

Rashidi, Runoko. "Tribute to a Great Man: Dr. Jan Rynveld Carew." *Global African Presence: The Global African Community, History Notes.* Available from <http://www.cwo.com/~lucumi/carew.html>.

Singham, Nancy. "Jan Carew—the Chicago Years." *Race and Class* 43, no. 3 (2002): 52–56.

Sivanandan, A. "Jan Carew, Renaissance Man." *Race and Class* 43, no. 3 (2002): 1–2.

University of Louisville, Liberal Studies Five-Year Project. "Scholar-in-Residence (2000): Jan R. Carew, Emeritus Professor, Northwestern University." Available from <http://www.louisville.edu/a-s/lbst/project/jcarew.html>.

NOVELS

Black Midas. New York: Periodicals Service Co., 1958; published in the United States as *A Touch of Midas,* New York: Coward-McCann, 1958.

The Wild Coast. London: Secker and Warburg, 1958.

The Last Barbarian. London: Secker and Warburg, 1961.

CHILDREN'S BOOKS

The Third Gift. Boston: Little, Brown, 1974.

Children of the Sun. Boston: Little, Brown, 1980.

POETRY

Streets of Eternity. 1952.

Sea Drums in My Blood. Trinidad: New Voices, 1981.

HISTORIES, ESSAY COLLECTIONS, MEMOIRS

Rape of Paradise. New York: A&B Books, 1984.

Grenada: The Hour Will Strike Again. Prague: International Organization of Journalists Press, 1985.

Fulcrums of Change: The Origins of Racism in the Americas and Other Essays. Trenton, N.J.: Africa World Press, 1988.

Ghosts in Our Blood: With Malcolm X in Africa, England and the Caribbean. New York: Lawrence Hill, 1994.

Moscow Is Not My Mecca, London: Secker and Warburg, 1964; published in the United States as *Green Winter,* New York: Stein and Day, 1965.

RHONDA FREDERICK (2005)

CAREY, LOTT

c. 1780
NOVEMBER 28, 1828

■■■

Lott Carey, America's pioneer missionary to Africa, was born in slavery around 1780 on the plantation of William A. Christian in Charles City County, some thirty miles south of Richmond, Virginia. In 1804 he was hired out to work in Richmond at the Shockoe tobacco warehouse. From the segregated gallery of Richmond's First Baptist

Church, Carey was converted to the Christian religion in 1807 by the preaching of John Courtnay, a white man. Courtnay baptized him, and he joined the church. Carey then determined to enter the ministry, and he learned to read and write. Permitted to preach to both blacks and whites in the area, Carey formed the African Missionary Society, which raised $700 in five years to send him and Collin Teague to Africa. At the tobacco warehouse he earned an extra $850 by 1813, with which he purchased his own and his children's freedom (his first wife had recently died).

In January 1820 (or possibly 1821) Carey and Teague sailed on the *Nautilus* for Africa. Teague retired after a year to Sierra Leone, but Carey was instrumental in establishing the colony of Liberia and forming a Baptist church in Monrovia, the colony's capital. He became the country's health officer, and in 1826 he was named vice agent of the colony under the American Colonization Society. Carey identified with the effort to build a black republic, stating "I am an African. . . . I wish to go to a country where I shall be estimated by my merits, and not by my complexion; and I feel bound to labor for my suffering race."

Carey was killed on November 28, 1828, in an accidental explosion of gunpowder while he was engaged in making cartridges to fight off attacking native Liberians. In 1897 the Lott Carey Baptist Foreign Missionary Society was established in his memory.

See also Missionary Movements

■ ■ *Bibliography*

Fitts, Leroy. *Lott Carey: First Black Missionary to Africa*. Valley Forge, Pa.: Judson Press, 1978.

LEROY FITTS (1996)

CARIBBEAN COMMISSION

▪▮▪

The Caribbean Commission began as the Anglo American Caribbean Commission on March 9, 1942, a cooperative effort of the United States and the United Kingdom to deal with the World War II emergency. Reorganized in 1945 as the Caribbean Commission, France and the Netherlands were included, but the life of the organization was terminated in 1957.

Concerns by British and American authorities about reports on the state of Caribbean misery—especially the Moyne Commission Report (1938), war conditions, and the impact of German submarine activity on the region made colonial defense a priority for the United States and Britain. In return for a ninety-nine year lease to establish naval and military bases in the region, fifty antiquated American naval destroyers were given to Britain. American bases were established in seven British Caribbean territories.

Each country had three representatives on the commission, one of which was designated cochair. The commission functioned as two national sections. The British Section was the Barbados-based Colonial Development and Welfare Organisation and the American section was administered from Washington, D.C., as a part of the Department of State.

Charged with the responsibility of attending to social and economic issues pertaining to the region and advising their respective governments, the commission undertook a survey of ways to cope with the basic social and economic problems of the region and formulated war emergency measures. From 1942 to 1945 the commission held seven formal meetings and organized two conferences.

The commission established two auxiliary bodies. The Caribbean Research Council was established in August 1943 to advise the commission on mutual problems of the member nations. The membership of the council included representatives from Britain, the United States, and Holland. The council established committees on agriculture, fisheries, forestry, and nutrition and later added committees on public health and medicine, industrial technology, building and engineering technology, and social services. The second auxiliary body was the West Indian Conference, a forum for the discussion of regional matters, which was first held in Barbados, March 21-30, 1944.

Over the fifteen-year period of its existence, the commission successfully directed the region's war survival strategy, identified a ten-point development program for the region that focused on the most critical issues in Caribbean development, and developed programs around them. Unemployment relief was offered through the American bases and a labor recruitment scheme. A Venereal Disease Control Center was established to provide free blood testing, and there were increased opportunities for education and training. The commission offered greater attention to regional matters, it provided the opportunity for the United States to play a larger role in the social and economic life of the region, it helped to foster increased contact between the American and British colonies, and it promoted greater information exchange and communication among the British West Indian territories. Ironically, one of its major contributions was that it provided an avenue for the growth and expression of nationalism in the region, a factor that contributed to its own demise.

■ ■ *Bibliography*

Anglo American Commission, "International Action and the Colonies." Fabian Publishers Ltd., Research Services No. 75, 1943 (CO 318/452/6 71265).

Corknan, Herbert. *Patterns of International Cooperation in the Caribbean, 1942–1969.* Dallas, Tex.: Southern Methodist University Press, 1970.

Frazier, Franklin and Eric Williams, eds. *The Economic Future of the Caribbean.* Dover, Mass.: Majority Press, 2004.

Report of the Anglo American Caribbean Commission to the Governments of the United States and Britain for the Year 1942-1943 (CO 318/421/7 71265 1943).

USA Section of the Anglo American Commission, "A Record of Progress in Facing Stern Realities." Washington, D.C., 1943.

D. RITA PEMBERTON (2005)

CARIBBEAN COMMUNITY AND COMMON MARKET (CARICOM)

■ ■ ■

In 1958 the West Indies Federation, which consisted of Barbados, Jamaica, Trinidad and Tobago, and the Windward and Leeward Islands under British control, was established with the hope of regional integration. It came to an end in 1962 with the independence of Jamaica and Trinidad and Tobago from Great Britain, but it led to the political leaders in the Caribbean hoping to strengthen their ties with a Common Services Conference that was called in mid-1962. The government of Trinidad and Tobago proposed the creation of a Caribbean Community that would consist of not only the ten members of the former federation but also of French Guiana, Suriname (formerly Dutch Guiana), Guyana (formerly British Guiana), and all the islands—both independent and nonindependent—in the Caribbean Sea. The prime minister of Trinidad and Tobago convened the first Heads of Government Conference in July 1963, which was attended by the leaders of Barbados, British Guiana, Jamaica, and Trinidad and Tobago. The July 1965 conference established a Free Trade Area, and in December 1965 the Caribbean Free Trade Association (CARIFTA) was established. The CARIFTA agreement came into effect May 1, 1968, with Anti-

gua, Barbados, Guyana, and Trinidad and Tobago participating. In July 1968 Dominica, Grenada, St. Kitts/Nevis/Anguilla, St. Lucia, and St. Vincent joined. Jamaica and Montserrat became members in August 1968, and Belize joined in May 1971.

At the seventh Heads of Government Conference in October 1972, the leaders decided to transform CARIFTA into a common market and establish the Caribbean Community. The members signed a draft in April 1973, and the Treaty of Chaguaramas, which established the Caribbean Community and Common Market (CARICOM), was signed at Chaguaramas, Trinidad, on July 4, 1973. It went into effect on August 1, 1973, among the independent countries of Barbados, Guyana, Jamaica, and Trinidad and Tobago. Eight other territories—Antigua and Barbuda, Belize, Dominica, Grenada, Monserrat, St. Kitts and Nevis, St. Lucia, and St. Vincent and the Grenadines—became full members on May 1, 1974. The Bahamas joined on July 4, 1993, Suriname on July 4, 1995. Haiti became the fifteenth member state on July 3, 2002. (However, Haiti's membership was put on hold with the ouster of President Jean-Bertrand Aristide in February 2004.) Associate members include Anguilla, the British Virgin Islands, the Turks and Caicos Islands, the Cayman Islands, and Bermuda. The fifteen member nations have a combined population of some twelve million.

CARICOM has concentrated on the promotion of cooperation, especially in human and social development, and in the integration of the economies of its members. The objectives of CARICOM include establishing a free-trade area within its member nations; improving the region's standard of living and work; full employment; accelerated, coordinated, and sustained economic development; expansion of trade and economic relations; enhanced levels of competitiveness; increased production and productivity; greater economic leverage and effectiveness; and the coordination of foreign and economic policies. The Conference of the Heads of Government, the decision-making forum and final authority for CARICOM, is made up of the heads of government of the member states, with their primary responsibility being to determine and provide policy direction. There are four minister councils within the community: The Council for Trade and Economic Development (COTED), the Council for Foreign and Community Relations (COFCOR), the Council for Human and Social Development (COHSOD), and the Council for Finance and Planning (COFAP).

The eighth conference in 1987 established the CARICOM Single Market and Economy (CSME) to promote economic issues and to allow goods, services, people, and capital to move throughout the community without tariffs

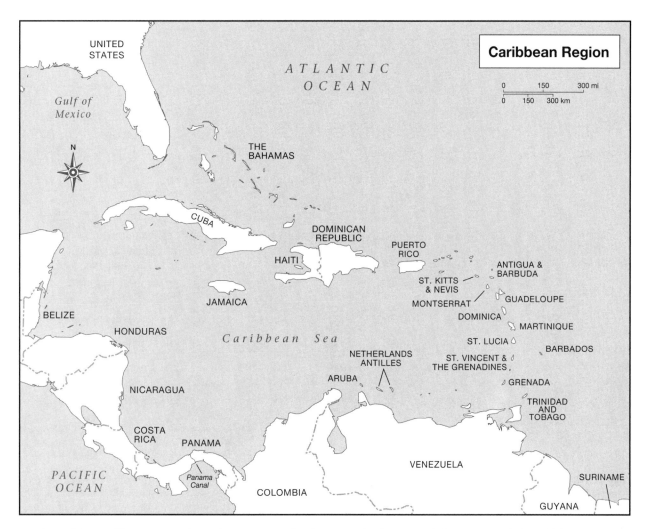

Members of the Caribbean Community and Common Market (CARICOM). The Treaty of Chaguaramas, which established CARICOM, was signed in Trinidad on July 4, 1973. Barbados, Guyana, Jamaica, and Trinidad and Tobago were the four pioneering member nations. Eight other territories, Antigua and Barbuda, Belize, Dominica, Grenada, Montserrat, St. Kitts and Nevis, St. Lucia, and St. Vincent and the Grenadines, were added the following year. The Bahamas and Suriname joined the community in the 1990s, with Haiti added as a fifteenth member state in 2002. MAP BY XNR PRODUCTIONS. THE GALE GROUP.

and restrictions; the CSME was included as part of the Treaty of Chaguaramas when it was revised in February 2002. In 1992 CARICOM established the Charter of Civil Society to recommend and develop a free press; a fair and open democratic process; respect for fundamental civil, political, economic, social, and cultural rights; the rights of women and children; respect for religious diversity; and greater government accountability. In July 1994 CARICOM established the Association of Caribbean States (ACS) to promote and implement policies and programs designed to utilize and develop the Caribbean region to attain cultural, economic, social, scientific, and technological advancement as well as promote trade and investment and various cooperative arrangements. The ACS consists of thirty-seven states and associated territories located in and around the Caribbean Basin. In 1999 the Heads of

Government also established a supreme court for the region known as the Caribbean Court of Justice (CCJ). Although the court has been in the planning stages since 1970, various disputes concerning its legal powers and authority have hindered its effectiveness. CARICOM has also mobilized a region-wide response against HIV/AIDS through the Pan-Caribbean Partnership Against HIV/AIDS (PANCAP), and its leaders also work to promote the Caribbean region as a tourist destination with more than twenty-five percent of the gross domestic product (GDP) currently provided by the tourism industry. The community also maintains a number of subsidiary organizations, including the Caribbean Disaster Emergency Response Agency (CDERA), the Caribbean Meteorological Institute (CMI), the Caribbean Environment Health Institute (CEHI), and the Caribbean Agriculture Research and De-

Colin Powell meets CARICOM ministers in Washington, D.C., 2003. *U.S. Secretary of State Colin Powell (center) poses with Caribbean Community (CARICOM) ministers prior to their meeting at the State Department. From left are Guyana Foreign Minister Samuel Insanally, Jamaican Foreign Minister Keith Knight, St. Vincent Deputy Prime Minister and Foreign Minister Louis Straker, Powell, Barbados Trade Minister Kerry Symmonds, Bahama Foreign Minister Fred Mitchell and CARICOM Secretary General Edwin Carrington.* © YURI GRIPAS/REUTERS/CORBIS

velopment Institute (CARDZ), among others. The headquarters of CARICOM is located in Georgetown, Guyana, and is headed by a secretary-general who is responsible for providing leadership to the development of the community.

CARICOM also has its own flag, which was approved by the Heads of Government Conference in November 1983. The flag features a blue background—the upper part being a light blue representing the sky and the lower part a dark blue representing the Caribbean Sea. The yellow circle in the center represents the sun. On it, printed in black, are two interlocking Cs (for Caribbean Community) in the form of broken links in a chain that symbolize both unity and a break with the community's colonial past. A narrow green ring around the sun represents the vegetation of the region.

See also West Indies Federation

■ ■ *Bibliography*

CARICOM Secretariat. *CARICOM: Our Caribbean Community—An Introduction.* Kingston, Jamaica: Ian Randle Publishers, 2005.

Charles, Jacqueline. "CARICOM Looks at Ways to Assert Influence in Region." *Miami Herald* (June 1, 2005).

Dowling, Jay. "Caribbean Common Market Has Broad Economic Agenda." *Business America* (March 23, 1992): 7.

Hall, Kenneth, ed. *Reinventing CARICOM: The Road to New Integration.* Kingston, Jamaica: Ian Randle Publishers, 2003.

Luxner, Larry. "CARICOM: 25 Years of a United Caribbean Voice." *Americas* (February, 1999): 56.

Nicholls, Colin. "The Caribbean Community." *UNESCO Courier* (October, 1986).

Pollard, Duke, and Kenneth Hall, eds. *The CARICOM System: Basic Instruments.* Kingston, Jamaica: Ian Randle Publishers, 2003.

Serbin, Andres. "Towards an Association of Caribbean States: Raising Some Awkward Questions." *Journal of Interamerican Studies and World Affairs* (winter, 1994). Available from

<http://www.findarticles.com/p/articles/mi_qa3688/
is_199401/ai_n8732131>.

CHRISTINE TOMASSINI (2005)

CARIBBEAN/NORTH AMERICAN WRITERS (CONTEMPORARY)

The work of Caribbean-American writers generally reflects a sense of rootedness in the American landscape while simultaneously expressing a connection to and knowledge of their Caribbean home cultures, be it Haiti, the Dominican Republic, Trinidad, or Jamaica. Poised between two cultures, this literature belongs equally to both spaces and reflects a Pan-Caribbean perspective. This includes Dominican American writers such as Junot Diaz, Angie Cruz, Loida Maritza Perez, Julia Alvarez, and Nelly Rosario; writers of Jamaican descent such as Patricia Powell, Colin Channer, Kwame Dawes, Claudia Rankine, Thomas Glave, Ifeona Fulani, Donna Hemans, and Shara McCallum; Haitian American writers such as Edwidge Danticat and Danielle Legros Georges; and Trinidadian writer Elizabeth Nunez. Many of these writers belong to the canon of American immigrant literature, yet they explore the tensions between Caribbean cultures in the region and the diaspora. Edwidge Danticat's *Breath, Eyes, Memory* (1994) and Julia Alvarez's *How the Garcia Girls Lost Their Accents* (1991) are novels about young women from the Caribbean coming of age in New York, where they must negotiate the cultural baggage brought from their respective homelands. Yet other novels by these authors, such as Danticat's *Farming of Bones* (1998) and Alvarez's *In the Time of Butterflies* (1994), explore a history of racial tensions in Haiti and Dominican Republic, which for Danticat culminates in the 1937 massacre of Haitian migrant laborers in the Dominican Republic, and for Alvarez concerns the making of a totalitarian president in the form of Rafael Molina Trujillo. In chronicling moments of contact, conflict, and even pleasure, these writers engage in a conversation about a Pan-Caribbean sensibility and sense of responsibility for shared regional histories.

From as early as the 1920s, with writers such as Claude McKay and Eric Walrond, early Caribbean/North American writing has been Pan-African and anticolonial in orientation—focusing on a larger black world outside of the United States and the Caribbean. In novels such as McKay's *Home to Harlem* (1928) and *Banjo* (1929), or Paule Marshall's *Praisesong for the Widow* (1983), writers have created spatial scenes where various black identities meet and discover what differences of nationality, class, and gender mean for their sense of racial connection. For McKay, socialism is the uniting factor, whereas for Marshall it is an Afrocentric spirituality.

Today's literature builds on these earlier themes, focusing on questions of diaspora and postcolonialism. Like McKay, the novels of Colin Channer (*Waiting In Vain* [1998] and *Satisfy My Soul* [2003]) deal with contemporary black diasporic subjects. Set in New York, London, and Jamaica, *Waiting in Vain* chronicles the romance of Fire, a London- and Jamaica-based Booker Prize–winning author, and Sylvia, a magazine editor who is a second-generation Caribbean-American living in Brooklyn. They meet by chance on a Manhattan street and proceed to fall in love—in spite of complications of geographical distance and the entanglements of past and present relationships. While they are both Jamaicans, class background makes all the difference. As an American immigrant of working-class Jamaican origins, Sylvia left Jamaica as a child and has never returned. In contrast, Fire is from a wealthy Jamaican family, maintains homes in London and Jamaica, and considers the latter his primary residence.

Adhering to the plot structure of the romance genre, class, geographical differences, and time spent abroad are rendered insignificant as the novel ends with the possibility of Sylvia and Fire's reconciliation. She leaves the safety of Brooklyn and goes to Jamaica in search of Fire. There she is received by the local community, which suggests the possibility of her re-integration in Jamaica, despite the years of her American absence. Significantly, while their romance starts in Brooklyn it gets resolved in Jamaica. The message here for Channer's Caribbean diasporic readers is that you can go home again, and that you will be welcomed.

Satisfy My Soul, in contrast, is a narrative of romantic failure and points to the limits of diaspora. While our contemporary moment of rapid globalization brings various black diasporic subjects together in one locale—Channer shows how distinctions of origins matter, since they shape one's worldview. Although the story begins in Jamaica, Channer goes to great length to make his characters more than Caribbean. The hero, Carey McCullough, a thirty-eight-year-old Cambridge-educated New York playwright, for example, is born in Harlem but raised in Cuba and Jamaica to a mother of Jamaican Jewish ancestry and a father who has Ghanian and southern black American roots. The heroine, Frances Carey, the owner of a small construction company in Kingston, has similar black Atlantic roots: born in Guyana, she moved to Jamaica at seventeen. But her parents are Ghanian and she still speaks Hora, her native Ghanaian language. More importantly, the narrative emphasizes that she also lived and worked in the United States as a jazz singer. While their roots and routes span the black Atlantic world, the novel still retains a Jamaican undercurrent. But rather than the romantic happy ending, this novel presents a love plot in which differences between lovers are irreconcilable.

Channer's treatment of cosmopolitan black characters who are at home in the world, yet who cannot resolve differences of interests to sustain a lasting love relationship, points to the limits of diaspora. These differences are predicated upon how various diasporic sites distinctly mark and make each subject. Black diasporic subjects carry their old world histories with them, and these histories complicate and often compromise how they relate to each other. In this novel, the diaspora does not become a space where people meet and reconcile differences, as in *Waiting in Vain*. Instead, it is a place where differences collide and people have to find a new language to communicate across the gulf of divergent imperial histories. It is the failure to create new modes of communication across ideological borderlines, in the end, that makes the gulf unbridgeable.

The relation between sexuality and national belonging is another theme explored by Caribbean-American writers. Michelle Cliff, Thomas Glave, and Patricia Powell, for example, address how a homosexual identity impacts one's sense of belonging to the nation-state. Powell's *Pagoda* (1998) tells the story of Lau A-yin Ling, who faces famine, clan fighting, and gender restrictions in nineteenth-century patriarchal China. Then, disguised as a young man, she travels to the West Indies. In her oceanic passage in search of freedom, Ling's true gender and sexual identity is uncovered by Cecil, the white shipmaster. With no law to protect her at sea, Cecil repeatedly rapes Ling aboard the ship, despite her numerous attempts to kill him. By the time they arrive in the new world, Ling is pregnant. After giving birth to her daughter, Lizabeth, Ling cloaks her female identity and assumes a Chinese maleness in order to survive as a Chinese single mother on the island. When Lizabeth is two years old, Cecil establishes Ling as a local male shopkeeper and renames her Lowe. To complete the masquerade, he brings Miss Sylvie, who appears to be a white creole, to play mother to Lizabeth and wife to Lowe. Another level of passing ensues here, as Miss Sylvie is, in fact, a black woman who was married to a white man. When her pregnancies result in visibly black babies, she kills her husband before he kills her for "darkening" and, therefore, bringing shame to his white patrilineage. Cecil joins these two nonblack, but "not quite white," women together in marital union, protecting the secrets of their racial and gender identities, while they secure his economic interests. Furthermore, with the profits he makes from his trafficking in enslaved and indentured women's bodies, Cecil sets them up in a house that "stood grandly on the very pinnacle of the hill," and from which they "gazed down at the villagers' mud-and-wattle, thatch-roofed hovels and huts" (p. 103). Based on public appearances, the villagers would have envied Lowe, a newly arrived Chinese immigrant, for so quickly forming relationships with that society's elite and living an idealized interracial heterosexual romance. What they do not yet know, however, is the private trauma Ling relives every day for her "apparent" privilege. This gender and sexuality passing, with the accompanying loss of body, language, history, and family is the drama that unfolds.

With this focus on the violated sexed body, Powell belongs to a new generation—a third wave—of Caribbean women writers. These women explore questions of sexual violence enacted against women and girls. In previous generations, these stories were protected through silence and concealment in national and family histories. In this post-postcolonial moment, these writers excavate those buried stories and explore the existing cultural narratives that enable various kinds of sexual trauma against women to continue relatively unchecked by the culture. Among these writers are Edwidge Danticat, Elizabeth Nunez, Nelly Rosario, Patricia Powell, Julia Alvarez, Angie Cruz, Shani Motoo, Dionne Brand, and Marlene Nourbese Phillip.

Through their fictional narratives, third-wave writers highlight that sex is one vehicle through which power is exercised and maintained over the minutest details of women's lives. Not content to have the politics of sexuality severed from other sociopolitical issues, trivialized, or rendered "merely" private, these writings address issues of domestic violence, sex work, and sexual abuse, making explicit the implications of these occurrences for women's experiences of citizenship, of belonging to a national community with rights of protection. Challenging dichotomous readings that celebrate Caribbean women's resistance on the one hand, or lament their victimization on the other, these writers show that women are not without power to reproduce sexual violence themselves. Such narrative emphases go against conventions of respectability and received narratives, and also allow for a more complicated understanding of the relationship between the individual body, the state, and society. Put another way, third-wave texts make explicit the linkages between the Caribbean female body, sexuality and citizenship.

At once (though not simply) queer, feminist, immigrant, Latino, African American, American minority literature, or science fiction, Caribbean North American writings further complicate our understanding of global black identities and what it means to be a Caribbean person in the twenty-first century.

See also African Diaspora; Danticat, Edwidge; Literature of the English-Speaking Caribbean; Marshall, Paule; McKay, Claude; Walrond, Eric Derwent; Women Writers of the Caribbean

■ ■ *Bibliography*

Alvarez, Julia. *How the Garcia Girls Lost Their Accents*. Chapel Hill, N.C.: Algonquin Books of Chapel Hill, 1991.

Alvarez, Julia. *In the Time of Butterflies*. Chapel Hill, N.C.: Algonquin Books, 1994.

Bell, Beverly. *Walking on Fire: Haitian Women's Stories of Survival and Resistance*. Ithaca, N.Y.: Cornell University Press, 2001.

Channer, Colin. *Waiting in Vain*. New York: One World/Ballantine, 1998.

Channer, Colin. *Satisfy My Soul*. New York: One World/Ballantine, 2003.

Chauncy, Miriam. *Searching for Safe Spaces: Afro-Caribbean Women Writers in Exile*. Philadelphia: Temple University Press, 1997.

Cliff, Michelle. *No Telephone to Heaven*. New York: Dutton, 1987.

Cobham, Rhonda. "Revisioning Our Kumblas: Transforming Feminist and Nationalist Agendas in Three Caribbean Women's Texts." *Callaloo* 16, no. 1 (Winter 1993): 44–64.

Cruz, Angie. *Soledad*. New York: Simon and Schuster, 2001.

Cruz, Angie. *Let it Rain Coffee*. New York: Simon and Schuster, 2005.

Danticat, Edwidge. *Breath, Eyes, Memory*. New York: Vintage Books, 1994.

Danticat, Edwidge. *The Farming of Bones*. New York: Soho Press, 1998.

Danticat, Edwidge. *The Dewbreakers*. New York: Knopf, 2004.

Davies, Boyce Carole. *Black Women, Writing, and Identity: Migrations of the Subject*. London and New York: Routledge, 1994.

Davies, Boyce Carole, and Elaine Savory Fido, eds. *Out of the Kumbla: Caribbean Women and Literature*. Trenton, N.J.: Africa World Press, 1990.

Dawes, Kwame. *Requiem: A Lament for the Dead*. Leeds, UK: Peepal Tree Press, 1996.

Dawes, Kwame. *Midland*. Columbus: Ohio University Press, 2000.

Diaz, Junot. *Drown*. New York: Riverhead Books, 1996.

Donnell, Alison, and Sarah Lawson Welsh. *The Routledge Reader in Caribbean Literature*. London, New York: Routledge, 1996.

Edmondson, Belinda. *Making Men: Gender, Literary Authority and Women's Writing in Caribbean Narrative*. Durham, N.C.: Duke University Press, 1999.

Fulani, Ifeona. *Seasons of Dust*. New York: Writers and Readers Publishing, 1997.

Glave, Thomas. *Whose Song? and Other Stories*. San Francisco: City Lights Books, 2000.

Glave, Thomas. *Words to Our Now: Imagination and Dissent*. Minneapolis: University of Minnesota Press, 2005.

Hemans, Donna. *River Woman: A Novel*. New York: Washington Square Press, 2003.

Kincaid, Jamaica. *Annie John*. New York: Farrar, Straus, Giroux, 1985.

Kincaid, Jamaica. *Lucy*. New York: Farrar Straus Giroux, 1990.

Marshall, Paule. *Brown Girl, Brownstones*. New York: Random House, 1959.

Marshall, Paule. *Praisesong for the Widow*. New York: Putnam, 1983.

Marshall, Paule. *Daughters*. New York: Plume Books, 1992.

Marshall, Paule. *The Fisher King*. New York: Scribner, 2001.

McCallum, Shara. *Song of Thieves*. Pittsburgh, Pa.: University of Pittsburgh Press, 2003.

McCallum, Shara. *The Water Between Us*. Pittsburgh, Pa.: University of Pittsburgh Press, 1999.

McKay, Claude. *Home to Harlem*. New York: Harper & Brothers, 1928.

McKay, Claude. *Banjo: A Novel Without a Plot*. New York: Harper & Brothers, 1929.

McKay, Claude. *A Long Way from Home*. New York, L. Furman, 1937.

Nunez, Elizabeth. *Bruised Hibiscus*. Seattle, Wash.: Seal Press, 2000.

O'Callaghan, Evelyn. *Woman Version: Theoretical Approaches to West Indian Fiction by Women*. New York: St. Martin's, 1993.

Perez, Loida Maritza. *Geographies of Home*. New York: Penguin, 2000.

Powell, Patricia. *The Pagoda*. New York: Alfred A. Knopf, 1998.

Powell, Patricia. *A Small Gathering of Bones*. New York: Beacon Press, 2003.

Rankine, Claudia. *Nothing in Nature is Private*. Cleveland, Ohio: Cleveland State University Poetry Center, 1994.

Rankine, Claudia. *The End of the Alphabet*. New York: Grove Press, 1998.

Rankine, Claudia. *Don't Let Me Be Lonely: An American Lyric*. Minneapolis, Minn.: Graywolf Press, 2004.

Rosario, Nelly. *Song of the Water Saints*. New York: Pantheon Books, 2002.

Sanon, Barbara. "Black Crows and Zombie Girls." In *The Butterfly's Way: Voices from the Haitian Dyaspora in the United States*, pp. 43–48. New York: Soho Press, 2001.

Smith, Faith. "Genders and Sexualities." *Small Axe 7*, March 2000, special issue.

Walrond, Eric. *Tropic Death*. New York, Boni & Liveright, 1926. Reprint, New York: Collier Books, 1972.

DONETTE A. FRANCIS (2005)

CARIBBEAN THEATER, ANGLOPHONE

To understand the nature of the development of Caribbean theater over the centuries, as well as the form of theater that is now evolving in the region, it is important to know something of the history of the Caribbean. The experience of colonization and the type of slavery that existed there have left an indelible mark on the creative impulses of the people. Theater in the Caribbean, therefore, must be seen as having various stages of development. These stages are defined by historical periods, beginning with the meeting of African and European cultures, then the period after Emancipation, followed by a more classical form of theater, and finally a period of ritualistic and popular expression.

The source of Caribbean drama is in the folklore, myth, and rituals of the people. There are two types of rituals: (1) the sacred rituals, which include a variety of social, spiritual, and religious actions performed privately by and for the participants who are integral to the ceremony; and (2) profane rituals, which are those that make everyday life meaningful, predictable, and comfortable. Spectators are allowed to watch these profane rituals, and they may even participate in them. Included in all these rituals are the religious practices of the Indians, the Chinese, and the other peoples who were brought to the Caribbean. Unlike the indentured laborers who were brought to the region with a promise of returning home, the Africans, who were chattel slaves, suffered a violent sense of dispossession after being prevented from returning to Africa. Loss, dispossession, alienation, and a lifetime of imposed poverty resulted in a search for a cultural identity, which is a major theme in the literature of the Caribbean.

In their early theatrical presentations, slaves took the opportunity to ridicule their oppressors, and to console themselves, by presenting the victorious efforts of small, cunning animals. They also sought relief in entertainment through drumming and dancing. This entertainment took place on days when they were free from work, such as Sundays, Christmas, and Easter, as well as on certain work-related holidays, such as the end of the sugarcane harvest. Many of the communal festivals of black people in the Caribbean—such as Papa Diable or Papa Jab in Trinidad, La Rose and La Marguerite in Saint Lucia, Jonkunnu in Jamaica and the Bahamas, Crop-Over in Barbados, Masquerade in Guyana, and even the short skits performed during the renditions of calypsos—have their origin in these entertainments.

Freedom and voting rights gave the masses the opportunity to question what had been presented to them as theater, providing a chance to found a theater that expressed their own aspirations. It was obvious that this would require that they ignore the theatrical fare given to them by the plantocracy. The first National Hero of Jamaica, Marcus Garvey, was the first proponent of black pride in black culture, and between 1930 and 1932 he produced four plays with large casts. Unfortunately, these plays have been lost to posterity. In 1941, Greta and Henry Fowler founded the Little Theatre Movement and introduced the Pantomime, based on the traditional English Pantomime. The Jamaica National Pantomime remains faithful to the structure of the traditional English Pantomime, presenting the same type of traditional characters and a pervading theme of good overcoming evil. Louise Bennett, the *grande dame* of Jamaican theater, was the leading Pantomime figure for many years. She played alongside Ranny Williams, and these two actors remain unforgettable icons of the Jamaica Pantomime. The Little Theatre Movement still produces the National Pantomime, though the social commentary, the content, and artistic form are more definitively Caribbean than when it was introduced by the Fowlers. Also in the 1940s, the Yard Theater was founded in Barbados, as was the Theatre Guild in Guyana.

In the early 1950s, Errol Hill (1921–2003), a leading Trinidadian playwright, called for a national theater that truly represented the cultural attitudes, expressions, and aspirations of the people of Trinidad and Tobago. Over the course of his life, he produced and directed over 120 plays and pageants in the West Indies, England, the United States, and Nigeria. He wrote eleven plays, of which *Man Better Man* is considered a Caribbean classic. The poet and playwright Derek Walcott, from Saint Lucia, made his appearance on the scene in the 1950s. A winner of the Nobel Prize in Literature in 1992, Walcott sometimes writes plays in verse, and his work, though firmly aligned to the ancient classical drama of Europe, is unmistakably Caribbean in content. He founded The Little Carib Theatre in Trinidad.

The 1950s also saw the appearance of a number of playwrights who were committed to presenting a mirror of society. "Yard" plays, as they were called, examined the conflicts of life in low-income communities, the tenement yard, and rural areas. Some of the playwrights involved in this movement were Barry Reckord from Jamaica; Slade Hopkinson from Guyana; and Errol Hill, Eric Roach, and Douglas Archibald from Trinidad. The Yard Theatre in Jamaica was part of this movement, and the Trinidadian playwright Marina Omowale Maxwell was its chief exponent. Unfortunately, yard theater had a rather short life span.

One of the outstanding modern Caribbean playwrights is Errol John (1924–1988) of Trinidad. Two of his plays, *The Tout* and *Moon on a Rainbow Shawl*, have become Caribbean classics. Other playwrights who wrote works that can be classified as social realism also came to the fore at this time. These writers dealt not only with the social issues affecting low-income communities, but with those important to a cross-section of Caribbean society. Among these playwrights are Basil Dawkins, Ginger Knight, Carmen Tipling, Pat Cumper, and Trevor Rhone from Jamaica; Stanley French from Saint Lucia; Ronald Amoroso from Trinidad; and Rudolph Wallace from St. Thomas. Of these playwrights, Trevor Rhone has received the widest international acclaim. His most famous work, written largely in the vernacular, is *Old Story Time,* which makes use of significant Caribbean folk forms. His other well-known works are *Smile Orange, School's Out, Two Can Play,* and the screenplay for the 1988 film *Milk and Honey.* He is also an actor, and his performance in his own play *Bellas Gate Boy* (2002) was a one-man *tour de force.*

Another playwright who is highly esteemed is Earl Lovelace (b. 1935) from Trinidad. He came into prominence first as a novelist. In both his novels and his plays he is deeply concerned about the human condition. Another prominent playwright is Dominican artist, actor, and director Alwin Bully. His most memorable plays are *Streak, Folk Nativity, Pio-Pio, McB* and *The Ruler of Hiroona.*

Under the aegis of the Little Theatre in Kingston, the Jamaica School of Drama was established in 1969, and a permanent home for the school was erected in 1976. This is the only theater school in the English-speaking Caribbean, and it has brought together theater practitioners from all over the region. It has, however, been plagued by a lack of funds from its inception. In 1979, Jean Small, a tutor at the school, devised a course titled "A Caribbean Laboratory," which explored Caribbean folk forms in order to arrive at a Caribbean theater aesthetic. The research done in this laboratory influenced much of the ritual theater that took place in that period. Dennis Scott, a poet, playwright, dancer, choreographer, and theater director, was the then director of the school.

One of the interesting outcomes of the work done at the Jamaica School of Drama was the formation in 1983 of Groundwork Theater, a company formed by graduates of the school. They performed in schools using the popular form of theater that marks this period of theater, particularly in Jamaica, in which the structure of the African ritual, the use of significant ritual objects, the function of ritual agents, and the use of sound and movement were all studied and applied to relevant everyday Caribbean

human issues. Scott displayed his adeptness in using ritual as an act that binds human communities in his outstanding play *An Echo in the Bone.* His other major play is *Dog.*

Following in this mode of ritual theater was the Trinidadian playwright Rawle Gibbons. His first full-length play, which made use of ritual, was *Shepherd,* which opened at the Jamaica School of Drama in 1981. Gibbons also became the director of the Centre for Creative and Festival Arts on the Saint Augustine Campus of the University of the West Indies. In 1991 he staged his calypso musical *Sing de Chorus,* which won five national Cacique Awards. The show is a docudrama on the development of calypso and Trinidadian society. Other ritual playwrights are Marina Omowale Maxwell, whose *Play Mas* is based on Trinidad's Carnival, while her *Hounsi Kanzo* is based on a Haitian ritual of consciousness. Zeno Constance Obi, a secondary school teacher, writes mainly for his student actors, and his play *The Ritual* has become the play of choice for teenagers. A splinter group of the Theatre Guild in Guyana commissioned the multitalented Guyanese playwright Michael Gilkes to write a play. The result was *Couvade,* which was performed at the first Carifesta, held in Guyana in 1972. The uniqueness of this play is that it makes use of an Amerindian ritual, and that it deals with the subject of Caribbean integration. In 1979 Gilkes settled in Barbados as a member of staff of the Cave Hill campus of the University of the West Indies. He became the founder and first artistic director of Stage One, the leading theatre company in Barbados.

Popular theater was a reaction to the middle-class proscenium-arch type of theater. There were two important factors that identified popular theater: (1) it was led by an academic with formal knowledge of theater; and (2) it utilized the culture and aesthetics of the working class. In Jamaica, Ralph Holness was the founder of a sub-genre of popular theater called "roots theater," which focused on the lives of the working-class populace and the inner city. These plays were performed in unconventional spaces, such as a cinema that was no longer used as such, a section of a bar, or a space in a restaurant close to a bar. The proximity to a bar seemed to be very important as an adjunct of the performance, and the intermission of the included light entertainment of singing and dancing. Roots theater placed emphasis on the use of nation language, such as the Creole languages of the region, and it was usually done in a humorous way. This theater of the masses spread all over the Caribbean.

In 1977 in Jamaica, under the Michael Manley government, an "Emergency Employment," or "Crash," program was introduced. A number of inner-city women found employment in this program as street sweepers.

Under the same government, the Bureau of Women's Affairs was set up, and that office decided to put on a show to celebrate the Annual Workers' Day. The street sweepers were invited to participate in this show, and when asked what they would like to do, thirteen of them decided that they wanted to act in memory of plays they had done as children in Sunday school. As they had no theater experience, the Jamaica School of Drama was approached to assist, and a member of staff there, Honor Ford Smith, volunteered to work with them. As the women could not read or write, she developed a form of oral theater using Jamaican Creole, the medium of expression with which they were most confident. The group dubbed themselves the Sistren Theatre Collective, and they were the first to proudly use Jamaican Creole in theater. Their first performance, *Downpression Get a Blow*, lamented the abandonment of a move to improve the conditions of factory workers.

The early work of Sistren was mainly improvisational, and the content of their plays was based on their life experiences. Their second major production *Bellywoman Bangarang*, produced in 1978, was an award-winning play that established Sistren as the new grassroots voice for women in the 1970s. Sistren's work concentrated on the plight of women, as well as the universality of women's issues. They became internationally recognized, although their plays were performed in Jamaican Creole using symbols, colors, dance forms, music, and ritual that came directly from their culture. An oral history project on their personal lives, their hardships, and their courage was documented by Honor Ford Smith in the publication *Lionheart Gal*. Some of their other important plays are *Bandool-oou Version*, and *Muffet Inna Alla Wi*. Hertencer Lindsay directed *QPH*, a play on the lives of three well-known women living in a retirement home. In 1980, Jean Small directed *Nana Yah* which was based on the life of the Jamaican National Heroine, Nanny of the Maroons, and from then on Sistren started creating plays on subjects outside of their personal lives but relevant to the lives of all women.

During the turbulent period of the 1970s in Jamaica, this type of activist theater had its place and was very popular, but with the change of government in the 1980s the mood changed and the freedom of expression that was experienced under the Manley government disappeared. Sistren had by this time acquired a home base, and they had created an income-generating screen-printing business. Their cushion covers, bags, curtains, and wall hangings depicted themes from their work. Unfortunately, as the activist leaders of the group moved on to other jobs, and as members of Sistren themselves started to look for opportunities outside of Jamaica, the original group fell apart

and the screen-printing work came to an end. Sistren now mainly conducts workshops in communities and schools, and only four of the original thirteen members are currently residing in Jamaica. A later production, directed by Jean Small, was *Mirro Mirro,* a play about women's sexuality and incest. In the 1990s, however, the audiences in Jamaica were searching for entertainments that offered relief from the stresses and strains of life, and serious discussions of women's issues were no longer appealing. The play, therefore, was not financially successful.

In Guyana in the 1990s, a few stalwarts, such as Al Creighton and Ron Robinson, kept theater activities going in spite of the inactivity of the Theatre Guild. Directors turned to the National Cultural Centre as the main theater space. Theater at the center gave rise to a large proletariat audience. The Link Show, a satirical commentary on current events in Guyana, is the only current annual production. A committee has been set up, however, with the support of the government, to refurbish the Theatre Guild.

In Jamaica, the commercial theater production company Jambiz International was formed in 1996. Their productions take place at the Centerstage Theatre, in Kingston, and they concentrate on humorous entertainment with actors such as Oliver Samuels, Glen Campbell, Christopher Daley, and Claudette Pious. Their main playwright is Patrick Brown. They also take their work to places such as London, New York, Miami, Atlanta, Los Angeles, and Toronto.

Most theater practitioners in the Caribbean cannot afford to be engaged on a full-time basis in theater. In Jamaica, the prolific playwright Basil Dawkins is one of the few practitioners who works professionally in the theater. Most of his plays are directed by Buddy Pouyat, and he regularly takes his productions to England, the United States, and other parts of the Caribbean region. His work analyzes serious current social issues in an entertaining manner. His plays feature such well-known actors as Charles Hyatt, Karen Harriott, Volier Johnson, and Leonie Forbes. In Grenada, the Heritage Theatre Company offers light fare in the form of situational theatrical performances. Grenada also stages an annual Spice Festival, which consists of productions in which laughter is the main ingredient. The Cultural Division of the Antigua government promotes theater activity and exports their productions to neighboring islands. In 2001, theater practitioners in Jamaica came together to form the Jamaica Association of Dramatic Artists (JADA), with the determination to improve the quality of theater in the island. In 2002, JADA organized their first Script Festival as a first step to acquiring a stock of quality plays.

A genre of theater that is becoming increasingly important in the Caribbean is storytelling. Louise Bennett, through her poetry and storytelling written in Jamaican Creole, has helped give the Jamaican people a sense of self and a cultural identity. The Trinidadian storyteller Paul Keens-Douglas has similarly used Trinidadian Creole in his poems and stories, and he has helped to establish storytelling as a respectable form of theater. Storytelling is maintained in Saint Lucia by George "Fish" Alphonse, while Ricardo Keens-Douglas has been an important practitioner in Grenada. In Guyana, Desrey Foster, an academic in the Amerindian Research Unit of the University of Guyana, is the only established Amerindian storyteller in the region. There are also other young storytellers in the region, such as Joan Andrea Hutchinson, Amina Blackwood-Meeks, and AdZiko Simba. Storytelling has influenced Jean Small's one-woman performances, and her *Black Woman's Tale* has been performed internationally.

Twelve of the Caribbean islands came together in 1997 to form the Caribbean Regional Alliance (CARA) which is the regional representative body to the International Amateur Theatre Association (IATA). The first CARA Theater Festival was held in Trinidad, hosted by the National Drama Association of Trinidad and Tobago. Since CARA was established, IATA has been forced to include Spanish as one of its working languages.

Since 2000, the University of the West Indies has been organizing an Inter-Campus Foreign Language Theatre Festival, which takes place each year at one of the three campuses of the University—Mona Campus in Jamaica, Saint Augustine Campus in Trinidad, and Cave Hill Campus in Barbados—and only Anglophone students who are studying a foreign language are allowed to participate.

See also Bennett, Louise; Creole Languages of the Americas; Garvey, Marcus; Hill, Errol; Walcott, Derek

■ ■ *Bibliography*

Allison, Helen. *Sistren Song: Popular Theatre in Jamaica.* London: War on Want, 1986.

Fido, Elaine. "Radical Woman: Woman and Theatre in the Anglophone Caribbean." In *Critical Issues in West Indian Literature: Selected Papers from West Indian Literature Conferences, 1981–1983,* edited by Erika S. Smilowitz and Roberta Q. Knowles. Parkersburg, Iowa: Caribbean Books, 1984.

Harrison, Paul Carter, Victor Walker, II, and Gus Edwards, eds. *Black Theatre: Ritual Performance in the African Diaspora.* Philadelphia, Pa.: Temple University Press, 2002.

Herskovits, Melville J. *The Myth of the Negro Past.* New York, 1941. Reprint, Boston: Beacon Press, 1990.

King, Bruce. *Derek Walcott and West Indian Drama.* Oxford, U.K.: Clarendon Press, 1995.

Ogunbiyi, Yemi. *Drama and Theatre in Nigeria: A Critical Source Book.* Lagos: Nigeria Magazine Books, 1981.

Omotoso, Kole. *The Theatrical into Theater: A Study of Drama and Theatre in the English-Speaking Caribbean.* London: New Beacon Books, 1982.

Stone, Judy. *Theatre.* Studies in West Indian Literature series. London: Macmillan, 1994.

JEAN SMALL (2005)

CARMICHAEL, STOKELY

JUNE 29, 1941
NOVEMBER 15, 1998

■ ■ ■

Born in Port of Spain, Trinidad, Stokely Standiford Churchill Carmichael, an activist, graduated from the Bronx High School of Science in 1960 and received a bachelor's degree in philosophy from Howard University in 1964. During his college years he participated in a variety of civil rights demonstrations sponsored by the Congress of Racial Equality (CORE), the Nonviolent Action Group (NAG), and the Student Nonviolent Coordinating Committee (SNCC). As a freedom rider, he was arrested in 1961 for violating Mississippi segregation laws and spent seven weeks in Parchman Penitentiary. After college, he worked with the Mississippi Summer Project, directed SNCC voter-registration efforts in Lowndes County, Alabama, and helped organize black voters through the Lowndes County Freedom Organization.

Elected SNCC chairman in 1966, Carmichael took an outspoken, militant stance that helped distance SNCC from the moderate leadership of competing civil rights organizations. A chief architect and spokesperson for the new Black Power ideology, Carmichael coauthored (with Charles V. Hamilton) *Black Power* (1967) and published a collection of his essays and addresses, *Stokely Speaks* (1971). He left his SNCC post in 1967. The next year he was made prime minister of the Black Panther Party; in 1969 he quit the Black Panthers and became an organizer for Kwame Nkrumah's All-African People's Revolutionary Party. Studies with Nkrumah of Ghana and Sékou Touré of Guinea confirmed his Pan-Africanism and, in 1978, moved him to change his name to Kwame Ture. For the last thirty years of his life he made Conakry, Guinea, his home, and he continued his work in political education, condemning Western imperialism, Zionism, and capitalism while promoting the goal of a unified socialist Africa. He died of prostate cancer in 1998.

See also Black Panther Party for Self-Defense; Congress of Racial Equality (CORE); Student Nonviolent Coordinating Committee (SNCC)

Stokely Carmichael (1941–1998). *Carmichael, one of the most influential leaders of the Student Non-Violent Coordinating Committee (SNCC) during the early 1960s, became the center of controversy when he articulated his thoughts about "Black Power" before assembled television cameras during a march in Mississippi in 1965.* AP/WIDE WORLD PHOTOS

Stokely Carmichael

"We are going to use the term 'Black Power' and we are going to define it because Black Power speaks to us."

FROM SPEECH ON BLACK POWER, UNIVERSITY OF CALIFORNIA–BERKELEY, JULY 28, 1966. REPRINTED IN JOHN BRACEY, AUGUST MEIER, AND ELLIOTT RUDWICK, EDS. *BLACK NATIONALISM IN AMERICA*. INDIANAPOLIS: BOBBS-MERILL, 1970, P. 470.

■ ■ *Bibliography*
Carmichael, Stokely, and Ekwueme Michael Thelwell. *Ready for Revolution: The Life and Struggles of Stokely Carmichael (Kwame Ture)*. New York: Scribner, 2003.

WILLIAM L. VAN DEBURG (1996)
Updated by author 2005

CARNEIRO, EDISON

AUGUST 12, 1912
DECEMBER 2, 1972

Edison Carneiro was born in Salvador, Bahia. In addition to earning a law degree in 1935, he dedicated his life to journalism, the study of black culture and folklore, and political militancy. At every step he sought to defend communist ideals and Brazil's Afro-descendant population.

During the 1930s, influenced by his family and by larger debates about the role of blacks in Brazilian society—especially works by Gilberto Freyre, Renato Mendonça, and Artur Ramos—Carneiro became one of the most well-known and effective advocates of Afro-Brazilian studies. In 1932 he presented two essays at the First Afro-Brazilian Congress in Recife, both of which previewed future interests: "A Situação do negro no Brasil" (The Situation of the Black in Brazil) and a study of African-influenced religion titled "Xangô."

Between 1936 and 1937, Carneiro prepared and published his first books, *Religiões Negras* (Black Religions) and *Negros Bantus: Notas de ethnographia religiosa e de folklore* (Black Bantus: Ethnographic Notes on Religion and Folklore). During the same period, he collaborated with Aydano Couto Ferraz and Reginaldo Guimarães to organize the Second Afro-Brazilian Congress, in Salvador. According to contemporary accounts, the second gathering was largely successful, despite criticisms made by Gilberto Freyre, the luminary scholar who organized the First Congress but publicly denounced the second for being disorganized.

In addition to Brazilian intellectuals, the conference in Salvador brought together foreign scholars such as Melville Herskovits, Donald Pierson, and (from Cuba) Salvador Garcia Agüero. Participants discussed themes ranging from religion, music, dance, class relations, race, and culture to assessments of the study of blacks in Brazilian history and culture. The conference produced a volume titled *O Negro no Brasil* (The Black in Brazil), published in 1940 by Civilização Brasileira.

The Second Congress was also notable for the participation and presentations made by leaders from Salvador's *terreiros*: communities dedicated to the worship of Candomblé, a popular African-derived religion. Those notable participants included Martiniano do Bonfim (during the late nineteenth century an informant for Nina Rodrigues, a leading researcher at the Bahia Medical School who took particular interest in Afro-Brazilian religion), Manoel Bernardino da Paixão, Manuel Vitorino dos Santos, and Eugênia Ana dos Santos. Dos Santos, better known as Donha Aninha, hosted a party for the conference's participants at the *terreiro* of her Axé do Opô Afonjá congregation.

The Second Congress also led to the founding of the "Union of Afro-Brazilian Sects of Bahia," which united all of the Bahian Candomblé communities. The federation's larger purpose was to fight persecution against Candomblé and to defend religious freedom. With the support of Carneiro, Martiniano do Bonfim won the presidency. The conference also helped alter the way that politicians and the press treated African-influenced religions in Bahia, a change affected largely by the writings of Carneiro and the increased exposure that religious and black studies had won in academic circles.

Carneiro's time in Bahian *terreiros* and his relationships with religious leaders allowed him to record important ethnographic observations during the 1930s. He also facilitated research by the likes of Donald Pierson, Ruth Landes, and Roger Bastide. At the onset of President Getúlio Vargas's dictatorial *Estado Novo* (New State), Carneiro found political refuge in the house of Donha Aninha. In the preface to *Negros Bantus,* Carneiro thanked the religious leaders, as well as the *capoeiristas* (practitioners of *capoeira*, a combination of martial art and dance) and samba musicians (samba combined musical streams from Africa, Europe, and the Americas, becoming by the 1920s and 1930s the de facto national rhythm), naming them all as the book's collective author. Carneiro's relationship with those whom he studied would mark his oeuvre for the rest of his career.

After moving to Rio de Janeiro in 1939, Carneiro continued writing while remaining active in academic and political circles. In addition to dozens of articles and encyclopedia entries, he published widely read books, such as *Candomblés da Bahia* (1948), *Antologia do Negro Brasileiro* (1950), *Linguagem Popular da Bahia* (1951), *O Negro em Minas Gerais* (1956), *A Sabedoria Popular* (1957), *Samba de Umbigada* (1961), *Ladinos e Crioulos* (1964), and *Dinâmica do Folclore* (1965). *Folguedos Tradicionais* was published posthumously in 1974.

With the organization of the Brazilian Folklore Movement in the late 1940s, and with increased government interest, Carneiro assumed a crucial role in national projects to preserve folklore. In 1961, he was named executive director of the Campaign in Defense of Folklore, leaving the post three years later after a coup established the military regime that would rule until 1985. Even after the coup, Carneiro remained an active intellectual, and in 1966 he traveled to Africa, chosen by the Ministry of Foreign Relations to represent Brazil at the First Black Art Festival in Dakar, Senegal.

Carneiro's interest in folklore is indicative of his larger desire to understand and explain the formation of Brazilian culture. To Carneiro, Africans and their descendants made enormous contributions to that culture, but in a 1953 article (included in *Ladinos e Crioulos*) he pushed his contemporaries to see "the Negro as a Brazilian with black skin" (Carneiro, 1964, p. 117). By doing so, he challenged the notions that black populations were isolated from the rest of Brazil and that studying them meant *only* studying Africa. The "Afro-Brazilian phase," which made blacks strangers in Brazil, would be definitively closed. Carneiro considered the search for a black cultural personality a "forced Americanization of the problem." Instead, he sought details about what he saw as a reciprocal relationship between whites and blacks in Brazil.

In 1962 Carneiro organized another conference, this time in order to discuss and implement strategies to protect and preserve samba music. The conference's participants declared samba to be a unique manifestation of Brazilianness (they called samba, among other things, the "legitimate expression of our people" and "one of the cultural manifestations that most clearly distinguishes our nationality") and felt the music to be threatened by the influence of international music. Participants issued a manifesto titled "Carta do Samba" which identified *samba* schools (associations that, in addition to serving as community centers throughout the year, organize parades and events during Carnival) as the guardians of traditional samba. Having already established numerous links between academic and nonacademic circles, Carneiro was well connected among the schools, just as he had been among Candomblé communities in Salvador during the 1930s. In 1960 he received honorary titles from three of the oldest and most famous samba schools: Portela, Mangueira, and Salgueiro.

See also Black Press in Brazil; Candomblé; Folklore; Race and Education in Brazil; Samba

■ ■ *Bibliography*

Carneiro, Edison. *Carta do Samba: aprovada pelo I Congresso Nacional do Samba, 28 de novembro/2 de dezembro de 1962.* Rio de Janeiro: Ministério da Educação e Cultura, Campanha de Defesa do Folclore Brasileiro, 1962.

Carneiro, Edison. *Ladinos e Crioulos, estudos sobre o negro no Brasil.* Rio de Janeiro: Civilização Brasileira, 1964.

Carneiro, Edison. *Religiões Negras, Negros Bantus,* 2d ed. Rio de Janeiro: Civilização Brasileira, 1981.

O Negro no Brasil. Congresso Afro-Brasileiro 2 (Bahia), 1940. Rio de Janeiro: Civilização Brasileira, 1940.

Oliveira, Freitas Waldir e Lima, Vivaldo Costa, ed. *Cartas de Edison Carneiro a Artur Ramos.* São Paulo, Brazil: Corrupio, 1987.

MARTHA ABREU (2005)
Translated by Marc Hertzman

CARNEY, WILLIAM H.

C. 1840
DECEMBER 9, 1908

▪▪▪

First black winner of the Congressional Medal of Honor, William Carney was born to a slave woman and her free husband in Norfolk, Virginia. When his master died, Carney, aged fourteen, and his mother were manumitted. Carney studied for a time at a school run secretly by a minister. He also worked at sea with his father. In 1856 Carney's family moved to New Bedford, Massachusetts. He joined a church there and studied for the ministry. In February 1863 Carney enlisted in the Fifty-Fourth Regiment of Massachusetts Volunteer Infantry, the first African-American regiment recruited by the United States Army.

On July 18, 1863, the Fifty-fourth Massachusetts led the charge against Fort Wagner on Morris Island, South Carolina. Carney caught the Union colors when the flag bearer was wounded by an exploding shell. Carney made his way alone to the outer wall of the fortress, until advancing Confederate troops forced him back. Although he was shot twice and had to crawl on his knees, he kept the flag aloft until he reached his company. While he crept back in retreat under fire, he was shot again before reaching safety. Upon reaching Union lines, Carney is reported to have said, "Boys, the old flag never did touch the ground."

The Battle of Fort Wagner signaled a turning point in the federal government's use of black troops. The Fifty-fourth Massachusetts dispelled doubts about the reliability of black soldiers; by the end of 1863 there were sixty African-American regiments in combat or being organized. After the war, the battle flag Carney had carried was enshrined in the Massachusetts statehouse.

Carney was discharged with the rank of sergeant in 1864. He lived for two years in California but eventually returned to New Bedford, where he worked as a mail carrier until 1901. He was a popular speaker at patriotic celebrations, including a convention of black veterans in 1887. For his valor Carney was the first African American cited for the Congressional Medal of Honor, on June 18, 1863, although he was not issued the medal until May 20, 1900. He retired in 1901 and moved to Boston, where he served as a messenger in the statehouse. He died in 1908.

See also Civil War, U.S.; Military Experience, African-American

▪▪ *Bibliography*

Quarles, Benjamin. *The Negro in the Civil War.* Boston: Little, Brown, 1953. Reprint, New York: Russell & Russell, 1968.

Westwood, Howard C. *Black Troops, White Commanders, and Freedmen During the Civil War.* Carbondale: Southern Illinois University Press, 1992.

SIRAJ AHMED (1996)
ALLISON X. MILLER (1996)

CARNIVAL IN BRAZIL AND THE CARIBBEAN

▪▪▪

The term *Carnival* refers generally to a wide range of festivities that are held in Europe and the Americas in the days before the Catholic observance of Lent. The festivities are a time when the normal restraints of society are abandoned and the hierarchy of social class is reversed or subverted. In the Americas the regions that received large numbers of African slaves developed some of the most famous and colorful Carnival celebrations that exist today. In those places Carnival, although it follows the Catholic calendar and has many strong roots in European traditions, has been shaped by the infusion of African traditions that slaves and their descendents brought to them. The music, instruments, themes, styles of singing and dance, traditions of masking, and many other discrete cultural elements show a link to an African past. The naming of kings and queens, which has a counterpart in European traditions, can be linked in the Americas to a practice from the time of slavery when communities of Africans named their own leaders, expressing a hierarchy in their own community that built on memories of different types of African social organization. These black kings and queens could be found throughout the Americas, from the Argentine and Uruguayan Candombe to the "Negro Election

Scene of Carnival in Brazil. *From Debret, Jean Baptiste,* Voyage Pittoresque et Historique au Bresil, ou Sejour d'un artiste francais au Bresil, depuis 1816 jusqu'en 1831 inclusivement, epoques de l'avenement et de l'abdication de S. M. D. Pedro 1er, fondateur de l'Empire bresilien. *Dedie a l'Academie des Beaux-Arts de l'Institut de France. Published 1834–1839.* ART AND ARTIFACTS DIVISION, SCHOMBURG CENTER FOR RESEARCH IN BLACK CULTURE, THE NEW YORK PUBLIC LIBRARY, ASTOR, LENOX AND TILDEN FOUNDATIONS.

Days" in the United States. In the twentieth century, many of these kings and queens came to be translated into Carnival figures that take to the streets in the upside-down world of Carnival.

Brazil has one of the most famous Carnival traditions in the world. Most people think of the Rio de Janeiro Carnival when they talk about this celebration in Brazil, but there are many different expressions of Carnival in Brazil, each with its own local character. In every case, however, Carnival has been shaped by the traditions of Africans and their descendents. In Rio de Janeiro, many different threads came together in the late nineteenth century to give birth to the music and dance of samba and the *batucadas* (percussion orchestras), dances, and parades that make the current Rio de Janeiro Carnival famous. The signature music and dance of the current-day Carnival celebration, samba, had its roots in the *lundu,* a popular dance of the African population. The dance was known for its

"breaking" of the body and circular movements of the hips, done to a polyrhythmic music, which directly linked *lundu* to its Afro-Brazilian predecessors such as the *batuque.* The dance became popular among many Brazilians of European descent, especially during the European pre-Lenten festivities called *entrudos* in the nineteenth century, when people would go out for several days and throw colored powders and water balloons at each other.

In the late nineteenth century the *lundu* evolved into a new dance craze, the *maxixe,* which soon swept throughout Brazil. At first the *maxixe* was danced in dance halls, but it soon emerged on to the streets when, during the 1880s, groups of blacks brought their *cucumbys* to the streets during the pre-Lenten celebration. The *cucumbys,* also known as *congos* and *congadas* in different regions of Brazil, were expressions that emerged from lay religious brotherhoods of blacks and that included the procession of kings and queens accompanied by ambassadors, who dressed as different "nations" of Africans and Indians. Processions of the *cucumbys* were most often associated with the Day of Kings (the feast day of the Epiphany), January 6, when many of the black lay-religious brotherhoods held their feast-day celebrations. They emerged in the pre-Lenten Carnival in the same year as the abolition of slavery, in 1888, probably to celebrate that victory. Soon the *cucumbys,* who had paraded with drums and various hand-percussion instruments, were mixing their movements with the *maxixe,* which led to the formation of the modern samba. In the 1930s, in large part because of a populist mayor, the descendents of Africans who lived in the shantytowns around Rio de Janeiro started their own "samba schools," and the Carnival of Rio de Janeiro as we know it was born.

Salvador, Bahia, has a reputation for a Carnival that emphasizes Afro-Brazilian themes. Like Rio de Janeiro, Carnival in nineteenth-century Salvador was marked by the *entrudo,* which was characterized by play and practical jokes. In the late 1880s, again corresponding with the abolition of slavery and in an attempt to get the unruly *entrudo* off the streets, the elite of Bahia started to sponsor Carnival clubs that celebrated the European past of Bahia. In response, descendents of Africans started to sponsor their own clubs that honored a noble African past, including African kings and their entourages. The first club to start was the Embaixada Africana (African Embassy) in 1895, which in its first year crowned King Babá-Anin and Ajahy, figures reminiscent of West African kings. The club paraded to the rhythm of African instruments, the *atabaque* and the *agôgô.* In 1898 the same club chose an Ethiopian king, whom they crowned in front of the Church of the Rosary, a nod to the lay religious brotherhoods that had for centu-

Black Kings and Queens in the Americas

The presence of black kings and queens in almost every Euro-American colony highlights the important role that concepts of kingship and hierarchy played in Africans' understanding of the world. African leaders, whether chiefs of small polities or kings of large states, held important ritual positions that mediated several levels of social, spiritual, and political relationships. When Africans were brought to the Americas, they reconstructed these social structures as best they could in the narrow nooks and crevices that the slave structure left open. In some cases the kings and queens may have been part of, or been descended from, royal families in Africa. In other cases they may have been elected, or chosen, by a particular community. When communities lasted longer than a generation, some black kings and queens in the Americas inherited their titles from relatives. All of these variations represented the reconstruction of African social structures in the Americas.

The two most common settings in which black kings and queens appeared in the Americas were in black social organizations and runaway slave communities. The social organizations took various forms. Whether in the black confraternities of Brazil and Spanish America, the *cabildos* of Cuba, or the "Negro Election Days" and Pinkster Festivals of British North America, records exist of black leaders—kings, queens, governors, and chiefs—presiding over black festivities. In many cases, however, their influence went beyond simply being "king for a day." The authorities in seventeenth century Mexico City closely associated the coronation of black kings and queens in confraternities with slave uprisings, and quickly moved to ban those organizations. In Brazil, where authorities saw confraternities as a form of social control, kings and queens would often be in their posi-

tions for life and would pass on their scepter and crown to a chosen successor. Sometimes these successions could be fraught with political intrigue and eventual recourse to the authorities. In small towns in the Brazilian backlands authorities would complain of the assumed power of the black kings and queens—some of whom were still slaves. The positions of kings and queens were so important throughout the Americas that they still survive, not only in the ubiquitous Carnival celebrations but also in confraternities of blacks and communities descended from them. As in the past, these kings and queens today are often much more than just "festive" royalty, they hold their positions for life and are respected and influential in their communities.

Slaves and free blacks that participated in these enclave communities found a way to interact with the dominant society, which constantly placed them at the bottom of the social structure. Many slaves, however, chose to flee intolerable conditions by running away and forming communities with fellow runaways. These communities, called *quilombos* and *mocambos* in Brazil, maroon communities in the Caribbean and the Guianas, and *palenques* in much of Spanish America also named leaders who often took the titles of kings, queens. Some of the most famous leaders have gone down in history as mythic heroes in the fight against slavery, such as Zumbi of the Quilombo dos Palmares in Brazil, and Nanny, the leader of the Windward Maroons of Jamaica. Although many maroon societies were destroyed or eventually assimilated into the modern nations in which they were located, examples of the hierarchical systems in these runaway communities still exist in a few places, such as among the Bush Negro groups in Suriname which still have their own tribal chiefs and village leaders.

ries crowned their black kings and queens. The Embaixada Africana was only one of many African clubs, which had names such as the African Merrymakers and the Sons of Africa.

Around 1905 began a period of repression of the African clubs, which threatened the new concept of order and progress of the Brazilian First Republic. In 1949 there

emerged a new type of Afro-Bahian Carnival group, *afoxés*, which used in their songs a secular version of the music of the Afro-Brazilian religion Candomblé. In 1975, as a result of the growing black consciousness movement, blacks in Bahia started the *blocos afros*, the first of which called themselves Ilê-Aiyê, or "House of Life" in Yoruba. Like their predecessors almost a century earlier, *blocos afros* be-

Paraders and Float pictured during the celebration of Carnival in Brazil. *Shaped by traditions that slaves and their descendants brought with them to the Americas, Carnival festivities are especially popular in Brazil.* © CLAUDIO EDINGER/CORBIS

came places to honor and teach about the African past, as well as to serve as a forum for criticizing racial inequality in Brazil.

Cuba has one of the strongest African cultural complexes of the Caribbean, and traditionally its Carnival celebrations have expressed those influences. In Santiago de Cuba, as elsewhere on the island, present-day Carnival traditions are based on the *cabildos,* mutual aid societies that were similar to the black lay religious brotherhoods of Brazil. In Cuba, the African *cabildos* tended to divide by "nations," each of which would choose its own royalty. Although they had long celebrated privately, after 1823 *cabildos* were given permission to parade publicly on the Day of Kings, January 6, and at that celebration each of the *cabildos* crowned its king and queen. The *cabildos* also participated in the Carnival celebrations and inspired the other major types of Carnival groups in Santiago, the *congas, comparsas,* and *paseos,* all of which continue to play important roles in Santiago's Carnival. Until the 1920s

there were two Carnival celebrations in Santiago, a pre-Lenten Carnival held in exclusive clubs and a Carnival held on the feast day of St. James on July 25. The summer Carnival was held by the workers to celebrate the end of the sugar harvest. In the 1920s the pre-Lenten festival ended in Santiago, leaving only the summer celebration. After the revolution, Fidel Castro officially changed the date of Carnival to July 26, near to the date of the already existing Carnival in Santiago, to commemorate the attack on the Moncada barracks that started the revolution. Even with the sponsorship and control of the state, the *cabildos* and their royalty still play a role in the Carnival of Santiago, most notably the Cabildo Carabalí Isuama and the Cabildo Carabalí Olugo, both of which trace their origin from the Igbo region of Nigeria. Afro-Haitian groups, such as the Tumba Francesa and Tajona, whose members are descendents of nineteenth-century Haitian immigrants to Cuba, also continue to participate in Carnival in Santiago with their kings and queens and their distinctive style of music and dance.

Trinidad, despite the British and Protestant influence on the island, boasts one of the most energetic Carnival celebrations in the Caribbean. More than any other place in the Caribbean, Trinidad has been the site of a riotous mixture of cultures and influences. Nonetheless, as elsewhere in the Western Hemisphere, its Carnival has been highly influenced by the African branch of its history. The traditions of masking (to "play mas'"), *canboulay* (*canne brûlée,* burning cane), and *calinda* (stick fighting) all emerge from strong African roots. Masking in Trinidad's Carnival descends in part from West African traditions of masking and masquerading, as do the stilt dancers. The *canboulay* tradition, which is the central aspect of the Trinidadian Carnival, reenacts the times when slaves were called to put out burning cane fields, and probably dates from before the abolition of slavery. Shortly after emancipation, which came on August 1, 1838, the whites stopped participating in Carnival altogether until the beginning of the twentieth century. In the nineteenth century *canboulay* bands, which also divided by African "nation," would each have their own kings, queens, and princes. By the 1880s Carnival centered on the predawn activities of the Monday before Lent, called *J'Ouvay,* when *canboulay* bands would gather, sing call-and-response songs, and engage in the *calinda.* Despite inevitable changes of the twentieth century, including the invention of the steel drum and the development of music such as *soco,* the traditions of masking, *J'Ouvay, canboulay,* and *calinda* remain central to the Trinidadian festival.

See also Festivals, U.S.; Samba

■■ *Bibliography*

Bettelheim, Judith, ed. *Cuban Festivals: A Century of Afro-Cuban Culture.* Princeton, N.J.: Markus Wiener, 2001.

Butler, Kim D. *Freedoms Given, Freedoms Won: Afro-Brazilians in Post-Abolition São Paulo and Salvador.* New Brunswick, N.J.: Rutgers University Press, 1998.

Chasteen, John Charles. "The Prehistory of Samba: Carnival Dancing in Rio de Janeiro, 1840–1917." *Journal of Latin American Studies* 28 (1996): 29–47.

Liverpool, Hollis Urban. "Origins of Rituals and Customs in the Trinidad Carnival: African or European?" *TDR: The Drama Review* 42 (1998): 24–38.

Mauldin, Barbara, ed. *¡Carnival!* Seattle: University of Washington Press, 2004.

Riggio, Milla C. "Resistance and Identity: Carnival in Trinidad and Tobago." *TDR: The Drama Review* 42 (1998): 6–24.

ELIZABETH KIDDY (2005)

CARROLL, DIAHANN

JULY 17, 1935

Singer and actress Diahann Carroll was born Carol Diahann Johnson in New York, the daughter of John Johnson, a subway conductor, and Mabel (Faulk) Johnson. Her mother had her take voice and piano lessons, and at the recommendation of a guidance counselor she enrolled in the High School of Music and Art. She modeled for *Ebony* and other magazines, and at fourteen, appearing under the name "Diahann Carroll," she won first prize on the popular television show *Arthur Godfrey's Talent Scouts.* Carroll enrolled at New York University but left during her first year after winning a talent contest on the television show *Chance of a Lifetime.* Over the following years she toured as a singer in various important hotels and nightclubs. Her light, swinging style was influenced by Frank Sinatra and Ella Fitzgerald. She released several albums, including *Fun Life* (1961).

In 1954 Carroll began an acting career when she was chosen for the role of Ottilie in Harold Arlen and Truman Capote's *House of Flowers.* While small, the role included the song "A Sleepin' Bee," which Carroll popularized. She received a Tony Award nomination for the role. The same year, she made her screen debut in a small role in the film *Carmen Jones.* She went on to perform in such films as *Porgy and Bess* (1959), *Paris Blues* (1961), and *Goodbye Again* (1961). She returned to Broadway in 1962 as the lead in Richard Rodgers's musical *No Strings,* for which she won a Tony Award. Twenty years later she again appeared on Broadway, this time in the drama *Agnes of God.*

In 1968 Carroll became the first African-American woman to have her own television series, when she starred in the series *Julia.* Carroll played a widowed mother who worked as a nurse. The role aroused a storm of opposition among some blacks, who felt that the character was too "white" and represented white liberal images of African Americans rather than being authentically black. Nevertheless the program was a success.

Carroll remained with the program for three seasons; then, tired of the controversy, she asked to be released from her contract. In a reversal of her image, Carroll next played a single ghetto mother in the film *Claudine* (1974), for which she was nominated for an Academy Award and won an NAACP Image Award. In 1976 she was inducted into the Black Filmmakers' Hall of Fame.

Starting in the 1970s, Carroll revived her singing career, starring in nightclubs and in such places as the Kennedy Center for the Performing Arts (1971). Her solo album *Diahann Carroll* (1974) won her a Grammy Award nomination.

During the late 1970s and 1980s Carroll also returned to television. In 1979 she appeared in the miniseries *Roots: The Next Generation,* and in the television film *I Know Why the Caged Bird Sings.* In 1984 she took the role of Dominique Devereaux on the television series *Dynasty,* thus becoming the first African American to star in a nighttime soap opera. Carroll felt that her portrayal of a character as conniving and mean-spirited as her white peers was both her best work and an important step forward for black actors. In the 1990s she appeared frequently on the TV series *A Different World,* as the mother of Whitley Gilbert. In 1999 she appeared in the movies *Having Our Say* and *Livin' for Love: The Natalie Cole Story.*

See also Fitzgerald, Ella; Television

■■ *Bibliography*

Carroll, Diahann, and Ross Firestone. *Diahann!: An Autobiography.* Boston: Little, Brown, 1986.

"Diahann Carroll: A Trailblazing Actress." *Lifetime Intimate Portrait.* Available from <http://www.lifetimetv.com> (April 17, 2002).

VASANTI SAXENA (1996)
Updated by publisher 2005

CARTER, JOHN

JANUARY 27, 1919

The politician and diplomat John Patrick Carter was born in the village of Cane Grove, British Guiana. He received

his secondary education at Queen's College from 1931 to 1938, after qualifying at the Government County scholarship examination that determined who would be eligible to attend that elite school. Carter's political awakening occurred in the 1920s when his mother took him to meetings of the Negro Progress Convention (NPC), a group that aimed to uplift black people, whom NPC leaders felt were oppressed like crabs in a barrel. As a student in London, where he studied law and qualified as a barrister with a Bachelor of Arts and a Bachelor of Laws degree in 1942, Carter's experience with the "English landlady" who refused to rent rooms to nonwhite students sensitized him to racial injustices in England and was the most significant reason he became involved in political activity. During his sojourn in England, Carter also joined the League of Coloured Peoples (LCP), whose membership at the time included all races, especially whites, as well as students from the colonies of Britain, all of whom were fighting for racial integration in Britain. Eventually, the aims of the LCP expanded to include self-government for the colonies.

Upon returning to British Guiana, Carter entered politics, became a member of the colony's Labour Party, and was elected to the Legislative Council in 1947, after Hubert Critchlow, the original winner of the constituency in question, was unseated as a result of a libel suit brought against him by the wife of a prominent attorney, whom Critchlow had accused of mistreating a black employee. In any event, Carter pursued a labor line as a politician, and although he and later People's Party Progressive (PPP) leader Cheddi Jagan supported each other initially, in the Legislative Council their paths eventually diverged as Jagan's more radical politics began to obtrude.

Carter also became assistant secretary of the LCP in Guiana, which at the time was seeking not merely to sensitize African Guianese regarding the issue of political independence but was also concerned with promoting their social, economic, educational, and political interests. Indeed, one manifestation of this concern occurred in January 1953, when along with other LCP leaders Carter protested against the appointment of a Guianese Royal Air Force Officer, who had served in World War II and had later qualified as a barrister, as a sergeant-major in the police force. This incident, which clearly involved a gross injustice as the disjuncture between academic qualifications and the occupational status of the job was one that was clearly based on race, was taken up with the attorney general, as a result of which the individual in question was seconded to the attorney general's office.

Also with fellow LCP leaders, Carter was involved in the formation of the National Democratic Party (NDP)—subsequently becoming an executive member of the party—which contested the 1953 general elections, the first to be held under universal adult suffrage, and which was won by the PPP. After the PPP ministers were dismissed, the constitution was suspended in October 1953, and a struggle for the leadership of the party ensued between Cheddi Jagan, the party leader, and Forbes Burnham, the chairman. Carter, who reportedly had heard the news of the suspension "with a heavy heart," traveled to England with a delegation of prominent political figures to consult with Colonial Office officials and to express the group's disenchantment with the PPP. While there, British officials suggested that although they were sympathetic to the delegation, it was in the latter's interest to organize politically to present a stronger opposition to the PPP and thereby enhance the prospects of democracy in Guiana. Perhaps with that in mind, and because Carter felt that he had more in common with the more moderate Burnham than with Jagan, and since the NDP and the People's National Congress (PNC), which came into being in 1958 with Burnham as its leader, were not too far apart on the issues, the two parties merged.

As a diplomat from 1966 to 1970, Carter was accredited to the United States as Guyana's first ambassador to that country, with additional accreditation to Canada and the United Nations; from 1970 to 1976, he was accredited to Great Britain as Guyana's high commissioner, with additional accreditation to France, West Germany, Netherlands, Austria, the Soviet Union, Sweden, Yugoslavia, and India; from 1976 to 1981 he was accredited to the People's Republic of China as Guyana's ambassador, with additional accreditation to Japan and North Korea; and finally from 1981 to 1983 he was accredited to Jamaica as Guyana's ambassador. For his services to the Guyana government, Carter was knighted by Britain's Queen Elizabeth.

See also Burnham, Forbes

■ ■ *Bibliography*

Seeraj, Sandra. "Sir John and Lady Sara Carter: A Story of Sterling Accomplishment, Distinguished Service and Enduring Love." *Guyana Chronicle* (November 21, 2004).

St. Pierre, Maurice. *Anatomy of Resistance: Anti-Colonialism in Guyana, 1823–1966.* London and Basingstoke: Macmillan, 1999.

MAURICE ST. PIERRE (2005)

CARTER, MARTIN

JUNE 7, 1927
DECEMBER 13, 1997

━┫┣━

The poet and political activist Martin Wylde Carter was born into a middle class family in Georgetown, Guyana (then British Guiana), on June 7, 1927. Committed to a life in the Caribbean, Carter was a founding member of the socialist and anticolonial People's Progressive Party (PPP). His first major publication, *To a Dead Slave* (1951), made him one of the first poets in the anglophone Caribbean to tie his colonial experience directly to his slave ancestry.

In 1953 Carter married Phyllis Howard. In the same year, the PPP won a landslide victory in the first universal suffrage elections, and Carter attended the World Festival of Youth in Romania. As he returned, the political landscape of British Guiana changed. Due to a perceived Communist threat, Britain declared a state of emergency in the colony and dismissed the PPP government. Carter was arrested on October 25, 1953, and detained at the U.S. airbase, Atkinson Field, for "spreading dissension." During this period, Carter published "University of Hunger" in the journal *Kyk-Over-Al,* writing in Creole, "is the university of hunger the wide waste / is the pilgrimage of man the long march." Released in January 1954, Carter was quickly reimprisoned for breaking laws that came in the wake of the state of emergency. Nevertheless, his poetry was on the move: *Poems of Resistance from British Guiana* (1954) was published in London by Lawrence and Wishart, who heralded Carter as "the foremost poet of the Caribbean."

Split between radical and moderate factions, in 1955 the PPP fragmented; Carter chose Cheddi Jagan's radical faction, only to leave the party a year later, having been accused of "ultra-leftism." By 1959 Carter was employed as an information officer at Bookers, the colony's major sugar producer, which was foreign controlled. But Carter was increasingly disappointed by his country's failure to recognize how race and colonialism had twisted Guyana's revolutionary prospects. His poem "Black Friday 1962" (named after a day of rioting and burning that took place in Georgetown) addresses the dreams and disappointments of insurrection. A year after Guyana became independent (in 1966), Linden Forbes Burnham of the People's National Congress (PNC) invited Carter to join the government as minister of information. In November 1970 he resigned, later saying that he could not accept this privileged position in the face of so much material want.

Carter was writer-in-residence at the University of Essex in 1975. From 1978 until his death he was employed by the University of Guyana as a writer and researcher. Although Carter was never again involved in party politics, he was increasingly critical of the PNC, participating in demonstrations against corruption and electoral fraud. Carter's poetry from this period provides an excoriating anatomy of a postcolonial country caught between hope and despair. When the academic and activist Walter Rodney was murdered in 1980, Carter wrote, "Assassins of conversation / they bury the voice / . . . I intend to turn a sky / of tears for you" ("For Walter Rodney").

In 1989 Carter's *Selected Poems* won the Guyana Prize for Literature, but a series of strokes in the early 1990s left him unable to write. In 1994 Carter received the Guyanese Order of Roraima for his "outstanding contribution to literature." In 1996 the Chilean government awarded him the Gabriela Mistral Gold Medal for his contribution to literature. Carter died on December 13, 1997. He is survived by his wife and their four children, and was given a state funeral and buried at the Place of the Seven Ponds in Georgetown.

See also Creole Languages of the Americas; Literature; Politics

■ ■ *Bibliography*

Brown, Stewart, ed. *All Are Involved: The Art of Martin Carter.* Leeds, England: Peepal Tree, 2000.

Carter, Martin. *Poems of Succession.* London: New Beacon, 1977.

Carter, Martin. *Selected Poems.* 2d ed. Georgetown, Guyana: Red Thread Women's Press, 1997.

GEMMA ROBINSON (2005)

CARVER, GEORGE WASHINGTON

C. 1864
JANUARY 5, 1943

━┫┣━

Born in Diamond, Missouri, scientist and educator George Washington Carver did not remember his parents. His father was believed to be a slave killed accidentally before Carver's birth. His mother was Mary Carver, a slave apparently kidnapped by slave raiders soon after he was born. He and his older brother were raised by their mother's former owners, Moses and Susan Carver, on their small, largely self-sufficient farm.

Denied admission to the neighborhood school because of his color, Carver was privately tutored and then

George Washington Carver at work in his laboratory at Tuskegee Institute in Alabama, c. 1920. Carver developed a crop rotation system and other innovations that greatly improved southern agriculture. PHOTOGRAPHS AND PRINTS DIVISION, SCHOMBURG CENTER FOR RESEARCH IN BLACK CULTURE, THE NEW YORK PUBLIC LIBRARY, ASTOR, LENOX AND TILDEN FOUNDATIONS.

moved to nearby Neosho to enter school in the mid-1870s. He soon realized he knew more than the teacher and left with a family moving to Fort Scott, Kansas. After witnessing a lynching there, he left that town and for over a decade roamed around the Midwest seeking an education while supporting himself by cooking, laundering, and homesteading.

In 1890 Carver enrolled in Simpson College in Indianola, Iowa, where he was an art major and the only African-American student. After his teacher convinced him that a black man could not make a living in art, Carver transferred to Iowa State College at Ames in 1891 to major in agriculture. Again the only black student on campus, Carver participated fully (except for dating) in extracurricular activities and compiled such an impressive academic record that he was hired as a botany assistant to pursue postgraduate work. Before he received his master

of agriculture degree in 1896, he was placed in charge of the greenhouse and taught freshmen students.

An expert in mycology (the study of fungi) and plant cross-fertilization, Carver could have remained at Iowa and probably would have made significant contributions in one or both fields. However, he felt an obligation to share his knowledge with other African Americans and accepted Booker T. Washington's offer to become head of the agricultural department at Tuskegee Normal and Industrial Institute in 1896.

When he arrived at Tuskegee, Carver intended to stay only a few years and then pursue doctoral work. Instead, he spent his remaining forty-six years there. Although he once considered matrimony, he never married and instead "adopted" many Tuskegee students as his "children," to whom he provided loans and guidance. For the first half of his tenure, he worked long hours in administration, teaching, and research. The focus of his work reflected the needs of his constituents rather than his personal talents or interests. As director of the only all-black-staffed agricultural experiment station, he sought answers to the debt problems of small-scale farmers and landless sharecroppers. Thus, in his teaching, extension work (carried on with a wagon equipped as a movable school), and agricultural bulletins, Carver preached the use of available and renewable resources to replace expensive, purchased commodities. He especially advocated the growing of peanuts as a cheap source of protein and published several bulletins with peanut recipes.

After twenty years at Tuskegee, Carver was respected by agricultural researchers but largely unknown to the general public. His rise to fame began with his induction in 1916 into Great Britain's Royal Society for the Arts and the growing realization of his usefulness by the peanut industry. In 1921 a growers' association paid his way to testify at tariff hearings in Congress. There his showmanship in demonstrating peanut products drew national press coverage. Two years later some Atlanta businessmen founded the Carver Products Company, and Carver won the Spingarn Medal of the NAACP. Although the company failed, it generated publicity. Then in 1933 an Associated Press release exaggerated Carver's success in rehabilitating polio patients with peanut-oil massages. Soon he was perhaps the best known African American of his generation.

The increasing publicity caught the attention of numerous people who found Carver's rise from slavery and his personality appealing. Articles began to appear describing the flowers in the lapels of his well-worn jackets and his rambles in the woods to commune with his "Creator," through which he expressed his devout but nonsectarian belief. Because he took no public stand on political or racial matters, many diverse groups could adopt him as a symbol of their causes. Thus, he was appropriated by advocates of racial equality, the "New South," religion, the "American Dream," and even segregation. His significant work as an agricultural researcher and educator was obscured by the myth of the "peanut wizard."

Relishing the publicity, Carver did little to correct the public record, aside from general statements of his "unworthiness" of the honors that came with increasing frequency. Some symbolic uses of his life helped to perpetuate white stereotypes of African Americans, but most of the publicity had a positive impact on both white and black Americans. Indeed, Carver became a potent tool for racial tolerance after the Commission on Interracial Cooperation and the YMCA began to sponsor his lecture tours of white college campuses in the 1920s and 1930s. On these tours, Carver added dozens of whites to his adopted "family." To them he was no "token black" but a trusted father figure to whom they wrote their innermost thoughts. Many, such as white clergyman Howard Kester, became outspoken advocates of racial justice.

Because of his compelling personality, Carver had a profound impact on almost everyone—black or white—who came in contact with him. His "special friends" ranged from white sharecroppers to Henry Ford. Most of his major publicists were true disciples of Carver's vision of the interrelatedness of all human beings and their environment. Because of his extreme frugality, he was also able to leave a substantial legacy by giving about sixty thousand dollars to establish the George Washington Carver Foundation, which continues to support scientific research at Tuskegee University. Although his scientific contributions were meager relative to his fame and he could not singlehandedly save the black family farm, Carver's work and warmth greatly enriched the lives of thousands.

See also Inventors and Inventions; Science; Tuskegee University

■ ■ *Bibliography*

Federer, William J. *George Washington Carver: His Life and Faith in His Own Words.* St. Louis, Mo.: Amerisearch, 2002.

Kremer, Gary R. *George Washington Carver in His Own Words.* Columbia: University of Missouri Press, 1987.

Mackintosh, Barry. "George Washington Carver: The Making of a Myth." *Journal of Southern History* 42 (1976): 507–528.

McMurry, Linda O. *George Washington Carver: Scientist and Symbol.* New York: Oxford University Press, 1981.

LINDA O. MCMURRY (1996)
Updated bibliography

CARY, MARY ANN SHADD

OCTOBER 9, 1823
JUNE 5, 1893

■ ■ ■

Teacher and journalist Mary Ann Shadd Cary was born in Wilmington, Delaware, the daughter of free blacks Abraham and Harriet Parnell Shadd. After attending a Quaker school in West Chester, Pennsylvania, she returned to Wilmington, where at age sixteen she opened a school, the first of several she was to establish during the following decades. After passage of the Fugitive Slave Law of 1850, Mary and her brother Isaac went to Windsor, Canada, where she founded a school for both black and white pupils. In 1856 she married Thomas F. Cary of Toronto. She resumed teaching in Chatham (1859–1864) under the auspices of the American Missionary Association.

Cary's most noteworthy achievements center on the *Provincial Freeman,* a weekly Canadian newspaper, published with varying regularity between 1853 and 1859. Although men (Samuel Ringgold War and the Rev. William P. Newman) served as titular editors, Cary's contemporaries recognized her as the real editor. She is generally acknowledged to be the first woman publisher of a newspaper in Canada and the first black newspaperwoman in North America. A crusading journalist, Cary became embroiled in particularly bitter quarrels—notably with Henry Bibb—over the issue of integration (the question of whether blacks were exiles or new citizens of Canada) and about the activities of the Refugee Home Society, whose land-purchase scheme, she claimed, offered no advantage over the Canadian government's offers and was sometimes more costly.

During the Civil War, Cary returned to the United States to recruit for the Union army, working in Indiana, Ohio, and Michigan. From 1869 to 1874 she taught public school in Detroit and in Washington, D.C., where she also served as a principal (1872–1874). An activist for women's suffrage, Cary addressed the annual convention of the National Woman Suffrage Association in 1878 and was founder of the Colored Women's Progressive Association (Washington, D.C.). She received her LL.B. degree from Howard University Law School in 1883; she was the first woman to receive the degree from that school and only the second black woman to earn a law degree.

In addition to her work for the *Provincial Freeman,* Cary was the author of an advisory pamphlet, *Hints to the Colored People of the North* (1849), espousing her ideals of self-help; of *A Plea for Emigration, or Notes on Canada West, in Its Moral, Social, and Political Aspect* (1852), a booklet describing opportunities for blacks in Canada; and (with Osborne Anderson, one of the five survivors of John Brown's raid) of *A Voice from Harpers Ferry* (1873). She contributed to Frederick Douglass's *New National Era* and John Wesley Cromwell's *Advocate* as well.

See also Douglass, Frederick; Journalism

■ ■ *Bibliography*

Rhodes, Jane. *Mary Ann Shadd Cary: The Black Press and Protest in the Nineteenth Century.* Bloomington: Indiana University Press, 1998.

Silverman, Jason H. "Mary Ann Shadd and the Search for Equality." In *Black Leaders of the Nineteenth Century,* edited by Leon Litwack and August Meier, pp. 87–100. Urbana: University of Illinois Press, 1988.

QUANDRA PRETTYMAN (1996)
Updated bibliography

CATHOLICISM IN THE AMERICAS

Numbering some two billion in all, one of every three people in the world today is Christian, half of them Catholic. Fifty percent of all Catholics live in the Americas, where the three countries with the largest Catholic populations in the world—Brazil, Mexico, and the United States—are located. In all, more than sixty percent of the population of the Americas is Catholic, with the highest numbers of African-descended Catholics being found in Brazil (forty million), Colombia (fifteen million), the Dominican Republic (eight million), and Haiti (six million). In all, eighty million of the five-hundred million Catholics in the Americas—or roughly sixteen percent—are of African descent, with three-fourths of this population residing in Latin America and the balance residing in the Caribbean and North America.

However, these figures are to some degree misleading, as millions of other blacks in the Americas practice African-derived religions such as Vodou, Santería, and Candomblé, which draw considerable symbolic and ritualistic substance from Catholicism. Therefore, Catholic influence in the Americas, among both African-descended and indigenous peoples, extends far beyond the confines of formal parish membership and dogmatic obedience. It is also important to take into account the complicity of the Roman Catholic Church in the epic horrors of the transatlantic slave trade that made the region the major part of the African diaspora that it is, for many slaves never embraced Catholicism sincerely, just as many of their descendants are concerned with the faith's healing potential rather than with being the kinds of orthodox believers that the Church hierarchy would prefer. Nevertheless, the vast majority of black Catholics in the Americas are (and always have been) sincere in their faith and find abundant meaning, solace, and hope in belonging to the world's largest religious community.

National Sanctuary of Our Lady of Aparecida, Aparecida do Norte, Brazil, 2004. *A black virgin, Our Lady of Aparecida, is the patroness of Brazil, which is home to the world's largest Catholic population, including more than 40 million Catholics of African descent.* AFP/GETTY IMAGES

Bulls, Sacraments, and Slavery in the "New World"

Christianity's long acceptance of slavery received its most momentous doctrinal sanction in the form of a series of papal bulls, beginning with *Romanus pontifex*, which was promulgated in 1455 to legitimate the plunder of the West Coast of Africa by the kingdoms of Portugal and Castile. The bull states that "The Roman pontiff . . . seeking and desiring the salvation of all, wholesomely ordains and disposes upon careful deliberation those things which he sees will be agreeable to the Divine Majesty and by which he may bring the sheep entrusted to him by God into the single divine fold, . . . [bestows] favors and special graces on those Catholic kings and princes, who . . . not only restrain the savage excesses of the Saracens and of other infidels, . . . but also . . . vanquish them and their kingdoms and habitations, though situated in the remotest parts unknown to us." Thirty-eight years later, Columbus's "discovery" of the Americas would drive the Vatican to promulgate other bulls that would have immense influence and forever shape this "New World," in large part by legitimating the transatlantic slave trade and requiring the baptism of African slaves into the "single divine fold." The most important of these pontifical documents was *Inter caetera*, promulgated by Pope Alexander IV in 1493. This document drew a line of demarcation from the Arctic Pole to the Antarctic Pole, passing between the Azores and Cape Verde, with all "islands and mainlands remote and unknown and not hitherto discovered by others" west of the line to Spain, and those east of the line to Portugal, "to the end that you might bring to the worship of our Redeemer and the profession of the Catholic faith their residents and inhabitants."

As early as 1502, Africans were shipped to the island of Kiskeya, which the Spanish had claimed and renamed Hispaniola. The first enslaved Africans in the Caribbean were imported from Latin Europe's slave market, which was already over half a century old in Portugal. Soon, the island became the first Catholic seat of power in the Americas, home to the New World's first Catholic church, the Cathedral of the Immaculate Conception in the capital city of Santo Domingo. In addition to Christianity, the

Archbishop Wilton Gregory, the first African-American president of the U.S. Conference of Catholic Bishops, addressing his colleagues at their annual conference, Washington, D.C., 2003. AFP/GETTY IMAGES

Spanish also brought forced labor and disease to this and other American colonies, which triggered a staggering spike in the morbidity rate for the indigenous populations. Some clerics, like Bartolomé de Las Casas, were horrified by this and argued for the rights of local victims of Euro-Catholic plunder. Others, like Juan de Sepulveda, countered that the indigenous peoples of the Americas were "a thick, servile people created inferior by God, who could legitimately be constrained for the benefit of the more evolved nations" (Bien-Aimé, pp. 564-565). After several decades devoted to the Amerindian's rights and liberation, Las Casas pleaded personally before the Spanish throne, and finally, in 1542, legislation was passed that banned the forced labor of indigenous peoples in the colonies. A similar law would be codified for Portugal's American colonies in 1570.

It is altogether regrettable that this missionary who devoted the better part of his life and talents to the hu-

manitarian concerns of the Amerindians was among the first to endorse the large-scale importation of enslaved Africans as replacement labor for the decimated indigenous population. However, it is stretching the point to suggest, as some commentators have, that Las Casas was chiefly responsible for initiating the transatlantic slave trade, for the Jeromite Fathers were also then petitioning for Africans to be enslaved and brought to the Americas. King Carlos I of Spain, moreover, had sanctioned the direct importation of slaves from Africa to New Spain as early as 1518, and by the 1530s there were already African slaves toiling in Brazil.

Despite such ecclesial promotion of slavery, many Africans quite ably managed to appropriate Catholic saints to bolster their resistance to the injustices of slavery, viewing the saints as new manifestations of the powerful spiritual beings they had known, venerated, and counted on in Africa. In Brazilian maroon communities (*quilombos*) such as Palmares, for example, statues of Catholic saints were featured in redoubt shrines in order to spiritually empower the antislavery resistance struggle. The most significant Maroon community in Colombia, meanwhile, took Saint Basil as its patron (*Palenque de San Bisilio*), while Maroon raiders in the early stages of the Haitian Revolution (e.g., Makaya and Romaine-la-Prophétesse) appealed to Catholic saints and biblical figures to bolster their charisma and chances on the battlefield. One of the most influential leaders of the Mexican independence struggle, furthermore, the Afro-Mexican Catholic priest José María Morelos y Pavon, saw his cause to be in large part a endeavor to raise oppressed Afro-Mexicans to positions of social and political equality. By 1812, Morelos's ultimately victorious army was comprised mostly of blacks and mulattoes. Also worthy of mention concerning Catholic resistance to slavery in colonial America is the contribution of some European Catholic missionaries, especially Jesuits, to the subversive cause, which was surely a key reason for their banishment from the Catholic New World in 1762.

Despite the Catholic Church's complicity in the brutality of the Atlantic plantation system, there were Catholic clerics who represented to enslaved Africans the compassionate side of Christianity in a heroic, and even saintly, manner. In 1610, the Spanish Jesuit Peter Claver arrived as a missionary in Cartagena, where he began a thirty-three-year ministry to African slaves, and where he became a rare abolitionist voice in one of the New World's busiest slave ports, declaring himself "a slave to the Negroes." His ministry extended onto plantations, and Claver is said to have converted 300,000 Africans to Catholicism. Around the same time, an Afro-Peruvian Dominican, Martin of Porres, demonstrated similar compassion in his establishment of an orphanage and children's hospital for Lima's poor. He also created a shelter for stray cats and dogs. Claver was canonized in 1888, and Porres in 1962, the first-ever black American saint.

While their contributions have been muted by the patriarchal and racist biases of much historical scholarship, black Catholic women in the Americas have also exhibited genuine saintliness. In spite of the evils engendered by the institutional Catholic Church on their people, both during the slave trade and during the institutionalized racism that followed in most of the Americas after abolition, these women successfully aspired to embody the true love of neighbor demanded by Jesus Christ in the Gospels. Mother Theresa Lange is one significant example. Born during the Haitian Revolution in Saint Domingue, her family fled the violence then raging in the French colony, settling for a time in Cuba before eventually immigrating to Balti-

more. There, in 1828, Mother Lange, a nun of the Oblate Order, founded the first black Roman Catholic order in the United States, the Oblate Sisters of Providence. The Order established the St. Frances of Rome Academy, the oldest continuously functioning black school in the United States, and it later founded similar educational institutions in other cities.

Until the 1570s, most African slaves in the Americas toiled in Peruvian and Mexican mines. The development of plantation economies, first in Brazil, and later in the Caribbean and in the United States, would change this. By the 1780s the French (as well as the British and Dutch) had established lucrative plantations so aggressively that Saint Domingue (the western third of Hispaniola, which was ceded to them by the Spanish in 1697) had become, in the words of historian Philip Curtin, "the pinnacle of achievement of the South Atlantic system as a whole" (Curtin, p. 75). Although Dutch and British colonies would likewise draw tens of thousands of slaves in this same period, among the northern European nations it was only France that would join Spain and Portugal in shaping the Catholic foundation of the Americas, including, of course, its African and African diasporic populations and dimensions. These three imperial powers brought about sixty percent of the approximately ten million African slaves who survived the Middle Passage and arrived in the New World.

In French and Spanish colonies, a series of legal codes obliged slave owners to deliver religious instruction to their slaves. In Brazil, meanwhile, the Portuguese never codified any parallel document to regulate the treatment of slaves, though even there the application of papal bulls, at least in theory, meant that all slaves should have been indoctrinated in the Catholic faith. For the French, the most significant of these documents was *le Code Noire,* which was promulgated at Versailles by King Louis XIV in 1685. The first eight articles of *le Code Noire* dealt specifically with religion, stipulating that slaves could practice no other religion but Roman Catholicism, and that they could only be baptized, married, and buried as Catholics. Modeled largely after the *le Code Noire,* a series of Spanish *codigos* culminated with the *Codigo Negro Carolina,* promulgated in Santo Domingo in 1784. Reflecting Europeans' clear grasp of Catholicism's great utility as putative divine sanction for the unspeakable injustices of New World slavery, *Codigo Negro Carolina* labeled Africans "superstitious and fanatics . . . inclined to poisonous acts," and explained that Catholic indoctrination was crucial to "assure internal and external security of the island because [Catholicism's] powerful influence has preserved Spanish colonies in the past."

Thus, slave owners in Spanish, French, and Portuguese America were doctrinally and legally bound to baptize into Catholicism, at the very least, roughly six million Africans and their descendants (more than half of all slaves in the New World) over a period of more than three hundred years. Yet, more often than not, the baptism of enslaved Africans was a nominal gesture. More often still, slaves who sought baptism of their own accord—and many did so on numerous occasions—understood the sacrament in decidedly African terms as a healing ritual rather than as any sacramental demarcation of religious conversion. Moreover, most planters were loathe to expend their own and their slaves time and energy in seeing to Africans' religious instruction, and thus the Catholicism of Africans and their descendants in the Americas developed in a climate that was abundantly fertile for the development of Afro-Catholic religious syncretism, especially in Brazil, Saint Domingue, and Cuba, where emerged the great African-derived religions of Candomblé, Vodou, and Santería, respectively.

AFRICAN CATHOLICS AND AFRICAN INNOVATION IN NEW WORLD CATHOLICISM

Soundly understanding the origins of black Catholicism in the Americas demands focusing some careful attention on the presence in the New World of Central Africans (who were already Catholic prior to being enslaved). The late-fifteenth century introduction by the Portuguese of Catholic saints in the kingdom of Kongo, and the baKongo's subsequent appropriation of the saints over the next quarter millennium, is, as much as any European Catholic culture, a taproot of Catholicism in the Americas. Given the strength and nature of the indigenous Kongolese ancestor and *bisimbi* (spirits of the soil and terrestrial waters) cults and the cosmology in which they were framed, Catholic saints—who, like ancestors, were white and would have to traverse waters (*nzadi*) were they ever to visit the world of the living (*nza yayi*)—resonated quite harmoniously with traditional Kongolese religious notions. Once Kongolese people learned about the lives of Catholic saints, they quite logically identified them with the ancestors. Ancestor/saint assimilation, furthermore, readily explains why in Kongo—and in Brazil, Haiti, Cuba, and elsewhere—All Saints' Day and All Souls' Day remain so wildly popular to this day. Although accuracy in estimating the number of Kongolese Catholic slaves who arrived in the Americas is elusive, it is safe to claim that tens of thousands were, if not ardent Catholics, quite exposed to Catholicism long prior to their enslavement. These Africans, in effect, were the first significant black Catholic community in the New World, and their influence remains far greater than scholarship has heretofore shown.

Perhaps nowhere was the Kongolese Catholic influence greater than in Saint Domingue, where more than half of all slaves imported during the last half of the eighteenth century were from Central Africa. Given that the Kingdom of Kongo had been exposed to Catholicism for roughly a quarter-millennium by this time, thousands of these slaves had been born, baptized, and raised Catholic prior to their enslavement. In effect, this meant that much of the development of popular Catholic devotions in Saint Domingue were in large part extensions of Kongolese Catholic traditions, and to this day in Haiti the most popular saints in the precolonial Kingdom of the Kongo—the Virgin Mary and Saint James the Greater—remain the most popular saint cults in the modern Caribbean nation. Furthermore, just as in the Kongo there was an acute shortage of ordained Catholic priests to administer the sacraments, forcing the Church to rely largely on catechists as its leaders, so too in Saint Domingue were Kongolese catechists instrumental in carrying on the faith in a religious field where orthodox sacerdotal leadership was scant and often dubious. As one colonial administrator in Saint Domingue remarked in 1761, it was "not uncommon to find them [African Catholics] acting as missionaries and priests." The value of such forms of initiative in sacerdotal Catholic leadership among Africans and their descendants was amplified, furthermore, during the decades following Haitian independence in 1804, as the Vatican refused to recognize the new republic, and thus declined to send it any priests until a concordat was signed with Port-au-Prince in 1860.

Enslaved Catholics from Central Africa also played significant roles in the origins of New World black Catholicism in the most important Portuguese and Spanish plantation colonies, namely Brazil and Cuba. According to legend, King Galanga (later named and recalled as "Chico Rei"), the leader of one small community near the mouth of the Congo River, was enslaved around 1720 and brought to Brazil. In time, Galanga managed to secure his freedom and began to build *Igreja Nossa Senhora Efigenia no Alto Cruz* (Church of Our Lady of Saint Efigenia of the High Cross), dedicated to one of the emergent patron saints of slaves. In Brazil, the mark of Kongolese Catholicism is also prominent in the vastly popular cult of Our Lady of the Rosary (whose feast some believe was initially established by Galanga), to whom African slaves once composed and sang hymns to the Marian icon as "Queen of the Kongo" and "Queen of Angola." Similarly, throughout Brazil, black religious societies (*irmandades*) have long fused Catholic devotions with memorial feasts for ancestral Kongolese kings, the first on record occurring in 1760.

Elsewhere, African religious societies were also a major influence on the development of black Catholicism

Father Charles Randolph Uncles

Born in Baltimore, Maryland, in 1859, Uncles was baptized as a Roman Catholic at the age of sixteen at St. Francis Xavier's Church, founded in 1863 by Archbishop Spalding for the exclusive use of blacks. Uncles attended Baltimore Normal School and taught in the Baltimore County Schools from 1880 to 1883. Unable to gain admittance to local Roman Catholic colleges and seminaries because of his race, Uncles traveled to Canada in 1883 to matriculate at St. Hyacinthe's College in Quebec. He graduated with honors in 1888 and returned to Baltimore to attend St. Mary's Seminary, whose all-white student body voted unanimously to allow him to enter.

On December 22, 1891, Uncles became the first black to be ordained a Roman Catholic priest in the United States. (Previous African-American priests had been ordained in Europe.) The ceremony took place in Baltimore Cathedral and was conducted by His Eminence James Cardinal Gibbons. After his ordination, Uncles served as a professor of English, Latin, and Greek at Epiphany Apostolic Church in Walbrook, Md., transferring to Newburgh, N.Y., when the college moved there in the 1920s. He was recognized as a Latin-language expert and published a Latin grammar. The Rev. Charles Uncles was a member of the Josephite Brothers, a society founded in England in 1871 with the specific purpose of serving as missionaries to emancipated blacks in the United States. He died in 1933.

LYDIA MCNEILL (2005)

in the Americas. Usually consecrated to a particular saint, these "brotherhoods" organized feast day processions and, as much as anything else, shaped the nature of popular Catholicism in places like Brazil and Cuba. Certain black saints, like Benedict of Palermo, Our Lady of Czestochowa, and Santa Ephigenia, gained much prominence on the popular level in this way, as did the Feast of the Magi throughout the Iberian New World. Black religious socie-

ties were perhaps most germane to African innovations in New World Catholicism in Cuba, where they were called *cabildos* or *cofradías.* Sanctioned by the Cuban Catholic Church and organized according to African ethnic origins as of the mid-seventeenth century, the primary religious function of the quasi-autonomous *cabildos* was to indoctrinate Africans into the Catholic faith, with saint veneration taking center stage in this regard. Besides nourishing black devotion to Catholic saints, *cabildos* also served as mutual aid societies for slaves and free blacks alike, providing health and burial services and sometimes managing to purchase manumission. But their lasting legacy for black religion in Cuba and beyond was their fertility for Afro-Catholic syncretism. With its belief in a single creator God and a pantheon of spirits and ancestors who intervene in their lives in the here-and-now, traditional West African, and particularly Yoruba, religion was structurally resonant with Catholic understandings of spiritual beings and ritual paraphernalia, such that Catholicism, far from being adopted by Africans merely as a mask to perpetuate their ancestral traditions, was quite fluidly adapted and adopted by them. Out of the *cabildos,* as a result, emerged the rich (and now global) Afro-Cuban religion of Santería.

FROM 1804 TO 2004

Beginning with Haiti in 1804 and ending with Cuba in 1888, American nations with large African-descended populations gained political independence from their respective European colonizers. The true independence of local Catholic hierarchies from European control, however, would in many places take much longer to be realized, as light-skinned archbishops and bishops from São Paolo to San Juan allied themselves with the economic and political elites that replaced European administrators. For much of its post-independence history in the Americas, the Catholic hierarchy has thus played a legitimating role for the elite and the status quo, providing invaluable religious sanction for the ravages of classist and racist oppression. Cognizant of the important role that African-derived religion played in the Haitian Revolution and in slave rebellions elsewhere, the Catholic hierarchy, whose local clergy were now under the authority of Rome rather than regional sees, soon became an agent of religious persecution against practitioners of Candomblé in Brazil, Santería in Cuba, and Vodou in Haiti. This often tragic trend would generally continue until after the Second World War, further alienating blacks from the institutional Catholic Church.

The resultant sociocultural imbalance and irrelevance of the Catholic hierarchy, along with the Eurocentric ritualism of the Latin Mass, eventually caused many Catholics

Group portrait of Catholic nuns and priests, Harlem, New York. PHOTOGRAPHS AND PRINTS DIVISION, SCHOMBURG CENTER FOR RESEARCH IN BLACK CULTURE, THE NEW YORK PUBLIC LIBRARY, ASTOR, LENOX AND TILDEN FOUNDATIONS.

in the Americas, especially those of the underclasses, to feel disenfranchised by their church. This opened the door for the extraordinary spread of Protestantism in the Caribbean and Latin America during the second half of the twentieth century. At the peak of the Protestant explosion in the 1970s and 1980s, several thousand Catholics were leaving their mother church—often for Pentecostal sects—every day. Obviously, from the Catholic standpoint, something had to be done to stem this massive outflow of apostates, and the changes in liturgy and doctrine forged at the Second Vatican Council (1962–1965) offered the means by which to resolve this crisis. In seeking to make the Catholic Church less archaic and alien to its global flock, and to bring it up to date (*aggiornomento*), the Council empowered local churches to enculturate Catholicism in ways that would help keep people in their pews. In Brazil this meant that the Mass was said in Portuguese, while in Colombia and the Dominican Republic it was said in Spanish, and in Haiti in French and Haitian

Creole. Even more important for New World Catholics of African descent, cultural and even religious expressions rooted in African traditions were integrated into communal rites, and thus the drums of Candomblé, Vodou, and Santería are beaten regularly in Catholic Masses today, from rural Colombian and Venezuelan parishes to the national cathedrals of Puerto Rico and the Dominican Republic.

Also inspired in part by the Second Vatican Council and subsequent regional episcopal conferences in Medellín, Colombia (1968) and Puebla, Mexico (1979), liberation theology began to inspire Catholics throughout Latin America and the Caribbean to embody a more socially-engaged form of Catholicism, one rooted in a "preferential option for the poor." The appeal of liberation theology to the disenfranchised masses of the region was powerful, as thousands of Catholics joined base church communities (*communidades eclisiales de base,* or CEBs) in response to a fresh commitment among many priests and theologians to ensure Catholic action on behalf of social justice for the downtrodden. In Brazil, where the Catholic left had been productive in social activism as early as 1959, some CEBs became important bases for black unity and consciousness. Although liberation theology would take root there somewhat later than in Brazil or Central America, nowhere were its fruits more impressive than in Haiti, where CEBs led a popular protest movement in 1986 that toppled the thirty-five-year dynastic Duvalier dictatorship. In 1990 a liberation theologian and Catholic priest, Jean Bertrand Aristide, was elected president in one of the largest margins of victory in any fair national election in the history of the Americas.

However, for all of its admirable accomplishments and its success in making the Catholic Church more concretely relevant to the poor of the Americas, liberation theology had lost much of its force by the end of the twentieth century, in part due to political repression and the fruitless martyrdom of many of its adherents. A slightly newer Catholic movement would also contribute to the decline of liberation theology in the Americas: the Catholic Charismatic Renewal. Being definitively Pentecostal in its theology, ecclesiology, and practice, the Renewal encourages rebirth in the Holy Spirit and inward spiritual transformation, rather than political engagement and street protests, as the means to improve the lives of the poor. Paralleling certain principal forms of ecstatic ritual and religious experience of traditional African religion and its New World manifestations, such as speaking in tongues, faith healing, and spirit possession, it is not surprising that millions of African-descended Catholics are finding the comfortable space for free spiritual expression in the Renewal that is lacking in most other forms of communal Catholic ceremony. Attracting throngs of adherents through its formidable blend of Pentecostal spirituality and Roman Catholic tradition, today the Renewal in Latin America could count roughly twenty-five million members, or approximately half of the world total, in the early twenty-first century. Some observers would argue that these figures fall far short of the actual reality, noting that in Brazil, for example, fully half of all Catholics are now Charismatics. Statistical concerns aside, there is no doubt that the Charismatic Renewal, having overtaken the CEB movement, is currently the most impressive and dynamic movement in the contemporary Latin American, Caribbean, and North American Catholic Church. Its revivals fill soccer stadiums from Lima to Caracas, while the annual National Charismatic Congress in Haiti draws over 100,000 believers, making it the second largest gathering in the country, after carnival.

Besides the resonance of the Renewal's animated and ecstatic rituals with traditional African spirituality, another factor surely helps explain the movement's extraordinary success in the course of merely three decades. For the poor of all ethnic backgrounds, it became increasingly apparent that for all of its activism and strides in consciousness, the CEB movement ultimately failed to achieve the kind of concrete liberation that they were so longing for. The CEBs, furthermore, never offered the parallel spiritual liberation or faith healing that is central to the Charismatic Renewal. For Charismatics, the promise of liberation lies not in street protests, voter registration, or literacy campaigns, but in direct ecstatic rebirth in the Holy Spirit. For the millions of African-descended Catholics in the Americas, most of whom can be counted among the region's marginalized, the solace, hope, and solidarity that Charismatic spirituality brings is certainly to be welcomed. However, CEB enthusiasts have lamented the Renewal's social agenda as being weak and misguided. This suggests, if history indeed unfolds in dialectical processes, that a synthesis of Charismatic spirituality with the social and political agenda of the CEB movement could well amount to the greatest triumph of black Catholicism in the Americas. Indeed, concrete signs suggest that something momentous could be on the verge of happening, half a millennium after Roman Catholicism first reached the shores of the New World, as more and more Charismatics seem to be rekindling their interest in social and political reform. For black Catholics throughout the region, so much will depend on such a synthesis, as noted so eloquently by Archbishop Wilton Gregory, the first-ever African-American president of the United States Catholic Bishops Conference, in his 2004 address to the Black Caucus of the United States Congress: "For us religious leaders to deliver a message of hope is crucial, because it will be a defeat for our nation if a new atmosphere of fear and mistrust were to choke the oxygen out of the God-given concern that each of us must bear for one another, especially the underprivileged and the deprived; a commitment that we Catholics call 'Christ's preferential love for the poor'."

See also Candomblé; Oblate Sisters of Providence; Protestantism in the Americas; Religion; Santería; Slave Religions; Toussaint, Pierre; Voodoo; Yoruba Religion and Culture in the Americas

■ ■ *Bibliography*

Bidegain, Ana María, ed. *Historia del Cristianismo en Colombia.* Bogotá: Taurus, 2004.

Bien-Aimé, Gabriel. *Eglise pour changer.* Port-au-Prince: Potest, 1987.

Brandon, George. *Santeria from Africa to New World: The Dead Sell Memories.* Bloomington: Indiana University Press, 1993.

Burdick, John. *Looking for God in Brazil: The Progressive Catholic Church in Brazil's Urban Brazil's Religious Arena.* Berkeley: University of California Press, 1996.

Chesnut, Andrew. *Competitive Spirits: Latin America's New Religious Economy.* New York: Oxford University Press, 2003.

Curtin, Philip. *The Atlantic Slave Trade: A Census.* Madison: University of Wisconsin Press, 1969.

Hayes, Diana L., and Cyprian Davis, eds. *Taking Down Our Harps: Black Catholics in the United States.* Maryknoll, N.Y.: Orbis, 1998.

Heywood, Linda M., ed. *Central Africans and Cultural Transformations in the American Diaspora.* New York: Cambridge University Press, 2002.

Rey, Terry. *Our Lady of Class Struggle: The Cult of the Virgin Mary in Haiti.* Trenton, N.J.: Africa World Press, 1999.

Sweet, James H. *Recreating Africa: Culture, Kinship, and Religion in the African-Portuguese World, 1441–1770.* Chapel Hill: University of North Carolina Press, 2003.

Thornton, John K. *Africa and Africans in the Making of the Atlantic World, 1400–1680.* New York: Cambridge University Press, 1992.

TERRY REY (2005)

CATLETT, ELIZABETH

APRIL 15, 1919

The youngest of three children, printmaker and sculptor Elizabeth Catlett was educated at Dunbar High School in Washington, D.C. Her father, John Catlett, taught at Tuskegee Institute and in the D.C. public schools. He died before her birth. Her mother, Mary Carson Catlett, worked as a truant officer.

Catlett graduated cum laude from Howard University School of Art in 1937, studying with James Herring, James Porter (drawing), James Wells (printmaking), and Lois Mailou Jones (design). In 1940 Catlett earned the M.F.A. degree from the University of Iowa. She studied with painter Grant Wood and changed her concentration from painting to sculpture. In 1941 her thesis project, a marble sculpture titled *Mother and Child,* took first prize in the American Negro Exposition in Chicago.

From 1940 to 1942 Catlett was head of the Art Department at Dillard University. Among her students was Samella Sanders (Lewis), who became a lifelong friend and her biographer. In the summer of 1941 Catlett studied ceramics at the Art Institute of Chicago. She met and married Charles White. Over six years they spent time in Chicago, where she worked at the South Side Art Center; New York, where she studied with sculptor Ossip Zadkine (1942 and 1943); and Hampton Institute, where she taught sculpture (1943). She came to believe that graphics was the appropriate medium to reach large, diverse audiences, and in 1944 she studied lithography at the Art Students' League in New York.

In 1945 Catlett received a Julius Rosenwald Foundation award to do a series on African-American women. She and White traveled to Mexico to work at the Taller de Gráfica Popular. She also studied sculpture at the Escuela de Pintura y Escultura with Francisco Zúñiga and wood carving with José L. Ruiz. After a brief period in New York when she divorced, she returned to Mexico. In 1947 she married Mexican artist Francisco Mora, and the two had three sons, Francisco, Juan, and David. The two artists remained part of the Taller de Gráfica Popular until 1966.

In 1958 Catlett became the first woman to teach at the National University of Mexico's School of Fine Arts. From 1959 until her retirement from teaching in 1976, she served as the head of the school's sculpture department.

Catlett's work combines realism and abstract art. Much of her work deals with African-American women: the mother-and-child theme is strong and recurring. Her art reflects her concern with the needs and aspirations of common people, the poor, and the oppressed. The influence of Mexican as well as African-American culture is evident. Her sculpture, which ranges from monumental to small, is in wood, bronze, stone, terra-cotta, or marble. Works on paper are lithographs, linocuts, woodcuts, collographs, and serigraphs. Among the most well known are *Sharecropper* (1968) and *Malcolm X Speaks for Us* (1969).

Beginning in 1940 Catlett's work has been shown in numerous solo and group exhibitions. It is included in over two dozen prestigious public collections and in many books, catalogs, periodicals, and film and video productions. She has received awards in several countries. Elizabeth Catlett correctly has been called a pioneer and one of the greatest artists of the twentieth century. In 2003 she received the Lifetime Achievement in Contemporary Sculpture Award from the International Sculpture Center. She and her husband live in Cuernavaca and New York City.

See also Art in the United States, Contemporary; Hampton Institute; Painting and Sculpture

■ ■ *Bibliography*

Lewis, Samella. *The Art of Elizabeth Catlett.* Claremont, Calif.: Hancraft Studios, 1984.

Lewis, Samella, and Richard Powell. *Elizabeth Catlett: Works on Paper, 1944–1992.* Hampton, Va.: Hampton University Museum, 1993.

Lewis, Samella, and Ruth Waddy. *Black Artists on Art*. Vol. 2. Los Angeles: Contemporary Crafts, 1971.

Sims, Lowery Stokes. *Elizabeth Catlett: Sculpture*. New York: June Kelly Gallery, n.d.

JEANNE ZEIDLER (1996)
Updated by publisher 2005

CAULWELL, EDGAR

See Hearne, John (Caulwell, Edgar)

CAYTON, HORACE

APRIL 12, 1903
JANUARY 22, 1970

▪ ▪ ▪

Sociologist and educator Horace Roscoe Cayton Jr. was born in Seattle, Washington, the son of activist and newspaper publisher Horace R. Cayton Sr. and Susie Revels Cayton, the daughter of former U.S. Senator Hiram Revels. Cayton dropped out of high school in his junior year and signed up as a messman on a coastal steamer, and in the four succeeding years traveled to California, Mexico, and Hawaii. At the age of twenty, he returned to Seattle. After enrolling in a Young Men's Christian Association (YMCA) preparatory school, he entered the University of Washington, supporting himself by working as a detective. In 1932 he graduated with a degree in sociology.

Invited by eminent sociologist Robert Park to the University of Chicago, Cayton became a research assistant and did graduate work there. In 1934 he became an assistant to the U.S. Secretary of the Interior and helped draft a study of black workers in Birmingham, Alabama. In 1935 he was named instructor of economics and labor at Fisk University in Nashville. In 1936 he returned to Chicago, where he headed a Works Project Administration (WPA) research project that focused on Chicago inner-city life. He also worked as a columnist for the *Pittsburgh Courier* and various magazines. In 1939 he and George S. Mitchell coauthored a book, *Black Workers and the New Unions*, which discussed prejudice in the labor movement and examined the integration of blacks into steel, railroad, and meatpacking unions. The following year, after a study tour in Europe financed by a Rosenwald Foundation grant, Cayton was named director of Chicago's Parkway Community House, a black settlement house and study center. During World War II, Cayton refused to serve in a segregated army and enlisted in the Merchant Marine.

Cayton's best-known scholarly work is *Black Metropolis: A Study of Negro Life in a Northern City* (1945), which he cowrote with St. Clair Drake. Focusing on African-American life in Chicago, the book was hailed as an original study of urbanization in the United States. It received the Anisfield-Wolf Award and was named the outstanding book on race relations for 1945 by the New York Public Library.

In 1950 Cayton left Parkway Community House and was briefly a research assistant for the American Jewish Committee. Some time later, he was hired as a researcher by the National Council of Churches. He continued to write scholarly articles on such subjects as the sociology of mental disorders and the psychology of prejudice. In 1955 he and Setsuko Matsanuga Nishi cowrote *The Changing Scene: Current Trends and Issues*, a discussion of the attitudes of different churches toward social work. During this period, he also served as the *Pittsburgh Courier*'s correspondent at the United Nations. In 1959 Cayton was hired as professor of sociology by the University of California at Berkeley, a position he retained until his death. He published an autobiography, *Long Old Road*, in 1964.

In the late 1960s, Cayton became interested in writing a biography of his friend, the writer Richard Wright (who had written the introduction to *Black Metropolis*). In 1968 he edited a special issue of *Negro Digest* devoted to Wright, and the next year traveled to France to do research for a biography. He died while in Paris, collecting material on Wright.

See also Black World/Negro Digest; Revels, Hiram Rhoades; Wright, Richard

■ ■ *Bibliography*

Fabre, Michel. "The Last Quest of Horace Cayton." *Black World* 19 (May 1970): 41–45.

Page, James A. *Selected Black American, African, and Caribbean Authors*. Littleton, Colo.: Libraries Unlimited, 1985.

GREG ROBINSON (1996)

CELIA

▪ ▪ ▪

Celia, a slave, stood trial in 1855 in Fulton, Missouri, for the murder of her master, Robert Newsom, a prosperous Callaway County farmer. The events that led to her arrest, her trial, and her ultimate fate provide a fascinating case study of the significance of gender in the slaveholding

South, illustrating the manner in which the southern legal system was manipulated to ensure the slaveholders' power over their human chattel while creating the illusion of a society that extended the protection of the law to its slaves.

Purchased a year after the death of Newsom's wife in 1849, Celia served as his concubine for five years, during which time she bore him two children. She lived in a brick cabin he built for her behind the farmhouse, where Newsom lived with two adult daughters, one of whom had two children of her own. By the mid-1850s, Newsom's two sons had established their own farms near that of their father. Sometime in 1854, Celia began a relationship with George, another of Newsom's slaves. When she became pregnant for the third time, George demanded that Celia cease to have sexual relations with her master. Celia appealed to the Newsom women to prevent their father from sexually abusing her. The daughters, however, were in no position to control the actions of their father, who continued to view sexual relations with Celia as his privilege.

On a June night in 1855, Newsom demanded sex of Celia, who responded by beating him to death with a club and disposing of his body by burning it in her fireplace. The family's efforts to find the missing father led George to implicate Celia in his disappearance, and under threat to her children, she confessed and was arrested and tried. Missouri law assigned her public council, led by John Jameson, a noted attorney and democratic politician. Jameson based his defense on the claim that Celia, under Missouri law, had the same right to use deadly force to defend her honor as did white women. This defense not only recognized the crime of rape against slave women, something the legal system of no southern state did; but it also threatened a slaveholder's control over the reproductive capabilities of female slaves. For precisely these reasons it was disallowed by the presiding judge, who agreed with the prosecution's traditional contention that a female slave had no right to use force to reject her master's sexual demands. A jury of local farmers convicted Celia, and the Missouri Supreme Court rejected her attorneys' appeal for a new trial. On December 23, 1855, Celia was hanged in Fulton.

See also Slavery and the Constitution

■ ■ *Bibliography*

McLaurin, Melton A. *Celia, A Slave.* Athens: University of Georgia Press, 1991.

State of Missouri Against Celia, A Slave. File 4496, Callaway County Court, October Term, 1855: Callaway County Courthouse, Fulton, Mo.

Williamson, Hugh P. "Document: The State of Missouri Against Celia, A Slave." *Midwest Journal* 8 (Spring/Fall, 1956): 408–420.

MELTON A. MCLAURIN (1996)
Updated bibliography

CEMETERIES AND BURIALS

One of the most direct and unaltered visual manifestations of the African influence on the culture of African Americans in the United States is found in the social behaviors associated with funerals. In many rural graveyards across the South, and in quite a few urban cemeteries in the North and Far West, too, black Americans mark the final resting places of their loved ones in a distinctive manner. While they use standardized stone markers and floral arrangements, the personal property of the deceased is frequently placed on the grave as well. Sometimes a single emblematic item, such as a glass pitcher or vase, sits atop the mounded earth, while in other places a grave may be covered with a veritable inventory of the dead person's household goods.

In addition to glass and ceramic containers (which might also serve as holders for flowers), one may also find cups, saucers, clocks, salt-and-pepper shakers, spoons, toothbrushes, lightbulbs, soap dishes, flashlights, razors, toys, cigar boxes, false teeth, marbles, and piggy banks. Such material assemblages do not merely contrast with the usual Euro-American ideal of a sedate cemetery landscape; they establish a link to customary practices known not only on southern plantations but in West and Central Africa.

In 1843 the daughter of a Georgia planter recalled that "Negro graves were always decorated with the last article used by the departed, and broken pitchers and broken bits of colored glass were considered even more appropriate than the white shells from the beach nearby. Sometimes they carved rude wooden figures like images of idols, and sometimes a patchwork quilt was laid upon the grave." This antebellum scene not only matches much of what can be found today in black graveyards but could be substituted for descriptions of African practice as well. E. J. Glave, who traveled through Zaire in 1884, wrote that "the natives mark the final resting-places of their friends by ornamenting their graves with crockery, empty bottles, old cooking pots, and so on, all of which articles are rendered useless by being cracked or penetrated with holes."

Another traveler in nearby Gabon observed, "Over or near the graves of the rich are built little huts, where are laid the common articles used by them in their life—pieces of crockery, knives, sometimes a table, mirrors, and other goods obtained in foreign trade." While the stability of these behaviors across such lengthy spans of time and space might at first seem astonishing, it must be recalled that funerary customs were one of the few areas of black life into which slave owners tended not to intrude. Thus, in spite of the massive conversion of Africans to Christian faiths, they retained many of their former rituals associated with the veneration of the dead.

They remembered, for example, that the spirit of the deceased person might linger near the body for a period of time before moving to the spirit world. Believing further that the needs of the spirit are similar to those of a living human, they maintained the belief that the potential fury of an individual's spirit could be soothed by presenting it with the various items that the individual had used while alive. One resident of the Georgia Sea Islands testified, "I don't guess you be bother much the spirits if you give-em a good funeral and put the things what belong to 'em on top of the grave." Another added, "Spirits need these [things] same as the man. Then the spirit rest and don't wander." Statements from other Deep South black communities support this belief in the lingering spirit and warn that "unless you bury a person's things with him, he will come back after them." Left unsaid here is a more threatening corollary belief that roaming spirits can exact a further toll; they could, if disturbed, cause another person's death.

Placing personal items on graves is, then, more than an emotional gesture aimed at providing the bereaved with the ritual means to reconnect with a loved one (although this behavior does indeed serve that function). For those who retain the African-derived belief in a soul with two parts—one that travels immediately to the afterworld and one that lingers for a while near the body—the burial mounds that bristle with bowls, lamps, mirrors, plaster statues, and other hardware not only keep the deceased at rest but contribute to the physical well-being of the community. However, for those African Americans whose beliefs are derived from a more orthodox Christian position, the vessels placed atop burial mounds (often broken just slightly) are explained simply as metaphors of death, and such proverbs as "The pitcher that goes often to the well shall at last be broken" are cited as a plausible rationale for their use as grave decorations.

In addition to personal objects, some African-American graves in the South are decorated with white seashells and pebbles. These suggest a watery environment at the bottom of either the ocean or a lake or river. While some might see the allusion to water as derived from the Christian association of water with salvation (as in the sacrament of baptism), these objects are more likely signs of the remembrance of African custom. In Kongo belief (in South Carolina, nearly 40 percent of all slaves imported between 1733 and 1807 were from the Kongo-speaking region), the world of the dead is understood to lie not only underground but also underwater. This place is the realm of the *bakulu*, creatures whose white color marks them as deceased. Shells and stones signal the boundary of this realm, which can be reached only by penetrating beneath two physical barriers. Their whiteness, moreover, recalls that at least in Central Africa, white, not black, is the color of death. Also found in black cemeteries are a number of other features traceable to Kongo sources: pipes driven into burial mounds to serve as speaking tubes that may allow beneficial communication with the deceased, statues of chickens that recall animal sacrifices offered to the deceased, and mirrors that are said to catch the flashing light of a spirit and hold it there. Any of these features alone might indicate only the action of a single imagination engaged in the task of decorating a loved one's final resting place. But when several occur together, as is so often the case in graveyards of the black Sea Islanders of South Carolina and Georgia, we have powerful evidence of allegiance to a venerable African tradition.

In the light of these signs (all of which may be interpreted as elements of cultural continuity), it is not surprising that black burial sites in the Bay Area of California should resemble those seen in South Carolina. When given the opportunity, any people will carry its heartfelt customs from place to place as indispensable cultural baggage. Nor is it strange that a Mr. Coffee machine should turn up in a black cemetery in Mississippi. Among the more tradition-minded of the African-American faithful, the significance of a modern-day coffeemaker in a graveyard is very clear: "Spirits need these same as the man."

See also African Burial Ground Project; Africanisms

■ ■ *Bibliography*

Garman, James C. "Viewing the Color Line Through the Material Culture of Death." *Historical Archaeology* 28, no. 3 (1994): 74–93.

Jones-Jackson, Patricia. *When Roots Die: Endangered Traditions on the Sea Islands.* Athens: University of Georgia Press, 1987.

Nichols, Elaine. *The Last Miles of the Way: African-American Homegoing Traditions, 1890–Present.* Columbia, S.C.: South Carolina State Museum, 1989.

Nigh, Robin F. "Under Grave Conditions: African-American Signs of Life and Death in North Florida." *Markers* 14 (1997): 158–189.

Puckett, Newbell Niles. *The Magic and Folk Beliefs of the Southern Negro.* Chapel Hill: University of North Carolina Press, 1926.

Thompson, Robert Farris, and Joseph Cornet. *The Four Moments of the Sun: Kongo Art in Two Worlds.* Washington, D.C.: National Gallery of Art, 1981.

Trinkley, Michael. *Grave Matters: The Preservation of African American Cemeteries.* Columbia, S.C.: Chicora Foundation, 1996.

Vlach, John Michael. *The Afro-American Tradition in Decorative Arts* (1978). Reprint, Athens: University of Georgia Press, 1990.

JOHN MICHAEL VLACH (1996)
Updated by author 2005

CENTRAL AFRICAN RELIGIONS AND CULTURE IN THE AMERICAS

"Central Africa," more properly "West-Central Africa," is the huge region inland from the Atlantic coastline delimited in the north by Cape Lopez in present-day Gabon and in the south by the Kunene River, now the border between Angola and Namibia. People from Central Africa formed a significant proportion of Africans in most black communities of the Americas throughout the period of the slave trade. Of the 11.1 million persons embarked as slaves from Africa to the Americas, 44 percent were from Central Africa. People from this area formed 89 percent of those sent in the early decades of the trade (1519–1650). Their presence declined to 29 percent in the period 1651–1725, then rose to 41 percent in 1726–1825 and 50 percent in 1826–1867.

Of all major slave-importing areas, the British Caribbean exhibited the lowest proportion of Central Africans among incoming bondspeople: about fifteen percent. At the other extreme were Brazil and Saint Domingue, where Central Africans constituted respectively about three-fifths and half the total. Cuba and Guadeloupe were intermediate cases, with a little under one-third of the newly enslaved from Central Africa. In French/British/Dutch South America and British North America (including Louisiana), the proportion was somewhat over one-fourth. Within each of these societies there were variations over time and by subregion. An extreme case is Brazil's Southeast after 1810, where three-fourths of forced migrants were Central Africans. In the American South, Louisiana and South Carolina received proportionately more Central Africans than other areas.

The cultural impact of Central Africans in the Americas may have been more than commensurate to their numbers. Central Africa was a relatively uniform "culture area," compared to the regions of West Africa. Then too, even after 1750, when the trade in human beings extended far into the interior, at least a large minority of enslaved Central Africans still came from closely related peoples near the coast: in particular, the Kongo (Bakongo) from the lower Zaire basin, the Mbundu from the hinterland of Luanda, and the Ovimbundu from the highlands behind Benguela. Thus, Central Africans sold into Atlantic slavery from different origins often quickly found that they had much in common, from language (all were speakers of West Bantu tongues, many mutually intelligible) to cosmology. In sum, their numbers, their general similarities, and the large core group among them from closely related cultures probably hastened the formation of new Central African communities in the Americas and strengthened their hand in negotiating differences with other displaced Africans.

A significant minority of Central Africans also brought with them an unusual resource for their encounter with European and Creole cultures: a prior knowledge of Christianity, acquired in their homelands. The Kingdom of Kongo, in the lower Zaire basin and northern Angola, adopted Christianity as the state religion in the early sixteenth century, and the Portuguese introduced it a century later into their spheres of influence in Angola. In the former region, lay catechists linked to the nobility were important in bringing Christian rituals and knowledge about Christ and the saints to the local level, even in the absence of missionaries. This was a Christianity reinterpreted from a Central African perspective, as one would expect in a part of Africa where religious movements have commonly experimented with foreign rituals and symbols, while subordinating them to indigenous understandings.

Among Central Africans carried to the Caribbean and to British North America, people shipped from the Zaire and points north generally predominated. The same applies to Central Africans carried to Brazil during the early decades of the trade and (to a lesser extent) after about 1820. In these cases, then, Kongo and near-Kongo culture left a strong imprint. Brazil during the eighteenth and early nineteenth centuries received Central Africans predominantly through Luanda and Benguela. Thus, in this period the Kongo influence in Brazil was weaker, but the

Portuguese colony was strongly marked by the presence of enslaved people from the Kongo-related Mbundu and Ovimbundu.

Emblematic of the encounter of enslaved Kongo, Mbundu, and Ovimbundu is the name they attributed to shipmates in the Middle Passage, regarded as siblings: *malungu,* meaning "ship" (literally "gigantic canoe") or, by extension, "partner in misfortune." Reflection on *malungu* and its referent, the slave ship, a vehicle of physical and social death, would have led bondspeople from these core Central African groups to discover that they shared the concept of *kalunga,* signifying "ocean (or large body of water)," "death," "the otherworld," and "the interface between this and the otherworld." Through *kalunga,* in turn, these people would have recognized a common cosmology, centered in a concern to propitiate ancestral and tutelary earth and water spirits (the latter called *bisimbi,* plural of *simbi,* among the Kongo) to maintain community health; in the diagnosis of individual and social disorders as frequently the product of witchcraft; and in the recourse to ritual specialists in "cults of affliction" (a phenomenon widespread in Central Africa) to counter witchcraft and effect cures, usually through the use of consecrated medicines (among the Kongo, *minkisi,* plural of *nkisi*) that captured the force of specific spirits. Among the Kongo at least, these holy objects were often spiritually empowered by being tied intricately with rope or thread; symptomatically, their verb for "tie" (*kanga*) was used to translate the Christian concept of "save" (as in "Christ saves").

In conversing about "cults of affliction," newly enslaved Kongo, Mbundu, and Ovimbundu would have realized that they all perceived drums to be eminent mediators with the spirit world, particularly the single-skin, long cylindrical drum made of a hollowed-out log, called *ngoma* by the Kongo. The subject of *ngoma* (at least among Kongo and Mbundu) would have led to reflections on dancing, which was commonly accompanied by drumming and call-response singing and practiced in a circle of participants that moved in a counterclockwise direction. Dancing, in turn, would have evoked ritual kick fighting, also practiced within a similarly moving circle. This counterclockwise motion and certain movements in kick fighting made explicit reference to what scholars have called the "Kongo cosmogram": a "cross" inscribed in a circle or reclining oval, with the horizontal east-west line representing the *kalunga* interface and the vertical north-south line connecting the high noon (masculine power) of this life, above, with the midnight (feminine power) of the other world, below. In this symbol of the cosmos, the outer circle or oval described the counterclockwise move-

ment of the sun, when seen from the southern hemisphere. Ritual kick fighters, within their moving circle, purposely adopted inverted positions—supporting their weight on their hands, with their feet in the air—thereby symbolically mirroring *kalunga* to draw on its power. More broadly, in Central African warfare "dancing" was deemed part of a spiritual preparation to confront the enemy, not just a means of honing one's combat skills.

In the Americas, abundant evidence indicates that some combination of Kongo, Mbundu, Ovimbundu, and related cultures was indeed at the core of most Central African communities. *Malungu,* as a metonym for "shipmate," entered European languages: directly in Brazil (Portuguese *malungo*), in translation in Haiti and Cuba, respectively as *batiment* ("ship") and *carabela* ("caravel"). More significantly, in Cuba the extensive ritual vocabulary of the "lengua congo" has been shown to be basically Kikongo, the language of the Kongo. In southeastern Brazil, the ritual vocabularies of Macumba and Umbanda, African-Brazilian religions described in Rio de Janeiro and São Paulo from the early twentieth century on, show considerable resonance with Kikongo and Kimbundu (the language of the Mbundu). The lexicon of the Cabula, a cult described around 1900 in Espírito Santo, is even more clearly related to these languages. The vocabulary of Petro cults in Haitian vodou includes clear references to Kongo spirit names (among them, *simbi*).

In Cuba, evidence of the heritage of Central African "cults of affliction" can be found in the Palo Monte cults and their practice still today of making *prendas*: spiritually empowered charms, commonly made in a pot, which clearly resemble in form and function Kongo *minkisi,* even to the point of being bound with thread in intricate patterns. In nineteenth-century Brazil such objects were also present, as were anthropomorphic charms (in the Cabula called *baculo,* the Kikongo word for "ancestor"). The Cabula itself had much in common with a community cult of affliction among the Kongo (most commonly referred to as *kimpasi*), in the delimitation of its sacred space (a Kongo cosmogram) and in the ritual death and rebirth through trance experienced by both its male and female initiates. During and after slavery in Saint Domingue/Haiti, North America, and Brazil, there are abundant references to small amulet-charms containing medicinal substances empowered by tightly wound thread, called *paquets congo* in Saint Domingue and French Louisiana. In Brazilian Macumba and Umbanda, as well as in Haitian vodou and Cuban Palo Monte, ritual marks drawn on a consecrated ground, on banners, or on charms (marks known in Brazil as *pontos riscados*—drawn "knots" or "stitches"), which demand esoteric knowledge to be interpreted, seem inspired by the Kongo cosmogram.

Vodou sacrifice in Haiti. *A Vodou priest takes blood from the neck of a recently sacrificed bull, offered to the Vodou spirit Ogou by a mambo (priestess) at the edge of a sacred pool of mud in Plaine du Nord, Haiti, July 23, 2004. Haitians gather there to honor the saint day of the hamlet's patron saint Jacques (St. James of Compestela) and also Ogou, the Vodou spirit of war and iron.* © DANIEL MOREL/CORBIS

With respect to dance, the *jongo/caxambu/batuque* in Brazil's Southeast is performed to the rhythm of the single-faced drum mentioned above, as well as sometimes to that of the friction drum (*puíta*), an instrument known to the three "core" Central African peoples. (Both drums are also found in Cuba, where they are associated with the "Congo" community.) The dance's variable choreography in western São Paulo and in the Paraíba Valley (respectively with and without the *umbigada,* the sudden meeting of the navels of the dancing couples), corresponds to the variants observed in the mid-nineteenth century among the Mbundu and Kongo, respectively. In the Paraíba Valley, its opening rituals, its performance within a circle of observers-participants moving counterclockwise, and the riddles posed by one master singer to the other—*pontos de demanda,* or challenge "knots" demanding to be "untied"—indicate its origins in Central African religious precepts. *Capoeira,* the now-secularized Brazilian kick dancing, whose performers still commonly assume "upside-down" positions, must initially have had similar religious connotations, as probably did its relative, "knocking and kicking," centered in South Carolina. The dancing en-

gaged in before battle by African slave rebels in South Carolina's Stono rebellion (1739), most of them from the region of the Kingdom of Kongo, almost certainly had this religious dimension.

Central Africans of diverse provenance in many, perhaps most areas of the Americas were able to form new, enlarged communities that provided them with a sense of cultural continuity, as well as a set of shared outlooks to confront the challenges of slavery. Yet, they also soon began building bridges to Africans of other origins, often aided in this by the discovery of significant shared understandings. The American ring shout is a case in point; although scholars have emphasized its Central African origins, they have also shown that counterclockwise movement in a circle (with participants keeping their feet constantly in touch with the ground) was typical of religious dancing in West as well as Central Africa. That it was not typical of dances of European origin further contributed to the ring shout's evolution as a central element of African-American identity. Another example is the Candomblé Angola in Salvador, Bahia. Here the deities have the attributes of those of the Candomblé of Yoruba origin, but Central African names (the spirit of thunder is *Nsasi*, which means "thunder" in Kikongo); furthermore, drum rhythms are identical to ones documented among the Kongo. A third example is Haitian vodou, which has separate Rada and Petro forms (reflecting strong initial influences, respectively, from Dahomey and Central Africa) yet an essential unity of ritual and cosmology.

Finally, the reinterpreted Christianity of many Central Africans also played a role in the formation of New World cultures and identities. It provided Africans (and Creoles) with polysemic symbols and rituals that could alternately provide an avenue for integration into a European-dominated society, a way of feigning such integration, a resource to reaffirm Central African identities (after all, the 1704 Antonian movement in the Kongo Kingdom appropriated Saint Anthony and Christ as native-born Kongolese), or even a common ground for unity between different African groups (something that has been argued for the case of pre- and postrevolutionary Saint Domingue).

See also Africanisms; Candomblé; Capoeira; Jongo; Social Dance; Voodoo

■ ■ *Bibliography*

Dianteuill, Erwan. "Les Amériques kôngo, Brésil, Cuba, Haïti." In *Le Geste kôngo*, Exhibition Catalog, Musée Dapper (September 18, 2002–January 19, 2003), orgs. Christiane Falgayrettes-Leveau and Robert Farris Thompson. Paris: Éditions Dapper, 2002.

Eltis, David. "The Volume and Structure of the Transatlantic Slave Trade: A Reassessment." *The William and Mary Quarterly* 58, no. 1 (January 2001): 17–46.

Gomez, Michael. *Exchanging Our Country Marks: The Transformation of African Identities in the Colonial and Antebellum South*. Chapel Hill: University of North Carolina Press, 1998.

Heywood, Linda M., ed. *Central Africans and Cultural Transformations in the American Diaspora*. Cambridge: Cambridge University Press, 2002.

Schwegler, Armin. "El vocabulario (ritual) bantú de Cuba. Parte I: Acerca de la matriz africana de la 'lengua congo' en *El Monte* y *Vocabulario Congo* de Lydia Cabrera," and "El vocabulario (ritual) bantú de Cuba. Parte II: Apéndices 1-2," respectively in *América Negra*, 16 and 19 (1998).

Slenes, Robert W. "'*Malungu, Ngoma*'s Coming!': Africa Hidden and Discovered in Brazil." In *Mostra do Redescobrimento: Negro de Corpo e Alma—Black in Body and Soul*, Catalog of Exhibition (April 23–September 7, 2002), org. Nelson Aguilar, pp. 221–229. São Paulo: Fundação Bienal de São Paulo/Associação Brasil 500 Anos Artes Visuais, 2000.

Sweet, James H. *Recreating Africa: Culture, Kinship, and Religion in the African-Portuguese World, 1441-1770*. Chapel Hill: University of North Carolina Press, 2003.

Thompson, Robert Farris, and Joseph Cornet. *The Four Moments of the Sun: Kongo Art in Two Worlds*. Washington, D.C.: National Gallery of Art, 1981.

Thornton, John, "Les racines du vaudou. Religion africaine et société haïtienne dans la Saint-Domingue prérévolutionnaire," *Anthropologie et Sociétés* 22, no. 1 (1998): 85–102.

ROBERT W. SLENES (2005)

CÉSAIRE, AIMÉ

JUNE 26, 1913

The Martinican poet, playwright, essayist, and politician Aimé Césaire emerged as one of the leading voices of the *Négritude* movement after World War II. Born in Basse-Pointe, in 1931 he was sent to the Louis-le-Grand secondary school in Paris on scholarship to prepare for entrance to the École Normale Supérieure, which he entered in 1935. In March of that year he published an article on "Black Youth and Assimilation" (Négreries: Jeunesse noire et assimilation") in the only surviving issue of *L'Étudiant noir*. Neither he nor L. S. Senghor used the term *Négritude* in that ephemeral student paper. The notions of African heritage that would eventually be called *Négritude* were initially culled from Leo Frobenius's book *Kulturgeschichte Afrikas*, in French translation *La Civilisation africaine* (1936), as both Césaire and Senghor later confirmed.

Césaire has had a tortured relationship with black America. In the decade prior to *Brown v. Board of Education* professors Mercer Cook and Edward A. Jones saw the young intellectual and poet of *Négritude* as a beacon to the race. (Césaire's thesis on the theme of the South in the work of black American writers received a mention in Cook's *Five French Negro Authors* in 1943.) From the first Congress of Negro Writers and Artists held in Paris in 1956 to the late 1960s, however, Césaire was held in suspicion by the black elite of the United States. In 1958 John A. Davis of Howard University, who led the U.S. delegation to the Paris conference and who had taken grievous offense at Césaire's depiction of black Americans as a colonized people within their own country, co-edited the volume *Africa from the Point of View of American Negro Scholars*. Davis assigned to Samuel Allen the difficult task of presenting to integrationists the originality of a poet who was a Marxist, a Communist delegate from Martinique to the French National Assembly from 1946 to 1956, and an atheist. The Black Power movement from the end of the 1960s through the 1970s, which would promote a new radicalized black elite—many of whom had Caribbean connections—overturned the view of Césaire held by their elders. From the late 1970s to the present a new generation of university-trained black intellectuals has developed a more sophisticated view of Césaire, which has followed the general trend toward diasporic and postcolonial studies.

Négritude is the central subject that has dominated discussion of Césaire in the United States. Poorly understood and usually reduced to a tag line such as "Black is Beautiful," the word and the concept emerged in Césaire's long poem *Notebook of a Return to the Native Land (Cahier d'un retour au pays natal)*, which was first published as a volume in New York by Brentano's in 1947. The poem in its pre-1956 editions demonstrates a fairly clear dialectical structure in which the speaker-hero first describes the sick state of his colonized native land; then, in a long middle section, the speaker makes an Orphic descent into his own and his island's social and psychic history; so as to be reborn in the upward-surging and much shorter final section of the poem. In conclusion, the speaker assumes a messianic leadership role. Césaire's concept of *Négritude*, unlike that of L. S. Senghor of Senegal with which it is too often confused, is thus a dynamic structure of a lyric and dramatic type that he has sometimes called Pelean (after the name of Martinique's volcano) because of the violent explosive imagery that characterized his poetry from the early 1940s to about 1960. The period from 1941 to 1948 marked Césaire's closest association with the Paris surrealists. The surrealist poetic features of his collections *Miraculous Weapons* (1946) and *Solar Throat Slashed* (1948) were so mystifying to American readers used to the style of Langston Hughes and Countee Cullen that his treatment of subjects such as lynching elicited no critical reaction. His poem on the brutal killing of young Emmett Till in Mississippi in August 1955 was published in the Paris journal *Présence Africaine* as "Message sur l'état de l'Union" ("State of the Union Address") in the February–March 1956 issue before being collected in *Ferrements (Ferraments*, 1960). It met the same fate.

The full flower of Césaire's heroic vision of *Négritude* is to be found in his lyrical oratorio *And the Dogs Were Silent (Et les chiens se taisaient)*, which was first published in English in 1990. In *Dogs* the sacrificial hero, called The Rebel, undergoes agony and death, which are meant to galvanize the community to collective action. Césaire told an early student of his theater that he had in mind the tragedies of Aeschylus as Nietzsche understood them in *The Birth of Tragedy*.

During the decade of the 1960s, as African and Afro-Caribbean societies—other than Césaire's own in the French West Indies—were gaining their independence, Césaire published no new poetry and turned to the theater. In his first play written for the stage, *The Tragedy of*

King Christophe (La Tragédie du roi Christophe, 1963), a minor character called Metellus embodies the agonism that characterized the speaker of the *Notebook* and the hero of *Dogs*. Unable to come to terms with the needs of political compromise, Metellus is killed by the future leaders of Haiti on the battlefield. This fate quite clearly signifies that Césaire's lyrical Rebel was to be abandoned on the threshold of politics as predominantly black societies emerged across the world. The Haitian Revolution in Césaire's work is usually summed up in a few lines extracted from the *Notebook*. *Toussaint Louverture* (1961) preceded *The Tragedy of King Christophe* by two years and explains many of the choices Césaire made in the events and characters depicted. *Toussaint Louverture* is divided into three sections, which represent the dialectical movement of history as Césaire then understood it: I—The Insurrection of the White Colonists; II—The Mulatto Revolt; III—The Black Revolution. The revolt of the mulattos was but the antithesis of the white reactionary insurrection; it triggered the only true revolutionary movement, that of the black ethnoclass. Thus, Césaire's dramatic hero had to be Christophe, the black emperor, rather than Dessalines (murdered by his generals), Pétion (a mulatto), or Toussaint (the Rebel who dies sacrificially in a French military prison).

The condemnation of the United States and the United Nations for complicity in the death of Patrice Lumumba in *Une Saison au Congo (A Season in the Congo*, 1965) did not elicit much sympathy from either black or white America. Nor did Césaire's preference for Malcolm X over Dr. Martin Luther King Jr. in *Une Tempête (A Tempest*, 1969) improve the playwright's standing in the eyes of the African-American establishment in the aftermath of the assassination of King. (Césaire told interviewers that he had King in mind in rewriting Shakespeare's Ariel and that Malcolm was his model for Caliban.) The elegiac tone of Césaire's final collection of verse, *moi, laminaire. . . (i laminaria. . .*, 1982) marked a critical engagement with the heroic pose of the hero of *Négritude*. It has been neglected by partisans of Afrocentrism, who have invested heavily in a mythic interpretation of Césaire's first phase to the detriment of a full understanding of his work's significance for the black Americas.

See also Afrocentrism; Chamoiseau, Patrick; Dessalines, Jean-Jacques; Haitian Revolution; Négritude; Toussaint-Louverture

■■ *Bibliography*

Allen, Samuel. "Tendencies in African Poetry." In *Africa from the Point of View of American Negro Scholars*, edited by Alioune Diop and John A. Davis, pp. 175–198. Paris: Présence Africaine, 1958.

Arnold, A. James. *Modernism and Negritude: The Poetry and Poetics of Aimé Césaire*. Cambridge, Mass., and London: Harvard University Press, 1981.

Arnold, A. James. "La réception afro-américaine de Césaire: un dialogue difficile aux États-Unis." In *Césaire 70*, edited by M.aM. Ngal and Martin Steins, pp. 141–161. Paris: Silex, 1984.

Arnold, A. James. "Negritude, Then and Now." In *A History of Literature in the Caribbean*. Vol. 1. *Hispanic and Francophone Literature*, edited by A. James Arnold, pp. 479–484. Amsterdam and Philadelphia: John Benjamins, 1994.

Césaire, Aimé. *A Season in the Congo*. Translated by Ralph Manheim. New York: Grove Press, 1968.

Césaire, Aimé. *The Tragedy of King Christophe*. Translated by Ralph Manheim. New York: Grove Press, 1969.

Césaire, Aimé. *The Collected Poetry*. Translated by Clayton Eshleman and Annette Smith. Berkeley: University of California Press, 1983 (bilingual edition).

Césaire, Aimé. *Lyric and Dramatic Poetry, 1946–1982*. Translated by Clayton Eshleman and Annette Smith. Charlottesville, Va., and London: University Press of Virginia, 1990.

Césaire, Aimé. *A Tempest; based on Shakespeare's* The Tempest—*Adaptation for a Black Theatre*. Translated by Richard Miller. New York: Theatre Communications Group, 1992 [1985].

Cook, Mercer. *Five French Negro Authors*. Washington, D.C.: Associated Negro Publishers, 1943.

A. JAMES ARNOLD (2005)

CHAGUARAMAS

In the summer of 1940, as the Nazi war machine launched its furious assault on France and Britain in an effort to inflict a decisive victory on its European opponents, the Franklin D. Roosevelt administration and the British wartime government, headed by Winston Churchill, negotiated an exchange of surplus destroyers and other military supplies for several naval bases in the British West Indian colonies and Bermuda. The exchange of notes between the two governments on September 2, 1940, marked a major turning point in Anglo-American relations and in the course of the war against the Axis powers. In effect, the British West Indian colonies had become a cornerstone of the "Special Relationship" that would be consolidated over the course of World War II and the Cold War that arose after 1945.

As part of the exchange the United States obtained the right to establish a military base in Chaguaramas on the northwest peninsula of Trinidad and Tobago—a relatively secluded region with easy access to the Caribbean Sea. The choice of the site was met with less than enthusiasm by the existing colonial administration, and, despite the reservations of the governor of the British colony, the area was ceded to American control for ninety-nine years. The wartime context did not disguise the Imperial government's lack of concern for local sentiment; in fact, it emphasized the arbitrary nature of colonial rule and the willingness of the United States to profit from Britain's increasing dependence upon American support for its war effort.

It was a decision that would return to haunt both the British and American governments when West Indian nationalists sought to achieve political independence from the British government in the 1950s and 1960s. The American attempts to retain the base in the 1950s were perceived as a symbol of the colonial order under which the rights and wishes of the inhabitants of the colony were treated dismissively. Chaguaramas also represented, in the eyes of West Indian nationalists, the heavy-handed effort by the United States to establish a new quasicolonial order in the West Indies in the waning years of British colonial rule.

The eruption of the Anglo-American–West Indian dispute over Chaguaramas occurred in 1956 as plans were being finalized to bring the West Indies Federation into existence. The British government and West Indian nationalists had agreed that the West Indies Federation would constitute the basis for the transfer of power in the Caribbean and the accession to independence by the colonies. In 1956 the issue of identifying a suitable site for the federal capital was entrusted by West Indian leaders to a group of British officials who were to identify a list of suitable sites. In Trinidad, a wide cross section of local opinion championed the island as the site for the federal capital, and in the 1956 national election campaign, Eric Williams, the leader of the victorious People's National Movement, endorsed the idea of Trinidad as the future capital. Unfortunately, the British commission was not impressed by Trinidad's appeal to its citizens, and its report ranked Trinidad as the third choice for the capital site. In explaining the low ranking for Trinidad, the commission's report was scathing about the colony's political life and disparaging in its specific references to the Indian community on the island. It was a decisive moment in the development of West Indian nationalism, and the commission's report was emblematic of the discomfiture that West Indian nationalism had created for British officials. In February 1957 the West Indian leadership decided to endorse Trinidad as the site of the future capital—a decisive rejection of the commission's report.

As a consequence, the West Indian leaders requested that the British government convene a tripartite meeting among the West Indies, the United Kingdom, and the United States to discuss: (1) releasing the naval base at Chaguaramas for the establishment of the federal capital, and (2) a defense agreement among the three parties. The West Indian leaders were making it clear that they would not accept the inequities of the agreement of 1940 and that they were prepared to renegotiate the American presence in Trinidad and the wider region.

Over the next three years the dispute would escalate as Eric Williams used the Chaguaramas issue to establish his credentials as a committed Trinidadian nationalist who was prepared to challenge both the United Kingdom and the United States on the legacies of the colonial order. Williams's challenge would force both the United States and Britain to agree to renegotiate the terms of the Chaguaramas lease and to accept that West Indian nationalism had redefined the terms of the Anglo-American relationship in the Caribbean. Just as important, it expanded the number of independent states in the Caribbean that stood as a model of political development in which people of African descent were key players (in marked contrast to the continued weight of Jim Crow on American life). The Chaguaramas issue formed part of the ongoing effort to consolidate the idea of freedom for African-descent populations in the Americas.

See also Caribbean Commission; International Relations of the Anglophone Caribbean; Peoples National Movement; West Indies Federation; Williams, Eric

■ ■ *Bibliography*

Fraser, Cary. *Ambivalent Anti-Colonialism: The United States and the Genesis of West Indian Independence, 1940–1964.* Westport, Conn.: Greenwood, 1994.

Mordecai, John. *The West Indies: The Federal Negotiations.* London: Allen & Unwin, 1968.

Ryan, Selwyn. *Race and Nationalism in Trinidad and Tobago.* Toronto: University of Toronto Press, 1972.

CARY FRASER (2005)

CHAMBERLAIN, WILT

AUGUST 21, 1936
OCTOBER 12, 1999

❙❙❙━━━━━━━━

Born in Philadelphia, basketball player Wilton Norman "Wilt" Chamberlain was one of nine children of William Chamberlain, a custodian/handyman, and Olivia Chamberlain, a part-time domestic. Large even as a child, he grew to seven feet one inch by the age of eighteen and developed great running speed and endurance. At Overbrook High School, he starred in track and field. Dubbed "Wilt the Stilt" and "The Big Dipper" for his great height, he became the premier high school basketball player of his era. The Philadelphia Warriors of the National Basketball Association (NBA) drafted him before he finished high school, but Chamberlain elected to go to college. After fierce competition among colleges, he chose to attend the University of Kansas. While at Kansas, he starred in track, and his amazing basketball skills and dominance led to many changes in the college rule book, including the widening of the foul lanes, in order to hamper him. Despite these impediments, in his first year with the varsity Chamberlain led Kansas to the National College Athletic Association (NCAA) finals. However, the constant harassment, fouling, and triple-teaming upset him, and after another year he left Kansas, saying basketball was no longer fun. Not yet eligible for the NBA, he spent a year touring with the Harlem Globetrotters (playing at guard!).

Chamberlain entered the NBA with the Philadelphia Warriors in 1959–1960 and was an immediate sensation. In his rookie year he broke eight NBA scoring and rebounding records, and was named both Rookie of the Year and Most Valuable Player. In 1960 he grabbed a record fifty-five rebounds in one game. The following season Chamberlain had the greatest individual scoring performance the game has ever seen. He scored 4,029 points, an average of 50.4 points per game, and on March 2, 1962, scored 100 points in a game.

Chamberlain went on to play a total of fourteen seasons with the Philadelphia/Golden State Warriors (1959–1965), the Philadelphia 76ers (1965–1968), and the Los Angeles Lakers (1968–1973). He won four MVP awards and was named to the All-Star team thirteen times (every year he was in contention). He revolutionized professional basketball, ushering in the era of the dominant centers, usually seven feet or taller. A sensational scorer during his early years, he relied on a graceful jump shot and popularized the "dunk" shot. His lifetime scoring totals—31,419 points and an average of 30.1 points per game—stood for many years. He also excelled at shot blocking and defense. While Chamberlain led his teams to NBA championships in 1967 and 1972, his teams lost several times in playoff finals, and fans unfairly derided him as a "loser." A controversial figure, he complained about the lack of recognition of his talents, stating "nobody roots for Goliath." In 1973 he left the Lakers and was hired as a player-coach by the San Diego Conquistadores of the American Basketball Association (ABA). The Lakers obtained an injunction in court forbidding him from playing, and he passed the year unhappily as a coach, leading the team to a 38–47 record, and then retired. He was elected to the Naismith Memorial Basketball Hall of Fame in Springfield, Massachusetts, in 1978.

After his retirement, Chamberlain, a volleyball enthusiast, helped start the International Volleyball Association and also sponsored track-and-field meets. At various times he pursued a performing career. He acted in the film *Conan the Destroyer* (1984) and appeared as himself in several commercials. During the 1960s he owned the Harlem nightspot Big Wilt's Small Paradise, and he later owned Wilt Chamberlain's Restaurants. He achieved considerable notoriety for his claims of extraordinary sexual promiscuity in his 1991 book, *A View from Above*. Whatever his exploits off the court, he remains one of the greatest basketball players of all time.

Chamberlain died unexpectedly of heart failure in 1999.

See also Basketball

■ ■ *Bibliography*

Chamberlain, Wilt. *The View from Above*. New York: Villard Books, 1991.

Chamberlain, Wilt, and David Shaw. *Wilt: Just Like Any Other 7-Foot Black Millionaire Who Lives Next Door*. New York: Macmillan, 1973.

Lynch, Wayne. *Season of the 76ers: The Story of Wilt Chamberlain and the 1967 NBA Champion Philadelphia 76ers*. New York: St. Martin's, 2002.

GREG ROBINSON (1996)
Updated by publisher 2005

CHAMBERS, GEORGE

OCTOBER 4, 1928
NOVEMBER 4, 1997

▪▪▪━━━━━━━━━━━

George Michael Chambers, the second prime minister of the Republic of Trinidad and Tobago, received his early education at Nelson Street Boys Roman Catholic School in Port of Spain, where he later attended Burke College and Osmond High School. He left school at an early age, taking up a job as an office boy in a solicitor's office. Later he pursued a correspondence course in general education from Wosley Hall, Oxford, and was employed in the legal department of a locally based foreign oil company.

He served as prime minister and political leader of the Peoples National Movement (PNM) from 1981 to 1986.

Until his appointment as prime minister, he was the least known by the public among the three deputy political leaders of the party. This was for want neither of experience nor ability. For having first entered politics in 1966, he had served since 1971 as the member of parliament for the constituency of St. Ann and on the Central Executive and General Council of the party. He was appointed minister of public utilities and housing in 1969 and minister of national security in 1970. From 1971 to 1975 he held the portfolios of minister of finance and minister of planning and development. From 1976 to 1981 he served as minister of agriculture, lands, and fisheries, and as minister of industry and commerce.

The first general elections contested by the PNM under his leadership saw the party winning twenty-four of thirty-six seats, although largely out of respect for his predecessor, Eric Williams. It proved challenging to succeed the latter, who had died in his fourth consecutive term in office and had exerted unparalleled influence over the country. Many viewed Chambers as less formidable and charismatic, especially as his was a humble and unassuming style. Most critical of him were the opponents of the PNM, who made every effort to portray him as a simpleton, lacking in intellect and ability.

Still, during Chambers' short tenure as prime minister, his was a significant contribution to the development of the party and nation. One of his objectives was to promote greater productivity among a population that had become complacent, fortified by the proceeds of an earlier oil boom. Chambers introduced various belt-tightening measures to bring inflation and unemployment under control after the country's economy was negatively affected by falling oil prices during the early 1980s. Yet, he maintained the anti-imperialist position the PNM had taken since the March for Chaguaramas in 1961, refusing to implement certain recommendations of the International Monetary Fund and dismissing the organization as a group of meddlesome international civil servants. He was a firm believer in Caribbean integration. Yet in the aftermath of a bloody palace coup against the Maurice Bishop regime in Grenada, he held out for a policy of nonintervention, despite a decision by some Caribbean neighbors to support a U.S.-led invasion of that island.

Chambers' policies were located in neither right-wing nor left-wing politics but in what was politically pragmatic at the time. However, he had come to power at a difficult period in the nation's social and economic history when, despite the slump in international economic activity and declining oil revenues, the expectations of the mass of the people remained high. Consequently, his austerity measures left many disgruntled, and in the national elections of 1986 the PNM suffered a humiliating defeat under his leadership, losing the general elections for the first time in thirty years.

Following this defeat, Chambers resigned his post as political leader of the party and retired to an almost completely reclusive life, though reportedly many continued to seek his advice and expertise regarding political matters.

Since his death, Chambers' critics have been far more generous concerning his abilities. There is now widespread consensus that he was an extremely competent but grossly underrated administrator, with better than average ability, and one of the best finance ministers of Trinidad and Tobago.

See also Peoples National Movement (PNM)

■ ■ *Bibliography*

Ghany, Hamid.*Kamal: A Lifetime of Politics, Religion and Culture.* San Juan, Trinidad and Tobago: Kamaluddin Mohammed, 1996.

Hackshaw, John M. *Party Politics and Public Policy.* Diego Martin, Trinidad and Tobago: Citadel Public Service, 1997.

Sutton, Paul. *Forged from the Love of Liberty.* Port of Spain, Trinidad and Tobago: Longman Caribbean, 1981.

MICHAEL F. TOUSSAINT (2005)

CHAMOISEAU, PATRICK

MARCH 12, 1953

▬ ▬ ▬ ────────────────────

Born in Fort-de-France, Martinique, Patrick Chamoiseau has become one of the island's most successful and celebrated authors and a leading figure in contemporary postcolonial and world literature. After studying law at universities in Martinique and Paris, he became a social worker. Since returning to live in Fort-de-France, he has continued his vocation as a probation officer working with young offenders. This proximity to Martinican society and culture has influenced his work.

Although he is principally known for his novels, Chamoiseau has ranged broadly into other genres. He has written autobiographical narratives, assembled a collection of folktales, and been at the forefront of the theoretical debates surrounding *créolité,* or creoleness. He has also written for the theater, contributed to discussions on contemporary Martinican and Caribbean politics, and collaborated on several photographic essays. A testament to his importance and appeal as a writer and commentator is the portion of his work, both fiction and nonfiction, that has been translated into other languages.

Chamoiseau began to draw serious attention as a novelist after the publication of his first two novels, *Chronique des sept misères* (*Chronicle of the Seven Sorrows,* 1986), and *Solibo magnifique* (*Solibo Magnificent,* 1988). His third novel, and perhaps the most successful to date, is *Texaco* (1992), for which he garnered France's most important and prestigious literary award, the Prix Goncourt. After the English translation of *Texaco* appeared in 1997, critical acclaim for his work began to take on new dimensions and his international stature as a writer grew. Other awards include the 1993 Prix Carbet de la Caraïbe for his novel *Antan d'enfance* (*Childhood*), and in 2002 he was the recipient of the Prix Spécial du Jury RFO for his novel *Biblique des derniers gestes* (2002).

Chamoiseau's fictional trademark is his integration of French Creole into his French prose, thereby emphatically affirming the socio-cultural importance of the Creole language and its connection to an authentic Martinican identity. It is this focus on language and orality that is also central to his theoretical work and the idea that it is not French, but rather Creole, that is the authentic linguistic representation of Martinique.

The subject and style of his fiction have closely mirrored the political and theoretical interventions of his essays. His most important, and likely most controversial, was the 1989 *Éloge de la créolité* (*In Praise of Creoleness*), a collaboration width writer Raphaël Confiant and linguist Jean Bernabé, which signaled the official launch of the *créolité* movement. In this seminal essay (in reality a manifesto), the authors argued that their identity was emphatically Creole; it was not singularly European, African, or Asian. This was important because it was a direct challenge to the *Négritude* movement founded in part by the Martinican writer and politician Aimé Césaire. The essay is, therefore, a move away from the black-white binary of *Négritude,* suggesting instead that politics, like literature, must reflect the complexities of multiracial histories and realities in places like Martinique and the wider Caribbean. This theory, with all of its political and cultural implications for contemporary Martinique, continues to be fiercely debated.

Nevertheless, Chamoiseau continues to be one of the most important and creatively provocative voices in Caribbean and world literature.

See also Creole Languages of the Americas; Literature of Martinique and Guadeloupe; Négritude

■ ■ *Bibliography*

Bernabe, Jean, Patrick Chamoiseau, and Raphaël Confiant. *Éloge de la créolité.* Paris: Gallimard, 1989.

Bongie, Chris. *Islands and Exiles: The Creole Identities of Post-Colonial Literature*. Stanford, Calif.: Stanford University Press, 1998.

Île en Île. "Patrick Chamoiseau." Available from <http://www.lehman.cuny.edu/ile.en.ile/paroles/chamoiseau.html>.

Watts, Richard. "'Toutes ces eaux!': Ecology and Empire in Patrick Chamoiseau's *Biblique des derniers gestes*." *Modern Language Notes* 118 (2003): 895–910.

THORALD M. BURNHAM (2005)

CHANEY, JAMES EARL

MAY 30, 1943
JUNE 21, 1964

▄▜▄

Civil rights activist James Chaney was born in Meridian, Mississippi, to Ben Chaney and Fannie Lee Chaney. His parents instilled a strong sense of racial pride in him, and in 1959 he, along with a group of his friends, was suspended from high school for wearing a button meant to criticize the local NAACP chapter for its unresponsiveness to racial issues. One year later he was expelled from school and began to work alongside his father as a plasterer. Chaney's experiences traveling to different job sites throughout Mississippi on segregated buses, at the same time that Freedom Rides mounted by civil rights organizations aimed at challenging segregated interstate transportation were occurring throughout the South, further spurred his activism. In 1963 he became directly involved in civil rights activities and joined the Congress of Racial Equality (CORE). One year later CORE joined forces with the Mississippi branches of the Student Nonviolent Coordinating Committee (SNCC), and the National Association for the Advancement of Colored People (NAACP) to form the Council of Federated Organizations (COFO) to spearhead a massive voter-registration and desegregation campaign in Mississippi called the Freedom Summer.

During his work with COFO, Chaney met Michael Schwerner, a white Jewish liberal who had been a New York City social worker before he joined CORE in 1963 and relocated to become a field worker in Mississippi, and Andrew Goodman, a young Jewish college student who had volunteered for the Mississippi Freedom Summer project. Assigned to work together in Meridian, on June 21, 1964, the three men went to Longdale—a black community in Neshoba County, Mississippi—to investigate the burning of a church that had been a potential site for a Freedom School teaching literacy and voter education. The Ku Klux Klan was firmly entrenched in large areas of Mississippi, and it was widely suspected that the Klan had burned the church down to prevent civil rights activities. As the three men were driving back to Meridian, they were detained by the police in Philadelphia, Mississippi. Chaney was arrested for speeding and Schwerner and Goodman were arrested as suspects in the church bombing. None of the men was allowed to make a phone call or pay the fine that would have facilitated his release from the Neshoba County jail.

The arrest of Chaney, Schwerner, and Goodman was no accident. Civil rights workers were constantly harassed by white night riders and local policemen who were often Klan members more committed to maintaining the racial status quo than to upholding justice. Schwerner was the first white civil rights worker to be stationed outside of Jackson, Mississippi. His activities and presence had made him well known to Meridian whites, and his success in initiating civil rights programs and his Jewish background had made him a target of the Klan, which had nicknamed him "Goatee" because he wore a beard. After Neshoba County Deputy Sheriff Cecil Ray Price confirmed that the car Chaney had been driving was registered to CORE, he alerted local Klan leader Edgar Ray Killen. Killen quickly organized a posse of Klansmen and formulated a plan of action with as many as twenty conspirators. Later that same night, Price released the three men from jail after Chaney paid the fine. They were followed out of town by a Klan posse, forcibly removed from their cars, driven to an isolated wooded area a few miles away, and killed. Their bodies were buried in an earthen dam in the immediate vicinity of Philadelphia, a burial site that had been chosen beforehand.

Attempts to locate Chaney, Schwerner, and Goodman had been initiated by COFO when the trio had not called or reached their destination at the allotted time. As it became increasingly apparent that harm had befallen them, COFO renewed its longstanding request for assistance from the Justice Department and mobilized a campaign among their membership to put pressure on governmental officials. Social violence against black people in Mississippi was commonplace, and despite the high proportion of lynchings that took place in Mississippi, no white person had ever been convicted of murdering a black person in the history of the state. The heightened interest in civil rights, and the likely involvement and disappearance of two white men, commanded national attention and federal response. Attorney General Robert Kennedy met with the families of the missing men, and FBI agents were dispatched to the scene to mount an extensive investigation. When the charred remains of Chaney's car were found a few days after the incident, Neshoba county was flooded with journalists who reported to the shocked nation the hostility of Mississippi whites who seemed to epitomize southern racism.

The FBI recovered the bodies of the three civil rights workers from the earthen dam on August 4, 1964, and four months later nineteen men were charged with the conspiracy. The federal government was forced to use a Reconstruction-era statute to charge the men with conspiring to deprive Chaney, Schwerner, and Goodman of their civil rights because the social consensus behind the lynch mob's actions made state prosecution for murder unlikely.

Recalcitrant judges, defense delays, and problems with jury selection hampered the due process of law for three years. In 1966 the U.S. Supreme Court stepped in to reinstate the original indictments after the case had been thrown out of court, and in February 1967 the long-delayed trial finally began. Despite various confessions and eyewitness accounts, only seven defendants, one of whom was Deputy Sheriff Price, were convicted nine months later. Only two men were given of the maximum sentence of ten years under the law. Two of the other men received sentences of six years, and three received three-year sentences. The conspirators were all paroled before serving full jail terms and most returned to the Mississippi area by the mid-1970s.

The murders of Chaney, Schwerner, and Goodman became a milestone in the civil rights movement. Although an important precedent for federal intervention on behalf of civil rights workers was set, this incident was memorialized by many in the civil rights movement, not only as an instance of southern injustice but as the result of many years of federal indifference to the plight of African Americans. In 2004, the fortieth anniversary of the murders, Ben Chaney, James's brother and head of the James Earl Chaney Foundation, spearheaded a grassroots campaign to reopen the case.

See also Congress of Racial Equality (CORE); Freedom Summer; National Association for the Advancement of Colored People (NAACP); Student Nonviolent Coordinating Committee (SNCC)

■ ■ *Bibliography*

Cagin, Seth and Dray, Philip. *We Are Not Afraid: The Story of Goodman, Schwerner, and Chaney and the Civil Rights Campaign for Mississippi.* New York: Bantam Books, 1988.

Huie, William Bradford. *Three Lives for Mississippi.* New York: WCC Books, 1965.

ROBYN SPENCER (1996)

Mary Eugenia Charles, Prime Minister of the Dominican Republic, 1983. RAY FISHER/GETTY IMAGES

CHARLES, EUGENIA

MAY 15, 1919

Mary Eugenia Charles became Prime Minister of Dominica in 1980. She remains the first and so far only elected female head of government, minister of finance and economic affairs, and minister of foreign affairs in the Commonwealth Caribbean. Charles successfully led the Dominica Freedom Party (DFP), which she cofounded in 1968, through three successive general elections. She became the leader of the parliamentary opposition in 1970, and her party won its first general election in 1980.

Charles's political leadership in the Caribbean is unprecedented. She is the only woman to have been the cofounder and leader of a political party—and to have held the aforementioned ministries simultaneously. In 1993 she resigned as political leader of the DFP, but she remained as prime minister until the 1995 general elections, when she retired from active politics, becoming the first Caribbean leader to retire undefeated.

Charles catapulted into national political prominence in 1968 when she mobilized a citizens' campaign against a repressive piece of legislation, the Seditious and Undesirable Publications Act. She led a group called the "Freedom Fighters" in a series of public meetings, in demonstrations outside the House of Parliament, and in the gathering of 3,317 signatures supporting the repeal of the legislation. This effort was unsuccessful, however, and even when Charles herself took power, she did not repeal the bill.

Before becoming politically active, Charles became, in 1949, the first woman lawyer in Dominica. She was called to the bar at the Inner Temple in London in 1949, after graduating from the University of Toronto in 1947 with an L.L.B. in law. She continued her legal education at the London School of Economics and Political Science.

Charles was a forceful, decisive, and confrontational leader who enjoyed the practice of politics and the exercise of political power. Her tenure was marked by concerted efforts to restore political and economic stability on the island, minimize deficits, reduce foreign debt, improve basic social services, and develop an economic infrastructure. To counter declining economic conditions, Charles introduced a controversial economic citizenship program designed to attract foreign investment. The program enabled an investor (and up to three dependents) to gain economic citizenship after a successful application and a deposit of 35,000 American dollars in a designated escrow account. However, the opposition, and many citizens, criticized the policy as a sale of citizenship.

Charles was relatively successful in introducing fiscal management and helping to halt the decline of the economy, especially after the country's main export and revenue earner, the banana industry, was devastated by two successive hurricanes. She was even more successful in restoring political stability after thwarting two coup attempts by disgruntled members of the disbanded defense force (they conspired with mercenaries on the second attempt to overthrow her administration).

Charles's lasting political legacy is her role in the U.S. invasion of Grenada in October 1983. As chair of the Organisation of Eastern Caribbean States (OECS), Charles insisted that the OECS had invited the Reagan administration to invade Grenada after the People's Revolutionary Government had been overthrown in a military coup and its popular prime minister, Maurice Bishop, had been assassinated. Charles stated that countries in the region shared a common bond, and they had therefore asked the United States to intervene to halt the spread of communism in the region. She gained international prominence by appearing in a nationally televised press conference at the White House with President Reagan to announce and support the deployment of United States forces in Grenada.

Throughout her career, Charles remained a staunch political conservative, and she was publicly critical of progressive and socialist Caribbean leaders, particularly Fidel Castro and Maurice Bishop. In honor of her service, she was knighted by Queen Elizabeth in 1991. In 2002 the London School of Economics named her as one of five distinguished Honorary Fellows, while the Caribbean Community conferred on her its highest honor, the Order of the Caribbean Community.

See also International Relations in the Anglophone Caribbean

■ ■ *Bibliography*

Barriteau, V. Eudine, and Alan Cobley, eds. "Enjoying Power: Eugenia Charles and Political Leadership in the Commonwealth Caribbean." Barbados: Centre for Gender and Development Studies, University of the West Indies, 2004.

Charles, Mary Eugenia. "My Experiences as the First Female Prime Minister in the Commonwealth Caribbean" (Inaugural Lecture, Caribbean Women Catalysts for Change). Barbados: Centre for Gender and Development Studies, University of the West Indies, 1995.

Higbie, Janet. *Eugenia: The Caribbean's Iron Lady.* London: Macmillan Caribbean, 1993.

V. EUDINE BARRITEAU (2005)

CHARLES, EZZARD

JULY 7, 1921
MAY 28, 1975

┫┣─────────────

Boxer Ezzard Charles was born in Lawrenceville, Georgia. When he was a child, his family moved to Cincinnati, where he became interested in boxing. By the time he was sixteen, he had taught himself the rudiments of boxing so well that he won forty-two amateur fights in a row—including two Golden Gloves and the AAU National Championship in 1939—before turning professional in 1940. His ascending career was interrupted by service in the U.S. Army, but after Joe Louis announced his retirement as undefeated world heavyweight champion in 1949, a title match was set up between Charles and Jersey Joe Walcott. Charles won the title in a fifteen-round decision on June 22, 1949. He held the title from 1949 to 1951, successfully defending it in 1950 against Joe Louis. Despite this victory, Charles did not receive the recognition many felt he deserved. He depended on his boxing skills and ability to score points rather than delivering one powerful knockout punch and thus was criticized by some for lacking a harsh fighting instinct.

Charles lost his heavyweight title on July 18, 1951, when he was knocked out by Joe Walcott in the seventh round of their third fight. Three years later, on June 17, 1954, he lost a grueling fifteen-round decision to Rocky Marciano, and in a rematch later that year Marciano knocked him out in the eighth round. Charles retired from boxing in 1956, with two brief, unsuccessful comeback attempts in 1958 and 1959. From 1940 to 1959 he fought in 122 bouts, winning 96 of them. In 1966 he was stricken with a muscle-debilitating disease, amyotrophic lateral sclerosis, and was confined to a wheelchair. Charles died on May 28, 1975, at the age of fifty-three. In 1987 he was named the ninth greatest heavyweight of all time by *The Ring*.

See also Boxing

■ ■ *Bibliography*

Rust, Art, Jr., and Edna Rust. *Art Rust's Illustrated History of the Black Athlete.* Garden City, N.Y.: Doubleday, 1985.

Obituary. *New York Times*, May 29, 1975, p. 38.

LINDA SALZMAN (1996)

Ray Charles (1930–2004). Charles's rich vocals, soulful piano style, and remarkable versatility as a performer and composer of gospel, blues, country, pop, and jazz music made him one of the most popular and influential musicians of the twentieth century. AP/WIDE WORLD PHOTOS. REPRODUCED BY PERMISSION.

CHARLES, RAY (ROBINSON, RAY CHARLES)

SEPTEMBER 23, 1930
JUNE 10, 2004

┣┥┣

Ray Charles's achievements mark him as one of the most important and influential U.S. musicians of the postwar period. He is often called the Father of Soul, both for his innovative blending of gospel, blues, and jazz, and for his enormous versatility as a singer, pianist, songwriter, composer-arranger, saxophonist, and band leader.

Born into a poor family in Albany, Georgia, Ray Charles Robinson was raised in Greenville, Florida. At the age of five he contracted glaucoma; it was left untreated and soon blinded him. His mother, Aretha, sent him to the School for the Deaf and Blind in Saint Augustine, where he spent the next eight years studying composition, learning to write musical scores in braille, and mastering various instruments (trumpet, alto saxophone, clarinet, organ, and piano). After his mother died in 1945, he left school to form a combo, and after he had saved enough money he moved to Seattle, where he played in a number of jazz trios, gradually developing a piano and vocal style heavily influenced by Nat "King" Cole. At around this time, Ray Charles dropped his surname in order to avoid being confused with prizefighter Sugar Ray Robinson.

Charles developed a significant following in Seattle and soon began to record for various labels. His first hits, "Baby Let Me Hold Your Hand" (1951) and "Kiss Me Baby" (1952) were recorded for the Swing Time label. In 1952 he began to record for Atlantic Records, where he made his first musical breakthrough with "I've Got a Woman" (1955), a blend—startlingly unconventional for the time—of coarse bluesy sexuality with the intense emotionality of gospel. Many of his musical ideas in this period were taken from gospel music, but his adaptations provoked much criticism for combining sexually explicit lyrics with the vocal techniques of "testifying." The style nevertheless provided Charles with some of his most successful songs, among them, "Hallelujah, I Love Her So" (1956), "The Right Time" (1959), and "What'd I Say" (1959).

As his fame increased, Charles increasingly found favor with white audiences. In 1959 he left Atlantic for ABC/Paramount; the move signaled a turn toward country-and-western music and popular standards. While his early recordings with ABC (such as "Georgia on My Mind," "Hit the Road Jack," and "I Can't Stop Loving You") are generally considered the equals of those of his Atlantic period, some critics charged that his music was gradually becoming conventional and uninspired. Nevertheless, throughout the 1960s Charles turned out scores of Top-Ten hits (including "You Are My Sunshine," "Let's Go Get Stoned," and "Here We Go Again"), and a number of successful LPs.

Charles's rise to fame was not without its struggles. Along the way he developed an addiction to heroin, and in 1955, 1961, and 1965 he was arrested for possession of narcotics. He never served a long prison term, but he stopped performing for a year after his last arrest, during which time he worked successfully to overcome his seventeen-year-long addiction, after which the record shows a steady series of successes and honors. In 1966 the U.S. House of Representatives passed a special resolution honoring Charles for his musical achievement. In the late 1960s he founded his own record label and music publishing firm. In 1979 Hoagy Carmichael's "Georgia on My Mind," perhaps Charles' best-known recording, was adopted as the official song of Georgia. In 1986 Charles was among the first ten artists inducted into the Rock and Roll Hall of Fame.

During his career, Charles appeared in several films, including *Blues for Lovers* (also known as *Ballad in Blue,* 1965) and *The Blues Brothers* (1980), and has performed on the soundtracks of many more, including *The Cincinnati Kids* (1965) and *In the Heat of the Night* (1967); his song "What'd I Say" was the subject of *Cosmic Ray,* an experimental film by Bruce Conner, in 1961.

Charles was also active in various social causes, including civil rights, African famine relief, and aid to the disabled. In 1985 he attributed the presence of several bombs found under a bandstand where he was to perform to his public statements opposing racism. In 1987 he made an appeal to Congress for federal aid for the deaf and established the Robinson Foundation for Hearing Disorders with an endowment of $1 million.

In addition to making frequent concert appearances and appearing in several popular commercials (most notably the phenomenally successful Diet Pepsi ads in the early 1990s), Charles remained active in producing and recording his own albums. His LP *Friendship* rose to number one on the country-and-western charts in 1985. In 1990 he performed with B. B. King in the Philip Morris Superband

and released an album, *Would You Believe?* His autobiography, *Brother Ray* (1978, with David Ritz), was re-released in a revised and updated edition in 1992. Charles won eleven Grammy Awards, the title of Commandeur de l'Ordre des Arts et des Lettres from the French Republic, a National Association for the Advancement of Colored People (NAACP) Hall of Fame Award (1983), and a Lifetime Achievement Award from the National Academy of Recording Arts and Sciences (1989).

Ray Charles died in 2004, the same year that *Ray,* a motion picture based on his life and starring Jamie Foxx, was released. The movie was a critical and box office success, with Foxx earning an Academy Award for best actor. Charles won five posthumous Grammy Awards in 2005 for his final album, *Genius Loves Company,* which features duets with many artists, including B. B. King, Willie Nelson, Elton John, Norah Jones, and Diana Krall.

See also Blues, The; Cole, Nat "King"; Gospel Music; Jazz

■ ■ *Bibliography*

Balliett, Whitney. *American Singers.* New York: Oxford University Press, 1979.

Brelin, Christa, and William C. Matney Jr., eds. *Who's Who Among Black Americans,* 7th ed. Detroit: Gale, 1992.

Lydon, Michael. *Ray Charles: Man and Music.* New York: Riverhead, 1998.

Marsh, Dave. "Ray Charles." In *The New Grove Dictionary of American Music,* edited by H. Wiley Hitchcock and Stanley Sadie. New York: Grove, 1986.

Shaw, Arnold. *Black Popular Music in America.* New York: Schirmer, 1986.

White, James L. *Ray: A Tribute to the Movie, the Music, and the Man.* New York: Newmarket, 2004.

ROBERT W. STEPHENS (1996)
Updated by publisher 2005

CHASE, ASHTON

JULY 18, 1926

■ I ■

Ashton Chase was born in Georgetown, British Guiana, and received his primary education at St. Andrews Scots School and his secondary education at what was then Alleyne High School. Possibly because Chase's grandmother was an executive in the British Guiana Labour Union (BGLU), the first union in the colony, which had come into existence in 1919, Chase was associated with trade union activity and served as assistant secretary of the

BGLU before his entry into the political arena in British Guiana. An early admirer of Hubert Nathaniel Critchlow, the father of trade unionism in the colony and founder of the BGLU, Chase later became a founding member of the Political Affairs Committee (PAC), initially a shadowy group that met in a house located in a suburb of Georgetown and that was beyond the gaze of colonial authorities. The PAC sought to analyze political and trade union social developments using political education as a major tool, and to mold and form political opinion from the perspective of scientific socialism.

The PAC, which was also designed to be an ad hoc entity, eventually morphed into the People's Progressive Party (PPP), the colony's first mass-based political party, which viewed trade unions as a focal point for rallying the masses, with Chase becoming one of its central figures. Chase became minister of labor, industry, and commerce in the first PPP government in 1953. He was instrumental in introducing a labor relations bill in September 1953 after a sugar workers' strike by the Guiana Industrial Workers' Union (GIWU), whose president was PPP minister of health Dr. Joseph Prayag Lachmansingh. The GIWU was seeking recognition by the powerful Sugar Producers' Association, which had recognized the Man Power Citizen's Association, then viewed as a company union. The strike, which had the support of PPP leaders, led to much concern from the Americans, who feared that what they regarded as a politically motivated strike action might spread to other territories. The British also deemed it necessary to provide emergency powers to the governor on short notice in order to preserve public safety and maintain essential services. However, while the labor relations bill also occasioned the ire of the local establishment, especially the business community, Chase felt that the government was on solid ground because the intention to introduce a bill of that nature had formed part of the PPP's election manifesto.

Though viewed as a moderate by the governor, the British removed Chase and the PPP government from office and suspended the constitution in October 1953. In Chase's view, the suspension of the constitution changed the character of politics in the colony and corrupted the thrust for change. Some people, unable to withstand the pressure, compromised with the demands of the political situation, which resulted in an upsurge of right-wing influence and the emergence of socialism without socialists, referring to the idea that socialism should be actualized by socialists, that is, by individuals who have read about, understand, and believe in the application of socialist principles so as to bring about improved social change. By making this observation, Chase was suggesting that this was no longer the case.

After the suspension of the constitution, Chase went to England in 1954, where he read law and was called to the bar at Gray's Inn in 1957, the same year that he graduated with a bachelor of laws degree with honors from London University. Following his return to Guiana, Chase served as a member of Parliament from 1964 to 1968, after which he never held political office. Chase was appointed senior counsel in 1985 after the death of President Forbes Burnham, who had long denied Chase that distinction. In 1991, though, he came out of political retirement to be the consensus presidential candidate in the 1992 general elections, conceivably the fairest election held since 1968. At the 1992 elections, however, the PPP led by Dr. Cheddi Jagan garnered the most votes, and Jagan then became President of the Republic of Guyana, after being out of office since 1964.

In addition to serving from 1970 to 1974 as a member of the Public Service Commission, from 1971 to 1973 Chase was vice president of the Guyana Economic Society. On various occasions he served as president of the Guyana Bar Association from the 1980s to 1998 and as a member of the Council of Legal Education (a body responsible for training attorneys in the Commonwealth Caribbean), including a period as the council's chairman from 1992 to 1998. An acknowledged expert on trade union law, after his retirement from politics Chase published *Trade Union Law in the Caribbean, Glimpses of the Growth of Trade Unions in the Commonwealth Caribbean,* and *Guyana—A Nation in Transit—Burnham's Role.*

See also International Relations of the Anglophone Caribbean

■ ■ *Bibliography*

Chase, Ashton. *A History of Trade Unionism in Guyana 1900 to 1961,* edited by Audrey Chase. Ruimveldt, Demerara: New Guyana Company, 1964.

Chase, Ashton. *133 Days towards Freedom in Guiana.* Georgetown: Guyana, n.d.

MAURICE ST. PIERRE (2005)

CHAVIS, BENJAMIN FRANKLIN, JR.

JANUARY 22, 1948

Born and raised in Oxford, North Carolina, the Rev. Dr. Benjamin F. Chavis, Jr., a civil rights activist, came from a long line of preachers. His great-great-grandfather, the Rev. John Chavis, was the first African American to be ordained a Presbyterian minister in the United States. Chavis first became involved in the struggle for civil rights at the age of twelve, when his persistence in seeking privileges at a whites-only library in Oxford started a chain of events that led to its integration. In 1967, while a student at the University of North Carolina (UNC) at Charlotte, Chavis became a civil rights organizer with the Southern Christian Leadership Conference (SCLC); he remained active with the organization until he graduated from UNC in 1969 with a B.A. in chemistry. After a year spent as a labor organizer with the American Federation of State, County, and Municipal Employees (AFSCME), he joined the Washington field office of the United Church of Christ's Commission for Racial Justice (UCCCRJ).

On February 1, 1971, Chavis was sent to Wilmington, North Carolina, in response to a request from Wilmington ministers for a community and civil rights organizer. The racial climate in Wilmington had become explosive when court-ordered desegregation began in 1969. In January 1971 black students began a boycott of Wilmington High School; Chavis was sent to help organize this student group. Within two weeks of his arrival, Wilmington erupted in a weeklong riot.

In March 1972, fourteen months after the riot ended, Chavis and fifteen former students were arrested for setting fire to a white-owned grocery store and shooting at firemen and policemen who answered the call. Chavis, eight other black men, and a white woman were convicted for arson and conspiracy to assault emergency personnel. Chavis and the nine other defendants became known as the Wilmington Ten. In 1975, after his appeals were exhausted, Chavis entered prison. Because of the weak nature of the evidence against them, Amnesty International designated them political prisoners in 1978, the first time the organization had done so for any U.S. convicts. Their case received national and international support.

In 1977 all three witnesses who testified against the Wilmington Ten admitted they had given false testimony and had been either pressured or bribed by the Wilmington police. Despite this new evidence, the defendants were denied the right to a new trial. Chavis, the last of them to be paroled, was released in 1980, having served more than four years of his thirty-four-year sentence at Caledonia State Prison. On December 4, 1980, a federal appeals court overturned the convictions, citing the coercion of prosecution witnesses.

While in prison, Chavis taught himself Greek, translated the New Testament, wrote two books (*An American Political Prisoner Appeals for Human Rights* in 1979 and *Psalms from Prison* in 1983) and earned a master of divinity degree magna cum laude from Duke University. After his release he earned a doctor of ministry degree from the Divinity School of Howard University. In 1986 Chavis became the executive director of the UCCCRJ. In this capacity, he focused on combating both what he calls "environmental racism"—the government and industry's practice of burdening poor and predominantly black neighborhoods with toxic waste dumps—and gang violence. In 1993 he became the seventh executive director of the National Association for the Advancement of Colored People; his election at age forty-five made him the youngest person ever to lead the organization. He pledged to revitalize the organization, whose aging membership had been a source of concern, and to sharpen its focus; he also cited the longer-term goal of expanding membership to include other minorities.

Chavis's policies during his tenure as executive director proved extremely controversial. In an attempt to reorient the NAACP toward young urban blacks, he held dialogues with militant black leaders, including Louis Farrakhan. In the summer of 1994 he acknowledged that he had used NAACP funds in an out-of-court settlement with a female NAACP staff member who accused Chavis of sexual harassment. Amid these and other charges of financial impropriety, the board of directors relieved Chavis of his position as executive director on August 20, 1994.

Following his resignation from the NAACP, Chavis joined the Nation of Islam as an organizer and close adviser of Louis Farrakhan. In 1995 Chavis was the principal organizer of the Million Man March. In February 1997 he announced his conversion to Islam, and he took the name Benjamin Chavis Muhammad. He was subsequently defrocked by the United Church of Christ. He was named by Farrakhan to lead Malcolm X's old mosque in Harlem.

In 2001, Chavis became president of the Hip-Hop Summit Action Network (HHSAN), an organization working for the rights of African Americans.

See also Civil Rights Movement, U.S.; National Association for the Advancement of Colored People (NAACP); Southern Christian Leadership Conference (SCLC)

■ ■ *Bibliography*

Chavis, Benjamin, Jr. "Foreword." In *Confronting Environmental Racism*, edited by Robert Bullard. Boston: South End Press, 1993.

Kotlowitz, Alex. "A Bridge Too Far? Ben Chavis." *New York Times Magazine* (June 12, 1994): 40–43.

MANSUR M. NURUDDIN (1996)
ALEXIS WALKER (1996)
Updated by publisher 2005

CHESIMARD, JOANNE DEBORAH BRYON

See Shakur, Assata

CHESNUTT, CHARLES W.

JUNE 20, 1858
NOVEMBER 15, 1932

Born in Cleveland, Ohio, to freeborn mulattoes, the writer Charles Waddell Chesnutt was raised mostly in Fayetteville, North Carolina, by his father, Andrew; his mother, Ann Maria, died when he was only thirteen. Though Chesnutt attended the Howard School and received a fairly sound general education, he proved to be a model autodidact, teaching himself advanced mathematics, ancient languages, history, and shorthand. His first teaching assignments—in Charlotte, North Carolina, and Spartanburg, South Carolina, from 1875 to 1877—served as a proving ground for what he had learned. He rose from being first assistant to the principal of the State Colored Normal School of North Carolina to become its principal in 1879, serving also as Sunday-school superintendent of the renowned Evans Chapel African Methodist Episcopal Zion Church.

Despite his success, Chesnutt was determined to escape the harsh racism of the South. In 1883, peddling his shorthand skills, he sought work with northern newspapers, such as the *New York Mail and Express.* However, he stayed in New York for only five months before moving on to Cleveland to try his luck in this city of his birth, soon to become his permanent place of residence. While working in the law offices of a railroad company, Chesnutt studied law, and in 1887 he passed the Ohio bar examination. Pleased with his accomplishments, he began operating a stenographic service for the courts, and he was well rewarded for his efforts. Having secured a foothold in this trade, he sent for his wife, Susan (whom he had married

in 1878) and his children, who were left behind in Fayetteville while he traveled from the South to the North and back again—a pattern of departures and returns that would later play a subtle role in most of his fiction.

Rankled by racist or insensitive southern white writers and their depictions of miscegenation and the black experience, Chesnutt vowed to render a more accurate and faithful account of the issues. In 1887 his tale of magic, witchcraft, and slavery, "The Goophered Grapevine," brought him to the nation's attention, though by now he had already published approximately sixteen short stories in a variety of magazines and newspapers. With the heavy-handed assistance of his publisher's editors, Chesnutt produced *The Conjure Woman* (1899), a collection of tales connected by their depiction of magical events and unified by their portrayal of the horrors of slavery, while also raising troubling questions regarding the complex attachments that linked ex-slaves to their slave forebears and to their masters. It was a stunning success, preceded a few months earlier by *The Wife of His Youth and Other Stories of the Color Line* (1899)—a collection of tales wherein irony and inexplicable coincidences, rather than magic, represent the controlling literary technique, and where blacks confront the lessons of the "color line," or color prejudice among blacks, which is as much about race as it is about kinship and familial affiliation. This collection was also very well received.

Though Chesnutt appears to have been steadfast against any temptation to pass as white himself, he often flirted with this topic in his fiction. Thus, the pathos aroused in his first novel, *The House Behind the Cedars* (1900), is created by the choice a young woman must make between passing as white, thereby enjoying the apparent benefits of white society, and remaining with her mother to live among those of the black race with whom she was raised, but among whom she would be forever blocked from enjoying the fruits due her as an American citizen.

In the wake of his early successes, Chesnutt closed his stenographic offices and devoted himself full-time to writing fiction. By now it appeared that he had joined that diverse group of regional writers called "local colorists." But with a compulsory life of Frederick Douglass (1899) behind him, his next literary efforts proved too realistic and bitter for his newfound audience. Though his readers may have been be moved by the sibling rivalry of two women, one black and one white, depicted in *The Marrow of Tradition* (1901), his second novel, the story of their kinship was eclipsed by the highly charged politics of the post–Civil War period, a polarized time that left little room for moderating sentiments in the North or the South. The plot depicts strange bedfellows brought together by political goals based more on postbellum fears than on any alliance they might have forged during the antebellum era or any indignity they might have suffered in common. Poor sales force Chesnutt to return to stenography in 1901, and he consequently remained sorely underrated during his lifetime.

As a witness to events that took place in the South during the 1890s, Chesnutt could no longer believe that paternalistic, well-meaning whites were able or willing to do anything more for blacks. In his last published novel, *The Colonel's Dream* (1905), a white colonel returns to his southern home with the belief that he can forestall the return to slave conditions into which many blacks and poor whites are falling. Having failed, the colonel returns north with the belief that blacks cannot win the war of "Redemption," as this era was dubbed, with or without the assistance of white patrons. With Reconstruction over, blacks were, during this nadir of their odyssey in America, on their own.

Chesnutt's light complexion, erudition, sophistication, and accomplishments, however, gave him an entrée into the upper ranks of Cleveland society, where he observed activities satirized in his highly ironic short story "Baxter's Procrustes." As one of the wealthiest black men in the city, Chesnutt was among the most successful political forces in Cleveland, though he never held political office. He often took the middle ground in racial affairs, whether the issue was between blacks and whites or among blacks—he was a member of both the National Association for the Advancement of Colored People (NAACP), founded in part by the militant W. E. B. Du Bois, and the Committee of Twelve, steered by the cautious and conciliatory Booker T. Washington.

Nevertheless, until his death, Chesnutt was so outspoken in defense of blacks against discrimination and illegal practices that in 1928 he was awarded the NAACP Spingarn Medal for the most "distinguished service" of any black person that year who had acted to advance the cause of blacks in America.

Besides his two published collections of short stories, Chesnutt wrote and/or published an additional twenty-nine short stories, sixteen "tales," ten "anecdotes," seven occasional poems, and numerous essays, articles, and book reviews. He continued to write and publish until 1930 ("Concerning Father" was his last short story), despite poor critical reception and sales, not to mention poor health. As Chesnutt's reputation grows, however, he will likely be seen as the first African-American master of the short story.

See also Literature of the United States

■ ■ *Bibliography*

Andrews, William L. "A Reconsideration of Charles Waddell Chesnutt: Pioneer of the Color Line." *CLA Journal* 19, no. 2 (1975): 137–151.

Andrews, William L. *The Literary Career of Charles W. Chesnutt.* Baton Rouge: Louisiana State University Press, 1980.

Chesnutt, Helen. *Charles Waddell Chesnutt: Pioneer of the Color Line.* Chapel Hill: University of North Carolina Press,, 1952.

McWilliams, Dean. *Charles W. Chesnutt and the Fictions of Race.* Athens: University of Georgia Press, 2002.

Render, Sylvia. *Charles W. Chesnutt.* Boston: Twayne, 1980.

Thompson, Gordon. *Charles W. Chesnutt, Zora Neale Hurston, Melvin B. Tolson: Folk and Non-Folk Representation of the Fantastic.* Ph.D. diss., Yale University, 1987.

Wonham, Henry B. *Charles W. Chesnutt: A Study of the Short Fiction.* New York: Twayne, 1998.

GORDON THOMPSON (1996)
Updated bibliography

CHICA DA SILVA

C. 1731
FEBRUARY 15, 1796

Francisca da Silva de Oliveira, known as Chica da Silva, was a slave who lived in Brazil in the eighteenth century at the height of diamond production. Her mythical figure has served to represent the sensuality of the black woman and the capacity for race mixing characteristic of Brazilian society. This slave woman became legendary for her relationship with the diamond contractor João Fernandes de Oliveira, who had the monopoly on extraction of ore in the region of the hamlet of Tejuco, today the city of Diamantina, in Minas Gerais.

The myth of Chica da Silva began to be built up by a nineteenth-century memorialist of Diamantina, who dedicated a few chapters of his book to the story of the slave and her relationship with the diamond contractor, although the author portrayed her in a negative way. At the beginning of the twentieth century, local writers began to add some positive features to the image of the legendary slave, describing her as a woman of rare beauty. Since then the character has been immortalized in poems, novels, television serials, and in the cinema with the film *Xica da Silva*, directed by Cacá Diegues, in 1976.

Francisca da Silva de Oliveira was the daughter of an African slave, Maria da Costa, who was born in the Costa da Mina, and the Portuguese Antonio Caetano de Sá. While still a slave, Chica had her first child, Simão, with her owner, the Portuguese doctor Manuel Pires Sardinha, who granted the boy his freedom on the occasion of his baptism. In 1753 she was bought by the judge João Fernandes de Oliveira, who had arrived in the hamlet to administer the diamond contract, bid for by his father in Lisbon. Soon afterward, in December of the same year, he granted Chica her freedom.

From 1755 to 1770 Chica and João Fernandes lived together as if they had been officially married. They had thirteen children, four boys and nine girls, but they never legalized their relationship, which would have been dishonorable for a white man, and such mixed marriages were discouraged by church and state. Having an average of one child every thirteen months transforms the sensual, lascivious, man-devouring image with which Chica was always associated.

The ex-slave tried to act like any lady of the local elite. She had her daughters educated at the best educational establishment of the Minas, which was intended only for the daughters of well-off families. Chica always sought the social placement of herself and her children in the bosom of the local elite. This was achieved by way of various expedients, not to be credited only to the importance and fortune of João Fernandes, as he had to return to Portugal in 1771 to resolve family disputes over the paternal inheritance and never returned. Since she had to depend only on herself, Chica found mechanisms to maintain her status, like other freedwomen of Tejuco. One of these was membership in several brotherhoods (*Irmandades*), which most often joined individuals of the same origin and social condition as a way of obtaining distinction and social recognition. These rules were not always respected, however, and some people of color succeeded in becoming members of societies that were usually exclusive to white people.

The proof of the importance and degree of social success that Chica obtained was the fact that Dona Francisca da Silva de Oliveira, as she was always addressed, and her children belonged to the principal brotherhoods, whether of white, brown, or black people. She was also the owner of many slaves and of a house near those of the important local people. This was a solidly built, large and airy two-story house with a backyard, which had its own chapel—the privilege of few—where two of her daughters would later marry.

Chiua died in Tejuco and was buried at the Church of São Francisco de Assis, whose brotherhood was normally reserved for the local white elite, a demonstration of her importance and prestige. All the priests of the hamlet gathered in ceremony around her body, which was accompanied to the grave by all the brotherhoods she belonged to, a way of demonstrating the distinction she had achieved in life. In contrast to the myth that emerged around her,

Chica da Silva was not the queen of the slaves or redemptress of her race, nor was she a shrew, a witch, or a seductress. She knew, as was common for freedwomen of the period, how to take advantage of the few possibilities that the system offered her. Her actions among the white elite of the hamlet of Tejuco were always aimed at diminishing the stigma that color and slavery had imposed on her and of promoting the social ascension of her descendents.

See also Folklore; Slavery

■ ■ *Bibliography*

Furtado, Júnia Ferreira. *Chica da Silva e o contratador dos diamantes: o outro lado do mito.* São Paulo: Companhia das Letras, 2003.

Higgins, Kathleen J. *Licentious Liberty in a Brazilian Gold-Mining Region.* University Park: Pennsylvania State University Press, 1999.

Russell-Wood, A. J. R. "Women and Society in Colonial Brazil." *Journal of Latin American Studies* 9, no. 1 (May 1977): 1–34.

Santos, Joaquim Felício dos. *Memórias do Distrito Diamantino,* 4th ed. Belo Horizonte: Itatiaia, 1976. Original publication, Rio de Janeiro: Typografia Americana, 1868.

Vasconcelos, Agripa. *Chica que manda.* Belo Horizonte: Itatiaia, 1966.

FILM

Diegues, Cacá, director. *Xica da Silva.* 117 min. Brazil: Globo Vídeo, 1976.

JÚNIA FERREIRA FURTADO (2005)

CHICAGO DEFENDER

The *Chicago Defender* was founded in 1905 by Robert Sengstacke Abbott, a journalist and lawyer from Georgia. He started the newspaper with almost no capital and worked out of the dining room of his landlady, who supported him during the first years of operation. The paper was initially a four-page weekly that Abbott peddled from door to door on the South Side of Chicago. Through his work with the *Defender,* Abbott began a new phase in black journalism. He did not appeal primarily to educated African Americans, as earlier black newspapers had, but sought to make the paper accessible to the majority of blacks. Although the *Defender* adopted a policy of muckraking and sensationalism, covering topics such as crime and scandal as well as prostitution in the black community, Abbott used the paper primarily as a vehicle for achieving racial justice. He refused to use the word *Negro* because of what he believed were its derogatory connotations, preferring the word *race*. The paper also took a militant stand against segregation and discrimination and encouraged blacks to protest. In 1907 it "pledge-[d] itself to fight against [segregation, discrimination, and disfranchisement] until they have been removed." It believed in the importance of political participation and stated that blacks should use their vote as leverage to win concessions from both the Republican and Democratic parties.

The *Chicago Defender* gained national prominence during the Great Migration during World War I, when large numbers of African Americans left the South to move North. The paper covered brutal incidents of racism in the South and encouraged African Americans to leave the rigid segregation, poor pay, and violence of the South. In 1915, in response to the rising incidence of lynching, the *Defender* advised, "If you must die, take at least one with you." It promised better-paying jobs and more freedom in northern cities. Although Abbott decried World War I as "bloody, tragic, and deplorable," he believed there were some benefits from it for African Americans, noting that "Factories, mills, and workshops that have been closed to us through necessity are being opened to us. We are to be given a chance."

Many black southerners wrote to the *Defender* asking for job-placement help. The *Defender* also tried to address the problems of migrants by helping form clubs that arranged reduced rates on the railroad. It counseled newly arrived African Americans, helped them find jobs, and sent them to the appropriate relief and aid agencies. To alleviate the acute housing shortage, the *Defender* supported the construction of housing for African Americans and opposed restrictive covenants. The paper was repeatedly attacked by white southerners, who attempted to control its distribution by preventing its sale in many southern towns, harassing and intimidating anyone who possessed a copy. Despite this, copies of the paper were distributed by railroad porters and shipped to more than 1,500 southern towns and cities. The circulation of the *Defender* increased dramatically during World War I, climbing from 33,000 in 1916 to 125,000 in 1918. Branch offices were opened across the country and around the world.

Like most newspapers, the *Defender* was hurt by the Great Depression. By 1935 circulation had dropped to 73,000. It continued to cover black civil rights issues, but also included cartoons, personals, and social, cultural, and fashion articles. In 1939, the year before he died, Abbott passed control of the paper to his nephew John Sengstacke. Under Sengstacke's leadership, the *Defender* continued to be an advocate for social and economic justice.

During World War II, its editors wrote, "In pledging our allegiance to the flag and what it symbolizes we are not unmindful of the broken promises of the past. We ask that America give the Negro citizen the full measure of the democracy he is called upon to defend." The paper covered the racial violence and riots during the war but made a special effort to see that its coverage was not provocative. Editors refused, for example, to publish photographs of the 1943 Harlem Riot. In 1945 its total Chicago and national circulation was 160,000. In 1956 the paper became a tabloid issued four times a week with a national weekend edition.

During the civil rights movement, the *Defender* took a strong stand in favor of racial equality. It criticized the Civil Rights Act of 1964 because it did "nothing" for the North. The paper advocated open housing and argued that "the nation must sooner or later come to the grim realization that residential segregation is the root cause of the racial unrest." In addition, the *Defender* supported nonviolent direct-action demonstrations and protests as a method of change. Of Chicago protests, the editors wrote, "The demonstrations, so loudly denounced by City Hall and most of the press, have proved their justification beyond the shadow of a doubt. . . . It was the demonstrations and the inflexible determination of Negro leadership as spearheaded by the Rev. Dr. Martin Luther King Jr. that caused the city of Chicago to acknowledge its mistakes and agree to rectify them." Although the *Defender*'s political tone had become more moderate by the early 1990s, it continued to cover both national and local news and speak out against what it considered unfair housing, employment, and educational policies.

See also Abbott, Robert Sengstacke; Journalism; Lynching; Migration

■ ■ *Bibliography*

Grossman, James. *Land of Hope: Chicago, Black Southerners, and the Great Migration.* Chicago: University of Chicago Press, 1989.

"Robert S. Abbott." *Contemporary Black Biography.* Detroit, Mich.: Gale, 2001.

Wolseley, Ronald. *The Black Press, U.S.A.* Ames: Iowa State University Press, 1971.

JOSHUA BOTKIN (1996)
Updated bibliography

CHICAGO RIOT OF 1919

See Red Summer; Riots and Popular Protests

CHILDREN'S LITERATURE

The portrayal of African Americans in mainstream American children's literature has been, on the whole, demeaning and unrealistic. From the inception of children's literature as a separate genre in the early nineteenth century, African Americans were presented by white authors as mindless, superstitious, and shiftless. This treatment was particularly evident in two nineteenth-century works, Thomas Nelson Page's *Two Little Confederates* (1888) and Joel Chandler Harris's *Free Joe and the Rest of the World* (1887). A further example of this kind of racism can be found in Helen Bannerman's *Little Black Sambo* (1928).

These stereotypical portrayals continued throughout the early decades of the twentieth century; however, by the late 1930s several works emerged that tried to convey the African-American experience in an informed manner. Among the first such efforts were African-American author Arna Bontemps's *You Can't Pet a Possum* (1936) and *Sad-Faced Boy* (1937). However, most of the material published for children during this period continued to depict stereotypes of African Americans.

By the mid- to late 1940s, books began to portray a slightly more realistic picture of blacks and began to address civil rights and other issues relevant to the African-American community. Carter G. Woodson, the father of modern black historiography, wrote several books for children in the 1940s documenting African-American heritage, among them *African Heroes and Heroines* (1944) and *Negro Makers of History* (1948). During the 1950s Langston Hughes wrote a series of educational books for children, among them *The First Book of Negroes* (1952), *Famous American Negroes* (1954), and *The First Book of Jazz* (1955). Pulitzer Prize–winning poet Gwendolyn Brooks wrote *Bronzeville Boys and Girls* (1956), a book of poems for children depicting the lives of the urban poor. (Brooks wrote another children's book, *The Tiger Who Wore White Gloves,* in 1974.) Other titles from this period include author Jesse Jackson's *Call Me Charley* (1945) and Dorothy Sterling's *Mary Jane* (1959).

By the 1960s, some well-written material portraying African Americans was being published. Examples include white author Ezra Jack Keats's *The Snowy Day* (1962) and Ann Petry's *Tituba of Salem Village* (1964). But in 1965 Nancy Larrick was still able to present significant evidence in her analysis of the literature that omissions and distortions were widespread. She surveyed sixty-three mainstream publishers who had published a total of 5,200 children's books between 1962 and 1964. Her investigation revealed that only 6.7 percent included a black child in either the text or the illustrations (Larrick, p. 64).

Larrick's article, coupled with the rise of the civil rights movement and the increased availability of funds for schools and libraries, motivated publishers to produce more materials about African Americans. In 1969 the Coretta Scott King Book Award was established in order to recognize African-American authors and illustrators for outstanding contributions to children's literature. As a result, more realistic portrayals began to emerge, presenting the diversity of black life, culture, and experience in both fictional and nonfictional works.

Louise Clifton wrote her first book for children, *Some of the Days of Everett Anderson,* in 1970; she has since written many books of poetry and stories for children that are widely praised as realistic portrayals of black children's experience and as valuable introductions to African-American heritage. During this period, June Jordan also began writing books for children and young adults that were acclaimed for their political relevance and for the intensity of their reproduction of the African-American experience; examples include *His Own Where* (1971), which was nominated for a National Book Award; *New Life: New Room* (1975); and *Kimako's Story* (1981). By incorporating elements of black southern folklore with a contemporary political consciousness, Julius Lester brought a special emphasis to his children's literature. His works for children and young adults include *To Be a Slave* (1968), which was nominated for a Newbery Medal; *Black Folktales* (1969); *The Knee-High Man and Other Tales* (1972); and *The Long Journey Home: Stories from Black History* (1972), a nonfiction collection of slave narratives that was a finalist for a National Book Award. International authors of children's literature also began to gain recognition in this period; a notable example is Chinua Achebe, the celebrated Nigerian author, whose best-known children's book is *How the Leopard Got His Claws* (1973). Other significant authors and illustrators from the period include Virginia Hamilton, Walter Dean Myers, John Steptoe, Eloise Greenfield, and the artist team of Leo and Diane Dillon.

This positive trend continued to the end of the next decade, as evidenced in the 1979 study conducted by Jeanne S. Chall, which updated Larrick's investigation. Chall's study indicated that in 4,775 children's books published between 1973 and 1975, 14.4 percent represented black characters in the text or illustrations—more than double the percentage found by Larrick in 1965 (McCann, p. 215).

As the civil rights movement waned in the late 1970s and 1980s, the publication of books on the African-American experience diminished. New African-American writers could no longer break into the mainstream easily, and even established authors found themselves struggling to find publishers. Despite this trend, additional new authors emerged. Ossie Davis, for example, wrote two books for children based on major figures in black history: *Escape to Freedom: A Play About Young Frederick Douglass* (1978) and *Langston, A Play* (1982). Mildred Taylor also entered the scene with *Song of the Trees* (1975) and the Newbery Award–winning *Roll of Thunder, Hear My Cry* (1976).

With the retrenchment of mainstream publishers in the 1980s, alternative presses emerged to fill the void. Black Butterfly Press, Just Us Books, and the Third World Press were among the few houses that published African-American authors who were shut out of the mainstream. By the 1990s these publishers had expanded in response to the public's demand for African-American materials. Mainstream publishers also again responded to the interest in these materials, so that in the early years of the twenty-first century, numerous African-American titles were found on the lists of major publishing houses.

With the increase of these publications, debate has arisen over whether non-African Americans can write effectively about the black experience. While the cultural background of an author/illustrator is important, the crucial issue is one of perspective (i.e., the author's mind-set and point of view in creating the work). An important consideration is whether, at the time of creation, the author/illustrator—regardless of his or her own cultural background—was thinking as a member of the group or as an outsider (Lachmann, p. 17). If the former perspective is operative, it allows the creator to produce sincere and meaningful portrayals of the subject. Examples of white authors and illustrators who have successfully portrayed the black identity include Ann Cameron, William Loren Katz, Ann Grifalconi, and Ezra Jack Keats.

A number of successful African-American titles were published in the 1990s, including Mildred Taylor's *Mississippi Bridge* (1990), Angela Johnson's *When I Am Old with You* (1990, winner of an Honorable Mention at the 1991 Coretta Scott King Book Awards), Eloise Greenfield's *Night on Neighborhood Street* (1991), and Rosa Parks's *Rosa Parks: My Story* (1992, with James Haskins). The literature now offers a rich complexity in depicting ethnic experience. This situation is beneficial not only to the African-American community but to the larger society because it furnishes insights that can help to further communication and understanding. This trend should serve to increase the quantity and quality of African-American literature for children.

In the new century authors such as Mildred Taylor, Ann Grifalconi, Patricia McKissack, Virginia Hamilton, Angela Johnson, and Walter Dean Myers continued to produce high-quality work reflecting the African-American Experience. Contemporary issues such as teen parenthood in Angela Johnson's *The First Part Last* (2005), incarceration in Walter Dean Myers's *Monster* (2001), gang violence in Barbara M. Joosse's *Stars in the Darkness* (2001), and family strength in Virginia Hamilton's *Time Pieces* (2005) gave voice to the reality of contemporary life.

Captivating African tales such as Ann Grifalconi's *The Village That Vanished* (2004) and Tamara Bower's *How the Amazon Queen Fought the Prince of Egypt* (2005) included exceptional illustrations. Patricia McKissack's *Precious and the Boo Hag* (2005) brought humor and suspense as a young girl followed her mother's advice and outwitted the scary monster, a not too subtle reminder for young readers to mind their elders.

The journey of African Americans from slavery through racism and prejudice is chronicled in Hariette Robinet's *Twelve Travelers, Twenty Horses* (2005) and Elisa Carbone's *Last Dance on Holladay Street* (2005), which graphically depict life in 1800s America. In *The Land* (2003) Mildred Taylor explains the genesis for racial feuds found in her earlier novels, giving voice to the struggles of the period. Toni Morrison's fictional dialogue and actual photographs result in an eloquent photo-essay, *Remember: The Journey to School Integration* (2004). Race relations and family strength are key elements in this world of harsh realities.

Contemporary big city life is captured in Barbara Joosse's *Hot City* (2004), while Jane Kurtz's *In the Small, Small Night* (2005) and Marie Fritz's *A Gift for Sadia* (2005) portray the adjustment of African children who migrated to America. Strength of character, perseverance in the face of hardship, and family love predominate. Stories written by, or about, African-American celebrities include Will Smith's *Just the Two of Us* (2005), George Forman's humorous *Let George Do It* (2005) and Chris Raschka's *John Coltrane's Giant Steps* (2002). Books that introduce both the writer and the works include Patricia McKissack's *Zora Neale Hurston: Writer and Storyteller* (2002), Caroline Lazo's *Alice Walker: Freedom Writer* (2000), and Doreen Rappaport's *Martin's Big Words: The Life of Dr. Martin Luther King, Jr.* (2001).

The decade that began in 2000 produced African-American children's literature of substance. These works, and hopefully more to come, are a dynamic segment of the children's literature market.

See also Bontemps, Arna; Brooks, Gwendolyn; Davis, Ossie; Folklore; Hughes, Langston; Literature; Morrison, Toni; Parks, Rosa; Slave Narratives; Woodson, Carter G.

■ ■ *Bibliography*

Broderick, Dorothy. *Image of the Black in Children's Fiction.* New York: Bowker, 1973.

Lachmann, Lyn Miller. *Our Family, Our Friends, Our World: An Annotated Guide to Significant Multicultural Books for Children and Teenagers.* New Providence, N.J.: Bowker, 1992.

Larrick, Nancy. "The All-White World of Children's Books." *Saturday Review* (September 11, 1965): 63–65, 84–85.

McCann, Donnarae, and Gloria Woodard. *The Black American in Books for Children: Readings in Racism.* Metuchen, N.J.: Scarecrow Press, 1985.

Norton, Donna E., Saundra E. Norton, and Amy McClure. *Through the Eyes of a Child.* 6th ed. Upper Saddle River, N.J.: Merrill, Prentice Hall, 2003.

Rand, Donna, and Toni Trent Parker. *African-American Children's Books.* New York: Wiley, 2001.

Rollock, Barbara. *Black Authors and Illustrators of Children's Books: A Biographical Dictionary.* 2nd ed. New York: Garland, 1992.

Sims, Rudine. *Shadow and Substance: Afro-American Experience in Contemporary Children's Fiction.* Urbana, Ill.: National Council of Teachers of English, 1982.

HEATHER CAINES (1996)
NORMA L. GRANT (2005)

CHILDRESS, ALICE

OCTOBER 12, 1920
AUGUST 14, 1994

Born in Charleston, South Carolina, playwright Alice Childress was reared in Harlem by her grandmother, Eliza Campbell. Childress grew up economically poor but culturally rich because her grandmother exposed her to the arts, fostered in her a desire for excellence, and introduced her to testimonials at the Salem Church in Harlem. It was her grandmother who encouraged her to write by creating a game that allowed her to develop fictional characters. She was forced to drop out of high school when her grandmother died. But she decided to educate herself by reading books borrowed from the public library.

Childress began her writing career in the late 1940s while involved in helping develop and strengthen the American Negro Theatre (ANT), where she studied acting and directing. Her decision to become a playwright was a natural outgrowth of her experiences at ANT. She wrote and produced thirteen plays, including *Florence* (1949), *Trouble in Mind* (1955; winner of an Obie Award in 1956 for the best original Off-Broadway play—the first time the award was given to a black woman), *Wedding Band: A Love Hate Story in Black and White* (1966; televised on ABC in

1974), *Wine in the Wilderness* (1969; produced on National Educational Television that year), *Mojo: A Black Love Story* (1970), and *Moms* (1987). Childress's plays treat the plight of the poor and the oppressed. She championed underdogs and showed their dignity and will to survive.

Childress was an equally dynamic novelist, having published five novels, including *Like One of the Family: Conversations from a Domestic's Life* (1937), *A Hero Ain't Nothin' but a Sandwich* (1973), *A Short Walk* (1979), *Rainbow Jordan* (1981), and *Those Other People* (1990). Her novels, like her plays, champion the poor and explore the inspiriting influences of the community.

In addition to the Obie she received in 1956, Childress received several honors and awards, including a John Golden Fund for Playwrights grant (1957), a Rockefeller grant (1967), and an appointment to Harvard's Radcliffe Institute for Independent Study (1966–1968).

See also American Negro Theatre; Drama

■ ■ *Bibliography*

Brown-Guillory, Elizabeth. *Their Place on the Stage: Black Women Playwrights in America.* Westport, Conn.: Greenwood Press, 1988.

Dugan, Olga. "Telling the Truth: Alice Childress as Theorist and Playwright." *Journal of African American History* (winter 2002): 146.

ELIZABETH BROWN-GUILLORY (1996)
Updated by publisher 2005

CHISHOLM, SHIRLEY

NOVEMBER 30, 1924
JANUARY 1, 2005

Shirley Chisholm was among the most significant black politicians of the twentieth century. Born Shirley St. Hill, in Brooklyn, she lived with her family in Barbados for some years before returning to the United States. She graduated cum laude from Brooklyn College in 1946 and earned a master's degree from Columbia University's Teachers College. After her marriage to Conrad Chisholm in 1949, she taught nursery school and became involved in the Democratic Party.

In 1960 Chisholm helped form the Unity Democratic Club in New York, and in 1965 she ran a successful campaign for a seat in the New York State Assembly. During her tenure there she helped establish the Search for Educa-

Shirley Chisholm (1924–2005). *The first African American woman elected to the U.S. House of Representatives, Chisholm was a candidate for the Democratic Party's nomination for President in 1972.* AP/WIDE WORLD PHOTOS. REPRODUCED BY PERMISSION.

tion, Equity, and Knowledge (SEEK) program to assist low-income students. She also helped win a maternity-leave policy for teachers.

In 1969 Chisholm won a seat in the House of Representatives, becoming the first African-American woman elected to Congress. While in the House she served on a number of committees, including Veterans' Affairs, Education and Labor, and House Rules. She was an outspoken opponent of the war in Vietnam and continued to fight for economic justice and women's rights.

In January 1972, Chisholm announced her candidacy for the Democratic nomination for president, becoming the first African American ever to do so. Although her campaign was unable to gain the support of the Congressional Black Caucus or the major women's groups with which she had long worked, Chisholm's effort was nonetheless groundbreaking.

Shirley Chisholm retired from Congress in 1982 and went on to teach at Mount Holyoke and Spelman colleges. She remained active in politics as the founder of the National Political Congress of Black Women and as its first president.

The story of Chisholm's rise in was recounted in *Chisholm '72: Unbought and Unbossed,* a documentary produced by Shola Lynch and Phil Bertelson in 2004. After suffering a series of strokes, Chisholm died at the age of eighty on January 1, 2005, in Ormond Beach, Florida.

See also Congressional Black Caucus; Politics in the United States

■ ■ *Bibliography*

Brownmiller, Susan. *Shirley Chisholm: A Biography.* Garden City, N.Y.: Doubleday, 1970.

Chisholm, Shirley. *Unbought and Unbossed.* Boston: Houghton Mifflin, 1970.

Chisholm, Shirley. *The Good Fight.* New York: Harper & Row, 1973.

Scheader, Catherine. *Shirley Chisholm: Teacher and Congresswoman.* Hillside, N.J.: Enslow, 1990.

JUDITH WEISENFELD (1996)
Updated by publisher 2005

CHRISTIANA REVOLT OF 1851

One of the major episodes of African-American resistance to enforcement of the Fugitive Slave Act of 1850, and the first in which blood was shed, occurred on September 11, 1851, near the tiny Quaker village of Christiana, Pennsylvania. That morning, Maryland slave owner Edward Gorsuch, several of his relatives, and three U.S. marshals bearing federal warrants surrounded the house of William Parker, a local black leader. The posse demanded the surrender of two of Gorsuch's slaves, who had run away from the Gorsuch farm two years before and were hiding inside Parker's home. Parker and his guests sounded an alarm to which local citizens responded. Although two Quakers advised the posse to retreat, Gorsuch refused, declaring, "My property I will have, or I'll breakfast in hell (Slaughter, 1991, p. 63)." Shots rang out, and when the smoke cleared, Gorsuch lay dead and three members of his party were wounded.

Within hours, the incident assumed national significance. A Lancaster, Pennsylvania, paper proclaimed: "Civil War—The First Blow Struck." One representative of the southern press, warning of secession, announced that "unless the Christiana rioters are hung . . .the bonds will be dissolved (Slaughter, 1991, pp. 220-221)." Sensing the event's political importance, President Millard Fillmore dispatched a company of U.S. Marines and some forty Philadelphia policemen to the village to apprehend those involved. After combing the countryside, they arrested more than thirty blacks and half a dozen whites. Even so, the five blacks most responsible for Gorsuch's death escaped; three—Parker, and Gorsuch's two runaway slaves—fled to Ontario. Although federal officials sought their extradition, Canadian authorities refused.

Hoping to make examples of the rioters, federal prosecutors charged them not only with resisting the Fugitive Slave Act but with treason. A federal grand jury indicted thirty-six blacks and two whites, some with tenuous links to the incident, and imprisoned them pending trial before the U.S. circuit court in Philadelphia. Federal attorneys used the trial of Castner Hanway, a white Quaker alleged to have directed the rioters in their attack on the posse, as a test case upon which to decide the fate of the other thirty-seven. The trial—which, ironically, convened on the second floor of Independence Hall—took on comic overtones. One defense attorney chided the government for arguing "that three harmless non-resisting Quakers and eight-and-thirty wretched, miserable, penniless negroes armed with corn cutters, clubs, and a few muskets . . .[had] levied war against the United States (Slaughter, 1991, p. 127)." The available evidence proved insufficient to substantiate the charges and, after acquitting Hanway in early December, the government dropped all remaining indictments and released the rioters.

The Christiana incident raised serious questions about the ability of the federal government to enforce the Fugitive Slave Act. But it did even more. Southerners were outraged by the results of the trial, and federal efforts to punish the rioters had increased sympathy for the abolitionists throughout the North. By galvanizing public opinion in both the North and the South on the question of enforcement of the law, the Christiana riot moved the nation closer to civil war.

See also Demerara Revolt; Malê Rebellion; Nat Turner's Rebellion; Stono Rebellion; Runaway Slaves in the United States

▪▪ *Bibliography*

Forbes, Ella. *But We Have No Country: The 1851 Christiana, Pennsylvania Resistance.* Cherry Hill, N.J.: Africana Homestead Legacy, 1998.

Slaughter, Thomas P. *Bloody Dawn: The Christiana Riot and Racial Violence in the Antebellum North.* New York: Oxford University Press, 1991.

ROY E. FINKENBINE (1996)
Updated bibliography

CHRISTIAN DENOMINATIONS, INDEPENDENT

▪▪▪

Independent black denominations are Protestant communions controlled entirely by blacks. The seven largest Independent black denominations are Baptist, Methodist, or Pentecostal and include the African Methodist Episcopal (AME) Church, the African Methodist Episcopal Zion (AMEZ) Church, the Christian Methodist Episcopal (CME) Church, the National Baptist Convention, U.S.A., Inc. (NBC), the National Baptist Convention of America, Unincorporated (NBCA), the Progressive National Baptist Convention (PNBC), and the Church of God in Christ (COGIC).

Independent black denominations of the nineteenth century formed as black members of predominantly white churches sought freedom from white governance and control, with racism being the initial catalyst for their formation. Thus from their inception African-American Protestant denominations acted as agents for the educational, political, economic, and social welfare of their black constituencies.

Independence took on two additional connotations from the late nineteenth century onward. First, independent inferred the differences in doctrine, decorum, and governance that fostered subsequent black religious independence movements. This is evidenced by splits occurring within Black Baptist and Methodist denominations and the eventual birth of autonomous black denominations such as the Church of God in Christ, whose history is traced uniquely to black religious leaders.

Independent also refers to the growth of loose inter- and nondenominational fellowships, whose founders and member churches trade doctrinal positions in favor of a more general emphasis on Bible-based sermons and attempts to overcome racial division. The media and Internet have provided denominations, fellowships, and individual churches with global access and worshippers of every persuasion with countless opportunities to observe, examine, or emulate the practices of others at home without censure or obligation.

Nondenominational ministries, especially those headed by popular ministers with television ministries, often bring together members from various traditions by providing safe space for adherents to participate in activities that individual churches may not sponsor. Despite the doctrinal competition that remains among independent black denominations, history affirms the growth of inter-faith initiatives, where member churches attempt to find common ground.

BLACK BAPTISTS: FOUNDERS OF THE FIRST INDEPENDENT BLACK CHURCHES

Black Baptists in the U.S. South are credited with establishing the first black congregations. Given slavery throughout the South and the fear of insurrection among slaveholders, Black Baptist congregations remained under white control until Emancipation. Thereafter, Black Baptists formed the National Baptist Convention, U.S.A., Inc. (NBC), the National Baptist Convention of America, Unincorporated (NBCA), and the Progressive National Baptist Convention (PNBC).

The first known Black Baptist, identified only as Quassey, was listed as one of fifty-one members of the Newton, Rhode Island, church in 1743. The Baptist congregation in Providence, Rhode Island, had nineteen black members in 1762, and blacks were first received into the First Baptist Church of Boston in 1772. Most Black Baptists were nonetheless in the South.

BLACK METHODISTS: FOUNDERS OF THE FIRST INDEPENDENT BLACK DENOMINATION

Black Methodists are credited with institutionalizing black religious independence. Free blacks in the North formed early Methodist churches, conferences, and denominations after growing weary of restrictions on their level of participation in church governance and proceedings.

Black Methodists generally refers to the African Methodist Episcopal Church (AME), the African Methodist Episcopal Zion Church (AMEZ), and the Christian Methodist Episcopal Church (CME). Five smaller communions exist as well, including the Union American Methodist Episcopal Church (UAME), the oldest of all Black Methodist denominations. Additional groups resulted from splits within the AME and AMEZ churches.

The Black Methodist Church emerged from the Methodist movement, which began in Oxford University in the 1720s and was named for its distinct "methods" of organization and spiritual discipline. The denomination's antislavery position enhanced the appeal of Methodism to African Americans, free and enslaved. The church later retreated from its position after 1785, but the number of black members continued to increase as African Americans embraced the church's earlier position and experienced the fervor of the Second Great Awakening at the turn of the century.

THE AFRICAN METHODIST EPISCOPAL CHURCH

Richard Allen, a former slave, initiated the separation of blacks from the Methodist Episcopal Church in 1787. Allen, Absalom Jones, and other black worshippers withdrew their membership from St. George's Methodist Episcopal Church in Philadelphia after being pulled from their knees while worshipping in a gallery that was off limits to blacks.

Allen also organized the Free African Society the same year for religious and secular purposes. Allen and Jones raised funds to build a church and intended to remain under the jurisdiction of the Methodist church. But when the edifice was completed, St. George's refused to send a minister there. Allen then moved to an old blacksmith shop that he owned. The structure was transformed into the mother church of the soon-to-be-founded AME denomination.

The Free African Society, the birthplace of Episcopal and Bethel AME churches, was duplicated by several like organizations in Pennsylvania, Maryland, Delaware, and New Jersey. After communicating with each other over a period of years and discussing their racial struggles within the Methodist church, representatives from five of the congregations came together at Bethel Church in 1816 to officially organize the African Methodist Episcopal Church. Richard Allen, ordained a deacon by Bishop Asbury in 1799, was then ordained an elder. At the same gathering he was elected bishop of the AME after Daniel Coker declined the office.

The Free African Society focused specifically on racial solidarity and abolitionist activity. Education was an equally important issue. Although early church leaders were not educated, they understood the positive impact education would have on the livelihood of the church and the progress of African people.

The organization focused on missions as well, increasing from a thousand members to approximately seven thousand within two years of its founding. It attracted thousands of new members in the South, where membership grew from 20,000 at the beginning of the Civil War to nearly 400,000 by 1884 and over 450,000 by 1896. The pattern of growth and expansion returned north and westward as African Americans migrated from the South in the early twentieth century. The AME has been the most effective of all black denominations in its overseas missionary efforts. The denomination claims one million members and over 22,000 churches in Africa and the Caribbean.

THE AFRICAN METHODIST EPISCOPAL ZION CHURCH

The AME Zion Church originated in the late eighteenth century when a delegation of black members separated from the white-controlled John Street Methodist Episcopal Church in New York City. In 1796, at the behest of Peter Williams, a former slave, one of the classes organized an African chapel in a cabinetmaker's shop that William Miller, another member, owned. Services were held there until a new edifice was built in 1800. In 1801 the chapel was incorporated as the "African Methodist Episcopal Church of the City of New York." It was required that church property be owned by the board of trustees and that only trustees of African descent act for the corporation. Membership was restricted to Africans, and voting on church matters was restricted to men.

The conference separated in 1816 and included Zion Church and Asbury African Methodist Episcopal Church in New York City. In October 1820 the two black churches adopted their own discipline and the name African Methodist Episcopal Zion. However, they opted not to join the conference over which Bishop Richard Allen presided.

Because of internal conflict and competition with "Allenites," the growth of the AME Zion Church was stunted prior to the Civil War. It began with 22 preachers and 1,400 members in 1821 and by 1860 numbered 4,600 with 105 preachers. By 1884 the church had grown to 300,000, with membership standing at 250,00 by in 1896. Foreign mission programs were established in South America, Africa, and the Caribbean. The church experienced a third wave of growth in the twentieth century as African Americans migrated northward and from rural to urban areas. Today, the African Methodist Episcopal Zion is the second largest black Methodist denomination. In 1989 it counted 1.2 million members in the United States, with an additional 100,000 in Africa and the Caribbean.

Known as "The Freedom Church," AME Zion claimed as members such abolitionists as Sojourner Truth, Harriet Tubman, and Frederick Douglass, who was licensed as an AME Zion preacher. Many members, pastors, and church officials were abolitionists and greatly involved with the Underground Railroad. Their commitment to social justice remains a characteristic of the church. The AME Zion Church was the first of all Methodist denominations, including the Methodist Episcopal Church, to ordain women. While whites have been admitted to membership and may hold any church office, their numbers remain small.

THE CHRISTIAN METHODIST EPISCOPAL CHURCH

The CME Church, unlike the AME or AME Zion, was born in the postslavery South with a different experience than its northern predecessors, as demonstrated in the name it selected. Initially called the Colored Methodist Episcopal Church in America, the name was changed in 1954 to Christian Methodist Episcopal Church. Although the AME Church in 1876 rejected a proposal to change its name from African to American, the CME changed the word "Colored" to "Christian" during the integrationist era.

The CME was affiliated with the Methodist Episcopal (ME) Church, South, the branch of white Methodism that emerged when the Methodist Episcopal church split over the issue of slavery. Their departure from the ME Church, South, was a protest of the segregated conditions and degrading treatment to which northern and southern blacks were subjected, as well as a declaration of self-determination. Their departure was particularly significant given that almost all of its members had been enslaved.

The separation from the ME church came with restrictions. As a condition of transferring ownership of properties to the new denomination, political activity was prohibited. Notwithstanding the criticism of many northern blacks, many recently emancipated southern blacks acquiesced to the restrictions. As the CME began under such limitations and lacked the tradition of the African societies and abolitionist movement, its early development appeared ultraconservative on political and social fronts.

Although the CME grew more slowly than the African churches, by 1890 its membership exceeded 103,000, 77 percent of whom were in Alabama, Georgia, Mississippi, and Tennessee. By 1945 it had expanded to eighteen states in the North and West, a process amplified by the emigration of blacks from the South during the two world wars and the Great Depression. The CME remains the smallest of the three black Methodist denominations. By 1989 membership stood at 900,000 in the United States and 75,000 overseas.

BLACK PENTECOSTALS: A NEW KIND OF INDEPENDENCE

With roots in the Holiness movement, an offshoot of Wesleyan Methodism, the Pentecostal movement is exceptional for the unprecedented level of interracial cooperation that occurred in its wake. White minister Charles Parham of Topeka, Kansas, began holding seminars on speaking in tongues in Topeka, where Lucy Farrow, Frederick

Douglass's niece, served as Parham's governess and became a missionary for the Pentecostal Movement, and in Houston, Texas, where William J. Seymour, a black Baptist preacher from Louisiana, listened in on messages from outside the classroom. Social customs of the time forbade his sitting in the same classroom with whites.

Influenced by Parham's teaching, Seymour journeyed to California and established the Azusa Street Mission, where he began to hold prayer meetings. Christians from throughout the world flocked to Los Angeles to witness the Azusa outpouring when participants began speaking in tongues. Among those attending the meeting was Charles Harrison Mason, cofounder with C. P. Jones of the Church of God in Christ. When Mason and Jones parted company over the question of tongues, Mason established a reorganized Church of God in Christ in 1907. The COGIC, therefore, did not evolve from racial division but rather theological interpretation, a characteristic that sets it apart from independent black churches of the nineteenth century. Pentecostals will celebrate the one-hundredth anniversary of the movement in 2006.

THE CHURCH OF GOD IN CHRIST (COGIC)

Under Mason's charismatic leadership, the COGIC became the fastest growing independent black religious organization in the country in the early twentieth century, although the organization was interracial at the outset. White ministers received ordination papers from Bishop Mason and worshipped among the COGIC for approximately ten years. Racial division prompted their egress and led to the formation of the Assemblies of God, a predominantly white Pentecostal body.

The COGIC has always been an urban movement with an affinity for attracting and affirming small and rural congregations. But it was a southern organization until the 1940s, when postwar and social changes sent black southerners to the Midwest, West, and Northeast. Early COGIC leaders placed great emphasis on land acquisition for church work. Property records affirm the steady rate of COGIC growth and expansion in the early twentieth century as southern and rural blacks migrated out of the South and into urban areas.

INDEPENDENT BLACK CHURCHES AND THE SUSTAINED QUEST FOR CIVIL RIGHTS AND CULTURAL AUTONOMY

Independent black churches have always emphasized the civil rights movement, with different denominations taking the lead on various political, social, and cultural fronts. In the antebellum period, the AME and AMEZ led the charge for social justice, focusing on abolition and the proposed colonization of Sierra Leone by American-born blacks. Independent black churches of the Reconstruction period focused on educating millions of former slaves and helping them navigate their political, social, and economic transition from bondage to freedom.

The AME had a track record of supporting black progress. But Black Baptists, particularly those affiliated with the Progressive Baptist Movement, became the dominant figures of resistance during the civil rights era, with Martin Luther King's ascendancy representing the zenith of Baptist participation in the quest for justice.

The COGIC denomination did not take an institutional position on the civil rights movement, but select COGIC members participated in key moments. Robert's Temple COGIC in New York City hosted Malcolm X's eulogy. Mamie Till Mobley, a COGIC adherent and the mother of Emmett Till, galvanized the movement by allowing photographs of her son's remains to be published in *Jet* magazine. Mason Temple COGIC, the headquarter church for the COGIC named for founder C. H. Mason, hosted rallies and musicals to support workers participating in the Sanitation Workers Strike in Memphis, Tennessee—the strike Martin Luther King was in town to support when he was assassinated. And Mason Temple was also the place King delivered his "mountaintop" speech, the last public address given before his assassination.

NEW CHANGES AND CHALLENGES

Although independent black denominations and fellowships continue to play a significant role in the African-American community, classic divides remain over the status of women and sexuality. Since the 1970s the black church has also been challenged by the appeal of the Nation of Islam to African-American men, a development underscoring the complex chasm between the black church and the contemporary struggles of black men. Despite new challenges, the black church remains a premier institution within the African-American community.

See also African Methodist Episcopal Church; African Methodist Episcopal Zion Church; African Orthodox Church; African Union Methodism; Allen, Richard; Christian Methodist Episcopal Church; Nation of Islam; National Baptist Convention, U.S.A.; National Black Evangelical Association; Pentecostalism in North America; Protestantism in the Americas

Bibliography

Cone, James H., and Gayraud S. Wilmore. *Black Theology: A Documentary History,* vol. 1, *1966–1979,* 2nd ed. Maryknoll, N.Y.: Orbis Books, 1993.

Cone, James H., and Gayraud S. Wilmore. *Black Theology: A Documentary History,* vol. 2, *1980–1992.* Maryknoll, N.Y.: Orbis Books, 1993.

Higginbotham, Evelyn Brooks. *Righteous Discontent: The Women's Movement in the Black Baptist Church, 1880–1920.* Cambridge, Mass., and London: Harvard University Press, 1993.

Jackson, Jerma A. *Singing in My Soul: Black Gospel Music in a Secular Age.* Chapel Hill and London: University of North Carolina Press, 2004.

Kossie-Chernyshev, Karen. "A Grand Old Church Rose in the East: The Church of God in Christ in East Texas." *East Texas Historical Journal,* 2003.

Kossie-Chernyshev, Karen. "Constructing Good Success: The Church of God in Christ and Social Uplift in East Texas." *East Texas Historical Journal,* spring, 2006.

Lincoln, C. Eric, Lawrence H. Mamiya. *The Black Church in the African American Experience.* Durham, N.C., and London: Duke University Press, 1990.

Rivers, Larry Eugene, and Canter Brown, Jr. *Laborers in the Vineyard of the Lord: The Beginnings of the AME Church in Florida, 1865–1895.* Gainesville: University Press of Florida, 2001.

Washington, Joseph R. *Black Sects and Cults.* Lanham, Md.: University Press of America, 1984.

KAREN KOSSIE-CHERNYSHEV (2005)

CHRISTIANITY

See Christian Denominations, Independent; Religion; *and articles on particular Christian denominations (e.g., Baptists)*

CHRISTIANITY IN FILM

African Americans have long recognized the power of popular culture and media to help shape the society's views on race. As a result of the explicit intent of the artists and in less conscious ways, popular culture has informed discussions about civil rights, politics, and economics. While literary, theatrical, journalistic, and radio representations of African Americans have been influential, motion pictures have held a particularly prominent place in the American imagination. Film scholars have noted that, from film's earliest days, the appearance of black skin on screen—either on black actors or white actors in blackface makeup—has signaled a complex set of issues about political and social power. The stereotypical images that civil rights activists and film scholars have identified—which generally mark African Americans as lazy, childlike, hypersexual, or superstitious, for example—function to invest race with moral meaning, justifying racial hierarchy. At the same time, black filmmakers have also used the medium to explore artistic, social, and political issues of importance in ways that do not rely on those stereotypes.

Representations of African-American religious beliefs and practices have been featured prominently in many early, Hollywood, and more recent independent films that focus on African-American life or feature African-American characters. The appearance of this subject matter over time reflects in part the historical and contemporary significance of religion for many African Americans, both in institutional forms and as a component of individual identity. Film historian Thomas Cripps argues that films about religion made by African Americans for black audiences constitute a distinct genre, and he notes that, "No other genre, except perhaps the American western, spoke so directly to the meaning and importance of shared values embraced by its audience (1996, p. 12)." In addition to this small subset of black religious films, one finds explorations of black religion across an assortment of genres. This variety points to the way in which African-American religion in film has provided an imaginative arena to explore a broad range of topics, including politics, class, skin color, regional issues, gender, and theology.

EARLY BLACK FILM

Film historians often cite white director D. W. Griffith's 1915 film *The Birth of a Nation* as transformative because of its compelling visuals and sophisticated use of cinema as a medium for storytelling. Griffith's extremely popular work, which was based on Thomas W. Dixon's 1905 novel *The Clansman: A Historical Romance of the Ku Klux Klan,* is also significant in film history because it made clear the utility of cinema to locate Christian white supremacy as the basis of American identity. Outraged by the racism and violence of the film, African Americans and concerned whites in the National Association for the Advancement of Colored People mounted an unsuccessful campaign to halt its exhibition in a number of cities. In addition to protesting formally, African Americans addressed the troubling perspective advanced in *The Birth of a Nation* by presenting alternative visions on film and, in a number of cases, their cinematic responses spoke to the religious implications of Griffith's perspective. In 1920 black director Oscar Micheaux, who produced almost forty films in the silent and sound eras, released *Within Our Gates,* which tells the story of Sylvia Landry, a black teacher in a southern school for black children. Responding to Griffith's justification of segregation and of Ku Klux Klan lynchings as necessary tools to restore the divinely ordained glory of the white nation, Micheaux presented a story of racial violence from the perspective of innocent and upstanding African Americans who seek nothing more than just pay for their labor and fair treatment as citizens. In addition to his critique of racial violence directed at African Americans, Micheaux directed his attention to questions of what African Americans at the time termed "racial uplift"—strategies for political, economic, and social development that would enable blacks to claim the full rights of citizenship.

Religious leadership proved an important part of Micheaux's vision, and *Within Our Gates* argues—through the character of Old Ned—that uneducated and manipulative ministers threaten black progress by diverting attention from more significant issues toward an unproductive quest for reward in heaven. Micheaux presented a similar and even more dangerous character in his 1925 *Body and Soul* in which Paul Robeson stars as the greedy, manipulative, and violent Rev. Isaiah Jenkins, whose reign of terror is enabled by the utter devotion of the congregation's women. While Micheaux called into question the frequent reliance of African Americans on clergy for leadership, he still provided a place for religion, and Christianity in particular, in racial uplift. Micheaux's theological response to Griffith's Christian white supremacy was to argue, through the character of Dr. V. Vivian in *Within Our Gates*, a model of appropriate commitment to racial uplift, that Christianity insists on racial equality and human rights for all.

The Birth of a Race (1919), directed by John W. Noble, responded directly to the religious implications of *The Birth of a Nation*. Although the film's title might lead viewers to expect a film that focuses on African-American achievements, *The Birth of a Race*'s approach to countering Griffith's presentation of the American nation as fundamentally Anglo-Saxon instead relates the history of the human race, using the Bible as its source. The film narrates the birth and development of humanity as a product of God's desire for peace. Produced in the shadow of World War I, Noble's film presents America's sacred history as a divinely ordained development of biblical sacred history and endorses African-American participation in the war, which it sees as benefiting "the Cause of Mankind" and God's ultimate desire for peace.

Later "race films"—intended for black audiences and produced by independent black filmmakers or in cooperation with white production companies—provide evidence that these artists were concerned about the past and future place of black religious institutions and their leaders in light of the social changes brought on by urbanization and the Great Migration. Some of these films are devotional and were produced from an explicitly religious perspective in an effort to evangelize and instruct about the dangers of the modern secular world. Others sought to provide a critique of black religious leadership, and yet other films simply included religious themes because black audiences found the familiar material entertaining.

Among the devotional films produced before 1950, those of African-American directors Eloyce King Patrick Gist and James Gist stand out as particularly geared toward engaging the viewer in an explicitly religious mode. Two of their surviving silent films made in the mid-1930s—*Hell-Bound Train* (c. 1929–1930) and *Verdict Not Guilty* (c. 1930–1933) focus on demonstrating the potential consequences for Christians of participation in worldly and sinful activities. In *Verdict Not Guilty* a woman's soul is brought before a heavenly court to answer for behavior during her life. While found innocent, she is subjected to Satan's attempts to claim her for himself by characterizing her as an irredeemable sinner. Similarly, in *Hell-Bound Train* the Gists presented their audience with examples of behaviors that they believed would lead the individual to hell, including gambling, drinking, dancing, listening to jazz music, abortion, and adultery.

African-American director Spencer Williams's films from the 1940s engaged many of the same themes as those found in the Gists' films but set the moral and religious messages in a variety of generic contexts, including melodrama, comedy, and musical. Two of his religious melodramas—*The Blood of Jesus* (1941) and *Go Down, Death* (1944)—pit devout churchwomen against the attempts of scheming men who scorn religion. In both cases religion triumphs in the end. Both films are also characterized by Williams's superimposition of one image over another to make present a variety of divine and demonic figures who interact with and attempt to influence the human characters. Even in a comedy, such as *Dirty Gertie from Harlem, U.S.A.* (1946), Williams engaged religious themes and provided a cautionary tale for viewers. A reworking of W. Somerset Maugham's 1924 story "Miss Thompson," *Dirty Gertie* interrogates the moral fortitude of black clergy, presenting Rev. Jonathan Christian as a sanctimonious and prim man who finds he cannot resist his desire for a nightclub dancer.

HOLLYWOOD FILMS

Representations of African and African-American religion have been common in Hollywood films, which have often characterized these beliefs and practices as savage, super-

Scene from Oscar Micheaux's **Within Our Gates: A Story of the Negro** *(1920). Micheaux's critique of racial violence was meant to counter the racist themes in D. W. Griffith's popular film* The Birth of a Nation. PHOTOGRAPHS AND PRINTS DIVISION, SCHOMBURG CENTER FOR RESEARCH IN BLACK CULTURE, THE NEW YORK PUBLIC LIBRARY, ASTOR, LENOX AND TILDEN FOUNDATIONS.

stitious, hysterical, or childlike. During the heyday of the studio system, Hollywood films frequently made use of images of African-derived and African-American religion to evoke laughter or terror and sometimes both within the same narrative. Vitaphone Varieties' short silent comedy *Revival Day with Slim Timblin* (1930), for example, takes the viewer into the world of the black church and lampoons the preaching styles and comportment of black ministers, using a white actor in blackface makeup in the lead role. Hal Roach's film *The Little Sinner* (1935), a short in the *Our Gang* series, relies for its comedy on a white character's terror in response to seeing members of a black congregation's river baptism. A scene in the Marx Brothers' *A Day at the Races* (1937) also enlists African-American religious culture in its humor, presenting black culture as authentic and joyful when set against the pretensions of wealthy whites. During this same period, film audiences frequently saw adventure films that focused on

a white explorer's encounter with savage black jungle peoples whose superstitious practices mark them as a danger to white civilization. Whether set in Africa or in the Caribbean, such films typically revolved around the rescue of a white woman from rape, cannibalism, or the threat of her surrender to "voodoo" or paganism. *Trader Horn* (1931), *White Zombie* (1932), *Kongo* (1932), *King Kong* (1933), *Black Moon* (1934), and *I Walked with a Zombie* (1943) typify such early films. Although they are set in contexts far from the United States, American ideas about the moral valence of race, which equates blackness with evil, informed these adventure films. Similar approaches to African-derived religions are present in later Hollywood films such as *The Believers* (1987), *Angel Heart* (1987), and *The Serpent and the Rainbow* (1988). These movies promote the view that the African-derived religions of vodou and Santería are profoundly dangerous and, as with the earlier generation of films, attempted to speak to the particular historical moment and to fears about African and Caribbean immigrants to the United States.

On a number of significant occasions in its early years, Hollywood turned its attention to "all-black cast" films, spurred on by the idea that black religious music, particularly spirituals, provided the best material to demonstrate the wonders of the new sound technology. In 1929 Fox released *Hearts in Dixie* and Metro-Goldwyn-Mayer *Hallelujah,* the first all-black cast Hollywood films. Even after sound had become a routine part of the movies, the studios continued to be interested in all-black cast films set in religious contexts. Warner Brothers followed in 1936 with a film adaptation of Marc Connelly's Pulitzer Prize–winning play, *The Green Pastures,* an attempt to present a black version of the Hebrew Scriptures, and Metro-Goldwyn-Mayer returned again in 1943 with *Cabin in the Sky,* also adapted from a Broadway show. While novel in the context of Hollywood because of their use of black casts, these films nevertheless attempted to fix African Americans in an imagined untroubled rural past, failing to note economic exploitation, racial violence, or political disfranchisement. Each of these early all-black cast films employed images of simple or superstitious black religion as a sign that the black masses were suited to a subordinate economic, political, and moral standing in America. These patterns held true in later films, even when the focus was not on an imagined all-black context.

CONTEMPORARY FILM

Hollywood's representational traditions of black religion had a long-term impact, and the absence of religious themes in later films by black filmmakers may be attributed, in part, to this legacy. The writers and directors of the male-oriented new black independent cinema of the 1980s and 1990s, for example, showed little interest in exploring religious belief and practice in their art. Spike Lee's 1992 biographical film, *Malcolm X,* engaged Malcolm's religious beliefs only briefly and, in charting his movement out of the Nation of Islam, emphasized political over equally important theological motivations. A number of films directed by black and white directors in the 1990s and early 2000s did take the opportunity to engage religious themes in ways that charted new territory with regard to the representation of black religious life. Charles Burnett's *To Sleep with Anger* (1990) is set in Los Angeles but presents a family with roots deep in the South and for whom belief in conjure—African-derived magical practices—remains strong. Julie Dash's 1991 *Daughters of the Dust* also concerns itself with conjure traditions among the Gullah people of the Sea Islands but uses the medium in novel ways in her attempt to represent African sensibilities about

memory, time, and place. In addition, Dash's work stands out because of her focus on African-American women's religious sensibilities as central to the formation of collective identity. *Eve's Bayou* (1997), written and directed by Kasi Lemmons, also interweaves magic into its exploration of secrets and family dynamics in 1960s New Orleans. A number of films in the period returned to explore the significance of Christianity for African Americans. In 1992 actor Blair Underwood directed *The Second Coming,* a short film in which he stars as a modern-day Jesus who is judged insane for declaring himself the son of God. The film takes on the contested issue of representing the race of the historical Jesus, as well as poses questions about how to make the Christian message relevant in modern times. White actor, writer, and director Robert Duvall, in his 1997 independent film *The Apostle,* surrounds white Pentecostal preacher Sonny Dewey with a largely black congregation in his search for personal redemption. Avoiding both the conventional Hollywood stereotypes of revivalist preachers and of black congregations, Duvall's work proved effective in imagining a religious landscape in which people engage each other's deep human frailties.

The increasing presence of African Americans behind the camera in Hollywood and in independent film, coupled with the interest among white directors familiar with black religion in presenting stories about African-American religious life, makes it likely that audiences will have access to a broader range of representations and more complex examinations of black religion in American film in the twenty-first century.

See also Film in the United States; Film in the United States, Contemporary; Religion; Representations of Blackness in the United States

■ ■ *Bibliography*

Bowser, Pearl, Jane Gaines, and Charles Musser, eds. *Oscar Micheaux and His Circle: African-American Filmmaking and Race Cinema of the Silent Era.* Bloomington: Indiana University Press, 2001.

Cripps, Thomas. "The Making of *The Birth of a Race:* The Emerging Politics of Identity in Silent Movies." In *The Birth of Whiteness: Race and the Emergence of U.S. Cinema,* edited by Daniel Bernardi. New Brunswick, N.J.: Rutgers University Press, 1996.

Snead, James. *White Screens, Black Images: Hollywood from the Dark Side.* Edited by Colin MacCabe and Cornel West. New York and London: Routledge, 1994.

Weisenfeld, Judith. "For the Cause of Mankind: The Bible, Racial Uplift, and Early Race Movies." In *African Americans and the Bible: Sacred Text and Social Texture,* edited by Vincent Wimbush. New York: Continuum, 2002.

Weisenfeld, Judith. "Saturday Sinners and Sunday Saints: The Nightclub as Urban Menace in 1940s Race Movies." In *Faith in the Market: Religion and The Rise of Urban Commercial Culture,* edited by John Giggie and Diane Winston. New Brunswick, N.J.: Rutgers University Press, 2002.

Weisenfeld, Judith. "'My Story Begins Before I Was Born': Myth, History, and Power in Julie Dash's *Daughters of the Dust.*" In *Representing Religion in World Cinema: Filmmaking, Mythmaking, Culture Making,* edited by S. Brent Plate. New York: Palgrave, 2003.

FILMOGRAPHY

Angel Heart, dir. Alan Parker. Carolco Entertainment/TriStar Pictures, 1987.

The Apostle, dir. Robert Duvall. Butcher's Run Films, 1997.

The Believers, dir. John Schlesinger. Orion Pictures, 1987.

The Birth of a Race, dir. John W. Noble. Birth of a Race Photoplay Corp., 1919.

Black Moon, dir. Roy William Neill. Columbia Pictures, 1934.

The Blood of Jesus, dir. Spencer Williams. Amegro Films/Sack Amusement Enterprises, 1941.

Body and Soul, dir. Oscar Micheaux. Micheaux Film Corp., 1925.

Cabin in the Sky, dir. Vincente Minnelli. Metro-Goldwyn-Mayer, 1943.

Daughters of the Dust, dir. Julie Dash. Geechee Girls, 1991.

A Day at the Races, dir. Sam Wood. Metro-Goldwyn-Mayer, 1937.

Dirty Gertie From Harlem, U.S.A., dir. Spencer Williams. Sack Amusement Enterprises, 1946.

Eve's Bayou, dir. Kasi Lemmons. Addis Weschler Pictures, 1997.

Go Down Death, dir. Spencer Williams. Sack Amusement Enterprises, 1946.

The Green Pastures, dir. Marc Connelly and William Keighley. Warner Brothers, 1936.

Hallelujah, dir. King Vidor. Metro-Goldwyn-Mayer, 1929.

Hearts In Dixie, dir. Paul Sloane. Fox Film Corp., 1929.

I Walked With a Zombie, dir. Jacques Tourneur. RKO Radio Pictures,1943.

King Kong, dir. Merrian C. Cooper and Ernest B. Schoedsack. RKO Radio Pictures,1933.

Kongo, dir. William Cowan. Metro-Goldwyn-Mayer, 1932.

The Little Sinner, dir. Gus Meins. Hal Roach Studios, 1935.

Malcolm X, dir. Spike Lee. 40 Acres and a Mule, 1992.

Revival Day with Slim Timblin, dir. Roy Mack and Tenny Wright. Vitaphone Varieties, no. 3679, 1930.

The Second Coming, dir. Blair Underwood. Quiet Fury Productions, 1992.

The Serpent and the Rainbow, dir. Wes Craven. Universal Pictures, 1988.

To Sleep with Anger, dir. Charles Burnett. SVS Films, 1990.

Trader Horn, dir. W. S. Van Dyke. Metro-Goldwyn-Mayer, 1931.

White Zombie, dir. Victor Halperin. United Artists Corp., 1932.

Within Our Gates, dir. Oscar Micheaux. Micheaux Film Corp., 1920.

JUDITH WEISENFELD (2005)

CHRISTIAN METHODIST EPISCOPAL CHURCH

▪▪▪

The Colored Methodist Episcopal Church in America (CME) was organized December 16, 1870, in Jackson, Tennessee, by former slaves who had been members of the Methodist Episcopal (ME) Church–South. After their emancipation, however, they realized that continued membership in the church of their former masters was neither desirable nor practical and requested their own separate and independent church "regularly established," as Isaac Lane said, "after our own ideas and notions." With careful attention to what was pointed to as the "desires of our colored members," the ME Church–South, provided the basic ecclesiastical, legal, and practical means that enabled them, in the words of Lucius H. Holsey, to establish their "own separate and distinct ecclesiasticism."

From 1866 to 1870 several hundred black preachers were ordained, an official periodical, *The Christian Index,* began publication, five black annual conferences were established, delegates empowered to set up their "separate ecclesiastical jurisdiction" were called to meet, the ordination of bishops was authorized, and transfer to the new church of all properties that had been used by slave congregations was sanctioned. On December 21, 1870, William H. Miles and Richard H. Vanderhorst—two black preachers elected bishops and ordained by Robert Paine, senior bishop of the ME Church–South—assumed the Episcopal oversight of the new jurisdiction, and an independent church of African Americans became a reality.

The CME Church soon emerged as one of the more influential churches in African-American communities throughout the South. Beginning with approximately seventy-eight thousand members, competent leaders, several hundred congregations, and title to hundreds of pieces of church property, it had, by the turn of the century, expanded beyond the Mason-Dixon Line following the migrations of African Americans to the North, Midwest, and the Pacific Coast. At the close of World War I, the CME Church was established wherever significant numbers of African Americans were located. After World War II, as CMEs found themselves in more racially inclusive communities and the civil rights struggle intensified, the term "colored" took on the stigma of discrimination and Jim Crow–ism. Consequently, in 1954 the name was changed to the Christian Methodist Episcopal Church. By 1990 it had more than 812,000 communicant members, congregations throughout the United States, and conferences in Nigeria, Ghana, Liberia, Haiti, and Jamaica.

The CME Church is the ecclesiastical outgrowth of the grafting of nineteenth-century Protestantism, as practiced by American Methodists, and African slave religion, as found in the peculiar institution of slavery. In confronting slavery, Protestant denominations endeavored to "save" the souls of slaves rather than free them from their bondage. Preaching the gospel to the slaves was the means to this end. The Methodists were highly effective in slave evangelism. Methodism, begun by John Wesley in England and established on the American continent in 1784 as the Methodist Episcopal Church, was appealing to slaves. Methodists preached a plain and simple gospel that gave meaning and hope to the desperate conditions of the slave experience, practiced styles of preaching and worship that encouraged the expression of deep feelings and strong emotions, and provided a system of licenses and ordination that enhanced the status of slave preachers.

Early American Methodists had opposed slavery, but as more southerners and slaves joined the church, irreconcilable conflicts developed, and in 1844 Methodism split over the slavery issue. The southern branch of Methodism promoted such an extensive program of slave evangelism that by the beginning of the Civil War more than 207,000 slaves—almost 50 percent of all slaves who embraced Christianity—were members of the ME Church–South. Among them were those who would organize the CME Church in 1870.

The Christianity that the slaves embraced, however, was reshaped in accordance with the realities of their slave experiences and the remnants of their African heritage. Residual elements of African religion such as belief in one Supreme Being, the union of the spiritual and the material, a strong affirmation of the present life, and certitude of life after death, molded the gospel preached to the slaves into African-American religion, the most powerful force of African-American life. Although the scion of African-American religion would flourish from the sap of orthodox Christian faith, it would nonetheless have a shape all its own. And it would sprout the varied branches of African-American religion, such as the CME Church, as former slaves, finally set free, established their separate churches, giving institutional meaning to the religion that had sustained them in the darkest days of slavery.

The CME Church perceived the social concerns of African Americans to be a significant part of its mission. CMEs have been in the vanguard of black America's "stride toward freedom" in demanding their own church, sharing in Reconstruction governments, protesting the enactment of Jim Crow laws, helping establish and support civil rights organizations, and participating fully in the civil rights struggle. It has been a leader in the education

of black youth as many of its early church buildings were used as schools. Twenty-one educational institutions have been under its auspices, and four colleges and a school of theology are presently under its sponsorship. CME churches helped to meet the needs of African Americans through ministries such as low-income housing projects, credit unions, senior citizens' homes, child care centers, Project Head Start, and antipoverty and drug prevention programs. The CME Church has been a pioneer participant in the ecumenical movement through the National Council of Churches, the World Council of Churches, and the National Congress of Black Churches.

Influential African Americans of the CME Church include William H. Miles, its first bishop; Lucius H. Holsey, the leader in establishing CME schools; Charles H. Phillips, the major influence in expanding the church; Helena B. Cobb, founder of an institute for black girls and an early proponent of women's rights; Channing H. Tobias, chairman of the board of the NAACP; John Hope Franklin, historian of African Americans; William Y. Bell, who served as dean of the School of Religion of Howard University; B. Julian Smith, a leader in the ecumenical movement; Joseph A. Johnson, Jr., a black theologian; and Alex Haley, author.

See also Franklin, John Hope; Haley, Alex; Slavery

■ ■ *Bibliography*

Lakey, Othal Hawthorne, *The History of the CME Church.* Memphis, Tenn.: CME Publishing House, 1985.

Phillips, C. H. *The History of the Colored Methodist Episcopal Church in America.* Jackson, Miss.: CME Publishing House, 1900.

OTHAL HAWTHORNE LAKEY (1996)

CHRISTIAN RECORDER

The *Christian Recorder,* the official organ of the African Methodist Episcopal (AME) Church, was established as the *Christian Herald* in 1848. It was renamed the *Christian Recorder* in 1852. During the nineteenth century, several AME clergymen served as editors of the weekly journal: Augustus R. Green (1848–1852); Molliston Madison Clark (1852–1854); Jabez Pitts Campbell (1854–1858); Elisha Weaver (1861–1867); Benjamin Tanner (1868–1884); Benjamin F. Lee (1885–1892); H. T. Johnson (1893–1902).

As an AME periodical, the *Christian Recorder* focused primarily on church matters and moral and religious topics in its early years. But as a voice for African Americans, it served a broader audience and addressed a wider range of community concerns. During the Civil War, the *Recorder* served as a communications link between black communities and their soldiers in the field. A weekly "Information Wanted" column helped reunite families torn apart by slavery, war, and economic distress. During Reconstruction, reports from AME clergymen working in southern missions provided information on the condition of the freedpeople.

Correspondence from black communities across the continent created a composite picture of American race relations in the decades following the Civil War. *The Christian Recorder,* as the oldest surviving publication of the black periodical press, provides a valuable historical record of African-American life and culture.

See also African Methodist Episcopal Church; Tanner, Benjamin Tucker

▨ ▨ *Bibliography*

Williams, Gilbert Anthony. *The Christian Recorder: Newspaper of the African Methodist Episcopal Church*: *History of a Forum for Ideas, 1854–1902.* Jefferson, N.C.: McFarland, 1996.

Wright, Richard R., Jr. *Encyclopedia of African Methodism,* 2nd ed. Philadelphia, 1948.

MICHAEL F. HEMBREE (1996)
Updated bibliography

CHRISTOPHE, HENRI

OCTOBER 6, 1767
OCTOBER 8, 1820

╊╋╉

Henri Christophe was born in 1767 in Grenada, in the Lesser Antilles. As a boy he worked as a sailor and accompanied a French naval officer to Savannah, Georgia, where he fought against the British in the American Revolution (1765–1783). He then found work as a chef at the Hotel de la Couronne in Le Cap, Haiti. Scholars disagree as to whether Christophe was born a free black or bought his way out of slavery through his employment as a chef. Regardless, in 1794, when he joined in the Haitian Revolution (1791–1804), he was not bound by slavery.

During the Haitian Revolution, Christophe served as one of General Toussaint L'Ouverture's chief officers. Under Christophe's leadership, troops in the North of Haiti expanded the revolution from an internal conflict to a full-scale assault on imperialism, fighting off the invasion of French general Charles-Victor-Emmanuel Leclerc in 1802. Christophe refused to allow Leclerc to dock in Le Cap until he received permission from L'Ouverture. Leclerc charged Christophe with rebellion and landed his forces anyway. In the meantime, Le Cap was evacuated and burned to the ground leaving Leclerc at a strategic disadvantage. However, the French were able to win a number of important engagements, and only months after having been the first to directly resist the French army, Christophe and his troops deserted. Christophe most likely deserted at this time because it appeared the French would not be defeated. Under the French, Christophe and his soldiers were used to suppress the Haitians who continued to resist the French. With time it became clear that the revolutionary forces were unlikely to be broken, and Christophe and his soldiers returned to fight on the Haitian side.

Independence was finally achieved on January 1, 1804, and Jean Jacques Dessalines became Haiti's first ruler. When Dessalines was assassinated in 1806, Christophe was elected to succeed him. Christophe refused to serve as president, however, because he believed the Haitian Constitution placed too many restrictions on the office. Instead, he attempted to seize Port-au-Prince and take unbridled control of Haiti. Mulatto General Alexandre Pétion and his forces stopped Christophe and forced him to retreat to the North. Christophe established a mostly black kingdom, while Pétion maintained control of the largely mulatto population in southern Haiti. The people of northern and southern Haiti engaged in a civil war, fed by regionalism and racism, before coming to an armed truce around 1809.

Christophe declared himself King Henri I in 1811 and set up a court that included hereditary barons and counts. He maintained a fear, however, that Haiti would again be invaded, and he saw to the construction of the Citadelle la Ferriere to defend Haiti. This massive fortress sits on top of a mountain near Cap Haïtian (formerly known as Le Cap) and was built over a period of thirteen years with walls up to twelve feet thick. It is claimed that as many as twenty thousand Haitians died in its construction, though this estimate remains unverified. The Citadelle served as a barracks capable of housing as many as ten thousand soldiers. According to his contemporaries, Christophe sometimes marched soldiers off the edge of the fortress to their deaths in order to display his authority.

Christophe's reign encompassed a number of important changes. He initially attempted to confront the war-ravaged Haitian economy through the maintenance of the plantation system complete with *corvé,* or compulsory labor. This, of course, proved far too similar to the slave system that had been successfully toppled, and it therefore met with widespread resistance. As autocratic as Christophe attempted to be, he could not ignore the demands of his subjects and was forced to embrace small landholding among the people. Christophe implemented an education system modeled primarily on the British school system, and he invited European teachers to settle in Northern Haiti. He also supported the abolition movement and courted Spain and England in the hopes of securing allies against possible French invasion.

Christophe expected the complete submission of the Haitian peasantry and became increasingly concerned at their growing disaffection for him. When unrest turned into rebellion, Christophe took his own life. He is said to have killed himself with a silver bullet, but, like many aspects of Christophe's life, this claim remains unconfirmed. His death allowed Jean-Pierre Boyer to reunite Haiti. Despite his authoritarian rule, Christophe played an important role in the independence of Haiti and remains a major figure of early Haitian history.

See also Dessalines, Jean-Jacques; Haitian Revolution; Toussaint-Louverture

■ ■ *Bibliography*

Fergusson, James. *A Traveller's History of the Caribbean.* New York: Interlink Books, 1999.

Fick, Carolyn. *The Making of Haiti: The Saint Domingue Revolution from Below.* Knoxville: University of Tennessee, 1990.

Nicholls, David. *From Dessalines to Duvalier: Race, Colour, and National Independence in Haiti.* New Brunswick, N.J.: Rutgers University, 1996.

Vandercook, John. *Black Majesty: The Life of Christophe, King of Haiti.* New York: Harper, 1928.

SEAN BLOCH (2005)

CINEMA

See Blaxploitation Films; Christianity in Film; Documentary Film; Film; Filmmakers

CIVIL RIGHTS CONGRESS

❙❙❙

The Civil Rights Congress (CRC) was founded in 1946 with the merger of the International Labor Defense, the National Negro Congress, and the National Federation for Constitutional Liberties—three organizations closely associated with the Communist Party, U.S.A. During the late 1940s and early 1950s the CRC fought for the civil rights and liberties of African Americans, labor leaders, and suspected communists. They believed that the defense of communists was the first line in the defense of civil liberties generally and sought to overturn the Smith Act (1940) and the McCarran Act (1950), both designed to stifle dissent and harass left-wing organizations.

Like the National Association for the Advancement of Colored People (NAACP), the CRC pursued legal cases to challenge the racism and inequality in American society. However, the CRC did not rely on legal strategy alone but combined it with political agitation, massive publicity campaigns, and large demonstrations to mobilize public opinion to demand an end to racist attacks. In the early 1950s the CRC launched a campaign to raise public awareness about the systemic violence and segregation that African Americans faced by presenting a petition to the United Nations that charged the U.S. government with genocide.

In one of the CRC's earliest cases, Rosa Lee Ingram, a black tenant farmer and widowed mother of twelve children, together with two of her sons, was convicted in 1947 of the murder of John Stratford and sentenced to death. Stratford, a white tenant farmer, had been sexually harassing Ingram when her sons came to her defense and hit Stratford on the head. The CRC, under the leadership of its women's auxiliary, Sojourners for Truth and Justice, fought a public battle to free the Ingrams. They filed a petition with the United Nations, named Rosa Ingram Mother of the Year, started the National Committee to Free the Ingram Family, which raised money for family members, and sent a delegation armed with 100,000 signatures to the Department of Justice and the White House. As a result of the CRC's efforts and the resulting press coverage, Rosa Ingram and her sons were freed in 1954.

In another well-publicized effort the CRC defended the Martinsville Seven, seven young black men in Virginia sentenced to death in 1949 by an all-white jury for raping a white woman. Civil rights organizations were outraged by the harshness of the sentence as well as the judge's refusal to grant a change of venue to ensure that the men received a fair trial. Deferring the legal case to the NAACP, the CRC focused on the publicity campaign. They conducted a massive international letter campaign, organized a prayer vigil, picketed the White House, held demonstrations in Richmond, and demanded a pardon from the governor. Although the NAACP and the CRC failed to save the lives of the Martinsville Seven, they succeeded in exposing the racism of the legal system in the United States.

The CRC fought tenaciously to defend the civil rights of the persecuted. They were not, however, strict civil libertarians. For example, they opposed free speech for the Ku Klux Klan and other racists, which brought them into conflict with an organization such as the American Civil Liberties Union. In addition, recurring tension with the NAACP made an alliance difficult, but at times the two organizations were able to achieve behind-the-scenes cooperation. Nevertheless, the CRC's unyielding opposition to racism won it support among some sectors of the African-American community. At its peak, the CRC reached a membership of ten thousand, with its strongest base in large cities. William Patterson, a lawyer and Communist Party leader, served as executive secretary of the organization during its existence. Other prominent leaders included Paul Robeson, Dashiell Hammett, and Louise Thompson Patterson.

The CRC was active during the McCarthy period, and the U.S. government tried persistently to repress the organization. In the mid-1950s the organization was under investigation by the Internal Revenue Service, New York State, and the House Committee on Un-American Activities. Government officials impounded CRC records, conducted an audit, and demanded lists of contributors. In 1954 the organization's leaders refused to give up the names of supporters and were arrested on contempt charges. Two years later, the Subversive Activities Control Board concluded that the CRC was "substantially controlled" by the Communist Party, U.S.A. Although many Communist party members and sympathizers were active in the CRC, the organization was always independent of the party. Nevertheless, in 1956 the CRC was forced to close its doors because of the increasing legal costs of the government investigations and a decline in the number of contributors. Despite its short-lived existence, CRC succeeded in bringing to international attention the injustice prevalent in the American legal system and the racism endemic to American society.

See also Communist Party of the United States; National Association for the Advancement of Colored People (NAACP); National Negro Congress; Patterson, William; Robeson, Paul

■ ■ *Bibliography*

Horne, Gerald. *Communist Front? The Civil Rights Congress, 1946–56.* Rutherford, N.J: Fairleigh Dickinson University Press; London and Cranbury, N.J.: Associated University Presses, 1987.

PREMILLA NADASEN (1996)
Updated bibliography

CIVIL RIGHTS MOVEMENT, U.S.

From the beginning of their involuntary servitude in the United States, Africans contested the exploitation of their labor, their unequal treatment, and their less-than-human status. Black slaves engaged in work slowdowns and sabotage, escapes, and rebellions, while enclaves of free blacks opposed racial discrimination through petitions, litigation, incipient political organization, communal self-defense, and nonviolent protest, including a boycott campaign from 1844 to 1855 that pressured Boston authorities to desegregate public schools.

Until 1910, 90 percent of blacks lived in the South, where legal slavery persisted until 1865. The Civil War accelerated black freedom struggles throughout the country as free blacks in Massachusetts clamored to enlist in Northern armies (where they served in a segregated regiment), while numerous slaves deserted their war-torn plantations. Under Northern occupation during Reconstruction, emancipated slaves asserted their rights as voters and public officials and engaged in nonviolent protests against segregated transport.

The specter of black political power and public assertiveness spurred countermovements of white guerilla warfare and racial terror, particularly in the Deep South. This, coupled with the corruption, war-weariness, and casual racism of national political leaders, led to the withdrawal of Northern armies and the consolidation of legalized segregation, much of which was modeled upon existing statute and nationwide practice. These "Jim Crow" laws triggered black resistance in every state of the former Confederacy, much of it centered on boycotts of segregated streetcars, but including efforts to sustain nascent black political organization. These actions postponed the spread of segregation in some cities, but ultimately they failed everywhere amid a surge of white violence and legal repression, including disfranchisement of most southern blacks by 1900. Segregation was legitimized nationally by the Supreme Court decision in *Plessy v. Ferguson* (1896) that upheld a Louisiana segregation statute for affording blacks "separate-but-equal" facilities.

The preeminent southern black spokesman, Booker T. Washington, accommodated these bleak trends by appealing to whites for economic cooperation and racial peace while publicly renouncing agitation for social and political rights. Heavily patronized by white elites across the country, Washington presided over the truncated field of black political action until his death in 1915. Outspoken activists such as editor and antilynching crusader Ida B.

Chain gang in Richmond, Virginia. *Under President Andrew Johnson's post–Civil War reconstruction government, black codes were used in an attempt to preserve some remnant of the status quo. "Vagrancy" laws targeted at former slaves forced them, like the man pictured here, into chain gangs and involuntary labor.* THE LIBRARY OF CONGRESS

Wells-Barnett were literally driven from the South. Wells would ultimately find a more receptive audience for her message overseas than she did in the United States.

Because of the long odds and mortal risks facing black dissidents in the South, organized agitation for civil rights in the early twentieth century became chiefly the province of northern blacks, such as Massachusetts attorney William Monroe Trotter and writer and scholar W. E. B. Du Bois. In 1905 Du Bois began a movement in Niagara Falls, New York, to urge redress of racial injustices. Poorly attended and funded, the Niagara Movement reformed into a new, interracial organization in the wake of white rioting in Springfield, Illinois, the city of Abraham Lincoln's youth. In 1910 the National Association for the Advancement of Colored People (NAACP) began its long crusade for racial equality, operating through the courts and the trenchant pen of Du Bois, the group's first black officer and the editor of a new journal, *The Crisis.*

The NAACP pinned its hopes upon educating elite public opinion into a more favorable dispensation toward blacks as fellow citizens. Its strategy focused on the courts, where it sought to chip away at the legal edifice of segregation. In the 1915 case *Guinn v. United States,* attorneys for the NAACP persuaded a unanimous Supreme Court to declare unconstitutional the "grandfather clause," by which some states had disfranchised blacks through harsh registration tests while exempting citizens—invariably whites—whose grandfathers had voted. Beginning in the 1930s the NAACP sued for equal school facilities for blacks, in accord with the Supreme Court sanction of separate-but-equal treatment, securing the desegregation of all-white law or graduate schools in Maryland, Missouri, and other states unable to convince federal courts of an equal commitment to black and white students.

These unusual victories neither exhausted the South's legal stratagems for denying blacks the ballot nor frontally challenged the institutional segregation that powerfully skewed the distribution of rights and recognition, opportunity and reward along racial lines. At the same time, the impact of black migrations out of the South and the economic and political crisis of the 1930s were forcing issues of black civic inclusion and political representation onto the national agenda. More than 500,000 blacks entered into new industrial unions by the end of the decade and 150,000 blacks were on the federal payroll by the end of the 1930s—triple the number when Herbert Hoover left office in 1932. Black voters in northern cities defected to the Democratic Party en masse, providing a counterweight to the party's dependency on the white South. Federal antilynching bills pushed by the NAACP passed the House of Representatives in 1937 and again in 1940, though each time succumbing to southern filibusters in the Senate.

A range of militant civic and political organizations began championing the cause of racial justice. The Provisional Committee for the Defense of Ethiopia (PCDE) against the Italian invasion of that country signaled the enduring mass appeal of race-based internationalism once arrayed under the banner of Garveyism. The Communist Party widened its popularity among blacks as its International Labor Defense (ILD) spearheaded the defense of the unjustly convicted Scottsboro boys in Alabama. The National Negro Congress and the Congress of Racial Equality (CORE), supported by such black newspapers as the *Pittsburgh Courier,* agitated for racial equality in the United States to the point of collective action.

In 1941, A. Philip Randolph, leader of the Brotherhood of Sleeping Car Porters union, formed the all-black March on Washington Movement (MOWM), which planned a massive march on the nation's capital to protest racial discrimination in the armed forces and defense industries. A young MOWM organizer, and later key strategist of the nonviolent civil rights movement, Bayard Rustin would describe this as the "symbolic inauguration" of the modern civil rights era. To persuade Randolph to call off the march, President Franklin Roosevelt in July 1941 created an advisory committee, the Fair Employment Practices Committee, to promote racial integration in munitions factories. A limited step, it was the first presidential order for civil rights since Reconstruction—and the first intended chiefly to quiet an emerging black mass movement.

World War II dramatically accelerated black struggles for democratic rights. Black activists and liberal intellectuals called for a "Double Victory" against fascism abroad and racism at home, sharply illuminating the contradiction between fighting a war against the vicious racial policies of Nazi Germany while sustaining a legalized racist order at home. Blacks in the United States consciously laid claim to the global promise of the 1941 Atlantic Charter, in which the Allies avowed that they were fighting for the rights of all peoples to self-determination. Millions of blacks worked in the armed forces and served in the munitions industry during these years, further augmenting

claims for full citizenship. In 1944 the NAACP won a significant legal victory against southern apartheid as the Supreme Court overturned the formal exclusion of blacks from party primary elections in the South in *Smith v. Allright.*

Despite these signs of progress, this was a period of intensifying racial conflict around employment, housing, and public space, particularly in centers of wartime production like Detroit, where a race riot in 1943 left thirty-four dead and where racially motivated hate strikes were a regular occurrence. VE Day yielded a resurgence of incidents of white terrorism in the South in response to a new assertiveness, particularly among returning black veterans, while such northern cities as Chicago were gripped during the 1940s and 1950s by violent racial conflicts around neighborhood boundaries and the integration of public housing.

The cold war between the United States and the Soviet Union had a contradictory impact upon the national arena of race relations formed by World War II. Competition for support from emerging nonwhite nations in the decolonizing world made evidence of American racism a damaging embarrassment. At the same time, domestic anticommunism was enlisted to retrench southern apartheid, with defenders of racial segregation sturdy proponents of anticommunist legislation in Congress. Vocal black liberals such as the NAACP's Walter White and Roy Wilkins were effective in linking the cause of cold war to civil rights, arguing that white supremacy was the "Achilles' heel" of U.S. claims to defend the "free world." Yet, prominent black leftists, critical of U.S. foreign policy, including Paul Robeson, Du Bois, Benjamin Davis, and Claudia Jones, were harassed by state agencies, opened to public vilification, and in some cases tried, imprisoned, or deported.

Under pressure to establish his legitimacy both at home and in the world arena, President Harry Truman appointed a committee to investigate violations of black rights. In 1946 he endorsed the resulting report, titled "To Secure These Rights," which prescribed a comprehensive federal assault on Jim Crow. In 1948 Truman acceded to a strong civil rights plank that liberal delegates had inserted in the Democratic national platform. He then weathered defections by a minority of southern whites to narrowly win a second term, aided by 70 percent of the northern black vote. Two years later he began desegregation of the armed forces to heighten military efficiency for the Korean War and to quiet restive black leaders threatening a mass boycott of military service.

By the late 1940s the NAACP's chief legal counsel, Thurgood Marshall, directly attacked the principle of seg-

March on Washington, August 28, 1963. With the Washington Monument in the background and facing the Lincoln Memorial, a crowd of more than 200,000 gathers on the mall in Washington, D.C. to hear Martin Luther King Jr. speak. © FLIP SCHULKE/CORBIS. REPRODUCED BY PERMISSION.

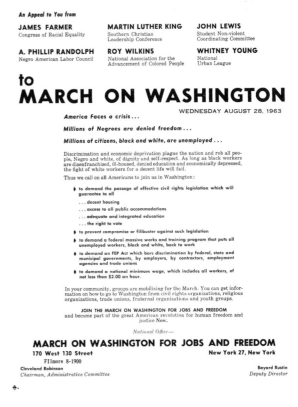

Flyer for the March on Washington, August 28, 1963. COURTESY OF MICHIGAN STATE UNIVERSITY LIBRARIES, SPECIAL COLLECTIONS

regation in public education. In several cases before the Supreme Court, Marshall argued that segregation denied blacks "equal protection of the laws" as guaranteed by the Fourteenth Amendment to the Constitution. In 1954 Chief Justice Earl Warren wrote for a unanimous Court, in *Brown v. Board of Education of Topeka, Kansas,* that in the area of public education "the doctrine of 'separate but equal' has no place."

By threatening white supremacy the *Brown* case intensified southern resistance to the civil rights agenda. The Ku Klux Klan and other hate groups experienced overnight revivals, congressmen and governors vowed "massive resistance," and state district attorneys sought injunctions to ban NAACP branches (they were entirely successful in Alabama by 1957). In May 1955 the Supreme Court tempered its original ruling in *Brown* by requiring no timetable for school desegregation, only that school

districts move "with all deliberate speed." Compliance proved minimal, and when President Dwight D. Eisenhower sent federal troops in 1957 to guard nine blacks attending a formerly all-white high school in Little Rock, Arkansas, the prolonged furor discouraged further national intervention for desegregation.

Despite its limited tangible impact, *Brown* did confer legitimacy on black activists, who prepared bolder assaults on segregation in the South. In December 1955 blacks in Montgomery, Alabama, organized a bus boycott after a former NAACP secretary, Rosa Parks, was arrested for refusing to yield her seat on a segregated bus to a white man. The boycott leader was a twenty-six-year-old northern-educated minister originally from Atlanta, the Rev. Dr. Martin Luther King, Jr. King gained national attention for the protest against segregation by invoking Christian morality, American ideals of liberty, and the ethic of nonviolent resistance to evil exemplified by Mohandas Gandhi of India in his campaign against British colonial rule. Like Gandhi, King advocated confronting authorities with a readiness to suffer rather than inflict harm, in order to expose injustice and impel those in power to end it. In November 1956, despite growing white violence, the boycott triumphed with aid from the NAACP, which secured a Supreme Court decision (in *Gayle v. Browder*) that overturned Montgomery's laws enforcing bus segregation.

Growing black restiveness in the South encouraged new civil rights initiatives. In January 1957 King organized the Southern Christian Leadership Conference (SCLC), a network of nonviolent civil rights activists drawn mainly from the black church. In September of that year Congress passed the first Civil Rights Act since Reconstruction; the act created a commission to monitor civil rights violations and authorized the Justice Department to guard black voting rights through litigation against discriminatory registrars. This act (and a follow-up measure in April 1960) nonetheless failed to curb the widespread disfranchisement of southern blacks.

The failure to implement federal civil rights edicts increasingly provoked blacks to disruptive protest and collective action. During the late 1950s blacks, often affiliated with local NAACP youth chapters, conducted scattered, short-lived sit-ins at lunch counters that served whites only. On February 1, 1960, a sit-in by four students at the Woolworth's lunch counter in Greensboro, North Carolina, triggered a host of similar protests throughout the South, targeting Jim Crow public accommodations from theaters to swimming pools. Strict conformity to the tenets of nonviolence characterized the demonstrators, many of whom courted arrest and imprisonment in order to dramatize the evils of segregation.

In April 1960 several hundred student activists gathered in Raleigh, North Carolina, at the invitation of Ella Baker, executive director of the Southern Christian Leadership Conference. Baker urged the students to preserve their grass-roots militancy by remaining independent of established civil rights groups, and they responded by forming the Student Nonviolent Coordinating Committee (SNCC, pronounced "snick"). By the summer of 1960 the sit-ins, which were often reinforced by boycotts of offending stores, had desegregated dozens of lunch counters and other public accommodations, mainly in southern border states.

Black protests intensified during the presidency of John F. Kennedy, a Democrat elected in 1960 with heavy black support. Kennedy directed the Justice Department to step up litigation for black rights, but he avoided bolder commitments that he feared would trigger southern white racial violence and political retaliation. Civil rights leaders therefore increasingly designed campaigns to pressure their reluctant ally in the White House. In May 1961 James Farmer, who had cofounded CORE nearly two decades earlier, led fourteen white and black CORE volunteers on a freedom ride through the South, testing compliance with

a Supreme Court order to desegregate interstate bus terminal facilities. White mobs abetted by police beat the riders in Birmingham, Alabama, on May 14; six days later federal marshals saved the riders from a mob in Montgomery.

Racial violence was unrelenting in these years. In October 1962 Kennedy sent federal marshals to protect a black student, James Meredith, who had registered at the all-white University of Mississippi at Oxford. After mobs killed two people at the campus and besieged the marshals, the president was forced to send troops to restore order. In early May 1963, police in Birmingham beat and unleashed attack dogs on nonviolent black followers of Dr. King, in full view of television news cameras. The resulting public revulsion spurred President Kennedy to address the nation on June 11, to confront a "moral issue" that was "as old as the Scriptures" and "as clear as the American Constitution." He urged Congress to enact a strong civil rights law that would allow racism "no place in American life."

A coalition of African-American groups, led by Randolph, Rustin, and King, along with their white allies in labor and peace and justice organizations, sponsored a March on Washington on August 28, 1963, to advance the civil rights bill then before Congress. Reflecting the growing national stature of the civil rights movement, the rally secured the participation of diverse political, cultural, and religious figures. Standing before the Lincoln Memorial, Dr. King told several hundred thousand blacks and whites at this event of his "dream" for interracial brotherhood.

When Lyndon B. Johnson succeeded to the presidency on November 22, 1963, he made passage of the civil rights bill his top priority and effectively linked this goal to the memory of the martyred President Kennedy. A broad-based federation called the Leadership Conference on Civil Rights coordinated the lobbying efforts of over a hundred groups on behalf of the legislation and centered on extraordinary activity by Protestant, Catholic, and Jewish ministers. On July 2, 1964, Johnson signed the omnibus Civil Rights Act, which barred segregation in public accommodations, ended federal aid to segregated institutions, outlawed racial discrimination in employment, sought to strengthen black voting rights, and extended the life of the United States Commission on Civil Rights.

SNCC remained in the vanguard of black activism in 1964 by organizing rural black voters in Mississippi, a state whose history was pockmarked with the casual murder of black people. About a thousand college students, most of them white, volunteered for the Freedom Summer project to further the nonviolent, integrationist ideals of the civil rights movement. The project workers set up "Freedom

Civil rights marchers, 1965. Walking fifty-four miles along Route 80 from Selma to the state capitol in Montgomery, Alabama, where they will demonstrate for African-American voting rights, the activists endure rain on the third day of their journey. AP/WIDE WORLD PHOTOS. REPRODUCED BY PERMISSION.

Schools" to give black children a positive sense of their history and identity, and an interracial party, the "Freedom Democrats," to give disfranchised blacks a political voice. The project also exposed the extreme dangers facing civil rights workers after a federal manhunt recovered the bodies of three volunteers—Michael Schwerner, Andrew Goodman, and James Chaney—murdered by a mob led by the deputy sheriff of Philadelphia, Mississippi. In late August the project workers helped the Freedom Democrats try to unseat Mississippi's entirely white delegation at the Democratic National Convention. Despite considerable northern support, their challenge failed because of strong resistance by President Johnson, who feared the loss of southern white voters in an election year. This harsh coda to the Freedom Summer spurred younger black activists to question alliances with white liberals and to stress instead the importance of black solidarity.

The fraying civil rights coalition rallied in 1965 behind Dr. King's campaign in Selma, Alabama, for equal voting rights. On March 7 black marchers setting out from Selma toward Montgomery suffered assaults by state and local police. The televised scenes of violence galvanized national support for protection of blacks seeking the ballot, a view that President Johnson reinforced in a special appearance before Congress on March 15. Ten days later twenty-five thousand black and white marchers reached Montgomery escorted by federal troops. On August 6, 1965, Johnson signed a strong Voting Rights Act, which authorized the attorney general to send federal examiners to supersede local registrars and regulations wherever discrimination occurred. The act also directed the attorney general to challenge poll taxes for state and local elections in the courts (the Twenty-fourth Amendment to the Constitution, adopted in 1964, had already banned such taxes in national elections).

With the passage of landmark national legislation, black movements for racial equality and social justice suffered new divisions and faced new strategic dilemmas. During a march with King through Mississippi in June 1966, SNCC's Stokely Carmichael criticized faith in nonviolence and white goodwill and demanded "black power," a slogan that alienated white liberals and worried established black leaders. The emphasis of the movement turned from the problem of de jure segregation to issues relating to de facto segregation: poverty, police brutality, and the unequal access to employment, education, housing, and transportation produced by the divide between black urban areas and white suburbs. Ghetto riots, including a six-day conflagration in South Central Los Angeles in August 1965, highlighted these issues and divided the movement and its supporters by shattering the aura of nonviolence.

Despite the Johnson administration's avowed commitment to waging a war on poverty, the escalating war in Vietnam increasingly monopolized its resources and attention. In the spring of 1967, King, drawing upon a long tradition linking black struggles in the United States with the global tribulations of a colonized world, sharply attacked the war in Vietnam as an unjust war that undermined the promise of "the Great Society" at home. While younger activists cautiously applauded, established black leaders publicly repudiated King's stance, with Johnson accusing him of betrayal bordering on sedition. The cold war civil rights consensus that had linked official progress on racial matters with support for U.S. foreign policy was broken.

On April 4, 1968, King was assassinated in Memphis, Tennessee, where he was supporting the unionization efforts of predominantly black sanitation workers. King's murder touched off riots that left Washington, D.C., in flames for three days. The following week, partly in tribute to the slain King, Congress passed the Civil Rights Act of 1968, which banned discrimination in the sale and rental of most housing.

The 1970s witnessed the emergence of expressly race-conscious government programs to redress the legacy of racial discrimination. In *Swann v. Charlotte-Mecklenburg* (1971), the Supreme Court acknowledged the failures of earlier approaches to school desegregation by sanctioning the busing of children to other neighborhoods as a tool to achieve racial balance. The federal government also promoted affirmative action to afford blacks (and, increasingly, other minorities and women) preference in school admissions and employment. These developments reflected the limitations of civil rights legislation in affording access to the economic mainstream; but they provoked fierce opposition. Violence in Boston and other cities over racial busing confirmed that the race problem was truly national rather than regional. And in *Regents of University of California v. Bakke* in 1978 the Supreme Court reflected the national acrimony over affirmative action by ruling five to four to strike down racial quotas in medical school admissions while allowing (by an equally slim margin) some race-conscious selection to achieve educational "diversity."

During the 1980s a conservative shift in national politics frustrated civil rights leaders, especially in the NAACP and the Urban League, who relied on federal activism to overcome state, municipal, and private acts of discrimina-

tion. Symbolically, Ronald Reagan, a Republican who won the presidency for the first of two terms in 1980, launched his presidential campaign in Philadelphia, Mississippi, with the promise to trim federal authority in racial matters. From 1981 to 1985 his administration reduced the number of lawyers in the Justice Department's Civil Rights Division from 210 to 57 and also vainly attempted to disband altogether the United States Commission on Civil Rights. On January 8, 1982, Reagan restored the federal tax exemptions for segregated private schools that had been ended in 1970. The following year the Supreme Court, by an eight-to-one vote, overturned this ruling as a violation of the Civil Rights Act of 1964; in 1986 Reagan appointed the lone dissenter, William Rehnquist, to be Chief Justice of the Supreme Court.

The Rehnquist Court increasingly chipped away at government safeguards of black rights, a pattern evident from several employment discrimination cases in 1989: In *Patterson v. McLean Credit Union* the Court ruled that the Civil Rights Act of 1866 protected blacks merely in contracting for jobs but did not protect them from racial harassment by employers; in *Wards Cove Packing Co. v. Atonio* the Court shifted the burden of proof from employers to employees regarding job discrimination; in *City of Richmond v. J. A. Croson Co.* the Court rejected a program setting aside 30 percent of city contracts for minority businesses in the absence of flagrant evidence of discrimination, although Richmond had a history of official segregation and although minority contractors held fewer than 1 percent of the city contracts in Richmond, where minorities constituted half the population; in *Price Waterhouse v. Hopkins* the Court exonerated an employer who had committed acts of racial discrimination but who also cited other, legitimate reasons for such actions. In October 1990 Republican president George H. W. Bush vetoed a civil rights bill that expressly restored the earlier, tougher curbs on job discrimination, and the Senate sustained his veto by a single vote. In November 1991 President Bush signed a milder version of this same bill while restating his opposition to quotas to promote minority hiring.

The central goal of the long civil rights movement that unfolded over the second half of the twentieth-century—full equality between blacks and whites—remains a distant vision. Residential segregation, seen in the persistence of inner-city black ghettos and white suburbs, has easily survived federal open-housing statutes. De facto segregation of churches, social centers, and private schools also remains routine; and wealth, too, is largely segregated along racial lines, with the median family income of blacks in 1990 barely three-fifths that of whites, and with blacks three times as likely to be poor. Since the

1980s, as a "war on drugs" replaced antipoverty at the center of urban policy agenda, black incarceration rates soared—over one millions African Americans are now incarcerated, approximately 50 percent of the U.S. prison population. Many civil rights leaders have urged comprehensive government remedies, but black political power remains limited with regard to national office holding and access to the circles that make foreign and domestic policy.

Despite its limitations, the civil rights movement has in key respects transformed American society. During the 1960s "whites only" signs that had stood for generations in the South suddenly came down from hotels, restrooms, theaters, and other facilities. School desegregation by the mid-1970s had become fact as well as law in over 80 percent of all southern public schools (a better record than in the North, where residential segregation remains pronounced). The federal government has also checked groups promoting racial hatred: Beginning in 1964 the FBI infiltrated the Ku Klux Klan so thoroughly that by 1965 perhaps one in five members was an informant; federal indictments and encouragement of private lawsuits helped reduce Klan membership from 10,000 in 1981 to less than 5,500 in 1987.

Protection of the suffrage represents the civil rights movement's greatest success: When Congress passed the Voting Rights Act in 1965 barely a hundred blacks held elective office in the country; by 1989 there were more than 7,200, including twenty-four congressional representatives and some three hundred mayors. Over 4,800 of these officials served in the South, and nearly every Black Belt county in Alabama had a black sheriff. Mississippi, long the most racially repressive state, experienced the most dramatic change, registering 74 percent of its voting-age blacks and leading the nation in the number of elected black officials (646). The unexpectedly strong showing by the Reverend Jesse Jackson in seeking the Democratic presidential nomination in 1984 and 1988 reflected the growing participation by blacks in mainstream politics. The release of Nelson Mandela and the crumbling of the apartheid regime in South Africa in the early 1990s was in part a product of international pressures for divestment that captured the imagination of younger activists and tapped wellsprings of the international solidarity that animated the black freedom movement from its inception.

In some ways the civil rights movement is a misnomer. There were in fact many movements dedicated to black freedom, social justice, and equality in the United States. Having leveled the formal barriers of a legal caste system during the early 1960s, the civil rights movement returned to older, more intractable problems of substantive equality of opportunity in all areas of American life.

The NAACP and the Urban League have for decades urged federal measures to reconstruct the inner cities, create jobs, extend job training to all poor Americans, and strengthen affirmative action to help minorities overcome a legacy of exclusion. Beginning in the 1980s, however, a growing minority of blacks have gained national influence (highlighted by the appointment of Clarence Thomas to the Supreme Court in 1991) by emphasizing private rather than government initiatives and by deploring quotas and other race-conscious programs as politically divisive. The movement for racial equality is now struggling to forge a program that can both unify black activists and also capture the nation's moral high ground and its reform impulses as convincingly as earlier civil rights campaigns.

See also Affirmative Action; Carmichael, Stokely; Congress of Racial Equality(CORE); Freedom Rides; Freedom Summer; Jim Crow; Marshall, Thurgood; Montgomery, Ala., Bus Boycott; National Association for the Advancement of Colored People; National Negro Congress; Niagara Movement; Southern Christian Leadership Conference; Student Nonviolent Coordinating Committee(SNCC); Trotter, William Monroe

▪ ▪ *Bibliography*

Howell, Raines, ed. *My Soul Is Rested: Movement Days in the Deep South Remembered*. New York: Penguin, 1983.

Kluger, Richard. *Simple Justice*. New York: Random House, 1977.

Sellers, Cleveland, with Robert Terrell. *The River of No Return: The Autobiography of a Black Militant and the Life and Death of SNCC*. New York: William Morrow, 1973.

Singh, Nikhil Pal. *Black Is a Country: Race and the Unfinished Struggle for Democracy*. Cambridge, Mass.: Harvard University Press, 2004.

Sitkoff, Harvard. *The Struggle for Black Equality, 1954-1980*. New York: Hill and Wang, 1981.

Von Eschen, Penny, *Race Against Empire: African Americans and Anti-Colonialism, 1937–1957*. Ithaca, N.Y.: Cornell University Press, 2000.

Weisbrot, Robert. *Freedom Bound: A History of America's Civil Rights Movement*. New York: Norton, 1991.

Williams, Juan, with the "Eyes on the Prize" Production Team. *Eyes on the Prize: America's Civil Rights Years, 1954–1965*. New York: Viking, 1987.

ROBERT WEISBROT (1996)
NIKHIL PAL SINGH (2005)

CIVIL WAR, U.S.

The dispute between white brothers that erupted into armed conflict in April 1861 was a turning point for American men and women of color. African Americans had fought in the nation's previous wars, but the Civil War was different. Much more was at stake, for themselves as well as for the country. At the beginning of the conflict, nearly four million enslaved people lived and labored as property, denied a birthright while making the nation (not just the South) richer. The nearly 500,000 African Americans who had known statutory freedom before the war had endured a second class status that denied them a political voice, refused them equal access to economic opportunity, and marginalized them socially. Aliens in their own homeland, they watched as immigrants sought and eventually received the fruits of American democracy, only to use their newly acquired citizenship to perpetuate long-established traditions of bigotry and injustice.

AIMS OF THE WAR

When the war came, African Americans recognized its long-term as well as its immediate implications for themselves. Long before the rest of the nation acknowledged the possibility, blacks saw the war as an opportunity to topple the socioeconomic foundation of the southern way of life. In striking a blow against slavery, they sought both liberation for the enslaved and an extension of rights that for so long had been denied to all African Americans. Black men and women, therefore, agitated for an expansion of the war's limited aim—preservation of the Union—while pressing for the right of black men to don the Union blue. But a nation fearful of even greater disunion, and doubtful of the ability and courage of black men, was not immediately prepared to accept them as soldiers. This was a white man's war, they believed, to be fought by them exclusively for the preservation of the Union.

While black men waited for the nation to recognize their value to the Union cause, they drilled and prepared themselves for service. Some of them responded to the army's rebuff by joining the navy, which historically had admitted black men into its ranks. Others managed to gain entry into all-white units, despite laws meant to exclude them. Attempts to organize black units early in the war, especially efforts by Senator James Lane of Kansas and Major General David Hunter in the Sea Islands off the coast of South Carolina, met with outright rejection or slow acceptance from the Lincoln administration. Hunter was forced to disband his units and official recognition of Lane's force was delayed until 1863.

"Contrabands," Culpepper, Virginia, 1863. Although initially there was no clear Federal policy regarding contrabands, as escaped slaves came to be known during the Civil War period, most union army units set up camps providing food, clothing, and shelter for former slaves. THE LIBRARY OF CONGRESS

With Lincoln's 1863 proclamation of freedom for enslaved people living and laboring in Confederate-controlled territory, the conflict became not simply a fight for the Union, but a war of liberation as well. This shift, along with a desire to strengthen Union forces, which had been depleted by a war of attrition, led to the admission of black men into the army. Ultimately, nearly 200,000 African Americans would serve in the army and navy, the majority of them former slaves. Approximately 50,000 of them were drawn from the North. In addition, former slaves and the free born who had fled the country following the passage of the Fugitive Slave Act of 1850, now returned to the United States to help liberate their people. These black soldiers were organized into segregated units under the division of United States Colored Troops and were commanded overwhelmingly by white officers.

DISCRIMINATION IN THE ARMED FORCES

Winning the struggle to enter the war, however, led neither to respect nor equal treatment. Instead of real soldiering, black men often found themselves erecting fortifications and engaging in fatigue duty. Moreover, black men suffered externally imposed disabilities that left them demoralized and resentful. For instance, they were paid roughly half what a white soldier of comparable rank received, making it difficult for the families of black soldiers

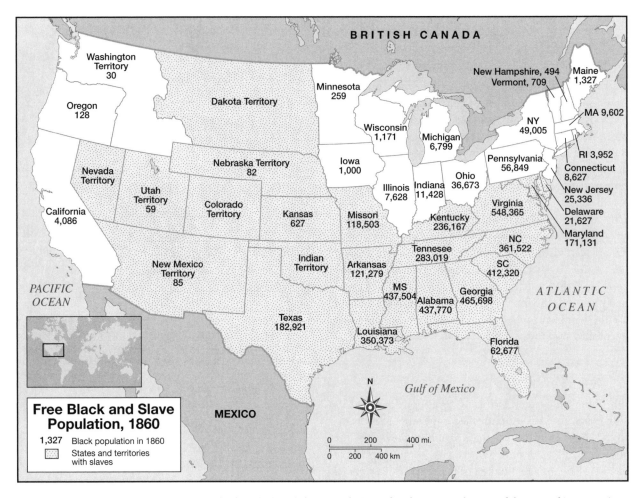

Map of the United States in 1860, showing the free black and slave populations of each state. At the start of the war, African Americans comprised about 14 percent of the nation's total population. Of that number, some 90 percent, or over four million persons, were slaves. MAP BY XNR PRODUCTIONS. THE GALE GROUP.

to survive and sometimes leading black soldiers to protest by stacking their arms or refusing to receive any pay until their grievances had been redressed. When the men of the Third South Carolina Volunteers stacked their arms in protest against their low pay, the leader of the protest was court-martialed and executed.

Black military men were especially vulnerable to the Confederate forces, who were determined to treat them as property, without regard for rules governing the treatment of captured enemy soldiers. The Confederacy considered all black troops slaves in insurrection, regardless of their status before the war. Hence, rebel forces executed some and sold others into slavery. The Fort Pillow Massacre of April 1864 provides a chilling example of the consequences of this policy. After having surrendered to Confederate forces led by General Nathan Bedford Forrest, Union troops, most of whom were African American,

were shot down. The incident outraged the black community and inspired black men to fight even more tenaciously, adopting the rallying cry "Remember Fort Pillow!"

In spite of discriminatory practices, black soldiers served in battle with valor and distinction. During the spring of 1863, at Port Hudson, Louisiana, they engaged in a desperate (and unsuccessful) assault against rebel units perched atop an 80-foot bluff. Two weeks later, at Milliken's Bend (near Vicksburg), inexperienced black soldiers stood firm as Confederate forces descended on their position. At Morris Island, South Carolina, in July of that same year, the famed 54th Massachusetts, under the most difficult of circumstances, advanced on Confederate forces positioned at Fort Wagner before a torrent of artillery fire forced the black soldiers to withdraw. And at the Battle of the Crater (Petersburg, Virginia) in July 1864, black units stormed the rebel position after white soldiers

The Union Army's 107th Colored Infantry, at Fort Corcoran, Washington, D.C. AP/WIDE WORLD PHOTOS. REPRODUCED BY PERMISSION.

failed to exploit effectively the breech in Confederate lines caused by Union underground mining. By the war's end valiant black soldiers and sailors had won two dozen Medals of Honor and had dispelled doubts about their courage under the most extreme of combat conditions.

CIVILIAN CONTRIBUTIONS TO THE WAR EFFORT

African-American contributions to the war effort extended beyond armed military service. Long before blacks were accepted as fighting men, military laborers provided valuable assistance in building fortifications and as teamsters, cooks, launderers, and orderlies. Southern blacks provided invaluable aid by serving as guides, scouts, and spies, often relaying detailed information on Confederate troop movements and activities. Many of them risked their lives smuggling escaping Union soldiers and sympathizers out of the Confederacy. The indomitable Harriet Tubman, who had escaped slavery and returned south to lead many others to freedom before the war, is perhaps the most cele-

brated of these "civilian soldiers." In addition to spying for the Union army, she traveled with troops up South Carolina's Combahee River, where she helped liberate hundreds of her people from bondage. Similarly, Robert Smalls won respect and admiration for his daring escape from slavery by piloting the Confederate boat *Planter* out of Charleston Harbor, securing the freedom of fifteen members of the crew and their families, including his own.

Although the majority of enslaved blacks trapped behind Confederate lines never took up arms against their owners, they used the disruptions of war to destroy the institution of slavery from within. Emboldened by the absence of so many able-bodied white men from the farms and plantations, they flouted the rules and customs that had governed their behavior. Insolence became commonplace and the threat of flight was employed to negotiate the terms and conditions of labor.

With a quiet militancy and considerable dignity, black men and women—soldier and civilian—used the Civil War to effect a revolution. African-American soldiers demanded that they be treated not just as men, but as men with equal standing. Noncombatants pressed for recognition of the right of all African Americans to full citizenship. They expected a grateful nation to honor the obligation it incurred from black sacrifice and loyalty during the war years.

Black soldiers and civilians measured the success of the war not simply in terms of objectives seized or positions successfully defended. Every black man who enlisted or received a commission, every opportunity for marching at the front of the assaulting army, every shackled man, woman, or child rescued from bondage placed people of color closer to their intended objective: preserving the Union, perhaps; winning universal freedom for the enslaved, undoubtedly; but equally important, attempting to bequeath to America a new national identity predicated on true equality and recognition of an African-American birthright.

See also Military Experience, African-American; Smalls, Robert; Tubman, Harriet Ross

▪ ▪ *Bibliography*

Berlin, Ira, Joseph P. Reidy, and Leslie S. Rowland, eds. *Freedom's Soldiers: The Black Military Experience in the Civil War.* New York: Cambridge University Press, 1998.

Glatthaar, Joseph T. *Forged in Battle: The Civil War Alliance of Black Soldiers and White Officers.* New York: Free Press, 1990.

Quarles, Benjamin. *The Negro in the Civil War.* 1953. Reprint, New York: Da Capo, 1989.

Smith, John David, ed. *Black Soldiers in Blue: African American Troops in the Civil War Era.* Chapel Hill: University of North Carolina press, 2002.

EDNA GREENE MEDFORD (2005)

CLARK, KENNETH BANCROFT

JULY 24, 1914

┣┃┫━━━━━

Born in the Panama Canal Zone, psychologist Kenneth Bancroft Clark, the son of Hanson and Miriam Clark, had a direct influence on the U.S. Supreme Court decision in the case of *Brown v. Board of Education of Topeka, Kansas,* in 1954. The Court cited Clark's psychological research on race relations in its favorable ruling outlawing segregation. Clark attended Howard University (B.A., 1935; M.S. 1936), and earned a Ph.D. from Columbia in 1940. He had a distinguished career at the City College of New York,

where he taught from 1942 to 1975, retiring as professor emeritus of psychology. During his City College career, he also served as visiting professor at Columbia, the University of California at Berkeley, and Harvard. A writer as well as scholar, Clark is the author of *Prejudice and Your Child* (1955), *Dark Ghetto: Dilemmas of Social Power* (1965), *Crisis in Urban Education* (1971), and, with Talcott Parsons, *The Negro American* (1966). He was also one of the chief organizers of Harlem Youth Opportunities Unlimited. He has been recognized for his scholarship and his contributions to the black community, most notably as the winner of the Spingarn Medal in 1961. Since his retirement from academia, he has served as president of Kenneth B. Clark and Associates, a consulting firm specializing in affirmative action in race relations.

See also *Brown v. Board of Education of Topeka, Kansas;* Spingarn Medal

▪ ▪ *Bibliography*

"Kenneth Bancroft Clark." *Notable Black American Scientists.* Detroit: Gale, 1998.

Meyers, Michael, and John P. Nidiry. "Kenneth Bancroft Clark: The Uppity Negro Integrationist." *Antioch Review* 62 (spring 2004): 265.

CHRISTINE A. LUNARDINI (1996)
Updated by publisher 2005

CLARK, SEPTIMA

MAY 3, 1898
DECEMBER 15, 1987

┣┃┫━━━━━

Educator and civil rights activist Septima Poinsette was born and reared in Charleston, South Carolina. Her mother, Victoria Warren Anderson, was of Haitian descent and worked as a laundress, and her father, Peter Porcher Poinsette, was a former slave who worked as a cook and a caterer. Her parents deeply influenced Poinsette and instilled in her a willingness to share her gifts and a belief that there was something redeeming about everyone. In addition, Poinsette's early education, which brought her into contact with demanding black teachers who insisted that students have pride and work hard, left a positive and lasting impression on her. Partly as a result of these influences, Poinsette pursued a career in education. In 1916 she received her teaching certificate from Avery Normal Institute, a private school for black teachers founded after the end of the Civil War by the American Missionary Association in Charleston.

Poinsette's first teaching position was on John's Island, South Carolina, from 1916 to 1919, because African Americans were barred from teaching in the Charleston public schools. She tried to address the vast educational, political, and economic inequities that faced John's Island blacks by instituting adult literacy classes and health education and by working with the NAACP. In 1919 she returned to Charleston to work at Avery and spearheaded a campaign against Charleston's exclusionary education system that resulted, one year later, in the overturning of the law barring black teachers from teaching in public schools. In May 1920 Poinsette married Nerie Clark, a back navy cook. She had two children, one of whom died at birth. After her husband died in 1924, Clark sent her other child, Nerie, Jr., to live with his paternal grandmother because she could not support him financially.

Shortly thereafter, Clark returned to Columbia, South Carolina, became active in various civic organizations, and continued her education, receiving a B.A. from Benedict College (1942) and an M.A. from Hampton Institute (1945). She led the fight for equal pay for black teachers in South Carolina. Her efforts attracted the attention of the NAACP, which initiated litigation and won a 1945 ruling mandating equal pay for black teachers in South Carolina. In 1947 Clark returned to Charleston to teach in public schools and continued her civic activities until she was fired in 1956 because of her membership in the NAACP. Unable to find another position in South Carolina, Clark moved to the Highlander Folk School in Monteagle, Tennessee, an interracial adult education center founded by Myles Horton in 1932 to foster social activism and promote racial equality. There Clark became director of education. Together with Horton and South Carolina black activists such as Esau Jenkins from John's Island, she devised educational strategies to challenge black illiteracy and encourage black voter registration. Clark, guided by the belief that literacy was integral to black equality, instituted the citizenship school program, an adult literacy program that focused on promoting voter registration and empowering people to solve their own problems through social activism.

The first citizenship school, founded on John's Island in 1957, was a success, and Clark traveled throughout the Deep South, trying to make links with other local activists to foster the expansion of the schools. In 1961 the citizenship school program was transferred to the Southern Christian Leadership Conference (SCLC) after the Tennessee legislature's persistent efforts to disrupt Highlander

activities resulted in the school's charter being revoked and its property being confiscated. Clark joined the SCLC to oversee the newly renamed Citizen Education Project, and by 1970 over eight hundred citizenship schools had been formed that graduated over 100,000 African Americans who served as a key grass-roots base for the civil rights movement throughout the Deep South. In 1971, however, she retired from SCLC because long-term commitment to the schools had faded.

Clark remained an outspoken spokesperson for racial, as well as gender, equality. She chronicled her life of activism in her autobiography, *Echo in My Soul*, in 1962. In 1966 she spoke at the first national meeting of the National Organization of Women (NOW) about the necessity of women challenging male dominance. In 1976 she was elected to the Charleston, South Carolina, school board. Three years later, she was awarded the Living Legacy award from President Jimmy Carter in honor of her continuing dedication to black empowerment through education. In 1987 she received an American Book Award for her second autobiography, *Ready from Within: Septima Clark and the Civil Rights Movement* (1986). Later that year, Septima Clark died in Charleston.

See also National Association for the Advancement of Colored People (NAACP); Southern Christian Leadership Conference (SCLC)

▪ ▪ *Bibliography*

Clark, Septima. *Echo in My Soul*. New York: Dutton, 1962.

Clark, Septima, with Cynthia Stokes Brown. *Ready from Within: Septima Clark and the Civil Rights Movement*. Navarro, Calif.: Wild Trees Press, 1986.

Crawford, Vicki, Jacqueline Rouse, and Barbara Woods, eds. *Women in the Civil Rights Movement: Trailblazers and Torchbearers 1941–1965*. Brooklyn, N.Y.: Carlson, 1990.

CHANA KAI LEE (1996)

CLARKE, AUSTIN

JULY 6, 1934

▪┃▪

Austin Ardinel Chesterfield Clarke, born in Barbados, is one of the most prolific Canadian writers of Afro-Caribbean descent; he is considered the godfather of Caribbean-Canadian writing. His body of work spans four decades of literary productivity (including ten novels, six short story collections, three memoirs, and a number of newspaper articles and essays) and helps to define and nuance discussions about the African diaspora, the immigrant experience, ethnicity, and the multicultural, international contexts of his writing. As the foremost writer on Afro-Caribbean/Canadian subjects, Clarke was the first to explore the conditions of labor and cultural adjustment for Caribbean women who moved to Canada to work as domestic helpers in the 1950s. The major themes of the Toronto trilogy (*The Meeting Point* [1967], *Storm of Fortune* [1971], and *The Bigger Light* [1975]), and his other Canadian-based novels and short stories, include cultural dislocation and adjustment, race, class and cultural hegemony, and issues of gender. In both his Canadian and Caribbean writing, Clarke explores the postcolonial dilemmas of identity, poverty, exile, belonging, and nationhood, while celebrating cultural resuscitation in the New World through Afro-Caribbean speech rituals.

Prestigious awards conferred on Clarke signify his lifelong contribution to the literary arts in Canada and the Caribbean. He won the 1999 W. O. Mitchell Prize for his outstanding body of work and for his mentorship of young writers, the 2002 Giller Prize, the Trillium Book Award, and the 2003 Commonwealth Writer's Prize for Best Book (for *The Polished Hoe)*. This novel, which chronicles the epic story of colonial atrocities on the lives of Afro-Caribbean peoples via the confessions of murder by the mistress of a plantation owner, represents the pinnacle of Clarke's literary efforts up to this point. Other accolades include the 1980 Casas de las Americas Prize (for *Growing Up Stupid under the Union Jack*), the 1998 Rogers Communications Writers' Trust Prize (for *The Origin of Waves*), 1999 nominations for the James Beard Award (for *Pigtails 'n Breadfruit: The Rituals of Slave Food: A Barbadian Memoir*), and the conferment of honorary doctorates and national awards in Canada and Barbados. In addition, his novel *The Question* (1999) was a finalist for the Governor General's Award.

Clarke's commitment to the African diasporic community goes beyond his literary engagement. His role as journalist, activist (he organized protests against South African apartheid and its subtle resonance in Canada), or representative of disadvantaged groups on civic boards confirm his impressive support of the causes and issues of Africans in the diaspora. Prior to his short, controversial reign beginning in 1975 as manager of the Caribbean Broadcasting Corporation in Barbados—which made him the satiric subject of a calypso song and led to the subsequent censorship of his political thriller, *The Prime Minister* (1977), based on that period—he had already made his mark at the Canadian Broadcasting Corporation. As a broadcast journalist, he brought to the Canadian public a magnified focus on the American civil rights movement through interviews with figures like Malcolm X and documentaries on places such as Harlem. Moreover, he stoutly debated cultural and racial issues in numerous newspaper articles in both Barbados and Canada, and he represented the disenfranchised on the Metro Toronto Library Board, the Ontario Board of Censors, and the Canadian Immigration and Refugee Board. From watchman to government advisor, stagehand to cultural attaché, from journalist to successful writer, and from janitor to eminent statesman, Clarke, the "lyrical Blues geographer," charts the African diasporic journey as both a life of struggle and a life of triumph (Walcott, p. 13).

See also Canada, Blacks in; Canadian Writers in English; Caribbean/North American Writers (Contemporary)

■ ■ *Bibliography*

Algoo-Baksh, Stella. *Austin C. Clarke: A Biography*. Toronto: ECW Press, 1994.

Brown, Lloyd W. *El Dorado and Paradise: Canada and the Caribbean in Austin Clarke's Fiction*. London, Canada: Centre for Social and Humanistic Studies, University of Western Ontario, 1989.

Clarke, Austin. *A Passage Back Home: A Personal Reminiscence of Samuel Selvon*. Toronto: Exile Editions, 1994.

Walcott, Rinaldo. "Preface." In *The Austin Clarke Reader,* edited by Barry Callaghan. Toronto: Exile Editions, 1996.

MICHAEL A. BUCKNOR (2005)

CLARKE, JOHN HENRIK

JANUARY 1, 1915
JULY 16, 1998

The historian John Henrik Clarke, a founding father of Afrocentrism, was born in Union Springs, Alabama. He moved to New York's Harlem in 1933. During the 1930s he attempted, unsuccessfully, to publish plays and poems and began his intensive reading of African and world history under the guidance of the African-American bibliographer Arthur Schomburg. Clarke also became involved in the Young Communists League. Although he never actually joined the Communist Party, he was long active in left-wing African-American groups, including the Harlem Writers Guild.

In 1941 Clarke entered the U.S. military, and he served throughout the war as a master sergeant in the Army Air Forces. During the postwar years, he taught African and Afro-American history at the New School for Social Research, worked as a columnist and writer, and began developing his thesis that black Americans were Africans who shared in Africa's advanced cultural and political legacy.

During the 1960s, Clarke was energized by the civil rights movement. In 1962 he began a twenty-year assignment as assistant editor of the newspaper *Freedomways.* He also became a close associate of Malcolm X and in 1964 drew up the charter for Malcolm X's Organization of Afro-American Unity. Clarke also continued his historical/literary pursuits, eventually writing twenty-three books. In 1966 he edited an anthology, *American Negro Short Stories,* and two years later compiled the anthology *William Styron's Nat Turner: Ten Black Writers Respond.* In 1970 Clarke became a professor of black studies at Hunter College. After retiring in 1986 he continued to lecture and write on Africa's legacy. With Yosef ben-Jochannan, he published *New Dimensions in African History: The London Lectures of Dr. Yosef ben-Jochannan and Dr. John Henrik Clarke* in 1991. Clarke also published two studies, *African People in World History* and *Christopher Columbus and the Afrikan Holocaust: Slavery and the Rise of European Capitalism* in 1993.

See also Afrocentrism; Communist Party of the United States; Harlem Writers Guild; Malcolm X; Schomburg, Arthur

■ ■ *Bibliography*

Adams, Barbara Eleanor. *John Henrik Clarke: Master Teacher.* Brooklyn, N.Y.: A&B Publishers Group, 2000.

Bourne, St. Clair. *John Henrik Clarke: A Great and Mighty Walk* (film). New York: Cinema Guild, 1995.

GREG ROBINSON (1996)
Updated bibliography

CLARKE, LEWIS G.

1815
1897

Lewis G. Clarke was a fugitive slave who became an ardent abolitionist. He was born in Madison County, Kentucky, one of ten children. Clarke had a white father and was owned by his grandfather, Samuel Campbell, who made unfulfilled promises to free Clarke's slave family.

An aunt who was notorious for her mistreatment of young slaves claimed Clarke as part of her dowry when he

was six, and he suffered the woman's cruelties for ten years. Then, in 1831 Samuel Campbell died and Clarke's family was broken up and sold at auction. Clarke became a field laborer. When he was inherited by a new owner, the man allowed Clarke to hire out his time; that is, Clarke worked for wages but gave his owner most of his earnings beyond a sum to cover living expenses.

In Clarke's first attempt to escape in August 1841, he assumed the role of master to a darker-skinned companion, but they soon gave up the attempt because neither could read. Two weeks later Clarke set off alone and reached Canada. He later returned to Oberlin, Ohio, in search of his brother Milton. He was in contact with the abolitionists there and became an antislavery advocate, speaking widely and effectively. By 1861 he was living in Canada, but he returned with his children to Oberlin in 1871 after the death of his wife. Clarke died in Lexington, Kentucky, and his body was returned to Oberlin for burial. Harriet Beecher Stowe based the character of George Harris in *Uncle Tom's Cabin* on Clarke.

See also Abolition; Runaway Slaves in the United States; Slave Narratives; Slavery

■ ■ *Bibliography*

Clarke, Lewis G. *Narrative of the Sufferings of Lewis Clarke, During a Captivity of More Than Twenty-Five Years, Among the Algerines of Kentucky, One of the So Called Christian States of North America.* Boston: D. H. Ela, 1845.

Volke, Betty. "Lewis G. Clarke." In *Dictionary of American Negro Biography,* edited by Rayford W. Logan and Michael R. Winston. New York: Norton, 1982.

ROBERT L. JOHNS (2001)

CLASSICAL MUSIC

See Music; Opera

CLAY, CASSIUS

See Ali, Muhammad

CLAY, WILLIAM LACY

APRIL 30, 1931

━ ▮ ▮ ▮ ━━━━━━━━━━━━━━━━━━━━━━━━━━

Born in St. Louis, Missouri, Congressman William Clay was the son of Luella and Irvin Clay, a welder. He attended the city's public schools, helping to support himself by working as a tailor and a salesman in a clothing store. He then attended St. Louis University, graduating with a B.A. in 1953. Following his graduation, Clay was drafted into the army. After his discharge in 1955, he returned to St. Louis and worked several years at such jobs as insurance salesman and bus driver. Meanwhile, he became active in civil rights efforts in association with the St. Louis branch of the Congress of Racial Equality (CORE) and the National Association for the Advancement of Colored People (NAACP). In 1959, with aid from group members, Clay was elected to the St. Louis Board of Aldermen. During his first term, he sponsored passage of the city's first Fair Employment Act. Reelected in 1963, he proposed an ordinance banning discrimination in public accommodations, but he resigned from the board shortly after and was selected for the more influential post of Democratic ward committeeman.

Clay became involved in political organizing while on the board of aldermen. In 1961 he was named business representative for the city branch of the state, county, and municipal employees' union. He also engaged in civil rights work and spent four months in prison in 1963 following a demonstration at the city's Jefferson Bank and Trust Company. In 1966 he became election coordinator for the local branch of the powerful steamfitters' union.

In 1968 a black majority congressional district opened up in St. Louis following redistricting. Clay won a five-person Democratic primary by 6,500 votes, then handily defeated his white Republican opponent in the general election to became Missouri's first black member of Congress. Initially Clay was assigned to the Education and Labor Committee, where he called for a raise in the minimum wage and for stronger fair employment laws. As head of the Labor-Management Relations Subcommittee, he began a long-standing effort to pass legislation requiring employers to hire back striking workers following settlement of labor disputes. As head of the Subcommittee on Pensions, Clay won changes in laws to allow workers to be vested in their retirement system after fewer years of experience.

In 1975 Clay was the target of investigations following charges that he had engaged in drug trafficking and evaded income taxes. Although exonerated of any drug charges by the Justice Department, he sharply criticized what he claimed were politically motivated attacks on his character. He was also embarrassed in 1992 by revelations that he had overdrawn 290 checks on his account in the House bank. Despite both attacks, Clay was easily reelected in both 1976 and 1992.

Long a member of the House Post Office and Civil Service Committee, Clay was named chair in December 1990, a post he held for four years. During his tenure he sponsored legislation extending job-safety protections to post office workers and worked to amend the Hatch Act to permit lobbying and voluntary political action by federal workers.

Clay is the author of *Thoughts on the Death Penalty* (1976), an investigation of capital punishment; and *Just Permanent Interests* (1992), a history of blacks in Congress.

Clay retired from Congress in 2000 to be replaced by his son, William Lacy Clay, Jr. In 2004 Clay published his autobiography: *Bill Clay: A Political Voice at the Grass Roots.*

See also Congress of Racial Equality (CORE); National Association for the Advancement of Colored People (NAACP)

■ ■ *Bibliography*

Christopher, Maurine. *Black Americans in Congress.* New York: Crowell, 1976.

Clay, William L. *Just Permanent Interests: Black Americans in Congress, 1870–1991.* New York: Amistad, 1992.

Clay, William L. *Bill Clay: A Political Voice at the Grass Roots.* St. Louis: University of Missouri Press, 2004.

GREG ROBINSON (1996)
Updated by publisher 2005

CLEAGE, ALBERT B., JR.

JUNE 13, 1911
FEBRUARY 20, 2000

━ ▮ ▮ ▮ ━━━━━━━━━━━━━━━━━━━━━━━━━━

Clergyman Albert B. Cleage, also known as Jaramogi Abebe Agyeman, was born on June 13, 1911, and graduated from Wayne State University (Michigan) in 1937 with a degree in sociology. He received a divinity degree from Oberlin College in 1943, the year he married Doris Graham. (One of the two daughters of this union is the noted author Pearl Cleage). The couple divorced in 1955.

After serving as a Congregational minister in Kentucky, California, and Massachusetts, Cleage became pastor of Saint Mark's Community Church in Detroit, which was renamed Central United Church of Christ in 1953. There he became increasingly involved in political and community activism and grew convinced that white resistance blocked black advancement and that blacks could depend only on their own efforts. In 1967 Cleage unveiled a 20-foot portrait of a black Madonna with Jesus at his church and changed its name to Shrine of the Black Madonna.

This church became the mother church of the Black Christian Nationalist Movement, which called for economic self-sufficiency in the black community and presented Jesus as a black revolutionary. Other churches across the country came to espouse the same philosophy, and the movement soon numbered 50,000 members. Cleage expounded on his theology in *The Black Messiah* (1968) and *Black Christian Nationalism* (1972). In the early 1970s he adopted the name Jaramogi Abebe Agyeman. Cleage's political organization, Black Slate, Inc., became influential in Detroit politics, particularly in the 1973 election of Coleman Young as Detroit's first African-American mayor.

See also Pan-African Orthodox Church (The Shrine of the Black Madonna); Young, Coleman Alexander

■ ■ *Bibliography*

"Albert Cleage is Dead at 88; Led Black Nationalist Church." *New York Times*, February 27, 2000.

Brennan, Carol. "Jaramogi Abebe Agyeman." In *Contemporary Black Biography*, Vol. 10. Detroit: Gale, 1995.

ROBERT L. JOHNS (2001)

CLEAVER, ELDRIDGE

AUGUST 31, 1935
MAY 1, 1998

╺╋╍╋╍

Writer and political activist Eldridge Leroy Cleaver was born in Wabbaseka, Arkansas, where he attended a junior college. From 1954 to 1957 and again from 1958 to 1966 he was incarcerated on drug and rape charges, and furthered his education while in prison. In 1965 Cleaver became the most prominent "Black Muslim" prisoner to break with Elijah Muhammad's Nation of Islam after Malcolm X's assassination. Just as FBI director J. Edgar Hoover had begun to target the Black Panthers as the nation's "greatest threat," Cleaver became the party's minister of information in 1966, calling for an armed insurrection to

overthrow the U.S. government and replace it with a black socialist government. During the late 1960s and early 1970s, he also was an assistant editor and contributing writer to *Ramparts* magazine.

In 1968 Cleaver published *Soul on Ice*, which remains his primary claim to literary fame. A collection of autobiographical and political essays in the form of letters and meditations, *Soul on Ice* articulated the sense of alienation felt by many black nationalists who refused to work within an inherently corrupt system. Cleaver viewed his own crimes as political acts and spelled out how racism and oppression had forged his revolutionary consciousness.

Later that year, while on parole, Cleaver was involved in a shootout with Oakland police during which a seventeen-year-old Black Panther, Bobby Hutton, was killed; Cleaver and a police officer were wounded. Cleaver's parole was revoked and he was charged with assault and attempted murder. Although he received worldwide support and was chosen to run as the presidential candidate for the Peace and Freedom Party (see Dick Gregory for discussion of another 1968 black antiwar presidential candidate), Cleaver feared for his safety if he surrendered to the authorities. He fled the country, jumping a $50,000 bail, and lived for the next seven years in Cuba, France, and Algiers. He also visited the Soviet Union, China, North Vietnam, and North Korea during these years of exile. But in 1975 he returned to the United States and struck a deal with the FBI. Although he faced up to seventy-two years in prison, he was sentenced instead to 1,200 hours of community service.

In 1978 Cleaver published *Soul on Fire*, a collection of essays on his newly acquired conservative politics, and in 1979 he founded the Eldridge Cleaver Crusades, an evangelical organization. In 1984 he ran as an independent candidate for Congress in the Eighth Congressional District in California. In the 1980s he lectured on religion and politics, and published his own poetry and polemical writings. In March 1994 his struggle with drugs came to national attention when he underwent brain surgery after he had been arrested in Berkeley, California, late at night with a serious head injury, in a state of drunkenness and disorientation. During this period he attended Harvard Law School, then returned to Berkeley, where he became a preacher. In his later years he spoke in prisons, schools, and churches about drug addiction and nonviolence. He was also a consultant to the Coalition for Diversity at the University of La Verne in Southern California. In the Pomona, California, area he spent many evenings giving poetry readings at local coffeehouses and in his spare time crafted ceramics.

Cleaver was a prolific writer and speaker and was seen by some in the late 1960s as a black leader capable of orga-

Poster for the Black Panther Party featuring "Eldridge Cleaver, Minister of Information." THE LIBRARY OF CONGRESS

nizing and leading a mass movement. *Soul on Ice* won the Martin Luther King Memorial Prize in 1970. Most of his work consists of nonfiction writing: *Eldridge Cleaver: Post-Prison Writings and Speeches* (1969), *Eldridge Cleaver's Black Papers* (1969), the introduction to Jerry Rubin's *Do It!* (1970), and contributions to *The Black Panther Leaders Speak: Huey P. Newton, Bobby Seale, Eldridge Cleaver, and Company Speak Out Through the Black Panther Party's Official Newspaper* (1976) and to *War Within: Violence or Nonviolence in Black Revolution* (1971). He also authored and coauthored numerous pamphlets for the Black Panther Party and the People's Communication Network. Some of his work has also appeared in anthologies such as the *Prize Stories of 1971: The O. Henry Awards*.

Cleaver had both his critics and his followers. There are those who felt that his commitment to violence and his use of rape as a political weapon in the 1960s had no place within society. Others have questioned the sincerity and credibility of his later volte-face to right-wing politics and fundamentalist Christianity, and Cleaver often felt compelled to explain and defend himself. According to him, combined with his growing disenchantment with communism and radical politics was a mystical vision resulting in his conversion to Christianity. When accused of

having mellowed with age, Cleaver replied, "That implies that your ideas have changed because of age. I've changed because of new conclusions."

See also Black Panther Party for Self-Defense; Gregory, Dick; Malcolm X; Muhammad, Elijah; Nation of Islam

■ ■ *Bibliography*

Baranski, Lynne, and Richard Lemon. *People* (March 22, 1982).

Cleaver, Kathleen. *Target Zero: Eldridge Cleaver, a Life in Writings.* New York: Palgrave Macmillan, 2005.

Hunter, Charlayne. "To Mr. and Mrs. Yesterday." *New York Times Book Review* (March 24, 1968): 3.

AMRITJIT SINGH (1996)
Updated by publisher 2005

CLEVELAND, JAMES
DECEMBER 5, 1931
FEBRUARY 9, 1991

Born in Chicago, gospel singer James Edward Cleveland was educated in public schools and began piano lessons at the age of five. Three years later he became a soloist in Thomas A. Dorsey's Junior Gospel Choir at Pilgrim Baptist Church. At age fifteen he joined a local group, the Thorne Crusaders, with whom he remained for the next eight years. He began composing, and at age sixteen wrote "Grace Is Sufficient," recorded by the Roberta Martin Singers and now a part of the standard gospel repertory.

After leaving the Thorne Crusaders, Cleveland served as pianist and arranger for Albertina Walker's Caravans and recorded with them. He later joined the Gospel Chimes and the Gospel All-Stars, and eventually organized the James Cleveland Singers. In 1963 he joined Rev. Lawrence Roberts and his choir at First Baptist Church in Nutley, New Jersey, to make a number of recordings beginning with "Peace, Be Still" (1962). Cleveland liked a treble sound and dispensed with the bass voice in the gospel choir. He also preferred the call-and-response delivery to singing in concert, and on choir recordings he played the role of preacher to the choir as congregation. He felt that gospel needed a congregation present and made all his choir recordings live.

During the 1950s and 1960s Cleveland wrote over five hundred songs, including "Oh, Lord, Stand By Me" (1952), "He's Using Me" (1953), "Walk On by Faith" (1962), and "Lord, Help Me to Hold Out" (1973). He continued to compose into the 1980s and scored a success with the Mighty Clouds of Joy recording of "I Get a Blessing Everyday" (1980).

The Cleveland style was one of half-crooning, half-preaching the verses and then moving into sung refrains. His hard gospel technique of singing at the extremes of his register created a contrast with the falsetto he employed. He was fond of the vamp—a section of the song, usually toward the end, when the choir repeated one phrase, over which he extemporized variations. Like Dorsey, Cleveland wrote and sang in the everyday language of his audiences, dealing with such common subjects as paying rent and buying food.

In August 1968 Cleveland formed the Gospel Music Workshop of America, an organization with several hundred thousand members by the mid-1980s. Each year's convention released a recording; one of the better known was with his protégée Aretha Franklin ("Amazing Grace," 1971), who studied his style when he was director of the Radio Choir at Detroit's New Bethel Baptist Church, where her father, Rev. C. L. Franklin, was pastor.

Known as the "Crown Prince of Gospel" and "King of Gospel," Cleveland won several gold records and three Grammy Awards, appeared at Carnegie Hall, worked with Quincy Jones in the TV production of *Roots,* and recorded the opera *Porgy and Bess* with Ray Charles and Cleo Laine. In 1980, along with Natalie Cole, he starred in the television special *In the Spirit,* filmed in England for Grenada Television (BBC). In November 1970 Cleveland organized and became pastor of Cornerstone Institutional Baptist Church in Los Angeles, with sixty charter members. At his death in 1991, membership totaled over seven thousand.

See also Charles, Ray (Robinson, Ray Charles); Dorsey, Thomas A.; Franklin, C. L.; Franklin, Aretha; Jones, Quincy

■ ■ *Bibliography*

Boyer, Horace Clarence. "A Comparative Analysis of Traditional and Contemporary Gospel Music." In *More than Dancing: Essays on Afro-American Music and Musicians,* edited by Irene V. Jackson, pp. 127–146. Westport, Conn.: Greenwood Press, 1985.

Heilbut, Anthony. *The Gospel Sound: Good News and Bad Times.* New York: Simon and Schuster, 1971. Reprint, New York: Limelight Editions, distributed by Harper & Row, 1985.

HORACE CLARENCE BOYER (1996)

CLUB ATENAS

The Club Atenas (Athens Club), founded in Havana in 1917, was the most influential civic and cultural organization among peoples of African descent in Cuba during the Republican period (1902–1958). Despite its elitist tendencies, the club provided a space for congregation and recreation and an important political advocacy group for Afro-Cubans in an era when racial discrimination governed many aspects of Cuban social life.

The Club Atenas was part of a long tradition of Afro-Cuban institution-building since the colonial period. In the era of slavery, African-based fraternal societies called *cabildos de nación* served mutual aid and recreational functions for slaves and free persons of color. After Emancipation, Afro-Cubans created new organizations called "colored societies" to cater to their social and educational needs during the transition from slavery to freedom. The colored societies expanded during the opening decades of the Cuban Republic, many of them led by upwardly mobile Afro-Cubans who saw their chances for equality and citizenship limited by racial discrimination. In 1917 an emerging class of Afro-Cuban professionals founded the Club Atenas as an institution that would further their interests and provide recreational opportunities in a society where most leisure activities were racially segregated. By naming the group after the mecca of ancient Greek civilization, the club's founders sought to lay claim to a Western cultural image.

The Club Atenas became the most influential of these Afro-Cuban societies because of the social and political stature of its members. Lawyers, doctors, dentists, professors, students, politicians, journalists, and other distinguished Afro-Cubans were the backbone of the organization. While full-fledged membership was reserved for males only, women participated in the group's activities through "women's sections." The club's class and gendered elitism made it a frequent target of criticism from social activists throughout its history.

The Club Atenas, like many other civic, political, and recreational associations in the African diaspora during this time, was dedicated to the goal of racial "improvement," the project launched by black aspiring classes in order to "uplift" the black masses from the vestiges of slavery. The club's preoccupation with uplift is exemplified in the association's "respectable" recreational activities, which included dances, costume parties, sport contests, concerts, and beach excursions. Club members danced to *danzones* (as opposed to *rumbas*), listened to classical music, and read the works of classical Western authors. Moreover, part of the club's project of racial improvement entailed establishing ties with prominent African Americans. By hosting African-American travelers to Cuba, and by profiling the works of writers such as Langston Hughes, the club sought to ally itself with what it saw as the vanguard of the global "colored race."

A major figure throughout the Club Atenas's history was Miguel Angel Céspedes. Born in the town of Camagüey in 1885, Céspedes's status as a lawyer, intellectual, and politician made him one of the more influential Afro-Cuban public figures during the Republican period. In the first decade of the century he was director of the Instituto Booker T. Washington, a trade school in Havana that was inspired by its namesake's program of industrial education for black youth. Years later he was among the founders of the Club Atenas and served several terms as president of the organization. It was through his position as president of Atenas that Céspedes developed his reputation as an Afro-Cuban leader. During the 1920s he was an outspoken critic and activist against racial discrimination, leading protests to oppose instances of racial violence against Afro-Cubans.

From the time of its inception until the mid-1950s, the Club Atenas was the most powerful Afro-Cuban society. However, the polarization of politics engendered by the revolutionary struggle against the Fulgencio Batista regime during the 1950s crippled the organization. After the revolution took power, an increasing number of Cubans argued that racially defined organizations such as Atenas had no place in a revolutionary society with a commitment to racial equality. Soon thereafter, the club became a casualty of the revolution's program of abolishing societies organized along racial lines. In 1961 the Club Atenas was forced to close its doors by the revolutionary government, seemingly with little protest. The club's old headquarters was converted into a day care center that still exists in Havana today.

See also Abakuá; Afrocubanismo

■ ■ *Bibliography*

Bronfman, Alejandra. *Measures of Equality: Social Science, Citizenship, and Race in Cuba, 1902–1940.* Chapel Hill: University of North Carolina Press, 2004.

de la Fuente, Alejandro. *A Nation for All: Race, Politics, and Inequality in Twentieth-Century Cuba.* Chapel Hill: University of North Carolina Press, 2000.

Guridy, Frank, A. "Racial Knowledge in Cuba: The Production of a Social Fact, 1912–1944." Ph.D. diss., University of Michigan, Ann Arbor, 2002.

FRANK A. GURIDY (2005)

COARTACIÓN

The frequency of manumission, the legal act of releasing a slave from his or her bondage, is often highlighted as a primary distinction between colonial Latin American slavery and its counterparts in the slave societies of the Caribbean and British North America. Manumission is important not only because of the potentially profound impacts it had in the lives of slaves, but also because the intricacies of its operation speak volumes about the institution of slavery in Latin America.

As Iberian (Spain and Portugal) imperial law did not guarantee slaves access to manumission, it is best understood as a customary right. Although the *Siete Partidas* (1348), the basis for colonial Iberian slave law, stipulated that "all laws of the world should lead towards freedom," this body of law only outlined the processes by which slave owners could free their chattel, stopping short of guaranteeing the right to emancipation for slaves. Nor did subsequent slave legislation for Spanish America—including the *Recopilación de Leyes de Indias* and the Royal Cedula of 1789—codify a slave's right to manumission.

Manumissions generally took one of three forms: (1) immediate freedom without compensation; (2) immediate freedom for payment; and (3) conditional freedom, contingent upon the completion of a specific term of service or upon the owner's death. The last type was often granted in the last will and testaments of masters, while the first two tended to be granted in formulaic manumission deeds called *cartas de libertad* (Spanish) or *cartas de alforria* (Portuguese), which were sworn out before a notary public. Self-purchase became increasingly important over time, as slaves actively pursued their freedom rather than relying on the generosity of their owners.

Many historians believe that a another option—*coartación* (Spanish) or *quartação* (Portuguese)—became increasingly important throughout Latin America after the middle of the eighteenth century. The process of *coartación*, which originated in eighteenth-century Cuba, consisted of the setting of a "just price," agreed upon by slave and master, for self-purchase. Once set, the price could not be raised, and slaves could make payments towards their manumission price until they reached the stipulated amount. Slaves in the process of purchasing themselves, known as *coartados* (Portuguese, *quartados*), remained in the service of their master until the total self-purchase price was met.

While *coartación* existed in both Spanish and Portuguese America, it appears to have developed slightly differently in those two contexts. In Spanish America, colonial

A sugar mill in Brazil, early 1800s. Slaves could work to earn money that could be applied to coartación, *or self-purchase at an agreed-upon price. From Debret, Jean Baptiste.* Voyage Pittoresque et Historique au Bresil, ou Sejour d'un artiste francais au Bresil, depuis 1816 jusqu'en 1831 inclusivement, epoques de l'avenement et de l'abdication de S. M. D. Pedro 1er, fondateur de l'Empire bresilien. *Dedie a l'Academie des Beaux-Arts de l'Institut de France. Published 1834–1839.* ART AND ARTIFACTS DIVISION, SCHOMBURG CENTER FOR RESEARCH IN BLACK CULTURE, THE NEW YORK PUBLIC LIBRARY, ASTOR, LENOX AND TILDEN FOUNDATIONS.

courts became involved in the process both in terms of setting a "just price" and in guaranteeing a slave's right to self-purchase. In other words, despite the fact that *coartación* was not guaranteed in Spanish American colonial law until 1843, when Cuban masters were required to *coartar* those slaves who offered a minimum down payment of fifty pesos towards self-purchase, slaves throughout Spanish America could theoretically avail themselves of the courts to set their manumission price and to guarantee that they were freed upon meeting their self-purchase price. In Brazil, however, the courts refused to serve as arbiters between masters and slaves precisely because the practice had no basis in law.

The importance of *coartación* may have been overstated within past treatments of slavery in colonial Iberian America. Quantitative studies for Mexico, Peru, Argentina, and Brazil (Bahia, Rio de Janeiro, and Minas Gerais) have found that only in colonial Buenos Aires and Minas Gerais were a majority of manumissions purchased, and

it is unclear what proportion of those manumissions resulted from *coartación*. Additionally, in regions of eighteenth-century Minas Gerais and nineteenth-century Cuba, approximately one percent of the total slave population was in the process of purchasing their freedom through *coartación*, while only six-tenths of one percent of the slave population achieved freedom annually via *coartación* in 1850s Cuba, when it became the primary means of liberating slaves.

The importance of purchased manumission requires discussion of a related topic: the slave *peculium,* or private fund. Throughout Latin America individual slaves could and did accumulate money that could be applied to self-purchase. However, the *peculium* is also best understood as a customary right because the *Siete Partidas* stipulated that slaves did not have the right to possess private property. Yet Spanish American courts did defend slaves' possession of property and money, so long as it was earned legitimately.

Manumission was a decidedly urban phenomenon, with the exception of rural slaves engaged in gold or diamond mining. Estimates of manumission rates in urban and mining contexts range from 0.33 to 1.5 percent of the slave population annually. In one extreme case, manumission rates may have been as high as three percent annually in the gold mining fields of colonial Colombia. Compared to the average rural field hand, the typical urban or mining slave probably had greater opportunities to accumulate money for self-purchase due to the specific waged occupations they filled (e.g., marketeering, waged day labor, prostitution, mining). This explains, in part, their greater access to manumission.

There is a surprising uniformity in terms of which slaves tended to be liberated throughout Latin America. Primarily, women received between fifty-five and sixty-seven percent of all manumissions. These numbers are made all the more impressive because women were generally a minority within the slave population itself. For example, in the city of Rio de Janeiro during the first half of the nineteenth century, women represented approximately forty percent of the slave population, but they received sixty-four percent of all manumissions. Children occupied a similarly advantaged position in terms of access to manumission, but rates throughout the Americas show much greater variability than was the case for manumission based upon gender.

Historians have offered numerous possible explanations for the advantages enjoyed by women and children in achieving liberty. They highlight their lesser market value compared to adult men, as well as the greater opportunities for women to accumulate money as marketeers or prostitutes that could theoretically be used to free themselves or their children. Alternatively, these patterns might reflect strategies of slave families for achieving freedom. Freeing women served to prevent their future offspring from being born into slavery, as only children born to slave mothers were slaves under Spanish and Portuguese law. In addition, adult children may have been more likely to free their slave mothers due to the matrifocal nature of most slave families. A dominant explanation for the preponderance of these two groups among freed slaves is that slave women were able to manipulate their sexuality to improve their own chances for freedom (and those of their children). It has also been suggested that women's domestic occupations within the household may have provided more opportunities for daily interactions with slave owners, and thus for stronger, more amiable relations between masters and slaves. This may, in turn, have translated into increased opportunities for freedom for slave women and their children. Clearly, all of these explanations point to the reality that gender played a key role in manumission.

A slave in Brazil being corrected by his master. *From Debret, Jean Baptiste.* Voyage Pittoresque et Historique au Bresil, ou Sejour d'un artiste francais au Bresil, depuis 1816 jusqu'en 1831 inclusivement, epoques de l'avenement et de l'abdication de S. M. D. Pedro 1er, fondateur de l'Empire bresilien. *Dedie a l'Academie des Beaux-Arts de l'Institut de France. Published 1834–1839.* ART AND ARTIFACTS DIVISION, SCHOMBURG CENTER FOR RESEARCH IN BLACK CULTURE, THE NEW YORK PUBLIC LIBRARY, ASTOR, LENOX AND TILDEN FOUNDATIONS.

Generally, American-born slaves (Creoles) had greater chances to be manumitted than did African-born slaves. Likewise, mixed-race slaves were more likely to be freed than were black slaves. However, these patterns are more likely explained by increased opportunities to achieve skilled positions within slavery and to cultivate relationships with masters than any other factor.

Female slave-owners were responsible for a significant portion of freed slaves, liberating between one-third and one-half of all slaves freed throughout Latin America. Furthermore, the proportion of slaves freed by women, compared to those freed by men, was much higher than the percentage of slaves that women actually owned. Men dominated economic life in colonial Latin America, and thus more men than women owned slaves, and men generally owned more slaves than did women.

The practice of manumission served to buttress the institution of slavery in important ways. Opportunities for manumission had obvious potentially positive ramifications for slaves, but it also served to empower masters, as the possibility of manumission served as an incentive to insure the good behavior of slaves. In theory, the possibility of manumission made slaves less resistive because they would not want to jeopardize their chances for manumission, and through coartación and conditional manumission, masters could insure faithful service from slaves during their prime working years.

As a result of manumission (and the subsequent natural growth of the families of those freed), Latin America was characterized by sizeable free populations of color. For example, in Salvador, Brazil, in 1835, free people of color represented nearly thirty percent of the total population, compared to twenty-eight percent for whites and forty-two percent for slaves. At the turn of the nineteenth century in Rio de Janeiro, free people of color accounted for twenty percent of the total population, while slaves accounted for thirty-five percent and whites for forty-five percent. In Spanish America, free people of color actually came to outnumber slaves in colonial Mexico by the middle of the seventeenth century, and in Peru and New Granada they outnumbered slaves by the end of the eighteenth century. These large populations of freed people did not undermine the integrity of slavery as an institution, however. Although this population faced significant racism, which prevented their complete incorporation into Spanish and Portuguese society, differences in status (free vs. slave), race and ethnicity, and occupation, among other factors, prevented the unification of slaves and free people of color against slavery and Europeans. Even in contexts where slaves were outnumbered by free people of color, slavery proved to be a very stable and enduring institution. It was not uncommon for ex-slaves and free people of color to own slaves themselves, although they were less likely to do so than whites.

See also Manumission Societies; Slavery

■ ■ *Bibliography*

Aimes, Hubert H. S. "Coartación: A Spanish Institution for the Advancement of Slaves into Freedom." *Yale Review* 17 (1909): 412–431.

Carniero da Cunha, Manuela. "Silences of the Law: Customary Law and Positive Law on the Manumission of Slaves in 19th-century Brazil." *History and Anthropology* 1 (1985): 427–443.

Higgins, Kathleen J. *"Licentious Liberty" in a Brazilian Gold-Mining Region. Slavery, Gender, and Social Control in Eighteenth-Century Sabará, Minas Gerais.* University Park: Pennsylvania State University Press, 1999.

Johnson, Lyman L. "Manumission in Colonial Buenos Aires, 1776–1810." *Hispanic American Historical Review* 59, no. 2 (1979): 258–279.

Karasch, Mary C. *Slave Life in Rio de Janeiro, 1808–1850.* Princeton, N.J.: Princeton University Press, 1987.

Klein, Herbert S. *Slavery in the Americas: A Comparative Study of Virginia and Cuba.* Chicago: University of Chicago Press, 1967.

Libby, Douglas Cole, and Clotilde Andrade Paiva. "Manumission Practices in a Late Eighteenth-Century Brazilian Slave Parish: São José d'El Rey in 1795." *Slavery and Abolition* 21, no. 1 (2000): 96–127.

Patterson, Orlando. *Slavery and Social Death: A Comparative Study.* Cambridge, Mass.: Harvard University Press, 1982.

Salmoral, Manuel Lucena. "El derecho de coartación del esclavo en la América Española." *Revista de Indias* vol. 54, no. 216 (1999): 357–374.

Schwartz, Stuart B. "The Manumission of Slaves in Colonial Brazil: Bahia, 1684–1745." *Hispanic American Historical Review* 54 (1974): 603–635.

Scott, Rebecca J. *Slave Emancipation in Cuba: The Transition of Free Labor, 1860–1899.* Princeton, N. J.: Princeton University Press, 1985. Reprint, Pittsburgh: University of Pittsburgh Press, 2000.

Sharp, William F. *Slavery on the Spanish Frontier: The Colombian, 1680–1810.* Norman: University of Oklahoma Press, 1976.

FRANK "TREY" PROCTOR III (2005)

COBB, W. MONTAGUE

OCTOBER 12, 1904
NOVEMBER 20, 1990

William Montague Cobb, a physician, was born in Washington, D.C., the son of William Elmer and Alexzine Montague Cobb. A graduate of Dunbar High School (1921), he pursued a liberal-arts program at Amherst College and earned an A.B. there in 1925. Cobb's special talent for science earned him the Blodgett Scholarship for work at the Marine Biological Laboratory in Woods Hole, Massachusetts, where he studied embryology in the summer of 1925. He entered Howard University Medical College that fall, earning an M.D. in 1929.

During his final year at Howard, Cobb taught embryology to medical students. This was the start of a lifelong career in teaching and research. Following a year's internship at Freedmen's Hospital, he enrolled in the doctoral program at Western Reserve University and was awarded a Ph.D. in anatomy and physical anthropology in 1932.

Cobb taught anatomy at Howard University for forty-one years. Starting as an assistant professor in 1932, he attained the rank of full professor in 1942. He served as chairman of the Department of Anatomy from 1947 to 1969. In 1969 he became the first to hold a distinguished professorship at Howard. Following his official retirement in 1973, he served as visiting professor at several institutions, including Stanford University, the University of Maryland, and Harvard University.

Cobb's research interests were wide-ranging. He contributed the chapter on the skeleton to the third edition (1952) of E. V. Cowdry's *Problems of Aging: Biological and Medical Aspects.* Other work of his was cited in *Gray's Anatomy,* Sir Henry Morris's *Human Anatomy,* and *Cunningham's Manual of Practical Anatomy.* He is said to have been the first black scientist cited in all three of these standard medical texts. Cobb's work on the "physical anthropology of the American Negro," published in the *American Journal of Physical Anthropology* and other periodicals, was recognized as authoritative.

Along with Julian H. Lewis, Cobb pioneered efforts to counteract the myths that had evolved among scientists concerning the biological inferiority of black people. In all, he published over six hundred articles in professional journals. His prominence brought him terms as president of the Anthropological Society of Washington (1949–1951) and of the American Association of Physical Anthropologists (1958–1960), at a time when it was almost unheard of for an African American to hold such posts within predominantly white organizations.

Cobb is perhaps best remembered, both within the medical community and beyond, for his civil rights activities. During the 1940s he represented the National Association for the Advancement of Colored People (NAACP) before the U.S. Senate in testimony supportive of a national health-insurance program. Under the auspices of the NAACP he prepared two seminal monographs, *Medical Care and the Plight of the Negro* (1947) and *Progress and Portents for the Negro in Medicine* (1948), which helped raise public awareness of how discriminatory practices had adversely influenced the access of blacks to health-care services and professional opportunities. Cobb served as NAACP president from 1976 to 1982.

In his capacity as president (1945–1947, 1951–1954) of the all-black Medico-Chirurgical Society of the District of Columbia, Cobb led two important campaigns: the racial integration of Gallinger Hospital (later, D.C. General Hospital) in 1948 and the admission, in 1952, of black physicians to membership in the all-white Medical Society of the District of Columbia. He also served a term as president of the National Medical Association in 1964. It was in his role, however, as editor of the *Journal of the National Medical Association* (1949–1977) that he found his primary forum, both for discussing contemporary issues of health-care access and for portraying the rich historical heritage to which blacks—going back beyond colonial America to prehistoric times—can lay claim.

See also Freedmen's Hospital; National Association for the Advancement of Colored People (NAACP)

■ ■ *Bibliography*

Cobb, W. Montague. *The First Negro Medical Society: A History of the Medico-Chirurgical Society of the District of Columbia.* Washington, D.C.: Associated Publishers, 1939.

Lawlah, John W. "The President-Elect." *Journal of the National Medical Association* 55 (November 1963): 551–554.

KENNETH R. MANNING (1996)

COCHRAN, JOHNNIE L., JR.
OCTOBER 2, 1937
MARCH 29, 2005

▮▮▮

Johnnie Cochran, a lawyer, civil libertarian, and philanthropist, gained national recognition as a defense lawyer in O. J. Simpson's murder trial. Cochran was born in Shreveport, Louisiana. His family later moved to Los Angeles, where he attended public schools before attending the University of California, Los Angeles (UCLA; B.A., 1959) and Loyola Marymount University School of Law (J.D., 1962).

Cochran began his public career in 1963 as a deputy city attorney for the city of Los Angeles. After entering private practice in 1965, Cochran returned to public service in 1978 to become the first African-American assistant district attorney of Los Angeles County. He returned to private practice in the early 1980s, eventually becoming the only Los Angeles attorney to receive both the Criminal Trial Lawyer of the Year and the Civil Trial Lawyer of the Year awards. In 2001, after heading several law firms, he founded The Cochran Firm, a bicoastal conglomerate devoted to personal injury and civil law. He was also involved with various legal teams exploring the issue of reparation for slavery and worked with the Innocence Project, which contests wrongful convictions using DNA evidence.

Among the influences on Cochran's career are Thurgood Marshall and Martin Luther King Jr.—particularly

King's belief that one must question the "official" version of events. Cochran represented (and successfully defended) many high-profile personalities, including Michael Jackson, Jim Brown, and Tupac Shakur. His media involvement included both print and television appearances (the latter as both newscaster and anchor). Cochran wrote *Journey to Justice* (1996), *Last Man Standing: The Tragedy and Triumph of Geronimo Pratt* (2000), and *A Lawyer's Life* (2002).

Cochran served as a member of the American College of Trial Lawyers, the International Academy of Trial Lawyers, and the Inner Circle of Advocates. His many awards included *National Law Journal*'s Trial Lawyer of the Year (1995), the Arizona Civil Liberties Union's Lifetime Achievement Award (2001), and the Association of Manhattan's Autistic Children's Humanitarian Award (2001). He established university scholarships at UCLA, the University of New Mexico, and Southern University, and funded and dedicated several community projects. Cochran died of a brain tumor in 2005 at the age of sixty-seven.

See also Jackson, Michael; King, Martin Luther, Jr.; Marshall, Thurgood; Simpson, O. J.

■ ■ *Bibliography*

Cochran, Johnnie, with David Fisher. *A Lawyer's Life.* New York: Thomas Dunne Books, 2002.

Londin, Jesse. "Johnnie Cochran." Available from <http://www.lawcrossing.com/article/index.php?id=335>.

"Johnnie Cochran." In *Contemporary Black Biography*, vol. 39, edited by Ashyia Henderson. Detroit: Gale, 2003.

"Johnnie Cochran." In *Notable Black American Men*, edited by Jessie Carney Smith. Detroit: Gale, 1998.

HELEN R. HOUSTON (1996)
Updated by author 2005

COKER, DANIEL

1780
1846

■■■

Born Isaac Wright in Maryland to an African slave father and an English indentured-servant mother, minister and abolitionist Daniel Coker received a rudimentary education while attending school as his white half-brother's valet. He escaped to New York while still a youth and took his new name to avoid detection. In New York Coker met Bishop Francis Asbury, who ordained him to the Methodist Church ministry around 1800. Coker returned shortly after to Baltimore and, with his freedom recently purchased, spoke out against slavery, writing an abolitionist pamphlet, *A Dialogue Between a Virginian and an African Minister,* in 1810. He became the leader of a society of black Methodists who desired independence from white Methodists because of discrimination, and ran the African School in connection with this society.

Coker's Methodist society evolved into the independent African Bethel Church. In 1816 delegates, including Coker and Richard Allen, from five black Methodist societies gathered in Philadelphia to establish the independent African Methodist Episcopal Church. Elected as the first bishop of the new denomination, Coker declined the post—perhaps because of dissension over his light skin color—and Allen became the first bishop. Coker returned to his Baltimore pastorate, but was expelled from the ministry from 1818 to 1819 for an unknown offense. He left for Africa in 1820 as a missionary with the assistance of the Maryland Colonization Society. After spending some time in Liberia, he settled in Sierra Leone, where he was the superintendent of a settlement for "recaptured" Africans and helped found the West African Methodist Church.

See also Abolition; African Methodist Episcopal Church

■ ■ *Bibliography*

Coker, Daniel. *Journal of Daniel Coker.* Baltimore, 1820.

Payne, Alexander. *History of the African Methodist Episcopal Church.* Nashville, Tenn.: Publishing House of the A.M.E. Sunday School Union, 1891.

TIMOTHY E. FULOP (1996)

COLE, NAT "KING"

MARCH 17, 1919
FEBRUARY 15, 1965

■■■

Singer and pianist Nathaniel Adams Cole was born in Montgomery, Alabama, and moved with his family to Chicago when he was two years old. His father, the Rev. Edward James Cole Sr., was a pastor at the True Light Baptist Church. His parents encouraged the musical talents of young Cole and his four brothers. All but one eventually became professional musicians. Cole had his earliest musical experiences in his father's church, where he sang and played the organ. While in high school, he played in the

Rogues of Rhythm, a band led by his brother Eddie, at a Chicago night spot called the Club Panama. In 1936 he played piano in a touring production of Noble Sissle and Eubie Blake's *Shuffle Along*. The tour ended in Long Beach, California, in 1937. Cole stayed in southern California and played piano in Los Angeles–area clubs.

In 1938 he organized a trio with Oscar Moore on guitar and Wesley Prince on bass. At about this time he adopted the name Nat "King" Cole. The trio began to gain popularity, largely due to Cole's sophisticated, swinging piano style. In 1943 Cole signed a contract with the newly organized record company Capitol.

On his first hit recording, "Straighten Up and Fly Right" (1943), Cole sang for the first time. The song, based on a sermon of his father's, was taken from a traditional black folktale. In 1944 Cole achieved a national reputation as a pianist, taking part in "Jazz at the Philharmonic," a series of touring jazz concerts.

Eventually, Cole's singing came to dominate his piano playing. His 1946 recording of "The Christmas Song," which added a string section to Cole's singing, was a turning point in his career. By 1949 he was recording primarily with orchestral accompaniment, and his piano playing was relegated to a secondary role. Cole achieved great success with such vocal recordings as "Mona Lisa" (1950) and "Unforgettable" (1951). His singing style was, like his piano playing, relaxed, disarming, and authoritative. His performances remained impressive, even with the most banal material, and they always retained their integrity, shunning both pseudodramatic straining for effects and coy mannerisms. His singing had an immense popularity with both white and black audiences. Cole's was the first black jazz combo to have its own sponsored radio program (1948–1949), and in 1956 and 1957 he became the first black performer to have his own series on network television. (The program was canceled, however, because of the difficulty in finding sponsors for it.) Cole also made several films, including *St. Louis Blues* (1958, a life of W. C. Handy), and *Cat Ballou* (1965).

In the early 1960s Cole was sometimes criticized by black activists for his failure to actively participate in the struggle for civil rights. He resented the accusations, noting that he had made substantial financial contributions to civil rights organizations. By this time, Cole was a headliner at Las Vegas casinos and was one of the most financially successful performers in popular music. He died of lung cancer in 1965, at the height of his popularity. He was the most successful black performer of the postwar era. Appreciation of his contribution to popular music has increased since his death, and his television show has been syndicated and many of his recordings reissued.

Cole's first marriage, to Nadine Robinson in 1937, ended in divorce. He married Maria Ellington (no relation to Duke Ellington) in 1948. They had four children, and also adopted Maria's niece. One of their children, Natalie Cole, has had a successful career as a pop singer. In 1991, Natalie Cole achieved considerable recognition for her album *Unforgettable,* an ingeniously recorded album of duets with her late father, which won Grammy Awards for best album and best song.

See also Blake, Eubie; Jazz; Jazz Singers; Music

■ ■ *Bibliography*

Cole, Maria, with Louie Robinson. *Nat King Cole: An Intimate Biography.* William Morrow, 1971.

Gourse, Leslie, *Unforgettable: The Life and Mystique of Nat King Cole,* St. Martins Press, 1991.

Haskins, James, with Kathleen Benson. *Nat King Cole: A Personal and Professional Biography.* Chelsea, Scarborough House, 1980.

ROBERT W. STEPHENS (1996)

COLEMAN, BESSIE
JANUARY 26, 1892
APRIL 30, 1926

Bessie Coleman was the first African-American female aviator. She was born in Atlanta, Texas, but her family moved to Waxahachie, Texas, when she was still an infant. When she was seven, her parents separated. Her father, who was a Choctaw Indian, returned to the reservation in Oklahoma, and her mother supported the large family by picking cotton and doing laundry, jobs in which her children aided her. Because she wanted Coleman to attend college, her mother allowed her to keep her income from her laundry work, but this money only financed one semester at the Colored Agricultural and Normal University in Langston, Oklahoma (now Langston University). After this semester, she returned to Waxahachie briefly; and between 1915 and 1917, she went to Chicago, where she took a course in manicuring and worked at the White Sox barbershop until the early years of World War I. She then managed a small restaurant.

Coleman became interested in the burgeoning field of aviation, which had entered the national consciousness as a consequence of its role in World War I, but aviation schools rejected all her applications on the basis of her race and/or gender, until Robert S. Abbott, founder and editor of the *Chicago Defender,* advised her to study aviation abroad. She took a course in French, went to Paris in November 1920, and attended an aviation school in Le Crotoy. She returned to the United States in September 1921 with a pilot's license and went back to Europe in 1922, this time obtaining an international pilot's license, the first African-American woman to earn these licenses. When she returned to the United States after her second sojourn in Europe, Coleman made a name for herself in exhibition flying, performing at shows attended by thousands. She barnstormed throughout the United States and became known as "Brave Bessie." She lectured in schools and churches on the opportunities in aviation wherever she performed, and she saved the money she earned from these lectures and performances in the hope of opening an aviation school for African Americans. On April 30, 1926, during a practice run in Jacksonville. Florida, Coleman's plane somersaulted out of a nosedive, and Coleman fell 2,000 feet (610 meters) to her death.

See also Abbott, Robert Sengstacke

■ ■ *Bibliography*

Gates, Henry Louis, and Cornel West. *The African-American Century: How Black Americans Have Shaped Our Century.* New York: Simon & Schuster, 2000.

King, Anita. "Brave Bessie: First Black Pilot." *Essence* (May 1976): 36; (June 1976): 48.

Rich, Doris L. *Queen Bess: Daredevil Aviator.* Smithsonian Institution Press, 1993.

Smith, Jessie Carney, ed. *Notable Black American Women.* Detroit: Gale Group, 1992.

SIRAJ AHMED (1996)
Updated bibliography

COLEMAN, ORNETTE

MARCH 9, 1930

┣━┫┣━┫

Born in Fort Worth, Texas, on a date that remains in dispute, jazz saxophonist and composer Ornette Coleman's early musical influences included gospel, rhythm and blues, and bebop. Coleman, whose father was a singer, began playing saxophone at age sixteen and had little formal music instruction. His earliest performances were in local churches, and he was expelled from his high school band for improvising during a performance of John Philip Sousa's "Washington Post March." Coleman at first played tenor saxophone in a honking rhythm-and-blues style influenced by Illinois Jacquet and Big Jay McNeely. His first professional work came in 1949 with the Silas Green Minstrels, a tent show that toured the South and Midwest. Coleman also traveled with blues singer Clarence Samuels and blues singer and guitarist "Pee Wee" Crayton. By this time he had been inspired by bebop to start playing with a coarse, crying tone and a frantic, unrestrained sense of rhythm and harmony. The reception in the jazz community to his controversial style kept him from working for a decade.

In 1950 Coleman moved to Los Angeles and began to recruit a circle of associates, including drummers Edward Blackwell and Billy Higgins, trumpeters Don Cherry and Bobby Bradford, bassist Charlie Haden, and pianist Paul Bley. He married poet Jayne Cortez in 1954; unable to support himself as a musician, he took a job as a stock boy and elevator operator at a Los Angeles department store. Despite his reputation as an eccentric who had unusually long hair, wore overcoats in the summer, and played a white saxophone, in 1958 he was invited to make his first recording, *Something Else!,* which included his compositions "Chippie" and "When Will the Blues Leave." Pianist John Lewis brought Coleman and Cherry to the Lenox (Massachusetts) School of Jazz in 1959, which led to a famous series of quartet performances at New York's Five Spot nightclub.

The albums Coleman made over the next two years, including *Tomorrow Is the Question, The Shape of Jazz to Come, This Is Our Music,* and *Free Jazz,* were vilified by traditionalists, who heard the long, loosely structured, collective improvisations and adventurous harmonies as worthless cacophony. However, among his admirers, those performances, which included his compositions "Focus on Sanity," "Peace," "Lonely Woman," and "Beauty Is a Rare Thing," were also recognized as the first significant development in jazz since bebop. Although modeled on the wit and irreverence of bebop, Coleman's pianoless quartets broke out of traditional harmonies, as well as rigid theme-and-improvisation structures. He began to call this style "harmolodics," referring to a musical system, since developed in a vast, unpublished manuscript, in which improvised melodies need not obey fixed harmonies.

In the 1950s Coleman was shunned by the jazz world, but in the 1960s he found himself hailed as one of the greatest and most influential figures in jazz. Yet Coleman, who was divorced from Cortez in 1964, scaled back his activities in order to study trumpet and violin. In the mid-1960s he most frequently appeared in trio settings (*At the Golden Circle,* 1965–1966), often including bassist David

Izenzon and drummer Charles Moffett. In 1967 Coleman became the first jazz musician to win a Guggenheim fellowship. During the late 1960s and early 1970s he often played with the members of his old quartet, plus tenor saxophonist Dewey Redman, with whom he had first become acquainted in Fort Worth (*Science Fiction*, 1971).

Coleman, who had been composing classical music since the early 1950s, also saw performances in the 1960s of his string quartet *Dedication to Poets and Writers* (1961), his woodwind quintet *Forms and Sounds* (1967), and *Saints and Soldiers* (1967), a chamber piece. Coleman's *Skies of America* symphony was recorded in 1972 with the London Symphony Orchestra. In 1973 he traveled to Morocco to record with folk musicians from the town of Joujouka.

Coleman's next breakthrough came in 1975, when he began to play a style of electric dance music that recalled his early career in rhythm-and-blues dance bands. Using Prime Time, a new core group of musicians that often included his son, Denardo, a drummer, born in 1956, Coleman recorded *Dancing in Your Head*, an album-length elaboration of a theme from *Skies of America*, in 1975, and *Of Human Feelings* in 1979. During this time he also founded Artists House, a collective that helped introduce guitarists James "Blood" Ulmer and bassist Jamaaladeen Tacuma.

The mid-1980s brought a revival of interest in Coleman. His hometown, Fort Worth, honored him with a series of tributes and performances, including the chamber piece *Prime Design/Time Design* (1983). A documentary by Shirley Clarke, *Ornette: Made in America*, was released in 1984, and he collaborated with jazz-rock guitarist Pat Metheny (*Song X*, 1985), and rock guitarist Jerry Garcia (*Virgin Beauty*, 1987). On *In All Languages* (1987) he reunited with his 1959 quartet, and in 1991 Coleman, who had composed and performed on the film soundtracks for *Chappaqua* (1965) and *Box Office* (1981), recorded the score for *Naked Lunch*. Coleman, who has lived in Manhattan since the early 1960s, continues to compose regularly, though performing and recording only sporadically with Prime Time. In 1997, the same year he received the French award of Commander of the Order of Arts and Letters, he wrote a jazz concerto grosso, "Skies of America."

In the early 2000s Coleman was touring as part of the Ornette Coleman Quartet, and the group released a CD, titled *Ornette!*, in 2004.

See also Cortez, Jayne; Jazz; Lewis, John; Music

■ ■ *Bibliography*

Davis, Francis. *In the Moment: Jazz in the 1980s*. New York: Oxford University Press, 1986.

Litweiler, John. *Ornette Coleman: The Harmolodic Life*. New York: Morrow, 1992.

Spellman, A. B. *Four Lives in the Bebop Business*. New York: Schocken, 1970.

Wilson, Peter Niklas. *Ornette Coleman: His Life and Music*. Berkeley, Calif.: Berkeley Hills Books, 1999.

BILL DIXON (1996)
Updated by publisher 2005

COLLINS, CARDISS

SEPTEMBER 24, 1931

Cardiss Robertson Collins was the first African-American woman to serve in the U.S. Congress. Born in St. Louis, Cardiss Robertson moved with her family to Detroit when she was ten years old. She studied accounting at Northwestern University and in 1958 married George Washington Collins, a local politician. Collins helped organize campaigns for her husband. Her own career in politics began when she became Democratic committeewoman in Chicago's twenty-fourth ward.

After U.S. Congressman George Collins died in 1972, Cardiss Collins resigned her position with the Illinois Department of Revenue, ran for his seat, and won handily. She took office on June 5, 1973. In 1979 she became the first woman to chair the Congressional Black Caucus. Two years later she became the first African American and the first woman to be appointed Democratic whip-at-large. In the mid-1980s she led inquiries into the employment practices of the airline industry. She also investigated college sports and pressed colleges and universities to meet the mandates of Title IX of the Educational Amendments of 1972 regarding female athletes. The NCAA yielded to her prodding and moved to bring about gender equity in sports. Collins introduced the Non-Discrimination in Advertising Act aimed to correct injustices against minority-owned media. In 1993 she co-authored the Child Safety Protection Act, which set standards for bicycle helmets and required warning labels on potentially dangerous toys.

Throughout her political career, Collins was a strong advocate of civil rights, the rights of women and the poor, and of universal health insurance. She wrote the resolution that designated October as National Breast Cancer Awareness Month.

After twenty-three years in Congress, Collins retired in 1996.

See also Congressional Black Caucus; Politics in the United States

■■ Bibliography

Abromowitz, Jack. "Accommodation and Militancy in Negro Life 1876–1916." Ph.D. diss., Columbia University, New York, 1950.

Gaither, Gerald H. Blacks and the Populist Revolt: Ballots and Bigotry in the "New South." Tuscaloosa: University of Alabama Press, 1977.

Goodwyn, Lawrence C. "The Populist Response to Black America." In Democratic Promise: The Populist Moment in America. New York: Oxford University Press, 1976.

JESSIE CARNEY SMITH (2001)
Updated by publisher 2005

COLÓN MAN

Caribbean men migrated to Panamá to work on its railroad (1850–1855), French-supported canal (1881–1898), and the successful United States canal (1904–1914). These Colón Men, taking the name of Panamá's port city, were defined by their migration to and work in the Central American country. Appearing in historical, literary, lyrical, and personal narratives, the figure's cockiness, possessions, cosmopolitanism, canal-forged masculinity, and even the illnesses he contracted distinguish him. Because of the significance of one of the Caribbean's largest internal migrations and the construction of the Panamá Canal, the Colón Man has come to signify the real and imagined possibilities of both.

This migration's import can be seen in the figure's dynamic representation in nineteenth- and twentieth-century narratives, representations that include the poorly depicted Caribbean worker in early histories, the thwarted lover in folk songs, and the ancestral figure in pan-Caribbean literature. The differences between these narratives suggest that Colón Men occupy both "factual" and "imaginable" spaces in the Caribbean imaginary. Thus, maintaining the collisions and parallels inherent in the various depictions of these laborers offers details about migrants and isthmian migration, about the ways canal work influenced these laborers, and about the communities shaped by these men's absence and presence.

Fictionalized Colón Men are cosmopolitan, ladies' men, Pan-Africanist, and rich; importantly, they are also unsuccessful lovers, loyal colonials, poor, and a mixture of all these characteristics. This ambivalence suggests that creative narratives make accessible aspects of the canal enterprise that are "undocumentable"—that is, inaccessible and/or devalued—in some canal histories. Colón Men went to Panamá to profit from their employers, but they also traveled with desires that had little to do with the United States or canal construction.

Historical narratives about the Panamá Canal reference workers from Jamaica and Barbados; songs that were popular during the construction period also prominently feature men from these two countries. Literature and workers' letters, however, feature migrants who traveled from Guadeloupe, the Bahamas, St. Lucia, Trinidad, Antigua, Grenada, Dominica, and St. Vincent. That this isthmian migration mainly comprised Afro-Caribbean men makes this pan-Caribbean national representation more startling. Of course, women, East Indian, Chinese, and other peoples occupied the region at the time, but very few migrated to Panamá, or inadequate documentation makes their presence hard to reconstruct.

Although economic reasons—both on the isthmus and within the Caribbean—partially explain migrants' reasons for leaving home, the range of Colón Man stories reveals more complex motivations. The chance to make money was a definite draw; however, the uses to which the money was put appeared to be more significant. Whether Colón Men used their "Panamá Money" to purchase shops, buy or improve property, or sport the latest jewelry and fashions, they were determined to project an image of a successful (though mostly mythic) migrant. In many cases this image was more important than the money.

For another population of Panamá Men, migration served as a form of resistance. When facing post-emancipation laws designed to limit the franchise, employment, and movement of formerly enslaved plantation workers, they left for the isthmus. Plantation owners pressured their governments to impose taxes on would-be migrants to stem this tide; however, this merely changed the character of migrant populations: more affluent, urban, skilled, and white-collar workers displaced rural, peasant, and unskilled ones.

Finally, the lure of adventure and the desire to accrue characteristics believed to be "manly" pulled Caribbean men to the isthmus. Former canal workers described their desire for "adventure and experience" and to test their "adult" status by challenging their parents, comments that speak to the power that these more-than-economic reasons held, as they often diminished the impact of stories about diseases in the Canal Zone. Even after confronting for themselves Colón's inadequate sewer systems, diseases, work-related injuries and deaths, and North American racism, Colón Men remained on the isthmus, went home to show off their finery, and returned to Panamá when their money ran low.

The U.S. Isthmian Canal Commission (ICC) hired Colón Men for various jobs. For example, Caribbean men worked as water or messenger boys, pick-and-shovel men, carpenters, plumbers, subforemen, machine operators, and in various white-collar jobs. Yet because of the ICC's rigidly held "color line," few black workers rose to the highest levels of employment; even those who did were subject to its silver/gold payment scale: white, U.S. citizens were paid in gold currency, and all others were paid in silver (hence the designation of "Silver Men" for the overwhelmingly black workforce and "Silver City" for the town where many of them lived).

See also Panama Canal

■■ *Bibliography*

Conniff, Michael L. *Black Labor on a White Canal: Panama, 1904–1981*. Pittsburgh, Pa.: University of Pittsburgh Press, 1985.

Cramer, Louise. "Songs of West Indian Negroes in the Canal Zone." *California Folklore Quarterly* 5 (1946): 243–272.

Frederick, Rhonda D. *"Colón Man a Come": Mythographies of Panamá Canal Migration*. Lanham, Md.: Lexington Books, 2005.

Lewis, Lancelot. *The West Indian in Panama: Black Labor in Panama, 1850–1914*. Washington, D.C.: University Press of America, 1980.

Newton, Velma. *The Silver Men: West Indian Labour Migration to Panama, 1850–1914*. Mona, Jamaica: Institute of Social and Economic Research of the University of the West Indies, 1984.

Petras, Elizabeth McLean. *Jamaican Labor Migration: White Capital and Black Labor, 1850–1930*. Boulder, Colo.: Westview, 1988.

Richardson, Bonham C. *Panama Money in Barbados, 1900–1920*. Knoxville: University of Tennessee Press, 1985.

Senior, Olive. "The Colon People." *Jamaica Journal* 11, no. 3 (1978): 62–71; 12, no. 4 (1978): 87–103.

Stuhl, Ruth C., ed. *Letters from Isthmian Canal Construction Workers*. Balboa Heights, Panama: Isthmian Historical Society, 1963.

Thomas-Hope, Elizabeth. "The Establishment of a Migration Tradition: British West Indian Movements to the Hispanic Caribbean in the Century after Emancipation." In *Caribbean Social Relations*, edited by Colin G. Clarke. London: University of Liverpool-Centre for Latin American Studies, 1978.

RHONDA FREDERICK (2005)

COLORED FARMERS ALLIANCE

■■■

The Colored Farmers Alliance, an agrarian organization founded in Texas in 1886, represented the largest network of black farmers, sharecroppers, and agricultural laborers in the South during the late nineteenth century. Fueling the region's black populist movement, the organization began by espousing self-help and economic cooperation, but it then took increasingly radical measures to improve economic conditions through lobbying efforts, boycotts, and strikes, meeting fierce resistance from white authorities, often joined by the segregated Southern Farmers Alliance.

Within five years, the Colored Alliance spread to every southern state, comprising an estimated membership of 1,200,000—of whom 300,000 were women. Many African Americans who joined the Colored Alliance were previously active in the Colored Agricultural Wheels, the Cooperative Workers of America, and the Knights of Labor. While the white Baptist minister Richard M. Humphrey served as the organization's general superintendent, most of its key leaders were black, including the Rev. Walter A. Pattillo of North Carolina and Oliver Cromwell of Mississippi. In 1891 the Colored Alliance launched a national cotton-pickers' strike, which was quickly suppressed by white planter militias. Members of the Colored Alliance turned to electoral politics, endorsing the Lodge Bill for federal supervision of elections, then helping to establish the People's Party. As the black populist movement grew and developed politically, the Colored Alliance began to dissolve. Black agrarian radicalism would resurface in the 1930s through the work of the Sharecroppers Union and the Southern Tenant Farmers' Union.

See also Labor and Labor Unions

■■ *Bibliography*

Ali, Omar H. "Black Populism in the New South, 1886–1898." Ph.D. diss., Columbia University. 2003.

Gaither, Gerald H. *Blacks and the Populist Revolt: Ballots and Bigotry in the "New South."* University of Alabama Press, 1977.

Goodwyn, Lawrence C. "The Populist Response to Black America." In *Democratic Promise: The Populist Moment in America*. New York: Oxford University Press, 1976.

OMAR H. ALI (1996)
Updated bibliography

COLTRANE, JOHN

SEPTEMBER 23, 1926
JULY 17, 1967

Born in Hamlet, North Carolina, jazz tenor and soprano saxophonist John William Coltrane moved with his family to High Point, North Carolina, when he was only a few months old. His father was a tailor, and his mother was an amateur singer. Coltrane received his first instrument, a clarinet, when he was twelve, although he soon began to play the alto saxophone, which was his primary instrument for a number of years.

After high school Coltrane moved to Philadelphia, where he studied at the Ornstein School of Music and the Granoff Studios, where he won scholarships for both performance and composition. He played in the Philadelphia area until 1945, when he entered the navy for two years, playing in navy bands. His exposure at this time to bebop and the playing of Charlie Parker proved a major and lasting influence on Coltrane's music. Coltrane was so awed by Parker's abilities on the alto saxophone that he switched to playing the tenor saxophone, on which he felt he wouldn't be intimidated by the comparison. When Coltrane returned to Philadelphia, he started playing in blues bands, and in 1948 he was hired by Dizzy Gillespie. But Coltrane began drinking heavily and using drugs, and in 1951 he lost his job with the Gillespie band.

The recognition of Coltrane as a major jazz figure dates from his joining the Miles Davis Quintet in 1955, an association that would last, on and off, until 1959. In 1957 Coltrane overcame his drinking and narcotics problem, in the process undergoing a spiritual rebirth. Also in 1957 he began to play with Thelonious Monk and recorded his first album as a leader, *Blue Train*. Other important albums from this period include *Giant Steps* and *Coltrane Jazz*, both from 1959.

Coltrane left Davis in 1959 and thereafter led his own ensemble. The key personnel in Coltrane's definitive quartet of the period, which stayed together from 1961 to 1965, included McCoy Tyner on piano, Elvin Jones on the drums, and Reggie Worhman on bass. Alto saxophonist Eric Dolphy played regularly with the ensemble until his death in 1964. In 1959 Coltrane started playing the soprano saxophone (an instrument that, except for Sidney Bechet, had been rarely used by jazz musicians). He soon recorded his most famous soprano sax solo, "My Favorite Things." Coltrane developed a distinctive soprano style, different from the one he favored on the tenor saxophone. His best-known works of this period include *A Love Supreme* (1964) and the collective free jazz improvisation *As-*

cension (1965). In 1965 Coltrane's band underwent another change. His regular band members included Rashied Ali on drums, Pharoah Sanders as a second tenor saxophone, and on the piano, his second wife, Alice Coltrane. With this ensemble, Coltrane explored free jazz improvisation until his death from cancer.

In the little more than ten years of his active career, Coltrane's music underwent a number of metamorphoses. He first achieved renown as bluesy hard-bop tenor saxophonist. After 1957 he began to develop a new approach in which his solos were filigreed with myriad broken scales and arpeggios played extremely rapidly—this became known as his "sheets of sound" approach. In 1961 Coltrane began to play solos of unprecedented length, often lasting twenty or thirty minutes. If some found these solos to be soporific and self-indulgent, others were mesmerized by their sweep and intensity, and Coltrane acquired a number of avid fans. His best solos in the early 1960s were often gentle and powerfully introspective. By the mid-1960s Coltrane was playing free jazz, where his former lyrical style was often replaced by a harsh and turbulent soloing.

Coltrane, often simply called "Trane," was by far the most popular jazz musician to emerge from the New York City jazz avant-garde of the late 1950s and 1960s. His personal and communicative style, his spiritual quest, and his early death, in addition to the virtuosity and grace of his solos, contributed to a Coltrane "cult" that has not abated in the decades since his passing. His influence on subsequent musicians, which has been immense, includes not only his musical ideas but his taking of extended solos and his view of jazz as an ongoing quest for spiritual knowledge and self-wisdom.

See also Davis, Miles; Gillespie, Dizzy; Jazz; Monk, Thelonious Sphere; Parker, Charlie

■ ■ *Bibliography*

Porter, Lewis. *John Coltrane: His Life and Music*. Ann Arbor.: University of Michigan Press, 1998.

Simpkins, C. O. *Coltrane: A Musical Biography*. New York: Herndon House, 1975.

Taylor, Cecil. "John Coltrane." *Jazz Review* (January 1959): 34.

Thomas, John. *Chasin the Trane: The Music and Mystique of John Coltrane*. Garden City, N.Y.: Doubleday, 1975.

WILLIAM S. COLE (1996)
Updated bibliography

COMBS, SEAN

NOVEMBER 4, 1969

Rapper, producer, songwriter, and entrepreneur Sean Combs was the son of a well-known street hustler who was murdered when Combs was three. Nicknamed "Puffy" for his exaggerated "huffing and puffing" displays of anger as a child, Combs attended Howard University in Washington, D.C., where he became a successful party and concert promoter. He returned to New York after two years and convinced Andre Harrell—then president of Uptown Records—to give him an internship. Combs worked ardently, and within a year Harrell promoted him to vice president of promotion.

At Uptown Combs established himself as a producer for Mary J. Blige and Jodeci. After an argument with Harrell in 1993, he formed his own label—Bad Boy Records. That year he negotiated a $15 million deal with Arista Records that granted him full creative control and distribution. His artists—Lil Kim, Notorious B.I.G., Total, and Mase—sold millions of albums, and his own 1997 album, *No Way Out,* sold over seven million copies. In 1997 he was responsible for nearly 60 percent of the year's hit pop songs.

While Combs is often criticized for his reliance on well-known samples, his musical and business accomplishments are undeniable. He owns two successful restaurants and a clothing line, and publishes *Notorious* magazine. His Daddy's House social program is a nonprofit charity organization that services inner-city children and the homeless. In 2001 Combs changed his stage name from Puff Daddy to P. Diddy.

See also Hip Hop Rap; Recording Industry

■ ■ *Bibliography*

Cable, Andrew. *A Family Affair: The Unauthorized Sean "Puffy" Combs Story.* New York: Ballantine, 1998.

"Sean 'Puffy' Combs." In *Contemporary Black Biography,* vol. 43. Detroit, Mich.: Gale, 2004.

Muhammed, Tariq K. "Hip-Hop Moguls: Beyond the Hype." *Black Enterprise* (December 1999): 79–85.

Ro, Ronin. *Bad Boy: The Influence of Sean "Puffy" Combs on the Music Industry.* New York: Pocket, 2001.

RACHEL ZELLARS (1996)
Updated by publisher 2005

COMEDIANS

In any culture, comedians serve complicated functions as both entertainers and social critics. For African-American comedians, this has been further complicated by the burden of American racism and the historical legacy of racial comedy in this culture. Racially grounded humor has been both a means of denigrating black people—reinforcing their degradation and justifying their oppression by white society—and a repository of folk wisdom, a popular tradition of criticism and self-criticism, and a means by which black people could affirm and enjoy their own view of the world. Black comedians have derived much of their humor from the precarious balance between these two tendencies.

African-American comedy as a professional genre originated with blackface minstrelsy, which remained the province of white performers until around the time of the Civil War. According to Robert Toll (1974), the performance of "alleged Negro songs and dances" in these shows emerged as a popular genre in the 1820s. When all-black troupes such as Callender's Georgia Minstrels were formed after the war, they continued to perform the same kind of material. These early black minstrels, unlike their white rivals, usually did not perform in burnt cork (except for the end men), so that the audience could recognize them as authentic African Americans. As the years passed, however, more and more of these performers reverted to using burnt cork.

The fact that many performers continued to use burnt cork as late as the 1920s and 1930s, supported by a predominantly black clientele, attests to the powerful and paradoxical legacy of the minstrel tradition. Other conventions of minstrelsy persisted in the styles of black comedians as well: for example, the use of ludicrous attire, grotesque facial expressions and body movements, and song-and-dance routines. Favorite minstrel subjects also persisted, such as linguistic maladroitness and misunderstandings, differences in racial behavior, romantic mismatches and misadventures, overindulgence in alcohol and other pleasures, and the common folk's views of current events. Black comedy teams often maintained the basic structure of minstrelsy, generating comic effects from the interaction between a "straight" person (the minstrel "interlocutor") and a foolish companion (the end men, Mr. Tambo and Mr. Bones). As scholars such as Constance Rourke (1931) and Walter Blair (1978) have demonstrated, these subjects and most minstrel conventions derived from old traditions of European comedy. Nevertheless, the racial elaborations of the traditions were distinctly American.

Dewey "Pigmeat" Markham. One of the leading black comedians of the 1920s and 1930s, Markham is best remembered for his routine "Heah Come de Judge," created in 1929. PHOTOGRAPHS AND PRINTS DIVISION, SCHOMBURG CENTER FOR RESEARCH IN BLACK CULTURE, THE NEW YORK PUBLIC LIBRARY, ASTOR, LENOX AND TILDEN FOUNDATIONS.

In the twentieth century, after the collapse of traditional minstrel shows, black performers continued to practice their craft on the TOBA circuit (Theater Owners Booking Association, which controlled tours of black theaters and clubs around the country) and in black musical comedies, such as *Shuffle Along* (1921) and *Hot Chocolates* (1929). Often performing in blackface, these comedians did skits, sang, and danced. The greatest of them was Bert Williams, a magnificent performer whose ability to range from the hilarious to the heartrending eventually made him the first black star of the Ziegfeld Follies.

The establishment of Harlem's Apollo Theater in 1934 was an important event for black performers. It provided a black equivalent of Carnegie Hall or the Grand Ole Opry: a venue where amateurs could gain recognition and where stars could compete for preeminence. In subsequent decades other venues, such as the Roberts Show Club in Chicago, performed a similar function. From the beginning, comedians were a staple at the Apollo. As in smaller clubs and theaters, they performed both as filler between acts and as headliners when they gained sufficient

popularity. One of the most popular acts of the 1930s was Butterbeans and Susie. This husband-and-wife team (Joe and Susie Edwards) specialized in risqué, sexually suggestive humor. Ted Fox (1983), a historian of the Apollo, describes their song "I Want a Hot Dog for My Roll" as typical of their material, which delighted their audiences and outraged censorious middle-class black critics.

Among their contemporaries at the Apollo, Fox lists Dewey "Pigmeat" Markham, Dusty Fletcher, Tim "Kingfish" Moore, and Jimmy Baskette. These men were among the leading comedians of the day. Their routines—again, often in blackface—included skits, songs, and dances, much in the minstrel tradition. Markham is best remembered for his routine "Heah Come de Judge," created in 1929, which was resurrected and popularized by Sammy Davis, Jr., on the television show *Laugh-In* in the 1960s. Markham also claimed to have invented "truckin'," a comic dance that is now best known from Robert Crumb's underground comic strips. No comedy routine of those years was better known or more loved than Dusty Fletcher's "Open the Door, Richard." Playing a bumbling drunk in minstrel attire attempting to enter a house, Fletcher would stagger repeatedly up a stepladder, falling off again and again, as he wailed piteously: "Open the door, Richard!" This line entered the vernacular as a self-sufficient punch line.

Jackie "Moms" Mabley is a crucial transitional figure, both because her popularity spanned from these early days through the 1970s and because stylistically she represented a new form of comedy. Like other early comics, Moms played a character, a "dirty old lady," who dressed in oversize, faded cotton dresses, baggy cotton stockings, large brogans—or, in later years, sneakers—and droopy hats. Her signature line was "An old man can't do nothing for me but show me which way a young man went." But Moms was a stand-up monologist rather than a skit performer. In this, she anticipated the dominant style of later comedians. Her forte remained sexual comedy about the failings of old men and the appeal of young ones, but in the 1960s she turned increasingly to political commentary. For instance, in the early 1960s she composed an "opera," rewriting the words of traditional songs and children's rhymes to praise the Rev. Dr. Martin Luther King, Jr., and satirize segregationists. She sang these songs in her gravelly voice, with a piano accompanist—naturally, a young man.

In the 1950s and 1960s the work of comedians was often disseminated on recordings called "party records." These records usually featured "adult" humor, and they ranged in style from madcap, minstrel-style skits by acts like Skillet and Leroy to the nightclub acts of comedians like George Kirby, Melvin "Slappy" White, and Redd

Jackie "Moms" Mabley. *One of the best loved and most enduring of black comics, Mabley entertained audiences from the 1920s through the 1970s with her witty and mordant observations on life.* PHOTOGRAPHS AND PRINTS DIVISION, SCHOMBURG CENTER FOR RESEARCH IN BLACK CULTURE, THE NEW YORK PUBLIC LIBRARY, ASTOR, LENOX AND TILDEN FOUNDATIONS.

Foxx. All of these performers used sexual humor, with Kirby inclined more toward wit and Foxx more toward raunchiness and profane language. Slappy White, Foxx's partner when the two began performing in the late 1940s, was simultaneously witty and raunchy. All three of these comedians made their reputations on the nightclub circuit and eventually made television appearances. Redd Foxx, the most popular of the group, gained mainstream success in the 1970s as star of the television series *Sanford and Son.* Compared with Foxx's scathing nightclub persona, the mildly naughty Fred Sanford was a pussycat.

A remarkable group of young stand-up comics emerged in the early 1960s, and most of them went on to very successful careers that included work in television and movies: Nipsey Russell, Godfrey Cambridge, Scoey Mitchell, Flip Wilson, and, most important, Dick Gregory, Bill Cosby, and Richard Pryor. Russell, noted for his quick, razor-sharp wit, was very popular in New York City. He soon developed a lucrative career as a headliner in Las Vegas nightclubs and as a regular on the television show *Hollywood Squares.* Cambridge, a very large man, combined gentleness, vulnerability, and moral fervor in his

routines about race relations, obesity, international politics, and contemporary culture. Like Dick Gregory, he was an outspoken supporter of the civil rights movement. Flip Wilson, due to the popularity of his weekly television comedy show in the early 1970s, became, for a time, perhaps the most familiar of all these comedians. On *The Flip Wilson Show,* he played a variety of amusing characters, most memorably a saucy woman named Geraldine.

Nonetheless, Gregory, Cosby, and Pryor are among the most talented and enduringly important of this group. One could hardly imagine three more sharply contrasting comedians: Gregory, the impassioned and blunt-spoken social activist; Cosby, the cool, politely middle-class comedian of family relations; and Pryor, the manic, whimsical, outrageous improviser on every aspect of human and animal life. Collectively, these three represent the finest achievements of modern African-American comedy.

Dick Gregory, more than any other comedian, has used his celebrity as an entertainer to advance social causes. His style employs deadpan understatement and understated exaggeration to great satirical effect. For example, he commented in one of his routines: "I know the South very well. I spent twenty years there one night." Gregory joined the voter-registration marches in Greenwood, Mississippi, in 1963, becoming the first celebrity to participate in that struggle. During the 1960s he was a popular speaker on college campuses and television talk shows. His unique ability to combine social satire and moral fervor with a compassionate humor regarding the foibles of people from all backgrounds made him a compelling, immensely popular comedian. In the 1970s Gregory began to devote most of his energy to research, writing, and consulting on issues of health, nutrition, and obesity.

Though not an activist, Bill Cosby has also made a significant social impact, both through the content of his television shows and through his philanthropy, as a donor of millions of dollars to Spelman and other black colleges. Cosby first gained national fame in the early 1960s as co-star of the television series *I Spy.* His brilliance as a comedian, however, was established by a series of recordings that revealed him to be a versatile, broadly appealing entertainer. Avoiding "blue" humor and political commentary, Cosby's albums focused on childhood, movies, animals, sports, and various whimsies, such as "Why is there air?"

His reminiscences about a childhood friend called Fat Albert eventually developed into a very successful television cartoon series. A significant amount of Cosby's work has been not only about but for children. The ultimate popularity of Fat Albert notwithstanding, however,

Comedian Bill Cosby. AP/WIDE WORLD PHOTOS. REPRODUCED BY PERMISSION.

Cosby's most famous routine of the 1960s was "Noah," a series of exchanges between God and Noah regarding the ark. When Noah, exasperated by animal care and neighbors' ridicule, threatens to dismantle the ark, God asks him: "How long can you tread water?" After a pause, Noah recants with his characteristic, deadpan refrain: "Riiight!" Like Dusty Fletcher's "Open the door, Richard," these lines quickly entered the vernacular.

In the early 1970s Cosby appeared with Sidney Poitier in a series of popular movies, including *Uptown Saturday Night.* Though entertaining, these did nothing to advance Cosby's reputation as a comic. In the 1980s he returned to television with *The Cosby Show,* a series about a physician, his lawyer wife, and their several children. This show was designed to break the stereotype of black families as ghetto-dwelling buffoons with unmarried parents. The backbone of the show, of course, was Cosby's wise and gentle humor, as he dealt with the family's problems and adventures. This was the most successful television show of the decade, gaining top ratings even in South Africa. It brought an unprecedented dignity to blacks in television comedy, and it introduced a new generation to the benevolently mischievous, family-oriented humor of Bill Cosby. Cosby decided to conclude the show in 1992.

Despite the brilliance of Dick Gregory and Bill Cosby, Richard Pryor must be acknowledged as the preeminent African-American comedian of the past two decades. The uniqueness of Pryor's comic genius lies not just with his extraordinary ability to make people laugh but, more important, with the emotional complexity of his humor. Pryor is the most frighteningly confessional of all comedians, and much of his humor derives from his own failed relationships, his personal fears, misfortunes, angers, and addictions. His unprecedented willingness to expose everything, combined with his childlike ability to find wonderment in common things, produces a comedy of breadth and profundity, encompassing emotions from moral horror to sheer exhilaration.

From the beginning of his career in the early 1960s, Pryor had the reputation of being a crazy, unpredictable performer, one who would do or say anything, no matter how profane or taboo. Even then, however, his routines were tempered by moments of poignant self-revelation. Pryor's reputation as America's top stand-up comedian was consolidated in the 1970s and 1980s with the release of several live performances as full-length theatrical films (and subsequently as LP recordings). In these concerts, Pryor demonstrates the full range of his art. He does impersonations of white people, women, dogs, monkeys, and children; he portrays Mudbone, an old black storyteller from the South; and he discusses his misadventures with women, his heart attack, his drug addiction, and even his horrible self-immolation in a freebasing accident.

After this close brush with death Pryor's comedy mellowed somewhat, causing some critics to complain that he had lost his comic edge. Nevertheless, his spellbinding narrative of his addiction, his accident, and his convalescence clearly epitomizes the combination of pain and humor, confession and moral reflection, that has always made him unique. Throughout his career, the conflict between desire and restraint has been central to Pryor's comedy. In his late work, this continues to be the case, except that he has gained a sharper understanding of moral consequences in the failure of restraint. By traditional aesthetic criteria, this discovery of wisdom must be considered a deepening and not a diminution of his art.

Of the African-American comedians to emerge since the 1970s, three are clearly preeminent: Arsenio Hall, Eddie Murphy, and Whoopi Goldberg. Hall, due to his nightly monologues on his popular late-night program, *The Arsenio Hall Show,* became the most familiar of the three as a stand-up comic. Early in his career, Hall toured with popular soul-music bands, including Patti LaBelle's, as a warm-up act. He gained national television exposure as a regular on *Solid Gold,* a popular soul-music show of the late 1970s and early 1980s. Hall's monologues were reminiscent of Johnny Carson's, drawing heavily on current news stories and celebrities. Aside from his television work, Hall received critical accolades for his comic roles in two Eddie Murphy films: *Coming to America* and *Harlem Nights*.

Eddie Murphy created an immediate sensation when he joined the cast of *Saturday Night Live* in the late 1970s. Distinguished by his exceptional talents as a mimic, Murphy created several memorable caricatures for the show, including portrayals of Buckwheat and Stevie Wonder. Several of those performances were compiled on a videocassette, *The Best of Saturday Night Live: Eddie Murphy*. In the 1980s Murphy gained stardom in a series of immensely popular movies, such as *Beverly Hills Cop* and *48 Hours*, that capitalized on his biting repartee and derisive cockiness. He also filmed a pair of live-performance movies, *Eddie Murphy Live* and *Raw*. Murphy's monologues focus primarily on family and sexual relations, but they lack the shifting perspectives and self-critical insight of Pryor's routines. The caustic edge of Murphy's humor has rarely been tempered by compassion.

Whoopi Goldberg incorporates elements of several earlier comedians. Goldberg's stage persona—dreadlocks, athletic shoes, guttural voice—brings to mind Moms Mabley. Like Richard Pryor, she portrays characters facing personal crises with a combination of humor and pathos. Like Dick Gregory, she has incorporated political activism into her career. Goldberg's one-woman show on Broadway in the early 1980s brought her instant acclaim. Her characters, such as a Valley girl who attempts abortion with a coat hanger and a black girl who wears a mop as a wig, yearning for blond hair, were at once funny, poignant, and politically charged. Goldberg's greatest triumph came with her portrayal of Celie in the movie *The Color Purple* (1985), but her first memorable comic role came in *Ghost* (1990), in which she played a phony psychic who suddenly begins to communicate with real ghosts. Though Goldberg brings flashes of brilliance to all her work, she has not consistently played roles commensurate with her talent.

During the 1990s several factors combined to produce a renaissance in comedy. The popularity of comedy clubs began in the major cities and soon spread to smaller cities and towns across the country. At the same time, new shows featuring stand-up comedy proliferated on television, especially on the new cable channels, which soon included a channel devoted entirely to comedy. African-American comedians have been a notable presence in these new venues. *Saturday Night Live* has continued to be an important showcase for emerging stars, such as Chris Rock and Chris Tucker, who have both earned starring roles in several high-profile Hollywood films. Tucker is a singular and zany comic actor whose style of manic, physical comedy harks back to Jerry Lewis. Rock, on the other hand, is a classic, straight-talking, sharp-witted stand-up comedian, reminiscent of Nipsey Russell.

The most significant black comedy show since Flip Wilson's show of the 1970s and Richard Pryor's brilliant but very brief show in 1977—it lasted only four episodes—was *In Living Color,* which began the first of its three seasons in 1990. This show was historically significant for several reasons. Its format, essentially the same as that of Rowan and Martin's *Laugh-In* from the 1960s, was not original. Indeed, the mix of skits, dialogues, and monologues, separated by dance or musical interludes, is the classic form of American comedy shows since the heyday of minstrelsy. But just as *Laugh-In* brought the music, dance, and fashions, the psychedelic colors and shifting shapes, the attitudes, and the aesthetic sensibilities of 1960s youth counterculture to the mass audience, *In Living Color* introduced a mass-market version of hip-hop culture to the television audience.

The show was also significant because the Fox network so conspicuously placed creative control in the hands of Keenan Ivory Wayans, who was host, executive producer, and lead writer for the show. This was a sharp contrast to the public debacle created by NBC executives in their inept handling of Richard Pryor's show. Network censorship became an embarrassingly pervasive theme of the show after its first episode. Whatever the reality behind the scenes may have been, *In Living Color* was presented to the public as a joyful, celebratory family enterprise, featuring the talented and seemingly endless Wayans clan (beginning with three brothers and a sister) along with their madcap, multiethnic posse. The show was a hit with the television audience, and it launched several major comedy careers, most notably those of Keenan Ivory Wayans, Damon Wayans, and Jim Carrey. Perhaps the most celebrated recurring feature on the show was "Men on Film," which sometimes became "Men on Art." It presented Keenan and Damon, in clownish attire and makeup, posed as homosexual critics on a cultural appreciation TV show. Full of outlandish double entendres and signifying glances, these hilarious skits became the show's signature, epitomized by Damon's catchphrase of ultimate approval: "I'll give that two snaps and a circle." This accolade was usually reserved for representations of male beauty, such as Michelangelo's *David*, which often appeared in these skits in all his nude glory, sporting a bow tie.

Regardless of their actual class backgrounds, most of the new comedians of the past decade evince a clear middle-class orientation in their performances. However, the revival of performance venues in black communities has allowed the development of comedians who are derived from and oriented toward a primarily black audience. Cedric the Entertainer and Mo'Nique are good examples. Cedric is a veteran of the black stand-up comedy circuit. He first became familiar to the television audience in a series of Bud Lite commercials. Subsequently, he has starred in several movies, most notably, *Barbershop*. His stage persona is a genial, cheerful, slightly nervous man, self-impressed with his own constant efforts to appear cool, yet always on the brink of becoming merely silly and pompous. Thus far, he has succeeded brilliantly at walking this dangerous tightrope.

Similarly, Mo'Nique has adopted the very risky stance of defining herself as proudly overweight. She defends the dignity and sexiness of "big girls," yet she also derives much of her humor from the common negative attitudes regarding obesity. At a time when obesity is becoming a rampant health problem for all Americans, and especially for black women, Mo'Nique has positioned herself in a worrisome area that is nonetheless ripe for comedy. Of course, embracing the "big girl" identity connects her with a long tradition of blueswomen, from Bessie Smith and Big Momma Thornton to Koko Taylor and Shemekia Copeland. It also resonates with Moms Mobley's persona as an old woman, which Moms began to cultivate long before she was truly old. Mo'Nique has now gained national celebrity as a hostess of the Apollo Theater's televised amateur night shows. She has been well received in this role. Her comic persona reminds us that painful truths can yield robust laughter.

All of these are highly accomplished comedians, yet all of them work within some particular niche of comedy. None of them has been able, in the manner of Richard Pryor, to encompass all the familiar modes of comedy with equal adeptness and to open up, as well, the wholly unexpected. When the *Dave Chappelle Show* began on Comedy Central in 2003, a new young star with exceptional range materialized before a delighted public. Chappelle's topics include race, relationships, identity, politics, and current events, as one might expect of any black comedian. However, he is also as zany and whimsical as Richard Pryor and Robin Williams: a manic, unpredictable, morally probing and satirically incisive comedian. In his first two seasons, his show has been extraordinarily successful, catapulting him to preeminence in the world of comedy. Unfortunately, just as he was set to begin filming, in the spring of 2005, for his third season, Chappelle abruptly disappeared. After many days of mysterious absence, he turned up in South Africa: he had decided to give himself an unplanned sabbatical. Whether he will continue his show and realize the potential of his astonishing talent remains to be seen.

For black comedians who came of age during the civil rights era, there was a sense of imperative to transcend racist stereotypes and to perform even comedy with intelligence and dignity. In this era of resurgent conservatism, comedians face a more complicated set of challenges. If opportunities diminish for black comedians to work, the pressures may increase for them to accept problematic arrangements or to perform in ways that they would not freely choose. Such has been the plight of black performers throughout modern history, and the inevitable tendency of conservative periods is to move backward. The commitment to perform with intelligence and dignity may be displaced by the imperative simply to find work. In any case, the greatest challenge for comedians will always be to create a humor that taps deep emotions and engages experience honestly, provoking a laughter intensified by moral passion and tempered with tears.

See also Apollo Theater; Cambridge, Godfrey MacArthur; Cosby, Bill; Foxx, Redd; Goldberg, Whoopi; Gregory, Dick; Mabley, Jackie "Moms"; Minstrels/Minstrelsy; Murphy, Eddie; Pryor, Richard; Walker, George; Williams, Bert; Wilson, Flip

▪ ▪ *Bibliography*

Blair, Walter, and Hamlin Hill. *America's Humor from Poor Richard to Doonesbury*. New York: Oxford University Press, 1978.

Ellison, Ralph. "Change the Joke and Slip the Yoke." In *Shadow and Act*. New York: Vintage, 1972, pp. 45–59.

Fox, Ted. *Showtime at the Apollo*. New York: Holt, Rinehart and Winston, 1983.

Haskins, Jim. *Richard Pryor: A Man and His Madness*. New York: Beaufort Books, 1984.

Levine, Lawrence. *Black Culture and Black Consciousness*. New York: Oxford University Press, 1977.

Rourke, Constance. *American Humor: A Study of the National Character*. New York: Harcourt, Brace and World, 1931.

Toll, Robert. *Blacking Up*. New York: Oxford University Press, 1974.

Travis, Dempsey. *An Autobiography of Black Jazz*. Chicago: Urban Research Institute, 1983.

Watkins, Mel. *On the Real Side*. New York: Simon and Schuster, 1994.

Williams, John A., and Denise A. Williams. *If I Stop I'll Die: The Comedy and Tragedy of Richard Pryor*. New York: Thunder's Mouth Press, 1993.

DAVID LIONEL SMITH (1996)
Updated by author 2005

COMIC BOOKS

In the early years of comic books, African Americans sometimes appeared as minor characters, usually in the demeaning guise of familiar stereotypes. Not until the 1960s did blacks begin to appear as important figures in mass-circulation comic books. African-American artists and writers, meanwhile, did not gain a significant presence in the comic book industry until the 1970s, and their numbers have remained very small.

In important respects, comic books have always reflected tendencies in other popular genres, including comic strips, radio shows, movies, and television. Thus, the depictions of black Americans in comic books have often reflected established popular cultural norms. In the 1940s, for example, Will Eisner's series *The Spirit* included a black sidekick named Ebony White. Reflecting the transition between traditional racial stereotypes and an incipient realism during that decade of World War II, Eisner drew Ebony with some stereotypical features, such as exaggerated lips, but also portrayed him as a sympathetic character, no more the butt of low humor than *The Spirit*'s other characters.

In the 1960s such television shows as *I Spy* and *Julia* began to incorporate black characters as educated middle-class professionals—for example, as intelligence agents and nurses. Correspondingly, the Spiderman comic book introduced Joe Robertson as city editor at the *Daily Bugle,* the newspaper where Spiderman's alter ego, Peter Parker, worked as a freelance photographer. This trend continued in the 1970s, especially in the Marvel Comics universe. For example, *Silver Surfer* #5 (1969) featured a black scientist named Al B. Harper who used his technical skills and ultimately sacrificed his life to help the Silver Surfer save humanity from extermination by the Stranger, an intergalactic misanthrope.

Marvel also introduced the first major black superhero, the Black Panther, in 1966. The ruler of a fictional African nation called Wakanda, T'Challa, the Black Panther, wore a skintight black costume that invoked his namesake and personal totem. Though he lacked true superpowers, the Panther possessed the enhanced strength, quickness, and agility that his name suggested. Wakanda maintained a combination of traditional culture and advanced technology; reflecting this cosmopolitanism, the Black Panther often traveled to America, becoming involved with superhero groups. He first appeared in *The Fantastic Four* No. 52 and eventually became a regular member of The Avengers. He gained his own series, titled *Jungle Action,* beginning in 1973.

Marvel's first and most successful black title, however, was Luke Cage, Superhero for Hire (1972). In an accident involving a combination of electric shock and immersion in chemicals, Cage acquired impenetrable skin and greatly magnified strength (though not "superhuman" power on the scale of Marvel's the Hulk or DC Comics' Superman). A comic book equivalent of popular "blaxploitation" movie heroes, Cage lived in Harlem and fought various criminals, usually working on a "for hire" basis. Later in the 1970s, as the popularity of martial-arts films began to eclipse blaxploitation, Marvel teamed Luke Cage with a martial-arts superhero, Iron Fist. The Luke Cage series was significant as the first major black feature to be drawn by a black artist, Billy Graham. Graham also drew some issues of the Black Panther series.

Subsequent black characters in Marvel Comics have included Black Goliath, who briefly had his own title; Storm, an African woman who joined the New X-Men, a group of mutant superheroes; and the Falcon, who became the partner of Captain America in the 1970s. There have been fewer black characters in DC comics, and nearly all have been minor figures. These have included John Stewart, who occasionally appeared in Green Lantern, and Mal, a sidekick of the Teen Titans. In the 1970s a special DC collectors' series included a duel between Superman and Muhammad Ali. In the 1980s DC introduced Cloak and Dagger, a pair of symbiotically linked superheroes. Cloak is a black man, Dagger a white woman.

Also worthy of note is *Sabre,* a series produced by Eclipse Publications, a small comics company. Created by Don MacGregor, who wrote the Black Panther series for Marvel, Sabre features a protagonist modeled visually on the rock guitarist Jimi Hendrix. This is not a superhero comic. Rather, it is a philosophical, postnuclear holocaust fiction, somewhat like the Mad Max movies. Sabre's adventures are secondary to his meditations, and, despite his appearance, his blackness has no ethnic content. The series originally appeared in an extended, black-and-white graphic-novel format, drawn by Paul Gulacy, in 1978. Subsequent issues have been in conventional full-color comic format, drawn by Billy Graham.

In the 1980s the proliferation of specialty comic book stores and other economic factors led to fundamental changes in the comics industry. The creation of new outlets undermined the power wielded by the major companies through their control of newsstand space. New comics companies developed, marketing their titles through specialty stores, often to more mature and selective clienteles than traditional comic books had targeted. This created opportunities for people with special genre interests (social realism, fantasy, science fiction, horror, etc.),

Black Superheroes

The names Storm, Black Panther, and Luke Cage may not invoke the same connotations as Superman, Batman, and Spiderman, but that is changing as black superheroes become more prevalent in mainstream comics and take on further starring roles. The first recurring black comic character was Ebony White, created by Will Eisner as a sidekick for Spirit, a crime-fighting detective. Ebony White was a poor taxi driver with overly large lips and exaggerated saucer-like eyes. Black superheroes have come a long way since this stereotypical sidekick.

Possibly the most famous black superhero is The Black Panther, created by Stan Lee and Jack Kirby in 1966 for Marvel Comics. The Black Panther is known as T'Challa, king of the imaginary African nation, Wakanda. He is a scientist as well as a superhero and wears a suit of all black. He first started as an adversary to the Fantastic Four and moved on to eventually become one of The Avengers. In 1973 he finally got his own series. The Black Panther is not a character defined by his skin color, but his adventures often do involve conflict between ancient and modern nations, racial issues, and ecological issues.

Since the emergence of The Black Panther, there have been many other black superheroes and characters in comics. Luke Cage (otherwise known as Power Man) was a street thug until he was framed and went to prison where he volunteered to be experimented on. The experiment left him with super strength and super powers. He showed up in Marvel Comics in 1972 as a "hero for hire." In 1977, DC Comics introduced its first black superhero, Black Lightning. Created by Tony Isabella, Jefferson Pierce (a.k.a. Black Lightning) was an Olympic athlete who returns to his old school to teach and decides to crusade against the school's rampant drug problem.

Other characters include Blade, a vampire hunter. Bishop and Storm, both members of the famed X-Men, Todd McFarlane's Spawn, and Battalion, part of Stormwatch. The Falcon is a street-level crime fighter who eventually teams up with Captain America. Cyborg is a member of the Teen Titans, a child genius named Victor Stone whose parents worked as scientists causing a freak accident and turning him into a cyborg. There are scores of black superheroes, both male and female represented in comics today. Instead of the stereotypical representations of the past, such as a grammatically challenged character used for comic relief, these action heroes are diverse and heroic.

women, ethnic minorities, and others to produce and consume a greater variety of comics than ever before. Even the major companies began to produce graphic novels and other special projects, designed for this new comic book market. In the early 1990s some independently produced black comic books have appeared, such as *Brotherman* by David, Jason and Guy Sims, and *Black Thunder* by Ernest Gibbs, Jr. African Americans currently working for the major companies include the writer Dwayne McDuffie and Marcus McLaurin, an editor at Marvel. These exceptions notwithstanding, black people remain underrepresented in the world of comic books, both as subject matter and as producers.

See also Comic Strips; Popular Culture

■ ■ *Bibliography*

Daniels, Les. Marvel: *Five Fabulous Decades of the World"s Greatest Comics.* New York: Abrams, 1991.

Riley, Rochelle. "The Dictator of Discipline: Superhero Brotherman." *Emerge* (February 1991): 24–26.

DAVID LIONEL SMITH (1996)
Updated by author 2005

COMIC STRIPS

From its very beginnings in 1895, the American comic strip has reflected the nation's rich ethnic mixture, with such features as *The Katzenjammer Kids* (1897–), *Alphonse and Gaston* (1902), *Bringing Up Father* (1911–), and *Abie* the *Agent* (1914–1940) focused on characters of German, French, Irish, and Jewish backgrounds, respectively. The African American, however, generally served as a background character in early comic strips and was consistently portrayed in the mainstream press in the stereotyped minstrel-show style that had become commonplace in the films, cartoons, advertising, and other media of the period. This was true even of the early work of the brilliant creator of *Krazy Kat,* George Herriman (1880–1944), who, it is now widely believed, was of African ancestry.

After the turn of the twentieth century, it became evident that the comic strip had become a permanent part of the newspaper, and many black newspapers encouraged the development of comic strips by black staff artists. These were often only for local consumption, but they were more sensitive to the nuances of black character and life. The best known and longest lived of them was *Bungleton Green* (1920–1963), which appeared in the *Chicago Defender.* The strip was first created by Leslie L. Rogers, and it continued under the hands of Henry Brown from 1929 to 1934, Jay Jackson from 1934 to 1954, and Chester Commodore until its end. Bung, the central character, was an inept opportunist and con man, much in the pattern of such mainstream characters as Mutt and Jeff and Barney Google, and the humor derived from his unsuccessful efforts to make a quick buck by hustling someone. Since his economic woes were not far from the situations of most of the strip's readers, Bung struck a responsive chord in his faithful following, who approved of his spunk, if not his methods. During the 1940s the strip became more of an adventure tale, though it eventually returned to the gag format. From time to time, it dealt in satiric and indirect ways with racial themes.

Other African-American strips to emerge in the wake of *Bungleton Green* in the 1930s were *Sunnyboy Sam* by Wilbert Holloway, *Bucky* by Sammy Milai, and *Susabelle* by Elton Fax, the last two beginning a tradition of features about black children drawn with honesty and humor. Oliver W. "Ollie" Harrington (1912–1995), who has been called one of America's greatest cartoonists, earned prominence and popularity in the black community in the mid-1930s through his candid cartoons about the character Bootsie for the *Amsterdam News,* and in the mid-1940s for the World War II adventure strip about a black aviator, *Jive Gray.* This strip was distributed nationally by the Continental Features Syndicate, which was established by the black entrepreneur Lajoyeaux H. Stanton and was one of the first to handle black features.

In the 1940s and 1950s, Mel Tapley's *Breezy* was about teenagers, Chester Commodore's *The Sparks* satirized middle-class black family life, and Tom Feelings' (1922–

2003) *Tommy Traveler in the World of Negro History* took its young hero back to witness some of the proud achievements of the black past. The panel *Cuties* by Elmer Simms Campbell (1906–1971) began mainstream syndication in 1943, but here, as in his work for *Esquire* and, later, *Playboy,* Campbell specialized in drawing beautiful white women in romantic situations. Most readers never knew he was black. The most important feature to appear at the time was *Torchy Brown* by Jackie Ormes, a distinctively drawn strip about an independent, aggressive, and attractive woman who becomes involved in fighting racism and sexism, among other social problems, in exciting adventure narratives. Torchy was a powerful role model for young black women.

The first African-American strip to achieve mainstream national distribution by a major syndicate was *Wee Pals* by Morrie Turner (b. 1923), in 1964. The California-born Turner had first drawn an all-black strip about children called *Dinky Fellas* (and modeled after *Peanuts*) for two black papers, the *Berkeley Post* and the *Chicago Defender,* in 1963. With the encouragement of Charles Schulz and Dick Gregory, the strip was integrated with children of different races and dispositions (Anglo-American, Asian, Native American, Chicano, and Jewish; intellectual, feminist, militant, etc.). The charm of Turner's style and his gently satiric treatment of racial and political themes made the strip a great success during the years of the civil rights movement, and he turned his characters to educational advantage by using them in children's books, television shows, and campaigns in support of social improvement and racial harmony.

Turner's success in breaking the racial barrier in mainstream syndication was emulated by two more features about children. *Luther* (named after the Reverend Dr. Martin Luther King Jr.) was begun by Brumsic Brandon Jr. (b. 1927) in 1968, with the intent of finding humor in the lives of working-class blacks in the urban ghetto, without gloss or glamour. In addition to Luther, it featured such young characters as Hardcore, Oreo, and the white teacher Miss Backlash. In 1970 the Jamaica-born Ted Shearer (1921–1996) began another racially mixed strip called *Quincy,* which was more sentimental and gentle-natured than *Luther.* Shearer's style was distinctive and the humor engaging, but *Quincy* was like too many other children's strips of the time and seldom reflected the social and economic problems of blacks. Both *Luther* and *Quincy* ended in 1986. Three integrated adventure strips appeared during this period, but none lasted very long: *Dateline Danger* began in 1968, *The Badge Guys* in 1971, and *Friday Foster* in 1972, the last featuring a glamorous black heroine.

After Turner, Brandon, and Shearer had demonstrated a national interest in comic strips about blacks, the syndicates soon began to search out African-American talents and nurture their work. Between 1980 and 1982, Ray Billingsley (b. 1957), a young cartoonist from North Carolina, created a popular feature about a black inner-city family called *Lookin' Fine*. Billingsley found more widespread success in 1988 with the appearance of *Curtis*. This strip also features a typical black family, but Billingsley succeeds in balancing the ethnic humor with generalized situations of family conflict. Occasionally, the strip ventures into controversial areas such as drugs, drinking, smoking, and discrimination (which sometimes generates letters to the newspaper editors from readers upset over the idea of treating such topics in the pages of the "funny papers").

While a young, hardworking black couple are at the center of *Jump Start* by Philadelphia-born Robb Armstrong (Joe is a policeman and Marcy a nurse), this strip, begun in 1988, takes in, through numerous subsidiary characters, an entire urban community. The stresses of their action-oriented careers and the strains of married life are major sources of comedy. In 1989 Stephen Bentley of Los Angeles began *Herb & Jamaal*, featuring two mature and experienced men, former high-school buddies, who have opened an ice cream parlor. The ethnicity of the strip resides less in its humor than in its authentic feel for black, streetwise, inner-city relationships. In 1991 Barbara Brandon, the daughter of Brumsic Brandon Jr., nationally syndicated a feature she had first developed in 1989 called *Where I'm Coming From*. Using an open panel style and talking heads rather than full figures (in order to reverse the traditional emphasis on the female body), Brandon had created a small community of women characters who observe social attitudes, politics, and gender behavior through the prism of their experience as black women in America. The humor is acerbic and often provocative to male readers, but it is nevertheless realistically and sensitively attuned to contemporary social issues. In 2005, Brandon announced that she was retiring the feature.

The provocative nature of Brandon's panel was taken a radical step further in 1999 by Aaron McGruder's brilliant comic strip *Boondocks*. Originating in a 1996 feature for the University of Maryland student newspaper, it addresses the problems of two black children from Chicago who find themselves living with their grandfather in the mainly white suburbs of Woodcrest. The character Huey Freeman adopts the role of the intellectual revolutionary, while Riley aspires to be a "gangsta." However, their diminutive size and lack of any power continually undermine their efforts. While racism more often than not is the topic of the humor, McGruder targets discrimination in all its forms and attitudes both within the black community and the larger white society. The Reverend Jesse Jackson and Black Entertainment Television (BET) are as likely to be ridiculed as U.S. Senator Jesse Helms and President George W. Bush for their hypocrisy and political stupidity. *Boondocks* is the first black strip to compete with Garry Trudeau's *Doonesbury*, which McGruder greatly admires, in its ability to generate controversy, letters of complaint to the editors, and subscription cancellations. McGruder has taken his angry message—that the right is corrupt, the left is naïve, and no one cares enough to make a difference—to animation, film, television, and the lecture platform as well.

A less provocative comic strip begun in 2003 is Darrin Bell's *Candorville*, in which a group of racially diverse, inner-city friends discuss such matters as bigotry, biracialism, poverty, and personal responsibility. Even so, the satire has a sharp and honest edge. It was launched in both English and Spanish versions.

Another sign of an African-American presence in the comics is the number of black characters that have been added to popular features since the 1960s. A selective list of these include Franklin in *Peanuts* by Charles Schulz, Lieutenant Jack Flap in *Beetle Bailey* by Mort Walker, Morrie (after Morrie Turner) in *Family Circus* by Bill Keane, Clyde and Ginny in *Doonesbury* by Garry Trudeau, and Oliver Wendell Jones and Ronald-Ann in *Bloom County* by Berkeley Breathed. While they may appear to be token presences, these are characters who have moved beyond stereotypes and become integrated in the larger community of the world of comic art.

See also *Chicago Defender*; Comic Books; Feelings, Thomas; Gregory, Dick

▪ ▪ *Bibliography*

Hardy, Charles, and Gail F. Stern, eds. *Ethnic Images in the Comics*. Philadelphia: Balch Institute, 1986.

Harvey, Robert C. "Encountering Aaron McGruder." *Comics Journal* 255 (September 2003): 104–115.

Horn, Maurice, ed. *The World Encyclopedia of Comics,* 2d ed. Philadelphia: Chelsea House, 1999.

Inge, M. Thomas, ed. *Dark Laughter: The Satiric Art of Oliver W. Harrington*. Jackson: University Press of Mississippi, 1993.

Stevens, John D. " 'Bungleton Green': Black Comic Strip Ran 43 Years." *Journalism Quarterly* 51, no. 1 (spring 1974): 122–124.

Stromberg, Fredrick. *Black Images in the Comics: A Visual History*. Seattle, Wash.: Fantagraphics Books, 2003.

M. THOMAS INGE (1996)
Updated by author 2005

COMMUNIST PARTY OF THE UNITED STATES

▪▪▪

When the Communist Party of the United States (CPUSA) was founded in 1921, few people realized the critical role it would play in African-American politics and culture. The product of several splinter groups emerging out of the Socialist Party's left wing in 1919, it was founded by people who—like the Socialists before them—viewed the plight of African Americans as inseparable from the class struggle. However, pressure from the newly formed "Third" International (that is, Comintern) and popular support for black nationalist movements within African-American communities compelled the CPUSA to reconsider its approach to the "Negro question." In 1921 V. I. Lenin assailed the American Communist leadership for neglecting the plight of black workers; one year later, Comintern officials insisted that African Americans were a "nationality" oppressed by worldwide imperialist exploitation and called on American Communists to work within Marcus Garvey's Universal Negro Improvement Association. In 1928 the Comintern, with input from Harry Haywood and South African Communist James La Guma, passed a resolution asserting that African Americans in the southern Black Belt counties constituted an oppressed nation and therefore possessed an inherent right of self-determination.

An emerging black left, deeply touched by the Bolshevik revolution as well as by postwar workers' uprisings and racial violence, also shaped the Communist position toward African Americans in the 1920s. The members of the African Blood Brotherhood (ABB), founded in 1918 by Cyril Briggs, eventually joined the CPUSA en masse during the early 1920s. Formed as a secret, underground organization of radical black nationalists, the ABB supported collective working-class action and advocated armed defense against lynching as well as racial equality and self-determination for Africans and peoples of African descent. After being absorbed by the CPUSA, the ABB ceased to exist as an independent entity. In its place the party in 1925 created the American Negro Labor Congress (ANLC), an organization led chiefly by ex-ABB leaders intent on building interracial unity in, and black support for, the labor movement. When the ANLC disintegrated after failing to gain popular support, it was replaced by the League of Struggle for Negro Rights in 1930. This proved to be somewhat more successful because of the popularity of its newspaper, the *Liberator*. Under the editorship of Cyril Briggs, it became a journal of black news tailor-made for the African-American community and a forum for radical black creative writers.

The self-determination slogan may have inspired a few black intellectuals already in the CPUSA, but it was not the key to building black working-class support during the 1930s. However, the party's fight for the concrete economic needs of the unemployed and working poor, its role in organizing sharecroppers in Alabama, its militant opposition to racism, and its vigorous courtroom battles in behalf of African Americans through the International Labor Defense (ILD) attracted a considerable section of America's black working class and intelligentsia. In particular, the ILD's defense of nine young black men falsely accused of raping two white women in Alabama, known as the Scottsboro Case, crystallized black support for the CPUSA in the 1930s.

Black support during this period typified black working-class life and culture, and many rank-and-file Communists were churchgoing Christians who combined the party's politics and ideology with black folk culture. Moreover, in spite of the Communist Party's highly masculine language of class struggle and self-determination, black women played central roles in both the leadership and the rank and file. African-American working women participated in and sometimes led relief demonstrations and marches to free the Scottsboro Boys, resisted evictions, confronted condescending social workers, and fought utilities shutoffs. The American Communist movement produced a significant group of black women leaders during the Great Depression and World War II, including Louise Thompson Patterson, Audley Moore, Bonita Williams, Claudia Jones, Dorothy Burnham, Moranda Smith, and Esther Cooper Jackson.

In 1935, in accordance with the Comintern's Seventh World Congress, the CPUSA called for a Popular Front against fascism, de-emphasized its Marxist ideology, and eventually supported Roosevelt's New Deal coalition. While southern Communists chose to play down race in order to build alliances with southern white liberals, the Popular Front led to more support from African Americans in the urban North. The party gained a larger black following in such places as Harlem and Chicago because of its opposition to Italy's invasion of Ethiopia in 1935, and when African-American radicals were unable to join Haile Selassie's army because of U.S. government restrictions against the enlistment of U.S. citizens in a foreign army, many closed ranks with the left and fought in the Spanish Civil War. Communists were also the primary force behind the National Negro Congress (1935–1946) and the Southern Negro Youth Congress (1937–1949), both of which represented hundreds of black organizations. Finally, during the Popular Front, black Communist labor organizers—among them, Hosea Hudson, Ebb Cox,

Benjamin J. Davis Jr. marching beneath a Communist Party banner in New York City. Davis, a member of the New York City Council from 1943 to 1947, was one of the few persons elected to public office as a member of the Communist Party. PHOTOGRAPHS AND PRINTS DIVISION, SCHOMBURG CENTER FOR RESEARCH IN BLACK CULTURE, THE NEW YORK PUBLIC LIBRARY, ASTOR, LENOX AND TILDEN FOUNDATIONS.

James Hart, and Ferdinand C. Smith—played a critical role in the formation of the Congress of Industrial Organizations (CIO), particularly in the steel, mining, marine transport, and meatpacking industries.

During this period the party attracted a considerable number of black artists, including Paul Robeson and Langston Hughes. Communist cultural critics collected African-American music, began to write jazz criticism, and insisted that black culture was the clearest expression of "American culture." This newfound appreciation of black culture opened up potential space for creative expression within CPUSA circles. Communist papers published poems and short stories by black writers and carried articles and cartoons on black history; CPUSA auxiliaries sponsored plays by black playwrights, art exhibits, benefit jazz concerts, and dances. Nevertheless, many projects were constrained by ideological imperatives or failed because of lack of support. In 1932, for example, the Soviet Union invited a group of twenty-two black artists, including Louise Thompson and Langston Hughes, to make a film about African-American life, but the Soviets soon abandoned the project.

The Nazi-Soviet Pact of 1939, the CPUSA's sudden shift to an extreme antiwar position, the Dies Committee's investigation into "un-American" activities, and the rising anticommunism among CIO leaders weakened the party's base of support on the eve of World War II, but its relationship to black workers and artists remained fairly strong, especially in Harlem. Between 1939 and 1940, for instance, black Communists led a boycott of the film *Gone with the Wind*, initiated a campaign to "End Jim Crow in Sports," collected ten thousand signatures to demand the integration of blacks in major league baseball, organized numerous plays and jazz concerts, and persuaded blues composer W. C. Handy to lecture at the Workers School.

When Communists shifted to a prowar position after Germany invaded Russia in 1941, the African-American leadership, for the most part, adopted an uncompromising stance vis-à-vis the war effort, insisting on a "double victory" against racism at home and fascism abroad. While the CPUSA essentially opposed the "Double V" campaign, arguing that too much black militancy could undermine the war effort, rank-and-file Communists continued to fight on the civil rights front throughout the war, demanding, among other things, the full integration of the armed forces and implementation of the Fair Employment Practices Committee. In spite of these measures, the party's opposition to the Double V slogan left many African Americans feeling that it had abandoned them for the sake of the war.

After the war Communists shifted to the "ultra left." The party again advocated class struggle and it sought to rebuild ties to black working-class communities, a strategy that included resurrecting the self-determination thesis. The Civil Rights Congress, led by Communist William L. Patterson, gained notoriety for its militant defense of African Americans falsely accused of crimes and Communists accused of "un-American" activities, and for its historic petition to the United Nations charging the U.S. government with genocide against African Americans in 1951.

The late 1940s and the early 1950s were an exciting time for black feminist theorizing and activism in the American Communist movement. For example, in 1949 the CPUSA's theoretical journal *Political Affairs* published Claudia Jones' seminal essay, "An End to the Neglect of the Problems of the Negro Woman!" The article strongly criticized "white chauvinism" within the party in particular and black women's marginal place within the left in general. The article also popularized the term "triple oppression"—race, class, and gender oppression—within the party. In 1951 Louise Thompson Patterson, with poet, actor, and progressive activist Beah Richardson, founded the Sojourners for Truth and Justice. This short-lived, all-black women's, progressive civil rights organization sought to give black women an independent voice in the left and in the emerging, postwar black freedom movement.

The left also served as an important cultural and political site where a small but vibrant community of black women artists and writers came together. For example, articles by playwright and journalist Lorraine Hansberry, playwright and novelist Alice Childress, and labor organizer Vicki Garvin appeared in Paul Robeson's *Freedom*, a black progressive newspaper published between 1950 and 1955. Novelist Rosa Guy took part in the progressive Harlem Writers Guild during the McCarthy period. And visual artists Margaret Burroughs and Elizabeth Catlett forged ties with progressives in Chicago, Mexico, and beyond during the 1940s and 1950s.

However, McCarthyite repression and the party's leftward turn in the wake of Secretary Earl Browder's expulsion and William Z. Foster's rise to power weakened the CPUSA considerably. The state arrested Communists for violating the Smith Act—including black leaders such as Henry Winston, Ben J. Davis Jr., Claudia Jones, William

"The Communist Party not only declares its support for social, economic, and political equality—for complete unconditional equality—for the Negroes, but the Communist Party fights for equality for the Negroes."

CLARENCE HATHAWAY
FROM SPEECH ON BLACK SELF
DETERMINATION, REPRINTED IN WILLIAM L.
VAN DEBURG. *modern black nationalism.* NEW
YORK UNIVERSITY PRESS, 1997, P. 61.

L. Patterson, James Jackson Jr., and Pettis Perry. This stifling cold war political climate isolated the CPUSA from politically mainstream African-American protest groups. McCarthyism also contributed to the demise of the Southern Negro Youth Congress, the Civil Rights Congress, and the Sojourners for Truth and Justice. As the state targeted the left, the party experienced its own factional disputes and expulsions. As the country moved right, the party under Foster moved farther left and further into isolation. By 1956 the CPUSA had become a shadow of its former self, never to achieve the status it had enjoyed in the 1930s and 1940s.

During the next three decades, black Communists and ex-Communists such as Jack O'Dell, Mae Mallory, Abner Berry, Audley "Queen Mother" Moore, and Hosea Hudson participated in various civil rights organizations, antiwar movements, labor unions, and black nationalist struggles. As an organization, however, the CPUSA maintained a significant black constituency only in New York City, Detroit, and California—with the latter regarded as a renegade state by the CPUSA Central Committee. While the national leadership attacked black nationalism during the height of the Black Power movement, the California cadre, under the guidance of leaders such as Charlene Mitchell and Dorothy Healey, not only gave support to various nationalist movements but established an all-black youth unit called the Che-Lumumba Club, in defiance of Central Committee directives. The movement to free Angela Davis, the last nationally renowned black Communist of the twentieth century, further strengthened the CPUSA's black support in California.

With the collapse of the Soviet Union in 1991, the CPUSA practically fell apart. Virtually every leading African-American cadre member, including Angela Davis, James Jackson, and Charlene Mitchell, quit the party altogether with the hope of reconstituting a new democratic left-wing movement. The late 1990s, however, saw a resurgence of activity in the Young Communist League (YCL). YCL members took part in graduate student labor, anti-sweat shop, and trade union organizing and in antiglobalization demonstrations. Despite these activities, the American Communist Party remains a marginal force in the U.S. left.

See also African Blood Brotherhood; Briggs, Cyril; Civil Rights Movement, U.S.; National Negro Congress; Politics in the United States

■ ■ *Bibliography*

Allen, James S., and Philip Foner, eds. *American Communism and Black Americans: A Documentary History, 1919–1929.* Philadelphia: Temple University Press, 1987.

Gore, Dayo Folayan. "To Light a Candle in a Gale Wind: Black Women Radicals and Post World War II U.S. Politics." Ph.D. diss., New York University, 2003.

Haywood, Harry. *Black Bolshevik: Autobiography of an Afro-American Communist.* Chicago: Liberator Press, 1978.

Horne, Gerald. *Communist Front? The Civil Rights Congress, 1946–1956.* London and Toronto: Associated University Presses, 1988.

James, Winston. "Dimensions and Main Currents of Caribbean Radicalism in America: Hubert Harrison, the African Blood Brotherhood, and the UNIA." In *Holding Aloft the Banner of Ethiopia: Caribbean Radicalism in Early Twentieth-Century.* London: Verso, 1998.

Kelley, Robin D. G. *Alabama Communists during the Great Depression.* Chapel Hill: University of North Carolina Press, 1990.

Kornweibel, Theodore, Jr. *"Seeing Red": Federal Campaigns against Black Militancy.* Bloomington: Indiana University Press, 1998.

Makalani, Minkah. "For the Liberation of Black People Everywhere: The African Blood Brotherhood, Black Radicalism, and Pan-African Liberation in the New Negro Movement, 1917–1936." Ph.D. diss., University of Illinois, Urbana-Champaign, 2004.

Maxwell, William J. *New Negro, Old Left: African-American Writing and Communism between the Wars.* New York: Columbia University Press, 1999.

McDuffie, Erik S. "Long Journeys: Four Black Women and the Communist Party, USA, 1930–1956." Ph.D. diss., New York University, 2003.

Miller, James, Susan D. Pennybacker, and Eve Rosenhaft. "Mother Ada Wright and the International Campaign to the Free the Scottsboro Boys, 1931–1934." *American Historical Review* 106, 2 (April 2001): 387–430.

Mullen, Bill V. *Popular Fronts: Chicago and African-American Cultural Politics, 1935–1946.* Urbana: University of Illinois, Press, 1999.

Mullen, Bill V., and James Smethhurst. *Left of the Color Line: Race, Radicalism, and Twentieth Century Literature of the United States.* Chapel Hill: University of North Carolina Press, 2003.

Naison, Mark D. *Communists in Harlem during the Depression.* Urbana: University of Illinois Press, 1983.

Shapiro, Linn. "Red Feminism: American Communism and the Women's Rights Tradition, 1919–1956." Ph.D. diss., American University, Washington, D.C., 1996.

Sherwood, Marika. *Claudia Jones: A Life in Exile.* London: Lawrence and Wishart, 1999.

Smethurst, James Edward. *The New Red Negro: The Literary Left and African American Poetry, 1930-1946.* New York: Oxford University Press, 1999.

Solomon, Mark. *The Cry Was Unity: Communists and African Americans, 1917–1936.* Jackson: University of Mississippi Press, 1998.

Weigand, Kate. "Claudia Jones and the Synthesis of Gender, Race, and Class." In *Red Feminism: American Communism and the Making of Women's Liberation.* Baltimore, Md.: Johns Hopkins University Press, 2001.

ROBIN D. G. KELLEY (1996)
ERIK S. MCDUFFIE (1996)
Updated by author 2005

COMMUNITY RADIO

The history of black public radio parallels the history of noncommercial radio, the oldest form of radio broadcasting in the United States. Philip A. Thompsen notes that "noncommercial radio arose from the radio broadcasting pursuits of college students, community groups, political parties, and non profit organizations" (Albarran, p. 133). The first noncommercial station in America, WHA, began as a radio experiment in the physics department of the University of Wisconsin in 1902, according to Thompsen.

BLACK PUBLIC RADIO EARLY HISTORY

Black public radio's early stages evolved on the campuses of the historically black colleges and universities. The missions of the black college stations were to train, educate, and inform, though their primary purpose was to educate students in radio. The radio station functioned as a learning laboratory that students programmed with the oversight of a faculty advisor. A strong commitment to public affairs programming emerged as a means to inform the local community, which was typically politically disenfranchised by commercial mass media. The local black community began to have a voice through the medium of black public radio.

In 1945 the Federal Communications Commission (FCC) designated one-fifth of the FM band from 88.1 and 91.9 megahertz for the exclusive use of noncommercial educational radio. The term *public radio* is sometimes used by listeners and holders of noncommercial educational FM licenses to refer to FM stations operating in this band. In fact, all AM and FM radio service in the United States is public.

Black noncommercial radio began in the early 1960s with WCSU-FM at Central State University in Ohio and KUCA at the University of Central Arkansas. North Carolina has the largest number of black noncommercial stations with seven. In 1967, the Public Broadcasting Act was signed into law by President Lyndon Johnson. The act created a federally funded radio service that would greatly increase public interest programming and relieve commercial broadcasters from FCC-mandated public service obligations. The passage of this law and the subsequent formation of the Corporation for Public Broadcasting opened opportunities for black colleges and universities to secure federal funding and establish noncommercial stations. It was in the early 1970s that black public radio began to flourish. Eighteen black college radio stations began broadcasting during the 1970s as a result of the passage of the Public Broadcasting Act and the federal funds made available through the Corporation for Public Broadcasting. Additionally, the description of "public radio" refers to black college stations with an affiliation to the Corporation of Public Broadcasting and National Public Radio.

CATEGORIES AND FORMATS OF BLACK PUBLIC RADIO

Black public radio consists of two categories: educational and community stations. These stations are primarily owned and operated by black colleges and universities. Within the classification of educational noncommercial stations licensed to the black colleges and universities is another form of radio broadcasting called cable or carrier current stations. These stations broadcast primarily on the college campus by closed-circuit cable connections or carrier currents. Carrier current stations are limited in power and not required to be licensed by the FCC. Carrier current stations are mainly operated by students.

Some historic black colleges and universities have both educational noncommercial and carrier current stations. Clark Atlanta University in Atlanta and Bethune Cookman College in Daytona Beach, Florida, have student-run carrier current stations and FM noncommercial stations. Carrier current stations located on the campuses of Clark Atlanta University, Tennessee State University, Bethune Cookman College, and Howard University are the most influential. Presently there are at least fifty-four terrestrial and carrier current/closed circuit black college

radio stations, with forty-two stations broadcasting over the air regularly.

The general format of most black public radio stations is a mixture of music, news, information, and public affairs. In addition, many of the black colleges have a regular schedule of gospel music aired daily. The most common formats of public radio stations are news, information programs, jazz, and classical music.

SERVING THE COMMUNITY

The majority of black public stations owned and operated by historically black colleges and universities play jazz music. However, some black college stations are changing to include contemporary and other music genres. At Wiley College in Marshall, Texas, the general manager of KBWC states, "The station was only a one-format station (jazz), and the community wanted more of a variety." Accordingly, in recent years the station has offered more of a variety, a mix of gospel, R&B, hip-hop, smooth jazz, blues, reggae, and old school. The inclusion of more music genres helped KBWC cater to the community it serves.

On the other hand some black public stations have extended the ideal of serving the community through more informational programming. Clark Atlanta University station WCLK produces its own public affairs programming for distribution to forty black public stations in urban areas, including Atlanta; Houston, Texas; Baltimore, Maryland; Memphis, Tennessee; Columbia, South Carolina; Richmond, Virginia; and Durham, North Carolina. The primary method of program distribution includes satellite communication, Integrated Services Digital Network (ISDN), and programs recorded on tape and compact disc. One of the most popular public affair programs is *Power Point* produced at Clark Atlanta University.

Recent advances in Internet technology increased black public radio's ability to distribute programming through a new method of program distribution called media on demand. Media on demand enables the listener to download a program on the Internet at any time from a specified content provider. Black public radio since its inception has attempted to provide programming to serve the local community whether it is music or information.

COMMUNITY RADIO STATIONS

Community radio stations by contrast are owned and operated by nonprofit foundations controlled by a local board of directors and operated by mostly volunteers. Black community stations were an outgrowth of a movement pioneered by the Pacifica Foundation in the 1950s.

The primary task of community radio stations is to provide programming that is an alternative to commercial radio stations. The most distinctive feature of the black community station is its commitment to sustain an independent, critical, and oppositional stance.

One of the first black community radio stations was WAFR in Durham, North Carolina, in 1971. The black community station rose as a means to facilitate access to the airwaves for black viewpoints and music typically ignored by commercial stations. Black community radio stations have adapted a wide range of organizational structures and program formats to meet the communication and informational needs of a particular community.

Listener support is the primary funding source for the black community stations. Federal funding through the Corporation for Public Broadcasting is limited because most community radio stations do not meet the minimum transmitting power requirement of 100 watts. In 1974 the National Federation of Community Broadcasters was founded to develop a national organization representing community broadcasters. The federation helped stations obtain their FCC licenses and set up a program exchange to facilitate sharing of programming tapes among stations. To date there are over 125 community radio stations, but of that number only ten are black controlled and operated.

Black-controlled community radio started on the west coast. KPOO in San Francisco was the first black-controlled community station, although it was actually established by white community activists in 1972. Other black-controlled community radio stations were founded by nonprofit foundations such as Pacifica, Radio Free Georgia, and the Students for a Democratic Society. In 1977 in Warren County, North Carolina, a black nonprofit organization called Sound and Print United established WVSP-FM. One of the most successful community radio stations is WPFW in Washington D.C., founded by the Pacifica Foundation and funded by listener support. WPFW is a powerful community radio station with a transmitting power of 50,000-watts and a broadcast coverage radius of over thirty-five miles.

THE NEW ROLE OF BLACK PUBLIC RADIO

Most of this country's broadcast media have been stripped of an authentic sense of place, culture, and experience. In this media environment, black public radio is one of the few trusted sources of information, dialogue, and culture in a rapidly changing international environment. Black public radio provides opportunities for new voices and innovative programming. Producers work independently crafting exceptional documentaries for black public radio, such as Radio Smithsonian Black Radio's *Telling It Like It*

Was. Other program productions, such as Clark Atlanta University's *Power Point* and the *Tavis Smiley Show*, were developed to fill the information void in the black community. Black public radio brought a position of strength by reinvigorating public radio's public vision and extending its core values to minority audiences.

Despite the financial challenges of federal funding cutbacks and dwindling listener support, black public radio stations provide a wide variety of innovative, interesting, and illuminating programs designed especially for the communities it serves, filling the information vacuum created by commercial radio because of dwindling news, cultural, and public affairs programming, as well as the focus on profits.

THE CHALLENGES OF BLACK PUBLIC RADIO

The changing political landscape of the United States also has had an effect on black public radio. Since the passage of the Public Broadcasting Act, the CPB has had to argue its case to every newly elected Congress. The climate for funding black public radio has not fared well. The black colleges and universities that hold a broadcast license are putting less money into the radio stations. Many stations dramatically slashed budgets and adopted alternative fund-raising methods to stay operational. Many of the early community stations, notably WAFR in Durham, North Carolina, are no longer broadcasting because of lack of financial support. Money has been the biggest challenge to black public radio.

Yet with both political and economic challenges black public radio remains resilient, with a focus toward a unified network. The road of a unified consortium is being paved through annual meetings of the African American Public Radio Futures Summit, which started in 1998. This group of some twenty-one powerful black college and community stations has mapped out strategies for the future of African-American public radio. The consortium, headed by radio stations at Clark Atlanta University, Morgan State, Jackson State, North Carolina Central, and Texas Southern universities, urged executives at NPR to bring Tavis Smiley on in order to appeal to African-American listeners. The black college consortium felt that this program was necessary for diversity and to provide information to the African-American community. The consortium of unified black college and universities within the Corporation of Public Broadcasting presented in 2001 a persuasive argument to bring the program to National Public Radio. In addition to program inclusion the consortium focuses on finance, audience research, technology, and development during its annual summit meetings.

On the Horizon

The future for black public radio in the new millennium is very promising. The FCC has conducted several engineering studies regarding interference and concluded that there is available spectrum space for new low-power FM (LPFM) stations. These stations are authorized for non-commercial educational broadcasting only and operate with an effective power of 100 watts or less. LPFM stations are available to noncommercial educational entities and public safety and transportation organizations but are not available to individuals or for commercial operations. Current broadcast licensees with interests in other media (broadcast or newspapers) are not eligible to obtain low-power FM stations. These stations would open the door for more broadcasting opportunities to African-American and other minority communities. The combination of digital technology with traditional broadcasting is helping public radio stations connect with the community better. Several black public radio stations, including WBGO-FM, WEAA-FM, WPFW-FM, and WWOZ-FM have websites and broadcast on the Internet.

In addition, the Corporation for Public Broadcasting is taking the initiative to fill the information void left by commercial radio by awarding public and community stations with grants to enhance listener and community service through the Internet. Black public and community stations are taking advantage of the technology and adding Web broadcasts to their broadcasts, thus making the smallest of stations accessible not only to their communities but to the world.

See also Radio

■■ *Bibliography*

Adams, Michael H. *Introduction to Radio: Production and Programming.* Dubuque, Iowa: Brown & Benchmark, 1995.

Adams, William C. "Marrying the Functions: The Importance of Media Relations in Public Affairs Planning." *Public Relations Quarterly* 40, no. 3 (1995): 7ff.

Albarran, Alan B., and Gregory G. Pitts. *The Radio Broadcasting Industry.* Boston: Allyn and Bacon, 2001.

Barlow, William. *Split Image: African Americans in the Mass Media,* 2nd ed. Washington, D.C.: Howard University Press, 1993.

Bozeman, Barry. "Public-Value Failure: When Efficient Markets May Not Do." *Public Administration Review* 62, no. 2 (2002): 145 ff.

Geller, Henry. "Promoting the Public Interest in the Digital Era." *Federal Communications Law Journal* 55, no. 3 (2003): 515 ff.

Hefner, David. "Changing Frequency: Newly Formatted Black College Radio Stations Work to Jazz Up Their Image, While Serving Campus and Community." *Black Issues in Higher Education,* October 9, 2003. Available from <http://www.blackissues.com/>.

Loomis, Kenneth D. "American Public Broadcasting: Will It Survive Adolescence?." *Journal of Broadcasting & Electronic Media* 45, no. 3 (2001): 522.

MacFarland, David T. *Future Radio Programming Strategies: Cultivating Leadership in the Digital Age,* 2nd ed. Mahwah, N.J.: Lawrence Erlbaum Associates, 1997.

Massey, Kimberly K. *Introduction to Radio: Production and Programming.* Dubuque, Iowa: Brown & Benchmark, 1995.

Sauls, Samuel J. *The Culture of American College Radio.* Ames: Iowa State University Press, 2000.

REGINALD D. MILES (2005)

Condé, Maryse
February 11, 1937

▪┼▪

Born in Guadeloupe, Maryse Condé, novelist and critic, is one of the most well-known twentieth-century Francophone Caribbean writers. Although she started her career writing plays, *Dieu nous l'a donné* (1972) and *Mort d'Oluwemi d'Ajumako* (1973), she is known mainly for her novelistic oeuvre. Her first novel, *Heremakhonon* (1976), the story of a young Guadeloupean woman who travels to West Africa in search of her mythical ancestors, is set against the backdrop of President Sekou Toure's political regime. It already contains most of the themes that would later become landmarks of Condé's fiction: the historical relationship between Africa and its diaspora in *A Season in Rihata* (1981); the relentless quest for identity, love, and freedom by black protagonists throughout the "monde noir" in *Les derniers rois-mages* (1992) and *La colonie du nouveau monde* (1993); the often iconoclastic challenging of black mythical figures and discourses in *La vie scélérate* (1987); the complexity of family ties and genealogical intricacies in *Désirada* (1997). However, it is with a historical saga of precolonial Africa that the French public came to know Condé when the Malian saga of *Segou* became a best-seller in France in 1985. The African continent, where she resided for about twelve years, remained a crucial source of inspiration for her, such as in *Histoire de la femme cannibale* (2003), figuring again a Guadeloupean female protagonist, this time residing in South Africa.

Critics often distinguish between Condé's "African" novels and her more Caribbean-inspired ones, such as *I, Tituba* (1986); *La vie scélérate* (1989); *Traversée de la mangrove* (1989), set entirely in a small community in Guadeloupe; or *Désirada* (1997) and *La belle créole* (2001), where Condé also experiments with the *policier* (detective) genre.

Some of the recurrent themes in Condé's fiction can be related to her own trajectory, particularly her nomadic existence between her native Guadeloupe, to France, where she studied in the 1970s, Africa, and the United States, where she resided and taught until she retired from academia in 2002. In this respect her fictional autobiography, published in 1999 under the title *Le cœur à rire et à pleurer: Contes vrais de mon enfance* (1999), translated as *Tales from the Heart: True Stories from My Childhood* (2001), reads as a meticulous historical and social account of the life of a young woman in colonial Guadeloupe and Paris. This intimate text is a good introduction for the new reader of Condé, since it sheds a personal light on the writer's life, philosophy, and thoughts. A prolific writer, Condé never fails to give a challenging, often provocative or controversial view of the issues and worlds so artistically evoked in her texts. These characteristics of her fiction can be found also in her work as a literary critic and commentator on, among others topics, globalization, postcolonialism, feminism, being Francophone, and the Francophone world. Condé also returned to dramatic writing with plays such as *The Tropical Breeze Hotel* (1988) and *In the Time of the Revolution* (1989), commissioned by the Conseil Général de la Guadeloupe for the commemoration of the French Revolution. Some of her plays have been widely staged. She also wrote several texts for younger readers: *Hugo le terrible* (1991) on the devastating hurricane that hit Guadeloupe in 1989 and *Haïti chérie* (1991) about the difficult life in Haiti and the tragic destiny of a young Haitian girl, who will eventually try to reach the U.S. coast.

Condé received numerous awards and prizes, in the United States (Puterbaugh, Marguerite Yourcenar), the Caribbean (Carbet), Germany (Liberatur), and France (Grand Prix Littéraire de la Femme, Prix de l'Académie Française). Her books, most of which are promptly translated into English by her husband, Richard Philcox, are taught in schools and universities all over the world.

See also Women Writers of the Caribbean and Latin America

■ ■ *Bibliography*

Callaloo 18, no. 3 (1995). Special issue.

Cottenet-Hage, Madeleine, and Lydie Moudileno, eds. *Une nomade inconvenante.* Guadeloupe: Ibis Rouge, 2002.

Pfaff, Françoise. *Entretiens avec Maryse Condé.* Paris: Karthala, 1993.

Pfaff, Françoise. *Conversations with Maryse Condé.* Lincoln: University of Nebraska Press, 1997.

World Literature Today 67 (1993). Special issue.

EXTENSIVE BIBLIOGRAPHY:
Book Review Index. Available from <http://www.lehman.cuny.edu/ile.en.ile/paroles/conde.html>; *Humanities Index; Index de la presse écrite française; The MLA International Bibliography.*

MICHELINE RICE-MAXIMIN (2005)
LYDIE MOUDILENO (2005)

CONE, JAMES H.
AUGUST 5, 1938

Theologian James Hal Cone was born in Fordyce, Arkansas, in 1938 and was raised in Bearden, Arkansas. He received degrees from Philander Smith College (B.A.), Garrett Theological Seminary (B.D.), and Northwestern University (M.A., Ph.D.). His intellectual, emotional, and racial identities developed out of two threads of his childhood experiences. First, the wholesome encouragement and support of the African Methodist Episcopal Church and Bearden's black community reinforced his fundamental sense of self-worth and his Christian convictions. Second, the negative effects of segregation and white racism left him with an intolerance for discrimination.

Born into a family of modest means (his father cut wood), Cone experienced poverty and grew to appreciate the problems of the poor in American society. His father became his decisive role model for what it meant to be a poor, proud African-American man in a predominantly white society.

Cone's theological reflections are products of both the Civil Rights and Black Power movements of the 1950s and 1960s. Although he earned his Ph.D. in 1965 and taught at Philander Smith College and Adrian College, Cone's theological creativity bore fruit with his first book, *Black Theology and Black Power* (1969). This text catapulted Cone, then a little-known college professor, to the prestigious and internationally recognized faculty at Union Theological Seminary in New York.

Black Theology and Black Power was the first scholarly work published on black theology. Cone contended that the 1960s Black Power movement was the revelation of Jesus Christ. Conversely, North American white churches represented the Antichrist and therefore were non-Christian. Similarly, all black churches siding with white Christianity were evil. Basically, religious institutions could find God's presence only in urban rebellions and community organizing among poor black Americans. Only when the poor obtained their full humanity could everyone be free; hence the universal dimension of black theology.

A further systematic treatment of the poor and the Christian faith appeared in Cone's next book, *A Black Theology of Liberation* (1970). This work marked the first attempt to develop a black theology by investigating major church doctrines through the eyes of the African-American poor. It made black religious studies into a systematic theology. In reaction to his overreliance on white religious systems of thought, *The Spirituals and the Blues: An Interpretation* (1972), Cone's third book, indicates black theology's major turn toward religious sources created by the African-American church and community. If black theology was a faith expression of poor African Americans, Cone believed, then such a theology must arise organically from the African-American experience itself.

His fourth text, *God of the Oppressed* (1975), marks Cone's second systematic black theology of liberation, this time based on his personal experiences and black resources.

Cone closed out the 1970s by coediting (with Gayraud Wilmore) *Black Theology: A Documentary History, 1966–1979* (1979). After *My Soul Looks Back* (1982), *For My People* (1984), and *Speaking the Truth* (1986), Cone published *Martin and Malcolm and America* (1991), a pioneering advancement of black theology into mainstream popular discussion.

In 1999, Cone published *Risks of Faith: The Emergence of a Black Theology of Liberation,* tracing the Civil Rights movement from the 1950s to the end of the twentieth century.

See also African Methodist Episcopal Church; Black Power Movement; Civil Rights Movement, U.S.

■ ■ *Bibliography*

Cone, James H. *For My People: Black Theology and the Black Church.* Maryknoll, N.Y.: Orbis Books, 1984.

Cone, James H. *Risks of Faith: The Emergence of a Black Theology of Liberation.* Boston: Houghton Mifflin, 1999.

Hopkins, Dwight N. *Shoes That Fit Our Feet: Sources for a Constructive Black Theology.* Maryknoll, N.Y.: Orbis Books, 1993.

Satya. "Malcolm and Martin: *Still* Teachers of Resistance: The *Satya* Interview with James H. Cone." Available from <http://www.satyamag.com>.

DWIGHT N. HOPKINS (1996)
Updated by publisher 2005

CONGOS OF PANAMA

The Congos of the Republic of Panama inhabit small villages and towns on the Caribbean coast of the isthmus and along the trans-Isthmian highway. While some present-day Congos are actual descendants of *cimarrónes*— Africans who liberated themselves by fleeing to the mountains and rainforests—most are inheritors of the cultural traditions developed by both the *cimarrónes* and enslaved Africans during the colonial period. Once free, the *cimarrónes* established *palenques,* or fortified villages, from which they set out on raiding parties against Spanish settlements and caravans.

During the colonial period, the term *Congo* was used more as a generic term for African, rather than as a definitive term referring to a specific ethnic or religious group. Africans from almost every region of the continent from which people were abducted passed through Panama on their way to forced labor in the gold and silver mines of Peru and other parts of the Americas. Some scholars in Panama, however, believe that a significant number of Africans who remained may have come from the region of the Kongo and Guinea. For the most part, however, the *cimarrónes* became a culturally mixed group, since they consisted of Africans from various ethnic groups who intermarried. They also married other blacks and mulattos who had been born in Panama, as well as indigenous people. The *lingua franca* for both the enslaved and the *cimarrónes* became an Africanized version of Spanish, which the enslavers had difficulty understanding. Recognizing their ability to communicate with each other without their enslaver1s knowledge, they created a jargon that consisted of double meanings, reverse meanings of some words, and some African words and phrases. This "language" was used by the *cimarrónes* and enslaved Africans to plan escapes, develop and manage an elaborate system of espionage, and organize acts of subterfuge.

Very often, the *cimarrónes*—adhering to the adage "my enemy's enemy is my friend"— collaborated with pirates in actions against the Spaniards. After several defeats, the Spaniards were forced to sign truces with the *cimarrónes,* recognizing their freedom and sovereignty over parts of the country. The *cimarrónes* then attempted to live normal lives and raise families in their *palenques.* Some palenques were more successful than others. In some cases, like the village of Palenque, palenques became towns that still exist today in Panama. The legacy of their linguistic subterfuge, however, has infused their history, culture, and customs with layers of idiosyncratic symbolism, paradigms, tropes, and metaphors that can best be described as a living art tradition.

Historians in Panama differ in their accounts of the origins of Congo traditions. At least two popular versions seem credible and can be substantiated by recorded data. The first theory links the present-day Congo celebrations to those held by the *cimarrónes* in commemoration of winning their freedom in the wars against the Spaniards. A second theory suggests that the origins are in the festive dancing and singing performances of enslaved Africans who assumed the role of court jesters, wearing European clothing backwards to entertain the Spaniards during Carnival. These Africans employed double meaning and reversals, however, and were actually mocking the Spanish.

While Congo traditions may have many points of origin, by the nineteenth century they were an integral part of Carnival in Panama. It is difficult to date with any degree of accuracy the beginning of Congo traditions because little attention has been paid to the history and cultural developments of the *cimarrónes*. In addition, many valuable documents were lost over the last three centuries due to the numerous raids of Panama City and Portobelo by pirates, the humid climate of the isthmus, and fires in public buildings. As a result, Congo customs today comprise a "living art tradition" that serves as an innovative way to tell the stories and oral history of the *cimarrónes*.

Congo traditions consist of a complex social structure, unscripted traditional performances with mythological personages, buffoonery, a language, music, dance, the culinary arts, and material culture. These traditions, however, are practiced during the Carnival season and on special occasions. Except for those instances, the Congos are not a separate or distinct ethnic group in Panama. In recent years, Taller Portobelo, an artist cooperative dedicated to preserving Congo culture in the village of Portobelo, has introduced a new Congo tradition in the visual arts.

The five most important characters in Congo society are: the queen, known as *María Merced*; the king, *Juan de Dioso*; *Pajarito* (little bird) who functions as a messenger of the group; the *Diablo Mayor* (the major devil) who represents the Spaniards; and the archangel who is the leader of seven angels, also referred to as *animas* (tortured souls). The king, queen, and *Pajarito* are the only members of the group who wear crowns. New characters have been added over the years as Congos take on new names and personas.

Congo drama is manifested in two very significant ways. First, as impromptu street theater, in which the Congos use the license of Carnival to assert their authority over the land. This is a reminder that their ancestors had dominion over their land. They stop cars and demand a tariff to pass through *Tierra Guinea* (Guinea land). They may demand that the *extranjero* (foreigner) buy them a bottle of beer or contribute food to their communal meal.

Should the *extranjero* refuse or insult them, she or he may be "arrested" and brought to trial, though all in good Carnival humor. The other significant dramatic event takes place on Ash Wednesday, when the *diablos* (the devils) assume the right to whip anyone in the village they wish and attempt to capture the angels. The Congos, who—along with the angels—are the benevolent figures in this drama, chase after the *diablos*, capture them, and then deliver them to the "priest" to be baptized. Finally their leader, the *Diablo Major* is captured, forced to renounce evil, and is baptized. He is then tied up and taken throughout the community to be "sold." Metaphorically, this act recalls the plight of their ancestors who were caught, baptized, and sold into slavery. This event, which also highlights the triumph of good over evil ends the Carnival season. The Congo flag is lowered and the village settles down to forty days of self-denial during Lent.

See also Maroon Societies of the Caribbean; Runaway Slaves in Latin America and the Caribbean

■ ■ *Bibliography*

Barnet, Miguel. *Biografía de un cimarrón.* Barcelona: Ediciones Ariel, 1968.

Bastide, Roger. *Las Américas negras: las civilizaciones africanas en el Nuevo Mundo.* Madrid: Alianza Editorial, 1969.

Dominguez, Rafael Rivera. "Los orígenes tribales del negro colonial panameño." *Hombre y Cultura, la Revista del Centro de Investigaciones Antropológicos de la Universidad de Panamá,* no. 5 (December 1966).

Gage, Thomas. *Thomas Gage's Travels in the New World,* edited by John Eric Sydney Thompson. Norman: University of Oklahoma Press, 1969.

Helms, Mary W. *Ancient Panama: Chiefs in Search of Power.* Austin: University of Texas Press, 1979.

Lipski, John M. *The Speech of the Negros Congos of Panama.* Philadelphia: John Benjamins, 1989.

Martínez, Yolanda. "Documentación Relativa a la Población Negro existen en el A.N.P. siglo XVIII y Mitad del siglo XIX." Thesis, Universidad de Panama, 1973.

Romero, Fernando. "El Rey Bayano y los negros panameōs en los medianos del siglo XVI." *Hombre y Cultura, la Revista del Centro de Investigaciones Antropológicos de la Universidad de Panamá* 3, no. 1 (December 1975).

ARTURO LINDSAY (2005)

CONGRESSIONAL BLACK CAUCUS

▪▪▪

The Congressional Black Caucus was a product of the growth in black political power in the 1960s and 1970s.

The creation of an institutional base for black Americans within the U.S. Congress had been encouraged by the passage of the Civil Rights Act of 1964 and the Voting Rights Act of 1965. In 1969 Rep. Charles Diggs (D-Mich.) formed the Democratic Select Committee (DSC), the precursor of the Congressional Black Caucus, as a means by which the nine black members of the House of Representatives could address their common political concerns. Later that year Diggs and his colleagues played a role in defeating the nomination of Clement Haynesworth to the U.S. Supreme Court, and they investigated the killings of Black Panther Party members in Chicago. They boycotted President Richard Nixon's 1970 State of the Union address and pressured Nixon into meeting with the DSC concerning civil rights, antidrug legislation, welfare reform, and Vietnam.

On June 18, 1971, at its first annual dinner in Washington, D.C., the group was formally organized as the Congressional Black Caucus (CBC), and Diggs became its first chairman. In March 1972 the CBC helped sponsor the National Black Political Convention in Gary, Indiana, but distanced itself from the convention because of it was dominated by militant activist groups. In June of that year, in order to make the 1972 Democratic National Convention more attentive to black concerns, the CBC drafted the Black Declaration of Independence and the Black Bill of Rights. The Black Declaration of Independence demanded that the Democratic Party and its nominee commit themselves to full racial equality. The Black Bill of Rights called for, among other items, a full-employment program, a guaranteed-annual-income system, an end to American military involvement in Vietnam and all African countries, and a setting aside of 15 percent of all government contracts for the use of black businesses. However, the CBC failed to win the official support of the Democratic Party or its nominee, George McGovern, for these demands.

In 1973 Rep. Louis Stokes (D-Ohio) succeeded Diggs as caucus chairman. Stokes worked to get individual CBC members greater seniority and more powerful committee chairs in Congress. Rep. Charles Rangel (D-N.Y.) became the CBC chair in 1974, serving until 1976. Over the next twenty years, Rangel became one of the leading congressional authorities on urban housing and narcotics control. During that same period, the CBC extended its influence both within and outside of Congress. CBC members became chairs of seven out of twenty-seven congressional committees. It developed nationwide networks of black voters and business leaders and "brain trust" networks addressing education, health, the justice system, and foreign affairs. In 1976 it established the Congressional Black Caucus Foundation, which conducts and funds studies relating congressional politics to the concerns of the black community. In 1977 the CBC established TransAfrica, headed by Randall Robinson, which became the major lobbying body in Washington on behalf of the antiapartheid movement in South Africa and of other African policy issues. The CBC was also involved in the successful efforts to pass the 1977 Full Employment Act, the 1982 Martin Luther King Holiday legislation, and the 1986 sanctions against South Africa.

The growth of black political power has expanded the size of the CBC. In 1992 an unprecedented forty African Americans were elected to Congress. This increase in size has tested and transformed the CBC in other ways as well. In 1993 Carol Moseley-Braun (D-Ill.) became the first black senator in fourteen years and one of ten black women in Congress. In 1990 Gary Franks (R-Conn.) became the first black Republican elected to the House of Representatives since 1932. A conservative Republican, Franks has been at odds with the policies of the CBC and has attacked it for its liberal slant and allegiance to the Democratic Party.

There has been a growing ideological diversity within the CBC, its chairs ranging from such centrists as Charles Rangel (D-N.Y.) and Edolphus "Ed" Towns (D-N.Y.) to such left-liberals as Ron Dellums (D-Calif.). In 1993 Kweisi Mfume (D-Md.) became chair and has been active in publicizing the activities of the CBC. He has also been its most controversial chair. In 1993 he advocated the formation of a "sacred covenant" between the CBC and the Nation of Islam with its leader, Louis Farrakhan. The other members of the CBC subsequently renounced this covenant, and Mfume eventually followed the rest of the Black Caucus in doing so.

Although controversial, Mfume helped to make the CBC more aggressive in influencing domestic and foreign policy. When the House of Representatives, without consulting the CBC, moved to give President Bill Clinton the line-item veto (a tool that governors had used in the past to keep civil rights measures out of legislative bills), Mfume led the CBC in blocking the effort. Mfume also helped change President Clinton's policy toward Haiti. His pressure persuaded Clinton to extend more aid to Haitian refugees, place stronger sanctions on Haiti's military government, and consider returning Haiti's democratic government to power by force.

The Congressional Black Caucus has become one of the most influential voting blocks within Congress. While it has been divided on certain issues, such as the 1993 North American Free Trade Agreement (NAFTA), on many other issues, such as health care, welfare reform, and crime, the CBC has emerged as a shrewd and pragmatic advocate for African-American interests.

In 2004 members of the CBC, in conjunction with Africa Action, spearheaded a petition urging the United States to take direct action to put an end to the genocide in Darfur, a region in western Sudan. Many thousands around the country signed the petition.

See also Anti-Apartheid Movement; Black Panther Party for Self-Defense; Dellums, Ron; Diggs, Charles, Jr.; Farrakhan, Louis; Nation of Islam; Rangel, Charles Bernard; Voting Rights Act of 1965

■■ *Bibliography*

Barnet, Marguerite Ross. "The Congressional Black Caucus." In *Congress Against the President: Proceedings of the Academy of Political Science*, edited by Harvey C. Mansfield. New York: Academy of Political Science, 1975.

Clay, William L. *Just Permanent Interests: Black Americans in Congress, 1870–1991*. New York: Amistad Press, 1992.

Ruffin, David C., and Frank Dexter Brown. "Clout on Capitol Hill." *Black Enterprise* 14 (October 1984): 97–104.

DURAHN TAYLOR (1996)
Updated by publisher 2005

CONGRESS OF NATIONAL BLACK CHURCHES, INC.

▮▮▮

The Congress of National Black Churches (CNBC), an interdenominational religious organization, is an umbrella organization of eight major African-American denominations that represents 65,000 churches and over 20 million individuals. Based in Washington, D.C., CNBC was founded in 1978 by Bishop John Hurst Adams of the African Methodist Episcopal Church to establish dialogue within the African-American community across denominational lines and to facilitate collective church action. It unites the following denominations: African Methodist Episcopal; African Methodist Episcopal Zion; Christian Methodist Episcopal; Church of God in Christ; National Baptist Convention of America, Inc.; the National Baptist Convention, USA, Inc.; National Missionary Baptist Convention of America; and Progressive National Baptist Convention, Inc. The board of directors of CNBC is made up of four representatives from each denomination and meets twice a year. A staff of approximately twenty people, headed by an executive director, implements policy and keeps the organization running on a day-to-day basis.

The platform of the CNBC has two goals. First, it strives to provide moral leadership for African Americans, enhance spirituality, and strengthen values. Second, the Congress operates as a social service agency, providing material assistance to meet the needs of the poor and augment the power of the African-American community. It holds seminars and awards fellowships to those interested in the ministry as a career. In the past the Congress initiated an Anti-Drug Campaign to provide assistance and information to community groups that want to rid their neighborhood of drugs, and it discussed the possibility of providing health insurance for larger numbers of African Americans. In 1993, in cooperation with Africare, it raised over $100,000 for the starving people of Somalia. According to Bishop Adams, the vision includes "organizing the institutional power of the black church to address the pragmatic needs of the black community. It is to use power to relieve pain; to use power to enhance possibilities."

One of CNBC's most well-known and successful ventures, which combines both these goals, is Project SPIRIT (Strength, Perseverance, Imagination, Responsibility, Integrity, and Talent). Launched in 1985, SPIRIT has as its central component an after-school tutoring and morale-building program. Other aspects of this project, which is designed to strengthen the black family, are a weekly session for parents on child rearing, and counseling sessions to prepare pastors to deal with family problems. Another major project of CNBC was the creation in 1984 of the Church Insurance Partnership Agency, an alliance between churches and insurance companies, which provides churches with property and liability coverage. More recently CNBC has begun a dialogue about sexuality to examine AIDS, sexually transmitted diseases, homosexuality, male-female relationships, and birth control within the black community. In the early 2000s, CNBC began working on other socially and politically important projects, including partnering with a major telecommunications company to expand access to the Internet and technology to underserved communities.

See also African Methodist Episcopal Church; African Methodist Episcopal Zion Church; Christian Methodist Episcopal Church; National Baptist Convention, U.S.A., Inc.

■■ *Bibliography*

"Economic Salvation." *Black Enterprise* (June 1984): 56.

"Health Debate Rages On." *Black Enterprise* (May 1992): 20.

Poinsett, Alex, and Avery Russell. "Black Churches: Can They Strengthen the Black Family?" *American Visions* (October 1988): 9–10.

Visions: The Congress of National Black Churches, Inc. (newsletter) 3, no. 1 (spring 1993).

PREMILLA NADASEN (1996)
Updated by publisher 2005

CONGRESS OF RACIAL EQUALITY (CORE)

With a political and ideological legacy that spans the decades from interracial nonviolent direct action in the 1940s and 1950s, militant black nationalist separatism in the late 1960s, and black capitalism in the 1970s, 1980s, and 1990s, the Congress of Racial Equality (CORE) is one of the most important civil rights organizations in the history of the United States. It was founded in Chicago in 1942 as the Committee of Racial Equality (the name was changed to the present one in 1943) by a group of ten white and five black student activists who were influenced by the Christian Youth Movement, rising industrial unionism, and the antiracist political activism of black and white communists in the 1930s. The founders of CORE were staunch believers in pacifism. Many of them were members of the Chicago chapter of the Fellowship of Reconciliation (FOR), an interracial and pacifist civil rights organization committed to social change through the transformation of racist attitudes, led by A. J. Muste (1885–1967). Deeply influenced by the strategies of social change championed by Indian activist Mahatma Gandhi as described in Krishnalal Shridharani's *War Without Violence* (1939), "CORE founders believed that through interracial organizing and nonviolent direct action they could attack racism at its core."

CORE was an informal, decentralized organization. Members drafted a "Statement of Purpose" and "CORE Action Discipline," both of which served as a constitution for the organization and proclaimed the members' commitment to working for social change through nonviolent direct action in a democratic, nonhierarchical organization. Guidelines for new members demanded familiarity with Gandhian ideas and active participation in the organization. Voluntary contributions from the members served as the organization's only source of funding. The leadership of CORE was shared by George Houser, a white student at the University of Chicago, and James Farmer, a black Methodist student activist. James Robinson, a white Catholic pacifist, and Bernice Fisher, a white divinity student at the University of Chicago, also provided inspirational and organizational leadership.

In their first year, CORE activists organized sit-ins and other protests against segregation in public accommodations, but white recalcitrance and a weak membership base left them with few victories. In 1942, at a planning conference to discuss organizational growth, CORE activists declared their commitment to expanding nationally by forming alliances with local interracial groups working to defeat racism through nonviolent direct action. Farmer argued that CORE would not grow as a mass-based activist organization unless it severed its ties to FOR and disassociated itself from the organization's pacifism. Under the rubric of FOR's Department of Race Relations, he and Bayard Rustin (1910–1987), a black FOR field secretary, traveled around the country and met with activists sympathetic to Gandhian ideology and fostered interest in forming CORE chapters among those present at FOR events.

As a result of their efforts, CORE had seven affiliates by the end of 1942. Most chapters were located in the Midwest; they contained fifteen to thirty members, who were usually middle-class college students and were predominantly white. Local groups retained primary membership affiliation and control over local funds. As a result, chapter activities varied widely and were not centrally coordinated. Chapters where pacifists dominated focused almost entirely on educating and converting racists, rather than on direct action. The repressive atmosphere of the South in the 1940s severely curtailed the activity of CORE's few southern affiliates. New York, Chicago, and Detroit were the most active and militant chapters, conducting training workshops in nonviolent direct action for volunteers in selected northern cities. They also organized sit-ins—a tactic pioneered by CORE activists—and picket lines at segregated restaurants, swimming pools, movie theaters, and department stores.

CORE had some success in integrating public accommodations and recreational areas, but it was clear to CORE's founders that to mount a sustained assault on racism they would have to create a stronger national structure. In 1943 Farmer was elected the first chairman of CORE, and Bernice Fisher was elected secretary-treasurer. By 1946, due to both the reluctance of local chapters to relinquish their independence or share their funds and to the infrequency of national planning meetings, CORE faced an organizational crisis. After much debate, CORE revamped its national structure: Farmer resigned and George Houser occupied the newly created leadership position of executive secretary. Houser played a central role in defining the ideology of CORE as editor of the CORElator, the organizational newsletter, and author of almost

CORE-sponsored protest. Demonstrators picket outside a Woolworth store in Harlem, protesting discrimination practices at Woolworth's lunch counters there and in Greensboro, Charlotte, and Durham, North Carolina. © BETTMANN/CORBIS. REPRODUCED BY PERMISSION.

all CORE literature. He focused CORE's organizational energy and limited resources on a closer coordination of local activities among its thirteen affiliates, with the ultimate goal of building a mass movement.

The culmination of Houser's efforts was CORE's first nationally coordinated action, the Journey of Reconciliation—a two-week trip into the Upper South to test the 1946 Morgan decision by the U.S. Supreme Court, which outlawed segregation in interstate travel. In April of 1947, sixteen men—eight white and eight black—traveled by bus through the region challenging segregated seating arrangements that relegated blacks to the back of the bus. The protesters were confronted by some violence and overt hostility, but in general they were faced with apathy from most whites, who were unaware of the Morgan decision. In many instances, black passengers on the bus followed suit when they saw racial mores being successfully challenged. The arrest of four of the protesters in Chapel

Hill, North Carolina—with three of them, Bayard Rustin, Igal Roodenko, and Joe Felmet, forced to serve thirty days on a chain gang—catapulted CORE and the Journey of Reconciliation to national attention.

In 1947, CORE took further steps to strengthen its organizational structure by creating an office of field secretaries to travel around the country to organize new CORE chapters. Two year later CORE's leadership created the National Council—a policymaking body with one representative from each local chapter—to improve communication between the local and the national chapters. In 1951, CORE hired James Robinson to coordinate fund-raising efforts. Despite these efforts, the early 1950s marked another period of organizational decline for CORE, as the number of affiliated chapters dropped from a high of twenty at the end of the 1940s and fluctuated around eleven during the early 1950s.

Weakened by continuing debates over the role of pacifism and the national organizational structure, CORE's growth was further stunted by anticommunism. Although CORE's executive committee had drafted a "Statement on Communism" in 1948, saying that it would not work with communists, CORE's civil rights activities were attacked as "subversive" and "un-American" in the hostile racial climate of the 1950s. At this organizational nadir, Houser resigned and the national structure was once again reorganized to divide his duties among three people: Billie Ames, a white activist from CORE's St. Louis chapter, became group coordinator and took charge of organizational correspondence; James Peck, a white Journey of Reconciliation veteran, was in charge of editing the CORE-lator; and James Robinson continued to serve as treasurer. Wallace Nelson, who had held the salaried position of field secretary, was replaced by four volunteers.

CORE found a renewed sense of purpose in the mid-1950s. In 1954, the *Brown v. Board of Education of Topeka, Kansas* decision declared separate but equal educational facilities unconstitutional. One year later, the Montgomery bus boycott mobilized thousands of African Americans to challenge segregated buses. CORE activists—as pioneers of the strategy of nonviolent direct action—provided philosophical resources to the boycott and dispatched LeRoy Carter, a black field-secretary, to Montgomery to provide support. Electrified by rising black protest, CORE decided to channel the majority of the organization's energy into expanding into the South.

To facilitate this expansion, there was a revival of the national staff. In 1957, James Robinson, whose tireless fund-raising efforts had boosted organizational finances, was appointed executive secretary. He worked closely with the National Action Committee, comprising influential members based in New York who made policy decisions. CORE created a staff position for a public relations coordinator, who was in charge of promoting CORE as a major civil rights organization alongside the NAACP and the Southern Christian Leadership Conference (SCLC), which was founded after the Montgomery bus boycott. In addition, the CORE-lator was transformed from an organizational organ into an informative news magazine that reported on the social movements emerging in the South.

Most importantly, CORE directly confronted its relationship to the black community for the first time. Although its predominantly white leadership structure remained firmly in place, African Americans such as James McCain, who was appointed field secretary in 1957, were sought out for prominent and visible positions. Publicity for CORE was also sought in the black press. Nonetheless, CORE's ideological commitment to interracialism continued to be unwavering. McCain, for example, worked closely with James Carey, a white field secretary, to demonstrate the viability of interracial organizing to potential new affiliates. However, the fundamental nature of the organization had begun to change. Interracialism—which had been defined since CORE's inception as racial diversity within chapters—was redefined on a regional level. To reflect the probability of minimal white support for CORE in the South, as well as the continued inability of majority white chapters on the West Coast to secure a black membership base, the interracial requirement for chapters was removed from the constitution. In addition, although CORE retained its base among white and black middle-class college students, its class and age composition was radically altered as many younger and poorer African Americans, with few ideological links to pacifism, joined its ranks.

By 1960 the number of CORE chapters had risen to twenty-four, with new chapters springing up in Virginia, Tennessee, South Carolina, Florida, and Kentucky. With a stable national structure, growing income, new constituencies, and increased visibility, CORE finally seemed poised to join the ranks of the major civil rights organizations. In February 1960, when four college students sat in at a lunch counter in Greensboro, North Carolina to protest segregation and ignited a wave of student protest that spread throughout the South, CORE activists scrambled to provide guidance. In Florida, CORE members pioneered the "jail-in" technique when five members chose to serve out their sentences rather than pay bail after being arrested for sitting in at a department store counter. One year later, CORE activists organized another "jail-in" in Rock Hill, South Carolina. This time, they received national attention, helping to galvanize the black community and setting a precedent of "jail–no bail" that became an important direct action strategy in the civil rights movement. In the North, affiliates started sympathy demonstrations for the student demonstrators and called for nationwide boycotts to attempt to place economic pressure on national chains to desegregate their facilities.

In May 1961, CORE mounted its most militant challenge to segregation: the Freedom Rides. Modeled on the earlier Journey of Reconciliation, the Freedom Rides were protests against segregated interstate buses and terminals in the South. Seven white and six black activists, including James Farmer (who had been appointed CORE executive director earlier that year), participated in the Freedom Rides. After successfully challenging segregation in Virginia and North Carolina, the Freedom Riders faced harassment, intimidation, and violence from racist southern whites in the Deep South. Two riders were attacked in Rock Hill, South Carolina; two were arrested in Winnesboro, South Carolina; and in a violent climax, riders were beaten and their bus bombed by a white mob near Birmingham, Alabama. After this event, which was recorded by the press for a shocked nation to see, CORE terminated the rides. Activists from the Student Nonviolent Coordinating Committee (SNCC) resumed the Freedom Rides in Mississippi, unleashing a white backlash so virulent that the Kennedy administration was forced to intervene with federal protection. Though SNCC activists—with some resentment on the part of CORE officials—took the leadership of the protest and received most of the credit for the remaining Freedom Rides, CORE continued to provide guidance to the freedom riders and stationed field secretaries in key southern cities to assist riders. Many CORE activists, including Farmer, rejoined the rides when SNCC continued them. The freedom riders finally triumphed in September 1961 when the Interstate Commerce Commission issued an order prohibiting segregated facilities in interstate travel.

The Freedom Rides placed CORE in the vanguard of the civil rights movement. As a result of the national attention that the rides had generated, James Farmer joined SNCC's John Lewis and the Reverend Dr. Martin Luther King Jr. of the Southern Christian Leadership Conference (SCLC) as national spokespersons for the civil rights movement. By the end of 1961, CORE—with fifty-three affiliated chapters, rising income, and increased visibility—was able to mount new activities. CORE was an active participant in the wave of direct action protest that swept through the South in 1962 and 1963. In 1962, CORE worked closely with the local NAACP to launch the Freedom Highways project designed to desegregate Howard Johnson hotels along North Carolina highways. Faced with retaliatory white violence, and locked into increasingly contentious competition with the other civil rights organizations, CORE broadened the scope of its activities. In 1962, CORE joined the Voter Education Project (VEP) initiated by President John F. Kennedy and mounted vigorous voter registration campaigns in Louisiana, Florida, Mississippi, and South Carolina.

CORE activists played a pivotal role in many of the leading events of the civil rights movement. In 1963, CORE joined the NAACP, SCLC, and SNCC in sponsoring the March on Washington. As a part of the Council of Federated Organizations (COFO), a statewide coalition of civil rights organizations engaged in voter registration, CORE played a crucial role in the Freedom Summer in 1964 in Mississippi. James Chaney and Michael Schwerner, two of three civil rights workers killed in June 1964 by racist whites in the infamous case that focused national attention on the South, were members of CORE.

By 1963, CORE activities—severely curtailed by arrests and racial violence—shifted from the South to the

Jackie Robinson marches with CORE executive director James Farmer in San Francisco, July 12, 1964. Former major league baseball star Robinson, center right, confers with James Farmer of the Congress of Racial Equality (CORE) as the two prepare to lead a massive parade during the peak years of the civil rights movement. The previous month, two members of CORE were among three civil rights workers killed in the infamous "Freedom summer" murders in Mississippi. © BETTMANN/CORBIS

North. Two thirds of CORE's sixty-eight chapters were in the North and West, concentrated mainly in California and New York. In the North, CORE chapters directly confronted discrimination and segregation in housing and employment, using tactics such as picketing and the boycott. As they began to address some of the problems of economically disadvantaged African Americans in the North—including unemployment, housing discrimination, and police brutality—they began to attract more working-class African-American members. To strengthen their image as a black-protest organization, leadership of northern chapters was almost always black, and CORE chapters moved their headquarters into the black community. As member composition changed and CORE acquired a more militant image, CORE's deeply held ideological beliefs and tactics of social change were increasingly challenged by black working-class members. These members were willing to engage in more confrontational tactics, such as resisting arrest, obstructing traffic, all night sit-ins, and other forms of militant civil disobedience. Drawing on different ideological traditions, they viewed nonviolence as a tactic to be abandoned when no longer expedient—not as a deeply held philosophical belief. They often identified with Malcolm X, who preached racial

Roy Innis poses with presidential candidate George W. Bush at CORE fundraiser in New York City, June 26, 2000. Born in St. Croix, U.S. Virgin Islands, Innis joined the Harlem chapter of the Congress of Racial Equality (CORE) in 1963, and was elected National Chairman of the organization in 1968. © CINIGLIO LORENZO/CORBIS SYGMA

pride and black separatism, rather than with Gandhian notions of a beloved community.

By 1964 the integrationist, southern-based civil rights coalition was splintering, and consensus over tactics and strategy within CORE was destroyed. Vigorous debates emerged within CORE about the roles of whites (by 1964, less than 50 percent of the membership) in the organization. Infused with heightened black pride and nationalism, angered by the paternalism of some white members, and believing that black people should lead in the liberation of the black community, many black CORE members pushed for the diminution of the role of whites within the organization; an increasingly vocal minority called for the expulsion of whites.

As CORE struggled for organizational and programmatic direction, old tensions between rank and file members of the national leadership resurfaced as local chapters, operating almost autonomously, turned to grass-roots activism in poor black communities. In the South, CORE activities centered on building self-supporting community

organizations to meet the needs of local communities. Activists organized projects that ranged from job discrimination protests to voter registration to securing mail delivery for black neighborhoods. In the North, CORE activists continued in the tradition of direct action. They fostered neighborhood organizations with local leadership, started community centers and job placement centers, and organized rent strikes and welfare rights protests.

In 1966 the National CORE convention endorsed the slogan of Black Power. Under the leadership of Farmer and Floyd McKissick—elected in 1963 as CORE national chairman—CORE adopted a national position supporting black self-determination, local control of community institutions, and coalition politics. In 1967 the word "multiracial" was deleted from the constitution, and whites began an exodus from the organization. One year later, Roy Innis, a dynamic and outspoken leader of CORE's Harlem chapter, replaced Farmer, and under the new title of national director took control of the organization. Innis staunchly believed in separatism and black self-determination and argued that blacks were a "nation within a nation." He barred whites from active membership in CORE and centralized decision-making authority to assert control over local chapter activities. By this point, however, CORE was a weakened organization with only a handful of affiliated chapters and dwindling resources.

Innis's economic nationalism and support for black capitalism led to an extremely conservative political stance for CORE on issues ranging from civil rights legislation and foreign policy to gun control and welfare. In 1970 he met with southern whites to promote separate schools as a viable alternative to court-imposed desegregation and busing. In the late 1970s and early 1980s, almost all CORE activities ground to a halt as Innis and CORE came under increasing criticism. In 1976 Farmer severed all ties with CORE in protest of Innis's separatism and his attempt to recruit black Vietnam veterans to fight in Angola's civil war on the side of the South-African-backed National Union for the Total Independence of Angola (UNITA). In 1981, after being accused by the New York State attorney general's office of misusing charitable contributions, Innis agreed to contribute $35,000 to the organization over a three-year period in exchange for not admitting to any irregularities in handling funds. In the early 1980s, former CORE members, led by Farmer, attempted to transform CORE into a multiracial organization, but Innis remained firmly in command. In 1987 Innis supported Bernhard Goetz, a white man who shot black alleged muggers on the subways in New York; and Robert Bork, a conservative Supreme Court nominee. CORE chapters have mounted only sporadic activities in the 1990s, but Innis—at this point, one of the leading black conservatives—has maintained visibility as national director of the organization.

See also *Brown v. Board of Education of Topeka, Kansas*; Farmer, James; Freedom Rides; Freedom Summer; Innis, Roy; McKissick, Floyd B.; National Association for the Advancement of Colored People (NAACP); Rustin, Bayard; Southern Christian Leadership Conference (SCLC); Student Nonviolent Coordinating Committee (SNCC)

■ ■ *Bibliography*

Bell, Inge Powell. *CORE and the Strategy of Nonviolence*. New York: Random House, 1968.

Farmer, James. *Lay Bare the Heart: An Autobiography of the Civil Rights Movement*. New York: Arbor House, 1985.Reprint, Fort Worth: Texas Christian University Press, 1998.

Meier, August, and Elliot Rudwick. *Black Protest in the Sixties*. Chicago: Quadrangle Books, 1970. Reprint, New York: Wiener, 1991.

Meier, August, and Elliot Rudwick. *CORE: A Study in the Civil Rights Movement*. New York: Oxford University Press, 1973.

Peck, James. *Cracking the Color Line: Nonviolent Direct Action Methods of Eliminating Racial Discrimination*. New York: CORE, 1960.

Van Deburg, William. *New Day in Babylon: The Black Power Movement and American Culture, 1965–1975*. Chicago: University of Chicago Press, 1992.

CAROL V. R. GEORGE (1996)
Updated by publisher 2005

CONSTANTINE, LEARIE

SEPTEMBER 21, 1901
JULY 1, 1971

Learie Nicholas Constantine was one of the best all-round cricketers in the world. Born in Diego Martin, Trinidad, Constantine was selected to the Trinidad and Tobago and the West Indies teams in 1922 and 1923, respectively. In 1928 he became the first member of the West Indies team to achieve 1,000 runs and 100 wickets in a season. He played on the West Indies team until he retired in 1940. The first black professional to play cricket for the Nelson team in the Lancashire League (1928–1937), he wrote many books on cricket, including *How to Play Cricket* (1954).

In 1946 Constantine received the M.B.E. (Member of the Order of the British Empire) for his work as a billeting officer in Nelson—where he lived for many years with his wife, Agatha, and daughter Gloria—and as a welfare officer in the British Ministry of Labour in Liverpool. In 1955 he was admitted to the bar in England, but he returned to Trinidad, where in 1956 he became one of the founding members and the first chairman (the highest office) of the People's National Movement led by Dr. Eric Williams. Because of his international reputation he attracted wide support for the party, which won the 1956 general elections. Constantine won the Legislative Council seat for Tunapuna and became the minister of communications, works, and, utilities, responsible for over half of all government expenditures.

In 1962, after Trinidad and Tobago gained independence, Constantine was appointed the first high commissioner to England (1962–1964). That same year he was knighted for his contribution to cricket. In his ambassadorial role he challenged the restrictions the British government placed on West Indian immigration. He also intervened in the Bristol transport strike in which white workers protested the appointment of blacks as bus conductors and drivers.

Constantine was honored many times by being appointed or elected to many prestigious institutions and boards. In 1963 he was given the unprecedented honor, as a junior barrister, of being elected an Honorary Bencher of the Middle Temple, London's prestigious legal association. Between 1966 and 1971 he served on the British Race Relations Board, which investigated cases of racial discrimination in England. He was known for his strong views against racial discrimination in England and South Africa, and he wrote the book *Colour Bar* (1954), an autobiographical work that dealt with racial prejudice in England. In 1967 he was honored by the town of Nelson as a Freeman of the Borough of Nelson. He was also the first black elected as rector—the third-ranking official—of St. Andrew's University in Scotland. At his installation as rector in 1968, he spoke on the theme "Race in the World."

Before his death on July 1, 1971, in London, he was appointed a governor of the British Broadcasting Corporation, for which he served as a broadcaster on many occasions. His capstone honor came in 1969 when he was given life peerage, as the first black man appointed to the House of Lords, as Baron Constantine of Maraval in Trinidad and Tobago and of Nelson in the County Palatine of Lancaster. He was buried in his native country, which posthumously gave him its highest national award, the Trinity Cross.

See also International Relations of the Anglophone Caribbean; Peoples National Movement (PNM); Williams, Eric

▪ ▪ *Bibliography*

Anthony, Michael. *Historical Dictionary of Trinidad and Tobago.* Lanham, Md.: Scarecrow Press, 1997.

Clarke, A. M. *Lord Constantine & Sir Hugh Wooding.* Freeport, Trinidad: HEM, 1982.

Giuseppi, Undine. *A Look at Learie Constantine.* London: Thomas Nelson, 1974.

Howat, Gerald. *Learie Constantine.* London: Allen & Unwin, 1975.

LEARIE B. LUKE (2005)

CONSTITUTION (U.S.), AMENDMENTS TO

See Fifteenth Amendment; Fourteenth Amendment; Thirteenth Amendment

CONYERS, JOHN

MAY 16, 1929

Congressman John Conyers Jr. was born in Detroit to John and Lucille Conyers. He graduated from Wayne State University (B.A., 1957) and Wayne State Law School (J.D., 1958). From December 1958 to May 1961 he served as a legislative assistant to Michigan representative John D. Dingell. During these years, he was also a senior partner in the law firm of Conyers, Bell & Townsend. In October 1961 Conyers was appointed by Gov. John B. Swainson to be a referee for the Workman's Compensation Department. When redistricting created a second black-majority congressional district in Detroit in 1964, Conyers entered the race. Running on a platform of "Equality, Jobs, and Peace," he won his first election by a mere 108 votes and became the second black to serve as congress representative from Michigan (he followed Democrat Charles C. Diggs Jr. from the Thirteenth District, who had been elected in 1954). In subsequent years, Conyers gained reelection by ever increasing margins, winning his fifteenth term, in 1992, with 84 percent of the vote.

In his long tenure as representative of Michigan's First District, and as a founding member of the Congressional Black Caucus (CBC), Conyers has worked to promote social welfare and civil rights causes. Soon after his arrival in Washington, he supported President Lyndon Johnson's Medicare program and the Voting Rights Act (1965). Just four days after the assassination of the Rev. Dr. Martin Luther King Jr. in April 1968, Conyers submitted a bill to create a national holiday on the birthday of the slain civil rights leader. Getting federal approval for the holiday proved to be an arduous task; fifteen years passed before President Ronald Reagan signed the bill into law on November 22, 1983. In the interim, Conyers had convinced a number of mayors and governors throughout the country to declare January 15 a local or state holiday.

While Conyers has advocated independent black political movements, he has avoided aligning himself with black separatists. At the National Black Political Convention held in Gary, Indiana, in March 1972, Conyers was critical of those who advocated forming an independent black political party, saying, "I don't think it is feasible to go outside the two-party system. I don't know how many of us blacks could be elected without white support."

During the 1980s Conyers was often an opponent of the administrations of Ronald Reagan and George Bush. He spoke out against Bush's efforts to keep Haitian refugees from entering the United States in 1992 and opposed the appointment of conservative African American Clarence Thomas to the Supreme Court. While a lifelong Democrat, Conyers was also at times critical of President Jimmy Carter, as he was when Carter dismissed UN ambassador Andrew Young. In fact, relations between Carter—who had also failed to support the King holiday bill—and Conyers grew so strained that the congressman launched a "dump Jimmy Carter for President" campaign on the eve of the 1980 primaries.

Conyers has served as chairman of the Government Operations Committee and has also served on the House Small Business Committee and the Speaker's Task Force on Minority Set-Asides. In 1998, as the ranking Democrat on the Judiciary Committee, Conyers was a vocal opponent of the impeachment of President Bill Clinton.

In 2002 Conyers was reelected to his nineteenth term in Congress. Conyers has spearheaded an effort to correct the voting system that eliminated thousands of African Americans from the voting lists in 2000 and has worked to improve living conditions in Haiti.

See also King, Martin Luther, Jr.; Politics in the United States; Thomas, Clarence; Voting Rights Act of 1965

■ ■ *Bibliography*

Ehrenhalt, Alan, ed. *Politics in America: Members of Congress in Washington and at Home.* Washington, D.C.: Congressional Quarterly, 1984.

"John Conyers, Jr." *Contemporary Black Biography,* Vol. 45. Detroit, Mich: Gale, 2004.

CHRISTINE A. LUNARDINI (1996)
Updated by publisher 2005

COOKE, HOWARD

NOVEMBER 13, 1915

Howard Felix Hanlan Cooke was born in the aptly named town of Goodwill, Saint James Parish, Jamaica, where he began a lifelong dedication to the freedom and welfare of his country. Cooke's commitment reached its peak in 1991, when he was appointed governor-general of Jamaica by Queen Elizabeth II.

Cooke was raised by his parents, David and Mary, in Goodwill, where he played cricket and football as a young man. After both public and private schooling, he attended Mico College in Kingston, where he earned his teaching certificate. After graduation, Cooke remained at Mico as a teacher until 1938. He also married, joined a teachers'

union, and became involved in politics at a time when many Jamaicans were unhappy with British rule. Particularly hard hit by economic woes, the country was rocked by rampant unemployment and rioting. Those favoring change established political parties affiliated with labor unions, and Cooke was a founding member of the People's National Party (PNP), which allied itself with the National Workers Union (the PNP's rival, the Jamaica Labour Party [JLP], was aligned with the Bustamante Industrial Trade Union). The British, who had been in control of the country since 1655, responded to the growing unrest by allowing Jamaicans to hold elections in 1944 under the system of universal adult suffrage. Although the PNP did not gain much of the country's newfound political power, it would wrestle control of the island's government from the JLP in 1955.

Cooke continued teaching while he pursued his political activities, serving as headmaster at Montego Bay Boys' School, Port Antonio Upper School, and Belle Castle All-Age School in the 1950s. In 1958, when Jamaica and its neighboring islands formed the West Indies Federation (WIF), Cooke served as a representative from the parish of Saint James. In 1961, however, Jamaica withdrew from the federation, followed by Trinidad and Tobago. The move triggered action by the British, who granted Jamaica and Trinidad and Tobago their independence. On August 6, 1962 Jamaica became an independent nation within the British Commonwealth. Cooke, as a prominent PNP member, became one of Jamaica's twenty-one newly appointed senators, serving until his election to Parliament in 1967.

As a member of Parliament, Cooke was appointed a minister of government in 1972, when the PNP gained control of the House, the Senate, and the office of prime minister. Over the next eight years Cooke headed the Pension, Labour, and Education ministries, instituting a number of reforms and initiatives and gaining the respect of his people. In 1978 he was named a Commander of the Order of Distinction, and he was given a commendation for distinguished service by the Commonwealth Parliamentary Association in 1980. Cooke served as president of the Senate for two years (1989–1991) and was elected to the executive board of the Commonwealth Parliamentary Association.

After completing his term as president of the Senate, Cooke was appointed by Queen Elizabeth II as Jamaica's governor-general in August 1991. The following year Prime Minister Michael Manley stepped down and another PNP member, Percival James (P. J.) Patterson, was installed as his successor. In 1991 Cooke was knighted by the queen and bestowed with the Grand Cross of Saint Michael and Saint George (GCMG) and the Order of the Nation (ON). He was awarded the Grand Cross of the Royal Victorian Order (GCVO) in 1994.

As a longtime supporter of education and the arts, Cooke has served on the Jamaica Cultural Development Commission, the Saint James Cultural Commission, and various other organizations. He has remained active in religious groups as well, serving as a senior elder and lay pastor of the United Church of Jamaica and the Cayman Islands, and as a lay pastor and chairman of the Cornwall Council of Churches. In addition, Cooke was a member of the Ancient Free and Accepted Order of Masons and received honorary doctorates from Western Carolina University and the University of the West Indies in 2003. In addition, from the 1960s through the 1990s Cooke worked in the insurance industry, holding management positions at Standard Life Insurance Company, Jamaica Mutual Life Assurance Company, and American Life Insurance Company.

See also Bustamante, Alexander; Jamaica Labour Party; Manley, Michael; Patterson, Percival James "P.J."; People's National Party; West Indies Federation

▪▪ *Bibliography*

"Sir Howard Cooke." Ministry of Foreign Affairs and Foreign Trade, Jamaica. Available from <http://www.mfaft.gov.jm/Leaders/GG.htm>.

Stalker, Peter. "Jamaica." In *Oxford A-Z of Countries of the World*. Oxford, U.K.: Oxford University Press, 2004.

Stephens, John D., and Evelyne Huber Stephens. "Jamaica." In *The Oxford Companion to the Politics of the World,* 2d ed., edited by Joel Krieger. Oxford, U.K.: Oxford University Press, 2001.

NELSON RHODES (2005)

COOK, MERCER

MARCH 30, 1903
OCTOBER 4, 1987

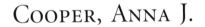

The son of composer Will Marion Cook and singer Abbie Mitchell, educator and ambassador Mercer Cook was born in Washington, D.C., and given the full name of Will Mercer Cook. He received his B.A. from Amherst College in 1925, a diploma from the University of Paris in 1926, and an M.A. and Ph.D. from Brown University in 1931 and 1936. He served as assistant professor at Howard University from 1927 until 1936; he then joined the faculty at

Atlanta University as a professor of French, where he taught for seven years. From 1943 to 1945 Cook was supervisor of English at the University of Haiti in Port-au-Prince, after which he returned to Howard University, where he taught until 1960. During these years he wrote and edited books in English and French, most prominently *Le Noir* (1934), *Portraits americains* (1939), and *Five French Negro Authors* (1943). He also translated Léopold Senghor's *African Socialism* (1959), Mamadou Dia's *The African Nations and World Solidarity* (1961), and Cheikh A. Diop's *The African Origins of Civilization* (1974).

In 1961 President John F. Kennedy appointed Cook ambassador to the Republic of Niger, a position he held for three years. From 1964 to 1966 he was the envoy to Senegal and Gambia. Cook also occupied leadership positions in the American Society for African Culture and the Congress of Cultural Freedom. In 1963 he represented the United States as alternate delegate to the United Nations General Assembly.

Cook returned to Howard University in 1966 to head its department of romance languages. In 1969 he coauthored with Stephen Henderson *The Militant Black Writer in Africa and the United States*. The following year he retired from active teaching. Cook died of pneumonia in Washington, D.C.

▪▪ *Bibliography*

Low, Augustus W., and Virgil A. Cliff, eds. *Encyclopedia of Black America*. New York: McGraw-Hill, 1981.

Rush, Theresa Gunnels. *Black American Writers Past and Present: A Biographical and Bibliographical Dictionary*. Metuchen, N.J.: Scarecrow Press, 1975.

Shockley, Ann Allen. *Living Black American Authors: A Biographical Directory*. New York: R. R. Bowker, 1973.

STEVEN J. LESLIE (1996)

COOPER, ANNA J.

AUGUST 10, 1858
FEBRUARY 27, 1964

Educator and writer Anna Julia Haywood was born a slave in Raleigh, North Carolina. While still a child, she was hired out as a nursemaid and developed a love for books and learning. In 1867 she entered St. Augustine's Normal and Collegiate Institute in Raleigh, where she soon began to tutor and teach other students. While there, she met George A. C. Cooper, a teacher of Greek. The couple married in 1877, but George Cooper died two years later.

In the fall of 1881 Anna Cooper entered Oberlin College. She received a B.A. in 1884 and an M.A. three years later. She taught for a short while at Wilberforce College in Ohio and at St. Augustine's in Raleigh before going to the M Street (now Paul Laurence Dunbar) High School in Washington, D.C., in 1887. In 1902 Cooper became principal of M Street High School.

Cooper believed that African Americans needed to pursue not only industrial training but academic education as well. During her tenure as head of M Street, she successfully expanded college prep courses, attracted academically oriented black students, and increased the proportion of M Street graduates attending Ivy League schools. Cooper's commitment to classical studies for African Americans clashed with Booker T. Washington's philosophies, which dominated black higher education at the time. Her unconventional approach resulted in charges of misconduct and insubordination. Because of the charges leveled against her, the school board decided not to reappoint her as principal in 1906. Cooper then taught for four years at Lincoln University in Missouri before returning to M Street to teach Latin.

At the age of fifty-three, Cooper began doing graduate work. She studied at La Guilde Internationale, Paris (1911–1912), and at Columbia University (1913–1916), working toward her Ph.D., which she received from the Sorbonne in Paris in 1925. Her dissertation, *"L'attitude de la France à l'égard de l'esclavage pendant la revolution"* (translated as "The Attitude of France Toward Slavery During the Revolution") was published in 1925.

Much of the rest of Cooper's career revolved around Frelinghuysen University in Washington, D.C., an institution of adult education offering evening classes in academic, religious, and trade programs. She served as president of Frelinghuysen from 1930 to 1940. Because of financial difficulties, the university lost its charter in 1937, becoming the Frelinghuysen Group of Schools for Colored Working People, and Cooper became its registrar. Cooper continued to be centrally involved with the school, offering her home for classes and meetings, when necessary.

Throughout her career Cooper was a staunch defender of African-American rights and a relentless proponent of education for females. She believed that race and sex were inseparable and that both racism and sexism affected the social status of black women. She also argued that the struggles of all oppressed people were "indissolubly linked" together. In her book *A Voice from the South*, published in 1892, she asserted that African-American women were a distinct political and social force and that they could act as spokespersons for their race and as advocates for women.

Anna Julia Cooper

"Only the BLACK WOMAN can say 'when and where I enter,' in the quiet, undisputed dignity of my womanhood, without violence and without suing, or special patronage, then and there the whole…race enters with me."

A VOICE FROM THE SOUTH (1892). INTRODUCTION BY MARY HELEN WASHINGTON, NEW YORK: OXFORD UNIVERSITY PRESS, IN COLLABORATION WITH THE SCHOMBURG CENTER FOR RESEARCH IN BLACK CULTURE, 1988.

Cooper believed that the key to achieving social equality for women was education, and she fought for women's collective right to higher education. During her early years at St. Augustine, she protested the exclusion of females from courses for ministerial studies and argued that boys and girls should have equal access to education. She believed that education would widen women's horizons and make them less dependent on marriage and love. She was one of the earliest advocates for women's rights and one of the most tenacious supporters of women's suffrage. Cooper was also the only woman elected to the American Negro Academy, was a participant in the 1900 Pan African Conference, and was elected to its executive committee.

Although Cooper never had children of her own, she adopted and raised five great-nieces and nephews. The death in 1939 of her niece and namesake, Annie Cooper Haywood Beckwith, who had lived with her since 1915 when she was six months old, devastated Cooper. Shortly after Beckwith's death in 1939, Cooper's public activity diminished. Nevertheless, she continued to write and work at home. She was a prolific writer, publishing on a wide variety of subjects, such as *Le Pélerinage de Charlemagne* (*Charlemagne's Pilgrimage*) (1925), *Equality of Race and the Democratic Movement* (1945), *The Life and Writings of the Grimké Family* (1951), and essays on "College Extension for Working People" and "Modern Education." Cooper died in her sleep in 1964 at the age of 105.

See also Education in the United States; Washington, Booker T.

■ ■ *Bibliography*

Cooper, Anna J. *A Voice from the South by a Black Woman of the South.* New York: Oxford University Press, 1988.

Gabel, Leona C. *From Slavery to the Sorbonne and Beyond: The Life and Writings of Anna J. Cooper.* Northampton, Mass.: Department of History, Smith College, 1982.

Hutchinson, Louise Daniel. *Anna J. Cooper, A Voice from the South.* Washington, D.C.: Smithsonian Institution Press, 1982.

Johnson, Karen Ann. *Uplifting the Women and the Race: The Lives, Educational Philosophies and Social Activism of Anna Julia Cooper and Nannie Helen Burroughs.* New York: Garland, 2000.

PREMILLA NADASEN (1996)
Updated bibliography

COPPIN, FANNY JACKSON

1837
JANUARY 21, 1913

The educator Frances "Fanny" Jackson Coppin was born a slave in Washington, D.C. When she was approximately twelve years old, her freedom was bought for $125 by her aunt Sarah Orr Clark, who saved the purchase price from her $6-a-month salary. Coppin went to live with another aunt in Newport, Rhode Island, but felt she was a strain on her relative's limited resources. At the age of fourteen, she went to live as a domestic servant with a white couple, using her salary to pay for a private tutor and piano lessons. In 1859 she entered the Rhode Island State Normal School in Bristol. From 1860 to 1865 she attended Oberlin College, where she earned a B.A. and was named class poet at graduation. While at the college, Coppin had sixteen private music students and established an evening adult-education class for freed blacks, which she taught voluntarily four nights a week. The publicity she received for this class prompted Oberlin to name her a student teacher for preparatory classes. She was the first African-American student named to this position.

In 1865 Coppin became principal of the girls' division of the Institute for Colored Youth in Philadelphia (later known as Cheyney State College). The institute had been founded in 1837 by the Society of Friends to counter anti-abolitionist claims that blacks were incapable of acquiring a classical education. In 1869 Coppin was named principal of the entire institute, becoming the first black American female to head an institution of higher learning.

In 1889 the institute opened an industrial department, for which Coppin had vigorously campaigned because she wanted to train black men and women in the technical skills and trades from which they were often excluded by trade unions. In her 1913 autobiography, *Reminiscences of School Life, and Hints on Teaching,* she wrote, "In Philadelphia, the only place at the time where a colored boy could learn a trade, was in the House of Refuge, or the Penitentiary!"

Coppin actively campaigned to earn women the right to vote. She wrote a column for the *Christian Recorder,* the newspaper of the African Methodist Episcopal (AME) Church. After her retirement in 1902, she traveled with her husband, an AME minister, as a missionary to South Africa. Coppin State College in Baltimore is named in her honor.

See also African Methodist Episcopal Church; Education in the United States

■ ■ *Bibliography*

Coppin, Fanny Jackson. *Reminiscences of School Life, and Hints on Teaching.* Philadelphia: AME Books, 1913.

Perkins, Linda M. *Fanny Jackson Coppin and the Institute for Colored Youth, 1865–1902.* New York: Garland, 1987.

JUALYNNE DODSON (1996)

COPPIN, LEVI JENKINS

DECEMBER 24, 1848
JUNE 25, 1924

A native of Fredrickstown, Maryland, Levi Jenkins Coppin spent his childhood in Baltimore and in Wilmington, Delaware. It took Coppin only a short time to rise in the African Methodist Episcopal (AME) Church after receiving his license to preach in 1876. Twelve years later the denomination chose him as editor of its major publication, the *AME Church Review,* a post he held until 1888, when he ran unsuccessfully for the bishopric. He then returned to Philadelphia, where he had previously resided, to serve as pastor of the historic Bethel Church.

Coppin became a bishop in the AME Church in 1900. From 1990 to 1904 he served in South Africa, where he worked to spread the influence of the denomination in that area and in Ethiopia. Coppin, a devoted Mason, also established the Masonic Lodge of Capetown, which had an affiliation with the Philadelphia Jurisdiction of the Prince Hall Masons. After his return to the United States, he served most of his remaining years in the South.

Coppin was a moderately conservative theologian on the issue of race. Although he counseled patience, hard work, and thrift, he did hold membership in social protest groups such as the Afro-American Council and the National Association for the Advancement of Colored People. Coppin is remembered best for the influence he had upon the church as editor of the *Review* and for his work in Africa.

See also African Methodist Episcopal Church

■ ■ *Bibliography*

Coppin, Levi Jenkins. *Observations of Persons and Things in South Africa, 1900–1904*. Part second, chap. 11—letters. Philadelphia: A.M.E. Book Concern, 1905.

Wright, Richard R. *The Bishops of the African Methodist Episcopal Church*. Nashville: A.M.E. Sunday School Union, 1963.

JIMMIE LEWIS FRANKLIN (1996)
Updated bibliography

CORE

See Congress of Racial Equality

CORNISH, SAMUEL E.

1795
NOVEMBER 6, 1858

┣┫┫

Abolitionist and newspaper editor Samuel Eli Cornish was born of free parents in Sussex County, Delaware, and raised in Philadelphia and New York City. He graduated from the Free African School in Philadelphia. Shortly thereafter he began training for the ministry under John Gloucester, pastor of the First African Church, Presbyterian, in Philadelphia. Licensed to preach as a Presbyterian minister in 1819, Cornish spent six months serving as a missionary to slaves on Maryland's Eastern Shore before returning to New York to organize the New Demeter Street Presbyterian Church. He was ordained in 1822 and continued there until 1828. Throughout his life Cornish remained involved in religious activities, working as a preacher and missionary to African Americans in New York, Philadelphia, and Newark, New Jersey; in 1845 or 1846 he organized Emmanuel Church in New York City, remaining as its pastor until 1847.

In addition to his role as a clergyman, Cornish was noted as a journalist. His most significant contribution was the founding of *Freedom's Journal,* the first African-American newspaper in the United States. Cornish began the weekly journal in New York on March 16, 1827, serving as senior editor, with another young African American, John B. Russwurm, holding the position of junior editor. As fathers of the African-American press, the two men stated in their first editorial that "we wish to plead our own cause. Too long others have spoken for us." Under Cornish's control, *Freedom's Journal* became a popular protest vehicle and an instrument for promoting racial pride, as well as an advocate of education and emancipation.

Cornish resigned as editor of the *Journal* in September 1827 and became an agent for the New York Free African schools, but under Russwurm's editorship the paper declined. In 1829 Cornish revived it, changing the name to the *Rights of All,* and sustained publication for one year. Cornish went on to serve in various positions in missionary and benevolent societies. From 1837 to 1839 he served as the sole or joint editor of the *Colored American.* In 1840 Cornish wrote *The Colonization Scheme Considered,* a powerful pamphlet against colonization, which he felt was unjust and failed to provide a solution to the problem of slavery.

In addition to his religious and journalistic efforts, Cornish served antislavery and other reform causes through a number of benevolent organizations. Among his other efforts, he helped found and served as an executive committee member of the American Anti-Slavery Society (1835–1837), was vice president of the American Moral Reform Society (1835–1836), and served on the executive committee of the New York City Vigilance Committee (1835–1837) and the American and Foreign Anti-Slavery Society (1840–1841; 1847–1848). By the 1850s, Cornish, who had been at one time both a founding member of the American Missionary Association and a fervent Garrisonian, grew impatient with anticlericalism and black exclusiveness in antislavery efforts. He remained active in American Missionary Society efforts as a member of the executive committee (1846–1855) and as vice president (1848–1858), but essentially ceased active participation in the abolitionist movement. In poor health in his later years, he moved to Brooklyn in 1855 and died there in 1858.

See also Abolition; *Freedom's Journal*; Religion; Russwurm, John Brown

■ ■ *Bibliography*

Bennett, Lerone, Jr. "Founders of the Black Press." *Ebony,* February 1987, 96–100.

Hutton, Frankie. *The Early Black Press in America, 1827–1860.* Westport, Conn.: Greenwood, 1993.

GREG ROBINSON (1996)

CORTEZ, JAYNE

MAY 10, 1936

■■■

The poet Jayne Cortez was born in Fort Huachuca, Arizona, and she moved with her family to Watts in Los Angeles when she was seven. Jazz was one of her earliest and most significant artistic influences. In 1954 she married the avant-garde saxophonist Ornette Coleman. The two were divorced in 1960, and Cortez soon began to pursue her childhood dream of becoming an actress. She studied drama and attended acting workshops, and it was around this time that she began to write poetry.

In 1963 she met James Forman, the executive secretary of the Student Nonviolent Coordinating Committee (SNCC), who persuaded her to go to Mississippi to help register voters. After spending the summer of 1963 in Greenwood and the summer of 1964 in Jackson, she was, by her own account, transformed: "I saw history being made."

Upon her return to California, Cortez founded the Watts Repertory Theater Company, a writers' and actors' workshop, and she began public readings of her poetry there. In 1967 she moved to New York City, where she founded Bola Press. Two years later she published her first collection of poetry, *Pissstained Stairs and the Monkey Man's Wares* (1969). In 1975 she married the artist Melvin Edwards, and from 1977 to 1983 she served as writer-in-residence at Livingston College of Rutgers University.

African imagery, poetic forms, and language are important facets of Cortez's work, which is collected in the volume *Coagulations: New and Selected Poems* (1984). However, it is music that most permeates Cortez's poetry. She abruptly changes line lengths and frequently repeats words and lines, establishing rhythms evocative of the spectrum of the African-American musical tradition, from the blues to experimental jazz. She often performs with her own jazz band, the Firespitters, which includes her son Denardo Coleman on drums. She has released several CDs of her poetry set to music, including *Borders of Disorderly Time* (2003). This interest in music also pervades her latest collection of poetry, *Jazz Fan Looks Back* (2002), which celebrates such artists as Louis Armstrong and Miles Davis.

In addition to her poetry, Cortez and Ghanian writer Ama Ata Aidoo founded the Organization of Women Writers of Africa, and in 1999 and 2004 she coordinated the "Yari Yari International Conference of Women Writers of African Descent." She also helped to organize "Slave Routes: The Long Memory," an international symposium that took place in New York City in 1999. Cortez continues to be a highly political poet, and she has traveled widely, reading her poetry in North America, Latin America, Africa, Europe, and the Caribbean.

See also Poetry, U.S.

■ ■ *Bibliography*

Bolden, Tony. "All the Birds Sing Bass: The Revolutionary Blues of Jayne Cortez." *African American Review* 35, no. 1 (2001): 61–71.

Brown, Kimberly N. "Of Poststructuralist Fallout, Scarification, and Blood Poems: The Revolutionary Ideology Behind the Poetry of Jayne Cortez." In *Other Sisterhoods: Literary Theory and U.S. Women of Color,* edited by Sandra Kumamoto Stanley. Urbana: University of Illinois Press, 1998.

Melhem, D. H. *Heroism in the New Black Poetry: Introductions and Interviews.* Lexington: University Press of Kentucky, 1990.

Nielson, Aldon Lynn. *Black Chant: The Languages of African American Postmodernism.* New York: Oxford University Press, 1997.

LOUIS J. PARASCANDOLA (1996)
Updated by author 2005

COSBY, BILL

JULY 12, 1937

■■■

Comedian and philanthropist William Henry "Bill" Cosby Jr. was born in Germantown, Pennsylvania, to William and Annie Pearle Cosby. After a stint in the Navy (1956–1960), Cosby studied at Temple University in Philadelphia but dropped out to pursue a career as a stand-up comic.

During the 1960s Cosby worked in network television as a comedian featured on late-night talk shows. In 1965 he became the first African-American network television star in a dramatic series when producers named him to co-star with Robert Culp in *I Spy* (1965–1968). Cosby's character, Alexander Scott, did not usually address his blackness or another character's whiteness. As with other forms of popular entertainment with black characters at the time, Cosby's character was portrayed in a manner in which being black merely meant having slightly darker skin. He won Emmy awards for the role in 1966 and 1967.

From 1969 through 1971 Cosby appeared as Chet Kincaid, a bachelor high school coach, on the situation

Comedian Bill Cosby, 1965. That year, in the series I Spy, *Cosby became the first African American to have a starring role in a television dramatic series. Co-starring with Robert Culp, Cosby won Emmy awards for his portrayal of the character Alexander Scott in 1966 and 1967.* THE LIBRARY OF CONGRESS

comedy series *The Bill Cosby Show.* Cosby portrayed Kincaid as a proud but not militant black man. The series was moderately successful. A few years later, Cosby and CBS joined forces in a television experiment, *Fat Albert and the Cosby Kids* (1972–1977), a cartoon series for children. The series set the course for television in the vital new area of ethics, values, judgment, and personal responsibility. By the end of its three-year run, *Fat Albert* had inspired a number of new directions in children's television.

In 1972 and 1973 Cosby starred in *The New Bill Cosby Show,* a comedy-variety series. Cosby's Jemmin Company, which he had recently established, produced the shows, allowing him to have more control over the productions. As he did in all his television series, Cosby made great use of other black artists who had had few opportunities to practice their craft elsewhere.

For a few months in late 1976, largely because of his success as a regular guest on the PBS educational series *The Electric Company,* where he demonstrated great skill at working with and entertaining youngsters, ABC hired Cosby to host a prime time hour-long variety series oriented toward children, *Cos.* It did not catch on with viewers, however, and was canceled after a few months.

In the fall of 1984 *The Cosby Show* began on NBC, featuring Cosby as Cliff Huxtable, an obstetrician living with his wife and four children in a New York City brownstone. Their fifth child, away at college most of the time, ap-

peared sporadically in featured parts. The show put black images on the screen that many people admired. The characters on *The Cosby Show* represented a real African-American upper-middle-class family, rarely seen on American television. Cosby sought black artists who had not been seen on network television in years for cameo roles (Dizzy Gillespie and Judith Jamison, for example). He also included black writers among his creative staff, and by the third year, he insisted on using a black director for some of the episodes. In its first year, *The Cosby Show* finished third in the ratings; from the second season through the fourth season, it was the number-one-rated show in the United States.

Conscious of the need to lead the networks toward more equitable treatment of African Americans, Cosby used his position to require that more doors be opened. He had a presence in almost every area of television programming: He was a mass volume spokesman and star presenter for advertisements and public relations image campaigns that included Jell-O, Coca-Cola, Delmonte, Kodak, and E. F. Hutton. He appeared in drama, action-adventure stories, comedies, and children's programs. In 1992 he also entered into prime-time syndication with Carsey-Werner Productions with a remake of the old Groucho Marx game series, *You Bet Your Life.* The show lasted only one season. That same year, however, Cosby made public his bid to purchase the National Broadcasting Corporation (NBC-TV), a television network worth $9 billion. Cosby was determined to call attention to the proliferation of negative images of black people and the titillation of viewers with sex and violence. All television viewers, he argued, were diminished by the spate of "drive-by images" that reinforced shallow stereotypes. In 1995 Cosby produced another unsuccessful syndicated series, *The Cosby Mysteries.* In 1996 he began a new hit series, *Cosby,* in which he played a working-class man from Queens, New York.

Throughout his career Cosby appeared at highly popular concert performances across the United States. His comedy focused on his own life as a reflection of universal human needs. He also produced more than twenty comedy/musical record albums, many of which won Grammy awards, including *Bill Cosby Is a Very Funny Fellow* (1963), *I Started Out as a Child* (1964), *Why Is There Air?* (1965), *Wonderfulness* (1966), *Revenge* (1967), *To Russell, My Brother, Whom I Slept With* (1968), *Bill Cosby* (1969), *Bill Cosby Talks to Children About Drugs* (1971), and *Children, You'll Understand* (1986). Cosby has written many best-selling books, including *The Wit and Wisdom of Fat Albert* (1973), *You Are Somebody Special* (1978), *Fatherhood* (1986), *Time Flies* (1987), and *Love and Marriage* (1989).

He has served on numerous boards, including those of the NAACP, Operation PUSH, the United Negro College Fund, and the National Sickle Cell Foundation.

Cosby, who in 1993 was listed in *Forbes* magazine as one of the four hundred richest people in the world with a net worth of more than $315 million, has been one of the most important benefactors to African-American institutions. In 1986 he and his wife gave $1.3 million to Fisk University; the following year they gave another $1.3 million to be divided equally among four black universities— Central State, Howard, Florida A & M, and Shaw; in 1988 they divided $1.5 million between Meharry Medical College and Bethune-Cookman College. In 1989 Bill and Camille Cosby announced that they were giving $20 million to Spelman College, the largest personal gift ever made to any of the historically black colleges and universities. In 1994 the couple donated a historic landmark building in downtown Washington, D.C., to the National Council of Negro Women to help them establish a National Center for African-American Women. Cosby himself has been the recipient of numerous awards, including the NAACP's Spingarn Medal (1985). He holds an M.A. (1972) and a doctorate (1976) in education from the University of Massachusetts at Amherst. In 1976 he also finally received a B.A. from Temple University. Cosby, who married Camille Hanks in 1964, has lived in rural Massachusetts since the early 1970s.

In 1997 Cosby's life was shattered when his son Ennis was robbed and murdered in Los Angeles. (Mikail Markhasev, a Russian immigrant, was convicted of the murder in 1998.) In the fall of 1997 Cosby was the target of an extortion plot by Autumn Jackson, an African-American woman who threatened to reveal that Cosby was her father unless he paid her. At Jackson's extortion trial, Cosby was forced to admit to an extramarital affair with Jackson's mother, but he denied he was Jackson's father. After Cosby's assertion was confirmed by DNA testing, Jackson was convicted. In 1998 he began a new television series, *Kids Say the Darnedest Things.*

In addition to his stand-up comedy, Cosby has produced movies, including *Men of Honor* (2000) and *Fat Albert* (2004), as well as numerous television shows. At the 2003 Emmy Awards, Cosby received the Bob Hope Humanitarian Award.

See also Comedians; Philanthropy and Foundations; Television

■ ■ *Bibliography*

Fuller, Linda K. The Cosby Show: *Audience, Impact, and Implications.* Westport, Conn.: Greenwood Press, 1992.

Lane, Randall. "Bill Cosby, Capitalist." *Forbes* (September 28, 1992): 85–86.

Smith, Ronald L. *Cosby: The Life of a Comedy Legend.* Amherst, N.Y.: Prometheus Books, 1997.

Zoglin, Richard. "Cosby Inc." *Time* (September 28, 1987): 56–60.

JANNETTE L. DATES (1996)
Updated by publisher 2005

COTTON CLUB

The Cotton Club, at Lenox Avenue and West 142nd Street in Harlem, first opened in 1920 as the Club Deluxe but took on new ownership and its permanent name in 1922. Owney Madden, who bought the club from heavyweight boxing champion Jack Johnson, intended the name Cotton Club to appeal to whites, the only clientele permitted until 1928. The club made its name by featuring top-level black performers and an upscale, downtown audience. It soon became a leading attraction for white tourists from high society who wanted to see the much publicized, risqué Harlem cultural life.

Following the death in 1927 of Andy Preer, leader of the house band, the Cotton Club Syncopators, Duke Ellington and his orchestra were brought in as replacements and began a four-year rise to prominence on the Cotton Club's stage. Soon after Ellington took over as bandleader, the Cotton Club Orchestra began to be broadcast nightly over a national radio network.

Responding to local protests, the club's management opened its doors to black patrons for the first time in the winter of 1928. Nonetheless, prices were kept prohibitively high and the club's audience remained virtually all white. The nightly revues, which were generally more popular than the orchestra, featured scantily clad, light-skinned women dancing to Ellington's "jungle music."

In 1931 Ellington and his orchestra left the club and were replaced by Cab Calloway's Missourians. Calloway, like Ellington, established himself as a major figure in mainstream jazz during his Cotton Club years. Calloway's Missourians remained the house band until 1934, when they were replaced by Jimmie Lunceford's acclaimed swing band. Most of the renowned jazz performers of the period appeared at the Cotton Club, including Louis Armstrong, Ethel Waters, and dancers Bill "Bojangles" Robinson and the Nicholas Brothers.

Following riots in Harlem in 1935, the club was forced to close due to a widespread perception among whites that the area was unsafe. It reopened downtown in

The Cotton Club. *The famed Harlem, New York, nightclub is seen here at night, with the illuminated marquee advertising performances by Cab Calloway and Bill Robinson.* HULTON/ARCHIVE. REPRODUCED BY PERMISSION.

1936, at 200 West 48th Street, where it remained until its final closing in 1940.

See also Calloway, Cab; Ellington, Duke; Harlem Renaissance; Jazz; Robinson, Bill "Bojangles" (Robinson, Luther)

■ ■ *Bibliography*

Charters, Samuel Barclay, and Leonard Kunstadt. *Jazz: A History of the New York Scene* (1962). New York: Da Capo, 1981.

Schuller, Gunther. *The Swing Era: The Development of Jazz, 1930–1945.* New York: Oxford University Press, 1989.

THADDEUS RUSSELL (1996)

COUNCIL ON AFRICAN AFFAIRS

■ ▪ ■

The Council on African Affairs (CAA), the most important Pan-Africanist group of the 1940s, was founded on January 28, 1937, by a group led by Paul Robeson and Max Yergan, a former YMCA secretary. Originally named the International Committee on African Affairs, it was a small information and lobbying group. Anticolonialist in nature, it was dedicated to increasing Americans' awareness of conditions in Africa, to expose the "ruthless exploitation of the people; repressive legislation . . . and the growing poverty of the Africans." For many years it was the only organization dedicated to African problems. It was funded largely by Frederick V. Field (of the Chicago department store family), who had communist leanings, as did many of the CAA's leaders. Its seventy-member board, however, included such noncommunist luminaries as Adam Clayton Powell, Jr., Alain Locke, Channing Tobias, Herbert Delany, and Mary McLeod Bethune. Two other board members, Ralph Bunche and Mordecai Johnson, decided shortly after joining that the CAA was too left wing in its politics and resigned. In 1941 the group had fourteen active committee members who met three times per year.

In 1942 the organization, renamed the CAA, set up offices at 23 West Twenty-sixth Street in New York City, and in August published its first two-page newsletter, *News of Africa*. In 1943 Alphaeus Hunton, a Howard University English professor, became the CAA's educational director. He began a monthly bulletin, *New Africa* (later called *Spotlight on Africa*), which was part of a program to influence mass opinion, especially on the U.S. role in Africa as exploiter of cheap labor and raw materials. In April 1944 the CAA sponsored a conference titled "Africa—New Perspectives" with Kwame Nkrumah of the Gold Coast (now Ghana) as the guest speaker.

During World War II Hunton and Yergan conferred with the U.S. State Department's Division of African Affairs about economic and political questions, advocating a program of postwar liberation and self-determination for African colonies. In 1945 CAA chairman Paul Robeson lobbied President Harry S. Truman and Secretary of State Edward Stettinius to support African decolonization at the United Nations Conference in San Francisco. Hunton was an accredited observer, and he attended meetings of the Ad Hoc Committee on Non-Self-Governing Territories. He prepared reports for UN delegates on South Africa. When Jan Smuts, the prime minister of South Africa, applied for permission to annex South West Africa, the CAA led the successful fight at the UN to block the measure.

By 1946 the CAA had seventy-two members, some 80 percent of whom were African Americans. Often the only source of information on Africa, the CAA provided news releases to sixty-two foreign and sixty-seven U.S. newspapers. Its *African Bibliography* was published from January 1945 to February 1950. It publicized apartheid, starvation, and exploitation of black Africans in South Africa, and supported the African National Congress. So influential was the CAA that *New Africa* was banned in British-held Kenya. CAA activities included mass meetings, picketing of the South African embassy, and a food drive.

The last big CAA event was an April 1947 meeting at the 71st Regimental Armory in New York. Paul Robeson spoke, comparing the United States unfavorably to the Soviet Union, citing the latter's aid to third-world countries.

That year, as the cold war heated up, the CAA was placed on the attorney general's list of subversive organizations.

In February 1948 a major schism occurred. Executive Director Max Yergan insisted that the CAA Council should declare its "nonpartisan" character, while Robeson and his followers claimed this would aid anti-Soviet reactionaries. The dispute was referred to a policy committee headed by W. E. B. Du Bois, who had become active in the CAA following his departure in 1948 from the National Association for the Advancement of Colored People (NAACP). In March the CAA board defeated Yergan's motion and censured him for alleged financial irregularities. Yergan claimed the CAA had been taken over by communists and formed his own rump faction. That summer, the CAA leadership expelled him. This action cost the organization the support of Powell, Tobias, Delany, and Bethune. Robeson remained as chairman, Du Bois became vice chairman, and Hunton became executive secretary. Louise Thompson Patterson, a prominent communist, became the director of organization, and with Robeson he organized fund-raising concerts and local chapters. The CAA became Robeson's power base, and supporters demonstrated in 1950 after he was denied a passport.

In 1953 the CAA was ordered to register under the McCarran Act as a subversive organization, and in 1955 Hunton was called before a federal grand jury to testify about whether the CAA was a foreign agent, given its ties with the African National Congress and the South African Indian Congress. Funding soon dried up, and in 1955 the CAA ceased most activities. The U.S. government's Subversive Activities Control Board finally shut it down for good in 1956.

See also Bethune, Mary McLeod; Du Bois, W. E. B.; National Association for the Advancement of Colored People (NAACP); Robeson, Paul; Yergan, Max

■ ■ *Bibliography*

Duberman, Martin B. *Paul Robeson*. New York: Knopf, 1988.

Horne, Gerald. *Black and Red: W. E. B. Du Bois and the Afro-American Response to the Cold War, 1947–1963*. Albany: State University of New York Press, 1986.

Hunton, Dorothy. *Alphaeus Hunton: The Unsung Valiant*. Self-published, 1986.

Lynch, Hollis R. *Black American Radicals and the Liberation of Africa: The Council on African Affairs, 1937–1955*. Ithaca, N.Y.: Africana Studies and Research Center, Cornell University, 1978.

ALANA J. ERICKSON (1996)

COUNT BASIE

See Basie, William James "Count"

COX, OLIVER CROMWELL

AUGUST 24, 1901
SEPTEMBER 4, 1974

Sociologist Oliver Cox was born in Port of Spain, Trinidad, the son of Virginia Blake and William Raphael Cox. His father, a customs officer and the captain of a revenue schooner, was too busy to supervise the education of Cox and his eight siblings, and so it was entrusted to his uncle, Reginald W. Vidale, a teacher and headmaster of Saint Thomas Boys' School in Port of Spain.

Cox came to the United States in 1919 to work and be educated. In 1925 he entered Lewis Institute in Chicago, where he majored in history and economics. He received an associate degree in the spring of 1927 and that fall entered Northwestern University, where he graduated with a bachelor of science in law in 1929. Shortly thereafter he was stricken with polio. He spent eighteen months recovering and thereafter always walked with crutches.

After abandoning the idea of practicing law in Trinidad, Cox decided to go into academic work, which would, he said, "not require too much legwork." In the fall of 1930 he entered the University of Chicago as a graduate student in economics, earning an M.A. in 1932. Soon after, however, he switched to sociology, claiming that economists had not explained the causes of the Great Depression. His dissertation, "Factors Affecting the Marital Status of Negroes in Chicago," was based on the study of a massive quantity of statistical data. Cox received his Ph.D. in August 1938.

Despite his degrees in both economics and sociology, Cox was unable, then as later, to find a job at a white institution. He took a position in the economics department at Wiley College in Marshall, Texas. After five years he accepted a more lucrative post at Tuskegee Institute in Alabama. Tuskegee's vocational approach to education frustrated him, however, and he joined the faculty of Lincoln University in Jefferson City, Missouri, in 1949. He stayed at Lincoln until 1970, when he joined the faculty at Wayne State University in Detroit, Michigan, where for a short time he was a distinguished visiting professor.

Cox is best known for his attack on the caste school of race relations, of which W. Lloyd Warner was the most articulate member. Cox argued, first in his article "The Modern Caste School of Race Relations" (1942) and at greater length in his major work, *Caste, Race, and Class* (1948) that to view race relations in America as analogous to caste systems such as that of Hindu India ignored historical differences in the development of the two systems and discounted the political and economic basis of American race relations. Cox insisted that racism in America was a product of class conflict. In later years, Cox elaborated his Marxist view of capitalism and race relations in three books: *Foundations of Capitalism* (1959), *Capitalism and American Leadership* (1962), and *Capitalism as a System* (1964). He underlined the importance of international trade and uneven global development in the history of European capitalism. Cox's final work, "Jewish Self-Interest and 'Black Pluralism'" (1974), dealt with the problem of black nationalism. His assertion that ethnic pluralism was promoted by Jews for their own benefit caused a storm of criticism.

Only at the end of his life did Cox achieve limited professional recognition. His work, despite its originality, remains curiously overlooked.

See also Tuskegee University

Bibliography

Blackwell, James, and Morris Janowitz, eds. *Black Sociologists: Historical and Contemporary Perspectives.* Chicago: University of Chicago Press, 1974.

Hunter, Herbert M., and Sameer Y. Abraham, eds. *Race, Class, and the World System: The Sociology of Oliver C. Cox.* New York: Monthly Review Press, 1987.

McAuley, Christopher. *The Mind of Oliver C. Cox.* Notre Dame, Ind.: Notre Dame University Press, 2004.

GREG ROBINSON (1996)
Updated bibliography

CRAFT, ELLEN AND WILLIAM

Ellen (1826–1891) and William (1824–1900) Craft were fugitive slaves who became known for their dramatic escape to freedom. Ellen Smith was born in Clinton, Georgia, the daughter of a mulatto slave, Maria, and her owner, Major James Smith. At eleven years of age, Ellen was given as a wedding gift to one of Smith's daughters living in Macon, Georgia. She soon met William Craft, a fellow slave and cabinetmaker, and within a few years they began

WILLIAM CRAFT.

ELLEN CRAFT.

Fugitive slaves Ellen and William Craft. In a carefully arranged plan for escape, Ellen, of fair complexion, disguised herself as an invalid white male traveling north to consult doctors; William impersonated her black slave. Journeying successfully to Philadelphia in 1848, the Crafts were driven into exile in England by the passage of the Fugitive Slave law two years later. PHOTOGRAPHS AND PRINTS DIVISION, SCHOMBURG CENTER FOR RESEARCH IN BLACK CULTURE, THE NEW YORK PUBLIC LIBRARY, ASTOR, LENOX AND TILDEN FOUNDATIONS.

to plot their escape from bondage. The couple were married in 1846.

Escape from the Deep South was a rare and dangerous undertaking, and the Crafts' plan was bold, creative, and worked out in detail. They first procured passes to visit friends during the Christmas season, when discipline was known to be lax. Their pass was good for several days, so they had time to travel some distance before their absence was noticed. Ellen had a fair complexion, and she posed as an invalid white male traveling north to consult doctors; William impersonated her black slave. She cut her hair, wrapped her head in a bandage, and practiced imitating a man's gait. As a final touch, she wore eyeglasses to disguise her appearance, and because she was illiterate, she held her writing arm in a cast to avoid having to sign her name. This part of the disguise would be crucial when they were forced to sign hotel registers.

The couple left for freedom on December 21, 1848, and traveled by train, steamer, and ferry through Georgia, South Carolina, North Carolina, Virginia, and Maryland, in a journey that involved several near discoveries. Finally, they arrived in Philadelphia, which was free territory, on Christmas day, 1848.

In Philadelphia, Ellen and William Craft stayed with free blacks and Quakers. They were befriended by abolitionist luminaries such as William Wells Brown (c.1814–1884) and William Lloyd Garrison (1805–1879), and the Crafts frequently lectured on their dramatic escape on the antislavery circuit. In 1850, however, national events changed their lives dramatically. In that year the Fugitive Slave Law was passed and the Crafts were literally hunted down in Boston by southern slavehunters and driven into exile in England. Their plight became a national issue when President Millard Fillmore insisted that if the laws of the land were not obeyed in Boston, and the Crafts not shipped back to the South, he would use the United States Army to force the issue.

While in England, the Crafts remained active in the abolitionist movement. They went on a speaking tour with abolitionist William Wells Brown, and in 1851 they took a post teaching at the Ockham School, a pioneering trade school that combined classroom work in traditional subjects with farming, carpentry, and other crafts. William Craft also gained a reputation as a public spokesman against slavery, and he made several trips back to the United States to speak out against the Confederacy during the Civil War. Ellen was active in the British and Foreign Freedmen's Aid Society, a missionary organization that organized "civilizing" work in British colonies in Africa and the Caribbean. The Crafts published the story of their escape from slavery, *Running a Thousand Miles for Free-*

ELLEN CRAFT, A FUGITIVE SLAVE.—(SEE NEXT PAGE.)

Fugitive slave Ellen Craft, in disguise. *From* Running a Thousand Miles for Freedom; *or,* The Escape of William and Ellen Craft from Slavery *(1860), by William Craft.* PHOTOGRAPHS AND PRINTS DIVISION, SCHOMBURG CENTER FOR RESEARCH IN BLACK CULTURE, THE NEW YORK PUBLIC LIBRARY, ASTOR, LENOX AND TILDEN FOUNDATIONS.

dom, while in London in 1860. Between 1863 and 1867, William was in Dahomey in West Africa with the Company of African-American Merchants, where he started a school and established commercial ties.

In 1868 the Crafts returned to the United States with two of their five children and settled in Bryan County, Georgia, where they opened an industrial school for black youths. They purchased a plantation in Woodville in 1871, where they continued their school and hired tenant farmers to grow rice, cotton, corn, and peas, which they sold in the Savannah area. By 1877 they had seventy-five pupils, but they were suffering from the financial burden of keeping up the school.

William became a leader in the local Republican Party, ran for the state senate in 1874, and in 1876 represented his district at the state and national Republican conventions. He also spent a good part of his time in the North, raising funds for the school and lecturing to church groups on conditions in the South. Ellen managed the plantation while he was away, negotiated the annual con-

tracts with tenants, and drove their crops to market. But the plantation never prospered, and northerners, in the mood for reconciliation with the South, were less forthcoming with donations to the experimental school. Rumors spread by the Crafts' enemies suggesting that they were living off the largess of naive northern philanthropists did not help their project, and they eventually gave up the school. Around 1890 they left the Woodville plantation and moved to Charleston, South Carolina, where they remained for the rest of their lives. In 1996, Ellen Craft was named a Georgia Woman of Achievement.

See also Abolition; Brown, William Wells; Runaway Slaves in the United States

▪▪ *Bibliography*

Blackett, R. J. M. *Beating the Barriers: Biographical Essays in Nineteenth-Century Afro-American History.* Baton Rouge: Louisiana State University Press, 1986.

Brusky, Sarah. "The Travels of William and Ellen Craft: Race and Travel Literature in the Nineteenth Century." *Prospects: An Annual Journal of American Cultural Studies* 25 (2000): 177–192.

Clift-Pellow, Arlene. "Ellen Craft." In *Notable Black American Women,* edited by Jessie Carney Smith. Detroit, Mich.: Gale Research, 1992.

McCaskill, Barbara. "'Yours Very Truly': Ellen Craft—The Fugitive as Text and Artifact." *African American Review* 28, no. 4 (1994): 509–529.

Sterling, Dorothey. *Black Foremothers,* 2d ed. New York: Feminist Press, 1988.

SABRINA FUCHS (1996)

CREOLE LANGUAGES OF THE AMERICAS
▪▪▪

Enslaved by the European superpowers of England, France, Spain, Portugal, and the Netherlands thousands of Africans primarily from the west coast of the continent were transported to the Americas. The fates of these people varied widely according to where they were located. In Surinam and a few other places, large numbers escaped the plantations to live in the bush, often in close contact with the native peoples of the region. In Haiti, slaves rose up against the French slave owners, ousted them and established their own sovereign state. In Barbados, Africans toiled alongside large numbers of indentured laborers from England and Ireland. New societies—characterized by new forms of art, kinship, politics and language—were forged from this contact between Africans, Europeans, and others.

For many people, the term *creole* is intimately associated with the language, people, and cuisine of Louisiana. Most linguists, however, use this term to designate a group of languages either on the basis of a common history or a shared set of linguistic features. A few linguists would say that whether one calls a language creole or not is purely a matter of historical accident (since, according to this line of argument, these languages have no more in common than do Chinese and French), while some refuse to use the term altogether. As this dilemma suggests, the "creole languages of America" represent a great challenge to current scholarship, and even the terms used to describe them are a matter of some controversy.

The word *creole* was, of course, not originally used to refer to language at all, but to people—a *criollo* was a person of Spanish descent born in the New World. Eventually, the word came to be used not only for people of European, African, and mixed ancestry born in the Americas, but also for the distinctive languages they spoke.

The term *creole* is used here to designate a broad swath of languages sometimes called *patois* (for instance in Jamaica), *pidjin* (in Hawaii), *Kweyol* (in St. Lucia), *Creolese* (in Guyana) and *dialect* (for instance, in the Sea Islands of Georgia and in many Caribbean Islands). What these languages have in common is that they emerged out of contact between speakers of a number of different languages in the context of plantation slavery and colonialism. Exactly how this happened is again a matter of some controversy. However, it seems relatively certain that in all cases, the result was a fairly extensive restructuring of the languages present at the time of such contact. In the case of Ndjuka (a language spoken in Suriname) restructuring was so extreme that it requires systematic linguistic investigation to find any residue of English in the language spoken today. In other cases, where the restructuring was less extensive, as in Barbados, a speaker of a relatively standard variety of English may be able to recognize a few words upon hearing the language as it is spoken, though there will be little hope of following a conversation.

For many years, linguists treated these languages as oddities and unworthy of serious study. A few early pioneers such as Hugo Schuchardt, John Reinecke, Lucien Rens, Uriel Weinreich, and Lorenzo Dow Turner recognized the importance of Creoles, but for the most part the languages went unstudied. Then, in the 1950s, a group of scholars gathered for the first conference on pidgins and creole in Mona, Jamaica. Since that time, a growing number of linguists have turned their attention to pidgins and creoles, not only in the Americas but also in Melanesia, Af-

rica, and the islands of Mauritius and Seychelles in the Indian Ocean. Today, a relatively small but tightly knit group of researchers, many of whom are themselves native speakers of a creole language, work at describing and understanding these languages through the application of modern linguistic techniques. The question of how these languages formed and developed continues to dominate the field.

VARIATION

All languages exhibit internal variation. Since the 1960s, sociolinguists have shown that this variation is not random but highly systematic. Creole languages are no exception. Indeed, due to their particular histories of contact and colonialism, creole languages often offer the most extreme cases of such variation.

Such variation has posed significant challenges for linguistic theory, and a number of alternatives have been developed to model it. While consideration of this research would take us too far afield, it is crucial to understand that variation is not the result of speaking "incorrectly." A creole language, like any other, may be spoken correctly or incorrectly, but this has nothing do with the rules of English (or French, etc.) grammar. Native speakers of Creolese (Guyanese Creole) often claim that their language has no rules—that it is simply "broken English." Many, however, would agree that

mi na worii goo [I didn't bother to go.]

is a perfectly good sentence, whereas

worii na goo mii

is not. Every language has its own rules, and native speakers use these rules to produce and understand sentences, as well as to decide what is acceptable and unacceptable.

LINGUISTIC FEATURES OF CREOLES

Creole languages tend to draw the bulk of their words from the superstrate—the language of the colonizer. Most of these languages developed in settings where there were many different native languages. The European language thus served as a bridge between people who did not share a common language. The European vocabulary was therefore particularly important.

In Barbados and a number of other early colonies, Africans worked for many years side by side with indentured servants from Ireland, Scotland, and western England. The European language that slaves learned was therefore derived from regional sources. Thus, there are many words in contemporary creole languages that have their source in the regional dialects of European languages. For instance, the Sranan word *wenke* (woman) derives from English wench, while the verb *bay/ba* (to give) in the French creoles derives from *bailer,* an archaism preserved in regional dialects. The early colonies were, in many ways, societies built around the sea, and nautical usage has provided many words to the Creoles of the Caribbean. In the Atlantic English creoles, for instance, *hais* (lift) comes from the English hoist.

All the creole languages of the Americas show some influence of the substrate languages (the original African languages) in their vocabulary. This influence ranges from a fairly significant proportion of words of African origin in the Surinamese creoles—perhaps as much as 5 percent in Saramaccan—to the much more limited influence on the varieties spoken in other places. Of course, the slaves who made up the early linguistic communities of the colonies spoke many different languages, so that relatively few words were likely to carry over into the common creole language. There are some exceptions, however, for example Berbice Creole Dutch mentioned below.

In his *Africanisms in the Gullah Dialect* (1949), African-American linguist Lorenzo Dow Turner recorded hundreds of words of African origin that had survived in Gullah. The bulk of these are used as personal names. A full 150 pages of Turner's book is devoted to recording these names and their sources in various African languages. The number of words listed as "used in conversation" is considerably smaller. This category of words includes, for instance, *bEble,* an Ewe word for deceit, as well as *ibi* (to vomit) from Yoruba. Some African words such as *nyam* (to eat/food) and *bokra/bakra* (white man) are particularly widespread, occurring in creoles with different lexical bases.

An early pioneer of creole studies, Frederic Cassidy (b. 1966), pointed out another way in which African words were preserved in creole vocabularies. He called this phenomenon "multiple etymology" which points to the fact that sometimes a word can be traced to more than one source, and that its current usage reflects this multiple etymology. Cassidy gave examples such as Jamaican *cuss-cuss,* or *kas-kas,* which may be traced to both English *cuss* and Twi *kasa-kasa* (argument).

Another process widely evidenced in creole languages is "calquing." Calques are produced when idioms or phrases in one language are translated word-for-word into the creole using the superstrate lexicon. For instance in Caribbean English creoles, *big-eye* means greedy. Parallel forms of this metaphor are found not only in Haitian (*gwo že*), but also in African languages such as Twi (*ani bre*) and Ibo (*aŋa uku*). All of these examples literally translate as "big" plus "eye".

One also finds influence in a variety of word-formation rules. For instance, reduplication is a process in which a word or part of a word is repeated, resulting in a distinct lexical item. Reduplication is associated with a variety of meanings such as intensification (e.g., *kwik-kwik*—as in *da bai a iit kwik kwik,* the boy eats very fast), distribution (e.g., *di piknii a waak wan-wan,* the children are walking one by one), and reiteration (e.g., *di pkinii a krai-krai,* the child is constantly crying).

Many other languages have contributed to the vocabularies of creole languages. In the Caribbean, the Amerindian languages of the Carib and Arawak people have contributed words such as the Carib *mabii* (root from which a drink is made) and the Arawak (possibly via Spanish) *ginip* (a little fruit). In Guyana, where the majority of the population today is of East Indian ancestry, Bhojpuri has contributed a large number of words to the lexicon of Guyanese Creole such as *baigin* (eggplant) and *kaharii* (curry pot).

PHONOLOGY

The sound systems of creole languages—their phonologies—differ according to the languages that contributed to their formation, though they also show a number of quite striking similarities. In general, there seems to be a preference for syllables without extensive clustering of consonants. This may be the result of substrate influence, though it may also be the product of second language learning in the contact situation. Holm (1988) notes that African languages such as Ewe, Vai, and Wolof have a basic CV (consonant–vowel) syllable structure. The basic CV syllable structure of many creole languages contrasts with a language like English which has a range of syllable types (e.g., CVC *bit,* CCVC *snap,* CCVCC *stink*).

Creole languages have been affected by a wide variety of phonological processes through which words from European languages have been adapted to the sound systems and phonotactic patterns of the creole. In aphesis, for example, one or more sounds are omitted at the beginning of the word, which results in words such as the Sranan *tan* (stand). Syncope involves the omission of one or more sounds in the middle of a word (e.g., Sranan *kosi,* from the English curtsy). Apocope, in which one or more sounds are omitted from the end of a word, has had a massive effect on creole languages—as in the Haitian *ris* (from the French *risqué*) and the Caribbean English Creole words *lan* (land), *hool* (hold), *las* (last), and *fos* (first). Epenthesis involves the insertion of a sound in the middle of a word. A vowel inserted in this way typically serves to break up a consonant cluster (e.g., Negerhollands *kini,* knee, from the Dutch *knie*). Paragogue, in which a sound is added at the end of a word, has operated across the lexicon of the Surinamese Creoles, resulting in Sranan words such as *bigi* (big), *dede* (dead), and *mofo* (mouth). The two vowels in the resulting Sranan words exhibit a feature known to linguists as vowel harmony (a characteristic of many West African languages).

Some creole languages have sounds known as co-articulated stops. These are quite rare across the world's languages (what linguistics call a "marked feature"), and their presence in creole languages is a clear inheritance from the West African languages spoken by slaves. Labio-velar co-articulated stops such as *gb* or *kp* occur in a number of Niger-Congo languages, and Saramaccan and Ndjuka also have these stops in words of African origin (e.g., *kpasi*, vulture, and *gbono-gbono*, moss).

GRAMMAR

Creole languages tend to be more highly analytic than the languages that contributed to their formation. This means that they tend to avoid inflectional morphology in favor of relatively short words, which are more or less invariant. In this they resemble languages such as Cantonese or Laotian more than Russian, Inuktitut, or Kwakiutl. This tendency toward analyticity is seen in many areas of the grammar. For instance, in many languages, whether an action or event took place in the past or will take place in the future (tense) is indicated by an inflectional ending (e.g., the *-ed* in *worked*). Another distinction often marked in the same way (by inflectional endings) is called aspect. Aspect indicates, among other things, whether the action is completed (bounded) or ongoing (e.g., the *-ing* in "John is walking"). Again, these distinctions are typically not marked through inflection in creole languages, but rather through a series of preverbal markers.

The tendency towards analyticity has sometimes been misunderstood as making creole languages "easier" or even "simpler." While there is some evidence that highly inflected languages are more difficult to learn (Marianne Mithun's 1989 study of the acquisition of Mohawk), it does not follow that highly analytic languages are easier or simpler. What the language does not convey through inflection it conveys through a complex combination of preverbal markers, and what it does not convey through highly specified semantic or grammatical categories, speakers may convey through adverbial specification or grammatical processes such as reduplication or pragmatic inference.

ENGLISH-BASED CREOLES

Perhaps the best known creole languages of the Americas within the English speaking world are those of the Anglo-phone Antilles (Jamaica, Barbados, Saint Vincent, Saint Kitts, etc.) and mainland South and Central America (Guyana, Belize, etc.). Gullah (spoken along the coast of Georgia and on the Sea Islands) should also be included here. That these form a group of interrelated languages can be shown through both linguistic and historical evidence. Certain islands such as Saint Kitts and Barbados were colonized very early. Colonies established later typically drew a larger proportion of their founding population from these islands. Thus, an early creole language was first established on one or two islands, and this provided the initial input to a number of other languages that emerged sometime later.

An important fact about these languages is that they typically co-exist with (standard) English. In all of the places named above, English is the official language of education and government. This means that English acts as the lexifier language, influencing the creole by providing a constant stream of new words. English also has exerted an influence on the grammar and phonology of these languages. Moreover, because the creole is in contact with the lexifier language, it is constantly compared to it. As a result, many speakers of the creole often do not recognize that they speak a different language but rather see themselves as speaking an incorrect version of the standard.

The following excerpts are from the small Grenadine Island of Bequia. They show some of the major grammatical features of the language, as well as the range of variation between different speakers.

Speaker 001 (Hamilton)

yu sii a faal dong an a hit dis fut hii an di boon kik out. So ai doz wak wid a piis o stik. Oonlii fo kiip dii fut bot— an a stil wok in mai grong. Til plantin mai kan an piiz az uujal. Karn ai don akostom. luk a ha rait- a piis a grong rait bai di walsaid wen aalyu komin dong. De we yu sii a waal de soo. You sho noo wa mos de soo. Rait de mi a wok.

[You see I fell down and I hit this foot here and the bone kicked out. So I walk with a piece of stick only to keep the foot. But—and I'm still working my ground, still planting my corn and peas as usual. Hm. Because I'm accustomed. Look I have a piece of ground right by the roadside when you're coming down there, where you see a wall there so. You should know what is there. Right there I work.]

Speaker 029 [LaPompe-Southside]

it streenj. Wans wii wor cheesin dii foulz an sombadi didn sii won an it et a gud lat an it fal dong, it star to staga an it fal dong. An—an Mamii see to mii "keerii it giv moma," da iz mai granmoda, "keerii it giv or." An wen ai keerii it giv or shii get a litl pen naif an shi hool dong di foul an shii kot open di cra, an shii teek out al di kasava, an shii chroo som wata, an shii wash it out, an shi stich it bak and di foul get op an goo abou ii biznis. Ya, ya as lang az dee kech it in taim dee alweez uusto duu dat.

[It is strange—once we were chasing the fowls and somebody didn't see one and it ate a good lot and it fell down. It started to stagger and it fell down. And—and mommy said to me, "carry it give momma," that is my grandmother, "carry it give her," and when I took it to her she took out a little pen knife and she held down the fowl and she opened the craw and she took out all the cassava and she splashed some water and she washed it out and she stitched it back and the fowl got up and went about his business. Yeah yeah as long as they caught it in time they always used to do that.]

These fragments provide a number of examples of tense and aspect. Whereas English relies primarily on tense—distinguishing actions and events that occurred *before* the time of speaking from those that did not—most English creoles rely more heavily on a basic aspectual distinction between perfective (unmarked) and imperfective (the marked option). Imperfectivity indicates that the action or event is one that is either in progress or done habitually. In Guyanese and Vincentian (along with other conservative or basilectal English creoles of the Eastern branch), imperfective is conveyed by the preverbal marker *a* or *da*, as in *rait de mi a wok* (Right there I work). These passages also illustrate the rather extreme grammatical variation that is characteristic of this community. Thus, imperfectivity (including the specific senses of progressivity and habituality) is marked in the following ways:

TABLE 1.

doz	*So ai doz wak wid a piis o stik.* [So I walk with a piece of stick.] (Habitual)
ø	*An a stil ø wok in mai grong.* [And I'm still working my ground.] (Habitual)
ø V+ing	*Til plantin mai kan an piiz az uujal.* [Still planting my corn and peas as usual.] (Habitual)
a	*Rait de mi a wok.* [Right there I work.] (Habitual)

were V+ing	*Wans wii wor cheesin dii foulz an sombadi didn sii won.* [Once we were chasing the fowls and somebody didn't see one.] (Past Progressive)
used to	*Dee alweez uusto duu dat.* [They always used to do that.] (Past Habitual)

Perfectivity, which "indicates the view of a situation as a single whole, without distinction of the various separate phases that make up that situation" (Comrie, 1976, p. 36) is usually expressed by the use of the unmarked verb. Taken in context, it is clear that these events and actions took place in the past. Thus, what a language like English conveys with tense, this one conveys with aspect. A final marker of aspect illustrated here is *don*—*I done accustom.* Notice that in many cases *don* is more or less equivalent to English "finish" (as in *di torkii don kuk,* The turkey has finished cooking.). Here, however, the word does not mean "finish" but rather something like "already." This illustrates a widespread phenomenon called grammaticalization found in all languages, whereby lexical items are gradually transformed into grammatical items and in the process undergo a change of meaning.

Another feature illustrated in the passages is the use of serial verbs. In the second passage, the mother tells her daughter to *keerii it giv mama.* Here two verbs ("carry" and "give") are combined to convey a complex meaning that is expressed by the combination of verb and preposition in English. This is a very common pattern in the Caribbean creoles. Typical examples are from Donald Winford (1993, see also Migge, 1998):

Mieri waak go a maakit. [Mary walked to the market.]

Jan bring moni gi shi. [John brought money for her.]

Di pikni tall paas mi. [The child is taller than me.]

In a serial verb construction, the second verb is used to express a grammatical relation—directional, benefactive, and comparative, respectively, in the above three examples).

THE CREOLE LANGUAGES OF SURINAME

Suriname is located between Guyana and French Guyana. Like its neighbors, it is a country of dense tropical rainforest and long, winding rivers. Although the official language of Suriname is Dutch, the coastal population speaks Sranan, an English-based creole, as the vernacular. In the interior, the descendants of escaped slaves—Maroons—speak their own creole languages: Ndjuka, Saramaccan, and Kwinti. Suriname was originally colonized by the English in 1651. However, in 1667 the territory was ceded to the Dutch. Although many English took their slaves with them on their departure (some to Jamaica, where a language clearly related to the Surinamese creoles exists as Maroon Spirit Language), some did not. The African slaves of English planters left behind in Suriname formed a linguistic community that was eventually to develop Sranan. Because the period of contact between African slaves and English speakers was so short, only a very small part of the English lexicon, grammar, and phonology made it into the new language. This meant that the emerging linguistic community drew heavily both on the universal structures of language and the African substrate. Sranan appears to have developed gradually through processes of both grammaticalization and continuous contact with the African languages spoken by newly arrived slaves. The result is a radical creole that resembles English only to a very limited extent.

In the interior, things were even more complicated. Whereas Ndjuka, like Sranan, is unambiguously English-derived, Saramaccan contains a high proportion of words of Portuguese origin. The explanation for this has been a matter of some controversy. Some creolists have claimed that Saramaccan is based in part on the language spoken by Jewish refugees who came to Suriname from Brazil. Others have suggested that Saramaccan inherited its Portuguese content from the original Portuguese pidgin purportedly spoken in the Angola area and Slave Coast, where the Dutch acquired most of their slaves from the 1640s until 1725. The weight of evidence, both historical and linguistic, seems to support a Brazilian rather than African origin for the Portuguese component of Saramaccan.

FRENCH-BASED CREOLES

A French-based creole language is spoken in a number of Caribbean islands, including Haiti, Guadeloupe, Martinique, Saint Lucia, Saint Barts, and Dominica. French Guiana is also home to a French lexicon creole called *Guyanais*. There are also remnants of French-based Creole in Grenada, Carriacou, and Trinidad. Finally, a French-based creole is also spoken in Louisiana.

These languages exhibit a number of striking similarities, both among themselves and to the other creole languages of the region. Similarities among the French creoles in the region may be due, at least in part, to the fact that between 1664 and 1763 planters throughout the French West Indies were legally obligated to import their slaves by way of Martinique. Although it is likely that the law was

sometimes violated, it appears that the creole of Martinique and Guadeloupe was transferred to Haiti and the Windward Islands during this period.

The articles of the French creoles have attracted a good deal of attention from creolists. In French, as in English, the article always precedes the noun, as in *l'eglisse* (the church), *le chat* (the cat), and *le chien* (the dog). In Haitian, however, the article follows the noun, as in *pen-a* (the bread), *banan-la* (the banana). This looks like a very straightforward transfer from substrate languages such as Fongbe. Noting the similarities between Haitian Creole (HC) and Fon, and how they differ from the French, Claire Lefebvre argues that such examples provide evidence for the relexification model of creole formation, in which creoles are generated when superstrate word forms are mapped onto the substrate grammar. However, it is not quite true to say that French provided no model at all for such structures in the creole. In French, an item homophonous with the feminine article (*la*) can follow a noun in a construction such as *Qui est ce monsieur-là?* (Who is that gentleman there?). Such structures were likely a pervasive feature of the dialectal varieties spoken by early French settlers (as they are today in vernacular varieties) and may have provided a model for the creole grammar. At the same time, this model provided by French vernacular varieties cannot account for the many correspondences between Haitian Creole and Fongbe.

DUTCH-BASED CREOLES

The Dutch were heavily invested in both the slave trade and plantation colonialism, and it is therefore no surprise to find that there have been a number of Dutch creoles. One of these, Skepi Dutch, is no longer spoken and is attested only by a few words lists. Another, Berbice Dutch Creole (BDC) is spoken by a handful of older people. Negerhollands, a creole once widely spoken in what are now the U.S. Virgin Islands, is also virtually extinct and spoken only by a few second-language speakers.

Before it became British, Guyana was under Dutch control. In the 1970s, a Guyanese linguist named Ian Robertson discovered that a Dutch-based creole was still spoken in the interior. This language was apparently once the vernacular of the Dutch-owned Berbice colony. As of 1993, the number of BDC speakers numbered only four or five.

Berbice Dutch Creole is of special interest because, unlike many other creoles, its substrate appears to have been quite uniform. As Ian Robertson writes, "the seminal African substratum input into Berbice Dutch Creole came from Eastern Ijo, with the Kalabari dialect perhaps the major contributor" (1993, p. 297). By a standard measure of the most common terms in the language, the Berbice Dutch Creole lexicon is 61 percent Dutch, 27 percent Ijo, 7 percent English and 5 percent other. This is quite remarkable given that the substrate contributed about 5 percent of the lexicon in other conservative creoles (e.g., Saramaccan). In terms of tense and aspect marking, Berbice Dutch Creole is quite unlike other creoles in having a marked perfective category (as opposed to an unmarked verb stem conveying this meaning), which is indicated by an inflectional element on the verb. In this and other respects Berbice Dutch Creole resembles not other creole languages but, rather, Eastern Ijo, the substrate. Robertson writes that the perfective suffix –te "appears to be a direct transfer from Eastern Ijo" (1993, p. 303).

IBERIAN-BASED CREOLES: PALENQUERO AND PAPIAMENTO

The relative scarcity of creoles based on Spanish has been a matter of debate for some time. The anthropologist Sidney Mintz has suggested "with considerable caution" that this might be explained by the fact that "the Hispano-Caribbean colonies were never dominated demographically by inhabitants of African origin" and further that in these colonies "movement from the social category of 'slaves' to that of 'freemen' was almost always *relatively* rapid and *relatively* continuous" (Mintz, p. 481). More recently, however, John McWhorter has challenged this apparently quite reasonable explanation and suggested a provocative alternative account. There is one clearly Spanish-based creole in the Americas: Palenquero, which is spoken by the older members of a community of approximately 2,500 people living in the isolated village of El Palenque de San Basilio on the Caribbean coast of Colombia. Another possible instance is Papiamento, which is spoken by approximately 200,000 people on the leeward Netherland Antilles (Curacao and Bonaire) and on Aruba. Unlike other creoles, Papiamento has a fairly well-established literary tradition, a spelling system, and it plays a role in the educational system. The language emerged in the seventeenth century and is based primarily on Portuguese and Spanish. In terms of tense and aspect marking, Papiamento differs from the prototypical creole pattern in having an overtly marked perfective category as well as a "past imperfective."

THEORIES OF CREOLE FORMATION

The question of how these languages originated is highly contentious, and a number of accounts have been developed. A theory of how creoles emerge must account for both the striking similarities and the important differences among these languages.

Most accounts of creole formation assume the following scenario: When African slaves were brought to New World and Indian Ocean plantations, they encountered the European languages of the masters and their indentured servants. However, this encounter was characterized by severely limited access to the relevant European language. Africans patched together what they could of the lexical, phonological, and grammatical structures of the language, but this process left gaping holes. This situation then led—either gradually or more or less spontaneously in conjunction with language acquisition—to significant reconstitution, reorganization, and restructuring. The most important attempts to explain how this restructuring took place can be divided into four main groups: monogenetic, universal, superstratal, and substratal.

MONOGENETIC THEORIES: THE POSSIBILITY OF AN AFRICAN ORIGIN. Many pidgins and creoles share a core of words from Portuguese. For instance, Jamaican, Guyanese Sranan, Tok Pisin, Krio, and many French creoles include the words *piknii* (child) from the Portuguese *pequenos* (little ones) and *sabi* (know) from the Portuguese *saber* (to know). A more restricted group (e.g., Sranan, Saramaccan) also have *ma* (but) from *mas* (but), *na* as a locative preposition from *na* (in the; used before singular feminine nouns), and *kaba* or *kba* as a completive marker from *acabar* (to complete, finish). On the basis of this widespread distribution of Portuguese lexical items, some early creolists suggested that all the creoles developed out of a Portuguese pidgin spoken on the west coast of Africa and in other places where the Portuguese traded in the fifteenth century (this included the Pacific region). In each territory, this contact vernacular was relexified by the local superstrate language (a kind of calquing).

More recently, John McWhorter has developed another monogenetic theory. He suggests that the Caribbean Creoles, as well as those of the Indian Ocean, originated in slave-trading forts along the west coast of Africa. According to this theory, English-based creoles originated as a proto-variety at Cormantin among castle slaves, and this language was then transported to Barbados. According to McWhorter, all this happened sometime between 1630 and 1650.

The early colonies of the seventeenth century comprised small settlements, homesteads, and farms. This period was not characterized by significant demographic disproportion between white and black or by excessive social distance. Rather, European indentured laborers and Africans worked side-by-side in close quarters. The limited access model simply does not apply to this period. It was on the basis of such historical evidence that the limited access model was significantly revised in the 1980s, with many creolists coming to argue that the varieties closest to English (or the lexifier) emerged first. These were then subject to a process of "basilectalization" or dilution and restructuring as the numbers of African people increased significantly in the eighteenth century. The problem with this account, according to McWhorter, is that Sranan must have formed before 1671 when the English left Suriname for Jamaica. The slaves they brought to Jamaica introduced a language very similar to Sranan, which is still spoken as a ritual register by Maroons (Maroon Spirit Language, or MSL). The MSL–Sranan connection suggests that these languages formed early in the seventeenth century and thus makes the revised "limited access" scenario problematic.

THE ROLE OF AN INNATE CAPACITY FOR LANGUAGE AND LANGUAGE UNIVERSALS. Among linguists, the theories that emphasize the role played by an innate human capacity for language have attracted the most interest. The most prominent advocate of such a view is Derek Bickerton. This basic idea has been around for as long as people have seriously studied these languages. The story goes as follows: In the initial stages of plantation slavery, Europeans tended to outnumber Africans. However this situation did not last long. After the initial settlement stage, plantations expanded massively and many thousands of Africans were imported. After a few decades, Africans greatly outnumbered the Europeans. The African population in these colonies was heterogeneous, and their own languages did not provide a viable vehicle for interethnic communication. As a result, a rudimentary pidgin developed based on the vocabulary of the European language. This language would have been adequate for organizing work on the plantation and for other rudimentary tasks, though it lacked the expressive capacity of a full-blown language. Not only was the lexicon severely limited, there was essentially no grammar. The general paucity of expressive resources reflected a learning environment in which access to the target language was severely limited. Moreover, whatever parts of the target language did make it into the pidgin were continually "diluted" as they spread throughout the population of nonnative speakers.

This meant that the inflections by which many languages express tense, aspect, and other important information were lost. When children were born into this community, the language they encountered was radically deficient and irregular. In order to construct a fully functional, natural language—a first language—children in this situation independently drew on their inborn capacity for language. They had to reconstruct a system for expressing distinctions of tense and aspect, for example. Because

they all drew on the same innate capacity for language, they produced similar creole languages—but because in each case they were dealing with different levels of dilution of different languages, they produced different languages. Bickerton supports his argument with data such as in Table 2.

Bickerton's theory is a sophisticated version of the life-cycle model of pidgins and creole development. It is a commonly held view that these languages originate in grammarless jargons—essentially just a collection of words. They may go on to become stabilized pidgins used only for trade and interethnic contact. Alternatively, they may be "nativized" when a generation of children learn them as a first language, at which point they are transformed into creoles (see Figure 1).

THE SUPERSTRATE: THE CONTRIBUTION OF EUROPEAN LANGUAGES. A number of scholars have suggested that many creoles owe much more to their superstrate languages than has been previously acknowledged. Theories that emphasize the superstrate were long associated with French scholars who examined the French of Reunion. More recently, a kind of superstrate model has been developed by Shana Poplack and Sali Tagliamonte in studies of African-American English. In part, this work was a reaction to research that tacitly assumed monolithic European languages, such as English, French, and Dutch. Scholars in this tradition rightly pointed out that the dialectal and regional versions of English that would have been spoken on seventeenth- and eighteenth-century plantations were quite varied and incorporated many features similar to the ones seen in contemporary creoles. This research has focused, however, on a limited set of languages, such as African-American English and Reunion French, which have been only moderately restructured.

THE SUBSTRATE: THE CONTRIBUTION OF AFRICAN LANGUAGES. Perhaps the most popular theory among creolists is one that emphasizes the role of substrate languages in the formation of creoles. Although there are a number of different accounts, West African languages provided a base of common grammatical structures, which were transferred to the creole through some kind of calque-like mechanism. Where one substrate language was dominant—such as Eastern Ijo for Berbice Dutch Creole, or Gbe for Sranan—its structures tended to get transferred. Where no particular substrate was dominant, structures common across them—such as serial verbs—were likely to get transferred.

There are a number of different substratal theories. Perhaps the most explicit is that developed by Claire Le-

	Hawaiian	Haitian	Sranan
Base form			
"He walked"	He walk	Li mache	A waka
"He loves"	He love	Li reme	A lobi
Anterior			
"He had walked."	He bin walk	Li té maché	A ben waka
"He loved."	He bin love	Li té rêmé	A ben lobi
Irreal			
"He will/would walk."	He go walk	L'av(a) maché	A sa waka
"He will/would love."	He go love	L'av(a) rêmé	A sa lobi
Nonpunctual			
"He is/was walking."	He stay walk	L'ap maché	A e waka
Anterior + irreal + nonpunctual			
("He would have been walking")	He bin go stay walk	Li t'av ap maché	A ben sa e waka

Table 2

febvre and her colleagues, known as "relexification." According to Lefebvre, exposure to the superstrate languages in the early days of plantation slavery provided access to "phonetic strings" (strings of sounds understood as a "word"). These did not necessarily correspond to French words (in fact they rarely did). For instance, the Haitian Creole word for water is *dlo* which is quite clearly a concatenation of the preposition *de*, the article *l'*, and the noun *eau*, forming *de l'eau* (water). These phonetic strings were then mapped onto the lexical entries of Africans' native languages.

While there appears to be some strong evidence for relexification, there are also problems with this theory. First, it works best when a given structure from Haitian Creole and Fongbe match, and the French is different, but this is not always the case. Moreover, relexificationists can be accused of failing to consider what kind of French would actually have been spoken in the contact situation. For the most part, their claims are based on the more-or-less standard French of today and not the regional, vernacular, and nonstandard dialects of the seventeenth and eighteenth centuries. Relexificationists also often do not consider the full range of substrate languages, focusing instead on the one they argue was dominant.

CREOLES, LANGUAGE ATTITUDES, AND NATIONAL LIFE

Creole languages vary greatly in terms of the status accorded to them. In Guyana, most people are deeply ambivalent about the language they speak. In rural villages, everybody speaks creolese, and a person speaking standard English is mocked and often not trusted. On the other hand, a person who is able to speak only the creole is sometimes characterized as stupid and ignorant. Such complex attitudes pose a challenge for those who wish to standardize and institutionalize the language in the service of national or international (i.e., Caribbean) integration.

In Guyanese education, the creole language is unrecognized, and it has no place in government except to the extent that politicians make use of it in presenting themselves to the people. Although writers sometimes use creole when writing dialogue, and sometimes in poetry, creole is basically absent from the newspapers, except where it is used in a story or to voice a character.

In contrast, entire newspapers are published in Haitian Creole, Papiamento, and Sranan. Indeed, when Jean-Bertrand Aristide came to power in Haiti he used Haitian Creole, not French, to address the people. This signaled a significant change in a country that was included as a prototypical example in Charles Ferguson's original discussion of diglossia. Perhaps the most extreme case is presented by a few of the formerly French colonies. In Saint Lucia and Dominica, where English is making significant inroads, the local language has been taken up and valorized by the cultural elite. In Saint Lucia, Kweyol has been invoked as a symbol of cultural heritage.

CREOLES AND AFRICAN-AMERICAN ENGLISH

A matter of great controversy since the 1960s is the relationship between the various Caribbean English Creoles and the variety of English spoken by many African Americans in the United States. In the 1970s a number of creolists argued that African-American English descended from a prior creole language that in many respects resembled the vernacular languages of Guyana and Jamaica. They pointed to similarities in the area of phonology (significant consonant cluster reduction), morphology (in the expression of past tense, for example) and vocabulary.

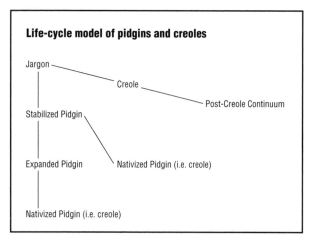

Life-cycle model of pidgins and creoles

Jargon

Creole

Post-Creole Continuum

Stabilized Pidgin

Expanded Pidgin

Nativized Pidgin (i.e. creole)

Nativized Pidgin (i.e. creole)

Figure 1

CONCLUSION

Although these languages show a number of significant similarities both in terms of their linguistic structures and the conditions within which they developed, they are also distinct in many ways. Each is a living tradition which is valued by its speakers not for its connections to Africa or for what it might reveal about the human mind, but for its capacity to effectively represent the natural, social, and political world, and at the same time serve as an efficient vehicle of communication.

See also English, African-American; Haitian Creole Language

 Bibliography

Bickerton, Derek. *The Roots of Language*. Ann Arbor, Mich.: Karoma, 1981.

Bickerton, Derek. "Creole Languages." *Scientific American* 249, no. 1 (1983): 116–122.

Bickerton, Derek. "The Language Bioprogram Hypothesis." *Behavioral and Brain Sciences* 7, no. 2 (1984): 173–188.

Bilby, Kenneth. "How the 'Older Heads' Talk: A Jamaican Maroon Spirit Possession Language and its Relationship to the Creoles of Suriname and Sierra Leone." *Nieuwe West-Indische Gids* 57 (1983): 37–88.

Cassidy, Frederic G. "Multiple etymologies in Jamaican Creole." *American Speech* 41, no. 3 (1966): 211–215.

Chaudenson, Robert. *Creolization of Language and Culture*. New York: Routledge, 2001.

Comrie, Bernard. *Aspect: An Introduction to the Study of Verbal Aspect and Related Problems*. Cambridge, UK: Cambridge University Press, 1976.

den Besten, Hans, Pieter Muysken, and Norval Smith. "Theories Focusing on the European Input." In *Pidgins and Creoles: An Introduction*, edited by Jacques Arends, Pieter Muysken, and Norval Smith, pp. 87–98. Amsterdam: J. Benjamins, 1995.

Devonish, Hubert. *Language and Liberation: Creole Language Politics in the Caribbean*. London: Karia, 1986.

Ferguson, Charles. "Diglossia." *Word* 15 (1959): 325–337.

Garrett, P. B. "'High' Kweyol: The Emergence of a Formal Creole Register in St. Lucia." In *Language Change and Language Contact in Pidgins and Creoles*, edited by John McWhorter, pp. 63–101. Amsterdam: John Benjamins, 2000.

Holm, John A. *Pidgins and Creoles*. Cambridge, UK: Cambridge University Press. 1988.

Hopper, Paul J., and Elizabeth C. Traugott. *Grammaticalization*, 2nd ed. Cambridge, UK: Cambridge University Press, 2003.

Kouwenberg, Silvia. "Berbice Dutch." In *Pidgins and Creoles: an Introduction*, edited by Jacques Arends, Pieter Muysken, and Norval Smith, pp. 233–243. Amsterdam: John Benjamins, 1995.

Lefebvre, Claire. "The Role of Relexification and Syntactic Reanalysis in Haitian Creole: Methodological Aspects of a Research Program." In *Africanisms in Afro-American Language Varieties*, edited by S. S. Mufwene, pp. 254–279. Athens: University of Georgia Press, 1993.

McWhorter, John H. *The Missing Spanish Creoles: Recovering the Birth of Plantation Contact Languages*. Berkeley: University of California Press, 2000.

Migge, Bettina. "Substrate Influence in Creole Formation: The Origin of Give-Type Serial Verb Constructions in the Surinamese Plantation Creole." *Journal of Pidgin and Creole Languages* 13, no. 2 (1998): 215–265.

Mintz, Sidney W. "The Socio-Historical Background to Pidginization and Creolization." In *Pidginization and Creolization of Languages*, edited by D. H. Hymes, pp. 481–496. Cambridge, UK: Cambridge University Press, 1971.

Mintz, Sidney W., and Richard Price. *The Birth of African-American Culture: An Anthropological Perspective*. Boston: Beacon Press, 1992.

Mithun, Marianne. "The Acquisition of Polysynthesis." *Journal of Child Language* 16, no. 2 (1989): 285–312.

Morgan, Marcyliena. "Theories and Politics in African American English." *Annual Review of Anthropology* 23 (1994): 325–345.

Mühlhäusler, Peter. *Pidgin and Creole Linguistics*. Oxford, UK: Blackwell, 1986.

Poplack, Shana. *The English History of African American English*. Malden, Mass.: Blackwell, 2000.

Poplack, Shana., and Sali Tagliamonte. *African American English in the Diaspora*. Malden, Mass.: Blackwell, 2001.

Price, Richard. *Maroon Societies: Rebel Slave Communities in the Americas*, 3d ed.. Baltimore, Md.: Johns Hopkins University Press, 1996.

Robertson, Ian. "The Ijo Element in Berbice Dutch and the Pidginization/Creolization Process." In *Africanisms in Afro-American Language Varieties*, edited by S. S. Mufwene, pp. 296–316. Athens: University of Georgia Press, 1993.

Sidnell, Jack. "Gender and Pronominal Variation in an Indo-Guyanese Creole-Speaking Community." *Language in Society* 28, no. 3 (1999): 367–399.

Sidnell, J. "Habitual and Imperfective in Guyanese Creole." *Journal of Pidgin and Creole Languages* 17, no. 2 (2002): 151–189.

Smith, Norval, Ian Robertson, and Kay Williamson. "The Ijo Element in Berbice Dutch." *Language in Society* 16, no. 1 (1987): 49–89.

Turner, Lorenzo Dow. *Africanisms in the Gullah Dialect*. Chicago: Chicago University Press, 1949.

Winford, Donald. *Predication in Caribbean English Creoles*. Amsterdam: John Benjamins, 1993.

Winford, Donald. "Re-Examining Caribbean English Creole Continua." *World Englishes* 16, no. 2 (1997): 233–279.

JACK SIDNELL (2005)

CRIMINAL JUSTICE SYSTEM

The American criminal justice system has shaped racial inequalities and been shaped by them. From 1619 until Emancipation, the vast majority of African Americans were enslaved. At Emancipation, approximately four million people were enslaved in the United States. This 250-year period saw the development of a system of laws and practices that often protected white people from conviction for crimes against African Americans. This legal system also regulated marriage and mobility in a restrictive manner for African Americans.

SLAVE CODES

In the South until slavery was abolished, policing was carried out by publicly or privately financed patrols. These patrols—called *paterollers*—policed the roads, woods, and public spaces in the plantation South. The earliest slave patrols were groups of owners in sixteenth-century Cuba, then a Spanish colony, who gathered to capture enslaved people who had fled their plantations. Over time, this amateur system was replaced by professionals—often themselves former bondsmen—who were paid a bounty for each fugitive they apprehended.

Whereas these early patrols focused their energies on enslaved people who had fled, the British colony of Barbados was the first to develop a system of laws to regulate the movement and behavior of all enslaved peoples. In reaction to an abortive rebellion in 1649, Barbados instituted a pass system. In addition to enforcing the pass system, which required enslaved people to carry passes explaining and authorizing their movement, Barbadian patrols also enforced laws that forbade enslaved people from carrying firearms and from moving around on Sundays. In 1661 Barbados created the first slave code in the British colonies in an "Act for the Better ordering and governing of Ne-

groes." As Sally Hadden notes, this act was based on the assumption that enslaved people were "heathenish brutish" and a "'dangerous kinde of people' who had to be controlled" (2001, p. 11).

This code was soon adopted by other British colonies, first in Jamaica and Antigua and then in the North American colony of South Carolina, founded in part by former Barbadian slave owners in 1670. South Carolina created its "Act for the Better Ordering of Slaves" in 1690. Designed primarily to limit the movement of free and enslaved black people to specific days and the carrying out of specific tasks, it also regulated behavior. Whites who apprehended an enslaved person without a pass were mandated by law to administer a whipping under the 1696 revision of the South Carolina Act. After the Stono Rebellion in 1739, patrolling became the exclusive duty of the militia. These codes soon spread to other North American colonies, including Georgia, Virginia, Louisiana, Kentucky, and Alabama.

In still other ways, the emerging criminal justice system played a central role in establishing racial inequality. The lives of the approximately 500,000 free African Americans in 1860 were heavily regulated by the criminal justice system. Laws in the slave states barred black people from serving on juries or serving as witnesses against whites. Maryland and Louisiana maintained a large free black population throughout the period, particularly in Baltimore and New Orleans. But in most states in the early nineteenth century, if someone wanted to free an enslaved person he or she was required to pay the freedperson's transportation out of the state.

CRIMINAL JUSTICE IN THE JIM CROW ERA

Through legislation, the antebellum criminal justice system codified the meanings of racial difference. After the Civil War, when slavery no longer existed, the codified meanings of racial difference underwent transformations through subtle and pernicious changes in criminal law. Through the convict-lease system, the southern criminal justice system managed to maintain many of the worst elements of slavery. In the convict-lease system, African Americans—including juveniles—could be leased out to labor contractors to engage in backbreaking labor for no compensation. As W. E. B. Du Bois would later argue, the convict-lease system was a "spawn of slavery" that did nothing to lower crime rates. Like the paterollers, post-Civil War criminal justice was designed primarily to maintain white racial supremacy by restricting the movement and behavior of African American people. As social reformers and journalists investigated and revealed these practices, the convict-lease system gave way to state-run prison farms. From Angola in Louisiana to Parchman Farm in Mississippi, former plantations turned prison farms became among the most profitable farms in the post-Reconstruction South. This segregated—or Jim Crow—system of punishment recreated the brutality and exploitation of slavery within the criminal justice system.

Extralegal practices of policing and punishment developed alongside this Jim Crow system of criminal justice. In the late nineteenth and early twentieth centuries, lynching was the most pernicious form of extralegal social control. Between 1877 and 1892, 728 documented lynchings took place. The charge of rape often accompanied lynching. Memphis journalist Ida B. Wells revealed that the premise that lynching was needed to curb an insatiable black male desire to have sex with white women obscured more credible underlying reasons. Perhaps her most important argument centered on the contention that "the whole matter is explained by the well-known opposition growing out of slavery to the progress of the race. . . .The South resented giving the Afro-American his freedom, the ballot box, and the Civil Rights Law" (Wells, p. 30). She saw lynching as a political act intended to maintain white economic, political, and social supremacy. The strategy was "kill the leaders and it will cow the Negro" (Wells, p. 34). In the absence of police protection, she urged every African American to learn that "a Winchester rifle should have a place of honor in every black home, and it should be used for that protection which the law refused to give" (Wells, p. 37).

Like paterollers, the convict-lease system, and prison farms, lynching served to maintain white supremacy through terror and violence. In couching the atrocity of lynching as a response to a rape or attempted rape, "Judge Lynch," as the practice was sometimes called, placed the extralegal practice within the language of law and order. As Ida B. Wells argued, however, lynching maintained racial oppression while claiming to protect citizens from organized violence. This ongoing link between policing and racial oppression resulted in a criminal justice system that could not be seen merely as a means of protecting law-abiding citizens from criminals. Rather, the criminal justice system was supportive of lawlessness in the case of lynching and, as the twentieth century opened, overzealous in its prosecution of African Americans, whom whites increasingly believed were associated with the problem of urban crime.

THE GREAT MIGRATION

Partly in response to continued discrimination, one million African Americans moved from the South to the North between 1915 and 1925. This became known as the

SOUTHERN HORRORS.
LYNCH LAW
IN ALL
ITS PHASES

MISS IDA B. WELLS,

Price, · · · Fifteen Cents.

THE NEW YORK AGE PRINT,
1892.

Cover page from Southern Horrors: Lynch Law in all its Phases *(1892), by Ida B. Wells. Wells's landmark study explored the motivations behind the lynching of blacks in the South.* PHOTOGRAPHS AND PRINTS DIVISION, SCHOMBURG CENTER FOR RESEARCH IN BLACK CULTURE, THE NEW YORK PUBLIC LIBRARY, ASTOR, LENOX AND TILDEN FOUNDATIONS.

Great Migration. African-American neighborhoods in cities like New York and Chicago often had high crime rates, in part because they housed vice districts that served a broad, multiracial, illicit market for drugs, prostitution, and gambling. During the 1920s, sociologists offered two competing explanations for the involvement of some African Americans in urban vice and crime. The first posited that overcrowding, poverty, and uprooting helped to produce an increase in criminality. The second, more popular explanation sought racialized explanations for what was called "Negro crime." In short, explanations alternated between blaming the ghetto environment and blaming the "innate criminality" of black people. Although the explanations differed, most whites agreed that the newly urban African-American population needed intensive policing. Almost immediately following the Great Migration, state and local police resources targeted African-American communities. A third explanation soon emerged, blaming saturation policing of black communities, discrimination throughout the criminal justice system, and racist stereotypes for the overrepresentation of black people in crime data and the prison system.

Despite changes in location and justification, the criminal justice system maintained white racial domination in a historically consistent manner. In 1931 national attention focused on nine young African-American men ranging in age from thirteen to twenty-one who became known as the Scottsboro Boys after they faced trial in Alabama on rape charges. When the "boys" were convicted and sentenced to death, many observers used the case as evidence that the old system of racially inspired justice remained firmly in place. The Supreme Court reversed their convictions in *Powell v. Alabama* (1932), but subsequent trials resulted in prison sentences of up to nineteen years for five of the defendants. Outrage at this treatment, however, inspired the formation of the National Association for the Advancement of Colored People (NAACP) Legal Defense Fund (LDF). Under Charles Hamilton Houston, vice dean of the Howard University Law School, the LDF joined the efforts of the civil rights movement to transform the criminal justice system during the post–World War II period.

THE CIVIL RIGHTS MOVEMENT AND THE CRIMINAL JUSTICE SYSTEM

In 1963, while incarcerated in a Birmingham, Alabama, jail, Martin Luther King Jr. wrote a justification of civil disobedience. His willingness to violate the laws that legitimized segregation stemmed from his belief that "all segregation statutes are unjust because segregation distort[s] the soul and damages the personality. . . .Thus it is that I can urge men to obey the 1954 decision of the Supreme Court, for it is morally right; and I can urge them to disobey segregation ordinances, for they are morally wrong" (King, p. 38). In both his practice and advocacy, King urged people to break unjust laws even as the movement worked to reshape the legal system in ways that advanced the cause of racial justice, as had, for example, the *Brown v. Board of Education* (1954) decision, which outlawed school segregation.

The LDF emerged as the most powerful proponent of changing the criminal justice system during the 1960s and 1970s. While the LDF became well known for its work on school desegregation, it worked equally hard on revising laws and practices that unfairly targeted African Americans. In the years following the assassinations of Martin Luther King Jr. and Robert F. Kennedy, the LDF joined Amnesty International and the American Civil Liberties Union in condemning the death penalty. These organizations insisted that the application of the death sentence— particularly in cases involving the rape of a white woman—constituted an arbitrary and racist double standard. Between 1930, the first year such statistics were collected, and 1969, state governments executed 445 men for rape. Of these, 40 were white, the rest African American (Bernstein, p. 16). The LDF succeeded in overturning the death sentences of over 600 death row inmates in a series of cases between 1967 and 1972.

During the late 1960s and 1970s, the argument that the criminal justice system played a crucial role in maintaining racial inequality intensified. Most notably, prisoners and former convicts voiced their concerns that racism had fundamentally influenced their incarceration. Malcolm X was joined by Huey P. Newton, George Jackson, Ericka Huggins, and Angela Davis in articulating the link between racial inequality and the policing of African-American communities. In 1967, according to Useem and Kimball (1989), 80 percent of the almost 300,000 prison inmates in the United States were people of color. These masses of incarcerated people raised more than their voices: On the East Coast, the Attica prison riots became the best known of the approximately 300 such disturbances in the United States between the late 1960s and early 1980s. Forty-eight of these were concentrated between 1968 and 1971.

The liberation of all black prisoners became a central demand of the struggle for social justice in the aftermath of the civil rights movement. As Huey P. Newton—the founder of the Black Panther Party, whose release from prison became a focus of Panther efforts—said at the eulogy for Jonathan Jackson and William Christmas, "There are no laws that the oppressor makes that the oppressed are bound to respect" (Newton, p. 322). Jonathan Jackson's older brother George soon became known for his book of prison letters, *Soledad Brother,* in which he observed that "there are still some blacks here who consider themselves criminals, but not many"(Jackson, p. 36).

These writers also articulated the view that police officers were a colonizing presence in black communities; that as agents of oppression, police officers were agents of the perpetuation of segregation and exploitation. As these arguments achieved widespread influence in the wake of urban uprisings in Los Angeles, Detroit, and northern New Jersey, police departments began actively recruiting African-American officers. There had long been some few African-American police officers, but they largely served in segregated "Negro divisions" or as one of several token figures in otherwise white departments. In an explicit effort to improve relations between black communities and police departments, African Americans were hired in large numbers in Chicago, Newark, Detroit, and Houston during the 1960s and 1970s. In other cities, African Americans were promoted to leadership positions. In some cases, they spoke out against racism in their ranks in order to expedite changes in the culture of police departments. In addition, some cities joined New York City in establishing civilian review boards to investigate citizen complaints against police departments. However, white-dominated police unions took legal action against both affirmative action policies and civilian review boards. Even where they existed, the presence of African-American officers and civilian review boards did little to change discriminatory practices at every level of the criminal justice system.

The appointment of African-American judges and prosecutors proceeded even more slowly than the racial integration of police departments. In 1977, 22 of 500 federal judges were African American (4.4%). In the area of jury service, the rate of inclusion for African Americans was also low. Although the exclusion of African Americans from juries was outlawed in 1875, African Americans continued to be excluded from juries through the use of peremptory challenges—a practice that allows prosecutors to eliminate individuals from the jury pool without needing to explain their reasons. This resulted in the underrepresentation of African Americans on juries in federal and state trials.

CRIMINAL JUSTICE SINCE THE 1970S

Since the 1970s, two factors have dominated explanations for the continued overrepresentation of African Americans in the criminal justice system. First, the war on drugs has disproportionately affected African Americans and other peoples of color. Although drug use occurs across racial lines and some studies suggest that drug use among whites is higher than among African Americans, African Americans are prosecuted, convicted, and incarcerated for drug and drug-related crimes at far higher rates than people from all other backgrounds. Second, while scholarly studies disagree on whether people from economically disadvantaged backgrounds are more likely to break laws, they agree that they are much more likely to enter into the criminal justice system when they do so. According to U.S. census data cited by Marvin Free (1996), between 1970 and 1990 the percentage of black families with incomes below the poverty line increased from 20.9 percent to 25.6 percent. During this same period, African-American overrepresentation in correctional facilities increased. These trends have led some criminologists to suggest that an improvement in African-American socioeconomic conditions must join fundamental changes in the criminal jus-

tice system—including the decriminalization of violations that unfairly target African Americans—in order to begin disentangling the legacies of racial inequality and criminal justice.

See also Black Panther Party; Davis, Angela; Houston, Charles Hamilton; Jackson, George Lester; Jim Crow; Lynching; National Association for the Advancement of Colored People (NAACP); Slave Codes

■ ■ *Bibliography*

Bernstein, Lee. "'. . .Give Me Death': Capital Punishment And The Limits Of American Citizenship." In *States Of Confinement: Policing, Detention, And Prisons*, edited by Joy James. New York: Palgrave, 2002.

Christianson, Scott. *With Liberty for Some: 500 Years of Imprisonment in America.* Boston: Northeastern University Press, 1998.

Cole, David. *No Equal Justice: Race and Class in the American Criminal Justice System.* New York: New Press, 1999.

DuBois, W. E. B. "The Spawn of Slavery: The Convict-Lease System in the South." *The Missionary Review of the World* 14 (1901): 737–745. Reprinted in *African American Classics in Criminology and Criminal Justice*, edited by Shaun L. Gabbidon, Helen Taylor Greene, and Vernetta D. Young. Thousand Oaks, Calif.: Sage, 2002.

Dulaney, W. Marvin. *Black Police in America.* Bloomington: Indiana University Press, 1996.

Free, Marvin D., Jr. *African Americans and the Criminal Justice System.* New York: Garland, 1996.

Hadden, Sally E. *Slave Patrols: Law and Violence in Virginia and the Carolinas.* Cambridge, Mass.: Harvard University Press, 2001.

Jackson, George. *Soledad Brother: The Prison Letters of George Jackson.* New York: Bantam, 1970.

King, Martin Luther, Jr. "Letter from a Birmingham Jail." *The Christian Century* 80, no. 24 (June 12, 1963): 767–773. Reprinted in *Imprisoned Intellectuals: America's Political Prisoners Write on Life, Liberation, and Rebellion*, edited by Joy James. Lanham, Md.: Rowman and Littlefield, 2003.

Newton, Huey P. "Eulogy for Jonathan Jackson and William Christmas." Delivered at Saint Augustine's Church, Oakland, Calif., August 15, 1970. Reprinted in *Off the Pigs! The History and Literature of the Black Panther Party*, edited by G. Louis Heath. Metuchen, N.J.: Scarecrow, 1976.

Oshinsky, David. *"Worse than Slavery": Parchman Farm and the Ordeal of Jim Crow Justice.* New York: Simon and Schuster, 1997.

Useem, Bert, and Peter Kimball, *States of Siege: U.S. Prison Riots, 1971–1986.* New York: Oxford University Press, 1989.

Wells, Ida B. "Southern Horrors: Lynch Law in All Its Phases," 1892. Reprinted in *African American Classics in Criminology and Criminal Justice*, edited by Shaun L. Gabbidon, Helen Taylor Greene, and Vernetta D. Young. Thousand Oaks, Calif.: Sage, 2002.

LEE BERNSTEIN (2005)

CRISIS, THE

The Crisis magazine is the official organ of the National Association for the Advancement of Colored People (NAACP) and was founded in 1910 by its first editor, W. E. B. Du Bois (1868–1963). The publication's original title for many years was *The Crisis: A Record of the Darker Races,* and its contents over time have continuously reflected its historical importance as the chronicler of African-American history, thought, and culture. The title, Du Bois later wrote, was the suggestion of William English Walling (1877–1936), a founder of the NAACP.

Du Bois said his object in publishing *The Crisis* was "to set forth those facts and arguments which show the danger of race prejudice, particularly as manifested today toward colored people. It takes its name from the fact [that] the editors believe that this is a critical time in the history of the advancement of men" (Du Bois, 1910, p. 10). The monthly issues contained subject matter ranging from literary works, editorial commentary, feature stories, and reports on NAACP activities to articles on current events. In the first decades, two regular features were "American Negroes in College" and "Along the NAACP Battlefront."

Du Bois served as editor for twenty-four years before retiring in 1934. By that time, *The Crisis* could boast among its contributors such luminaries as George Bernard Shaw, Mahatma Gandhi, Sinclair Lewis, Langston Hughes, and James Weldon Johnson. Although founded with the objective of being the official organ of the NAACP, it was also intended to be as self-supporting as possible. But when Du Bois retired as editor in 1934, its circulation had dropped from 100,000 (1918) to only 10,000. His successor as editor was Roy Wilkins (1901–1981), who served in that role until 1949 before being succeeded by James W. Ivy, who was at the helm during the peak years of the civil rights era, until his retirement in 1966.

During the transition years, *The Crisis* shifted its focus from the issues of wartime discrimination against African Americans in the U.S. armed forces, lynchings, and other manifestations of Jim Crow policies, to the courts, where rights were being upheld in voter registration, school desegregation, and housing discrimination. By 1988, circulation had risen to 350,000 subscribers. The magazine's basic editorial philosophy changed little over time from that established by Du Bois, but it had attracted enough major national corporate advertisers to place it on solid financial footing. Moreover, the NAACP had changed its policy to require both members and nonmembers to pay the subscription fee.

The Crisis continues with contributors from all walks of African-American life, including leadership in the clergy, academe, business, law, medicine, and other professions. It continues the tradition of serving as the cultural and social "record of the darker races."

See also Du Bois, W. E. B.; Jim Crow; National Association for the Advancement of Colored People (NAACP)

■ ■ *Bibliography*

Du Bois, W. E. B. "Opinion." *The Crisis* 1, no. 1 (1910): 10.

Du Bois, W. E. B. *The Autobiography of W. E. Burghardt Du Bois.* New York: International, 1968.

Emery, Edwin, and Michael Emery. *The Press and America*, 4th ed. Englewood Cliffs, N.J.: Prentice-Hall, 1978.

CLINT C. WILSON II (1996)

CRITCHLOW, HUBERT NATHANIEL

DECEMBER 18, 1884
MAY 14, 1958

Hubert Nathaniel Critchlow, OBE, was born to James Nathaniel and Julia Elizabeth Critchlow in Georgetown, British Guiana. Critchlow is renowned as the "Father of the Trade Union Movement" in Guyana for his pioneering role in organizing workers. After an early education at Bedford Wesleyan School, Georgetown, at age fourteen he became an engineer apprentice at the Demerara Foundry. However, his initial work experiences consisted of a series of low-paying jobs under abject conditions. He was an electric car motorman, cigar maker, bottle washer, office boy, gold miner, and a dockworker for Bookers Brothers Ltd., the sugar plantation colonial conglomerate. Critchlow, well known for his track-and-field prowess, was also a footballer and cricketer. Still, it was as a trade union activist that Critchlow made his greatest contributions to Guyana and the Caribbean.

Critchlow was the origin of trade union activism in the country. On November 28, 1905, he organized and led the dockworkers of Sandbach Parker & Co. Ltd., another colonial conglomerate, on a strike to protest deplorable working conditions. At a time of social unrest in the colony, Critchlow's actions served to unite urban working-class and rural estate workers against colonial officials and companies' management. Although the police on that occasion fired into the crowd of marching workers Critchlow led, the next year he organized a similar protest.

In 1917 and 1918 Critchlow was again at the helm of workers protesting for higher wages. For this action, he lost his job and was unable to secure further waterfront employment. On January 11, 1919, he formed the British Guiana Labour Union (BGLU), the first of its kind in British Guiana. Its membership was approximately 13,000 in the early years, at a time when the population of the country was estimated at 295,000. Critchlow served as general secretary of the union until his resignation in 1952. From 1924 to 1932 Critchlow attended several labor and workers conferences held in England, Germany, and Russia. Under his guidance the BGLU initiated the British Guiana and West Indian Labour Congress, a regional meeting of trade unionists.

Critchlow's most significant accomplishments include the 1922 introduction of a Rent Restriction Bill in the British Guiana Legislative Council. The bill's success led to the designation of July 3, 1922, as "Critchlow Day." In 1923 Critchlow supported petitions urging the colonial government to address increasing unemployment and rising consumer prices in the colony. He also advocated the introduction of national health insurance, old-age pensions, a girls' industrial training school, and a children's court. In addition to waterfront workers, Critchlow also demonstrated concern for domestics, nurses, carpenters, and shop assistants, who worked for long hours at low wages. He was instrumental in obtaining an eight-hour workday for dock and stevedore laborers and in the passage of the Workmen's Compensation Act. Moreover, under his leadership the BGLU demanded of the colonial administration the extension of the franchise to women, universal adult suffrage, labor representation in the legislative council, and self-government.

Critchlow served on the Discharged Prisoners Aid Committee, the Advisory Committee to the Rent Assessor, Georgetown, the Ex-Servicemen Committee, Poor Law and Local Government Boards, the Old Age Pensions Board, and the Public Works Advisory Committee. When the first British Guiana Trade Union Congress registered on April 8, 1941, Critchlow was the secretary. In 1943 he was appointed the first labor representative in the British Guiana Legislative Council. One year later, in 1944, he became the first labor leader appointed to the executive council of the British Guiana legislature. He was a government nominee to the Georgetown Town Council and also a member of the Arbitration Tribunal, under Sir Clement Malone, which inquired into a wage dispute concerning waterfront workers in Grenada, West Indies.

By December 1951 Critchlow was elected to the Legislative Council as a member of the British Guiana Labour Party. In 1951 he was awarded the Order of the British Empire (OBE). Critchlow influenced a new era in the country's history—the coming of the trade union movement. For example, by 1931 the British Guiana Workers League was formed and in 1937 the Man Power Citizens' Association was founded. Tributes to his contributions in improving labor conditions and the lives of workers include a statue of him on the lawns of the Public Buildings, the seat of the country's government, and the establishment of the Critchlow Labour College. Appropriately, the headquarters of the BGLU is named Critchlow House.

See also Labor and Labor Unions

■ ■ *Bibliography*

Ashton, Chase. *A History of Trade Unionism in Guyana, 1900–1961*. Georgetown, Guyana: New Guyana Company, 1966.

Hyacinth, Thomas. "Hubert Critchlow, Trade Unionist." In *African-Guyanese Achievement 1: 18. 155th Anniversary of African Slave Emancipation*. Georgetown, Guyana: Free Press, 1993.

"Mr. Hubert Nathaniel Critchlow Is Dead: Unique Chapter in History of Colonial Trade Unionism Closed." *Daily Argosy* (Georgetown, British Guiana; May 15, 1958).

"Outstanding African-Guyanese, Hubert Critchlow, OBE." *Emancipation, The African-Guyanese Magazine* (2000–2001): 36.

Who Is Who in British Guiana, 1945–1948. Georgetown, British Guiana: *Daily Chronicle*, 1948.

Woolford, Hazel M. "The Origins of the Labour Movement." In *Themes in African-Guyanese History*. Georgetown, Guyana: Free Press, 1998.

"Workers to Mourn Critchlow with Reverence." *Daily Chronicle* (Georgetown, British Guiana; May 16, 1958).

BARBARA P. JOSIAH (2005)

CRITICAL MIXED-RACE STUDIES

■ ■ ■

Critical mixed-race studies is a burgeoning scholarly approach to race, culture, and ethnicity. While its proponents hold widely varying opinions, they share a commitment to placing at the forefront of analysis the historical and present-day significance of race mixing, racial border crossing, and interracial life in the United States and elsewhere. Topics of particular interest within this line of inquiry include individual and collective identity, sexuality, marriage, and adoption. Like its counterpart, African-American studies, most scholars in this field take as a given that a complex legacy of racism lingers, that "the problem of the color-line," as W. E. B. Du Bois called it (1903, p. 3), persists, even though scientists have proven "race" to be a biological fallacy. There is, in fact, as much genetic variance within races as between races. Nor is race a reliable index for culture or for people's beliefs and practices, as these vary greatly among members of so-called races as well. While blacks are defined (in a U.S. context) as having African ancestry, the vast majority also have ancestors who were white, Native American, Asian, or some other "race." That is, they are racially mixed. Moreover, most Americans are familiar with the "one-drop rule," also called the law of *hypodescent*, which classifies interracial persons as black if they have any African ancestors, however distant in history and however few in number. Historically, the one-drop rule was applied far less than is perceived to be the case, however. Even though blacks are mixed, and mixed people with African ancestry are black, debates about the racial and cultural status of mixed-race subjects are ongoing and can be traced a long way back. These debates have permeated the realms of legal classification, census taking, and grassroots movements (i.e., the growing "mixed-race movement"), along with other discursive, popular, and ideological domains. The engagement of, and intervention into, these debates is one facet of critical mixed-race studies.

The negotiation of black-white interconnections is another dominant strand of critical mixed-race studies, though its practitioners might choose to examine any possible racial and cultural mixtures and their ramifications. Some in this field believe that the primacy of black-white mixing within critical mixed-race studies is problematic in its eclipsing other, equally significant manifestations of racial and cultural crossover, such as that between whites and Native Americans or Asian Americans, or between Native Americans and Asian Americans. Critical mixed-race studies overlaps with African-American studies in its concern with matters of race, racism, culture, and identity, but it is distinct in its focus on racial mixing—that is, on the fact that people from different racial backgrounds have interacted and reproduced throughout history, whether by choice, coercion, or force (as in the case of rape). Critical mixed-race studies confronts the reality that, as a result of extensive human intermixing, so-called racial groups cannot easily be divided into neat categories. While there is consensus that some fall in between socially constructed categories, debates ensue about whether this in-between space is a new category unto itself. Certainly, pervasive racial intermingling and color-line crossing raise the question of whether the color line is really a line at all. And critical mixed-race studies scholars share an interest in the vantage point from this would-be color line itself, rather than from one side of it or the other. What point of view

emerges—what lessons reveal themselves—if race and culture, past and present, are assessed from the location of racial crossover, of mixing, of in-between spaces, of intercultural contact zones? Applying such a lens can give rise to useful revisions of history and more accurate reinterpretations of social reality. Though it should be said that some African-American critical writings have already noted the frequency with which the racial divide has always been crisscrossed, with these color-line transgressions long operating as a site of political strategy, a site for the implementation of antiracist visions and agendas.

Critical mixed-race studies accounts for the degree to which racial contact zones can be fraught with conflict and risk. But interracial cooperation, collaboration, and cohabitation are also aspects of American reality that often go unacknowledged, given the emphasis on the black-white binary as the predominating racial schema, and given widespread notions of the workings of power and oppression as straightforwardly white over black. Within critical mixed-race studies, racial dichotomies are problematized, treated not as a matter of black or white (or red or yellow or brown, etc.), but rather as a matter of spectrums, of multiplicity, of heterogeneity, and above all of complexity. Despite racism as an overarching reality, race mixing has always occurred. The rape of slave women by slave owners was one dominant form in which race mixing took place, but it is less well known that there have always been freely chosen interracial unions as well.

Antimiscegenation laws—legislation against interracial marriage and interracial sexual relations—came about because of both racism and the rampant race mixing that was taking place historically. These laws were taken off the books only as recently as 1967, with the U.S. Supreme Court's *Loving v. Virginia* court case, a case that figures prominently within critical mixed-race writings. Interracial marriage between whites and all nonwhite races, and in some cases between various nonwhite races, has been outlawed in various places and at various times in U.S. history. But the mandates against black-white intimacy seem to have been the most strenuously enforced and obsessed over by those who were invested in such things, as many were, due to prevailing social, political, and economic forces, and due to the depth and magnitude of racism. Racism fueled the logic that mixing with other groups contaminated, debased, and ruined whiteness. Many, however, felt that mixing was an equally bad idea for all races given the supposedly inferior nature of the progeny, seen as inferior for being impure, a mongrel race. As Robert J. C. Young writes in his book *Colonial Desire*, no one in the annals of human history has been so maligned and "so demonized as those of mixed race" (1995, p. 180).

Biological or other ties to nonblack groups might appear to be beneficial to a person socially designated as black, but critical mixed-race studies proponents would question whether this is necessarily the case. Certainly much has been made of light-skinned privilege, the relative social, political, and economic advantages that can accrue to black people who are fair in complexion. Some have noted the preference shown by some whites for light-skinned blacks in employment practices, politics, the media, and the like. There are also troubling histories of black people themselves excluding darker blacks from membership in the black elite. Efforts to determine a person's "blackness" have included the administering of tests to assess whether a person was lighter in color than a brown paper bag, whether blue veins were visible on the underside of their wrists, and whether a comb or a pencil would pass effortlessly through their tresses. Persons who did not pass these tests would be barred from the proceedings to which they sought admittance. Many of mixed parentage "failed" such tests, for many were not light skinned with straight hair. And even those with the requisite coloring and coiffeur could be barred from the black elite precisely for being the offspring of a white person. To have a white parent, historically, was literally to confront assumptions of one's illegitimacy, as decreed by antimiscegenation laws. Having racially divergent parentage also conjured up a slew of anti–mixed-race prejudices that operated alongside of and in addition to antiblack ones.

The disadvantages that accrue to interracial subjects are another concern of critical mixed-race studies. One is the general incomprehension one incurs when one's identity is "both/and" in a context where "either/or" thinking continues to dominate. Hybrid persons are seen as enigmatic, anomalous, as an assault on a common-sense logic that insists on categorizing and sorting people. Some have noted that stereotypes of mixed people being especially attractive, exotic, or occupying "the best of both worlds" serve to objectify, fetishize, and emphasize "otherness." Interracial persons are frequently asked the million-dollar critical mixed-race studies question, "What are you?" by curious intimates and strangers alike, who are unabashed in seeking assistance in their efforts to pigeonhole them. The crisis of classification mixed-race people can inspire, the confusion they can generate at the level of public perception, gets projected back onto them—*they* must be confused. In the past, such reactions were even more extreme. Black-white mixed people specifically were seen as high-strung with jangled nerves and a tendency toward flightiness and shallowness. This was attributed in part to the two warring, irreconcilable bloods said to be coursing in their veins, some of which was flowing in one direction, the rest in another, wreaking havoc on body and psyche.

They were also seen as weak, effete, effeminate, and prone to mental illness. They were purported to be sexually impotent, with scientific thought holding officially, as recently as the early 1900s, that black-white persons were unable to reproduce—like the mule from which, according to myth, the word *mulatto* derives (a mule being the infertile offspring of a donkey and a horse).

Black mixing with nonwhites gives rise to still other cultural considerations and forms of prejudice. In Itabari Njeri's essay "Sushi and Grits" (1993), a woman of Japanese, Native-American, and African-American descent speaks of being taunted for being a "half breed," but more specifically for eating the sushi her mother put in her school lunch and for swinging her long hair in a way some of her peers perceived as inappropriate for a "black" girl. She became a staunch mixed-race movement advocate as a result. Critical mixed-race studies can itself be seen as a kind of intellectual mixed-race movement, one that is concerned with critiquing and complicating prevailing paradigms of race, culture, and ethnicity, whether those often employed within African-American studies or elsewhere. Eschewing a monolithic approach, critical mixed-race studies emphasizes racial hybridity, overlap, and crossover. It centralizes the many manifestations, past and present, of an interracial reality.

See also Black Studies; Identity and Race in the United States; Intellectual Life

▪ ▪ *Bibliography*

Du Bois, W. E. B. *The Souls of Black Folk* (1903). New York: Vintage, 1990.

Ifekwunigwe, Jayne. *Scattered Belongings: Cultural Paradoxes of "Race," Nation, and Gender*. New York: Routledge, 1999.

Kennedy, Randall. *Interracial Intimacies: Sex, Marriage, Identity, and Adoption*. New York: Pantheon, 2003.

Njeri, Itabari. "Sushi and Grits: Ethnic Identity and Conflict in a Newly Multicultural America." In *Lure and Loathing: Essays on Race, Identity, and the Ambivalence of Assimilation*, edited by Gerald Early. New York: Penguin, 1993.

Root, Maria. *The Multiracial Experience: Racial Borders as the New Frontier*. Thousand Oaks, Calif.: Sage, 1996.

Sollors, Werner. *Neither Black nor White yet Both: Thematic Explorations of Interracial Literature*. New York: Oxford University Press, 1997.

Spencer, Rainier. *Spurious Issues: Race and Multiracial Identity Politics in the United States*. Boulder, Colo.: Westview, 1999.

Stephens, Gregory. *On Racial Frontiers: The New Culture of Frederick Douglass, Ralph Ellison, and Bob Marley*. New York: Cambridge University Press, 1999.

Young, Robert, J. C. *Colonial Desire: Hybridity in Theory, Culture, and Race*. New York: Routledge, 1995.

Zack, Naomi. *Race and Mixed Race.* Philadelphia: Temple University Press, 1993.

NAOMI PABST (2005)

CRITICAL RACE THEORY

━ ❙ ❙ ❙ ━━━━━━━━━━━━━━━━━━━━━━━━━━━━━

The critical race theory (CRT) movement developed in the mid-1970s as lawyers, law students, and legal scholars who were sympathetic to the social justice movements of the 1960s witnessed a backlash against the advances of the previous decade. Critical race theory intended to address the most insidious forms of racism and unearth the multiple sources of racial inequality through a critical examination of laws, social practices, and institutions.

Critical race theorists seek to challenge racial inequality by questioning the underlying biases present in the practices and norms of American law, specifically liberalism, integrationism, rationalism, and the notion of an objective Constitution. Although the movement began with law professors and students, it is interdisciplinary. It uses theories and methods of economics, history, sociology, pedagogy, literature, narrative theory, and cultural studies. It has drawn scholars from a range of disciplines, although it remains centered in law and legal academia.

Critical race theory scholars write on an array of subject matters, from very specific case or doctrine analyses to theoretically broad examinations of race in society. However, some principles are consistent across the field. Critical race theorists reject the idea that integration necessarily means equality. They believe in interrogating what are often considered to be objective norms, such as "merit" or "color blindness," to see if they entail racial bias, and they believe in working against the subordination of people of color by placing at the fore perspectives and experiences that are often submerged.

Critical race theory found its intellectual origins in the crossroads of several movements: critical legal studies, a scholarly movement in which the law was considered to be an instrument for maintaining the status quo rather than a set of abstract rational principles; the civil rights and Black Power movements, with their interests in redress, self-determination, and socially engaged thought; and radical feminism, with its observations about the relationship between power and social roles. While it is often suggested that CRT was self-consciously born out of student movements at Harvard Law School, the movement appears to have coalesced from multiple origins and diverse actors with shared concerns. Seminal scholars in the critical race theory movement include Derrick Bell and Alan Freeman (who together made up the first generation of CRT scholars), Patricia Williams, Charles Laurence, Neil Gotanda, Robert Williams, Mari Matsuda, Kimberle Crenshaw, Angela Harris, Francisco Valdes, Margaret Montoya, Richard Delgado, and Jean Stefanic.

CRT has been criticized by detractors from several angles. Some have said that the personal narratives of law professors of color have figured too centrally in the work, while empirical data has been minimal. Others have said that CRT critiques structures of inequality but provides few answers on to how to address them, and still others have challenged it for venturing too far afield of traditional legal writing, even as the work is still principally found in law reviews that are not widely accessible.

CRT scholarship is extremely diverse. While some authors have innovatively used narrative, including personal narrative or fiction, as an argumentative technique, others have used traditional social science methodologies. And while CRT principally provides a critical lens through which to interpret social realities, a great deal of CRT scholarship also makes arguments about how certain legal doctrines should be interpreted or changed. Such arguments have been used in courts as well as in other fields of scholarly inquiry and by activists.

The first CRT conference was held in Madison, Wisconsin, in 1989. Since then dozens of meetings, conferences, and retreats have been held with CRT as a focus. A number of CRT scholars, including Derrick Bell and Patricia J. Williams, have become public figures who have impacted the national conversation about race, and many critical race theorists work in their local communities as practicing attorneys or grassroots activists. Critical race theory has become a subject for many university courses, in which students are encouraged to examine race critically using a wide range of materials.

In addition to finding its origins in several movements, CRT has also led to the development of other movements. Although historically CRT was principally concerned with African Americans, in the 1990s new voices began to emerge in CRT, giving birth to LatCRIT, a Latino-focused critical race theory, and Asian American Jurisprudence, as well as a convergence of queer theory and CRT. Additionally, critical race feminism has emerged, in which the specific gendered experience of women of color is centralized as a subject of concern. In recent years, CRT scholars have increasingly been looking to how race operates internationally, and specifically toward how to address global structures of racial inequality.

See also Black Studies; Civil Rights Movement, U.S.; Critical Mixed-Race Studies

■ ■ *Bibliography*

Bell, Derrick. *Faces at the Bottom of the Well: The Permanence of Racism.* New York: Basic Books, 1993.

Bell, Derrick. *Afrolantica Legacies.* Chicago: Third World Press, 1997.

Brown, Dorothy. *Critical Race Theory: Cases, Materials, and Problems.* St. Paul, Minn.: West Group, 2003.

Crenshaw, Kimberle, Neil Gotanda, Gary Peller, and Kendall Thomas, eds. *Critical Race Theory: The Key Writings that Formed the Movement.* New York: New Press, 1996.

Delgado, Richard, and Jean Stefanic, eds. *Critical Race Theory: The Cutting Edge,* 2d ed. Philadelphia: Temple University Press, 1999.

Delgado, Richard, and Jean Stefanic, eds. *Critical Race Theory: An Introduction.* New York: New York University Press, 2001.

Valdez, Francisco, Jerome McCristal Culp, and Angela Harris, eds. *Crossroads, Directions and a New Critical Race Theory.* Philadelphia: Temple University Press, 2002.

Williams, Patricia J. *The Alchemy of Race and Rights.* Cambridge, Mass.: Harvard University Press, 1991.

Williams, Patricia J. *Seeing a Color-Blind Future: The Paradox of Race.* New York: Farrar, Straus and Giroux, 1997.

Wing, Adrien Katherine, ed. *Global Critical Race Feminism: An International Reader.* New York: New York University Press, 2000.

Wing, Adrien Katherine, ed. *Critical Race Feminism: A Reader.* New York: New York University Press, 2003.

IMANI PERRY (2005)

CRITICISM, FEMINIST

See Feminist Theory and Criticism

CRITICISM, LITERARY

See Literary Criticism, U.S.

CROCKETT, GEORGE WILLIAM, JR.

AUGUST 10, 1909
SEPTEMBER 7, 1997

George William Crockett Jr. was born in Jacksonville, Florida, received his B.A. degree from Morehouse College in 1931 and his law degree from the University of Michigan in 1934, and became a champion of civil rights. In 1939 he became the first African-American attorney at the United States Department of Labor. President Franklin D. Roosevelt appointed him hearings officer of the Fair Employment Practices Committee in 1943. In 1944 he became head of the United Auto Workers Fair Employment Practices Office and returned to private practice in Detroit in 1946.

In 1949 Crockett undertook the defense of eleven Communists charged under the Smith Act; for his vigorous defense he was sentenced to four months in jail for contempt of court and narrowly escaped disbarment. In 1964 Crockett again demonstrated his commitment to civil rights by becoming director of Project Mississippi for the National Lawyers Guild. He sought election to Detroit Recorder's Court in 1960, winning a six-year term and later a second term in 1972.

As a judge, Crockett was noted for his lenient treatment of first-time offenders and his concern for civil rights. In 1969 a policeman was killed outside a black church where a meeting of black separatists was underway. The police stormed the church and arrested 140 people. Crockett went to the police station, declared court in session, and began freeing those he deemed held without probable cause. Almost all were released.

Crockett's popularity with blacks in Detroit was demonstrated by his election to the House of Representatives in 1980 with 98 percent of the vote. He served six terms.

See also Civil Rights Movement, U.S.; Politics in the United States

■ ■ *Bibliography*

Brennan, Carol. "George Crockett, Jr." In *Contemporary Black Biography,* Vol. 10. Detroit: Gale, 1996.

Thomas, Robert McG., Jr. "George W. Crockett Dies at 88; Was a Civil Rights Crusader." *New York Times,* September 15, 1997.

ROBERT L. JOHNS (2001)

CROUCH, STANLEY

DECEMBER 14, 1945

Critic and essayist Stanley Crouch was born in Los Angeles, where he was raised by his mother, Emma Bea Crouch, a domestic. During his boyhood he became fascinated by jazz music. In 1965, after attending school and junior college in Los Angeles, he was inspired by the Watts riot to become involved in the Black Power and black arts movements, and he joined the Watts Repertory Theatre Company as an actor and writer. In 1968 Crouch was hired by California's Claremont College as an instructor, and he later became the first full-time faculty member of the Black Studies Center.

By 1975 Crouch left Claremont and moved to New York. Disenchanted with black nationalism, he became a disciple of writers Ralph Ellison and Albert Murray, who celebrated the centrality of blacks in a pluralistic American culture. He joined the staff of the weekly *Village Voice* as a jazz and cultural critic, where he remained until 1989. At the *Voice* Crouch became controversial for his forthright critiques of modern jazz, African-American literature, and other subjects. *Notes of a Hanging Judge* (1990), a collection of his *Voice* columns, was a finalist for the National Book Award.

During the 1990s Crouch worked as a freelance scholar and essayist and functioned as an advisor to the Lincoln Center Jazz Program. In 1993, Crouch won a prestigious MacArthur Foundation "genius" grant of $296,000. He joined the New York *Daily News* as a columnist in 1995. *Always In Pursuit: Fresh American Perspectives,* a collection comprised mostly of his *Daily News* columns, was published in 1998.

Crouch was further honored as the 2002–2003 Louis Armstrong Visiting Professor of Jazz Studies at Columbia University. His collection *The Artificial White Man: Essays on Authenticity* was published in 2004.

See also Intellectual Life; Jazz; Journalism; Literary Criticism, U.S.

▓ ▓ *Bibliography*

Crouch, Stanley. *Always in Pursuit: Fresh American Perspectives.* New York: Pantheon, 1998.

Crouch, Stanley. *The Artificial White Man: Essays on Authenticity.* New York: Basic Civitas Books, 2004.

Crouch, Stanley, and Playthell Benjamin. *Reconsidering the Souls of Black Folk.* Philadelphia: Running Press, 2002.

GREG ROBINSON (1996)
Updated by publisher 2005

"INCIDENTS OF HOPE FOR THE NEGRO
RACE IN AMERICA."

A THANKSGIVING SERMON

November 26th, 1895.

BY

ALEX. CRUMMELL,

RECTOR EMERITUS OF ST. LUKES' CHURCH,

WASHINGTON, D. C.

Title page from Alexander Crummell's Incidents of Hope for the Negro Race in America: A Thanksgiving Sermon, November 26, 1895. THE LIBRARY OF CONGRESS

CRUMMELL, ALEXANDER

MARCH 3, 1819
SEPTEMBER 19, 1898

Nationalist, abolitionist, and missionary Alexander Crummell was the son of Boston Crummell, who had been kidnapped from his homeland in Temne country, West Africa, and enslaved in New York. Boston Crummell was never emancipated, his son later wrote, but obtained his freedom simply by announcing to his master that "he would serve him no longer." Boston Crummell married Charity Hicks, a freeborn woman from Long Island, New York, and established an oyster house in lower Manhattan. It was in the Crummell home that the African-American newspaper *Freedom's Journal* was founded.

The Crummells were members of the Protestant Episcopal Church, and Alexander came early under the influence of Rev. Peter Williams Jr. Williams was a supporter of back-to-Africa movements and had been friendly with the repatriationists Paul Cuffe and John Russwurm. Crummell attended school in Williams' church and in the African Free School until his early teens, when he enrolled in the Noyes Academy in Canaan, New Hampshire. Shortly after it opened, the academy was closed by mob violence and Crummell resumed his studies at the Oneida Institute in Whitesboro, New York.

Encouraged by Williams to become a candidate for ordination, Crummell applied to the General Theological Seminary in New York City but was rejected. He informally attended lectures at Yale University and studied privately with clergymen in New England. While in New England he married Sarah Mabritt Elston of New York, ministered to congregationists in New Haven and Providence, and worked as a correspondent for the *Colored American*. Crummell was ordained to the Episcopal priesthood in 1842 and labored with small congregations in Philadelphia and New York. He went to England in 1848, ostensibly to raise funds for his parish; almost immediately, however, he began preparing with a tutor to enter Cambridge University. His familial obligations and lecturing activities detracted from his academic performance, and he failed his first attempt at the university examinations, but he was among the eleven out of thirty-three candidates who passed an additional examination, and he was awarded the bachelor's degree in 1853.

Wanting to bring up his children "under black men's institutions," he embarked on his missionary career in West Africa under the auspices of the Protestant Episcopal Church. Over the ensuing decades he was often in conflict with his immediate superior, Rev. John Payne, the bishop of Cape Palmas, especially when Crummell attempted to organize another diocese in the Liberian capital city of Monrovia. Crummell at first showed little interest in working with the native population. Many of his writings during these years addressed such statesmanlike topics as "God and the Nation" and "The Relations and Duties of Free Colored Men in America to Africa." These, along with a number of his other essays on black-nationalist themes, were collected for his first book, *The Future of Africa* (1862).

Between 1853 and 1872, Crummell spent sixteen years in Liberia, although he returned to the United States twice during those years to raise money. The assassination of Liberian president Edward James Royce and threats against Crummell's own life led to his hasty and final departure in 1872. Sarah Crummell died in 1878 and he was remarried, to Jennie M. Simpson, on September 23, 1880. Crummell established Saint Luke's Episcopal Church in Washington in 1879 and retained the pastorate until 1894, when he retired. He continued to write and lecture actively until his death in 1898. Among his important writings during the Washington years were "The Destined Superiority of the Negro" and "The Black Woman of the South, Her Neglects and Her Needs" (1883). These and other sermons were collected in his books *The Greatness of Christ and Other Sermons* (1882) and *Africa and America* (1891).

Crummell's theological writings are dominated by the idea that salvation cannot be achieved solely by the accep-

Alexander Crummell

"The greatness of a people springs from their ability to grasp the conception of being. It is the absorption of a people, of a nation, of race, in large majestic and abiding things which lifts them up to the skies."

CIVILIZATION: THE PRIMAL NEED OF THE RACE AND ATTITUDE OF THE AMERICAN MIND TOWARD NEGRO INTELLECT. IN AMERICAN NEGRO ACADEMY. OCCASIONAL PAPERS, 3:3–7. WASHINGTON, D.C.: THE ACADEMY, 1897.

tance of grace. He believed that God works actively in history and that the good are punished and the evil rewarded in this life. Crummell was contemptuous of enthusiastic revivalism and believed that the struggle for salvation must remain an arduous task, even after the Christian has experienced conversion. Although a notorious Anglophile and hostile to the cultural expressions of the black masses, he never wavered in his black-nationalist chauvinism, apparently seeing no contradictions in his position. His essay "The Destined Superiority of the Negro" revealed his confidence that the African race was a chosen people.

In the year before his death, Crummell organized the American Negro Academy, which was dedicated to the pursuit of the higher culture and civilization for black Americans. He influenced W. E. B. Du Bois, whose sentimental and somewhat inaccurate eulogy, "Of Alexander Crummell," was reprinted in *The Souls of Black Folk* (1903). Other Crummell protégés were William H. Ferris and John E. Bruce, both of whom became prominent Garveyites during the 1920s.

Crummell's papers are widely scattered. The main repository is in the Schomburg Collection of the New York Public Library. A number of important letters are in the American Colonization Society Papers in the Library of Congress and in the Domestic and Foreign Missionary Society Papers in the Archives of the Episcopal Church at Austin, Texas. Additional important materials are in the Massachusetts and Maryland State Historical Societies.

See also Abolition; Bruce, John Edward; Cuffe, Paul; Du Bois, W. E. B.; *Freedom's Journal*; Missionary Movements; Religion; Russwurm, John Brown

Bibliography

Moses, Wilson J. *Alexander Crummell: A Study of Civilization and Discontent.* New York: Oxford University Press, 1989.

Oldfield, John. *Alexander Crummell and the Creation of an African-American Church in Liberia.* Lewiston, Maine: E. Mellon, 1990.

Rigsby, Gregory U. *Alexander Crummell: Pioneer in Nineteenth Century Pan-African Thought.* New York: Greenwood, 1987.

Scruggs, Otey M. *We the Children of Africa in This Land.* Washington, D.C.: Howard University, 1972.

WILSON J. MOSES (1996)

CRUSE, HAROLD

MARCH 18, 1916

Relatively little is known of the life of writer and educator Harold Wright Cruse, who is known primarily for his authorship of a single influential book, *The Crisis of the Negro Intellectual* (1967). He was born in 1916 in Petersburg, Virginia, where his parents separated when he was young. He moved with his father to New York, where the elder Cruse became a cleaning supervisor on the Long Island Railroad. Cruse studied in New York's public schools and worked at a variety of jobs after his graduation. He dates his intellectual life from 1940, when he attended a book party/lecture by author Richard Wright in Harlem. Cruse served in the quartermaster division of the army during World War II. Following his discharge, he attended City College of New York on the GI Bill but dropped out after less than a year.

During the following fifteen years Cruse became involved in Harlem left-wing circles, although he has long refused to give details of his involvement with the Communist Party. He attempted to write articles and plays and held a variety of part-time jobs. Eventually, he became a bitter opponent of the Communist Party. Around 1963 he began work on *The Crisis of the Negro Intellectual,* which he completed four years later. The book was a massive historical study that criticized many black leaders and thinkers for their failure to give expression to nationalist consciousness. Cruse argued that Harlem culture had been dominated by a "clique" of writers and artists affiliated with left-wing groups such as the Communist Party, which had systematically opposed the creation of black intellectual or cultural autonomy. As a result, they had no black intellectual or political program to offer as an alternative to integration and assimilation into white America. The book, published in the midst of the Black Power movement, stirred up enormous controversy among both blacks and whites. In 1968 Cruse published a book of essays on black nationalism, *Rebellion or Revolution?*

In the fall of 1968 Cruse was hired as a visiting professor by the University of Michigan in Ann Arbor. The following year he helped found the university's Center for Afro-American and African Studies. In 1977 he became the first African-American professor without an academic degree to be named full professor at an American university. In 1982 he published a second full-length work, *Plural but Equal,* a critique of the effects of integration on African-American education and life. In 1987 he was named professor emeritus.

In 2002 *The Essential Harold Cruse: a Reader,* edited by William J. Cobb, was released.

See also Black Power Movement; Communist Party of the United States; Wright, Richard

Bibliography

Cruse, Harold. *The Crisis of the Negro Intellectual.* New York: Morrow, 1967. Reprint, New York: Morrow, 1984.

Cruse, Harold. *Plural but Equal: A Critical Study of Blacks and Minorities and America's Plural Society.* New York: Morrow, 1987.

Cruse, Harold. *The Essential Harold Cruse: a Reader.* Edited by William J. Cobb. New York: Palgrave, 2002.

GREG ROBINSON (1996)
Updated by publisher 2005

CUFFE, PAUL

JANUARY 17, 1759
SEPTEMBER 9, 1817

The merchant and emigrationist Paul Cuffe was born on Cuttyhunk Island in the Massachusetts Bay Colony to Cuffe Slocum, a former slave who had purchased his freedom, and Ruth Moses, a Wampanoag Native American. Growing up near the busy port of New Bedford, Massachusetts, Cuffe shipped out on whaling expeditions while still a teenager. On one voyage, at the beginning of the American Revolution, his ship was seized by the British in the Bay of Mexico and Cuffe was imprisoned in New York City for three months. After returning to Massachusetts in 1776, he resumed self-education and farming before returning to a maritime career.

Early in his life Cuffe—like most of his nine siblings, he used his father's African name as a surname—showed disdain for racial discrimination. In 1780 he and his brother John refused to pay taxes to protest a clause in the state constitution that forbade blacks suffrage. Their petition to the Massachusetts General Court alluded to the injustice of taxation without representation. Although Cuffe was again briefly imprisoned, this time by Massachusetts authorities for civil disobedience, the bold action successfully reduced the family's taxes.

On February 25, 1783, Cuffe married Alice Pequit. They had seven children. Throughout the American Revolution, Cuffe continued his maritime activities, captaining several boats to Nantucket Island past patrolling British privateers. He began family-based businesses, which included farming, fishing, and whaling, as well as coastal and international commerce. He built at least seven vessels at his Westport, Massachusetts, docks, including the schooner *Ranger*, the bark *Hero*, the brig *Traveler*, and the ship *Alpha*. His own ship's crews were identified by their African ancestry, customarily drawn from extended family members, mainly the offspring of his sister Mary and her Native-American husband, Michael Wainer. Cuffe amassed a fortune in trade, despite ostracism and periodic encounters with arriving slavers. His property in 1806 was valued at approximately $20,000, making him Westport's wealthiest resident.

In 1808 Cuffe was received into the Society of Friends. He became a devout Quaker, contributed over $500 toward the building of meetinghouses, and entered into business ventures with leading Friends such as William Rotch Jr. Religious affiliations also linked Cuffe to the Anglo-American abolitionist movement to end the transatlantic slave trade. Cuffe received requests from members of the Royal African Institution to visit Sierra Leone, England's West African asylum for ex-slaves. The possibility of Cuffe's involvement in resettling American blacks in Africa became the subject of letters between James Pemberton, Benjamin Rush, and James Brain of the Pennsylvania and Delaware Abolition Societies, and William Wilberforce, Thomas Clarkson, and Zachary Macauley of Britain's abolitionist coalition in Parliament.

Cuffe made two trips to Sierra Leone. The first left Westport on January 1, 1811, with a crew of nine black sailors. Disembarking on the West African coast from his brig *Traveler*, Cuffe became intrigued with the possibilities of beginning a three-way trade among the United States, England, and Sierra Leone. The trade route, he imagined, would bond together African descendants and their benefactors on three continents. On this trip, Cuffe also sailed to England, where he protested the effects of Britain's trading monopoly upon aspiring black settler merchants. Nevertheless, he was warmly received by English abolitionists and lionized by the British press as the "African Captain."

Cuffe's efforts—he hoped to bring skilled immigrants for settlement on annual trips to Africa—were inhibited by the War of 1812, during which both the United States and England forbade trade with one another. Cuffe's petitions to allow continuance of his peaceful traffic, which he made both to the United States Congress and to the British Parliament, were refused.

After the war's end, Cuffe sailed again for Sierra Leone—this time leaving on December 10, 1815, with nine families consisting of thirty-eight people. Two of the families were headed by Congolese and Senegalese men returning home. America's urban black elite, particularly Philadelphia's James Forten, Absalom Jones, and Richard Allen, endorsed Cuffe's emigration scheme.

Upon his return to the United States, Cuffe became increasingly convinced of the need for a mass emigration of blacks. He even gave his support to the American Colonization Society—an organization led by white southerners and widely suspected by abolitionists—after they courted his endorsement. Cuffe's death in 1817 came before he could fulfill his own emigration plan, which he hoped would lessen the plight of black Americans and bring a measure of prosperity to Africa. He is considered by some to be the father of black nationalism.

See also Abolition; Allen, Richard; Forten, James; Jones, Absalom

▪ ▪ *Bibliography*

Diamond, Arthur. *Paul Cuffe.* New York: Chelsea House, 1989.

Harris, Sheldon H. *Paul Cuffe, Black America, and the African Return.* New York: Simon & Schuster, 1972.

Salvador, George. *Paul Cuffe, the Black Yankee, 1759–1817.* New Bedford, Mass.: Reynolds-DeWalt, 1969.

Thomas, Lamont D. *Paul Cuffe, Black Entrepreneur and Pan-Africanist.* Urbana: University of Illinois Press, 1988.

LAMONT D. THOMAS (1996)

CULLEN, COUNTEE
MARCH 30, 1903
JANUARY 9, 1946

It has been difficult to place exactly where poet, novelist, and playwright Countee Cullen was born, with whom he spent the very earliest years of his childhood, and where

Countee Cullen (1903–1946). Pictured here in a portrait by Carl Van Vechten, Cullen rose to fame in the early years of the Harlem Renaissance, winning more major literary prizes than any other African American writer during the 1920s. THE LITERARY ESTATE OF CARL VAN VECHTEN. REPRODUCED BY PERMISSION.

he spent them. Scholars variously cite New York City and Baltimore as his birthplace, but Cullen himself, on his college transcript at New York University, listed Louisville, Kentucky, as his place of birth. A few years later, when he had achieved considerable literary fame during the era known as the New Negro or Harlem Renaissance, he was to assert that his birthplace was New York City, a claim he continued to make for the rest of his life. Both Cullen's second wife, Ida, and some of his closest friends, including Langston Hughes and Harold Jackman, all said he was born in Louisville, although one Cullen scholar, Beulah Reimherr, claims in her M.A. thesis that Ida Cullen gave her husband's place of birth as Baltimore. As James Weldon Johnson wrote in *The Book of American Negro Poetry* (1931), "There is not much to say about these earlier years of Cullen—unless he himself should say it." And Cullen—revealing a temperament that was not exactly secretive but private, less a matter of modesty than a tendency toward being encoded and tactful—never in his life said anything more clarifying.

What we know for certain is that he was born on March 30, 1903, and that sometime between his birth and 1918 he was adopted by the Rev. Frederick A. and Carolyn Belle (Mitchell) Cullen of the Salem Methodist Episcopal Church in Harlem. It is impossible to state with any degree of certainty how old Cullen was at the time or how long he knew the Cullens before he was adopted. Apparently he went by the name of Countee Porter until 1918. He became Countee P. Cullen by 1921, and eventually just Countee Cullen. According to Harold Jackman, the adoption was never really "official"; that is to say, it was never formally consummated through the proper state-agency channels. It is difficult, indeed, to know whether Cullen was ever legally an orphan at any stage in his childhood.

Frederick Cullen was one of the pioneer black activist-ministers; he moved his Salem Methodist Episcopal Church from a storefront mission—where it was in 1902, when he first arrived in New York City—to the site of a former white church in Harlem in 1924, where he could boast of a membership of over 2,500. Since Countee Cullen himself stated in his 1927 anthology of black American poetry, *Caroling Dusk,* that he was "reared in the conservative atmosphere of a Methodist parsonage," it is clear that his foster father, particularly, was a strong influence. The two men were very close, often traveling abroad together. But as Cullen evidences a decided unease in his poetry over his strong and conservative Christian training and the attraction of his pagan inclinations, his feelings about his father may have been somewhat ambivalent. Frederick Cullen was, on the one hand, a puritanical Christian patriarch, and Countee was never remotely that. On the other hand, it has been suggested that Frederick was also something of an effeminate man. (He was dressed in girl's clothing by his poverty-stricken mother well beyond the acceptable boyhood age for such a practice and was apparently effeminate in his manner as an adult.) Some scholars, especially Jean Wagner, have argued that Countee Cullen's homosexuality, or decidedly ambiguous sexual nature, may have been attributable to his foster father's contrary influence as both fire-breathing Christian and latent or covert transsexual. To be sure, in his poetry Cullen equated paganism with various sensual postures, including homosexuality. Cullen was a devoted and obedient son, and the fact that the Cullens had no other children made this attachment much easier to achieve.

Cullen was an outstanding student both at DeWitt Clinton High School (1918–1921)—where he not only edited the school's newspaper but also assisted in editing the literary magazine, *Magpie,* and wrote his first poetry that achieved notice—and at New York University (1921–1925), where he wrote most of the major work that was to make up his first two volumes, *Color* (1925) and *Copper Sun* (1927). It was also while at NYU that he wrote *The Ballad of the Brown Girl* (1927). In high school Cullen won his first contest, a citywide competition, with the poem "I

ENCYCLOPEDIA of AFRICAN-AMERICAN CULTURE and HISTORY
second edition

567

Have a Rendezvous with Life," a nonracial poem inspired by Alan Seeger's "I Have a Rendezvous with Death." If any event signaled the coming of the Harlem Renaissance, it was the precocious success of this rather shy black boy who, more than any other black literary figure of his generation, was being touted and bred to become a major crossover literary figure. Here was a black man with considerable academic training who could, in effect, write "white" verse—ballads, sonnets, quatrains, and the like— much in the manner of Keats and the British Romantics (albeit, on more than one occasion, tinged with racial concerns), with genuine skill and compelling power. He was certainly not the first African American to attempt to write such verse, but he was first to do so with such extensive education, with such a complete understanding of himself as a poet, and producing poetry that was not trite or inferior. Only two other black American poets before Cullen could be taken so seriously as self-consciously considered and proficient poets: Phillis Wheatley and Paul Laurence Dunbar.

If the aim of the Harlem Renaissance was, in part, the reinvention of the native-born African American as a being who could be assimilated while decidedly retaining something called a "racial self-consciousness," then Cullen fit the bill better than virtually any other Renaissance writer. And if "I Have a Rendezvous with Life" was the opening salvo in the making of Cullen's literary reputation, then the 1924 publication of "Shroud of Color" in H. L. Mencken's *American Mercury* confirmed the advent of the black boy wonder as one of the most exciting American poets on the scene. After graduating Phi Beta Kappa from NYU, Cullen earned a master's degree in English and French from Harvard (1927). Between high school and graduation from Harvard he had become the most popular black poet—virtually the most popular black literary figure—in America. It was after one of his poems and his popular column appeared in *Opportunity* magazine that A'Lelia Walker (heiress of Madame C. J. Walker's hair-care-products fortune) named her salon, where the black and white literati gathered in the late 1920s, the Dark Tower.

Cullen won more major literary prizes than any other black writer of the 1920s: the first prize in the Witter Bynner Poetry Contest in 1925; *Poetry* magazine's John Reed Memorial Prize; the Amy Spingarn Award of *The Crisis* magazine; second prize in *Opportunity* magazine's first poetry contest; second prize in the poetry contest of *Palms*. He was the second African American to win a Guggenheim Fellowship. His first three books—*Color, Copper Sun,* and *The Ballad of the Brown Girl*—sold well and made him a hero for many blacks. Lines from Cullen's

Title page from Caroling Dusk, *Cullen's 1927 anthology of black American poetry.* SPECIAL COLLECTIONS LIBRARY, UNIVERSITY OF MICHIGAN. REPRODUCED BY PERMISSION.

popular poems, such as "Heritage," "Incident," "From the Dark Tower," and "Yet Do I Marvel," were commonly quoted.

Cullen was also at the center of one of the major social events of the Harlem Renaissance; on April 9, 1928, he married Yolande Du Bois, the only child of W. E. B. Du Bois, in one of the most lavish weddings in black New York history. This wedding was to symbolize the union of the grand black intellectual patriarch and the new breed of younger African Americans who were responsible for much of the excitement of the Renaissance. It was an apt meshing of personalities, as both Cullen and Du Bois *père* were conservative by nature and ardent traditionalists. That the marriage turned out so disastrously and ended so quickly—Yolande and Cullen divorced in 1930— probably adversely affected Cullen. (He remarried in 1940.) Cullen published *The Black Christ and Other Poems* in 1929, receiving lukewarm reviews from both black and white presses. He was bitterly disappointed that "The

Black Christ," his longest and in many respects his most complicated poem, the product of over two years' work, was considered by most critics to be his weakest and least distinguished.

From the 1930s until his death, Cullen wrote a great deal less, partly hampered by his job as a French teacher at Frederick Douglass Junior High (his most famous student was James Baldwin). But he wrote noteworthy, even significant work in a number of genres. His novel *One Way to Heaven,* published in 1934, rates among the better black satires and is one of the three important fictional retrospectives of the Harlem Renaissance, the others being Wallace Thurman's *The Infants of the Spring* and George Schuyler's *Black No More;* his translation of *The Medea* is the first major translation of a classical work by a twentieth-century black American writer; the children's books *The Lost Zoo* and *My Lives and How I Lost Them* are among the more clever and engaging books of children's verse, written at a time when there was not much work published for children by black writers; and his poetry of the period includes perhaps some of his best, certainly some of his more darkly complex, sonnets. He was also working on a musical with Arna Bontemps called *St. Louis Woman* (based on Bontemps's novel, *God Sends Sunday*) at the time of his death from high blood pressure and uremic poisoning.

For many years after his death, Cullen's reputation was eclipsed by those of other Harlem Renaissance writers, particularly Langston Hughes and Zora Neale Hurston, and his work had gone out of print. Later, however, there was a resurgence of interest in his life and work, and his books were reissued.

See also Baldwin, James; Bontemps, Arna; Du Bois, W.E.B.; Dunbar, Paul Laurence; Harlem Renaissance; Hurston, Zora Neale; New Negro; Schuyler, George S.; Thurman, Wallace; Walker, A'Lelia; Walker, Madam C. J.; Wheatley, Phillis

■ ■ *Bibliography*

Bontemps, Arna, ed. *The Harlem Renaissance Remembered.* New York: Dodd, Mead, 1972.

Davis, Arthur P. *From the Dark Tower: Afro-American Writers, 1900 to 1960.* Washington, D.C.: Howard University Press, 1974.

Early, Gerald, ed. *My Soul's High Song; The Collected Writings of Countee Cullen, Voice of the Harlem Renaissance.* New York: Doubleday, 1991.

Ferguson, Blanche F. *Countee Cullen and the Negro Renaissance.* New York: Dodd, Mead, 1966.

Huggins, Nathan. *Harlem Renaissance.* New York: Oxford University Press, 1971.

Johnson, James Weldon. *The Book of American Negro Poetry,* 2nd ed. New York: Harcourt, Brace & World, 1931.

Perry, Margaret. *A Bio-bibliography of Countée P. Cullen, 1903–1946.* Westport, Conn.: Greenwood, 1971.

Wagner, Jean. *Black Poets of the United States: From Paul Laurence Dunbar to Langston Hughes.* Translated by Kenneth Douglas. Urbana: University of Illinois Press, 1973.

GERALD EARLY (1996)

DADDY GRACE

See Grace, Sweet Daddy

DALTON-JAMES, EDITH

FEBRUARY 1, 1896
NOVEMBER 5, 1976

Edith Dalton-James was one of the pioneering women of Jamaica during the first half of the twentieth century. She moved beyond merely pursuing a profession tailor-made for women of her times to challenge the status quo by entering the world of politics, the world of men. She was known for her dedication to education and public service and her desire to see Jamaicans become a free and independent people. She believed that women had a significant role to play in the process.

Dalton-James was born of John William and Jeanette Walcott in Townhead (near Savanna-la-Mar), Westmoreland. Her father was a mechanical engineer. In 1919 she married Spencer Wesley James, son of Haughton James, a teacher. The marriage produced a son (Dr. Seymour W. James, Jr.) and two daughters (Marebelle James Mowat and Dr. Joyce James). She was a member of the Anglican Church.

Dalton-James attended school in her community where her performance got her into Shortwood Teachers College before the normal age of matriculation. She attended the college from 1911 to 1914 and graduated with honors. She taught at Unity and Half Way Tree schools with her husband before serving as principal of Chetolah Park Primary School beginning in 1951. She was a schoolteacher for forty years, twenty of which she spent at Chetolah Park. While at Chetolah Park, she attended the London Institute of Education, University of London, and graduated with honors.

She was first and foremost an educator and served Jamaica well in this area. Her investment in the educational system of Jamaica is seen in the offices she held in related local and international organizations, allowing her to voice her position on issues such as corporal punishment in schools. She served four terms as president of the Jamaican Union of Teachers (JUT), three times as president of the Caribbean Union of Teachers, and was a life member of both these associations. She was a uniting force in education in her native land and was instrumental in the development of the Jamaica Teachers Association (JTA, formerly the JUT, which was formed in 1894). Her prowess and pioneering spirit is seen in the fact that she was the only assistant teacher who sat on the Board of Education, and she was the first woman and classroom teacher to become president of the JUT/JTA in 1949. When she became president in 1949, there were several small teachers' associations. She called a joint conference of teachers that resulted in the formation of the Joint Executives of Teachers' Associations (JETA). This eventually became the Jamaica Teachers' Association. She served as vice chair of the Teachers' Mutual Aid Society and was manager of the Teachers' Book Centre, of which she was a founding member. She sat on the advisory board of the Moneague Teacher Training College and Jamaica Advisory Council. She served the Caribbean Union of Teachers as president for two terms, sat on the committee of the International Council for Teachers Education, and was active in the World Conference of the Teaching Profession. She fought for the cause of teachers, and the JTA recognized her work and worth by mounting a plaque in their headquarters building on Church Street in her honor.

Dalton-James carried a vision for a better Jamaica and was not satisfied to operate only in the classroom and through educational associations. She was active in community work and served in a number of social and charitable associations. An important part of her community outreach was her pet project, adult literacy. She also served the Junior Centre of the Institute of Jamaica, the City Mission Orphanage, the Mass Wedding Committee, the Convalescent Society, the Save the Children Fund, and the Women's Liberal Club.

Dalton-James was interested in public affairs and entered politics when adult suffrage was granted. She became a founding member of the People's National Party (PNP) in 1939, was made a life member in 1962, and ran three times as a candidate for the House of Representatives. She was elected to the House of Representatives Legislative Council in 1944. She served until 1949 when she lost her seat to another woman. She again became a member of the Legislative Council from1959 to 1962. She was to influence other women such as Daphne Campbell, who was a political activist in the 1940s.

Dalton-James's contribution to public affairs and her fellowmen was widely recognized. In 1953 she was awarded the Queen's Coronation Medal, and in 1958, the insignia of the Most Excellent Order of the British Empire (MBE). In 1971 the University of the West Indies conferred on her the honorary Doctor of Laws, and in 1975 the Jamaican government conferred on her the Order of Distinction (Commander Class). Her community service was recognized when in 1977 a community complex on Slipe Pen Road, Kingston, was named in her honor. The complex houses a basic school, a day care center, a library, and a community college. Edith Dalton-James's life commitment was to the cause of teachers, education, and her country. She lived her motto: "work hard; study continuously; service for reward or no reward."

See also Education in the Caribbean; People's National Party

■ ■ *Bibliography*

B/N File, Dalton-James, Edith. National Library of Jamaica.

"Edith Dalton-James Dies." *Daily Gleaner,* November 6, 1976.

"Edith Dalton-James Dies." *The Star,* November 5, 1976.

"Edith Dalton-James Gets Insignia for Commander of Order of Distinction." *Jamaica Daily News,* January 17, 1976.

Guy, Henry A., et al. *Women in the Caribbean.* Kingston, Jamaica: Henry A. Guy, 1966.

"Mrs Dalton-James Buried." *Jamaica Daily News,* November 11, 1976.

"Mrs Dalton-James Seen as 'Woman of the Hour.'" *Daily Gleaner,* September 9, 1958.

ALERIC J. JOSEPHS (2005)

DANCE

See Ballet; Breakdancing; Capoeira; Dance, Diasporic; Tap Dance; Social Dance; Theatrical Dance

DANCE, DIASPORIC
▬▬▬

African diasporic dance denotes those dances and dance traditions Africans brought with them and passed on to their descendants during the great "scattering," or diaspora. Beginning with the slave trade to Portugal in the fifteenth century and lasting well into the nineteenth century, between ten and thirteen million Africans were enslaved and displaced throughout the Americas. With them came African worldviews that meshed the material and spiritual worlds and incorporated music and dance into life's every aspect.

Preserved through an oral tradition, passed from generation to generation and body to body, these dances have survived as characteristic traits, entire rituals, and spiritual traditions, thus creating a basic vocabulary of movement principles common throughout the entire diaspora. They survived because they were the easiest to conceal and the hardest to erase.

These principles are part of what can be called an African cultural continuum or aesthetic— ways of speaking, moving, and approaching artistic expression that have roots firmly planted in Africa yet are clearly transformed by Africans' experiences in the Americas. These principles have shaped much of what is seen as uniquely American forms of expression and have been fundamental in creating American vernacular dance. International dance crazes such as the Charleston, cakewalk, Lindy Hop, bossa nova, and twist sprang forth from the loins of African diasporic dance. Theatrical forms of dance have felt its touch as well, influencing the fields of ballet, modern dance, and the Broadway stage.

THE ROLE OF DANCE IN AFRICAN CULTURES

Art historian Robert Farris Thompson states in *African Art in Motion: Icon and Act* (1974) "Africa . . . introduces a different art history, a history of *danced* art" (p. xii).

More than three times the size of the continental United States, Africa is home to hundreds of different cultural groups and over seven hundred distinct languages. The music and movement styles of Africa are as diverse as its peoples. Yet comparative studies show that there are commonalities that cross ethnic and cultural lines and grow out of a shared conceptual approach to art. In *African Rhythm and African Sensibility* (1979), John Miller Chernoff maintains that people in Africa "do not so much observe rituals in their lives, as they ritualize their lives" (p. 160). Music and dance are inextricably linked, a multidimensional community event that integrates dance, instrumental music, song, literature, and visual arts.

AFRICANISMS

Old dances made anew—reinvented and renamed, evolving and merging with other types of movement while never losing certain characteristics—these traits, or "Africanisms," become part of the hallmark of African diasporic dance. These African-derived movement characteristics can be described as polyrhythmic and multicentered music and movement, orientation toward the earth, call and response, improvisation, functionality, circularity in movement, formation and community, repetition, and spiritual transport, or "flash of the spirit."

Rhythm is made visible through movement that breaks the body into various points of interest or centers with overlapping *polyrhythms,* often with the hips as the central focus. Its bent-kneed, full-footed contact stance is the embodiment of a "get-down quality" or *orientation toward the earth,* exhibited also through descent in posture

and musical tone as intensity increases. Angularity in the elbows, torso, and legs—knees bent, hips riding above the rhythmic steps, close to the ground—ensure that legs are seldom straight and the feet leave the ground only to return again.

In *call and response,* dancers "answer" the call of the drum with a movement response, be it a specific rhythmic pattern that signifies a particular movement of dance or the dialogue between the lead drummer and dancer during solos. Throughout the South, gandy dancers moved railroad ties in a unified rhythmic response to the chants of the lead "caller."

Improvisation is an essential part of expression, implying a connection to the divine that inspires the dancer to do the impossible. A sense of *functionality* prevails so that gestures become symbol, a means of spiritual transport, to pass on to others cosmic principles or the values of a society.

Circularity in movement, formation, and community, expressed in the saying "Let the circle be unbroken," reflects a cosmology that sees the continuity of life and our connection to those passed on before us. Form is secondary to motion, and circular formations encourage little separation between participant and observer. One dances with and for the community. Movements are repeated, building toward a climactic end. This use of *repetition* raises energy and increases intensity.

AFRICAN-AMERICAN ORIGINS

Although African traders, soldiers, and diplomats prior to the fifteenth century migrated to Europe, the Middle East, and Asia, bringing their cultures with them, it was not until the European transatlantic slave trade that the dissemination of African culture was so extensive. Dispersed throughout North America, the Caribbean, and South and Central America, these Africans, who came primarily from West and Central Africa and Mozambique, would make up the largest forced migration in history.

During the weeks and months of the Middle Passage, slave traders would often "dance the slaves" in an attempt to keep them somewhat healthy. Chained together naked in filthy shallow berths, slaves were forced on deck to "dance"—that is, jump up and down while still chained, encouraged by the cat-o'-nine-tails, a particularly brutal type of whip.

One of the earliest and most important dances to appear in the Americas was the ring shout. This ancestral dance became a powerful tool for Christian conversion, as well as survival and resistance. It was as sacred as prayer and provided Africans with a way of worship, even as they converted to Christianity. Counterclockwise shuffling of the feet, close to the ground and never crossing but sustaining the rhythm, accompanied by singing, hand clapping, stomps, and an occasional broom handle upon the floor, the shout symbolized the very meaning of being African in the Americas.

During the 1800s, Place Congo, once a site for informal gatherings of Africans, Indians, and Creoles, was designated as Congo Square by the mayor of New Orleans, Louisiana, the only place where African Americans, free or enslaved, were allowed to gather to dance, and only before sunset on Sundays.

Growing largely out of public interest in African American culture, the minstrel show becomes the most widespread form of entertainment in the United States from the 1840s to the 1890s. Largely a northern entertainment, these performances by white performers in blackface, or "blackened up" with burnt cork and makeup, were based on imitation and mockery of African-American music, dance, and performance styles. Idealizing plantation life with caricatured portrayals of African Americans, these minstrel shows become the basis of some of the longstanding stereotypes of African Americans. The minstrel show also provided one of the first performance venues for African Americans.

It took one extraordinary performer, William Henry Lane, to break this standard. Lane, born a free black in Providence, Rhode Island, came to notoriety for his exquisite dancing, which mixed the rhythmic foot patterns of Irish step dancing with African movement vocabulary and the syncopation of flatfooted buck dances. Often considered the father of American tap dance, Master Juba, as Lane was called, "ingeniously combined the Irish jig and reel with African-derived movements and rhythms to lay the foundation for what we know as American tap dance," as stated by dance historian Jacqui Malone in *Steppin' on the Blues* (1996, p. 54).

Another dance made popular by the minstrel stage was the cakewalk, first created as a dance of derision by African Americans mocking the mannerisms of slaveholder society, and then imitated by minstrel performers, unwittingly imitating the imitators. It became the first international dance craze, often accompanied by the syncopated piano rolls of ragtime music at the turn of the century.

TWENTIETH-CENTURY FORMS

Dances like the black bottom and the Charleston, observed in African-American communities, become international dance crazes. The Lindy Hop, so named after

Charles Lindbergh's successful flight across the Atlantic, emerged from the dance halls of Harlem and spread across the United States like wildfire. The Lindy Hop included both acrobatic partnering lifts and its characteristic breakaway—partners "breaking away" to insert their own improvised steps, such as the shorty George or hucklebuck—giving rise to the jitterbug. The jitterbug became the emblem of the 1950s, danced to another music evolved from the blues: rock and roll.

On the Broadway stage, American tap dance was the predominant style of dance used in musicals of the 1930s and 1940s. Brilliant tap artists such as the Nicholas Brothers, Bill "Bojangles" Robinson, John Bubbles, and Jeni LeGon were innovators in the art form, serving as coaches and unnamed choreographers in movie musicals such as *Orchestra Wives* and *Gentlemen Prefer Blondes*. Evolving out of the buck dances of African-American slaves and meshed with the stepping traditions of Irish immigrants, tap dance focuses on the feet as percussive instruments, involving intricate rhythms performed for the ear as well as the eye. Young choreographers such as Savion Glover have reinvigorated the form, infusing it with the heavy rhythms of hip-hop and urban style.

Stepping, born on the campuses of the historically black colleges and universities, began as a bonding ritual for young African-American college students in black fraternities in the 1920s. This uniquely African-American dance form, characterized by elaborate syncopated stomps, hand clapping, and verbal play, had its roots in military-style marching, children's hand-clapping games, South African gumboot dances, cheerleading, and patting traditions. Step shows, showcasing choreographed step routines of the various black Greek organizations, have grown to be hugely popular intercampus events, involving students across both cultural and ethnic lines.

Toward the end of the twentieth century, a new urban culture burst forth from African-American and Latino communities in New York City. Rooted in grassroots Africanized urban music/dance culture and practiced at house parties, playgrounds, and dance halls, hip-hop developed into a global phenomenon, shaping music, dance, fashion, poetry, and visual arts.

Breaking was a social dance form that included "popping and locking," "up and down rock" (stylized mock fighting modeled after Asian martial arts movement), and the dance-like movements of the Afro-Brazilian fighting form *capoeira*. Renamed *break dancing* by the media, breaking borrowed elements from earlier dance forms, such as the aerial and ground Lindy, the Charleston, cakewalk, jitterbug, double-dutch jump rope, and stepping. Elaborate graffiti mural paintings appeared everywhere,

Contestants for the Cakewalk Crown, c. 1890s. *First created as a dance of derision by African Americans mocking the mannerisms of slaveholder society, the Cakewalk gained popularity when it was imitated by minstrel performers, becoming an international dance craze by the early years of the twentieth century.* PHOTOGRAPHS AND PRINTS DIVISION, SCHOMBURG CENTER FOR RESEARCH IN BLACK CULTURE, THE NEW YORK PUBLIC LIBRARY, ASTOR, LENOX AND TILDEN FOUNDATIONS.

emblazoned across subway cars and city buildings, as the fashion world exploded with baggy, low-slung pants, sneakers, and baseball caps.

AMERICAN CONCERT DANCE

On the concert stage, innovators such as choreographers Edna Guy, Hemsley Winfield, and Asadata Dafora (Horton) meshed African-American sacred and secular dance traditions with modern dance in the early 1930s. Horton, originally from Sierra Leone, fused African and Western performance styles to create concert dances drenched in African movement principles yet stylized for the concert stage. Edna Guy, a student of modern dance pioneer Ruth St. Denis, created works based on African-American spirituals and, with fellow choreographer Hemsley Winfield, gave the first Negro art dance concert at the Ninety-

Second Street YMHA in 1937. In the 1940s choreographer Katherine Dunham brought forward African-American and Afro-Caribbean social and traditional folkloric dance and ritual forms through her choreography, at the same time as Pearl Primus began her research of rural southern migrant communities. Primus's choreography was embedded with elements observed in sacred and secular dance traditions, and after completing her Rosenwald Fellowship in Africa, she became one of the preeminent teachers of African dance in the United States.

Generations of dancers have followed in the footsteps of these trailblazing women. Choreographers, performers, and artists have continued to reinvent and reshape African dance forms, including modern dancers Alvin Ailey, Dianne McIntyre, and Bill T. Jones; tap dancers Savion Glover and Gregory Hines; ballet choreographer Alonzo King; and hip-hop artist Rennie Harris, among others.

CONCLUSION

African diaspora dance is part of an African cultural continuum that has, from the beginning, altered American dance from within. It developed out of the circumstances of slavery, the socioeconomic marginalization of African Americans, and the presence of European influences. Rather than dying out, it has persisted, deeply imprinting American dance expression with traditional African dance characteristics. From the pulpit to the concert stage, African diaspora dance continues to express the values of a people and infuse American culture.

See also Africanisms; Ballet; Dunham, Katherine; Tap Dance; Theatrical Dance

▪▪ *Bibliography*

Chernoff, John Miller. *African Rhythm and African Sensibility.* Chicago and London: University of Chicago Press, 1979.

Dixon Gottschild, Brenda. *Digging the Africanist Presence in American Performance, Dance, and Other Contexts.* Westport, Conn.: Praeger, 1998.

Emery, Lynne Fauley. *Black Dance: From 1619 to Today.* 2nd ed. Princeton, N.J.: Princeton Book Co., 1988.

Floyd, Samuel A., Jr. *The Power of Black Music: Interpreting Its History from Africa to the United States.* New York: Oxford University Press, 1995.

Glass, Barbara. "Introduction." In *When the Spirit Moves: African American Dance in History and Art* (exhibition catalog), edited by B. Glass. Wilberforce, Ohio: National Afro-American Museum and Cultural Center, 1999.

Malone, Jacqui. *Steppin' on the Blues: The Visible Rhythms of African American Dance.* Urbana and Chicago: University of Illinois Press, 1996.

Perpener, John O., III. *African-American Concert Dance: The Harlem Renaissance and Beyond.* Urbana and Chicago: University of Illinois Press, 2001.

Stuckey, P. Sterling. *Slave Culture: Nationalist Theory and the Foundation of Black America.* New York: Oxford University Press, 1987.

Thompson, Robert Farris. *African Art in Motion: Icon and Act.* Los Angeles: University of California Press, National Gallery of Art, 1974.

ROBIN MARIE WILSON (2005)

DANCEHALL

▪▬▪

The musical style known as "dancehall" derives its name from the Jamaican dance hall, a cultural institution that has historically nurtured all major genres of that country's recorded popular music. While dancehall first emerged in the late 1970s as a distinct style, its real explosion occurred in the early 1980s, coinciding with the widespread use of digital music technology by Jamaican record producers.

The contemporary roots of the dancehall movement are evident in the "toasting" records of disc jockeys, or DJs, produced during the "roots reggae" era of the 1970s. The half-spoken, half-sung improvisations known as "DJ toasting," exemplified by U-Roy and Big Youth, were a standard accompaniment used by DJs when playing reggae records to live audiences, and toasting soon became an integral part of recorded reggae. However, the DJ became much more central to reggae culture in the dancehall era, overlapping with the influence that DJ toasting had on the birth of hip-hop culture in America.

The initial domestic underground impact of dancehall in Jamaica is inextricably linked with the work of the producer Henry "Junjo" Lawes, whose early 1980s recordings helped establish both the genre in general and the careers of many of its better-known proponents, such as Yellowman. However, this phase was a precursor to the wave of digital dancehall that broadened the genre's mass appeal and significantly increased the number of available recordings, many of which utilized either the same or very similar rhythm tracks. The spread of affordable digital music technology beyond the recording studio accelerated and solidified dancehall. Producers could create rhythms more cheaply because the programmable technology freed them from both the need for session musicians and the expense of hiring a professional recording studio. The economics of dancehall production were therefore as important as the audiences' demand for the records. The crucial turning point for dancehall was Wayne Smith's massive 1985 hit "Under Mi Sleng Teng," a minimalist song overseen by producer King Jammy, which eventually led to the recording of over 400 versions.

As a result of dancehall's rapid rise in international popularity, and its notable lyrical and instrumental differences from "roots" reggae, deep divisions have arisen within reggae communities. Key observers often note that the 1980s transformation of reggae was far from being exclusively musical, but was also integrally connected to political and economic circumstances. This was an economically impoverished era characterized by widespread violence, and the conservative foreign and domestic policies of the United States and Great Britain (under President Ronald Reagan and Prime Minister Margaret Thatcher, respectively), coupled with the domestic conservatism of the Jamaican leader Edward Seaga (prime minister, 1980–1989), stimulated rebellion against major social ills and the establishment identified with worsening them. This environment fostered a lack of creative innovation and a large-scale recycling of rhythms. Moreover, the philosophical and political ideals featured in many roots reggae lyrics were initially replaced by "slackness" themes that highlighted sex rather than spirituality. The lyrical shift also coincided with a change in Jamaica's drug culture from marijuana to cocaine, arguably resulting in the harsher sonic nature of dancehall, which was also referred to as *ragga* (an abbreviation of ragamuffin), in the mid-1980s.

The centrality of sexuality in dancehall foregrounded lyrical sentiments widely regarded as being violently homophobic, as evidenced by the controversies surrounding Buju Banton's 1992 hit, "Boom Bye Bye." Alternatively, some academics argue that these viewpoints are articulated only in specific Jamaican contexts, and therefore should not receive the reactionary condemnation that dancehall often appears to impose on homosexuals. While dancehall's sexual politics have usually been discussed from a male perspective, the performances of X-rated female DJs, such as Lady Saw and Patra, have helped redress the gender balance. By the early 1990s, with the emergence of performers such as Luciano offering a blend of reggae styles, dancehall became more philosophical, although X-rated lyrics maintained their popularity.

Dancehall has gradually become a global popular music commodity, with record sales closely linked to an ongoing alliance with the hip-hop world. The development of transnational corporate ties has also affected its popularity, as key independent record labels have been able to increase distribution through major established companies. Following the signing of Lieutenant Stitchie to Atlantic Records in 1987 (the first signing of a dancehall DJ by a major record label), commercial peaks have included the early 1990s success of Shabba Ranks (the first internationally successful Jamaican DJ) and the twenty-first-century impact of Shaggy, Beenie Man, and Sean Paul.

See also Reggae

■ ■ *Bibliography*

Alleyne, Mike. "International Crossroads: Reggae, Dancehall, and the U.S. Recording Industry." In *Globalisation, Diaspora and Caribbean Popular Culture,* edited by Christine Ho and Keith Nurse. Kingston, Jamaica: Ian Randle, 2005.

Cooper, Carolyn. *Noises in the Blood: Orality, Gender, and the "Vulgar" Body of Jamaican Popular Culture.* London: Macmillan, 1993.

Larkin, Colin. *The Virgin Encyclopedia of Reggae.* London: Virgin Books, 1998.

Salewicz, Chris, and Adrian Boot. *Reggae Explosion: The Story of Jamaican Music.* New York: Harry N. Abrams, 2001.

Stolzoff, Norman C. *Wake the Town and Tell the People: Dancehall Culture in Jamaica.* Durham, N.C.: Duke University Press, 2000.

MIKE ALLEYNE (2005)

DANCE THEATER OF HARLEM

■ ■ ■

The Dance Theater of Harlem (DTH), a classical dance company, was founded on August 15, 1969, by Arthur Mitchell and Karel Shook as the world's first permanent, professional, academy-rooted, predominantly black ballet troupe. Mitchell created DTH to address a threefold mission of social, educational, and artistic opportunity for the people of Harlem, and to prove that "there are black dancers with the physique, temperament and stamina, and everything else it takes to produce what we call the 'born' ballet dancer." During its official 1971 debut, DTH triumphantly debunked opinions that black people could not dance ballet. By 1993 DTH had become a world-renowned company with forty-nine dancers, seventy-five ballets in its repertory, an associated school, and an international touring schedule.

DTH's extensive repertory has included technically demanding neoclassic ballets (George Balanchine's 1946 *The Four Temperaments*); programmatic works (Arthur Mitchell's 1968 *Rhythmetron* and Alvin Ailey's 1970 *The River* to music by Duke Ellington); and pieces that explore the African-American experience (Louis Johnson's 1972 *Forces of Rhythm* and Geoffrey Holder's 1974 *Dougla* created in collaboration with DTH conductor-composer Tania Leon). DTH also excels in its own versions of classic ballets, including a sumptuous, Geoffrey Holder–designed production of Stravinsky's *Firebird* (1982) choreographed by John Taras, and a stunning Creole-inspired staging of *Giselle* (1984) created by Arthur Mitchell, designer Carl Mitchell, and artistic associate Frederic Franklin. This highly acclaimed *Giselle* set the Romantic-era story in the society of free black plantation owners in pre–Civil War Louisiana. DTH is perhaps best known for its revivals of dramatic ballets, including Agnes de Mille's 1948 *Fall River Legend* and Valerie Bettis's 1952 *A Streetcar Named Desire,* both of which have starred principal ballerina Virginia Johnson. Other important classical dance artists associated with DTH include Lydia Arbaca, Karen Brown, Stephanie Dabney, Robert Garland, Lorraine Graves, Christina Johnson, Ronald Perry, Walter Raines, Judith Rotardier, Paul Russell, Eddie J. Shellman, Lowell Smith, Mel Tomlinson, and Donald Williams.

A scene from the Dance Theater of Harlem production of the ballet Firebird. Since its premier performance in 1971, the Dance Theatre of Harlem has become a world-renowned dance company, performing both traditional classical ballets and new works inspired by the African-American experience. © JACK VARTOOGIAN/ FRONTROWPHOTOS

In 1972 the DTH school moved to its permanent home at 466 West 152nd Street, where training in dance, choreography, and music supplemented outreach programs bringing dance to senior citizens and children of the Harlem community with special needs. The international celebrity achieved by DTH began with a Caribbean performance tour in 1970, an engagement at the Spoleto Festival in 1971, and an auspicious 1974 London debut at Sadler's Wells Theatre. In 1988 DTH embarked on a five-week tour of the USSR, playing sold-out performances in Moscow, Tbilisi, and Leningrad, where the company received a standing ovation at the famed Kirov Theatre. In 1992 DTH successfully performed in Johannesburg, South Africa.

In 1990, faced with a $1.7 million deficit, DTH was forced to cancel its New York season and lay off dancers, technicians, and administrative staff for a six-month period. Mitchell and the board of directors responded with increased efforts to enlarge corporate support and strengthen their African-American audience base. In 1994 DTH completed a $6 million expansion and renovation project, which doubled classroom and administrative space and confirmed the DTH commitment to provide access to the disciplined training necessary for a career in classical ballet. However, financial problems continued. In February 1997 the company was paralyzed by a three-week strike. In 2004 the company faced an overwhelming deficit that forced extended layoffs for much of its staff.

See also Ailey, Alvin; Ballet; Ellington, Edward Kennedy "Duke"

■ ■ *Bibliography*

Kendall, Elizabeth. "'Home' to Russia: Dance Theatre of Harlem on Tour in the Soviet Union." *Ballet Review* 16, no. 4 (winter 1989): 3–49.

Maynard, Olga. "Dance Theatre of Harlem: Arthur Mitchell's 'Dark and Brilliant Splendor.'" *Dance Magazine* (May 1975): 52–64.

THOMAS F. DEFRANTZ (1996)
Updated by author 2005

DANDRIDGE, DOROTHY

c. NOVEMBER 1923
SEPTEMBER 8, 1965

▮▮▮

The daughter of a minister and a stage entertainer, the actor and singer Dorothy Dandridge was born in Cleveland, Ohio, and was groomed for a stage career by her mother, Ruby Dandridge, who separated from her husband and began touring the country as a performer shortly after Dorothy, her second daughter, was born. While still a child, Dandridge sang, danced, and did comedy skits as part of her mother's show. When their mother settled in Los Angeles, she and her older sister, Vivian—together they had been billed as "The Wonder Kids"—attended school and appeared in bit parts in films, including the Marx Brothers comedy *A Day at the Races* (1937). During the 1940s, Dorothy and Vivian joined with another young African-American woman, Etta Jones, to form an act called "The Dandridge Sisters," and the three embarked on a tour with the Jimmie Lunceford band. Dandridge met her first husband, Harold Nicholas (of the Nicholas Brothers dancing team), while she was performing at the Cotton Club in Harlem. A brain-damaged daughter, Harolyn, was born to the couple before they divorced.

During this time, Dandridge managed to secure a few minor Hollywood roles, appearing in such films as *Drums* of the Congo (1942), *The Hit Parade of 1943* (1943), *Moo Cow Boogie* (1943), *Atlantic City* (1944), *Pillow to Post* (1946), and *Flamingo* (1947). The early 1950s witnessed the flowering of her movie career, as she acquired leading roles in the low-budget films *Tarzan's Perils, The Harlem Globe-Trotters,* and *Jungle Queen* (all made in 1951). Dandridge, who was exceptionally beautiful, worked actively at cultivating a cosmopolitan, transracial persona, brimming with sexual allure. She also became increasingly well known as a nightclub singer. Indeed, Dandridge's performances at New York's La Vie En Rose in 1952 were in such demand that the club—then on the brink of bankruptcy—was saved from financial collapse. She was one of the first African Americans to perform at the Waldorf-Astoria's Empire Room, and she appeared at such prestigious clubs as Ciro's (Los Angeles), the Cafe de Paris (London), the Copacabana (Rio de Janeiro), and the Chi Chi (Palm Springs).

Dandridge's big break as a motion picture actress came in 1954, when she secured the title role in Otto Preminger's all-black production *Carmen Jones,* a role for which she became the first black actor to be nominated for an Oscar for a performance a leading role. That she had achieved celebrity stature was evidenced by her appearances on the cover of *Life,* as well as in feature articles in other national and international magazines. However, three years were to pass before Dandridge made another film, largely because, in racist Hollywood, she was not offered roles commensurate with her talent and beauty, and she felt she could no longer settle for less. Her next film, *Island in the Sun* (1957), was the first to feature an interracial romance (between Dandridge and white actor John Justin); the film was poorly received, however, as were *The Decks Ran Red* (1958), *Tamango* (1959), and *Malaga* (1962), all of which touched on interracial themes. Although Dandridge won acclaim in 1959 for her portrayal of Bess (opposite Sidney Poitier) in Otto Preminger's film of *Porgy and Bess,* she received fewer and fewer film and nightclub offers as time passed. After divorcing her second husband, the white restaurant-owner Jack Dennison, she was forced to file for bankruptcy and lost her Hollywood mansion. Her sudden death in 1965 was attributed to an overdose of antidepressants; she was forty-one years old. Dandridge's autobiography, *Everything and Nothing,* was published posthumously in 1970; in 1977, she was inducted into the Black Filmmakers Hall of Fame. In 1999, a film biography of her life, *Introducing Dorothy Dandridge,* starring Halle Berry, was produced for television by HBO Pictures.

See also Film in the United States; Poitier, Sidney

■ ■ *Bibliography*

Bogle, Donald. *Dorothy Dandridge: A Biography.* New York: Amistad, 1997.

Dandridge, Dorothy, and Earl Conrad. *Everything and Nothing: The Dorothy Dandridge Tragedy.* New York: Abelard-Schuman, 1970.

Sylvester Melvin R. "Dorothy Dandridge: The Tragic Life of an Actress Called the Dream Goddess." Available from <http://www.liu.edu/cwis/cwp/library/african/movies.htm>.

Schoell, William. *Heartbreaker: The Dorothy Dandridge Story.* Greensboro, N.C.: Avisson Press (Avisson Young Adult Series), 2002.

PAMELA WILKINSON (1996)
Updated bibliography

DANTICAT, EDWIDGE

JANUARY 19, 1969

■ ■ ■

Edwidge Danticat was born in Port-au-Prince, Haiti. Her parents emigrated to the United States when she was only two years old, leaving her and a younger brother in the custody of their aunt and uncle. The two children had to wait until 1981 to be reunited with their parents, who were living in Brooklyn, New York. Sent to an American public school, she started writing in English to develop her mastery of the language. While attending Barnard College, some of her short stories were published in the magazines *Essence* and *Seventeen.* In 1991 she became involved with the National Coalition for Haitian Refugees (NCHR), speaking at public meetings in defense of Haitian boat people and other illegal immigrants.

In 1994 Danticat published her first novel, *Breath, Eyes, Memory.* The novel tells about the experience of migration and adjustment in the United States from a child's perspective, and it explores mother-daughter relationships and female bonding. The work was widely acclaimed upon publication, and it has generated numerous critical studies.

Danticat's second book, *Krik? Krak!* (1995), a collection of short stories, was a finalist for the National Book Award and received the Pushcart Short Story Prize. The stories of the collection, anchored around the imaginary provincial town of Ville-Rose, reveal a writer experimenting with style and technique. In 1998 Danticat published *The Farming of Bones,* a compelling novel about the 1937 slaughter of Haitian cane workers in the Dominican Republic. In June of that same year, *Breath, Eyes, Memory* was selected as a featured book on the *Oprah Winfrey Show* as part of Oprah's Book Club.

Danticat has also edited two anthologies: *The Beacon Best of 2000: Great Writing by Women and Men of All Colors and Cultures* and *The Butterfly's Way: Voices from the Haitian Diaspora* (2001), a collection of writings by Haitians living in the United States. Other publications include a book on Carnival in Haiti, *After the Dance: A Walk Through Carnival in Jacmel, Haiti* (2002); a children's story, *Behind the Mountains* (2003); her third novel, *The Dew Breaker* (2004); and a historical young-adult novel, *Anacoana* (2005).

Danticat's books have been translated into French, Spanish, German, and Dutch, and in 1999 she received the Prix Carbet (a coveted French Caribbean literary prize) for *La Récolte douce des larmes,* the French translation of *The Farming of Bones.* Because she writes in English, it took some time for her to find acceptance among Haitian writers living in Haiti. However, they have come to recognize her as a "go-between" and the most talented writer of the young generation.

Danticat is also very committed to the Haitian community, both in Haiti and the United States. She collects books for Haitian schools and visits the special sections of American schools to which Haitian migrant children are often relegated.

See also Caribbean/North American Writers (Contemporary); Literature of Haiti; Women Writers of the Caribbean

■ ■ *Bibliography*

N'Zengou-Tayo, Marie-José. "Rewriting Folklore: Traditional Beliefs and Popular Culture in Edwidge Danticat's *Breath, Eyes, Memory* and *Krik? Krak!" MaComère* 3 (2000): 123–140.

Shea, Renee H. "The Dangerous Job of Edwidge Danticat: An Interview." *Callaloo* 19, no. 2 (Spring 1996): 382–389.

MARIE-JOSÉ N'ZENGOU-TAYO (2005)

DASH, JULIE

OCTOBER 22, 1952

■┼┼━━━━━━━━━━━━━━━━━

The filmmaker Julie Dash was born and raised in New York City. She began studying film as a teenager in 1969 at the Studio Museum of Harlem. After receiving a B.A. in film production from the City College of New York, Dash moved to Los Angeles to attend the Center for Advanced Film Studies at the American Film Institute (she is the youngest person ever to receive a fellowship to attend this institution). She later did graduate work at the University of California at Los Angeles.

Dash's films are sensitive, complex portrayals of the dilemmas confronting a diverse group of black women. While at the American Film Institute, she directed *Four Women,* an experimental dance film inspired by the Nina Simone song of the same title. The film won the 1977 Golden Medal for Women in Film at the Miami International Film Festival. In addition, she directed *Diary of an African Nun,* based on a short story by Alice Walker, during her time at the institute. This film was the 1977 winner of the Director's Guild Award. Her 1983 black-and-white short *Illusions,* the story of a fair-skinned black female film executive set in 1942, was nominated for a Cable ACE Award in art direction and is permanently archived at Indiana University and at Clark College in Atlanta.

In 1986 Dash relocated to Atlanta from Los Angeles and began work on *Daughters of the Dust.* Generally regarded as the first feature-length film by an African-American woman, *Daughters of the Dust* opened in 1992 to critical acclaim. Its nonlinear narrative, focusing on the Gullah culture of the South Carolina Sea Islands, centers on the lives of African-American women. They are the bearers of the culture, tellers of the tales, and most important, spectators for whom she created the film. Dash's approach to filmmaking has been "to show black women at pivotal moments in their lives . . . [to] focus on and depict experiences that have never been shown on screen before."

Dash then moved to London to collaborate on a screenplay with Maureen Blackwood, a founding member of Sankofa Film and Video, a collective of young black British filmmakers. She also began work on a series of films depicting black women in the United States from the turn of the twentieth century to the year 2000. In 2002, Dash directed the highly acclaimed television movie *The Rosa Parks Story,* about the woman credited with spawning the modern civil rights movement. The movie was nominated for Black Reel and Directors Guild of America awards.

See also Film in the United States, Contemporary

■ ■ *Bibliography*

Baker, Houston. "Not Without My Daughters." *Transition* 57 (1992): 150–166.

Davis, Zeinabu Irene. "An Interview with Julie Dash." *Wide Angle* 13, nos. 3 and 4 (1991): 120–137.

Klotman, Phyllis Rauch. "Julie Dash." In *Screenplays of the African-American Experience* edited by Phyllis Klotman, pp. 191–195. Bloomington: Indiana University Press, 1991.

Mills, David. "A Dash of Difference." *Washington Post*, February 28, 1992, p. C1.

Ryan, Judylyn S. "Outing the Black Feminist Filmmaker in Julie Dash's *Illusions*." *Signs* 30, No. 1 (Autumn, 2004): 1319–1344.

FARAH JASMINE GRIFFIN (1996)
Updated by publisher 2005

DA SILVA, BENEDITA

C. 1943

Benedita da Silva was born in the *favela* (shantytown) Praia do Pinto in the barrio of Leblon in the city of Rio de Janeiro, Brazil. She moved with her family a few months later to another favela, Chapéu Mangueira, situated on a hill overlooking Copacabana Beach. Her adopted father, José Tobias de Sousa, worked in construction, and her mother, Maria da Conceiçao de Sousa, washed clothes. The de Sousas had thirteen children, only eight of whom survived infancy, and Benedita was the only one who learned how to read and write. Because the family lived in poverty, Benedita was forced to earn money starting at age seven. She shined shoes, sold candies in the streets, and worked as a live-in maid, as a school janitor, and in a leather factory. In her thirties, she worked as a clerk in the Department of Transportation of Rio de Janeiro and supplemented her income as a nurse's aid at the Miguel Couto Hospital. In 1980 Benedita earned her high school degree, and only a year later she graduated from the State University of Rio with a degree in social work.

Benedita married three times. She married her first husband, Nilton Aldano da Silva, at age sixteen; he was ten years older than her. The couple had four children, two of whom died within days of their birth. After Nilton's death in 1981, she married Aguinaldo Bezerra dos Santos, a community leader in Chapéu Mangueira. In 1988, however, Aguinaldo died suddenly. Benedita married again in October 1993. Her third husband was Antônio Pitanga, a popular actor and city councilor in Rio de Janeiro.

Benedita's experiences as a black child, a wife, and a mother shaped her political activism. Elected president of the community association for Chapeu Mangueira in 1978, she was the first female to hold the position. Influenced by the ideas of liberation theology and the progressive ideas of the Brazilian educator Paulo Freire, she became a vigorous proponent of educational opportunity for all Brazilians. During her political career, Benedita has led efforts to assure that domestic workers receive a minimum wage, to make gender discrimination illegal, to end mass

Reverend Jesse Jackson, U.S. civil rights leader, campaigns with Rio de Janeiro state Governor Benedita da Silva in Rio, 2002. Da Silva, an international spokeswoman for women's and human rights who helped found Brazil's Workers Party in 1980, became the first black female senator in the history of Brazil in 1994. She was defeated in the 2002 gubernatorial elections. © REUTERS/CORBIS

sterilization of women, to defend female prisoners from violent abuse, to provide access tohealthcare, and to protect the reproductive rights of women.

In 1980 Benedita helped found the Workers Party (*Partido dos Trabalhadores*). Two years later, campaigning with the slogan "I am [proud to be] black, a woman, and from the favela," she was elected to the City Council of Rio de Janeiro, the first black woman to attain this position in the history of Brazil. This success was followed by a series of stunning electoral victories as a representative of the state of Rio de Janeiro. In 1986, she was elected to the Federal Chamber of Deputies, and she was re-elected in 1990. Four years later she won election as Brazil's first black female senator. Then, in 1998, she became vice-governor (deputy governor) of the state of Rio de Janeiro.

When Governor Anthony Garotinho ran for the presidency of Brazil in March 2002, Benedita took up the governorship. Although she was defeated in the gubernatorial election of October 2002, she was soon after appointed

Minister of Social Welfare by Brazil's president, Luiz Iná-cio Lula da Silva. She headed this ministry until January 2004. Since her resignation, Benedita has spoken on behalf of women's rights and human rights around the world. In February 2005, she visited Atlanta, Georgia, to establish the Benedita da Silva Foundation in that city. The foundation seeks improve social conditions and increase educational opportunities for Afro-Brazilians, particularly women marginalized children, and the poor.

In a nation that has been portrayed as a "racial democracy," Benedita's career has vividly shown the harsh struggles faced by Afro-Brazilians. Although she has endured racist slander and discrimination, she has been unceasing in her defense of the rights of Afro-Brazilians (estimated to number more than half of Brazil's 186 million inhabitants), women, and native people (estimated at 734,000 in the 2000 census). Benedita's extraordinary journey and contributions are a testament to her determination to survive and succeed in spite of the desperate circumstances into which she was born.

See also Politics and Politicians in Latin America

■ ■ *Bibliography*

City of God. DVD. Directed by Fernando Meirelles and Kátia Lund. Miramax Films, 2002.

Da Silva, Benedita, with Medea Benjamin and Maisa Mendon-ça. *Benedita da Silva: An Afro-Brazilian Woman's Story of Politics and Love.* Oakland, Calif.: Institute for Food and Development Policy, 1997.

DALE TORSTON GRADEN (2005)

DAS NEVES, EDUARDO

1874
1919

┣━┃━┃━━━━━━━━━━━━━

The musician Eduardo Sebastião das Neves was born in 1874, most likely in the outskirts of Rio de Janeiro, the same city in which he died in 1919. Of African descent, he was by his own definition a *crioulo,* an antiquated term used to refer to Brazilian-born blacks. The word may carry strongly racist meanings, but, as in the case of das Neves, was also appropriated by blacks, similar to the multiple contemporary uses of *nigger* in English. He became a famous singer and a famous guitar player just after the abolition of slavery in 1888. He sang numerous musical styles, including *lundu, modinha, marcha, seresta, samba, valsa,* and *maxixe,* performing on stages in Rio de Janeiro and throughout Brazil. Turn-of-the-century newspaper accounts describe das Neves as squandering his earnings, and he died poor, but he enraptured crowds with his guitar.

The lyrics of his song "O Crioulo," written in Rio de Janeiro in 1900, present a kind of autobiography and reveal the confidence that das Neves had in his own abilities. The song begins by declaring his superior knowledge of the guitar, which he claimed to have possessed from his earliest days and maintained as he learned and grew, even while mixing in mischief. His success was such, the song continues, that when he picked up a musical instrument, "all the little brown girls loved watching the *crioulo* play his music" (das Neves, 1926, p. 64).

Until 1902, when he was discovered by Casa Edison—an influential purchaser and vendor of sheet music and records—the "Crioulo Dudu," as he like to be called, shared the hard life of the city's thousands of other poor workers. In 1892 he served in the National Guard, achieving the title of captain and defending President Floriano Peixoto during an uprising in 1893. Soon afterwards, he joined the fire department, but he was fired after various reprimands for insubordination. At the age of twenty-one, he worked as a brakeman on the railways. In "O Crioulo," he explains that he left the rails after a strike because his boss "did not like his *ginga,*" a kind of strut, which also implies here attitude (das Neves, 1926, p. 64). Beginning in 1895, he dedicated himself completely to his guitar and public performances.

With the popular publishing company Editora Quaresma, das Neves published four books of songs, many of which appear to have been written by him. He selected others from various regional and slave traditions in Brazil. In the preface of one book, *O Trovador da Malandragem* (1902), with songs produced between 1889 and 1902, he complained that other artists often used his work without recognizing his contributions. As he made clear, his songs were "sung by everyone everywhere, from fancy parlors to street corners, at all hours of the night" (das Neves, 1926, p. 3).

Among the often humorous and irreverent verses sung and written by das Neves, many deal with daily problems in Rio de Janeiro (e.g., urban reform, the rising cost of public transportation, mandatory vaccinations, hunger, squalid living conditions, taxes, street fighting), celebrations of the nation (e.g., an anthem written to Santos Dumont, the hero of Brazilian aviation, and other public figures), and satires about noble figures (especially barons and bishops) and social practices (such as festivals and patronage relationships). Some deal directly with race relations and challenge what were then widely-held racist theories suggesting the inferiority of black and mixed-race Brazilians. There are also tales of romance with *iaiás* (a word used during the nineteenth and early twentieth centuries to refer to wives and daughters of slaveholders), encounters with women, and descriptions of flashy, self-styled *crioulos* and various black figures from the times of slavery. From the serious to the whimsical, the musical genres that das Neves played were not just produced and played by Afro-Brazilians, but instead were composed and performed by numerous writers and artists and disseminated in theaters, circuses, and cafés.

However, by identifying the value of nonwhites in his work, das Neves made manifest the important role that musical production played for Afro-Brazilians who were fighting racial oppression and attempting to realize their dreams during a period of low literacy rates and levels of education. However limited, the rise and recognition of the "Crioulo Dudu" in Brazilian music—which grew steadily during the late nineteenth and early twentieth centuries—reveals a strategy employed by Afro-Brazilians to assert themselves in a nation not inclined to accept them.

See also Music in Latin America; Samba

■ ■ *Bibliography*

Abreu, Martha. "Outras histórias de Pai João: conflitos raciais, protesto escravo e irreverência sexual na poesia popular, 1880-1950." *Afro-Asia,* no. 31 (2004).

Das Neves, Eduardo. *O Trovador da Malandragem.* Rio de Janeiro: Livraria Quaresma Editores, 1902, 1926.

Guimarães, Francisco (O Vagalume). *Na roda de samba.* (Originally published in 1933.) Rio de Janeiro: Funarte, 1978.

Tinhorão, José Ramos. *Cultura Popular, Temas e Questões.* Rio de Janeiro: Ed. 34, 2001.

MARTHA ABREU (2005)

DAVIS, ALLISON

OCTOBER 14, 1902
NOVEMBER 21, 1983

The educator William Allison Davis was born in Washington, D.C., and attended Williams College in Williamstown, Massachusetts, graduating in 1924. The following year he received an M.A. in English from Harvard University. Soon after, he switched his focus to anthropology; he received an M.A. in anthropology from Harvard in 1932. From 1933 to 1935 he was a field researcher for social anthropologist W. Lloyd Warner, studying class/caste relations in a southern town. The project ultimately resulted in the well-known study *Deep South* (1941). In 1935 Davis was hired as professor of anthropology at Dillard University in New Orleans, and in 1939, after a brief period at Yale University, he moved on to the University of Chicago, where he was named an assistant professor by the university's Center for Child Development. Soon after, Davis and his colleague John Dollard collaborated on *The Children of Bondage: The Personality Development of Negro Youth in the Urban South* (1940), a study of the destructive psychological effects of segregation on southern black children. In 1942 Davis received his Ph.D. in education from the University of Chicago and was named an assistant professor of education. Over the following years he did exhaustive research on racial bias in intelligence testing, and in 1948 he published his most notable book, *Social-Class Influences upon Learning,* in which he argued that black children's lower scores on IQ tests were not based on their lower intelligence, but resulted from middle-class cultural bias in the questions posed.

In 1948 Davis was granted tenure and promoted to full professor at the University of Chicago, the first African American to hold such a position at a major integrated university. During the next twenty years, he continued his work in psychology and education. He devised the Davis-Ellis intelligence test, a relatively bias-free measure of mental development, and wrote several important studies of the influence of social and class factors in the education of children, including *Psychology of the Child in the Middle Class* (1960) and *Compensatory Education for Cultural Development* (1964), as well as numerous articles in professional journals.

Davis received many tributes for his work. He was the first scholar from the field of education elected to the American Academy of Arts and Sciences. In 1965 he was elected a Distinguished Professor at the University of Illinois. In 1966 he was appointed the President's Commission on Civil Rights, and in 1968 served as vice-chair of the U.S. Labor Department's Commission on Manpower Retraining. In 1970 he became the University of Chicago's first John Dewey Distinguished Service Professor.

Davis retired from teaching in 1978 and was named professor emeritus. He devoted his last years to writing *Leadership, Love, and Aggression* (1983), a study of the psychological forces governing four African Americans—Frederick Douglass, W. E. B. Du Bois, the Rev. Dr. Martin Luther King Jr., and Richard Wright—and the role of anger and love in their leadership efforts. In November

1983, shortly after the book was published, Davis died following heart surgery. In 1993 the U.S. Postal Service honored him with a postage stamp.

▪ ▪ Bibliography

Davis, Allison. *Leadership, Love, and Aggression.* San Diego, Calif.: Harcourt Brace Jovanovich, 1983.

GREG ROBINSON (1996)

DAVIS, ANGELA

JANUARY 26, 1944

Political activist Angela Yvonne Davis lived in a section of Birmingham, Alabama, known as "Dynamite Hill" because of the violent attacks by white night riders intent on maintaining the residential demarcation line between blacks and whites. Both of her parents were educators, worked actively for the National Association for the Advancement of Colored People (NAACP), and taught their children not to accept the socially segregated society that existed at the time. She attended Brandeis University, where she was influenced by the teachings of Marxist philosopher Herbert Marcuse. After graduating in 1961, she spent two years in Europe, where she was exposed to student political radicals. Her own radicalism, however, came into focus with the murder in 1963 of four young black Sunday school children in a Birmingham, Alabama, church bombing. In California, where she went to pursue graduate study with Marcuse (who was now at the University of California at San Diego), Davis began working with the Student Nonviolent Coordinating Committee (SNCC), the Black Panthers, and the Communist Party, of which she became a member in 1968.

Hired in 1969 by UCLA to teach philosophy, Davis not long after was fired by the board of regents and then-governor Ronald Reagan because of her Communist Party affiliation. Ultimately, her case went to the Supreme Court, which overturned the dismissal. By that time, however, Davis herself was in hiding as a result of an incident at the Soledad state prison. In August 1970 George Jackson, a prisoner and member of the Black Panthers, assisted by his brother Jonathan, attempted to escape using smuggled guns. Both brothers were killed and some of the guns were traced to Davis. Fearful for her safety and distrustful of the judicial system, Davis went underground. For two months she was on the FBI's Ten Most Wanted list before being apprehended and incarcerated. She remained in jail for sixteen months before being tried for murder and conspiracy. In June 1972 she was acquitted of all charges against her.

Davis resumed her academic career at San Francisco State University and again became politically active, running as the Communist Party candidate for vice president in 1980 and 1984. In 1991 she joined the faculty of the University of California, Santa Cruz, as professor of the history of consciousness. She left the Communist Party in 1991 but remained politically active. In 1995 she was a prominent feminist critic of the Million Man March. She is the author of several books, including *If They Come in the Morning* (1971), *Women, Race, and Class* (1983), *Women, Culture, and Politics* (1989), and *Blues Legends and Black Feminism* (1998). In 2003, Davis took a searing look at the prison system in her work, *Are Prisons Obsolete?* Her autobiography, *Angela Davis: An Autobiography*, originally published in 1974, was reissued in 1988.

See also Black Panther Party for Self Defense; Communist Party of the United States

▪ ▪ Bibliography

Davis, Angela. *Are Prisons Obsolete?* New York: Seven Stories Press, 2003.

Lanker, Brian. *I Dream a World: Portraits of Black Women Who Changed America.* New York: Stewart, Tabori & Chang, 1989.

CHRISTINE A. LUNARDINI (1996)
Updated by publisher 2005

DAVIS, BENJAMIN O., JR.

DECEMBER 18, 1912
JULY 4, 2002

Benjamin Oliver Davis Jr., son of the first African-American general in the U.S. Army, had a long and distinguished career of his own in the U.S. Air Force. Following his long military service, he spent a number of years working as an important administrator in the Department of Transportation.

The younger Davis was born in Washington, D.C., and he spent many of his early years watching or participating in his father's military activities. In the 1920s he lived with his parents and attended school in Tuskegee, Alabama, and Cleveland, Ohio. One of his most vivid memories from those days involved his father facing down a Ku Klux Klan march while the family lived at Tuskegee. As an adolescent, Davis Jr. was an excellent scholar and displayed leadership qualities. He was one of the few African-American students at Central High School in Cleveland and was elected president of his graduating class. He attended college at Western Reserve University (Cleveland, Ohio) and the University of Chicago, but then decided on a military career. Despite the handicaps that had faced his father, he felt that it was a profession where he could advance on his merits. In 1932 his father asked the assistance of Oscar DePriest, a congressman from Illinois, who nominated Davis Jr. to the United States Military Academy. He subsequently passed the entrance examination and entered West Point in 1932.

Life at the military academy had change little since the last African American had graduated in the 1880s. The presence of blacks was resented, and almost all the cadets ignored Davis. The only time he had any companionship was when he was allowed to leave West Point. During his years at the academy he began to develop an interest in flying, an area the Army had closed to African Americans. When he graduated in 1936, ranking thirty-fifth in a class of 276, he requested assignment to the Army Air Corps. The Army refused because there were no African-American flying units and they would not assign a black officer to a white unit. During the next few years he performed a variety of duties, similar to those of his father. In 1938 he received an appointment as professor of military science at Tuskegee Institute. Two years later he was detached to work as an aide to his father, who was then commanding the 2nd Cavalry Brigade at Fort Riley, Kansas.

His interest in flying never waned, and in 1941 he received his opportunity. Bowing to pressure, the army decided to allow African Americans into the Army Air Corps, established a flight-training program at Tuskegee Institute, and ordered Davis to command the first class. After he graduated in 1942, he was rapidly promoted to the rank of major and given command of the 99th Pursuit Squadron, the first African-American air unit. In April 1943 the unit was transferred to North Africa, and in June it flew its first combat mission. Most of the ensuing missions were rather routine, but not everyone was persuaded of their effectiveness. A number of white officers were convinced that no African-American air unit could ever measure up to the quality of the white units.

Later in the year Davis was ordered back to the United States and assigned command of the 332nd Fighter Group, a larger all-black flying unit. More important, he was able to answer the many questions that army staff officers posed about the effectiveness of the 99th Squadron. Enough of these officers were convinced to the extent that they decided to continue the African-American flying program and transferred the 332nd to the Italian theater. During the last year of the war, Davis was promoted to the rank of colonel, flew sixty combat missions (mainly escorting bombers) and received several awards, including the Distinguished Flying Cross. At the end of the war he returned to the United States and was placed in command of the 477th Composite Group. Among the problems he had to face in his new assignment were segregated base facilities, poor morale, and continued evidence of the detrimental impact of segregation.

During the next few years Davis continued to deal with those problems while advocating an end to segregation. When President Harry S. Truman issued Executive Order 9981 in 1948, ending racial discrimination in the armed forces, Davis became a key officer in the Air Force. He helped draft desegregation plans and put them into practice at Lockbourne Air Base. Subsequently he was assigned to the new Air War College. During the Korean War he served at the Pentagon as deputy for operations in the Fighter Branch. Later he was given a variety of command assignments throughout the world, including Formosa, Germany, and the Philippines. In 1965 he was promoted to lieutenant general, the first African American to reach that rank. He retired from the Air Force in 1970.

During the following years he served in a variety of positions within civilian government. For several months in 1970 he was director of public safety in Cleveland, Ohio, but found he could not work well with Mayor Carl Stokes. Adapting to the world of urban politics proved to be quite difficult for a man who had spent the previous thirty years in the military. In June 1970, Davis became a member of the President's Commission on Campus Unrest. From 1970 to 1975 he served as an administrator in the Department of Transportation. As assistant secretary of transportation, he headed the federal programs developed to deal with air hijacking and highway safety. In 1978 he became a member of the Battle Monuments Commission, a position his father had held twenty-five years earlier. During the next few years he remained busy with a variety of activities, including programs designed to tell people about the role of African Americans in aviation, and the writing of his autobiography, which was eventually published in 1991. In 1998 he was awarded an honorary promotion to the rank of general.

Davis died of complications from Alzheimer's disease on July 4, 2002.

See also Military Experience, African-American

■ ■ *Bibliography*

Davis, Benjamin O., Jr. *Benjamin O Davis., Jr., American: An Autobiography.*Washington, D.C.: Smithsonian Institution Press, 1991.

Nalty, Bernard C. *Strength for the Fight: A History of Black Americans in the Military.* New York: Free Press, 1986.

MARVIN E. FLETCHER (1996)
Updated by publisher 2005

DAVIS, MILES

MAY 26, 1926
SEPTEMBER 28, 1991

One of the most influential musicians in America in the 1950s and 1960s, jazz trumpeter and composer Miles Davis was a restlessly innovative performer, a central figure in several post-bebop jazz styles, including cool, hardbop, modal, fusion, and electric jazz. Born in Alton, Illinois, Miles Dewey Davis III grew up in East St. Louis. His mother was a classically trained pianist and violinist. Davis received his first trumpet at the age of thirteen from his father, a successful dentist. In high school he studied with Elwood Buchanan, and trumpeter Clark Terry also served as a mentor. Davis began playing dates in the St. Louis area in his mid-teens, and in 1943 and 1944 he played with Eddie Randle's Rhumboogie Orchestra. He also performed with Adam Lambert's Six Brown Cats in Chicago and with Billy Eckstine in St. Louis before moving to New York in 1944. Davis's ostensible reason for going to New York was to study at the Juilliard School, but he gained his real education in the jazz clubs of Harlem and Fifty-second Street.

Once in New York, Davis began associating with the young musicians beginning to popularize bebop. He made his first recordings in 1945 with vocalist Rubberlegs Williams. Later that year he recorded with alto saxophonist Charlie Parker ("Billie's Bounce," "Now's the Time"). Parker became Davis's mentor and roommate, and over the next few years the two made many important and influential bebop recordings, including "Yardbird Suite," "Ornithology," "A Night in Tunisia," "Donna Lee," "Chasin' the Bird," and "Parker's Mood." On these recordings Davis distinguished himself by his intimate tone and sparse, hesitant style of improvisation. During this time Davis was a fixture on Fifty-second Street, performing and recording with pianist Tadd Dameron, pianists Bud Powell and Thelonious Monk, vocalist Billy Eckstine, and saxophonist Coleman Hawkins. He first recorded as a band leader in

Miles Davis (1926–1991), New York City, 1986. Davis was one of the most innovative musicians of the twentieth century, standing at the forefront of a number of modern jazz movements. PHOTOGRAPH BY JON SIMON. CORBIS/BETTMANN. REPRODUCED BY PERMISSION.

1947 ("Milestones" and "Half Nelson," with Parker on tenor saxophone), and the next year he left Parker to form an experimental nine-piece group in collaboration with arranger Gil Evans. The ensemble, which included a French horn and tuba and featured advanced harmonies and unusual compositional forms, was short-lived, performing at the Royal Roost nightclub for only two weeks. Nonetheless, its recordings from 1949–1950 ("Move," "Venus de Milo," "Boplicity," and "Israel") spawned the cool jazz movement of the 1950s and became particularly popular upon their 1954 re-release in LP form as *The Birth of the Cool.*

Despite a period of heroin addiction from 1949 to 1953, Davis continued to perform and record in a cool style, often with saxophonist Sonny Rollins ("Morpheus," "Dig," "The Serpent's Tooth," "Tune Up," and "Miles Ahead"). His career took another leap forward with the 1954 recording of "Walkin'." That recording, with its more extroverted approach, inaugurated hard bop, a rugged and bluesier version of bebop. In 1955 Davis formed his first significant quintet, including tenor saxophonist

John Coltrane, bassist Paul Chambers, pianist Red Garland, and drummer Philly Joe Jones. They recorded the landmark *Round About Midnight* (1955) and performed and recorded until 1957, when Davis added alto saxophonist Cannonball Adderley to the group. In 1957 Davis went to France to record the soundtrack for Louis Malle's film *Elevator to the Gallows.* Back in the United States the next year, Davis recorded *Milestones,* which introduced the concept of modal jazz, in which modes or scales, as opposed to chord changes, determine a song's harmonies. In 1959 Davis recorded perhaps his greatest record, *Kind of Blue,* which included the modal compositions "So What," "All Blues," and "Freddie Freeloader," with an ensemble that included drummer Jimmy Cobb and pianists Wynton Kelly and Bill Evans. In the late 1950s Davis also renewed his association with arranger Gil Evans. They produced three acclaimed orchestral works, *Miles Ahead* (1957), *Porgy and Bess* (1958), and *Sketches of Spain* (1959–1960). During this time Davis achieved his mature instrumental style, delicate and tentative on ballads, boldly lyrical on up-tempo numbers.

Davis's trumpet style resembled, in a famous description, "a man walking on eggshells," but he was often belligerent and profane, on stage and off. He refused to announce titles, walked off the stage when sidemen soloed, and rarely acknowledged applause. Nonetheless, he openly demanded the respect he felt was appropriate to jazz musicians. During the 1950s Davis also became an internationally known public figure noted for his immaculate attire, his interest in sports cars, and for taking up boxing as a hobby.

In 1960 Adderley and Coltrane left the ensemble, which underwent a number of personnel shifts until 1963, when Davis hired pianist Herbie Hancock, bassist Ron Carter, and drummer Tony Williams. With saxophonist Wayne Shorter's arrival the next year, Davis began featuring churning, lengthy improvisations built around Shorter's quirky compositions (*E.S.P.,* 1965; *Miles Smiles,* 1966).

During the late 1960s Davis became disenchanted with the poor reception his music found among black audiences, and he began to search for a new, more commercially appealing style. He found inspiration in the funk rhythms of James Brown and Sly Stone, as well as in Karlheinz Stockhausen's vast electric-mystic soundscapes. Davis added Keith Jarrett and Chick Corea on electric pianos and John McLaughlin on electric guitar to his regular ensemble and recorded *In a Silent Way* (1969) and the best-selling *Bitches Brew* (1969), albums that introduced the style that has become known as jazz-rock or "fusion," using loud rock instruments and funk rhythms to accom-

pany extended solo and group improvisations. Davis continued in this vein on *Big Fun* (1969), *Live-Evil* (1970), *On the Corner* (1972), *Agharta* (1975) and *Pangea* (1975). Although Davis gained many fans of rock music, jazz fans were perplexed and unsympathetic. Health problems due to drug abuse and a 1972 car accident convinced Davis to retire in 1975.

In 1980 Davis returned to music, but to the disappointment of many of his fans he continued using popular forms of electric instruments. In his best performances Davis still communicated with the intensity and fire he had in the 1950s, but his recordings, including *The Man with the Horn* (1981), *Star People* (1982), *Tutu* (1986), and *Amandla* (1989), were largely panned by critics, who were particularly harsh on his undistinguished accompanists. Davis, who lived in New York and Malibu, continued to perform and record in the late 1980s and early 1990s. In 1982 Davis married his third wife, the actress Cicely Tyson; they were divorced in 1989.

Davis published an outspoken memoir, *Miles, the Autobiography,* in 1989. After many years of battling alcoholism, drug addiction, and circulatory and respiratory ailments, Davis died in 1991 in New York.

See also Brown, James; Coltrane, John; Eckstine, Billy; Hancock, Herbie; Jazz; Parker, Charlie; Monk, Thelonious Sphere

■ ■ *Bibliography*

Carr, Ian. *Miles Davis: The Definitive Biography.* New York: Thunders Mouth Press, 1982.

Chambers, Jack. *Milestones,* 2 vols. Toronto, Ontario, Canada: University of Toronto Press, 1983, 1985.

Cole, Bill. *Miles Davis: A Musical Biography.* New York: Morrow, 1974.

Davis, Miles, with Quincy Troupe. *Miles, the Autobiography.* New York: Simon and Schuster, 1989.

Szwed, John. *So What: The Life of Miles Davis.* New York: Simon and Schuster, 2002.

WILLIAM S. COLE (1996)
Updated bibliography

DAVIS, OSSIE

DECEMBER 18, 1917
FEBRUARY 4, 2005

■ ■ ■

Actor and playwright Ossie Davis was born in Cogdell, Georgia, to Kince Charles Davis, a railroad construction worker, and Laura Cooper Davis. After finishing high school in Waycross, Georgia, he hitchhiked north and attended Howard University. In 1937 Davis left Howard and went to New York City, where he worked at odd jobs before joining Harlem's Rose McClendon Players in 1939.

Davis was drafted into the army in 1942, and after his discharge in 1945 he again pursued his acting career. In 1946 he successfully auditioned for Robert Ardrey's *Jeb,* in which he starred opposite actress Ruby Dee. Davis and Dee were married in 1948.

In 1953 Davis wrote *Alice in Wonder,* a one-act play produced in Harlem that dealt with the politics of the McCarthy era. Blacklisted for left-wing associations, Davis and Dee supported themselves by staging readings at colleges. In 1955 Davis starred in a television production of Eugene O'Neill's *The Emperor Jones,* and two years later appeared on Broadway opposite Lena Horne in *Jamaica!*

In the 1960s Davis achieved broad success in the performing arts. In 1960 he replaced Sidney Poitier and appeared with Ruby Dee in Lorraine Hansberry's play *A Raisin in the Sun.* The following year, his play *Purlie Victorious,* a satire on southern racism, opened on Broadway to an enthusiastic response. Davis also wrote and starred in the film version of *Purlie Victorious,* entitled *Gone Are the Days* (1963). He appeared in several other films during this period, including *The Cardinal* (1963), *The Hill* (1964), *The Scalphunters* (1968), and *Slaves* (1969). He also appeared on several television shows, wrote an episode for the popular series *East Side/West Side,* and narrated National Education Television's *History of the Negro People* (1965). In 1969 Davis was nominated for an Emmy award for his performance in the Hallmark Hall of Fame special *Teacher, Teacher.* That same year Davis directed, cowrote, and acted in the film *Cotton Comes to Harlem,* based on a novel by Chester Himes.

During these years, Davis continued his political activities. In 1962 he testified before Congress on racial discrimination in the theater and joined the advisory board of the Congress of Racial Equality (CORE). The following year he wrote a skit for the 1963 March on Washington, and in 1965 he delivered a eulogy at the funeral of his friend, Malcolm X. In 1972 he served as chairman of the Angela Davis Defense Fund. While Davis has strong affinities with black nationalism, he has nonetheless rejected black racism and separatism.

Through the 1970s, 1980s, and early 1990s, Davis continued his performing career, notably in a radio series, the *Ossie Davis and Ruby Dee Hour* (1974–1976); in the public television series *With Ossie and Ruby* (1981); in the role of Martin Luther King, Sr., in Abby Mann's television miniseries *King* (1977); and in the Spike Lee films *Do the Right Thing* (1989), *Jungle Fever* (1991), and *I'm Not Rappaport* (1996). Throughout the early 1990s, he was a semiregular on the television series *Evening Shade.* Davis also has written several children's books, which include plays based on the lives of Frederick Douglass and Langston Hughes, and a novel, *Just Like Martin* (1992), about a southern boy, inspired by the life of the Rev. Dr. Martin Luther King, Jr. In 1998 Davis celebrated his fiftieth wedding anniversary with Ruby Dee by publishing a joint memoir, *With Ossie and Ruby Dee: In This Life Together.* His play *A Last Dance for Sybil* was produced off-Broadway in 2002. Davis continues to take on roles in films and television shows, including episodes of such series as *JAG, Third Watch,* and *Touched by an Angel.*

In December 2004 the Kennedy Center honored Davis with a lifetime achievement award. Davis died at age eighty-seven on February 4, 2005.

See also Congress of Racial Equality (CORE); Hansberry, Lorraine; Himes, Chester; Lee, Spike; Malcolm X; Poitier, Sidney

■ ■ *Bibliography*

Davis, Ossie, and Ruby Dee. *With Ossie and Ruby Dee: In This Life Together.* New York: Morrow, 1998.

Landay, Eileen. *Black Film Stars.* New York: Drake, 1973.

McMurray, Emily J., and Owen O'Donnell, eds. *Contemporary Theater, Film and Television.* Detroit: Gale, 1992.

SUSAN MCINTOSH (1996)
GREG ROBINSON (1996)
Updated by publisher 2005

DAVIS, SAMMY, JR.

DECEMBER 8, 1925
MAY 19, 1990

Singer, dancer, and actor Sammy Davis Jr. was born in Harlem in New York and began performing with his father, a vaudeville entertainer, before his fourth birthday. Davis made his first film, *Rufus Jones for President* (1933) when he was eight years old. By the time he was fifteen, he had traveled widely throughout the United States as a full partner in the Will Mastin Trio, comprised of Davis, his father, and Davis's adopted "uncle" Will Mastin. Although they often played at white venues, the trio was compelled to eat and room at Negro establishments; yet Davis, who had received an informal education at the hands of family and friends, was unprepared for the virulent racism he encountered upon joining the army in 1943. During his tenure in the military, he produced and performed in shows with other service personnel, including the singer and songwriter George M. Cohan, Jr.

Following World War II Davis returned to the Will Mastin Trio. The group played to segregated audiences and, despite their rising popularity, were forbidden to sleep or socialize in the hotels and casinos where they worked. Davis began recording songs for Capitol Records in 1946; one of his first cuts, "The Way You Look Tonight," was named Metronome's Record of the Year. An extremely versatile performer, adept at tap dancing, singing, impersonations, and comic and serious acting, he received his first big break when Frank Sinatra asked the trio to open for his show at Manhattan's Capitol Theater. Davis went on to perform at Slapsie Maxie's and Ciro's in Los Angeles and at the Copacabana in New York, in addition to appearing on *The Ed Sullivan Show* and Eddie Cantor's *The Colgate Comedy Hour.*

In November 1954 Davis, who had become a celebrity with white and black audiences alike, was involved in a near-fatal car accident while driving from Las Vegas to Los Angeles. He lost his left eye and was hospitalized for several months; during this time, he was visited by a rabbi, who urged him to reflect on the consequences of the accident and the meaning of his previous actions. After a period of intense study, Davis, who claimed to have found an "affinity" between blacks and Jews as oppressed peoples, converted to Judaism.

Davis's popularity was much enhanced by his brush with death. He performed in Philadelphia, Chicago, and Los Angeles before taking the lead role in *Mr. Wonderful,* a musical comedy that opened on Broadway in 1956. Two years later Davis, who had been nicknamed "Mr. Wonderful" after the Broadway show, was featured in a serious dramatic role in the movie *Anna Lucasta.* In the 1959 film version of *Porgy and Bess,* Davis gave a memorable performance as the character Sportin' Life. That year, he married Loray White, an African-American dancer whom he later left for the Swedish actress Mai Britt. Davis's interracial romance with Britt was highly publicized, and the couple married in 1960.

Davis is perhaps best known for the films he made during the 1960s, when he worked and socialized with the "Rat Pack," a group of Hollywood actors that included Sinatra, Dean Martin, Peter Lawford, and Joey Bishop, who were featured, along with Davis, in such films as *Oceans Eleven* (1960), *Sergeants Three* (1962), *Robin and the Seven Hoods* (1964), *Salt and Pepper* (1968), and *One More Time* (1970). Davis also appeared in such films as

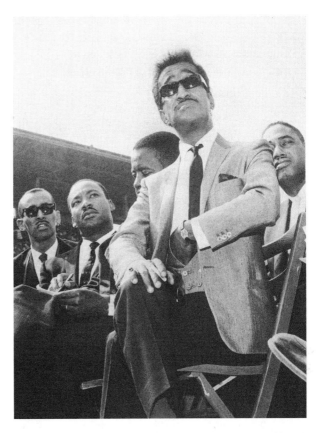

Sammy Davis Jr. on a speaker's platform at Wrigley Field with Martin Luther King Jr. May 28, 1963. *Striking a Napoleonic pose, Davis was among 35,000 in attendance at the freedom meeting in Chicago. The popular entertainer was awarded a Spingarn Medal by the NAACP in 1968 for his work to promote civil rights.* © BETTMANN/CORBIS

Johnny Cool (1963), *A Man Called Adam* (1966), *Sweet Charity* (1969), and the German remake of *The Threepenny Opera* (1964), in which he sang "Mack the Knife." In addition, he continued to perform in clubs and on Broadway, where he was praised for his rendering of the title character in *Golden Boy,* Clifford Odets's play about an African-American boxer struggling to free himself from the constrictions of ghetto life. Davis appeared on television in numerous comic and guest-artist roles, as well as in serious dramatic series like the *Dick Powell Theatre* and *General Electric Theater.* In 1966 he hosted a television variety and talk show called *The Sammy Davis Jr. Show,* which ran for less than a year. He also continued to record albums and produced such hit songs as "Candy Man," "Hey There," "Mr. Bojangles," and "The Lady Is a Tramp."

Throughout the 1960s Davis worked to promote civil rights and African-American/Jewish relations by giving benefit performances and substantial donations. His first autobiography, *Yes I Can,* was published in 1965; three years later, he was awarded the Spingarn Medal by the

NAACP for his work in civil rights. Davis's marriage to Mai Britt ended in 1968, and two years later, he married African-American actress Altovise Gore. In 1971 he was awarded an honorary doctorate of fine arts by Wilberforce University in Ohio. A controversy erupted the following year when Davis, a registered Democrat and supporter of left-wing causes, allowed himself to be photographed with President Richard Nixon at the 1972 Republican Convention; he publicly endorsed Nixon for a time but then renounced their affiliation in 1974.

During the early 1970s Davis, by then almost as well known for his extravagant spending habits and hard-drinking lifestyle as for his stage presence and vitality, began to experience liver and kidney problems, for which he was eventually hospitalized in 1974. However, he rebounded fairly quickly and was back onstage a few months later in a revue called *Sammy on Broadway*. From 1975 to 1977 he starred in the television show *Sammy and Company*. He performed regularly on the Las Vegas club circuit, and in 1979, became the first recipient of *Ebony* magazine's Lifetime Achievement Award.

Davis's second autobiography, *Hollywood in a Suitcase*, was published in 1980; throughout the decade he continued to appear, albeit less frequently, in films, on television, and onstage. In 1986 he received an honorary degree from Howard University. Two years later he embarked on a national tour with Frank Sinatra, Dean Martin, and Liza Minnelli. Davis was featured in the movie *Taps* (1989), a tribute to showbiz entertainers, and published a third autobiographical work, *Why Me?* (1989), before dying of throat cancer in the spring of 1990.

See also Film; Tap Dance; Theatrical Dance

■ ■ *Bibliography*

Davis, Sammy, Jr. *Yes I Can.* New York: Farrar, Straus and Giroux, 1980.

Davis, Sammy, Jr., and Jane and Burt Boyar. *Sammy: An Autobiography: With Material Newly Revised from Yes I Can and Why Me.* New York: Farrar, Straus and Giroux, 2000.

Early, Gerald, ed. *The Sammy Davis, Jr. Reader.* New York: Farrar, Straus and Giroux, 2001.

Fishgall, Gary. *Gonna Do Great Things: The Life of Sammy Davis, Jr.* New York: Scribner, 2003.

Haygood, Wil. *In Black and White: The Life of Sammy Davis, Jr.* New York: Knopf, 2003.

Mortiz, Charles, ed. *Current Biography Yearbook.* New York: H. W. Wilson, 1978.

Silber, Arthur. *Sammy Davis, Jr.: Me and My Shadow: A Biographical Memoir.* Valley Village, CA: Samart, 2002.

JESSE RHINES (1996)
Updated bibliography

DeCarava, Roy

December 9, 1919

━■■■━━━━━━━━━━━━━━━━━━━━━

The photographer Roy DeCarava was born in New York's Harlem. He was raised by his mother and graduated with a major in art from the Straubenmuller Textile High School in 1938. While still in high school he worked as a sign painter and display artist and in the poster division of the Works Projects Administration (WPA) in New York City. In his senior year he won a competition to design a medal for the National Tuberculosis Association's high school essay contest and upon graduation received a scholarship for excellence in art.

Supporting himself as a commercial artist, DeCarava studied painting at Cooper Union with Byron Thomas and Morris Kantor from 1938 to 1940, and lithography and drawing at the Harlem Art Center from 1940 to 1942. He attended the George Washington Carver Art School in 1944 and 1945, studying painting with Charles White. In 1946 his serigraph won the print award at the Atlanta University Fifth Annual Exhibition of Painting and Sculpture (a national juried exhibition for black artists), and the following year he had a one-man show at the Serigraph Gallery in New York.

In 1946 DeCarava began to use photography as a way to sketch ideas for paintings, and by 1947 he had decided to concentrate exclusively on it. Although he lacked formal training, DeCarava approached photography as "just another medium that an artist would use"; he quickly established a distinctive style and chose a subject—the people of Harlem—that engaged him deeply and productively. Some of his strongest work dates from the late 1940s and early 1950s, including *Graduation* (1949) and *Gittel* (1950). His first photographic exhibition was in 1950 at New York's Forty-Fourth Street Gallery, and that year he sold three prints to the Museum of Modern Art. In 1952 DeCarava became the tenth photographer and among the earliest black artists to be awarded a Guggenheim Fellowship. Continuing his work in Harlem during the fellowship year, DeCarava produced over 2,000 images; he wanted to show, he said, "[African Americans'] beauty and the image that we presented in our being." In 1955 four of his photographs appeared in the Museum of Modern Art's famous *Family of Man* exhibition and best-selling book. In the same year, 141 photographs were published with a text by Langston Hughes in their much-acclaimed classic *The Sweet Flypaper of Life* (1955), a tale of everyday events in the lives of a fictional yet representative Harlem family.

DeCarava formed his style at a time in photographic history when the social documentary ethos of the 1930s

Photographer Roy DeCarava. DeCarava, best known for his deeply evocative images of the African-American experience in Harlem, poses at his Brooklyn home. PHOTOGRAPH BY MARIN CABRERA. AP/ WIDE WORLD PHOTOS.

Roy DeCarava, 1940. An art student at Cooper Union, DeCarava poses with one of his prize-winning designs. PHOTOGRAPHS AND PRINTS DIVISION, SCHOMBURG CENTER FOR RESEARCH IN BLACK CULTURE, THE NEW YORK PUBLIC LIBRARY, ASTOR, LENOX AND TILDEN FOUNDATIONS.

was giving way to a more formalist aesthetic, which especially appreciated a photographer's manipulation of the unique qualities of the medium. He was influenced by the French photographer Henri Cartier-Bresson, whose theory of the "decisive moment" credits formal organization equally with factual content in conveying essential meaning in a photograph. Like Cartier-Bresson, DeCarava uses a small camera, avoids contrived settings, often shooting in the street, and achieves important, often metaphorical, effects through composition, as in *Sun and Shade* (1952) and *Boy Playing, Man Walking* (1966). Indeed, DeCarava has taken pains throughout his career to foster interpretations that see more in his style than literal and programmatic documentary. His titles are always brief and uninflected, and he insists that his work is not political and that "the definition of truth is a personal one." Dismayed that so few galleries showed photography as a fine art, DeCarava operated the Photographer's Gallery from 1954 to 1956, exhibiting work by such artists as Berenice Abbott, Harry Callahan, and Minor White.

DeCarava felt keenly that black people were not seen as "worthy subject matter" for art; he was determined that African Americans be portrayed in ways that were "serious," "artistic," and "human." His dual commitment—to

content representing the beauty and diversity of the African-American experience and to full formal mastery of his medium—has deeply influenced younger photographers, who have seen him as the first to develop the black aesthetic in photography. From 1963 to 1966, he directed the Kamoinge Workshop for black photographers and chaired the Committee to End Discrimination against Black Photographers of the American Society of Magazine Photographers. In 1968 DeCarava picketed the Metropolitan Museum of Art's controversial *Harlem on My Mind* exhibition, protesting its emphasis on documentary, rather than artistic, representation of the Harlem community. In 1972 DeCarava received the Benin Award for contributions to the black community.

DeCarava's work was included in six group shows at the Museum of Modern Art during the 1950s and 1960s, and he had a one-man show at the Studio Museum in Harlem in 1969. In 1958 he gave up commercial art to support himself as a freelance photographer for magazines, advertising agencies, museums, and nonprofit organizations. From 1968 to 1975, DeCarava was a contract photographer for *Sports Illustrated* magazine, and in 1975 he was appointed associate professor of art at Hunter College, attaining the rank of City University distinguished professor in 1989.

DeCarava's impressive exhibition record continued in the 1970s and 1980s with solo shows at the Museum of Fine Arts in Houston, the Corcoran Gallery of Art in Washington, D.C., and the Museum of Modern Art in Sweden. *The Sound I Saw,* an exhibition of 100 jazz photographs at the Studio Museum in Harlem, was accompanied by a publication of the same title (1983). In 1982, the Friends of Photography published *Roy DeCarava: Photographs,* a major monograph with eighty-two pictures.

In the course of his career DeCarava has traveled and photographed in Paris, London, Stockholm, and Bangkok. His developing interest in abstraction has suggested to some critics that he feels an increasing emotional detachment from his subjects. Most viewers, however, have appreciated the artist's occasional experiment with blur or soft focus in later work as evidence of his ongoing creative exploration of his medium.

A retrospective of DeCarava's works was held at New York's Museum of Modern Art in 1996. More recent photographs were exhibited in a commercial gallery showing at Ariel Meyerowitz (New York City) in 2004.

See also Art; Harlem, New York; Photography, U.S.

■ ■ *Bibliography*

Coleman, A. D. "Roy DeCarava: 'Thru Black Eyes.'" In *Light Readings: A Photography Critic's Writings, 1968–1978.* New York: Oxford University Press, 1979, pp. 18–28.

DeCarava, Sherry Turner. "Celebration." In *Roy DeCarava: Photographs.* Carmel, Calif.: Friends of Photography, 1981, pp. 7–20.

Fraser, C. Gerald. "For Roy DeCarava, 62, It's Time for Optimism." *New York Times,* June 6, 1982.

Rachleff, Melissa. "The Sounds He Saw: The Photography of Roy DeCarava." *Afterimage* 24, no. 4 (January–February 1997).

Robinson, Fern. "Masterful American Photographer Roy De-Carava." *American Visions* 14, no. 6 (December 1999).

Stange, Maren. "Shadow and Substance." *Art in America* 84, no. 3 (March 1996).

Wallen, Ruth. "Reading the Shadows: The Photography of Roy DeCarava." *Exposure* 27, no. 4 (Fall 1990): 13–26.

FILMS

Blue, Carroll. *Conversations with Roy DeCarava.* 58 minutes. New York: First Run/Icarus Films, 1983.

MAREN STANGE (1996)
Updated bibliography

DECEMBER, WILLIAM

See Williams, Billy Dee (December, William)

DECLARATION OF INDEPENDENCE

■ ■ ■

The Declaration of Independence is the formal statement of independence from Britain made by the Continental Congress through which the thirteen American colonies became the United States of America. It was passed and signed well over a year after the outbreak of the American Revolutionary War. The patriot leadership had initially insisted that they were fighting for the redress of grievances and that they sought reconciliation with Britain. Thomas Jefferson and George Washington claimed that they did not consider independence until well into 1775. In addition, several colonies specifically instructed their delegates not to consent to independence in the closing months of 1775 and the beginning of 1776. However, independence soon became a practical necessity, both in order to give the state governments official sanction to exercise authority and in order to permit the negotiation of treaties with foreign countries. The movement gained added momentum from popular outrage at British military tactics, including their use of slaves and mercenaries, and from the realization that there was no chance of mediation by King George III. Thomas Paine articulated the most compelling case for independence in his widely read pamphlet, *Common Sense,* published in January 1776.

Richard Henry Lee proposed a series of resolutions for independence in the Continental Congress on June 7, 1776, stating that "these United Colonies are, and of right ought to be, free and independent States, that they are absolved from all allegiance to the British Crown, and that all political connection between them and the State of Great Britain is, and ought to be, totally dissolved." After four days of debate, Congress appointed a committee to draft a declaration consisting of members from the northern, middle, and southern colonies. The committee included John Adams of Massachusetts, Benjamin Franklin of Pennsylvania, Thomas Jefferson of Virginia, Robert R. Livingston of New York, and Roger Sherman of Connecticut. They delegated the task of making the first draft to Jefferson and submitted to Congress on June 28: "A Declaration by the Representatives of the United States of America, in General Congress Assembled." The motion for independence passed on July 2, with the single abstention of New York. There followed a debate and amendments to Jefferson's draft, and the final draft, titled "The Unanimous Declaration of the 13 United States of America," was approved on July 4.

According to a later account by John Adams, the committee chose Thomas Jefferson to write the Declaration because he had a reputation for his literary skills and because he was from Virginia, which was the largest state in the union, with about a quarter of the total population. Jefferson's primary concern was to justify the reasons for declaring independence from Britain. The great body of the text is therefore a long litany of grievances, for which Jefferson personally blamed George III. This was because he wanted to establish that a state of tyranny existed to legitimate the rebellion: "The history of the present King of Great Britain is a history of injuries & usurpations, all having in direct object the establishment of an absolute tyranny over these states. To prove this, let facts be submitted to a candid world."

The opening paragraphs of the Declaration are its most well-known section. It asserts the broader principles that Jefferson, as he asserted in a letter to Henry Lee, May 8, 1825, "intended to be an expression of the American mind and to give to that expression the proper tone and spirit" (Ford, vol. 10, p. 343). The second paragraph most famously includes the assertion "that all men are created equal," it proclaims the doctrine of natural and inalienable rights that governments must protect, including "life, liberty and the pursuit of happiness," and it states that government is based on the "consent of the governed." Although debate continues among historians about the source of the ideas contained in the Declaration, it is widely held that Jefferson was particularly indebted to the writings of John Locke. Indeed, there is such strong similarity with passages in Locke's *Second Treatise on Government* that Richard Henry Lee charged that Jefferson plagiarized from Locke. The Scottish Enlightenment thinkers Frances Hutcheson and Lord Kames also influenced Jefferson, together with the thought of English republicans and "Country" Whigs, the seventeenth- and eighteenth-century opposition writers and politicians like Lord Bolingbroke. Jefferson later recalled that he turned to neither book nor pamphlet while writing the Declaration, since he did not consider it his role to invent new ideas altogether or to offer sentiments that had never been expressed before.

In the minds of modern readers, the lofty ideals of the document might seem at odds with the reality of social conditions at the time they were written. The claim "that all men are created equal" particularly seems at variance with the presence of slaves, who accounted for a fifth of the total population in 1776. Indeed, such sentiments appear hypocritical from the pen of one who was himself a tobacco planter and slave owner. While Jefferson denounced slavery throughout his life, historians disagree about his sincerity. He had included in the original draft of the Declaration a passage condemning George III for the slave trade, but this section was deleted at the behest of southern representatives in the Continental Congress. And he did exclude slavery in his draft of an ordinance for the Northwest Territories. As president of the United States, Jefferson played a major role in the abolition of the slave trade in 1808. Towards the end of his life, he wrote nothing was more certainly written in the book of fate than that slaves would eventually be free. However, he did not emancipate his own slaves, unlike George Washington. Furthermore, he was unable to conceive of a biracial society, believing that blacks and whites could not live under the same government. In his *Notes on the State of Virginia* (1785), in which he condemned the slave trade, he wrote of his "suspicion" and "opinion" that blacks were mentally and physically inferior to whites. He proposed a gradual plan of emancipation but advocated that free blacks be resettled elsewhere.

Whatever Jefferson's intentions, his use of abstract universal principles in the Declaration of Independence has facilitated the demands of those seeking equality. Martin Luther King, Jr. described it as a promissory note to black people in his "I Have a Dream" speech. Nevertheless, the laudable ideals that it expresses did not prevent manifest inequalities, especially between the races. Slavery was abolished throughout much of the Caribbean and South America before it was officially outlawed by the Thirteenth Amendment of the Constitution in the United States.

See also Banneker, Benjamin; Fifteenth Amendment; Fourteenth Amendment; Slavery and the Constitution; Thirteenth Amendment

■ ■ *Bibliography*

Becker, Carl L. *The Declaration of Independence: A Study in the History of Political Ideas.* New York: Harcourt, Brace. 1922. Reprint, New York: Knopf, 1942.

Ford, Paul Leicester, ed. *The Writings of Thomas Jefferson,* 10 vols. New York: G. P. Putnam's Sons, 1892–99.

Jayne, Allen. *Jefferson's Declaration of Independence: Origins, Philosophy, and Theology.* Lexington: University Press of Kentucky, 1998.

Maier, Pauline. *American Scripture: Making the Declaration of Independence.* New York: Knopf, 1997.

Onuf, Peter S. *Jefferson's Empire: The Language of American Nationhood.* Charlottesville: University Press of Virginia, 2000.

Wills, Gary. *Inventing America: Jefferson's Declaration of Independence.* Garden City, N.Y.: Doubleday, 1978.

ANDREW JACKSON O'SHAUGHNESSY (2005)

DEE, BILLY

See Williams, Billy Dee (December, William)

DEE, RUBY

OCTOBER 27, 1924

▪▪▪

Born Ruby Ann Wallace in Cleveland, Ohio, actress Ruby Dee and her family soon moved to New York City and settled in Harlem. After graduating from high school, Dee attended Hunter College, and from 1941 to 1944 she prepared for a stage career at the American Negro Theater. In 1943 she made her Broadway debut with Canada Lee in Harry Rigsby and Dorothy Heyward's *South Pacific* (not to be confused with the later Rodgers and Hammerstein musical of the same name). She had her first starring role on Broadway in *Jeb*, alongside Ossie Davis. Two years later she married Davis, who subsequently appeared with her in several productions. Her notable New York theater performances include *A Raisin in the Sun* (1959); *Purlie Victorious* (1961); *Boseman and Lena* (1971), for which she won a 1971 Obie Award; and *Wedding B*and (1972–1973), for which she won a Drama Desk Award (1974).

Dee's film debut was in the role of Rachel Robinson in *The Jackie Robinson Story* (1950). She went on to perform in *St. Louis Blues* (1957), *A Raisin in the Sun* (1961), *Gone Are the Days* (1963), and *Buck and the Preacher* (1971). In 1965 she joined the American Shakespeare Festival in Stratford, Connecticut, and was the first black actress to play major roles in the company. In 1975 Dee and Ossie Davis received a special award from Actor's Equity for "outstanding creative contributions both in the performing arts and in society at large." Dee collaborated on the screenplay for *Uptight* in 1968 and wrote the Off-Broadway musical *Twin-Bit Gardens* (1979).

Together with Ossie Davis, Dee has long been a participant in civil rights efforts. She has served on national committees of the National Association for the Advancement of Colored People (NAACP) and the Southern Christian Leadership Conference, and has performed in numerous fund-raising benefits. In the late 1960s she hosted benefits for the Black Panther Party and the Young Lords. In 1970 Dee and Davis were presented with the Frederick Douglass Award by the New York Urban League. Her other activities include reading for the blind, raising money to fight drug addiction, and helping black women study drama through the Ruby Dee Scholarship in Dramatic Art, established in the late 1960s. A frequent reader of poetry and drama in national tours, she has also written several books of poetry and short stories, including *Glowchild* (1972), *My One Good Nerve* (1987), *Two Ways to Count to Ten* (1988), and *Tower to Heaven* (1991). Dee has contributed columns to the *New York Amsterdam News,* and she was the assistant editor of the magazine *Freedomways* in the early 1960s.

Dee has been seen in the films *Cat People* (1982) and *Do the Right Thing* (1989). Television appearances include her Public Television Series *With Ossie and Ruby* (1981), the Negro Ensemble Company's production of *Long Day's Journey into Night* (1983), and the Hallmark Hall of Fame production *Decoration Day* (1991), for which she was awarded an Emmy. In 1990 Dee wrote the script and starred in the American Playhouse production *Zora Is My Name,* a one-woman show based on the life and work of Zora Neale Hurston. In 1998 Dee and Davis celebrated their fiftieth wedding anniversary by publishing a joint memoir, *With Ossie and Ruby Dee: In This Life Together.* Dee received a Lifetime Achievement Award at the Kennedy Center for Performing Arts in December, 2004. Her husband Ossie Davis died two months later at the age of 87.

See also Black Panther Party for Self-Defense; Davis, Ossie; Hurston, Zora Neale; National Association for the Advancement of Colored People (NAACP); Southern Christian Leadership Conference (SCLC)

■ ■ *Bibliography*

Davis, Ossie, and Ruby Dee. *With Ossie and Ruby Dee: In This Life Together.* New York Morrow, 1998.

Mapp, Edward. *Directory of Blacks in the Performing Arts,* 2nd ed. Metuchen, N.J.: Scarecrow Press, 1990.

SUSAN MCINTOSH (1996)
Updated by publisher 2005

DE JESUS, CAROLINA MARIA

MARCH 14, 1914
FEBRUARY 13, 1977

Born illegitimate and impoverished in the Brazilian state of Minas Gerais, Carolina Maria de Jesus had to overcome a series of seemingly insurmountable obstacles throughout her lifetime just to survive. During her childhood, de Jesus had few educational opportunities, taking only two years of formal schooling. As a young adult she migrated to São Paulo, South America's industrial megalopolis, where as an unemployed single parent she struggled to eke out a living for herself and her three children. Eventually, she moved into a shack in one of the city's worst *favelas* (slums).

There, around 1955, de Jesus began keeping a crudely written account of the brutal reality of her day-to-day existence in a community populated by society's outcasts. In these journal entries she documented the grinding poverty, illiteracy, and unemployment that characterized the lives of her neighbors, calling attention to a host of social problems—prostitution, adultery, incest, alcoholism, physical violence, foul language—that these ills engendered. She constantly worried that her children would succumb to the pernicious influence of this hazardous environment. While hunger remained an ever-present theme, de Jesus also offered opinions on such topics as politics, social conditions, religion, and morality, and she communicated her pride in being Brazilian and black. Over the next several years she continued to jot down observations and impressions, little realizing that her insider perspective on the sights, sounds, and smells of the *favela* would one day appear in print and break all records for book sales in Brazil.

For de Jesus, writing was a pastime and a way to vent her frustrations. She routinely remarked on what she ate and when she bathed—far from mundane matters to those in her predicament—and cherished the occasions when her stomach was full and when, if she had been fortunate enough to obtain soap, she could attend to personal hygiene. She also detailed the drudgery of drawing water at the *favela*'s common spigot and having to roam the city streets every day to collect paper and scrap metal she could sell in order to get money for food.

In 1958 a young reporter, Audálio Dantas, met de Jesus by chance while on assignment. Upon learning that she kept a journal, he quickly recognized the uniqueness and sociological importance of these writings and the human-interest potential in her story. After winning de Jesus's confidence, he began editing her handwritten manuscripts (she wrote on the clean pages of used notebooks she had retrieved from garbage bins). Following the appearance of journal excerpts in Dantas's newspaper, she became an overnight sensation. In 1960 the diary was published in book form as *Quarto de Despejo*, and the following year it appeared in English as *Child of the Dark*. The book soon had a worldwide readership. The original title, a phrase designating a room in the back of a house reserved for short-term storage of trash, garbage, and other disposable items, was de Jesus's crude but effective way of accentuating the abject poverty in which she lived. If, according to this "house" metaphor, slum dwellers occupied the trash room or garbage dump, then middle-class Brazilians resided in the parlor or living room. The stark contrast explicit in this comparison provides convincing evidence of de Jesus's class consciousness and literary sensibility.

Using book royalties, de Jesus was able to realize her lifelong ambition of purchasing a house in a middle-class neighborhood. During this transition period—one of great turmoil in her life—she continued to write, and in 1961 a second volume of diary entries, entitled *Casa de Alvenaria*, was released. This new installment, the title of which alludes to the sturdy, masonry-constructed house of her dreams, offers a fascinating glimpse into her ill-fated attempts to enter mainstream Brazilian life. In these entries her humanity is on display as she recounts her struggles, triumphs, and failures, making no attempt to hide her emotions. This sequel garnered little attention, and, like de Jesus herself, it was soon forgotten, until 1997 when the University of Nebraska Press translated and published it with the title *I'm Going to Have a Little House.*

In her second diary, de Jesus wrote about the elation and disappointments she experienced on book-signing tours throughout Brazil, her inability to adjust to living in a new neighborhood, and her annoyance at being accosted by strangers asking for money. Eventually, she decided to leave her chaotic middle-class urban existence and start a new life in the countryside on the outskirts of the city. There, de Jesus spent the remainder of her life, and although she relapsed into poverty, she did not re-experience the destitute conditions of her former life. When she died in 1977, her passing went virtually unnoticed.

De Jesus also composed poems, childhood memoirs, a novel, and other works, but she never succeeded in winning the favor of Brazilian literary elites. Nevertheless, her writings serve as enduring reminders of the richness of the testimonial narrative tradition in Latin America.

See also Literature; Women Writers of the Caribbean

■ ■ *Bibliography*

Arrington, Melvin S., Jr. "From the Garbage Dump to the Brick House: The Diaries of Carolina Maria de Jesus." In *South Eastern Latin Americanist* 36, no. 4 (1993): 1–12.

de Jesus, Carolina Maria. *Child of the Dark: The Diary of Carolina Maria de Jesus*. Translated by David St. Clair. New York: Dutton, 1962.

de Jesus, Carolina Maria. *I'm Going to Have a Little House: The Second Diary of Carolina Maria de Jesus*. Translated by Melvin S. Arrington Jr. and Robert M. Levine. Lincoln: University of Nebraska Press, 1997.

Levine, Robert M., and José Carlos Sebe Bom Meihy. *The Life and Death of Carolina Maria de Jesus*. Albuquerque: University of New Mexico Press, 1995.

University of Miami, Center for Latin American Studies. "Carolina Maria de Jesus Project." Available from <http://www.as.miami.edu/las/project.htm>.

MELVIN S. ARRINGTON JR. (2005)

DELANEY, JOSEPH

SEPTEMBER 13, 1904
NOVEMBER 20, 1991

▮▮▮

Painter Joseph Delaney was born in Knoxville, Tennessee. Both he and his older brother Beauford Delaney became painters of contemporary urban African-American life. Joseph Delaney came north after high school, living briefly in Cincinnati, Detroit, Pittsburgh, and Chicago, working at odd jobs along the way. He was captivated by the social life of Chicago in the early 1920s and remained in that city until 1928, shining shoes, washing windows, waiting tables, and meeting many of the jazz musicians who would become subjects for his paintings. In 1925 he began a three-year term with the National Guard; when he returned to Knoxville for a year in 1928, he organized the city's first Boy Scout troop and sold insurance.

Delaney settled in New York City in 1929 and enrolled at the Art Students League, where he was a student of Thomas Hart Benton and a classmate of Jackson Pollock. During the 1930s he was a muralist for New York's Federal Art Project (1936–1939), taught art in Brooklyn and Harlem, and cataloged textiles, Chippendale furniture, and Paul Revere silver for the Index of American Design.

Delaney's paintings include portraits and street scenes of New York; his most famous works are *V-J Day, Times Square* (1945) and *Penn Station at Wartime* (1945). Both scenes capture the movement of crowds in the metropolis while concentrating on each individual's unique facial expression and physical constitution. His works, which depict the constancy of everyday routines during moments of historical significance, tell a story through the stylistic tendencies of regional realism and German expressionism, influenced by Thomas Hart Benton and Jackson Pollock respectively. While the paintings communicate a concrete sense of place, presenting viewers with recognizable New York terrain and highly individualized characters, the linked elongated figures and the flattened perspective are informed by expressionist techniques.

Delaney exhibited individually through the 1940s at numerous galleries, and during the 1960s and 1970s his work was included in large exhibits that spanned the history of African-American visual arts in the United States. These included The Evolution of Afro-American Artists: 1800–1950 at City College of New York (1968), Invisible Americans, Black Artists of the 1930s at the Studio Museum in Harlem (1969), Fragments of American Life at Princeton University (1975), and Two Centuries of Black Art, which was produced by the Los Angeles County Museum of Art and traveled throughout the United States (1977). Until his death, Delaney continued to operate a studio in Manhattan and showed his paintings at the annual Greenwich Village Art Show near Washington Square in New York.

■ ■ *Bibliography*

Driskell, David C. *Two Centuries of Black American Art*. New York: Knopf, 1976.

Feinstein, Sam. "Joe Delaney." *Art Digest* (March 15, 1953): 31.

Fine, Elsa Honig. *The Afro-American Artist: A Search for Identity*. New York: Hacker Art Books, 1982.

Stock, Ellen. "Roamin' Fever." *New York* (May 26, 1975): 63.

JANE LUSAKA (1996)

DELANY, MARTIN R.

MAY 6, 1812
JUNE 24, 1885

▮▮▮

Abolitionist and writer Martin Robison Delany was born in Charles Town, Virginia (now Charleston, West Virginia); his mother was free, his father a slave. Delany grew up in Chambersburg, Pennsylvania, and was educated at the school of the Rev. Louis Woodson in Pittsburgh. His mentor was the well-to-do John B. Vashon. In 1843 Delany married Catherine Richards and began his career as a medical doctor and abolitionist. From 1843 to 1847 Delany published the first African-American newspaper west of the Alleghenies, *The Mystery*. In 1847 he joined Frederick Douglass as coeditor of the newly founded *Rochester North Star,* in which his letters provide valuable commentary on antebellum free blacks.

In the 1840s Delany and Douglass criticized the American Colonization Society's advocacy of emigration of free African Americans to Liberia, which Delany, like most blacks, saw as forcible exile. But as the decade ended, Delany and Douglass grew apart. Delany left the *North Star* in 1849, advocating more black self-reliance than Douglass, who welcomed the support of white reformers. The strengthening of the federal Fugitive Slave Laws and his frustration with his fellow blacks prompted Delany to withdraw from reform in 1850 and attend the Harvard Medical School until he was forced out in 1851.

The crisis of the 1850s distressed northern blacks, many of whom fled to Canada to avoid reenslavement and harassment. Four years before moving his family from Pittsburgh to Chatham, Canada West (now known as Ontario), Delany published the first book-length analysis of the economic and political situation of blacks in the United States: *The Condition, Elevation, Emigration, and Destiny of the Colored People of the United States, Politically Considered* (1852), which is cited for its nationalism and advocacy of emigration out of the United States. In 1859 the *Anglo-African Magazine* and in 1861–1862 the *Weekly Afro-American* published his only novel, *Blake, or the Huts of America,* in serial form.

During the 1850s Delany moved from cautious endorsement of emigration within the Americas to planning African-American colonies in West Africa. He organized emigration conferences in 1854, 1856, and 1858, and in 1854 he published *The Political Destiny of the Colored Race,* a pamphlet that recommended emigration. In late 1858 he sailed to West Africa, visiting Alexander Crummell in Liberia in 1859. In December of that year, in the company of Robert Campbell, a teacher at the Institute for Colored Youth in Philadelphia, he signed a treaty with the Alake of Abeokuta, in what is now western Nigeria, providing for the settlement of educated African Americans and the development of commercial production of cotton using free West African labor. Before the first group of settlers could leave for West Africa, however, the Civil War broke out and the plan never materialized.

In 1863 the War Department reversed its refusal to enroll black volunteers in the Union army, and Delany became a full-time recruiter of black troops for the state of

Massachusetts. One of the earliest volunteers in the Fifty-fourth Regiment of Massachusetts Volunteer Infantry was Toussaint Louverture Delany, his oldest son. (The Delanys had named each of their seven children after a famous black figure.) In early 1865 Martin Delany was commissioned a major in the Union army, the first African American to be made a field officer. He finished the war in the South Carolina low country and began to work for the Bureau of Refugees, Freedmen, and Abandoned Lands (Freedmen's Bureau).

Immediately after the war, Delany was a popular speaker among the freedpeople, for he symbolized both freedom and blackness. But as the years passed and the South Carolina Republican Party became the party of the poor and black, Delany also began to question its ability to govern South Carolina as a whole. He went into the real estate business in Charleston and drifted into conservatism. By the mid-1870s he was criticizing South Carolina blacks and white carpetbaggers (he, too, was a carpetbagger) for demagoguery and corruption. In 1874 he ran unsuccessfully for lieutenant governor on the slate of the Independent Republicans, a coalition of conservative Republicans and moderate Democrats. By 1876 he was supporting the candidacy of the Democratic candidate for governor, Wade Hampton III, who had been the richest slave owner in the South before the war. Hampton and the Democrats were elected and by 1879 had purged the state of all black officeholders, including Delany.

At sixty-seven Delany once again dedicated himself to emigration, this time to Liberia, with the ill-fated Liberian Exodus Joint-Stock Steamship Company. His last acts were the publication of *Principia of Ethnology: The Origin of Races with an Archaeological Compendium of Ethiopian and Egyptian Civilization* and selling his book on a lecture tour. He died in Wilberforce, Ohio.

See also Bureau of Refugees, Freedmen, and Abandoned Lands; Civil War, U.S.; Crummell, Alexander

▪ ▪ *Bibliography*

Griffith, Cyril E. *The African Dream: Martin R. Delany and the Emergence of Pan-African Thought.* University Park: Pennsylvania State University Press, 1975.

Levine, Robert S., *Martin Delany, Frederick Douglass, and the Politics of Representative Identity.* Chapel Hill: University of North Carolina Press, 1997.

Miller, Floyd J. *The Search for a Black Nationality: Black Emigration and Colonization.* Urbana: University of Illinois Press, 1975.

Painter, Nell Irvin. "Martin Delany and Elitist Black Nationalism." In *Black Leaders of the Nineteenth Century,* edited by

August Meier and Leon Litwack. Urbana: University of Illinois Press, 1988.

Ullman, Victor. *Martin R. Delany: The Beginnings of Black Nationalism*. Boston: Beacon Press, 1971.

NELL IRVIN PAINTER (1996)
Updated bibliography

DELANY, SAMUEL R.

APRIL 1, 1942

Born in Harlem in comfortable circumstances, science fiction writer and critic Samuel R. Delany graduated from the Bronx High School of Science and briefly attended City College of New York. Despite serious dyslexia, he embarked early on a literary career, publishing his first novel, *The Jewels of Aptor,* in 1962. Delany has been a rather prolific writer, and by the time of his eighth novel, *The Einstein Intersection* (1967), he had already achieved star status in science fiction. He was the first African American to devote his career to this genre. Delany won the Nebula—one of science fiction's two most prestigious awards—in 1967, twice in 1968, and again in 1969. He received the other major science fiction award, the Hugo, in 1968 and 1989 (the latter for his autobiography). Today, he is considered to be one of the wide-ranging masters of the field, having produced books of sword-and-sorcery fantasy as well as science fiction. In addition, he has established himself as a rigorous and erudite theorist and critic of what he calls "the science fiction enterprise."

From a perspective of African-American literary history, Delany is noteworthy in part because he was the first significant black figure in a field with which, previously, African Americans at best had had a tangential relationship. Still, he was not the first writer to introduce black themes or characters into science fiction; indeed, he has written of how startled he was to discover, deep into the novel, that the hero of Robert Heinlein's *Starship Troopers* (1959) was non-Caucasian. Early in his own career, in fact, Delany's blackness certainly was not evident to the majority of his readers. However, his real importance depends, first, upon the way his work has focused on the problematic aspects of desire, difference, and the nature of freedom. In his four-volume Nevèrÿon fantasy series (1983–1987), these themes are played out in a mythical past. In *The Tides of Lust* (1973) and *Dhalgren* (1975), the site is a kind of mythical present; and in *Triton* (1976) and *Stars in My Pocket Like Grains of Sand* (1984), the setting is the far future. Many of the same concerns found in his fiction are articulated in his autobiography, *The Motion of Light in Water* (1988). Delany's second major contribution is his successful meshing of postmodern critical thought with the discourses of science fiction and fantasy. He has brought to these often scorned forms a narrative depth and linguistic sophistication they had seldom previously displayed.

In 1961 Delany married the poet Marilyn Hacker. The two separated in 1975. They have a daughter, Iva Alyxander, born in 1974. Delany taught at the State University of New York at Buffalo, the University of Wisconsin in Milwaukee, Cornell University, and the University of Massachusetts at Amherst. Delany was also a fellow at the University of Michigan's Institute for the Humanities in 1993. He joined the faculty of Temple University in 2001 as a professor of English and creative writing.

See also Butler, Octavia; Literature of the United States

▪ ▪ *Bibliography*

Delany, Samuel R. *The Straits of Messina*. Seattle: Serconia Press, 1989.

Fox, Robert Elliot. *Conscientious Sorcerers: The Black Postmodernist Fiction of LeRoi Jones/Amiri Baraka, Ishmael Reed, and Samuel R. Delany*. Westport, Conn.: Greenwood Press, 1987.

The Review of Contemporary Fiction 16, no. 3 (Fall 1996): 90–171.

ROBERT ELLIOT FOX (1996)

DELLUMS, RON

NOVEMBER 24, 1935

Congressman Ronald Vernie Dellums was born and raised in Oakland, California. He received undergraduate degrees from Oakland City College and San Francisco State University before earning an M.S.W. degree in psychiatric social work from the University of California at Berkeley. He served on the Berkeley City Council from 1967 to 1971 and in 1970 mounted a successful campaign for Congress. Dellums's victory in the Democratic primary over longtime representative Jeffrey Cohelan, a white liberal who was slow to oppose the Vietnam War, was largely due to his militant opposition to the war in a district that was a center of the peace movement. Dellums's Eighth District, which encompasses Berkeley, Oakland, and the surrounding suburbs, was 70 percent white in 1993 and the eighth best-educated district in the nation. But the district also includes West Oakland and East Oakland, two of the largest and poorest black ghettoes in the western United States. The district has been described as "a mixture of poverty and intellectual ferment."

Dellums's unique constituency has enabled him to maintain his stance as one of the nation's most radical national politicians. The legislation he sponsored included bills to impose sanctions against apartheid South Africa, to remove restraints on abortion and marijuana, to create a national health care system, and to grant amnesty to all Vietnam War resisters. Unlike most of his legislation, the South African sanctions bill actually passed, after fifteen annual submittals, in 1986. Dellums has been a consistent and unabashed gadfly from the left. In 1977 he shocked Congress with his characterization of the American class system: "America is a nation of niggers. If you are black, you're a nigger. Blind people, the handicapped, radical environmentalists, poor whites, those too far to the left are all niggers."

Dellums was the leading congressional dove and consistently opposed expansion of the military and U.S. intervention abroad. He was the first to introduce legislation to preclude funding for the MX, Pershing II, Midgetman, and B-1 weapons programs. In 1991 he was one of very few members of Congress to remain opposed to the war in the Persian Gulf after it began. Because of his seniority on the House Armed Services Committee, he became chair of the committee in 1993. He also served as chair of the Congressional Black Caucus from 1989 to 1991. Dellums retired from Congress in February 1998.

See also Congressional Black Caucus

■ ■ *Bibliography*

Clay, William L. *Just Permanent Interests: Black Americans in Congress, 1870–1991.* New York: Amistad, 1992.

Dellums, Ronald V., and H. Lee Halterman. *Lying Down with the Lions: A Public Life from the Streets of Oakland to the Halls of Power.* Boston: Beacon Press, 2000.

Swain, Carol M. *Black Faces, Black Interests: The Representation of African Americans in Congress.* Cambridge, Mass.: Harvard University Press, 1993.

THADDEUS RUSSELL (1996)
Updated by publisher 2005

DEMERARA REVOLT
▐ ▐ ▐

In August 1823 slaves in the British colony of Demerara, part of present-day Guyana, stopped working, seized the arms of their owners, and demanded their freedom. Led by a slave named Quamina and his son Jack, an estimated twelve thousand slaves from thirty-seven plantations participated in an uprising that would later become the largest slave revolt in British Guianese history.

After gaining possession of the colony from the Dutch two decades before the revolt occurred, the British immediately pushed Demerara toward a monoculture economy based on sugar production. While the majority of the colony's white population lived in Georgetown, the rest managed an unhealthy, overworked slave population that outnumbered whites by twenty to one. In 1823 Parliament ordered Demerara to improve the condition of its slaves. The slave population misunderstood the decree, firmly believing that Parliament granted them their freedom and that Demerara planters continued to enslave them illegally.

On August 18, 1823, slaves on Success and Le Resouvenir plantations quickly spread throughout the colony. Led largely by Christianized slaves who worshiped at Le Resouvenir's Bethel Chapel, the rebels attempted to succeed through peaceful methods and opted to imprison Demerara's whites rather than murder them. Some participants demanded their immediate freedom from slavery, while others wanted two or three days a week away from the fields to attend religious services, work their provision grounds, and go to the market. Others rebelled against the separation of families by sale and the punishment many endured from plantation managers who felt their slaves were too Christian.

Within twenty-four hours, the revolt spread as far east as Mahaica and as far west as Georgetown. To quell the rebellion, the colony declared martial law and deployed regular troops, as well as civilian militiamen. Although the rebels succeeded in their efforts at first, the tide turned on the third day. That day, troops led by Lieutenant-Colonel Leahy met over three thousand slave rebels at Bachelor's Adventure plantation. Leahy commanded the slaves to surrender and return to their estates. They refused, and Leahy's troops opened fire. The massacre sparked a turning point in the revolt, leading to a drop in rebel morale, as well as desertion. The majority abandoned the revolt and returned to their estates, while Leahy's troops traveled the countryside, freeing the white population and killing slaves.

Fearing that fugitive rebels might incite another revolt, the white community organized expeditions into the plantation backlands in search of escaped insurgents. These expeditions, aided by Amerindian slave hunters, continued for several weeks and led to the deaths of many participants. During one of these expeditions, an Amerindian found and shot Quamina in his refuge behind Chateau Margot plantation. His son Jack turned king's evidence and was deported to Saint Lucia. In all, over two hundred slaves were killed, while dozens more were executed. Those spared death received a thousand lashes and hard labor.

Martial law continued long after the rebellion ended, largely as a justification for the expeditions. Furthermore, martial law allowed for the trial of Reverend John Smith, an English clergyman who ministered to the slaves of Success and Le Resouvenir estates. Demerara planters accused Smith of being the main instigator of the revolt. Consequently, Demerara courts sentenced him to death. Smith, later called the Demerara Martyr by the colony's slaves, died in prison of consumption before he was hanged.

The Demerara revolt of 1823 was by far the largest slave rebellion in British Guianese history and one of the largest revolts in Caribbean history. Only the Haitian Revolution and the Jamaican Rebellion of 1831, or "The Baptist War," had larger numbers of insurgents. Despite testimony from the whites captured by the rebels stating that their captors treated them humanely, news of a Creole-led rebellion in Demerara spread throughout the Caribbean and England. As a result, the revolt cemented the belief that Creole slaves were more rebellious than African-born slaves, a sentiment born out of the Creole-led revolt in Barbados just seven years earlier. Although the goal of the revolt was to bring emancipation, England did not end slavery in her colonies until 1834. In the short term, the revolt changed little for Demerara's slaves. The surviving participants were executed, and the colony returned to business as usual. The revolt itself, however, caught the attention of the English, who long thought that Demerara planters were the most benevolent toward their slaves. More importantly, the revolt caught the interest of England's abolitionists, who incorporated the Demerara revolt into their antislavery campaign.

See also Christiana Revolt of 1851; Haitian Revolution; Malê Rebellion; Nat Turner's Rebellion; Stono Rebellion

■ ■ *Bibliography*

Costa, Emilia Viotti da. *Crowns of Glory, Tears of Blood: The Demerara Slave Rebellion of 1823*. Oxford: Oxford University Press, 1994.

Craton, Michael. "Proto-Peasant Revolts? The Late Slave Rebellions in the British West Indies, 1816–1832." *Past and Present* 85 (1979): 99–125.

Schuler, Monica. "Ethnic Slave Rebellions in the Caribbean and the Guianas." *Journal of Social History* 3 (1970): 374–385.

COLLEEN A. VASCONCELLOS (2005)

DEMOCRATIC PARTY

See Political Ideologies; Politics in the United States

DEMOGRAPHY

The approximately 150 million people of African descent who inhabit the Americas are concentrated on the coastal rim of Brazil, the eastern and southern parts of the United States, and the Caribbean region, helping to create a geographical pattern characterized by some people as the "Black Atlantic." Yet important concentrations of these peoples are found throughout the Western Hemisphere, the result of a continuing dispersion or movement of black peoples that continues in the twenty-first century.

With relatively few exceptions, blacks in the Americas are descendants of the slaves transported from Africa in the transatlantic slave trade that lasted from the early sixteenth century to the late nineteenth century. The origins of this trade were nearly simultaneous with the exploration and conquest of the Americas by Europeans. Blacks actively resisted enslavement from the start; as early as 1505, African slaves escaped into the mountains of what is now the Dominican Republic, thereby establishing a free black presence in the Americas that predates the landing of the Pilgrims at Plymouth Rock by more than a century.

In 1969 the historian Philip Curtin, having researched censuses, ship records, and similar documents, estimated that a total of 9.6 million African slaves were brought across the Atlantic in the four centuries of the slave trade. Subsequent academic work has revised these figures, usually upwards. Taken altogether, these studies reveal the broad contours of the Atlantic slave trade. The overwhelming majority of slaves were from West and West Central African, from Senegal south to Angola. The main destination for African slaves (nearly 40%) was Brazil. African supply patterns and the labor requirements and economic cycles for tropical and subtropical plantation staple crops in the Americas led to an uneven flow of slaves, rather than a continuous movement. The overall numbers of slaves brought to particular regions did not necessarily predict population totals of later years; very high slave imports into the Caribbean, for example, were almost always reduced by the tragically high slave death rates in the region.

Liberation and emancipation movements of the nineteenth century, from Haiti's successful rebellion of 1803 to the last slave emancipations in Brazil and Cuba in the

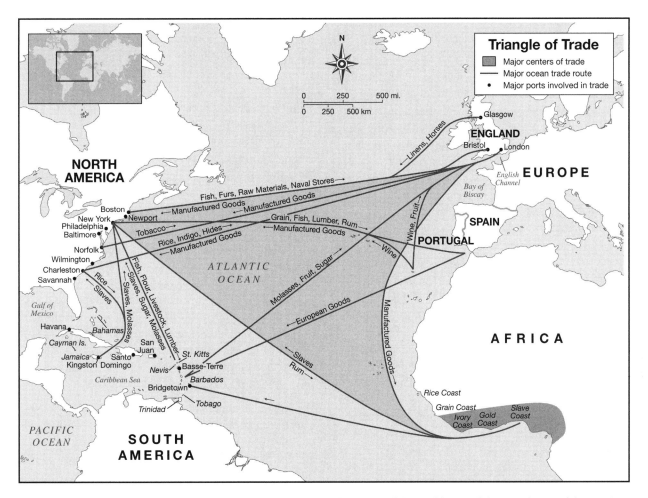

The "triangle of trade" outlines the movement of slaves from Africa to the islands of the Caribbean and the coastal areas of the Americas, partly in exchange for manufactured goods from Europe. In this triangle, slaves were not only a primary commodity, they also produced, by means of their forced labor, many of the crops and products that were traded. MAP BY XNR PRODUCTIONS. THE GALE GROUP.

1880s, led to increased mobility. Since that time, black individuals, families, and groups, have moved from country to city, from one region to another, and internationally. These movements defy simple classification, reflecting at once coercion, opportunity, dissatisfaction, and personal choice, and they have complicated explanations for subsequent black population patterns in the Western Hemisphere and elsewhere.

A further complication is the impossibility of designating a common meaning of who is and is not "black." The intermixing of those of pure African descent with others in the Americas has led to an almost infinite gradation of skin colors and other physical attributes among individuals, so that an individual considered "black" in the United States may not be so designated in Jamaica or Brazil. These varying attributes or features also lead to difficulties and ambiguities in self-identity that often change over time, greatly complicating the tasks of census takers.

NORTH AMERICA

The 2000 population census of the United States enumerated 281 million people, of whom 36.4 million (nearly 13%) considered themselves black. Among black Americans, 55 percent resided in the South, 18 percent in both the Midwest and the East, and 9 percent in the West. In the District of Columbia, 61 percent of the residents were black, and the states with the highest black percentages were Mississippi (37%), Louisiana (33%), South Carolina (30%), Georgia (29%), and Maryland (29%).

Whereas the prototypical black American of the early twenty-first century lives in a southern town or small city, the greatest concentrations are in the large urban areas. The 2000 census counted 2.3 million black people (accounting for 28.5% of the city's total population) in New York, while Chicago had over one million black residents. Among the largest cities in the country, Detroit (82%), Philadelphia (44%), and Chicago (37%) had the largest percentages of black people. In Baltimore, Memphis, Washington D.C., and New Orleans over 60 percent of the population was black.

The census data gathered in 2000 contributed to a national statistical profile showing that blacks (36% of males were under eighteen) were younger than non-Hispanic whites (24%). At the other end of the age spectrum, only 7 percent of black males lived past age 65 and were therefore able to collect full social security benefits, whereas their non-Hispanic white counterparts were twice as likely to live beyond 65. A lower percentage of black families were headed by married couples than whites; 43 percent of black families were headed by a single woman and 9 percent of black families headed by a single man. An estimated 32.9 million people in the United States lived below the poverty line, among them 23 percent of blacks (8.1 million) and 8 percent of whites (15.3 million).

The statistical contours of the black American populace delineated by the 2000 census data were, of course, the cumulative result of decades of demographic history. The United States population census of 1790, which showed a total human population of almost four million, enumerated over 757,000 African Americans, roughly 19 percent of the total. And although studies of British colonial demographic history are complicated by conflicting and unreliable data, scholars agree that, beginning around the 1730s, the black population of British North America (later the United States) showed a high rate of natural increase, especially when compared with the British West Indies.

Roughly 95 percent of the blacks enumerated in the 1790 census were slaves, about the same percentage as in 1810, by which time the black population of the United States had nearly doubled to 1,378,000. This dramatic rise came from a combination of slave imports (until the trade was abolished in 1807) and natural increases. In the next half century, as plantation cotton came to dominate the U.S. Gulf Coast states all the way to Texas, the black slave population grew accordingly. In 1870, the year of the first U.S. census taken since slave emancipation in 1862, the black American population had grown to 4,880,000.

This figure grew in the next half century, and in 1920 there were 10,463,000 blacks in the United States. Yet because of the remarkably high immigration rates of Europeans into the United States in the latter part of the nineteenth century, the percentage of African Americans in 1920 was just under 10 percent, down from the nearly 20 percent in colonial days. The early and middle decades of the twentieth century saw an expansion of black America into the country's heartland. From border states such as Kentucky and Missouri, African Americans began migrating north in substantial numbers during World War I, followed by larger numbers from the Deep South in subsequent decades to Chicago, Detroit, and other industrial cities. The overall percentages of blacks in the country's total population increased somewhat by the end of the century; the 1980 U.S. census enumerated a total of 226.5 million Americans, of whom 26.5 million (11.7%) were black; there were 30 million African Americans (12.1%) among the overall total of 249 million in 1990; and in 2000, the census counted almost 35 million African Americans (12.3%) among the 281 million U.S. residents.

Black immigrants coming to the United States have augmented natural population increases in the latter decades of the twentieth century and into the twenty-first. Notably, Caribbean peoples have come in the thousands—some to Miami and other large cities, but the great majority to New York. Perhaps two million black people of Caribbean descent inhabited the New York area at the start of the twenty-first century, but any such figure is an estimate because many have come without formal documentation and because there is much back-and-forth movement between the Caribbean and New York.

Perhaps one million Canadians are black. The 2001 census, enumerating nearly 30 million Canadians, included "Black" as a category, but it also included categories such as "Jamaican," "Haitian," and "West Indian," which include black people. Blacks have lived in Canada since colonial days. Their numbers were increased by the Underground Railroad traffic in the 1800s during U.S. slavery. In the latter decades of the twentieth century, thousands of black West Indian immigrants settled mainly in the eastern part of Canada, with English-speakers concentrated in Ontario and French-speakers in Quebec. A few tens of thousands of noticeably black peoples live in the coastal areas of Mexico's Vera Cruz state and also in the Pacific "Costa Chica" zone of Guerrero and Oaxaca states. An important presence of descendants of black slaves in Mexico has been reduced, however, apparently through absorption into the larger population.

THE CARIBBEAN AND CENTRAL AMERICA

Probably two-thirds of the 35 to 40 million people inhabiting the Caribbean region in the early twenty-first century are of African descent. The region's relatively small population does not square with the estimate that 50 percent of all African slaves brought to the Western Hemisphere during the four centuries of the slave trade came to the Caribbean. The slaves' high death rates in the region, and their subsequent inability to sustain their own populations, came from overwork, an alien disease environment,

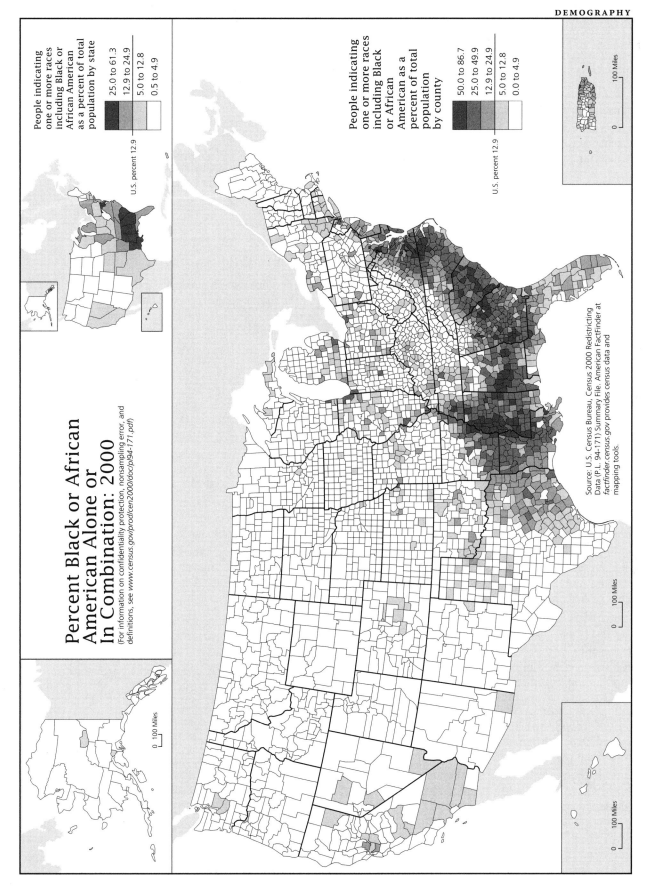

People indicating one or more races including Black or African American as a percent of total population by state

25.0 to 61.3
12.9 to 24.9
5.0 to 12.8
0.5 to 4.9

U.S. percent 12.9

Percent Black or African American Alone or In Combination: 2000

(For information on confidentiality protection, nonsampling error, and definitions, see *www.census.gov/prod/cen2000/doc/pl94-171.pdf*)

100 Miles

People indicating one or more races including Black or African American as a percent of total population by county

50.0 to 86.7
25.0 to 49.9
12.9 to 24.9
5.0 to 12.8
0.0 to 4.9

U.S. percent 12.9

100 Miles

Source: U.S. Census Bureau, Census 2000 Redistricting Data (P.L. 94-171) Summary File. American FactFinder at *factfinder.census.gov* provides census data and mapping tools.

0   100 Miles

0   100 Miles

Map depicting Blacks as a percentage of total population by U.S. county, 2000. *At the time of the 2000 census, about 55% of black Americans resided in the South.* U.S. CENSUS BUREAU and precarious food sources that often depended upon imports.

Although most people in the Caribbean are black and consider themselves so, the region is characterized by ethnic and racial complexity. An estimated 62 percent of Cuba's 11 million people are black or Mulatto. Well over 90 percent of the 2.5 million Jamaicans and 7 million Haitians are black. The 11 percent black population among the nearly 9 million people in the Dominican Republic, Haiti's neighbor on the eastern side of the island of Hispaniola, does not include the nation's very high percentage of mixed-blood peoples. Only 8 percent of the 3.8 million Puerto Ricans counted in the 2000 U.S. population census considered themselves "Black," yet an additional 11 percent were of "some other race." Among the islands of the eastern Caribbean, most people are black—on some of the smallest islands almost every person could be classified as Afro-Caribbean. Yet among the 1.5 million Trinidadians, only half are of African ancestry; this is because of the presence of hundreds of thousands who descend from indentured laborers from India.

Caribbean demography is further complicated by high rates of migration. Since British slave emancipation in the 1830s, black men and women have traveled away—permanently and temporarily—in quest of better opportunities elsewhere, to improve conditions at home, as an antidote to the boredom of insularity, and for many other reasons. The probable majority of these movements have been within the Caribbean itself, resulting in enclaves of outsiders residing on nearly every island. But Caribbean migrants have moved internationally as well. When attractive prospects elsewhere have combined with economic distress at home, these migrations have taken on sizable proportions. Tens of thousands of black West Indians traveled to work on the Panama Canal in the early twentieth century and to Cuban and Dominican sugar cane fields thereafter. Similar numbers have migrated to Europe since the mid-twentieth century.

The historically recent movements of black peoples from the Caribbean to New York and elsewhere in the United States has reinforced an earlier African presence that is centuries old and has greatly affected American culture. Early-twentieth-century labor and cultural movements (such as the Harlem Renaissance) were heavily influenced by black Caribbean migrants. Music and sport in the United States in the late twentieth century would be very different without black West Indians. Important personalities all along the black American political spectrum—including Harry Belafonte, Shirley Chisholm, Louis Farrakhan, Malcolm X, and Colin Powell—trace their heritage to the Caribbean.

Caribbean migrants have also traveled to work destinations in Central America, both as individuals and as groups of laborers. In some cases they have encountered black descendants of earlier enslavement there. The resulting black presence in Central America is most noticeable along the Caribbean rim of the isthmus. In any case, population estimates of Afro–Central American peoples are contested and unreliable. Conservative estimates for other black populations in the region are Honduras: 110,000; Nicaragua: 379,000; Costa Rica: 103,000; and Panama: 379,000.

SOUTH AMERICA

As one would assume from historical slavery estimates, by far the largest numbers of Afro–South Americans are Brazilian. Brazil's estimated total population of 182 million in 2003 included 6 percent black and 38 percent of mixed black ancestry—percentages that many consider too low, owing to a widespread desire to be considered white for purposes of socioeconomic advancement. Like most people in the country, Afro-Brazilians are mainly urban dwellers, and high percentages of black people reside in the enormous cities of southern Brazil; an estimated 25 percent of the 18 million people residing in São Paolo are of African descent, and 66 percent of Rio de Janeiro's 10 million people are black. In the same way that many U.S. blacks continue to inhabit the nineteenth-century tobacco and cotton zones of the U.S. South, many Afro-Brazilians reside in the former sugar cane zones in the northeastern part of the country. Bahia (or Salvador), the principal city in that region, and Brazil's third largest urban area at 2.5 million people, is estimated to have a black populace nearing 80 percent.

Brazilian demographic data show a distressing disparity in well-being between whites and blacks, and thereby run counter to exuberant claims that the country is a "racial democracy." Infant mortality rates among white Brazilians are 37 per 1000 live births, but 62 per 1,000 for Afro-Brazilians; white life expectancy is 66 years, while for blacks it is 59; and literacy rates are 85 percent for whites but only 65 percent for blacks. Brazilian education, income, and employment figures show similar disparities between blacks and whites.

After Brazil, Colombia (with an estimated total population of 41 million in 2001) has the largest black populace in South America. An estimated 7 million (18% of all Colombians) are of African ancestry, and probably two-thirds of them are mixed-blood peoples. Black Colombians descend from slaves brought by the Spaniards to work in colonial mines and plantations. Early in the twenty-first century, Afro-Colombians inhabit the nation's Caribbean coastal areas and the Cauca and Magdalena river valleys farther south. In both Venezuela (where 2.3 million people of black ancestry reside) and Ecuador (1.2 million blacks), people of African ancestry make up about 3 to 5 percent of national populations. An estimated 750,000 blacks live in Peru, and smaller numbers of Afro–South Americans are found elsewhere on the continent.

A numerically tiny yet culturally significant black group lives in the rainforests of northern South America. The so-called "Bush Negro" peoples of interior Suriname inhabit river settlements inland from the coastal zone of the small country. Numbering only a few thousand, they are direct descendants of slaves who escaped from Dutch colonial plantations. Their material culture is thus heavily influenced by their African heritage, and their oral history tells of their escapes from plantation control and a centuries-long resistance to European domination. These small African village settlements along the rapids of Suriname's rivers are thereby a living microcosm of the historical sweep of a black African presence in the Western Hemisphere for five hundred years.

See also African Diaspora; Identity and Race in the United States; Migration; Mortality and Morbidity, Latin America and the Caribbean; Mortality and Morbidity, United States; Slave Trade

■ ■ *Bibliography*

Conniff, Michael L. and Thomas J. Davis, eds. *Africans in the Americas: A History of the Black Diaspora*. New York: St. Martin's Press, 1994.

Curtin, Philip D. *The Atlantic Slave Trade: A Census*. Madison: University of Wisconsin Press, 1969.

Farley, Reynolds. *Growth of the Black Population: A Study of Demographic Trends*. Chicago: Markham, 1970.

Graham, Richard, ed. *The Idea of Race in Latin America, 1879–1940*. Austin: University of Texas Press, 1990.

Haines, Michael R. and Richard H. Steckel, eds. *A Population History of North America*. Cambridge, U.K.: Cambridge University Press, 2000.

Hine, Darlene Clark and Jacqueline McLeod, eds. *Crossing Boundaries: Comparative History of Black People in Diaspora*. Bloomington: Indiana University Press, 1999.

Klein, Herbert S. *The Atlantic Slave Trade*. New York: Cambridge University Press, 1999.

McKinnon, Jesse. "The Black Population: 2000." U.S. Census report, pp. 1–12. Available from <http://www.census.gov/prod/2001pubs/c2kbr01-5.pdf>.

Palmer, Colin A. *Slaves of the White God: Blacks in Mexico, 1570–1650*. Cambridge, Mass.: Harvard University Press, 1976.

Price, Richard. *First-Time: The Historical Vision of an Afro-American People*, 2d ed. Chicago: University of Chicago Press, 2002.

Reichmann, Rebecca, ed. *Race in Contemporary Brazil: From Indifference to Inequality*. University Park: Pennsylvania State University Press, 1999.

Reid, Ira De A. *The Negro Immigrant: His Background, Characteristics, and Social Adjustment, 1899–1937*. New York: Columbia University Press, 1939. Reprint, New York: Arno Press, 1969.

Richardson, Bonham C. *The Caribbean in the Wider World, 1492–1992: A Regional Geography*. Cambridge, U.K.: Cambridge University Press, 1992.

Waters, Mary C. *Black Identities: West Indian Immigrant Dreams and American Realities*. Cambridge, Mass.: Harvard University Press, 1999.

BONHAM C. RICHARDSON (2005)

DENBOW, CLAUDE H. A.

MARCH 28, 1911
JANUARY 6, 1979

Claude Hicks Augustus Denbow epitomized the mission of his alma mater, Howard University, in providing "leadership for America and the global community." The son of Sarah Louisa and Charles Denbow, chief county sergeant major of police, he attended Leonora Primary School, West Coast Demerara, and the prestigious Queen's College in Georgetown, Guyana, where he excelled academically. In the early 1930s he was unable to obtain employment at the Royal Bank of Canada, Georgetown, likely because he was a dark-skinned African Guianese, so he became a conductor with the Transport and Harbours Department before attending Howard University, beginning in 1935. Denbow was a brilliant undergraduate student and was awarded a chemistry scholarship to attend the College of Dentistry in 1937. He returned home in 1942 and began a career as a dentist. He was also a politician and community leader.

Denbow practiced dentistry for thirty-one years. As president of the British Guiana Labour Union from 1945 to 1952, he was instrumental in improving labor conditions in the colony. He chaired the Waterfront Enquiry Commission (the Denbow Commission) from 1969–1970, which investigated the working conditions of waterfront workers and resulted in significant reforms. Denbow was a founding member of the National Democratic Party in 1943, the forerunner of the United Democratic Party of 1947 that merged with Forbes Burnham's People's National Congress in 1958 and led British Guiana from colonial status to independence from Great Britain as Guyana.

As leader of British Guiana's branch of the League of Coloured Peoples (LCP), founded by Dulcina Armstrong in 1937, Denbow endeavored to fulfill the organization's aims, including instilling in the peoples of African descent racial consciousness and pride, promoting and protecting the general interests of its members, and cooperating and affiliating with sympathetic organizations. The LCP was formed in England in 1931 by Jamaican-born Dr. Harold A. Moody with the assistance of the African Americans Drs. Charles Wesley Harris and St. Clair Drake, along with Jamaican Joel Augustus Rogers, a self-educated historian, to fight the racism that people of color encountered there.

From 1944 to the 1960s, Denbow initiated and organized the LCP's Annual Exhibition and Fair, which showcased local talent, skills, and crafts. The event attracted and promoted African, Caribbean, and African-American artists and entertainers and raised funds for the purchase of the Harold Arundel Moody LCP Hall. Apart from functioning as the organization's headquarters and as a venue for dances, ice-cream banquets, and concerts, it accommodated a school from kindergarten to high school grades, serving its members and children countrywide. It also provided space for co-op savings societies, credit unions, penny banks, and affairs held by the juvenile and women's sections.

Denbow encouraged the study of African culture and languages, and LCP funds provided scholarships for members or their children to study abroad. A scholarship granted to E. V. Liverpool enabled him to train at Boni College, West Africa, as a teacher of the Ibo language. In 1950 Denbow's invitation to King Eze II of Oweri, Nigeria, to visit the country created controversy because some East Indians and the British governor publicly questioned if Eze was indeed royalty and deserved welcome as such. Denbow immediately solicited help from Dr. Ralph Bunche at the United Nations, who had taught him when he was a Howard undergraduate, in making the visit possible. The visit is captured in the 1954 publication *Seven Amazing Days*. Mary McLeod Bethune emphasized that "this book is most vital since it portrays the great potentials of mankind through the experiences of real people . . . through the inspiration of their own pride in themselves and in the accomplishments of their kind" (Bethune, 1954).

Denbow maintained linkages with African Americans, including George S. Schuyler of the *Pittsburgh Courier*. He visited the United States in 1950 and was a guest on Schuyler's *Negro World Program* on radio station WLIB. Still, Denbow's greatest contribution to Guyana and the African diaspora was his launching of one of the first newspapers by a Howard University alumnus from the Caribbean. The *Sentinel*, the LCP's organ, was published beginning on April 30, 1950. On August 21, 1950, Howard's president, Dr. Mordecai W. Johnson, belatedly acknowledged Denbow's invitation to write a column on Africa in the inaugural edition of the newspaper. He praised Denbow for his "efforts towards improving conditions touching people of African descent" and congratulated him for his "insight, vision, and industry." Dr. Johnson regarded Denbow as a "credit to Alma Mater."

Denbow's marriage to Catherine Mood Griffith in 1943 produced two sons: Charles, a heart specialist at the University of the West Indies Hospital, Jamaica, and Claude Jr., a law professor at the university's Trinidad campus.

See also Burnham, Forbes; Howard University; People's National Congress

▪ ▪ *Bibliography*

"African Royalty to Set Foot on BG Soil Saturday: Historic Event for Colony." *Sentinel* (August 6, 1950).

Bethune, Mary McLeod. In *Seven Amazing Days in the Life of Eze A. Ogueri II*, compiled by the League of Coloured Peoples, British Guiana. Boston: House of Edinboro, 1954.

Denbow, Claude H. "Class of 1941." *Howard University Bulletin. The Dentoscope* 18 (July 31, 1938): 37–39.

"Dr. Denbow Interviewed by George S. Schuyler." *Sentinel* (November 5, 1950).

"Dr. Denbow Returns from Business Trip: Had Enjoyable Stay in U.S.A." *Sentinel* (November 12, 1950).

Foreign Service Despatch, American Consulate, Georgetown, The Department of State, Washington, Decimal File (1910–1963), Memorandum of British Guiana Branch of League of Colored People, July 13, 1944, and 741D.00/8-261, August 2, 1961, Record Group 59, National Archives at College Park (Archives 11), Md.

"He Is King" and "HRH. Eze Anyuara Receives Biggest Welcome Ever: Historic Event in BG." *Sentinel* (December 31, 1950).

"Howard University President Writes Dr. Denbow." *Sentinel* (September 24, 1950).

Interviews with Sir John Patrick Carter, QC, KB, CCH, OR, by Barbara P. Josiah. Bethesda, Md., 2003–2004.

Public Record Office (The National Archives), London, Colonial Office (CO) 111-1950-51/820/8, *Reports and Correspondence* 6655/10, British Guiana. 1950 Visit by King Eze Ogueri of Obibi, Nigeria.

"They Met at Lake Success." *Sentinel* (September 30, 1950).

BARBARA P. JOSIAH (2005)

DE PASSE, SUZANNE

1946?

The entertainment executive Suzanne de Passe grew up in Harlem. She guards her private life carefully, and as a result little is known about her early life and career. De Passe apparently was working as a booking agent at the Cheetah Disco in New York when she met Berry Gordy, then the head of Motown Records. Her strong criticisms of Motown's business operations, delivered directly to Gordy, earned her a position as his creative assistant. Until 1972 she served as road manager, costume designer, and choreographer for the Jackson Five, then Motown's newest sensation. She was also responsible for signing the Commodores, who went on to become one of Motown's most popular singing groups during the 1970s.

In the 1970s de Passe became increasingly involved with Motown's theater, television, and film productions. In 1971 she helped write *Diana*, the first production by Motown's television and theatrical division. That project was so successful that the next year Gordy named de Passe corporate director of Motown's Creative Production division and vice president of Motown's parent corporation, positions that allowed her to work almost exclusively in television and film. De Passe was nominated for an Academy Award for co-writing the Motown-produced film *Lady Sings the Blues* (1972).

In the late 1970s Gordy began to entrust de Passe with the fastest-growing and most profitable divisions of Motown. In 1977 she was promoted to vice president of Motown Industries, another television and film subsidiary, and in 1981 she was named president of Motown Productions. Under de Passe, the budget for the company grew from $12 million in 1980 to $65 million in 1989. She won Emmy Awards for *Motown 25: Yesterday, Today, Forever* (1982–1983) and *Motown Returns to the Apollo* (1984–1985).

By the early 1980s de Passe was considered one of the rising black female Hollywood executives. In 1985 her reputation soared further after she paid $50,000 for the rights to *Lonesome Dove*, the Larry McMurtry novel about a nineteenth-century cattle drive. The project had been rejected by every major Hollywood studio. De Passe sold the telecast rights for *Lonesome Dove* to CBS for $16 million, and by 1989 she had produced an eight-hour program that won seven Emmy Awards and drew one of the largest audiences ever for a television miniseries. In 1990 de Passe produced *Motown 30: What's Goin' On*.

In the early 1990s de Passe started a new company, de Passe Entertainment, and produced the five-hour miniseries *The Jacksons: An American Dream* (1992). During the same period she also served as co-executive producer of the film *Class Act*. Scoring another hit, she joined with Hallmark Entertainment in 1998 to produce the well-received four-hour miniseries "The Temptations." In 2004 de Passe announced plans for another such effort, to be produced jointly with NBC. Based on Berry Gordy's autobiography *To Be Loved: The Music, the Magic, the Memories of Motown,* the docudrama will relate the phenomenon of Motown from the perspective of its founder.

Considered one of the most powerful black female executives in Hollywood, de Passe won a 1989 Essence Award, and was inducted into the Black Filmmaker's Hall of Fame in 1990. That same year, de Passe received a Micheaux Award for her contributions to the entertainment industry.

See also Gordy, Berry; Jackson Family; Recording Industry

■ ■ *Bibliography*

"Motown Executive Brings Western to TV." *Afro-American* (February 4, 1989): 3.

Mussari, Mark. *Suzanne de Passe: Motown's Boss Lady.* Ada, Okla.: Garrett Educational, 1992.

JONATHAN GILL (1996)
Updated by publisher 2005

DEPRESSION, THE GREAT

See Great Depression and the New Deal

DEPRIEST, OSCAR STANTON

MARCH 9, 1871
MAY 12, 1951

Congressman and businessman Oscar DePriest was born in Florence, Alabama, the child of former slaves. In 1878, as part of the Exodusters migration, the family emigrated to Kansas to escape poverty. DePriest went to Chicago in 1889 and worked as a painter and decorator, trades that led him to become a building contractor and later a successful real estate broker. He also turned out to be a tireless political organizer and established himself as a valuable member of the powerful Republican Party organization. The party slated him in 1904 for his victorious first race for a public position, a place on the Cook County Board of Commissioners. He won reelection in 1906, but his loss two years later sidelined him from political office until he won election as Chicago's first black alderman in 1915.

Rapid migration of African Americans to Chicago from the South drove up property values in the segregated South Side Black Belt, and DePriest capitalized on the resulting real estate opportunities to amass a considerable fortune. These new immigrants would also refuel DePriest's political career as he became the central black leader in Republican mayor William ("Big Bill") Thompson's machine—a formidable organization held together by patronage, generosity in political appointments, and extraordinary party loyalty among blacks. DePriests's big political break came in 1928 with the death of his mentor, Congressman Martin Madden. DePriest insisted that the party support his candidacy for Madden's old seat, and with its backing the district's swelling black majority elected him. When, in 1929, DePriest took his seat in the 71st Congress as the first African-American U.S. representative from a northern state, it was the first time in twenty-eight years that the House had had a black member.

In Congress, DePriest was an energetic, controversial figure who had little success in enacting his frequently introduced civil rights measures. His colleagues defeated his antilynching bill, a measure prohibiting government job discrimination in the South, a proposal to have blacks served in the House restaurant, and a plan for transfer of jurisdiction in criminal cases when a defendant feared local racial or religious prejudice. His most outstanding achievement was an amendment that Congress enacted in March 1933 to prohibit discrimination in the Civilian Conservation Corps. He also secured greater government support of Howard University and was a strong supporter of immigration restriction to preserve jobs for African Americans.

DePriest survived the first Democratic electoral sweeps of 1930 and 1932, but he lost two years later to a black Democrat, Arthur Mitchell, as African-American voters in Chicago gave up their traditional loyalty to the party of Abraham Lincoln and turned to the Democrats. DePriest resumed his real estate career, lost to Mitchell again in 1936, and served once more as a Chicago alderman between 1943 and 1947. He died of a kidney ailment in 1951.

See also Mitchell, Arthur

▪ ▪ *Bibliography*

Christopher, Maurine. *Black Americans in Congress.* New York: Crowell, 1976.

Drake, St. Clair, and Horace R. Cayton. *Black Metropolis: A Study of Negro Life in a Northern City* (1945). New York: Harper & Row, 1962.

Logan, Rayford W., and Michael R. Winston, eds. *Dictionary of American Negro Biography.* New York: Norton, 1982.

STEVEN J. LESLIE (1996)

DESSALINES, JEAN-JACQUES
c. 1758
OCTOBER 17, 1806

▪▪▪

Jean-Jacques Dessalines's origins are somewhat unclear. He was most likely born a slave in Grande-Riviere-du-Nord, Haiti, but there is also speculation that he was born in West Africa around 1758. In either case, he lived out the early part of his life as a slave to a free black, serving as a coachman. He escaped slavery in 1791 and joined the Haitian Revolution (1791–1804). Through his aptitude for military science and leadership he quickly earned the confidence of Toussaint L'Ouverture, commander of the revolutionary forces, and became his second in command.

During the revolution, Dessalines proved himself to be a brilliant general. In 1802 he and his soldiers captured the fort at Crete-a-Pierrot, where they fended off twelve thousand French troops before escaping through enemy lines. Yet only months later Dessalines followed Henri Christophe, another of L'Ouverture's principle officers, and deserted to the French side. Shortly after the defections, L'Ouverture was captured and shipped to the French Alps, where he died in prison.The Haitian people continued to fight against the French, and Dessalines soon came back to their side. After returning to fight against the French, he ruthlessly squashed any opposition to his leadership. This earned him a reputation for brutality and eventually led to his ascendance to control of the Haitian army. He assumed command of the revolutionary army on July 5, 1803, and led the final charge to independence. On November 18, 1803, the revolutionaries scored a decisive victory over General Rochambeau's army at the Battle of Vertieres, forcing Napoleon to abandon his claims—not only to Haiti, but also to Louisiana and other French territories in the Americas. Haitian independence was achieved on January 1, 1804.

After independence, Dessalines attempted to consolidate his power over the war-ravaged state. Ironically this resulted in his sometimes emulating Napoleon. On September 22, 1804, Dessalines had himself crowned Emperor Jacques I. Among his first acts was changing the name of Haiti from its colonial moniker of Saint Domingue to its modern Arawak-derived name. A product of the Atlantic slave system, Dessalines maintained a bitter hatred of whites. During the revolution, Dessalines equated independence with the elimination of whiteness from Haiti, and he even established the style of the modern Haitian flag by ripping the white section out of the French tri-color flag. After the revolution, Dessalines ordered the extermination of all remaining whites, though some clergymen, as well as the Poles and Germans who had defected from the French army, were spared. Though they were phenotypically white, these soldiers were considered black in the Haitian racial schema, which was and is intimately connected to class.

On the economic front, Dessalines oversaw the emergence of the peasantry that would drive subsequent Haitian history. Postrevolutionary Haitians desired a tangible realization of their freedom, and land provided the basis for a sustainable future. Dessalines made cultivation the basis for land ownership thereby acquiescing to the desires of the people. This was a serious blow to the many mulattoes who had benefited from the French defeat by purchasing or confiscating large French plantations as the war wore on. In the aftermath of the war, Dessalines instituted a policy nationalizing all lands that had formerly been held by the French, and he issued a decree in February 1804 that nullified all gifts and sales of land made by the French during the war. This was quickly followed by the confiscation of more than five hundred properties in thewestern part of the country. The threat of enforcing this law in the mulatto-controlled South led to the uprisings that eventually resulted in the assassination of Dessalines. On October 17, 1806, he was ambushed in Port-au-Prince and killed by a group of mulatto officers. His body was mutilated. The period following his assassination was one of civil war between northern Haiti, under the black leader Henri Christophe, and southern Haiti, under the mulatto Alexandre Pétion.

The legacy of Dessalines, the "father of Haiti," is extensive. The anniversary of his death is commemorated each year as a national holiday. While the commitment of Dessalines to the peasantry ultimately resulted in his death, it earned him the continued reverence of the Haitian people. His invocation of the link between race and class set the tone for future black nationalism in Haiti.

See also Christophe, Henri; Haitian Revolution; Toussaint-Louverture

■ ■ *Bibliography*

Dupuy, Alex. *Haiti in the World Economy: Class, Race, and Underdevelopment Since 1700.* Boulder, Colo.: Westview, 1989.

Fick, Carolyn. *The Making of Haiti: The Saint Domingue Revolution from Below.* Knoxville: University of Tennessee Press, 1990.

LaCerte, Robert. "The Evolution of Land and Labor in the Haitian Revolution, 1791–1820." In *Caribbean Freedom,* edited by H. Beckles and V. Shephard, pp. 42–47. Kingston, Jamaica: Ian Randle, 1993.

Nicholls, David. *From Dessalines to Duvalier: Race, Colour and National Independence in Haiti.* Rev. ed. New Brunswick, N.J.: Rutgers University Press, 1996.

SEAN BLOCH (2005)

DETROIT RIOTS (1943 AND 1967)

See Riots and Popular Protests

DIALECT POETRY

Although it had been written by white and black poets alike, dialect poetry emerged as a significant part of African-American writing in the mid-1890s with the success of its first well-known black practitioner, Paul Laurence Dunbar, and it played a dominant role in African-American poetry until World War I. It figured prominently in black-edited newspapers and periodicals and in virtually all of the many collections of verse by the black poets of the time. Among its leading creators, in addition to Dunbar, were James Edwin Campbell, Daniel Webster Davis, James D. Corrothers, James Weldon Johnson, Elliot Blaine Henderson, and Fenton Johnson.

Much of the earliest African-American dialect poetry was inspired by, and a response to, the highly successful work of white plantation-tradition writers, who, evoking nostalgic images of the Old South, used dialect in a way that furthered negative racial stereotypes. This plantation-tradition background was apparent in the work of black dialect poets, who drew on it thematically and wrote in a dialect that—rarely going beyond fairly conventionalized misspellings—owed more to that white literary tradition than to actual folk speech. The opening of Dunbar's "Lover's Lane" was fairly typical in its language and tone: "Summah night an' sighin' breeze, / 'Long de lovah's lane; / Frien'ly, shadder-mekin' trees, / 'Long de lovah's lane."

Some dialect poets even came close to their white counterparts in both nostalgia and the use of stereotypes. Davis, for example, penned a tribute to the slave-owning plantation mistress, "Ol' Mistis," fondly describing life on the plantation and including such lines as "Ub all de plezzun mem'riz' / Dar's one dat fills my heart, / 'Tiz de thought ub dear ol' Mistis, / An' 'twill nebber frum me part."

But most dialect poets, including Dunbar and even Davis, sought to use the problematic plantation-tradition background in a way that rescued both the form and its subjects from the more demeaning aspects of the tradition on which they drew. These poets often made use of actual folk sources, subtly subverting the stereotypes white writers portrayed, as in Dunbar's "An Ante-bellum Sermon," in which a slave preacher turns a message of heavenly freedom into a barely disguised anticipation of the day "when we'se rec'onised as citiz'—/ Huh uh! Chillun, let us pray!" or even working to create a dialect poetry of protest against racial oppression, as when Elliot Blaine Henderson wrote of black American life in a South where "Dey lynch him on de lef' / An' dey lynch him on de right." In so doing, the poets moved dialect poetry away from caricature and even, in the view of some writers and critics of the time, toward the presentation of a distinctive African-American cultural heritage rooted in the folk life of the rural South.

Following World War I, dialect poetry lost much of its prominence in African-American literature. Many writers, especially during the Harlem Renaissance, became more troubled by the form's lingering association with plantation-tradition writing while agreeing with the famous 1922 statement of James Weldon Johnson, rejecting his own earlier work, that dialect poetry was severely constrained as a form, limited to little more than humor and pathos. Still, a few poets, notably Langston Hughes, experimented with it. And, toward the end of the Renaissance period, with the 1932 publication of Sterling Brown's *Southern Road*, dialect poetry—which Brown strongly defended against Johnson's strictures—received a major, if somewhat isolated, re-elaboration.

It would be difficult to argue for any direct connection between the dialect tradition and contemporary African-American poetry. Nevertheless, many of the impulses that took shape within that older body of writing have been notable in more recent work as well. Beginning particularly with the black arts movement in the 1960s, a number of poets have sought to put distinctively African-American forms of speech to poetic use. Their work, having a flavor that is both urban and militant, is very different from the dialect poetry of Dunbar or even Brown. Growing out of an urban milieu and out of specifically urban speech, this later vernacular poetry represents a self-conscious rejection of dominant literary models and of dominant cultural models. Still, the earlier dialect poets remain important precursors to this more contemporary work. Above all, they help emphasize the length of a tradition into which it fits, a tradition marked by recurring efforts to create a distinctively African-American literature and cultural identity through the possibilities inherent in the representation of a unique folk life and a unique folk speech.

See also Black Arts Movement; Brown, Sterling Allen; Dunbar, Paul Laurence; Harlem Renaissance; Hughes, Langston; Johnson, James Weldon

■ ■ *Bibliography*

Bell, Bernard W. *The Folk Roots of Contemporary Afro-American Poetry*. Detroit, Mich.: Broadside Press, 1974.

Gates, Henry Louis. "Dis and Dat: Dialect and the Descent" and "Songs of a Racial Self: On Sterling A. Brown." In *Figures in Black: Words, Signs, and the "Racial" Self*, pp. 167–195, 225–234. New York: Oxford University Press, 1989.

Redding, J. Saunders. *To Make a Poet Black*. Chapel Hill: University of North Carolina Press, 1939; reprint, Ithaca, New York: Cornell University Press, 1988.

DICKSON D. BRUCE JR. (1996)

DIASPORIC CULTURES IN THE AMERICAS

From 1492 on radical changes took place in the Americas as the European conquest and the ensuing colonial period brought ideas of race into the classification and treatment of all peoples. Those of European descent occupied the top of a pyramid that placed people classed as Indians and Africans as slaves and lesser beings on the bottom. In the late nineteenth century concepts of culture either fused with or replaced the idea of "race" but preserved the same system of ranking and classification that worked to the advantage of the few and the detriment of many others.

CULTURE

Four approaches to culture are in vogue in the twenty-first century: the *elitist*, the *hegemonic-diffusionist*, the *historical*, and the *paradigmatic*. The first affirms that only some people in a given society are cultured (as in high culture), while others are not. Those others exist in "subculture," something below that of the elite. From this perspective, cultured people are formally educated, speak language correctly, and worship in a well-known religious manner. By contrast, other people, especially Native Americans and African Americans, are seen as illiterate or unable to learn correctly, speak dialects, and practice "cults."

The second concept is associated fundamentally with the anthropology of the early twentieth century. In this hegemonic-diffusionist approach, associated especially with Melville J. Herskovits and later with Robert Farris Thompson, cultural elements are diffused from specific distant origins. In such diffusion the pristine and authentic becomes retained as corrupt retentions and reinterpretations. To understand the ways of life of an African-American people, one searches the "high" donor cultures of Africa (as though they have remained essentially unchanged for centuries) for elements "found" in the Americas. The result is a view of all African diasporic cultural systems in the Americas as syncretic hodgepodges. By this scheme, the self-liberated Saramaka people of Suriname and French Guiana (Guyane), and more recently Brazil, rank "high" in the "scale of intensity of Africanisms," but the self-liberated Afro-Lowlanders of Ecuador, Colombia, and Panama are said to "lack" Africanisms and by implication to be "without authentic culture" and "acculturated." African Americans of the United States were ranked by Herskovits at the very bottom of the scale of intensity, thereby denying their past, present, and future contributions to the cultural systems of the Americas.

The third concept, *historical,* is well stated by Daniel Boorstin: "'Culture' (from the Latin *cultus* for 'worship') originally meant reverential homage. Then it came to describe the practices of cultivating the soil, and later it was extended to the cultivating and refinement of mind and manners. Finally, by the nineteenth century 'culture' had become a name for the intellectual and aesthetic side of civilization" (1983, p. 647). In 1977, at the First Congress of Black Culture in the Americas, held in Cali, Colombia, black people confronted self-styled intelligentsia and insisted on the Spanish definite article "*la*" before the Spanish word *cultura* and initiated a foundational concept of *la cultural negra,* black cultural systems that are sophisticated, existential, experiential, and adaptable. They constitute entwined processes of tradition, history, and modernity moving toward higher and higher levels of black civilization in the Americas. The idea here of *emergent culture* is just as important as history, tradition, and legacy, and it is far from any concept of bits and pieces of Africa retained, and much culture lost.

A critically important dynamic in this perspective is that of *cultural continuity.* Culture is always changing.

People make it as it is and interpret their own lifeways dynamically. People are not at the periphery of culture but at its center, its generative heart. There are also, as Amiri Baraka makes clear in his discussion of "the changing same," remarkable continuities in cultural systems as well. Examples include some of the art forms of the Saramaka people and the marimba music of the Afro-Ecuadorian and Colombian lowlanders. This historical perspective differs significantly from the imperialist-diffusionist, however, because it draws on *paradigmatic* approaches to decide what to study.

Stated briefly, the paradigmatic perspective stresses an understanding of what real people living their own way of life take to be significant. One studies how culture unfolds in real life in real places and works outward from people-in-action to broader and more distant systems to make comparisons, without evaluating the "degree" or "intensity" or "level" of culture. Taken together, historical and the paradigmatic approaches establish a contemporary critical perspective in the social sciences and the humanities. They are used in the remainder of this article.

HISTORY

African-American systems of life and thought are profoundly cultural. They are clearly African descended and African diasporic. Any study of Afro-American cultural systems must comprehend commonalities of experience and especially of local interpretations of experiences at specific places in given periods in time, and also some degree of cultural construction of a meaningful historical past that may be obliterated, or highly distorted, by written literature. In *Silencing the Past* (1995), Michel-Rolph Trouillot discusses two dimensions of history that must always be considered: that which happened (an event such as a forced passage from Africa across the Atlantic Ocean to be sold in a slave market in the Americas, or the myriad revolts, rebellions, and movements of self-liberation of Africans in the Americas) and the *stories told about the event.* When stories are not told, or are not remembered, or are hidden, history is silenced. The stories themselves must be opened up and studied to be reasonably sure that they reflect events critical to the real cultural histories of people, not bent and distorted to the canons of a rigid educational system.

For example, in 1991 a dramatic discovery was made in Lower Manhattan in New York City: A graveyard was unearthed by construction workers. It was found to contain the bodies of African people—men, women, and children—buried there from the 1600s through 1794. Although clear evidence of the importance of enslaved Africans in the development of New York City existed, it was ignored and silenced by historians and archivists. Eventually, African-American archaeologist Michael L. Blakey received permission and funds to excavate the site and demonstrated that the presence of Africans constituted "the earliest and largest African cemetery found in North America." Africans were fundamental to the building of New York City, but their lives and deaths were not written into history, even though their presence was quite clear in the archives of New York City. An estimated twenty thousand Africans were buried near what is now Wall Street. They were brought to New Amsterdam in 1626, so were part of the founding of New York. Indeed, *"Ian Rodriguez, a free black trader, had set up the first long-term trading post in Manhattan prior to the establishment of the Dutch colony, making a person of African descent Manhattan's first foreign (i.e. nonindigenous) businessman"* (Blakey, 2001, pp. 222–223, emphasis added).

Stories such as this one, well documented in the official city archives, go far to contradict U.S. educational stereotypes, such as the one that says slavery began in the South and existed until Northerners freed black people there. After the passage of the Fugitive Slave Act of 1850, which obligated Northerners to return escaped Southern slaves to their owners, revolts and movements of self-liberation increased throughout the northern United States, where slavery also existed.

Another story—that an enduring ideology of a history of slavery and a cultural legacy of deprivation per force predates a sense of freedom for black people in the Americas—must also be contested. In 1712 in New York City, for example, enslaved African-American people rose up and killed at least nine whites (Bennett, 1964, p. 101). In the Americas, wherever slavery existed self-liberation also occurred (Laguerre, 1989; Taussig, 1980; Whitten and Torres, 1998). The true stories reveal the early presence of black people where national educational literature says they never were, and that freedom of African and African-European peoples in the Americas may precede, or coexist with, systems of enslavement.

SPACE, TIME, AND AFRICAN-DESCENDED PEOPLE

We reflect now on the breadth of the African diaspora and important dimensions of the history of African-descended people. We must first set aside notions of cultural or racial purity of the few and contamination of the rest. The African diaspora does not begin in the Americas, and certainly not in North America, as is so often supposed, nor is Africa divorced from Europe and Christianity prior to the horrors of the European-sponsored Middle Passages that

brought Africans to the Americas against their will to build the very systems that may now deny their existence.

In 711, as the Muslim conquest of Iberia began, black soldiers were present in the Islamic forces. Further north, according to the historian Folarin Shyllon, Irish records suggest that during a Viking raid on Spain and North Africa in 862, a number of Africans were captured and some carried to Dublin, where they were known as "blue men." In the tenth century, black Africans who fought alongside North African Moors made up a significant part of the conquering army of the Iberian Peninsula.

By the eleventh and twelfth centuries (and on into the sixteenth) images of black Africans were present in European monumental art and architecture, Christian iconography, and heraldic shields throughout western Europe. Between the fourth and fourteenth centuries, representations of Africans appear in religious works involving the land of Ethiopia, the coming of the Magi to confirm the birth of Christ, the realm and person of Prester John in India or Africa, the queen of Sheeba, St. Maurice, and the meaning of Old Testament legends and prophecies about the cosmic relationship between darkness and light.

In the mid-fifteenth century, sailors under the command of the Portuguese entrepreneur Prince Henry the Navigator began purchasing diverse people at ports in West Africa and shipping them to Lisbon for sale throughout Europe. As Prince Henry's sailors color-coded their chattel, Africans previously known on the Iberian Peninsula by multiple cultural and ethnic designations such as Biafara and Mandingo, in all their diversity, were designated by a single color term, *negro* (black). Such pejorative and dangerous labeling of diverse African peoples ironically coincided with large-scale conversions of Africans to Christianity in the region of the Congo and by the emergence of "racially mixed" people in the coastal towns of West Africa.

The multiple cultural heritages and histories of Afro-Americanity stem from African and European sources, including, after 1492, indigenous contributions (e.g., Whitten and Corr, 2001). Cultural systems were suppressed tremendously by slavery but rejuvenated, recreated, and revitalized by revolt and revolution, wherein Maroons (from the American Spanish–Arawak word *cimarrón*) came to stand for the core values of freedom itself, a concept built into African-American cultural systems across the entire hemisphere. Most of the prominent black areas of eastern and northern South America, Central America, and the Caribbean stem directly from creative processes of rebellion, self-liberation, and sovereign territoriality that were initiated and sustained by African-American people.

They include various regions of Brazil; the *yungas* (deep Andean valleys) of Bolivia; the northwest coast of Ecuador; the Pacific and Atlantic coasts and Cauca Valley of Colombia; the Venezuelan *llanos* (plains) and northern coastal crescent; the interior of the Guianas, including Amazonas; the Darién, coasts, and interior of Panama; the Mosquitia of Honduras and Nicaragua; the west coast of Guatemala, Belize, Honduras, and Nicaragua; the mountains of Haiti and the Dominican Republic; the Jamaican Blue Mountains and Red Hills regions; the Cuban eastern highland region; and the list goes on. When combined with similar lists from Canada and the United States and fused with the reality of extensive travel of African Americans across the entire continent, the image of profound continuities and innumerable radical changes is sustained and fortified.

MAROON PEOPLE IN HISTORY AND CONTEMPORARY CULTURE

To begin to understand African-American cultures in the Americas from intertwined paradigmatic and historical perspectives, we turn now to two dynamic, contemporary peoples, each with deep roots in multiple pasts: the Afro-Lowlanders of Esmeraldas Province, northwest Ecuador, and the Saramaka Maroons of Suriname, French Guiana, and more recently Brazil. The latter were regarded by Melville J. Herskovits (1941) as the most African in the Americas, while the former long languished in historical and cultural scholarship by an apparent "lack" of African cultural features (e.g., Whitten, 1974/1996; Rahier, 1999). Both cultural systems are highly dynamic and have made and are making their presence felt in their respective nations. One does not find them represented in textbooks on the history of the Americas, as taught in high schools, nor are they represented as exemplars of cultural dynamics in the innumerable introductory texts to anthropology, ethnology, or history used in colleges and universities. The formal education system of the United States silences their past and their present.

AFRO-LOWLANDERS OF NORTHWEST ECUADOR. Esmeraldas, so named for its three-tiered canopied rain forest in northwest Ecuador, became home to self-liberated African and Afro-Hispanic people in the mid-1500s (Lane, 2002). Different groupings seized their freedom in the north and south of the province after fortuitous shipwrecks, intermarried with indigenous people, became the dominant force in the Emerald Province, and resisted all attempts by the Spanish military and the Roman Catholic Church to subdue and subvert them. In 1599 direct descendants of one grouping of the original Maroons, fifty-six-year old

don Francisco de Arobe and his two sons, don Pedro and don Domingo (ages twenty-two and eighteen, respectively), journeyed to Quito to pay homage to the Spanish court (Lane, 2002). Their portrait was painted by an indigenous artist, Andrés Sánchez Gallque, in a magnificent work entitled *Esmeraldas Ambassadors*. Today, a restored version of this painting hangs in the Museo de Américas, Madrid. Kris Lane captures the elegance of these Esmeraldan lords in this manner:

> The men's noses, ears, and lips are studded with strange crescents and balls and tubes of gold. Beneath starched white ruffs flow finely bordered ponchos and capes of brocaded silk, their drape lovingly rendered by the painter: here a foil-like blue, there bronze, now bright orange against velvety black. Only don Francisco's poncho appears to be woolen, perhaps fashioned from imported Spanish broadcloth. The three are further adorned with matching shell necklaces, and don Francisco holds a supple, black felt hat with a copper trim. Don Domingo holds a more pedestrian sombrero. . .and all three appear to be wearing fitted doublets of contemporary, late-Renaissance European style. These are all but hidden, nestled beneath flowing Chinese overgarments, which are, in turn, cut in a distinctly Andean fashion. (2002, p. xi)

The African-American ambassadors from the Emerald land constituted in 1599 a global presence in a parochial Spanish court of the Americas. Over 460 years have passed since the first moments of *cimarronaje* (marronage) in Esmeraldas, and over four centuries have gone by since the aesthetic moment of magnificent representation of three of the elite of the earliest Afro-indigenous American republic. Through three hundred years of colonial rule that featured European-dominated gold lust, slavery of indigenous and African peoples, and a shift from a Renaissance to a baroque ethos, Afro-Hispanic Esmeraldanians endured (Lane, 2002). They fought in the wars of liberation and later in the Ecuadorian Liberal Revolution. In 2005 they regard themselves proudly as the true Christians of Ecuador. They manifest some of the most Spanish and the most African music and storytelling in the Americas, and they are among the poorest people in modern twenty-first-century Latin America.

In the twenty-first century the cultural system of these Afro-Ecuadorians is rich in its diversity and deep in its African, European, and indigenous legacies. During the conquest and colonial era the Spanish divided up the people of their vast empire into two republics: that of the Spanish, and that of the *indios*. No place was ever created under colonial rule for black people, *los negros,* nor was a construction of blackness, *lo negro,* recognized. Afro-Latin American people created their own niches, environmental adaptations, ideologies, and cosmologies. Among the core features of blackness in Ecuador, as in Colombia, Panama, Venezuela, and elsewhere in Latin America and the Caribbean, is the enduring emphasis on *freedom.* One is either free or not. There is no middle ground (Price, 1996; Whitten and Torres, 1998).

In 1992 blackness in Ecuador clearly emerged as a national quality spanning coastal, Andean, and Amazonian regions. Its ethnic nationalist expression was called *négritud,* coined initially (as *négritude*) by the Martinique writer Aimé Césaire. As the movement surged under such cultural rubrics as "the advancement of the black community," and identification of the movement among white and black intellectuals was expressed by the representations *afro-ecuatorianos(as)* (Afro-Ecuadorians) and *afro-latinoamericanos(as)* (Afro-Latin Americans), varied associations between those so identifying and the surging indigenous movement came into being. As the concept of Afro-indigenous peoples also became salient in national discourse, the concept of *zambaje* entered the Ecuadorian literary lexicon. *Zambo(a),* long a term of identity and reference in Esmeraldas and elsewhere in the Americas, signifies freedom and dignity; it refers to the genetic blending of African peoples with indigenous peoples, the epitome of such blending historically embodied in the painting of the three cosmopolitan ambassadors and lords from Esmeraldas, described above. Significantly, perhaps, in the restoration of the Museo de Américas' painting, the features of *zambaje* described by Lane were transformed to very black, denying thereby the representation and significance of mixed heritage of the Afro-indigenous *cimarrones.* Once again, history was silenced, this time through powerful museum imagery.

Christianity pervades the cosmology of the Afro-Esmeraldians. Some aficionados of Afro-Americana and other scholars and activists are bothered by the self-assertion of black people in this area that they are true Catholic Christians, people who resisted subversion by the imperialism of the Roman Catholic Church and resisted the ideology and praxis of inquisitorial curates. Esmeraldians nonetheless cooperate with priests, nuns, and brotherhoods who respect their beliefs and practices. *Respect* is a key to understanding the resilience of black people of Esmeraldas, as elsewhere. Those who respect people and their customs may move freely in and out of the Afro-Esmeraldanian world, but those who seek to deprecate or humiliate their persons and their lifeways may find them uncooperative and unresponsive. Respect and freedom are

clearly tied together in the twenty-first century as in the sixteenth through the twentieth, and before.

Salient cultural features of the black lowlanders that go back into deep antiquity and stretch into the present with the promise of a dynamic future include the marimba dance, featuring the most African musical and rhythmic styles in the Americas; the songs of praise (*arrullos*) to saints, with origins in both Africa and Iberia; and wakes and second wakes for adults with strong roots in Moorish Iberia and North Africa.

La tropa. This cultural performance—called the troop (or troops)—is the most dramatic ceremony held in the province of Esmeraldas and in the neighboring departments of Nariño, Cauca, and Valle, Colombia. It is a forceful enactment of the capture, crucifixion, and resurrection of Jesus Christ that some take to be an extended dramatic metaphor for the formation of an Afro-indigenous Maroon settlement and the resurrection of Christ within it. *La tropa* is enacted during the week leading up to Easter Day and ends with a secular parade, sometimes called Belén, on Easter Sunday. *La tropa* brings outmigrants back home from urban areas to small villages such as Güimbí on the Güimbí River and Selva Alegre (Rahier, 1999) on the Santiago River. Community ties are very important to many outmigrants, who spend considerable sums of money and take up to two or three weeks from their urban lives to make their way up the coast of Ecuador, and thence upriver by launch or canoe, to attend this important and dramatic communal event.

The *la tropa* ceremony begins in the fringes of the community as groups of soldiers with shotguns, machetes, spears, and knives run off in directed squads to search for the lost or hidden Christ, but they find only the biblical thief, Barabbas. They then march in step on the church and enter it, march within it, and eventually enact the killing of Christ, his removal from the cross, the reign of the devil on Saturday, the bringing of the forest into the Catholic Church within the black and free village, and perhaps the liberation of the people of the forest and of the true free church from oppression of crown, church, and later state (Rahier, 1999). During this ceremony women sing sacred hymns of praise to Christ and to the assembled "sinners." The *tropa* formation itself, composed strictly of adult men, marches in a stylized manner to a drumbeat not used in any other ritual. The stylized manner of marching and walking to and from the church and within the church has been recorded on film and audiotape since the 1940s.

On Easter Sunday, after the enactment of Christ's resurrection, women take over the entire ceremony and lead the participants to and fro through main streets, back streets, and house yards to the songs of praise of the *arrullos* and to national popular music. This street parade, called Belén ("Bethlehem," and also "bedlam"), is led and controlled by women, just as in the hymns and dances to saints and to deceased children. Members of marimba bands participate and are controlled by women, who dance, sing, and shake tube rattles or maracas. With the beginning of the Belén the transformation from sacrality and connectivity with the realm of the divine to secularity and severance from that realm is instantaneous. Life in the realm of the human, which is connected to hell (Quiroga, 2003)—with its myriad of dangers—is fully restored in festivity and joy.

> Barrio de los negros Barrio of blacks de calles oscuras of dark streets preñadas de espantos, bursting with spooks que llevan, que asustan, that carry off, that frighten, que paran los pelos that make hairs stand [rise] en noches sin luna on moonless nights Barrio encendido, Inflamed barrio de noche y de día by night and by day infierno moreno, dark hell, envuelto en las llamas enveloped in the flames de son y alegría of rhythm and happiness. (Preciado Bedoya, 1961/1983, pp. 121–122)

MAROONS OF THE GUIANAS. Marronage began in a burst of freedom off the coast of Ecuador in the mid-1500s, led by both Africans and *ladinos*, black people of Afro-Hispanic descent. It was preceded by the first such movements in Hispaniola (contemporary Haiti and the Dominican Republic) in 1502, which continued. Enslaved Africans fled to the forested mountains in the interior, known as *haiti* in the Taíno (Arawak) indigenous language, merged with indigenous Taíno people, and began to raid and trade with new slaveholding colonists. Such movements became salient in African-American stories about their cultural origins and vigorously denied by white historians (Price, 1996; Trouillot, 1995).

Self-liberation in the Guianas (Guyana, Suriname, Guyane) took place on highly profitable sugar plantations operated by white European owners and overseers. As Sally Price and Richard Price note, "Between the mid-seventeenth and late eighteenth centuries, the ancestors of the present-day Maroons escaped from the coastal plantations on which they were enslaved, in many cases soon after their arrival from Africa, and fled into the forested interior, where they regrouped into small bands" (1999, p. 15). In Suriname, the Saramaka people tell the stories of First-Time (*fesi ten*) to commemorate not only such monumental events but also to evoke the dangers therein. In one case, at the plantation run by a Sephardim Jewish Brazilian named Imanüel Machado, two relatively newly arrived Africans, first Lanu by himself, and then his younger brother Ayako with his sister and sister's baby daughter, fled the local plantation atrocities and escaped into the rain forest hinterland where, after trials and tribulations, they founded the Matjáu clan of the contemporary and historical Saramaka cultural nationality. The soul of Lanu, it is said, returned to Africa, while the souls of his siblings remained in the Americas as founders of the Saramaka people.

It was supposed to be impossible to escape from the plantations, but these Maroons did so because, as a First-Time story goes, Ayako saw that following the brutal killing by a plantation overseer of his sister's son, he would have no kinspeople left when (as seemed to be inevitable) the overseer killed his sister's daughter the next day. Thus, not only was the concept of freedom at any cost established in the cultural system of the Saramaka, but the seeds of African-American structural matriliny were sown there, to mature eventually into an incredibly full social system of matrilineal descent reminiscent of West African systems but forged in the crucible of self-liberation and the often silenced wars of black liberation in the Americas.

Saramaka people and the five other Maroon peoples—Kwinti, Matawai, Ndyuka, Paramaka and Aluku—raided plantations to liberate more of their African congeners and fought a war of one hundred years against the Dutch, which they won. They were then instrumental in establishing the peace of 1762, which lasted until 1986. Richard Price studied the cultural system of First-Time while undertaking long-term ethnography with the people, where he listened with care to Maroon tellers, who located their own ancestry in the tales of significant events. Then, unlike most anthropologists, he worked in Dutch archives (the Algemeen Rijksarchief of The Hague), and there he found references to the very events that the Saramaka preserved orally, ritually, and in many other ingenious cultural ways, in their own historicities. Later, however, when he returned to the archives in Holland, he found that the documents were missing. Again, the Dutch silenced the past that the Saramaka tellers maintained in a reverential manner.

Maroon arts of the Guianas are particularly rich, and reminiscent of Africa in their tales, sense of historicity, kinship system, drumming, and especially the aesthetics of wood carving by men and the quilts and carved gourds made by women. But the timing for direct transmission ("diffusion") from Africa to the Americas is all wrong. The arts of the Suriname Maroons are not to be taken as "retentions" or "survivals" or "relics" of Africa, as followers of the hegemonic-diffusion position would, did, and still hold. They are African-American creations that resemble African forms through a series of cultural and aesthetic templates first forged among *different* African people and reconstituted from deep aesthetic patterns in the Americas. They share broad African traditions found especially in West and Central Africa (Price and Price, 1999, p. 280), but it was and is their creative use of such complex but recognizable aesthetic templates in the Americas, some influenced by Native American arts and crafts, that forged the African American cultural systems of Suriname, as elsewhere.

In *Maroon Arts* (1999) Sally Price and Richard Price address this issue, as they have been doing since the 1970s. To understand cultural systems of African Americans we must understand continuity-in-change, what Amiri Baraka (who was once known as Leroi Jones) called "the changing same." By so doing we appreciate culture in its own right, as created by real people in real places, and abandon the archaic search for traces of a lost past and a lost culture. Such a perspective, together with that of the real power of professional silencing of salient voices and suppressing of historical evidence that is disturbing to entrenched educational systems, opens African-American Studies to new vistas of understanding. As Price and Price note:

> Where scholars once strained to discern the stylistic essences of particular arts in particular cultures, they are now directing their gaze more frequently toward the doorways where artistic and aesthetic ideas jostle with each other in their passage from one cultural setting to the next. Where the emphasis was once on abstracting back from an overlay of modernity to discover uncorrupted artistic traditions, modernization now lies at the heart of the enterprise, providing a springboard for explorations of cultural creativity and self-affirmation. (1999, p. 6)

DIFFERENCES AND SIMILARITIES

This entry makes broad statements, buttressed by long-term serious ethnographic research with two distinct peoples from western and eastern South America (the Afro-Lowlanders of Ecuador and the Saramaka of Suriname). The same sort of description could be written of hundreds of different African-American people in the Americas, who share legacies of enslavement and self-liberation, who speak many languages, and some of whose ritual activities and religious beliefs and practices are fairly well known, if often distorted (Haitian Vodoun, Brazilian Candomblé, Cuban Santería).

With regard to similarities in the two case presentations, the concept and practice of *freedom* undergirds secular and religious ideology in both systems, as it does in the rest of the Americas. Another foundational concept is that of the viability of *soul,* not as something detached from the body but as an enduring and empowering concept of expanded brotherhood and sisterhood across innumerable boundaries and barriers. Expression of complex ideas through rhythm and stylized motion together with considerable improvisation in text and performative modes also characterizes both peoples, as in other African-American systems in the Americas.

Reverential homage to ancestors takes a very different, indeed opposite, track in the two dynamic cultural systems, but even here there are similarities. The Saramaka place themselves in huge matrilineal (but not matriarchal) systems with ascendant male authority. But the ancestors can be dangerous, so little by little they are "forgotten" and the torts that may have been made from one clan or lineage member to another in recent and past times are somewhat diffused of an awful power of spiritual revenge. In the Pacific Lowlands of Ecuador, there are no unilineages, and a complex network system of kinship exists, also reminiscent of African systems. Ancestors are *dismissed at death,* but lingering worries hang on that they may return in a vengeance mode, either as a real ancestor or as one transformed into a dangerous spirit, ghost, or ghoulish creature. In both cases, which in some ways seem so very different, the closeness of the living and the dead combine with a world of sentient spirit, water, and forest beings to create a rich if at times frightening image of contemporary existence.

Finally, to add one more feature of comparison, in both systems people have, because they initiated their own heritage and ideology of freedom and defended it against many adversaries, learned to live effectively in two radically different economic systems: the global, expanding, and contracting money economy dictated by world demands of capital gain, and the local, sustainable system of subsistence life that provides their basis for survival.

See also African Diaspora; Identity and Race in the Americas

■ ■ *Bibliography*

Bennett, Lerone, Jr. *Before the Mayflower: A History of the Negro in America, 1619–1964.* Baltimore: Penguin, 1964.

Blakey, Michael L. "The Study of New York's African Burial Ground: Biocultural and Engaged." In *African Roots/ American Cultures: Africa in the Creation of the Americas,* edited by Sheila S. Walker. Lanham, Md.: Rowman & Littlefield, 2001.

Boorstin, Daniel J. *The Discoverers: A History of Man's Search to Know His World and Himself.* New York: Vintage, 1983.

Herskovits, Melville J. *The Myth of the Negro Past.* Boston: Beacon, 1941. Reprint, 1958.

Laguerre, Michel. *Voodoo and Politics in Haiti.* New York: St. Martin's Press, 1989.

Lane, Kris. *Quito, 1599: City and Colony in Transition.* Albuquerque: University of New Mexico Press, 2002.

Lewis, Marvin A. *Afro-Hispanic Poetry, 1940–1980: From Slavery to "Négritud" in South American Verse.* Columbia: University of Missouri Press, 1983.

Preciado Bedoya, Antonio. "Jolgorio" (1961). In *Afro-Hispanic Poetry, 1940–1980: From Slavery to "Négritud" in South American Verse,* edited by Marvin A. Lewis. Columbia: University of Missouri Press, 1983.

Price, Richard. *First-Time: The Historical Vision of an Afro-American People.* Baltimore: Johns Hopkins University Press, 1983.

Price, Richard, ed. *Maroon Societies: Rebel Slaves Communities in the Americas.* 3rd ed. Baltimore: Johns Hopkins University Press, 1996.

Price, Richard, and Sally Price. *The Root of Roots: Or, How Afro-American Anthropology Got its Start.* Chicago: Prickly Paradigm, 2003.

Price, Sally, and Richard Price. *Maroon Arts: Cultural Vitality in the African Diaspora.* Boston: Beacon, 1999.

Quiroga, Diego. "The Devil and Development in Esmeraldas: Cosmology as a System of Critical Thought." In *Millennial Ecuador: Critical Essays on Cultural Transformations and Social Dynamics,* edited by Norman E. Whitten. Iowa City: University of Iowa Press, 2003.

Rahier, Jean Muteba, ed. *Representations of Blackness and the Performance of Identities.* Westport, Conn.: Bergin and Garvey, 1999.

Taussig, Michael. *The Devil and Commodity Fetishism in Latin America.* Chapel Hill: University of North Carolina Press, 1980.

Trouillot, Michel-Rolph. *Silencing the Past: Power and the Production of History.* Boston: Beacon, 1995.

Whitten, Norman E., Jr. *Black Frontiersmen: Afro-Hispanic Culture of Ecuador and Colombia.* Cambridge, Mass.: Schenkman, 1974. Reprint, Prospect Heights, Ill.: Waveland, 1996.

Whitten, Norman E., Jr., ed. *Millennial Ecuador: Critical Essays on Cultural Transformations and Social Dynamics.* Iowa City: University of Iowa Press, 2003.

Whitten, Norman E., Jr., and Rachel Corr. "Contesting the Images of Oppression: Indigenous Views of Blackness in the Americas." North American Congress on Latin America (NACLA) Special Issue: *The Social Origins of Race, Race and Racism in the Americas,* Part I, 34, no. 6 (2001): 24–28, 45–46.

Whitten, Norman E., Jr., and Diego Quiroga. "Afro-Hispanic Pacific Lowlanders of Ecuador and Colombia." *Encyclopedia of World Cultures.* Vol. 7: *South America.* New Haven, Conn.: Human Relations Area Files Press; Boston: G. K. Hall, 1994.

Whitten, Norman E., Jr., and Arlene Torres, eds. *Blackness in Latin America and the Caribbean: Social Dynamics and Cultural Transformations.* 2 vols. Bloomington: Indiana University Press, 1998.

NORMAN E. WHITTEN JR. (2005)

DICKSON, MOSES

APRIL 5, 1824
NOVEMBER 28, 1901

The political and fraternal leader Moses Dickson was born in Cincinnati, Ohio, and supported himself as a barber from an early age. He took a position on a steamboat in 1840, and his travels through the South over the next three years gave him the opportunity to witness slavery firsthand.

Dickson was profoundly affected by what he saw, and determined to do whatever he could to abolish the slave system. He later claimed to have met with eleven other black men in Saint Louis in August 1846 to found a secret organization known as the Twelve Knights of Tabor, or the Knights of Liberty. According to Dickson, this organization claimed 47,000 members at its peak and was actively preparing to do battle against slavery when its work was suspended in 1856 in anticipation of an impending war between the North and the South. Dickson also claimed that the organization helped as many as 70,000 slaves escape to freedom through the Underground Railroad. In the absence of any other evidence for the order's existence, however, Dickson's account is regarded with skepticism.

Dickson fought in the Civil War, returning in 1864 to Missouri, where he became active in local politics. He was a delegate to every Republican State Convention in Missouri from 1864 to 1878, and served as an elector for Ulysses S. Grant in 1872. He was also a leading member of the Equal Rights League, an organization that worked to secure the franchise and equality before the law for African Americans in the state. Dickson lobbied for improved education for ex-slaves and their children, and he was one of the founders of the Lincoln Institute (now Lincoln University) in Jefferson City, Missouri, serving as the institution's vice president and as a trustee. In 1866 he joined the African Methodist Episcopal (AME) Church, in which he was licensed to preach the following year. In 1878, he became president of the Refugee Relief Board of Saint Louis, which provided food and clothing to thousands of people on their way to resettlement in Kansas and elsewhere.

A prominent fraternalist, Dickson served as Grand Master of the Missouri lodge of the Prince Hall Masons. In 1871 he founded a new fraternal order, the International Order of the Twelve Knights and Daughters of Tabor. He wrote an elaborate ritual for this order, combining elements drawn from Masonry and Methodism, and he encouraged members to practice Christianity, education, temperance, self-reliance, and economic self-improvement. The organization also provided its members and their families with material assistance in cases of illness or death. In 1907, six years after Dickson's death, the order claimed 100,000 members in thirty states and several foreign countries. Moses Dickson died in St. Louis, where he had lived for many years.

See also African Methodist Episcopal Church; Fraternal Orders

■■ *Bibliography*

Aptheker, Herbert. *A Documentary History of the Negro People in the United States.* New York, 1951.

Greene, Lorenzo John, Gary R. Kremer, and Anthony F. Holland. *Missouri's Black Heritage.* St. Louis, 1980.

Pipkin, J. J. *The Story of a Rising Race: The Negro in Revelation, in History and in Citizenship.* St. Louis, 1902.

Walton, Lester. "Moses Dickson: The Great Negro Organizer and Fraternal Leader." *The Colored American Magazine* (April 1902): 354–356.

LYDIA MCNEILL (1996)
DANIEL SOYER (1996)

DIDDLEY, BO (MCDANIEL, OTHA ELIAS)
DECEMBER 30, 1928

▮▮▮

Bo Diddley, a rhythm-and-blues singer and guitarist, was born Otha Ellas (or Elias) Bates in McComb, Mississippi. Shortly after his birth he was sent to Chicago to live with his cousins, whose last name, McDaniel, he then adopted. He began studying the violin while still a child. In his early teens he also taught himself to play the guitar, and he was soon playing in informal bands. He also played trombone in Chicago's Baptist Congress Band. He attended Foster Vocational High School, and after graduating he made his living as a boxer and construction worker. In 1946 he married Ethel Mae Smith. During this time he performed with the Langley Avenue Jive Cats, a rhythm and blues ensemble that included the guitarist Earl Hooker.

In the 1950s he adopted the name Bo Diddley, apparently in reference to the diddley bow, a one-string guitar.

He has also suggested that his name was slang for a mischievous youngster. In 1955 he recorded the songs "Bo Diddley" and "I'm a Man," appeared on Ed Sullivan's television show, and soon became a significant figure in Chicago's blues scene. His other important recordings from this time include "Crackin' Up" (1959) and "Say Man" (1959). In the 1960s Bo Diddley gained an international reputation for his electrifying live performances, but his recordings, including "You Can't Judge a Book by Its Cover" (1962), "Boss Man" (1966), and "Ooh Baby" (1967), were never hits.

Bo Diddley's notoriety derives largely from a signature syncopated rhythm, related to the "shave and a haircut" and "hambone" figures, which he has used in most of his songs. He has also cultivated a reputation as a powerful and outrageous singer, famous for shouting, growling, and howling boastful lyrics filled with sexual innuendo. His stark and earthy, yet highly experimental, guitar playing, combining Chicago electric blues and Afro-Cuban influences, was a prime influence on British rock bands in the 1960s. Bo Diddley appeared in three films during this time, *The Big T.N.T. Show* (1966), the documentary *The Legend of Bo Diddley* (1966), and *Keep on Rockin'* (1969).

Since the 1960s Bo Diddley has maintained a busy schedule. He has performed all over the world, hailed as one of the pioneers of rock and roll. His recordings include *Black Gladiator* (1971), the soundtrack for the animated film *Fritz the Cat* (1971), The *London Bo Diddley Sessions* (1973), and *I'm a Man* (1977). Bo Diddley's connection with British rockers has continued, including tours with The Clash in 1979 and Rolling Stones guitarist Ron Wood in 1988. In the 1980s Bo Diddley recorded for his own record label, Bokay Productions, a record distribution company based in Hawthorne, Florida. He also occasionally performed with Offspring, a group led by his daughter. He performed at George H. W. Bush's presidential inauguration in 1989, and again at Bill Clinton's inauguration in 1993.

Bo Diddley was honored with a Lifetime Achievement Award from the Rhythm and Blues Foundation at the Seventh Annual Pioneer Awards in 1996. He has his own "Star" on the Hollywood Walk of Fame, and is a member of the Rock and Roll Hall of Fame (inducted in 1987). In 1999 Diddley released *Road Runner Live,* and he has continued performing into the early years of the twenty-first century.

See also Rhythm and Blues

■ ■ *Bibliography*

Loder, Kurt. "Bo Diddley Interview." *Rolling Stone* (February 12, 1987): 76–78.

Tucker, Neely. "Bo Diddley." *Living Blues* 77 (December 1987): 17–21.

JONATHAN GILL (1996)
Updated by publisher 2005

DIGGS, CHARLES, JR.

DECEMBER 2, 1922
AUGUST 24, 1998

Born in Detroit, Congressman Charles Coles Diggs Jr. was the only child of Mayne Jones and Charles Coles Diggs. The senior Diggs was a Michigan legislator and the owner of the state's largest funeral home. Diggs Jr. studied at the University of Michigan and Fisk University. During World War II he served as a Tuskegee airman, reaching the rank of lieutenant. After his discharge in 1945, he attended Wayne State University in Detroit, where he obtained a degree in mortuary science. He then went to work in his father's funeral home.

In 1950 Diggs's father, who had been imprisoned for taking bribes, won reelection to his Michigan state senate post in a special election, but the legislature refused to seat him. Diggs Jr. ran for the seat in a special election, defending his father's record. He won both the primary and the general election by large margins. In the legislature Diggs allied himself with the policies of Gov. G. Mennen Williams, a friend of the labor movement. In 1951 and 1952 Diggs took night law courses at the Detroit School of Law.

In 1954 Diggs ran for the House of Representatives from Michigan's 13th District. He defeated incumbent George O'Brien in the Democratic primary and defeated a Republican challenger in the general election, becoming Michigan's first African-American congressman. Once in the House of Representatives, Diggs pressed for civil rights legislation and enforcement. In 1956 he introduced the measure to establish a Civil Rights Commission. Later, in 1971, he became a founder of the Congressional Black Caucus. In the 1960s Diggs backed successful measures to lower the voting age to eighteen and to aid minority businesses. In 1972 he was one of the organizers of the National Black Political Convention in Gary, Indiana, an unsuccessful attempt to unify African Americans politically and to form an alternative political party. Diggs established himself on the House District of Columbia Committee, helping to win the district home rule. In 1973 he was named chair of the District Committee.

Diggs also specialized in foreign affairs, particularly in Africa. A champion of foreign aid, in 1959 he became the first African-American member of the House Foreign Affairs Committee, and he later served as chair of the Committee's Africa Subcommittee. Named by President Richard Nixon to the U.S. delegation to the United Nations, he resigned in December 1971 to protest U.S. support of South Africa and Portuguese involvement in Africa.

In 1978 Diggs, by then the senior black representative, was convicted of mail fraud and payroll kickbacks involving his office employees. His constituents elected him to a thirteenth term, and he appealed his conviction. Under pressure, he resigned his committee chairmanships, and on July 31, 1979, the House formally censured Diggs, 414–0, for his conduct. On June 3, 1980, the Supreme Court refused to hear Diggs's appeal. He resigned his seat and went to prison in Alabama, where he served seven months. Following his release he served as an aide to the Congressional Black Caucus and practiced his mortician trade in Maryland. In 1987 he ran unsuccessfully for the Wayne County Commission in Michigan, but that same year he regained the state mortuary license he had lost with his conviction.

Charles Diggs died in 1998. More than six hundred people attended a ceremony in Maryland celebrating his civil rights record.

See also Congressional Black Caucus

■ ■ *Bibliography*

Christopher, Maurine. *Black Americans in Congress.* New York: Crowell, 1976.

"Diggs Released from Prison." *New York Times,* March 7, 1981, p. 38.

"Hundreds Pay Tribute to Late Rep. Charles Diggs' Civil Rights Record at Maryland Ceremony." *Jet,* September 21, 1998, p. 18.

STEVEN J. LESLIE (1996)
Updated by publisher 2005

DIGITAL CULTURE

In the mid-1990s, a confluence of factors—including exponentially increasing microchip processing power, the diffusion of personal computing, the largesse of venture capitalists, and the conception of the World Wide Web—culminated in a thoroughgoing transformation of American society. Dubbed the "information revolution," the digitalization of ever-larger segments of American life irreversibly changed modes of communication, circuits of commerce, methods of governance, and rhythms of work and leisure.

However, the social power of new information technology was neither universally nor equally distributed in the United States. The "digital divide," a phrase coined in 1995 by an Ohio reporter and popularized as the subtitle of a 1999 National Telecommunications and Information Administration report entitled *Falling Through the Net,* soon became shorthand for a host of inequities that attended the emergence of the United States as an information society, including disparities in language (English remains the lingua franca of the Internet); accessibility to computer hardware and software; the availability of the basic telephony infrastructure that supports networked computing, especially in rural areas; and the age of those most likely to log on.

For the most part, however, the phrase "digital divide" connotes the uneven access to information technology that exists among different racial and ethnic communities—in particular, between African Americans, who report the lowest rates of personal computer and Internet usage, and other social groups. Although this gap is steadily diminishing, black Americans remain somewhat less likely than Latinos, and appreciably less likely than whites and Asian Americans, to regularly use the Internet. In 2002, for example, 45 percent of African Americans had Internet access compared with 60 percent of whites and 54 percent of Latinos.

Although the digital divide paradigm, which measures the adoption of networked computing to the exclusion of other technologies, succinctly describes a new frontier of race-based social stratification, it also at times obscures the diversity of African-American digital culture. Encompassing the Internet and World Wide Web, yet ranging beyond them, African-American digital culture can be said to include multiple forms of technical *and* artistic creation, a proliferating network of virtual communities, and a unique standpoint on contemporary technoculture that stems from black diasporic experience. And, though black digital culture is characterized by the use of new techniques and media, it also extends an already rich tradition of aesthetics and critical reflection.

Bill Gates, Steve Jobs, and Tim Berners-Lee—the captains of computer science and industry whose combined efforts ushered in the information revolution are now legendary. Other founding figures are less renowned, but their labors were no less important. Among these are African-American entrepreneurs, engineers, programmers,

and creatives who played a role in the conception of the hardware and software architecture that supports information society and who continue to contribute to its growth. Nigerian-American computer scientist and engineer Philip Emeagwali, for instance, has been called "a father of the Internet." In 1982 Emeagwali conceived of a globe-shaped network of interlinked microprocessors spanning the planet that has been credited with prefiguring the idea of the Internet, a similarly expansive international network of computers. Mark Dean, an IBM executive, also contributed to the foundation of the information society: Working with a collaborator, he devised a flexible plug-in technology that opened up personal computers (PCs) to an array of peripheral devices such as headphones, speakers, and printers. First used commercially in 1984, this technical innovation enabled personal computers to evolve from business tools into technologies of leisure and entertainment as well. PC culture was further pushed in this direction with the introduction of programs that enabled the evolution of the Internet and the World Wide Web from text-based mediums to multimedia platforms—including images, animation, text, and sound. Two such programs were Macromedia Director and Shockwave, which were built on the backbone of the Lingo scripting language developed by African-American computer scientist and engineer John Henry Thompson.

The creation of a hardware-software information infrastructure readied the way for new configurations of the black community. An early pioneer in this effort was Brooklyn-based computer aficionado and businessman Omar Wasow. In 1993 Wasow founded New York Online (NYO), a dynamic virtual gathering place for people of color in the New York metropolitan area. This undertaking became the inspiration for his pathbreaking subsequent project, blackplanet.com. Soon after its founding in 1999, blackplanet.com, a website fostering online community among people of African descent, became one of the most popular sites on the Web; the site continues to draw an impressive audience. Other websites popular among African Americans include africana.com, a joint venture between Harvard University academics K. Anthony Appiah and Henry Louis Gates Jr. and the Microsoft Corporation that features original reporting and cultural criticism across the African diaspora; the multichannel arts and entertainment site seeingblack.com; and the politically oriented blackcommentator.com.

While recent technological advances provided a vehicle for novel forms of African-American community, these developments also inspired social observers to theorize African-American engagement with technology. Sometimes grouped together under the general rubric of Afrofuturism, cultural critics Mark Dery and Greg Tate and novelists Samuel R. Delany and Octavia Butler, among others, observed a tradition of technical experimentation and futurist themes in African-American culture that both anticipated and found continued expression in black digital culture. Black critical reflection on new technologies spans utopian and dystopian perspectives, including parts of Ralph Ellison's *Invisible Man* in which the nameless narrator becomes a cog in the machine of modern life; labor activist James Bogg's optimistic essay "The Negro in Cybernation," which opines that technology might help create the conditions for social equality; the Black Panther Party's Vietnam War–era lament that "The Spirit of the People is Greater Than the Man's Technology"; and the symbolism in black music genres such as techno and funk that likens the experience of black Americans to that of space travelers, cyborgs, and robots.

The innovative music production techniques pioneered by black American hip-hop artists, as documented by scholar Tricia Rose in her *Black Noise* (1994), also partake of this Afro-futurist spirit, as do the creations of artists like Keith and Mendi Obadike, whose art transports interrogations of black identity into the digital realm with multimedia projects. The Obadike's *The Interaction of Coloreds* project, for example, uses the familiar image of the color dialog box, familiar to users of word-processing software, to simultaneously comment on information society and the politics of color caste in American society.

Digital culture comprises the ways in which new technologies figure—literally, figuratively, and virtually—in black experience. Black technoculture reveals that the "digital divide" is but one perspective on African Americans' interactions with new technologies. Moreover, there is a longer continuum of black theory and practice around technology that proliferates and finds novel form in contemporary digital culture.

See also New Media and Digital Culture

■ ■ *Bibliography*

Afrofuturism: Special issue of *Social Text* (Summer 2002).

Dery, Mark. "Black to the Future." In *Flame Wars: The Discourse of Cyberculture*, edited by Mark Dery. Durham, N.C.: Duke University Press, 1994.

"The Ever-Shifting Internet Population: A New Look at Internet Access and the Digital Divide." Pew Internet and American Life Project, April 16, 2003. Available from <http://www.pewinternet.org/pdfs/PIP_Shifting_Net_Pop_Report.pdf Study>.

National Telecommunications and Information Administration. *Falling Through the Net: Defining the Digital Divide.* Washington, D.C.: U.S. Department of Commerce, 1999.

Rose, Tricia. *Black Noise: Rap Music and Black Culture in Contemporary America.* Middletown, Conn.: Wesleyan University Press, 1994.

Williams, Ben. "Black Secret Technology: Detroit Techno and the Information Age." In *Technicolor: Race, Technology and Everyday Life*, edited by Alondra Nelson and Thuy Linh N. Tu with Alicia Headlam Hines. New York: New York University Press, 2001.

ALONDRA NELSON (2005)

DILLARD UNIVERSITY

Dillard University, a historically black college located in New Orleans, Louisiana, grew out of two institutions, Straight College and New Orleans University. Straight College (originally Straight University) was founded by the American Missionary Association in 1869 to educate emancipated African Americans. Straight featured both secondary and undergraduate programs and briefly housed a Law Department. New Orleans University, created by the Methodist Episcopal Church, was originally called the Union Normal School. Following the end of Reconstruction, Union was transformed into an undergraduate institution, New Orleans University, while the Gilbert Academy was established under university auspices as a secondary school. Shortly thereafter, a medical department and nursing school were added, and the Sarah Goodridge Hospital and Nursing Training School (later Flint-Goodridge Hospital) was set up as a teaching institution. Although the medical school closed in 1911, Flint-Goodridge Hospital remained affiliated with the university until 1983.

In 1930 Straight College and New Orleans University merged. The new institution was named Dillard University in honor of James Hardy Dillard, a pioneering educator of African Americans in the South. Will W. Alexander, the director of the Commission on Interracial Cooperation and a leading southern white liberal, was named acting president. Following Alexander's departure in 1937, the distinguished educator Albert Dent became Dillard's first African-American president. During these years a student theater group, the Dillard Players, became nationally known. By 2003, Dillard had more than 2,300 students and nearly 150 full-time faculty directing 31 major programs of study. In addition to its academic and athletic programs, it sponsors a notable yearly conference on Black-Jewish relations.

See also Bethune-Cookman College; Bond, Horace Mann; Catlett, Elizabeth; Fisk University; Howard University;

Lincoln University; Morehouse College; Spelman College; Tuskegee University; Wilberforce University

■ ■ *Bibliography*

Dent, Jessie Covington. *Reminiscences of Dillard University: The Early Years.* New Orleans: Author, 1991.

GREG ROBINSON (1996)

DINKINS, DAVID

JULY 10, 1927

Born and raised in Trenton, New Jersey, politician David Norman Dinkins served in the Marine Corps during World War II. In 1950 he graduated from Howard University and later entered Brooklyn Law School, where he received a degree in 1956. From 1956 through 1975 Dinkins worked as an associate and partner in a law firm.

In the early 1960s Dinkins joined Harlem's George Washington Carver Democratic Club, then headed by the powerful city councilman J. Raymond Jones. He soon took an active interest in local politics and was elected to the New York State Assembly in 1965 and as a New York State Democratic Party district leader in 1967. He lost his assembly seat as a result of redistricting after only one term but continued his political career as Harlem's district leader. In 1972 Dinkins became the first African-American president of the Board of Elections, but he resigned a year later in protest when the department failed to enact registration reforms.

In 1973 Dinkins was appointed deputy mayor for planning and development under newly elected Mayor Abraham Beame. His attempt to become New York City's first black deputy mayor was ended when he disclosed that he failed to pay income taxes for the four previous years. He withdrew his nomination and paid heavy fines, but he continued his career despite this setback. In 1975 he was named city clerk, a position he would hold for ten years. He twice ran for Manhattan borough president, in 1977 and 1981, losing both times to Andrew Stein. Dinkins finally won the office in 1985 and served for one term.

In 1989 Dinkins ran for mayor against incumbent Edward I. Koch. Dinkins presented himself as a civil alternative to the acrimonious Koch and as someone who could better handle the city's racial problems, which he accused the three-term mayor of exacerbating. He defeated Koch in the Democratic primary and in the election defeated Republican Rudolph Giuliani by a slim margin, thereby becoming the first African-American mayor in New York City's history. His tenure as mayor had its share of budgetary and political problems. He earned the reputation of a cautious and careful administrator who proved reasonably adept in negotiating the treacherous complexities of New York City's racial and ethnic politics, but he was widely criticized as ineffective and biased in his handling of black boycotts of Korean-American shop owners in 1992 and in his response to the Crown Heights riot in 1993. Following his narrow defeat for reelection by Rudolph Giuliani in 1993, Dinkins began teaching at Columbia University and hosted a weekly public affairs radio program.

A former tennis player, Dinkins was inducted into the United States Tennis Association (USTA) Eastern Section Tennis Hall of Fame in 1993. Serving a fourth consecutive term as a Director at Large of the USTA in 2005, Dinkins continued teaching as Professor in the Practice of Public Affairs at Columbia University.

See also Mayors; Politics in the United States; Tennis

■ ■ *Bibliography*

"David N. Dinkins." In *Notable Black American Men.* Detroit, Mich.: Gale, 1998.

Moritz, Charles, ed. *Current Biography Yearbook 1990.* New York: H. W. Wilson, 1990.

JAMES BRADLEY (1996)
Updated by publisher 2005

DISEASES, TROPICAL

See Tropical Diseases

DIVINATION AND SPIRIT POSSESSION IN THE AMERICAS

The *orishas* (also spelled *orisa* and *orixá*), the guardian spirits of Yoruba religions, originally settled in the city of Ile Ife (in present-day Nigeria). There they established all of the ancient Yoruba arts, including farming, smithing, sciences, and divination. Each orisha, upon his or her passing, became the divine patron of the individual art he or she had mastered. The creator god, Olodumare, asked the orisha Orumila to stay on earth to advise humans regarding the dangers of daily life through the art of divination. Since then, divination has been used in Africa—and eventually in the New World—as the way for humans to receive advice from the orishas in matters that range from the spiritual to the physical. However, as time has passed, the orishas have availed themselves of man's own advances (e.g., in the arts of medicine, law, finances, etc.) and directed their believers to an expert in specific fields. This has been the most important change in the divination process since its creation.

The character of divination is predominantly private, while that of spirit possession is usually communal. Spirit possession or mounting (as in climbing on a horse), is common to most ancient belief systems, benefiting one person or an entire community through the energy that is believed to come from the spirits. This energy, known as *axé* or *aché,* is achieved through trance. Two elements are necessary for the propitiation of a trance: drumming and dance. At a speed of 200 to 220 beats per minute, drumming induces a state of altered consciousness. The drums employed for these rituals have been consecrated to particular deities. Dancing adheres to similar parameters, with an endless repetition of simple steps done to prepare for a trance. Particular rhythms are associated to each divinity. Once mounted, trancers dance the characteristic steps and movements of the visiting spirit. Another manifestation of trance is a sudden change from the mother tongue to one of the Yoruba dialects.

Spirit possession can be observed in the rituals of four of the major African-based religions in America: Candomblé, Santería, Umbanda, and Vodou. Eventually, these religions meshed with the Catholic beliefs of the colonizers and were enriched by the cosmology and trance traditions of the pre-Columbian inhabitants of the Americas, such as the Caribs, Arawaks, and Tainos.

CANDOMBLÉ

Candomblé has two realms, the spiritual (or *orun*), and the earthly (or *aiê*). *Orun* is composed of nine concentric energy circles of ever-increasing power. Olorum, the main god, presides where the energy is highest. Closest to Orolum is the *irumale,* then the ancestors or *eguns,* and finally the *orixás.* These circles surround *aiê.* The level inhabited by the *orixás* has an energy level similar to that of Earth, thus facilitating transit during possession rituals.

The *pai-* or *mãe-de-santo* (fathers and mothers) occupies the highest position within the religion. The high priest is assisted by the *iaôs,* also known as *filhos-* and *filhas-de-santo,* or sons and daughters. Possession occurs predominantly through filhas during rituals held in their temples (*terreiros*). Trance occurs within the context of religious festivities conducted in the *barracão,* the meeting room for public ceremonies. When possession seems imminent a drummer plays a dissonant note as if to precipitate the event. The *orixás* announce their identity by uttering Yoruba expressions associated with their individual personality; for example, those possessed by Omula will shout *Atotô!* The trancers then start to act out the *orixá's* personality.

During this activity, the congregation dances in concentric circles. In this manner their individual energies are channeled into the ritual's focal point. The possessed worshiper is placed at that focal point when the first signs of spirit possession appear. Another manifestation of trance is a sudden change from the mother tongue to one of the Yoruba dialects. After possession occurs, the individual is taken to an adjacent room and dressed in the color-coded garments and attributes associated with the deity. Returned to the *barracão* wearing the proper regalia, the *orixá* begins to provide personal advice, warnings, admonitions, and guidance to devotees. The character of this advice is general in nature; individualized advice is received only via divination.

In the early hours of morning, the body of the possessed filhas experiences a secondary trance in which the *orixá* changes to a childhood state, called *erê.* In this state the *orixá* tends to be obscene, playful, and boisterous. This type of trance signals the ending of the festivities. Once the *santo* leaves the body it has occupied during the festivities, the vehicle person has no recollection of the events that ensued during the trance and does not remember any message given by the *orixá.*

Communication between *orun* and *aiê* is achieved with the intervention of the *pai-de-santo.* The first step of divination is the identification of the client's guardian deities, of which there are usually two. Of the many divination methods brought from Africa to Brazil, the *jogo de búzios,* or shell toss, remains paramount. The priest begins the ritual with salutations and invocations to the *orixás* in a mixture of Yoruba and Portuguese. Sixteen cowry shells are tossed into a small wooden board adorned with sacred necklaces. The formation and position, open or closed, of the cowries will determine which *odu,* or myth, is applicable to the problem at hand. A second toss, this time using only four shells, is done to verify the answer obtained during the first toss. Other materials employed in divination to communicate with the *orixás* include small fruits and grains favored by the deity summoned.

SANTERÍA

Possession in Santería (often referred to as *Regla de Osha*) is also known as *mounting,* as in climbing atop a horse. Commonly limited to members of the priesthood class, however, it is not restricted to initiates alone. Mounting in non-initiates can signal a calling into the priesthood class to serve under the possessing orisha, called a *santo.* Mounting occurs within the content of a religious festivity (*bembé*). The events that follow the coming of the orisha are very similar to those described in Candomble.

There are two types of divination in Santería. One of them, *diloggun,* can be performed by all priests and priestesses while *ekuele* or *ifa* is reserved for the high priests alone. In *diloggun,* cowry shells or coconut pieces are the vehicle of communication with the *orishas.* As a result, coconut consumption is forbidden to initiates. The coconut used in divination is broken into pieces, from which the officiating priest chooses four. Small portions from each are removed to equal the number associated with the orisha to be consulted, and the pieces are placed on the deity's soup tureen. Chants are then sung in honor of Olodumare, the supreme being, the orishas, the priest's godparents, the client's godparents (in the event they exist), and the ancestors, or *eguns.* Following this ritual, the santero (priest) asks permission to perform the divination from all of the previously mentioned spirits and deities, and from Biague, the first diviner who employed coconut pieces in divination. A strict ritual ensues, whereby the four pieces are passed over the client's head, shoulders, chest, hands, knees, and feet, while the santero requests that the coconut pieces tell the truth. Once this ritual is finished, the pieces are cast into a special rug used only for divination. Each question is then repeated for verification purposes. The coconut pieces can fall with the white side up or with the dark outer cover up, in any of the mathematical combinations possible for the number four. A *letra* (letter) with its own particular meaning is associated to each of the five possible combinations. Each letter has its own name: *Alafia, Otagüe, Eyife, Okana Sorde* and *Oyekun.* The *santos* also employ the coconut to communicate with a particular adherent, though on those occasions questions are not formulated before casting the pieces into the mat.

A similar approach is followed when using the cowry shells for divination. The bottom of each shell is removed for stability, and the way the shells fall determines the *orisha's* message. The number of shells employed is sixteen, a sacred amount in the religion. In their absence, larger shells, (*ayes*), small black stones, (*ota*), and even human vertebrae are used as substitutes. The different numeric combinations, *odús,* are identified by individual names.

Odús are associated with several stories (*appatakis*) from the lives of the orishas. It is up to the priest, who must memorize all of these stories, to choose the one that carries a message applicable to the condition or situation experienced by the person undergoing the divination.

Only the highest priests within the religion, the *babalaos,* can perform the most reliable form of divination in Santería. This type leaves no room for mistakes, since it involves direct communication with Olodumare. Two modalities are available: the *Ekuele* and the *Tablet of Ifá.* The Ekuele is made up of two chains, fourteen to sixteen inches long. Hooked to these chains are pieces of metals, seeds, and a variety of small objects. Only one chain is employed per day. Part of a priest's morning rituals is to throw the ekueles into the divination matt, which allows Olodumare to decide which one will be used that day.

Ifá's Tablet (*Opon Ifá*) has two components, a round tablet and sixteen palm nuts. The heads of the orishas who control the four cardinal points are engraved in the tablet. Occasionally, the tablet is rectangular in shape, and in those cases the number of palm nuts increases to seventeen. The ritual begins with invocations like those employed for divining through coconut and cowries. The ritual develops in the following manner: the priest holds all the nuts in the right hand and allows them to slide through his fingers. The resulting combinations and *letras* depend on the number of shells that escape and those that remain in the priest's hand. The process is repeated eight times in order to obtain an *odu.*

UMBANDA

With a cosmos organized somewhat differently than that of the other three religions discussed in this article, the dynamics of spirit interaction and possession in Umbanda also vary. Here, the cosmos is divided into three spaces: the underworld, earth, and the ancestral realm, home to good spirits. *Exús* and *Quinbanda* spirits inhabit the underworld but venture to earth to harm humans, which harm is undone by the enlightened spirits. Among the enlightened spirits are the *Caboclos,* unacculturated Amazonian natives, and *Pretos Velhos,* elderly enslaved Africans. The latter perform their good deeds on earth as a means to ascend to a higher level of spiritual awareness. *Orixás* also take part in trance, depending on the type of Umbanda practiced at the individual center. The most important forms of Umbanda practiced are *Kardecista* (spiritism), Oriental, and Africana (African). Trances occur within the context of public celebrations, held in tents or rooms of worship (*terreiros*).

Umbanda ritual is conducted in a rectangular white room divided in two. This is a sacred place, with an altar and a public place for the congregation. The altar holds representations of *Pretos Velhos, Caboclos,* Catholic counterparts of the *orixás,* and glasses of water (known in spiritism as *Grave*). A ritual cleansing (*defumacão*) is followed by invocations dedicated to God and to more festive deities, as members of the congregation join the celebrants in clapping hands as they invite the spirits of *Caboclos* and *Pretos Velhos* to *vem trabalhar* (come to work).

Possession begins when the mediums stop dancing and start to convulse and perspire. Immediately after this, they assume the facial and bodily demeanors of the spirits who have entered their bodies. Once settled inside the mediums' bodies, the spirits proceed to greet one another, special members of the congregation, and important visitors. Divination is central to this ritual. An attendant gives numbers for consultation with the different spirits. Consultations aim at resolving the physical and spiritual problems of members of the congregation. At times this consultation involves the transferring of an evil spirit, or *exú,* from the body of a parishioner to that of a medium. These exorcists claim to have protection against the negative vibrations of the *exús.*

Spirit possession varies according to the type of Umbanda practiced at each *centro.* Those with a Kardecian orientation are visited by divinities of the spiritism pantheon: spirits of Arabs, Aztecs, Chinese, and Hindus. Here, trance is subdued and is accompanied by religious classical music, such as the "Ave Maria." In the more African *centros* it is *orixás* who come down to earth. The ritual is more elaborate and includes all of the elements of trance described in Candomblé and *Regla de Osha.*

In Umbanda, the male *chefes* (leaders) and male mediums, or spiritists, attests to the religion's Kardecian influence. Brazilian *machismo* still prevails in the religion, to the extent that only in the more Afro-Brazilian practices will a male possessed by a female *orixá* be allowed to display an overt feminine demeanor without risking expulsion from the *centro.*

Vodou

Because *Le Bon Dieu,* or *Bondye* (the good god) is well disposed towards man, the religion of Vodou focuses on the *loas* (spirits and divinities) who are closer to mankind. Music, dance, and animal sacrifices are important parts of the spirit possession experience.

Trance occurs through the *serviteurs,* members who serve as vehicles. The loas' presence at the ceremonies is understood by the *fideles* (worshipers) as a positive answer to their prayers and requests. Once a *loa* has entered the body of a *serviteur* the *fideles* can observe the physical manifestations of the *loa*'s character in the person possessed. It is then that the spirit communicates with the worshipers, either on an individual or collective basis. In many cases, the saint or loa is offered one of its favorite animals, which is then sacrificed by the *serviteur,* manifesting the *loa,* in trance. The animal is then given cooks who prepare their meat for the loas and the fideles. Only in Vodou has trance been openly associated with political actions. The slave uprising organized by Mackandal in Saint Domingue (Haiti) in 1757–1758, was one such instance, for Mackandal claimed to be the representative of an African divinity. Also important was the August 14, 1791, *Petro* ritual, a form of vodou that allegedly triggered the Haitian Revolution by empowering slaves through possession rituals. In such a spiritual state the slaves emerged victorious over the Napoleonic army in spite of their inferior numbers and lack of sophisticated weaponry.

As in the other religions the Vodou priest, or *houngan,* is responsible for both trance induction and divination. Communicating with the loas is also very important in Vodou. Playing cards and bones are employed, alternating with the techniques used in Candomblé and *Regla de Oshá:* seeds or coconut pieces, obí, cowry shells, and Ifá. In Vodou, Ifá is performed with the aid of palm nuts or with a chain of eight half-seed shells, called *opelé.* Trance is not to be confused with the Petro practice of zombification, which is induced by ingestion of particular substances that produce an altered state in humans. Zombification does not involve communion with the loas, nor does it affect the congregation in a positive manner. Zombification occurs when a person ingests a mixture of herbs and toxins especially prepared by a vodou sorcerer (the mixture may also be applied to the skin). The signs and symptoms follow a progression from feeling sick to generalized body weakness, ending in a decrease of vital signs to levels barely compatible with life. Once this occurs the individual is aware of his or her surroundings but is unable to react to them. At the mercy of the sorcerer, the victim might even be buried alive, only to be disinterred days later and given the antidote. This particular ritual, often performed as punishment, constitutes a show of power.

See also Candomblé; Folk Religion; Orisha; Myal; Religion; Santería; Voodoo; Yoruba Religion and Culture in the Americas

■ ■ *Bibliography*

Bisnauth, Dale. *A History of Religions in the Caribbean.* Kingston, Jamaica: Kingston Publishers, 1989.

Bourguignone, Erika. *Trance Dance.* Dance Perspective Foundation, 35. New York, 1968.

Brandon, George. *Santeria from Africa to the New World: The Dead Sell Memories.*Bloomington: Indiana University Press, 1993.

Brown, Diana DeG. *Umbanda: Religion and Politics in Urban Brazil,* 2d ed. New York: Columbia University Press, 1994.

Conner, Randy P. *Queering Creole Spiritual Traditions: Lesbian, Gay, Bisexual, and Transgender Participation in African-Inspired Traditions in the Americas.* Binghamton, N.Y.: Harrington Park Press, 2004.

Cros Sandoval, Mercedes. *La Religion Afrocubana.* Madrid, Spain: Playor, S.A., 1975.

Desmangles, Leslie G. *The Faces of the Gods: Vodou and Roman Catholicism in Haiti.* Chapel Hill: University of North Carolina Press, 1992.

Heaven, Ross. *Vodou Shaman: The Haitian Way of Healing and Power.* Rochester, Vt.: Destiny Books, 2003.

Murphy, Joseph. *Santería: African Spirits in America,* 2d ed. Boston: Beacon Press, 1993.

Nicholls, David. *From Dessalines to Duvalier: Race, Colour and National Independence in Haiti,* 3rd ed. New Brunswick, N.J.: Rutgers University Press, 1996.

Sanchez, Julio. *La Religion de los Orishas: Creencias y Ceremonias de un Culto Afro-Caribeño.* Hato Rey, P.R.: Ramallo Bros. Printing, 1978.

Voeks, Robert A. *Sacred Leaves of Candomblé: African Magic, Medicine, and Religion in Brazil.* Austin: University of Texas Press, 1997.

Wafer, Jim. *The Taste of Blood: Spirit Possession in Brazilian Candomblé.* Philadelphia: University of Pennsylvania Press, 1991.

JOSÉ ANTONIO LAMMOGLIA (2005)

DIVINE, FATHER

See Father Divine

DIXON, MELVIN

MAY 29, 1950
OCTOBER 26, 1992

Born in Stamford, Connecticut, novelist and poet Melvin Dixon received his B.A. from Wesleyan University in 1971 and his Ph.D. in American Studies from Brown University in 1975. He taught African-American literature, modern drama, and creative writing at Fordham University, Williams College, Queens College of the City University of New York (CUNY), and the CUNY Graduate Center, where he was professor of English from 1986 to 1992. As a critic Dixon helped to shape the emergent field of com-

parative African-American literary studies. His major critical work, *Ride Out the Wilderness: Geography and Identity in Afro-American Literature,* was published in 1987. He also translated two important volumes from the French: Geneviève Fabre's *Drumbeats, Masks, and Metaphor* (1983), a seminal study of contemporary African-American theater, and *The Collected Poems of Léopold Sédar Senghor* (1987).

In addition to his success as a critic, Dixon was an award-winning creative writer. His collection of his own verse, *Change of Territory* (1983), reflects his spiritual itinerary and development as a black writer; drawing upon diverse travels and sojourns in France, the Antilles, and Senegal, these poems reenact his pilgrimage to many different African-American historical sites. His first novel, *Trouble the Water* (1989)—which received the Charles H. and N. Mildred Nilon Excellence in Minority Fiction Award—poetically chronicles the dramatic homecoming of a black protagonist to his southern roots. By contrast, his second novel, *Vanishing Rooms* (1991), is a terse story set in New York about the agonies and rewards of love and friendship; it is one of the few major works in the African-American literary tradition that focuses on issues of black male homosexuality. Shortly before his death in 1992, Dixon completed a volume of poetry titled *Love's Instruments,* about his experience of living with AIDS. He also completed an authorized translation of the complete poems of Léopold Sédar Senghor.

See also Literary Criticism, U.S.; Literature of the United States

■ ■ *Bibliography*

Fabre, Michel. *From Harlem to Paris: Black American Writers in France, 1840–1980.* Urbana: University of Illinois Press, 1991.

McHenry, Susan. Review of *Vanishing Rooms,* by Melvin Dixon. *Black Issues Book Review* 3, no. 3 (May 2001): 24.

Pinson, Hermine D. "Geography and Identity in Melvin Dixon's 'Change of Territory.'" *MELUS* 21, no. 1 (spring 1996): 99–111.

MICHEL FABRE (1996)
Updated bibliography

DOCUMENTARY FILM

Documentary film has played a central role in the long-standing African-American tradition of presenting the lives and struggles of Black people as a means to achieve social justice. As a result, it owes a tremendous debt to African-American slave narratives, journalism, and photography. African-American documentary generally refers to artistically crafted, nonfiction films made by and about people of African descent but may also include films about African Americans by individuals of other backgrounds.

In Klotman and Cutler's *Struggles for Representation: African American Documentary Film and Video* (1999), Pearl Bowser describes the mission of African-American documentary as "recording the highs and lows of ordinary folk, as well as extraordinary moments in Black history and culture as seen from within" (1999), p. 31. From early twentieth-century newsreels through the 1970s Black documentary film movement to contemporary experimental films, Black America has produced many of the most prolific and masterful documentary filmmakers in cinema history.

INVENTING AFRICAN-AMERICAN DOCUMENTARIES

African Americans began to use moving pictures to document their lives as soon as film technology became available in the early twentieth century. Black photographers like Addison Scurlock, Peter P. Jones, Jennie Louise Touissant Welcome, Ernest Touissant Welcome, and Arthur Laidler Macbeth used their photographic expertise to become some of the world's first documentary filmmakers. In addition to making their own films, these artists, along with other Black photographers like James Van Der Zee, created the photographs that continue to enrich African-American documentaries.

Many consider *A Day at Tuskegee* (1910) the first comprehensive African-American documentary. Political leader and Tuskegee Institute founder Booker T. Washington commissioned George W. Broome and the National Negro Business League to document Tuskegee's history. The acclaimed film opened at Carnegie Hall in New York City and was the first to reveal documentary's political potential.

Prior to World War I, several African-American film companies emerged to produce fictional and documentary films, which often screened together in theaters, schools, and churches. Early documentaries, like narrative "race movies," attempted to challenge the growing number of racist films by documenting impressive activities and achievements of African Americans. Peter P. Jones Photoplay Ltd.'s elaborate *Dawn of Truth* (1915) combined a number of Jones's shorts into one of the earliest historical survey documentaries.

Most early African-American documentaries were newsreels and short subjects that, because they have deteriorated or been lost, are now known to us only through references in written texts. However, these images are still being discovered. Ethnographic film footage by African-American anthropologist/novelist Zora Neale Hurston was recently found, and more lost films promise to emerge.

With the advent of sound in the 1920s and the controlling influence of the Hollywood studio system, the cost of film production became prohibitive for many artists. Despite this, filmmakers like Edward Lewis, William Alexander, and Carlton Moss sustained the emerging African-American documentary industry.

In the 1930s Edward Lewis created a number of documentary series that would foreshadow theme-based formats, like *Eyes on the Prize*, to emerge decades later. William Alexander founded The All-America Newsreel Company, which generated hundreds of newsreels. Alexander worked with the Office of War and Information, where he created *A Call to Duty* (1946) and focused media attention on African Americans in the military. After the war Alexander spent several decades in Africa, where he produced documentaries about emerging African nations.

The topic of African Americans in the military was one of the first and most popular in African-American documentaries. During World War II, *The Negro Soldier* (1944) became one of the most significant African-American documentaries ever produced. The War Department commissioned Carlton Moss to create the film, which was aggressively promoted by the National Association for the Advancement of Colored People (NAACP) and eventually shown to thousands of white as well as black troops. A number of other films about African Americans in the military were created during this period, and Moss continued to make documentaries until his death in 1997.

Many of these early African-American documentary filmmakers struggled in isolation and anonymity. However, their work helped define the medium and proved documentary's political and cultural potential, soon to be realized by their successors.

VISIONS OF A MOVEMENT: DOCUMENTARY ACTIVISM

In the 1960s the civil rights movement inspired documentary artists of all races to use film to represent, preserve, and propel impending social change. By the 1970s the ensuing Black Power movement's emphasis on preserving Black history and the emergent Black independent film movement combined with the training and inspiration provided by documentary institutions like *Black Journal*

Actor Gabriel Casseus (l) and former major league baseball star Maury Wills (r) pose with director Spike Lee at the premiere of Lee's documentary film Jim Brown: All-American, *April 17, 2002, in Beverly Hills, California. Lee is among several prominent African American filmmakers who have used the documentary to chronicle black life, politics, and the civil rights movement in the United States.* LEE CELANO/GETTY IMAGES.

and Blackside, Inc. to produce an unprecedented number of African-American documentaries.

Madeline Anderson's *Integration Report #1* (1961) documented the nation's first sit-ins and arguably launched the second wave of the contemporary Black documentary film movement. The 1960s also saw documentaries by former actor William Greaves; Gordon Parks, of *Shaft* (1971) fame; and journalist St. Clair Bourne, who previously wrote for William Alexander's newsreels. All of these men would continue to make significant contributions to cinema throughout the rest of the century.

A steady stream of Black documentaries began in 1969 when Greaves became executive producer of the *Black Journal.* Following the 1967 race riots, President Lyndon B. Johnson's Kerner Commission mandated improvements in media representations of African Americans. The result was the 1968 Public Broadcasting Service (PBS) program *Black Journal,* which soon hired Greaves as executive producer. Greaves turned *Black Journal* into an Emmy- award-winning documentary and news pro-

gram that set the highest standard for all nonfiction media production and launched a generation of Black filmmakers including Madeline Anderson, St. Clair Bourne, Kathleen Collins, Lou Potter, Jacqueline Shearer, and Tony Brown (who in 1976 turned the program into *Tony Brown's Journal*). PBS continues to serve as a home for African-American documentaries, and Greaves, who has made more than two hundred documentaries, has emerged as one of the most prolific filmmakers of any race.

Although it was not broadcast until 1987, the 1970s also set the stage for the Oscar-nominated *Eyes on the Prize*, a documentary series about the civil rights movement by Henry Hampton, founder of Blackside, Inc. Blackside made many other documentaries in the 1970s while creating *Eyes on the Prize*, and the company later produced the Emmy-award-winning *Eyes on the Prize* II (1990). Blackside, Inc., like *Black Journal*, trained important filmmakers, including Orlando Bagwell, Carroll Parrot Blue, Louis Massiah, and Sam Pollard. Blackside has also created successful documentary series on African-American science, poverty, and faith.

REINVENTING AFRICAN-AMERICAN DOCUMENTARY

Changes in society and technology from the 1980s to the present have been reflected in documentaries. Video has made documentary filmmaking more affordable. In the last several decades successes in Black independent film, combined with increased access to university film training, have inspired hundreds of African-American documentaries.

While African-American women and gay filmmakers have always made documentaries, in recent years their numbers and visibility have grown, as have the number of films addressing gender and sexuality. Black artists of all backgrounds are making increasing numbers of personal, essay, and experimental films.

Inspired by Black feminist discourses, African-American women filmmakers created a movement within a movement, documenting black women's lives through innovative combinations of history, poetry, and performance. In the 1970s and early 1980s Camille Billops, Cheryl Fabio Bradford, Ayoka Chenzira, Julie Dash, Zeinabu Irene Davis, Alile Sharon Larkin, Barbara McCullough, O. Funmilayo Makarah, Michelle Parkerson, Debra J. Robinson, Kathe Sandler, and Sandra Sharp were among the first documentary filmmakers to explicitly address the experiences of Black women.

This wave of Black women's documentaries continues to inspire filmmakers of both genders. *Suzanne, Suzanne*

(1982) by Billops and James Hatch initiated a focus on personal family politics. Chenzira's *Hairpiece: A Film for Nappy Headed People* (1984) made her the first African-American woman animator, Parkerson's films popularized biographies of Black women artists, and Dash applied her documentary training to narrative film, becoming the most successful Black woman independent filmmaker in the world.

In the 1980s and early 1990s, award-winning documentaries like Marlon Riggs's *Tongues Untied* (1989) and Isaac Julien's *Looking for Langston* (1989) candidly explored the complexity of Black gay identities, a theme also engaged by the films of Cheryl Dunye, Shari Frilot, Donna Golden, Thomas Allen Harris, and Cyrille Phipps.

William Greaves's *Symbiopsychotaxiplasm* (1968) was one of the first experimental documentaries in film history, and beginning in the 1980s numerous Black documentaries regularly employed experimental elements. As of the early twenty-first century, hundreds of black experimental film and digital projects were reinventing the style, structure, and content of documentary filmmaking. Documentaries by Isaac Julien, John Akumphrah, and other members of the British Sankofa and Black Audio Film Collective documented African-American subjects and were expanding African Diaspora documentary film.

The late twentieth- and early twenty-first century witnessed the emergence of documentaries about hip-hop culture, including numerous profiles of Tupac Shakur. Several hip-hop documentaries, such as Lauren Lazin's Oscar-nominated *Tupac: Resurrection* (2003), have enjoyed theatrical releases, which few documentaries receive, and high domestic and international DVD/Video sales to become some of the most successful documentaries ever made.

During this period, cable television networks began to create new distribution avenues for documentaries. However, PBS networks remain the most committed distributors of African-American documentary films. Documentary has always informed the style and content of African-American fiction films, contributing to what Valerie Smith calls the "documentary impulse" in urban cinema (1998). In fact, the narrative film and television careers of important contemporary filmmakers began in the 1970s documentary film movement. In addition to artists already mentioned, these include Gil Noble, Haile Gerima, Warrington Hudlin, Carol Munday Lawrence, Monica J. Freeman, Philip Mallory Jones, Stan Lathan, William Miles, and others. In recent years, successful African-American fiction filmmakers, like Charles Burnett (*Nat Turner: A Troublesome Property*, 2003) and Spike Lee (*Four Little Girls*, 1997), have reversed this process by

making documentaries, further revealing the dynamic relationship between African-American fiction and nonfiction film art.

U.S. president Woodrow Wilson famously described the racist classic *Birth of a Nation* (1914) as "history writ with lightening." However, it is the work of African-American documentary filmmakers that truly deserve this description for bringing America's complex racial and cultural heritage to cinematic life. For more than a century, the creative activists of documentary film have merged art, history, and politics, and they continue to march for freedom with cameras in their hands.

See also Film in Latin America and the Caribbean; Film in the United States; Film in the United States, Contemporary; Filmmakers in the Caribbean; Filmmakers, Los Angeles School of; Urban Cinema

▪ ▪ *Bibliography*

Bobo, Jacqueline, ed. *Black Women Film and Video Artists.* New York: Routledge, 1998.

Bogle, Donald. *Toms, Coons, Mulattoes, Mammies & Bucks: An Interpretive History of Blacks in American Films*, 4th Edition. New York: Continuum International Publishing Group, 2001.

Bowser, Pearl. "Pioneers of Black Documentary Film." In *Struggles for Representation: African American Documentary Film and Video*, edited by Phyllis R. Klotman and Janet K. Cutler. Bloomington: Indiana University Press, 1999.

Bowser, Pearl, Jane Gaines, and Charles Musser, eds. *Oscar Micheaux and His Circle: African-American Filmmaking and Race Cinema of the Silent Era.* Bloomington: Indiana University Press, 2001.

Cham, Mbye B. and Claire Andrade-Watkins, eds. *Blackframes: Critical Perspectives on Black Independent Cinema.* Cambridge, MA: MIT Press, 1988.

Cripps, Thomas. *Making Movies Black: The Hollywood Message Movie From World War II to the Civil Rights Era.* New York: Oxford University Press, 1993.

Fusco, Coco, ed. *Young, British and Black: The Work of Sankofa and Black Audio Film Collective.* Buffalo, N.Y.: Hallwalls/Contemporary Arts Center, 1988.

Klotman, Phyllis R. and Janet K. Cutler, eds. *Struggles for Representation: African American Documentary Film and Video.* Bloomington: Indiana University Press, 1999.

PBS African American World. "Reference Room: Books and Films." Available from <http://www.pbs.org/wnet/aaworld/reference/books.html>.

Rony, Fatimah Tobing. *The Third Eye: Race, Cinema and Ethnographic Spectacle.* Durham, NC: Duke University Press, 1996.

Smith, Valerie, ed. *Representing Blackness: Issues in Film and Video.* New Brunswick, N.J: Rutgers University Press, 1997.

Smith, Valerie. "The Documentary Impulse in U.S. African American Film." In *Black Popular Culture*, Gina Dent, editor. New York: The New Press, 1998.

Taylor, Clyde. "Paths of Enlightenment: Heroes, Rebels and Thinkers." In *Struggles for Representation: African American Documentary Film and Video*, editors Phyllis R. Klotman and Janet K. Cutler. Bloomington: Indiana University Press, 1999.

Willis, Deborah. *Reflections in Black: A History of Black Photographers, 1840 to the Present*. New York: W. W. Norton & Company, 2000.

DIONNE BENNETT (2005)

DODGE REVOLUTIONARY UNION MOVEMENTS

See League of Revolutionary Black Workers

DODSON, OWEN

NOVEMBER 28, 1914
JUNE 2, 1983

■┼■

Born in Brooklyn, New York, Owen Vincent Dodson, an educator and writer, received his B.A. from Bates College in Lewiston, Maine, in 1936 and an M.F.A. from Yale University in 1939. He began his career in education as drama director at Spelman College, where he worked from 1938 until 1941. In this early phase of his career he also served as an instructor and director of drama at Atlanta University (1938–1942) and at the Hampton Institute in Virginia (1941–1942). His teaching career was briefly interrupted by his enlistment in the navy (1942–1943). In 1947 Dodson joined the faculty at Howard University. In 1949 he led the Howard University Players on what was both the first State Department–sponsored European tour by a black theater company and the first European tour of any American college theater group; their success influenced Congress to establish a nationally funded cultural exchange program. Dodson directed, produced, and taught drama at Howard for the next twenty-three years, eventually becoming chair of its drama department (1960–1969). He also lectured at Vassar and Kenyon Colleges and at Cornell University and served as poet-in-residence at the University of Arizona from 1969 to 1970. After his retirement, he returned to New York City, where he died of a heart attack at age sixty-eight.

Dodson was a versatile and prolific writer whose works reflect his acute concern for the problems of racism and injustice while at the same time evincing a belief in the basic goodness of humanity and in the redemptive power of love. His poetry, in which he characteristically adapts traditional European forms such as the sonnet to the rhythms of black street language, was published in three volumes: *Powerful Long Ladder* (1946), *The Confession Stone* (1968; revised as *The Confession Stone: Song Cycles*, 1970) and *The Harlem Book of the Dead* (1978, with James VanDerZee and Camille Billops). He contributed verse, short stories, and nonfiction to numerous anthologies and periodicals. He also wrote novels, including the semi-autobiographical *Boy at the Window* (1951; published in paperback as *When Trees Were Green*, 1967) and its sequel, *Come Home Early, Child* (1977). Together with composer Mark Fax he wrote two operas, *A Christmas Miracle* (1955) and *Till Victory Is Won* (1967).

Dodson also wrote many plays, including the popular *Divine Comedy* (1938), a portrait of religious chicanery first produced at Yale University, and *New World A-Coming: An Original Pageant of Hope* (1944), a work celebrating the black American contribution to the war effort, first produced at Madison Square Garden. His other plays include *The Shining Town* (1937), *The Garden of Time* (1939), *Bayou Legend* (1946), and *The Third Fourth of July* (1946, with Countee Cullen).

Dodson's work brought him a number of awards, including a General Education Board fellowship (1937), a Rosenwald fellowship (1945), a Guggenheim fellowship (1953), a *Paris Review* prize for his short story "The Summer Fire" (1956), an honorary doctorate from Bates College (1967), and a Rockefeller Foundation fellowship (1968).

See also Education in the United States; Poetry, U.S.

■■ *Bibliography*

Hatch, James V. *Sorrow is the Only Faithful One: The Life of Owen Dodson*. Urbana: University of Illinois Press, 1993.

Hatch, James V., Douglas A. M. Ward, and Joe Weixlmann. "The Rungs of a Powerful Long Ladder: An Owen Dodson Bibliography." *Black American Literature Forum* 14 (1980): 60–68.

Metzger, Linda, ed. *Black Writers: A Selection of Sketches from Contemporary Authors*. Detroit, Mich.: Gale, 1989.

ALEXIS WALKER (1996)

DOMESTIC WORKERS

■┼■

Domestic workers (also called domestic servants and household workers) are those who are paid to perform personal or domestic service within households other than their own. In the Americas, wherever there have been significant numbers of Africans or persons of African descent, some of them have been involved in and associated with domestic work; and where there have been blacks performing domestic work, these have primarily been black female domestic workers, "doing the dirty work." However, the paid domestic work performed by black female workers has its antecedents in the slavery that so marked and shaped the black experience in the Americas. The links between "domestic slavery" and "domestic work" for black female workers are as strong as they are poignant.

Without a doubt, in most slave societies, the focus of the slaveholders was on productivity and economic gain; enslaved African labor was deployed with those twinned goals, and their commensurate benefits, in mind. However, enslaved Africans and their descendants were also used to provide personal service for those who had invested in their bodies: these were the domestic slaves. In the areas of the region where the enslaved black populations were large (the Caribbean, Brazil, the southern United States), there were slaves who functioned almost exclusively as domestic workers, constituting between five and fifteen percent of the enslaved population. In places where the enslaved black populations were smaller or where slaveholders owned five or fewer slaves (e.g., in New England or British North America), the domestic slaves also performed heavy agricultural work. In those places where enslaved Africans were few, and where they were a minority among aboriginal slaves (e.g., New France), they spent most of their lives performing domestic service. Yet like their counterparts elsewhere, they were constant symbols of the slaveholders' prosperity and power.

Enslaved persons who were chosen to perform domestic labor were sometimes selected because of their perceived affinity for and skill in providing the sort of personal service that was required. But sometimes the choice of a domestic worker was made on the grounds of race and color: there was an abiding belief that enslaved persons who were of lighter complexion were less able to withstand the rigors of agricultural labor, so they were "saved" by domestic work. What was at issue with the cadre of lighter colored slaves (mulattos or "coloreds" in the Caribbean) was that they were part white and, by virtue of that, believed to be more delicate. In truth, very often they were the children of the slaveholders or their white employees. The "colored domestic slaves" then, represented many aspects of the slave societies where they were forced to work, and they often operated as a buffer group between the masses of enslaved blacks and the white slaveholding class.

They both resulted from and represented the (often violent) sexual contact between the races (even where that contact was illicit). Their circumstances were, indeed, curious; they performed domestic work for households that were sometimes headed by their biological fathers, who owned them.

During the nineteenth century, as slavery was slowly abolished across the hemisphere, the transition from forced labor to paid domestic work did not mean an end to the association between the formerly oppressed state of slaves and the personal service that domestic workers were hired to perform after slavery. In societies where social and economic categorizations ran along the same fault lines as did racial groupings, many domestic workers were triply disadvantaged: they were poor, they were almost always black, and the vast majority of them (more than 90%) were women.

Whether during the period of slavery or for many decades after its end, the tasks that black female domestic workers had to perform were not easy: often food preparation was over an open flame (with numerous reports of injury), laundry was done by hand in water that the worker had to fetch, the house was cleaned with cloths and rags (often on hands and knees), and child care consisted of an ongoing series of demands. All of these tasks were carried out according to the demands and standards of employers who watched, "supervised," and criticized every small detail. The symbolic and real relations of exploitation and subordination were clear.

In many ways, the domestic-service sector ran counter to the developments that were taking place in many other occupations; by its location, poor remuneration, conditions of work, and labor relations, domestic service seemed decidedly precapitalist. While other types of employment were affected by the increasingly applied template of "modernity," which separated workers from workplaces that were also households, domestic workers continued to labor in the home.

The remuneration that domestic workers commanded was very often among the lowest among workers. Part of the challenge that domestic workers faced was the fundamental categorization of their work as not productive—their labors were often excluded from national account statistics, and in some circumstances they were labeled as earners and consumers, but not as producers. Their situation was further complicated by the variety of wages that many domestic workers received—cash wages, cash in kind (e.g., food, housing, clothing), and often combinations of these types of wages. Where the cash nexus characterized other working experiences as "modern," this haphazard way of paying domestic workers not only indicated remnants of precapitalist labor conditions, but it marked those who received (often discarded) goods as payment as dependents whose circumstances had not greatly improved over those of their foremothers.

The conditions of work that many black female domestic workers experienced were determined by their geographical locations, the positions that they were employed to fill, and whether they were "live-in" or "live-out" servants. Workers who operated in urban areas were sometimes relieved of some of the harsher aspects of rural domestic work (e.g., fetching water, procuring firewood) because many urban employers enjoyed higher material standards than their rural counterparts. The positions that domestic workers filled helped to determine exactly what was involved in their daily tasks. However, few domestic workers were treated as skilled workers; the majority tended to be drawn from a large labor force, expendable and invisible.

It is in the area of labor relations—that curious employer-employee connection—that the precapitalist nature of domestic work was most apparent. In some societies in the Americas, that relationship was defined by long histories of paternalism, prescribed by law and custom, that gave the "master" control over all who were in his house. Thus, while the laws might have changed, the attitudes remained long in place. Since these societies were affected by the ideologies of race and hierarchy, the emphasis on difference and the expectations of deference made the circumstances of black female domestic workers exceedingly complex. Where both employer and employee were black or colored, they used other means, such as uniforms, to differentiate and separate themselves.

In the attempt to control the activities and actors within their households, many employers sought to recruit young, unattached female domestic workers, whom they thought would be most easily controlled. They attempted to determine how their employees should live (where they should go, what they should do, who they should spend time with) because, for many employers, domestic workers gave "dignity" to their households, and since the workers represented those households, their behavior needed to be controlled. In response to these attempts, some domestic workers accepted the proscriptions, while many others resisted them by the only means they could—they left their jobs.

Domestic workers were often in the vanguard of the movement out of the depressed social and economic circumstances that so many black persons in the Americas continued to experience. In their attempts to better their circumstances, many migrated from rural areas into urban centers. During the Great Migration of the early 1900s,

thousands of blacks in the United states migrated from the rural south to the cities of the north. However, this movement did not necessarily alleviate the unemployment and underemployment that blacks were trying to address. Some workers even crossed international borders in search of better circumstances. Within the Caribbean, some women migrated to territories (for example to Aruba) that were able to offer jobs and levels of remuneration not available in their own countries. Having left their families behind to labor in isolation, these women found that they were no more "at home" in their places of employment, even after decades of work.

Since the twentieth century, by various schemes and means, there has been a steady flow of black women out of the Caribbean and into North America to perform domestic work. Some of them have arrived on government-supported schemes (e.g., to Canada), after extensive screening to make sure that they are the "right type" to provide personal service, and many arrive on their own auspices. Even more recently, some of the women willing to take these jobs, which closely define their status in the country, were not domestic workers in their home countries, but were professionals who are now willing to work as servants in order to leave economic and personal difficulties behind. The situation is similar among those who go to the United States, for even as many African-American women move out of domestic work, their place is taken by a silent army of "undocumented" black female domestic workers from the Caribbean. Having made the decision to migrate, many of these former professionals find that the remuneration and conditions of work leave them barely able to survive.

Still largely relegated to the bottom of hierarchies constructed along lines of class, race, or gender, black female domestic workers are increasingly organized. They continue to struggle for the reward and respect that their hard work, unacknowledged and often unrecorded, ought to provide.

See also Economic Condition, U.S.; Labor and Labor Unions

■ ■ *Bibliography*

Aymer, Paula L. *Uprooted Women: Migrant Domestics in the Caribbean.* Westport, Conn., London: Praeger, 1997.

Anderson, Bridget. *Doing the Dirty Work: The Global Politics of Domestic Labour.* London, New York: Zed Books, 2000.

Bakan, Abigail B. and Daiva Stasiulis. *Not One of the Family: Foreign Domestic Workers in Canada.* Toronto: University of Toronto Press, 1997.

Bunster, Ximena and Elsa M. Chaney. *Sellers and Servants: Working Women in Lima, Peru.* New York: Praeger, 1985.

Chaney, Elsa M. and Mary Garcia Castro, eds. *Muchachas No More: Household Workers in Latin America and the Caribbean.* Philadelphia: Temple University Press, 1987.

Chang, Grace. *Disposable Domestics: Immigrant Women Workers in the Global Economy.* Cambridge, Mass.: South End Press, 2000.

Clark-Lewis, Elizabeth. *Living In, Living Out: African American Domestics in Washington, D.C., 1910–1940.* Washington, D.C.: Smithsonian Institution Press, 1994.

Dudden, Faye E. *Serving Women: Household Service in Nineteenth-Century America.* Middletown, Conn.: Wesleyan University Press, 1983.

Gray, Brenda Clegg. *Black Female Domestics during the Depression in New York City, 1930–1940.* New York: Garland, 1993.

Katzman, David. *Seven Days a Week: Women and Domestic Service in Industrializing America.* New York: Oxford University Press, 1978.

Rollins, Judith. *Between Women: Domestics and Their Employers.* Philadelphia: Temple University Press, 1985.

Romero, Mary. *Maid in the U.S.A.* New York, London: Routledge, 1992.

Silvera, Makeda. *Silenced: Talks with Working Class Caribbean Women about Their Lives and Struggles as Domestic Workers in Canada.* Toronto: Sister Vision, 1989.

Sutherland, Daniel E. *Americans and Their Servants: Domestic Service in the United States from 1800 to 1920.* Baton Rouge: Louisiana State University Press, 1981.

Tucker, Susan. *Telling Memories among Southern Women Domestic Workers and Their Employers in the Segregated South.* Baton Rouge: Louisiana State University Press, 1988.

MICHELE A. JOHNSON (2005)

DOMINGO, W. A.

1889
FEBRUARY 14, 1968

▉▮▉

Born in Kingston, Jamaica, editor and activist Wilfred Adolphus Domingo was the youngest son of a Jamaican mother and a Spanish father. He was orphaned soon after birth, and he and his siblings were raised by their maternal uncle. Domingo attended Kingston Board School, then took a job as a tailor in Kingston. He wrote newspaper articles and joined the National Club in lobbying for home rule for Jamaica, becoming the club's second assistant secretary. There Domingo met and became close with the first assistant secretary, Marcus Garvey. In 1912 Domingo came to the United States, settling in Boston, where he intended to enroll in medical school. In 1913 he left Boston and moved to New York, where he began working for Ja-

maican freedom. In 1917 he formed the British Jamaican Benevolent Association, and he became associated with the Socialist Party shortly thereafter.

In 1918 Garvey asked Domingo, who had been peripherally involved in the activities of Garvey's Universal Negro Improvement Association (UNIA), to find him a publisher for a UNIA newspaper. Domingo obliged and wrote two lead editorials for the first issue of the new *Negro World.* Soon after, Garvey hired him as editor of the journal. Domingo was not passionate about Garvey's back-to-Africa ideology, although he later claimed to have invented the newspaper's tag line, "Africa's Redemption." Instead, he turned the paper into a forum for a discussion of socialist ideas. Domingo warned white labor leaders to unite with black workers or become a tool of strikebreaking capitalists. In the summer of 1919 Garvey, displeased, charged Domingo before the UNIA Executive Committee with writing editorials that diverged from the group's program. Domingo resigned and soon became a bitter critic of Garvey. He began a short-lived socialist paper, the *Emancipator.* After it failed he began working for A. Philip Randolph's black socialist newspaper, the *Messenger.* In 1923 Domingo broke with Randolph, whom he accused of anti–West Indian prejudice. He joined Cyril Briggs's newspaper, the *Crusader,* and became active in the African Blood Brotherhood.

After 1923 Domingo returned to Jamaica, where he spent several years working as a food importer. In later years he became active in the Jamaican independence movement, helping to found the Jamaica Progressive League in 1936 and later joining the People's National Party (PNP). He spent the early 1940s in Jamaica, then returned to New York, where he became an enemy of the PNP. Domingo suffered a paralyzing stroke in 1964 and died four years later.

See also Garvey, Marcus; *Messenger, The*; *Negro World*, People's National Party; Political Ideologies; Universal Negro Improvement Association

■ ■ *Bibliography*

Hill, Robert A., ed. *The Marcus Garvey and Universal Negro Improvement Association Papers,* vol. 1, appendix I. Berkeley: University of California Press, 1983.

GREG ROBINSON (1996)

DOM OBÁ II D'ÁFRICA

c. 1845

July 8, 1890

❚❚❚

The popular Afro-Brazilian leader Dom Obá II D'África was born Cândido da Fonseca Galvão, in Lençóis, in the interior of the then province of Bahia. Dom Obá was the son of a freed African slave. He was also an African prince, thought to be the grandson of Aláàfin Abiodun, the founder of the Yoruba Empire.

A warrior prince, Dom Obá was a volunteer with the Brazilian forces in the Paraguayan War (1865–1870). In recognition of his bravery, he was made an honorary officer in the army. After being demobilized, Dom Obá settled in Rio de Janeiro, the Brazilian capital, where he fought for the rights of the poor and for the abolition of slavery.

To the white elite, Dom Obá was considered a "half-crazed" figure whom the Brazilian emperor, Dom Pedro II, was misguided enough to receive at the palace. To Rio's slaves and people of color, however, he was revered as a true African sovereign. His followers paid him a tithe, they would fall to their knees before him, and they gathered in public places to listen to his articles, which were published in the popular press, being read aloud.

Having an alternative view of the Brazilian society and its historical process, Dom Obá was, at least in theory, a monarchist standing above all political parties. He was, in his own words, "a conservative to conserve what is good," as well as "a liberal to repress the murders that have taken place in the current time on the orders of certain potentates" (Dom Obá II D'África, 1885, p. 5).

The struggle against racism was a crucial element in the thought and political practice of Dom Obá. He believed that "it is right that Brazil should give up the question of colour, because the real question is value and when a man has value one should not look at what colour he is" (Dom Obá II D'África, 1887, p. 4). In his articles, the prince spoke on behalf of "the Blacks and Pardos" (people of mixed race). He also came out with apparently original formulations, arriving at an aesthetic perception remarkably similar to the "black is beautiful" approach developed in the United States in the 1960s. Dom Obá encouraged his followers to feel that black was not only beautiful, but "superior to the finest diamonds."

See also Yoruba Religion and Culture in the Americas

■ ■ *Bibliography*

Dom Obá II D'África, "As vivas razões da constituição da lei que nos rege e nos faz respeitá-la." *Jornal Do Commercio* (February 1885): 5.

Dom Obá II D'África, "Ao universo imploro a suplicada saudação"(II). *O Carbonário*, (May 30, 1887): 4.

Moraes Filho, Mello. *Quadros e Crônicas.* Rio de Janeiro, Brazil: Garnier Livreiro-Editor.

Silva, Eduardo. *Prince of the People: The Life and Times of a Brazilian Free Man of Colour.* London: Verso, 1993.

EDUARDO SILVA (2005)

DORSEY, THOMAS A.

July 1, 1899

January 23,1993

❚❚❚

Born in Villa Rica, Georgia, the oldest of three children of Rev. Thomas Madison and Etta Plant Dorsey, gospel composer Thomas Andrew Dorsey obtained his education in the public schools of Villa Rica and Atlanta. His first piano teacher was his mother, from whom he learned enough by age eight to play the pump organ for church services at which his father preached. In his early teens he began piano lessons, four times weekly, with a Mrs. Graves, from whom he learned not only piano technique and musical reading but enough music theory to be able to jot down musical ideas he was already creating. He was encouraged in this aspect of musicianship by the band members who accompanied acts at the 81 Theater, a vaudeville house on Atlanta's Decatur Street, where, since age eleven, he had worked selling soda pop. It was in this capacity that, at age thirteen, he met the legendary Ma Rainey. Other performers he met who were to influence him were pianists Eddie Heywood and Ed Butler, and the comedy team Butterbeans and Susie. Shortly thereafter, Dorsey began playing the house-party circuit in Atlanta.

Desiring a better musical education, Dorsey migrated to Gary, Indiana, in 1916, where he worked in a steel mill and played piano in various jazz bands. After returning to Atlanta for the winters of 1917 and 1918, he settled permanently in Chicago in 1919, where he studied for a short while at the Chicago Musical College. From 1923 until 1924 he served as pianist and arranger for Les Hite's Whispering Serenaders. During this time he composed "Riverside Blues" (1923), recorded by King Oliver's Creole Jazz Band. Around 1924 Dorsey organized his own group, the Wildcats Jazz Band, at the request of J. Mayo ("Ink") Williams of Paramount Records. This group accompanied Ma Rainey on recordings and on tour. While he accompanied

Rainey irregularly for a number of years, Dorsey also began a successful association with Tampa Red (born Hudson Whittaker) in 1925. This duo produced the 1928 hit "Tight Like That." It was during this time that Dorsey became known as "Georgia Tom" and "Barrelhouse Tom" because of the raunchy nature of the songs he played.

Although he continued to play in and conduct jazz and blues bands throughout the 1920s, Dorsey's interest was steadily growing toward the new gospel music created by the southern Pentecostal churches and a prominent form of music in Chicago at this time.

Dorsey then wrote his first gospel song, "If I Don't Get There," which was published in the National Baptist Convention's *Gospel Pearls*. Despite this new conviction, Dorsey returned to the blues world until 1928, when he suffered a nervous breakdown. His second conversion to Christianity—he had been converted as a child in Georgia but in the terminology of the African-American church of the era "backslid" when he began to play secular music—occurred in Chicago, at the 1932 annual meeting of the National Baptist Convention, the largest organization of African-American Christians. During the convention, Rev. A. W. Nix of Birmingham, Alabama, delivered a stirring gospel rendition of Edwin O. Excell's "I Do, Don't You?" Not only did Dorsey join the church again, but he decided that he wanted to dedicate his life to writing gospel music.

In 1930 Dorsey renounced secular music and became a full-time gospel musician, composing gospel pieces and peddling "song sheets" throughout Chicago. The response was discouraging and he was often the butt of jokes. Notwithstanding these initial rejections, Dorsey organized one of the first gospel choirs at Chicago's Pilgrim Baptist Church in 1931, where his accompanist was the young Roberta Martin and whose future members included Eugene Smith, leader of the Roberta Martin Singers, and James Cleveland, later known as the "Crown Prince of Gospel." The next year Dorsey opened the first publishing house for the exclusive sale of gospel music by African-American composers in the country. The same year, along with Sallie Martin and others, he organized the National Convention of Gospel Choirs and Choruses, which, along with Cleveland's Gospel Music Workshop of America (organized in 1968), annually draws the largest number of gospel musicians and music lovers in the United States. In addition to Martin, Dorsey was aided in the early gospel movement by composers Theodore R. Frye and Kenneth Morris and singer Willie Mae Ford Smith. In 1932 Dorsey and Frye traveled from Chicago to Indianapolis to organize a gospel choir. When Dorsey arrived in Indianapolis, a telegram informed him that his wife had given birth to a child but had

not survived. Dorsey returned to Chicago, only to find that his newly born daughter had died as well. In his grief, he sat alone in a dark room for three days, emerging to write the song that—after "Amazing Grace"—is the second most popular song in African-American Christendom, "Precious Lord, take my hand, lead me on, let me stand. / I'm tired, I'm weak, I am worn, through the storm, through the night / Lead me on to the light, take my hand, precious Lord, lead me home."

Dorsey taught this song to his choir at Pilgrim Baptist, and in less than a year it had moved into the folk category, with congregations singing all three stanzas without the benefit of sheet music. Since then, it has been translated into more than fifty languages, and Dorsey conducted it throughout the world.

"Precious Lord" is not unlike most of Dorsey's compositions, in that the text is that of the poor, disfranchised African-American Christian but also speaks to all people. He had a special penchant for imbuing his songs with catchy phrases, such as "I'm Going to Live the Life I Sing About in My Song," "If We Ever Needed the Lord Before, We Sure Do Need Him Now," and the song written for Mahalia Jackson, who served as his song demonstrator from 1935 to 1946, "There Will Be Peace in the Valley for Me." His melodies were simple, supported by harmonies that did not detract from the text. Dorsey was so instrumental in the development of gospel music that there was a period during the 1930s and 1940s when gospel songs were referred to as "Dorseys." For his contributions he was early on dubbed the "Father of Gospel."

Although only a few of Dorsey's songs helped to initiate new trends in gospel music, he is nevertheless remembered as the most important person in gospel music to date. He organized gospel music's first chorus and its first annual national convention, founded its first publishing house, established the gospel-music concert tradition, and in recognition of this, he was celebrated in the 1982 documentary *Say Amen, Somebody*.

See also Gospel Music; Jazz

▪ *Bibliography*

Boyer, Horace Clarence. "Analysis of His Contributions: Thomas A. Dorsey, 'Father of Gospel Music.'" *Black World* 23 (1974): 20.

Harris, Michael W. *The Rise of Gospel Blues: The Music of Thomas Andrew Dorsey in the Urban Church.* New York: Oxford University Press, 1992.

Heilbut, Anthony. *The Gospel Sound: Good News and Bad Times.* New York: Simon and Schuster, 1971. Reprint, New

York: Limelight Editions, distributed by Harper & Row, 1985.

HORACE CLARENCE BOYER (1996)
Updated bibliography

DOS PRAZERES, HEITOR

SEPTEMBER 23, 1898
OCTOBER 4, 1966

Eduardo Alexandre dos Prazeres, a clarinetist in the Brazilian National Guard Band, had enormous pride in his origins. He saw heroic resistance in the stories of slaves who fought to liberate and affirm their African roots. His own name—Prazeres (Pleasures)—represented to him the ability to find light and joy even in the darkest situations. This pride turned into enormous satisfaction on the day his son, Heitor dos Prazeres, was born. Heitor would carry the family name and his father's pride into the twentieth century. (Famous Brazilians are often referred to by their first name or by a nickname.)

One day in 1908, Heitor left his house in Rio de Janeiro early. He had a can of shoe polish and a leather rag slung over his shoulder, and he carried a *cavaquinho* (a four-stringed instrument, resembling a ukelele) in his other hand. The instrument was a present from the famous musician and close family friend "Uncle" Hilário Jovino (also known by his nickname, Lalau de Ouro), one of the founders of Rio de Janeiro's *ranchos* (carnival groups from the late nineteenth and early twentieth centuries). The instrument would become his constant companion and faithful partner in creations like the *chorinho* "Cadenciado"—his first composition, written when he was twelve years old—and it helped him gain the nickname "Lino do Cavaquinho." (The *chorinho* was a popular musical genre at the turn of the century, played with string and wind instruments and marked by improvisation and rapid and changing melodies.)

In addition to his work polishing shoes, Heitor worked as a newspaper boy, a carpenter's assistant, and a furniture polisher. But he continued to work on his music, and by 1910 he was participating in the gatherings at Tia Ciata's house, where participants cultivated African-Brazilian religious practices and musical rhythms like *candomblé*, *jongo*, *lundu*, *cateretê*, and *samba*. Among the stars that participated in those gatherings were Lalau de Ouro, José Luiz de Moraes (a.k.a., Caninha), João Machado Guedes (João da Baiana), José Barbosa da Silva (Sinhô), Getúlio Marinho (Amor), Ernesto Joaquim Maria dos Santos (Donga), Saturnino Gonçalves (Satur), and Alfredo da Rocha Viana (Pixinguinha), each of whom became icons of Brazilian popular music.

The development of these sounds took place in the area that Heitor is popularly credited for naming "Little Africa," which extended from the city's ports to the Cidade Nova neighborhood, with its geographical heart at the famous plaza Praça Onze. It was in Little Africa where Heitor spent countless hours, became a respected *samba* musician, and helped found the first *samba* schools (carnival groups that succeeded the *ranchos* and gained limited government patronage beginning in the 1930s.)

Heitor's complete oeuvre includes more than three hundred compositions ranging from sacred (Candomblé, Umbanda, and Christian hymns) to popular (waltzes, *choros*, *sambas*, *canções*, marches, *rancheiras*, *baiões*, *rumbas*, and *mambos*). Of these works, 219 were recorded, the most important of which are "Pierrô Apaixonado," "Lá em Mangueira," "Gosto que me Enrosco," "Mulher de Malandro," "Vou ver se Posso," "A Tristeza me Persegue," "Canção do Jornaleiro," "Olinda," "Carioca Boêmio," and "Consideração."

After the death of his wife in 1937, Heitor began to dedicate himself to painting. He taught himself his new trade, and his initial objective was simply to decorate the walls of his house and illustrate sheet music. His artistic production through 1940 was dominated by depictions of rustic, rural scenes of nineteenth-century Rio de Janeiro, images he transferred to the canvas by relying on little more than his intuition.

In 1943, at the urging of his friend Augusto Rodrigues, he participated in an exposition organized by the Royal Air Force to benefit victims of the Second World War. In the following years, he took part in various expositions, both in Brazil and abroad. In 1951 he was honored at the First Bienal in São Paulo, winning third place among national artists with *Moenda*, a painting inspired by the daily life of sugar planters. Today, the work hangs in São Paulo's Museum of Contemporary Art.

The mark of Heitor's self-taught work rests in its uninhibited artistic creativity. Like other naïf artists, he portrayed an intensely personal vision of the world, replete with color and marked by careful but unique brush strokes. In Brazil, the art naïf movement gained momentum after 1937, in large part due to the work of Heitor and Cardosinho, both of whom were also inspired by contemporary European artists.

In 1950 the writer Rubem Braga said about Heitor, "His paintings are flowers which bloom from his music and his life" (Braga, p. 14). In 1961, a *Time* magazine contributor wrote, "A modest, quiet, and unassuming man,

Heitor dos Prazeres is, as we are seeing, a name which deserves respect and attention. The victories he has won in music and in painting are the result of his own hard work."

See also Art; Candomblé; Jongo; Music; Samba; Tia Ciata

■ ■ *Bibliography*

Braga, Rubem. *Três Primitivos*. Rio de Janeiro: Ministério da Educação/Serviço de Documentação, série Os Cadernos de Cultura n§ 63, 1953.

"Heitor dos Prazeres." *Time* (Portuguese-language supplement; December 10, 1961).

Prazeres Filho, Heitor dos, and Alba Lírio. *Heitor dos Prazeres: sua Arte e seu Tempo*. Rio de Janeiro: ND Comunicação, 2003.

WALTER PINTO (2005)
HEITORZINHO DOS PRAZERES (2005)
Translated by Marc Adam Hertzman

DOS SANTOS, JOÃO FRANCISCO

See Madame Satã (dos Santos, João Francisco)

DOUGLAS, AARON

MAY 26, 1899
FEBRUARY 24, 1979

Born in Topeka, Kansas, Aaron Douglas, a painter and educator, graduated from Topeka High School in 1917, then earned his B.F.A. from the University of Nebraska in 1922. While he taught art at Lincoln High School in Kansas City, Missouri (1923–1925), his social circle included future civil rights leader Roy Wilkins, future classical music composer William Levi Dawson, and Ethel Ray (Nance), who became Charles S. Johnson's assistant at *Opportunity* magazine. Ray and Johnson persuaded Douglas to postpone study in France to work in New York. Douglas soon became one of the leading artists of the New Negro movement, developing a geometric, monochromatic style of depicting African Americans in dynamic silhouettes by synthesizing formal and symbolic elements of West African sculpture with European-American traditions and modern design into a hard-edged, art deco–like style.

In 1925 Douglas earned three important distinctions that launched his career—first prize for a front cover illustration of *Opportunity*, first prize in drawing (for *The African Chieftain*) from *Crisis* magazine, and a commission to illustrate Alain Locke's anthology, *The New Negro*. The following year, Douglas married his high school classmate, educator Alta Sawyer, and illustrated *The Emperor Jones* and the short-lived magazine of African-American art and literature *Fire!!* In 1927 he illustrated *Plays of Negro Life*, edited by Locke and Montgomery Gregory, and *God's Trombones: Seven Sermons in Negro Verse* by James Weldon Johnson. Six works in the latter book, along with a portrait, were exhibited at the Harmon Foundation in 1928. Over the next decade, Douglas would illustrate books by Charles S. Johnson, Claude McKay, Paul Morand, and Andre Salmon, as well as numerous magazine covers.

In the late 1920s Douglas studied privately with Fritz Winold Reiss, a German-American artist whose modernist work Douglas had admired in the New Negro issue of *Survey Graphic* (edited by Locke in March 1925). Reiss and Locke encouraged Douglas to look to African art for inspiration and develop his own racially representative work. Through their influence Douglas received a one-year scholarship (1928–1929) to the Barnes Foundation in Merion, Pennsylvania, where he studied both African and modern European art.

In 1930 Douglas painted heroic murals of African-American culture and history in the library at Fisk University in Nashville, the Sherman Hotel in Chicago, and Bennett College in Greensboro, North Carolina. In 1931 he went to Paris for one year to study independently and with Charles Despiau and Othon Friesz at the Académie Scandinave. While Douglas worked diligently, only one piece from his time abroad is known: *Forge Foundry*, a black-and-white illustration published in the French journal *Revue du monde noir* (1931).

In the 1930s Douglas based himself in New York as an arts leader and muralist. The year after he was elected president of the Harlem Artists' Guild (1935), he addressed the First American Artists Congress. With sponsorship from New Deal art programs and various grants, Douglas completed several murals, most notably *Aspects of Negro Life*, at the 135th Street Harlem Branch of the New York Public Library (1934); those for the Hall of Negro Life exhibited at the Texas Centennial Exposition (1936); and *Education of the Colored Man*, at the Atlanta City Housing Project (1938). In 1938 Douglas received a travel fellowship to the American South and Haiti from the Julius Rosenwald Fund. He exhibited his paintings of Haitian life at the American Contemporary Art Gallery in New York the following year.

In 1939 Douglas began teaching art at Fisk University, where he served as professor and chair of the Department of Art Education for nearly three decades. During this period, he often divided his time between Nashville and New York, where he completed his M.A. in art education at Columbia University Teachers College in 1944 (his fraternal affiliations included Sigma Pi Phi and Kappa Alpha Psi) and received a Carnegie teaching grant in 1951. From the 1930s until the 1950s, the Douglases frequently entertained artists and writers at their home at 409 Edgecombe Avenue, known as "the White House of Harlem" because the building's residents included prominent intellectuals and civil rights leaders. Douglas painted many of their portraits, in addition to landscapes.

As founder of the Carl Van Vechten Gallery (1949) at Fisk, Douglas acquired a major gift from Georgia O'Keeffe, the Alfred Steiglitz Collection (1949), as well as an important series of portraits of African Americans, the Winold Reiss Collection (1952), and he brought numerous artists to the university for lectures and exhibitions. Noted for these achievements and his art, Douglas was honored by President John F. Kennedy at a White House reception commemorating the centennial of the Emancipation Proclamation in 1963. In 1972 he became a fellow of the Black Academy of Arts and received its outstanding achievement award. The following year, Fisk University awarded Douglas an honorary degree of Doctor of Fine Arts. After retiring as professor emeritus in 1966, Douglas lectured widely and continued to paint until his death in 1979.

Douglas's work has appeared in many major American museums and galleries and in university and community center exhibitions. Additional solo exhibitions were held at D'Caz-Delbo Gallery (1933); University of Nebraska, Lincoln (1941); People's Art Center, St. Louis (1947); Chabot Gallery, Los Angeles (1948); Riley Art Galleries, New York (1955); University of California, Berkeley (1964); and Mulvane Art Center, Topeka, Kansas (1970).

See also Art; *Crisis, The*; Johnson, Charles Spurgeon; Johnson, James Weldon; Locke, Alain Leroy; McKay, Claude; New Negro; *Opportunity: Journal of Negro Life*; Painting and Sculpture; Wilkins, Roy

■ ■ *Bibliography*

Driskell, David, David Levering Lewis, and Deborah Willis Ryan. *Harlem Renaissance: Art of Black America.* New York: Abrams, 1987.

Huggins, Nathan Irvin. *Harlem Renaissance.* New York: Oxford University Press, 1971.

Igoe, Lynn Moody, with James Igoe. *250 Years of Afro-American Art: An Annotated Bibliography.* New York and London: Bowker, 1981.

Kirschke, Amy Helene. *Aaron Douglas: Art, Race, and the Harlem Renaissance.* Jackson: University of Mississippi Press, 1995.

Lewis, David Levering. *When Harlem Was in Vogue.* New York: Penguin, 1979.

THERESA LEININGER-MILLER (1996)
LINDA NIEMAN (1996)

DOUGLASS, FREDERICK

FEBRUARY 1817?
FEBRUARY 20, 1895

Born Frederick Augustus Washington Bailey to Harriet Bailey, a slave, and an unacknowledged father (perhaps his master, Aaron Anthony) in Tuckahoe, Maryland, abolitionist, journalist, orator, and social reformer Frederick Douglass—he assumed this name in 1838 when he escaped north to freedom—soon became the most famous African American of the nineteenth century. Separated from his family while young, he was a personal slave to several whites during his formative years. Consequently, at an early age he learned self-reliance and began honing the arts of survival. At the same time, he found a sense of belonging through his relationships with various families and individuals, white and black, who liked and encouraged the bright and precocious youth. Ultimately, the lure of freedom and equality proved irresistible and propelled him on an extraordinary journey of both individual achievement and service to his people and his nation.

Taken in 1826 to Baltimore—where, as an urban slave, he could expand his horizons greatly—Douglass taught himself how to read and write with the witting and unwitting assistance of many around him. Similarly, this more open urban environment, with its large and expanding free African-American population, further whetted his desire to learn as much as possible about freedom, including runaway slaves and the abolitionist movement.

Around the age of thirteen, Douglass converted to Christianity, but over time he became increasingly disillusioned with a religious establishment that compromised with and supported evil and injustice, especially slavery and racial prejudice and discrimination. Also around that age, he purchased his first book, *The Columbian Orator*, which deepened not only his understanding of liberty and equality but also the enormous power of rhetoric, as well as literacy. Indeed, throughout his life he firmly believed in the power of the written and spoken word to capture and to change reality.

As a rapidly maturing eighteen-year-old developing spiritually and intellectually as well as physically, he revealed an intensifying longing to be free that led him to plan an unsuccessful runaway scheme with several fellow slaves. Several months previously he had fought and defeated Covey, the "Negro breaker"—one versed in subduing unruly slaves—another sign of the depth of that longing. He later portrayed his triumph over Covey as a turning point in his struggle to become a free man. With the aid of Anna Murray, a free African-American woman in Baltimore with whom he had fallen in love, he escaped to freedom. They moved to New Bedford, Massachusetts (1838); Lynn, Massachusetts (1841); Rochester, New York (1847); and Washington, D.C. (1872).

In the North Douglass found it very hard to make a living as a caulker because of racial discrimination, and he often had to resort to menial jobs. Anna worked hard as well, creating a comfortable domestic niche for a family that eventually included five children: Rosetta, Lewis Henry, Frederick Jr., Charles Remond, and Annie. Frederick's speeches within the local black communities brought him to the attention of the mostly white abolitionists allied with William Lloyd Garrison, and in 1841 they asked him to join them as a lecturer. An increasingly powerful lecturer and draw for the Garrisonian Massachusetts Anti-Slavery Society, Douglass learned a great deal from his work with such people as Garrison and Wendell Phillips. Most importantly, he adopted their pacifism and moral suasionist approach to ending slavery and was deeply influenced by their interrelated perfectionism and social reformism. As a good Garrisonian he argued for disunion and rejected the political approach to ending slavery as a compromise with a proslavery constitution.

Douglass also began to come into his own as an activist and a thinker. Drawing upon his experiences as a slave, he lambasted slavery and its notorious effects, most notably antiblack prejudice and discrimination in both North and South. As the living embodiment of a small measure of success in the enormous struggle against slavery, he spoke eloquently with uncommon authority. In 1845 his *Narrative of the Life of Frederick Douglass, an American Slave* was published, and its huge success, followed by a successful speaking tour of Great Britain, heightened his celebrity immeasurably. Ever conscious of his public persona and his historical image, he carefully crafted both. *My Bondage and My Freedom* (1855) and *Life and Times of Frederick Douglass* (1881; revised 1892), fuller autobiographies, were likewise crucial in this regard.

Douglass's stirring narrative and equally stirring oratory derived much of their power and authenticity from his deep-seated engagement with the plethora of issues confronting blacks north and south, free and slave. His strong involvement in the national Negro convention

A recruitment poster soliciting Black soldiers to fight for the Union army in the American Civil War. The poster features signatures including that of African American abolitionist Frederick Douglass, who urged President Abraham Lincoln to accept black troops in the Union Army, then recruited actively among blacks for men to support the union cause. HULTON ARCHIVE/GETTY IMAGES

movement, as well as with various state and local black conferences, furthered his impact and by 1850 made him the principal spokesman for his race. His fierce commitment to egalitarianism, freedom, and justice similarly led him to embrace the women's-rights movement, notably women's suffrage, and to become one of the most important male feminists of the nineteenth century. He attended the first Women's Rights Convention, in Seneca Falls, New York, in 1848; on the day of his death, February 20, 1895, he had earlier attended a meeting of the National Council of Women.

Shortly after his return from Great Britain in 1847, Douglass embarked upon a distinguished career in journalism. He edited the *North Star* (1847–1851), *Frederick Douglass' Paper* (1851–1860), *Douglass' Monthly* (1859–1863), and, for a time, the *New National Era* (1870–1874). Complementing the other aspects of his varied public voice and extending its reach and influence, Douglass's work as a journalist furthered his use of the printed word as a tool for agitation and change. Stressing self-reliance, hard work, perseverance, education, and morality, Douglass exemplified the embrace by many African Americans of middle-class values and the American success ethic. Likewise, invoking America's revolutionary tradition, he emphasized the imperative of full black liberation within the confines of the American nation. After 1851, when he formally broke with the Garrisonians and accepted political action against slavery as viable and necessary, he became more politically engaged. By the outbreak of the Civil War, he supported the Republican Party.

The tumultuous events of the 1850s convinced Douglass, like untold numbers of his compatriots, that war was unavoidable, the Union cause just, and slave emancipation inevitable. He urged his audience, most notably President Abraham Lincoln, to further ennoble the Union cause by accepting black troops into the Union army and treating them fairly. He exhorted his people to support fully the Union cause and to struggle ceaselessly to ensure that Union victory would mean emancipation and the necessary conditions for black progress. His often arduous efforts to recruit black Union troops, who braved strong white hostility and mistreatment, showed him grappling intensely with the central and complex issue of African-American identity. African Americans, he cogently argued, honored their group as well as national heritage and mission through vigorous support of an abolitionist Union cause.

Douglass emerged from the war even more widely known and respected. He continued to urge his nation to deal justly and fairly with his people, even after the nation reneged on its insufficient and short-lived efforts to do so during Reconstruction. While many blacks questioned his continuing allegiance to the Republican Party, Douglass valiantly—albeit unsuccessfully—endeavored to help the party rediscover its humanistic and moral moorings. Appointed to serve as the United States marshal for the District of Columbia (1877–1881), recorder of deeds for the District of Columbia (1881–1886), and chargé d'affaires for Santo Domingo and minister to Haiti (1889–1891), he remained a stalwart Republican.

Over the years Douglass's status as a comfortable middle-class elder statesman tended on occasion to blind

Statue of Frederick Douglass, Rochester, New York. *Dedicated by New York State governor Theodore Roosevelt in 1898, the statue of Douglass, later moved to Highland Park, was the first public monument to an African American.* PHOTOGRAPHS AND PRINTS DIVISION, SCHOMBURG CENTER FOR RESEARCH IN BLACK CULTURE, THE NEW YORK PUBLIC LIBRARY, ASTOR, LENOX AND TILDEN FOUNDATIONS.

Frederick Douglass

"This Fourth of July is *yours*, not *mine. You* may rejoice, I must mourn, to drag a man in fetters into the grand illuminated temple of liberty, and call upon him to join you in joyous anthems, were inhuman and sacrilegious irony."

"WHAT TO THE SLAVE IS THE FOURTH OF JULY" SPEECH, ROCHESTER, NEW YORK, JULY 5, 1852.

him to the harsh conditions confronting rural, impoverished, and migrant blacks. Still, as in his fiery condemnation of the alarming growth in the number of lynchings of black men in the 1880s and 1890s (often upon the false accusation of an attack on a white woman), it was clear that his commitment to justice never wavered. Likewise, while many women's-rights advocates criticized him for supporting the Fifteenth Amendment, which failed to enfranchise women as it enfranchised black men, Douglass contended that the greater urgency of the black male need for the vote and its greater likelihood of passage made support imperative. After its passage he continued his efforts on behalf of women's rights and sought to heal the rift within the movement.

When Douglass married Helen Pitts, his white secretary, in January 1884, a year and a half after the death of his first wife, they endured much criticism from many blacks and whites, including close family members. Nonetheless, Douglass, the quintessential humanist, steadfastly articulated his commitment to a composite American nationality, transcending race, as an integral component of his vision of a democratic and egalitarian country. When others criticized him for a lack of race spirit, Douglass, refusing to be imprisoned within a racialist universe, claimed ultimate allegiance to the human race.

Yet Douglass also fully understood and vividly personified his people's struggle from slavery to freedom, from obscurity and poverty to recognition and respectability. His enduring legacy to his people and all Americans is best captured in his lifelong and profound dedication to the imperative of agitation and concerted action: "If there is no struggle," he declared, "there is no progress."

See also Abolition; Free Blacks, 1619-1860

■ ■ *Bibliography*

Andrews, William L., ed. *Critical Essays on Frederick Douglass.* Boston: G. K. Hall, 1991.

Blassingame, John W., et al., eds. *The Frederick Douglass Papers.* New Haven, Conn.: Yale University Press, 1979.

Blight, David W. *Frederick Douglass' Civil War: Keeping Faith in Jubilee.* Baton Rouge: Louisiana State University Press, 1989.

Douglass, Frederick. *Life and Times of Frederick Douglass: Written by Himself* (1892). New York: Crowell, 1962.

Douglass, Frederick. *Narrative of the Life of Frederick Douglass, an American Slave, Written by Himself* (1845). New York, 1968.

Douglass, Frederick. *My Bondage and My Freedom* (1855). New York: Arno Press, 1969.

Douglass, Frederick. *The Life and Writings of Frederick Douglass.* 5 vols. New York, 1975.

Martin, Waldo E., Jr. *The Mind of Frederick Douglass.* Chapel Hill: University of North Carolina Press, 1984.

Martin, Waldo E., Jr. "Frederick Douglass: Humanist as Race Leader." In *Black Leaders of the Nineteenth Century,* edited by Leon Litwack and August Meier, pp. 59–84. Urbana: University of Illinois Press, 1988.

McFeely, William S. *Frederick Douglass.* New York: Norton, 1990.

Preston, Dickson J. *Young Frederick Douglass: The Maryland Years.* Baltimore, Md.: Johns Hopkins University Press, 1980.

Quarles, Benjamin. *Frederick Douglass* (1948). Englewood Cliffs, N.J.: Prentice-Hall, 1968.

Russell, Sharman Apt. *Frederick Douglass: Abolitionist Editor.* Philadelphia: Chelsea House, 1987.

Sundquist, Eric J., ed. *Frederick Douglass: New Literary and Historical Essays.* New York: Cambridge University Press, 1990.

WALDO E. MARTIN JR. (1996)
Updated bibliography

DOVE, RITA

AUGUST 28, 1952

▬▬▬

Poet Rita Dove was born in Akron, Ohio. She graduated summa cum laude from Miami University in Oxford, Ohio, in 1973, then spent the following year in Tübingen, Germany, as a Fulbright scholar. In 1975 she enrolled in the Writers' Workshop at the University of Iowa, where she received her Master of Fine Arts degree two years later. In 1981 Dove joined the English department at Arizona State University, where she continued to teach creative writing until 1989. In that year she accepted a position at the University of Virginia, which named her Commonwealth Professor of English in 1992.

Dove's first volume of poems, *Yellow House on the Corner,* was published in 1980. It was followed in 1983 by *Museum,* which displays a more conscious awareness of the conventions of artistic and historical practice. Three years later, Dove published *Thomas and Beulah* (1986), two versions of the story of two ordinary African Americans. The volume, which loosely narrates the lives of Dove's grandparents, was awarded the Pulitzer Prize in Poetry in 1987. *Thomas and Beulah* was a turning point in Dove's career for more reasons than its award-winning status. Not coincidentally, its narrative style emerged just after Dove's first published foray into fiction, *First Sunday* (1985), a collection of stories. Dove also published one novel, *Through the Ivory Gate* (1992), the story of a black woman whose work as a puppeteer evokes painful childhood memories of disturbing cultural significance. What *First Sunday* and *Through the Ivory Gate* may lack in believable dialogue and depth of characterization is made up for in the echoes of *Grace Notes* (1989). In the poems in this collection, each moment is filled by the persistent ringing of carefully culled metaphor.

More public attention has fallen on Dove's career than on that of any other contemporary African-American poet. Recognized for her virtuoso technical ability, Dove represents a generation of poets trained in university writers' workshops who are sometimes chastised for their formal competence at the expense of emotional depth. Dove has distinguished herself in her capacity to filter complex historical and personal information through precise selections of poetic form. In this, she is most closely allied to black poets such as Gwendolyn Brooks, Michael S. Harper, and Robert Hayden. Her unusual range of subject matter, thematically and geographically, has earned her a reputation as a black writer unafraid to set African-American culture within a global context. Dove's gifts as a poet were most fully acknowledged in 1993 when she was appointed Poet Laureate of the United States, the first black writer and the youngest poet ever to have been so honored.

Dove has continued reaping honors, including the 1996 National Humanities Medal, the 2001 Duke Ellington Lifetime Achievement Award, and the 2003 Emily Couric Leadership Award. She has also been awarded honorary doctorates from more than twenty colleges and universities across the United States. From 2000 to 2002, she wrote a weekly poetry column in the *Washington Post*. In 2004 Dove published *American Smooth,* a collection of poetry.

See also Literature of the United States; Poetry, U.S.

■ ■ *Bibliography*

Ingersoll, Earl G, ed. *Conversations with Rita Dove.* Jackson: University Press of Mississippi, 2003.

Rampersad, Arnold. "The Poems of Rita Dove." *Callaloo* 9, no. 1 (winter 1986): 52–60.

Taleb-Khyar, Mohamed B. "An Interview with Maryse Condé and Rita Dove." *Callaloo* 14, no. 2 (spring 1991): 347–366.

GINA DENT (1996)
Updated by publisher 2005

DOVE, ULYSSES

JANUARY 17, 1947?
JUNE 11, 1996

Modern dancer and choreographer Ulysses Dove was born in Columbia, South Carolina, the eldest of three children. He began dance study with Carolyn Tate while a premedical student at Howard University. He transferred to the University of Wisconsin to study with Xenia Chlistowa of the Kirov Ballet, and in 1970 he graduated from Bennington College with a degree in dance. Upon moving to New York, Dove joined the Merce Cunningham Dance Company and also performed with Mary Anthony, Pearl Lang, and Anna Sokolow. In 1973 he joined the Alvin Ailey American Dance Theater, where he quickly rose to the rank of principal dancer acclaimed for his commanding presence, bright clarity of movement, and truthful dramatic intensity.

Dove turned to choreography at Ailey's urging and created the 1980 solo "Inside" for Judith Jamison. He left the Ailey company that year to begin a significant freelance career choreographing dances for the Basel Ballet, Swedish Cullberg Ballet, Dutch National Ballet, London Festival Ballet, American Ballet Theater, New York City Ballet, and Groupe de Recherche Choréographique de l'Opéra de Paris, where he spent three years as assistant director. Several Dove ballets have found their definitive, punchy interpretations in performances by the Ailey company, including "Night Shade" (1982), "Bad Blood" (1984), "Vespers" (1986), "Episodes" (1987), and "Vespers" (1994). His final projects included "Red Angels," which was premiered by the New York City Ballet in 1994, and "Twilight," made for that company and premiered May 23, 1996. His choreography was marked by its relentless speed, violent force, and daring eroticism.

See also Ailey, Alvin; Ballet

■ ■ *Bibliography*

Lewis, Julinda. "Inside: A Dance." *Dance Scope* 14, no. 3 (1980).

Supree, Burt. "Ulysses Dove: Beginning Again, Again." *Village Voice,* July 17, 1984.

THOMAS F. DEFRANTZ (1996)

DOZENS, THE

The dozens—also referred to as "playing the dozens," "sounding," "joning," or "woofing"—is a verbal game of insult and boasting involving at least two participants and an audience. The dozens are played by males and females across all age groups. Insults can be rhymed or unrhymed, although adult versions rely less on rhyme and more on improvisation. Audience participation is integral, since observers issue the verbal praise that regulates the contest to either a peaceful or violent resolution.

The dozens can be "clean" or "dirty." Performers of the clean or ordinary dozens insult intelligence, achievements, or appearance, as in this example: "Your lips are so big, they call them soup coolers." Performers of the dirty dozens use obscene language to boast of sexual conquests, frequently of the contender's family members, as in the following: "I fucked your mother between two cans. Up jumped a baby and hollered, 'Superman'" (Abrahams, 1990, p. 301). The retort "Your mama!" is considered a shorthand form of the dirty dozens.

Early researchers pinned Freudian explanations for the dozens to their perceptions of a dysfunctional community. These patterned insults were interpreted as release valves for a racially repressed group (Dollard, 1990) or as strategies for African-American males to build masculine identities within a matriarchal society (Abrahams, 1990). Later research targeted functional values, citing the dozens's role in promoting community norms and teaching verbal strategies for resolving actual conflicts (Garner, 1983).

The origins of the dozens are uncertain. However, analogs include the verbal duels or "joking relationships" of various African ethnic groups and the derisive exchanges in West Indian calypso and African-American rap music. Before scholarly attention was accorded them, the dozens were recorded by blues performers such as Memphis Minnie McCoy, Sweet Peas Spivey, and Lonnie Johnson. The consensus of researchers and performers is that the dozens are entertaining exercises that display cultural competency. Along with other speech acts such as preaching, signifying, and rapping, the dozens demonstrate the high value placed on verbal skills across the African diaspora.

See also Blues, The; English, African-American; Rap

■ ■ *Bibliography*

Abrahams, Roger D. "Playing the Dozens." *Journal of American Folklore* 75 (1962): 209–220. Reprinted in *Mother Wit from the Laughing Barrel:* edited by Alan Dundes. Jackson: University Press of Mississippi, 1990.

Dollard, John. "The Dozens: Dialect of Insult." *American Imago* 1 (1939): 3–25. Reprinted in *Mother Wit from the Laughing Barrel; Readings in the Interpretation of Afro-American Folklore,* edited by Alan Dundes. Jackson: University Press of Mississippi, 1990.

Garner, Thurmon. "Playing the Dozens: Folklore as Strategies for Living." *Quarterly Journal of Speech* 69 (1983): 47–57.

Mufwene, Salikoko, John R. Rickford, Guy Bailey, and John Baugh, eds. *African-American English: Structure, History, and Use.* New York: Routledge, 1998.

CASSANDRA A. STANCIL (1996)
Updated bibliography

DRAKE, ST. CLAIR

JANUARY 2, 1911
JUNE 14, 1990

▮▮▮————————

Sociologist St. Clair Drake was born in Suffolk, Virginia, where his father was a Baptist pastor in small rural parishes. Although Drake knew his father only during his first thirteen years, the elder Drake had a decisive influence on his son's later development. John Gibbs St. Clair Drake had been born in Barbados but studied for the Baptist ministry in Lynchburg, Virginia. During World War I, Reverend Drake followed his congregation to Pittsburgh, where many had migrated to work in the steel mills.

In Pittsburgh the family lived in a "middle class" house, with access to a well-stocked library. There Drake formed his habit of wide reading on many subjects. He attended a school where he was the only African-American child, and listened, fascinated, to discussions of religion and race between his father and other preachers.

His parents were divorced in 1924, and Drake accompanied his mother back to Virginia. He attended Booker T. Washington High School in Staunton, Virginia, where he had his first encounters with southern segregation.

From 1927 through 1931 Drake attended Hampton Institute in Virginia, where he was an outstanding student. Central to his subsequent career was the influence of a young professor, W. Allison Davis, who introduced him to anthropology. After graduating, Drake taught high school in rural Virginia, traveling to Philadelphia every summer and investing his small earnings in a few books on anthropology. During those summers he worked and studied with the American Friends Service Committee, a Quaker organization.

In the summer of 1931 Drake demonstrated the quiet courage that remained characteristic of him. Some of the Friends initiated a "peace caravan," and Drake and his friend, Enoch Waters, traveled with it through the South, attempting to win support for disarmament and international cooperation. Remarkably, the trek did not terminate in disaster.

In 1935, while still teaching in Virginia, Drake became a member of a research team that was making a social survey of a Mississippi town. Davis had questioned whether the ideas of the white anthropologist W. Lloyd Warner concerning class and caste were applicable to blacks and whites in the South. The outcome was Drake's earliest published research, which was incorporated into Davis's *Deep South.* Working with senior anthropologists, Drake conducted much of the research and prepared the manuscript for publication. After *Deep South,* Drake's closeness to those whom he studied caused him always to describe himself as a "participant-observer."

In 1937 Drake entered the University of Chicago on a Rosenwald Fellowship for further studies in anthropology. Intermittently, he continued to study there over the next fifteen years. In 1942 he married Elizabeth Johns, a white sociologist. *Black Metropolis,* his best-known work, appeared in 1945. Coauthored with Horace Cayton, it is a pathbreaking work of description and analysis of African-American life in Chicago.

In 1946 Drake joined the faculty of the newly established Roosevelt College (later University) in Chicago, where he remained until 1968. This college had been created as a protest against the racially restrictive Central YMCA College, its predecessor.

Drake was increasingly interested in Africa and the African diaspora. His doctoral dissertation for the University of Chicago, "Value Systems, Social Structure, and Race Relations in the British Isles," involved one year of research of the "colored" community of Cardiff, Wales, placing that community into the larger context of Africa and the South Atlantic. During that year in Britain, Drake became a close associate of George Padmore, the West Indian Pan-Africanist and adviser to Kwame Nkrumah. After Ghana's independence, from 1958 to 1961, Drake became professor of sociology at the University of Ghana, while still holding his professorship at Roosevelt University.

In 1969 Drake accepted a long-standing invitation to become professor of sociology and anthropology and director of African and Afro-American Studies at Stanford University in California. The Stanford period was most notable for the publication of the vast and erudite *Black Folk Here and There* (two volumes, 1987–1990). Using an enormous array of sources, it presents the thesis that prejudice against blacks is a relatively recent phenomenon, arising first during the Hellenistic period.

See also Anthropology and Anthropologists; Cayton, Horace; Davis, Allison

■ ■ *Bibliography*

Drake, St. Clair. "In the Mirror of Black Scholarship. W. Allison Davis and *Deep South.*" *Harvard Educational Review,* Monograph #2 (1974): 42–54.

Drake, St. Clair. Autobiographical manuscripts held in the Schomburg Collection, New York Public Library.

FRANK UNTERMYER (1996)

DRAMA

African-American drama draws from at least two sources: the heritage of Africa and that of Europe. On the North American continent, those cultures met, interacted with Native American traditions and a new physical environment, and produced a culture that, while related to both Africa and Europe, is nonetheless distinct from both. For the historian of African-American drama, this heritage poses a series of complex questions: What kinds of events count as drama, in that Europeans have come to define drama primarily as a written text, while Africans have placed more value on the communicative capacity of such ephemeral elements as dance, music, and spectacle? If one focuses on written forms, then for whom have black playwrights written? What are the indicators—in terms of content and/or style—that signify the choice of a primarily black, white, or mixed audience? How have dramatists coded or masked their intentions so as to speak to these different audiences simultaneously?

If emphasis is placed on performance rather than upon a written script, then African-American drama begins on the slave ships, when Africans were forced to sing and dance in order to ensure their health and salability and to provide entertainment for white crewmen. Slave narratives and travelers' accounts attest to the fact that plantation owners encouraged their property to perform because they thought that occasional merry-making increased productivity and lessened the possibility of revolt, and because they seemed genuinely fascinated by the musical idioms, gestures, and the black body itself, all of which were radically different from what they knew of European tradition.

Long before black men were allowed on American stages, a caricature stage Negro made an appearance. The English dramatist Isaac Bickerstaff introduced a lazy, rambunctious West Indian slave in *The Padlock* in 1769; in 1795 the white American James Murdoch followed suit with *The Triumph of Love,* in which a stupid buffoon known as Sambo delighted audiences and initiated a derogatory stereotype that the American public seemingly will not let die. To counter this representation with spectacles more pleasing to "ladies & gentlemen of color," a free black man named Mr. Brown (first name unknown) opened the African Grove Theatre in lower Manhattan in New York City in 1821. This first, professional black theater company mounted productions of Shakespeare, dance and pantomime interludes, and *King Shotaway* (1823), thought to be the first play written and performed by African Americans. Though no script remains today, records indicate that it concerned a slave insurrection in the Caribbean. Produced within a year of the Denmark Vesey slave insurrection in Virginia, the play roused the ire of white spectators to the extent that a group of rowdies intent on "wanton mischief" destroyed the theatre building and forced the company's closure in 1823. With its demise, Ira Aldridge, who had been inspired to join the group after seeing the West Indian actor James Hewlett in *Richard III,* left for Europe where he eventually won gold medals from the Prussian and Austrian heads of state for his superior artistry in Shakespearean tragedies as well as in popular comedies. Sadly, Aldridge became the first of a long line of African-American expatriate artists who found greater acceptance abroad than at home.

The Sambo stereotype would solidify in the 1840s into the minstrel show. According to conventional theater history, minstrelsy began in 1828 when a young white performer named Thomas D. Rice observed an old, deformed Negro singing and dancing. He is said to have borrowed the man's entire performance (including his clothing), thereby initiating what would become an extremely popular form of entertainment—and a pattern of exploitation repeated by many other white performers who reaped great profit from their imitations of black art. More recent scholarship, however, argues that minstrelsy originated not with Rice and his colleagues who claimed that they were accurately depicting real African-American customs, but with black people themselves. In gathering to sing and dance, enact stories, and mock the cultured pretensions of their masters, slaves were creating a form in which improvisation and ecstatic response based upon the interactions of those assembled were more important than a fixed or written text wherein all elements are related to each other by an inviolable logic that does not give any space to the unplanned or unexplained. They were pioneering a form in which language was treasured for its power to stimulate the imagination and emotions. Given slave conditions, they were projecting a metaphysical stance and style that enabled them to survive with their intelligence, humor, and dignity relatively intact. But in performing for white observers, these slaves masked their behavior so that the owners could interpret their efforts as black incompetence rather than as a critique of what appeared to the slaves as white ridiculousness. Thus, white minstrel performers were offering white audiences a parody of black behavior that was, unbeknownst to them, already a parody of white customs. By the 1860s when black men were allowed to perform onstage, audiences had grown so accustomed to the black-face image that African Americans had to black up—adding yet another layer of parody.

Because of its topicality, improvised quality, and general construction as entertainment aimed at the masses,

the minstrel show is usually not considered drama. Yet, it was particularly significant for what would follow, because any playwright wishing to represent African Americans onstage would have to confront the enduring legacy of minstrelsy's grinning darky. Furthermore, it signaled that performance modes rooted in African-American culture were likely to be characterized by masking, evocative language, improvisation grounded in a mastery of technique, episodic structure shaped as much by performer-audience interactions as by logic, as well as by ecstasy, and an ethical/aesthetic stance that seeks to affirm the humane even while it holds opposites in balanced tension.

Masking is at the core of *The Escape; or a Leap for Freedom* by William Wells Brown, who is generally considered the first African American to have a play published. First read from Northern, abolitionist platforms in 1857 by Brown, who was a successful fugitive, this text appears double-voiced, offering contradictory representations to audience members. Undoubtedly, abolitionist attendees at a reading agreed with the representation of slave owners as exploitative and religiously hypocritical, and they sympathized with the mulatto couple who, in fine diction, vow to seek freedom. They probably also found comic relief in Cato, the stereotypical buffoon who uses nonsensical words, pursues gluttonous pleasures, and apes white mannerisms. But Cato is also a trickster who, when beyond his owners' presence, sings freedom songs (in standard English) and cunningly schemes to turn every situation to his own advantage. Thus, when freedom is almost at hand, he jettisons the grinning mask, helps the runaway couple, and makes his own leap to freedom. In his trickstering, Cato seems to represent an independent spirit that will not be contained by social conventions not of his own making. That position could hardly have been a comforting prospect to those Northerners who, despite their antislavery convictions, believed in black inferiority, and yet, presumably it accurately reflected one attitude found among pre–Civil War blacks. Though the figure of the manipulative buffoon found no place in the theaters patronized by whites, its appearance in one of the earliest black plays identifies masking as an important African-American survival strategy. It is a representation to which African Americans have periodically returned in the musical comedies of Bert Williams and George Walker (*Abyssinia,* 1906; *Bandanna Land,* 1908), and in dramas as different as Garland Anderson's *Appearances* (1925), LeRoi Jones's (Amiri Baraka's) *The Slave* (1964), Douglas Turner Ward's *Day of Absence* (1965), and Ed Bullins's *The Gentleman Caller* (1969).

The use of theater as an arena for advancing social change continued in the first decades of the twentieth century, when W. E. B. Du Bois and others organized the pageant *The Star of Ethiopia*. Seeking to teach history to both blacks and whites, Du Bois and his pageant master Charles Burroughs crafted a series of tableaux linking Egyptian and Yoruba cultures with African-American heroes like Nat Turner and with the quest for freedom. Between 1913 and 1925, this pageant involved approximately three thousand people as performers and was performed in four cities before more than thirty thousand people. Not only did the pageant mobilize often competitive community energies, foster racial pride, and indulge a love of spectacle, but it also provided a model of nonprofessional, socially charged art that others would utilize. Thus, for example, inhabitants of Los Angeles mounted "50 Years of Freedom" in 1915 to combat the negative imagery of D. W. Griffith's film *The Clansman*, and in 1974, people dressed in Ku Klux Klan outfits appeared in San Francisco City Hall chambers as part of an effort to ban the display of regalia of groups advocating hate and genocide.

Angelina Weld Grimké's *Rachel* is the first twentieth-century full-length play written, performed, and produced by blacks. In this sometimes melodramatic coming-of-age play, a high-spirited young woman rejects marriage and the possibility of motherhood because she fears that future generations will be unable to escape the racism she has personally experienced. The production provoked a storm of controversy when sponsored by the District of Columbia branch of the National Association for the Advancement of Colored People (NAACP) in 1916, because it implicitly defied the NAACP philosophy of racial progress led by an educated, black elite, whom Du Bois had termed "the talented tenth." For some, the play reduced art to the level of propaganda. Thus, when Alain Locke, one of the leading theoreticians and promoters of the Harlem Renaissance, and educator Montgomery Gregory founded Howard University's dramatic art department in 1921, they explicitly espoused an aesthetic that privileged technical beauty or art over social concerns. W. E. B. Du Bois took a different position, arguing both in his writings and his organization of the amateur Krigwa Players that the two were not so easily separated. Though short-lived (1925–1927), this drama group was significant because it extended Du Bois's efforts and those of Charles Johnson to foster formal cultural production and increase readership through contests and publication in the NAACP and Urban League magazines, Crisis and Opportunity. Additionally, the theater's manifesto propounded a standard of evaluation that would be echoed in the militant sixties. Namely, an authentic black theater had to be "about us. . .by us. . .for us. . .and near us."

Also differing with Locke's and Montgomery's emphasis on art divorced from a strong social referent were a number of women who won most of the drama prizes in the Crisis and Opportunity contests sponsored between 1925 and 1927. Protest against lynching, the lack of birth-control information, and racial discrimination against returning black World War I veterans were some of the issues that women like Alice Dunbar Nelson, Georgia Douglas Johnson, Mary Burrill, and May Miller dramatized in plays like *Mine Eyes Have Seen* (1918), *Sunday Morning in the South* (1925), *Safe* (c. 1929), *Blue-Eyed Black Boy* (c. 1930), *Nails and Thorns* (1933), *They That Sit in Darkness* (1919), and *Aftermath* (1919). The antilynching dramas are of particular importance because these women, largely deprived of leadership roles in organizations like the NAACP or the Urban League, seemingly viewed the stage as an arena for advancing an important social agenda. Their work formed a continuum with the direct, antilynching campaigns launched by Ida B. Wells and other black women active in the Women's Club movement from the turn of the century to the early decades of the twentieth century. Additionally, the antilynch play was a genre in which black women predominated, producing more plays than either black men, white women, or white men.

The Great Depression of the 1930s largely stymied African-American efforts to establish their own theaters. One outlet for theatrical interests was the black church, where folk dramas such as "The Old Ship of Zion," "Heaven Bound," or "In the Rapture" began. Popular throughout the Midwest, East, and South, these dramas took their plots from the Bible. Often a given church would mount the same play over a number of years, so that novelty of story line was not an objective. Rather, dramatic appeal rested in the improvisational space allotted to comic by-play, the artistry with which spirituals were rendered, and the affirmation of a sense of communal solidarity in terms of both religious emotions aroused by the actual event and the creative energies marshalled in preparing costumes, sets, and participants for performance. The aesthetic evident in these folks dramas has parallels with such African traditions as festivals, for in both instances a community, sharing a set of beliefs and symbols, gathers to enact itself in a performance balancing fixed and fluid elements. That is, the broad parameters of a known plot, familiar spirituals, and performers whose personalities both onstage and offstage are known to the community are balanced against fluid performance specifics like the particular placement and rendition of individual songs and narrative episodes, the spontaneous extension of humorous moments, and the emotional dynamic between audience and performers. Through this symbolic practice, a value system is reaffirmed, and the individual is offered an opportunity to experience his or her relationship to a community. Started during the Great Depression, folk dramas like *Heaven*

Bound, Noah's Ark, or *The Devil's Funeral* can still be witnessed in some black Baptist and fundamentalist churches.

The government inadvertently became another sponsor for dramatic activity during the Depression. Faced with the collapse of financial markets and the unemployment of millions of Americans, in 1935 the federal government established a relief program known as the Works Progress Administration. It included the Federal Theatre Project (FTP) that during its four years of operation annually employed some thirteen thousand theater workers who performed before approximately 65 million people in theaters, parks, schools, hospitals, and churches. With black units in twenty-two cities, FTP not only offered work to black performers, but also provided many of them with their first formal training in acting, directing, writing, and technical design. Offerings ran the gamut from adaptations of mainstream plays to musicals and dramas addressing contemporary social issues. One of its most popular shows with white and black audiences was a "voodoo" *Macbeth* directed by Orson Welles for the New York Negro unit of FTP. In setting this classic in the tropics, Welles was not only continuing the practice of making Shakespeare accessible to people with varying degrees of formal education, but he was also furthering a theatrical convention in which aspects of African-related culture are used to make mainstream fare more exotic or appealing. "Voodoo" *Macbeth* was soon followed by *Swing Mikado,* a jazz version of the Gilbert and Sullivan light opera; in more recent years, black "remakes" of white standards have resulted in such musicals as *The Wiz* (1975; adapted from *The Wizard of Oz*) and Lee Breuer's *The Gospel at Colonus* (1983; adapted from the fifth-century Greek drama *Oedipus at Colonus*).

In addition to delightful spectacles, the FTP also produced serious drama that questioned the fabric of American life. One such drama, *Big White Fog* by Theodore Ward, is a good example of a play that speaks simultaneously to both white and black audiences. Its realistic style with an immediately recognizable physical setting, operation of cause-and-effect within family relationships, and the hero's movement toward greater self-knowledge locates the text within the mainstream of American dramaturgy. The play's cultural specificity resides in it focus on the competing promises of Marcus Garvey's Back-to-Africa movement, a black capitalism derived from Booker T. Washington, and socialism within the context of the Depression. Furthermore, its dramatization of intraracial (as well as interracial) color prejudice adds powerful depth, because it captures a reality known painfully well by African Americans, but for the most part hidden from the view of the larger society. Produced first in 1938 by the

FTP black unit in Chicago, it aroused a certain degree of controversy because of its seeming support of communism. It was subsequently remounted in New York in 1940 by the short-lived Negro Playwrights Company, which Ward had helped to organize along with other playwrights like Langston Hughes and Abram Hill (*On Striver's Row,* 1940; *Walk Hard,* 1944). Theodore Ward subsequently found critical praise and limited audience success with his historical drama about Reconstruction, *Our Lan'.* Begun in 1941, it was first produced off-Broadway at the Henry Street Settlement Playhouse in 1946.

Further fueling conservative concern about art and politics was a form of experimental theater known as the Living Newspaper. The format was initially conceived by FTP director Hallie Flanagan, who, like many other white American artists had been impressed by the theatrical experimentation she witnessed in Germany and Russia in the 1920s. The Living Newspaper hired unemployed workers to research current events that were then enacted by large casts in an episodic, panoramic fashion with minimal sets or costumes, in effect producing a kind of theatricalized newsreel. One of the first Living Newspapers to run afoul of its government sponsors was *Ethiopia,* which was closed after an initial preview because of fears that its powerful dramatization of Benito Mussolini's invasion of the African nation of Ethiopia would provoke protests and jeopardize relations with the Italian government, with which the nation was then at peace. Politics also seems to have been the explanation for not producing Abram Hill and John Silvera's script *Liberty Deferred* (1938), which utilized many of the Living Newspaper techniques to dramatize the African-American history. Though FTP fare was very popular with the American public, it nonetheless drew the suspicions of congressmen who regarded this first attempt at subsidized public art as a haven for allegedly anti-American, communist sympathizers. With the economy improving as the nation moved toward active participation in World War II, the Dies Committee killed the Federal Theatre Program in 1939.

Langston Hughes's *Don't You Want to Be Free?* (1937) stands in marked contrast to Ward's *Big White Fog.* While Ward's play had been sponsored by the Federal Theatre, Hughes's was produced by his own leftist-affiliated Harlem Suitcase Theatre. Like much of the agitprop, or agitation-propaganda play writing of the Great Depression, his play utilizes minimal scenery, a small pool of actors to play a large number of roles, and direct address to the audience, designed to encourage them to undertake a specific action. In this case, the text argues for an acceptance of working-class solidarity across racial barriers. The play's distinctiveness is marked by its use of poetry, gospel and blues songs, dance, and vignettes to suggestively chronicle black history from Africa to the United States. The validation of culture that Hughes had begun in experimenting with poetic form in *The Weary Blues* (1926) was here extended to the theater; his use of an episodic structure, knitted together and propelled by the emotional energy of black music as well as by the evocative intensity of language, provided a model that more contemporary playwrights like Amiri Baraka and Ntozake Shange would emulate in the 1970s. Hughes's later deployment of religious experience, which found commercial success in *Black Nativity* (1961), helped inaugurate the contemporary gospel drama genre, practiced by such artists as Vinnette Carroll with *Your Arms Too Short to Box with God* (1975) and Ken Wydro and Vi Higgensen with *Mama I Want to Sing* (1980).

World War II (1939–1945) brought in its wake increased militancy at home and abroad, as African Americans agitated for fair-employment practices, the elimination of restricted housing, and an end to segregated schools, and as Africans mobilized to gain their independence from colonial masters. This new aggressiveness was mirrored in Lorraine Hansberry's *A Raisin in the Sun* (1959). Using Langston Hughes's poetic query, "What happens to a dream deferred?", the young playwright explored the conflicting aspirations of the Youngers, a Chicago tenement family eagerly awaiting the arrival of a $10,000 insurance check paid upon the death of the father. Thirty-year-old Walter Lee's dream of owning a liquor store and hence of functioning as a man in terms espoused by the American middle class clashes with Mama's desire to purchase a comfortable house with a small garden, while Beneatha's medical studies and humanist philosophy come into conflict with her brother's chauvinism and her mother's religiosity. Sister-in-law Ruth's decision to seek an illegal abortion marks the battering that the older generation's Southern, sharecropping values have taken in the industrial North. Paradoxically, Mama's spiritual faith, rooted in the American slave experience, is congruent with Asagai's progressive social commitment based in contemporary, African anticolonial movements, for in wooing Beneatha, this Nigerian student speaks of the necessity of belief in human potential and the consequence struggle for human betterment.

Produced five years after the historic *Brown v. Board of Education of Topeka, Kansas,* decision outlawing segregated schools, *A Raisin in the Sun* seemed to signal the nation's willingness to live up to its credo of equality. It constituted a number of landmarks: the first time that an African-American woman's work had been produced at the Ethel Barrymore Theatre on Broadway; the directorial debut of African-American Lloyd Richards in such a prestigious venue; widespread recognition for actors Claudia McNeil, Ruby Dee, Sidney Poitier, and Diana Sands; and encouragement for other artists to articulate their visions of black America. In addition, it won the New York Drama Critics Circle Award, beating out such mainstream competitors as Tennessee Williams's Sweet Bird of Youth, Eugene O'Neill's A Touch of the Poet, and Archibald MacLeish's J.B. Thus, the play's ending was interpreted, for the most part, as a ringing endorsement of integration. But at the time of its twenty-fifth-anniversary production in 1984, optimism had waned; the reinsertion of the character of the chatty neighbor, who brings news of a racial bombing, along with the final action of the play, namely Mama's retrieving her sickly plant for the family's move into a white neighborhood, clarified Hansberry's call for continued struggle for dignity.

In both its content and structure, Raisin speaks to the white mainstream and to black audiences. In fact, critics have compared this drama to the Depression-era *Awake and Sing* (1935), written by the white author Clifford Odets, because not only do both feature families dominated by women, but they also deploy ethnic slang and the metaphors of a cramped physical environment as a sign of moral constriction and of money from an insurance check as the vehicle for exercising personal integrity. Ephemeral, performance-based yet nonetheless significant elements, along with the written text, serve, however, to simultaneously locate this drama within an African matrix. Rather than arguing, as did critics influenced by the federally sponsored Moynihan Report on black families, that Mama is an emasculating matriarch because the Youngsters do not conform to the 1950s norm of the nuclear family, one can more profitably understand them as fitting the pattern of an extended African family in which great respect is due elders. At moments of extreme crisis, Mama and Walter Lee each evoke the dead patriarch's memory in halting, yet repetitive linguistic rhythms (that are merely suggested in the written script) seemingly to gain access to his moral support in their decision making. Their actions in these instances are akin to African customs of conjuring the spiritual energies of departed relatives in order to solve current, material problems. Similarly, Beneatha and Walter Lee's fanciful creation of a dance welcoming African warriors home from battle constitutes a writing of culture on the body that provides them a dignity denied them by the American environment; as such, it conforms to African assertions that knowledge is kinesthetic and subjective as well as cerebral.

If Hansberry's hero could be aligned with the southern Civil Rights Movement in his attempt to find a place within the American mainstream, then LeRoi Jones's (a.k.a. Amiri Baraka) protagonists in *Dutchman* and *The Slave* were related to the Nation of Islam and its fiery spokesman Malcolm X, for at the time of the plays' premieres in 1964, spectators saw these characters as determined to destroy the social system. In the former drama, a twentyish African-American man and older, white woman engage in a bizarre dating game on a subway car that never reaches its final destination. Claiming to know both everything and nothing concerning Clay's life history, this stranger named Lula alternately describes a tantalizing sexual liaison that they will enjoy and hurls racial taunts at the would-be poet until he sheds his polite, middle-class demeanor and acknowledges a deep hatred of white America. But Clay fails to act upon his murderous knowledge, preferring instead to use art as a safety valve that tempers rebellious impulses. Once Lula has exposed this rage, she kills Clay and enlists the aid of the hitherto passive onlookers in throwing his body off the train. Like the mythic captain of the Flying Dutchman, who was fated to sail the world looking for absolution for his crimes, Lula begins to seek out another young black male as the play closes. Seemingly, the play functioned as a cautionary tale demonstrating to blacks that death was the price for inaction upon their justifiable anger and warning whites of the rage they could expect if they continued to deny full citizenship to African Americans. Largely unnoted at the time was the text's gender politics, which accuses the white woman rather than fingering the actual holders of oppressive power in the United States.

In contrast, the black man is no longer the victim and the white man is visible in *The Slave*. Walker has invaded the home of his white former wife in order to take his daughters to safety behind the lines of his revolutionary army advancing on the city—or, so he alleges, because it seems as though Walker's real purpose is to exorcise those feelings that bind him to Grace and Easley, Grace's present (white) husband and Walker's former professor. In the ensuing literal and figurative battle, Walker kills Easley, a beam fatally hits Grace, and Walker departs, apparently leaving the children upstairs crying.

But social psychiatrist Frantz Fanon, whose writings on anticolonial struggles in Algeria provided intellectuals in the 1960s with an important framework for conceptualizing Black Power movements, has argued that it is easier to proclaim rejection than to reject. Fanon's analysis is pertinent to the Baraka text, for despite his aggressive stance, Walker agonizes that he has no language with which to construct a new world, his sole epistemology or frame of reference is a Western system that enforces hatred of black people.

The ambiguity of his position has, in fact, been signaled at the outset by a prologue in which an actor,

dressed as a stereotypical old field slave, addresses viewers directly, arguing that whatever he and they understand as reality may be a lie told for survival purposes. What is needed, he suggests, is a superstructure that will enable communication among blacks and whites by ensuring that their common language has the same undeniable referents; otherwise, a black man's legitimate quest for control over his destiny may be understood by a white man as senseless terrorism. The rest of the play then argues that this enabling structure is violence, undertaken by the exploited black masses in defense, as Fanon argued, against the violence waged upon them by the state. But as a playwright, Baraka is caught in a problematic position, for his primary tool of communication with audiences is language itself, suspect because of its inherent capacity to simultaneously convey multiple references and values. Yet, given the extra-theatrical, social backdrop of armed confrontations waged by groups like the Black Panther Party, most spectators and readers at the time of the drama's initial productions focused their attention on the text's revolutionary rhetoric rather than its ambivalence.

At the heart of both these plays is an examination of hegemony or the power of a ruling class to enforce throughout the entire society perspectives that maintain its privileged status through noncoercive means like education, the arts, or certain everyday practices. In *Dutchman* the dominance of the elite, as embodied in Lula, is maintained in part because art functions as a passive mode of resistance that deflects direct confrontation. In *The Slave* and subsequent dramatic works like *Four Black Revolutionary Plays, Arm Yrself or Harm Yrself* (1967), or *The Motion of History* (1977), art is defined as counterhegemonic; it is seen as a weapon that can be utilized to attack sociopolitical hierarchies. In rejecting, as Du Bois had done previously, the opposition of art to propaganda, Amiri Baraka became a major proponent of the Black Arts Movement (1964–1974), functioning as a role model for a younger generation eager to assert a positive sense of their black identity.

In an atmosphere of civil rights demonstrations and urban rebellions, entitlement programs designed to bring about what President Lyndon Johnson termed "the Great Society," Vietnam war protest, and the beginnings of a renewed feminism, African-American drama, with its implicit critique of the dominant social structure, briefly flourished. Playwrights like Ed Bullins, Richard Wesley, Clay Goss, Ron Milner, Ben Caldwell, Sonia Sanchez, and Marvin X followed Baraka's example. Artists like Robert Macbeth, Barbara Ann Teer, and Woodie King, Jr. established companies that advocated a black nationalist position (New York's the New Lafayette, National Black Theatre, and Concept East in Detroit respectively), while more moderate practitioners like Douglas Turner Ward, Hazel Bryant, C. Bernard Jackson, John Doyle, and Nora Vaughn, and such companies as the Negro Ensemble, the Richard Allen Cultural Center in New York, the Inner City Cultural Center in Los Angeles, and the Grassroots Experience and Black Repertory Group Theatre in the San Francisco Bay Area also found governmental funding and receptive audiences for their efforts.

Another of the most prolific playwrights of this period was Ed Bullins, who has written in a variety of styles, including comedy (*The Electronic Nigger*, 1968), theater of the Absurd (*How Do You Do?* 1965), fictionalized autobiography (*A Son Come Home*, 1968), and a realism whose seemingly photographic accuracy does not reveal the playwright's evaluation of his source material (*Clara's Ole Man*, 1965). Unlike virtually any other black dramatist before him, Ed Bullins placed onstage—and thereby validated—in plays like *Goin' a Buffalo* (1966), *In the Wine Time* (1968), and *The Taking of Miss Janie* (1975) lower-class hustlers, prostitutes, pimps, and unemployed teens as well as lower-middle-class community college students, veterans, musicians, and would-be artists and intellectuals, virtually all of whom aggressively pursue an individually-oriented materialism shorn of any rhetoric of concern for a shared, common good.

In disavowing the espoused social values of the American mainstream, Bullins's playwriting style in his full-length dramas also demanded a mode of criticism that was outside the Aristotelian-derived, mainstream preference for tightly organized, linear dramatic structures. Thus, these dramas may be more productively analyzed in terms of jazz, a musical idiom that originated among African Americans and was until relatively recently held in low regard by the American public. Like a jazz composition in which individual musicians improvise a solo or "riff" off a shared melodic line, a play such as *The Fabulous Miss Marie* (1971) has a basic narrative concerning a group of black Los Angelenos who party unconcernedly while a civil rights demonstration is being broadcast on television. The seemingly endless rounds of drinking, meandering conversations, verbal sparring, and sexual repartee function as a base line from which action is periodically stopped in order for individual characters to step from the shadows into a spotlight and address the audience directly with their own solos on the theme of trying to "make it" in the United States.

Adrienne Kennedy is another playwright whose work demanded different critical tools. Like Baraka, Kennedy confronts, in plays like *The Owl Answers* (1965) and *Rat's Mass* (1963), questions of representation and identity for-

mation, offering a black woman's account of the cultural schizophrenia induced by American racial constructions. Thus, protagonists like Sarah in *Funnyhouse of a Negro* (1963) are paralyzed by devotion to European culture, symbolized in this text by Queen Elizabeth and the Duchess of Hapsburg, and by psychosexual confusion centered on a father figure, associated here with blackness, encroaching jungles, civilizing missions in Africa, and contradictorily, the anticolonialist Congolese hero Patrice Lumumba. Adding to the ambiguity is Kennedy's consistent decision to distribute the female protagonist's story amongst a number of different characters, thereby producing an identity or voice that does not come together in a single, coherent whole. Though her earliest plays were produced during the same time period as Baraka's, the ideological demand for positive valorization of "the black experience" in the sixties' Black Arts and Black Power movements meant that her frighteningly powerful dramatizations of the anguished sensibility Du Bois had termed "double consciousness" won a few supporters among African-American theatergoers. Notwithstanding, her highly abstract style found positive response within the limited circles of the white avant-garde in New York. Given subsequent critiques of identity and relationships of domination and marginality launched from theorists of feminism, literary deconstruction, postcoloniality, and postmodernism, a space has been cleared, and Kennedy's work is presently garnering from white and black critics alike the attention it deserves.

Exploding on the theatrical scene in 1976 with *for colored girls who have considered suicide/when the rainbow is enuf*, Ntozake Shange builds upon examples set by Hughes, Baraka, and Kennedy in black theater as well as those offered by Europe's Antonin Artaud and Bertolt Brecht. Coining the term "choreo-poem," Shange creates a total theater in which unscripted elements like music and dance become equal partners with the written word—i.e., poetry. Thus, in *for colored girls . . .* not only do the women talk about their encounters with men, but they also utilize 1960s Motown tunes, Afro-Cuban rhythms, nonsensical chants, and gospel cadences in order to break out of a social world in which they have been devalued as "a colored girl an evil woman a bitch or a nag." With this first text, Shange placed African-American women's experiences of rape, abortion, domestic abuse, sexual desire, and self-affirmation center stage, and she helped fuel an intense debate within black communities concerning the relevance of feminism—understood at that time as the preoccupation of white, middle-class women—to the lives of African Americans. Seeking in *Spell #7* (1979) to confront the power of the minstrel mask that has determined representations of blacks in American popular imagination she crafts a provocative theater whose implications refuse to remain within the illusionary space created by drama. Shange has continued in texts like *Boogie Woogie Landscapes* (1979), *From Okra to Greens/ A Different Kinda Love Story* (1978), and *The Love Space Demands: A Continuing Saga* (1992) to utilize poetry, music, and dance in a nonlinear fashion to explore ways in which a sense of personal integrity and nobility can be harmonized with the realities of racist and sexist social constructions of black (female) identity. Playwrights like Alexis Deveaux, Aishah Rahman, and George C. Wolfe have followed Shange's lead in experimenting with dramatic form, while the last has parodied the feminist content of Shange's dramas in *The Colored Museum* (1986).

Closer to the American mainstream's penchant for realism is August Wilson, who has benefited from a virtually unique, creative collaboration with Lloyd Richards, the same director who brought Hansberry's *A Raisin in the Sun* to Broadway some thirty-five years earlier. Each of his plays has been "workshopped" (read aloud by professional actors and a director, critiqued, and re-written) at the National Playwrights Conference of the Eugene O'Neill Theater, run by Richards, before receiving productions (and further revisions) and national media attention at various, mainstream regional theaters and on Broadway.

A skilled storyteller, Wilson has taken on the challenge of writing a play for each decade of the twentieth century. Thus, *Ma Rainey's Black Bottom* (1984) focuses on the renowned 1920s blues singer and her band, who, through their casual reminiscences, reveal a collective history of discrimination. *Fences* (1985) centers on an overbearing man's relationship to his son and other family members at the point in the 1950s when African Americans were being allowed entry into white, professional sports organizations; and *Joe Turner's Come and Gone* (1986) dramatizes the search by various boardinghouse occupants for a sense of wholeness and sustaining purpose in the first decade of the twentieth century, when thousands of rural black people moved north seeking employment in an industrializing economy. In *The Piano Lesson* (1987), set in the 1930s, a brother and sister fight for possession of the family's piano, which seems to symbolize conflicting ideas concerning uses of the past in charting present courses of action; while set against the backdrop of Malcolm X's militancy of the 1960s, *Two Trains Running* (1990) features the regular patrons of a modest diner who pursue their own dreams of advancement by playing the numbers (i.e., illegally betting on the outcome of horse races) or consulting Aunt Esther, a local fortune teller whose alleged, advanced age happens to correspond to the numbers of years African-Americans have lived in the United States.

Like the novelist Toni Morrison, August Wilson crafts a world in which the pedestrian often assumes grand, mythic proportions, nearly bursting in the process the neat, explanatory rationales implicit in the genre of dramatic realism. Characters regularly fight with ghosts, make pacts with the Devil, or talk to Death; seemingly, they quest for a spiritual center or standpoint from which to confront a material world hostile to their presence. Arguing the importance of blues music in shaping the identity of African Americans, Wilson seems to create characters whose very lives are a blues song: improvisatory, ironic, yet simultaneously affirmative, grounded in a bedrock of belief in the possibility of human integrity.

Seemingly with the post-sixties integration of some public school systems, (sub)urban neighborhoods, job sites, and mass media, the hybrid character of African-American—and indeed, American—culture has accelerated. Those comfortable with a postmodernism that often finds its inspirations in a global eclecticism of "high" and "low" cultures, can enjoy such African-American performance artists as Robbie McCauley (*My Father and the Wars*, 1985; *Sally's Rape*, 1991), and Laurie Carlos who, in the tradition of Ntozake Shange, work individually and collaboratively to fuse personal narratives with larger feminist issues. Also termed a performance artist, Anna Deavere Smith offers in her *On the Road: A Search for American Change* series solo performances of edited interviews with people, both famous and obscure, on topics like gender and racial tensions in professional organizations, urban neighborhoods, and on university campuses. She has also focused on the increasingly multicultural, fractious character of American cities, for her *Fires in the Mirror: Crown Heights, Brooklyn and Other Identities* (1992) and *Twilight: Los Angeles, 1992* (1994), in which she performs the words of more than thirty women and men within an hour and a half, challenges audiences to grapple with notions of community in the context of competing demands for racial and economic justice. They can also sample dramas by Suzan-Lori Parks (*The Death of the Last Black Man in the Whole Entire World*, 1990; *Imperceptible Mutabilities in the Third Kingdom*, 1989), who cites the white, American expatriate writer Gertrude Stein and "The Wild Kingdom" television program among her influences; or work by Eric Gupton, Brian Freeman, and Bernard Branner (*Fierce Love: Stories from Black Gay Life*, 1991), collectively known as AfroPomoHomo, a shortening of the identificatory tags, African-American, postmodernist, and homosexual. Or, spectators can attend a concert by Urban Bush Women, Bill T. Jones/Arnie Zane Dance Company, or David Rousseve, whose mixture of modern dance choreography, pedestrian gestures, athleticism, and narrative communicated through both movement and spoken text blur conventional Western distinctions between drama and dance. What all these artists share is a sensibility that does not reach for some grand, master truth. Rather, juxtaposing elements as diverse as European high art, Georgia Sea Island chants, television programs, West African religions, and popular music, they recognize that African-American identity is varied, and no one can claim to represent black authenticity without doing violence to other perspectives found in these communities.

Indeed, for those theatergoers in the 1990s who find the choreopoem form of an Ntozake Shange, the mythic reach of an August Wilson, or the puzzling symbolism of a Suzan-Lori Parks not to their liking, other options are available. They can attend a performance of *Beauty Shop*, *Living Room*, or *Beauty Shop, Part 2*, all of which have been written, produced, and directed by Shelly Garrett. Starting in 1987 with the intention of simply creating dramatic pieces that would leave audiences exhausted with laughter, Garrett is said to have targeted his attentions primarily toward an underserved population of black women, ages 25 to 54 who watch soap operas and rarely frequent theater. Thus, his scripts are closer to TV sitcoms in their representations of everyday life; stereotypes abound, with the women portrayed as materialist, classist, sexually repressed or rapacious. Men are represented as self-centered sex objects, financially secure but dull, or flamboyant homosexuals outgossiping the most catty (yet hilarious) women. Seemingly, considerable advertising on black-oriented radio stations, the dramas' verbal play, the performers' zestful aura, a mixture of some recognizable truths, and cheerful confirmation of spectators' misogynist and homophobic attitudes have attracted thousands of spectators, enabling Garrett to tour at least fifty cities nationwide for more than two years with one show. But those disturbed by what they may perceive as rampant sexuality in these shows also have an option in the commercial arena, for producers have created a religious version, like Michael Mathews's *I Need a Man* (1993), wherein some of these lively stereotypes undergo spiritual conversion aided by the performance of gospel music. As with much black art, the form is elastic, so that local, gospel radio personalities occasionally make guest appearances onstage during the performance; the predictability of plot and character types is offset by the dynamics of the performer-viewer interactions. Whether participants undergo a religious experience in this highly commercialized venue depends, as it does in church, upon their own belief systems and sensibilities.

In the 1990s, approximately 200 companies were dedicated to the production of African-American theater and drama. As the foregoing account suggests, audiences can experience a wealth of themes, perspectives, and styles, all of which seek to articulate aspects of African-American culture. This diversity is indeed a cause for celebration. Yet, given the nation's difficult economic conditions that promise no easy solution, the arts in general and black and other so-called minority expressive cultures in particular will be under intense pressure to obtain the financial resources that enable artistic production. Perhaps artists from earlier generations would have spoken of the economic constraints upon their work, too, and advised their descendants that the challenge remains constant: To create a tasty "soul" food of dramatic fare, one must utilize the diverse materials at hand, seasoning them with attention to technique, intelligence, passion, an occasional bit of humor, openness to inspiration, and most important, grace under pressure.

See also Aldridge, Ira; Black Arts Movement; Bullins, Ed; DuBois, W. E. B.; Jones, LeRoi (Amiri Baraka); Joplin, Scott; Kennedy, Adrienne; Literature of the United States; Minstrels/Minstrelsy; Parks, Suzan-Lori; Shange, Ntozake; Walker, George; Wilson, August

▪ ▪ *Bibliography*

Abramson, Doris E. *Negro Playwrights in the American Theatre, 1925–1959.* New York: Columbia University Press, 1969.

Boskin, Joseph. *Sambo: the Rise and Demise of an American Jester.* New York: Oxford University Press, 1986.

Brown-Guillory, Elizabeth, ed. *Their Place on the Stage: Black Women Playwrights in America.* New York: Greenwood Press, 1988.

Brown-Guillory, Elizabeth, ed. *Wines in the Wilderness: Plays by African American Women from the Harlem Renaissance to the Present.* New York: Greenwood Press, 1990.

Carter, Steven R. *Hansberry's Drama.* Urbana: University of Illinois Press, 1991.

Craig, E. Quita. *Black Drama of the Federal Theatre Era: Beyond the Formal Horizons.* Amherst: University of Massachusetts Press, 1980.

Fabre, Genevieve. *Drumbeats, Masks, and Metaphor.* Translated by Melvin Dixon. Cambridge, Mass.: Harvard University Press, 1983.

Fanon, Frantz. *Black Skin, White Masks.* Translated by Charles Lam Markmann. New York: Grove Press, 1967.

Fanon, Frantz. *The Wretched of the Earth.* Translated by Constance Farrington. New York: Grove Press, 1963.

Fletcher, Winona L. "Witnessing a 'Miracle': Sixty Years of 'Heaven Bound' at Big Bethel in Atlanta." *Black American Literature Forum* 25, no. 1 (Spring 1991): 83–92.

Harrison, Paul Carter. "Introduction: Black Theater in Search of a Source." In *Kuntu Drama: Plays of the African Continuum.* New York: Grove Press, 1974, pp. 5–29.

Harrison, Paul Carter. *Totem Voices: Plays from the Black World Repertory*. New York: Grove Press, 1989.

Hatch, James V., ed. *Black Theater, U.S.A.: Forty-Five Plays by Black Americans, 1847–1974*. New York: Free Press, 1974.

Hatch, James V., ed. *The Roots of African American Drama*. Detroit: Wayne State University Press, 1991.

Hill, Errol, ed. *The Theatre of Black Americans*. New York: Applause, 1990.

Mitchell, Angela. "Cheap Laughs: Bad Taste, Big Bucks." *Emerge* 4, no. 5 (March 1993): 49–51.

Mollette, Carlton, and Barbara Mollette. *Black Theatre: Premise and Presentation*. 1986. Reprint. Briston, Ind.: Wyndham Hall Press, 1992.

Neal, Larry. *Visions of a Liberated Future: Black Arts Movement Writings*. New York: Thunder's Mouth Press, 1989.

Perkins, Kathy A. *Black Female Playwrights: An Anthology of Plays Before 1950*. Bloomington: Indiana University Press, 1989.

Rampersad, Arnold. *The Life of Langston Hughes, Volume 1, 1902–1941: I, Too, Sing America*. New York: Oxford University Press, 1986.

Sanders, Leslie Catherine. *The Development of Black Theater in America*. Baton Rouge: Louisiana State University Press, 1988.

Scott, Freda L. "The Star of Ethiopia: A Contribution Toward the Development of Black Drama and Theater in the Harlem Renaissance." In Amritijit Singh, William S. Shiver, and Stanley Brodwin, eds. *The Harlem Renaissance: Revaluations*. New York: Garland, 1989.

Turner, Darwin T., ed. *Black Drama in America: An Anthology*. Washington, D.C.: Howard University Press, 1994.

Wiggins, William H., Jr. "Pilgrims, Crosses, and Faith: The Folk Dimensions of 'Heaven Bound'." *Black American Literature Forum* 25, no. 1 (Spring 1991): 93–100.

Wilkerson, Margaret B. *9 Plays by Black Women*. New York: New American Library, 1986.

Wilkerson, Margaret B. "Redefining Black Theatre." *The Black Scholar* 10, no. 10 (July/August 1979): 322–342.

Williams, Mance. *Black Theatre in the 1960s and 1970s*. Westport, Conn.: Greenwood Press, 1985.

Woll, Allen. *Black Musical Theatre: From "Coontown" to "Dreamgirls."* Baton Rouge: Louisiana State University Press, 1989.

SANDRA L. RICHARDS (1996)

DRED SCOTT V. SANDFORD

━┃┃┃━

In the *Dred Scott* decision of 1857 the U.S. Supreme Court ruled, by a 7–2 vote, that free blacks were not citizens of the United States and that Congress lacked the power to prohibit slavery in the western territories.

Scott was a Virginia slave, born around 1802, who moved with his master, Peter Blow, to St. Louis in 1830.

Blow subsequently sold Scott to Dr. John Emerson, an army surgeon, who took Scott to Fort Armstrong in Illinois, a free state, and Fort Snelling in the Wisconsin Territory, where slavery was prohibited by the Missouri Compromise. In 1846, after Emerson's death, Scott sued for his freedom (and that of his family). In 1850 a St. Louis court ruled that Scott became free by residing in Illinois and the Wisconsin Territory. In 1852 the Missouri Supreme Court, articulating the South's proslavery ideology, rejected precedents of its own that went back more than twenty-five years and reversed the lower court decision:

> Times are not as they were when the former decisions on this subject were made. Since then not only individuals but States have been possessed of a dark and fell spirit in relation to slavery, whose gratification is sought in the pursuit of measures, whose inevitable consequence must be the overthrow and destruction of our government.

Thus, Missouri would not recognize the freedom a slave might obtain by living in a free state.

In 1854 Scott began a new suit in United States District Court against John F. A. Sanford, a New Yorker who became the executor of Emerson's estate after Emerson's widow, the initial executor, remarried. Scott claimed he was a citizen of Missouri, suing Sanford in federal court because there was a diversity of state citizenship between the two parties. Sanford answered with a plea in abatement, arguing that no black, free or slave, could ever sue as a citizen in federal court. Federal District Judge Robert W. Wells ruled that if Scott was free, he was a citizen of Missouri for purposes of a diversity suit. However, Wells's ruling after the trial was that Scott was still a slave. Scott then appealed to the U.S. Supreme Court. At issue was more than his status: The Missouri Supreme Court's decision challenged the constitutionality of the Missouri Compromise. The central political issue of the 1850s—the power of the federal government to prohibit slavery in the territories—was now before the Supreme Court.

The ardently proslavery Chief Justice Roger B. Taney used *Dred Scott v. Sandford* (Sanford's name was misspelled by a clerk during the filing of the case) to decide this pressing political issue in favor of the South. Taney asserted that (1) the Missouri Compromise was unconstitutional because Congress could not legislate for the territories; (2) freeing slaves in the territories violated the Fifth Amendment prohibition on taking of property without due process; and (3) blacks, even those in the North with full state citizenship, could never be U.S. citizens. Taney asked: "Can a negro, whose ancestors were imported into

> ## Justice Roger Taney
>
> "We think they [Blacks] . . . are not included, and were not intended to be included, under the word 'citizens' in the Constitution, and can therefore claim none of the rights and privileges which that instrument provides for and secures to citizens of the United States."
>
> DRED SCOTT V. SANDFORD, 60 U.S. 393 (1856).

this country, and sold as slaves, become a member of the political community formed and brought into existence by the Constitution of the United States, and as such become entitled to all the rights, privileges, and immunities guaranteed by that instrument to the citizens?" Taney answered his own question in the negative. He asserted that at the nation's founding blacks were considered "beings of an inferior order, and altogether unfit to associate with the white race, either in social or political relations; and so far inferior, that they had no rights which the white man was bound to respect; and that the negro might justly and lawfully be reduced to slavery for his benefit." Taney thought his lengthy decision would open all the territories to slavery and destroy the Republican Party. In essence, he had constitutionalized racism and slavery. America, in Taney's view, was thoroughly a "white" nation.

Justice Benjamin Robbins Curtis of Massachusetts protested Taney's conclusions. Curtis noted: "At the time of the ratification of the Articles of Confederation [1781], all free native-born inhabitants of the States of New Hampshire, Massachusetts, New York, New Jersey, and North Carolina, though descended from African slaves, were not only citizens of those States, but such of them as had the other necessary qualifications possessed the franchises of electors, on equal terms with other citizens." Curtis concluded that when the Constitution was ratified, "these colored persons were not only included in the body of 'the people of the United States,' by whom the Constitution was ordained and established, but in at least five of the States they had the power to act, and doubtless did act, by their suffrages, upon the question of adoption." Curtis also argued that under a "reasonable interpretation of the language of the Constitution," Congress had the power to regulate slavery in the federal territories.

Northern Republicans and abolitionists were stunned and horrified. Horace Greeley, writing in the *New York Tribune,* called Taney's opinion "atrocious," "abominable," and a "detestable hypocrisy." The *Chicago Tribune* was repelled by its "inhuman dicta" and "the wicked consequences which may flow from it." Northern Democrats, on the other hand, hoped the decision would destroy the Republican Party by undermining its "free soil" platform and by finally ending the national debate over slavery in the territories. The *New York Journal of Commerce* hopefully declared that the decision was an "authoritative and final settlement of grievous sectional issues."

Ultimately, it was neither authoritative nor final. By 1858 northern Democrats faced a politically impossible dilemma. Their answer to the problem of slavery in the territories had been popular sovereignty—allowing the settlers to vote slavery up or down. But Taney's opinion denied both Congress and the settlers of a new territory the power to prohibit slavery. This made popular sovereignty meaningless. Stephen A. Douglas, the most prominent proponent of popular sovereignty, told his Illinois constituents that settlers could still keep slavery out of most of the territories by not passing laws that would protect slave property. This simply led to southern demands for a federal slave code for the territories and a split within the Democratic Party in 1860.

Republicans made Taney and the decision the focus of their 1858 and 1860 campaigns. Abraham Lincoln argued in his "house divided" speech (1858) that Taney's opinion was part of a proslavery conspiracy to nationalize slavery. He predicted "another Supreme Court decision, declaring that the Constitution of the United States does not permit a state to exclude slavery from its limits." He told Illinois voters that "we shall lie down pleasantly dreaming that the people of Missouri are on the verge of making their state free; and we shall awake to the reality, instead, that the Supreme Court has made Illinois a slave state."

Such arguments helped lead to a Republican victory in 1860. During the Civil War the Lincoln administration gradually reversed many of Taney's assertions about the status of blacks. This Republican policy culminated with the adoption of the Fourteenth Amendment, which explicitly overruled *Dred Scott,* declaring, "All persons born or naturalized in the United States . . . are citizens of the United States and of the State wherein they reside."

See also Slavery and the Constitution

■ ■ *Bibliography*

Ehrlich, Walter. *They Have No Rights: Dred Scott's Struggle for Freedom.* Westport, Conn.: Greenwood Press, 1979.

Fehrenbacher, Don E. *The Dred Scott Case: Its Significance in American Law and Politics.* New York: Oxford University Press, 1978.

Finkelman, Paul. *An Imperfect Union: Slavery, Federalism, and Comity.* Chapel Hill: University of North Carolina Press, 1981.

Finkelman, Paul. *Slavery in the Courtroom.* Washington, D.C.: Library of Congress, 1985.

Finkelman, Paul. *Dred Scott v. Sandford: A Brief History with Documents.* New York: St. Martin's, 1997.

Potter, David M. *The Impending Crisis: 1848–61.* New York: Harper & Row, 1976.

PAUL FINKELMAN (1996)
Updated bibliography

DREKE, VÍCTOR

MARCH 10, 1937

╺┤┝┤┝╸

Víctor Dreke Cruz is one of the heroes of Cuba's African story. Born in 1937 to a working-class family in the town of Sagua la Grande in Cuba's Villa Clara province, he joined the struggle against the dictatorship of Fulgencio Batista (1952–1958), rising to the rank of captain (the second highest rank, immediately below commander) in Fidel Castro's rebel army. After Castro assumed power in January 1959, Dreke served in the country's elite antiguerrilla force. In December 1962, at age twenty-five, he was promoted to the rank of commander.

In April 1965 Dreke left Havana on a secret mission. Cuba's interest in sub-Saharan Africa had quickened in late 1964. This was the moment of the great illusion, when the Cubans (and many others) believed that revolution beckoned in Africa. Guerrillas were fighting the Portuguese in Angola, Guinea-Bissau, and Mozambique, while in Congo Brazzaville a new government was loudly proclaiming its revolutionary sympathies. Above all, in Congo Leopoldville (the Democratic Republic of the Congo), an armed revolt had been spreading with stunning speed, threatening the survival of the corrupt pro-American regime that Presidents Dwight Eisenhower and John F. Kennedy had laboriously put in place. To save the Congolese regime, the Lyndon Johnson administration raised an army of a thousand white mercenaries in a major covert operation that provoked a wave of revulsion even among African leaders friendly to the United States. The Cubans saw the conflict as more than an African problem; as Che Guevara put it, "Our view was that the situation in the Congo was a problem that concerned all mankind" (Guevara, p. 41).

At the request of the Congolese rebels, Castro agreed to send a group of military instructors. (The Cuban approach to guerrilla warfare required instructors to fight with their students.) Che Guevara led the column, and Dreke was his second in command. But Central Africa was not ready for revolution. By the time the Cubans arrived in the Congo, the mercenaries had broken the resolve of the rebels. The story of Che's column is not one of great battles, but of 120 people thrust into an impossible situation in a totally alien world, who retained their humanity until the end. Guevara could only preside over the agony of the rebellion until the rebels' collapse left him no choice but to withdraw in November 1965. A few weeks later, in a secret document in which he assessed each of the men who had served under him in the column, Che honored Dreke with unusual praise: "He was, throughout our stay, one of the pillars on which I relied," he wrote. "The only reason I am not recommending that he be promoted is that he already holds the highest rank" (Gleijeses, p. 88).

After returning from the Congo, Dreke headed the bureau that trained Cubans going on military missions abroad and foreigners who came to Cuba for instruction in guerrilla warfare. In 1967, he left on a second African mission. By then the main focus of Havana's attention in Africa was Guinea-Bissau, where rebels were fighting for independence from Portugal. They were "Africa's most successful liberation movement," according to U.S. State Department reports (Gleijeses, p. 185). Until the colony won its independence in 1974, Cuban instructors helped operate the rebels' more sophisticated weapons, plan military strategy, and conduct military operations on the ground. Their contribution was, in the words of Nino, the senior rebel commander, "of the utmost importance." Dreke headed the Cuban military mission in Guinea-Bissau in 1967–1968 with great distinction, and he left a lasting impression on the men who served with him, Cubans and Guineans alike. "Dreke has always been a role model," a Cuban volunteer recalled, "very simple, very austere." He was, said Nino, "an exceptional leader" (Gleijeses, pp. 191, 196).

After returning to Cuba, Dreke held several high positions in the army, while also earning a law degree in 1981. After retiring from the army in 1990, he worked in Africa for two Cuban government corporations involved in trade and construction, and he was appointed ambassador to the Republic of Equatorial Guinea in 2003.

See also International Relations of the Anglophone Caribbean; Politics

■■ *Bibliography*

Anderson, Jon Lee. *Che Guevara: A Revolutionary Life.* New York: Grove Press, 1997.

Dreke, Víctor. *From the Escambray to the Congo: In the Whirl-wind of the Cuban Revolution.* New York: Pathfinder, 2002.

Gálvez, William. *El sueño africano del Che. Qué sucedió en la guerrilla congolesa?* Havana: Casa de las Américas, 1997.

Gleijeses, Piero. *Conflicting Missions: Havana, Washington, and Africa, 1959–1976.* Chapel Hill: University of North Carolina Press, 2002.

Guevara, Ernesto. *Pasajes de la guerra revolucionaria: Congo,* edited by Aleyda March. Barcelona: Grijalbo, 1999.

PIERO GLEIJESES (2005)

DREW, CHARLES RICHARD

DECEMBER 6, 1904
APRIL 1, 1950

The surgeon Charles Richard Drew was born and raised in Washington, D.C., graduating from Dunbar High School in 1922. In 1926 he received a B.A. from Amherst College. Drew was a first-rate basketball player, and upon graduation he was given an award as best athlete of the college. Between 1926 and 1928 he taught biology and chemistry at Morgan College (now Morgan State University) in Baltimore, where he also served as football coach and as director of athletics.

In 1928 Drew began medical studies at McGill University Medical School in Montreal, Canada. He excelled in medical science courses; won the annual prize in neuroanatomy; was elected to Alpha Phi Omega, the medical honorary scholastic fraternity; and received a prize for the top score in a medical exam competition. In 1933 Drew earned an M.D. and a Master of Surgery degree. He spent the next two years as an intern and a resident in medicine at Royal Victoria and Montreal General Hospitals.

As a McGill medical student, Drew was introduced to research on the chemical composition of blood and blood groups by John Beattie, a British medical researcher. A major problem then facing medical science was that quantities of whole, fresh blood large enough to match blood group types between blood donor and blood receiver were not readily available. Drew was bothered by the deaths of seriously ill or injured patients due to blood loss. Learning more about blood and how to preserve it over long periods of time became a research interest that Drew carried with him when he left Montreal to assume a teaching position at Howard University's College of Medicine in 1935.

In 1938 Drew received a research fellowship from the Rockefeller Foundation for study at Columbia-Presbyterian Hospital in New York City. He and John Scudder undertook research that led to the finding that it was blood plasma (the liquid portion of the blood, devoid of blood cells), rather than whole blood, that needed to be preserved for transfusions. Drew established an experimental blood bank at Columbia-Presbyterian Hospital. In 1940 he was awarded a doctorate at Columbia University with a thesis on "Banked Blood."

Returning to Howard University in 1940, Drew devoted himself to training medical students in surgery. His teaching was abruptly interrupted, however, by a call for blood plasma needed by wounded soldiers on the battlefields of Europe during World War II. The Blood Transfusion Association in New York City asked Drew to help. He was given leave from his instructional duties at Howard University to accept an assignment in the fall of 1940 as medical director of the Blood for Britain Program, which supplied blood for the British Red Cross. Under Drew's guidance, dried plasma was flown across the Atlantic Ocean to England. Once England had established its own banks, a larger blood program for U.S. military forces was developed. The American Red Cross and the Blood Transfusion Association jointly conducted this program, and Drew became its medical director.

In 1941 the military established a system of refusing blood donations from nonwhites to be used by whites. Blood donated by blacks was stored separately and given only to blacks. As director of the Red Cross Blood Bank Program, Drew took a strong stand against the racial separation of banked blood. As a result, he was asked to resign his directorship position, which he did. He then returned to teaching surgery at Howard University, where he became professor and head of the department of surgery, as well as surgeon-in-chief at Freedmen's Hospital.

On March 31, 1950, after working a long day that included performing several operations, Drew agreed to drive with other colleagues to a medical conference in Tuskegee, Alabama. He dozed at the wheel, and the car went off the road near Burlington, North Carolina, and overturned. Though stories abound that his medical emergency was ignored because of his race, he received prompt medical attention. He died from injuries resulting from the accident.

Drew gained much recognition during his lifetime. He was named Diplomate of Surgery by the American Board of Surgery in 1941; was a recipient of the Spingarn Medal from the NAACP in 1944; was granted honorary

Doctor of Science degrees from Virginia State College (1945) and Amherst College (1947); and was elected as a Fellow of the International College of Surgery (1946).

See also Howard University; Science

■ ■ *Bibliography*

Cobb, W. Montague. "Charles Richard Drew, M.D., 1904-1950." *Journal of the National Medical Association,* 42 (July 1950): 239–245.

Wynes, Charles E. *Charles Richard Drew: The Man and the Myth.* Urbana: University of Illinois Press, 1988.

ROBERT C. HAYDEN (1996)

DREW, TIMOTHY

See Noble Drew Ali

DU BOIS, SHIRLEY GRAHAM
NOVEMBER 11, 1896
MARCH 27, 1977

Writer and political activist Shirley Graham Du Bois was born Lola Bell Graham in 1896 near Indianapolis, Indiana, the daughter of an African Methodist Episcopal Church (AME) minister. She studied music at the Sorbonne and Harvard University, and from 1929 to 1931 she headed the music department at Morgan College in Baltimore. In 1931 she enrolled at Oberlin College, where she earned bachelor's and master's degrees. In 1932 her opera *Tom-Tom* was staged at the Cleveland Stadium. She became director of the Chicago unit of the Federal Theatre Project and then received a Rosenwald Fellowship for creative writing, which she used for study at Yale from 1938 to 1940.

Graham directed YWCA theater groups until the National Association for the Advancement of Colored People (NAACP) employed her as a field secretary in New York, a position she held from 1942 until 1944. During this period she began her series of biographies for young adults of noteworthy African Americans. Graham held a Guggenheim Fellowship in 1945–1947 and a National Institute of Arts and Letters Award in 1950. On February 14, 1951, she married her longtime friend and adviser, W. E. B. Du Bois, and devoted her energies to causes he championed.

At the invitation of President Kwame Nkrumah, the couple moved to Ghana in 1961, the year she also became a founding editor of *Freedomways.* From 1964 to 1966 Graham was the organizing director of Ghana television. When a coup toppled Nkrumah, she moved to Cairo. The U.S. Department of Justice would not permit her to return to the United States, citing her membership in numerous subversive groups. She died of cancer in Beijing in 1977.

See also Du Bois, W. E. B

■ ■ *Bibliography*

Brown-Guillory, Elizabeth. "Shirley Graham Du Bois." In *Black Women in America: An Historical Encyclopedia,* edited by Darlene Clark Hine. Brooklyn, N.Y.: Carlson, 1993.

Horne, Gerald. *Race Woman: The Lives of Shirley Graham Du Bois.* New York: New York University Press, 2000.

CHRISTINE A. LUNARDINI (1996)
Updated bibliography

DU BOIS, W. E. B.
FEBRUARY 23, 1868
AUGUST 27, 1963

Historian, sociologist, novelist, and editor William Edward Burghardt Du Bois was born in Great Barrington, Massachusetts. His mother, Mary Burghardt Du Bois, belonged to a tiny community of African Americans who had been settled in the area since before the American Revolution; his father, Alfred Du Bois, was a visitor to the region who deserted the family in his son's infancy. In the predominantly white local schools and Congregational church, Du Bois absorbed ideas and values that left him "quite thoroughly New England."

From 1885 to 1888 Du Bois attended Fisk University in Nashville, where he first encountered the harsher forms of racism. After earning a B.A. (1888) at Fisk, he attended Harvard University, where he took another B.A. (1890) and a doctorate in history (1895). Among his teachers were psychologist William James, philosophers Josiah Royce and George Santayana, and historian A. B. Hart. From 1892 to 1894 he studied history and sociology at the University of Berlin. His dissertation, "The Suppression of the African Slave-Trade to the United States," was published in 1896 as the first volume of the Harvard Historical Studies.

From 1894 to 1896 Du Bois taught at Wilberforce University in Ohio, where he met and married Nina

W. E. B. Du Bois. *Director of publications and research for the fledgling National Association for the Advancement of Colored People in 1910, Du Bois was also the founding editor of the NAACP's official media organ, the monthly* Crisis *magazine.* THE LIBRARY OF CONGRESS

Gomer, a student, in 1896. The couple had two children, Burghardt and Yolande. In 1896 he accepted a position at the University of Pennsylvania to gather data for a commissioned study of blacks in Philadelphia. This work resulted in *The Philadelphia Negro* (1899), an acclaimed early example of empirical sociology. In 1897 he joined the faculty at Atlanta University and took over the annual Atlanta University Conference for the Study of the Negro Problems. From 1897 to 1914 he edited an annual study of one aspect or another of black life, such as education or the church.

Appalled by the conditions facing blacks nationally, Du Bois sought ways other than scholarship to effect change. The death of his young son from dysentery in 1899 also deeply affected him, as did the widely publicized lynching of a black man, Sam Hose, in Georgia the same year. In 1900, in London, he boldly asserted that "the problem of the Twentieth Century is the problem of the color line." He repeated this statement in *The Souls of Black Folk* (1903), mainly a collection of essays on African-

American history, sociology, religion, and music, in which Du Bois wrote of an essential black double consciousness: the existence of twin souls ("an American, a Negro") warring in each black body. The book also attacked Booker T. Washington, the most powerful black American of the age, for advising blacks to surrender the right to vote and to a liberal education in return for white friendship and support. Du Bois was established as probably the premier intellectual in black America, and Washington's main rival.

Du Bois's growing radicalism also led him to organize the Niagara Movement, a group of blacks who met in 1905 and 1906 to agitate for "manhood rights" for African Americans. He founded two journals, *Moon* (1905–1906) and *Horizon* (1907–1910). In 1909 he published *John Brown,* a sympathetic biography of the white abolitionist martyr. Then in 1910 he resigned his professorship to join the new National Association for the Advancement of Colored People (NAACP) in New York, which had been formed in response to growing concern about the treatment of blacks. As its director of research, Du Bois founded a monthly magazine, *The Crisis.* In 1911 he published his first novel, *The Quest of the Silver Fleece,* a study of the cotton industry seen through the fate of a young black couple struggling for a life of dignity and meaning.

The Crisis became a powerful forum for Du Bois's views on race and politics. Meanwhile, his developing interest in Africa led him to write *The Negro* (1915), a study offering historical and demographic information on peoples of African descent around the world. Hoping to affect colonialism in Africa after World War I, he also organized Pan-African Congresses in Europe in 1919, 1921, and 1923, and in New York in 1927. However, he clashed with the most popular black leader of the era, Marcus Garvey of the Universal Negro Improvement Association. Du Bois regarded Garvey's "back to Africa" scheme as ill considered and Garvey as impractical and disorganized.

Du Bois's second prose collection, *Darkwater: Voices from Within the Veil* (1920), did not repeat the success of *The Souls of Black Folk* but captured his increased militancy. In the 1920s *The Crisis* played a major role in the Harlem Renaissance by publishing early work by Langston Hughes, Countee Cullen, and other writers. Eventually, Du Bois found some writers politically irresponsible; his essay "Criteria of Negro Art" (1926) insisted that all art is essentially propaganda. He pressed this point with a novel, *Dark Princess* (1928), about a plot by the darker races to overthrow European colonialism. In 1926 he visited the Soviet Union, then nine years old. Favorably impressed by what he saw, he boldly declared himself "a Bolshevik."

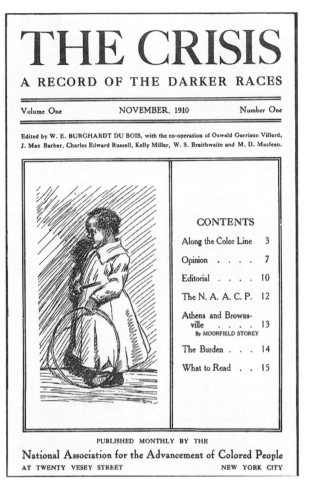

THE CRISIS

A RECORD OF THE DARKER RACES

Volume One   NOVEMBER, 1910   Number One

Edited by W. E. BURGHARDT DU BOIS, with the co-operation of Oswald Garrison Villard, J. Max Barber, Charles Edward Russell, Kelly Miller, W. S. Braithwaite and M. D. Maclean.

CONTENTS

Along the Color Line   3

Opinion   7

Editorial   10

The N. A. A. C. P.   12

Athens and Browns-
    ville   13
        By MOORFIELD STOREY

The Burden   .   .   .   14

What to Read   .   .   15

PUBLISHED MONTHLY BY THE

National Association for the Advancement of Colored People
AT TWENTY VESEY STREET   NEW YORK CITY

The cover for Volume One, Number One (November, 1910) of The Crisis: A Record of the Darker Races, *the monthly journal founded and edited by W. E. B. Du Bois.*

W.E.B. Du Bois

"...One even feels his two-ness—an American, a Negro; two souls, two thoughts, two unreconciled strivings, two warring ideals in one dark body, whose dogged strength alone keeps it from being torn asunder."

THE SOULS OF BLACK FOLK. CHICAGO:
A.C. MCCLURG AND CO., 1903.

The Great Depression increased Du Bois's interest in socialism but also cut the circulation of *The Crisis* and weakened his position with the leadership of the NAACP, with which he had fought from the beginning. In 1934 he resigned as editor and returned to teach at Atlanta Univer-

sity. His interest in Marxism, which had started with his student days in Berlin, dominated his next book, *Black Reconstruction in America* (1934), a massive and controversial revaluation of the role of the freedmen in the South after the Civil War. In 1936 Du Bois commenced a weekly column of opinion in various black newspapers, starting with the *Pittsburgh Courier.* He emphasized his continuing concern for Africa with *Black Folk: Then and Now* (1939), an expanded and updated revision of *The Negro.*

In 1940 Du Bois published his first full-length autobiography, *Dusk of Dawn: An Essay Toward an Autobiography of a Race Concept,* in which he examined modern racial theory against the major events and intellectual currents in his lifetime. In 1944 his life took another dramatic turn when he was suddenly retired by Atlanta University after tension grew between him and certain administrators. When the NAACP rehired him that year, he returned to New York as director of special research. In 1945 he was honored at the Fifth Pan-African Congress in Manchester, England, and published a bristling polemic, *Color and Democracy: Colonies and Peace.* A year later, he produced a controversial pamphlet, "An Appeal to the World," submitted by the NAACP on behalf of black Americans to the United Nations Commission on Civil Rights. In 1947 came his *The World and Africa,* an examination of Africa's future following World War II.

By this time Du Bois had moved to the left, well beyond the interests of the NAACP, which generally supported the Democratic Party. In 1948, when he endorsed the Progressive Party and its presidential candidate, Henry Wallace, he was fired. He then joined Paul Robeson, who was by this time firmly identified with radical socialism, at the Council on African Affairs, which had been officially declared a "subversive" organization. In 1950 Du Bois ran unsuccessfully for the U.S. Senate from New York on the American Labor Party ticket. Also that year, in another move applauded by communists, he accepted the chairmanship of the Peace Information Center, which circulated the Stockholm Peace Appeal against nuclear weapons.

Early in 1951 Du Bois and four colleagues from the Peace Information Center were indicted on the charge of violating the law that required agents of a foreign power to register. On bail and awaiting trial, he married Shirley Lola Graham, a fellow socialist and writer (his first wife had died in 1950). At the trial in November 1951, the judge heard testimony, then unexpectedly granted a motion by the defense for a directed acquittal. Du Bois was undeterred by his ordeal. In 1953, he recited the Twenty-third Psalm at the grave of Julius and Ethel Rosenberg, executed as spies for the Soviet Union. For such involvements, he found himself ostracized by some black leaders and organizations. "The colored children," he wrote, "ceased to hear my name."

Returning to fiction, he composed a trilogy, *The Black Flame,* about the life and times of a black educator seen against the backdrop of generations of black and white lives and national and international events (the trilogy comprised *The Ordeal of Mansart,* 1957; *Mansart Builds a School,* 1959; and *Worlds of Color,* 1961). After the government lifted its ban on his foreign travel in 1958, Du Bois visited various countries, including the Soviet Union and China. In Moscow on May 1, 1959, he received the Lenin Peace Prize.

In 1960 Du Bois visited Ghana for the inauguration of Kwame Nkrumah as its first president. He then accepted an invitation from Nkrumah to return to Ghana and start work on an *Encyclopedia Africana,* a project in which he had long been interested. In October 1961, after applying (successfully) for membership in the Communist Party, he left the United States. He began work on the project in Ghana, but illness the following year caused him to go for treatment to Romania. Afterward, he visited Peking and Moscow. In February 1963 he renounced his American citizenship and officially became a citizen of Ghana. He died in Accra, Ghana, and was buried there.

See also Communist Party of the United States; Council on African Affairs; Cullen, Countee; Great Depression and the New Deal; Harlem Renaissance; Hughes, Langston; National Association for the Advancement of Colored People (NAACP); Niagara Movement; *Pittsburgh Courier*; Universal Negro Improvement Association; Robeson, Paul; Washington, Booker T.

■ ■ *Bibliography*

Aptheker, Herbert. *Annotated Bibliography of the Published Writings of W. E. B. Du Bois.* Millwood, N.Y.: Kraus-Thomson, 1973.

Lewis, David Levering. *W. E. B. Du Bois: Biography of a Race 1868–1919.* New York: Henry Holt, 1993.

Rampersad, Arnold. *The Art and Imagination of W. E. B. Du Bois.* Cambridge, Mass.: Harvard University Press, 1976; New York, Schocken Books, 1990.

Willis, Deborah. *A Small Nation of People: W. E. B. Du Bois and African American Portraits of Progress.* New York: HarperCollins, 2003.

ARNOLD RAMPERSAD (1996)
Updated bibliography

DUB POETRY

The word "dub" in "dub poetry" is borrowed from recording technology, where it refers to the activity of adding and/or removing sounds. "Dub poetry," which is usually in Jamaican Creole, incorporates a music beat, often a reggae beat. It is often performed to an accompaniment of instrumental music, recorded or live. Although dub poets sometimes publish books, most of their work is designed for presentation live and is marketed in recordings. Some "dub poets" prefer not to be called by that name: They say they are simply poets, that some of what they write is manifestly not "dub poetry," and that, even in performance mode, they sometimes draw on musical forms that are not reggae or dub.

Dub poetry invites comparison with oral performance in any culture. In tracing its lineage, some commentators begin with African griots. Some point to more immediate connections—with Jamaican DJs of the 1970s, figures such as U. Roy, I. Roy, and Big Youth. "The 'dub-lyricist,'" wrote Linton Kwesi Johnson, "is the DJ turned poet. He intones his lyrics rather than sings them. Dub-lyricism is a new form of (oral) music-poetry" (Johnson, p. 398).

Early in 1979 a group of young poets in Jamaica began to promote the term "dub poetry" (adumbrated by Johnson) to identify work then being presented by Oku Onuora, Michael Smith ("Mikey"), and others. They paid frequent tribute to Jamaican poet Louise Bennett for having shown that Jamaican Creole can be the vehicle of significant art. Onuora (formerly Orlando Wong) was inspired by Bob Marley and the Wailers and other Jamaican reggae artists; he also learned from Langston Hughes, The Last Poets, Gil Scott-Heron, Kamau Brathwaite, and others steeped in the rhythms of black music.

The pioneer theorist on dub poetry, Onuora initially talked about its form: In a dub poem, he argued, reggae rhythms can be heard even when the poem is presented with no instrumental backing. By 1986 he was also highlighting sociopolitical content: "Dub poetry simply mean to take out and to put in, but more fi put in more than anything else. We take out the little isms, the little English ism and the little highfalutin business and the little penta-metre. . . . It's . . . dubbing in the rootsical, yard, basic rhythm that I-an-I know. Using the language, using the body. It also mean to dub out the isms and schisms and to dub consciousness into the people-dem head" (into the people's thinking; Morris, pp. 37-38).

Expressions such as "rootsical" (grounded, relating comfortably to poor black people), "I-an-I" (we), "isms and schisms" (pretentious ideologies and ideological disputes), and "consciousness" (progressive black consciousness) do not necessarily identify the speaker as Rastafarian, for Rastafarian influence is widely diffused. It is true, however, that a number of well-known dub poets are Rastafarian or have passed through a Rastafarian phase.

Like Rastafari and the Black Power movement (another major influence), dub poetry typically seeks to promote black consciousness and to confront injustice. Politically focused, it does not often explore subtle shifts of feeling or ambiguities of self-discovery. Some critics have noted with disapproval what they adjudge to be its limited emotional range and its tendency to rely on direct statement. Others commend dub poets for rhetorical force and political clarity and are critical of commentators who, invoking broad categories such as "performance poetry," seem inclined to blunt the political force of "dub." Various academics, including Gordon Rohlehr in *Voiceprint* (1989) and Carolyn Cooper in *Noises in the Blood* (1993), have praised particular pieces or poets, without seeming to endorse dub poetry in general as Christian Habekost does in *Verbal Riddim* (1993), which is an invaluable source of information.

Well known "dub poets"—though some resist the category—include Mutabaruka, Oku Onuora, the late Mikey Smith, Yasus Afari, Cherry Natural (Jamaica), Linton Kwesi Johnson, Benjamin Zephaniah (resident in the United Kingdom), Jean Binta Breeze (Jamaica and the U.K.), Lillian Allen, and Afua Cooper (based in Canada). Each is a compelling performer whose work has been available in recordings and in print. In 2002 *Mi Revalueshanary Fren: Selected Poems* by Linton Kwesi Johnson was published as a Penguin Modern Classic.

See also Bennett, Louise; Literature of the English-Speaking Caribbean; Rastafarianism; Reggae

■■ *Bibliography*

Brown, Stewart, Mervyn Morris, and Gordon Rohler, eds. *Voiceprint: An Anthology of Oral and Related Poetry from the Caribbean.* Burnt Mill, U.K.: Longman, 1989.

Cooper, Carolyn. *Noises in the Blood: Orality, Gender, and the "Vulgar" Body of Jamaican Popular Culture.* London: Macmillan, 1993. Durham, N.C.: Duke University Press, 1995.

Habekost, Christian. *Verbal Riddim: The Politics and Aesthetics of African-Caribbean Dub Poetry.* Amsterdam-Atlanta: Editions Rodopi B.V., 1993.

Johnson, Linton Kwesi. "Jamaican Rebel Music." *Race and Class* 17, no. 4 (1976): 398.

Morris, Mervyn. *Is English We Speaking and Other Essays.* Kingston, Jamaica: Ian Randle Publishers, 1999.

MERVYN MORRIS (2005)

DUNBAR, PAUL LAURENCE

JUNE 27, 1872
FEBRUARY 9, 1906

Paul Laurence Dunbar, the child of ex-slaves, was the first African-American writer to attain widespread fame for his literary activities. Known chiefly for his dialect poetry, Dunbar also broke new ground in several ways for the further development of an African-American literary tradition.

Born and raised in Dayton, Ohio, Dunbar showed early signs of literary ambition. He served as editor of his high school newspaper and at the same time began a short-lived newspaper of his own, the *Dayton Tattler,* focusing on matters of interest to the black community. Like most young black men, and despite a good school record, he confronted upon graduation a world with few opportunities and had to take work as an elevator operator; but he also became increasingly dedicated to his literary activity, especially to poetry. Encouraged by several white friends in Dayton as well as by the noted popular poet James Whitcomb Riley, Dunbar published locally his first book of poetry, *Oak and Ivy,* in 1892. However, he achieved real fame in 1896, when an expanded and revised collection, *Majors and Minors*—also published mainly for a local audience—came to the attention of the prominent American writer William Dean Howells. Howells admired it and saw to the publication that year of a larger volume, *Lyrics of Lowly Life,* by the established American firm Dodd, Mead. It was the first of five major collections to be published by the company during Dunbar's lifetime.

Singled out for praise by Howells, and serving as the basis for Dunbar's fame, was his dialect verse. Fitting broadly into the popular, mainly white-authored, plantation-tradition literature of the time, Dunbar's dialect poetry created a sentimental portrait of African-American folklife in the antebellum South, treating a variety of themes, from love and courtship to social life and folk ideas. Although the dialect Dunbar used owed more to its literary antecedents than to actual folk speech, he also drew heavily on folk traditions for his own subjects and themes and thus often succeeded in giving real life to the form, freeing it from the stereotypes that dominated the works of white practitioners. The publication of this work, together with successful public readings of it throughout the United States and abroad, made Dunbar among the most popular poets, regardless of race, in America at the turn of the twentieth century.

A postcard portrait of Paul Laurence Dunbar (1872–1906), proclaiming him the "Poet Laureate of the Negro Race." PHOTOGRAPHS AND PRINTS DIVISION, SCHOMBURG CENTER FOR RESEARCH IN BLACK CULTURE, THE NEW YORK PUBLIC LIBRARY, ASTOR, LENOX AND TILDEN FOUNDATIONS.

Dunbar's success with dialect poetry had a powerful impact on black American literature during its time. He had few black predecessors in the form—although such early black dialect writers as James Edwin Campbell and Daniel Webster Davis were his exact contemporaries—but as his fame grew, so did the volume of dialect poetry in African-American literature. It began to appear frequently in black newspapers and magazines, and few collections of African-American poetry over the next two decades lacked at least some examples of dialect verse. Many were dominated by it.

Dunbar himself was ambivalent about his success with the dialect form. He wrote a great deal of poetry in standard English and felt that this was his most important work. Much of this verse is significant, especially for its time, as Dunbar not only addressed such contemporary issues as southern racial injustice and violence but broke notably from conventions of piety and gentility that had

earlier dominated poetry by black Americans. Still, it was the dialect poetry that critics, black and white, praised during Dunbar's lifetime, a fact that the poet found greatly frustrating. His frustration spilled over into a personal life marked by real difficulties, including problems in his marriage to the talented writer Alice Moore Dunbar and the alcoholism and chronic ill health, culminating in tuberculosis, that led to his early death.

Although Dunbar made his reputation as a poet, his literary production during his brief life showed real diversity. It included a large number of short stories that appeared in popular magazines and in four major collections published by Dodd, Mead. Much of this short fiction complemented the popular dialect poetry, some of it written entirely in dialect and most of it featuring dialect-speaking folk characters. A few stories, however, moved in directions of protest, or of exploring issues of urbanization and cultural conflict. Dunbar also did some writing for the theater, including the highly popular musical comedy *Clorindy,* on which he collaborated with the composer William Marion Cook.

But some of his most important work, outside his poetry, lay in his novels. Dunbar published four novels; one, *The Love of Landry* (1900), was a sentimental work set in the American West, but the other three focused on questions of culture and identity in ways that allowed him to explore the issues affecting him as an individual and as an artist. These included *The Uncalled* (1899), tracing a young man's efforts to deal with pressures exerted on him to enter the ministry; *The Fanatics* (1901), a tale of Civil War–era Ohio; and *The Sport of the Gods* (1902), describing the travails of a black family forced to flee the South and to make its way in the more complex setting of urban New York. Only the last novel featured black protagonists, and it has often been considered the pioneering work in literary realism by a black writer. But all, excepting *The Love of Landry,* looked significantly and innovatively at the kinds of forces, cultural and psychological, that confront and constrain the individual in an effort to create a satisfying personal identity, and looked, at least implicitly at the meaning of race in American life.

Dunbar's work did not always fare well in the hands of critics in the years after his death. Not without justification, many found too much of the dialect work, despite the writer's efforts to the contrary, to be uncomfortably close to that of white plantation-tradition writers, contributing to the same stereotypes the plantation tradition helped to spread. But Dunbar's influence and originality remain important milestones in the subsequent evolution of an African-American literary tradition.

See also Dunbar-Nelson, Alice; Literature of the United States

▦ ▪ *Bibliography*

Baker, Houston A., Jr. "The 'Limitless' Freedom of Myth: Paul Laurence Dunbar's *The Sport of the Gods* and the Criticism of Afro-American Literature." In *Blues, Ideology, and Afro-American Literature: A Vernacular Theory,* pp. 114–138. Chicago: University of Chicago Press, 1984.

Martin, Herbert Woodward, and Ronald Primeau, eds. *In His Own Voice: The Dramatic and Other Uncollected Works of Paul Laurence Dunbar.* Athens: Ohio University Press, 2002.

Martin, Jay, ed. *A Singer in the Dawn: Reinterpretations of Paul Laurence Dunbar.* New York: Dodd, Mead, 1975.

Revell, Peter. *Paul Laurence Dunbar.* Boston: Twayne, 1979.

Wagner, Jean. *Black Poets of the United States from Paul Laurence Dunbar to Langston Hughes.* Translated by Kenneth Douglas. Urbana: University of Illinois Press, 1973, pp. 73–125.

DICKSON D. BRUCE JR. (1996)
Updated bibliography

DUNBAR-NELSON, ALICE

JULY 19, 1875
SEPTEMBER 18, 1935

▬▮▮▬——————————————

Writer Alice Dunbar-Nelson was born Alice Ruth Moore in New Orleans, Louisiana. From her father, Joseph Moore, a sailor who never lived with the family, she inherited the light-colored skin and hair that enabled her to pass as white when she wished. Her mother, Patricia Wright Moore, an ex-slave who was part black and part Native American, supported the family as a seamstress. After attending public schools, Dunbar-Nelson graduated from the teachers' training program at Straight College (now Dillard University) in her hometown in 1892. In addition to her teaching she worked as a stenographer and bookkeeper for a black printing firm. She was interested in theater, played the piano and cello, and presided over a literary society. In 1895 *Violets and Other Tales,* her first collection of stories, essays, and poetry, was published.

In 1896 Dunbar-Nelson moved with her family to West Medford, Massachusetts. The following year she moved to New York, where she taught public school in Brooklyn while she helped her friend Victoria Earle Matthews found the White Rose Mission (later the White Rose Home for Girls in Harlem), where she also taught. On March 8, 1898, she married the poet Paul Laurence Dunbar and moved to Washington, D.C., where he lived. Their romance had been conducted through letters. He first wrote to her after seeing her picture alongside one of her poems in a poetry review. At their first meeting they agreed to marry.

Although it was a stormy marriage, it significantly aided Dunbar-Nelson's literary career. In 1899 her husband's agent had her second collection, *The Goodness of St. Roque,* published as a companion book to Dunbar's *Poems of Cabin and Field.* The couple separated in 1902 and Dunbar-Nelson moved to Wilmington, Delaware, where she taught English at the Howard High School. Paul Dunbar died in 1906. In 1910 Dunbar-Nelson married a fellow teacher, Henry Arthur Callis, but that union soon dissolved. In 1916 she married Robert J. Nelson, a journalist with whom she remained until her death in 1935.

Dunbar-Nelson's writings, published continually throughout her life, displayed a wide variety of interests. After studying English literature as a special student at Cornell University, she published "Wordsworth's Use of Milton's Description of Pandemonium" in the April 1909 issue of *Modern Language Notes.* She also published several pedagogical articles, including "Is It Time for the Negro Colleges in the South to Be Put into the Hands of Negro Teachers?" (*Twentieth Century Negro Literature,* 1902) and "Negro Literature for Negro Pupils" (*The Southern Workman,* February 1922). *The Journal of Negro History* published her historical essay "People of Color in Louisiana" in two parts; the first appeared in October 1916 and the second in January 1917. From 1920 to 1922 she and Nelson published and edited the *Wilmington Advocate.* In addition, she reviewed contemporary literature and delivered political analyses in columns for the *Pittsburgh Courier* (1926, 1930) and the *Washington Eagle* (1926–1930).

In 1920 Dunbar-Nelson lost her job at Howard High School because of her political activity on behalf of women's and civil rights. That year she founded the Industrial School for Colored Girls in Marshalltown, Delaware, which she directed from 1924 to 1928. From 1929 to 1931 she served as executive secretary of the American Inter-Racial Peace Committee, a subsidiary of the American Friends (Quakers) Service Committee. She used this position to organize the National Negro Music Festival in 1929 and to engage in a ten-week cross-country speaking tour in 1930. In 1932 she moved to Philadelphia, where her husband was a governor appointee to the Pennsylvania Athletic Commission. Her lifelong interest in the African-American oral tradition prompted her to publish *Masterpieces of Negro Eloquence* in 1914 and *The Dunbar Speaker and Entertainer* in 1920. She was a member of the Delta Sigma Theta sorority and the Daughter Elks. Dunbar-Nelson is often considered a poet of the Harlem Renaissance. Her two most anthologized poems are "Sonnet" (often called "Violets"), and "I Sit and Sew." Her diary, published in 1984, is an invaluable source of information about her life.

See also Dunbar, Paul Laurence; Harlem Renaissance; Literature of the United States

■ ■ *Bibliography*

Brooks, Kristina. "Alice Dunbar Nelson's Local Colors of Ethnicity, Class, and Place." *MELUS* 23, no. 2 (1998): 3.

Hull, Gloria T. *Color, Sex, and Poetry: Three Women Writers of the Harlem Renaissance.* Bloomington: Indiana University Press, 1987.

Hull, Gloria, T., ed. *Give Us Each Day: The Diary of Alice Dunbar-Nelson.* New York: Norton, 1984.

MICHEL FABRE (1996)
Updated bibliography

DUNHAM, KATHERINE

JUNE 22, 1909

Born in Chicago and raised in Joliet, Illinois, choreographer and dancer Katherine Dunham did not begin formal dance training until her late teens. In Chicago she studied with Ludmilla Speranzeva and Mark Turbyfill, and danced her first leading role in Ruth Page's ballet *La Guiablesse* in 1933. She attended the University of Chicago on scholarship (B.A., social anthropology, 1936), where she was inspired by the work of anthropologists Robert Redfield and Melville Herskovits, who stressed the importance of the survival of African culture and ritual in understanding African-American culture. While in college she taught youngsters' dance classes and gave recitals in a Chicago storefront, calling her student company, founded in 1931, "Ballet Nègre." Awarded a Rosenwald Travel Fellowship in 1936 for her combined expertise in dance and anthropology, she departed after graduation for the West Indies (Jamaica, Trinidad, Cuba, Haiti, Martinique) to do field research in anthropology and dance. Combining her two interests, she linked the function and form of Caribbean dance and ritual to their African progenitors.

The West Indian experience changed forever the focus of Dunham's life (eventually she would live in Haiti half of the time and become a priestess in the vodoun religion), and caused a profound shift in her career. This initial fieldwork provided the nucleus for future researches and began a lifelong involvement with the people and dance of Haiti. From this Dunham generated her master's thesis (Northwestern University, 1947) and more fieldwork. She lectured widely, published numerous articles, and wrote three books about her observations: *Journey to Accompong* (1946), *The Dances of Haiti* (her master's thesis, published in 1947), and *Island Possessed* (1969), underscoring how African religions and rituals adapted to the New World.

And, importantly for the development of modern dance, her fieldwork began her investigations into a vocabulary of movement that would form the core of the Katherine Dunham Technique. What Dunham gave modern dance was a coherent lexicon of African and Caribbean styles of movement—a flexible torso and spine, articulated pelvis and isolation of the limbs, a polyrhythmic strategy of moving—which she integrated with techniques of ballet and modern dance.

When she returned to Chicago in late 1937, Dunham founded the Negro Dance Group, a company of black artists dedicated to presenting aspects of African-American and African-Caribbean dance. Immediately she began incorporating the dances she had learned into her choreography. Invited in 1937 to be part of a notable New York City concert, Negro Dance Evening, she premiered "Haitian Suite," excerpted from choreography she was developing for the longer *L'Ag'Ya*. In 1937–1938 as dance director of the Negro Unit of the Federal Theater Project in Chicago, she made dances for *Emperor Jones* and *Run Lil' Chillun,* and presented her first version of *L'Ag'Ya* on January 27, 1938. Based on a Martinique folktale (*ag'ya* is a Martinique fighting dance), *L'Ag'Ya* is a seminal work, displaying Dunham's blend of exciting dance-drama and authentic African-Caribbean material.

Dunham moved her company to New York City in 1939, where she became dance director of the New York Labor Stage, choreographing the labor-union musical *Pins and Needles.* Simultaneously she was preparing a new production, *Tropics and Le Jazz Hot: From Haiti to Harlem.* It opened February 18, 1939, in what was intended to be a single weekend's concert at the Windsor Theatre in New York City. Its instantaneous success, however, extended the run for ten consecutive weekends and catapulted Dunham into the limelight. In 1940 Dunham and her company appeared in the black Broadway musical *Cabin in the Sky,* staged by George Balanchine, in which Dunham played the sultry siren Georgia Brown—a character related to Dunham's other seductress, "Woman with a Cigar," from her solo "Shore Excursion" in *Tropics.* That same year Dunham married John Pratt, a theatrical designer who worked with her in 1938 at the Chicago Federal Theater Project, and for the next forty-seven years, until his death in 1986, Pratt was Dunham's husband and her artistic collaborator.

With *L'Ag'Ya* and *Tropics and Le Jazz Hot: From Haiti to Harlem,* Dunham revealed her magical mix of dance and theater—the essence of "the Dunham touch"—a savvy combination of authentic Caribbean dance and rhythms with the heady spice of American showbiz. Genuine folk material was presented with lavish costumes, plush settings, and the orchestral arrangements based on Caribbean rhythms and folk music. Dancers moved through fantastical tropical paradises or artistically designed juke joints, while a loose storyline held together a succession of diverse dances. Dunham aptly called her spectacles "revues." She choreographed more than ninety individual dances and produced five revues, four of which played on Broadway and toured worldwide. Her most critically acclaimed revue was her 1946 *Bal Nègre,* containing another Dunham dance favorite, "Shango," based directly on vodoun ritual.

If her repertory was diverse, it was also coherent. *Tropics and Le Jazz Hot: From Haiti to Harlem* incorporated dances from the West Indies as well as from Cuba and Mexico, while the "Le Jazz Hot" section featured early black American social dances, such as the juba, cakewalk, ballin' the jack, and strut. The sequencing of dances, the theatrical journey from the tropics to urban black America implied—in the most entertaining terms—the ethnographic realities of cultural connections. In her 1943 *Tropical Revue,* she recycled material from the 1939 revue and added new dances, such as the balletic "Choros" (based on formal Brazilian quadrilles) and "Rites de Passage," which depicted puberty rituals so explicitly sexual that the dance was banned in Boston.

Beginning in the 1940s, the Katherine Dunham Dance Company appeared on Broadway and toured throughout the United States, Mexico, Latin America, and especially Europe, to enthusiastic reviews. In Europe Dunham was praised as a dancer and choreographer, recognized as a serious anthropologist and scholar, and admired as a glamorous beauty. Among her achievements was her resourcefulness in keeping her company going without any government funding. When short of money between engagements, Dunham and her troupe played in elegant nightclubs, such as Ciro's in Los Angeles. She also supplemented her income through film. Alone, or with her company, she appeared in nine Hollywood movies and in several foreign films between 1941 and 1959, among them

Carnival of Rhythm (1939), *Star-Spangled Rhythm* (1942), *Stormy Weather* (1943), *Casbah* (1948), *Boote e Risposta* (1950), and *Mambo* (1954).

In 1945 Dunham opened the Dunham School of Dance and Theater (sometimes called the Dunham School of Arts and Research) in Manhattan. Although technique classes were the heart of the school, they were supplemented by courses in humanities, philosophy, languages, aesthetics, drama, and speech. For the next ten years many African-American dancers of the next generation studied at her school, then passed on Dunham's technique to their students, situating it in dance mainstream (teachers such as Syvilla Fort, Talley Beatty, Lavinia Williams, Walter Nicks, Hope Clark, Vanoye Aikens, and Carmencita Romero; the Dunham technique has always been taught at the Alvin Ailey studios).

During the 1940s and 1950s, Dunham kept up her brand of political activism. Fighting segregation in hotels, restaurants, and theaters, she filed lawsuits and made public condemnations. In Hollywood she refused to sign a lucrative studio contract when the producer said she would have to replace some of her darker-skinned company members. To an enthusiastic but all-white audience in the South, she made an after-performance speech, saying she could never play there again until it was integrated. In São Paulo, Brazil, she brought a discrimination suit against a hotel, eventually prompting the president of Brazil to apologize to her and to pass a law that forbade discrimination in public places. In 1951 Dunham premiered *Southland,* an hour-long ballet about lynching, though it was only performed in Chile and Paris.

Toward the end of the 1950s Dunham was forced to regroup, disband, and reform her company, according to the exigencies of her financial and physical health (she suffered from crippling knee problems). Yet she remained undeterred. In 1962 she opened a Broadway production, *Bambouche,* featuring fourteen dancers, singers, and musicians of the Royal Troupe of Morocco, along with the Dunham company. The next year she choreographed the Metropolitan Opera's new production of *Aida*—thereby becoming the Met's first black choreographer. In 1965–1966 she was cultural adviser to the President of Senegal. She attended Senegal's First World Festival of Negro Arts as a representative from the United States.

Moved by the civil rights struggle and outraged by deprivations in the ghettos of East St. Louis, an area she knew from her visiting professorships at Southern Illinois University in the 1960s, Dunham decided to take action. In 1967 she opened the Performing Arts Training Center, a cultural program and school for the neighborhood children and youth, with programs in dance, drama, martial arts, and humanities. Soon thereafter she expanded the programs to include senior citizens. Then in 1977 she opened the Katherine Dunham Museum and Children's Workshop to house her collections of artifacts from her travels and research, as well as archival material from her personal life and professional career.

Dunham has received numerous awards acknowledging her contributions. These include the Albert Schweitzer Music Award for a life devoted to performing arts and service to humanity (1979); a Kennedy Center Honors Award (1983); the Samuel H. Scripps American Dance Festival Award (1987); and induction into the Hall of Fame of the National Museum of Dance in Saratoga Springs, New York. (1987). That same year Dunham directed the reconstruction of several of her works by the Alvin Ailey American Dance Theater and *The Magic of Katherine Dunham* opened Ailey's 1987–1988 season. Later awards include the Presidential Medal of Arts, the French Legion of Honor, the Southern Cross of Brazil, the Grand Cross of Haiti, an NAACP Lifetime Achievement Award, Lincoln Academy Laureate, and the Urban Leagues' Lifetime Achievement Award.

In February 1992, at the age of eighty-two, Dunham again became the subject of international attention when she began a forty-seven-day fast at her East St. Louis home. Because of her age, her involvement with Haiti, and the respect accorded her as an activist and artist, Dunham became the center of a movement that coalesced to protest the U.S. deportations of Haitian boat-refugees fleeing to the United States after the military overthrow of Haiti's democratically elected President Jean-Bertrand Aristide. She agreed to end her fast only after Aristide visited her and personally requested her to stop.

Boldness has characterized Dunham's life and career. And, although she was not alone, Dunham is perhaps the best known and most influential pioneer of black dance. Her synthesis of scholarship and theatricality demonstrated, incontrovertibly and joyously, that African-American and African-Caribbean styles are related and powerful components of dance in America.

See also Ailey, Alvin; Ballet

■ ■ *Bibliography*

Aschenbrenner, Joyce. *Katherine Dunham: Dancing a Life.* Urbana: University of Illinois Press, 2002.

Beckford, Ruth. *Katherine Dunham: A Biography.* New York: Marcel Dekker, 1979.

Dunham, Katherine. *A Touch of Innocence.* New York: Harcourt Brace, 1959.

Perron, Wendy. "One Woman Revolution Katherine Dunham." *Dance Magazine* 74, no. 8 (August 2000).

SALLY SOMMER (1996)
Updated by publisher 2005

DURHAM MANIFESTO

On October 20, 1942—during World War II—a group of southern black leaders convened in Durham, North Carolina, to address the problem of increasing racial tension in the South. The convention, called the Southern Conference on Race Relations, was organized at the suggestion of Jessie Ames, a white moderate and an active member of the Commission on Interracial Cooperation (CIC). Ames, fearing that the voices of white and black southern moderates were being drowned out by more radical blacks and white supremacists, urged Gordon Blaine Hancock, a black sociologist and a moderate on racial issues, to convene the meeting. Ames expressed her hope that the black leaders would propose a "New Charter of Race Relations" for the South that would win the approval and support of white moderates, thereby restoring the role of the increasingly weak CIC and salvaging the possibility of interracial cooperation.

After some disagreement among the organizers (a group of black Virginians) over whether to include northern leaders, Hancock and the others decided to limit the conference to southern blacks. Of the eighty southern black leaders invited to attend the Durham conference, fifty-two accepted. Many of the attendees, including Charles Spurgeon Johnson of Fisk University, Benjamin E. Mays of Morehouse College, and Rufus E. Clement of Atlanta University, were former members of the CIC who had become disenchanted with the hesitant attitude of southern white moderates. In addition to Hancock, who served as the director of the conference, two other blacks from Virginia, Luther Porter Jackson and P. B. Young, the owner and editor of the *Norfolk Journal and Guide,* assumed leadership positions.

On December 15, 1942, the conference issued the Durham Manifesto, a statement outlining the leaders' demands for improving the position of African Americans in the South. In this statement of purpose, the delegates voiced their fundamental opposition to segregation but avoided a frontal attack on such issues as the desegregation of schools and public accommodations, which might appear to white southerners as calls for social equality. Instead the leaders expressed their belief that it was more important for the conference to address the "current problems of racial discrimination and neglect." Among the leaders' demands were calls for equal pay and opportunities for blacks in industry, the abolition of poll taxes and white primaries, the protection of civil rights, and a federal antilynching law. The leaders also implored white moderates to take a more active role in helping blacks combat racial discrimination in the South.

White moderates responded by organizing their own conference to address the black leaders' demands, and in June 1943 the two groups met at a collaborative conference in Richmond, Virginia, where they agreed to disband the CIC and replace it with the new Southern Regional Council. Many of the white leaders, however, objected to the Durham statement as too aggressive. When the conference finally drafted a common platform, it, like the Durham Manifesto, continued to avoid a direct confrontation on the issue of segregation. Although the Durham Manifesto failed to receive the full support of white moderates, it marked a major step forward in articulating an antisegregationist stance by southern black moderates.

See also Hancock, Gordon Blaine

■■ *Bibliography*

Gavins, Raymond. *The Perils and Prospects of Southern Black Leadership: Gordon Blaine Hancock, 1884–1970.* Durham, N.C.: Duke University Press, 1977.

Logan, Rayford Whittingham, ed. *What the Negro Wants.* Chapel Hill: University of North Carolina Press, 1944.

LOUISE P. MAXWELL (1996)

DU SABLE, JEAN BAPTISTE POINTE

c. 1750
1818

Jean Baptiste Pointe Du Sable (also spelled Au Sable, De Sable, and De Saible), the founder of Chicago, is thought to have been born in Saint-Domingue (now Haiti) to an African mother and a French mariner father. After his mother's death, his father sent him to Paris, where he was educated. After his stay in Paris, Du Sable worked as a seaman on his father's ships. How he came to North America is not known. According to one account, he immigrated to French Canada and became a fur trapper; another says he immigrated to Louisiana.

What is certain is that by 1779 Du Sable had traveled north to the Chicago River area, where he established trading posts on the sites of Peoria, Illinois, and Michigan City, Indiana. That year he also established a trading post at the mouth of the river, at a place local Indians called *Checagou*, the site of present-day Chicago. He returned that fall to Peoria, where his support of the Americans during the Revolutionary War angered the powerful Mackinac tribe, who were allies of Great Britain. Du Sable was arrested for espionage by British authorities, but his reputation was sufficiently impressive that not only was he released the following year but the British made him a trader for supplies for their fort and hired him to manage their own trading post.

In 1784, after the British left the region, Du Sable returned to Checagou, where he reestablished his trading post and built a cabin, the first house ever built in Chicago. Du Sable decorated it with French furniture and some twenty-three paintings, plus other luxury items. He lived in the region for sixteen years and married a Potawotomi Native American woman named Catherine, with whom he had two children.

In 1800, after an unsuccessful attempt at being elected chief of the Potawotomi, Du Sable suddenly sold his lucrative Chicago business and land holdings for about $1,200 and moved back to Peoria. Despite owning eight hundred acres of property there, a claim later upheld in a U.S. court, Du Sable lost his money and declared bankruptcy in 1814. Ironically, his land holdings in Chicago are now worth more than a billion dollars. Du Sable subsequently moved to St. Charles, Missouri, near St. Louis, where he died in poverty in 1818. His grave was discovered in St. Charles in 1991.

As the first permanent non–American Indian resident of the area, Du Sable is honored as the founder of Chicago. Plaques and a large high school in the city bear his name. The Du Sable Museum of African-American History, the oldest private nonprofit black museum in America, opened in 1961. In 1987 a portrait of Du Sable appeared on a postage stamp.

See also Black-Indian Relations

■■ *Bibliography*

Bennett, Lerone. "The Black Man Who Founded Chicago." In *Ebony* (November 1977): 64–78.

Katz, William. *Black People Who Made the Old West.* New York: Crowell, 1977.

MANSUR M. NURUDDIN (1996)
GREG ROBINSON (1996)

DUVALIER, FRANÇOIS

APRIL 14, 1907

APRIL 21, 1971

▮ ▮ ▮

François Duvalier was born on April 14, 1907, in Port-au-Prince, Haiti. As a child he was afflicted with yaws, a potentially disfiguring skin condition marked by sores, lesions, and pain in the bones and joints. Duvalier was one of a great many Haitian children plagued by yaws, but he was one of only a small number who had the opportunity to study at the Lycée Petion, where he studied under Dumarsais Estimé before going on to earn his medical license in 1934. As a doctor, Duvalier spearheaded a successful campaign to eradicate yaws and gained the famous nickname "Papa Doc."

Duvalier maintained an interest in politics and ethnology. He was part of a group of black intellectuals known as the Griots whose writings claimed a unique spiritual prowess attached to blackness and connected oppression to white and mulatto governments. Duvalier was a member of Mouvement Ouvrier Paysan (MOP), a popular black nationalist party led by Daniel Fignolé. In 1946 Duvalier was appointed minister of public health following the election to the presidency of his former teacher, Dumarsais Estimé. The Estimé government professed an adherence to *noirisme,* a black nationalist rhetoric closely connected to the *Négritude* and Griot movements. In 1950 Estimé provoked a coup by attempting to maintain the presidency through a constitutional amendment.

Duvalier was forced into the interior to hide out during the tenure of Colonel Paul Magloire (1907–2001) who became president shortly after the coup. Magloire remained in office until 1956, when he attempted to extend his presidency and was overthrown in another coup. This was followed by a series of six governments, all of which failed to gain enough support to endure longer than a few months. In 1957 Duvalier returned to the political scene and ran for president as the heir to Estimé's *noiriste* legacy. He gained the support of the military and a large segment of the black majority and was elected president later that year.

While in office, Duvalier constructed an image based upon a number of important Haitian personas. In an attempt to present himself as a patriarch, Duvalier looked to "the father of Haiti," Jean-Jacques Dessalines (1758–1806), for legitimacy. He named the army barracks after Dessalines and often compared himself to the famous ruler. Duvalier also campaigned with Estimé's widow and claimed to "take up the banner of *estimisme*" in order to reemphasize his link to the popular *noiriste* government of Estimé and its promises of modernization, autonomy, and black power. But Duvalier is best known for presenting himself as something of a *houngan,* or vodou priest. In particular he was connected with Gede, the *lwa* (spirit) most associated with death and comedy. Duvalier recognized the importance of vodou to the average citizen and was therefore quick to connect himself to it. He also attempted to control the egalitarian and potentially revolutionary possibilities of the religion through the manipulation of houngans throughout Haiti. Duvalier appointed many houngans to the upper positions of his personal army, the Tontons Macoutes. The term *Tonton Macoute* is Creole for "Uncle Basket," the "Bogeyman" of Haitian folklore. The Tontons Macoutes were recruited from the masses, operated as secret police, and owed personal loyalty to Duvalier. They dealt out violent retribution to Duvalier's political foes and were renowned for their brutality. Other presidents, such as Elie Lescot (ruled 1941–1946), had employed a personal guard, but never as effectively as "Papa Doc."

Duvalier's Tontons Macoutes were in part a response to the Haitian army, which had removed many presidents from office. To further secure his position vis-à-vis the army, Duvalier frequently switched the appointments of officers so that the military leadership remained fluid, which allowed him greater control of the forces. He also appointed lower-ranking black soldiers to high positions, and they often rewarded him with their loyalty. Based on his adoption of popular imagery, the infamous cruelty of the Tontons Macoutes, and the weakening of internal military opposition, Duvalier declared himself "president for life" in 1964. He remained in this dictatorial position until his death on April 21, 1971. Earlier that year he amended the constitution to allow his son Jean-Claude to take control of the presidency.

The Duvalier presidency was one of the highest periods of out-migration in Haitian history. Duvalier's authoritarian regime and the often arbitrary violence of the Tontons Macoutes led large numbers of Haitians to seek refuge, primarily in the United States, Canada, Jamaica, and the Dominican Republic. While Duvalier improved the condition of a number of previously immobile poor, black Haitians, the overall conditions under Duvalier were fairly desperate and the average Haitian suffered under his reign.

See also Dessalines, Jean-Jacques; Estimé, Dumarsais; Magloire, Paul; Négritude

François Duvalier (1907–1971). Duvalier reads his acceptance speech during a ceremony in which he was sworn in as the thirty-fourth president of Haiti in 1957. Declaring himself "president for life" in 1964, the authoritarian leader reigned in that dictatorial position until his death. © BETTMANN/CORBIS

▪ ▪ *Bibliography*

Abbott, Elizabeth. *Haiti: The Duvaliers and Their Legacy.* New York: McGraw-Hill, 1988. Rev. ed., New York: Simon and Schuster, 1991.

Diederich, Bernard, and Al Burt. *Papa Doc: The Truth about Haiti Today.* New York: McGraw-Hill, 1969.

Farmer, Paul. *Aids and Accusation: Haiti and the Geography of Blame.* Berkeley: University of California, 1992.

Fergusson, James. *Papa Doc, Baby Doc: Haiti and the Duvaliers.* Oxford: Basil Blackwell, 1987.

Mintz, Sidney. *Caribbean Transformations.* Chicago: Aldine, 1975. Reprint, New York: Columbia University, 1989.

SEAN BLOCH (2005)

EASTON, HOSEA

SEPTEMBER 1, 1798

1837

In 1837 the abolitionist Hosea Easton published one of the earliest analyses of slavery by an African American, *Treatise on the Intellectual Character, and Civil and Political Condition of the Colored People of the United States*. Although it addressed the issues facing African Americans in a comprehensive fashion, it attracted little enduring attention.

Easton came from a distinguished family of mixed African, white, and Native American heritage. His father, James (1854–1830), was a skilled ironworker in North Bridgewater (now Brockton), Massachusetts. James Easton established a manual training school for young black men; its failure after nearly ten years of existence, coupled with the failure of James Easton's business, embittered Hosea.

Hosea Easton's early years are obscure, but by 1828 he was active in Boston and taking his position among the elite. His first publication was a "Thanksgiving Day Address" to the black population of Providence, Rhode Island (1828). He was a delegate to the first National Col-

ored Convention, held in Philadelphia in 1831, as well as to subsequent conventions. In 1833 he became pastor of Talcott Street Congregational Church in Hartford, Connecticut. Racial tensions and violence in the city ran high, and in 1836, just after he became pastor of the Colored Methodist Episcopal Zion church, the building was burned.

Easton perceived clearly the limited extent to which self-help and uplift within the black community could improve the situation. His *Treatise* addressed whites and called on them to realize the deleterious effects of racism and to take steps to repair the damages it caused. The work appeared shortly before his death.

See also Abolition; Antebellum Convention Movement

▪ ▪ *Bibliography*

Price, George R., and James Brewer Stewart, eds. *To Heal the Scourge of Prejudice: The Life and Writings of Hosea Easton.* Amherst: University of Massachusetts Press, 1999.

ROBERT L. JOHNS (2001)

EBONY

Published by the Johnson Publishing Company, *Ebony* has the largest circulation of any African-American periodical. Founded in 1945, it grew out of an attempt by publisher John H. Johnson to please two staff members who wanted to start an entertainment magazine, *Jive*. Johnson agreed to a three-way partnership on the project, but the two staffers were unable to put up money, so Johnson assumed full ownership. Johnson changed the style of the proposed magazine into one whose philosophy would be to highlight the positive side of African-American life, emphasizing black pride and achievements rather than oppression and poverty. Recognizing the widespread appeal of photos, Johnson planned a monthly glamour magazine on glossy paper, in the style of the popular weekly *Life*, filled with pictures of prominent and successful blacks. The new magazine, which Johnson named *Ebony* (after the beautiful and strong black wood), was planned during World War II, but because of paper restrictions, the first issue did not appear until November 1, 1945. Johnson had pledged to accept no advertisements until circulation reached 100,000; the magazine was an immediate success and the first ads appeared in the May 1946 issue. By May 1947, when *Ebony* became the first African-American periodical large enough to be audited by the Audit Bureau of Circulation, its circulation had reached 309,715. Despite its prestige and large circulation, however, poor advertising revenues made it unprofitable until Johnson secured advertising contracts from white firms previously reluctant to purchase space in African-American publications.

Ebony has drawn some criticism over the years for the showy, escapist nature of its features and its emphasis on the activities of wealthy blacks, although the magazine took a more activist direction starting in the era of the civil rights movement. Over time, the magazine has added sections on cooking, health, and gossip. The enormous success of *Ebony* has inspired numerous competitors over the years, and the magazine has had numerous spin-offs, including the periodicals *Ebony Man,* the now defunct *Ebony Jr.,* the Ebony Fashion Fair traveling fashion show, and the syndicated television program *Ebony/Jet Showcase.*

In the 1990s the magazine's circulation was about 1.9 million, of which 12 percent were white, and *Ebony* was distributed in some forty countries, including many in Africa. African-American stars came out in force in 1996 to celebrate fifty years of the magazine in a TV special titled *Celebrate the Dream: 50 Years of Ebony Magazine.*

Ebony presented a redesigned look and new features with its issue of July 2003, the journal's first major update in more than two decades. Circulation in 2004 was estimated at about 1.6 million.

See also *Black World/Negro Digest; Jet;* Journalism

■ ■ *Bibliography*

Graves, Earl. "Johnson Celebrates 50th," *Black Enterprise* 23 (November 1992): 26.

Jackson, Jesse. "Growing Up with *Ebony.*" *Ebony* 51, no. 1 (November 1995): 50th anniversary issue.

Johnson, John H., and Lerone Bennett Jr. *Succeeding Against the Odds,* Chicago: Johnson Publishing Co., 1989.

GREG ROBINSON (1996)
Updated by publisher 2005

ECKSTINE, BILLY

JULY 8, 1914
MARCH 8, 1993

Popular singer and bandleader William Clarence "Billy" Eckstine was born in Pittsburgh, the youngest of three children. His family moved several times in his early childhood, and he attended high school in Washington, D.C. He later attended the St. Paul Normal and Industrial School in Lawrenceville, Virginia, and Howard University.

Eckstine began his career in show business as a singer and nightclub emcee in Buffalo, Detroit, and Chicago. In 1939 he was hired as the main vocalist for the big band of Earl "Fatha" Hines. While with Hines, he introduced Dizzy Gillespie, Charlie Parker, and Sarah Vaughan to the Hines band. After a number of hit recordings, including "Jelly, Jelly" (1940) and "Skylark" (1942), he left Hines in 1943.

In 1944 Eckstine organized his own big band, with personnel that included many up-and-coming bebop musicians, including Dizzy Gillespie, Miles Davis, Charlie Parker, Dexter Gordon, and Art Blakey. When, for financial reasons, he was obliged to abandon the band in 1947, he became a solo singer. His smooth baritone was particularly well-suited for ballads. In the late 1940s and early 1950s his popularity rivaled that of Frank Sinatra. He was one of the first black singers to transcend the race market and to become a national sex symbol.

Eckstine spent the next several decades as a performer in nightclubs, often accompanied by pianist Bobby Tucker. He also appeared in such films as *Skirts Ahoy* (1953), *Let's Do It Again* (1975), and *Jo Jo Dancer: Your Life Is Call-*

ing (1986). "Mr. B," as he was widely known, occasionally played the trumpet but was primarily known as a singer. He influenced several generations of African-American singers, including Joe Williams, Arthur Prysock, and Lou Rawls. He died in Pittsburgh.

See also Blakey, Art (Buhaina, Abdullah Ibn); Davis, Miles; Gillespie, Dizzy; Jazz; Parker, Charlie; Vaughan, Sarah

■ ■ *Bibliography*

Burn, Jim. "The Billy Eckstine Band." *Jazz Monthly* 13, no. 11 (1968): 6.

Dance, Stanley. *The World of Earl Hines.* New York: Scribner, 1977. Reprint, New York: Da Capo, 1985.

Gibson, F. "The Billy Eckstine Band." *Jazz Journal* 23, no. 5 (1970): 2–3.

Southern, Eileen. "'Mr. B' of Ballad and Bop." *The Black Perspective in Music* 7 (1979): 182–190; 8 (1980): 54–60.

Travis, Dempsey J. *An Autobiography of Black Jazz.* Chicago: Urban Research Institute, 1983.

EDDIE S. MEADOWS (1996)
Updated bibliography

ECONOMIC CONDITION, U.S.

▌▌▌————————————

Despite the impression of economic progress and success conveyed via the media by talk-show host Oprah Winfrey, basketball legend Michael Jordan, and business mogul Robert Johnson, the general economic status of African Americans in the United States is best characterized as a condition of persistent disparity. Relative economic outcomes for black Americans consistently lag behind those of whites collectively and most other nonblack segments of the U.S. population.

Most of the U.S. population, approximately 80 percent of the total, self-reports its race as white in recent decennial censuses. This, however, masks major variation in economic outcomes among them. In Census 2000, for example, white males ages 25 to 64 who declared Irish ancestry reported annual mean earnings of $37,029, white males who declared English ancestry reported annual mean earnings of $37,995, and white males who declared Russian ancestry reported annual mean earnings of $48,176. All of these reports were at least $10,000 higher than the $26,637 annual mean earnings reported by black males ages 25 to 64.

All groups of men reporting a white racial identity and European ancestry earned more than black males. In fact, virtually all of the thirty-five white, European ethnic groups in the 1980, 1990, and 2000 censuses reported earnings outcomes at or above the national mean.

For females, racial disparities in annual earnings were not as large, but generally white females with European ancestry still earned more than black women. White females who declared Irish ancestry reported annual mean earnings of $27,376; white females who declared English ancestry reported annual mean earnings of $27,405, and white females who declared Russian ancestry earned $34,586. For 25- to 64-year-olds, black women's mean annual earnings were $23,809.

Coupled with lower earnings when at work, blacks in the United States suffered far greater exposure to joblessness. Racial differences are pronounced, even when educational attainment is taken into account.

In 2004 the Bureau of Labor Statistics (BLS) estimated that annual unemployment rates for white men and white women 16 years of age and older were 5 percent and 4.7 percent respectively. In contrast, for black men and black women in the same age category the rates were more than twice as high, 11.1 percent and 9.8 percent respectively.

The gap for teens was even greater. In 2004 white males 16 to 19 years of age had an unemployment rate estimated at 16.3 percent by the BLS; white females 16 to 19 years of age had a rate of 13.6 percent. But for black males ages 16 to 19 the unemployment rate was 35.6 percent, and for black females it was 28.2 percent.

Data from 2002 is the most recent available from BLS that provides information for education-adjusted unemployment rates by race for persons 25 years of age and older. For whites with less than a high school degree the unemployment rate was 7.5 percent, with a high school degree it was 4.5 percent, with some college education it was 4.2 percent, with an associate degree it was 3.5 percent, and with a bachelor's degree it was 2.7 percent. Again, in contrast, in 2002 for blacks 25 years of age and older with less than a high school degree the unemployment rate was 13.6 percent, with a high school degree it was 8.8 percent, with some college it was 8.8 percent, with an associate degree it was 6 percent, and with a bachelor's degree it was 4.2 percent.

Thus, a black college graduate had almost the same odds of exposure to joblessness as a white high school graduate—and greater odds of exposure to joblessness than whites with some college education or an associate degree. And blacks with some college education had a greater likelihood of being unemployed than whites with less than a high school degree.

The racial disparity in education-adjusted unemployment rates suggests that discriminatory practices remain central to maintaining black disadvantage in U.S. labor markets. Evidence of the ongoing significance of discrimination in employment is compelling. The best available statistical inquiries indicate that there was a dramatic decline in labor market discrimination affecting both earnings and occupational status in the decade immediately following passage of the Civil Rights Act of 1964. Thereafter, however, black men have continued to suffer fairly stable 12 to 15 percent losses in earnings due to labor market discrimination relative to all men in the United States. Correspondingly, they also have incurred 8 to 10 percent losses in occupational status, measured by the Occupational Score (OCCSCORE) index, from 1980 through 2000.

Although the statistical procedures used by economists generally do not detect discriminatory losses for black women in earnings relative to all women, those procedures do find evidence of 5 to 6 percent discriminatory losses in occupational status again measured by OCCSCORE between 1980 and 2000. Furthermore, direct tests of discrimination via audit studies and résumé controls—utilizing both trained actors seeking jobs and utilizing correspondence tests, where race is signaled to prospective employers by the use of names—consistently expose significant levels discrimination against both black men and black women.

So even if blacks attain equivalent or superior credentials as whites, whites are still beneficiaries of racial privilege in U.S. labor markets. Higher levels of educational attainment improve an individual African American's labor market position vis-à-vis other African Americans, but they do not insulate him or her from labor market discrimination. Indeed, there is some preliminary evidence that indicates that the magnitude of discriminatory deficits in earnings and occupational status rises as black educational attainment increases.

The historical record is revealing in this regard. Between 1880, a mere fifteen years after the end of slavery in the United States, and 1910, African Americans underwent a spectacular increase in literacy. The black literacy rate rose from less than 30 percent in 1880 to close to 70 percent by 1910. As literacy rose, the magnitude of discriminatory losses in occupational prestige also grew substantially. Thus, the consolidation of Jim Crow practices went hand-in-hand with improved black skills. Discrimination began to function more intensively to exclude blacks from white terrain as the skills basis for exclusion eroded.

Far more pronounced than racial differences in earnings are racial differences in wealth. The Survey of Income and Program Participation provides data from 1988 that demonstrates that the mean net worth of white families was $127,237, while mean black family net worth was only $31,678. This would constitute a black-white mean wealth ratio of 25 percent. During the same year the black-white household income ratio was 63 percent. According to Thomas Shapiro (2001), even taking "the average black household and [endowing] it with the same income and age and with comparable occupational, educational, and other attributes as the average white household still [would leave] a $25,794 racial gap in financial assets."

At every income/education level blacks have significantly lower levels of wealth than whites. The racial gap in wealth is so vast that it renders it misleading to treat black and white families with similar income, educational, or occupational status levels as equivalently middle class. The black middle class is decidedly wealth poor in comparison with the white middle class.

By 1993 black median net worth was only 9.7 percent of white median net worth ($4,418 versus $45,740). A study conducted by the Pew Hispanic Center found that by 2002 the median net worth of a black household was $6,000, while median white wealth was $88,000, barely an 8 percent ratio.

Why does this matter? Wealth provides the capacity to take advantage of windfall opportunities, to pursue the option of self-employment, to ensure that one's offspring receive a quality education especially if public schools are unsatisfactory, to protect one's family in times of emergency, and to have access to homeownership, the major source of equity for most American families.

The racial gap in wealth is not attributable to greater black profligacy in spending. If anything the most recent research on consumption behavior indicates that, after adjusting for income, the black savings rate is at least as high as the white savings rate. The major source of personal wealth today is intergenerational transfers, in the forms of in vivo (transfers of wealth made by living relatives) transfers and inheritances; these transfers constitute large, non-merit sources of pecuniary resources.

While inheritances among those who have the capacity to provide them are larger, in vivo transfers are vital for maintaining and increasing wealth because of the timing of such transfers during the course of the life cycle. Major in vivo transfers occur at graduation, marriage, the birth of the child, or as down payments at the initial purchase of a home.

The magnitude of in vivo transfers and inheritances made by blacks are much smaller than those made by whites. M. O. Wilhelm (2001) has estimated not only that a much smaller proportion of blacks receive inheritances

Western Migration

After the Civil War, Reconstruction began social, but not economic, reform in the South. By the 1870s African Americans still seemed to be facing a bleak future despite Emancipation having been declared a decade earlier. Southern legislatures passed laws forbidding blacks to own land and other measures to restrict the freedoms of African Americans. Hate groups such as the Ku Klux Klan formed during this time as whites feared retribution for years of slavery, thus producing an environment even more hostile to blacks. Some African Americans began to feel that true freedom could be gained only through emigrating out of the South.

As a result, many African Americans went westward. African American laborers worked as cattlemen, cleared the land, built homes and raised crops and livestock.

One of the most well-known African-American westerners is Bill Pickett, whom some dub "the greatest cowboy of his day." He was born in Texas in 1870 and left school in the fifth grade to become a ranch hand. With his four brothers, he started the Pickett Brothers Bronco Busters and Rough Riders Association, performing rodeo shows all over the United States and Canada.

Oklahoma became a popular destination for African Americans during the late nineteenth and early twentieth centuries. Several all black towns were established after the Civil War, including Boley, Oklahoma, with more than 5,000 residents by 1905. Early settlers here were accorded the privileges of owning their own businesses, governing their own communities, and owning homes without the threat of white hostility present in the South.

From the beginning of the U.S. migration westward, African Americans were part of it either as freed people or as slaves. Along with everyone else immigrating to the west, emigrating free blacks were looking for a better way of life. The West provided hope for more freedom and diminished racial tension.

ERIC LINDERMAN

than whites (6 percent versus 24 percent) but also that the mean black inheritance is $41,985, while the mean white inheritance is $144,652. The racial incidence of in vivo transfers in a given year is similar at about 20 percent, but, according to Wilhelm, the black mean transfer is $805 while the white mean transfer is $2,824.

Blacks provide smaller inheritances and in vivo transfers because blacks have less wealth in the first place. Thus, the wealth gap is a cumulative product of intergenerational racial inequality. It originates with the failure of the nation to provide ex-slaves with an initial foundation in land ownership with the abrogation of the commitment to provide each freedman family of four with forty acres. The commitment evinced in General Sherman's Special Field Order No. 15, the first Freedman's Bureau Act, and the Southern Homestead Act went unfulfilled. Indeed, as Joe Feagin has observed in *Black Commentator*, the homestead legislation provided white families, including new immigrants, with access to public land and wealth between the 1860s and 1930s. Forty-six million white Americans received 246 million acres of land; only four thousand African Americans acquired land under the Homestead Act.

The commitment to forty acres per family of four would have provided 4 million ex-slaves with 40 million acres of land. By dint of their own determination and perseverance, blacks accumulated 15 million acres of land by the start of the twentieth century, still a shortfall of 25 million acres from the original promise. But the seizure of black-owned property by theft, fraud, and outright land taking by white terrorists became the norm throughout the first half of the century to such an extent that by the 1980s black land ownership had declined to 1 million acres. Some prosperous black communities literally were exterminated in white massacres, for example, Wilmington, North Carolina (1898), Tulsa, Oklahoma (1921), and Rosewood, Florida (1923).

The systematic denial of access to wealth and the systematic deprivation of wealth accumulated created the conditions in which blacks collectively have had fewer resources to endow upon subsequent generations. This is what has produced and sustained the gap in wealth, the most palpable and virulent dimension of racial economic inequality in the United States. A serious commitment to addressing the economic condition of black Americans will require contemplation of substantive procedures for engineering a racial redistribution of wealth.

See also Education in the United States; Entrepreneurs and Entrepreneurship; Literacy Education; Politics; Reparations

■ ■ *Bibliography*

Bertrand, Mary, and Sendhil Mullainathan. "Are Emily and Greg More Employable Than Lakisha and Jamal?" *American Economic Review* 94, no 4 (September 2004): 991–1013.

Darity, William, Jr., and Patrick Mason. "Evidence on Discrimination in Employment: Codes of Color, Codes of Gender." *Journal of Economic Perspectives* 12, no. 2 (spring 1998): 63–91.

Darity, William, Jr., and Samuel Myers Jr. "Racial Economic Inequality in the USA." In *The Blackwell Companion to Sociology,* edited by Judith Blau. Oxford: Blackwell Publishers, 2001.

Darity, William, Jr., Jason Dietrich, and David Guilkey. "Racial and Ethnic Inequality in the United States: A Secular Perspective." *American Economic Review* 87, no. 2 (May 1997): 301–305.

Gittleman, Maury, and Edward N. Wolff. "Racial Differences in Patterns of Wealth Accumulation." *Journal of Human Resources* 39, no. 1 (winter 2004): 193–227.

Shapiro, Thomas N. "The Importance of Assets: The Benefits of Spreading Asset Ownership." In *Assets for the Poor: The Benefits of Spreading Asset Ownership,* edited by Thomas N. Shapiro and Edward Wolff. New York: Russell Sage Foundation, 2001.

Wilhelm, Mark O. "The Role of Intergenerational Transfers in Spreading Assets." In *Assets for the Poor: The Benefits of Spreading Asset Ownership,* edited by Thomas N. Shapiro and Edward Wolff. New York: Russell Sage Foundation, 2001.

"Wealth of a White Nation." Published in *Black Commentator* (October 21, 2004). Available from <http://news.ncmonline.com/news/view_article.html>.

Winbush, Raymond. "The Earth Moved: Stealing Black Land in the United States." In *Should America Pay? Slavery and the Raging Debate over Reparations,* edited by Raymond Winbush. New York: HarperCollins, 2003.

Wolff, Edward. "Recent Trends in Wealth Ownership, from 1983 to 1998." In *Assets for the Poor: The Benefits of Spreading Asset Ownership,* edited by Thomas N. Shapiro and Edward Wolff. New York: Russell Sage Foundation, 2001.

WILLIAM DARITY JR. (2005)

EDELMAN, MARIAN WRIGHT

JUNE 6, 1939

The daughter of Arthur Jerome Wright, minister of Shiloh Baptist Church, and Maggie Leola Wright, a community activist, Marian Edelman, an attorney and the founder of the Children's Defense Fund, was born and raised in Bennetsville, South Carolina. She attended Spelman College, from which she graduated as valedictorian in 1960. During her senior year Edelman participated in a sit-in at City Hall in Atlanta. Responding to the need for civil rights lawyers, Edelman entered Yale Law School as a John Hay Whitney Fellow in 1960. After graduating from law school in 1963, she became the first black woman to pass the bar in Mississippi. From 1964 to 1968 she headed the NAACP Legal Defense and Education Fund in Mississippi, where she met her husband, Peter Edelman, a Harvard Law School graduate and political activist. In 1971 she became director of the Harvard University Center for Law and Education. She was also the first black woman elected to the Yale University Corporation, where she served from 1971 to 1977.

Edelman is best known for her work with the Children's Defense Fund (CDF), a nonprofit child advocacy organization that she founded in 1973. The CDF offers programs to prevent adolescent pregnancy, to provide health care, education, and employment for youth, and to promote family planning. In 1980 Edelman became the first black and the second woman to chair the Board of Trustees of Spelman College. She has been the recipient of numerous honors and awards for her contributions to child advocacy, women's rights, and civil rights, including the MacArthur Foundation Prize Fellowship (1985), the Albert Schweitzer Humanitarian Prize from Johns Hopkins University (1988), and the Presidential Medal of Freedom (2000). Edelman has published numerous books and articles on the condition of black and white children in America, including *Children Out of School in America* (1974), *School Suspensions: Are They Helping Children?* (1975), *Portrait of Inequality: Black and White Children in America* (1980), *Families in Peril: An Agenda for Social Change* (1987), *The Measure of Our Success: A Letter to My Children and Yours* (1992), *Guide My Feet: Meditations and Prayers on Loving and Working For Children* (1998), and *I'm Your Child, God: Prayers for Children and Teenagers* (2002).

■ ■ *Bibliography*

"Marian Wright Edelman." In *Contemporary Black Biography*, vol. 42. Detroit, Mich.: Gale, 2004.

Ploski, Harry A., and James William, eds. *The Negro Almanac: A Reference Work on the African American*, 5th ed. Detroit, Mich.: Gale, 1989.

Smith, Jessie Carney, ed. *Notable Black American Women*. Detroit, Mich.: Gale, 1992.

SABRINA FUCHS (1996)
Updated by publisher 2005

EDUCATION

━┃┃┃━━━━━━━━━━━━━━━━━━━━━━━━━━━━━━

This entry contains two distinct essays covering the topic of education from differing geographic perspectives.

EDUCATION IN THE CARIBBEAN
Carl C. Campbell

EDUCATION IN THE UNITED STATES
Garrett Albert Duncan

EDUCATION IN THE CARIBBEAN

The Spanish introduced formal schooling in the Caribbean in the sixteenth century. Although African slaves were present in the early Spanish Caribbean settlements, they were seldom in a majority anywhere in the Caribbean until the end of the eighteenth century. Schools for slaves did not exist, though some African slaves might have been literate in Arabic. The few schools in the Spanish Antilles were for the children of rich settlers and privileged persons of mixed racial descent. The major achievement in education during this period was the formation in 1538 of the Roman Catholic–owned University of Santo Domingo in Hispaniola, which today is the oldest university in the western hemisphere. Still, it was the norm for rich settlers to send their sons to Spain for education.

THE OTHER EUROPEAN COLONIES, 1620S TO 1840S

Sugar plantation economies with black African slave majorities were first established by the English, French, and the Danes in the 1620s. From then until the late eighteenth century there were no schools for slaves in these colonies, and little schooling for the free population.

The French and the humanitarian revolutions, which occurred between the 1790s and the slave emancipations in the 1840s, brought improvements in schooling though the latter weakened the Roman Catholic Church. The rebellious slave societies were open to various antislavery ideologies. If slaves were to be freed, they were believed to be in need of religious instruction. Protestant missionaries were allowed more space to provide this service, and they began to take haphazard opportunities to teach Bible reading. In a few towns, a handful of children of privileged slaves began to visit part-time schools, and eventually the idea of schools for slaves was countenanced by liberal French metropolitan governments in the early nineteenth century, and by the Danish authorities in the 1840s just before Emancipation. Full-curriculum day schools were never possible, but an incipient breakdown of the rule that literacy was incompatible with slavery was occurring. Writing and arithmetic did not yet enter the picture. In Haiti, however, where slavery was defeated by the slaves, a completely new revolutionary opportunity for full-curriculum day schools of ex-slaves had been created. Everywhere in this revolutionary era, the free colored population claiming full equality with whites wanted more local public colleges.

MAJOR DEVELOPMENTS IN THE NINETEENTH CENTURY

There were major advances in education from the mid-nineteenth century to the start of the twentieth century. During this period, momentous developments significantly changed the context in which schools and formal education developed. There was the independence of Haiti (1804) and the Dominican Republic (1865); the threatening independence movements in Cuba and Puerto Rico; and, of course, slave emancipations that occurred in the other empires.

The task of governments in Haiti, with a black majority, was to construct from scratch a system to serve the new black nation. But Haitian governments only made provisions for a small elite of coloreds and blacks, leaving the black masses in the countryside uneducated. In the Dominican Republic, where blacks were in a minority, the task was rather to integrate them into the schools for whites. There were few schools, however, and the country was so turbulent that education made little progress. Nonetheless, the professional education of the elites in law and medicine in these countries was provided for better than in colonial times.

In Cuba and Puerto Rico the problem was to integrate the black ex-slave minority into the schools for the whites. Many schools for the free population had been destroyed by the independence wars in Cuba. These schools and their teachers, especially the private schools, became polit-

Queen's Royal College, Port-of-Spain, Trinidad. Founded in 1870 under the British colonial government, the college is now part of the free secondary school system in Trinidad. Dr. Eric Williams, the first prime minister of Trinidad and Tobago, is listed among the distinguished graduates of the school. © NEIL RABINOWITZ/CORBIS

icized as teachers and students took a stand for or against independence, and Spanish governors hired or fired teachers according to their known political views. In Haiti, the Dominican Republic, Cuba, and even Puerto Rico, the question of the role of schools in nation building was blatantly posed. Schools were expected by nationalist politicians as well as Spanish loyalists to foster patriotism and nationalism—even for the mother country, Spain.

Neither the black rural majority in Haiti nor the black minorities in the Dominican Republic, Cuba, and Puerto Rico generated their own schools, except in the case of some Afro-Cuban societies in the early twentieth century. Generally, what this meant is that the African cultural elements found no place in schools organized for the blacks; instead, schools continued to work relentlessly for the Europeanization of the population.

In the sugar plantation colonies with black slave majorities, the major challenge was to establish a new educational provision for the black masses, and some major successes were recorded. Emancipation provided the first opportunities for the governments of the British, French,

and Danish colonies to develop a system of mass provision of full-curriculum primary day schools, including writing and arithmetic. Religious instruction was still the lifeblood of these schools, representing a key element in the search for new bases of social consensus.

The British, French, and Danish governments gave moral and financial support to new schools. In the post-Emancipation nineteenth century, governments accepted the responsibility of funding schools, and government inspection and control via boards of education came into existence at that time. Governments also formed open, if problematic, partnerships with churches to provide schools. The Roman Catholic Church was turned out of such a partnership in Martinique and Guadeloupe in the later nineteenth century. Generally speaking, the intention was not to provide upward social mobility, but social peace and continued economic production.

Primary school was all that existed for all but the few who were to become the new black and colored teachers, the vanguard of a new lower middle class. These teachers did not attend secondary schools, however, but went to teacher training colleges, usually run by the churches. As in slavery days, secondary schools were for the whites (or near whites) who had the means and ambition to study abroad or become junior civil servants. The best secondary schools aspired to be Latin grammar schools, and indeed without Latin grammar no school was truly a secondary school.

Despite the social and racial chasm between primary and secondary schools, some black and colored boys began to enter secondary schools—where custom, not laws, provided the racial barriers against them. Inevitably, postslavery societies became more responsive to academic talent, and secondary schools were the most public arena of academic competition even in Cuba and the Dominican Republic, which had universities. A few secondary schools in the British colonies submitted their work to overseas examiners in England, using these examinations to set high standards of work and to judge the winners (often talented black and colored boys) of scholarships to English universities.

Secondary schools worked as powerful agents of European civilization. Their curriculum was often a direct replica of that of the metropolitan schools and was designed to prepare students for university work. As in slavery days, sending children away for an education remained a primary policy of all who could afford it. In Haiti the lycées took their inspiration from France, and in Martinique and Guadeloupe the official policy of assimilation, accepted then by the aspiring black and colored middle class, drew the post-Emancipation lycées into a very close relationship with the lycées in France. The enormous prestige of secondary schools, which continued well into the twentieth century, was cemented in the nineteenth century in the face of a system that provided little beyond primary schools for the masses.

The secondary schools of the islands offered no technical or vocational subjects, thought then to be wholly inappropriate for such schools. Even primary schools had a "bookish" nature, but there were more voices in favor of exposing boys in primary schools to agricultural work, if not to agricultural skills. But the clerics and parents were unhappy with this direction for schools, and as in Europe, the inferiority of agricultural education and trade training was recognized by their exclusion from formal schools.

MAJOR DEVELOPMENTS IN THE TWENTIETH CENTURY

The second half of the twentieth century saw the expansion of secondary education for the masses and the opening of more universities. It was a century of progress and improvement in which Caribbean countries narrowed the gap between their educational institutions and those of western Europe and North America. In 1900 secondary education was reserved for whites or near whites, or for those who could pay for it; by the 1960s it was almost a right of all children; in 1900 the Caribbean had two or three universities; by the 1980s it had scores of universities, with Cuba, Puerto Rico, and the Dominican Republic each having several. And while in 1900 the European churches were the major providers of education, which was thought of mostly as service for the personal advancement of individuals, by the 1970s governments had become the major providers in most territories and education was for national development.

Some remarkable developments occurred in the interplay between the newest imperial power in the Caribbean, namely the United States of America, and the Greater Antilles (excepting Jamaica). In various invasions and occupations, and in the case of the Danish islands and Puerto Rico through acquisitions, the United States imposed its education models on Caribbean territories for the first time. This Americanization worked to expand primary schools, to increase the participation of women and girls as students and teachers, and to include agriculture and trades as worthy element in schools. The U.S. insistence on the primacy of technical-vocational education in Haiti in the 1920s evoked great resentment among Haitians, while the use of the English language for instructional purposes in schools became a focus of resistance by Puerto Ricans. The Danish West Indian islands were too small to resist Americanization effectively. United States influence in education continued everywhere in the twentieth century as the most potent source of the Europeanization of the Caribbean.

As in the nineteenth century, political turbulence in Haiti, Cuba, the Dominican Republic, and Puerto Rico created situations in which teachers and students sometimes supported, but more usually stood against, certain regimes or dictators. In this sense, education was very politicized in these territories. In the colonies of the French, British, or Dutch, teachers and students stayed out of politics generally, while student disturbances on university campuses in Havana or the Dominican Republic were not uncommon. The political involvement of University of the West Indies students in Jamaica and Trinidad in the Black Power politics of the late 1960s was really exceptional and not sustained. Also, the greater secularization of life in the twentieth century loosened the hold of some European churches on the Caribbean populations. It was still exceptional, though, for governments to reject these churches completely as partners in the formal provision of schools. This was done most resoundingly by the Cuban Revolution of the 1960s. The Roman Catholic Church remained a vital element in a few territories, and dictators in the Dominican Republic managed to use its schools as part of their mechanism of suppression.

The Caribbean country to depart most fundamentally from its nineteenth-century path was Cuba under Fidel Castro. The socialist revolution allowed radically new education models to be developed. Cuba abolished private schools and put in new programs at all levels, from the mass literacy campaign of 1961 to the reorganization of the universities in the 1970s. Work-study programs appeared in almost all schools, secondary schools were built in the countryside and made to produce goods, and the universities were made to concentrate on science and technology. The hope was to produce a new socialist person, and education was free for all who supported the revolution.

The British territories did not experience a revolution and had to build on educational foundations inherited from their imperial masters. But they too sought a measure of decolonization in education after independence: They reduced the role of the churches, secondary education was democratized, schoolbooks and curricula were redone to reflect local themes and interests, and the traditional classical grammar school education was partly de-emphasized to make way for technical-vocational subjects. All these changes left the education models in the British Caribbean well within the colonial framework of the past, but notably decolonized.

In the decolonization of education, the solutions could vary greatly from island to island. The redefinitions of education in Cuba before and after the Castro revolution had nothing to do with blackness or Africanness. Neither did the fierce cultural resistance of many Puerto Ricans to Americanization involve any cultural strivings after blackness or Africanness. All the Spanish-speaking territories identified themselves as white or colored Creole societies in which citizens of African descent had no official cultural existence apart from the Hispanic mainstream culture. However, in the Caribbean societies with black majorities there were feeble attempts to introduce elements of blackness or Africanness into schools. But the ascendancy of metropolitan educational culture remained intact even in Haiti.

Schools also faced criticisms that they were too "bookish," and one of the major twentieth-century trends was towards the greater inclusion of technical-vocational subjects into schools. School gardens became a feature of primary schools in British colonies especially in the first half of the twentieth century. The notion that education was a factor in development that came to the fore after

World War II made technical-vocational education seem all the more important. But this kind of education was still treated as inferior. The traditional grammar school curriculum of secondary schools, even after reforms eliminating Latin, remained stubbornly in the mainstream of what was thought to be proper secondary education. Although it was not always easy to fit girls into technical-vocational education, a major twentieth-century trend was the rise in participation of girls in all levels of education.

See also Education in the United States; Educational Psychology and Psychologists

■■ *Bibliography*

Bacchus, M. K. *Utilization, Misuse, and Development of Human Resources in the Early West Indian Colonies.* Waterloo, Ontario: Wilfred Laurier University Press, 1990.

Brutus, Edner. *Instruction publique en Haiti 1492–1945.* Port-au-Prince: Imprimerie d'état, 1948. Reprint, 1979.

Campbell, Carl. "Education in the Caribbean 1930–1990." In *General History of the Caribbean;* Vol. 5: *The Caribbean in the Twentieth Century,* edited by Bridget Brereton. Paris and London: UNESCO and Macmillan, 2004.

de los Santos, Danilo. "El pensamiento y la institution educativa en la sociedad Dominicana." *Eme-Eme: Estudios Dominicanos* 33 (1977): 14–68.

Fergus, Howard. *A History of Education in the British Leeward Islands, 1838–1945.* Mona, Jamaica: University of the West Indies Press, 2003.

Gallo, Garcio, Fidel Castro, Oscar Reno, and Elio Enriquez, eds. *La Educacion en Cuba.* Buenos Aires: Editorial Convergencia, 1975.

Logan, Rayford. "Education in Haiti." *Journal of Negro History* 4 (1930): 401–460.

Lopez Yustos, Alfonso. *Historia documental de la educacion en Puerto Rico, 1503–1970.* San Juan, Puerto Rico: Sandemann, 1985.

Tardieu-Dehoux, Charles. *L'education en Haiti de la periode coloniale a nos jours.* Port-au-Prince, Haiti: Imprimerie Henri Deschamps, 1980.

CARL C. CAMPBELL (2005)

EDUCATION IN THE UNITED STATES

The education of African Americans in the United States predates the creation of the Bureau of Refugees, Freedman, and Abandoned Lands that was established by an act of Congress in 1865 to assist newly emancipated slaves to become self-sufficient in all areas of life. As Bureau agents fanned across the South to assess conditions, they discov-

Busing. *Police on motorcycles escort school buses down a street in South Boston, September 16, 1974. Court-ordered busing of students to achieve integrated schools was highly controversial in many urban areas.* AP/WIDE WORLD PHOTOS. REPRODUCED BY PERMISSION.

ered that black southerners had already created the rudiments of an educational system for themselves. That this was the case may be understood within the larger context of the curious history that education has played in the lives of Americans of African descent. For instance, as early as 1787, black parents petitioned the Massachusetts state legislature on behalf of their children to obtain equal educational rights for them. These Bostonians made their case on the grounds that their young were being denied access to the very school that they, like their fellow white citizens, shared the tax burden of supporting. The request, although denied, was an augur of the desire—and the struggle—that would characterize the black quest for education for the next two hundred plus years.

The above example also indicates that even as education is inextricably tied to notions of freedom, justice, and citizenship, it is also linked to the oppression of subordinated racial groups in the United States. Since the beginning of formal schooling in the United States, a dominant view that citizenship should be limited to free whites informed popular attitudes about the role that education should play in the lives of Americans of African descent and other people of color. The majority of white citizens

in the American South believed that educating captive Africans would render them unfit for servitude and make it impossible to subordinate them or to retain them as slaves (Woodson, 1919). Such views were not at all unfounded. There were examples aplenty in colonial and antebellum America that pointed to the insight, courage, and sense of responsibility that education instilled among those fortunate enough to have access to it. Consider, for example, the case of the late eighteenth-century poet Phillis Wheatley. Arriving to the New England colonies as a young captive Senegalese, Wheatley would become renowned for her elegies, captured in the 1773 collection published as *Poems on Various Subjects, Religious and Moral*. Although poems written during her early years suggested that Wheatley identified wholesale with her white captors, those written during the later years of her life pointed to a change in her consciousness. For instance, Wheatley provided a subtle, and peculiar, critique of New World slavery in the following elegy:

But how, presumptuous shall we hope to find
Divine acceptance with th' Almighty mind—
While yet (o deed Ungenerous!) they disgrace
And hold in bondage Afric's blameless race?

Let virtue reign—And thou accord our prayers
Be victory ours, and generous freedom theirs.
(Wheatley, 1773, p. 238).

Conflicting views of the role and purpose of black education have characterized the nearly 400-year struggle around the schooling of Americans of African descent in the United States. On one end of the ideological and programmatic spectrum was the advocacy of an education to extend the practice of freedom and democracy to black communities. Along these lines, the quest for black liberation was realized through a two-pronged approach to education. According to noted educational historian James D. Anderson, "the short-range purpose of black schooling was to provide the masses of ex-slaves with basic literacy skills plus the rudiments of citizenship training for participation in a democratic society. The long-range purpose was the intellectual and moral development of a responsible leadership class that would organize the masses and lead them to freedom and equality" (1988, p. 31).

On the other end of the ideological and programmatic spectrum was the advocacy of an education for black students to ensure the maintenance of white supremacy. Such was especially true during the post-Reconstruction era. An observation made by W. E. B. Du Bois, reported in a 1918 issue of *The Crisis*, is typical of the second-class education provided to black children and youth during this period. Here, Du Bois decried the material disparities he found in the education of black and white students in Butte, Montana, public schools:

> What, now, is the real difference between these two schemes [white and black] of education? The difference is that in the Butte schools for white pupils, a chance is held open for the pupil to go through high school and college and to advance at the rate which the modern curriculum demands; that in the colored, a program is being made out that will land the boy at the time he becomes self-conscious and aware of his own possibilities in an educational *impasse*. He cannot go on in the public schools even if he should move to a place where there are good public schools because he is too old. Even if he has done the elementary work in twice the time that a student is supposed to, it has been work of a kind that will not admit him to a northern high school. No matter, then, how gifted the boy may be, he is absolutely estopped from a higher education. This is not only unfair to the boy but it is grossly unfair to the Negro race. (Du Bois, 1995, p. 263)

As indicated, black communities have long advocated for themselves an education for liberation—that is, one that promotes their full participation in the civic and economic life of the nation or that provides the means for self-sufficiency. Yet, as also indicated, the goals of black communities notwithstanding, white power interests have historically used the material and political resources at their disposal to exercise tremendous control over the direction of the education of black children and youth.

BROWN AND EDUCATIONAL JUSTICE

Education took on decisive meanings for black students in 1954 when the U.S. Supreme Court rendered its decision in *Brown et al v. Board of Education of Topeka, Kansas*. This landmark education ruling provided the legal basis for equal education for all subordinated racial groups, not the least being the black infant plaintiffs at the center of the celebrated case. *Brown* was sweeping in its mandate to shape race and education in the United States. The Supreme Court, though, did not provide clear guidelines to end *de jure* public school segregation and the imprecision of the ruling, captured in the order to proceed in the dismantling of segregated schools "with all deliberate speed," all but guaranteed that the desegregation of public schools would occur at a snail's pace. For instance, some of the white communities affected by the ruling attempted to close public schools rather than allow black students to attend them. Others adopted "freedom of choice" plans that permitted students to choose the schools they wanted to attend. Predictably, freedom of choice plans generally resulted in continued segregation of public educational facilities. Even in instances where authorities attempted in good faith to implement plans to desegregate schools, these efforts were often undermined by state-level action.

As a result of white resistance to the Supreme Court's 1954 ruling, little dismantling of *de jure* segregation in public schools occurred during the decade after *Brown*. In addition, *Brown*'s implications for nonsouthern schools were even less clear. The segregation of schools in northern, western, midwestern, and southwestern regions of the country occurred largely as the result of housing patterns that allegedly were not the result of direct state action, although researchers later found evidence that demonstrated the complicity of both local and federal governments in maintaining the color line (e.g., Massey and Denton, 1993). It wasn't until 1973, in *Keyes v. School District of Denver*, that the U.S. Supreme Court expanded *Brown* to include the dismantling of de facto segregation in public schools.

Despite the often-violent resistance to desegregation, the constitutional impact of *Brown* was enormous and lasting in creating educational opportunities for black students in the United States. For instance, the Supreme

A "Head Start" program classroom. Conceived as an eight-week summer program in 1965, Head Start is now a comprehensive child development program that increases the school readiness of young children in low-income families. PHOTOGRAPH BY SHELLEY GAZIN. CORBIS-BETTMANN. REPRODUCED BY PERMISSION.

Court's ruling resulted in a dramatic increase in the number of desegregation suits filling lower court dockets. In addition, the *Brown* ruling had extralegal, or indirect, effects that shaped education in the United States, even those that perhaps went beyond the intention of the landmark 1954 decision. In upholding the Equal Protection Clause of the Fourteenth Amendment in its rendering of *Brown*, the Supreme Court largely affirmed civil and political rights, also known as *first generation rights*. However, once black students gained access to predominately white schools, especially institutions of higher education, they not only pressed for their civil and political rights guaranteed by *Brown*, they also demanded that schools recognize their social, cultural, and economic rights. These latter rights are also called *second generation rights* and are affirmed by the United Nations' Universal Declaration of Human Rights (1948), to which U.S. courts are not bound.

Black students' exercise of second generation rights manifested itself, among other things, in the establishment of black studies programs at colleges and universities throughout the United States. The first such program was established at San Francisco State University in 1968, and many others soon followed, including the institution of

black studies at Harvard, Yale and Ohio State, to name a few, in 1969. In addition, the increase in the number of black students on college campuses was the impetus behind the establishment of other organizations and programs to support these students, as well as to recruit and prepare those in precollege settings for success in higher education, especially in the areas of science and engineering. In 1971, for instance, two undergraduates at Purdue University founded the Society of Black Engineers, now the National Society for Black Engineers (NSBE), to improve the recruitment and retention of black students in the field. NSBE now has a membership of 15,000 members, 17 precollege programs, and 268 student and 50 alumni/technical professional chapters.

Curricular and institutional changes at American colleges and universities that resulted from the increased presence of black students stimulated similar changes in U.S. public elementary and secondary schools as well. These changes are evident in yearly observances of Black History Month and the establishment of black student unions, as well as in the adoption of multicultural curricula in K–12 schools. Demands for multicultural education in K–12 schools also contributed to changes in the content of textbooks and, recursively, in how schools and colleges

Home schooling, Transylvania, Louisiana, 1939. *An African-American mother teaches her two children in their sharecropper's home. Often under such circumstances, children would attend school from November to March, helping with work in the fields during the remainder of the year.* PHOTOGRAPHS AND PRINTS DIVISION, SCHOMBURG CENTER FOR RESEARCH IN BLACK CULTURE, THE NEW YORK PUBLIC LIBRARY, ASTOR, LENOX AND TILDEN FOUNDATIONS.

of education and state departments of education certificated teachers and administrators, especially those preparing to work in school districts with large minority student populations.

RACE AND EDUCATION IN POST–CIVIL RIGHTS AMERICA

Even as the *Brown* decision contributed to unprecedented improvements in the condition of black education in the United States, it did not completely resolve the 400-year struggle that shaped the efforts of black students to obtain quality schooling in America. For example, as a federal legal intervention into the education of black students, *Brown* never fully equalized the resources that black students received, especially in terms of per student funding. Huge racial disparities persist in public education, largely

as a result of the ways schools in the United States are funded. Most local funding derives from property taxes; it follows that in wealthier white districts, property values and, hence, property taxes are much higher than those in less affluent and poor districts where black students are concentrated. In the 1990s this resulted in funding disparities in which New York State, for example, spent $38,572 per student in its richest school district, a sum that was seven times more than that of its poorest district, $5,423. The disparity was even greater in Texas, where the wealthiest schools spent as much as thirteen times more on students ($42,000 per pupil) than the state's poorest district, which spent $3,098 per pupil (Gordon, 1998).

In addition, *Brown* contributed to the mass displacement of black educators in teaching and administrative positions in K–12 public schools (Ethridge, 1979). In the

Supporters and opponents of school vouchers rally outside the Supreme Court building in Washington, D.C. The twenty-first century debate centers on programs in some cities allowing students to use publicly funded vouchers to attend private schools. PHOTOGRAPH BY RICK BOWMER. AP/WIDE WORLD PHOTOS. REPRODUCED BY PERMISSION.

absence of these educators, many students of color who integrated K–12 public schools often encountered second-generation discrimination and other challenges to obtain quality education (Meier, Stewart, and England, 1989). Second-generation discrimination refers to unjust education practices, such as the resegregation of students in previously desegregated schools and the disproportionate punishment of black students. As implied, these forms of injustice often stem from the failure of white teachers and administrators to recognize or respect the self-determination of their black students.

With respect to resegregation, integrated schools typically sort students into homogeneous subsets by ability groupings. This generally results in the concentration of white students in honors and gifted classes and of students of color in lower tracks, remedial courses, and special education programs. Although disparities in measures of academic attainment between black and white students began to narrow in the 1970s and 1980s, they began to widen in the 1990s and into the first decade of the twenty-first century, resulting in widely publicized reports of a "racial achievement gap" in public schools. The racial achievement gap reflects variances in standardized test scores that

indicate that white and some Asian American students consistently outperform their black and Latino peers.

The 2000 National Assessment of Educational Progress (NAEP), the "nation's report card," shows disparities among racial and ethnic groups. For example, in the area of mathematics, two-thirds of black and more than half of Latino and Native American eighth graders are performing below basic levels of achievement compared to a quarter of their white and Asian American peers. Similar disparities are evident in the area of science. For example, according to the NAEP's science results for 1996, three-quarters of black, two-thirds of Latino, nearly half of Native-American, and more than a third of Asian-American students performed below basic achievement levels in contrast to a quarter of white students that did so. The percentages in the below-basic category actually increased for all groups in grade twelve, with even greater disparities indicated between white students and their Asian-American and Native-American peers.

Racial academic disparities mirror significant differences in the quality of instruction that students receive, especially when it comes to the use of computer technologies. For example, in 1998 more teachers reported using computers primarily for drill and practice with their black eighth-grade students (42%) than they did with their white (35%), Asian-American (35%), or Latino (35%) eighth-graders. In contrast, fewer of these teachers reported using simulations and applications or learning games as their primary computer tools with black students (14% and 48%, respectively) than they did with their white (31% and 57%), Asian-American (43% and 57%), and Latino (25% and 56%) students (Wenglinsky, 1998). Some educational experts, such as Linda Darling-Hammond, point out that these differences result from the different levels of expertise among the teachers that are typically assigned to black and white students. Educational experts such as Asa Hilliard and Theresa Perry argue that these differences stem from the different expectations that teachers have for black and white students.

Racial gaps in the way that discipline in public schools is meted out also persist in the United States. These gaps increased in the late 1990s and the early 2000s as a result of the adoption by districts of "zero-tolerance" policies to curb real and imagined violence in American schools (Gordon, 1998). Widespread reports and highly publicized incidents of the expulsion of black students in the late 1990s refueled concerns in communities of color about educational justice and prompted the prominent civil rights leader Jesse Jackson to observe that, with increasing frequency, "school districts [are choosing] penal remedies over educational remedies when it comes to disciplining students" (*Washington Post*, 1999, p. A3). While, in general, poorer students are more likely to be suspended than wealthier students, researchers have found that black students from the wealthiest families were suspended at almost the same rate as white students from the poorest families (Gordon, 1998). Interestingly, a 2005 Yale study found that, nationally, prekindergarten students were expelled three times as often as students in K–12 settings and, predictably, that black prekindergarten students were twice as likely to be expelled as were their white and Latino preschool peers (Gilliam, 2005).

Finally, despite integration gains in the 1970s and 1980s, public schools became more segregated in the 1990s and the early years of the twenty-first century. Urban and fringe city school districts are being populated by increasingly multicultural populations of students of color from working-class and poor families, and more affluent suburban schools are being populated by homogeneous bodies of white students from middle-class families (Orfield and Yun, 1999). The reversal of school integration is attributable both to failed attempts to integrate schools at the local level as well as to significant Supreme Court rulings such as *Milliken v. Bradley* (1974) that removed the powers of federal courts to impose interdistrict remedies between cities and surrounding suburbs to desegregate city schools. Lastly, the resegregation of schools in the 1990s and 2000s occurs within a broader political context of changing public investments where states are increasingly spending more on criminal justice than they are on public education (Ziedenberg and Schiraldi, 2002). Indeed, during the opening years of the twenty-first century, states on average spent three times more on corrections than they did on public schools (Children's Defense Fund, 2004). Such public policy decisions have resulted in what Jonathan Kozol has called the "savage inequalities" that plague urban and rural schools, leaving them in the new millennium to provide their largely black student populations with what Robert Moses has called a "sharecropper's education."

RACE AND EDUCATION IN THE TWENTY-FIRST CENTURY

Echoing a view expressed by W. E. B. Du Bois at the beginning of the twentieth century, the eminent American historian John Hope Franklin noted that the problem of the color line will also be part of the legacy and burden of the twenty-first century (Franklin, 1993). Perhaps nowhere is Franklin's observation more evident than in the area of education. The matter of the education of black students has resurfaced in the late 1990s and into the new millennium both to unify and to divide Americans. For example, the issue of school privatization has made for strange bedfellows in the political arena where liberal black civic and religious leaders have joined with conservative white politicians and foundations to support the establishment and public funding of vouchers. Most notable of these are the programs established in Milwaukee, Wisconsin, and Washington, D.C., that allowed students, mostly black, to use publicly funded vouchers to attend private schools. The same period has also seen the unprecedented inroads made by for-profit educational companies into public schools, particularly through the establishment of charter schools in predominately black educational systems. In a similar vein, in higher education, ethnic studies programs have yet to find complete acceptance or legitimacy in colleges and universities. In addition, there have been numerous attempts, some of them successful, to dismantle affirmative action gains.

At the same time, there is still broad support for race-conscious educational policies, such as diversity, multiculturalism, bilingual education, and school funding in the arenas of K–12 schooling and higher education. Also, a number of black communities have rallied around their schools, and some predominately black school districts have experienced a renaissance in the education of their students. In some instances, measures have been taken to establish Afrocentric schools within public school districts. Notable among these are the Paul Robeson Academy and the Malcolm X Academy in Detroit, Michigan, and the Malcolm X African American Immersion Middle and the Martin Luther King African-American Immersion Elementary schools in Milwaukee, Wisconsin.

Despite recent challenges to affirmative action in higher education, a number of colleges and universities and other institutions in the United States have redoubled their efforts to increase the number of black students and faculty members in academia. The U.S. Supreme Court's preservation of the narrow use of affirmative action in higher education in its 2003 *Grutter v. Bollinger* ruling also lends renewed hope and support for the struggle of black communities in the United States to obtain educational justice for their students. However, whether or not such conditions will be realized within the twenty-five-year period expressed by Justice Sandra Day O'Connor in rendering the majority opinion in *Grutter* is one of the central questions confronting the education of black students in the twenty-first century.

See also Affirmative Action; *Brown v. Board of Education of Topeka, Kansas*; Civil Rights Movement, U.S.; Du Bois, W. E. B.; Education in the Caribbean; Educational Psychology and Psychologists

■ ■ *Bibliography*

Anderson, James D. *The Education of Blacks in the South, 1860–1935.* Chapel Hill: University of North Carolina Press, 1988.

Aptheker, Herbert, ed. *A Documentary History of the Negro People in the United States,* Vol. 1: *From Colonial Times Through the Civil War.* New York: Citadel, 1951–1994.

Baldwin, James. "A Talk to Teachers" (1963). In *City Kids, City Teachers: Reports from the Front Row,* edited by William Ayers and Patricia Ford. New York: New Press, 1996.

Children's Defense Fund. *The State of America's Children, 2004.* Washington, D.C.: Author, 2004.

Darling-Hammond, Linda. *The Right to Learn: A Blueprint for Creating Schools that Work.* San Francisco: Jossey Bass, 1997.

Du Bois, W. E. B. "Does the Negro Need Separate Schools?" *Journal of Negro Education* 4 (1935): 328–335.

Du Bois, W. E. B. *The Education of Black People: Ten Critiques, 1906–1960.* New York: Monthly Review Press, 1973.

Du Bois, W. E. B. "Negro Education" (1918). In *W. E. B. Du Bois: A Reader,* edited by David Levering Lewis. New York: Henry Holt, 1995.

Ethridge, S. B. "Impact of the 1954 *Brown vs Topeka Board of Education* Decision on Black Educators." *The Negro Educational Review* 30, no. 4 (1979): 217–232.

Fordham, Signithia. *Blacked Out: Dilemmas of Race, Identity, and Success at Capital High.* Chicago: University of Chicago Press, 1996.

Franklin, John Hope. *The Color Line: Legacy for the Twenty-First Century.* Columbia: University of Missouri Press, 1993.

Gilliam, Walter S. *Prekindergarterners Left Behind: Expulsion Rates in State Prekindergarten Systems.* New Haven, Conn.: Yale University Child Study Center, 2005.

Gordon, Rebecca. *Education and Race: A Journalist's Handbook.* Oakland, Calif.: Applied Research Center, 1998.

Jencks, Christopher, and Meredith Phillips, eds. *The Black-White Test Score Gap.* Washington, D.C.: Brookings Institution, 1998.

Kozol, Jonathan. *Savage Inequalities: Children in America's Schools.* New York: Crown, 1991.

Massey, Douglas, and Nancy Denton. *American Apartheid: Segregation in the Making of the Underclass.* Cambridge, Mass.: Harvard University Press, 1993.

Meier, Kenneth J., Joseph Stewart Jr., and Robert E. England. *Race, Class, and Education: The Politics of Second-Generation Discrimination.* Madison: University of Wisconsin Press, 1989.

Morris, Aldon D. *The Origins of the Civil Rights Movement: Black Communities Organizing for Change.* New York: Free Press, 1984.

Morris, Vivian Gunn, and Curtis L. Morris. *The Price They Paid: Desegregation in an African American Community.* New York: Teachers College Press, 2002.

Moses, Robert, and Charles E. Cobb Jr. *Radical Equations: Math Literacy and Civil Rights.* Boston: Beacon, 2001.

National Center for Education Statistics (NCES). Available from <http://nces.ed.gov/>.

Ogbu, John. *Black American Students in an Affluent Suburb: A Study of Academic Disengagement.* Mahwah, N.J.: Lawrence Erlbaum, 2003.

Orfield, Gary. "Public Opinion and School Desegregation." *Teachers College Record* 96, no. 4 (1995): 654–670.

Orfield, Gary, and John T. Yun *Resegregation in American Schools.* Cambridge, Mass.: Civil Rights Project, Harvard University, 1999.

Perry, Theresa, Claude Steele, and Asa Hilliard. *Young, Gifted, and Black: Promoting High Achievement Among African-American Students.* Boston: Beacon, 2003.

Siddle Walker, Vanessa. *Their Highest Potential: An African American School Community in the Segregated South.* Chapel Hill: University of North Carolina Press, 1996.

Washington Post. "Study: Racial Disparity in School Discipline." (December 17, 1999): A3

Washington, Booker T. *Up from Slavery: An Autobiography* (1902). New York: Carol, 1989.

Watkins, William. *The White Architects of Black Education: Ideology and Power in America, 1865–1954.* New York: Teachers College Press, 2001.

Wenglinsky, Harold. *Does it Compute? The Relationship Between Educational Technology and Student Achievement in Mathematics.* Princeton, N.J.: Educational Testing Service, 1998.

Wheatley, Phillis. *Poems on Various Subjects, Religious and Moral.* London: A. Bell, Aldgate, 1773. Reprinted in *The Col-*

lected Works of Phillis Wheatley, edited by J. C. Shields. New York: Oxford University Press, 1988.

Woodson, Carter Godwin. The Education of the Negro Prior to 1861. 2d ed. New York: A&B Books, 1919.

Woodson, Carter Godwin. The Miseducation of the Negro. Philadelphia: Hakim's, 1933.

Ziedenberg, Jason, and Vincent Schiraldi. Cellblocks or Classrooms? The Funding of Higher Education and Corrections and its Impact on African American Men. Washington, D.C.: Justice Policy Institute, 2002.

GARRETT ALBERT DUNCAN (2005)

EDUCATIONAL PSYCHOLOGY AND PSYCHOLOGISTS

Since the inception of the field of educational psychology in the early 1900s, researchers have focused on attention, memory, teaching, and learning, and on experimental approaches to these topics. While much of the seminal research in the field has been conducted on European-American subjects, and the literature reflects this focus, interest in African Americans has waxed and waned at various times over the last one hundred years. Key topics of research with regard to African Americans have included the differential performance of blacks and whites on intelligence tests and, more recently, the black-white gap in academic achievement and ways of promoting school success among African-American students.

Early in the last century, in an emerging debate on what was then called "Negro education," scholars argued about the educability of people of African descent, questioning whether they were innately inferior in intelligence. Edward Thorndike, the founder of educational psychology, and his students stressed the importance of educational measurement. Using intelligence (IQ) tests originally developed in France and adapted for U.S. populations, researchers sought to determine intelligence "scientifically." In 1913 A. C. Strong published one of the first studies that purported to show hereditarily determined racial differences in intelligence. This was the beginning of a series of studies that would be used to justify claims of mental inferiority of African Americans.

Horace Mann Bond, an African-American educator and researcher, and other African-American social scientists in the 1920s were instrumental in refuting many of these claims. Bond used findings from intelligence tests administered to white soldiers by the U.S. Army to argue

William B. Shockley, 1956. Co-winner of the 1956 Nobel Prize in Physics for his work in the development of the transistor, Shockley became avidly interested in a controversial topic for which he had no special training: the genetic basis of intelligence. During the 1960s, in a series of articles and speeches, he argued that people of African descent have a mental capacity that is genetically inferior to those of Caucasian ancestry. His hypothesis became the subject of intense and acrimonious debate during the tumultuous years of the Civil Rights movement. AP/WIDE WORLD PHOTOS. REPRODUCED BY PERMISSION.

against racial explanations for differences in intelligence. The median score of white soldiers from four southern states corresponded to the mental age of a twelve-and-a-half-year-old child; northern white soldiers on average scored higher. Such variations within a single racial group showed, according to Bond, that intelligence tests are less a measure of innate ability than a measure of such factors as environment and education.

From the 1930s through the 1960s hereditary explanations for differences in intelligence largely fell out of favor. Psychologists argued that there were intractable problems in the design of intelligence tests, including failure to control for the influence of subjects' economically unequal backgrounds. Moreover, they argued, the meaning of the test scores was debatable. And the validity of race as a scientific category was increasingly coming into question.

Instead, scholarly attention turned to the influence of environment on intelligence. As detailed in recent work by James Banks, the educational and social science theories, concepts, and research of the early 1960s depicted African Americans as culturally deprived. Scholars favoring the cultural deprivation or "culture of poverty" paradigm posited that low-income populations lacked the socialization experiences that would enable them to acquire the knowledge, skills, and attitudes of the middle class. Though these skills and attitudes were rarely measured, educational reform driven by this ideology aimed to transform many of the early socialization experiences of "disadvantaged" children. An array of programs such as Head Start were created with this goal in mind.

In 1966, however, Johns Hopkins University sociologist James S. Coleman wrote a landmark report that suggested, among other things, that remedial programs could not effectively combat the "culture of poverty" as long as children returned to culturally deprived homes. Meanwhile, noted geneticists Arthur Jensen and William Shockley turned the discussion once again toward the question of innate differences. In 1969 Jensen published a seminal article in the *Harvard Educational Review,* arguing that compensatory programs would not work for African Americans because of their supposed deficits in cognitive abilities. Though the scientific merit of his work has been widely debated, Jensen has continued to focus on differences between black and white IQ scores for more than thirty years and has become one of the most cited educational psychologists.

From the 1970s through the 1990s intelligence as measured by standardized tests remained a popular topic in the field of African-American educational psychology. Claims of innate differences in intellect received renewed attention with the 1994 publication of Richard Herrnstein and Charles Murray's *The Bell Curve.* Critics of this controversial work argue that IQ tests actually measure subjects' assimilation of white middle-class culture rather than their general abilities. Asa Hilliard, a noted African-American educational psychologist and historian, has argued against the use of IQ tests in general, citing their cultural biases. He contends that the problem of how much an individual can learn is complex and cannot be understood from the perspective of a single subdiscipline of psychology, that is, intelligence testing.

Critics of Jensen's research have also cited the problem of cultural bias in IQ tests. In one study, for example, Jensen compared the performance of black children to that of white children who were younger, in some cases by two or more years. High correlation between the test scores of these two groups served as the basis for his claim

that black children lag in cognitive development and that this is likely the result of heritable differences in general ability. African-American psychologist Janet Helms has argued that the developmental lag Jensen apparently found may have been due to differences in acculturation rather than in intellectual ability. That is, white children may learn their own culture two years earlier than black children vicariously learn white culture, which is also the culture of the test.

UNDERSTANDING THE ACHIEVEMENT GAP

Though biological explanations for differences in group performance are now widely rejected, many measures point to a persistent educational achievement gap between African-American and European-American children. In 2001, for example, whites outperformed blacks in math and reading at every grade level on the National Assessment of Educational Progress (NAEP). Various explanations have been advanced to account for the apparent discrepancy. In addition to purported differences in innate ability, as noted above, these hypotheses focus on poverty; actions and attitudes of parents and teachers; school-related inadequacies, ranging from differences in resources to inattention to the cognitive styles of African-American youth; an "oppositional culture" among blacks; and discrimination.

Several of these factors are clearly correlated with educational achievement within racial groups as well as between them. Within every American ethnic and racial group, children in higher socioeconomic brackets score better on standardized tests than children in lower brackets, and they are more likely to finish high school and attend college. Socioeconomic status has been shown to be an important predictor of differences in academic achievement among African-American children, with black children from poor backgrounds performing less well on average than those from more affluent backgrounds. The question that has not yet been clearly resolved by research, with adequate controls for different factors, is the extent to which socioeconomic differences account for the observed differences between racial groups. High expectations in parents and teachers also have been positively related to children's achievement, both in the general population and among black children in particular. Moreover, when African-American parents are involved in schools, such as by volunteering in the classroom, their children's academic skills and achievement improve.

African-American educational psychologists Barbara Shade, Wade Boykin, and Janice Hale attribute differences in black-white achievement in part to group differences in cognitive or learning styles (subsumed in the category "behavioral style" in the work of Hilliard). They argue that cognitive style accounts for group differences in a variety of cognitive, perceptual, and personality variables, which in turn influence the ways in which individuals perceive, organize, and interpret information. Scholars have noted, however, that important variations in cognitive style exist within the African-American population. For example, while some research suggests that African Americans typically exhibit "field dependence," tending to perceive things in relation to other objects in a given domain, it is clear that some blacks exhibit high levels of "field independence," tending to perceive things analytically and in isolation. Such intragroup differences have cast doubt on the claim that groups have particular cognitive styles. Some scholars believe that group differences in cognitive styles do exist in a broad sense but that class background may contribute to differences within groups.

John Ogbu, a Nigerian-born anthropologist, offers an alternative explanation for the gap in achievement. Since the slavery era, he contends, African Americans have developed a culture in opposition to that of whites. African-American students' low performance, according to this hypothesis, reflects their perception of academic achievement as "acting white."

One of the first scholars to examine social aspects of the schooling experiences of black children was Inez Beverly Prosser. The first African-American woman to earn a doctorate in educational psychology, she received her degree from the University of Cincinnati in 1933. Her dissertation, "The Non-Academic Development of Negro Children in Mixed and Segregated Schools," showed, although with modest results, that children in segregated schools fared better than those in mixed schools as measured by several social and personality variables, including introversion and extraversion.

In 1939 prominent African-American psychologist Kenneth Clark, along with his wife Mamie Clark, began a series of studies of African-American preschool and elementary school children in segregated, semi-segregated, and integrated groups. Among the instruments used were white and black dolls, identical except for skin color. When asked to "show me the doll that you like best," the black children displayed consistent preference for the white dolls, leading the Clarks to conclude that the children were developing a negative self-image and that segregation was taking a psychological toll. Kenneth Clark's testimony was influential in the landmark *Brown v. Board of Education* decision of 1954 that found racially segregated schooling unconstitutional.

Both the Prosser and Clark studies foreshadowed more recent research that cites discrimination as an im-portant factor that hinders the cognitive performance of African-American children. Claude Steele and his colleagues have argued that both socioeconomic status and genetic differences are insufficient explanations for underachievement by African-American children. Instead, they emphasize the role of negative stereotypes. According to this view, African Americans bear a psychological burden caused by society's stereotypes of black inferiority in achievement domains, and they may feel threatened by the risk of confirming these stereotypes. If this "stereotype threat" is strong enough, it interferes with social interaction and intellectual performance and can even lead to decisions to withdraw from participation in certain domains.

PROMOTING BLACK CHILDREN'S SCHOOL SUCCESS

It is clear from the literature that no single factor causes the gap in academic achievement. In an effort to explore the myriad contextual factors that can lead to successful cognitive development, educational psychologists have begun to study specific cases of excellence in teaching and learning that have fostered academic success among African-American children.

One of the most noted ethnographic case studies is that of African-American educator Gloria Ladson-Billings, who looked at effective teaching in an African-American community. Based on her observations, Ladson-Billings contends that teachers can promote academic success for African-American children by adopting culturally relevant pedagogical strategies. These include (a) allowing students to be apprenticed into a learning community rather than studying subject matter in isolation; (b) allowing students' real-life experiences to become "official" curriculum; (c) broadening the concept of literacy to incorporate both literature and oratory; (d) treating students as competent; (e) providing instruction that helps students move from what they already know to what they need to know; (f) extending students' thinking and abilities by first assessing their initial knowledge of the subject matter, and (g) having in-depth knowledge of their students and subject matter.

The literature on effective schooling for all racial groups has underscored the importance of strong leadership, accountability, academic focus, and orderliness. These and other school-related factors have been associated with high achievement among African American students. A case study of Providence–St. Mel, an independent, all-black school in Chicago, details the factors that have led to a one hundred percent college admission rate at the school. They include high expectations, praise, cooperative learning, caring teachers, tangible rewards, and extensive test preparation. School success or failure is attributed to a student's level of effort rather than to innate ability. The school encourages its students to envision constructive identities for themselves—as doctors, for example—and to learn about and take pride in their African-American heritage.

Early childhood educator Janice Hale, in *Learning While Black,* argues that promotion of academic success for African-American children requires building an infrastructure for educational accountability like those often created by parents in schools serving white middle-class students. Drawing on thirty years of experience working with schools that mainly serve black children, as well as on her own son's schooling experience, she calls for creation of a school culture in which every child is treated as part of a family. The school in turn must be part of a larger community in which concerned citizens are engaged to support families and the mission of the schools.

See also Education; Ogbu, John; Social Psychology, Psychologists, and Race

▪▪ *Bibliography*

Berliner, David C. "The 100-Year Journey of Educational Psychology: From Interest, to Disdain, to Respect for Practice." In *Exploring Applied Psychology: Origins and Critical Analyses,* edited by Thomas K. Fagan and Gary R. VandenBos. Washington, D.C.: American Psychological Association, 1993.

Bond, Horace Mann. "What the Army 'Intelligence' Tests Measured." *Opportunity* 2 (1924): 197–202.

Graham, Sandra. "Most of the Subjects Were White and Middle Class: Trends in Published Research on African Americans in Selected APA Journals, 1970–1989." *American Psychologist* 47, no. 5 (May 1992): 629–639.

Hale, Janice. *Learning While Black: Creating Educational Excellence for African American Children.* Baltimore, Md.: Johns Hopkins University Press, 2001.

Hilliard, Asa G., III. "Either a Paradigm Shift or No Mental Measurement: The Nonscience and Nonsense of the Bell Curve." *Cultural Diversity and Mental Health* 2, no. 1 (1996): 1–20.

Jensen, Arthur. "How Much Can We Boost I.Q. and Scholastic Achievement?" *Harvard Educational Review* 39 (February 1969): 1–123.

Ladson-Billings, Gloria. *The Dreamkeepers: Successful Teachers of African American Children.* San Francisco: Jossey-Bass, 1994.

Lee, Carol D., and Diana Slaughter-Defoe. "Historical and Sociocultural Influences on African American Education." In *Handbook of Research on Multicultural Education,* edited by James A. Banks and Cherry A. McGee Banks. San Francisco: Jossey-Bass, 2004.

Ogbu, John. "Collective Identity and the Burden of 'Acting White' in Black History, Community, and Education." *Urban Review* 36, no. 1 (2004): 1–35.

Pressley, Michael, Lisa Raphael, J. David Gallagher, and Jeannette DiBella. "Providence–St. Mel School: How a School That Works for African American Students Works." *Journal of Educational Psychology* 96, no. 2 (2004): 216–235.

Winston, Andrew, ed. *Defining Difference: Race and Racism in the History of Psychology.* Washington, D.C.: American Psychological Association, 2004.

BRENDESHA TYNES (2005)

EGIPCÍACA, ROSA

1718
1765

┫┃┣

Rosa Egipcíaca da Vera Cruz is certainly the eighteenth-century black African woman about whose life there exist the most documentary details and writings—in Africa, in the Afro-American diaspora, and in Brazil. She was the first Afro-Brazilian woman to have written a book, of which there remain some manuscript copies, and two dozen of her letters survive. She was considered at the time as "the holiest saint in heaven," whom whites, mestizos, and blacks, including all the family of her master and respectable Catholic priests, adored on their knees, kissing her feet, venerating her relics, and calling her "the Flower of Rio de Janeiro." Rosa founded a convent for ex-prostitutes, most of them black and mestizo women, the chapel of which, although remodeled, remains to this day in the same place in central Rio. She was imprisoned by the Inquisition of Lisbon on the charge of being a false saint.

Rosa Egipcíaca was born to the Koura Nation ("Courana"), on the Costa de Mina, close to where Lagos is today in Nigeria. She came to Rio de Janeiro on a slave ship in 1725 at age six. At the age of twelve she was sexually abused by her master and sold to the Captaincy of Minas Gerais, earning a living as a prostitute in the village of Inficcionado until she was twenty-nine, when she started to have supernatural visions and was exorcized by an old Portuguese Catholic priest. Examined by a group of theologians, she was accused of being a witch and was brutally whipped on the pillory in Vila de Mariana, after which the right side of her body was paralyzed for the rest of her life. She fled with her guardian priest to Rio de Janeiro, where she began to receive spiritual guidance from the Franciscans, who believed in her visions and encouraged her Christian virtues in their wish to have a black model of holiness for Brazil's slaves.

Rosa Egipcíaca learned to read and wrote 250 pages of a book titled *Sacred Theology of the Love of God Shining*

Light of the Pilgrim Souls, in which she said that the infant Jesus came every day to feed on her breast and, in gratitude, combed her hair; that the Lord had exchanged his heart with hers, and that Jesus, transubstantiated, was in her bosom; that she had died and been resuscitated; that Mary was the mother of mercy and that she, Rosa Egipcíaca, was the mother of justice, on whose will it depended whether souls went to heaven or hell; and that she was the wife of the Holy Trinity, the new redeemer of the world. In 1754 she founded the Convent of Our Lady of Childbirth, where numerous devotees venerated her as the holiest saint in heaven. She prophesized that there would be a new flood and that her nunnery would become an ark of salvation that would take her disciples to Portugal, where she would marry the mysterious King Dom Sebastião and give birth to a redeemer of mankind. Arrested by the Inquisition, she spent several years in Lisbon's jails, where she always maintained that her visions were true. She was not condemned to death by burning, but it is unknown how her life ended.

Rosa Egipcíaca da Vera Cruz is the Afro-Brazilian woman who best typifies the diversity and force of Catholic Afro-Brazilian syncretism. All the details of her life are found in three documents conserved in the Torre do Tombo, the Portuguese national archives in Lisbon, and published in Luiz Mott's *Rosa Egipcíaca: Uma Santa Africana no Brasil* (1993).

See also Catholicism in the Americas

■ ■ *Bibliography*

Mott, Luiz R. B. *Rosa Egipcíaca: Uma Santa Africana no Brasil* (Rosa Egipcíaca: An African Saint in Brazil). Rio de Janeiro: Bertrand, 1993.

LUIZ MOTT (2005)

ELDERS, JOYCELYN

AUGUST 13, 1933

━┃━┃━┃━

Born in Schaal, Arkansas, Minnie Joycelyn Jones, who would become U.S. surgeon general, was the eldest daughter of Haller and Curtis Jones. She attended Philander Smith College in Little Rock, Arkansas, where she received her B.A. in 1952. Wishing to become a doctor, she joined the U.S. Army and trained in physical therapy at the Brooke Army Medical Center at Fort Sam Houston, Texas. In 1956 she left the army and enrolled at the University of Arkansas Medical School, one of the first African Americans to attend, and received her M.D. degree in 1960, the same year she married Oliver Elders. Joycelyn Elders served an internship in pediatrics at the University of Minnesota, then returned to the University of Arkansas in 1961 for her residency period. Elders was ultimately named chief resident, and also received an M.S. in biochemistry in 1967. In 1971 the University of Arkansas Medical School hired Elders as an assistant professor in pediatrics and five years later named her a full professor. Over the succeeding years, she published 138 articles, mostly on child growth problems and diabetes.

In 1987 Arkansas governor Bill Clinton named Elders as the Arkansas Health Commissioner. Her advocacy of making birth control information and condoms available in schools as ways of fighting teenage pregnancy and AIDS caused a storm of controversy. Conservative critics decried her supposedly permissive attitudes toward sex and her implementation of a kindergarten-to-college health education program that included sex education as well as the usual information about hygiene, substance abuse, and other matters.

In 1993 Clinton, by then president of the United States, appointed Elders U.S. surgeon general. Despite conservative opposition in Congress over her advocacy of abortion rights and sex education, she was confirmed and was sworn in on September 10, 1993. During her first year as surgeon general, Elders faced continued opposition by conservatives to her advocacy of condom distribution and sex education in schools and stirred debate through several controversial stands, such as her support of the medical and compassionate use of marijuana, her warnings to parents against purchasing toy guns for children, and most notably her proposal that the question of legalizing drugs in order to "markedly reduce" the nationwide crime rate be studied. Her supporters claimed that opponents of the administration were simply using Elders as a target, and her courageous, forthright style made her a hero to thousands of African Americans and whites throughout the United States. In the wake of continuing controversy, however, President Clinton asked for her resignation; she left the surgeon general's office on December 30, 1994. Since her resignation, Elders has worked as an endocrinologist at the University of Arkansas Medical School. Her autobiography, *Jocelyn Elders, M.D.,* was published in 1996.

In 2002 the American Medical Women's Association inducted Elders into the International Women in Medicine Hall of Fame.

■ ■ *Bibliography*

Barnes, Steve. "The Crusade of Dr. Elders." *New York Times Magazine* (October 15, 1989): 38–41.

Elders, Jocelyn, and David Chanoff. *Jocelyn Elders, M.D.: From Sharecropper's Daughter to Surgeon General of the United States of America.* New York: Morrow, 1996.

Rosellini, Lynn. "The Prescriptions of Dr. Yes." *U.S. News and World Report* (July 26, 1993): 60–61.

GREG ROBINSON (1996)
Updated by publisher 2005

ELLINGTON, EDWARD KENNEDY "DUKE"

APRIL 29, 1899
MAY 24, 1974

╶┤┝┤╾

One of the supreme composers of the twentieth century, Edward Kennedy Ellington was born into a comfortable middle-class family in Washington, D.C. The son of a butler, Ellington received the nickname "Duke" as a child because of the care and pride he took in his attire. As he grew older, his aristocratic bearing and sartorial elegance made the nickname stick. Although he took piano lessons starting in 1906, he was also a talented painter, and before he finished high school he was offered an NAACP-sponsored painting scholarship for college. By this time, however, his interests were again turning toward music, especially ragtime and stride piano. By 1918, when Ellington married Edna Thompson, he was leading a band that played popular tunes in a ragtime style at white "society" events. To support his wife and son, Mercer, who was born in 1919, Ellington also worked as a sign painter.

In 1923, encouraged by pianist Fats Waller, Ellington moved to New York to be the pianist and arranger for the Washingtonians. When the leader of the ensemble, Elmer Snowden, left in 1924, Ellington took over and led the band in his first appearances on record. The Washingtonians had extensive stays at the Club Hollywood, later called the Kentucky Club, from 1924 to 1927. In this formative period, Ellington's key influence was the trumpeter Bubber Miley (1903–1932), whose guttural, plunger-muted style added a robust, blues-tinged element to Ellington's previously genteel compositions and arrangements. Miley's growling, mournful solos inspired Ellington's most important compositions in the 1920s, including "East St. Louis Toodle-O" (1926), "Black and Tan Fantasy" (1927), and "The Mooche" (1928). Another important composition from this period, "Creole Love

Call" (1927), features a wordless obbligato by vocalist Adelaide Hall.

On December 4, 1927, Ellington's band debuted at Harlem's Cotton Club, an all-white nightclub. The engagement lasted on and off for four years and gave Ellington a national radio audience, as well as the chance to accompany a variety of chorus and specialty dance numbers and vocalists, often portraying "primitive" and "exotic" aspects of African-American culture. It was in this environment that he perfected the style, marked by energetic climaxes and haunting sonorities, that became known as his "jungle music."

The Cotton Club engagement made Ellington one of the best-known musicians in jazz, famed not only for his eminently danceable tunes, but also for compositions that attracted the attention of the classical music world. During the 1930s the orchestra toured the United States extensively, and they made trips to Europe in 1933 and 1939. Ellington's 1930s recordings, which achieved a great success among both white and black audiences, include "Ring Dem Bells" (1930), "Mood Indigo" (1930), "Rockin' in Rhythm" (1931), "It Don't Mean a Thing If It Ain't Got That Swing" (1932), "Sophisticated Lady" (1932), "Daybreak Express" (1933), "Solitude" (1934), "In a Sentimental Mood" (1935), trombonist Juan Tizol's "Caravan" (1937), "I Let a Song Go out of My Heart" (1938), and "Prelude to a Kiss" (1938). Ellington's early 1940s band is often considered the best he ever led. Bolstered by tenor saxophonist Ben Webster, bassist Jimmy Blanton, and Ellington's assistant, composer and arranger Billy Strayhorn, the orchestra recorded a number of masterpieces, including "Ko-Ko" (1940), "Concerto for Cootie" (1940), "In a Mellow Tone" (1940), "Cotton Tail" (1940), "Perdido" (1942), and "C-Jam Blues" (1942), as well as Strayhorn's "Chelsea Bridge" (1941) and "Take the A Train" (1941). Ellington also recorded in groups led by clarinetist Barney Bigard, trumpeters Cootie Williams and Rex Stewart, and saxophonist Johnny Hodges.

In the 1940s Ellington became increasingly interested in extended composition. Though he was the greatest master of the four-minute jazz composition, he chafed against the limitations of the length of a 78-rpm record side. As early as 1934 he wrote the score for the short film *Symphony in Black,* and the next year recorded *Reminiscing in Tempo,* a contemplative work taking up four sides. His greatest extended composition was the fifty-minute *Black, Brown and Beige,* which premiered at Carnegie Hall on January 23, 1943. This work, which included the hymnlike "Come Sunday" passage, depicted African Americans at work and at prayer, with vignettes on aspects of history from emancipation to the development of Harlem

Time magazine cover featuring "Jazzman Duke Ellington," August 20, 1956. GETTY IMAGES

as a black community. Other extended works from this period include *New World-a-Comin'* (1943), *The Liberian Suite* (1947), and *The Tattooed Bride* (1948). Ellington continued to issue shorter recordings, but there were fewer memorable short compositions after the mid-1940s, though "The Clothed Woman" (1947) and "Satin Doll" (1953) were notable exceptions. In addition to composing and conducting, Ellington was an excellent pianist in the Harlem stride tradition, and he recorded memorable duets with the bassist Jimmy Blanton in 1940.

During the bebop era of the late 1940s and early 1950s, Ellington's band declined in influence. However, their performance at the 1956 Newport Jazz Festival, featuring the saxophonist Paul Gonsalves's electrifying solo on "Diminuendo and Crescendo in Blue," reaffirmed their reputation and earned Ellington a cover article in *Time* magazine. After this, Ellington took the orchestra to Europe, Japan, the Middle East, India, South America, and Africa. The orchestra also made albums with Louis Armstrong, Coleman Hawkins, Count Basie, Ella Fitzgerald, and John Coltrane, and Ellington recorded as part of a trio with the drummer Max Roach and the bassist Charles

Mingus. Among his many later extended compositions are *Harlem* (1951), *A Drum Is a Woman* (1956), *Such Sweet Thunder* (1957), *The Queen's Suite* (1959), *The Far East Suite* (1967), and *Afro-Eurasian Eclipse* (1971). Ellington also composed film scores for *Anatomy of a Murder* (1959) and the Oscar-nominated *Paris Blues* (1961). He composed music for ballets by the choreographer Alvin Ailey (1931–1989), including *The River* (1970) and *Les Trois rois noirs*, which has a section dedicated to the Reverend Dr. Martin Luther King Jr. and was composed in Ellington's final years and premiered in 1976. In his last decade, Ellington also wrote religious music for three events he called "Sacred Concerts" (1965, 1968, 1973). These were vast productions that evoked his strong sense of spirituality through gospel and choral music, dancing, and thankful hymns.

Starting with the 1943 *Black, Brown and Beige,* many of Ellington's extended works were tributes to his African-American heritage and demonstrations of his pride in the accomplishments of African Americans. His many shorter depictions of Harlem range from the elegiac "Drop Me Off in Harlem" (1933) to the boisterous "Harlem Airshaft" (1940). Perhaps his most personal tributes are his two musicals, *Jump for Joy* (including "I Got It Bad and That Ain't Good," 1942), and *My People* (1963), both dealing with the theme of integration. The latter includes the song "King Fit the Battle of Alabam."

Ellington's music was collaborative. Many of his works were written by band members, and many more were written collectively, by synthesizing and expanding riffs and motifs into unified compositions. Ellington's compositions were almost always written with a particular band member's style and ability in mind. His collaborator Strayhorn remarked that, while Ellington played piano, his real instrument was his orchestra. Ellington was an exceptionally original musical thinker whose orchestral sound was marked by instrumental doublings on reeds, ingenious combinations of instruments, and the carefully crafted use of a variety of muted brasses. The diversity of the band was remarkable, containing an extraordinary variety of masterful and distinctive soloists, ranging from the smooth, sensuous improvisations of saxophonist Johnny Hodges to the gutbucket sounds of trumpeter Cootie Williams and trombonist "Tricky Sam" Nanton.

In the ever-changing world of the big bands, the Ellington orchestra's core roster seldom changed. The most important of his band members, with their tenures parenthetically noted, include trumpeters William "Cat" Anderson (1944–1947, 1950–1959, 1961–1971), Bubber Miley (1924–1929), Rex Stewart (1934–1945), Arthur Whetsol (1923–1924, 1928–1936), and Cootie Williams (1929–

1940, 1962–1973); violinist and trumpeter Ray Nance (1940–1963); trombonists Lawrence Brown (1932–1951, 1960–1970), Joe "Tricky Sam" Nanton (1926–1946), and Juan Tizol (1929–1944, 1951–1953); alto saxophonists Otto Hardwick (1923–1928, 1932–1946), Johnny Hodges (1928–1951, 1955–1970), and Russell Procope (1946–1974); tenor saxophonists Paul Gonsalves (1950–1970, 1972–1974) and Ben Webster (1940–1943, 1948–1949); baritone saxophonist Harry Carney (1927–1974); clarinetists Barney Bigard (1927–1942) and Jimmy Hamilton (1943–1968); vocalists Ivie Anderson (1931–1942) and Al Hibbler (1943–1951); drummer Sonny Greer (1923–1951); bassist Jimmy Blanton (1939–1941); and composer and arranger Billy Strayhorn (1939–1967).

During his lifetime, Ellington was celebrated as a commanding figure in American culture. He cherished the many awards and honorary degrees he earned, including the Spingarn Medal (1959) and eleven Grammy Awards. Ellington remained gracious, though many were outraged by the refusal of a 1965 Pulitzer Prize committee, firmly opposed to recognizing "popular" music, to give him a special award for composition. In 1970 Ellington was awarded the Presidential Medal of Freedom by President Nixon and was feted with a seventieth-birthday celebration at the White House. He died of cancer on May 24, 1974.

Since Ellington's death, his orchestra has been led by his son, Mercer, himself a trumpeter and composer of note. In 1986 Duke Ellington became the first African-American jazz musician to appear on a U.S. postage stamp. Since the 1980s there has been a growing interest in Ellington among scholars, particularly in the extended compositions, and among jazz fans, who have had access to a wealth of previously unreleased recordings. Such attention, which hit a peak in 1999, the centennial of his birth, inevitably confirms Ellington's status not only as the greatest composer and bandleader in jazz, but as a figure unique in the history of twentieth-century music.

See also Cotton Club; Jazz; Jazz in African-American Culture; Music in the United States; Spingarn Medal

■ ■ *Bibliography*

Collier, James Lincoln. *Duke Ellington.* New York: Oxford University Press, 1987.

Dance, Stanley. *The World of Duke Ellington.* New York: Scribner's, 1970.

Ellington, Duke. *Music Is My Mistress.* Garden City, N.Y.: Doubleday, 1973.

Hasse, John Edward. *Beyond Category: The Life and Genius of Duke Ellington.* New York: Simon & Schuster, 1993.

Lambert, Eddie. *Duke Ellington: A Listener's Guide.* Lanham, Md.: Scarecrow Press, 1999.

Lawrence, A. H. *Duke Ellington and His World: A Biography.* New York: Schirmer, 1999.

Nicholson, Stuart. *Reminiscing in Tempo: A Portrait of Duke Ellington.* Boston: Northeastern University Press, 1999.

Steed, Janna Tull. *Duke Ellington: A Spiritual Biography.* New York: Crossroad, 1999.

Tucker, Mark. *Ellington: The Early Years.* Urbana: University of Illinois Press, 1991.

Tucker, Mark, ed. *The Duke Ellington Reader.* New York: Oxford University Press, 1993.

Williams, Martin. *The Jazz Tradition,* 2d rev. ed. New York: Oxford University Press, 1993.

Yanow, Scott. *Duke Ellington,* foreword by Billy Taylor. New York: Friedman/Fairfax, 1999.

MARTIN WILLIAMS (1996)
Updated bibliography

ELLISON, RALPH

MARCH 1, 1914
APRIL 16, 1994

Author Ralph Ellison was born to Lewis and Ida Millsap Ellison in Oklahoma City, Oklahoma, a frontier town with a rich vernacular culture. As a child he worked at Randolph's Pharmacy, where he heard animal tales and ghost stories. The local all-black high school provided rigorous training in music, and the Aldridge Theatre featured many of the leading blues, ragtime, and jazz musicians of the day. Ellison played in high school jazz bands and in 1933 enrolled as a music major at Tuskegee Institute, Alabama. He involved himself in the other arts as well and on his own discovered T. S. Eliot's *The Waste Land,* where he found a range of allusions "as mixed and varied as that of Louis Armstrong."

At the end of his third college year, Ellison went to New York to earn money. He never returned to Tuskegee. He met Langston Hughes, whose poetry he had read in high school, and Richard Wright, who urged him to write for *New Challenge,* which Wright was editing. Ellison wrote a review for the magazine in 1937, his first published work. In 1938 he took a Works Progress Administration job with the New York Writer's Project and worked at night on his own fiction. He read Hemingway to learn style.

Ellison wrote book reviews for the radical periodicals *Direction, Negro Quarterly,* and *New Masses,* which in 1940 printed at least one review by him every month. His first short stories were realistic in the manner of Richard Wright and presented fairly explicit political solutions to the dilemmas of Jim Crow. By 1940 he had begun to find his own direction with a series of stories in the Huck Finn/Tom Sawyer mold—tales of black youngsters who were not so much victims as playmakers in a land of possibility. "Flying Home" (1944) offers wise old Jefferson as a storyteller whose verbal art helps lessen the greenhorn Todd's isolation and teaches him a healthier attitude toward the divided world he must confront. That story set the stage for Ellison's monumental 1952 novel *Invisible Man,* which received the National Book Award the following year.

Set between 1930 and 1950, *Invisible Man* tells of the development of an ambitious young black man from the South, a naïf who goes to college and then to New York in search of advancement. At first Invisible Man, unnamed throughout the novel, wants to walk the narrow way of Booker T. Washington, whose words he speaks at his high school graduation as well as at a smoker for the town's leading white male citizens. At the smoker he is required to fight blindfolded in a free-for-all against the other black youths. In this key chapter, all the boys are turned blindly against one another in a danger-filled ritual staged for the amusement of their white patrons. That night the young man dreams of his grandfather, the novel's cryptic ancestor/wise man, who presents him with "an engraved document" that seems an ironic comment on his high school diploma and its costs. "Read it," the old man tells him. "'To Whom It May Concern,' I intoned. 'Keep This Nigger Boy Running.'"

Whether a student in the southern college or a spokesman in New York for the radical political movement called the Brotherhood (modeled on the Communist Party of the 1930s or some other American political organization that exploited blacks and then sold them out), Invisible Man is kept running. Quintessentially American in his confusion about who he is, he maddashes from scene to scene, letting others tell him what his experience means, who he is, what his name is. And he is not only blind, he is invisible—he is racially stereotyped and otherwise denied his individuality. "I am invisible," he discovers, "simply because people refuse to see me. Like the bodiless heads you see sometimes in circus sideshows, it is as though I have been surrounded by mirrors of hard, distorting glass. When they approach me they see only my surroundings, themselves, or figments of their imagination—indeed, everything and anything except me."

After encounters with remarkable adults—some wisely parental, some insane but brilliant, some sly con men—he learns to accept with equipoise the full ambiguity of his history and to see the world by his own lights. "It took me

Ralph Waldo Ellison (1914–1994). Ellison won the National Book Award for his novel Invisible Man *(1952). A Bildungsroman that begins with a setting in the South, the novel graphically depicts the humiliating, often violent treatment the nameless hero suffers at the hands of Southern white men who "educate" him and black men in Harlem who "use" him.* GETTY IMAGES

a long time," he says, "and much painful boomeranging of my expectations to achieve a realization everyone else appears to have been born with: That I am nobody but myself. But first I had to discover that I am an invisible man!" He had to find out that very few people would bother to understand his real motives and values; perhaps not all of these mysteries were knowable, even by himself. And yet in this novel of education and epiphany, Invisible Man decides he can nonetheless remain hopeful: "I was my experiences and my experiences were me," he says. "And no blind men, no matter how powerful they became, even if they conquered the world, could take that, or change one single itch, taunt, laugh, cry, scar, ache, rage or pain of it."

Rich in historical and literary allusions—from Columbus to World War II, from Oedipus and Br'er Rabbit to T. S. Eliot and Richard Wright—*Invisible Man* stands both as a novel about the history of the novel and as a meditation on the history of the United States. In doing so, it presents a metaphor for black American life in the twentieth century that transcends its particular focus. It names not only the modern American but the citizen of the contemporary world as tragicomically centerless (but somehow surviving and getting smarter): *Homo invisibilis.* It is Ellison's masterwork.

Shadow and Act (1964) and *Going to the Territory* (1987) are collections of Ellison's nonfiction prose. With these books he established himself as a preeminent man of letters—one whose driving purpose was to define African-American life and culture with precision and affirmation. The essays on African-American music are insider's reports that reflect Ellison's deep experience and long memory. Whether discussing literature, music, painting, psychology, or history, Ellison places strong emphases on vernacular culture—its art, rituals, and meanings—and on the power of the visionary individual, particularly the artist, to prevail. These books offer a strong challenge to social scientists and historians to consider African-American life in terms not just of its ills and pathologies but of its tested capacity to reinvent itself and to influence the nation and the world.

See also Hughes, Langston; Literature of the United States; Wright, Richard

■ ■ *Bibliography*

Benston, Kimberly, ed. *Speaking for You: The Vision of Ralph Ellison.* Washington, D.C.: Howard University Press, 1985.

Burke, Bob, and Denyvetta Davis. *Ralph Ellison: A Biography.* Oklahoma City: Oklahoma Heritage Association, 2003.

Jackson, Lawrence. *Ralph Ellison: Emergence of Genius.* New York: Wiley, 2002.

O'Meally, Robert G. *The Craft of Ralph Ellison.* Cambridge, Mass.: Harvard University Press, 1980.

ROBERT G. O'MEALLY (1996)
Updated bibliography

EMANCIPATION

This entry is comprised of two unique essays differing mainly in their geographical focus.

EMANCIPATION IN LATIN AMERICA AND THE CARIBBEAN
Christopher Schmidt-Nowara

EMANCIPATION IN THE UNITED STATES
David W. Blight

EMANCIPATION IN LATIN AMERICA AND THE CARIBBEAN

The process of slave emancipation in Latin America and the Caribbean was protracted and tortuous, beginning in the late eighteenth century with the Haitian Revolution, an event with profound consequences for slave regimes everywhere in the New World, and finally coming to an end with the abolition of Brazilian slavery in 1888. During that century, slavery was more pervasive than ever before in terms of the number of slaves working in the Americas, while also being more vulnerable given the rise of abolitionist movements, the spread of antislavery sentiment, and the numerous military and political crises that gave slaves opportunities both to escape enslavement and to take up arms against the institution. A comprehensive discussion of all the twists and turns in Latin American and Caribbean emancipation is impossible in these pages. Instead, this brief entry will offer a broad description of the forces that set the stage for emancipation and highlight them with specific examples from several countries, such as Haiti, Cuba, Brazil, and Jamaica. Though there was great variation in slave regimes and in the pressures leading to slavery's destruction across this geographically, economically, and politically diverse region, one overarching typology of slave emancipation will suggest the varieties of experience: on the one hand, emancipation via anticolonial rebellions, on the other emancipation through the legal process of abolition, keeping in mind that this division was not hard and fast and that in some cases both causes were at work in the same country.

ANTICOLONIAL REBELLION AND SLAVE EMANCIPATION: HAITI AND SPANISH AMERICA

African slavery was one of the central and most venerable institutions of the European empires in the Americas. The Spanish and Portuguese had turned early to the African slave trade, already flourishing in late medieval Europe, as they staked out colonies in the New World during the sixteenth century. While the sugar plantations of northeastern Brazil (Pernambuco and Bahia) were important destinations, so too were the great mining colonies of the Spanish empire, Peru and Mexico. In the seventeenth and eighteenth centuries, other European rivals forced their way into the region, particularly the Caribbean. The British and French, and to a lesser degree the Dutch, created rich plantation economies in colonies like Barbados, Jamaica, and Saint Domingue (Haiti). Spain, too, eventually

Emancipation in Barbados, January 1, 1833. *Slaves march through the streets, with cymbals, drum, and concertina, to celebrate their freedom.* GETTY IMAGES

turned to the production of sugar through the use of slave labor, transforming Cuba and Puerto Rico into major producers in the late eighteenth and early nineteenth centuries. Slavery was thus widespread and well entrenched in the Americas by the late eighteenth century. Any challenge to the colonial status quo would thus involve some challenge to slavery as well. This nexus was immediately apparent in the Haitian Revolution.

By the late eighteenth century, the French colony of Saint Domingue, on the western end of the island of Hispaniola, was the largest producer of cane sugar in the world. A small white population, divided between great planters and smaller property owners, shopkeepers, and professionals, ruled alongside a towering slave population, largely African-born (Dubois, 2004). There was also a significant population of people of color, in many cases freed by European fathers and at times well prepared to take a predominant position in the colony through education and the inheritance of wealth, though they found their prerogatives increasingly curtailed in the second half of the century. Many free people of color were planters in their own right, though usually of coffee as opposed to sugar.

Others filled positions in the colonial militia or the *maréchausée*, the gendarmerie dedicated to tracking down runaway slaves. They were accustomed to bearing arms and identified strongly with the dominant colonial culture.

When revolution broke out in France in 1789, the *gens de coleur* saw the new regime as a potential ally against the "aristocrats of the skin" who sought to disbar them from the full enjoyment of their liberty through racial discrimination, which had grown more onerous since mid-century. They found numerous advocates in France but also had to confront the vexing question of slavery and an abolitionist society, the Société des Amis des Noirs, founded in 1788 and dedicated to the gradual abolition of colonial slavery. By the later eighteenth century, more and more enlightened Frenchmen had come to see New World slavery as a gross injustice. They also saw it as a powder keg ready to explode at any moment.

Thus, at the inception of the French Revolution, the questions of race, slavery, emancipation, and citizenship were dramatically posed. When it became clear that the whites of Saint Domingue and their French allies would enforce white supremacy, several free colored leaders— such as Vincent Ogé—returned to the colony and took up arms to force their claims. They were quickly defeated, horribly tortured, and executed, but new openings would present themselves as both the colony and metropolis were divided. While the dominant groups fought among themselves, slaves in the northern part of the colony apparently saw the opportunity to assert their own demands for freedom. Inspired by diverse African and European ideas of justice and freedom, a huge slave rebellion erupted in 1791 across the hinterland of the city of Le Cap and eventually spread to other parts of the colony.

Rivals saw in this colonial unrest a chance to advance their own cause. Both the British and the Spanish dispatched large forces to the Caribbean, hoping to incorporate the rich colony into their own empires. Spain, for example, from the adjoining colony of Santo Domingo, supported Toussaint-Louverture, a well-educated former slave who, according to legend, was a reader of the Abbé Raynal, a *philosophe* who had predicted the violent destruction of New World slavery by a black Spartacus.

Ultimately, Toussaint defied his Spanish patrons. In 1793 he switched his allegiance from Spain to France in exchange for the legal abolition of slavery, ratified by the revolutionary government in France in 1794. For the next several years, he was the de facto governor of the colony, which he successfully defended for France against the Spanish and English. In 1802 France sought to restore slavery in its colonies. Though the French were successful in their other Caribbean colonies and able to capture Toussaint, other rebel generals like Henri Christophe and Dessalines defeated a large European expedition and proclaimed the independence of the new nation, Haiti, in 1804.

By 1804 there were two independent nation-states in the Americas: the United States and Haiti. The fate of slavery was a crucial issue in the fight for independence and the consolidation of the new regimes. The United States reasserted the privileges of slave owners, though in the face of significant internal opposition. Haiti wiped out the colonial planter class and asserted the priority of slave emancipation. The wars of national liberation in the Americas always involved conflict over the survival of slavery, but the outcome was far from uniform. The same would hold true in the colonies of the Iberian monarchies a few years later.

If the French Revolution of 1789 and the ensuing struggle for dominance in different corners of the Atlantic opened the way for the destruction of slavery and colonialism in Saint. Domingue, it had a similar impact on Spain's American empire. Information about the Haitian Revolution circulated throughout the Atlantic world, inspiring would-be rebels against the established order, despite the efforts of planters and government officials to silence it. Moreover, events in Europe continued to exert important and unpredictable influence. When France invaded the Iberian Peninsula in 1808, the empires of Spain and Portugal suddenly found themselves thrown into profound crisis. The invasion had differing effects on slavery in the two empires. The Portuguese court embarked for Rio de Janeiro under British escort and remained there until 1822. With Rio as the new capital of the empire and the protection of the hegemonic economic and naval power, Brazilian ports enjoyed greater freedom, urban and plantation slavery boomed, and political order reigned, at least in the short term.

In contrast, a political vacuum opened in Spain and its overseas empire. The Spanish court fell captive to the French, and the country was submerged in a violent resistance to the occupying force between 1808 and 1814. The overthrow of the Bourbon monarchy led to an acute crisis of political legitimacy in the colonies. Many patriots saw this as the moment to fight for independence; in doing so, they unintentionally shattered the colonial social order from the Río de la Plata in the south to Mexico in the north.

Slaves and slavery figured centrally in the independence struggle (Andrews, 2004). Both loyalist and patriotic forces mobilized slaves to fight on their sides during the protracted wars for independence. Loyalists could draw on old precedents by promising freedom in exchange for a term of military service. Such a compromise had existed throughout the colonial period and recognized the basic legitimacy of slavery as an institution in Spanish America, while also honoring the mechanisms for acquiring freedom enshrined in Spanish law since the Middle Ages. Throughout the nineteenth century, from the first wars against Venezuelan patriots in 1809 to the final wars against Cuban patriots between 1868 and 1880, Spain was able to attract military recruits from the slave population, trading freedom for service to the king and nation, as it had done throughout the old regime. Patriot armies often tried to strike a similar bargain—many of their initial leaders were slave owners themselves, such as Simón Bolívar in Venezuela and Carlos Manuel de Céspedes in Cuba—yet found it harder to defend the persistence of slavery in the context of liberal and republican aspirations, the breakdown of traditional forms of order, and the spread of the language of liberation.

From all corners of South America, where slavery was most widespread and where the battles were fiercest, slaves flocked to patriot armies, using the language of national liberation to forward their demands for liberty. Free people of color also saw great promise in the revolutionary movements. For example, the Afro-Colombian population of Cartagena de Indias, long the major depot for the slave trade to Spanish America, enthusiastically supported the uprising against Spanish rule with the hope of achieving political equality under the new regime. Many were inspired by the spread of knowledge of the Haitian Revolution. Demands for equality and some vision of racial democracy pervaded revolutionary and postcolonial Spanish America as popular groups—slaves included—mobilized for independence and embraced liberal and republican ideologies. Under such conditions, efforts to formalize racial inequality as the Spanish colonial regime continued to do or to reinvigorate bonded labor were virtually impossible. Revolutionary leaders had to capitulate. Simón Bolívar, who led the struggle for independence in South America admitted: "It seems to me madness that a revolution for freedom expects to maintain slavery" (quoted in Blanchard, 2002, p. 514). With the important exception of Brazil, all Latin American states abolished slavery once they threw off colonial rule, though in most cases they compromised by granting freedom to slave combatants and passing gradual emancipation laws that extinguished slavery in countries such as Peru, Venezuela, and Colombia by midcentury.

Cuba offers a slight variation to this process. The colony did not rebel against Spain in the 1810s and 1820s as most of the empire did. Rather, given the huge growth of

Slaves on a West Indies plantation receiving news of their emancipation. © BETTMANN/CORBIS

the slave population (Cuba became by far the largest slave society in Spanish American history), local elites decided to collaborate with the metropolis. The first movement for independence came only in 1868. As in other parts of the Spanish America earlier in the century, leaders such as Céspedes had to address the question of emancipation, his hand forced by the slaves who fled their masters to join the insurgency against Spanish rule. Once more, antislavery and anticolonialism were conjoined, national independence holding out the promise of liberty and racial equality. In this case, however, Spain responded with its own emancipation laws, finally abolishing slavery altogether in 1886. Nonetheless, the fights against colonial rule and racism would remain fused in the Cuban independence movement for the rest of the century (Scott, 2000).

ABOLITIONISM AND EMANCIPATION IN THE BRITISH WEST INDIES AND BRAZIL

We can see that even where anticolonial rebellions forced emancipation for many of the enslaved in Haiti and Spanish America, including Cuba, that the legal process of emancipation was still important. The French metropolis confirmed the abolition of slavery in Saint Domingue in 1794 (though confirming a right already effectively claimed by many of the enslaved themselves after the uprising of 1791); Spain passed laws that emancipated many Cuban slaves in the later nineteenth century to counter the anticolonial insurgency; and in independent Spanish America, some slave combatants claimed freedom for themselves, but many slaves were emancipated only later in the century under the auspices of laws passed by the new states. However, the importance of rebellion stands out when we look at other Caribbean and Latin American slave societies where governments, both colonial and national, exerted considerable control over the pace of slavery and emancipation.

Such was the case in Brazil and the British Caribbean colonies. In the latter, emancipation was legislated in stages by the metropolitan parliament under significant pressure from popular antislavery movements that arose in the later eighteenth century, inspired by nonconformist sects such as Quakerism and by conflicts over the nature of work and property in an emerging market society (Davis, 1975; Drescher, 1999). The strategy of British abolitionists was gradualist; they demanded first the suppression of the slave trade to the British colonies, a measure passed by the parliament in 1806. Again in the face of widespread popular demands, the parliament passed an emancipation law that took effect in 1834, though with the major restriction that freed slaves must serve an apprenticeship with their former masters. This qualification of liberation set the tone for the struggles over the limits of freedom that would follow final emancipation in 1838 (Holt, 1992).

Brazil, like the United States, was an independent New World country that held out persistently against the forces of emancipation unleashed in the later eighteenth century (Conrad, 1972). The major American importer of African slaves during the long history of the Atlantic slave trade, Brazil relied heavily on slave labor in most sectors of the economy (the extent of which is hinted at by the French painter Jean-Baptiste Debret in his renderings of daily life in mid-nineteenth-century Rio de Janeiro). Upon achieving independence from Portugal in 1822, largely without armed violence, the new country experienced a boom in slave imports to the Northeastern sugar regions. By midcentury, slavery was also on the rise in the southeastern coffee regions of Rio de Janeiro and São Paulo.

However, the supply of forced labor became increasingly tenuous. Under intense British naval pressure Brazil abolished the slave trade in 1850 (the British were also pressuring Spain to suppress the slave trade to Cuba and Puerto Rico). Planters in the southeast began to purchase slaves from the stagnant northeastern sugar regions, but a crisis loomed. In 1871 the Brazilian government passed a gradual emancipation law that called for the *very* protracted abolition of the institution. But slaves and abolitionists eventually took matters into their own hands to expedite the process. Mass flight from plantations, organized efforts to obstruct the internal slave trade, and increasingly ebullient and defiant public demands for abolition ultimately led to final emancipation in 1888, a century after the unpredictable struggle to destroy slavery had taken root in the Atlantic world.

See also Coartación; Emancipation in the United States; Haitian Revolution; Slavery

■ ■ *Bibliography*

Andrews, George Reid. *Afro-Latin America, 1800–2000.* New York: Oxford University Press, 2004.

Blanchard, Peter. "The Language of Liberation: Slave Voices in the Wars of Independence." *Hispanic American Historical Review* 82 (2002): 499–523.

Conrad, Robert Edgar. *The Destruction of Brazilian Slavery, 1850–1888.* Berkeley: University of California Press, 1972.

Davis, David Brion. *The Problem of Slavery in the Age of Revolution, 1770-1823.* Ithaca, N.Y.: Cornell University Press, 1975.

Drescher, Seymour. *From Slavery to Freedom: Comparative Studies in the Rise and Fall of Atlantic Slavery.* New York: New York University Press, 1999.

Dubois, Laurent. *Avengers of the New World: The Story of the Haitian Revolution.* Cambridge, Mass: Belknap Press, 2004.

Holt, Thomas C. *The Problem of Freedom: Race, Labor, and Politics in Jamaica and Britain, 1832–1938.* Baltimore, Md.: Johns Hopkins University Press, 1992.

Scott, Rebecca J. *Slave Emancipation in Cuba: The Transition to Free Labor, 1865–1899,* 2d ed. Pittsburgh: University of Pittsburgh Press, 2000.

CHRISTOPHER SCHMIDT-NOWARA (2005)

EMANCIPATION IN THE UNITED STATES

Few events in American history can match the drama and the social significance of black Emancipation in the midst of the Civil War. Since the early seventeenth century, when African-born slaves were first brought ashore in Virginia, through the long development of the South's plantation economy and its dependence upon slave labor, emancipation had been the dream of African-American people. From the age of the American Revolution when northern states freed their relatively small numbers of slaves to the time of increasing free black community development in the North, emancipation became a matter of political and religious expectation. To be a black abolitionist, a fugitive slave desperately seeking his or her way through the mysterious realities of the Underground Railroad, or one of the millions of slaves cunningly surviving on southern cotton plantations was to be an actor in this long and agonizing drama. The agony and the hope embedded in the story of emancipation is what black poet Francis Ellen Watkins tried to capture in a simple verse written in the wake of John Brown's execution in 1859 and only a little over a year before the outbreak of the Civil War:

Make me a grave where'er you will,
In a lowly plain, or a lofty hill,
Make it among earth's humblest graves,
But not in a land where men are slaves.

Soon, by the forces of total war, which in turn opened opportunities for slaves to seize their own freedom, emancipation became reality in America. Black freedom became the central event of nineteenth-century African-American history and, along with the preservation of the Union, the central result of the Civil War.

On Emancipation day, January 1, 1863 (when Abraham Lincoln's Emancipation Proclamation was to go into effect), "jubilee meetings" occurred all over black America. At Tremont Temple in Boston, a huge gathering of blacks and whites met from morning until night, awaiting the final news that Lincoln had signed the fateful document. Genuine concern still existed that something might go awry; the preliminary proclamation had been issued in September 1862, a mixture of what appeared to be military necessity and a desire to give the war a new moral purpose. Numerous luminaries from throughout antebellum free black leadership spoke during the day; the attorney John Rock, the minister and former slave John Sella Martin, the orator and women's suffragist Anna Dickinson, author William Wells Brown, and Boston's William Cooper Nell as presiding officer were among them. The most prominent of all black voices, Frederick Douglass, gave a concluding speech during the afternoon session punctuated by many cries of "Amen."

In the evening, tension mounted and anxiety gripped the hall, as no news had arrived from Washington. Douglass and Brown provided more oratory to try to quell the changing mood of doubt. Then a runner arrived from the telegraph office with the news: "It is coming!" he shouted. "It is on the wires!" An attempt was made to read the text of the Emancipation Proclamation, but great jubilation engulfed the crowd. Unrestrained shouting and singing ensued. Douglass gained the throng's attention and led them in a chorus of his favorite hymn, "Blow Ye the Trumpet, Blow." Next an old black preacher named Rue led the group in "Sound the loud timbel o'er Egypt's dark sea, Jehovah has triumphed, his people are free!" The celebration lasted until midnight, when the crowd reassembled at pastor Leonard A. Grimes's Twelfth Baptist Church—an institution renowned among black Bostonians for its role in helping many fugitive slaves move along the road to liberty—to continue celebrating.

From Massachusetts to Ohio and Michigan, and in many Union-occupied places in the South where ex-slaves were now entering the Yankee army or beginning their first year as free people, such celebrations occurred. Full of praise songs, these celebrations demonstrated that whatever the fine print of the proclamation might say, black folks across the land knew that they had lived to see a new day, a transforming moment in their history. At a large "contraband camp" (center for refugee ex-slaves) in Washington, D.C., some six hundred black men, women, and children gathered at the superintendent's headquarters on New Year's Eve and sang through most of the night. In chorus after chorus of "Go Down, Moses" they announced the magnitude of their painful but beautiful exodus. One newly supplied verse concluded with "Go down, Abraham, away down in Dixie's land, tell Jeff Davis to let my people go!" Many years after the Tremont Tem-

ple celebration in Boston, Douglass may have best captured the meaning of Emancipation day for his people: "It was not logic, but the trump of jubilee, which everybody wanted to hear. We were waiting and listening as for a bolt from the sky, which should rend the fetters of four millions of slaves; we were watching as it were, by the dim light of stars, for the dawn of a new day; we were longing for the answer to the agonizing prayers of centuries. Remembering those in bonds as bound with them, we wanted to join in the shout for freedom, and in the anthem of the redeemed." For blacks the cruel and apocalyptic war finally had a holy cause.

The emancipation policy of the Union government evolved with much less certitude than the music and poetry of jubilee day might imply. During the first year of the war, the Union military forces operated on an official policy of exclusion ("denial of asylum") to escaped slaves. The war was to restore the Union, not to uproot slavery. But events overtook such a policy. Floods of fugitive slaves began to enter Union lines in Virginia, in Tennessee, and along the southern coasts. Thousands were eventually employed as military laborers, servants, camp hands, and even spies. Early in the war, at Fortress Monroe, Virginia, in May 1861, the ambitious politician-general Benjamin F. Butler declared the slaves who entered his lines "contraband of war." The idea of slaves as confiscated enemy property eventually caught on. In early August 1861, striking a balance between legality and military necessity, the federal Congress passed the First Confiscation Act, allowing for the seizure of all Confederate property used to aid the war effort. Although not yet technically freed by this law, the slaves of rebel masters came under its purview and an inexorable process toward black freedom took root. Into 1862 the official stance of the Union armies toward slaves was a conflicted one: exclusion where the slaveholders were deemed "loyal," and employment as contrabands where the masters were judged "disloyal." Such an unworkable policy caused considerable dissension in the Union ranks, especially between abolitionist and proslavery officers. But wherever Union forces gained ground in the South, the institution of slavery began to crumble.

By the spring and summer of 1862 Congress took the lead on the issue of emancipation policy. In April it abolished slavery in the District of Columbia, and a large sum of money was allocated for the possible colonization of freed blacks abroad. The Lincoln administration, indeed, pursued a variety of schemes for Central American and Caribbean colonization during the first three years of the war. The sheer impracticality of such plans and stiff black resistance notwithstanding, this old idea of black removal from America as the solution to the revolutionary implica-

"We were waiting and listening as for a bolt from the sky, which should rend the fetters of four million slaves."

FREDERICK DOUGLASS ON THE MEANING OF EMANCIPATION DAY FOR AFRICAN AMERICANS.

tions of Emancipation died hard within the Lincoln administration and in the mind of the president himself. But Lincoln, as well as many other Americans, would be greatly educated by both the necessity and the larger meanings of Emancipation. A black newspaper in Union-occupied New Orleans declared that "history furnishes no such intensity of determination, on the part of any race, as that exhibited by these people to be free." And Frederick Douglass felt greatly encouraged by an evolving emancipation movement in early 1862, whatever its contradictory motives. "It is really wonderful," he wrote, "how all efforts to evade, postpone, and prevent its coming, have been mocked and defied by the stupendous sweep of events."

In June 1862 Congress abolished slavery in the western territories, a marvelous irony when one remembers the tremendous political crisis over that issue in the decade before the war, as well as the alleged finality of the Dred Scott Decision of 1857. In July Congress passed the Second Confiscation Act, which explicitly freed slaves of all persons "in rebellion," and excluded no parts of the slaveholding South. These measures provided a public and legal backdrop for President Lincoln's subsequent Emancipation Proclamation, issued in two parts, maneuvered through a recalcitrant Cabinet, and politically calculated to shape Northern morale, prevent foreign intervention (especially that of the British), and keep the remaining four slaveholding border states in the Union. During 1862 Lincoln had secretly maneuvered to persuade Delaware and Kentucky to accept a plan of compensated, gradual emancipation. But the deeply divided border states bluntly refused such notions. In the preliminary proclamation of September 21, 1862, issued in the aftermath of the bloody battle of Antietam (a Union military success for which Lincoln had desperately waited), the president offered a carrot to the rebellious South: in effect, stop the war, reenter the Union, and slavery would go largely untouched. In his State of the Union address in December, Lincoln dwelled on the idea of gradual, compensated Emancipation as the way to end the war and return a willful South to the Union. None of these offers had any chance of acceptance at this point in what had already become a revo-

lutionary war for ends much larger and higher than most had imagined in 1861.

Lincoln had always considered slavery to be an evil that had to be eliminated in America. It was he who had committed the Republican Party in the late 1850s to putting slavery "on a course of ultimate extinction." At the outset of the war, however, he valued saving the Union above all else, including whatever would happen to slavery. But after he signed the document that declared all slaves in the "states of rebellion . . . forever free," Lincoln's historical reputation, as often legendary and mythical as it is factual, became forever tied to his role in the emancipation process. Emancipation did indeed require presidential leadership to commit America to a war to free slaves in the eyes of the world; in Lincoln's remarkable command of moral meaning and politics, he understood that this war had become a crucible in which the entire nation could receive a "new birth of freedom." The president ultimately commanded the armies, every forward step of which from 1863 to 1865 was a liberating step, soon by black soldiers as well. On one level, Emancipation had to be legal and moral, and, like all great matters in American history, it had to be finalized in the Constitution, in the Thirteenth Amendment (passed in early 1865). But black freedom was something both given and seized. Many factors made it possible for Lincoln to say by February 1865 that "the central act of my administration, and the greatest event of the nineteenth century," was Emancipation. But none more than the black exodus of self-emancipation when the moment of truth came, the waves of freedpeople who "voted with their feet."

The actual process and timing of Emancipation across the South depended on at least three interrelated circumstances: one, the character of slave society in a given region; two, the course of the war itself; and three, the policies of the Union and Confederate governments. Southern geography, the chronology of the military campaigns, the character of total war with its massive forced movement of people, the personal disposition of slaveholders and Union commanders alike, and the advent of widespread recruitment of black soldiers were all combined factors in determining when, where, and how slaves became free. Thousands of slaves were "hired out" as fortification laborers, teamsters, nurses, and cooks in the Confederate armies, eventually providing many opportunities for escape to Union lines and an uncertain but freer future. Thousands were also "refugeed" to the interior by their owners in order to "protect" them from invading Yankee armies. Many more took to the forests and swamps to hide during the chaos of war, as Union forces swept over the sea islands of the Georgia or South Carolina coast, or the dense-

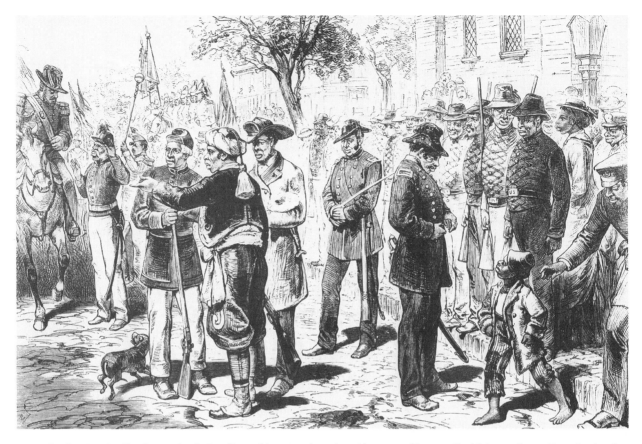

Emancipation Day in Charleston, South Carolina. *African Americans in uniform assemble near Citadel Square for an Emancipation Day procession and celebration.* PHOTOGRAPHS AND PRINTS DIVISION, SCHOMBURG CENTER FOR RESEARCH IN BLACK CULTURE, THE NEW YORK PUBLIC LIBRARY, ASTOR, LENOX AND TILDEN FOUNDATIONS.

ly populated lower Mississippi Valley region. Many of those slaves eventually returned to their plantations, abandoned by their former masters, and took over agricultural production, sometimes under the supervision of an old driver, and sometimes by independently planting subsistence crops while the sugarcane rotted.

Many slaves waited and watched for their opportunity of escape, however uncertain their new fate might be. Octave Johnson was a slave on a plantation in St. James Parish, Louisiana, who ran away to the woods when the war came. He and a group of thirty, ten of whom were women, remained at large for a year and a half. Johnson's story, as he reported it to the American Freedmen's Inquiry Commission in 1864, provides a remarkable example of the social-military revolution under way across the South. "We were four miles in the rear of the plantation house," said Johnson. His band stole food and borrowed matches and other goods from slaves still on the plantation. "We slept on logs and burned cypress leaves to make a smoke and keep away mosquitoes." When hunted by bloodhounds, Johnson's group took to the deeper swamp. They "killed eight of the bloodhounds; then we jumped into

Bayou Faupron; the dogs followed us and the alligators caught six of them; the alligators preferred dog flesh to personal flesh; we escaped and came to Camp Parapet, where I was first employed in the Commissary's office, then as a servant to Col. Hanks; then I joined his regiment." From "working on task" through survival in the bayous, Octave Johnson found his freedom as a corporal in Company C, Fifteenth Regiment, Corps d'Afrique.

For many slaves, the transition from bondage to freedom was not so clear and complete as it was for Octave Johnson. Emancipation was a matter of overt celebration in some places, especially in Southern towns and cities, as well as in some slave quarters. But what freedom meant in 1863, how livelihood would change, how the war would progress, how the masters would react (perhaps with wages but perhaps with violent retribution), how freedpeople would find protection in the conquered and chaotic South, how they would meet the rent payments that might now be charged, how a peasant population of agricultural laborers deeply attached to the land might now become owners of the land as so many dreamed, and whether they would achieve citizenship rights were all ur-

Watch meeting, December 31, 1862. The painting Waiting for the Hour *depicts African Americans in church on New Years Eve, 1862, the night before the Emancipation Proclamation took effect.* PAINTING BY HEARD AND MOSELEY. PRINTS AND PHOTOGRAPHS DIVISION, LIBRARY OF CONGRESS.

gent and unanswered questions during the season of Emancipation. Joy mixed with uncertainty, songs of deliverance with expressions of fear. The actual day on which masters gathered their slaves to announce that they were free was remembered by freedpeople with a wide range of feelings and experience. Some remembered hilarity and dancing, but many remembered it as a sobering, even solemn time. A former South Carolina slave recalled that on his plantation "some were sorry, some hurt, but a few were silent and glad." James Lucas, a former slave of Jefferson Davis in Mississippi, probed the depths of human nature and ambivalence in his description of the day of liberation: "Dey all had diffe'nt ways o' thinkin' 'bout it. Mos'ly though dey was jus' lak me, dey didn' know jus' zackly what it meant. It was jus' somp'n dat de white folks an' slaves all de time talk 'bout. Dat's all. Folks dat ain' never been free don' rightly know de feel of bein' free. Dey don' know de meanin' of it." And a former Virginia slave simply recalled "how wild and upset and dreadful everything was in them times."

But in time, confusion gave way to meaning, and the feel of freedom took many forms. For many ex-slaves who followed Union armies freedom meant, initially, life in contraband camps, where black families struggled to sur-

vive in the face of great hardship and occasional starvation. But by the end of 1862 and throughout the rest of the war, a string of contraband camps became the first homes in freedom for thousands of ex-slaves. At La-Grange, Bolivar, and Memphis in western Tennessee; at Corinth in northern Mississippi; in "contraband colonies" near New Orleans; at Cairo, Illinois; at Camp Barker in the District of Columbia; on Craney Island near Norfolk, Virginia; and eventually in northern Georgia and various other places, the freedpeople forged a new life on government rations and through work on labor crews, and received a modicum of medical care, often provided by "grannies"—black women who employed home remedies from plantation life. For thousands the contraband camps became the initial entry into free labor practices, and a slow but certain embrace of the new sense of dignity, mobility, identity, and education that freedom now meant. Nearly all white Northerners who witnessed or supervised these camps, or who eventually administered private or government work programs on confiscated Southern land, organized freedmen's aid societies and schools by the hundreds, or observed weddings and burials, were stunned by the determination of this exodus despite its hardships. In 1863, each superintendent of a contraband camp in the

The first page of the original Emancipation Proclamation.
AP/WWP/NATIONAL ARCHIVES

G. G. Fish, Pinx.   J. P. Soule, Photo.
Entered according to Act of Congress, in the year 1863, by John Sowle, in the
clerk's office of the District Court for the District of Massachusetts.
EMANCIPATION.
Published by John Sowle, 14 Summer St., Boston.

An 1863 propaganda drawing depicts "Emancipation" surrounded by slaves wrapped in the United States flag.
PHOTOGRAPHS AND PRINTS DIVISION, SCHOMBURG CENTER FOR RESEARCH IN BLACK CULTURE, THE NEW YORK PUBLIC LIBRARY, ASTOR, LENOX AND TILDEN FOUNDATIONS.

western theater of war was asked to respond to a series of interrogatives about the freedmen streaming into his facilities. To the question of the "motives" of the freedmen, the Corinth superintendent tried to find the range of what he saw: "Can't answer short of 100 pages. Bad treatment—hard times—lack of the comforts of life—prospect of being driven South; the more intelligent because they wished to be free. Generally speak kindly of their masters; none wish to return; many would die first. All delighted with the prospect of freedom, yet all have been kept constantly at some kind of work." All of the superintendents commented on what seemed to them the remarkable "intelligence" and "honesty" of the freedmen. As for their "notions of liberty," the Memphis superintendent answered: "Generally correct. They say they have no rights, nor own anything except as their master permits; but being freed, can make their own money and protect their

families." Indeed, these responses demonstrate just what a fundamental revolution Emancipation had become.

Inexorably, Emancipation meant that black families would be both reunited and torn apart. In contraband camps, where women and children greatly outnumbered men, extended families sometimes found and cared for each other. But often, when the thousands of black men across the South entered the Union army, they left women and children behind in great hardship, sometimes in sheer destitution, and eventually under new labor arrangements that required rent payments. Louisiana freedwoman Emily Waters wrote to her husband, who was still on duty with the Union army, in July 1865, begging him to get a furlough and "come home and find a place for us to live in." The joy of change mixed with terrible strain. "My children are going to school," she reported, "but I find it very hard

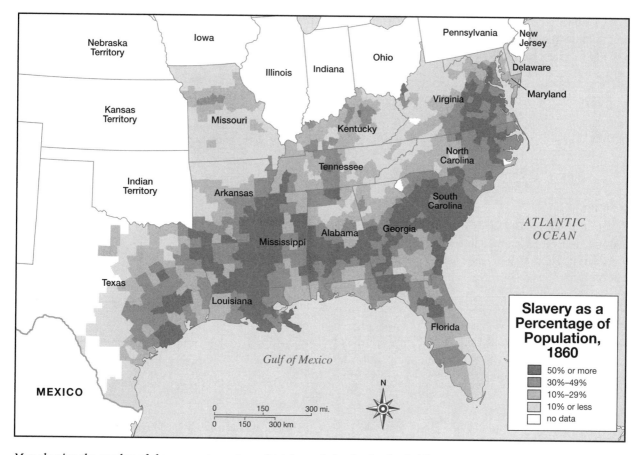

Map showing the number of slaves as a percentage of total population in the slaveholding states of the U.S., 1960. MAP BY XNR PRODUCTIONS. THE GALE GROUP.

to feed them all, and if you cannot come I hope you will send me something to help me get along. . . . Come home as soon as you can, and cherish me as ever." The same Louisiana soldier received a subsequent letter from Alsie Thomas, his sister, reporting that "we are in deep trouble—your wife has left Trepagnia and gone to the city and we don't know where or how she is, we have not heard a word from her in four weeks." The choices and the strains that Emancipation wrought are tenderly exhibited in a letter by John Boston, a Maryland fugitive slave, to his wife, Elizabeth, in January 1862, from Upton Hill, Virginia. "[I]t is with grate joy I take this time to let you know Whare I am i am now in Safety in the 14th regiment of Brooklyn this Day i can Adres you thank god as a free man I had a little truble in giting away But as the lord led the Children of Isrel to the land of Canon So he led me to a land Whare Fredom Will rain in spite Of earth and hell . . . i am free from al the Slavers Lash." Such were the joys of freedom and the agonies of separation. Boston concluded his letter: "Dear Wife i must Close rest yourself Contented i am free . . . Write my Dear Soon . . . Kiss Daniel For me." The rich sources on the freedmen's experience

do not tell us whether Emily Waters ever saw her husband again, or whether the Bostons were reunited. But these letters demonstrate the depth with which freedom was embraced and the human pain through which it was achieved.

The freedpeople especially gave meaning to their freedom by their eagerness for education and land ownership. In the Sea Islands of South Carolina, the Port Royal Experiment was a large-scale attempt, led by Northern philanthropists interested as much in profits as in freedmen's rights, to reorganize cotton production by paying wages to blacks. But amid this combination of abolitionists' good works and capitalist opportunity, thousands of blacks of all ages learned to read. So eager were the freedmen to learn that the teachers from the various freedmen's-aid societies were sometimes overwhelmed. "The Negroes will do anything for us," said one teacher, "if we will only teach them." Land ownership was an equally precious aim of the freedmen, and they claimed it as a right. No one ever stated the labor theory of value more clearly than Virginia freedman Bayley Wyat, in a speech protesting the eviction of blacks from a contraband camp in 1866: "We has a right to the land we are located. For Why? I tell you. Our wives, our children, our husbands, has been sold over and over again to purchase the lands we now locates upon; for that reason we have a divine right to the land. . . . And den didn't we clear the land, and raise de crops ob corn, ob cotton, ob tobacco, ob rice, ob sugar, ob everything?" The redistribution of land and wealth in the South would remain a largely unrealized dream during Reconstruction, and perhaps its greatest unfinished legacy. But armed with literacy, and an unprecedented politicization, Southern blacks accomplished much against great odds in the wake of Emancipation.

By the end of the war in 1865, the massive moving about of the freedpeople became a major factor in Confederate defeat. Thousands of white Union soldiers who witnessed this process of Emancipation became, despite earlier prejudices, avid supporters of the recruitment of black soldiers. And no one understood just what a transformation was under way better than the former slaveholders in the South, who now watched their world collapse around them. In August 1865 white Georgian John Jones described black freedom as the "dark, dissolving, disquieting wave of emancipation." That wave would abate in the turbulent first years of Reconstruction, when the majority of freedmen would resettle on their old places, generally paid wages at first, but eventually working "on shares" (as sharecropping tenant farmers). Reconstruction would bring a political revolution to the South, a great experiment in racial democracy, led by radical Republicans in the federal government and by a new American phenomenon: scores of black politicians. This "disquieting wave" would launch black suffrage, citizenship rights, civil rights, and widespread black officeholding beyond what anyone could have imagined at the outset of the Civil War. That the great achievements in racial democracy of the period 1865–1870 were betrayed or lost by the late nineteenth century does not detract from the significance of such a passage in African-American history. Many of the twentieth-century triumphs in America's never-ending search for racial democracy have their deep roots in the story of Emancipation and its aftermath.

See also Coartación; Emancipation in Latin America and the Caribbean; Slavery

■ ■ *Bibliography*

Berlin, Ira, et al., eds. *Freedom: A Documentary History of Emancipation, 1861–67.* Series 1, vol. 1, *The Destruction of Slavery.* Series 1, vol. 3, *The Wartime Genesis of Free Labor.* Series 2, *The Black Military Experience.* New York: Cambridge University Press, 1982–1990.

Clark-Lewis, Elizabeth, ed. *First Freed: Washington, D.C., In the Emancipation Era.* Washington, D.C.: Howard University Press, 2002.

Foner, Eric. *Nothing but Freedom: Emancipation and Its Legacy.* Baton Rouge: Louisiana State University Press, 1983.

Guelzo, Allen C. *Lincoln's Emancipation Proclamation: The End of Slavery in America.* New York: Simon and Schuster, 2004.

Litwack, Leon F. *Been in the Storm So Long: The Aftermath of Slavery.* New York: Knopf, 1979.

DAVID W. BLIGHT (1996)
Updated bibliography

EMIGRATION

See Migration

ENGLISH, AFRICAN-AMERICAN

■ ■ ■ ━━━━━━

African American English (AAE), which is not slang, is a form of communication for some African Americans in the United States. It has been one of the most widely discussed varieties of English since the 1960s. Different topics have been covered in research on AAE: its legitimacy and status as a dialect or language, its origin, and its effects on reading. Some of these topics have been hotly debated and have received media coverage.

FROM ARGUMENTS ABOUT LEGITIMACY TO VIEWS ABOUT ORIGIN

Research in the1960s affirmed the legitimacy of AAE by explaining that it was not a deficient mode of speech used by culturally deprived speakers. Early work, such as that by Marvin Loflin and William Labov, showed that AAE had clearly definable patterns of sentence structure, sound combinations, meaning, and vocabulary. Since then, AAE has been characterized as a rule-governed system, although some people have negative attitudes toward it and call it bad English.

As evidence was being presented to support claims about the legitimacy of AAE, linguists were raising questions about the development of AAE—whether it originated as a plantation Creole such as Gullah (spoken in the coastal Carolinas and Georgia) (Rickford and Rickford, 2000), which would have been influenced by African languages, or whether it developed like other dialects of English. Early debates about the provenance of AAE focused on African and Creole origins in research by linguists such as Lorenzo Dow Turner, William Stewart, David Dalby, and J. L. Dillard and later by Charles DeBose and Nicholas Faraclas. Arguments in support of English origins were made by Raven McDavid and Virginia McDavid and later by Salikoko Mufwene, Shana Poplack, and others. Historical research on AAE has expanded to include proposals about gradual development of AAE as a result of contact between Africans and colonial settlers in the South (Winford, 1997). In this research, linguists analyze ex-slave narratives, which have been taken to be representative of early AAE, and historical documents about plantation life in the United States.

Systems of Sounds, Sentences, and Meaning

Much research on AAE has been on language used by adolescent males, but males and females of all ages use it. Speakers know rules of putting sounds and words together. Some speakers use a wide range of AAE rules, while others do not.

AAE consists of systems of sounds, sentence structure, meaning, and vocabulary items and related information. It has been argued that parts of the sound system of AAE share similarities with that of West African languages, in which there is no *th* sound. In words in AAE in which the *th* sound would be produced at the beginning of the word, it is pronounced as *th* in *thing* or as *d* in *dese* ("these"). When the *th* sound would be produced in the middle of the word, it is pronounced as *f* in *bafroom* ("bathroom") or *v* in *brover* ("brother"). At the end of the word, it can be pronounced as *t, f,* or *v*, as in *mont* ("month"), *norf* ("north"), or *smoov* ("smooth"), respectively. The sound depends on the position of the *th* in the word and the voicing property of the *th*; speakers do not haphazardly pronounce *t, d, f,* or *v* instead of *th*. Voicing is a technical term that is used to distinguish the two different *th* sounds: the *th* sound in *bath* and the *th* sound in *bathe*. Given the voicing property of *th, bath* would be pronounced with an final *f* ("baf"), and *bathe* would be pronounced with a final *v* ("bav").

In AAE, inflected *be* (e.g., *is*), which marks present tense, does not have to occur in sentences in many cases, as in *The boy_not running*. However, it must occur if it is the first person singular form (*I'm running.*). Habitual *be,* which is different from inflected *be,* indicates that some activity occurs habitually, as in *Those athletes be running fast* ("Those athletes usually run fast."). This *be* is never inflected and is a source of confusion for non-AAE speakers, who incorrectly assume that AAE speakers are misusing inflected *be* when they use habitual *be*.

Often the general public confuse AAE with slang, which has a short life span and is generally used by adolescent to young adult speakers. AAE is not slang, although slang is a component of AAE just as it occurs in all dialects and languages. Slang generally refers to vocabulary items, words, and phrases; however, AAE is a system of communication—including sounds, sentence structure, component parts of words—not just a compilation of cool words and phrases. Some slang items, which may signal identification with a group, are used exclusively in African-American communities or started off in such communities and were adopted by mainstream America. An African American in the adolescent to young adult age group may use *She was all up in my grill* to mean "She was staring at me while I was talking to someone else" or "She was getting on my case, asking a series of questions." One reason people often define AAE as slang is that they make the link between African-American youth and hip-hop and thus take the language of hip-hop, which includes slang and innovative uses of words and phrases, to be AAE. Hip-hop artists may use AAE, but that cannot be determined just on the basis of their use of slang (e.g., "bling bling" to refer to expensive jewelry). In cases in which slang items in African-American communities cross over into the mainstream, African-American users generally abandon the old terms and coin new ones. Slang may be used in secular environments (e.g., *get your roll on,* "to cruise in an expensive car") and in religious contexts (e.g., *get your praise on,* "to praise God"). Other slang items are associated with regions, such as the New Orleans *whoadie* ("friend").

Some words used by people in African-American communities differ from slang in that they are long lived and used by speakers of all ages. *Kitchen* ("hair at the nape of the neck") and *saditty* ("conceited") are old words that are used by speakers of all age groups in AAE-speaking communities throughout the United States.

Because AAE differs from mainstream English and other English varieties in certain ways, questions have been raised about whether it is a separate language. Such questions have socio-political implications; however, it is clear that AAE has its own rules, and some of them overlap with rules of other varieties of English. From a linguistic standpoint, languages and dialects are equal in that they are rule-governed. (See Green, 2002, for further discussion of these patterns.)

Discourse and Rhetorical Strategies

Discourse and rhetorical strategies reflect the link between language and culture. Speakers of AAE understand rules of putting sounds together to form words and words together to form sentences, but they also know that there are rules of speaking that have social and cultural relevance. Topics in this area range from discourse marked by indirectness (Morgan, 2002) to speech events such as toasting, or paying tribute to oneself. In some instances, speakers make their points by indirectness, and the message may carry social, cultural, and historical information. As is the case with the dozens, the goal may be to insult or signify on an interlocutor, so extreme exaggerations may be made about family members, in particular "yo mama." An adult may say, "Common sense ain't so common" in the presence of a group intending to aim the remark at a person who has not displayed good judgment. In one conversation, a speaker directed his comment at another male. The first male asked whether the other had ever gotten a manicure and went on to talk about all the benefits, including a finger massage. The second male looked at his fingers and replied, "No, I don't get my nails did." The second male intentionally used a common phrase *get my nails did* with the past (*did*), not past participle (*done*) form, to signify on the first male. He indirectly indicated that getting his nails done was inappropriate for him and that the first male was engaging in bourgeois behavior. The interlocutors knew that *get my nails did* was used by some African-American females to refer to getting their nails done professionally.

Language and gender has not been widely researched in the AAE speech community with respect to social practice or linguistic patterns. Women use AAE on all levels; they are prime users of language (Smitherman, 1995). Troutman (2001) notes that African-American women's language includes a range of features from the general African-American speech community, such as signifying, and from the African-American women's speech community, such as assertiveness, "smart talk," and "sweet talk."

FEATURES OF AAE IN POPULAR CULTURE

Features of AAE are evident in popular culture. Patterns from the grammar of AAE occur in rap, so habitual *be* is used by some rappers. Also, some vocabulary items in rap make their way into the slang component of AAE. For instance, *bling bling* and *fo' shizzle* ("for sure") first occurred in rap and then made their way into speech of adolescents to young adults. In some cases, vocabulary items in rap undergo broadening such that their meanings move from specific to general. For instance, *gangsta* or *g* could be used in a greeting as a general term for a male without reference to gangster behavior. Two rhetorical strategies that are used in rap are boasting and toasting. Rappers use a braggadocio tone to boast about their verbal prowess and ma-

terial possessions. As more women enter the rap scene, they are also noted for mastering these verbal strategies. Toasting is certainly not just a property of rap or a strategy used by males. Chaka Kahn's "I'm Every Woman" is a toast that showcases the artist's talents and power.

AAE IN LITERATURE AND MEDIA

Different strategies are used to portray characters in literature and the media as speaking AAE. Eye dialect can be used to make the characters' language look like dialect or to distance it from mainstream English. This spelling technique may represent an AAE sound pattern, as in *bof* ("both"), or it may not reflect any change in pronunciation, as in *enuf* ("enough"). Some authors use strategies other than spelling techniques in representing the language of AAE speakers. Zora Neale Hurston, a twentieth-century African-American author, used sound, sentence structure, vocabulary, and meaning patterns in AAE, and it is necessary to understand linguistic and cultural meaning to get the gist of her characters' messages. For instance, *come* followed a verb ending in *–ing* (e.g., "come pulling") indicates speaker indignation, so when John in *Jonah's Gourd Vine* says, "She de one come pullin' on me," he is communicating indignantly that the woman had the audacity to pull or grab him. In John Edgar Wideman's *Brothers and Keepers,* AAE is used in contrast to "good English." Wideman associates rhetorical strategies such as rapping and trash talking, a form of bragging, with AAE and its users. Also, habitual *be* is used by AAE speakers in that book.

One marker that is used to signal black speech in the media is habitual *be*. Although the use and meaning of habitual *be* are not well understood by members outside of the AAE-speaking community, it is well known that the marker has a prominent place in AAE. It is used frequently in *Fresh*, a film about the coming of age of a streetwise adolescent. At times, the marker is used ungrammatically—in ways in which it is not used in AAE—and this suggests that its mere presence is intended to signal black street speech. Also, slang items are used in the media in representations of AAE. They occur in Spike Lee's movie *Bamboozled*, especially in the speech of a prominent white executive who tries to convince those around him that he is legitimately linked to the African-American community. African-American characters in Malcolm D. Lee's film *The Best Man* use language that is appropriate for them. One character who arguably has "street" and worldly experience uses habitual *be*. The characters also use slang items such as *cheese* ("money") and *get her lil swerve on* ("for her to have fun") and rhetorical strategies such as signification.

AAE SPEAKERS AND EDUCATION

Since the 1960s the relationship between AAE and education has been addressed in the literature. Two important events, *Martin Luther King Junior Elementary School Children v. Ann Arbor School District Board* (1979) and the 1996 Oakland, California, Ebonics controversy, called attention to the effect of AAE on students' success in school. In *King*, the judge acknowledged that AAE served as a barrier to education when teachers did not take it into consideration in teaching its speakers. The media misrepresented the situation in Oakland; however, that school system recognized that AAE is rule-governed and that it is beneficial to make students aware of the difference between AAE and mainstream English. (See Baugh, 2000; Perry and Delpit, 1998; and Wolfram, 1999, for more discussion.)

One issue that continues to be in the forefront of study of AAE and education is the relationship between reading and use of AAE. This issue is crucial because of the low reading performance of many African-American youth. Some school systems have addressed this problem by implementing mainstream English proficiency programs that are used to help students distinguish AAE and classroom English and use them in appropriate settings. Understanding that AAE is systematic is useful in combating negative attitudes towards the variety and its users and teaching speakers more effectively.

See also Creole Languages of the Americas

▪ ▪ *Bibliography*

Baugh, John. *Beyond Ebonics*. New York: Oxford University Press, 2000.

Green, Lisa J. *African American English: A Linguistic Introduction*. New York: Cambridge University Press, 2002.

Labov, William. *Language in the Inner City: Stories in the Black English Vernacular*. Philadelphia: University of Pennsylvania Press, 1972.

Morgan, Marcyliena. *Language, Discourse and Power in African American Culture*. New York: Cambridge University Press, 2002.

Perry, Theresa, and Lisa Delpit. *The Real Ebonics Debate: Power, Language and the Education of African American Children*. Boston: Beacon Press, 1998.

Rickford, John R., and Russell John Rickford. *Spoken Soul*. New York: Wiley, 2000.

Smitherman, Geneva. *Talkin' That Talk: Language, Culture and Education in African America*. New York: Routledge, 2000.

Troutman, Denise. "African American Women Talking That Talk." In *Sociocultural and Historical Contexts of African American English*, edited by Sonja L. Lanehart. Philadelphia: John Benjamins Publishing Company, 2001.

Winford, Donald. "On the Origins of African American English—A Creolist Perspective Part 1: The Sociohistorical Background." *Diachronica* 14 (1997): 305–344.

Wolfram, Walt. "Repercussions from the Oakland Ebonics Controversy—The Critical Role of Dialect Awareness Programs." In *Making the Connection: Language and Academic Achievement among African American Students,* edited by Carolyn Temple Adger, Donna Christian, and Orlando L. Taylor, pp. 61–80. McHenry, Ill.: Center for Applied Linguistics and Delta Systems Co., 1999.

LISA GREEN (2005)

ENTREPRENEURS AND ENTREPRENEURSHIP
▬▪▬

African economic practices in food production and distribution provided the basis for the initial entrepreneurial expression of black people in the United States. A vibrant commercial culture existed in western and central Africa during the transatlantic slave trade era. The economic structures of African societies were exceedingly sophisticated. Internal market systems proliferated, regulated by central authorities at the national, regional, and local levels. International trade—including trade in slaves—was controlled by kings and wealthy merchants, while local economies required the participation of men and women as producers, wholesalers, and retailers in markets overseen by guilds.

1619–1789

Africans who were brought to the United States as slaves first made use of the surplus commodities from their own provision grounds—land either allotted to them or surreptitiously appropriated by them for food growing and, occasionally, tobacco cultivation—to create local produce markets where goods were sold or bartered. These were the first businessventures that provided slaves with money. Successful slave entrepreneurs could earn enough money to purchase freedom for themselves and their families and subsequently acquire land. In mid-seventeenth-century Virginia the Anthony Johnson family secured its freedom and opened a commercial farm producing tobacco for both local and international markets. The Johnsons also had a number of indentured servants and slaves.

Although there were relatively few free blacks with holdings in land or slaves, their numbers did increase during the eighteenth century. In colonial cities African Americans were particularly active as entrepreneurs in the food-service industry, first as market people and then as street food vendors and cook- and food-shop owners. In 1736, in Providence, R.I., Emanuel Manna Bernoon opened the first African-American catering establishment with the capital from his wife's illegal whiskey distillery business. One of the leading caterers of nearby Newport was "Dutchess" Quamino, a pastry maker who conducted her business in a small house. The catering activities of blacks in these towns placed Rhode Island at the center of African-American enterprise and contributed significantly to the state's early development as a resort area.

One of the most renowned innkeepers in eighteenth-century America was Samuel Fraunces (1722–1795). While there is some dispute whether Fraunces was of African descent, there is no doubt that he was a West Indian who migrated to New York City in the 1750s. His tavern and inn, which opened in 1761, earned him a reputation as a leading restaurateur with "the finest hostelry in Colonial America." Four years later Fraunces established Vaux-Hall (named after the famous English pleasure gardens), a resort with hanging gardens, waxworks, concerts, fireworks, and afternoon dances, which set the standard for pleasure gardens in colonial America; during the 1780s, when New York City was the nation's capital, Fraunces' Tavern in lower Manhattan served as a meeting place for the new government and was the site of George Washington's farewell to his troops.

A number of northern blacks were successful tradesmen or artisans. Peter Williams, Sr., who was born a slave in New York and helped found the African Methodist Episcopal Zion Church in 1800, was a successful tobacconist. With the profits from his earnings, Williams purchased his freedom in 1786. African-born Amos Fortune (1710–1801) purchased his freedom at age sixty and established a successful tannery business with a clientele that extended to New Hampshire and Massachusetts.

Black entrepreneurs were also to be found at the American frontier. In 1779 Jean Baptiste Pointe Du Sable established a trading post on the site of what later became the city of Chicago. In addition to importing merchandise from the East, Du Sable owned a bake house, mill, dairy, smokehouse, and lumberyard. His mercantile activities serviced a wilderness hinterland with a two-hundred-mile radius.

Beginning in the late eighteenth century, blacks developed enterprises in sports and music. In Newport, R.I., African-born Occramer Marycoo, later known as Newport Gardiner (1746–?), established a successful music school based on his reputation as a musician and composer. In 1780 Gardiner cofounded the African Union Society, which kept community records, found training and jobs for black youth, and supported members in time of finan-

cial need. Gardiner led thirty-two other African Americans to Liberia, with support from the American Colonization Society, in 1826. The most famous late-eighteenth-century black sports figure was boxer Bill Richmond (1763–1829), who achieved recognition in both America and England. Born a slave in New York, Richmond left for London during the Revolution, where his fame in boxing grew. Upon retiring from the ring, he established a popular inn in London known as the Horse and Dolphin and opened a boxing academy.

1790–1865

The entrepreneurial efforts of African Americans became increasingly pronounced in the early national and antebellum years. Throughout this period African-American entrepreneurs were prominent in crafts and personal services, which required limited capital for the development of enterprise. Blacks also established profitable businesses in transportation, manufacturing, personal services, catering, restaurants and taverns, real estate, finance, commercial farming, merchandising, mining, and construction. Unlike later black entrepreneurs, most antebellum businessmen had a consumer base that was primarily white. By the advent of the Civil War, at least twenty-one black entrepreneurs had accumulated holdings of over $100,000.

A prominent figure in transportation and commodity distribution was Paul Cuffe (1759–1817), a native of New Bedford, Mass., who founded a shipping line, owned several vessels, and held an interest in several others. Cuffe purchased his first ship in 1785 and had constructed a wharf and warehouse by 1800. His shipping enterprises extended from whaling to coastal and transatlantic trade vessels, which carried cargo and passengers to the West Indies, Africa, England, Norway, and Russia. Cuffe's most notable voyage was undertaken in 1815, when he transported thirty-eight African Americans to Sierra Leone at his own expense. He died two years later and left an estate valued at $20,000. Like Cuffe, the Philadelphia entrepreneur James Forten (1766–1842) actively supported the abolitionist movement and agitated for the rights of free blacks. Forten, whose estate was valued at $100,000, invented a new sail-making device and ran a factory that employed over forty workers, both white and black. Other antebellum inventors and manufacturers included Henry Boyd (c. 1840–1922) and William Ellison (1790–1861). Boyd, a native of Cincinnati, patented a bedstead and employed some thirty people in his bed-making factory. Slave-born William Ellison of South Carolina established a successful cotton gin factory after he was freed. He invented a device which substantially increased the gin's efficiency, and his market extended to most of the South's cotton-producing regions. He invested his profits in slaves and real estate holdings.

Antebellum blacks became leading innovators in the personal-service and hair-care industry, establishing luxurious barbershops, bathhouses, and hotels. In Mississippi, where there were fewer than a thousand free blacks and over four hundred thousand slaves, slave-born William Johnson (1809–1851) purchased his freedom and founded a successful barbershop and bathhouse in Natchez. Johnson used his profits to develop other enterprises, such as money brokerage, real estate leasing, a toy shop, a drayage business, and agriculture. He owned slaves, some of whom worked in his barbershop and on his plantation, while others were hired out. The most successful hairdresser in the North was Joseph Cassey of Philadelphia, whose estate was valued at $75,000 in 1849. Cassey's wealth also included profits from moneylending enterprises.

Another prominent African American in the hair-care business and an early African-American philanthropist was Pierre Toussaint (1766–1853), a Haitian immigrant who became one of New York's leading hairdressers. Toussaint was generous in his support of the Roman Catholic church and the education of young men studying for the priesthood. During the 1840s the three Remond sisters, Cecilia, Maritcha, and Caroline Remond Putnam—members of a prominent African-American abolitionist and business family (their mother was a successful caterer)—established the exclusive Ladies Hair Works Salon in Salem, Mass. In addition to promoting the sale of Mrs. Putnam's Medicated Hair Tonic and other products both locally and nationally (through mail-order distribution), they opened the largest wig factory in the state.

Black entrepreneurs also flourished in the clothing industry, as African-American tailors and dressmakers became leading designers in American fashion. Perhaps best known was Mary Todd Lincoln's dressmaker, Elizabeth Keckley (1818–1907), who employed twenty seamstresses at the height of her enterprise.

During the antebellum period Philadelphia and New York became the leading centers for black catering businesses. The most prominent caterers of Philadelphia were Robert Bogle, Peter Augustine, the Prossers, Thomas Dorsey, Henry Minton, and Eugene Baptiste. Much of the $400,000 in property owned by free Philadelphia blacks in 1840 belonged to caterers. New York's Edward V. Clark was listed as a jeweler in the R. G. Dun mercantile credit records; yet he operated a successful catering business, which included lending out silver, crystal, and china for his catered dinners. In 1851 Clark's merchandise was valued at $5,000.

During the War of 1812, Thomas Downing established a famous oyster house and restaurant on Wall Street, which became a noted attraction for foreign tourists and the haunt of the elite in business and politics. In 1844 Thomas's son, George T. Downing (1819–1903), founded the Sea Girt Hotel, housing businesses on the first floor and luxury rooms above. Twelve years after the Civil War, Downing expanded his food-service business to Washington, D.C., where he was known as "the celebrated colored caterer."

Samuel T. Wilcox of Cincinnati, who established his business in 1850 and relied primarily on the Ohio and Mississippi riverboat trade, was the most successful black entrepreneur in wholesale food distribution. Before the Civil War Wilcox's annual sales exceeded $100,000; his estate was valued at $60,000. Solomon Humphries, a free black in Macon, Ga., owned a grocery valued at $20,000. In upstate New York William Goodridge developed a number of diverse enterprises, including a jewelry store, an oyster company, a printing company, a construction company, and a large retail merchandise store, while running a train on the Columbia Railroad. In 1848, Goodridge earned a reported business capital of $20,000 in addition to real estate holdings in both New York and Canada. In Virginia the slave Robert Gordan managed his owner's coal yard and established a side business whose profits amounted to somewhere around $15,000. After purchasing his freedom, Gordan used the capital to start a profitable coal business in Cincinnati and by 1860 reported annual earnings of $60,000 from coal and real estate profits.

The extractive industries proved to be a source of wealth for slave-born Stephen Smith (1797–1873), a Pennsylvania lumber and coal merchant, bank founder, and investor in real estate and stock who was known as "Black Sam." The R. G. Dun mercantile credit records list his wealth at $100,000 in 1850 and $500,000 in 1865. Smith, whose wife ran an oyster house, obtained his start in business as the manager of his owner's lumberyard. William Whipper (1804–1876), Smith's partner in the lumber business from 1835 to 1836, started out in the steam-scouring business. Whipper, who, like Smith, had extensive real estate holdings, was a cashier in the Philadelphia branch of the Freedman's Savings Bank from 1870 to 1874, with reported assets (registered in the 1870 census) amounting to $107,000. Both men were leaders in abolitionist activities and provided financial support to black institutions.

Eight of the wealthiest antebellum African-American entrepreneurs were slaveholders from Louisiana who owned large cotton and sugar plantations. Marie Metoyer

(1742–1816), also known as Coincoin, the daughter of African-born slaves, was freed in 1796 at the age of forty-six and acquired several hundred slaves as well as ten thousand acres of land. The Metoyer family's wealth amounted to several hundred thousand dollars. Urban black businessmen and women in Louisiana also owned productive slaves: CeCee McCarty of New Orleans, a merchant and money broker who owned a train depot and used her slaves as a traveling sales force, accumulated $155,000 from her business activities. Most of the wealthy black entrepreneurs lived in New Orleans: the Soulie Brothers, Albin and Bernard, accumulated over $500,000 as merchants and brokers; Francis La Croix, a tailor and real estate speculator, declared assets of $300,000; and Julien La Croix, a grocer and real estate speculator, reported assets totaling $250,000.

The developing frontier continued to provide entrepreneurial opportunities to African Americans. William Leidesdorff, a rancher and businessman in San Francisco during the last years of Mexican rule, died in debt in 1848; shortly afterward, gold was discovered on his property, and the value of his estate leaped to well over a million dollars. While still a slave, "Free" Frank McWorter (1777–1854) established a saltpeter factory in Kentucky during the War of 1812. Profits from the mining of crude niter, the principal ingredient used in the manufacture of gunpowder, enabled McWorter to purchase freedom for his wife in 1817 and for himself two years later. After he was freed, McWorter expanded his saltpeter enterprise and engaged in commercial farming and land speculation activities. In 1830 he moved to Illinois, where in 1836 he founded the town of New Philadelphia, the first town promoted by an African American, though both blacks and whites purchased New Philadelphia town lots. By the time he died, McWorter had been able to free a total of sixteen family members from slavery.

Antebellum blacks, both slave and free, profited significantly from the construction industry. The most resourceful slave entrepreneur in this field was Anthony Weston, who built rice mills and improved the performance of rice-thrashing machines. By 1860 Weston's property in real estate and slaves—purchased in his wife's name, since she was a free black—was valued at $40,075. Slave-born Horace King (1807–1885) worked as a covered-bridge builder in Alabama and Georgia. After being freed in 1846, King established a construction company that was eventually expanded to include construction projects for housing and commercial institutions. After King's death the company was renamed the King Brothers Construction Company and overseen by his sons and daughter.

Binga State Bank, Chicago, 1925. Chicago's first black-owned bank was founded by entrepreneur Jesse Binga in 1908 and became incorporated as a state bank in 1921. The Image is from John Taitt's Souvenir of Negro Progress, 1779–1925. GENERAL RESEARCH AND REFERENCE DIVISION, SCHOMBURG CENTER FOR RESEARCH IN BLACK CULTURE, THE NEW YORK PUBLIC LIBRARY, ASTOR, LENOX AND TILDEN FOUNDATIONS.

1865–1929

By the time the Civil War ended in 1865, over twenty-five hundred African-American businesses had been established by slaves and free blacks. Despite the difficulties that blacks experienced with regard to continuing social, political, and economic inequalities, the end of slavery did bring about a much wider range of prospects for budding African-American entrepreneurs. It was during this time that the first black millionaires emerged.

Health and beauty-aid enterprises, real estate speculation, and the development of financial institutions such as

Staff of the Dunbar National Bank, Harlem, c. 1920. *The black-owned bank was Harlem's first to be managed and staffed by African Americans.* PHOTOGRAPHS AND PRINTS DIVISION, SCHOMBURG CENTER FOR RESEARCH IN BLACK CULTURE, THE NEW YORK PUBLIC LIBRARY, ASTOR, LENOX AND TILDEN FOUNDATIONS.

banks and insurance companies provided the basis for the wealth accumulated by many of the most successful black entrepreneurs. The food– and personal-service industries continued to be sources of income. Durham, N.C., and Atlanta, Ga., became the commercial centers for black America. The numbers of blacks involved in business steadily increased: In 1890, 31,000 blacks were engaged in business; their numbers rose to 40,455 in 1900 and to 74,424 in 1920.

Many leading black entrepreneurs of this era were either slave-born or had slave-born parents. Others had only limited formal educations and often started as unskilled workers or laborers. A number of African-American businesses were farm related. In 1900 Junius C. Graves, who owned five hundred acres of Kansas land valued at $100,000, became known as the Negro Potato King. Perhaps the most successful black entrepreneur of the Reconstruction era was Benjamin Montgomery (1819–1877), a

slave of Joseph Davis (brother of the Confederate president, Jefferson Davis). In 1866 Joseph Davis sold his cotton plantations to Montgomery for $300,000. In addition to establishing a retail store on the Davis plantation in 1842, Montgomery had managed the Davis plantation from the 1850s on. In 1871 Dun gave Montgomery—who continued to run both enterprises with his sons as commission merchants—an A credit rating, ranking his family among the richest planter merchants and noting: "They are negroes, but negroes of unusual intelligence & extraordinary bus[iness] qualifications." The Montgomerys registered a net worth of $230,000 in 1874 but suffered severe setbacks several years later when crops failed and cotton prices declined. In 1881 the family was unable to make payments on interest and capital and the property reverted to the Davis family by auction. In 1887 Benjamin Montgomery's son Isaiah Montgomery migrated to Mississippi and founded the all-black town of Mound Bayou, where black enterprise was encouraged and where, in 1904, Charles Banks (1873–1923) founded the Bank of Mound Bayou and the Mound Bayou Loan and Investment Company.

By the turn of the century, some of the most successful black entrepreneurs had already begun to discover a national black consumer market. In 1896 Richard H. Boyd, a Baptist minister (1843–1922), established the National Baptist Publishing House in Nashville, Tenn., with a printing plant that covered half a city block. In 1910 the annual company payroll amounted to $200,000. Under Boyd's management the publishing house earned $2.4 million in just under ten years and by 1920 was one of the largest black businesses in the nation. But Boyd did not limit his business enterprises to religious publishing. His holdings included the One Cent Savings and Bank Trust, which he founded in 1904 (and which became the Citizens Savings Bank and Trust in 1920), the *Nashville Globe* (established in 1905), the National Negro Doll Company (1909–1929), the National Baptist Church Supply Company, and the Union Transportation Company. Union Transportation owned five steam-driven buses and fourteen electric buses, carrying twenty passengers each. This company was founded in 1905 to support a black bus boycott in response to the segregated streetcar ordinance that Nashville had passed that year. By 1993 four generations of Boyds had continued their ownership of the publishing house and Citizens Bank; as of that year the assets of the bank alone totaled $118.3 million.

Urban real estate investment and speculation ventures continued to be the major source of wealth for some of the leading black entrepreneurs during this era. In New Orleans Thomy La Fon (1810–1893), whose real estate activities began before the Civil War, left an estate valued at over $700,000. In St. Louis slave-born James Thomas (1827–1913) used the profits from his exclusive barbershop to invest in real estate; his property holdings exceeded $400,000 by 1879. In Memphis slave-born Robert Church (1839–1912) accumulated over $700,000 from real estate investments and speculation. His first enterprises were a bar, gambling hall, and pawnshop. Church Park, which he developed on Beale Street as a recreation center, included an auditorium used for annual conventions of black organizations and a concert hall that featured black entertainers. Church also founded the Solvent Bank and Trust Company.

The late nineteenth century marked the founding of large-scale black banks and insurance companies. In 1899 slave-born John Merrick (1859–1919) of Durham founded the North Carolina Mutual and Provident Company, which as of 1993 still ranked first on *Black Enterprise*'s list of black-owned insurance companies with assets of nearly $218 million. Merrick had little formal education and was a barber by trade; his initial business activities included a chain of barbershops as well as real estate investments. He also founded a land company, the Mechanics and Farmers Bank (1907), and the Durham Textile Mill. Indeed, while Chicago and New York were only emerging as important centers of African-American enterprise in the early decades of the twentieth century, Durham's black business district had come to be known as the Capital of the Black Middle-Class. "At the turn of the century," John Sibley Butler noted, "commentators were as excited about North Carolina as they are today about the Cuban-American experience in Miami." Atlanta was also rapidly rising to prominence as a center for black business. Slave-born Alonzo Franklin Herndon (1858–1927), who founded the Atlanta Life Insurance Company in 1905, left an estate valued at more than $500,000. Herndon's real estate investments and lavishly appointed barbershops—which catered to an elite white clientele—provided profits for the start-up and expansion of Atlanta Life.

In some cases, the overly rapid expansion of business enterprises led to bankruptcy. Atlanta businessman Edward Perry (1873–1929) established the Standard Life Insurance Company in 1913 and the Citizens Trust Bank in 1921. With the income from his Service Realty Company and Service Engineering and Construction Company, both founded in the 1920s, Perry purchased land on Atlanta's west side and constructed some five hundred homes. By 1925 he had established eleven different businesses together valued at $11 million and providing employment for twenty-five hundred people. Perry lost all of his holdings within four years. His contemporaries blamed his bankruptcy on imprudent expansion, limited capital reserves, and injudicious business decisions. An insurance company founder and winner of the NAACP's Spingarn Medal in 1927, Anthony Overton (1865–1945) was another black businessman whose success in the early decades of the century was followed by bankruptcy in the depression years.

Real estate, an enterprise crucial to the growth of northern black communities, offered similar opportunities for rapid expansion, sometimes with disastrous results. Jesse Binga (1865–1950) began his real estate operations on the south side of Chicago in 1905. Three years later he founded the first black-owned bank in the North, which in 1921 became the Binga State Bank. In 1929 he constructed the five-story Binga Arcade to revitalize the deteriorating black business district. Later that year, when his bank failed, Binga's wealth was assesssed at more than $400,000; he was convicted of fraudulent bank practices in 1933 and spent three years in jail. Like Herman Perry and James Thomas, Binga spent the rest of his life in poverty and obscurity. The same fate befell Harlem's Phillip A. Payton, Jr. (1876–1917), who organized a consortium of black investors to found the Afro-American Realty Company in 1904. Within two years the company controlled $690,000 in rental properties. Payton was largely responsible for opening Harlem as a community to African Americans; subsequently, however, his stockholders charged him with fraudulent practices, and he went bankrupt.

Hair and beauty care, a less risky industry, proved especially profitable for black entrepreneurs. Annie M. Turnbo-Malone (1869–1957), founder of the Poro Company (1900) and a pioneer in the manufacture of hair- and skin-care products, is considered the first self-made American female millionaire. She began her business in Lovejoy, Ill., and eventually expanded to St. Louis, where she built a five-story manufacturing plant in 1917. The plant housed Poro College, a beauty school with branches in most major cities. In 1930 Turnbo-Malone moved her operations to Chicago and purchased a square city block on the South Side. She franchised her operations and, with national and international markets, reportedly provided employment opportunities for some seventy-five thousand people.

C. J. Sarah Breedlove Walker (1867–1919) was a Poro agent before she initiated her own hair-care products and cosmetics business in St. Louis in 1905. The "Walker system" for hair included an improved steel hot comb that revolutionized hair straightening for black women. The business strategies of the company—which employed over five thousand black women as agents who disseminated information on the Walker hair-care system in a marketing and employee-incentive program that utilized a national and international network of marketing consultants—presaged the practices of modern cosmetics firms.

The World War I era also witnessed the growth of black-owned publishing businesses. In 1905 Robert Abbott (1870–1940) founded the *Chicago Defender*, the first black newspaper with a mass circulation. The *Defender* used sensationalized news coverage to attract a large audience and was outspoken in its condemnation of racial injustice. By 1920 it had a circulation of over 200,000, with national circulation exceeding local sales. At Abbott's death the *Defender* was valued at $300,000. Abbott's successor, his nephew John H. Sengstacke, went on to establish Sengstacke Enterprises, which, with the *Defender* and ten other papers, became the largest black newspaper chain in America.

As media opportunities grew, African Americans became increasingly visible in the entertainment industry.

One of the most successful black entrepreneurs in this field was Harry Herbert Pace (1884–1943). After founding Pace and Handy Music (1917), a sheet music company whose publications included W. C. Handy's "St. Louis Blues," he founded the New York-based Black Swan Record Company (1921), the first record company owned by an African American. Black Swan's first success was Ethel Waters's "Oh Daddy" in 1921, which sold 600,000 copies in six months. Pace, who wanted to tap a national market for his records, refused to record Bessie Smith because he thought her music "too colored." By 1923 Black Swan was cutting six thousand records a day. Pace sold the company, at a hefty profit, to Paramount later that year. In addition, Pace's creative management and financial strategies promoted the growth of several black financial institutions, including Robert Church's Memphis Solvent Savings Bank (whose assets he increased from $50,000 to $600,000 in the years from 1907 to 1911) and Herman Edward Perry's Standard Life Insurance Company. In 1929 Pace engineered the merger of three northern black insurance companies to form Supreme Liberty Life Insurance.

Even as African-American entrepreneurs were branching out into new lines of business, many remained active in the catering and hotel fields. James Wormley (1819–1884), a caterer and restaurateur who built the five-storied Wormley's Hotel (1871) in Washington, D.C., ranked among the most fashionable black hoteliers. Wormley's hotel was patronized by leading politicians and foreign dignitaries, and he left an estate exceeding $100,000 in assets. In Philadelphia the tradition of catering, long an African-American resource, reached a pinnacle with the Dutrieulle family. Their catering business, established by Peter Dutrieulle (1838–1916) in 1873, lasted for almost a century, flourishing under the management of his son Albert (1877–1974) until 1967.

African Americans also profited in new areas of the food industry. C. H. James & Company of Charleston, W.V., a wholesale food processing and distribution enterprise founded in 1883, lasted for four generations of family ownership. From the time of its inception, the company's suppliers and buyers were primarily white; it was initially headed by Charles Howell James (1862–1929) and included a traveling dry goods retail operation. However, once the family decided to abandon the retail operation (in 1916) and limit the enterprise solely to the distribution of wholesale produce, the profits escalated to over $350,000. After a brief period of bankruptcy—caused by the stock market crash of 1929—the company was resuscitated by Edward Lawrence James, Sr. (1893–1967), and began to show a profit by the end of the 1930s. The company's survival was due largely to innovations in wholesale food dis-

The Motown Museum. *Working from his home on West Grand Boulevard in Detroit, pictured here, entrepreneur Berry Gordy formed The Motown Record Company in 1959. By the end of the following decade, Motown Records had grown to become the largest independent record label in the world.* LAYNE KENNEDY/CORBIS. REPRODUCED BY PERMISSION.

tribution methods. Now headed by Charles H. James III (1959–), it remains one of the most successful black businesses in the country.

Up to the onset of the Great Depression, black entrepreneurial efforts were concentrated primarily on the service industry, since in most cases African Americans could not gain access to the capital markets and financial resources needed for developing industrial enterprises. The

few blacks who attempted to capitalize on the demand for such modern industries as auto manufactures, movie production, and airline companies did not succeed. Nevertheless, the Great Migration of the early twentieth century caused a dramatic rise in northern urban black populations, and entrepreneurs were quick to seize the opportunities afforded by a new and rapidly expanding African-American consumer base. This growth was not matched in the South, where Jim Crow laws and societal racist practices restricted black enterprise to the same, increasingly depleted markets.

1930–1963

During the Great Depression the number of black businesses declined from 103,881 in 1930 to 87,475 in 1940. Among the few who prospered in those years was Texan Hobart T. Taylor, Sr., who used family money from farm property to start a cab company in 1931. The company continued to flourish during World War II, and Taylor added considerably to his wealth by investing the proceeds in rural and urban real estate. By the 1970s Taylor's assets were valued at approximately $5 million.

The food-processing industries remained a fairly stable resource for black entrepreneurs before, during, and after World War II. In the late 1930s California businessman Milton Earl Grant started companies in rubbish hauling and hog raising. In 1947 he founded the Broadway Federal Savings and Loan Association in Los Angeles. By 1948 Grant had grossed some $200,000 from the sale of hogs; he invested the profits in real estate, and by 1970 his holdings exceeded more than $1.5 million. In Buffalo, N.Y., Cornelius Ford founded the C. E. Ford Company, a cattle brokerage firm, during the 1920s. Ford's business survived the depression and in the 1950s was yielding over $1 million annually from livestock trade and sales. His company was one of the chief buyers for Armour and Company for some twenty-five years. In addition, Ford became president of the Buffalo Livestock Exchange (the fifth largest in the nation), speculated in the Canadian cattle market, and leased railroad yards from New York Central.

George McDermmod, a potato chip maker and chief executive officer of Community Essentials, established a manufacturing plant in Crescent City, Ill., and a distribution plant in Detroit during the 1940s. As of 1950 McDermmod was selling his products to fourteen hundred dealers in nine states with gross business receipts amounting to over $100,000 annually. In Chicago Kit Baldwin established an ice-cream company that catered primarily to the black community and was reporting annual business receipts of $75,000 by the late 1940s. During this same period Detroit entrepreneur Sydney Barthwell established a drugstore chain of nine stores and manufactured ice cream. In 1948 Barthwell reported a staff of eighty full-time employees and gross business receipts in excess of $1.5 million.

The hair-care and cosmetic-manufacturing business also continued to attract black entrepreneurs. In Harlem Rose Morgan and Olivia Clark established the Rose Meta

House of Beauty in 1947. Three years later they were earning $3 million from the sale of cosmetics and hair-care products in national stores and via international mail. Morgan and Clark's chain of beauty shops proliferated in major American cities as well as in Monrovia, Liberia; Cayenne, British Guiana; Puerto Rico; Cuba; and Jamaica. In New York City alone, their three shops employed three hundred people.

One of the most successful and wealthiest black entrepreneurs of the World War II era was S. B. Fuller (1905–1988), whose Chicago business empire, Fuller Products, comprised health and beauty aids as well as cleaning products and real estate. Fuller's many investments included the famous Regal Theater, the *Pittsburgh Courier*, Fuller Guarantee Corporation, the Fuller Department Store, and various livestock operations. In 1947 he secretly purchased a cosmetic factory owned and operated by whites. By 1960 Fuller, who had begun his career in 1935 as a door-to-door salesman, reported a payroll of five thousand employees, white and black, and a three-hundred-product line that brought in over $10 million in sales. However, when Fuller's ownership of the cosmetic factory—the products of which were tailored to the needs of southern white consumers—was discovered in the early 1960s, his cosmetics were boycotted by whites, and he was unable to raise sufficient capital to offset his loses. In 1964 the SEC charged Fuller with the sale of unregistered securities and forced him to pay $1.5 million to his creditors. Although Fuller Products was resurrected from bankruptcy in 1972, it never recovered as a major black business.

Another financier who rose to prominence after the depression was Arthur George Gaston (1892–1996) of Birmingham, Ala. Gaston's business activities began with the founding of a burial society, which he incorporated in 1932 as the Booker T. Washington Insurance Company. Seven years later, with the proceeds from life and health insurance sales, Gaston established the Booker T. Washington Business College, the Gaston Motel, and the Gaston Construction Company. In 1952 he expanded his holdings with the Vulcan Realty and Investment Corporation, a real estate firm that financed the construction of office and apartment buildings, as well as the development of housing subdivisions. Gaston's Citizens Federal Savings and Loan Association—ranked seventeenth on the 1993 *Black Enterprise* list of financial companies—was founded in 1957. Additional enterprises included Booker T. Washington Broadcasting and a soft-drink bottling company. In 1987 Gaston sold ownership of his insurance, radio, and construction companies to the employees. In 1993 the Booker T. Washington Insurance Company ranked sixth on the *Black Enterprise* list of insurance companies, with assets over $43 million.

Robert L. Johnson. *In 1979, entrepreneur Johnson founded Black Entertainment Television (BET). BET became the first black-controlled company to be listed on the New York Stock Exchange in 1991. By the end of that decade, the company had become one of the largest minority-owned businesses in the United States.* AP/WIDE WORLD. REPRODUCED BY PERMISSION.

The 1940s and 1950s witnessed an increase in manufacturing opportunities for African-American entrepreneurs. The Grimes Oil Company of Boston, a petroleum products distributor, was founded in 1940 by Calvin M. Grimes; as of 1993, its sales had reached $37 million. In 1949 Dempsey Travis founded the H. G. Parks Sausage Company in Baltimore. Subsequently, in 1990, Travis initiated the development of a middle-class townhouse project on Chicago's South Side.

1964–2005

The 1960s marked the emergence of a national network of large black businesses, many of which were founded on minute initial capital outlays. Johnson Publications began in 1942 with an investment of $250; the H. J. Russell Construction Company began in 1952 with a $150 truck; Berry Gordy started Motown for $700 in 1958. As the civil rights movement gathered momentum in the late 1950s and early 1960s, it became easier for blacks to obtain more substantial business financing; however, undercapitalized joint ventures persisted as a major method in the founding and development of new enterprises by African-American entrepreneurs. With few exceptions enterprises founded by black entrepreneurs remain relatively small private or family-owned companies. As of 2005 only seventeen of the *Black Enterprise* top 100 industrial/service businesses employed more than a thousand people.

In 1964, for the first time in the history of this country, the federal government took steps to provide assistance to black entrepreneurs by creating the Office of Minority Business Enterprises (OMBE), a division of the Small Business Administration (SBA), which was overseen in turn by the Department of Commerce. In 1969 President Richard M. Nixon issued executive order no. 11458, calling for the "strengthening of minority business enterprise"; by 1976 surveys showed that over two-thirds of the top black businesses had been started with support from the SBA. However, under Presidents Reagan and George H. W. Bush progress toward business parity for blacks was visibly slowed.

While African-American businesses have continued to tap an African-American consumer market, black entrepreneurs have slowly expanded sales to include mainstream national and international markets. One ironic consequence of black economic success has been that some of the most profitable black-owned companies—such as Johnson Products and Motown Records—have since been acquired by larger, white-owned organizations. The first black company to have its stock publicly traded was the Johnson Products Company, which was founded by George E. Johnson (1927-) in 1954; it was listed for the first time on the American Stock Exchange in 1969. Johnson Products greatly increased its sales when it introduced a non-lye-based hair relaxer, Ultra-Sheen (developed by George Johnson), into the market in 1966. During the late 1960s Johnson developed another best-selling hair product, Afro-Sheen, in response to the newly popular Afro hair style; so successful were these and other items that his company controlled the market in black hair products throughout the mid–1960s and into the early 1970s. By the mid–1970s, however, a series of setbacks—mostly in the form of competition from new black- and white-owned companies—cost Johnson the leading market share; in 1989 he lost control of the company to his ex-wife, Joan B. Johnson, who then sold Johnson Products to IVAX for $67 million dollars in 1993. In its final year as a black company, Johnson Products ranked twentieth in the *Black Enterprise* top 100 of 1992, registering $46.2 million in sales.

The most prominent rival for Johnson Products was Edward G. Gardner's (1925-) Soft Sheen Products, established in 1964. Soft Sheen's most successful product, Care Free Curl, was introduced in 1979. Like Johnson, Gardner also had to compete with white companies—most notably Revlon and Alberto Culver—which controlled 50 percent of a $1 billion black hair-care market in 1988. By this time black enterprises were seriously theatened with losing the market to white corporations that had only recently entered the field. Black manufacturers launched an aggressive campaign to prevent white companies from gaining control and received support from Jesse Jackson's Operation PUSH, as well as from John H. Johnson, publisher of *Ebony* and *Jet* magazines, and *Essence* founder Edward T. Lewis, both of whom refused to accept advertisements from white-owned companies in their publications. The white cosmetic giants escalated their strategies; by 1993 only five of the nineteen cosmetic companies in the black hair-care market were African-American owned. Black hair-care products remain an extremely profitable field,

but in 2005 only Bronner Brothers cracked the *Black Enterprise* top 100 industrial/service companies list, at seventy-third.

Berry Gordy's company, Motown Records, a subsidiary of Motown Industries, was the largest and most successful African-American enterprise in the entertainment field and the first to profit from the introduction of black music into the mainstream consumer market. Gordy's eight record labels, which recorded such groups as the Supremes and the Temptations, produced numerous hits on the pop and R&B charts. Almost from its inception Motown included Motown Productions, Hitsville, and the music publishing company Jobete. Most of Motown's holdings were sold to MCA Records for $61 million in 1988, and the company's listing was removed from *Black Enterprise.*

Motown's success served as a catalyst for African-American participation in the entertainment industry. Dick Griffey Productions, a concert-promotion and record company founded in 1975, has continued to flourish in recent years. Its founder, Dick Griffey (1943–) expanded into international markets by investing the company's proceeds in the African Development Public Investment Corporation, as well as in an African commodities and air-charter service, which he founded in 1985. In 2000 Dick Griffey Productions ranked forty-eighth on *Black Enterprise*'s listing with sales of $61 million, while in 1993 the African Development Corporation, registered sales of $57.8 million and ranked twenty-second.

Perhaps the most successful African-American entrepreneur of the postwar era was John H. Johnson (1918–), the owner of Johnson Publications. Johnson's business empire extends to various media corporations, Fashion Fair (a cosmetic company), radio stations, and television production companies. Founded in the 1970s, Fashion Fair has become the largest black-owned cosmetic company of the 1990s.

Black enterprise was greatly stimulated by an increasingly diversified African-American reading audience. Essence Communications, the parent company of *Essence,* a black woman's magazine, was founded in 1970 by four African-American men. Edward T. Lewis (1940–), the company's publisher and CEO, also established a direct-mail catalogue business before joining with J. Bruce Llewellyn and Percy Sutton in the purchase of an American Broadcasting Company (ABC) affiliate TV station in Brooklyn. In 1993 Essence Communications reported $71.1 million in sales.

In 1970 Earl G. Graves (1935–) launched *Black Enterprise,* a publication designed to address African-American interests in business and to report on black economic development. Soon afterward, Graves expanded his business interests by acquiring both a marketing and research company and EGG Dallas Broadcasting. In 1990 he joined Earvin "Magic" Johnson in purchasing the Washington, D.C., Pepsi-Cola franchise, of which Graves was CEO. In 1998, they sold the franchise back to the parent company. Earl G. Graves, Limited, ranked sixty-fourth on the *Black Enterprise* listing in 2005, with sales of $57.8 million.

By the 1970s black entrepreneurs had managed to gain access to capital markets and were able to invest their wealth in a variety of business ventures. Some of the earliest black advertising agencies included the Chicago-based Proctor & Gardner Advertising, founded in 1970 by Barbara Gardner Proctor (1932-), and Burrell Communications Group, founded by Thomas J. Burrell (1939-) in 1971. In 2005 Burrell's client list included such megafirms as Coca-Cola, McDonalds, and Sears and registered assets in excess of $200 million.

One of the most promising businessmen to emerge during this period was New Yorker J. Bruce Llewellyn (1927–), who purchased FEDCO Foods Corporation, a Bronx chain of ten supermarkets, for $3 million. Llewellyn sold FEDCO for $20 million in 1984; the next year he joined basketball star Julius Erving and actor Bill Cosby in purchasing the Philadelphia Coca-Cola Bottling Company. Four years later Llewellyn bought Garden State Cable Television. By 1993 Garden State's assets registered $96 million. In 2005, Philadelphia Coca-Cola reported sales of $450 million, making it the sixth most profitable company on the *Black Enterprise* top 100 list.

Entertainment entrepreneur Percy E. Sutton (1920–) pursued a political career (he was Manhattan borough president for several years) in addition to founding the Inner City Broadcasting Company in 1970. Sutton, who controlled the Inner City Cable and the Apollo Theater Group, expanded his interests with Percy Sutton International, which has built manufacturing plants in such countries as Nigeria. In 1989 Sutton estimated his net worth at $170 million.

Black participation increased significantly in the area of finance. Perhaps the most profitable business enterprise was the TLC Group, established by securities lawyer Reginald Lewis (1942–1993). Lewis purchased the McCall Pattern Company for $1 million in cash and $24 million in borrowed money; four years later he sold the company for $63 million. Aided by financing from Manufacturers Hanover Trust and Drexel Burnham Lambert, he then engineered a $985 million leveraged buyout of Beatrice International Companies, a large multinational corporation. Beatrice became the first billion-dollar black company, and in 1993 ranked first on the *Black Enterprise* top 100

list with $1.7 billion in sales (five times as much as the second company on the list). At its peak in 1996, TLC Beatrice had sales of $2.2 billion and was number 512 on *Fortune* magazine's list of 1,000 largest companies.

Construction and land development executive Herman J. Russell (1930–), founder and CEO of H. J. Russell & Company of Atlanta, Ga., started out in 1952 as the owner of the H. J. Russell Plastering Company, a small private business. In 1959, Russell established the H. J. Russell Construction Company, which specialized in building single-family homes and duplexes. His involvement in large-scale private-sector commercial projects began in 1969, when he was commissioned to construct the thirty-four story Equitable Life Assurance Building in Atlanta. In the 1970s Russell obtained financing from the Department of Housing and Urban Development (HUD) in order to construct twenty-nine housing projects with four thousand units for low- and middle-income families, while he maintained ownership of the properties. Other large-scale construction projects followed: the Atlanta Stadium, the Atlanta City Hall Complex, the Martin Luther King Community Center, and the Carter Presidential Center. In joint-venture projects with white construction companies, Russell built the parking deck for Atlanta's Hartsfield Airport, the Georgia Pacific fifty-two-story office building, and the addition to the Atlanta Merchandise Mart. He also joined with another African-American-owned construction company, C. D. Moody Construction, to place the winning bid for the $209 million Olympic Stadium contract in Atlanta for the 1996 games.

Russell has expanded his conglomerate to include many diverse businesses. H. J. Russell & Company is the parent company of several subsidiary firms, including Williams-Russell and Johnson, an engineering, architecture, and construction management firm. Russell also owns Russell-Rowe Communications, an ABC affiliate in Macon, Ga. In addition, the City Beverage Company and the Concessions International Corporation, which oversees food concessions in several major airports, are owned by Russell. In 1972 he secured the management rights to Atlanta's Omni sports-convention complex and a 10 percent ownership share of the National Basketball Association's Atlanta Hawks, anticipating by almost two decades the 37.5 percent interest, $8 million purchase of the Denver Nuggets by black entrepreneurs Bertram Lee and Peter Bynoe (1989).

During the past three decades many black athletes and entertainers have assumed entrepreneurial management positions by using their million-dollar salaries to develop new enterprises both inside and outside the sports and entertainment industries. For example, former Green

Bay Packer football player Willie D. Davis (1934–) went on to earn an M.B.A. from the University of Chicago and found his own business, Willie Davis Distributing Company, in 1970. He sold the highly successful company (averaging annual sales of $25 million) in the late 1980s. Among Davis's multimillion-dollar enterprises are part ownership of five radio stations, significant shares in several companies, and the Alliance Bank of Culver City, Calif. Another successful athlete was football star Gale Sayers, who founded Crest Computer Supply in 1984, and by 1993 became the owner of a company whose annual sales amounted to $43 million. In 1999, George Foreman, boxer turned entrepreneur, put his name on a grill made by Salton. Salton purchased the rights to use his name for $127.5 million, plus $10 million in stock. By 2005, over 60 million George Foreman Grills were sold. Foreman helps to market and sell the grills and has also started a line of clothing and cleaning products.

One of the few very successful female entertainment entrepreneurs is television talk-show host Oprah Winfrey. In 1992 Winfrey became the highest paid U.S. entertainer, with earnings of $98 million. She has amassed a fortune of more than $250 million by controlling syndication of her talk show and founding the Harpo Production Company, a movie investment firm. In 2005, Harpo Inc. had $275 million in sales.

Another successful entrepreneur in the entertainment field is Robert Johnson (1946–), founder and CEO of Black Entertainment Television (BET). Johnson knew that the power of television could be a useful tool in promoting black businesses and culture. After graduating from Princeton University with a master's degree in public administration, Johnson worked as a lobbyist for the National Cable Television Association. In 1978, he began developing his plan to create the first cable television network aimed at African Americans. BET launched in January of 1980, eleven years later it became the first black-controlled company listed on the New York Stock Exchange. BET is now a number one brand in African-American media, reaching more than 65 million U.S. homes. Johnson also acquired the Charlotte Bobcats (an NBA expansion franchise) in 2004, making him the first African American to be principal owner of a major-league sports franchise.

Naomi Sims (1949–), one of America's first successful black models, capitalized on the black hair-care-product market by designing and manufacturing wigs that approximated the hair texture of black women. In 1973 she established the Naomi Sims Collection. With sales of $5 million the first year, Sims expanded distribution to include an international market. A cosmetic line, Naomi Sims Beauty Products, Limited, was introduced in 1986,

and by 1988 sales from those products exceeded $5 million.

Historically, black entrepreneurs have participated in the clothing industry as tailors and dressmakers but seldom as manufacturers of mass apparel. In 1989 Carl Jones (1955–) formed the first African-American-owned clothing manufacturing firm, the Los Angeles-based Threads 4 Life Corporation, doing business as Cross Colours. Cross Colours, which reported sales of $93 million in 1993, capitalized on the urban hip-hop, Afrocentric focus in dress, which came to prominence in the early 1990s. The company now has five clothing lines, including Cross Colour Classics, a line tailored to older and more conservative buyers. Jones's innovative Cross Colours Home, a home-furnishing line in which African fabrics and African-designed bed and table linens are featured prominently, is sold in Marshall Fields, I. Magnin, and Macy's

New Jersey-based H. F. Henderson Industries, founded in 1954 by Henry F. Henderson (1928–), is an example of black participation in America's high-tech industries. Henderson specializes in automatic weighing systems, although most of the revenue for the company—which earned a reported $25.7 million in 1993—comes from defense contracts for the design and manufacture of control panels for the U.S. military. He began expanding his business in the 1970s with the Small Business Association's 8(a) program and a $125 million government contract; by the mid–1980s government contracts amounted to 50 percent of his business, with the private domestic sector accounting for 25 percent and the remaining 25 percent coming from an international market that included the People's Republic of China, Japan, Canada, Spain, and England.

Increasingly, black entrepreneurs are tapping markets on a global scale. Henderson, Sutton, Griffey, and George H. Johnson have all found international markets for their products. Soft Sheen's global expansion has taken place under the leadership of Edward G. Gardner's son, Gary, who purchased Britain's black-owned Dyke and Dryden, an import and manufacturing company that specializes in the distribution—primarily in Africa—of black personal-care products. Soft Sheen West Indies was also established in Jamaica. In the 1960s and '70s entrepreneur Jake Simmons Jr. (1901–1981), had used his earnings from the southwestern petroleum industry to invest in oil leases in West Africa.

Despite the development of multimillion-dollar businesses by African-American entrepreneurs, black business-participation rates remain low; only 4 percent of all companies in the United States are black owned. Publicly traded black companies remain few; indeed, only sixteen black companies in the United States (and twenty-one in the Caribbean) have taken this route. In 1971 Parks Sausage of Baltimore went public; it was taken over by a white private investment group in 1977 but was reacquired by the former black owners in 1980. In 1993 its sales reached almost $23 million. Robert Johnson, the founder of the Black Entertainment Channel, placed his company in public trading in order to expand his holdings. "It's time for African-Americans to think of company control in terms other than just percentage of black ownership," Johnson explained. "We should start thinking in terms of black control through the creation of value."

The future of privately held black businesses in the early twenty first century remains unclear, though there are some promising statistics. There are one million African American owned businesses in the United States, which account for over $100 billion in annual sales. Instead of the traditionally owned businesses in the service sector, such as beauty shops, the fastest growing sectors are now legal services, real estate, and business services. According to U.S. Census figures, between 1975 and 1995, the number of black professionals, technicians, administrators and managers nearly tripled, and the number of black college graduates doubled.

It has been argued that in the 1990s and 2000s access to capital and strategic alliances has led some black-owned companies to either go public or become amalgamated within larger, interracial concerns. Whether exclusive black ownership of black enterprises will remain central to the black economy is one of many questions black entrepreneurship will face.

See also Abbott, Robert Sengstacke; Black Entertainment Television (BET); *Chicago Defender*; Cuffe, Paul; Du Sable, Jean Baptiste Pointe; Economic Condition, U.S.; Forten, James; Free Blacks, 1619–1860; Gordy, Berry; Mound Bayou, Mississippi; North Carolina Mutual Life Insurance Company; *Pittsburgh Courier*; Toussaint, Pierre; Walker, Madam C. J.; Winfrey, Oprah; Women Traders of the Caribbean

■ ■ *Bibliography*

Amos, Wally, and Leroy Robinson. *The Famous Amos Story: The Face That Launched a Thousand Chips.* Garden City, N.Y.: Doubleday, 1983.

Bailey, Ronald. *Black Business Enterprise.* New York: Basic Books, 1971.

Bates, Timothy. *Banking on Black Enterprise.* Philadelphia: University Press of America, 1993.

Bates, Timothy, and William Bradford. *Financing Black Economic Development.* New York: Academic Press, 1979.

Butler, John Silbey. *Entrepreneurship and Self-Help Among Black Americans: A Reconsideration of Race and Economics.* Albany: State University of New York Press, 2005.

Cross, Theodore. *Black Capitalism.* New York: Atheneum, 1969.

Du Bois, W. E. B. *The Negro in Business.* Atlanta, Ga.: Atlanta University Press, 1899.

Du Bois, W. E. B. *Economic Co-operation Among Negro Americans.* Atlanta, Ga.: Atlanta University Press, 1907.

Gatewood, Willard. *Aristocrats of Color: The Black Elite, 1880–1920.* Fayetteville: University of Arkansas Press, 2000.

George, Nelson. *Where Did Our Love Go? The Rise and Fall of the Motown Sound.* New York: St. Martin's Press, 1987.

Green, Shelley, and Paul Pryde. *Black Entrepreneurship in America.* New Brunswick, N.J.: Transaction, 1990.

Hamilton, Kenneth Marvin. *Black Towns and Profit: Promotion and Development in the Trans-Appalachian West.* Urbana: University of Illinois Press, 1991.

Harmon, J. H., Jr. Arnett G. Lindsay, and Carter G. Woodson. *The Negro as a Businessman.* 1929. Reprint. College Park, Md.: McGrath, 1969.

Harris, Abram L. *The Negro Capitalist: A Study of Banking and Business Among Negroes.* 1936. Reprint. College Park, Md.: McGrath, 1968.

Henderson, Alexa Benson. "Henry E. Perry and Black Enterprise in Atlanta, 1908–1925." *Business History Review* 61 (Summer 1987): 216–242.

Henderson, Alexa Benson. *Atlanta Life Insurance: Guardians of Black Economic Dignity.* Tuscaloosa: University of Alabama Press, 1990.

Hund, James. *Black Entrepreneurship.* Belmont, Calif.: Wadsworth, 1970.

Johnson, Frank J. *Who's Who of Black Millionaires.* Fresno, Calif., 1984.

Johnson, John H., and Lerone Bennett Jr. *Succeeding Against the Odds.* New York: Warner Books, 1989.

Kinzer, Robert, and Edward Sagarin. *The Negro in American Business: Conflict Between Separatism and Integration.* New York: Greenberg, 1950.

Litvan, Laura M. "The Changing Face of Ownership." *Investor's Business Daily,* June 25, 1996.

Oak, Vishnu V. *The Negro's Adventure in General Business.* Westport, Conn.: Negro Universities Press, 1970.

Ofari, Earl. *The Myth of Black Capitalism.* New York: Monthly Review Press, 1970.

Osborne, Alfred. "Emerging Entrepreneurs and the Distribution of Black Enterprise." In *Managing Take-off in Fast Growth Companies: Innovations in Entrepreneurial Firms.* New York: Praeger, 1986.

Pierce, Joseph A. *Negro Business and Business Education: Their Present and Prospective Development.* 1947. Reprint. New York: Plenum Press, 1995.

Schweninger, Loren, ed. *From Tennessee Slave to St. Louis Entrepreneur: The Autobiography of James Thomas.* Columbia: University of Missouri Press, 1984.

Schweninger, Loren. *Black Property Owners in the South, 1790–1915.* Urbana: University of Illinois Press, 1991.

Smith, Cheryl A. *Market Women: Black Women Entrepreneurs—Past, Present, and Future.* Westport, Conn.: Praeger, 2005.

Walker, Juliet E. K. *Free Frank: A Black Pioneer on the Antebellum Frontier.* Lexington: University Press of Kentucky, 1983.

Walker, Juliet E. K. "Racism, Slavery, and Free Enterprise: Black Entrepreneurship in the United States Before the Civil War." *Business History Review* 60 (1986): 343–382.

Walker, Juliet E. K. "Entrepreneurs, Slave." In the *Dictionary of Afro-American Slavery.* New York: Greenwood Press, 1988.

Walker, Juliet E. K. "Prejudices, Profits, Privileges: Commentaries of 'Captive Capitalists': Antebellum Black Entrepreneurs." *Economic and Business History* 8 (1990): 399–422.

Walker, Juliet E. K. "Entrepreneurs [Women] in Antebellum America." In *Black Women in America: An Historical Encyclopedia.* Brooklyn, N.Y.: Carlson, 1993.

Washington, Booker T. *The Negro in Business.* 1907. Reprint. Chicago: Afro-Am Press, 1969.

Weare, Walter B. *Black Business in the New South: A Social History of the North Carolina Mutual Life Insurance Company.* Durham, N.C.: Duke University Press, 1993.

Whitten, David O. "A Black Entrepreneur in Antebellum Louisiana." *Business History Review* 45 (1971): 210–219.

JULIET E. K. WALKER (1996)
Updated by publisher

ENVIRONMENTAL RACISM

Environmental racism—defined as "any environmental policy, practice, or directive that differentially affects or disadvantages (whether intended or unintended) individuals, groups, or communities based on race or color" by Robert Kuehn in his article titled "A Taxonomy of Environmental Justice"—became identified as a significant problem for blacks and other people of color during the last decades of the twentieth century. Most activists and many academics use the terms *environmental racism* and *environmental injustice* interchangeably. Some government agencies and industry groups are likely to employ the term *environmental equity*, a term coined by a U.S. Environmental Protection Agency (EPA) working group, because they believe it lends itself most readily to scientific risk analysis and avoids the more charged and controversial terms *racism* and *justice.*

Focused protests in black neighborhoods against environmental pollution began during the late 1970s. The phrase *environmental racism* was first documented in 1982 when African-American protesters, led by Rev. Walter Fauntroy (b. 1933) and Rev. Benjamin Chavis (b. 1948),

captured national media attention by launching mass demonstrations against the proposed construction of a landfill for highly toxic PCBs (polychlorinated biphenyls) in the very poor, and predominantly black, Warren County, North Carolina. Fauntroy, the District of Columbia delegate to Congress in 1982, commissioned a U.S. General Accounting Office study, which found that three of the four commercial hazardous waste facilities in EPA Region 4 (which includes North Carolina) were in African-American areas, while the fourth was in a low-income area.

Meanwhile, the issue of environmental racism was receiving the attention of scholars, including Robert Bullard, a pioneer in the environmental justice movement. Bullard's 1983 research found that twenty-one of Houston's twenty-five solid-waste facilities were located in predominantly African-American neighborhoods, even though African Americans made up only twenty-eight percent of the city's population in 1980. In 1987 the Commission for Racial Justice of the United Church of Christ published an influential national study that documented a close and significant relationship between race and the location of commercial hazardous waste facilities and uncontrolled toxic waste sites. This report, titled, "Toxic Wastes and Race in the United States," concluded that race was consistently the most significant variable in the location of these sites.

Many black communities throughout the United States struggled in the 1980s and 1990s against the placement of toxic waste plants and other polluting facilities close to their neighborhoods. Such struggles occurred in South Central Los Angeles; Alsen, Louisiana; Richmond, California; Halifax, Virginia; and Chester, Pennsylvania. In Africa, the Ogoni people battled to stop the environmental injustice inherent in Shell Oil's exploration activities in Nigeria.

Perhaps, the movement against environmental racism has gained the most prominence within the United States due to the work of certain key leaders of the environmental justice movement. Armed with studies documenting the disproportionate impact of pollution on low-income communities of color, these black community leaders and academics pressured President Bill Clinton to sign in early 1994 the Executive Order on Environmental Justice, which requires all federal agencies to "make achieving environmental justice part of its mission by addressing, as appropriate, disproportionately high and adverse human health or environmental effects of its programs, policies, and activities on minority populations and low-income populations." Since 1994, however, environmental justice activists have been bitterly disappointed with the performance of the federal government with respect to both the letter and intent of the Executive Order. Furthermore, while several state governments have acknowledged the problem of environmental injustice and launched initiatives to combat it, most activists have been disappointed with the results. Similarly, legal challenges to environmental decision-making in federal government agencies based on racial discrimination or environmental injustice have been unsuccessful. Therefore, most activists and students of the struggle against environmental racism in the early twenty-first century would likely argue that mobilizing residents to be more powerful participants in environmental decision-making forums is the most effective strategy for combating this problem.

▪ ▪ *Bibliography*

Bullard, Robert D., ed. *Confronting Environmental Racism: Voices from the Grassroots.* Boston, Mass.: South End Press, 1993.

Cole, Luke W. and Sheila R. Foster. *From the Ground Up: Environmental Racism and the Rise of the Environmental Justice Movement.* New York: New York University Press, 2001.

Kuehn, Robert. "A Taxonomy of Environmental Justice." In *Environmental Justice: Law, Policy, and Regulation,* edited by Clifford Rechtschaffen and Eileen Gauna, vol. 6. Durham, N.C.: Carolina Academic Press, 2002.

JAMES STERLING HOYTE (2005)

EPISCOPALIANS

Although the first African-American Episcopal Church, St. Thomas African Episcopal Church in Philadelphia, was consecrated on July 29, 1794, with Absalom Jones as the first priest, the history of the African-American affiliation with the Episcopal Church began with the baptism of African slave children in seventeenth-century Virginia, Maryland, and the Carolinas, where most eastern seaboard planters belonged to the Church of England. Whereas some devout masters baptized slave children, others, suspecting that Christianity might legally or morally undermine their slaves' subordinate status, expressed indifference to religious training for slaves and resisted slave conversions. In spite of resistance in the colonies, several Anglican missionaries began training and baptizing slaves as early as 1695. The Church of England Christianized slaves and Native Americans through the English Society for the Propagation of the Gospel in Foreign Parts (SPG), which was founded in 1701. The first schools for blacks in the colonies were organized by the SPG in the early eighteenth century. Through the SPG, the Church of England became the first church to take Christianity to slaves in the British North American colonies and became the earliest denomination to train blacks to be missionaries.

During the colonial period the Church of England and the SPG established Sunday schools and catechetical schools for missionary training and adult education of slaves. Since baptism and religious instruction depended upon the masters' and mistresses' attitude, SPG efforts to induce masters to send slaves to regular catechetical instructions met with inconsistent results. Whereas some masters encouraged slave baptism and conversion, many other colonists and Anglican ministers continued to ignore the religious lives of slaves throughout the colonial period. Other colonists apprehensively questioned SPG activities, rejected slave presence at the communion table, and doubted the qualifications of African Americans for Christian salvation and church participation.

Although at mid-century the Church of England carried out the most extensive work of any denomination among slaves in the southern colonies, the American Revolution disrupted the church's work and led to the complete reorganization of the Church of England in America into a separate denomination, the Protestant Episcopal Church of America, in 1787. In addition to losing the momentum and experience of seven decades of work among slaves, the church lost the most influential catalyst for bringing slaves into the Episcopal Church: the large number of Anglican southern aristocrats who were British sympathizers and loyalists. This contributed to the decay and disestablishment of the church in the southern states and the subsequent decline of its membership and the rise of the Baptists and Methodists.

Whereas in the colonial period black participation in the Anglican Church had been centered among slaves in eastern seaboard cities and on plantations, antebellum black Episcopalians were predominantly free blacks living in northern cities who saw themselves as role models of black achievement, activism, and independence for other blacks, and as members of a higher social class, differentiated from the masses of illiterate, rural slaves.

Given the identification of the Episcopal Church with the middle and upper classes, the bulk of the antebellum free black community rejected the Episcopal Church in favor of affiliation with the Methodists and Baptists, whose egalitarian message and ease of conversion offered greater access to membership and the ministry. Catechetical teaching and literacy requirements inhibited black membership in the Episcopal Church and especially denied African Americans access to the Episcopal ministry. With no literacy requirements for membership in Methodist and Baptist churches, blacks could not only join these denominations but also become ministers to their own people. While Episcopalians recoiled at the emotional expressiveness of black worship in song, dance, and shout, the Methodist and Baptist evangelical traditions included these same worship styles. Free to lead their own congregations, black ministers could preach a message of liberation, and their congregations could claim this niche of cultural and political autonomy.

For the vast majority of antebellum blacks who were slaves, Methodist and Baptist membership and ministry were infinitely more accessible than Episcopalian affiliation on the expanding frontiers of plantation slavery. The farmers, planters, and slaves of Alabama, Mississippi, Tennessee, and other new states did not inherit the Anglican traditions of the eastern seaboard colonial aristocracy. Instead, they were claimed by the Second Great Awakening of Methodist and Baptist revivalism, which not only brought slaves into Christianity in large numbers but also provided fertile ground for the invisible slave church, led by black ministers and embraced by slaves who created African-American religious traditions.

By the end of the Civil War these developments— limited access to membership and the ministry, rejection of African and evangelical traditions, and early geographic containment of the church on the eastern seaboard— placed black Episcopalians wishing to proselytize the freed slaves in the disadvantageous position of being in a church that required a highly literate ministry, that rejected African folk traditions, that afforded African Americans little independence or autonomy compared to the black Baptist church or the independent black Methodist denominations, and that appealed to northern urban black communities rather than the majority of blacks in the rural South. Nonetheless, some of the most important leaders of African-American cultural and religious life were Episcopal priests, including James Holly (1829–1911) and Alexander Crummell (1819–1898), both of whom, somewhat surprisingly given their denominational background, became ardent black nationalists.

In the two decades following the Civil War, the Episcopal Church's Freedman's Commission operated schools, hospitals, and churches but failed to compete effectively against the missionary campaign launched by the predominantly black denominations, whose membership swelled. To make matters worse, the black membership of the Episcopal Church drastically declined during Reconstruction when the Episcopal Church failed to accept black Episcopalians' demands for black ministers. For example, in South Carolina between 1860 and 1868 black membership in the Episcopal Church declined from three thousand to fewer than three hundred.

By the 1880s a slight increase in black membership from the small but growing black middle class in southern cities alarmed southern Episcopalians who had embraced the widespread reestablishment of white supremacy and segregation of the post-Reconstruction South. In 1883 the Sewanee Conference of Southern Bishops met in Sewanee, Tennessee, and unanimously authorized diocesan segregation and placed the care of black congregations and ministers under missionary organizations. In response to this and other forms of church discrimination, Alexander Crummell, rector and founder of St. Luke's in Washington, D.C., founded the Conference of Church Workers Among Colored People in 1883 and the Women's Auxiliary to the Conference in 1894. Although the Negro Conference failed in its appeal to the General Convention to change the Sewanee Canon's endorsement of church segregation, it succeeded in getting the General Convention to appoint a Church Commission for Work Among the Colored People. The meetings of the Conference of Church Workers Among Colored People also provided black Episcopalians a forum in which they could meet each other, share their grievances, and formulate solutions to their ambiguous and limited role in the church.

As black Episcopalians entered the twentieth century, they confronted an ironic, complex dilemma that discouraged growth of black membership: Whereas their own predominantly white denomination continued to discriminate against them by denying black clergy and laypersons full voting rights on diocesan councils and in the General Convention, the black denominations saw the majority of black Episcopalians as elite, privileged, and snobbish. From the 1880s to the 1930s the Episcopal Church did not decide if black communicants should be separated into racial dioceses and missionary districts with their own bishops or if they should remain in a diocese and be given equal representation and perhaps a black suffragan bishop (a bishop without the right to become archbishop). In 1903 the Conference of Colored Workers asked that black churches be placed under the general church rather than the diocesan conventions composed of the same local white leaders who supported and upheld secular racial segregation and discrimination. Requests for redress of the inequality within the church at the 1905 General Convention went unanswered and revealed that sentiments among northern white Episcopalians were little better than those of the Sewanee Conference. Northern dioceses questioned African-American ordinations and promoted the idea of placing black congregations under the supervision of white parishes or under the direction of the bishop.

The question of independence was even more complicated because black churches were not self-supporting.

Black clergy salaries and black school supplies were paid for by the Domestic and Foreign Missionary Society or the American Church Missionary Society and their auxiliaries until 1912. In 1918 Edward T. Demby and Henry B. Delany became the first black suffragan bishops.

By 1921 the Episcopal Church had two black bishops, 176 black ministers, 288 African-American congregations, and 31,851 communicants concentrated along the eastern seaboard from New York to Georgia. The church had failed to respond adequately to requests for a black ministry, although it had established schools during the late nineteenth century—not only primary and secondary schools but also schools to train teachers, ministers, and missionaries to go to Africa. Like the churches, the schools also had a welfare status and received at least half of their funding from the American Church Institute for Negroes, Inc., the agency that disbursed general church funds for black education. In spite of extensive efforts in support of black education, these schools created few black members, churches, or ministers. Black students felt no necessary allegiance to or affiliation with the Episcopal Church. Rather, their training led to secular jobs and their membership remained with the predominantly black denominations. After decades of training blacks, the church continued to impede African-American ordinations and to maintain the dependent status of black congregations as subordinate churches.

The large urban African-American migrations following World Wars I and II failed to increase the numbers of black Episcopalians. Rather, the rural folkways of black southerners estranged black Episcopalians even more from the black southern working class that filled northern cities. As ever larger numbers of black southerners entered the urban North, black Episcopal scholars and clergy attacked the spontaneous, emotional music and folk traditions of rural black southern church culture in the Methodist and especially the Baptist churches.

The civil rights movement of the 1950s and 1960s and the Black Power movements of the 1960s and 1970s evoked increasing racial consciousness among blacks within predominantly white denominations, including Episcopalians. Black Episcopalians confronted their historical dual identity crisis—one within the Episcopal church where black members and clergy had felt alienated, excluded, and invisible for almost two centuries, and the other in trying to identify with other black Christians, especially those in independent black churches.

Black Episcopalians responded to this new climate of racial awareness by forming the Episcopal Society of Cultural and Racial Unity and the General Convention Special Program in 1967. Formed out of the merger of the Conference of Colored Church Workers and Summer Schools of Religious Education, the Union of Black Episcopalians was founded in 1968 to confront the historically diminished role of African Americans in the Episcopal Church. More than twenty chapters in the United States serve 150,000 black members out of 3,500,000 Episcopalians. In 1972 the Union of Black Episcopalians had the church establish the Absalom Jones Theological Institute at the Interdenominational Theological Center in Atlanta. In 1973 the General Convention formed the Commission for Black Ministries, now the Office of Black Ministries, which compiles a directory of black clergy, convenes the Black Diocesan Executives, and acts as a clearinghouse for African-American clergy. In 1981 the church published an official supplementary hymnal, *Lift Every Voice and Sing: A Collection of Afro-American Spirituals and Other Songs*. Since the 1960s a large influx of black Anglicans from the Caribbean and the development of new liturgies directed toward black parishioners have revitalized the African-American presence in the Episcopal Church.

Whereas the National Baptist Convention could claim a tradition of independence and the largest black Methodist denominations could embrace a strong tradition of protest, it seemed that the black Episcopal tradition could claim neither independence nor protest. Beginning in the 1960s black Episcopalians affirmed the strains of independence and protest within the African-American religious traditions by celebrating being Episcopalian and black. In recent years women have taken a more active role in the church. In 1976 the social activist, lawyer, and poet Pauli Murray became the first black female priest in the Episcopal Church; in 1980 Barbara Harris—a black woman—became the first female Episcopal bishop. Black Episcopal clergy joined the National Council of Black Churches in its attack on white domination of the National Council of Churches and in its efforts to improve the lives of urban blacks. Since 1973 the Episcopal liturgical calendar has included the celebration of Absalom Jones, the first black Episcopal priest.

See also Baptists; Crummell, Alexander; Holly, James T., Protestantism in the Americas

■ ■ *Bibliography*

Bennett, Robert A. "Black Episcopalians: A History from the Colonial Period to the Present." *Historical Magazine of the Protestant Episcopal Church* 22 (1979): 312–321.

Bragg, George F. *Afro-American Church Work and Workers*. Baltimore, Md., 1904.

Bragg, George F. *History of the Afro-American Group of the Episcopal Church*. Baltimore, Md.: Church Advocate Press, 1922.

Brydon, George MacLaren. *The Episcopal Church Among the Negroes of Virginia*. Richmond: Virginia Diocesan Library, 1937.

Hewitt, John. *Protest and Progress: New York's First Black Episcopal Church Fights Racism*. New York: Routledge, 2000.

Hood, R. E. "From a Headstart to a Deadstart: The Historical Basis for Black Indifference Toward the Episcopal Church, 1800–1860." *Historical Magazine of the Protestant Episcopal Church* 51 (1982): 269–296.

Lewis, Harold T. *Yet With a Steady Beat: The African American Struggle for Recognition in the Episcopal Church*. Harrisburg, Penn.: Trinity Press International, 1996.

Shattuck, Gardiner H. *Episcopalians and Race: Civil War to Civil Rights*. Lexington: University Press of Kentucky, 2000.

Spencer, Jon Michael. "The Episcopal Church." In *Black Hymnody: A Hymnological History of the African-American Church*. Knoxville: University of Tennessee Press, 1993, pp. 165–181.

LILLIE JOHNSON EDWARDS (1996)
Updated bibliography

EQUIANO, OLAUDAH

C. 1750

APRIL 30, 1797

▌▐▐

The autobiographer Olaudah Equiano, also known as Gustavus Vassa, was born the son of an Ibo chieftain in Benin, now part of Nigeria. He was eleven when he and his sister were kidnapped and sold to white slave traders on the coast. He was subsequently shipped to Barbados and, later, Virginia, where he was sold to a British naval officer whom he served for nearly seventeen years. On board ships and during brief intervals in England, he learned to read and write and converted to Christianity. His autobiography relates his several adventures at sea off the Canadian coast during the Seven Years' War and with Admiral Boscawen's fleet in the Mediterranean. To his dismay, his master, who had promised him his freedom, sold him to an American shipowner, who employed him in trading runs—sometimes with slaves as cargo—between the islands of the West Indies and the North American coast. In this capacity, Equiano witnessed murders and cruel injustices inflicted on blacks, both free and enslaved.

In 1766 Equiano was at last able to purchase his freedom, but he elected to remain a seaman, although he passed some periods in England. Among other adventures, he sailed on the Phipps expedition to the Arctic in 1772–1773, and he later worked as a manservant on a tour of the Mediterranean and as an assistant to a doctor treating the Miskito Indians in Nicaragua. After 1777 he remained largely land-bound in the British Isles and assumed increasingly active roles in the antislavery movement. In 1787 he was appointed commissioner of stores for the resettlement of free Africans in Sierra Leone, but he was dismissed after accusing a naval agent of mismanagement. His efforts to join an African expeditionary group or to do African missionary work also met with failure.

In 1789 Equiano published his autobiography under the title *The Interesting Narrative of Olaudah Equiano, or Gustavus Vassa the African, Written by Himself*. Three years later he married Susannah Cullen, an Englishwoman with whom he would have two children. Although several of his accounts have since been questioned, he saw nine editions of the book printed in his lifetime, thereby drawing invitations to lecture throughout the British Isles. Because Equiano infused his autobiography with antislavery views and identified enslaved blacks with biblical Hebrews, his work is generally regarded as a truer precursor of slave narratives written between 1830 and 1860 than other eighteenth-century African-American autobiographies.

See also Free Blacks, 1619–1860; Slave Narratives

■ ■ *Bibliography*

Edwards, Paul. "Equiano's Narrative." Introduction to *The Life of Olaudah Equiano, or Gustavus Vassa the African*, edited by Paul Edwards. Harlow, U.K.: Longman, 1994.

Equiano, Olaudah. *The Interesting Narrative of the Life of Olaudah Equiano, or Gustavus Vassa, the African, Written by Himself*, edited by Werner Sollors. Norton Critical Edition. New York: Norton, 2001.

Ogude, S. E. "Facts into Fiction: Equiano's Narrative Revisited." *Research in African Literatures* 13 (1982): 31–43.

Walvin, James. *An African's Life: The Life and Times of Olaudah Equiano, 1745–1797*. London: Cassell, 1998.

EDWARD MARGOLIES (1996)
Updated bibliography

ESTIMÉ, DUMARSAIS

APRIL 21, 1900

JULY 20, 1953

▌▐▐

Dumarsais Estimé was born on April 21, 1900, in Verettes, a village in the Artibonite Valley of Haiti. He attended public schools and became a schoolteacher at the Lycee Petion. Among Estimé's students was François "Papa Doc" Duvalier (1907–1971). Estimé later ventured into politics and secured the posts of secretary of education, secretary of labor, and secretary of agriculture under President Stenio Vincent between 1930 and 1941. When widespread protests led to the removal of President Elie Lescot, who held power between 1941 and 1946, Estimé ran for president.

Estimé was one of many *noiristes*, Haitians who considered blacks to be the historical defenders of the nation's liberty and sought empowerment through opposition to white and mulatto rule. Inspired by popular disaffection with mulatto dictatorships and the black nationalism of *noirisme*, Estimé ran on the slogan "A Black Man in Power." Because he was the primary *noiriste* candidate from the North, he enjoyed the support of a large segment of the peasantry. He planned to liberate Haiti from U.S. domination, legislate greater freedoms, and embrace modernization as the panacea to the plight of workers and the peasantry. On August 16, 1946, Dumarsais Estimé was elected president of Haiti.

Estimé's election became known as the "revolution of 1946." His cabinet included Daniel Fignolé (1915–1986), the charismatic leader of *Mouvement Ouvrier Paysan* (MOP), as minister of education and François Duvalier as minister of public health. Among the first acts of the Estimé administration was the drafting of a new constitution that put strict limitations on foreign businesses (though less so on the tourist industry) and protected freedom of the press, allowing an opposition voice. The constitution equated citizenship with blackness, defining a Haitian as "any person of the black race born of a Haitian." In addition, the constitution reasserted the Haitian claim to the island of Navassa, located thirty-two miles southwest of Haiti. Both Haiti and the United States maintained an unresolved claim to Navassa, and Estimé's assertion of Haitian ownership continued this trend. Estimé also attempted to reinvigorate tourism. He courted Pan American Airways and Hilton Hotels and considered the possibility of a casino in Port-au-Prince. He also organized the International Exposition of 1949.

In 1950 Estimé proposed legislation to alter the constitution and extend his term of office. The Senate voted against him, but the Haitian public organized demonstrations in order to pressure the Senate to change their stance. With the public behind him, Estimé signed a decree to dissolve the Senate, but the military prevented its publication. The door was opened, and a coup instituted by a military junta that included Colonel Paul Magloire forced Estimé to resign and seek exile in New York, where he died three years later, on July 20, 1953.

Noirisme had brought Estimé to power, and within it the general public perceived the antidote to the class antagonism that inundated the nation. If blacks and mulat-

tos could unite under the name *black* then presumably they could be mutually uplifted. This possibility, which Estimé had made tangible again, would continue to drive Haitian politics and result in the election of François Duvalier in 1957.

See also Duvalier, François; Magloire, Paul

■ ■ *Bibliography*

Pamphile, Leon. *Haitians and African Americans: A Heritage of Tragedy and Hope.* Gainsville: University Press of Florida, 2001.

Paquin, Lyonel. *The Haitians: Class and Color Politics.* Brooklyn, N.Y.: Multi-Type, 1983.

Plummer, Brenda Gayle. *Haiti and the United States: The Psychological Moment.* Athens: University of Georgia Press, 1992.

SEAN BLOCH (2005)

ETHNIC ORIGINS

Africans may have crossed the Atlantic Ocean before the 1492 voyage of Christopher Columbus (1451–1506) by way of the Canary current. The current passes the coast of Senegal and proceeds across the ocean to the north coast of South America and the southern Caribbean and could easily carry even small watercraft from West Africa to America. Some scholars have suggested that such voyages, either accidental or intentional, took place in ancient times, though the most solid reference is to a voyage of exploration in the early fourteenth century by Mansu Qu, ruler of Mali. In 1312 Qu's successor, Mansa Musa, told Egyptian authorities that Qu had wished to explore the "Western Ocean" (Atlantic) and had shipped a large expedition to do so. The expedition never returned, however, undoubtedly because the wind and current system of the South Atlantic does not offer a ready means to return to Africa.

It wasn't until the fifteenth century that European navigators began to institute regular navigation between both Europe and Africa and between the Old World continents and the Americas. Portuguese navigators were regular visitors to West Africa by the middle of the fifteenth century, and they were visiting the entire coast by the end of the century.

Although one of their primary motives to sailing to Africa was to locate the sources of the trans-Saharan gold trade, early Portuguese sailors also began raiding the African coast, They captured fishermen and other coastal people, who did not expect seaborne raiders to attack them. However, they soon responded with their own naval craft, and in a series of encounters successfully defeated a number of Portuguese raids. In the aftermath of these early armed conflicts, the Portuguese crown, working through Diogo Gomes, negotiated a series of peace agreements with the rules of the Senegambian coast: the Portuguese would cease raiding in return for peaceful exchange. In the following years, Africans in Senegambia, and elsewhere along the coast where Europeans met other African states, peaceful transactions included the purchase of slaves as well as other goods. During these centuries, the slave trade grew from about 5,000 per year in 1500 to more than 60,000 per year in the late eighteenth century.

Between 1450 and 1850 some twelve to fifteen million Africans were transported across the Atlantic and sold in the New World. Many were captured and enslaved in Africa by African armies fighting either wars between the various African states (about two hundred sovereign polities were involved in the slave trade) or in civil wars within those states. Another substantial group was enslaved illegally in Africa by bandits and other criminal elements and sold illicitly to African and European middlemen for eventual transport. Others were enslaved as the result of judicial actions taken by African authorities as punishment for crimes, both by the enslaved and often by family, friends, and associates of the guilty party. In a few cases, European shippers raided African coastal locations, joined their forces with African armies or bandits, or tricked Africans into boarding their ships to be transported away. In Angola, however, following the founding of the Portuguese colony in 1575, many thousands of Africans were enslaved as a result of the activities of Portuguese-led armies, especially in a series of wars in the seventeenth century, but intermittently in the eighteenth century as well.

TRACING AFRICAN-AMERICAN ROOTS

About half of the slaves purchased or acquired by Europeans in Africa were destined for Brazil, another 40 percent for the Caribbean, and only about 5 percent came to British North America and the United States. Those who were brought to North America had as their ancestral homelands a wide area of western, central, and eastern Africa. They represented numerous cultures and languages, probably as many as fifty.

In recent decades, in part inspired by Alex Haley's *Roots* (1976), a fictional account of his heritage, and by scholarship on African retentions, there has been renewed interest in tracing the origins of contemporary African Americans to the specific cultures that fed the slave trade.

Similar interest in the African heritage is prominent in Brazil, especially in the Brazilian embrace of its African-inspired religious heritage and the writings of the prominent intellectual Gilberto Freyre on African influences in all aspects of Brazilian life. Cuban scholars and intellectuals have shown similar interest, both from the religious and cultural angles. The extent to which groups of African slaves were influenced by their distinctive heritage and how the various cultural legacies of Africa were in time combined and submerged have been a subject of intense debate.

In some ways the apparent cultural and linguistic diversity of African Americans can be misleading, for at any one time, either in Africa or in their destinations in the New World, only a few African cultural groups were dominant among those enslaved. For example, Brazil imported slaves from the Senegambia region in the sixteenth century, but in the early seventeenth century almost the entire African slave trade came from Angola. Portuguese slave ships rarely if ever took slaves from the Bight of Biafra area (though they did from the neighboring Slave Coast region), but English, French, and Dutch took them in large numbers, resulting in a considerable presence of people designated as *Ibos* (a term for the group of people living in the lower Niger region) in their respective colonies.

In North America, there was substantial regional diversity during its period of greatest imports from 1690 to 1810. Most of the slaves coming to the Chesapeake region arrived between 1680 and 1770, while those imported to South Carolina arrived over a much longer period, from about 1720 to 1810. Louisiana, on the other hand, imported some slaves between 1719 and 1743, and then none until a major burst after 1777 through the early nineteenth century. However, North America was in some measure exceptional, for most slave regimes had such dismal records of reproduction that they continued importing Africans from their earliest founding (or at least their earliest employment of slave labor on a large scale) and the end of the slave trade. Estates founded by Hernán Cortés (1485–1547) in Mexico, for example, imported new Africans from the early sixteenth century until the nineteenth century. Indeed, North America was the only region to have a self-reproducing and growing population of enslaved people, thus limiting the numbers of imported Africans and allowing a much larger native-born population to shape the resulting cultural mix.

The population of African descent in the Americas derives primarily from several nodes of import. Because North American slave populations were self-reproducing, the major North American slave trade was internal, from older plantation areas to newer ones, typically in the Deep

South. These factors explain why the period of importation of Africans was relatively brief and why North America imported only about 5 percent of all slaves exported from Africa.

American importers drew slaves from all parts of west and west central Africa and a few from as far afield as Madagascar, off the southeast coast of Africa. In many areas of North America, however, slave imports were dominated by a particular African exporting region. This was because the shippers who supplied slaves to American buyers often had customary relations with a limited group of African sellers, and people from those regions tended to predominate.

Frequently within the English trade, North American importers were in competition with importers from the Caribbean, who often favored slaves from particular regions and retained them in the Caribbean. Often this was because there was widespread belief among planters that slaves of particular ethnicities were more suitable for certain types of labor; this placed a premium on them and drove up the price for those who wished to export them from the colony. Thus, for example, Jamaica retained a large number of slaves from the Gold Coast, and North America received relatively few people from this region, even though British shipping had good connections and purchased thousands of slaves on the Gold Coast every year.

DISTRIBUTION OF AFRICANS

The African exporting area was traditionally divided by European shippers into three large regions. The first was Upper Guinea, which corresponded to the coast from Senegal down to roughly Liberia. Next came Lower Guinea, corresponding to the coast from eastern Ivory Coast to eastern Cameroon. The last was Angola, which commenced in modern Gabon and extended down to the central coast of Angola. These three regions were in turn subdivided into coasts. Upper Guinea had two major coasts: Senegambia on the north down to the Gambia River and Sierra Leone from Gambia down to Liberia. Lower Guinea had the Gold Coast from eastern Ivory Coast to the Volta River, the Slave Coast from the Volta to the eastern part of Nigeria, and the Bight of Biafra comprising the complex of rivers and deltas of eastern Nigeria and Cameroon. Terminology varied—Sierra Leone might be called the Rivers of Guinea by French or Portuguese shippers, for example—but the general boundaries remained quite stable throughout the long period of the Atlantic trade.

Although these coastal designations were created and maintained by European shippers, they did correspond to African cultural and political realities. Each coast possessed a complex commercial network reaching down to a group of related Atlantic ports, and each network, in turn, was also a zone of frequent communication that included cultural and political interaction. Thus, slave-trading patterns in Africa tended to produce a fairly predictable mixture of people from the hinterland area supplying the coast. By knowing from which coast a shipload of slaves came, both modern historians and eighteenth-century American slave owners could predict within fairly narrow limits from which African cultural groups the people derived.

The distribution of Africans varied in different parts of North America. Angolans and Senegambians predominated in South Carolina and Louisiana. In the Chesapeake area, there were fewer Angolans and Senegambians and more people from the Gold Coast and Bight of Biafra. People from Sierra Leone constituted a significant proportion of arrivals in South Carolina, but they were virtually absent in the Chesapeake area; people from the Slave Coast were important in Louisiana but not in South Carolina or the Chesapeake area. Historians have not yet fully investigated the implications of this regional diversity for the development of African-American culture.

Similarly, the distribution of slaves in the British Caribbean was different from that in North America, with Caribbean plantations receiving considerably more imports from the Gold Coast region and fewer from Senegambia. Brazil, on the other hand, derived the lion's share of its African population from Angola or from the Slave Coast, which Portuguese sources designated as *Mina*. The French Caribbean tended to have Africans from Central Africa and from the Slave Coast, though their trade in Senegambia was extensive.

DIVISIONS AMONG AFRICAN AMERICANS

The people who came to America from each of these coasts were known to American slave owners as being divided into a fairly large number of nations or countries whose membership was determined by cultural criteria such as language or facial and body markings. Comparisons between the detailed surveys of these nations that were conducted by eighteenth-century writers and modern African history researchers reveal that there is a trend to identify an African nation using constructs that were not the same as those used by the Africans themselves. Eighteenth-century Africans organized their lives by village, family, and grouping, or state, but did not recognize linguistic or cultural criteria as a primary element of their identity. A larger frame of reference for Africans was an adherence to either Islam or Christianity. Many Africans from a broad band of West Africa stretching from Senegal down to Sierra Leone and deep into the interior were Muslims, while most central Africans in Kongo and its southern neighbors in the Portuguese colony of Angola were Christians. In both regions, Africans had combined elements of their previous religious traditions with Christianity and Islam, often to the dismay of priests or visitors from more orthodox regions. Because of the regional patterns of enslavement, North America received a large number of slaves who followed either Christianity or Islam, and proportionately lower numbers of people who practiced other traditional African religions than might be found in the Caribbean.

However, there is good reason to believe that Africans in the Americas recognized cultural and linguistic divisions among themselves, and often were less concerned about the political divisions that may have been more prevalent in their homelands. Thus, Akan-speaking people from the Gold Coast region might form close bonds with other Akans, even if they were from different, and perhaps even rival, political groups. In this way, those in Jamaica or Antigua might recognize themselves as members of the *Coromantee* nation,, a term that was not used in Africa to identify either a language or any other group but was widely used in British America.

WARS, BANDITRY, AND THE ENSLAVEMENT PROCESS

The presence of these various African nations in America was a result of commercial, political, and military events in Africa. Historians have very little information about these processes because so many of the people were enslaved in areas where no contemporary written records were kept. Even where there are African records, such as in some parts of Muslim West Africa and in Kongo, relatively little light is shed on the enslavement process. One of the most important sources of the enslavement process are interviews conducted by interested parties, such as missionaries in the Americas, in which Africans provided some information about their own enslavement. None of these sources, however, provide us with statistical information that allows us to determine for sure which process was most prevalent at what times and places. Some people were enslaved because of poverty, others through judicial processes, but it appears that by far the most important reasons for African enslavement were wars and banditry.

In Senegambia, enslavement in the eighteenth century followed two models. The first of these was wars among the states of the Senegal Valley, particularly a cycle of conflict between Bawol and Kajoor that often involved their allies or neighbors. Further inland, a similar rivalry matched the states of Segu (on the Niger River) and

Kaarta, farther north. These states fought each other and also raided far to the north. In addition to these wars, which were among states indigenous to the area, there were raids conducted from the north by the Moors, who were linked to Morocco and had ambitions in the Senegal Valley region.

A second mode of enslavement came from banditry. Senegambian bandits were often off-duty soldiers. The *ceddo,* royal slaves who governed and staffed the armies of the states, routinely conducted raids on the population of the area. While these raids were illegal, authorities often cooperated with the soldiers in the acquisition and sale of slaves. The *sofa,* professional soldiers of Segu and Kaarta, engaged in the same pattern of unofficial and illegal enslavement with official collusion. Popular resentment against this activity was strong, and on two occasions, in the 1670s and again in the 1770s, popular movements with Islamic leadership revolted against the leadership, although without long-term success. In the first of these, Nasr al-Din, a religious leader from the nomadic society of the desert advanced religious reform both among his own people and among the common people of the Senegal Valley. The group was strongly opposed to the oppressive wars waged against common people by the political elites, but was overcome by local rulers when Nasr al-Din was killed in battle. In the second movement, Abd al-Kadir led people from the valley of Senegal in a reform movement that sought to eliminate, among other things, the sale of Muslim slaves to Christian buyers, an action that greatly affected the slave trade for a time.

The many Bambara (African people of the upper Niger) slaves who were imported to Louisiana in the early eighteenth century probably were obtained through the wars and raids of the Senegambian region, as were the many Senegambians who appear in the inventories of the last part of the eighteenth century. Because the Bambaras were nearly the totality of the people brought to Louisiana from Africa during the first French period, they played a major role in defining the culture of this region.

In Sierra Leone, small-scale piracy was widespread on the many creeks and rivers of the coast where forests provided hideouts for raiders. This piracy coexisted with petty wars, but the most important source for eighteenth-century enslavement was the holy war (jihad) of the Muslim Fulbe cattle herders of Futa Jallon following 1726. While in its initial stages, the jihad was aimed at redressing grievances of the Fulbe and establishing a reformed Islamic polity; in time it became a source of wars, as the new state in Futa Jallon raided its neighbors and sent the fruits of its efforts overseas on the slave ships. The timing of the arrival of Sierra Leonean slaves in South Carolina suggests that the wars of the jihad period played a major role in the burst of exports from the region.

Before the late seventeenth century, the Gold Coast was divided into dozens of small states. Wars were frequent in the area, often occasioned by commercial disputes and unpaid debts. European trading companies, which came to the coast to buy gold, often became involved in the disputes both in an effort to settle their own commercial affairs and also to act as mercenaries hired by African states. It was only in the late seventeenth century, with the rise of larger imperial states in the interior, that the region became a major supplier of slaves to the Atlantic region. The rise of the states of Denkyira, Asante, and Akwamu in the 1670s and later occasioned wars of expansion by these states, which were able to mobilize large armies, forced the coastal states to operate in conjunction with each other to meet the challenge. Although the petty disputes and wars continued into the eighteenth century, major wars in which tens of thousands of people were captured and exported became more important as the interior kingdoms fought coastal states and each other. By the 1720s Asante had emerged as the most powerful state in the area, but warfare was still common. Many of the areas that Asante had conquered revolted frequently, and Asante itself was beset with civil wars—especially upon the death of a ruler, as occurred in the 1750s.

Slaves from the Gold Coast, who were widely known in English-speaking America as Coromantees (from one of the exporting ports), were particularly valued for their strength and spirit in the West Indies. Their relatively limited numbers in America everywhere outside of the Chesapeake area reflected the greater purchasing power of the West Indian planters. On the other hand, their largely military enslavement made Coromantees capable of rebellion, and indeed, they were behind a large number of plots, conspiracies, and rebellions in both the West Indies and North America (such as the New York Slave Revolt of 1712, the Saint John's revolt of 1733, and Tackey's War in Jamaica in 1760–65).

The pattern of the Gold Coast was repeated on the nearby Slave Coast. Indeed, mercenaries from the Gold Coast were often involved in the politics of the petty states of the coast in the late seventeenth century. However, the rise of the kingdom of Dahomey in the 1680s increased the frequency of large-scale wars in the area. Almost every year Dahomey launched a campaign toward the coast and against the Mahi and the Nagos, loosely structured confederations of states that lie east and west of Dahomey's core. Slaves were taken from the Mahi and the Nagos if the Dahomean armies were successful, or from Dahomey itself if the campaigns failed, as they frequently did. The

Empire of Oyo, lying inland from Dahomey, occasionally intervened in the affairs of its coastal neighbors in an attempt to control Dahomey, its nominal vassal since the 1720s, or to act in conjunction with it. Oyo also conducted its own wars, about which few details are known, and many of the people captured or lost in these campaigns were also exported.

Remarkably, few Slave Coast slaves found their way to North America except for those who arrived through French shipping in Louisiana. British shippers maintained posts on the Slave Coast, and slaves from these posts formed a portion of the population in Jamaica and other West Indian islands. They were not notable, however, in the cargos arriving at any North American port.

Relatively few slaves were taken from the coastal areas of the Bight of Biafra, although piracy along its many rivers and creeks was quite common. Instead, people who were enslaved from the interior were exported from the coastal ports. Many of these interior slaves were designated as *Ibos* in English-speaking America and often as *Calabars* in Romance-language-speaking areas. The river network of the region provided cheap and easy transportation, while the population density of the interior regions was probably the greatest of any in Atlantic Africa.

In the early eighteenth century the kingdom of Benin, which dominated the western part of the area, underwent a lengthy civil war between government factions that lasted into the 1730s. Benin exported many of the victims of these wars through its own port of Ughoton, while many others found their way to other ports such as Warri or New Calabar on the main channel of the Niger River. New Calabar, one of the major exporting ports of the area along with its neighbor Bonny, drew most of its slaves from the Igbo areas that lie up the rivers in the interior. The autobiography of Olouadah Equiano, enslaved around 1760, provided a description of the area from which he originated. As he described it, people were enslaved as a result of many inter-town wars or were captured by pirates who operated along the rivers and from bases in the thickly wooden regions. In the Cross River region, which was served by the port of Old Calabar, a religious association called the Arochukwu often contributed to the supply of slaves. (The Arochukwu was an oracle that settled disputes and had branches over a wide network.) In addition to their religious services, for which they often demanded slaves in payment for adjudication, the association operated a more conventional trading network. Sometimes the oracle or its agents were reputed to kidnap people as well as engage in religious and commercial operations.

The central African coast was involved in the Atlantic economy from the late fifteenth century. Initially most slaves originated from the Kingdom of Kongo, acquired by the wars of expansion in that country in the early and middle sixteenth century. Later in the century, the Kingdom of Ndongo joined the trade and attracted enough Portuguese merchants that the Portuguese crown decided to establish a colony at Luanda (with the permission of Kongo) in 1575 to control it. However, in a series of wars between Portugal and Ndongo after 1579, the Portuguese managed to carve out a colony along the Kwanza River that served as their base and colony. When governors of the early seventeenth century made an alliance with the Imbangala, free-booting raiders from south of the Kwanza, they were able to launch a series of devastating attacks on Ndongo. This set off a half century of ferocious fighting that may have resulted in the capture of half a million slaves before the warring was over in the late seventeenth century.

In the eighteenth century, the Angola coast was largely supplied by the civil war in the kingdom of Kongo. Although there was an active slave trade from the ports of Luanda and Benguela, relatively few slaves exported from these ports or from the hinterland they served in the Kimbundu speaking interior found their way to North America. Instead, they were primarily shipped to Brazil; a few were smuggled to Kongo's ports and taken as slaves by French shippers. A few English crafts worked this coast in the late eighteenth century.

Dynastic disputes of the late seventeenth century lay at the root of Kongo's civil war. Although they were never quite resolved by force, some of these disputes were settled by monarchs in 1715, in the 1760s, the mid-1780s, after 1794, and again in 1805. The violent episodes of royal contest were interspersed with periods of smaller-scale violence because authority was not very centralized. Local wars enforcing shaky authority figures were frequent. This civil unrest and subsequent breakdown of authority led to the rise of bandits who either allied themselves with those in power or operated on their own.

Just as Muslim reformers in Senegambia sought to mobilize popular support to oppose the oppression of the military bandits and state officials in their area, so the Christian kingdom of Kongo had its own movement of reform. Led by Beatriz Kimpa Vita, who claimed to be possessed by Saint Anthony, the movement sought an end to the civil wars and the enslavement that resulted; it also sought the restoration of Kongo under a new mystical Christian leadership. Although the movement succeeded in occupying the capital, the leader was soon captured and burned at the stake as a heretic in 1706.

After 1750 captives from the civil war in Kongo were joined by increasing numbers of people enslaved from both the north and the east of the kingdom. The slaves from the north seem to have been captured during the petty wars between commercial states, while the slaves from the east were taken as a result of the emergence and raiding of the Lunda Empire, which extended its authority—or at least its ability to raid—as far as the Kwango River by 1760. All of these slaves from Kongo or elsewhere were sold to merchants who served North America and the English, French, and Dutch colonies of the Caribbean largely through ports north of the Zaire River, often under the kingdom of Loango.

Africans from more southerly regions were taken either from the various civil wars or Portuguese military campaigns, which were often quite intense after 1700, in the Central Highlands region of Angola.. The Portuguese relocated their fortress of Caconda from the coast to the highlands and subsequently pursued wars along the eastern and southern edge of the highlands. In addition, several new kingdoms like Viye and Mbailundu emerged in the eighteenth century, creating a cycle of warfare that often spread the slave trade to regions that had not participated in the trade very extensively before. In the later eighteenth century, the Portuguese became involved in their politics, helping to impose rulers on Mbailundu in the lengthy Mbailundu War of the 1770s.

Angolans made up a significant portion of the slaves imported into all American regions, but they were particularly numerous in Louisiana and South Carolina. Because so many had served in wars, they, like the Gold Coast Coromantees, were often implicated in revolts and rebellions in America. Angolans led the Stono Rebellion in 1739, and they also played an important role in other revolts in America such as those in Brazil and Haiti.

AFRICAN CULTURE IN AMERICA

Africans who arrived in America came with specific cultural backgrounds that related to their region of origin in Africa. This was particularly true of their linguistic background, for their ability to communicate with other people was limited at first to those of their own ethno-linguistic group. Unlike African social organization, which tended to be based on kinship and locality or citizenship in a state, the social organization of Africans in America was based on common languages. American *nations* or *countries,* as they were called in contemporary records, formed social and mutual self-help groups from among people of their own background to bury their dead or to celebrate occasional holidays. Where marriage registers allow us to follow the role of ethnicity in making marriage choices, it was common for people of the same nation to marry each other. They sometimes formed shadow governments with kings and queens, either independently or, in Spanish and Portuguese America, through membership in lay organizations created by the Catholic Church. In North America, this phenomenon was manifested in royal elections in New York and Negro Election Day in New England. The presence of these ethnic social groups helped to preserve African culture in America. They also provided a cross-estate network, which could allow coordinated action in larger areas and sometimes played an important role in conspiracies and revolts. Thus, ethnic networks were especially prominent in Tackey's War in Jamaica in 1760–65, which involved virtually only Coromantees, while runaway communities in Brazil often grouped themselves by ethnicity and sometimes either fought with or allied with other groups, as took place in the early eighteenth century in Minas Gerais.

See also African Diaspora; Africanisms; Diasporic Cultures in the Americas; Equiano, Olaudah; Migration; Slavery; Slave Trade

■ ■ *Bibliography*

Eltis, David. *Economic Growth and the Ending of the Transatlantic Slave Trade.* New York: Oxford University Press, 1987.

Eltis, David; Stephen D. Behrendt, David Richardson, and Herbert Klein, eds. *The Trans-Atlantic Slave Trade: A Database on CD-ROM.* Cambridge: Cambridge University Press, 1999.

Inikori, J.E., ed. *Forced Migration: The Impact of the Export Slave Trade on African Societies.* New York: Africana Publishing Co., 1982.

Klein, Herbert. *The Atlantic Slave Trade.* Cambridge: Cambridge University Press, 1999.

Lovejoy, Paul. *Transformations in Slavery: A History of Slavery in Africa, 2nd ed..* Cambridge: Cambridge University Press 2000.

Rodney, Walter. *A History of the Upper Guinea Coast, 1545–1800.* Oxford: Clarendon Press, 1970.

Thornton, John. *The Kingdom of Kongo: Civil War and Transition, 1641–1718.* Madison: University of Wisconsin Press, 1983.

Thornton, John. *Africa and Africans in the Making of the Atlantic World, 1400—1880, 2nd ed.* Cambridge: Cambridge University Press, 199.

Thornton, John. *Warfare in Atlantic Africa, 1500–1800.* London: UCL Press, 1999.

JOHN THORNTON (1996)
Updated by author 2005

EUGENICS

See Race, Scientific Theories of

EUROPE, JAMES REESE

FEBRUARY 22, 1881
MAY 9, 1919

Born in Mobile, Alabama, composer and conductor James Reese Europe spent his formative years in Washington, D.C., where his father held a position with the U.S. Postal Service. The family was unusually musical; his brother, John, became a noted ragtime pianist, and his sister, Mary, was an accomplished concert pianist, choral director, and music teacher in the Washington public schools. James Europe attended M Street High School and studied violin, piano, and composition with Enrico Hurlie of the Marine Corps Band and Joseph Douglass, grandson of Frederick Douglass. Other musical influences included Harry T. Burleigh (especially his arrangements of African-American spirituals), organist Melville Charlton, and composer Will Marion Cook.

Like Cook and Burleigh—who had both studied with the celebrated Bohemian composer Antonín Dvořák while he was directing the Prague National Conservatory of Music—Europe accepted Dvořák's assessment of the importance of African-American folk music as a basis for an American national music. He did not believe, however, as did many at the time, that popular forms of musical expression were necessarily vulgar or lowbrow and therefore lacked potential musical value. He was a consistent champion of African-American music and musical artistry at every level and in any form, including those (like jazz) that had yet to emerge fully.

After moving to New York City in 1903, Europe established himself as a leading composer and music director in black musical theater, contributing to such productions as John Larkins's *A Trip to Africa* (1904), Ernest Hogan's *Memphis Students* (1905), Cole and Johnson's *Shoo-fly Regiment* (1906–1907) and *Red Moon* (1908–1909), S. H. Dudley's *Black Politician* (1907–1908), and Bert Williams's *Mr. Lode of Koal* (1910). In April 1910 Europe and several fellow professionals (including Ford Dabney, William Tyers, and Joe Jordan) formed the Clef Club, a union and booking agency that substantially improved the working conditions for black musicians in New York City. Europe was elected president and conductor of the club's concert orchestra, a 125-member ensemble whose unusual instrumentation (consisting primarily of plucked or strummed instruments) he felt to be better suited to the performance of authentic African-American music than that of the standard symphony orchestra. The orchestra's 1912 Concert of Negro Music at Carnegie Hall was a historic event, and Europe and the orchestra repeated their appearance on New York's most famous stage in 1913 and 1914.

In addition to developing "an orchestra of Negroes which will be able to take its place among the serious musical organizations of the country," Europe realized the practical importance to black musicians of taking advantage of the increasing demand for popular music to support the expansion of nightlife. From 1910 to 1914 he built the Clef Club (and later, the Tempo Club) into the greatest force for organizing and channeling the efforts of black musicians in New York, providing musicians for vaudeville orchestras, hotels, cabarets, and dance halls, as well as for private society parties and dances. In 1913, as a result of his success in providing dance orchestras for the eastern social elite, Europe was recruited as musical director for the legendary dance team of Vernon and Irene Castle. Between them, they revolutionized American social dancing by making the formerly objectionable "ragtime" dances (turkey trots and one-steps, which had been derived from traditional African-American dance practice) widely acceptable to mainstream America. The most lasting of the Castle dances, the foxtrot, was conceived by Europe and Vernon Castle after a suggestion by W. C. Handy. Europe's association with the Castles led to a recording contract with Victor Records, the first ever for a black orchestra leader.

Late in 1916 Europe enlisted in the Fifteenth Infantry Regiment (Colored) of New York's National Guard and was commissioned as a lieutenant. Largely as an aid to recruitment, he organized a regimental brass band that became, when the Fifteenth was mobilized and sent overseas, one of the most celebrated musical organizations of World War I. As a machine-gun company commander, Europe also served in the front lines and was the first black American officer in the Great War to lead troops into combat. Upon his return to the United States in early 1919, he was hailed as America's "jazz king" for incorporating blues, ragtime, and jazz elements into his arrangements for the band. He received another recording contract and embarked upon a nationwide tour. During a performance in Boston, however, Europe was cut in a backstage altercation with a mentally disturbed member of the band. The injury did not appear serious at first, but his jugular vein had in fact been punctured, and he died before the bleeding could be stopped. Europe's funeral was the first public funeral ever held for an African American in New York City; he was buried with full military honors in Arlington National Cemetery.

Although Europe was not a composer of major concert works, his more than one hundred songs, rags, waltzes, and marches include several ("On the Gay Luneta," "Castle House Rag," "Castle Walk," "Hi There," "Mirandy") that exhibit unusual lyricism and rhythmic sophistication for their day. But it was as an organizer of musicians, as a conductor who championed the works of other African-American composers, and as an arranger and orchestrator that his genius was most pronounced and his influence the greatest. In this regard Europe may properly be seen as an original catalyst in the development of orchestral jazz, initiating a line of development that would eventually lead to Fletcher Henderson and Duke Ellington. Among the many individuals who acknowledged his pioneering influence were Eubie Blake, Noble Sissle (whose epoch-making 1921 musical *Shuffle Along* helped restore black artistry to the mainstream of American musical theater), and composer George Gershwin.

See also Blake, Eubie; Burleigh, Harry; Jazz; Musical Theater

■ ■ *Bibliography*

Badger, R. Reid. "James Reese Europe and the Prehistory of Jazz." *American Music* 7 (1989): 48–68.

Badger, R. Reid. *A Life in Ragtime.* New York: Oxford, 1995.

Harris, Stephen L. *Harlem's Hell Fighters: The African-American 369th Infantry in World War I.* Washington, D.C.: Brassey's, 2003.

Welborn, Ron. "James Reese Europe and the Infancy of Jazz Criticism." *Black Music Research Journal* 7 (1987): 35–44.

R. REID BADGER (1996)
Updated bibliography

EVERETT, RONALD MCKINLEY

See Karenga, Maulana

EVERS, CHARLES

SEPTEMBER 11, 1922

Born in 1922 to an impoverished farm family in Decatur, Mississippi, civil rights leader James Charles Evers gained national prominence in 1969 when he was elected mayor of Fayette, Mississippi. Fayette was then a town of two thousand, of whom twelve hundred were African American. Evers's victory helped open the way for many black candidates who had long desired political office but who had been restricted by racial discrimination. Since Reconstruction, white southerners had prevented African Americans not just from campaigning for public office but even from exercising their constitutional right to vote. Evers became the first black mayor since Reconstruction of a biracial Mississippi town.

In 1971 the Mississippi Democratic Party unanimously nominated Evers as its candidate for governor. Although he lost the election, he was the first African American in the history of the state to be a gubernatorial candidate. From 1973 to 1981 and from 1985 to 1987, Evers served again as mayor of Fayette.

Evers first attained national recognition when he replaced his slain younger brother, Medgar Evers (widely believed to have been assassinated by a white supremacist), as Mississippi field secretary for the National Association for the Advancement of Colored People (NAACP). The elder brother, who had been in business in Chicago, returned to his home state to devote his life to the nonviolent struggle for racial equality and social justice. Toward these ends, Evers successfully led numerous boycotts and voter-registration drives. He has also served as Jefferson County, Mississippi, chancery clerk administrator. In 1997 Evers published his autobiography, *Have No Fear: The Charles Evers Story*.

See also Civil Rights Movement, U.S.; Evers, Medgar; National Association for the Advancement of Colored People (NAACP)

■ ■ *Bibliography*

Berry, Jason. *Amazing Grace: With Charles Evers in Mississippi*. New York: Saturday Review Press, 1973.

Evers, Charles, and Grace Haskell, eds. *Evers*. New York: World, 1971.

Evers, Charles, and Andrew Szanton. *Have No Fear: The Charles Evers Story*. New York: Wiley, 1997.

LOIS LYLES (1996)
Updated by publisher 2005

EVERS, MEDGAR

JULY 2, 1925
JUNE 12, 1963

▐▐▐

The civil rights activist Medgar Wylie Evers was born in Decatur, Mississippi, served in World War II, graduated

Civil rights leader Medgar Evers (1925–1963). *Evers was shot and killed outside his home in Mississippi after returning from an integration rally.* AP/WIDE WORLD PHOTOS. REPRODUCED BY PERMISSION.

from Alcorn Agricultural and Mechanical College, and became an insurance agent. Refused admission to the University of Mississippi's law school, he became the first Mississippi field director of the National Association for the Advancement of Colored People (NAACP).

Evers's job entailed investigating the murders of blacks in Mississippi, including that of Emmett Till; local police generally dismissed such cases as accidents. A clear target for violence, Evers bought a car big enough to resist being forced off the road, roomy enough to sleep in where motels were segregated, and powerful enough for quick escapes. His family owned guns and kept the window blinds drawn. Evers received daily death threats but always tried reasoning with callers.

He led voter registration drives and fought segregation; organized consumer boycotts to integrate Leake County schools and the Mississippi State Fair; assisted James Meredith in entering the University of Mississippi; and won a lawsuit integrating Jackson's privately owned buses. He also began a similar effort with Jackson's public parks.

In May 1963, Evers's house was bombed. At a June NAACP rally he declared, "Freedom has never been free. . . . I would die, and die gladly, if that would make a better life for [my family]."

On June 12, Evers arrived home in the middle of the night. His wife heard his car door slam, then heard gunshots. He died that night; his accused murderer was acquitted, despite compelling evidence against him. Evers was buried at Arlington National Cemetery.

See also Civil Rights Movement, U.S.; Meredith, James H.; National Association for the Advancement of Colored People (NAACP); Till, Emmett Louis

■ ■ *Bibliography*

Evers, Myrlie, with William Peters. *For Us, the Living.* Garden City, N.Y.: Doubleday, 1967.

Morris, Willie. *The Ghosts of Medgar Evers: A Tale of Race, Murder, Mississippi, and Hollywood.* New York: Random House, 1998.

Wilbert, Lauren. "Medgar Evers' Death Commemorated at Arlington Cemetary." *Knight Ridder/Tribune News Service,* June 16, 2003, p. K5684.

Williams, Juan. *Eyes on the Prize: America's Civil Rights Years, 1954–1965.* New York: Viking, 1987.

ELIZABETH FORTSON ARROYO (1996)
Updated bibliography

EXODUSTERS

See Migration/Population, U.S.

EXPERIMENTAL THEATER

▪▪▪ ━━━━━━━━━━━━━━━━━━━━━━━━━━━

Experimental theater after the black arts movement is a loosely-related body of work that offers new ways of experiencing drama, reconsidering history, and interpreting black identity. Indebted to the theatrical, poetic, and performance trends of the black arts movement, especially its political and aesthetic innovations, experimental theater has both worked with and against the anti-assimilationist impulses of the black arts movement to create work that explores how black theater should engage with the world. Whereas the artists of the black arts movement sought to define a doctrine of black art as a collective vision, experimental theater relies on individual artists to articulate their own.

Despite this attention to individual vision, experimental theater embraces many elements of the black arts

movement theater, including the "nonobjective," African-American history, black vernacular, poetry, and interdisciplinary art collaboration. The nonobjective was a strategy for challenging an audience's passive engagement with the theater by providing an opportunity for them to "live through" the event they had come to see. In Ed Bullins's play *The Theme Is Blackness* (1973), the nonobjective was realized as a performance of blackness—which in this case was the absence of light. When seated, the audience was told that the night's theme was blackness. All lights were turned out for twenty minutes. Lights were then turned up to announce a curtain call for blackness and turned out once more. Amiri Baraka's *Slave Ship* (1969) exposed audiences to the sounds and smells of Africans being tortured during their journey across the Atlantic. Instead of focusing on enacting a story, the nonobjective created a visceral experience that would stay with the audience after the performance.

Black arts movement theater also mined African-American history to expose the truth about slavery, segregation, and racial violence inflicted on African Americans. Because plays were written to appeal primarily to younger African-American audiences, black vernacular was featured prominently to connote the youth, social intelligence, and political awareness of characters. Poetry also thrived during the black arts movement. Independent presses such as Dudley Randall's Broadside Press in Detroit and Haki Madhubuti's Third World Press in Chicago published new voices to great international acclaim. Strong theatre and poetry communities helped to foster collaboration with artists from other disciplines including music and the visual arts. The Nuyorican Poets Café in New York, founded in 1973 by Miguel Algarin, served as an incubator for this kind of work. Eventually works that combined theater, poetry, dance, music, and visual art came to signify the broad aesthetics of experimental theater.

Experimental theater was also influenced by other artistic movements during the 1960s and 1970s, especially "happenings" and feminist performance art. Happenings, also called "the painter's theater," emerged in New York and echoed the impulses in abstract expressionist painting through presentations of public spectacle and action. Unlike traditional theatrical events, happenings did not require there to be a distinction between the actors and audience. Instead it was the crowd's response to an array of visual, aural, or textual stimuli that determined the meaning of the event. Happenings encouraged discussions about how art exists in time. Feminist performance art also help to define "live art" through the presentation of action-oriented art. Influenced by the activism of the civil

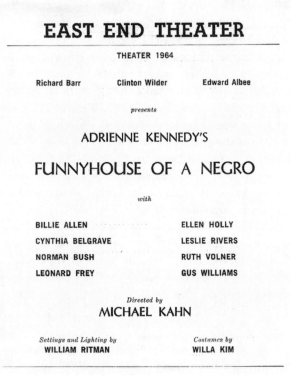

EAST END THEATER

THEATER 1964

Richard Barr   Clinton Wilder   Edward Albee

presents

ADRIENNE KENNEDY'S

FUNNYHOUSE OF A NEGRO

with

BILLIE ALLEN	ELLEN HOLLY
CYNTHIA BELGRAVE	LESLIE RIVERS
NORMAN BUSH	RUTH VOLNER
LEONARD FREY	GUS WILLIAMS

Directed by
MICHAEL KAHN

Settings and Lighting by   *Costumes by*
WILLIAM RITMAN   **WILLA KIM**

Playbill for Funnyhouse of a Negro, 1964. Adrienne Kennedy's first one-act play addressed experiences of racial confusion and ambivalence. PLAYBILL® IS A REGISTERED TRADEMARK OF PLAYBILL INCORPORATED, N.Y.C. ALL RIGHTS RESERVED. REPRODUCED BY PERMISSION.

rights and antiwar movements, feminist performance art aimed to challenge entrenched ideas about gender, sexuality, and women's rights. During the 1970s conceptual artists Adrian Piper, Judy Chicago, and Yoko Ono pulled performance works out of gallery spaces and academic institutions where they were most commonly seen and brought them into the communities in which they were most relevant. Many of these works were about breaking taboos associated with women's bodies. For example, Hannah Wilke and Carolee Schneeman attempted to reclaim female power and identity through performances involving nudity and obsessive self-admiration. Feminist performance art also addressed gender inequities in the art world and brought attention to the ways various people had been excluded from participating in it. Repercussions from this movement reverberated across cultures and helped to create an audience for new works in experimental theatre, especially those created by African-American women.

KEY ARTISTS/WORKS

At once culturally rooted and innovative, experimental theater has been shaped by a variety of artists working across genres, including Adrienne Kennedy, Ntozake Shange, Robbie MacCauley, Laurie Carlos, Bill T. Jones, Suzan-Lori Parks, and Paul D. Miller, also known as "DJ Spooky."

The lyrical dramas of Adrienne Kennedy (b. 1931) were largely overlooked by other black playwrights during the black arts movement, but since then she has emerged as one of the most important and undervalued voices in experimental theater. Her first one-act play, *Funnyhouse of a Negro* (1964), addressed experiences of racial confusion and ambivalence and was largely tragic in its depiction of a young woman's failed attempt to reconcile conflicts between her black and white ancestors. Other works addressing similar themes include *A Movie Star Has to Star in Black and White* (1976), *The Owl Answers* (1966), and *The Ohio State Murders* (1991). Kennedy's carefully wrought, poetic one-act plays borrow from films and other literary texts, including her own plays, in order to offer portraits of identity that reveal personal and psychological crises of racial identification. Her fragmentary and cinematic approach to autobiography reveals how the constant threat of violence shapes the real and imaginary worlds within the black experience.

Kennedy's plays helped to re-center the African-American woman as a vital subject for investigating culture and gender during a time when the particularity of the black woman's experience had been largely ignored. African-American women had also been excluded from much of the feminist performance art and theater taking place during the 1970s and would as a result have much to say over the next several decades. By the time that Ntozake Shange's (b. 1948) Obie-award-winning choreopoem, *For Colored Girls Who Have Considered Suicide, When the Rainbow is Enuf,* opened in 1975, theater by and about black women was starting to be acknowledged for its broad vision politically and aesthetically. *For Colored Girls* was told through dance, poetry, and song, and it revealed sensitive portraits of young, black women facing the repercussions of racial and gender bias, violence against women, and misogyny within the black community. The play was revolutionary in that it presented characters whose lives had never before been seen on stage.

Robbie MacCauley (b. 1942) performed in Shange's *For Colored Girls* and Kennedy's *A Movie Star* early in her career and eventually moved on to writing and directing her own work. Her 1991 piece *Sally's Rape* examines "the silences around racism in America that have gotten nailed in place" while recounting the life and survival of her

A scene from For Colored Girls Who Have Considered Suicide/ When The Rainbow is Enuf. *Ntozake Shange's 1977 Obie Award-winning play centers on a series of twenty poems dealing with the lives of black women.* PHOTOGRAPH BY MARTHA SWOPE. REPRODUCED BY PERMISSION.

great-great-grandmother, a slave on a Georgia plantation. This provocative piece expects participation from the audience during the most climatic scene. MacCauley stands naked on an auction block, inviting the audience to bid on her body. With this, she brings attention to the sale and sexual abuse of her great-great grandmother and, ultimately, the audience's complicity with this history. *My Father and the Wars* (1992) addresses her relationship with her father and his military service. *Indian Blood* (1994) also considers an ancestral relationship, this time her grandfather's participation in the genocide of his own people. MacCauley has called these pieces metaphors for an African-American family surviving against racism.

Like MacCauley, Laurie Carlos (b. 1949) starred in Shange's *For Colored Girls*. Her work integrates movement, language, and music to uncover what Africanness means for African Americans: A character in one of her early pieces asks the question "Is we still black? Still black?" Her 1992 work, *White Chocolate for My Father,* explores stories of racial persecution through Carlos's own matriar-

chal line. Ritual is often a powerful component of her pieces, which also show how language has the ability to injure and heal. Other original works inspired by real women's experiences include *Organdy Falsetto* (1986), *The Cooking Show* (1997), and *Marion's Terrible Time of Joy* (2003), which blends poetry, art, and food to explore the mingled borders of African and Indian origins. As a director and dramaturge, Carlos has helped to shape the artistic direction of many black independent theater companies, including Urban Bush Women in New York and Penumbra in Minnesota, which is also the longest-running black theater in the United States.

Whereas dance was not considered a significant component of black arts movement theater, choreographers such as Carlos, Jawole Willa Jo Zollar of Urban Bush Women, Rennie Harris, and dancer/choreographer Bill T. Jones (b. 1952) have expanded the dimensions of experimental theater to include dance as a primary means of storytelling. Jones's career began in Binghamton, New York, in 1971 after he met Arnie Zane. They founded the Ameri-

Bill T. Jones. *Jones, the acclaimed dancer and cofounder of the Bill T. Jones/Arnie Zane Dance Company, is pictured here in 1996, performing his dance Ballad, which is set to the poems of Dylan Thomas.* © JOHAN ELBERS 1997. REPRODUCED BY PERMISSION.

can Dance Asylum in 1973. In 1982 they created the Bill T. Jones/Arnie Zane Dance Company, which created pieces dealing with sexuality, racism, and power structures that maintain discrimination. Some of the company's key works include *Intuitive Momentum* (1982), *Secret Pastures* (1984) with sets by Keith Haring, and *History of Collage* (1988). When Zane died of AIDS in 1988, Jones took over full artistic direction of the company and created such pieces as *Last Supper at Uncle Tom's Cabin/Promised Land* (1990), *The Mother of Three Sons* (1990), and *Still Here* (1994). As part of *Still Here,* Jones created workshops for survivors of serious illnesses. Their voices were woven in and out of the performance and gave a sense of history told through individual lives. Through these community discussions and his own personal experiences, Jones articulated a vocabulary of movement to represent coping strategies for survival.

Playwright Suzan-Lori Parks (b. 1964) addresses the question of individual survival through dark and poetic satires of the American experience. Her 1999 play, *In the Blood,* contemporizes Nathaniel Hawthorne's 1850 novel *The Scarlet Letter,* only this time Hester is a homeless black woman living with her five children on the streets of New York. This parody addresses racism, gender, and social injustice and questions double-standards of morality. *Venus: A Play* (1996) recounts the exploitation of Saartje Benjamin, otherwise known as the Venus Hottentot, through her own eyes. In 2001 Parks won the Pulitzer Prize for *Topdog/Underdog,* which tells the story of two brothers, Lincoln and Booth, whose names portend a lifetime of sibling rivalry and resentment. Other major plays include *Imperceptible Mutabilities in the Third Kingdom* (1989), *The Death of the Last Black Man in the Whole Entire World* (1990), *Devotees in the Garden of Love* (1992), and *The America Play* (1993).

Whereas much theatrical innovation has taken place within the traditional stage environment, a new generation of multimedia artists are creating work that is impacting African-American drama at large. Paul D. Miller (b. 1970) is best known under the moniker of his "constructed persona" as "DJ Spooky that Subliminal Kid." His live remix of DW Griffith's *Birth of a Nation* (1915), titled *Rebirth of a Nation* (2004), recuts the film's original narrative and infuses it with new short films by Bill T. Jones. The score includes sampled and scored music remixed for the occasion of each screening. The piece allows audiences to interrogate the distinctions between cinematic manipulations of narrative and their acceptance or rejection of that manipulation.

Whether experimental theater is highly conceptual and or rich with personal history, it offers audiences the opportunity to follow an individual artist's aesthetic and political journey through the nuances of the black experience and leaves each artist to articulate his or her own ideas about what it is that makes theater black.

See also Drama; Kennedy, Adrienne; Parks, Suzan-Lori; Performance Art

■ ■ *Bibliography*

Algarin, Miguel, and Bob Holman, eds. Voices *from the Nuyorican Poets Café.* New York: Owl Books, 1994.

Elam, Harry J., and David Krasner. *African American Performance and Theater History: A Critical Reader.* Oxford, UK: Oxford University Press, 2001.

Goldberg, Rosalee. *Performance: Live Art since 1960.* London: Harry N. Abrams, 1998.

Hay, Samuel A. *African American Theater: An Historical and Critical Analysis.* Cambridge, UK: Cambridge University Press, 1994.

Jones, Bill T. *Last Night on Earth.* New York: Pantheon Books, 1995.

Kennedy, Adrienne. *The Adrienne Kennedy Reader.* Minneapolis: University of Minnesota Press, 2001.

Mahone, Sydne. *Moon Marked and Touched by the Sun.* New York: Theatre Communications Group, 1994.

Parks, Suzan-Lori. *The America Play and Other Works.* New York: Theatre Communications Group, 1995.

Parks, Suzan-Lori. *Venus: A Play.* New York: Theatre Communications Group, 1997.

Parks, Suzan-Lori. *Red Letter Plays.* New York: Theatre Communications Group, 2000.

Parks, Suzan-Lori. *Topdog/Underdog.* New York: Theatre Communications Group, 2002.

Williams, Saul. *S/he.* New York: MTV Books, 1999.

WENDY S. WALTERS (2005)

FANON, FRANTZ

JULY 20, 1925

DECEMBER 6, 1961

▮▮▮

Frantz Fanon was born on the French Caribbean island of Martinique. His father was a customs clerk, and his mother supplemented the family's income by running a variety store out of their home. There were eight children in this middle-class black family—four boys and four girls. Fanon attended the island's lycée, where he studied with the influential *Négritude* poet Aimé Césaire (1913–), who said that it was both beautiful and good to be black. It was during these years that the Nazi-controlled Vichy government of France (1940–1944) sent five thousand raucous white sailors to Martinique. Fanon escaped to the island of Dominica in 1943, where he joined the French Resistance and fought in North Africa and Europe. He returned to Martinique after the war with two decorations for bravery and the conviction that racism was a problem of European civilization in general, not only Vichy France. He then went to Paris to study dentistry, but he instead chose to study psychiatry in Lyon. It was there that he met and married Marie-Josèphe (Josie) Dublé, a Marxist journalist, with whom he had a son. (He also had a daughter from

a previous, short-lived relationship with a Martiniquan woman.) Fanon earned his medical degree in 1951, and the following year he received his license to serve as director of any psychiatric ward in the French-speaking world. In 1953 he accepted a post as the director of psychiatry at the Blida-Joinville Hospital in Algeria.

Fanon's psychiatric practice is legendary. He implemented a system of humanistic therapy, the success of which his fellow physicians attributed to his energy and charisma. Everything changed, however, at the advent of the Algerian War (1954–1962). Fanon secretly joined the Algerian rebels, the Front des Libération Nationale (National Liberation Front, or FLN), at the outset, but he resigned from his post in 1956 and made his membership in the FLN public. He became an outlaw in France and its colonies, which led to several attempts on his life over the next three years. Yet he managed to remain active as a medical researcher and writer, while serving as a negotiator for the FLN. By 1960 his health had deteriorated considerably, and he was diagnosed with leukemia. He went to the Soviet Union in search of treatment, but the Soviet physicians informed him that the best treatment was in the United States, in Bethesda, Maryland. After planning some projects and completing his last book, *Les damnés de la terre* (The wretched of the earth, 1961) he went to Bethesda, where he was detained for ten days without treatment by the Central Intelligence Agency (CIA). He developed pneumonia and died on December 6, 1961.

Fanon completed three books in his lifetime. His first, *Peau noire, masques blancs* (Black skin, white masks, 1952) offers his sociogenic theory of racial identity and oppression. This theory foregrounds contemporary theories of the role of society in the development of racial identity and prejudices. In this book, Fanon argues that mainstream psychology cannot alleviate the alienation of black people because it offers no livable model of a normal black adult. He urges people in colonized nations to fight against oppressive social systems and become questioning, critical human beings.

L'an v de la révolution algérienne (Year five of the Algerian revolution, translated into English as *Studies in a Dying Colonialism,* 1959), Fanon's second book, defends his view that colonized people must seize their freedom. His main point is that fighting for national independence awakens new ways of living in the world of colonized people. This means changing traditions, developing new relationships with technology (the radio), medicine, the family, and former white settlers.

The theme of seizing freedom returns in Fanon's most famous work, *The Wretched of the Earth.* Colonized people, he contends, face either demanding but not seizing their freedom and being welcomed by their colonizers as "nonviolent," or fighting for their freedom and being called "violent" by their opposition. He advocates the latter, arguing for the therapeutic value of violence. He also criticizes third world elites for propping themselves up as mediators with the old regimes and creating a neocolonial condition in which they become its new pillagers rather than building up their nation. The new struggle, then, is to fight this elite in the hope of achieving a genuine postcolonial society. Fanon closes the book with a call to build up the nation's material infrastructure (its roads, reservoirs, hospitals, and schools), and he asks colonized people to develop new ways of knowing and understanding themselves as human beings, to "shed our skin and set afoot a new humanity" (Fanon, 1961/1991; quotation translated by Lewis R. Gordon).

Finally, a collection of essays that includes his very prescient "Racism and Culture" was compiled and edited by his widow, Marie-Josèphe Fanon, and published in English in 1967 as *Toward the African Revolution.* Fanon's four books have been an influential legacy that continues to grow, though the author died when he was only thirty-six years of age. Leaders of the Black Panthers in the United States called *The Wretched of the Earth* "the textbook of the Revolution." The field of postcolonial studies has benefited significantly from his critique of colonialism,

and his discussion of race and colonialism in the Caribbean has made him one of the most influential thinkers on contemporary Caribbean culture and society.

See also Anti-colonial Movements; Psychology and Psychologists: Race Issues

■ ■ *Bibliography*

Bulhan, Hussein Abdilahi. *Frantz Fanon and the Psychology of Opression.* New York: Plenum, 1985.

Fanon, Frantz. *Wretched of the Earth.* Translated by Constance Farrington. New York: Grove Press, 1965.

Fanon, Frantz. *Studies in a Dying Colonialism.* Translated by Haakon Chevalier. New York: Monthly Review Press, 1965.

Fanon, Frantz. *Toward the African revolution: Political essays.* Translated by Haakon Chevalier. New York: Monthly Review Press, 1967.

Fanon, Frantz. *Black Skin, White Masks.* Translated by Charles Lam Markman. New York: Grove Press, 1967.

Fanon, Frantz. *Les damnés de la terre.* Preface by Jean-Paul Sartre. Paris: François Maspero, 1961; reprint, Paris: Éditions Gallimard, 1991.

Gibson, Nigel C. *Fanon: The Postcolonial Imagination.* Cambridge, UK: Polity Press, 2003.

Gibson, Nigel C., ed. *Rethinking Fanon.* Amherst, N.Y.: Humanity Books, 1999.

Gordon, Lewis R. *Fanon and the Crisis of European Man: An Essay on Philosophy and the Human Sciences.* New York: Routledge, 1995.

Gordon, Lewis R., T. Denean Sharpley-Whiting, and Renée T. White, eds. *Fanon: A Critical Reader.* Oxford: Blackwell, 1996.

Sekyi-Out, Ato. *Fanon's Dialectic of Experience.* Cambridge, Mass.: Harvard University Press, 1996.

Zahar, Renate. *Frantz Fanon: Colonialism and Alienation.* Translated by Willfried F. Feuser. New York: Monthly Review Press, 1974.

LEWIS R. GORDON (2005)

FARD, WALLACE D.

BIRTHDATE UNKNOWN
DISAPPEARED C. 1934

❚❚❚

Little is known about the mysterious religious and political leader Wallace D. Fard, credited with founding the Nation of Islam. Only the years of 1930 to 1934 are clearly documented. He claimed to have been born in Mecca, a member of the tribe of Kureish, to which the Prophet Muhammad belonged, and to have been educated in England and at the University of California. His detractors claimed he had been jailed in California for dealing in narcotics. Neither of these accounts of his life was ever confirmed.

Fard appeared in Detroit sometime before 1930, peddling silks and raincoats and declaring that he was on a mission to secure justice, freedom, and equality for American blacks. He professed that he was an Islamic prophet and that redemption would come through Islam. Fard quickly gained a following, especially among recent immigrants from the South who were undergoing severe economic hardship. In 1930 he set up permanent headquarters for what he called the "Lost-Found Nation of Islam" in the Temple of Islam. He also organized the Fruit of Islam, a defense corps; the Muslim Girls Training Corps Class; and the University of Islam, a radically unconventional elementary and high school that Muslim children attended instead of public schools. Fard began the practice of substituting X for black Muslims' last names—disavowing their identities as slaves. The names were intended to be replaced later by their "original" Arabic names.

Fard asserted that blacks were the first people on earth, indicating their superiority to whites, whom he castigated as devils. Fard was a reputed nationalist, calling for racial separatism and self-determination in the form of an independent black republic within current U.S. borders.

The Nation of Islam gained mainstream public attention in Detroit in November 1932 when one of its members, Robert Karriem, "sacrificed" his boarder, a fellow Nation member, by plunging a knife into his heart. Press reports tried to link this crime to his involvement in the Nation of Islam. The movement, however, continued. After converting an estimated eight thousand Detroit blacks to the Nation of Islam, Fard disappeared in late 1933 or 1934. His followers used the mysterious circumstances of Fard's disappearance to deify him further, maintaining that he was God, although his successor as the Nation's head, Elijah Muhammad (1897–1975), claimed to have accompanied him to the airport when he was deported.

While Wallace Fard clearly was important in the 1930s, his legacy in the large and influential Nation of Islam is more significant. Although his tenure with the organization was short, he continued to be revered as its spiritual leader. The Nation of Islam stated in an official publication in 1942, "We believe that Allah appeared in the person of Master W. Fard Muhammad, July 1930; the long-awaited 'Messiah' of the Christians and the 'Mahdi' of the Muslims."

See also Malcolm X; Muhammad, Elijah; Nation of Islam

■ ■ *Bibliography*

Evanzz, Karl. *The Judas Factor: The Plot to Kill Malcolm X.* New York: Pub Group West, 1992.

White, John. *Black Leadership in America: From Booker T. Washington to Jesse Jackson.* New York: Addison-Wesley Pub. Co., 1990.

SIRAJ AHMED (1996)

FARMER, JAMES

JANUARY 12, 1920
JULY 9, 1999

Civil rights leader and educator James Farmer was born in Holly Springs, Mississippi, where his father was a minister and professor at Rust College. The family moved when Farmer's father took a post at Wiley College in Marshall, Texas. Farmer grew up in Marshall and was educated at Wiley College and at Howard University, where he received a bachelor of divinity degree in 1941. During this time he became interested in the philosophy of nonviolence espoused by Mahatma Gandhi in his movement for India's independence. Farmer refused to become ordained to serve a segregated Methodist congregation (he was committed to interracial forums), and his pacifist ideas and opposition to army segregation led him to oppose the wartime draft. Exempted from service by his ministerial background, Farmer dedicated himself to pacifist and civil rights causes.

Shortly after graduating from Howard in 1941, Farmer took a job as race-relations secretary of the pacifist group Fellowship of Reconciliation (FOR). In 1942, while living in Chicago, he drew up plans for a civil rights group operating on Gandhian principles, and set up an organization with aid from some University of Chicago students. Farmer became the first executive director of the Chicago-based organization named the Congress of Racial Equality (CORE). Farmer was a committed integrationist, and CORE's early leadership was predominantly white. The congress remained small, and in 1946 Farmer tired of bureaucratic struggles with FOR and gave up his leadership role to work as a labor organizer for trade unions, and later as a civil rights campaigner for the National Association for the Advancement of Colored People (NAACP). He remained involved with CORE as a field worker.

In 1960, after the Montgomery bus boycott and sit-ins had made nonviolent protest a widespread civil rights tool, Farmer returned to leadership of CORE, by now based in New York City. In spring of 1961 he organized the first Freedom Rides, which were designed to desegregate buses and terminals in the South and publicize denials of civil rights. During the effort Farmer was jailed for forty days—the first of many such imprisonments during the days of the civil rights movement as CORE contingents participated in strikes, sit-ins, voter-education programs, and demonstrations, both in the South and in the North. As CORE's national director, Farmer was one of the foremost leaders of the civil rights movement and participated in its major campaigns. His eloquent speaking voice and manner made him a popular lecturer and debater. He wrote many articles and essays, and his 1965 book *Freedom, When?* dealt with the problem of institutionalized inequality and the debate over nonviolence as a protest tactic.

One of Farmer's significant efforts during his years in CORE was his ongoing attempt to improve the position of blacks in the job market and in labor unions. Realizing that African Americans faced disadvantages in schooling and training, Farmer pushed the idea of "compensatory" action by employers and government, including programs for the hiring of numbers of black workers proportionate with a labor pool, and their training in job skills, when necessary. These ideas were a major ingredient in the formation of affirmative action policies.

By 1966, as CORE turned away from its original integrationist goals and nonviolent tactics in civil rights action, Farmer decided to leave the organization. For two years he taught social welfare at Lincoln University in Pennsylvania. In 1968 Farmer, who had long been active in New York's Liberal Party, ran for Congress in Brooklyn on the Liberal and Republican tickets but was defeated by African-American Democrat Shirley Chisholm.

The following year Farmer faced a storm of criticism when he accepted the post of assistant secretary of Health, Education, and Welfare (HEW) in Richard Nixon's Republican administration. Farmer, who felt blacks should reach out to all political parties, was given the job of increasing minority participation in government. He soon grew dissatisfied with his role in HEW, however, and resigned in 1971.

In 1972 Farmer set up the Council on Minority Planning and Strategy, a black think tank, but was unable to secure sufficient funding. In 1975 he became active with the Fund for an Open Society, and from 1977 through 1982 he served as executive director of the Coalition of American Public Employees. Starting in 1982 and continuing through the early 1990s, he taught at Mary Washington College in Fredericksburg, Virginia. He continued to be a strong speaker for black equality, although he remained out of the political arena. In his later years Farmer

developed retinal vascular occlusion, a rare eye disease, and lost all vision in one eye and some vision in the other. Still, he managed to complete a volume of memoirs, *Lay Bare the Heart*, in 1985. Farmer's forceful leadership and eloquence combined with his dedication to nonviolent principles made him one of the central figures of the civil rights movement in the 1960s.

In 1998 Farmer was awarded the Presidential Medal of Freedom. He died in 1999, and in 2001 a memorial in his honor was unveiled on the campus of Mary Washington College.

See also Congress of Racial Equality (CORE); Howard University; Montgomery, Ala., Bus Boycott

■ ■ *Bibliography*

Farmer, James. *Lay Bare the Heart: An Autobiography of the Civil Rights Movement.* New York: New American Library, 1985.

Meier, August, and Elliot Rudwick. *CORE: A Study in the Civil Rights Movement.* New York: Oxford University Press, 1973.

Rosen, Sumner M. "James Farmer, 1920–1999." *Social Policy* 30, no. 2 (1999): 47.

STEVEN J. LESLIE (1996)
Updated by publisher 2005

FARM WORKER PROGRAM

━┫┣━━━━━━━━━━━━━━━━━━━

From 1943 to 1947, under the terms of intergovernmental agreements with British West Indian governments, the U.S. government recruited and transported approximately seventy thousand Jamaicans, Barbadians, and Bahamians to the United States for agricultural employment. The stimulus for the agreements came from American farmers, especially large growers, who complained to the federal government that they were experiencing a shortage of farm labor. Many rural men and women entered the armed forces during World War II, while others escaped the low wages of farmwork for the better wages offered in the expanding defense industry. As men and women deserted the farms, farmers became increasingly concerned about their dwindling supply of labor, and although there was no severe scarcity of domestic workers, the federal government was convinced to create an emergency program to alleviate labor shortages on farms.

Concurrent with American growers' struggle to recruit labor, the Caribbean was experiencing extreme economic devastation and political upheaval. In the late 1930s, high levels of unemployment and sociopolitical unrest led to riots throughout the Commonwealth Caribbean. Colonial administrations had only begun to propose remedies to the problems that gave impetus to the riots when World War II began. Additionally, wartime restrictions on shipping created food shortages and devastated the tourist industry in the Bahamas and on other islands, thereby exacerbating the already high levels of unemployment. These conditions encouraged Caribbean administrations and colonial authorities in Great Britain to support the American plan to transport West Indians to the United States for farmwork.

Jamaican officials were hopeful that the proposed American farmworker program would employ thousands of men between the ages of twenty-five and forty-four, the demographic with the highest unemployment rate. Such a program would alleviate some of the island's unemployment problems. They also expected the farmworkers' compulsory savings and remittances home to be an additional benefit, particularly as the money the farmworkers earned in a few months in the United Sates would take an entire year to earn in Jamaica. In fact, between the launching of the farm labor program in 1943 and its termination in 1947, West Indian farmworkers remitted to their home islands more than $40 million.

For these reasons, the United States successfully secured agreements with the government of the Bahamas (on March 16, 1943) and the government of Jamaica (on April 2, 1943) to bring West Indian labor to the United States. These two agreements established the British West Indies (BWI) Temporary Alien Labor Program. Barbadians were initially excluded because of the greater distance involved and additional transportation costs. The Barbadian governor urged their inclusion, however, and by 1944, Barbadians were employed on U.S. farms. Jamaicans always accounted for the largest number of Caribbean foreign workers in the United States, second only to the Mexican *braceros* (workers) employed on the West Coast.

The first Bahamian men and women arrived in the United States in April 1943 and one month later Jamaicans joined them (only men were recruited from Jamaica). In 1943 more than eleven thousand Jamaican men were employed in the United States. They were dispersed throughout fourteen states, including approximately 1,150 in Connecticut, 2,700 in Indiana, 950 in Michigan, 1,600 in New Jersey, and 2,000 in New York. In 1945, roughly 33,000 Jamaicans were employed in thirty-eight of the forty-eight states. Jamaican men worked on seasonal crops, which required significant hand labor in cultivation and harvest. Most were employed along the eastern sea-

board from Florida to Maine. Workers harvested rhubarb, asparagus, peas, spinach, and beets in Pennsylvania; picked strawberries, spinach, onions, and potatoes in New York and New Jersey; worked on tobacco farms in Connecticut; and even helped bring in the sugar beet crops in Idaho and Michigan. During each contract period, Jamaican men were relocated from one locality to the next, with most ending the season cutting cane in Florida.

Since the fall of 1943, Jamaican men have cut cane in Florida. When the first 1943 intergovernmental agreement between Jamaica and the United States was signed, however, Jamaican men were not allowed to receive employment in southern states. Given the racial climate in the American South, colonial officials feared for the well-being of Jamaican men. However, pressure exerted by large citrus and sugarcane growers eventually led to a reversal of this policy. The first Jamaican men arrived in Clewiston, Florida, in early October 1943 via Michigan, and men later poured in from Connecticut and other New England states, where employment in the winter months was impracticable. The Jamaican men sent to Florida were contracted to work for the United States Sugar Corporation, a large agricultural company known for its Jim Crow–style working conditions and extremely low wages. Those that protested the corporation's unfair treatment or excessively low wages were subject to unlawful imprisonment, repatriation, and physical abuse.

According to the intergovernmental agreement, West Indian farmworkers were employed by the U.S. government, not individual farmers, and they were thus guaranteed basic protections. Each worker signed a contract with the U.S. government detailing the government's obligations. The agreements stated that workers would receive a minimum of thirty cents an hour, be provided employment for at least 75 percent of the time, be housed in sanitary facilities maintained or approved by the U.S. government, and receive "all necessary food, health and medical care and other subsistence living facilities." Despite the contract provisions, however, workers complained that housing, food, and wage standards were frequently disregarded. In the summer of 1943, some Jamaicans employed with small Michigan beet growers were housed in fairground cattle exhibition sheds; in 1944, in Ohio, the men were housed in garages. Those not housed with their employers were placed in government camps called Farm Labor Supply Centers. These facilities were not permanent structures and usually were very basic accommodations, in either Army-issued tents or prefabricated wooden huts. The quantity and quality of the food served in the camps was also a point of great frustration. Because of wartime rationing, certain food items, especially the products Jamaican men liked the most—meat, sugar, and rice—were in very short supply. Yet, more than any other issue, dissatisfaction over wages was the most contentious. Jamaican men's contract stated, "there shall be no strikes, lockouts, or stoppages of work during the period of employment," but they frequently organized work stoppages and used other creative tactics to force farmers to improve their wages and comply with contract standards.

On April 28, 1947, Congress terminated the wartime British West Indies Temporary Alien Labor Program, although the program did not officially conclude until December 31, 1947. On January 1, 1948, the wartime program was replaced by a system of individual contracts between American employers and Jamaican men. Employers wanting Jamaican farmworkers could, with authorization from the Immigration and Naturalization Service, recruit within Jamaica or other West Indian islands. The disadvantage of the post-1947 agreements was that each contract was concluded after separate negotiations with individual employers. In 1952 this temporary system received permanent sanction when the Department of Labor, under section H-2A of the new Immigration Nationality Act, authorized American employers to contract with West Indian men for farm work. The H-2A program permitted American farmers to hire foreign workers if they could prove that no domestic workers wanted the jobs, and it gave employers complete discretion in where and how to recruit workers. Since 1952, American employers have recruited in Jamaica, St. Lucia, St. Vincent, Dominica, and Barbados, although Jamaicans have remained the largest group of West Indian farmworkers. Many have continued to pick citrus fruits and cut sugarcane in Florida, while others pick apples in New York and New England. Under the H-2A provisions, problems of housing, food, wages, and general mistreatment of Jamaican farm workers continue to beleaguer the program into the twenty-first century, just as they did during World War II.

■ ■ *Bibliography*

Hahamovitch, Cindy. "'In America Life Is Given Away': Jamaican Farmworkers and the Making of Agricultural Immigration Policy." In *The Countryside in the Age of the Modern State: Political Histories of Rural America*, edited by Catherine McNicol Stock and Robert D. Johnston. Ithaca, N.Y.: Cornell University Press, 2001.

Manuel-Scott, Wendi N. "Soldiers of the Field: Jamaican Farm Workers in the United States during World War II." Ph.D. diss., Howard University, Washington, D.C., 2003.

Rasmussen, Wayne D. *A History of the Emergency Farm Labor Supply Program, 1943–1947.* Agriculture Monograph No. 133. Washington, D.C.: U.S. Department of Agriculture, Bureau of Agricultural Economics, 1951.

Wood, Charles H., and Terry L. McCoy. "Caribbean Cane Cutters in Florida: Implication for the Study of the Internationalization of Labor." In *The Americas in the New International Division of Labor,* edited by Steven Sanderson. New York: Holmes and Meier, 1985.

WENDI N. MANUEL-SCOTT (2005)

FARRAKHAN, LOUIS

MAY 17, 1933

■ ■ ■

Louis Eugene Walcott was born in the Bronx, New York, but was raised in Boston by his West Indian mother. Deeply religious, Walcott faithfully attended the Episcopalian church in his neighborhood and became an altar boy. With the rigorous discipline provided by his mother and his church, he did fairly well academically and graduated with honors from the prestigious Boston English High School, where he also participated on the track team and played the violin in the school orchestra.

In 1953, after two years at the Winston-Salem Teachers College in North Carolina, Walcott dropped out to pursue his favorite avocation of music and made it his first career. An accomplished violinist, pianist, and vocalist, he performed professionally on the Boston nightclub circuit as a singer of calypso and country songs. In 1955, at the age of twenty-two, Malcolm X recruited him for the Nation of Islam. Following its custom, he dropped his surname and took an X, which meant "undetermined." However, it was not until he had met Elijah Muhammad, the supreme leader of the Nation of Islam, on a visit to the Chicago headquarters that Louis X converted and dedicated his life to building the Nation. After Louis X proved himself for ten years, Elijah Muhammad gave him his Muslim name, "Abdul Haleem Farrakhan," in May 1965. As a rising star within the Nation, Farrakhan also wrote the only song, the popular "A White Man's Heaven is a Black Man's Hell," and the only dramatic play, Orgena ("A Negro" spelled backward), endorsed by Muhammad.

After a nine-month apprenticeship with Malcolm X at Temple No. 7 in Harlem, Minister Farrakhan was appointed as the head minister of the Boston Temple No. 11, which Malcolm founded. Later, after Malcolm X had split with the Nation, Farrakhan was awarded Malcolm's Temple No. 7, the most important pastorate in the Nation after the Chicago headquarters. He was also appointed national spokesman or national representative after Malcolm left the Nation in 1964 and began to introduce Elijah Muhammad at Savior Day rallies, a task that had once belonged to Malcolm. Like his predecessor, Farrakhan is a dynamic and charismatic leader and a powerful speaker with an ability to appeal to masses of black people.

In February 1975, when Elijah Muhammad died, the Nation of Islam experienced its largest schism. Wallace Dean Muhammad, the fifth of Elijah's six sons, was surprisingly chosen as supreme minister by the leadership hierarchy. In April 1975 Wallace, who later took the Muslim title and name of Imam Warith Deen Muhammad, made radical changes in the Nation of Islam, gradually moving the group toward orthodox Sunni Islam. In 1975 Farrakhan left the New York Mosque. Until 1978 Farrakhan, who had expected to be chosen as Elijah's successor, kept silent in public and traveled extensively in Muslim countries, where he found a need to recover the focus upon race and black nationalism that the Nation had emphasized. Other disaffected leaders and followers had already formed splinter Nation of Islam groups—Silas Muhammad in Atlanta, John Muhammad in Detroit, and Caliph in Baltimore. In 1978 Farrakhan formed a new organization, also called the Nation of Islam, resurrecting the teachings, ideology, and organizational structure of Elijah Muhammad, and he began to rebuild his base of followers by making extensive speaking tours in black communities. Farrakhan claimed it was his organization, not that of Wallace Muhammad, that was the legitimate successor to the old Nation of Islam.

In 1979, Farrakhan began printing editions of *The Final Call*, a name he resurrected from early copies of a newspaper that Elijah Muhammad had put out in Chicago in 1934. The "final call" was a call to black people to return to Allah as incarnated in Master Fard Muhammad or Master Fard and witnessed by his apostle Elijah Muhammad. For Farrakhan, the final call has an eschatological dimension; it is the last call, the last chance for black people to achieve their liberation.

Farrakhan became known to the American public through a series of controversies that were stirred when he first supported the Rev. Jesse Jackson's 1984 presidential campaign. His Fruit of Islam guards provided security for Jackson. After Jackson's offhand, seemingly anti-Semitic remarks about New York City as "Hymietown" became a campaign issue, Farrakhan threatened to ostracize *Washington Post* reporter Milton Coleman, who had released the story in the black community. Farrakhan has also become embroiled in a continuing controversy with the American Jewish community by making anti-Semitic statements. Farrakhan has argued that his statements were misconstrued. Furthermore, he contends that a distorted media focus on this issue has not adequately covered the achievements of his movement.

Farrakhan's Nation of Islam has been successful in getting rid of drug dealers in a number of public housing projects and private apartment buildings; a national private security agency for hire, manned by the Fruit of Islam, has been established. The Nation has been at the forefront of organizing a peace pact between gang members in Los Angeles and several other cities. They have established a clinic for the treatment of AIDS patients in Washington, D.C. A cosmetics company, Clean and Fresh, has marketed its products in the black community. Moreover, they have continued to reach out to reform black people with the Nation's traditional dual emphases: self-identity, to know yourself; and economic independence, to do for yourself. Under Farrakhan's leadership, the Nation has allowed its members to participate in electoral politics and to run for office, actions that were forbidden under Elijah Muhammad. He has also allowed women to become ministers and public leaders in the Nation, which places his group ahead of all the orthodox Muslim groups in giving women equality. Although the core of Farrakhan's Nation of Islam continues to be about twenty thousand members, his influence is much greater, attracting crowds of forty thousand or more in speeches across the country. His group is the fastest growing of the various Muslim movements, largely through the influence of such rap groups as Public Enemy and Prince Akeem. International branches have been formed in Ghana, London, and the Caribbean.

In the United States throughout the 1990s, however, Farrakhan remained an immensely controversial figure. In January 1995 newspapers revealed that Qubilah Shabazz, the daughter of Malcolm X, had plotted with a gunman to assassinate Farrakhan. He responded by expressing sympathy for Shabazz, and he helped persuade federal officials to allow Shabazz to plea-bargain. Later that year, Farrakhan's plans for a Million Man March on Washington drew national attention. In October 1995 he delivered the keynote speech at the march, and he called for black men to repent for their treatment of their wives and to organize in their communities. In March 1996 he drew widespread condemnation following a trip to the Middle East that included stops in Iran, Libya, Syria, and Nigeria, and for his announcement that Libyan dictator Muammar Qadhafi had contributed one million dollars to the Nation of Islam.

In the late 1990s Farrakhan was treated for prostate cancer, a disease that caused the death of his good friend and fellow activist Kwame Ture (Stokely Carmichael) in 1998. Complications with his own treatment with implanted radioactive seeds caused extensive bleeding and resulted in a near death experience for Farrakhan. He was transformed by this experience and began to moderate his views and to move closer to Sunni Islam. Members of the

Nation of Islam leader Louis Farrakhan addresses a crowd of demonstrators, 2002. *Speaking on the issue of reparations for the injustices of slavery, Farrakhan joins in a rally and protest on the National Mall in Washington, D.C.* GETTY IMAGES

Nation of Islam were taught how to do the formal Arabic prayers, prostrating themselves as other Muslims, and to hold the Friday Jum'ah prayer service. They also follow the Islamic lunar calendar for the month of the Ramadan celebration instead of fasting only during the month of December, as Elijah Muhammad taught them in order to counteract the influences of Christmas. Beginning in 2001 Imam Warith Deen Muhammad and Minister Louis Farrakhan have held joint prayer services during the last weekend of February, the traditional time for the Nation's Savior's Day celebration. Although they have developed friendly relationships, they have decided not to merge their respective movements.

See also Fard, Wallace D.; Islam; Malcolm X; Muhammad, Elijah; Nation of Islam

■ ■ *Bibliography*

Essien-Udom, E. *Black Nationalism: A Search for an Identity in America.* Chicago: University of Chicago Press, 1962.

Farrakhan, Louis. *Seven Speeches by Minister Louis Farrakhan.* Newport News, Va.: Ramza Associates & United Brothers Communications Systems, 1974.

Farrakhan, Louis. *A Torchlight for America.* Chicago: FCN Publishing, 1993.

Lincoln, C. Eric. *The Black Muslims in America.* Boston: Beacon Press, 1963.

Lomax, Louis F. *When the Word Is Given.* New York: Signet, 1963.

Mamiya, Lawrence H. "From Black Muslim to Bilalian: The Evolution of a Movement." *Journal for the Scientific Study of Religion* 21, no. 2 (1982): 138–151.

Marsh, Clifton E. *From Black Muslims to Muslims: The Transition from Separatism to Islam, 1930–1980.* Metuchen, N.J.: Scarecrow Press, 1984.

Muhammad, Warith Deen. *As the Light Shineth from the East.* Chicago: WDM Publishing, 1980.

LAWRENCE H. MAMIYA (1996)
Updated by author 2005

FATHER DIVINE

C. 1880
SEPTEMBER 10, 1965

▪▪▪

Father Divine, a minister in New York City's Harlem and other locations, was born George Baker to ex-slaves in Rockville, Maryland. He endured poverty and segregation as a child, and at age twenty he moved to Baltimore, where he taught Sunday school and preached in storefront churches. In 1912 he began an itinerant ministry, focusing on the South. He attracted a small following and, pooling his disciples' earnings, moved north and purchased a home in 1919 in the exclusively white Long Island community of Sayville, New York. He opened his doors to the unemployed and homeless.

By 1931, thousands were flocking to worship services in his home, and his white neighbors grew hostile. In November 1931 they summoned police, who arrested him for disturbing the peace and maintaining a public nuisance. Found guilty, he received the maximum fine and a sentence of one year in jail. Four days later, the sentencing judge died.

The judge's sudden death catapulted Father Divine into the limelight. Some saw it as evidence of his great powers; others viewed it as sinister retribution. Although Father Divine denied responsibility for the death, the incident aroused curiosity, and throughout the 1930s the news media continued to report on his activities.

Father Divine's Peace Mission movement grew, establishing extensions throughout the United States and in major cities abroad. He relocated his headquarters to Harlem, where he guided the movement, conducted worship services, and ran an employment agency. During the Great Depression, the movement opened businesses and sponsored a national network of relief shelters, furnishing thousands of poor people with food, clothes, and jobs.

Father Divine's appeal derived from his unique theology, a mixture of African-American folk religion, Methodism, Catholicism, Pentecostalism, and New Thought, an ideology based on the power of positive thinking. He encouraged followers to believe that he was God and to channel his spirit to generate health, prosperity, and salvation. He demanded they adhere to a strict moral code, abstaining from sexual intercourse and alcohol, and disciples cut family ties and assumed new names. His worship services included a banquet of endless courses, symbolizing his access to abundance. His mind-power theology attracted many, especially those suffering from racism and economic dislocation, giving disciples a sense of control over their destinies in a time filled with chaos and confusion.

His social programs also drew followers. Although rigid rules governed the movement's shelters, they were heavily patronized. An integrationist, Father Divine campaigned for civil rights, attracting both African-American and Euro-American disciples. Challenging American racism, he required followers to live and work in integrated pairs.

With economic recovery in the 1940s, Father Divine's message lost much of its appeal; membership in the movement declined and Peace Missions closed. In 1946 he made headlines with his marriage to a white disciple named Sweet Angel, and he spent his declining years grooming her for leadership. Upon his death in 1965, she assumed control of the movement, contending that Father Divine had not died but had surrendered his body, preferring to exist as a spirit. The movement perseveres with a small number of followers and businesses in the Philadelphia area.

See also Catholicism in the Americas; Folk Religion; Pentecostalism in the United States; Religion

■ ■ *Bibliography*

Watts, Jill. *God, Harlem U.S.A.: The Father Divine Story.* Berkeley: University of California Press, 1992.

Weisbrot, Robert. *Father Divine and the Struggle for Racial Equality.* Urbana: University of Illinois Press, 1983.

JILL M. WATTS (1996)

FAUSET, JESSIE REDMON

APRIL 27, 1884
APRIL 30, 1961

▪▪▪

Jessie Redmon Fauset was a writer, a teacher, and the literary editor of the *Crisis*, the official journal of the National Association for the Advancement of Colored People (NAACP). Fauset published the early writings of Arna Bontemps, Langston Hughes, and Jean Toomer, and she promoted the work of poets Georgia Douglas Johnson and Anne Spencer. But, although she is more often remembered for her encouragement of other writers, she was herself among the most prolific authors of the Harlem Renaissance. In addition to her poems, reportage, reviews, short stories, and translations that appeared regularly in the *Crisis*, she published four novels in less than ten years.

Born in what is now Lawnside, New Jersey, Fauset grew up in Philadelphia. Her widowed father, a minister, was the primary influence on her childhood. Her outstanding academic record won her admission to Cornell University, where she was elected to Phi Beta Kappa; she graduated in 1905. She taught high school French and earned an M.A. from the University of Pennsylvania. W. E. B. Du Bois hired her for the *Crisis* in 1919.

Her contributions to the *Crisis* were numerous and diverse, including biographical sketches of blacks across the diaspora, essays on drama and other cultural subjects, and reports on black women activists and political causes. One of the few women to participate in the 1921 Pan-African Congress, Fauset recorded her vivid impressions of that meeting. Several of her best essays describe her travel to Europe and North Africa during 1925 and 1926. She reviewed and translated works by Francophone writers from Africa and the Caribbean.

Although she subtitled one of them "A Novel without a Moral," all of Fauset's books convey strong messages. *There Is Confusion* (1924) depicts the struggle of an educated, idealistic young woman to achieve her professional goal of becoming a concert singer without compromising her personal and racial pride. Fauset's best novel, *Plum Bun* (1929), uses the subject of "passing" to explore issues of race and gender identity. Its protagonist, another aspiring artist, learns that no success is worth betraying one's selfhood. In the foreword to *The Chinaberry Tree* (1931), Fauset explains that her purpose is to write about the "breathing-spells, in-between spaces where colored men and women work and love and go their ways with no thought of the 'problem'" (Fauset, p. xxxi). Rather than racial differences, Fauset concentrates on things blacks and whites have in common; this emphasis is itself a form of protest. But as her final novel, ironically titled *Comedy: American Style* (1934), demonstrates, she did not ignore the problems of racism and sexism endemic to early twentieth-century American life. In general, however, Fauset's novels present sentimental resolutions to the complex problems they raise.

After resigning from the *Crisis* in 1926, Fauset returned to teaching. In 1929 she married businessman Herbert Harris, and they later moved to Montclair, N.J. She ceased thereafter to play a public role. Yet even after her death, in 1961, her example continued to inspire. Not only had she probably published more than any black American woman before her, her fiction confirmed that not all the drama in African-American life revolved around interracial conflict.

See also Bontemps, Arna; *Crisis, The*; Du Bois, W. E. B.; Harlem Renaissance; Hughes, Langston; Literature; National Association for the Advancement of Colored People (NAACP); Pan-Africanism; Toomer, Jean

■ ■ *Bibliography*

Fauset, Jessie Redmon. *The Chinaberry Tree*. New York: Frederick A. Stokes, 1931.

McDowell, Deborah E. Introduction to *Plum Bun* by Jessie Redmon Fauset. Boston: Beacon Press, 1990.

Sylvander, Carolyn W. *Jessie Redmon Fauset, Black American Writer*. Troy, N.Y.: Whitston, 1981.

CHERYL A. WALL (1996)

FEBRUARY REVOLT

In the early months of 1970, thousands of Afro-Trinidadians marched up and down the roads and public spaces of Trinidad and Tobago shouting "Black Power," "Power to the People," and other related slogans. The Black Power movement (or the "Black Power Revolution" as it was termed by some commentators) was part of an international movement of African peoples protesting their continued marginalization—both in countries with white majorities and in those such as Trinidad and Tobago that had black majorities and were led by blacks. In what has been termed the February Revolt, Afro-Trinidadians expressed their profound disapproval with the way resources, material and symbolic, were being allocated in the society. The protests continued and grew larger in March and April before the government eventually declared a state of emergency and jailed the leaders of the demonstrations. Sections of the army also mutinied on April 21, 1970, before surrendering several days later to the government.

In Trinidad and Tobago, young blacks were protesting the fact that, although self-government and political independence had been won from the British in 1962, the engines of the economy (the oil refineries, the banks and insurance companies, and several other critical firms) remained in foreign hands, even though some had been juridically "localized." The protestors also lamented the fact that the industrialization strategy known as "Operation Jobs" that was being pursued by the ruling People's National Movement (PNM), depended heavily on direct foreign investment, which was capital intensive and did not create the number of jobs that had been promised.

There were also complaints that, political, or "flag," independence notwithstanding, many of the key symbols of the society, and the manner in which power and status were defined and allocated, continued to reflect the old socioeconomic order based on the sugar plantation and foreign-owned oil. A few blacks had been co-opted at the management level but they allegedly remained "Afro-Saxons," a pejorative term used to describe English loyalists in the tropics, also known as "Black Britishers."

The prime minister of the country at the time, Dr. Eric Williams, was a distinguished black scholar who had written the classic book, *Capitalism and Slavery* (1944), as well as *The Negro in the Caribbean* (1942). Both of these books had led his supporters to regard him as the providential messiah who would lead his people to the promised land. He had also authored several radical pamphlets, such as *Massa Day Done* (1961), in which promises were made to restructure the old colonial order. By 1970, however, this promised social revolution, though underway, was not visible enough to many impatient young blacks, who believed that Williams had either sold out the country or abandoned all that he had once stood for.

In response to the challenge posed by the marchers and a mutinous army, Williams repressed the movement by declaring a state of emergency and arresting many of its leaders. He then proceeded, however, to implement many of the policies that the protesters had demanded. Ironically, the movement provided Williams with the leverage he needed to force the private sector to broaden and deepen local participation in the economy. Williams went on to boast that he was the "biggest black power in the land," and that he supported all the positive things that the movement stood for.

Williams was of the view that his Afrocentric critics were not sufficiently aware of what the PNM had done between 1956 and 1970. As he declared in a nationwide broadcast on March 23, 1970:

> We have consciously sought to promote black economic power. We have ... created 1,523 black small farmers over the country; we have encouraged small businesses in manufacture and tourism. ... We have brought free secondary education within the reach of thousands of disadvantaged families who could not dream of it in 1956. ... Our Public Service ... is staffed today almost entirely by nationals, mainly black. We have unceasingly sought to control or at least to alleviate the unemployment which we inherited, and which has increased with the tremendous rise in the birth rate. We have created no fewer than 68,200 new jobs between 1956 and 1969.

Williams, however, came out fully in support of the programmatic agenda of Black Power, particularly its demand for economic power and black dignity. He urged the nation to "proceed to work more positively than ever towards the economic and social upliftment of the black disadvantaged groups in our society of both African and Asian origin, as the only way to achieve the genuine national integration to which so many of us are dedicated. If anyone wishes to continue to march and demonstrate, by all means let him do so. ... But I urge that this should be done without violence."

Also of consequence was the greater willingness on the part of blacks to acknowledge their blackness and to cease "atoning" for being of African provenance. The change in dress and hairstyles (including what the author Vidya Naipaul referred to as "threatening hair") was part of this process, as was the growing tendency to regard native cultural offerings as valid.

The system of social stratification also changed significantly after 1970. In the colonial era, and even in the post-independence period, foreign and local whites were at the top of the social pyramid, the Chinese and mulatto element was in the middle, and blacks and Indians were at the bottom. The caste system had begun to fray at the edges in the 1950s, but the basic outlines of the system had remained. Beginning in 1970, however, the pace of change in the social order accelerated considerably—particularly after 1973, when a dramatic rise in oil prices revived the economy. Revenue from higher oil prices provided the government with the funding to implement some of the changes called for by black radicals.

See also Black Power Movement; Peoples National Movement; Williams, Eric

■ ■ *Bibliography*

Meighoo, Kirk Peter. *Politics in a "Half Made Society": Trinidad and Tobago, 1925-2001.* Kingston, Jamaica: Ian Randle, 2003.

Oxaal, Ivar. *Race and Revolutionary Consciousness: a Documentary Interpretation of the 1970 Black Power Revolt in Trinidad.* Cambridge, Mass.: Schenkman, 1971.

Ryan, Selwyn D. *Race and Nationalism in Trinidad and Tobago: a Study of Decolonization in a Multiracial Society.* Toronto: University of Toronto Press, 1972.

SELWYN RYAN (2005)

FEDERAL WRITERS' PROJECT

▬ ▬ ▬

The Federal Writers' Project (FWP) was an arm of the New Deal's Works Project Administration (WPA) that gave employment between 1935 and 1939 to some 4,500 American writers, 106 of them (as of 1937) African-American. The great majority of FWP writers were hired to work on the American Guide Series, a collection of state guidebooks describing the distinctive folkways and histories of the country's different regions, both rural and urban.

A number of prominent African-American writers participated in the FWP. The Illinois project hired Margaret Walker, Richard Wright, Willard Motley, Frank Yerby, William Attaway, Fenton Johnson, Arna Bontemps, and Katherine Dunham. The New York projected hired Wright, Claude McKay, Ralph Ellison, Tom Poston, Charles Cumberbatch, Henry Lee Moon, Roi Ottley, Helen Boardman, Ellen Tarry, and Waring Cuney. Zora Neale Hurston briefly directed the Florida project, and Charles S. Johnson contributed to the Tennessee state guide.

Because federal funding was cut off in 1939, after which various FWP projects reverted to individual states, much FWP material never saw publication. But in addition to the sections on Negro history in several state guides, a number of important studies of black culture were generated by FWP writers from FWP-based research. Urban studies include: McKay, *Harlem: Negro Metropolis* (1940); Wright, *Twelve Million Black Voices* (1941); Ottley and William Weatherby, *New World A-Comin': Inside Black America* (1943); Ottley, *The Negro in New York: An Informal History* (1967); Bontemps and Jack Conroy, *Anyplace but Here* (1966); St. Clair Drake and Horace Cayton, *Negro Metropolis: A Study of Negro Life in a Northern City* (1945); Moon, *Balance of Power: The Negro Vote* (1948); and Gilbert Osofsky, *Harlem: The Making of a Ghetto* (1965).

Rural studies, drawn from the FWP's massive interviewing project of over two thousand ex-slaves from eighteen states, include the North Carolina project's *These Are Our Lives* (1939); the Savannah project's *Drums and Shadows: Survival Studies among the Georgia Coastal Negroes* (1940); Roscoe Lewis, *The Negro in Virginia* (1940); Benjamin Botkin, *Lay My Burden Down: A Folk History of Slavery* (1945); Charles L. Perdue, *Weevils in the Wheat: Interviews with Virginia Ex-Slaves* (1976); and George P. Rawick's nineteen-volume *The American Slave: A Compos-*

ite Autobiography (1972), subsequently supplemented (1977, 1979) by twenty-two additional volumes.

The materials gathered in the slave narrative collection, while flawed, continue to be widely used in studies of U.S. slavery. Sterling Brown, the FWP's national editor of Negro affairs, encountered resistance from various state project heads who were reluctant to hire black interviewers or to adhere to Brown's goal of eliminating "racial bias . . . [that] does not produce the accurate picture of the Negro in American social history" (Gabbin, 1985, p. 69). But Brown received support from other project directors and managed to insert substantial material about African-American history and culture into many state guides, as well as to foster the ex-slave interviewing project.

Some historians of slavery insist that because most of the FWP interviewers were white, the former slaves engaged in a self-censorship that "lead[s] almost inevitably to a simplistic and distorted view of the plantation as a paternalistic institution where the chief feature of life was mutual love and respect between masters and slaves" (Blassingame, 1975, p. 490). Other historians, however, argue that "a blanket indictment of the interviews is as unjustified as their indiscriminate or uncritical use" and that the interviews constitute "the single most important source of data used to examine the 'peculiar institution' and its collapse" (Yetman, 1984, pp. 189, 209).

In addition to contributing to the state guides and the slave narrative collection, a number of African-American writers wrote and published works of their own during their FWP tenure. Hurston published *Their Eyes Were Watching God* (1937), *Tell My Horse* (1938), and *Moses, Man of the Mountain* (1939); Attaway worked on *Blood on the Forge* (1941); Wright published *Uncle Tom's Children* and wrote *Native Son* (both in 1940); Bontemps published *Drums at Dusk* (1939); and Walker wrote an unpublished novel about Chicago ghetto life, *Goose Island,* as well as an early draft of *Jubilee* (eventually published in 1966).

The FWP experience did not simply provide these writers with financial support but significantly shaped the content and perspective of their writing. The project provided Hurston with recording equipment and transportation, enabling her to deepen her already established interests as a folklorist. Attaway's *Blood on the Forge* and Wright's *Twelve Million Black Voices,* which depict the cultural dislocation of southern sharecroppers in the industrial North, reflect central concerns of the Illinois project. Wright's *Native Son* was profoundly shaped by the FWP-based urban sociology of Cayton and Drake's emerging Chicago School. Ellison's *Invisible Man* (1953), which treats black experience as both distinctly African American and broadly human, reflected the FWP's characteristic insistence that the United States is a harmonious blend of distinct cultural particularities.

The work performed by black writers in the FWP showed the project's preoccupation with the nation's diverse folkways. The FWP's distinct approach to diversity cannot be fully understood, however, apart from the influence of the cultural politics espoused by the left—specifically, the Communist Party of the United States—in the era of the Popular Front (1935–1939). The FWP was not, as was claimed in 1939 by House Un-American Activities Committee head Martin Dies, "doing more to spread Communist propaganda than the Communist Party itself" (Penkower, 1977, p. 195). But a number of FWP writers, black and white, worked in the orbit of the left. The admixture of localism and universalism pervading many works of the FWP was strongly influenced by the cultural left's pluralistic project of seeking the "real America" in "the people."

See also Black Arts Movement; Bontemps, Arna; Brown, Sterling Allen; Cayton, Horace; Communist Party of the United States; Drake, St. Clair; Dunham, Katherine; Ellison, Ralph; Folklore; Great Depression and the New Deal; Harlem Renaissance; Hurston, Zora Neale; Literature of the United States; McKay, Claude; Slave Narratives; Wright, Richard

■ ■ *Bibliography*

Blassingame, James W. "Using the Testimony of Ex-Slaves: Approaches and Problems." *Journal of Southern History* 41 (1975): 473–492.

Gabbin, Joanne V. *Sterling A. Brown: Building the Black Aesthetic Tradition*. Westport, Conn.: Greenwood, 1985.

Hirsch, Jerrold. *Portrait of America: A Cultural History of the Federal Writers' Project*. Durham: University of North Carolina Press, 2003.

Mangione, Jerre. *The Dream and the Deal: The Federal Writers' Project, 1935–1943*. Boston and Toronto: Little, Brown, 1972.

Penkower, Monty Noam. *The Federal Writers' Project: A Study in Government Patronage of the Arts*. Urbana: University of Illinois Press, 1977.

Yetman, Norman R. "Ex-Slave Interviews and the Historiography of Slavery." *American Quarterly* 36 (summer 1984): 181–210.

BARBARA CLARE FOLEY (1996)
Updated bibliography

FEELINGS, THOMAS

MAY 19, 1933
AUGUST 25, 2003

▮ ▮ ▮

Born in New York and raised in the Bedford-Stuyvesant neighborhood of Brooklyn, author and illustrator Tom Feelings graduated from the George Westinghouse Vocational School in 1951 and the School of Visual Arts, where he studied cartooning from 1951 to 1953 and illustration from 1957 to 1960. His education was interrupted by four years in the air force, in which Feelings served in the graphic arts division.

In 1958, while still in school, Feelings published a comic strip, "Tommy Traveler in the World of Negro History," in the *New York Age*. The strip, featuring a boy educating himself about black history, was celebratory, pedagogic in intent, and directed largely at children—concerns that dominate all of Feelings's art. Upon graduation, he sought freelance work while occupying himself drawing pictures of black people and places in and around his Brooklyn neighborhood.

In 1960 Feelings joined the African Jazz Art Society, a group of musicians and artists inspired by the teachings of Marcus Garvey. In 1964, unable to establish a freelance career, largely because black illustrators found it difficult to get assignments, Feelings emigrated to Ghana. He worked as an illustrator at the Government Printing House and also did freelance commissions. The Ghana experience changed Feelings's illustrative style: His previous drawings had been somber and mostly monochromatic; his new pictures were colorful and livelier. Following the 1966 coup in Ghana, the press where Feelings worked was closed and he lost his job. He returned briefly to the United States, then headed the children's book project at the Ministry of Education, in Guyana, from 1971 to 1974.

After returning to the United States, Feelings lived mostly in New York and illustrated more than twenty books, winning numerous awards and citations in the process. In 1968 he illustrated Julius Lester's *To Be a Slave*. *Mojo Means One: Swahili Counting Book* (1971) and *Jambo Means Hello: Swahili Alphabet Book* (1974), both works authored by his wife at the time, Muriel Feelings, seek to introduce the young African-American reader to a traditional, simple, communal black America. His 1972 autobiography, *Black Pilgrimage*, looks at what it means to be black and a minority in the United States as compared to being part of a majority in independent Africa.

In 1982 Feelings was awarded a National Endowment for the Arts (NEA) Visual Arts Fellowship. *Now Sheba*

Sings the Song, a series of drawings of black women done over twenty-five years, accompanied by a poem by Maya Angelou, was published in 1987. In 1990 Feelings became the artist-in-residence at the University of South Carolina in Columbia. *Soul Looks Back in Wonder,* his first full-color picture book, along with poems with uplifting messages chosen from some of the best African-American poets, appeared in 1993. Like almost all of Feelings's output, it celebrates the African and African-American experience for the benefit of a young audience. The last book that Feelings both wrote and illustrated, *The Middle Passage: White Ships/Black Cargo* (1995), is considered by many commentators to be his masterpiece. A moving depiction of the journey of enslaved African Americans on slave ships bound for North and Central America, *The Middle Passage* was awarded the Coretta Scott King Book Award for illustration in 1996.

On May 18, 2003, family and friends joined Feelings for his seventieth birthday celebration—the first birthday party he had ever had. Feelings passed away on August 25, 2003, after a bout with cancer, leaving behind a picture of a legacy.

See also Angelou, Maya; Garvey, Marcus; Lester, Julius; Literature in the United States

■ ■ *Bibliography*

Dunbar, Ernest. *The Black Expatriates: A Study of American Negroes in Exile.* New York: Dutton, 1968.

Feelings, Tom. *Black Pilgrimage.* New York: Lothrop, Lee & Shepard, 1972.

Feelings, Tom. *The Middle Passage: White Ships/Black Cargo.* New York: Dial, 1995.

Harrison, Barbara, and Gregory Maguire, eds. *Innocence and Experience: Essays and Conversations on Children's Literature.* New York: Lothrop, Lee & Shepard, 1987.

Major Authors and Illustrators for Children and Young Adults, 2nd ed. Detroit, Mich.: Gale, 2002.

QADRI ISMAIL (1996)
Updated by publisher 2005

FEMINIST THEORY AND CRITICISM

While the term *black feminism* originated in the 1970s, the central tenets of black feminist ideology date back to the mid-nineteenth century. Black feminists in both the nineteenth and early twentieth centuries argued that the inter-section of race, class, and gender in their lives, commonly referred to as the "double bind," inevitably shape the political and ideological projects led by and for black women. Late-twentieth-century black feminists have expanded the concept of the "double bind" to include other forms of discrimination—such as sexual harassment and homophobia—that impact the daily lives of African-American women. For example, many black feminists have argued that they cannot fight one form of oppression, be it sexism, racism, classism, or homophobia, but must, because of their intersecting sociopolitical identities, challenge all or some combination of these forms of discrimination. Furthermore, black feminists have resisted for generations the separatism of their white feminist counterparts who have not traditionally included racism and classism as part of the women's rights agenda while simultaneously questioning the patriarchal beliefs of their African-American male leaders who often choose to ignore sexism in the fight for racial justice. Additionally, black feminists argue that their quest to eliminate racism and patriarchy must be deeply rooted in and connected to the freedom of all African-American people. As such, this community-centered concept has led to debates among black feminists to forgo the term *black feminist* and replace it with the seemingly more holistic, more multicultural term of *womanist.*

Black feminism has three underlying tenets: first, that black men have often asserted their "rights to be men" by restricting these same rights for black women; second, that black male leaders often consider it inappropriate for black women to playing a leading role in fighting for black freedom and justice; third, that mainstream feminism in the United States, from the suffragists to pro-choice advocates, define feminism by excluding the needs and rights of women of color and poor women. In regards to the first challenge, the emphasis on racial unity has resulted in black women being called "race traitor" when they critique or challenge black male authority. For example, the term "race traitor" was widely applied to black feminists who supported Desiree Washington in the rape trial against Mike Tyson; who criticized Clarence Thomas's nomination to the U.S. Supreme Court; or who protested the gender exclusion of the Million Man March. In all three cases black feminists who spoke out against sexism and tried to address the multiple forms of oppression evident in these events were accused of forfeiting their racial identity by blindly following white feminists at the expense of black people. In response to the perennial exclusion of black women from positions of leadership in civil rights and social justice programs, black feminists argue that these values stem from deeply patriarchal and heterosexist attitudes in the African-American community regarding "appropriate" women's behavior. Black feminists argue that these sexist belief systems within the African-American community unfairly relegate black women to subservient roles within the fight for racial justice. However, while black feminists contend that sexism and homophobia within the black community creates an antiblack feminist bias, they also articulate the third tenet of black feminism, which argues that mainstream feminism primarily addresses the needs of white, middle-class, well-educated women. As a result, black feminists have challenged white feminists to include the voices and experiences of women of color and working-class women as fundamental to the feminist project.

Black feminism can trace the roots of the "double bind" ideology back to the early-nineteenth century. Because most nineteenth-century African-American women were enslaved, free black women joined the abolitionist movement to help manumit their fellow black sisters. In early 1831, Maria Stewart published the essay titled "Religion and the Pure Principles of Morality, the Sure Foundation on Which We Must Build" in the abolitionist newspaper *The Liberator*. This essay was significant not only because it was the first political manifesto written by an African-American woman but also because Stewart revealed that black women faced a unique set of problems in slavery because of their doubly oppressed status as slave and woman. In 1861 Harriet Jacobs, under the pseudonym Linda Brent, published the slave narrative *Incidents in the Life of a Slave Girl*. *Incidents* was the first slave narrative to provide a detailed account of the life of a slave woman. In her autobiography Jacobs revealed that she, like most enslaved African-American women and girls, was especially vulnerable to sexual exploitation by her slave master. Moreover, in contrast to Frederick Douglass's 1845 *Narrative of Frederick Douglass, an American Slave,* Jacobs also recognized that black women were less likely to escape slavery than black men because they were the primary caretakers of their children. As such, enslaved black women had fewer options than black men and substantially fewer rights than white women. Like Jacobs, abolitionist Sojourner Truth focused on black women's rights in her antislavery speeches. Sojourner Truth is best known for her 1851 speech, popularly referred to as "Ain't I a Woman?" that she delivered at a women's rights convention in Akron, Ohio. In this speech, Sojourner challenged white feminists to expand their definitions of womanhood to include free and enslaved African-American women, while simultaneously critiquing men for refusing to grant all women equal rights. Immediately after the Civil War, Truth continued to politic on behalf of black women, arguing that because black men and women work equally hard, black women and black men should have equal rights and both be guaranteed the right to vote.

By the end of the nineteenth century, black women, like white women, still did not have the right to vote. However, the period 1890 to 1920 is now seen as the "Women's Era" of African-American history because of an increase in activism and political visibility of black women in society. Black women created organizations that demanded women's suffrage and focused on a range of social and political issues that affected black communities. Antilynching activism, brought to national attention by journalist and activist Ida B. Wells-Barnett, opposed not only the widespread lynching of black men but also the sexual stereotyping of black women as immoral in contrast to chaste white women, whom lynching supposedly vindicated. In 1892 Anna Julia Cooper wrote the first black feminist book, *A Voice from the South.* Cooper's basic premise was that black women and black men experienced severe oppression during slavery, with the result that neither sex had gained any significant advantage over the other. Consequently, Cooper did not believe that men were innately more suited for racial uplift than black women. In fact, she believed that when black women fought against injustice, they framed race issues around the needs of working-class men, women, and children. This was the message behind one of the most famous passages in *A Voice from the South*: "Only the Black Woman can say 'where and when I enter, in the quiet undisputed dignity of my womanhood, without violence and without suing or special patronage, then and there the whole Negro race enters with me.'"

In 1896 African-American women founded the National Association of Colored Women's Clubs (NACWC), in response to a white journalist's insulting letter about African-American women. The NACWC brought together more than one hundred black women's clubs and became the black woman's primary vehicle for race leadership. Clubwomen, who subscribed to the strictest model of "respectability," believed that it was their responsibility to teach poorer African-American women middle-class traits of housecleaning, child care, and etiquette. The national motto, "Lifting as We Climb," addressed concerns of class and social uplift. Leaders in the black women's club movement such as Josephine St. Pierre Ruffin, Mary Church Terrell, and Anna Julia Cooper, formed the clubs to enact municipal, civic, and educational reform. These activities coalesced with their desire for increased political visibility and the vote. In the end, the "Women's Era" embodied the ideology that the problems of the race revolved around the problems of its women.

Between 1923 and 1926, black women blues singers rose to national prominence. While the African-American woman activists in the "Women's Era" believed that they should model middle-class attitudes for working-class women, black women blues singers such as Bessie Smith and Gertrude "Ma" Rainey derived their black feminist identity from and within African-American poor and working-class communities. One significant ideological difference between these two strands of black feminism was the treatment of black women's sexuality. For the most part, black feminists of the "Women's Era" addressed issues of black female sexuality by disproving the stereotypes that black women were innately sexually promiscuous and unrespectable. However, in both their song lyrics and public persona, blues women were significantly more explicit about sexual desire. Given the stringent social norms regarding black female sexuality from both within and outside the African-American community, when artists like Gertrude Rainey and Bessie Smith sang about women's sexuality, they put forth a model of black feminism based on an open defiance of patriarchy and male sexual dominance. By embodying the traits of independence, tenacity, and sexuality, blues women redefined the woman's "sphere" of domesticity to include those women who worked on the road traveling and singing.

Black women's participation in the civil rights movement during the 1950s and 1960s was crucial, although few were recognized for their leadership. In fact, frustration with male dominance in the civil rights and black nationalist movements as well as dissatisfaction with the narrowness of white feminists' agendas were among the reasons that black women continued to confront the impact of gender oppression in their own lives. Even though Ella Baker was one of the most significant civil rights leaders, her pivotal leadership and contributions to the civil rights movement were ignored until very recently. In 1956, Baker, along with Stanley Levinson and Bayard Rustin, formed "In Friendship," a fund-raising group that supported southern civil rights organizations that were spawned by the 1955 Montgomery bus boycott. Nonetheless, she often felt that the patriarchal attitudes of the black men in the civil rights movement made it substantially harder for her to ascend to and keep her position of leadership. Although Baker was instrumental in organizing the Southern Christian Leadership Conference with Dr. Martin Luther King Jr. and other black ministers in 1957, she eventually disagreed with their concept of a strong central leadership. In line with the community-centered approach of black feminist thought, Baker was convinced change must begin at the grassroots level rather than through centralized power. As a result, in 1960 Baker helped organize many of the varied student organizations that had been involved in the early sit-in movement, eventually fostering the creation of the Student Nonviolent Coordinating

Committee (SNCC). During the early 1960s SNCC became involved in the Freedom Rides, which set out to desegregate buses, and also participated in the voter registration drive, Mississippi Freedom Summer of 1964.

The late 1960s and early 1970s were particularly challenging for black women activists who felt alienated by the mainstream feminist movement, civil rights organizations, and the Black Panther Party. As a result, black feminists, much like their early predecessors, realized that they had to create their own organizations and write their own political manifestos in order to challenge the daily discriminations African-American women experienced. On behalf of working- and middle-class black women, in 1973 the National Black Feminist Organization (NBFO) supported the African-American woman's right to work at a living wage; argued that she must have access to quality education, job training, and health care; and demanded protection for her reproductive rights, specifically her right to refuse sterilization. Similar to the leaders of the black women's club movement, members of the National Welfare Rights Organization (1967) and the NBFO did not differentiate race, class, and gender but instead focused on their intersections, serving the masses of African-American women who were multiply afflicted by American racism and sexism. In 1977 a group of radical black feminists in Boston, who were inspired by the NBFO, created the Combahee River Collective. The Combahee River Collective, named after the Combahee River that Harriet Tubman used to help more than seven hundred slaves escape slavery, issued a position paper that analyzed the intersection of oppression in black women's lives and asserted the legitimacy of feminist organizing by black women. While the "Black Feminist Statement" continued the black feminist tradition of addressing the exclusion of black women from gender-based or race-based political organizations, the document was an even more radical statement of black feminism because it was explicitly socialist, addressed homophobia, and called for sisterhood among black women of various sexual orientations.

Unlike the black feminists of the "Women's Era" who understandably depicted black women as respectable and virtuous, the black feminists of the late 1960s and early 1970s explicitly, quite like the blues women who preceded them, attended issues of black female sexuality. These modern black feminists expanded the definition of black female sexuality to include issues of birth control, forced sterilization, same-sex relationships, autonomous sexual desire, and sexual assault. As such, these black feminists expanded the definition of black women's oppression from the "double bind" to intersectional and multifaceted. Toni Cade Bambara's 1970 edited collection *The Black*

Woman explored these themes even more. Her anthology opened up a dialogue about black female sexuality that later books, most notably Toni Morrison's *Sula* (1974), Ntozake Shange's *For Colored Girls Who Have Considered Suicide When the Rainbow Was Enuf* (1975), Gayl Jones's *Corregidora* (1975), Michele Wallace's *Black Macho and the Myth of the Superwoman* (1979), and Alice Walker's *The Color Purple* (1982), explored in-depth. Additionally, the early commitment of black lesbian feminists such as Audre Lorde, Pat Parker, Margaret Sloan, and Barbara Smith were crucial to the foundation of the black feminist movement in the 1970s because they unequivocally argued against the multiple layers of oppression that black women faced both outside of and within the African-American community. Arguing against black nationalist liberation models that African-American families desperately needed to reinstate men as the head, Audre Lorde's classic text, *Sister Outsider*, skillfully illustrates that the intersections of sexism, racism, classism, and homophobia in the lives of black women needed to be challenged in order for all African Americans to be free.

In the 1980s, bell hooks and Alice Walker provided pivotal texts on black feminism. bell hooks's *Ain't I Woman* (1981) provided an extensive historical analysis of how race, gender, and class intersect to shape and to oppress the lives of black women. Like the Combahee River Collective's "Black Feminist Statement," hooks defined black feminism as a survival mechanism that African-American women have and continue to need to use to challenge their multifaceted oppression. In her controversial novel *The Color Purple,* Alice Walker sparked new debates about sexism in the African-American community. While *The Color Purple* explored the negative impact of southern segregation on the lives of African-American families, Walker primarily focused on how African-American women survived and confronted the sexism they experienced within their own families and communities. Like Michelle Wallace and Ntozake Shange, Walker was widely criticized for her portrayal of black men as sexist and abusive toward African-American women. In response, Walker addressed the sexism implicit in these critiques, but also argued that *The Color Purple* explored the variety of relationships—familial, sexual, and platonic— that provided the foundation for contemporary black feminist projects. In Walker's specific case, the woman-centered relationships that she created in *The Color Purple* inspired her coinage of the term "womanist" to describe the black feminist movement. In the introduction to *In Search of Our Mother's Gardens,* Walker noted that a womanist is "a Black feminist or feminist of color. . . . A woman who loves other women, sexually and/or nonsexually. Appreciates and prefers women's culture, women's emotion-

al flexibility (values tears as natural counterbalance of laughter), and women's strength. . . . Committed to the survival and wholeness of entire people, male and female. Not separatist, except periodically, for health."

In the 1990s African-American feminists continued to organize and openly challenge sexism and racism on the national scene and within the African-American community. In 1991 a grassroots group called "African American Women in Defense of Ourselves" gathered more than sixteen hundred signatures for a widely circulated ad in response to the hearings to appoint Clarence Thomas as a justice to the U.S. Supreme Court. In 1995, amid controversy, black feminists spoke out about the patriarchal assumptions of the male-only Million Man March. While in the twenty-first century, black feminists continue to view sexism and racism as the major challenges that afflict African-American women, twenty-first-century black feminists, or "third wave" black feminists, now confront popular culture, mass media, and globalization in their black feminist projects. Given the severe criticism that hip-hop music and culture is both misogynistic and homophobic, "hip-hop feminism" appears almost oxymoronic. However, as Joan Morgan skillfully reveals in her 1999 book, *When Chickenheads Come Home to Roost: A Hip Hop Feminist Breaks It Down*, while the black feminism of the hip-hop generation is radically different from that of previous generations, the need for black feminism movement is equally as strong. Like its predecessors, hip-hop feminism has a radical critique of how racism and sexism affect the daily lives of black women. However, hip-hop feminists have the privileges of the feminist and civil rights movements while being the "first to have the devastation of AIDS, crack, and Black-on-Black violence" (p. 61). Morgan argues that the result of this paradox of both privilege and despair requires a new type of black feminism, "a feminism committed to 'keeping it real.' We need a voice like our music—one that samples and layers many voices, injects its sensibilities into the old and flips it into something new, provocative, and powerful." In addition to Joan Morgan, filmmaker Aishah Shahidah Simmons (2003) believes that a black feminist movement is needed now more than ever. However, while her definition of black feminism incorporates the central tenets of black feminism, she, like Morgan, grounds her feminism in a critique of popular culture and mass media. She counters the negative depictions of African-American women in music videos, television, and films by implementing her coined term, "Afrolez" which is a "femcentric multimedia arts project committed to using the moving image, the written and spoken word to counteract the negative impact of racism, sexism, homophobia, and classism on the lives of marginalized and disenfranchised people, with a particular emphasis black women and girls."

Black feminism is both an ideological and a political project that challenges the varied forms of oppression that impact African-American women. From the nineteenth century to the twenty-first century, African-American feminists have recognized that their unique place in America society as both "woman" and "black" ensures that they will be doubly afflicted by racism and sexism. However, like any other political movement, black feminists hold on to their central tenets while they adapt their rhetoric and create projects that address the changing sociopolitical situations. From the "double bind" model to the multilayered oppression paradigm, black feminists argue that American democracy can only be realized when the most oppressed and marginalized members of society are free from the burden of oppression.

See also Baker, Ella J.; Bambara, Toni Cade; Blueswomen of the 1920s and 1930s; Civil Rights Movement, U.S.; Lorde, Audre; National Association of Colored Women's Clubs; Truth, Sojourner; Walker, Alice; Wells-Barnett, Ida B.

■ ■ *Bibliography*

Carby, Hazel. *Reconstructing Womanhood: The Emergence of the Afro-American Woman Novelist.* New York: Oxford University Press, 1987.

Collins, Patricia Hill. *Black Feminist Thought: Knowledge, Consciousness, and the Politics of Empowerment.* Boston: Unwin-Hyman, 1991.

Davis, Angela Y. *Blues Legacies and Black Feminism: Gertrude "Ma" Rainey, Bessie Smith, and Billie Holiday.* New York: Pantheon Books, 1998.

Dawson, Michael C. *Black Visions: The Roots of Contemporary African-American Political Ideologies.* Chicago: University of Chicago Press, 2001.

Giddings, Paula. *When and Where I Enter: The Impact of Black Women on Race and Sex in America.* New York: William Morrow, 1984.

Higginbotham, Evelyn Brooks, "African-American Women's History and the Metalanguage of Race." *Signs* 17 (1992): 251–274.

hooks, bell. *Ain't I a Woman: Black Women and Feminism.* Boston: South End Press, 1981.

Lorde, Audre. *Sister/Outsider: Essays and Speeches.* Freedom, Calif.: The Crossing Press, 1984.

Morgan, Joan. *When Chickenheads Come Home to Roost: A Hip Hop Feminist Breaks It Down.* New York: Simon and Schuster, 1999.

Simmons, Aishah. "Using Celluloid to Break the Silence about Sexual Violence in the Black Community." In *Violence in the Lives of Black Women: Battered, Black, and Blue,* edited by Carolyn M. West. New York: Haworth Press, 2003.

Walker, Alice. *In Search of Our Mother's Gardens: Womanist Prose.* San Diego: Harcourt Brace Jovanovich, 1983.

White, Deborah Gray. *Too Heavy a Load: Black Women in Defense of Themselves, 1894–1994.* New York: Norton, 1999.

SALAMISHAH MARGARET TILLET (2005)

FESTIVALS, U.S.

■ ■ ■

From early colonial times to the present day, African Americans have created and observed an impressive calendar of celebratory and commemorative events: jubilees, festivals and anniversaries, "frolics" and seasonal feasts, fairs and markets, parades, and pilgrimages—not to speak of more private or secret ceremonies, such as church meetings and revivals, family reunions, baptisms and funerals, and spiritual cults. These customs have received the casual or sustained attention of travelers, visitors, and local observers. They have been praised or disparaged, extolled as the epitome of a festive spirit that should prevail in any society and as the expression of an enduring, authentic culture, but they have also been dismissed by some as primitive, low-brow manifestations of a subculture; an unsophisticated, burlesque imitation of mainstream life; or, at best, an adaptation or appropriation of Euro-American customs.

This festive mood with which African Americans have been credited has encouraged the persistence of many prejudices and stereotypes fostered by the minstrel tradition, which represented blacks as a happy-go-lucky, careless, lighthearted people, prone to dancing and singing. This inclination for mirth has been interpreted as a sign that the predicament of slaves and their descendants should not be such a burden to the white mind, and that their sufferings and the wrongs committed against them have been exaggerated.

Yet African-American celebrations, with all their unacknowledged complexities of forms and functions, are powerful symbolic acts that express—vehemently and with exuberance—not acquiescence to fate but needs, desires, and utopian will, as well as disenchantment, anger, and rebelliousness. Communal, playful, or carnivalesque in character, they are events through which the community endeavors to build its identity, in self-reflective scrutiny and in constant confrontation with "the black image in the white mind." These feasts not only give the lie to and articulate the pain of certain truths, including the ambivalence of a dream always deferred, they also define unexamined propositions in performances infused with subtle ironies and double entendre.

CORONATION FESTIVALS

Among the "hallowdays" observed by northern slaves and free blacks, the coronation festivals, or "negro elections," set the pattern for many civic feasts and festivals. Once a year in colonial New England, slaves were allowed to accompany their masters to election festivities where whites organized the election of their governors. In the 1750s, blacks started to organize their own similar celebrations, in which a leader—preferably African-born and of known royal ancestry, quick-witted, and ready of speech—was elected king or governor, a title that endowed him with authority among both blacks and whites. (The title "king" or "governor" was used by blacks according to each New England colony's specific status: governors were elected in colonies that were relatively autonomous, whereas kings were elected in colonies more closely tied to England.) According to this custom, which endured through the 1850s, bondsmen confronted their African origin—the king was intermediary to the ancestors. Bondsmen also expressed their desire to have their separate institutions and to prove their ability for self-government.

Elections were prepared for by weeks of debates and meetings. A strong political message was conveyed to the community and to white rulers in a spirit that blended parodic intent and high seriousness. By ritually transferring power from the hands of the masters to those of one of their fellows, slaves were paving the way for their emancipation. Election days were perhaps the first freedom celebrations that combined the memory of the freedom and power Africans enjoyed before their capture—with an anticipation of the freedom to come. The official recognition of African royalty and gentility reversed old stereotypes, which associated Africanness with savagery and lack of culture. The king was regarded as a civilized "negro" (the term "black" was not in usage as a noun then), composed and refined. These elections, prompted by the desire to counter forces of fragmentation and to ease conflicts, sought a consensus and struck a note of unity.

Coronation festivals were also indicative of white-black relations. The elected was often the slave of a prominent master, and slaves devised strategies to gain the support of masters to organize their ceremonies. The wealthier the slave owner, the greater the chance of having a grand festival, and, conversely, the greater the display, the stronger the evidence of the master's influence. While these feasts increased antagonism between blacks and poor whites, they offered an occasion to redefine slave-master relations, based on mutual claims and obligations. Negro kings held many roles—as opinion leaders, counselors, justice makers, and mediators who could placate black in-

surgency or white fearfulness when faced with such a display of autonomy and self-rule.

There were other occasions when blacks gathered around a self-appointed leader, such as Pinkster, another well-known festival. Derived originally from the Dutch Whitsuntide celebration called *pfingster*, which the "Africs" took over in the late eighteenth century, Pinkster reached its peak in the early 1800s in Albany, New York. There, the choice of a hill as the site for the celebration had many symbolic meanings. From the top of this hill, blacks could look down on the world—an interesting reversal of the usual situation, as well as a mock imitation of the hills on which rulers like to set their capitols. Pinkster Hill was close to the place where many executions of blacks (accused in 1793 of having set fire to the city) had taken place. It was also close to a burial ground, a military cemetery, and an all-black cemetery.

Thus, death presided over the festivities, reminding blacks of the limits set on their freedom, of punishments inflicted on black rebels, of the failure to acknowledge or reward the achievements of black soldiers who had participated in the nation's wars, and of the intricate game of integration and segregation. The epitaphs and names inscribed on the graves in the black cemetery emphasized the enduring character of African customs and rites. Cemeteries may have been the ultimate freedom sites, since only in death could blacks reach the absolute freedom they were celebrating.

Coronations and Pinkster exemplify a significant trend in the role granted to feasts: the official recognition of blacks' special gift for creating festive performances—and their capacity for infusing it into other groups (Native Americans, Germans, Dutch, and French attended the Pinkster). Feasts thus offered an arena for interaction and for the dream of a utopian and pluralistic order in a society divided by many social and political conflicts. Feasts were also an ironic comment on a republic that claimed to be dedicated to freedom but could still enslave part of its population, as well as a demonstration of the resilience of victims whose spirits could not be crushed.

EMANCIPATION CELEBRATIONS AND THE FOURTH OF JULY

Throughout the postrevolutionary era and in the antebellum years, African Americans evolved a tradition of emancipation celebrations that charted the different stages toward gradual, then complete, liberation. The future that was at stake was not only that of slaves and freed blacks, it was also the destiny of the nation and its aspiring democracy. These yearly occurrences were not marginal to black life; they were a political manifestation of jeremiad and claim making that was pursued deliberately, was announced and debated in the press, and involved major institutions, societies, and associations (churches, societies for mutual relief, temperance and benevolent societies, freemasons, etc.).

Emancipation celebrations were occasions for public appearances in marches and parades or at universal exhibitions. Many leaders, both religious and political, seized these opportunities to address the world in sermons, speeches, orations, or harangues, developing race pride and race memory. They assessed the contribution of black people in the building of the nation, their progress, their capacity for self-government, and their commitment to liberty as a universal right. These feasts were not merely opportunities to celebrate on a large scale, they also held out a promise to fashion new roles in a better world and to wield new power. In addition, they heralded a season of change, from enslavement and invisibility to liberation and recognition.

Both freedom and power were present in the ceremonies, not as mere allegorical figures but as fully developed ideas whose force needed to be conveyed to large audiences. Images and symbols were evolved and played out—in words, gestures, movements, and visual forms, with much ado and a will to adorn. The talents and gifts of black folks were put to use in a collective effort to stir and arouse consciousness and encourage action.

In the black calendar of feasts, Independence Day was the most controversial and bleakest celebration. The solemnities of the Fourth of July encouraged African Americans to organize their own separate ceremonies and formulate their own interpretation of the meaning of these national commemorations. One is reminded of Frederick Douglass's famous 1852 address, "What Is to the American Slave Your Fourth of July?" Many black leaders urged their members not to observe that unholy day and proclaimed that persecution was not over and final emancipation still out of reach. July 4 thus became a menacing and perilous day, one on which blacks were more tempted to plan insurrection than to celebrate the republic. It was also a day when they were most exposed to violence, riots, arrests, and murder, as in New York in 1834 or New Hampshire in 1835. It is no wonder that they looked for other sites and landmarks to construct an alternative memory.

After 1808, January 1 was adopted as a day of civic celebration, in commemoration of the official end of the slave trade. Yet, as in similar feasts, thanksgiving was tempered by ardent protest, and rejoicing by mourning and memories of the hardships of the Middle Passage. January 1 induced a heightened consciousness of Africa, where the black odyssey had begun. Africa became the central symbol and the subject of heated debate, especially when the colonization movement encouraging free blacks to return to Africa divided the community.

Curiously, January 1 never became a black national holiday. It was celebrated for only eight years in New York, was abandoned in the 1830s in Philadelphia, and only after general emancipation was proclaimed on January 1, 1863, did it assume new significance. The strengthening of the "peculiar institution," the development of the dreaded domestic slave trade, and the illegal perpetuation of both the domestic and the foreign trade, may explain the decline in popularity of this memorial celebration. Blacks in many states chose instead the days when emancipation law was passed into their state constitutions, such as July 14 in Massachusetts. After 1827, New York blacks institutionalized July 5 as their freedom day, setting it apart from the American Fourth of July.

The abolition of slavery in the British West Indies by an act of Parliament on August 1, 1834, brought new hopes, and henceforth this memorable date became a rallying point for all freedom celebrations and for the black abolitionist crusade. State emancipations were indicted for having brought little improvement in the conditions of slaves and free blacks. The rights of blacks were trampled in the North, where racial violence and tensions continued to rise, while in the South slavery was entrenched more solidly than ever.

England and Canada became the symbols of the new celebration—the former was praised for setting an example for the American republic, while the latter was hailed as the land of the free and a refuge for the fugitives. Black orations became more fiery, urging the righting of wrongs and of all past errors. Orations also called for self-reliance, respectability, and exemplary conduct among blacks, for a distrust of whites, and for a stronger solidarity with the newly freed population of the West Indies and between the slaves and free blacks in the United States.

BIG QUARTERLY AND OTHER LOCAL CELEBRATIONS

Increasingly, blacks sought sites that would commemorate events or figures more related to the African-American diaspora or to their community and its own distinctive history. Sometimes towns set the calendars—Baltimore for the Haitian Revolution, Cleveland for Nat Turner's Rebellion, and Boston in the late 1850s for Crispus Attucks. In 1814, Wilmington, Delaware, created its own celebration, Big Quarterly, which was observed for many years. Held at the close of the harvest season, it honored the founder of the Union Church of Africa, Peter Spencer.

Similar to religious revivals and patterned after the early meetings of the Quakers, Big Quarterly celebrated the struggles endured by leaders to achieve full ecclesiastical autonomy. This feast can be seen as the prototype of many religious services; it included praying, singing, the clapping of hands and stomping of feet, the beating of drums and tambourines, the playing of guitars, violins, and banjos. There was also a characteristic use of space at such gatherings. The feast began in the church, then moved outside on the church grounds, and it finally moved out to the open—Baltimore's famous French Street, for instance—where, late in the century as the feast grew more popular (in Baltimore attendance reached 10,000 in 1892; 20,000 in 1912), revival preachers urged repentance from sin and wandering minstrel evangelists played spirituals on odd instruments.

It was then also that educated "colored people" criticized the celebrations for giving way to weird cult practices and worldly pleasures, and for being outdated relics of old slavery times. In antebellum days, this religious feast was closer to a freedom celebration. Occurring in a region where slave-catching activities were intense, where slaves—who had to have a pass from the master to attend—were tempted to escape to Philadelphia or to the free states, Big Quarterly became a "big excursion on the Underground Railroad," with the presence among the pilgrims, who became potential fugitives, of both vigilant spies and marshals in addition to helpful railroad conductors.

In Syracuse in 1851 another major festival emerged in protest against the 1850 Fugitive Slave Law and honoring the rescue of a slave named Jerry. Jerry Rescue Day, which established Syracuse as the slaves' City of Refuge, embodied the spirit of defiance and of bold resistance to "iniquitous power" and to an infamous act that prevailed in the prewar years. Significantly, black leaders, rebels, warriors, and fugitives became heroic figures in celebrations and were chosen because they could demonstrate the unending fight against tyranny and for freedom. The oratory became more exhortative, the mood more impatient and indignant.

Freedom celebrations culminated in the early 1860s in Emancipation Jubilees and in the famous "Juneteenth," still observed today in Texas and surrounding states. In Texas, emancipation was announced to slaves eighteen months after its proclamation. This oddity of American history explains why Juneteenth, and not January 1, became a popular celebration in that area.

THE TRADITION OF CELEBRATION

Thus, from Election Day to freedom celebrations, African Americans created a ritual tradition of religious and community life. Momentous appearances in public places became challenges to the established order, calling attention to the danger of overlooking or forgetting iniquities, setbacks, and sufferings, as well as heroic acts. By reiterating a commonality of origin, goals, and strivings, feasts served to correct the inconsistencies of history and to cement a unity that was always in jeopardy.

Feasts also emphasized the necessary solidarity between the enslaved and the free, between African-born and American-born black people. Although most celebrations occurred in the North, they were symbolically and spiritually connected with slaves in the South, and a dense network of interaction was woven between various sites, places, and times. Former celebrations were often referred to and used as examples to follow or improve upon. The feasts themselves became memorable events to be passed on for generations to come and to be recorded in tales, song, and dance and in physical, verbal, kinetic, or musical images. The festive spirit became ingrained in African-American culture as something to celebrate in black speech, where it is inscribed in the literature and the arts that bear incessant testimony to the tradition.

The tradition created by colonial and antebellum celebrations has continued into the twenty-first century, still in anticipation of a freedom and justice that general emancipation failed to accomplish. Numerous associations founded after the Civil War resorted to ceremonial and commemorative rites to continue to enforce the idea of freedom, and they patterned their meetings and conventions on earlier gatherings. Freedom celebrations remained a model for the great marches and demonstrations—the protest against the 1917 riots, the parades of the Garvey movement, or the marches of the civil rights movement. The persistence of the tradition attests to the participation of African Americans in the struggle for democracy and to the crucial significance of these ritual stagings in cultural, intellectual, and political life.

Yet civil celebrations underwent some dramatic changes. More and more they became occasions of popular rejoicings. Boisterous festivity, screened out at first, crept in. Abundance and plentifulness replaced the earlier sobriety. As they grew in scope (the most popular were in urban centers, where the population was largest), they sometimes lost their original meaning and became essentially social occasions for convivial gatherings. It was the orator's and leader's duty and the role of the black press to remind participants of the seriousness of the purpose, and they did so with authority and eloquence. Nevertheless, the celebrations sometimes got out of control. With the changes brought by migration and demographic shifts, by the development of the media and of mass culture, and by the impunity of profit-seeking sponsors, some feasts turned into large commercial and popular events and lost their civil and political character, while others continued to meet white opposition and censure.

Rituals played an important role in celebrations and, whatever the occasion, shared certain features. They included the same speeches, addresses, or sermons; parades, marches, or processions; anthems, lyrics, and songs; banquets or picnics; dances and balls. They used all black people's skills—from the oratorical to the culinary, from the gift to adorn to polyrhythmic energy—to create their own modes, styles, and rhythms, always with an unfailing sense of improvisation and performance. And as they drew more people, many folkways, many rites of ordinary life (the habit of swapping songs, of cracking jokes, or "patting juba"), found their way into the ceremonies, blending memories of Africa with New World customs and forms, in a mood that was both solemn and playful, sacred and secular, celebratory and satiric. In many respects also, feasts were a privileged space for the encounters between cultures, favoring reciprocal influences, mergings and combinations, syncretism and creolization.

CARNIVAL

Nowhere is the creolization of cultures more evident than in the Carnival tradition, which emerged in the New World in Brazil, Trinidad, Jamaica, and the other islands. Found in its earlier forms mostly in the South, it continues its modern forms in the great Caribbean festivals of Brooklyn and Toronto. These carnivals, perceived as bacchanalian revelry or weird saturnalia, were often associated with a special season and with rites of renewal, purification, or rebirth. Usually seen as more African—and therefore as more "primitive" and exotic, more tantalizing than the more familiar Anglo-European feasts—they have elicited ambiguous responses, ranging from outright disparagement on moral and aesthetic grounds (indecency and lewdness are judged horrid and hideous) to admiration for the exuberant display of so many skills and talents.

These "festivals of misrule" were often banned or strictly regulated by city ordinances and charged with bringing disturbances and misconduct—boisterous rioting and drunkenness, gambling, and undue license of all sorts. The same criticism, phrased in similar words, was leveled by some members of the black community itself, especially those concerned with respectability and with the dignity of the "race," every time they suspected any feast

of yielding too much to the carnivalesque propensity of their people.

Yet the carnivalesque is always present in festive rituals to correct excesses—of piety, fervor, power—and as an instrument of emancipation from any form of authority. In the African-American quest for liberation, it became an essential means of expression, allying humor, wit, parody, and satire. It had ancient roots in African cultures; and in North American society, where the weight of puritanism was strong, where work, industriousness, sobriety, and gravity were highly valued and had become ideological tools to enforce servitude, the Carnival tradition became part of the political culture of the oppressed. Artistically it developed also as a subversive response to the Sambo image that later prevailed in the minstrel tradition. It created, as coronation festivals did, possibilities for the inversion of stereotypes, and it challenged a system of representation that was fraught with ideological misinterpretations. Paradoxically, black carnivalesque performances may have nourished white blackface minstrelsy, providing it with the artistic devices on which it thrived.

JONKONNU. The most notorious manifestations of the tradition are perhaps to be found in the North Carolina JonKonnu (John Canoe) Festival or in the Zulu and Mardi Gras parades of New Orleans. JonKonnu probably originated in Africa on the Guinea coast; was re-created in Jamaica in the late seventeenth century; spread through the Caribbean, where it was widely observed; and was introduced by slaves in the United States in isolated places—on plantations like Somerset Place or in city ports like Wilmington, North Carolina, or Key West, Florida. Meant to honor a Guinean folk hero, the festival became an elaborate satirical feast, ridiculing the white world with unparalleled inventiveness and magnificence.

The festival could last weeks, but it climaxed on Christmas Day and was attended by huge crowds. The procession, which took a ragman and his followers from house to house and through the streets, came to be known as a unique slave performance. "Coonering," as it was called, was characterized most of all by spectacular costumes and by extravagant dance steps to the music of "sinful" tunes. The rags and feathers, the fanciful headdress and masks, the use of ox or goat horns and cow and sheep bells, and the handmade instruments wove a complex web of symbolic structure, ritualization, and code building. The dressing in white skin encouraged slaves to claim certain prerogatives, even to organize revolts. In many feasts an implicit analogy was established between the "beaten" skin of the (often forbidden) drums and that of whipped slaves.

Christmas, the season of merrymaking and mobility that favored big gatherings and intense communication, became a dreaded time for planters who tried to stifle the subversive and rebellious spirit of coonering and to change a disquieting performance into a harmless pageant. Still held today, but now mostly controlled and observed by whites, it has lost part of its magnificence. In its heyday in antebellum America, JonKonnu was an artistic and political response of the slave population to its situation; it echoed in its own mode the freedom celebrations of the North. The lampooning liberty and grotesque parody of southern festivals turned them into arenas in which to voice anger and protest.

THE ZULU PARADE. In New Orleans, when Carnival came into existence in the late 1850s, blacks were not supposed to participate. The Zulu parade, which grew out of black social life, was created by a section of the population concerned about publicly asserting its status. It developed into a wholly separate street event, a parody of the white Krewes. The African Zulu, a new king of misrule, precedes Rex and mocks his regal splendor. The Carnival figures—shrunken heads of jungle beasts, royal prognosticator, or voodoo doctor—the masked or painted faces, and the coconuts emphasize both the African and minstrel motifs. Neither elite nor low-brow, neither genuinely African nor creole, the Zulu parade came under attack as too burlesque. Later, in the 1960s, it was criticized as exemplifying an "Uncle Tom on Wheels" and not fitting the mood of the times.

Yet the Zulu is a complex ritual that brings together several traditions: satire and masking, minstrelsy and vaudeville, brass bands, song, and dance. Another version of the coronation festival, the Zulu fuses elements of the European carnival with African, Caribbean, and Latin American practices. It establishes African Americans' rights to participate in the city's pageant, not as mere onlookers or indispensable entertainers whose various skills as musicians and jugglers had often been used to increase the glamour of white parades, but as creators and full-fledged citizens who could demonstrate both their role in the city's history and their potential role in its future.

INDIAN MASKING. The Mardi Gras Indians, consisting of ritual chiefs, each with a spy, flag boys, and followers, march in mock imitation of the king's court and follow secret routes through the city. They enact their own rituals of violent physical and verbal confrontations between tribes. These wild warriors chant disquieting songs and speak in tongues, accompanied by haunting drumbeats and an array of other percussive sounds as old as ancestral memories (in preference and contrast to the orderly military music of the official bands). They dance weird dance steps (e.g., the famous spy dance) and wear elaborate costumes made of beads, sequins, rhinestones, ribbons, and lace.

The tradition of Indian masking is old—originally found in Brazil, it appeared in the Caribbean in 1847. Meant to celebrate the Indian's fighting spirit and resistance, it also relates to communal rites of ancestral worship and to Dahomean ceremonial dances also found in jazz funerals. It is no accident that Mardi Gras Indians perform in the same area of New Orleans where jazz emerged out of the brass bands of Congo Square dances. Their festival may be a resurgence of the early drum gatherings that started in 1730 near the marshes of Congo Square, a market site where slaves bought merchandise from Native Americans and danced to African beats.

Today, the black Indians also appear on another festive day, March 19, at the intermission of the Lenten season. St. Joseph Day, originally an Italian Catholic feast that stylized altar building, blends the cult of saints (St. Joseph, "Queen Esther") with that of Indian heroes (Black Hawk) as well as that of voodoo spirits. Thus, religious and pagan rites, cult and carnival practices, indoor ceremonies and outdoor parades complement each other, converge, and merge.

Later in the year, Easter Rock, another feast that is still observed in rural Louisiana, celebrates the resurrection and similarly blends pagan and Christian elements. Its hero and emblem is both son and sun. The Son of God's rise from the dead is likened to that of the sun "rocking from the earth." All night long, prayer, "the shout," and dance herald and accompany the rocking of the sun/son.

Although the South has been the cradle of a diverse black carnivalesque tradition, in the prejazz and jazz ages another form of Carnival celebration found its way to the North. The modern West Indian festivals of Brooklyn in New York City and of Toronto, Canada, give further evidence of a process of Caribbeanization that has always been at work and that repeatedly intensified during periods of great migration. The importation of slaves from the Carib Basin, the arrival of many slaves from Santo Domingo after the Haitian Revolution in the early nineteenth century, and the late twentieth-century West Indian migration to the United States have all in various degrees brought many changes to "black" celebrations. They have intensified the creolization that brought together people of African, Hispanic, Indian, and French descent. The recent festivals are also generating a pan–West Indian consciousness that expresses itself artistically through costumes, masks, music, and dance. On a much-contested terrain, they enact their own rituals of rebellion, resistance and protest, inclusion and exclusion. Chaotic, playful, or violent, Carnival offers a delicate balance between many complementary or contradictory elements.

African-American celebratory performances are special occasions to celebrate freedom; they consist of various cycles of ritualized events that have rich semantic and symbolic meaning, fully a part of African-American and American history and culture. They invite us to reconsider stereotyped representations of "the race" and to revise the assumptions upon which conceptions of important figures, events, and places have themselves become objects of celebration and commemorative fervor. They are potent weapons and arenas through which to voice anger, strivings, and desire. They are efficacious and eloquent tools to educate, exhort, or indict. They are witty parodies and satires that help distance reality and change "mentalities." Crucial agents of change, celebratory performances demonstrate a people's faith in words and ideas, in the force of collective memory and imagination, in the necessity of finding powerful display. These entertaining and instructive ceremonies exhibit a gift for adornment and an inventiveness that emphatically proclaim the triumph of life over all the forces that tend to suppress or subdue "the souls of black folk."

See also Africanisms; Carnival in Brazil and the Caribbean; Civil Rights Movement, U.S.; Emancipation; Minstrels/Minstrelsy; Voodoo

■ ■ *Bibliography*

Abrahams, Roger, and John Szwed, eds. *Discovering Afro-America*. Leiden, Netherlands: Brill, 1975.

Blassingame, John W. *The Slave Community: Plantation Life in the Antebellum South*. New York: Oxford University Press, 1972.

Genovese, Eugene D. *Roll, Jordan, Roll: The World the Slaves Made*. New York: Pantheon, 1974.

Levine, Lawrence W. *Black Culture and Black Consciousness*. New York: Oxford University Press, 1977.

Southern, Eileen. *The Music of Black Americans*. New York: Norton, 1971.

Stuckey, Sterling. *Slave Culture*. New York: Oxford University Press, 1987.

GENEVIÈVE FABRE (1996)

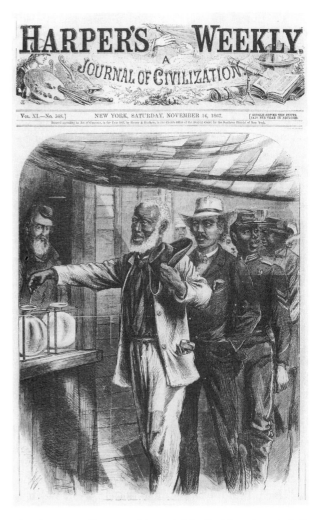

The First Vote. *The cover of Harper's Weekly, November 16, 1867, depicts an African-American freedman casting his ballot. Under the Reconstruction Act passed by Congress that year, Southern states were required to extend suffrage to black men. The fifteenth amendment, ratified in 1870, provided a constitutional guarantee for the voting rights off all African Americans, North and South.* PHOTOGRAPHS AND PRINTS DIVISION, SCHOMBURG CENTER FOR RESEARCH IN BLACK CULTURE, THE NEW YORK PUBLIC LIBRARY, ASTOR, LENOX AND TILDEN FOUNDATIONS.

FIFTEENTH AMENDMENT
■ ■ ■

The Fifteenth Amendment to the U.S. Constitution provides that voting rights shall not be abridged by the federal government or any state "on account of race, color, or previous condition of servitude." The amendment reflected the federal government's emergence during Reconstruction as the guarantor of civil rights against state intrusion.

Having granted most southern black men the right to vote, at least temporarily, by the Military Reconstruction

THE FIFTEENTH AMENDMENT.
CELEBRATED MAY 19th 1870.

Political poster celebrating the ratification of the fifteenth amendment, 1870. The amendment provided a constitutional guarantee that "the right of citizens of the United States to vote shall not be denied or abridged by the United States or by any State on account of race, color, or previous condition of servitude." Nevertheless, many state officials circumvented the intent of the legislation by using devices such as literacy tests and poll taxes to prevent black citizens from exercising their right to vote. PHOTOGRAPHS AND PRINTS DIVISION, SCHOMBURG CENTER FOR RESEARCH IN BLACK CULTURE, THE NEW YORK PUBLIC LIBRARY, ASTOR, LENOX AND TILDEN FOUNDATIONS.

acts of 1867, the Republican majority in Congress wanted to render black suffrage nationwide and permanent. Congressman George S. Boutwell of Massachusetts proposed a constitutional amendment in January 1869. Controversy arose over the wording, with many supporters of civil rights fearing that a vague amendment would permit later disenfranchisement through indirect means.

Other Republicans, however, insisted that northern states be able to restrict suffrage on the basis of literacy and education, often for nativist reasons. In addition, some congressmen feared granting unrestricted authority in this area to the federal government. In response to such concerns, a relatively limited form of the amendment passed Congress in February 1869, over vehement Democratic opposition. It was ratified by the states in March 1870,

aided by the presence of Reconstruction governments in most southern states.

A more radical amendment, calling for an end to disenfranchisement based on "race, color, nationality, property, education, or religious beliefs," was rejected, as were feminist calls for women's suffrage. Furthermore, the amendment did not guarantee the right of blacks to hold office.

As proponents of the more radical amendment had feared, southern Democratic state governments did almost eliminate black voting through poll taxes, literacy tests, residency requirements, and similar means. The Fifteenth Amendment, however, did permanently secure voting rights in the northern states, several of which did not permit black voting at the time. The amendment was also of long-term significance in that it declared equal suffrage an ideal, if not a reality, in the nation's fundamental law. The effort to actually secure black suffrage took more than this amendment. The National Association for the Advancement of Colored People (NAACP) fought successfully against the many abridgments to black suffrage in the early twentieth century, but it was not until the Voting Rights Act of 1965 that the vast majority of eligible southern blacks were registered to vote.

See also National Association for the Advancement of Colored People (NAACP); Voting Rights Act of 1965

■ ■ *Bibliography*

Foner, Eric. *Reconstruction: America's Unfinished Revolution, 1863–1877.* New York: Harper and Row, 1988.

Hyman, Harold M. *A More Perfect Union: The Impact of the Civil War and Reconstruction on the Constitution.* Boston: Knopf, 1973.

Maltz, Earl M. *Civil Rights, the Constitution, and Congress, 1863–1869.* Lawrence: University of Kansas, 1990.

Malveoux, Julianne. "Are Our Voting Rights at Risk?" *Black Issues in Higher Education* 21, no. 2 (March 2004): 38.

MICHAEL W. FITZGERALD (1996)
Updated bibliography

FILM
■·■·■

This entry consists of three articles. The first article examines the history of African descended peoples in film in Latin America and the Caribbean—with emphasis on Cuba and Brazil—noting similarities and differences with the history of African-American film in the United States. "Film in the United States" covers the history of African-American film through the 1970s. "Film in the United States, Contemporary" is an overview of African-American film in the United States since the mid-1980s.

FILM IN LATIN AMERICA AND THE CARIBBEAN
Darién J. Davis

FILM IN THE UNITED STATES
Thomas Cripps

CONTEMPORARY FILM IN THE UNITED STATES
Paula J. Massood

FILM IN LATIN AMERICA AND THE CARIBBEAN

Cinema has played an important role in the representation and diffusion of culture throughout the Americas since its arrival at the turn of the nineteenth century. Filmmakers have utilized the silver screen for a variety of purposes, from propaganda to entertainment to raising social consciousness. As in other areas of American life, Africans and their descendants have played significant roles in the development of the cinematic tradition in Latin American and the Caribbean. They have made important contributions as scriptwriters, producers, editors, directors, researchers, and actors despite discriminatory practices that limited their access and opportunities. At the same time, however, weak Latin American and Caribbean economies have provided few opportunities for filmmakers of all ethnicities.

Despite these obstacles, Brazil and Cuba, two countries with significant black populations, have produced scores of feature films that have garnered national and international praise. In addition, experimental and documentary filmmakers in Latin American have made a number of important works that speak to national and local experiences. Unfortunately, even high-quality Latin American and Caribbean films cannot attract the audiences that the highly advertised Hollywood blockbuster films often do. Nor has Latin America or the Caribbean developed internationally influential black directors. This has little to do with talent and much to do with language barriers, access to global communication systems, and limited publicity.

An assessment of film production in three broad geocultural divisions—Brazil; the Caribbean Basin; and Mexico and Spanish South and Central America—will help one understand the varied experience of the people of the African diaspora in film. Shaped by international and national social, political, and aesthetic trends, cinema has nonetheless contributed to pan-African consciousness. Indeed, feature films and documentaries about black culture and history have also played an important role in raising the awareness of the impact of the African diaspora throughout the Americas.

BRAZIL

Latin America's largest economy and most populous country is also home to the region's largest African-American population (depending on the method of organization of data). Even conservative statistics show more than fifteen million black Brazilians, whose contributions have been more visible in popular culture than in other areas. Their influence in Brazil's film industry began in the early stages with personalities such as director-writer-actor Benjamin de Oliveira. In general, however, Afro-Brazilians constitute a small fraction of the working directors, producers, technical staff, and actors in the country.

Black directors and writers have suffered from limited access to federal, state, and private funds necessary to make films in Brazil. Nevertheless, Brazil has produced several important directors, although none have produced a body of work that allows comparison to North American directors. The Afro-Brazilian writer, producer, and director José Cajado Filho (1912–1966) worked on a number of important films in the late 1940s and early 1950s, although the work of other black directors, such as Odilon López and Waldir Onofre (b. 1934), deal more specifically with racial issues.

Influenced by the theatrical revue and popular music and culture, Brazilian film production began at the turn of the nineteenth century and continued into the 1930s, under the watchful eyes of President Getúlio Vargas. In the 1940s, film entrepreneurs created the Hollywood-like film production companies, Cinédia and Vera Cruz. However, they soon fell into bankruptcy because they lacked the Hollywood distribution apparatus. The 1950s saw the emergence of a new cinema movement, cinema novo, that was interested in film with social relevance at a time when Brazil was experiencing rapid economic expansion under President Juscelino Kubitschek (1955-1960). In search of their national roots, many of the films looked at the ethnic and social groups often denied visibility in the official neo-colonial history, including Afro-Brazilians.

In 1969, the state created the first government film agency, EmbraFilme, that was responsible for financing, distributing, and promoting national films throughout the Brazil. In the 1980s, Brazilian film production continued to expand, due in part to its international recognition and the increase in sales receipts. This allowed the government film agency EmbraFilme to expand its operations, a trend that continued until the Collar presidency's budget cuts, which badly hurt film production from 1992-1996. Since then, Brazilian cinema has experienced a renaissance, and Afro-Brazilians are playing an important part in it.

At the beginning of the twenty-first century, the São Paulo group Dogma Feijoada (Bean Stew Dogma), led by Jeferson De and other black filmmakers, including Noel Carvalho, Billy Castilho, Rogério, Daniel Santiago, and Agenor Alves, aims to create a black cinema that both represents the multiplicity of the black experience and speaks directly to black audiences. Although inspired by the Danish group Dogme 95 and black American directors, Dogme Feijoada is firmly rooted in the Brazilian experience. Jeferson De's *Distraida para a morte* (Distracted to Death, 2001) and Ari Cândido Fernandes's *O Rito de Ismael Ivo* (The Ritual of Ishmael Ivo, 2003) are two of the first films that represent Dogma Feijoada's goals. In addition, a number of documentaries have been made by Afro-

Brazilians—from Zózimo Bulbul to Joel Zeto Araújo—on topics from slavery to modern life.

Black actors and actresses have played important roles in both the cinema and in television series and *novelas*, or soap operas. The pioneering work of Benjamin de Oliveira, one of Brazil's first clowns and a silent movie actor, leads the list of talented Afro-Brazilians, which includes the writer and producer Haroldo Costa, veteran actors and actresses such as Léa Garcia, Ruth de Souza, Milton Gonçalves, Zezé Motta, as well as younger artists, such as Lázaro Ramos, Taís Araújo, and the young actors and actresses from the Rio de Janeiro theatrical group Nós do Morro.

Despite the growing opportunities, Brazilian feature films about race and the African diaspora are largely shaped by an eclectic group of white filmmakers, many of whom (Nelson Pereira dos Santos, Carlos "Cacá" Diegues, Hector Babenco, Fernando Meirelles, Helvécio Ratton, and others) have garnered critical acclaim for their work. Major Brazilian films on race and on black Brazilians can be divided into four major categories: (1) slavery; (2) miscegenation and syncretism; (3) popular culture and celebration; and (4) class dynamics and marginality. Some films overlap into various categories.

Few Brazilian films on slavery were made before the 1950s, with the exception of Antônio Marques Filho's 1929 A *Escrava Isaura* (The Slave Isaura), based on Bernardo Guimarães 1875 novel of the same name (and remade in 1949 by Eurides Ramos). A *Escrava Isaura* is emblematic of a host of films that purportedly support black causes, such as abolition, while not necessarily embracing the notion of black liberation and self-sufficiency. To Guimarães and other abolitionists, the case of Isaura is tragic because she is well educated and "looks white," sentiments that allow Brazilians of the time, and consequently the film to sidestep issues of black suffering and liberation.

Some three decades later *Sinhá Moça* (The Landowner's Daughter, 1953) and *João Negrinho* (1958) provided viewers with more complex representations of abolition. Based on the nineteenth-century work by Maria Dezonne Pacheco Fernandes, *Sinhá Moça*, directed by Tom Payne and Oswaldo Sampãio, is a dramatic period piece about the abolition of slavery, although the film centers on the conflict between a slave-owning father and his abolitionist daughter. At the same time, the film offers complex views and performances by many talented actors, particularly Ruth de Souza (b. 1921), one of the pioneers of the Teatro Experimental do Negro (TEN) founded by Afro-Brazilian activist Abdias do Nascimento. The film also received a number of important national and international awards.

The Afro-Brazilian response to slavery is the focus of three of Cacá Diegues's (b. 1940) films: *Ganga Zumba*

(1964), *Xica da Silva* (1976), and *Quilombo* (1984). A member of the socially committed Cinema Novo movement, Diegues has treated black themes and employed black actors and actresses throughout his career. *Ganga Zumba*, which relies heavily on historical sources as well as myth, lore, and fantasy, recreates the life of Ganga Zumba, a nephew of Zumbi, the famous leader of Palmares, the seventeenth-century escaped-slave community turned republic. The history and dynamics of Palmares is the subject of Diegues's *Quilombo. Xica da Silva,* on the other hand, tells the story of the mulatto slave Xica (played by the black actress Zezé Motta) and her alliance with João Fernandes, a Portuguese diamond official who was sent to Vila Rica (Ouro Preto in the state of Minas Gerais) in the eighteenth century. The film emphasizes the plight of black women held in bondage although it utilizes the stereotype of the sensual black woman in a problematic manner. At the same time the film illustrates the limits of sexual union in achieving social ascent. Also important in this category is Walter Lima Junior's *Chico rei* (Chico the King, 1985). The film chronicles the capture of Galanga, a member of a royal Congo family, his baptism in Brazil as Francisco (Chico), and his eventual liberation and challenge to the colonial government.

While slavery and abolition constitute an important theme in Brazilian historical and cultural studies, many more films have explored issues of miscegenation and syncretism, two forces which many scholars believe have been fundamental to the Brazilian character. At the same time, this reality has often been misused to promote patriotism and deflect attention from social change. Thus, it is not surprising that many Brazilian films treat miscegenation or syncretism as a *de facto* part of the Brazilian cultural landscape, while others focus on the problems and challenges of syncretism and miscegenation more explicitly, as in the case of *Xica* or *A Escrava Isaura.*

The complexities of miscegenation and whitening is highlighted in *Macunaíma,* Joaquim de Pedro Andrade's 1969 satirical adaptation of Mario de Andrade's work of the same name. The film employs satire to provide insight into racial attitudes and the desire of many Brazilians to become white, but it is not as critical as the U.S. film *Imitation of Life* (1934, remade in 1959), whose African-American female protagonist attempts to pass for white.

Rather than focusing explicitly on race, as in the U.S. film *Guess Who's Coming to Dinner?*(1967), directed by Stanley Kramer, Brazilian films often present racial intermingling and mixing with class complexities. Films such as Carlos Manga's 1953 *Dupla de Barulho* (A Great Pair), with Grande Otelo and Oscarito, and Waldir Onofre's *As aventuras amorosas de um padeiro* (The Amorous Adventures of a Baker, 1977) lighten interracial tensions with humor. Furthermore, Onofre's film about the adventures of two working-class men and a white woman from the middle class is more about class dynamics in a Rio neighborhood.

Still, as in U.S. movies such as Spike Lee's *Jungle Fever* (1991), and following in the tradition of Diegues' *Xica,* a certain fatalism often dooms interracial relations in Brazilian films, despite historical examples to the contrary. This is the case in Odilon Lopez's *Um e Pouco, Dois e Bom* (One Is Not Enough, Two Is Good, 1971), in the more complex *Tenda dos Milagres* (*Tent of Miracles,* 1977), and in *Na boca do mundo* (*In the Mouth of the World,* 1979). Antonio Pitanga's *In the Mouth of the World* centers on a love triangle among a black worker (Antônio), a white bourgeois woman (Clarisse) with whom he has an affair, and his mulatto girlfriend (Terezinha). Race and class intersect with urban and rural tensions in this film, which ends in the death of the main character and a surprising alliance between Clarisse and Terezinha.

The portrayal of intra-class racism and prejudice is not as pervasive in Brazilian films as they are in American films. Nelson Pereira dos Santos exposes this issue (among many) in *Tenda dos Milagres* through a complex plot that deals with middle-class intermarriage and the obsession of a white professor who tries to hide his African ancestry. Paradoxically, the film also celebrates miscegenation, rather than black rights and liberation, as a solution to racism—an ideology that has its roots in the nineteenth century and that gained an internationally renown spokesmen in Gilberto Freyre and Jorge Amado (the author of the novel on which the film is based). While literature and cinematographic texts have historically focused on alliances of European men and women of color, Carlota Camuarti's 1996 dramatic farce *Carlota Joaquina* departs from this trend in its depiction of Infanta Carlota Joaquina, who is lured by the Brazilian racial mixing experience and takes a black lover.

Religious miscegenation or syncretism is treated in a number of Brazilian films, including *Tenda dos Milagres,* Glauber Rocha's *Barravento* (1962), Anselmo Duarte's *O Pagador de Promesas* (*The Given Word,* 1962), and Nelson Pereira dos Santos' *O Amuleto de Ogum* (*Ogum's Amulet,* 1974). *O Pagador de Promesas* and *Tenda dos Milagres* focus directly on syncretism and illustrate the tensions and prejudice of white society, while *Barravento* examines the Afro-Bahian religion Candomblé on its own terms, although not without exposing the limitations of organized religion. In *O Amuleto de Ogum,* Pereira dos Santos' explores the Afro-Brazilian religion Umbanda, while exposing racism and class prejudice in a small town in the

Northeast. The Brazilian-Nigerian coproduction of *A Deusa Negra* (1978), directed by the Nigerian filmmaker Olá Balogún, provides a rare cross-Atlantic glimpse into the religious and familiar continuity through the Yoruba-based religion Candomblé. *Samba da Criação do Mundo* (*Samba of the Creation of the World,* 1979) attempts to give a Yoruba rendition of the world's creation and Afro-Brazilian religious values, themes covered in a number of documentaries and shorts from Brazil, the United States, and Europe.

African religious practices such as Candomblé and Umbanda have not only had an impact on religion in Brazil but also on other national and local customs from dance and music to dress and food. In the silent film era, Afro-Brazilian musicians such as Pixinguinha, Donga, and others played live music during screenings. Others composed and played in orchestras for the carnival revue films of the 1930s and 1940s and the melodramas and slapstick comedies called *chanchadas* that showcased the talents of Grande Otelo, one of the pioneering Afro-Brazilian performers. Afro-Brazilian musicians have also been at the center of a number of documentaries, such as Leon Hirszman's 1969 *Nelson Caviquinho* and Andrucha Waddington's *Viva São João!* (Long Live St. John!, 2002), which features singer-songwriter Gilberto Gil.

Although filmmakers recognized the contributions (if not central role) of blacks to Brazilian popular music, they were visibly absent from the 1930s carnival films such as *Alô Alô Carnaval* and *Alô Alô Brasil*. This changes somewhat with the making of Luis de Barrow's *Samba em Berlim* (1943), featuring Grande Otelo and Nilo Chagas, and other films such as *Rio Zona Norte* (1957), with Grande Otelo, Angela Maria, and a host of other Afro-Brazilian performers. For its time, the internationally acclaimed French production of Marcel Camus's *Orfeu Negro* (*Black Orpheus,* 1959), which was based on the Vinicius de Moraes play *Orfeu da Conceíção*, was a rare assembly of talented black actors and performers. Only in 1999 did Carlos Diegues create his own rendition of the play, simply titled *Orfeu,* starring Afro-Brazilian Tony Garrido from the musical group Cidade Negra.

Black poverty and marginality also represent major themes in Brazilian cinema. While music, revelry, and religion constituted important aspects of the realist dramas of Cinema Novo, black discontent and revolt were essential in films such as Nelson Pereira dos Santos's *Rio 40 graus* (1955) and *Rio Zona Norte* (1957) as well as Roberto Farias's 1962 *Assalto ao trem pagador* (Assault on the Pay Train), based on an actual 1960 train robbery. Despite the title, Farias provides an engrossing story about the relationship among the multiracial robbers, interweaving is-

sues of race and class. Tião, one of the black thieves, stands in contrast to Grilo Peru, one of the white robbers, who not only iterates the only explicit racial slur in the film but also is able to spend his money conspicuously without drawing attention to himself. *Assalto ao trem pagador* boasts a talented multiracial cast that brought the film more critical acclaim than others films dealing with the inhabitants of the *favelas* (shantytowns, or slums). Also worthy of mention is Leon Hirszman's *Eles Não Usam Black-Tie* (1981), which deals with labor conflicts in São Paulo. Black characters play principal roles in the film, but race does not necessarily play a factor in the drama.

The twenty-first century has brought a host of impressive films that focus critically on poverty and marginality—and on black responses to them. Helvecio Ratton's *Uma onda no ar* (2002) presents the development and triumph of an alternative radio station (Radio Favela) created by four Afro-Brazilians in the *favelas* of Belo Horizonte in the state of Minas Gerais. Hector Babenco's 2003 production of *Carrindiru*, an epic on the São Paulo prison system of the same name, continues in the tradition of the politically committed movies of Cinema Novo. New directors such as Fernando Meirelles with his two films *Domésticas* (Maids, 2000) and *Cidade de Deus* (City of God, 2002), and the New York–based Brazilian filmmaker Karim Aïnouz's *Madame Satã* (2002), show the influence of Hollywood while appealing to a new generation of Brazilian filmgoers. In the tradition of Brazilian film, race and class are intimately interconnected, but the fact that the main characters in all three films are marginalized black characters indicates the need to explore, as Dogma Feijoada intimates, more diverse experiences of Afro-Brazilians.

Many Brazilian documentary filmmakers have exposed contemporary issues and problems related to the Afro-Brazilian world in ways that feature films have not. Compared to U.S. filmgoers, contemporary Brazilian documentaries have garnered a massive following, thanks, in part, to film festivals in Rio de Janeiro, Brasilia, Recife, and Miami that showcase Brazilian feature films and documentaries. The Bank of Brazil Cultural Center's "It's All True" festival and the Moreira Salles Institute's festival, which focus exclusively on documentaries, have been instrumental in providing spaces for this genre.

The black filmmaker Zózimo Bulbul's 150-minute film *Aboilção* (Abolition, 1988), which often meanders, nonetheless represents an important document that registered a personal perspective on the celebration of the one-hundredth anniversary of the abolition of slavery. Sections of the 1992 release of Orson Welles's unfinished *It's All True* (which gave the name to the Bank of Brasil-sponsored festival), deals with black influences in Brazil in the 1930s. Of the many important documentaries to come out of Brazil at the beginning of the twenty-first century, two deserve special mention. Joel Zito Araujo's *A negacāo do Brasil* (Denying Brazil, 2000) examines the struggles of black actors in Brazil, particularly how racial taboos, prejudice, and stereotypes have limited their roles in the television industry. The riveting *Ônibus 174* (2002) explores the tragic life of Sandro do Nascimento, a young black man who hijacked a bus in Rio de Janiero in June 2000. The film's innovative analysis interconnects issues of race, poverty, the media, the state, and police brutality Some of these issues are also present in New York-based filmmaker Tania Cypriano's powerful *Oda Ya! Vida com AIDS* (2001) which focuses on how AIDS has effected the black community, as well as education and the positive celebrations of human sexuality.

The aforementioned feature films and documentaries indicate that Brazilian cinema has experienced important social advancements. Yet, black filmmakers and actors remain underrepresented. This is particularly troubling in films made for television, as Brazilians have more access to this medium than to the cinema. In many ways, however, the diversity of black characters and themes present in Brazilian cinema is richer than in any other American nations.

THE CARIBBEAN BASIN

Despite their shared history and parallel African influences, the multilingual and politically independent nations of the Caribbean Basin (including the coastal regions of South and Central America) stand in contrast to Portuguese-speaking Brazil, which is unified both politically and linguistically. The population of Brazil is greater than the population of all the nations of the Caribbean Basin combined. Moreover, of all the Caribbean nations, Cuba is the only country that has developed an important film industry, and that only occurred after 1960. The former French, English, and, to a lesser extent, Dutch island colonies—all with black majorities—have nonetheless inspired foreign filmmakers. The islands have provided exotic backdrops to a host of Hollywood films, from *The Satanic Dr. No* (1963) to the cross-diaspora but also exoticizing *How Stella Got Her Groove Back* (1998), directed by Kevin Rodney Sullivan. Examples that explore the autonomous cultures of the Caribbean include Robert Rossen's *Island in the Sun* (1957); Gillo Pontecorvo's *Burn!* (1969), loosely based on the events of the Haitian Revolution; and a host of indigenous, European, and North American documentaries.

The French and English Caribbean have produced few feature films, although the Jamaican Perry Henzel's 1972 movie *The Harder They Come* helped to bring images of the poor black neighborhoods of Kingston to the silver screen along with the vibrant reggae music that has inspired the world. The French Caribbean has produced a number of important filmmakers including the Haitians Raoul Peck (*Haitian Corner*, 1988; *Lumumba*, 2000), Rassoul Labuchin (*Anita*, 1982), and the prolific Christian Lara from Guadeloupe. The Martinican director Euzhan Palcy's quiet portrayal of poverty and the lack of educational opportunities in a Martinican neighborhood in *Rue Cases Negres* (Sugar Cane Alley, 1983) brought her wide acclaim, ultimately leading to work in Hollywood on *A Dry White Season* (1989), a social drama set in South Africa. Guadeloupe-born Christian Grandman examines relationships among a number of marginalized Caribbean characters in a town outside of Pointe-a-Pitre in his 2000 film *Excluídos (Tètt Grenné)*.

Outside of Cuba, the making of feature films in the Spanish Caribbean is rare. Some exceptions include Efraín López Neris's *A Life of Sin* (1993) the story of the Puerto Rican prostitute Isabel la Negra (filmed in English); Leon Ichaso's *Piñero* (2001), the story of the Nuyorican poet Miguel Piñero, featuring black Nuyoricans who knew Piñero; or Angel Muñiz's *Nueba Yol* (1996), which was inspired by the immigrant experience of Dominicans in New York.

Many talented Caribbean actors have also played a vital role in the region's cultural production, but the majority are not known internationally. Those who have been able to cross over to international markets are often limited to specific language markets. This is the case with actors who work on productions directed by filmmakers such as Felix de Rooy from Curação and Pim de la Parra from Suriname (both are based in Holland). English-speaking actors with Caribbean connections, such as Harry Belafonte and Sidney Poitier, have also had an important impact on films in the United States in a variety of ways, although the same cannot be said of talented Afro–Puerto Ricans, Afro-Dominicans, or Afro-Cubans.

FILMMAKING IN CUBA

Before 1959, Cuban film production had been irregular and uneven. After the success of the Castro-led revolution, Cuba's film production was aided by the creation of the Cuban Institute for Cinematographic Art and Industry (ICAIC), and the Cuban Broadcasting Institute. Cubans engaged intellectuals throughout Latin America and the Caribbean in forging a new Latin American cinema, inspired by revolutionary ideals. They created what the filmmaker Julio García Espinosa, one of the founders of ICAIC, described as an "imperfect cinema"—which by its nature was supposed to be anti-Hollywood. From the

1960s to the 1980s, the ICAIC produced a steady stream of feature films, documentaries and docudramas as well as animated and more experimental film genres. Afro-Cubans have helped shaped the Cuban film industry, although, as in Brazil, they are not as visible as one might expect.

Directors such as Sergio Giral (b. 1973) and Sara Gomez (1943–1974), two well-known directors from the early era of ICAIC, have been followed by an enthusiastic group of young directors and writers, including Gloria Rolando, Tony Romero, and Rigoberto López. Actors and actresses have been equally important in bringing Cuban stories to the silver screen. Actresses such as Adelá Legrá, Assenech Rodriguez, and Daisy Granados (b. 1942) have played multiple roles in Cuban film since the 1960s. Granados, considered by many to be the grande dame of Cuban cinema, often plays roles in which racial identity is ambiguous or seemingly unimportant, although she also played the mulatta title character in *Cecilia* (1982). Other Afro-Cuban veteran actors include Mario Balmaseda, Miguel Benavides, and Tito Junco. Unfortunately, the Cuban economic crisis precipitated by the collapse of the Soviet Union in 1989 have meant that many young would-be actors and filmmakers have had to abort their careers in film or find work abroad. Moreover, as in Brazil, few black actors have appeared in central roles in nonhistorical feature films.

From the beginning of the revolution, however, Afro-Cubans and themes of the African diaspora have figured prominently in Cuba's film production. One important example is Sabá Cabrera Infante's 1961 short documentary film *P.M.,* which includes scenes from Havana's nightlife. In the film, black Cubans (and some white Cubans) are shown dancing and drinking in a local bar in Havana. The government's censoring of the film marked an important shift in the relationship between intellectuals who had supported the revolution and the Castro government. Although Cuba's film production industry emerged under the watchful eyes of censors bent on promoting revolutionary ideas and themes, many Cuban filmmakers succeeded in bringing their critical vision to the silver screen. Cuban films also promoted Third World solidarity, as in Tomás Gutiérrez Alea's *Cumbite* (1964), based on the Jaques Roumain novel about the life of sugar-cane cutters in Haiti. As in the case of Brazil, four broad categories, with socialist modifications, can help one to understand the filmography of race and Afro-Cubans in Cuba (although all four engage more explicitly with notions of nationhood, or *cubanidad*). These categories in Cuba are: (1) slavery; (2) miscegenation and racial intermingling; (3) music and culture; and (4) race, class, and nationhood.

Slavery lasted longer in Cuba than in any other Spanish colony, making Cuba the most culturally African of the Spanish-speaking nations of the Caribbean Basin. Thus, slavery and abolition figure prominently in the Cuban filmography. Indeed any film that treats the nineteenth century would be remiss without references to slavery. The majority of Cuban films that deal with slavery can be viewed through a Marxist revolutionary lens, with explicit class analysis, while at the same time they reconstruct important Cuban historical realities.

Tomás Gutiérrez Alea's 1977 *La Última Cena* (The Last Supper) deals explicitly with slavery and race relations. Based on an eighteenth-century incident, the film presents the story of a pious and supposedly well-meaning slave owner who decided to treat his slaves better by instructing them in the values of Christianity and by inviting them to participate in the feast of the celebration of Passover. The result is explosive, as the slaves rebel, burning the plantation and attempting to escape.

Afro-Cuban director Sergio Giral began his career with *The Other Francisco* (1975), a film that engages and deconstructs official interpretations of Cuban history. The film reinterprets Anselmo Suarez y Romero's nineteenth-century antislavery Romantic novel *Francisco,* written some twenty years before *Uncle Tom's Cabin* (1852). While the novel focuses on Francisco's desperation that eventually leads to suicide, the film emphasizes Francisco's role in fighting the system and attempting to secure his freedom. Giral also directed a number of documentaries and feature films including *Maluala* (1979) and *Maria Antonia (1991),* the latter an innovative reading of the Afro-Cuban goddess of beauty Ochún.

The nineteenth century saw the decline of slavery at a time when most of the Latin American societies were becoming increasingly more mestizo (mixed race). Syncretism and racial intermingling figure prominently in Cuban films, and in many respects represent de facto Cuban culture, making the term "Afro-Cuban" problematic at best. Huberto Solás's *Cecilia* (1982), based on the nineteenth-century novel *Cecilia Valdés* by Cirilo Villaverde, points to the problems of miscegenation in a society dominated by European values and is in many ways similar to *A Escrava Isaura*. Cecilia is part of a third-generation Cuban family that has slowly become more white. In the attempt to escape her black past, Cecilia must ultimately face tragic consequences. Solás' *Miel para Ochún* (Honey for Oshun, 2001) examines the issue of black heritage in a more provocative and politically charged manner. The main character, a white Cuban exile, returns to Cuba to find his mother, whom he barely remembers and whom he believes abandoned him. He not only comes into contact with

Afro-Cuban culture, but he finds that his mother is Afro-Cuban, and thus a part of his lost past. The intertextual dialogue with earlier Cuban films such as *Lucía* (1969), also directed by Solás, and Tomás Gutiérrez Alea's *Memories of Underdevelopment* (1968) cannot be overlooked. Particularly interesting is the choice of the actress Adelá Legrá to portray the Cuban mother in *Honey for Oshún*. Legrá had previously portrayed a peasant woman who becomes a part of revolutionary culture in the epic *Lucía*. In *Honey for Oshun*, Legrá is the character who represents the maternal figure whom the exiled protagonist seeks.

Despite Cuba's Marxist focus on class analysis, and its spurring of official religion, the Afro-Cuban religion Santería has flourished under the revolution and has even been commodified for a growing tourist economy. Cuban films have treated Santería as an integral part of Cuban culture, though often in passing or as a part of the Cuban landscape, as in Tomás Gutiérrez Alea's *Strawberry and Chocolate* (1994). Alea's treatment of race in *Strawberry and Chocolate* and *Memories of Underdevelopment* deserves special mention. On the one hand, blacks and blackness are equated in these films with undesirable Dionysian elements of Cuban culture from which the protagonists of both films wish to distance themselves. On the other hand, black actors in Cuba and throughout Latin American are often limited to roles representing stereotypes, such as the uncontrolled dancers and musicians in the opening scene of *Memories of Underdevelopment* or the *santero* in *Strawberry and Chocolate*.

Other feature films have provided lengthy examinations of African cultural influences. A departure from the political and committed new cinema of Cuba is Manuel Octavio Gómez's eclectic 1982 musical *Patakín*. This film provides a modern reading of two Yoruba deities in conflict: Changó, the god of thunder (represented by a man who lives off of his wife) and Oggún, the deity of war and guardian of arms and metals (represented by a hard-working machinist). Although drawing on popular idioms, the film, which was billed as Cuba's first musical, was more comedy than drama, and was not successful in engaging Cuban audiences.

The films *Miel para Ochún* and *La vida es Silbar* (Life Is to Whistle, 1998) address Afro-Cuban cultural influences and their relationship to larger national issues in a more profound manner. In the former, the search for the character's mother is explicitly and implicitly tied to the search for Oshún, the goddess of sweetness and beauty, at a critical time in Cuba's divided history. In the multilayered *Guantanamera* (1951), Alea integrates Afro-Cuban mythology throughout the narrative to comment critically on the Cuban political situation, death, and, ultimately, life in Cuba at the end of the 1990s—although the major characters are not black.

Afro-Cuban customs and rituals have also been explored in many Cuban documentaries and shorts. Gloria Rolando's *Oggún* (1992), for example, provides viewers with an understanding of the Afro-Cuban god of the same name. Through the multilayered testimony of Lázaro Ross, the lead singer of the Conjunto Folclórico Nacional de Cuba and a devotee of Oggún, Rolando presents viewers with stories that allow them to understand Santería, which remains vital to Cubans both inside and outside of Cuba. The Afro-Cuban filmmaker Rigoberto López's *Yo soy del son a la salsa* explores the development of the musical form *salsa* from its beginnings in Cuba as *son*. Luis Felipe Bernaza's *Hasta la Reina Isabel baila el danzón* (Even Queen Isabel Dances the Danzón, 1991) is a docudrama that combines live interviews with surrealistic recreations, satirizing many popular Cuban beliefs. The director includes scenes from Yoruba ceremonies and an innovative rendition of the Afro-Cuban poet Nicolás Guillén's famous work "Sensemayá." Especially important in helping to raise awareness of many of the forgotten Afro-Cuban musical veterans was Wim Wenders's widely acclaimed 1999 documentary *Buena Vista Social Club*. The film follows the making of a music CD and world tour of American musician Ry Cooder with legendary but forgotten Cuban musicians such as Compay Segundo, Ibrahim Ferrer, and Omara Portuondo. The 1997 CD compiled by Ry Cooder was responsible for reviving the careers of all the musicians involved. The protagonists of the equally moving Danish-Cuban music documentary *Lágrimas Negras* (1997) directed by Sonia Herman Dolz, have not been as commercially successful. Cuba has also produced many documentaries on Afro-Cuban legendary musical figures such as Chano Pozo and Joseito Fernandez. José Sánchez-Montes's endearing documentary *Bola De Nieve* (2003), for example, provides a brief biography of the life of one of Cuba's musical treasures. There are also a handful of documentaries on African-American musicians, including Dizzie Gillespie and Harry Belafonte, who both visited Cuba.

As in Brazil, issues of race and class have been intimately intertwined, although in a way that is more ideologically tied to the discussion of integration, national sovereignty, and revolutionary consciousness. Cuba's first female director, Sarah Gómez Yara (1943–1974), was an Afro-Cuban pioneer who had directed a number of short documentaries before her acclaimed docudrama *De Cierta Manera* (One Way or Another, 1977), which was codirected by Tomás Gutiérrez Alea and Julio García Espinosa. Gómez provides a poignant look at the culture of marginality prior to the Cuban Revolution, as well as the challenges of the revolution and the transition to a socialist society. The film is particularly important because of its focus on the ritual of the male-only Abakuá society, which was regarded by many in the Castro regime as antirevolutionary.

Following in the footsteps of Gómez, Gloria Rolando's *Roots of My Heart* (2001) deserves particular mention because of its attempt to treat Cuba's race war of 1912. At that time, members of a Cuban black political party, the Independents of Color, clashed with government forces when parties based on color were declared illegal. The result was the massacre of thousands of Afro-Cubans and decades of silence about the event, which made discussions of racial discrimination all but taboo. Rolando was the first filmmaker to break the silence on this watershed event in Cuban history. She constructed the story from the perspective of a contemporary woman in search of answers about her great grandparents. Other historical perspectives can be gleaned from short documentaries (although many were made with few resources).

Si me comprendieras (If You Only Understood, 1998), by Rolando Díaz, is one of the first Cuban films to openly and frankly discuss Cuban racism, emigration, and Cuba's international historical and contemporary presence in missions abroad. The film begins with a Cuban director assembling his cast for a new film project. In search of a black female dancer and singer, he takes to the street with his video camera. The film follows the film crew from behind the camera as they encounter and talk with Cuban women and possible candidates. From this perspective, audiences receive a glimpse into filmmaking in Cuba, as well as perspectives on attitudes towards women and black Cubans.

The Cuban immigrant communities in the United States and the swelling exile communities in the post–1959 era (particularly on the East Coast), have meant that, like Puerto Rico and the Dominican Republic, Cuban cultural production cannot be limited to the island. This is true of music and literature, but it is also true of film.

Particularly important from the African diaspora perspective is Pam Sporn's modest but revealing documentary *Cuban Roots/Bronx Stories* (2000), which highlights the experience of one black Cuban family while underscoring the diversity in the Cuban exile community. Cuban films in general have revealed a multiplicity of experiences, although the record indicates that, as in Brazil, films in which blacks figure prominently have more often than not dealt with historical themes of slavery and abolition or concentrated on documentaries related to cultural contributions. Complex portrayals where ordinary black Cubans take center stage are rare, although this practice is all too common in other Spanish-speaking countries as well.

MEXICO AND SPANISH SOUTH AND CENTRAL AMERICA

Over the last two centuries, Africans and their descendants have had an impact on the Spanish-speaking peoples of South and Central America in a variety of ways. The black population in Mexico and Argentina, although significant as late as the nineteenth century, do not constitute a major visual presence at the beginning of the twenty-first century. Moreover, many Argentines and Mexicans are oblivious to the African influence on their past, although that influence in Buenos Aires and the Mexican states of Vera Cruz, Guerrero, and Oaxaca has been fairly well documented. Maria Luisa Beberg's film *Camila* (1984) provides a brief glimpse at black servitude in the affluent O'Gorman household under the dictator Juan Manuel Rosas (ruled 1835–1852), but Argentine feature films rarely make references to or include Argentine blacks. In general, documentaries have more successfully challenged the national myths of whiteness and the official silence on the subjects of race and the African presence in feature films. *Afroargentines* (2002), by Diego Ceballos and Jorge Fortes, chronicles the marginalization and cultural legacy of blacks in Argentina, for example, while Lorena Fernandez's *Sodad* (2002) focuses on the Cape Verdian community in that country.

In Mexico, the now classic *Angelitos negros*, the 1948 Mexican remake of the Fannie Hurst novel *Imitation of Life* (Hollywood versions were made in 1934 and 1959), deals explicitly with race. In Joselito Rodríguez's Mexican version, the prejudiced main character (played by a blond Ana Luisa de la Fuente), has no idea that her black maid is actually her mother, and when she finds out her attitude towards her changes. Ironically, a Cuban (Rita Montaner) plays the main black character, Ana Luisa's mother. The film dealt with issues that resonated throughout the region and was immensely successful in Mexico and throughout Latin America, though it was not inspired by a Mexican reality. To date Roberto Olivares' 2004 film, *African Blood*, is a rare, albeit short documentary that explores Mexico's African roots in the states of Oaxaca and Guerrero.

Colombia, Peru, and Venezuela have all been influenced by the African diaspora, though rarely has that influence engendered national debates. Moreover, since the early 1990s, economic and civil strife have made film production difficult in all three countries. Carlos Hugo Christensen's earlier *La Balandra Isabel llegó está tarde* (The Yacht Isabel Arrived This Afternoon, 1949) represents an important cinematographic contribution to the filmography of the African diaspora. Adapted from the Guillermo Memeses's story of the same name, the film provides a rare portrait of urban Afro-Venzuelan culture narrated from the perspective of a black prostitute. In Colombia, a handful of documentaries have explored the country's African legacy, particularly the *palenques* (escaped slave communities). The 2002 British-Colombian coproduction of *Resistencia: Hip-Hop in Colombia,* directed by Tom Feiling, looks at hip-hop culture in Colombia and the response of various artists to the civil war that has ravaged the country for decades.

In the Andean region, which is without a strong film tradition, documentaries and docudramas such as Carlos Ferrand's docudrama *Cimarrones* (1982) treat the themes of slavery and rebellion. This docudrama looks at slavery and the relationship between Africans and Native Americans under Spanish rule. More recently, the Alberto Durant feature *Coraje* (1998) focuses on the extraordinary figure of María Elena Moyano, an Afro-Peruvian activist from the neighborhood of Villa El Salvador, on the outskirts of Lima. Like the majority of Latin American films with central black characters, *Coraje* is not about blackness, per se, but about Moyano's role as a grassroots activist and community leader caught between the terrorist activities of the Shining Path guerrillas and the inattentive government. The documentary on the renowned singer and activist Susana Baca in the joint Peruvian-Belgian film *Susana Baca: Memoria Viva* (2002) continues the focus on Afro-Peruvian women.

The vibrant and diverse black communities that make up Central and South America face similar infrastructure problems that limit film production. A host of other documentaries about the African experience in the Americas provide glimpses into local enterprise, however. They include small budget productions such as the Rafael Deugenio's sixteen-minute *Candombe* (1993), about the Afro-Uruguayan musical tradition. U.S.-based production companies and joint Latin American–U.S. ventures have added to the growing list of documentaries, including the Empowerment Project's *The Panama Deception* (1992), which features interviews with a number of Afro-Panamanian community leaders and commentators, attesting to the varied and diverse African presence through the Americas. However, much of that influence in Spanish South America and Mexico has yet to be explored on film.

The peoples of the African diaspora have had an impact, directly or indirectly, on every American nation. Government commitment to funding film production has provided the necessary backbone to the Brazilian and Cuban film industries, although foreign and private investment has also been critical. Documentaries, with their lower production costs, have highlighted important issues about the African experience in the Americas. Historical films aside, until recently Latin American filmmakers were not as likely to treat issues of prejudice and racial discrimination as central issues, at least when compared to their North American counterparts. Ironically, this has begun to change at a time when North America has seen a number of black actors play roles that are not racially predetermined and when interracial alliances are becoming more common on the silver screen. The welcome addition of a number of Afro-Latin American filmmakers, actors, and other professionals has benefited the region's film production, as has cross-national collaboration. These two developments will be fundamental to the exploration of black themes and issues in the future.

See also Documentary Film; Film in the United States; Filmmakers in the Caribbean; Representations of Blackness in Latin America and the Caribbean

■ ■ *Bibliography*

Cham, Mbye, ed. *Ex-Iles: Essays on Caribbean Cinema.* Trenton, N.J.: Africa World Press, 1992.

Chanan, Michael. *The Cuban Image: Cinema and Cultural Politics.* Bloomington: Indiana University Press, 1985.

García Osuna, Alfonso J. *The Cuban Filmography, 1897 through 2001.* Jefferson, N.C.: McFarland, 2003.

Johnson, Randall, and Robert Stam, eds. *Brazilian Cinema,* expanded edition. New York: Columbia University Press, 1995.

King, John. *Magical Reels: A History of Cinema in Latin America.* New York: Verso, 1990.

Rodrigues, João Carlos. *O Negro Brasileiro e o Cinema,* 2nd ed. Rio de Janeiro: Pallas, 2001.

Stam, Robert. *Tropical Multiculturalism: A Comparative History of Race in Brazilian Cinema and Culture.* Durham, N.C.: Duke University Press, 1997.

DARIÉN J. DAVIS (2005)

FILM IN THE UNITED STATES

Motion pictures and large numbers of African Americans arrived in American cities simultaneously in the late nineteenth century. Black Americans came to cities in flight from the southern peonage that had replaced the institution of slavery after the Civil War. Their Great Migration in turn coincided with a similar migration from Europe. Movies, in their "primitive" days, when techniques of cutting and editing as a means of conveying a narrative had not yet been perfected, became the first medium of mass communications for the poor, teeming populations that filled northeastern cities toward the end of the nineteenth century.

Movies had played the Cotton States Exposition in Atlanta in 1895, and in the following year opened at Koster and Bial's music hall in New York. Strikingly, in these early years African Americans often appeared on the screen in unmediated, unedited form and therefore devoid of some of the worst stereotypes with which they had been maligned by decades of southern novels, advertising logos, and popular songs. A shot of, for example, black soldiers watering their horses or dockers coaling a ship appeared on the screen untrammeled by the pejorative images of the past.

These topical vignettes were the result of a rage for news of events in the corners of the world. Thomas Edison filmed life in the Caribbean; others caught black "buffalo soldiers" on their way to the Spanish-American War, tribal ceremonies in Africa, and Theodore Roosevelt on safari.

Gradually after the turn of the century, the medium changed, both technically and economically. As the prospects for a profitable future opened up, producers began to cultivate more sophisticated techniques that allowed them to edit scenes into narratives along the lines set down by novelists and dramatists. The trend pointed toward a future cinema that would play to middle-class rather than poor audiences, in picture palaces rather than storefront nickelodeons, and at length rather than in the brief snippets with which the medium had begun its life.

For African Americans this meant a resumption of many conventions inherited from the nineteenth-century melodramatic, comic, and musical stage. Indeed, in 1903 William S. Porter brought *Uncle Tom's Cabin* to the screen, complete with overambitious attempts at spectacle—cakewalks, pursuits across ice floes, and even a race between miniature steamboats. Tom himself was more a figure drawn from the sentimental stage than Harriet Beecher Stowe's staunch hero.

Other restorations of familiar racial material gradually dominated the screen just as the medium began to emerge from a primitive, limited visual rhetoric. In *A Bucket of Cream Ale* (1904), a stock, obstreperous black-faced servant appeared; *The Fights of Nations* (1907) featured a razor fight; and comedies about chicken thieving and life in "coontown" became routine. From 1911 through 1915 movies sentimentalized the Civil War during the five years of its semicentennial. Rarely was there an opportunity for a genuine black portrayal to show through in *A Slave's Devotion* (1913), *Old Mammy's Secret Code* (1913), or *For the Cause of the South* (1914). Typical of the era was D. W. Griffith's *His Trust* (1911) and its se-

quel, a tale of the Civil War in which a slave is first entrusted with managing his master's estate while the latter is away fighting and then, after the master dies a hero's death, gives his own "savings" toward sending the master's daughter to finishing school so that she may meet and marry someone in her class.

It was at this moment that African Americans took their first steps toward an indigenous cinema. Local black entrepreneurs in Lexington, Kentucky, as early as the first decade of the century booked all-black films in their theaters. By 1912, William Foster in Kansas made *The Railroad Porter* with a black audience as his target. About the same time in Florida, James Weldon Johnson wrote two scripts for a company bent upon making films with an African-American angle.

Unfortunately for small-time entrepreneurs, the economic setting of moviemaking had begun to rationalize into competing oligopolies, even "trusts," in which ever-fewer sellers drove out competition for customers, who gradually included more demanding middle-class, urbane tastemakers. Edison's Motion Picture Patents Trust, for example, formed a pool of patents through which it hoped to control the entire nation's film output by licensing the use of cameras and projectors. In such a richly capitalized economic field, African Americans only a half century removed from slavery had little chance.

THE BIRTH OF A NATION

Then in 1915, D. W. Griffith—after years spent learning filmmaking and extending its range into techniques unforeseen in the primitive years—released his Civil War epic *The Birth of a Nation*. An evocative combination of conventional racial attitudes, a celebration of the Civil War and of the forbearance of the white South during Reconstruction, and a genuinely avant-garde piece of filmmaking, *The Birth of a Nation* galvanized African Americans and their white allies into a nationwide protest campaign. At issue were two major factors: first, its depiction of Reconstruction as a tale of black cupidity, corruption, and vindictiveness toward the prostrate white South, and second, the unprecedented nationwide advertising campaign, which further heightened the film's impact. It was this combination that nettled blacks. Most literate Americans believed the account of Reconstruction as portrayed therein, complete with its venal freedmen who did the bidding of scalawags and carpetbaggers (Woodrow Wilson had retold it in his multivolume history of the nation), but the couching of it in a blaring ad campaign and in an emotionally charged movie made the difference.

The NAACP fruitlessly conducted a national campaign against the movie, demanding cuts of scenes that "slandered" blacks, advocating strict legal codes against maligning races and groups, and instigating a plan to make its own movie, to be titled *Lincoln's Dream*. But despite the protesters' best efforts, by the end of 1915 *The Birth of a Nation* could be seen almost anywhere its makers wished, and *Lincoln's Dream* foundered for want of an "angel."

Nonetheless, the struggle against Griffith's film confirmed a number of African Americans in their embracing of a strategy of making movies alternative to those of the mainstream. Even Booker T. Washington, the famous founder of Tuskegee Institute and a reputed accommodationist in racial matters, took up the idea of making black movies. At first he feared that the makers of *The Birth of a Nation* might profit from the notoriety that would follow from a vigorous black protest, but soon, through his secretary Emmett J. Scott, he committed resources to a film eventually titled *The Birth of a Race*.

THE BIRTH OF A RACE

Washington and Scott's movie seemed to possess everything: the endorsement of national worthies of the Republican Party; a script that traced the progress of humankind, while allocating a prominent place in it for African Americans; and a panel of rich angels led by Julius Rosenwald, a Sears and Roebuck vice president. But things fell apart. First, Washington died on November 15, 1915. Then, acting on rumors of unscrupulous practices among the project's Chicago fund-raisers, Rosenwald and other prestigious figures withdrew. And finally, with the onset of World War I, the thrust of the already episodic movie veered wildly from a pacifist theme to its ideological opposite—a justification of the American entry into the war. Thus, after almost three years of scrabbling for money, shooting in Tampa, and cutting through the thicket of cross-purposed story lines, the project changed. And yet the completed movie reached a level of accomplishment never previously attained by black moviemakers. They had actually completed a feature-length film, albeit one burdened by seemingly endless title frames that slowed its pace and shouldered aside its African-American premise in favor of militaristic themes.

THE LINCOLN COMPANY

Moreover, readers of the black press noticed. Indeed, one man in particular, a postman in Omaha named George P. Johnson, saw the film as more than a grand flop. Together with his brother Noble Johnson, a contract player at Universal, he assembled a circle of black investors in Los Angeles into the Lincoln Company. From 1916 to 1922 they turned out an impressive string of films (of which only a fragment survives), all of them celebrations of the black aspiration embedded in one of the company's titles: *The Realization of a Negro's Ambition*.

Indeed, aspiration was emblazoned on the Johnsons' battleflags. It marked or guided everything they made, whether tales of black "buffalo soldiers" fighting Mexican *insurrectes* along the border or go-getters scoring successes in capitalist circles that few blacks would have had access to in the reality of American life. The Johnsons' rivals during the booming 1920s not only followed their example but extended its reach. Among these were the Frederick Douglass Company (with its Republican namesake on its letterhead), Sidney P. Dones's Democracy Company, and regional operations such as Gate City in Kansas, Ker-Mar in Baltimore, and Norman in Jacksonville and later Boley, Oklahoma. In the pages of the African-American press appeared dozens of announcements of additional companies, most of which did not survive long enough to see their first film to the screen.

Some studios, such as Norman, were conduits for the investments of white "angels" or were in fact white firms. Robert Levy's Reol Studio, for example, was a white-owned company that made films from well-known black classics such as Paul Laurence Dunbar's *The Sport of the Gods*. To some extent this rush of activity merely testified to the wealth that had reached even black strata of urban life during the 1920s. But it also suggested the presence of a maturing film culture, drawing in a sector of the black population that was not only well off enough to buy tickets but also literate enough to read the growing amount of advertising copy, reviews, and show-business gossip that had begun to fill the pages of the African-American press.

THE BLACK AUDIENCE

In other words, an audience had been formed by the black migrations to the urban centers of America, both North and South. The names of the theaters signaled the identity of the audience. No Bijous, Criterions, or Paramounts there but rather a Douglass or an Attucks to honor famous heroes, a Lenox, Harlem, or Pekin to provide linkages to increasingly well-known centers of black urban culture. This sort of social, institutional, and cultural density suggested the nature of this newly arrived audience: urban, literate, employed, affiliated in a circle of lodges and clubs, and church members. In short, the audience constituted a thin layer of bourgeoisie to whom movies spoke of aspiration, racial pride, and heroism, and cautioned against the evils of drink and sloth—much like a Booker T. Washington commencement address with pictures.

Advertisement for **The Burden of Race.** *Reol Productions made movies featuring black actors for African-American audiences, including this 1921 film about a young black man who falls in love with a white woman. The success of such commercial ventures is an indication of the size of potential audiences formed by the migration of African Americans to northern cities during the early decades of the twentieth century.* PHOTOGRAPHS AND PRINTS DIVISION, SCHOMBURG CENTER FOR RESEARCH IN BLACK CULTURE, THE NEW YORK PUBLIC LIBRARY, ASTOR, LENOX AND TILDEN FOUNDATIONS.

We can sense these social traits not only from the themes of the movies themselves but also from the critics who wrote about them: D. Ireland Thomas in the *Mississippi Valley,* Lester Walton of the *New York Age,* Theophilus Lewis in several papers in the New York area, Billy Rowe in the *Pittsburgh Courier,* Romeo Daugherty in the *Amsterdam News,* Fay Jackson for Claude A. Barnett's Associated Negro Press service, and other regulars on the Afro-American chain and even smaller papers. Augmenting their own acute criticism that seemed to be maturing toward a genuine African-American posture toward cinema were the syndicated columnists, who wrote gossipy copy for the *Los Angeles Sentinel* and the *California Eagle*— Ruby Berkeley Goodwin, Harry Levette, and Lawrence LaMar.

MICHEAUX AND THE COLORED PLAYERS

Playing to this emerging audience in the 1920s were the elite of "race" film companies, either staunchly black firms such as that of Oscar Micheaux or white firms with a feel for the audience, such as David Starkman's Colored Players in Philadelphia. Micheaux, a peripatetic author who sold his own novels from door to door, entered the movie business in 1919 after a failed negotiation with Lincoln to produce his autobiographical novel *The Homesteader.* For much of the ensuing quarter century and more, he audaciously if not always artfully reached for effects and messages left untouched by his forebears. In his *Body and Soul* (1924) he featured the singer Paul Robeson in his only appearance in a race movie. In *Within Our Gates* (1921) he put his own spin on the infamous Leo Frank murder case in Atlanta. And throughout his career Micheaux played on themes of racial identity, often hinging his plots upon revelations of mixed parentage.

The Colored Players differed from Micheaux's group in that they not only calculatedly played to urban, eastern audiences but seemed to have a capacity for putting every dollar on the screen, with handsomely—even densely—dressed sets and more polished levels of acting. They did Dunbar's *A Prince of His Race* (1926), a black version of the temperance tract *Ten Nights in a Bar Room* (1926), and an original screenplay entitled *The Scar of Shame* (1927).

More than any other race movie, *The Scar of Shame* addressed the concerns of the urban black middle class. Although it teased around the theme of color-caste snobbery among African Americans, its most compelling argument was a call to rise above the lot that blacks had been given and to strive for "the finer things" despite adversity. But at the same time, as critic Jane Gaines (1987) has argued, their poor circumstances were given them not by a natural order but by a white-dominated system that blacks knew as the real puppeteer working the strings off camera.

HOLLYWOOD'S BLACKS

For its part, Hollywood in the 1920s rarely departed from conventions it had inherited from southern American racial lore. Its high moments included *In Old Kentucky* (1926), in which the black romance was in the hands of the enduring clown Stepin Fetchit. In most movies blacks merely lent an atmosphere to the sets: Sam Baker as a burly seaman in *Old Ironsides*, Carolynne Snowden as an exotic dancer in Erich von Stroheim's Ruritanian romances, and so on. The decade also produced its own obligatory version of *Uncle Tom's Cabin*.

But with the coming of the cultural crisis wrought by the Great Depression of 1929 and after, blacks and whites shared at least fragments of the same depths of despair and were thrust together in the same bread lines and federal programs such as the Works Project Administration (WPA). In Hollywood the result was a run of socially and artistically interesting black roles and even a couple of tolerable all-black homages to the hard life the race lived in the South: *Hallelujah!* and *Hearts in Dixie* (both in 1929).

At the same time, Hollywood had also matured into a corporate system that had rationalized moviemaking into a vertically integrated mode of production, distribution, and exhibition. The result was a manufactured product marked by so many family traits that it could be labeled by some historians "the classic Hollywood movie." Typically, such movies told an uncomplicated tale in which engaging characters embarked on a plot that obliged them to fill some lack, solve a mystery, or complete a quest resulting in a closure that wrapped all the strands into a fulfilling dénouement.

Unavoidably, the African-American roles that filled out these plots owed more to the conventions of the moviemaking system than to the authentic wellsprings of everyday black life. Moreover, supporting this industrial/aesthetic system were the proscriptions set forth by Hollywood's self-censorship system, the Production Code Administration, or "the Hays Office." These dos and don'ts discouraged full black participation in any plot forbidding racial slander or miscegenation, so that almost no African-American "heavy" or villain could appear. Nor could any black person engage in any sort of close relationship other than that of master and servant.

Stepin Fetchit, for example, enjoyed a flourishing career during the Great Depression, but one severely limited in its range. In *The World Moves On* (1934) he had a rare opportunity to play a soldier in the French army, but only as a consequence of following his master into combat; in *Stand Up and Cheer* (1934) he joined the rest of the cast in fighting off the effects of the depression but was absent from pivotal scenes that centered on the white principals; and in the middle of the decade he appeared in a brief string of rural fables as a sidekick to Will Rogers's folksy Judge Priest or David Harum. Women had their moments as wise or flippant servants, notably Louise Beavers in *Imitation of Life* (1934) and Hattie McDaniel in *Alice Adams* (1935). Such a role eventually won McDaniel the first Oscar ever won by an African American: her "Mammy" in *Gone with the Wind* (1939). Whenever the script called for a character of mixed heritage, such as Tondelayo in *White Cargo* or Zia in *Sundown,* the Hollywood self-censorship system, the Hays Office, pressed the studios toward the cautious choice of casting white actors in the roles.

For African Americans, the combination of an increasingly factorylike Hollywood system and a lingering economic depression provided only scant hope of improved roles. And yet the coming of sound film technology opened a window of opportunity for black performers.

Already, theatrical audiences had been introduced to African-American musical performance in the form of rollicking revues such as the *Blackbirds* series and Marc Connelly's Pulitzer Prize–winning fable *The Green Pastures,* which he had drawn from Roark Bradford's book of tales, *Ole Man Adam and His Chillun.* Fleetingly, two major Hollywood studios—Fox and Metro—had responded with *Hearts in Dixie* and *Hallelujah!* And both the majors and the independents offered hope for an African-American presence in sound films in the form of a rash of short musical films that lasted well past the decade.

Movie still from **The Call of His People.** *Adapted by Aubrey Bowser from his story* The Man Who Would Be White, *this 1922 Reol Productions film tells the story of a black man who passes for white in order to get ahead in business.* PHOTOGRAPHS AND PRINTS DIVISION, SCHOMBURG CENTER FOR RESEARCH IN BLACK CULTURE, THE NEW YORK PUBLIC LIBRARY, ASTOR, LENOX AND TILDEN FOUNDATIONS.

The most famous of these one- or two-reel gems were Bessie Smith and Jimmy Mordecai's *St. Louis Blues* (1929)—which used not only W. C. Handy's title song but incidental choral arrangements by J. Rosamond Johnson, who, with his brother James Weldon, had written the "Negro National Anthem," "Lift Ev'ry Voice and Sing"— and Duke Ellington's films *Black and Tan* and *The Symphony in Black* (1929 and 1935, respectively). Throughout the decade and beyond, stars of the jazz scene—Cab Calloway, Louis Armstrong, and the Nicholas Brothers, among others—appeared in these shorts, which culminated with Lena Horne, the duo pianists Albert Ammons and Pete Johnson, and the pianist Teddy Wilson in *Boogie Woogie Dream* (1944). By then such films had attracted the attention of white aesthetes such as the photographer Gjon Mili, who cast Illinois Jacquet, Sid Catlett, Marie Bryant, and others in his *Jammin' the Blues* (1946), which became a *Life* magazine Movie of the Week.

LATE RACE MOVIES

As for race-movie makers, the times were harder. Of the African Americans only their doyen, Oscar Micheaux, worked through the entire decade of the 1940s, albeit as a client of white capital sources such as Frank Schiffman, manager of the Apollo Theater. Now and again a newcomer such as William D. Alexander's All America firm or George Randol with his *Dark Manhattan* (1947) entered the field, but race movies too had matured into a system led mainly by white entrepreneurs such as Ted Toddy of Atlanta, Alfred Sack of Dallas, Bert and Jack Goldberg of New York, and Harry and Leo Popkin of Hollywood, whose loose federation was modeled on the classic Hollywood system.

As a result, race movies soon imitated Hollywood genres such as the gangster film and the western. *Paradise in Harlem* (1940), for example, featured a tale of a black gang bent upon taking over Harlem. The community, led by an actor (Frank Wilson), mounts a jazz version of *Othello* as a fund-raiser, and the play is so compelling that even gangsters are won over by its seductive beat and a black-themed Shakespeare. Westerns—*Two Gun Man from Harlem, Bronze Buckaroo,* and *Harlem Rides the Range*—also borrowed their formulas from Hollywood, particularly their satisfying closures that promised happy lives to the good people of the cast.

THE IMPACT OF WORLD WAR II

No political event affected moviemaking more profoundly than did World War II. Even before the war reached America, Hollywood responded to it by forming an Anti-Nazi League and by cleansing its movies of the worst of racist traits, much as David O. Selznick tried to do when he told his writer to place African Americans "on the right side of the ledger during these Fascist-ridden times" as they began work on *Gone with the Wind*. Indeed, so successful was he that blacks were divided in their response to the Southern epic for which Hattie McDaniel became the first black ever to win an Oscar. In less splashy movies a similar impact of the war was felt. John Huston and Howard Koch included a strong black law student who stands up to a ne'er-do-well daughter of the southern gentry in their movie of Ellen Glasgow's Pulitzer Prize–winning novel in *In This Our Life*. And Walter White of the National Association for the Advancement of Colored People (NAACP) helped to adapt Walter Wanger's *Sundown* (1941) to fit the changing politics brought on by the war.

The war provided a cultural crisis that weighed upon African Americans in several ways: The Allies' war aims included anticolonialism, the nation needed black soldiers and war workers, and black journalists campaigned to insist on such linkages, as the *Pittsburgh Courier* did in calling for a "Double V," a simultaneous victory over foreign fascism and domestic racism. Together with the NAACP, liberals within the Office of War Information and the Pentagon joined in a campaign to make appropriate movies. Two new trends resulted: government propaganda such as *The Negro Soldier, Wings for This Man,* and *Teamwork,* which asserted a black place in the war effort, and Hollywood films such as *Crash Dive, Sahara, Bataan,* and *Lifeboat,* which often integrated the armed forces before the services themselves acted to do so. Along with federal measures such as a Fair Employment Practices Commission, the movies contributed to a new political culture that reintroduced the issue of racism to the arena of national politics.

After the war filmmakers emerged from their military experience to form a new documentary film culture bent upon making films of liberal advocacy, much as they had done during the war. The NAACP continued to lead this movement by urging wartime agencies to send their surplus films to schools, trade unions, and civil rights groups, constituting audiovisual aids for, as Roy Wilkins of the NAACP said, "educating white people now and in the future." Thus, informational films such as *The Negro Soldier* entered the civilian marketplace of ideas. In the same period a wartime antiracist tract by Ruth Benedict and Gene Weltfish became *The Brotherhood of Man,* an animated cartoon endorsed and distributed by the United Auto Workers. Another film of the era was *The Quiet One,* an account of a black boy of the streets who enters Wiltwyck School, an agency charged with treating such children. The fact that it enjoyed an unprecedented run in urban theaters perhaps contributed to Hollywood's decision to resume attention to the racial issues it had taken up during the war.

By 1949 Hollywood majors and some independent companies that had sprung up following the war produced peacetime versions of the war movies. The results were mixed. Louis DeRochemont's "message movie" *Lost Boundaries* focused on a New England village "black" family that had been passing as white, thereby blunting the main point, racial integration; Stanley Kramer's *Home of the Brave* did somewhat better by introducing a black soldier into an otherwise white platoon; Dore Schary's *Intruder in the Dust* faithfully rendered William Faulkner's book into film, including its portrayal of African Americans as icons of a sad past who could teach white people the lessons of history; Darryl F. Zanuck's *Pinky* provided a closure in which a black nurse learns the value of building specifically black social institutions; and Zanuck's *No Way Out* carried the genre into the 1950s, focusing tightly on a black family and neighborhood and their willingness to defend themselves against the threat of racism.

POSTWAR HOLLYWOOD

Taken as a lot, these message movies perpetuated the integrationist ideology that had emerged from the war and gave Sidney Poitier, James Edwards, Juano Hernandez, and others a foothold in Hollywood. Indeed, if anything, Hollywood only repeated itself in the ensuing decade, hobbling efforts to press on. Poitier, for example, after a few good films in the integrationist vein—*The Blackboard Jungle* (1954), *The Defiant Ones* (1959), and *Lilies of the Field* (1963)—was given few challenging scripts. Typical of the era was Alec Waugh's novel *Island in the Sun,* a book specifically about racial politics in the Caribbean, bought by 20th Century-Fox only to have its most compelling black spokesman written entirely out of the script. Black women fared little better, mainly because they were assigned only a narrow range of exotic figures, such as Dorothy Dandridge's title role in the all-black *Carmen Jones* (1954).

Not until the era of the civil rights movement—when such events as the Greensboro, North Carolina, student sit-ins of 1960 became daily fare on national television—would Hollywood try to catch up with the pace of events and TV's treatment of them. Even then, the most socially challenging themes were in movies made outside the Hollywood system, on East Coast locations or even in foreign countries. These included Shirley Clarke's harsh film of Harlem's streets *The Cool World* (1964); Gene Persson and Anthony Harvey's London-made film of Amiri Baraka's *Dutchman* (1967); Larry Peerce's cautionary tale about the stresses of interracial marriage, *One Potato Two Potato* (1965); Marcel Camus's Afro-Brazilian movie of the myth of Orpheus and Eurydice, *Orfeo Negro* (1960); and Michael Roemer's *Nothing but a Man* (1964), a pastoral film that was named by *Black Creation* magazine as the "greatest" of black movies.

Parallel to the civil rights movement, Hollywood itself experienced key changes in its institutional structure. Its production system became less vertically integrated and more dependent on sound marketing; federal laws began to require the active recruiting of blacks into studio guilds and unions from which they had been excluded by "grandfather clauses"; the old Hays Office censorship gave way to legal challenges and eventually to a liberalized system of ratings; and television assumed the role of seeking the steady audiences that B movies once had done. All these factors would alter the ways Hollywood treated race, but television had a particular impact.

In the 1960s television shows *East Side/West Side, The Store Front Lawyers, Mod Squad,* and *Julia,* social workers, idealistic attorneys, dedicated cops, and self-sacrificing hospital workers struggled on behalf of their clients, often against the social order itself. Television news and documentaries provided a tougher image for Hollywood to strive to emulate. Daily camerawork from southern streets and courtrooms recorded the agony of the region as it resisted African-American challenges to the status quo. The documentaries, whether on commercial or public television, occasionally emerged from black origins, such as William Greave's *Black Journal.* "TV Is Black Man's Ally," said the *Los Angeles Sentinel,* while *Variety* reported a new black stereotype: an "intensely brooding, beautiful black rebel."

"BLAXPLOITATION" FILMS

Hollywood had little choice but to take the point, particularly since several studios were close to collapse. They stood on the verge of what came to be called the era of blaxploitation films. Black youth flocked to this cycle of jangling, violent, and shrilly political movies. Timidly at first, the majors fell to the task. But first, there were easily digestible crossover movies, such as the pastoral tales *Sounder* and *The Learning Tree* (both 1968), the latter an autobiography by the photographer Gordon Parks Sr. Then came the urban, picaresque heroes most often thought of as "blaxploitation" icons, who combined the cynicism of 1940s film noir style with the kinetic yet cool mode of the black streets. The most famous and probably the highest earner of rentals was Parks's MGM film *Shaft* (1970). The movies that followed, such as Melvin Van Peebles's *Sweet Sweetback's Baadasssss Song* (1971), constituted calls for direct and sometimes violent retribution against brutal police and exploitative mobsters.

Other movies in the cycle tried to remake white classics by reinventing them in African-American settings—*Cool Breeze* (from *The Asphalt Jungle*), *Blacula* (*Dracula*), *The Lost Man* (*The Informer*). Some were derived from original material angled toward blacks, such as the cavalry western *Soul Soldier*.

Still another genre—"crossover" movies—sought a wider sector of the market spectrum in the form of material such as biographies of performers—Billie Holiday, Leadbelly (Huddie Ledbetter)—who had enjoyed followings among whites.

Yet whatever their uneven merits, the blaxploitation movies lost touch with the market. Their place was taken by Chinese martial-art fables, the work of purveyors such as Raymond Chow and Run Run Shaw, featuring impossibly adept warriors whose revenge motifs touched a nerve in the psyches of black urban youth. Soon the domestic makers of blaxploitation movies lost their market entirely so that African Americans reached the screen only as functionaries in conventional Hollywood features—police, physicians, and the like—or in prestigious, even reverent treatments of classics or successes from other media, such as Eli Landau's movie of Kurt Weill and Maxwell Anderson's South African musical *Lost in the Stars,* Charles Fuller's *A Soldier's Story,* and E. L. Doctorow's *Ragtime.*

BLACK INDEPENDENT FILM

Nonetheless, the era had revealed a previously unmeasured black marketplace that seemed ready for either the raffish or the political. Moreover, the combined impact of a thin wedge of black in the Hollywood guilds, an increase in African Americans' numbers in the university film schools, and the opening of television as a training ground resulted in a greater number of filmmakers and, eventually, a steady flow of independently made black films. Madeleine Anderson's combination of journalism and advocacy; St. Clair Bourne's access to black institutions, as in *Let the Church Say Amen;* Haile Gerima's syncretism of the pace and rhythms of East African life and the stuff of African-American life, mediated by film school experience, resulting in his *Bush Mama;* and William Miles's classically styled histories such as *Men of Bronze* and *I Remember Harlem* reflected the catholicity of the movement.

In addition to this focused sort of journalism of advocacy, the 1980s also resulted in a black cinema of personal dimensions, represented by Ayoka Chenzira's *A Film for Nappy Headed People,* Charles Burnett's *Killer of Sheep,* Kathleen Collins's *The Cruz Brothers* and *Miss Malloy,* and Warrington Hudlin's *Streetcorner Stories* and *Black at Yale.*

By 1990 one of this generation of filmmakers, Spike Lee, had—most notably because of his flair for self-advertisement and for shrewd dealing with established Hollywood—crossed over into the mainstream system. A product of film school as well as the most famous African-American association of the craft, the Black Filmmakers Foundation, Lee managed to glaze his movies of black life with a certain universalist charm that earned the sort of rentals that kept Hollywood financing coming. Somehow he conveyed the urgency, extremity, and drama of the arcana of black life—courtship, Greek letter societies, neighborhood territoriality, the tensions of interracial marriage—into a crescendo of ringing cashboxes. From *She's Gotta Have It, School Daze, Do the Right Thing,* and *Jungle Fever,* he moved toward being entrusted with a Holy Grail of black filmmakers, a biography of Malcolm X that had been stalled for almost a quarter of a century by fears that its protagonist's memory and mission would be violated if placed in the wrong hands.

More than at any other moment in African-American film history, Lee's access to black life, classical training, black associations, and commercial theaters promised the continued presence and vision of African Americans in cinema rather than a reprise of the peaks and troughs of faddishness that had marked all previous eras of the medium.

The most insidious threat to their work continued to be that which touched everyone in Hollywood, not only the latest generation of African-American moviemakers: the unyielding fact that Hollywood was a system, a way of doing business that obliged newcomers to learn its conventions and the rules of its game. This was how fads and cycles were made: An innovative spin placed upon a familiar genre revivified it, drew new patrons into the theaters, and inspired a round of sequels and imitators that survived until the next cycle drew attention to itself. After all, even the most dedicated outlaws, Oscar Micheaux and Melvin Van Peebles, either borrowed money from the system or used it to distribute their work. Unavoidably their benefactors expected to shape their products to conform to the codes of conduct by which all movies were made.

Spike Lee and his age-cohorts were particularly successful, since many of them had gone to film school where learning the trade meant in many ways learning the Hollywood system. Lee's *Malcolm X* was a case in point. In order to celebrate, render plausible, and retail his hero and his image, Lee was drawn into the dilemma of not only making a Hollywood "bioepic" but also marketing it as if it were a McDonald's hamburger. The result was remarkably faithful to its Hollywood model: Its protagonist is carried along by his own ambition, revealing slightly clayed feet, as though more a charming flaw than a sin, faces implacable adversaries, is misunderstood by his friends and family, undergoes a revelatory conversion experience, is cast out by his coreligionists for having done it, and finally meets a martyr's death and a last-reel apotheosis. This formula, as stylized as a stanza of haiku poetry, in the hands of Lee was transformed into a vehicle for carrying a particularly reverential yet engaging black political idiom to a crossover audience.

Could Lee's successors and age-mates not only endure but also prevail over their medium? Lee himself fretted over their future: "We seem to be in a rut," he told a black film conference at Yale in the spring of 1992. His concern was directed not so much at the Hollywood establishment but rather to the young African-American filmmakers who had followed him to Hollywood: John Singleton, who at age twenty-three had made *Boyz N the Hood;* Matty Rich, who while still a teenager had made *Straight Out of Brooklyn;* and Lee's own cameraman, Ernest Dickerson, who had made *Juice;* each one of them set in a black ghetto, each centered on a protagonist at risk not so much from forces outside his circle but from within, and each marked by a fatalism that precluded tacking on a classic Hollywood happy ending.

Indeed, forces of daunting economic power seemed to hover over the new black filmmakers even as old-line Hollywood producing companies turned out attractive packages in which black themes and characters held a secure place. First, despite various gestures, the studios had hired woefully few black executives so that every project was pitched to persons uncommitted to its integrity. Second, the topmost owners of the system were more remote than ever, as in the case of the Japanese firm Sony, which owned both Columbia Pictures and Tri-Star. Third, each new film, upon its release, faced a round of rumors of impending violence that would mar its opening. Fourth, some movies drawn from black material seemed lost in the welter of ghetto movies, much as Robert Townsend's chronicle of the careers of a black quintet of pop singers, *The Five Heartbeats,* sank from view without having reached the audience it deserved. Fifth, some black films, such as Julie Dash's *Daughter of the Dust,* a rose-tinted history of an African-American family in the Sea Islands of the Carolina low country, were so unique in texture, pace, and coloring that they were played off as esoteric art rather than popular culture. Sixth, Hollywood itself seemed ever more capable of portraying at least some aspects of black life or at least drawing black experiences into closer encounters with white. John Badham's *The Hard Way* (1992) featured the rapper LL Cool J as an undercover policeman of such depth that the actor felt "honored" to play him. Black critics almost universally admired the quiet depth of Danny Glover's role as a steady, rock-solid tow-truck driver in *Grand Canyon* (1992). And in the work of Eddie Murphy at Paramount (where he sponsored "fellowships" designed to add to the talent pool of minority writers) and in other movies such as *White Men Can't Jump,* the absurdities of race and racism in America were portrayed with arch humor.

At its height during the gestation period of Lee's *Malcolm X,* the trend toward a Hollywood-based African-American cinema seemed problematic and open either to a future of running itself into the ground as the moviemakers of the Super Fly era had done, falling prey to cooptation by the Hollywood system, or constantly searching out new recruits who might be the answer to Susan Lehman's rhetorical query in her piece in *GQ* (February 1991): "Who Will Be the Next Spike Lee?"

Although African Americans have been shut out of many of the major film awards over the years, progress was made in 2001 when Halle Berry and Denzel Washington won Academy Awards for Best Actress and Best Actor respectively. At the 2002 Academy Awards, Sidney Poitier received an Honorary Lifetime Achievement Award.

See also Berry, Halle; Blaxploitation Films; Dash, Julie; Film in Latin America and the Caribbean; Filmmakers, Los Angeles School of; Lee, Spike; Micheaux, Oscar; Urban Cinema; Washington, Denzel

■ ■ *Bibliography*

Bogle, Donald. *Toms, Coons, Mulattoes, Mammies & Bucks.* New York: Viking, 1973.

Bourne, St. Clair. *The Making of Spike Lee's Do the Right Thing* (film). New York, 1989.

Carbine, Mary. " 'The Finest Outside the Loop': Motion Picture Exhibition in Chicago's Black Metropolis, 1905–1928." *Camera Obscura* 23 (May 1990): 9–42.

Cripps, Thomas. "Native Son in the Movies." *New Letters* 28 (winter 1972): 49–63.

Cripps, Thomas. *Black Shadows on a Silver Screen* (film). Washington, D.C., 1976.

Cripps, Thomas. *Slow Fade to Black: The Negro in American Film, 1900–1942.* New York: Oxford University Press, 1977.

Cripps, Thomas. *Black Film as Genre.* Bloomington: Indiana University Press, 1978.

Cripps, Thomas. "*Casablanca, Tennessee Johnson,* and *The Negro Soldier*—Hollywood Liberals and World War II." In *Feature Films as History,* edited by K. R. M. Short, pp. 138–156. Knoxville: University of Tennessee Press, 1981.

Cripps, Thomas. "Movies, Race, and World War II: *Tennessee Johnson* as an Anticipation of the Strategies of the Civil Rights Movement." *Prologue: The Journal of the National Archives* 14 (summer 1982): 49–67.

Cripps, Thomas. "Winds of Change: *Gone with the Wind* and Racism as a National Issue." In *Recasting: Gone with the Wind in American Culture,* edited by Darden Asbury Pyron, pp. 137–153. Miami: University Presses of Florida, 1983.

Cripps, Thomas. "Making Movies Black." In *Split Image: African Americans in the Mass Media,* edited by Jannette L. Dates and William Barlow, pp. 125–154. Washington, D.C.: Howard University Press, 1990.

Cripps, Thomas. "*Sweet Sweetback's Baadasssss Song* and the Changing Politics of Genre Film." In *Close Viewings: Recent Film,* edited by Peter Lehman, pp. 238–261. Tallahassee: Florida State University Press, 1990.

Gaines, Jane. "The Scar of Shame: Skin Color and Caste in Black Silent Melodrama." *Cinema Journal* 26 (summer 1987): 3–21.

Hall, Stuart. "Gramsci's Relevance for the Study of Race and Ethnicity." *Journal of Communications Inquiry* 10 (summer 1986): 5–27.

hooks, bell. "Black Women Filmmakers Break the Silence." *Black Film Review* 2 (summer 1986): 14–15.

Klotman, Phyllis Rauch. *Frame by Frame: A Black Filmography.* Bloomington: Indiana University Press, 1979.

Klotman, Phyllis Rauch. *Screenplays of the African American Experience.* Bloomington: Indiana University Press, 1991.

Klotman, Phyllis Rauch, and Janet K. Cutler, eds. *Struggles for Representation: African American Documentary Film and Video.* Bloomington: Indiana University Press, 1999.

Leab, Daniel J. *From Sambo to Superspade: The Black Experience in Motion Pictures.* Boston: Houghton Mifflin, 1975.

Maynard, Richard A., ed. *The Black Man on Film: Racial Stereotyping.* Rochelle Park, N.J.: Hayden Book Co., 1974.

Merod, Jim. "A World Without Whole Notes: The Intellectual Subtext of Spike Lee's Blues." *Boundary* 2 (1991): 239–251.

Patterson, Lindsay, ed. *Black Films and Filmmakers: A Comprehensive Anthology.* New York: Dodd, Mead, 1975.

Peavy, Charles D. "Black Consciousness and the Contemporary Cinema." In *Popular Culture and the Expanding Conscious-*

ness, edited by Ray B. Browne, pp. 178–200. New York: Wiley, 1973.

Sampson, Henry T., ed. *Blacks in Black and White: A Source Book on Black Films.* Metuchen, N.J.: Scarecrow Press, 1977.

Taylor, Clyde. "Visionary Black Cinema." *Black Collegian* (October/November 1989): 226–233.

Waller, Gregory A. "Another Audience: Black Moviegoing in Lexington, Ky., 1907–1916." *Cinema Journal* 31 (winter 1992): 3–44.

Woll, Allen L., and Randall M. Miller, eds. *Ethnic and Racial Images in American Film and Television: Historical Essays and Bibliography.* New York: Garland, 1987.

THOMAS CRIPPS (1996)
Updated by publisher 2005

CONTEMPORARY FILM IN THE UNITED STATES

African-American film from the mid-1980s must be seen in the context of blaxploitation film from the 1970s. Blaxploitation was perhaps one of the most famous—and infamous—African-American film movements of the twentieth century. Its narratives of black characters and street culture were tremendously successful with both black and white audiences, from the surprising early achievements of Melvin Van Peebles's *Sweet Sweetback's Baadasssss Song* (1971) to later additions such as *Cleopatra Jones* (directed by Jack Starrett, 1973) and *Foxy Brown* (directed by Jack Hill, 1974). From the very beginnings, however, blaxploitation came under political and industrial attack. For groups such as Jesse Jackson's Operation PUSH and the Coalition Against Blaxploitation (CAB), the genre merely continued Hollywood's long history of caricaturing and stereotyping people of African descent. For Hollywood producers, blaxploitation was an easily reproducible formula, and it wasn't long before what was originally an African-American cultural expression of resistance was appropriated by the industry, thus pushing to the margins the black personnel and stories that originally made the genre successful. By the mid-1970s the film industry, bowing to criticism and pursuing other film forms, ceased production of blaxploitation films.

Very little African-American film (made by black personnel, starring black characters, and featuring black subject matter) was produced in the wake of blaxploitation, and the exceptions occurred primarily in the independent sector; for example, the Los Angeles school of filmmakers produced a number of shorts and features from the mid-1970s to the mid-1980s. In New York William Greaves was producing nonfiction and fiction films such as *Nationtime: Gary* (1973), *From These Roots* (1974), and *Symbiopsychotaxiplasm: Take One* (1971). At the same time, Holly-

wood was experiencing a transition. Blaxploitation films aided in saving the industry from financial ruin, but by the mid-1970s, the industry had shifted into the production of big-budget blockbuster films. It was argued by industry insiders that films with black characters and stories could not provide significant returns on the large-scale outlay of funds needed to produce blockbusters. In effect, the industry argued that black film was a bad investment.

African-American feature filmmaking languished until the mid-1980s, when a number of young writer-directors began making films that changed the direction of black film (and of Hollywood as a whole) by the end of the decade. Filmmakers such as Spike Lee, Warrington Hudlin, Reginald Hudlin, and Robert Townsend marked a break from previous filmmakers because they were college educated (many from film programs) and highly knowledgeable about both American and international film movements. In this way they were part of a larger phenomenon in American film that included such filmmakers as Martin Scorsese, Frances Ford Coppola, Brian De Palma, Charles Burnett, and Haile Gerima, all of whom were emerging from film school and self-consciously changing American film aesthetics. Filmmakers such as Lee, the Hudlins, and Townsend were also literate in African-American film history, film representation, and politics, and many of their early efforts interrogate and redefine black film representation by offering alternatives to Hollywood treatments of black subject matter. For example, Lee's debut, *She's Gotta Have It* (1986), a low-budget, independent feature, was a meditation on the experiences of an independent, articulate, middle-class black woman in Brooklyn. Warrington Hudlin began as a documentary filmmaker, making *Black at Yale* (1974) and *Street Corner Stories* (1977) before teaming with his brother Reginald to produce *House Party* (1990), a middle-class teen comedy featuring hip-hop stars Kid and Play. Robert Townsend's *Hollywood Shuffle* (1987) offered a satirical (and somewhat autobiographical) examination of Hollywood's demeaning casting practices in its story of a black actor's experiences trying to maintain his dignity while attempting to find acting work. Each filmmaker went on to influence black popular culture in a number of ways: Lee's expanding body of work as a director and producer has changed American and global film aesthetics, along with introducing a variety of African-American talent to Hollywood; Townsend has provided an alternative vision of the middle-class black family for thousands of television audiences; and Warrington Hudlin's work with the Black Filmmaker Foundation (which he established in 1978) helps support emerging filmmakers through the development and distribution of their work.

Spike Lee. *The film director Spike Lee (center) is seen here with actors John Canada Terrell (left) and Redmond Hicks on the set of his 1986 motion picture* She's Gotta Have It. AP/WIDE WORLD PHOTOS. REPRODUCED BY PERMISSION.

Perhaps enticed by the success of this first wave of young black filmmakers, and sparked by the critical climate engendered by Lee's *Do the Right Thing* (1989), a controversial film about one day on a block in Bed-Stuy, Brooklyn, Hollywood began to take notice of new black film. This interest was sparked further by the release of Matty Rich's *Straight Out of Brooklyn* (1991), a low-budget coming-of-age story set in the borough's Red Hook neighborhood. Like *Sweetback* twenty years earlier, Rich's film was made with a tiny budget and reaped tremendous returns. Soon, a number of films were released with common characteristics: They were made by mainly young African-American men and they focused on coming-of-age stories set in the inner-city communities of south-central Los Angeles, Brooklyn, and Harlem. Perhaps the best known films of what would eventually be referred to as the "'hood" film, the "gangsta" film, or "New Jack cinema" are John Singleton's *Boyz N the Hood* (1991), an examination of a young man's attempts to define himself and stay alive in an urban environment defined by poverty, criminality, governmental disinterest, and police abuse, and Mario Van Peebles's *New Jack City* (1991), a revisionist gangster film focusing on the rise and fall of a drug lord in Harlem.

Singleton's and Van Peebles's films were followed by a number of others with similar stories, self-conscious aesthetics, and performers from rap and hip-hop: for example, Ernest Dickerson's *Juice* (1992), a story of four friends in Harlem; and Allen and Albert Hughes' *Menace II Society* (1993), a caustic and highly reflexive rejoinder to Singleton's earlier film. There were also a few variants of the formula featuring female protagonists, most notably F. Gary Gray's *Set It Off* (1996) and Leslie Harris's *Just Another Girl on the IRT* (1991), a lesser-known independent film that is one of the rare feature-length examinations of the experiences of young women coming of age in urban areas.

The fact that 'hood films were attractive to Hollywood—because of their low budgets, their high returns (through film and video rentals and highly profitable soundtrack sales), and the appearance of diversity they provided an industry under attack by the NAACP—worried many scholars and critics who feared that 'hood films would be appropriated by the industry like blaxploitation films had been before them. Moreover, some argued that the films' explicit violence and depiction of criminalized men with nihilistic streaks and women whose

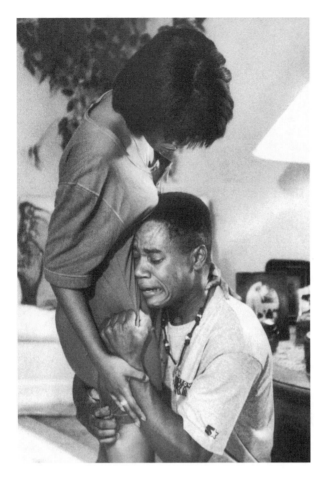

Scene from **Boyz N the Hood.** *The actors Nia Long and Cuba Gooding Jr. share an intimate moment in John Singleton's 1991 coming-of-age film set in a Los Angeles ghetto.* COLUMBIA/THE KOBAL COLLECTION

roles were limited to drug addicts and single mothers presented a one-dimensional depiction of the African-American community. Soon the genre began to be criticized in film as well, as in such satires as *CB4* (Tamra Davis, 1993) and *Don't Be a Menace to South Central While Drinking Your Juice in the Hood* (Paris Barclay, 1996), and in Spike Lee's more explicit critiques of rap (particularly gangsta rap) culture in *Clockers* (1995) and *Bamboozled* (2000).

One of the important ways in which 'hood films differed from blaxploitation is that there existed a greater range of African-American filmmakers and films during the 1990s, and this diversity stretched across industrial context and genre. While most of the African-American films associated with this time were produced with Hollywood support, a number of lesser-known filmmakers successfully released films through alternative financing (and sometimes distribution) outlets. Some of the features were made by veteran filmmakers first associated with the Los

Angeles school of filmmakers in the late-1960s and the 1970s: Charles Burnett's *To Sleep With Anger* (1991), Julie Dash's *Daughters of the Dust* (1991), Haile Gerima's *Sankofa* (1993), and Zeinabu irene Davis's *Compensation* (1999). Independent films were also released by a younger generation of filmmakers, including Wendell B. Harris and Cheryl Dunye, whose visions did not conform to Hollywood's preferred formula for African-American subject matter. Harris's *Chameleon Street* (1991) is based on the true-life experiences of Wendell Douglas Street, a man who impersonated a reporter, a lawyer, and a student in an attempt to find his own identity. The film's self-conscious aesthetics, drawing at once from experimental fiction and documentary realism, garnered critical praise and film-festival accolades upon release. Dunye's *Watermelon Woman* (1996) is likewise a self-conscious examination of gender, sexuality, and history; its mockumentary style notwithstanding, it offers a valuable history lesson about so-called race-film (films made for black audiences and shown in mostly segregated theaters) production companies during the early twentieth century.

The release of feature films by Leslie Harris, Julie Dash, Zeinabu irene Davis, and Cheryl Dunye suggest another characteristic of contemporary African-American film: the emergence of women directors as feature filmmakers. Many of the directors, including those listed above, along with Ayoka Chenzira (*Alma's Rainbow*, 1993), Cauleen Smith (*Drylongso*, 1998), and Bridgett M. Davis (*Naked Acts*, 1999), worked with varying stages of independence, often funding their films through private donations and public grant monies. Other directors chose relationships with Hollywood; for example, Darnell Martin (*I Like It Like That*, 1994), Gina Prince-Bythewood (*Love and Basketball*, 2000), and Kasi Lemmons (*Eve's Bayou*, 1997, and *The Caveman's Valentine*, 2001) made larger-scale films with more recognizable performers such as Omar Epps, Lynn Whitfield, and Samuel L. Jackson. The films may differ in budget and quality, yet they are connected by a concern with placing black female experiences of differing generations, geographies, and historical moments onscreen, thus filling a void in American cinema in existence since the late nineteenth century. The films examine women, history, the family, and issues of representation by almost exclusively focusing on black women, indicating a new direction for black feature filmmaking in a post-'hood film context. (Many of these same filmmakers, including Chenzira, Dash, Davis, Dunye, and Smith, had been exploring these issues in short films prior to the 1990s.)

The diversity of late-twentieth-century African-American film extends from behind the camera to the

Movie still from **Bamboozled, 2000.** *Tommy Davidson and Damon Wayans appear in director Spike Lee's film, in which a modern-day minstrel show, complete with blackfaced performers, becomes a hit on television.* NEW LINE/THE KOBAL COLLECTION/LEE, DAVID

types of films being made. Curtailing the fear that 'hood films would become the next blaxploitation, many directors first associated with the 'hood released a variety of works in other genres: For example, Matty Rich made a period piece (*The Inkwell,* 1994); John Singleton made a period piece (*Rosewood,* 1997), a college film (*Higher Learning,* 1995), action films (*Shaft,* 2000, and *2 Fast 2 Furious,* 2003), and a late return to the 'hood film (*Baby Boy,* 2001); Mario Peebles made a western (*Posse,* 1993) and an action film (*Panther,* 1995, among others; and the Hughes brothers have ventured into action films (*Dead Presidents,* 1995) and the horror genre (*From Hell,* 2001). Meanwhile, other young directors defined themselves with films in a variety of genres, such as the film noir (Carl Franklin's *One False Move,* 1992, and *Devil in a Blue Dress,* 1995), the romance (Theodore Witcher's *love jones,* 1997), the romantic comedy (Reginald Hudlin's *Boomerang,* 1992; Rick Famuyiwa's *The Wood,* 1999, and *Brown Sugar,* 2002; and Malcolm D. Lee's *The Best Man,* 2001), the comedy (F.

Gary Gray's *Friday,* 1995; Tim Story's *Barbershop,* 2002; and Malcolm D. Lee's *Undercover Brother,* 2002), and the drama (Denzel Washington's *Antwone Fisher,* 2002).

At the end of the twentieth century, and sparked by the success of such filmmakers as the Hudlins, Lee, Townsend, Dash, and Singleton, African-American film extended to a broad range of subjects, with many filmmakers directing films with mixed casts for crossover audiences, thus complicating the already contested borders of black film. Many times, but not always, these so-called crossover films feature African-American performers as leads or as seminal parts of teams; examples include Singleton's *Shaft* and *2 Fast 2 Furious,* Anton Fuqua's *Training Day* (2002), F. Gary Gray's *The Italian Job* (2003), and Cheryl Dunye's *My Baby's Daddy* (2004). Some veteran directors, such as Bill Duke (*The Cemetery Club,* 1992), Lee (*Summer of Sam,* 1999, *25th Hour,* 2002), and the Hugheses (*From Hell*) made films featuring white actors as leads, suggesting the incremental acceptance of black directors within Hollywood's ranks. The rise in the number of African-American directors making films for television networks such as BET, HBO, Showtime, and USA further complicates twenty-first-century definitions of black film. While part of a more general trend in network broadcasting, made-for-TV films offer an impressive array of black talent, including Julie Dash (*Funny Valentines,* 1999, *Love Story,* 2000, *The Rosa Parks Story,* 2002), Charles Burnett (*Nightjohn,* 1996, *The Wedding,* 1998, *Finding Buck McHenry,* 2000), Cheryl Dunye (*Stranger Inside,* 2001), Maya Angelou (*Down in the Delta,* 1998), and Forrest Whitaker (*Strapped,* 1993, *Black Jaq,* 1998). The networks have provided black directors, particularly African-American women, with the chance to continue making films, an opportunity that remains rare in Hollywood where funding for a second film is often impossible to secure.

By the end of the 1990s, contemporary African-American film had moved beyond the boundaries of the 'hood films that were so popular at the beginning of the decade, and even further beyond blaxploitation films from the 1970s. Black film in the twenty-first century is varied, stretching across genre, budget, and format (shorts and features). African-American filmmakers work in Hollywood and in the independent sector, a thriving area, particularly since more affordable formats, such as video and digital video, have enabled many more visual artists to explore the once cost-prohibitive area of filmmaking. What remains to come, however, is the release of a big-budget Hollywood blockbuster featuring African-American characters, stories, and technical personnel; for example, Lee struggled to make *Malcolm X* (1992) on a $20 million budget, while Singleton made *2 Fast 2 Furious,* an action film with crossover appeal, for $76 million. In this continuing reluctance to invest in African-American film, Hollywood remains politically and ideologically entrenched in the 1970s.

See also Blaxploitation Films; Burnett, Charles; Dash, Julie; Documentary Film; Film in the United States; Filmmakers, Los Angeles School of; Lee, Spike; Urban Cinema; Washington, Denzel

■ ■ *Bibliography*

Bobo, Jacqueline, ed. *Black Women Film and Video Artists.* New York: Routledge, 1998.

Boyd, Todd. *Am I Black Enough for You?: Popular Culture from the 'Hood and Beyond.* Bloomington: Indiana University Press, 1997.

Diawara, Manthia. *Black American Cinema.* New York: Routledge, 1993.

Dyson, Michael Eric. *Reflecting Black: African-American Cultural Criticism.* Minneapolis: University of Minnesota Press, 1993.

Fuchs, Cynthia, ed. *Spike Lee Interviews.* Jackson: University of Mississippi Press, 2002.

George, Nelson. *Buppies, B-Boys, Baps, & Bohos.* New York: HarperCollins, 1992.

Guerrero, Ed. *Framing Blackness: The African American Image in Film.* Philadelphia: Temple University Press, 1993.

Guerrero, Ed. *Do the Right Thing.* London: BFI, 2001.

hooks, bell. *Outlaw Culture: Resisting Representations.* New York: Routledge, 1994.

hooks, bell. *Reel to Real: Race, Sex, and Class at the Movies.* New York: Routledge, 1996.

Klotman, Phyllis R., and Janet K. Cutler, eds. *Struggles for Representation: African American Documentary Film and Video.* Bloomington: Indiana University Press, 1999.

Massood, Paula J. *Black City Cinema: African American Urban Experiences in Film.* Philadelphia: Temple University Press, 2003.

Reid, Mark A. *Redefining Black Film.* Berkeley: University of California Press, 1993.

Reid, Mark A., ed. *Spike Lee's Do the Right Thing.* London: Cambridge University Press, 1997.

Rhines, Jesse Algeron. *Black Film/White Money.* New Brunswick, N.J.: Rutgers University Press, 1996.

Smith, Valerie, ed. *Representing Blackness: Issues in Film and Video.* New Brunswick, N.J.: Rutgers University Press, 1997.

Snead, James, Colin MacCabe, and Cornel West. *White Screens/ Black Images: Hollywood From the Dark Side.* New York: Routledge, 1994.

Wallace, Michele. *Invisibility Blues: From Pop to Theory.* New York: Verso, 1990.

Watkins, S. Craig. *Representing: Hip Hop Culture and the Production of Black Cinema.* Chicago: University of Chicago Press, 1998.

PAULA J. MASSOOD (2005)

FILMMAKERS, LOS ANGELES SCHOOL OF

■ ■ ■

The Los Angeles school of filmmakers, also known as the "LA Rebellion," refers to a group of African-American and African filmmakers who worked under the auspices of the graduate film program in the Theater Arts Department at UCLA from the late 1960s to the early 1980s. Its members included Charles Burnett, Haile Gerima, Billy Woodbury, Alile Sharon Larkin, Ntongela Masilela, Jamaa Fanaka, Larry Clark, Ben Caldwell, Carroll Parrott Blue, Zeinabu irene Davis, and Julie Dash. Members of the LA school were interested in developing a revolutionary African-American film aesthetic that broke with the Hollywood conventions that had distorted black subject matter since the technology's inception. Unlike African-American filmmakers working in Hollywood, many of whom were involved in the production of blaxploitation films, members of the LA school expressed an explicitly political agenda that extended beyond profit and the superficial interrogation of representation; instead, they were concerned with breaking down what they saw as the internal colonization of African Americans, and they saw film as the primary tool to meet their goal. Rather than replicating Hollywood's emphasis on classical realism, often mistaken for or equated with a mimetic reproduction of reality, the LA school formulated a self-conscious, revolutionary cinema, one that, according to Ntongela Masilela, would be "a film form unique to their historical situation and cultural experience, a form that could not be appropriated by Hollywood" (Masilela, 1993, p. 108).

The LA school filmmakers were inspired by a diverse cross-section of political, industrial, and artistic influences: the black arts movement, the Black Panthers, the writings of Amilcar Cabral and Frantz Fanon, the approach to film production and exhibition practiced by early African-American independent filmmaker Oscar Micheaux, and the revolutionary "Third" cinemas emerging from Latin American and African countries, particularly Cuba and Brazil, most of which were in the midst of their own political, social, and aesthetic revolutions. Many of the LA school filmmakers adapted the revolutionary filmmaking techniques and politics of Third Cinema in an attempt to free their audience, according to Clyde Taylor, "from the mental colonization that Hollywood tries to impose on its audiences, black and white" (Taylor, 1985, p. 167). A similar rhetoric was used by Melvin Van Peebles, whose *Sweet Sweetback's Baadasssss Song* (1971) was the precursor to many blaxploitation films. Sweetback's mythic qualities, his virility and his agency, were an attempt to recode Hollywood representations of a disempowered or tamed black masculinity most closely linked with Sidney Poitier and the social protest films from the 1950s and 1960s. Notwithstanding *Sweetback*'s experimental form and empowered protagonist, the film's politics were not a model for the LA school filmmakers because *Sweetback*'s fantasy elements, its hyper-sexualized lead character, and its misogyny, like blaxploitation as a whole, were contrary to their goals. Instead, LA school films focused on "family, women, history, and folklore" within the urban milieu of post–Watts rebellion Los Angeles.

No unifying LA school aesthetic exists, and unlike many Latin American and African film movements from the same time, the filmmakers associated with UCLA did not produce a manifesto outlining their goals or prescribing an overarching film aesthetic. Yet, the LA school filmmakers were united in their self-conscious approach to story and technique. Much of this can be linked to the influences that the filmmakers drew from Latin American films such as Octavio Getino and Fernando E. Solanas's *Hour of the Furnaces* (1968) or Tomás Gutiérrez Alea's *Memories of Underdevelopment* (1968), but it can also be traced to other cinematic sources, such as Soviet cinema from the 1930s, Italian neorealism from the 1940s, and the French New Wave from the 1950s, all of which provided models of reflexive, low-budget fiction filmmaking. Additionally, some LA school filmmakers drew upon contemporary documentary filmmaking practices such as cinema verité and direct cinema, both of which were self-conscious attempts to question the implied truth of the nonfiction form. Burnett, in particular, was influenced by British social documentarians from the 1930s. Early British documentaries by such filmmakers as John Grierson and Basil Wright (on the faculty at UCLA and Burnett's mentor) developed a model of nonfiction film advocacy that focused on the working class and, for the first time in film history, provided its subjects with a voice. These various influences were, according to Paul Willeman, "examples of an artisanal, relatively low-cost cinema working with a mixture of public and private funds, enabling directors to work in a different way and on a different economic scale from that required by Hollywood and its various national-industrial rivals" (Willeman, 1989, p. 5), and they suggested the direction that many LA school filmmakers would choose: the establishment of a low-budget, socially active film movement that engaged with its immediate context in a language drawing upon diasporic conventions of storytelling.

Charles Burnett's *Killer of Sheep* (1977) is a good example of the thematic and stylistic diversity utilized by the LA school. The film focuses on a working-class family in Los Angeles that is struggling to maintain its economic and personal integrity in impoverished conditions. The film's main character, Stan, works during the day at a job in an abattoir that desensitizes him and distances him from his wife and children. The film combines an aesthetics of documentary immediacy—location shooting, moving camera, sync-sound—with more experimental and nonnarrative inserts of Stan's experiences in the slaughterhouse and with local children playing in empty lots and on the streets of Watts (also shot on location). The combination of narrative and nonnarrative sections provide both an urgency and poignancy to Stan's experiences while also suggesting the ways in which the experiential dilemma detailed in the film is much larger than just one person: It is experienced by the entire community.

In the links it makes between Stan's dilemma and the community's situation, *Killer of Sheep* explores themes that were common to many LA school films: the focus on the group over the individual, and the global over the local. One of the many critiques leveled at such blaxploitation films as *Sweetback, Shaft,* and *Superfly* was that the films focused on individual gain over community development and that many valorized individuals (drug dealers, pimps) who were seen as aiding in the destruction of African-American neighborhoods. LA school films redefined blaxploitation's narrative focus on the individual hero: Gerima's *Bush Mama* (1976), for example, extends its examination of African-American urban angst from one family to the experiences faced by impoverished black mothers forced into a debilitating social services system. Woodberry's *Bless Their Little Hearts* (1984) references, as *Killer of Sheep* did, the enervating effects of urban poverty and racism on African-American urban communities through the experiences of one family in Watts. In a different way, Julie Dash's *Illusions* (1984) self-consciously addresses the responsibility shouldered (and often ignored) by filmmakers through the story of an African-American studio executive passing for white during World War II, again suggesting that the individual and the social are intimately linked.

While the LA school shared a common political vision and a similarity in theme, its films were diverse in format and style, ranging from shorts to features and from conventional narratives to experimental fiction and nonfiction works. Gerima's *Bush Mama*, for example, is constructed around an experimental narrative, with Gerima often choosing to evoke certain moods and political positions through juxtaposed images and sounds rather than through expository dialogue. The film creates an audiovisual collage of Watts, encouraging the audience to participate in the life of its main character, Dorothy, as she experiences the frustrations of single motherhood, reliance on state support, and life in an urban police state. The film, like most of Ethiopian-born Gerima's output, expands its focus from a strictly American context through its references to the independence struggle in Angola at the time, thus suggesting a diasporic link between African-American urban life and subjugated communities on the African continent.

Many LA school filmmakers incorporated their concern with community into their own professional collaborations, thus embodying in person what they attempted to create onscreen. For example, besides writing, directing, and editing *Killer of Sheep*, Burnett wrote Woodberry's *Bless Their Little Hearts*, was the cinematographer for Gerima's *Bush Mama* and Larkin's *A Different Image* (1982), was the camera operator for Larry Clark's *Passing Through* (1977), and served as an additional photographer for Dash's *Illusions*. Moreover, many of the filmmakers collaborated with the same performers: Barbara O. Jones (sometimes credited as Barbara O) appeared in Gerima's *Child of Resistance* (1972) and *Bush Mama* (1976), Dash's *Diary of an African Nun* (1977) and *Daughters of the Dust* (1991), and Davis's *A Powerful Thang* (1991); Cora Lee Day appeared in *Bush Mama, Daughters of the Dust,* and Clark's *Passing Through;* Adisa Anderson in *A Different Image* (as Michael Adisa Anderson) and *Daughters of the Dust;* and Kaycee Moore in *Killer of Sheep, Bless Their Little Hearts,* and *Daughters of the Dust.* Part of this collaboration was due undoubtedly to financial exigency and circumstance, but it is also a clear indication of the support that existed between the filmmakers and other personnel.

Many of the filmmakers associated with the LA school continued to make films in the 1990s, most notably Charles Burnett (*To Sleep with Anger*, 1990), Julie Dash (*Daughters of the Dust*, 1991), Haile Gerima (*Sankofa*, 1993), and Zeinabu irene Davis (*Compensation*, 1999). In these later feature films, the directors developed many of the themes and alternative aesthetics that first concerned the LA school; for example, most of the films continue the focus on family, history, and folklore. The filmmakers continued to work outside of Hollywood, independently funding their films through a combination of public and private sources. Each, excluding Burnett (whose *To Sleep with Anger* was distributed by Samuel Goldwyn), also chose alternative distribution channels to reach diverse and appropriate audiences. Gerima, who self-distributes his films (and others, such as *Killer of Sheep*, from the LA school) through Mypheduh Films, is perhaps the best example of the LA school's continuing industrial and aesthetic legacy: independence and the development of a unique "film form . . . that could not be appropriated by Hollywood" (Masilela, 1993, p. 108).

See also Blaxploitation Films; Burnett, Charles; Dash, Julie; Documentary Film; Film in the United States; Film in the United States, Contemporary; Urban Cinema

▪▪ Bibliography

Bambara, Toni Cade. "Reading the Signs, Empowering the Eye: *Daughters of the Dust* and the Black Independent Cinema Movement." In *Black American Cinema*, edited by Manthia Diawara, pp. 118–144. New York: Routledge, 1993.

Diawara, Manthia. "Black American Cinema: The New Realism." In *Black American Cinema*, edited by Manthia Diawara, pp. 3–25. New York: Routledge, 1993.

Grant, Nathan. "Innocence and Ambiguity in the Films of Charles Burnett." In *Representing Blackness: Issues in Film and Video*, edited by Valerie Smith, pp. 133–155. New Brunswick, N.J.: Rutgers University Press, 1997.

Guerrero, Ed. "Negotiations of Ideology, Manhood, and Family in Billy Woodberry's *Bless Their Little Hearts*." *Black American Literature Forum* 25, no. 2 (1991): 315–322.

Klotman, Phyllis Rauch, ed. *Screenplays of the African American Experience*. Bloomington: Indiana University Press, 1991.

Masilela, Ntongela. "Black American Cinema: The New Realism." In *Black American Cinema*, edited by Manthia Diawara, pp. 107–117. New York: Routledge, 1993.

Masilela, Ntongela. "Women Directors of the Los Angeles School." In *Black Women Film and Video Artists*, edited by Jacqueline Bobo, pp. 21–41. New York: Routledge, 1998.

Massood, Paula J. *Black City Cinema: African American Urban Experiences in Film*. Philadelphia: Temple University Press, 2003.

Reid, Mark A. *Redefining Black Film*. Berkeley: University of California Press, 1993.

Taylor, Clyde. "Decolonizing the Image: New U.S. Black Cinema." In *Jump Cut: Hollywood, Politics, and Counter Cinema*, edited by Peter Steven, pp. 166–178. New York: Praeger, 1985.

Willeman, Paul. "The Third Cinema Question: Notes and Reflections." In *Questions of Third Cinema*, edited by Jim Pines and Paul Willeman, pp. 1–29. London: BFI Publications, 1989.

PAULA J. MASSOOD (2005)

FILMMAKERS IN THE CARIBBEAN
▬▬▬

The first film screenings in the Caribbean were held in 1895, a little more than a year after the emergence of film, and soon led to the development of cinemas throughout the region. Going to the cinema would prove to be a popular local pastime, as films increasingly captured the imagination of the Caribbean people. Almost all films were made outside the region, but some pioneering film directors lived in Cuba and Puerto Rico, and a few lived in the English-speaking Caribbean. It was only from the 1950s onward that the Caribbean began to produce films on a consistent basis—first documentaries made mainly by government film units and later independently produced feature films.

CUBA

Only a few blacks can be found among the major filmmakers in Cuba, the region's foremost film-producing country. Sara Gómez is important, as she was not only the first black Cuban to direct a feature film but also the first woman. She trained as a musician before joining the Instituto Cubano de Arte e Industria Cinematográficos as an assistant director to Cuban filmmakers Tomás Guitiérrez Alea and Jorge Fraga. Between 1964 and 1974 she directed ten short documentaries before making her first and only feature film, *De Cierta Manera* (1974). This innovative film combined documentary and dramatic sequences, real people and professional actors, to describe the role of African-influenced religions and male chauvinism in postrevolutionary Cuba. Gómez died of asthma while the film was being edited, and it was completed under the supervision of Alea and Julio García Espinosa.

Sergio Giral grew up in New York before returning to Cuba after the revolution. He made the short fictional film *La juala* (1964), the experimental documentary *La muerte de J. J. Jones* (1966) about a North American soldier fighting in Vietnam, and *Qué bueno canta usted* (1973) on the singer Beny Moré. He directed the feature films *El otro Francisco* (1974), *Rancheador* (1976), *Manuela* (1979), *Plácido* (1986), and *Maria Antonia* (1990), which focused on the history and culture of the Afro-Cuban population and the impact of sugar and slavery on the development of Cuban society. Most of these films were adaptations of famous Cuban novels or plays and reflected Giral's interest in exploring the multiple readings of major events in Afro-Cuban history.

Rigoberto López is one of Cuba's foremost documentary directors and has made films in Spain, Africa, and throughout the Caribbean. In Cuba, he worked first as an assistant director to Sergio Giral and Sara Gómez before producing such documentaries as *El mensajero de los dioses* (1989), which focused on santería, and *Yo soy, del son a la salsa* (1996), which illustrated the growth of salsa music. In 2003 he directed his first feature film, *Roble de olor*, exploring the issue of race in a story about the relationship between a German merchant and a freed slave in nineteenth-century Cuba.

Gloria Rolando's documentaries also celebrate the African presence in Cuba. She works almost entirely in video and has produced a number of short films on such topics as the presence of the West Indian community in Cuba in *My Footsteps in Baragua* (1995), santería in *Oggun: An Eternal Presence* (1991), and Carnival with *El alacrán* (2000). She heads an independent filmmaking group, Imágines del Caribe.

HAITI

Haitian cinema has been dominated by the work of Raoul Peck, who, like many other Caribbean filmmakers, operates from outside of the region, where he has access to funding and distribution. Peck grew up in Haiti and the Congo, and his work reflects a commitment to these countries. He directed his first full-length feature, *Haitian Corner*, in 1987, while he was a film student in Berlin. Peck's work has mainly focused on political issues, as can be seen in his feature *L'Homme sur les quais* (1993), about the Duvalier regime as seen through the eyes of a young girl, and two films on the first prime minister of the Congo, Patrice Lumumba: the full-length documentary *Lumumba: La Mort du prophète* in 1991, and the award-winning feature *Lumumba* in 2000.

Elsie Haas has established herself as a leading documentary filmmaker and has directed a number of films that explore Haiti and its culture, especially *Des saints et des anges* (1984), *La Ronde des tap-tap* (1986), and *La Ronde des vodu* (1987).

THE DUTCH ANTILLES

Producer/scriptwriter Norman de Palm from Aruba and director/designer Felix de Rooy from Curaçao have produced some of the most important Caribbean films. Their first feature, *Desiree* (1983), was their graduation project from New York University film school, and they went on to found Cosmic Illusions, a film and theater production company based in Amsterdam. Their other two films were shot in Curaçao. *Almacita di desolato* (1986) is a mythical story of Afro-Caribbean folklore and the fight between good and evil, and *Ava and Gabriel* (1990) is a critical depiction of such issues as race, class, religion, and sexuality in the Dutch colony of Curaçao in 1948.

MARTINIQUE AND GUADELOUPE

The French Antilles has produced a number of filmmakers of African descent, with Martiniquans Gabriel Glissant and Jean-Paul Césaire making short films and documentaries in the 1970s, and Guadeloupean Sarah Maldoror, with her feature film *Sambizanga* (1972), best known for her

Film director Euzhan Palcy. *Born on the French West Indian Island of Martinique, Palcy was the first black woman to direct a Hollywood studio film* (A Dry White Season, *1989). Among the most accomplished of Caribbean directors, Palcy lists among her credits a number of films exploring the history and culture of that region.* PHOTOGRAPH BY DAVID JAMES. THE KOBAL COLLECTION. REPRODUCED BY PERMISSION.

work in Angola. The most prolific filmmaker is Guadeloupe's Christian Lara, whose first feature was *Chap'la* (1977). Other early films include *Mamito* (1980), *Vivre libre ou mourir* (1980), *Adieu foulard* (1981), and *Bitter Sugar* (1997), an innovative treatment of slavery in the Caribbean. However, it is the Martiniquan filmmaker Euzhan Palcy who has made the greatest impact as a director. She received international recognition as the first black woman to direct a Hollywood studio film, *A Dry White Season* (1989), set in apartheid South Africa in 1976, but it was her first film *Rue Cases Nègres* (1983), adapted from Joseph Zobel's novel of postslavery plantation life, that established her as one of the foremost Caribbean directors. *Siméon* (1992), Palcy's other feature film set in Martinique, focuses on the growth of French Caribbean music and features the local group Kassav.

Guy Deslauriers, also from Martinique, has directed films that explore French Antillean history and culture, such as *L'Exil du roi Behanzin* (1995), about the king of

Dahomey, who in 1894 was exiled to Martinique after defending his country against the French; *Le passage du milieu* (1999), a impressionistic look at the inhumanities of the slave trade; and *Biguine* (2003), the story of two black musicians in nineteenth-century Martinique.

THE ENGLISH-SPEAKING CARIBBEAN

The question of who is an Afro-Caribbean filmmaker becomes rather delicate when considering filmmaking in the English-speaking Caribbean. It would be foolhardy not to consider Perry Henzell's pioneering *The Harder They Come* (1972), Jamaica's quintessential Caribbean feature film, because it was made by a white Jamaican. In addition, several of the other Jamaican-made films were made by white outsiders, all working with local crews and striving to give their movies a Caribbean flavor. Similarly, an Indian-born filmmaker, Harbance Kumar, made Trinidad's first two feature films, *The Right and the Wrong*, and *The Caribbean Fox*, both in 1970. And to add even more diversity, American-born Hugh Robertson, who was married to a Trinidadian, made *Bim* in 1974, highlighting the tensions between the African and Indian communities as it portrayed one man's struggle to come to terms with the society that has alienated him.

Jamaica has produced by far the most Caribbean films, thanks in part to its aggressive marketing and to the international appeal and popularity of reggae, the music that seems to drive every one of its films. The flagship *The Harder They Come* started the trend. With singing star Jimmy Cliff in the lead, the film portrayed the life of a budding singer turned criminal as a result of unscrupulous exploitation in the record industry and the drug trade.

Trevor Rhone, who is co-credited for the screenplay of *The Harder They Come*, provided a follow-up of sorts to that film with *Smile Orange* in 1975, based on his original play by the same name. This film did not have the same impact as the first one, but it went a long way toward establishing a body of work that could readily be called Jamaican/Caribbean cinema. The next milestone for an Afro-Jamaican was *Children of Babylon* (1980) by Lennie Little-White. Trained, like Perry Henzell, outside of Jamaica, Little-White is committed to developing an indigenous film industry. His film, ironically, suffered from being too polished, since by then international audiences had come to expect a particular brand of Third World filmmaking.

Trinidad, after the two Harbance Kumar films and *Bim*—a film that Trinidadians readily claimed as their own although it had been made by an African American—did produce some low-budget films by Indo-Trinidad directors Kamalo Deen and Tony Maharaj, and Gerard Jo-

Reggae singer Jimmy Cliff in a scene from **The Harder They Come, 1973.** *Cliff starred in Perry Henzell's film about corruption and exploitation in the Jamaican music business.* INTERNATIONAL FILMS/NEW WORLD/THE KOBAL COLLECTION

seph co-produced *Men of Gray II: Flight of the Ibis* in 1996. This graduate school project grew into a full-length martial arts action movie but made little impact in the Caribbean. However, the talented Horace Ové made a significant contribution to the work of diaspora-based filmmakers. Having migrated to England, Ové was keenly interested in the plight of West Indian immigrants there. The problems they faced were highlighted both in his early documentaries and in his feature films *Pressure* (1975) and *Playing Away* (1986). Both these films made use of talented immigrants seeking to make a new home away from the Caribbean. Unfortunately, they were not great successes in the Caribbean.

Filmmaking by Caribbean directors has been problematic at best. Some have made valiant efforts, but after the initial curiosity of seeing a movie made by a local filmmaker, the public shows little interest in keeping the work alive beyond occasional appearances at film festivals. An

example of this is *Guttaperc* (1998), directed and produced by Andrew Millington, the first feature-length movie by a Barbados national. It was politely received, but distribution problems led to its disappearing from the local scene and to apparent oblivion.

Filmmaking by Afro-Caribbeans remains largely a labor of love, for the logistical problems are almost overwhelming. Apart from Cuba, which has established a film institute and film school, most of the Caribbean countries are too preoccupied with more pressing economic matters to commit money to the relatively high-cost undertaking of filmmaking. Foundation help is sparse and usually doled out for documentaries. Private industry looks at the poor returns on previous efforts and prefers to err on the side of caution, thus remaining in the shadow of Hollywood productions. Talented filmmakers are now increasingly working in the area of video production, and the work of Banyan Productions and Robert Yao Ramesar in

Trinidad augurs well for the future. Unfortunately, the same spirited nationalism that has doomed attempts at a pan-Caribbean political federation also emerges in matters of art and culture. Films made in Cuba and Martinique are hardly shown in Trinidad; films from the Dutch Antilles are more likely to be shown in Holland than in the Caribbean. Cuba—followed by Jamaica—has staged an annual film festival to showcase new productions. One can only hope that such efforts will eventually spread throughout the entire Caribbean and inspire local filmmakers to produce a body of work that will take its rightful place on the international stage.

See also Film in Latin America and the Caribbean; Palcy, Euzhan; Peck, Raoul

■ ■ *Bibliography*

Cham, Mbye, ed. *Ex-Iles: Essays on Caribbean Cinema.* Trenton, N.J.: Africa World Press, 1992.

James, Conrad, and John Perivolaris. *The Cultures of the Hispanic Caribbean.* Gainesville: University Press of Florida, 2000.

King, John. *Magical Reels: A History of Cinema in Latin America.* New York: Verso, 2000.

Martin, Michael, ed. *Cinemas of the Black Diaspora: Diversity, Dependence, and Oppositionality.* Detroit, Mich.: Wayne State University Press, 1995.

Warner, Keith Q. *On Location: Cinema and Film in the Anglophone Caribbean.* London: Macmillan Caribbean, 2000.

Yearwood, Gladstone. *Black Film as a Signifying Practice: Cinema, Narration, and the African American Aesthetic Tradition.* Trenton, N.J.: Africa World Press, 2000.

KEITH Q. WARNER (2005)
BRUCE PADDINGTON (2005)

FISHER, RUDOLPH

MAY 9, 1897
DECEMBER 26, 1934

Rudolph John Chauncey Fisher, a fiction writer, dramatist, and essayist, was born in Washington, D.C., the youngest child of a Baptist minister. He lived briefly in New York City as a small boy but was raised and educated largely in Providence, Rhode Island, where he graduated from Classical High School and Brown University. An undergraduate of many talents, he was chosen by fellow students to be Class Day orator and by the faculty to be commencement speaker. He wrote his first published short story, "The City of Refuge" (1925), in his final year at Howard Medical School, initiating simultaneous vocations in literature and science. When Fisher's internship ended at Freedman's Hospital in Washington, D.C., a National Research Council Fellowship brought him to New York City in 1925 to work in bacteriology with Dr. Frederick P. Gay at the College of Physicians and Surgeons of Columbia University. In the mid-1920s, during Harlem Renaissance, he consolidated his medical and literary careers with scientific articles in the *Journal of Infectious Diseases* and the *Proceedings of the Society of Experimental Biology and Medicine* and short stories in the *Atlantic Monthly, Survey Graphic,* and *McClure's* magazine. He married Jane Ryder in 1925, and their son Hugh was born in 1926.

One of the more prolific writers of the Harlem Renaissance, Fisher produced in less than a decade fifteen published and seven unpublished short stories, two novels, half a dozen book reviews, a magazine feature article, and a play—while at the same time maintaining a medical practice, administering a private X-ray laboratory, and chairing the Department of Roentgenology at the International Hospital in Manhattan. Harlem is at the center of his literary work. "I intended to write whatever interests me. But if I should be fortunate enough to be known as Harlem's interpreter," he said in response to a radio interviewer's question on WINS in 1933, "I should be very happy." *The Walls of Jericho* (1928), his first novel, interweaves genre elements of color-conscious 1920s Harlem fiction—such as country-rooted southern migrants, slick Harlemites, and West Indians with their distinctive dialects and repartee; block-busting scenarios; racist uplifters of the race; rival lovers and their Arcadian conflicts; and passing—and brings it all together amid the converging vectors of social and racial distinction at a Harlem ball. His other novel, *The Conjure Man Dies* (1932), is regarded as an early example of a detective novel published in book form by an African-American author.

Fisher's place among the writers of the Harlem Renaissance rests, however, on the excellence of his short fiction. His short stories focus on tensions between West Indians and native-born Americans ("Ringtail"); alienation and reconciliation ("Fire by Night" and "The Backslider"); divisions between youth and age, the modern and the traditional, spirituals and blues ("The Promised Land"); and black consciousness and jazz in a battle of the bands ("Common Meter"). In these stories, he conveys what the scholar and writer Arthur P. Davis called a "fuller" picture of Harlem life viewed with "an understanding and amused eye" (Davis, 1974), and what the writer Sterling Brown termed "a jaunty realism . . . less interested in that 'problem' than in the life and language of Harlem's poolrooms, cafes, and barbershops" (Brown, 1969).

Two short stories in particular, "The City of Refuge" and "Miss Cynthie" (1933)—both anthologized in *The Best American Short Stories*—are Fisher's most highly regarded achievements. "The City of Refuge" concerns the arrival in Harlem of King Solomon Gillis, "a baby jess in from the land o' cotton . . . an' ripe f' the pluckin.'" Gillis is betrayed by everyone who seems to befriend him, yet when he is arrested by a black policeman, the symbol of Harlem's possibility he saw when he first arrived, Gillis, who "plodded flat-footedly" on "legs never quite straightened," can stand "erect" and "exultant" as he submits to an icon of black authority. In "Miss Cynthie," Fisher's last published work, he matches his undisputed ability to evoke locale and character with what the writer Robert Bone called a newly discovered sense of "how to interiorize his dramatic conflicts, so that his protagonists have the ability to grow" (Bone, 1988). Miss Cynthie struggles to embrace the success of the grandson she hopes is a doctor or at least an undertaker, but who turns out to be a song-and-dance virtuoso.

In 1934, Rudolph Fisher underwent a series of operations for an intestinal disorder—associated by some sources with his early work with X-rays—and he died on December 26 of that year.

See also Harlem Renaissance; Literature of the United States

■ ■ *Bibliography*

Bone, Robert. "Three Versions of Pastoral." In *Down Home: A History of Afro-American Short Fiction from Its Beginnings to the End of the Harlem Renaissance*. New York: Putnam, 1975.

Brown, Sterling. "The Urban Scene." In *Negro Poetry and Drama, and The Negro in American Fiction*. New York: Atheneum, 1969.

Davis, Arthur P. "Rudolph Fisher." In *From the Dark Tower: Afro-American Writers, 1900-1960*. Washington, D.C.: Howard University Press, 1974.

Gable, Craig. "Rudolph Fisher: An Updated Selected Bibliography." *Bulletin of Bibliography* 57 (2000): 13–19.

Gosselin, Adrienne Johnson. "Harlem Heteroglossia: The Voice of Nobody's 'Other.'" In *Multicultural Detective Fiction: Murder from the "Other" Side,* edited by Adrienne Gosselin, pp. 325–349. New York: Garland, 1999.

Löbbermann, Dorothea. "Harlem as a Memory Place: Reconstructing the Harlem Renaissance in Space." In *Temples for Tomorrow: Looking Back at the Harlem Renaissance,* edited by Geneviève Fabre and Michel Feith. Bloomington: Indiana University Press, 2001.

McCluskey, John, Jr. "Introduction." In *The City of Refuge: The Collected Stories of Rudolph Fisher*. Columbia: University of Missouri Press, 1987.

Perry, Margaret. "The Brief Life and Art of Rudolph Fisher." In *The Short Fiction of Rudolph Fisher*. New York: Greenwood, 1987.

Rudolph Fisher Newsletter (RFN): Online News and Resources for Rudolph Fisher and the Harlem Renaissance. Available from <http://www.fishernews.org>.

Tracy, Steven C. "The Use of Sacred and Secular Music in Rudolph Fisher's 'The Promised Land.'" In *Saints and Sinners: Religion, Blues and (D)evil in African-American Music and Literature*, edited by Robert Sacré. Liège, Belgium: Société Liégeoise de Musicologie, 1996.

Soitos, Stephen F. *The Blues Detective: A Study of African American Detective Fiction*. Amherst: University of Massachusetts Press, 1996.

JAMES DE JONGH (1996)
Updated bibliography

FISK JUBILEE SINGERS

The Fisk Jubilee Singers, a student choral group of former slaves at Fisk University in Nashville, Tennessee, was organized in 1867 by George L. White, Fisk's treasurer and vocal-music teacher. After several local appearances, the eleven-member group of men and women traveled north to raise money for the financially beleaguered young school. Barely meeting expenses and suffering prejudice and discrimination, the Singers worked their way through the Congregational and Presbyterian churches of Ohio. They began to achieve success with their appearance on November 15, 1871, at Oberlin College at a meeting of the National Council of Congregational Churches, constituents of the American Missionary Association, which had founded Fisk.

The Jubilee Singers' repertory of anthems, operatic excerpts, popular ballads, and temperance songs impressed their audiences, in part with the realization that African Americans could sing European music. The singers received their greatest popular response, however, when they sang spirituals, and it can be said that they introduced a white audience to black music. They made plantation hymns popular and even caused them to be written down and preserved. Endorsed by Henry Ward Beecher of Brooklyn's Church of the Pilgrims, the singers began winning praise and raising money in Connecticut and Massachusetts, especially with an audience of forty thousand at the World's Peace Jubilee in Boston in 1872. In Washington, D.C., a later Fisk Jubilee Singers group sang for President Ulysses S. Grant.

During a tour of the British Isles, the group sang for Queen Victoria and with the Moody and Sankey evangelistic campaign. They were popular with Quakers and other former abolitionists, as well as with both the aristocracy (Prime Minister William Gladstone invited them to lunch) and common people (they sang for an audience of six thousand in Charles Spurgeon's London tabernacle). Imitations of this group were legion. In 1875 Fisk graduated its first collegiate class and completed construction of Jubilee Hall, its first permanent building, paid for by the Jubilee Singers' tours. The Jubilee Singers continue to exist today at Fisk University.

See also Fisk University

■ ■ *Bibliography*

Marsh, J. B. T. *The Story of the Jubilee Singers with Their Songs.* Boston: Houghton, Osgood, 1881.

DORIS EVANS MCGINTY (1996)

FISK UNIVERSITY

Fisk University is a private, coeducational, independent liberal arts institution in Nashville, Tennessee. It was founded in October 1865 by Erastus Milo Cravath, field secretary for the American Missionary Association (AMA); John Ogden, superintendent of education, Freedmen's Bureau, Tennessee; and the Rev. Edward P. Smith, district secretary, Middle West Department, AMA, at Cincinnati. Cravath and Smith had been sent to Nashville by the AMA to establish an elementary school for freedmen in the area. The two men joined forces with Ogden, who was named principal of the Fisk School, or the Fisk Free Colored School, when it opened on January 1, 1866, in former Union hospital barracks. The buildings and land had been purchased with much financial and moral support from the assistant commissioner of the Freedmen's Bureau for Tennessee and Kentucky, Gen. Clinton Bowen Fisk, for whom the school was named. The American Missionary Association and the Freedmen's Bureau also helped to fund the school.

Although at first it functioned mainly as an elementary and normal school, Fisk was incorporated as Fisk University on August 22, 1867, following the founders' desires for a "first-class college" to educate black teachers. The college curriculum was organized by Adam K. Spence, a Scottish-born professor of foreign languages who left the University of Michigan in 1870 to replace Ogden as principal. Fisk graduated its first four college students in 1875, awarding them the B.A. degree for successfully completing courses in such liberal arts subjects as classical and foreign languages, mathematics, natural sciences, philosophy, history, and political science. In keeping with Fisk's religious orientation, weekly Bible classes were also required.

Fisk's income derived primarily from sporadic donations, as well as what could be raised from the modest tuition rates. Under Spence's leadership it experienced dire financial problems and often had to delay salary payments to its hardworking and dedicated teaching staff, which was originally composed primarily of white missionaries sent by the AMA. The buildings were deteriorating and in need of repair. George L. White, Fisk's treasurer and self-taught music instructor, set out on October 6, 1871, with a group of nine of his best students for a fund-raising singing tour of the North and East. White named the group the Jubilee Singers. The Jubilee Singers introduced "slave songs" or spirituals to audiences and returned the following year with $20,000 to purchase a forty-acre campus site. Groundbreaking ceremonies were held July 1, 1873, for the erection of Jubilee Hall, now a historic landmark. The Singers remain a Fisk tradition.

In 1875, Erastus Milo Cravath became the first president of Fisk University when the position of principal was eliminated and the AMA gave up direction of the institution, transferring titles and buildings to the Fisk trustees. Spence continued at Fisk as professor of Greek until 1900. He joined other members of Fisk's white faculty in enrolling his own child at the increasingly reputable university.

Under Cravath's presidency Fisk's reputation grew, and as early as 1875 black professors joined the staff. Among the students who came from the North to study at Fisk was W. E. B. Du Bois, one of the university's most famous alumni, who received his B.A. in 1888. When Cravath died in 1900, Fisk had graduated more than four hundred students who spread Fisk's fame across the United States in their careers as lawyers, professors, businessmen, ministers, and editors.

During the presidency of James G. Merrill (1900–1908), Fisk added a summer school for black teachers who wanted to improve their training, as well as many new science courses. When Merrill resigned, Fisk was again experiencing money troubles, since philanthropies at that time were more interested in investing in vocational and industrial schools such as the Tuskegee Institute. Many educators followed the line of reasoning that favored a "practical" education for blacks—training to enter the workforce. But Fisk remained staunchly in favor of offering the best liberal arts education it could to blacks in order to produce leaders for the black community.

Under the administration of George A. Gates, president from 1909 to 1912, Fisk established the social science department for which it would become well known. It also began to receive considerable donations from such philanthropists as Andrew Carnegie, Julius Rosenwald, and John D. Rockefeller. These donations were largely results of tireless campaigning on behalf of the university by Booker T. Washington, whose wife and son were alumni of Fisk.

The presidency of Fayette Avery McKenzie, who took office after Gates's untimely death, brought with it an expansion of the curriculum and raising of standards, as well as a $2 million endowment campaign. By July 19, 1924, McKenzie was successful in securing half of the endowment. Although the school showed growth, McKenzie's dictatorial administration and strict student discipline led in 1924 and 1925 to one of the first student rebellions on a black college campus. Du Bois fueled the fire of the revolt by speaking out to other alumni against McKenzie. McKenzie was especially resented for his ingratiating behavior toward prominent white citizens of Nashville and his insistence on unobtrusive, passive behavior from the black students even in the face of antiblack violence. McKenzie resigned on April 16, 1925.

Thomas Elsa Jones, a Quaker missionary, became the last white president in 1926. His years are viewed as one of the most productive periods in Fisk history. He eradicated the stricter regulations imposed on students until then. The $2 million endowment was attained. Black faculty increased to more than one half, and the first black dean, Ambrose Caliver, was named when Jones took office. Jones placed emphasis on increasing graduate studies at the university and attracting research-oriented professors. One of these professors was Charles Spurgeon Johnson, who became the head of the department of social science in 1928 and established the Institute of Race Relations at Fisk in 1944, drawing white and black leaders to campus annually for intensive three-week conferences. In 1947 Johnson became Fisk's first black president, replacing Jones, who had resigned to become president of his alma mater, Earlham College. Johnson's administration ended abruptly in 1956 when he died of a heart attack.

During these formative years Fisk garnered a number of historical firsts among black colleges and universities. It was the first black college to gain full accreditation by the Southern Association of Colleges and Schools (1930); to be on the approved list of the Association of American Universities (1933); to establish a university archive (1948); to be approved by the American Association of University Women (1951); to be granted a chapter of the honorary society Phi Beta Kappa (1952); and to be accredited for membership in the National Association of Schools of Music (1954).

The 1960s brought an expansion in educational programs and buildings. A centennial celebration was held in

1966, and James Raymond Lawson, an alumnus and scientist, was inaugurated as president, replacing Stephen Junius Wright, Jr., who had been named president after Johnson's death. Enrollment reached 1,559 in 1972, the largest in the university's history. In 1977 the Department of the Interior designated the campus as a historical site in the National Register of Historical Places by the National Parks Service.

Ironically, in the early 1970s school desegregation had an adverse effect on Fisk's finances, for government funding was cut back and competition for students increased as formerly segregated schools lured potential black applicants. In July 1975 Fisk's financial situation reached a crisis point as 11 percent of full-time faculty and forty staff members were laid off. Those remaining took a 20 percent salary abatement.

With the resignation of Lawson that same year, the school was without a president until 1977, when Walter Jewell Leonard, an attorney, was selected. Inheriting serious financial woes, Leonard's administration was also a target of faculty and student disgruntlement. Student enrollment dropped and a number of faculty resigned.

When a cold homecoming day on November 12, 1983, found dormitories without heat, it became public that the Nashville Gas Company had discontinued service in April because of an overdue bill of $157,000. The financial crisis worsened as the Nashville Electric Service threatened to cut off the university's electricity if $140,000 of their bill was not paid immediately. At the same time the Internal Revenue Service was threatening to put a lien on Fisk's property, since the university owed $500,000 in back payroll taxes. When Leonard suddenly resigned on November 23, 1983, the school, which had been $2.2 million in debt at his inauguration, owed some $2.8 million.

The crisis alarmed the nation, and leaders rallied to "save Fisk." President Ronald Reagan donated $1,000, and the U.S. Secretary of Education, Terrel H. Bell, created a task force from the public and private sectors to review the financial difficulties facing Fisk University. As in 1871 Fisk once again withstood the tide of financial disaster, receiving scores of donations from alumni and friends. Henry Ponder, an economist, took the reins of the beleaguered institution in July 1984 as the tenth president, and set out to pare back to a bare-bones operation.

Despite financial hardships, the university has continued to maintain its position as a flagship among historical black colleges and universities with a tradition of academic excellence. Fisk's $10 million Alfred Stieglitz Collection of Modern Art, presented to the university in 1949 by Georgia O'Keeffe, widow of Stieglitz, as well as its library of valuable research collections and rare books, attracts visi-

A meeting of the Young Men's Christian Association (YMCA) at Fisk University. PHOTOGRAPHS AND PRINTS DIVISION, SCHOMBURG CENTER FOR RESEARCH IN BLACK CULTURE, THE NEW YORK PUBLIC LIBRARY, ASTOR, LENOX AND TILDEN FOUNDATIONS.

tors from all over the world. Fisk alumni, among some of the most distinguished in the nation, include Du Bois, historian Charles H. Wesley, Congressman William Levi Dawson, and novelist Frank Yerby. Enrollment is in excess of eight hundred students.

In 2004 former U.S. Energy Secretary Hazel O'Leary was named president of the university, the fifth president in less than ten years.

See also Dillard University; Fisk Jubilee Singers; Howard University; Lincoln University; Morehouse College; Spelman College; Tuskegee University

■ ■ *Bibliography*

Collins, L. M. *One Hundred Years of Fisk University Presidents.* Nashville, Tenn.: Fisk University Press, 1989.

Richardson, Joe M. *A History of Fisk University, 1865–1946.* Tuscaloosa: University of Alabama Press, 1980.

ANN ALLEN SHOCKLEY (1996)
Updated by publisher 2005

FITZGERALD, ELLA

APRIL 25, 1918
JUNE 15, 1996

▐▐▐

In a career lasting half a century, jazz vocalist Ella Fitzgerald's superb pitch and diction, infallible sense of rhythm, and masterful scat singing all became part of the fabric of American music, and she was recognized as one "First Lady of Song." While her background and technique were rooted in jazz, she was always a popular singer, with a soothing yet crystalline sound that brought wide acclaim. Born in Newport News, Virginia, she came north as a child to Yonkers, New York, with her mother. In 1934, on a dare, she entered a Harlem amateur-night contest as a dancer but became immobile with stage fright when called on to perform. Instead, she sang two songs popularized by the Boswell Sisters, "Judy" and "The Object of My Affection," and won first prize.

After she had won several more amateur competitions, an opportunity came in February 1935, when she appeared at the Apollo and was spotted by Bardu Ali, the master of ceremonies for Chick Webb's band, who persuaded Webb to hire her. Fitzgerald began performing with Webb's band at the Savoy Club and cut her first record, "Love and Kisses," with them in June 1935. Inspired by a nursery rhyme, Fitzgerald cowrote and recorded "A-Tisket, A-Tasket" with Webb's group in 1938; it became one of the most successful records of the swing era and transformed the young singer into a national celebrity.

When Webb died suddenly in 1939, Fitzgerald assumed nominal leadership of his band, which broke up two years later. During the 1940s she gained prominence as a solo performer through hit records that showcased her versatility. Influenced by Dizzy Gillespie and bebop, in 1947 she recorded, "Oh, Lady Be Good" and "How High the Moon," two songs that utilized her scat singing, the wordless vocal improvising that became her signature style. By the early 1950s she had appeared around the world with the star-studded Jazz and the Philharmonic tours organized by Norman Granz, a record producer and impresario who became her manager in 1954. Under his supervision and on his Verve label, she recorded *The Cole Porter Songbook* in 1956, followed by anthologies devoted to George and Ira Gershwin, Duke Ellington, Irving Berlin, and other popular composers. Heavily arranged and cannily designed to promote both songwriter and performer, Fitzgerald's "songbooks" extended her appeal.

By the 1960s Fitzgerald was one of the world's most respected and successful singers. In the following years, she became something of an institution, regularly honored. She was named "Best Female Vocalist" by *Down Beat* magazine several times, and she won more Grammy Awards than any other female jazz singer. Following heart bypass surgery in 1986, she suffered from erratic health, but she intermittently recorded and gave concerts until her death in 1996.

See also Jazz; Jazz Singers; Music

■■ *Bibliography*

Colin, Sid. *Ella: The Life and Times of Ella Fitzgerald.* London: Trafalgar Square, 1986.

Gourse, Leslie. *The Ella Fitzgerald Companion: Seven Decades of Commentary.* Woodbridge, Conn.: Schirmer Books, 1998.

Kliment, Bud. *Ella Fitzgerald.* New York: Chelsea House, 1988.

Pleasants, Henry. "Ella Fitzgerald." In *The Great American Popular Singers.* New York: Simon and Schuster, 1974, pp. 168–180.

BUD KLIMENT (1996)
Updated by publisher 2005

FLAKE, FLOYD H.
JANUARY 30, 1945

Minister and former congressman Floyd H. Flake was born in Los Angeles and earned a B.A. degree from Wilberforce University in 1967 and a doctorate from United Theological Seminary in 1995. From 1970 to 1973 Flake was associate dean at Lincoln University in Pennsylvania. There he became alarmed by the failure of the recently integrated schools to educate young African Americans. Flake went to Boston University as dean of students, university chaplain, and director of the Martin Luther King Jr. Afro-American Center. In 1976 he took over Allen African Methodist Episcopal Church in Queens, New York.

Flake built up the church and increased its membership. He also involved himself and the church in the community and it became one of the major sources of new housing in the community through projects like the Allen A.M.E./Hall Estates, which in 1996 opened fifty new houses near the church-sponsored senior citizens center. His philosophy is expressed in his book, *The Way of the Bootstrapper: Nine Action Ways for Achieving Your Dreams* (1999).

In 1986, Flake was elected to the House of Representatives and held his seat until he resigned in the middle of 1997, just after he dedicated a $23 million cathedral for his church. Floyd attracted national attention when he threw his support to the Republican-backed school voucher plan in early 1997. He also showed that he was comfortable with the Republican Party's stress on "traditional family values" by opening his pulpit to presidential candidate George W. Bush. In May 2000 he announced that he was taking a position with Edison Schools, Inc., a large for-profit school management company.

See also African Methodist Episcopal Zion Church

■■ *Bibliography*

Brennan, Carol. "Floyd H. Flake" In *Contemporary Black Biography*, edited by Shirelle Phelps, vol. 18. Detroit, Mich.: Gale, 1998.

Flake, Floyd H., and M. Elaine McCollins Flake. *Practical Virtues: Everyday Values and Devotions for African American Families.* New York: HarperCollins, 2003.

Hicks, Jonathan P. "Rep. Flake Breaks with Party to Back School Vouchers." *New York Times,* March 12, 1997.

Traub, James. "Hopefuls; Street Toughs; Power Brokers; Networkers; Strivers; Grande Dames; Musclemen; Exiles; Reformers; Purists; Clones; Big Mouths; Outsiders; Air Kissers; Fanatics; Gossips; Nightclubbers: Floyd Flake's Middle America." *New York Times Magazine,* October 19, 1997.

Wyatt, Edward. "Floyd Flake to Take Post with Education Company." *New York Times,* May 3, 2000.

ROBERT L. JOHNS (1996)
Updated by publisher 2005

FLIPPER, HENRY O.

MARCH 21, 1856
MAY 3, 1940

▄▄▄

The son of Festus and Isabella Flipper, Henry Ossian Flipper, the first African-American graduate of West Point, was born a slave in Thomasville, Georgia. Festus, a shoemaker and carriage trimmer, managed to save enough money to purchase the freedom of his wife and children; in 1865 he brought the family to Atlanta. Henry and his brothers were educated in American Missionary Association schools and attended Atlanta University. In 1873, his first year in the university's collegiate department, Henry applied for and received an appointment to the United States Military Academy at West Point. He was not the first African American appointed to West Point: Michael Howard and James Webster Smith entered the academy in 1870, but both were dismissed prior to graduation. Flipper, however, endured four years of ostracism and persecution. On June 15, 1877, he became the first black cadet to earn a commission, graduating fiftieth in his class of seventy-six. In 1878 Flipper published *The Colored Cadet at West Point,* an autobiographical account of his experiences at the academy.

That same year Flipper was assigned to the all-black Tenth Cavalry Regiment and served in Texas and the Indian Territory. In 1881, while serving as post commissary at Fort Davis, Texas, he was brought before a general court-martial and charged by his commanding officer, Col. William R. Shafter, with the embezzlement of $3,791.77 in commissary funds and with "conduct unbecoming an officer and a gentleman." Although he was acquitted of the first charge, the court found him guilty of the second. On June 30, 1882, he was discharged from the army. Flipper claimed he was innocent of any misconduct and believed that his dismissal was motivated by white prejudice.

As a civilian, Flipper worked in Mexico and the American Southwest as a mining engineer and as a special agent of the Department of Justice in the Court of Private Land Claims. He became a recognized authority on Spanish and Mexican land law. While serving as an engineer for the Greene Gold-Silver Company in Chihuahua, Mexico, Flipper befriended Albert B. Fall. In 1919 Fall, then in his second term as a U.S. senator from New Mexico, asked Flipper to come to Washington, D.C., as a translator for the subcommittee on Mexican internal affairs of the Senate Committee on Foreign Relations. Two years later Fall was appointed secretary of the interior in the Harding administration and named Flipper as an assistant. In 1923 Flipper left Washington to work as a consultant for the Pantepec Oil Company in Venezuela. During his seven years there, he published an important translation of that country's mining and land law. In 1930 Flipper retired to Atlanta to live with his brother Joseph, a bishop in the African Methodist Episcopal Church. He died of a heart attack in 1940.

Flipper spent most of his life trying to clear his name, but despite the many political connections he was able to make in the West and in Washington, D.C., his efforts were in vain. Finally, in 1976 the army granted him a posthumous honorable discharge, and on May 3, 1977, West Point unveiled a bust commemorating its first black graduate. An annual award is given in his name to an outstanding cadet, and a section of the West Point library honors him.

President Clinton granted Flipper a presidential pardon fifty-nine years after his death. The ceremony, although largely symbolic, took place on February 19, 1999. Flipper's descendants attended the ceremony along with military officers. Also in attendance was Gen. Colin L. Powell, retired Chairman of the Joint Chief of Staffs, who said that he kept a picture of the lieutenant on his desk for inspiration. At the ceremony President Clinton said, "This good man now has completely recovered his good name."

See also Military Experience, African-American

▪▪ *Bibliography*

Carroll, John M., ed. *The Black Military Experience in the American West.* New York: Liveright, 1977.

Flipper, Henry O. *The Colored Cadet at West Point.* 1878. Reprint. New York: Arno, 1969.

Harris, Theodore D., ed. *Negro Frontiersman: The Western Memoirs of Henry O. Flipper.* El Paso: Tex.: Western College Press, 1963.

Johnson, Cecil. "Clearing the Name of a West Point Grad." *Knight Ridder/Tribune News Service* (February 25, 1999): K6807.

Katz, William L. *The Black West.* Seattle, Wash.: Open Hand, 1987.

New York Times, May 4, 1977, p. B-2.

BENJAMIN K. SCOTT (1996)
Updated bibliography

FOLK ARTS AND CRAFTS

The folk arts and crafts created by African Americans are, perhaps, the least acknowledged of their cultural traditions. Worldwide recognition of black achievement in music and dance has overshadowed significant accomplishments in the area of material culture, so that while black Americans are seen as gifted performers, they are rarely described as even adequate producers of objects.

VERNACULAR TRADITIONS

In times past, black artisans were numerous, and they are to be credited with making a wide array of artifacts, particularly in the southern states. It is important to recall that during the preindustrial era, most rural people made things, such as tools, utensils, containers, clothes, food, houses, and toys. Whether as slaves or as free people, blacks created a multitude of necessary, useful, and sometimes beautiful, objects.

The reasons why African Americans would be skilled at making domestic arts and crafts are not hard to fathom. On plantations they often had little choice when they were ordered to learn particular trades by their owners. But more often, because they were provided with so few domestic items, they either had to make most of their furnishings and utensils or do without them. After Emancipation the folk arts and crafts that blacks had developed in the plantation setting continued to prove useful. Reduced to a condition of near servitude by continued racial exploitation and poverty, African-American artisans used their traditional skills to get themselves and their families through tough times, and some still do so today. Folk arts and crafts have always played dual roles in the black community, serving both as a means of making a living and as a means for creative self-expression. While many items of folk art and craft produced by African Americans are indistinguishable in form, technique, and style from works produced by white Americans, there is a stream of African inspiration that runs through traditional black material culture in the South. The most distinctive works of African-American black folk art, in cultural terms, are those that manifest a linkage to African origins. This article surveys selected examples of those works with the strongest African connections.

BASKETRY

Coiled-grass baskets have been produced in the United States by black artisans for more than three centuries. Once integral items on plantations, particularly along the so-called Rice Coast that once extended from North Carolina to Florida's northern border, the craft is today most publicly on display in and around Charleston, South Carolina, where hundreds of "sewers" work fashioning baskets. Using sweetgrass, rush, pine needles, and strips of leaves from the palmetto tree as their primary materials, they produce a seemingly limitless variety of forms that they sell on street corners, in the central open-air market, and at more than fifty stands along the main highway entering the city.

What one sees here are "show baskets," a subgenre within this tradition that was initiated probably in the mid-nineteenth century. Included under this category are all sorts of decorative containers: flower baskets, serving trays, purses, sewing baskets, casserole holders, umbrella stands, and cake baskets. As is evident from this partial inventory, the show basket is intended to be used in the home where it will be prominently displayed. As these items are made, then, to be fancy, basketmakers explore, at every opportunity, new creative possibilities in form and decoration. A show basket is a highly personalized artwork shaped extensively by individual imagination.

However, as the matriarch basket maker Mary Jane Manigault explains, "All baskets begin as a hot plate," meaning that all works, no matter how imaginative and seemingly without precedent, trace back to a common ancestry rooted in basic forms and techniques. Thus, all coiled baskets start out as a disk form. The oldest African-American coiled baskets were "work baskets." They were made with bundles of stiff rushes and often sewn with strips of oak. With coils generally an inch in diameter, these were tough, durable baskets intended to be used outside, either in the fields or in the farmyard. They are easily distinguishable from the lighter, more delicately formed show baskets. Most work baskets were large, heavy, round containers made to carry produce; they all had flat bottoms and straight walls that flared out slightly from the base. One specialized work basket, the fanner, was a large tray about two feet in diameter, with a low outer rim. Primarily an implement for processing the rice harvest, it was also used as a basic kitchen tool. Rice could not be properly cooked unless it had first been fanned to separate the kernels from the husks.

These baskets were but one element in a set of African practices upon which the production of rice was based. Planters specifically sought out slaves from the rice-growing regions of West and Central Africa, people who came with not only a knowledge of rice cultivation, but also the basic technology for its harvest and preparation as food. While planters were generally wary about allowing overt African expressions among their slaves, they tolerated this mode of basketry when they realized that it basically enhanced the productivity of their estates.

Unwittingly, then, these planters actually facilitated the maintenance of a decidedly African tradition. While the end of the plantation era was, understandably, accompanied by a decline of the work basket tradition, it did not cause coiled basketry to disappear altogether. These baskets remained a feature of home craft on small black farms in the area, and from 1910 to 1950 there was an attempt at the Penn School on St. Helena Island to revive the practice. While this particular effort ended with disappointing results, the tradition was able to flourish in the Charleston area, where show baskets became exceedingly popular among tourists who assiduously sought them as souvenirs of their visits.

The basket making tradition was necessarily transformed as artisans shifted from a rural to an urban venue, where artisans made baskets more often for sale than for domestic use. Yet venerable traditions were still honored. The sewing baskets and serving trays were old-time baskets, too, even if their origins did not trace all the way back to Africa, as did those of the work baskets. But the entrepreneurial energies that were released in this commercial effort led mainly to freewheeling displays of personal imagination. Soon basketmakers were as proud of new unprecedented forms that they called "own style baskets" as they were of more conventional flower baskets or clothes hampers.

But even within this spirited and open-ended creativity, there are still signs of historical memory. Fanner baskets, for example, can occasionally be found for sale in the Charleston market, albeit as lightweight show-basket facsimiles. But more important, the techniques for coiling and stitching remain unchanged regardless of the type of basket. This continuity of process allows contemporary basket makers to place themselves in the flow of a tradition that traces back through time and space to African roots. The personal satisfaction that these artisans derive from making coiled baskets is amplified by a keen awareness of that history, and as a result they are all the more motivated to preserve this custom.

BOATBUILDING

That African-American competence in agriculture was matched by maritime abilities should not be surprising. Most African slaves were captured, after all, from either coastal or riverine environments, and thus they had extensive experience with a variety of small craft. When set to work on plantations, often located near coasts or along prominent rivers, these Africans had ample opportunity

to display their navigation skills. Eighteenth-century commentators were quick to acknowledge how adept slaves were in paddling log canoes, which often proved difficult to maneuver in swift currents and to keep upright. In the Charleston area, black watermen working out of hewn dugouts called "pettiaugers" (an Anglicized version of the French *pirogues*) had by 1750 achieved almost complete domination of the local fishing trade. White people depended on black boating skills from Georgia to Maryland, as slaves literally provided the backbone for the local transportation system at a time when there were few roads.

In this context, slaves also built boats, and while their surviving descriptions tend to be somewhat vague with respect to details, it seems that West Indian watercraft, and thus, in some measure, African-derived maritime traditions, provided the basic models. The pettiauger was a well-known Caribbean vessel with a hull consisting of a log dugout extended by the addition of extra planks. Fitted with sails for open-water voyaging, it could also by propelled by teams of oarsmen. Boats of this sort are described repeatedly as the usual type of plantation "barge" used to ferry people, supplies, and produce. A second type of plantation vessel was a canoe hewn from a single log. Derived from either African or Native American precedents, it was less than twenty feet in length and relatively light due to the thinness of the hull. This was an excellent vessel for navigating the shallow marshes and streams surrounding the barrier islands of the South Carolina and Georgia coasts. The plantation mistress Fannie Kemble recorded in 1838 that two slave carpenters on her Butler Island estate had made such a canoe, which they sold for the sum of sixty dollars. A type of multi-log dugout, common to the waters of the Chesapeake Bay, is credited to a slave from York County, Virginia, remembered only as Aaron. In form, this craft—a log canoe with a hull shaped from as many as nine logs—seems related to the West Indian pettiaugers.

In Virginia and Maryland, African Americans were extensively involved in a full range of shipbuilding trades as ship's carpenters, caulkers, sail makers, and blacksmiths. A remarkable account from the *Raleigh Star* in 1811 describes how a brig launched in Alexandria, Virginia, was "drafted by a coloured man belonging to Col. Tayloe and under his superintendence built from her keel to her topmast." Here the design sources were unquestionably Anglo-American, but the fact that a slave was given such broad authority suggests that he was working in a context in which most of the men under his command must have been slaves as well. This event suggests that blacks might have been able to do quite well as shipbuilders had they simply been afforded the chance. But there were few opportunities because African-American watermen were diverted mainly to fishing and oyster dredging, where they would be employed for their brawn rather than their designing and woodworking skills.

Musical Instrument Making

In the testimony of former slaves there is frequent mention of homemade musical instruments. Litt Young from Mississippi recalled exciting events around 1860, when "Us have small dances Saturday nights and ring plays and fiddle playin' and knockin' bones. There was fiddles made from gourds and banjos from sheep hides." The inventory here of stringed and percussive instruments identifies two of the main classes of musical instruments frequently made by African-American artisans. To Young's short list one can add rattles, gongs, scrapers, fifes, whistles, panpipes, and drums. All of these had verifiable African antecedents—as did many of the songs that were played on them and the dances they were intended to accompany.

Drums, which were so essential to both African musical performance and to religious and healing rituals, were frightening to slave holders, for they realized that these instruments could be used to send private messages that they would not be able to decipher. Laws were passed in South Carolina after the Stono Rebellion of 1739, and later in other colonies, banning the playing of drums expressly to eliminate this means of communication. But such prohibitions were less than effective as deterrents, and well into the nineteenth century, slaves, particularly those who were more recently arrived from Africa, were still making drums. They commonly affixed some type of animal skin with thongs or pegs across the open end of a hollowed log or large gourd. Apparently such drums were made often enough that even as late as the 1930s elderly blacks living in the coastal regions of Georgia could still describe the practice in detail. Even though the custom was fast fading into obscurity by that time, a few of these informants claimed that they had made drums themselves.

The banjo is a very old black folk instrument that continues to enjoy considerable popularity among white aficionados of so-called country music. This is an instrument that, according to no less an authority than Thomas Jefferson, black people "brought hither from Africa." In the earliest examples, the body of the instrument was shaped from a gourd sliced in half lengthwise and then covered with a stretched animal skin. A fretless neck was inserted at one end and four gut strings were run from its top to the base of the gourd. Today's banjos, made in factories, are different in every respect, except that they continue to have membrane-covered drums underneath the strings. Thus, when the instrument is strummed one can

still hear the distinctive combination of melodic tone and percussive thrump that was present in the original plantation instruments. The mainstay of African-American folk music through the early twentieth century, when it was largely supplanted by the blues guitar, the banjo is rarely played today by black musicians, and the only reported contemporary makers of banjos with gourd bodies are white.

The experience among fife makers, however, is more positive. In the delta area of northwestern Mississippi, a small number of families continue to play fifes—or, as they might say, "blow canes"—as the entertainment at local picnics and barbecues. These people make their fifes as well. The process seems relatively simple: A foot-long section of bamboo cane is hollowed out and a mouth hole and four finger holes are pierced into it with a red-hot poker. There is considerable difficulty in calculating the correct placement for the holes so that notes of the correct pitch can be played. Considerable experimentation is required, since each piece of cane has a slightly different tonal range. In Mississippi, the fife is played as the lead instrument together with an ensemble of drums; it is a performance that resonates with similar performances among the Akan peoples of Ghana.

Pottery

Slave potters made two very different types of wares. The earliest were earthenware vessels shaped by hand and fired to very low temperatures in open bonfires. These pots, recovered from the sites of many eighteenth-century plantations in South Carolina and Virginia, consisted mainly of small, round-bottomed bowls suitable for eating and drinking and larger round-bottomed cooking vessels. For decades these sorts of vessels were believed to be Native American in origin, and they therefore were labeled as "Colono-Indian wares." Subsequent investigation has shown that, given the sheer quantity of Colono shards at the sites of slave occupation and their relative absence in Indian villages during the same period, there can be no other conclusion than that this type of pottery was being made by slave artisans. Comparisons with African wares lend further support to the claim of slave manufacture, so that some of this eighteenth-century earthenware is now referred to as Afro-Colono pottery.

Many plantation-made bowls have a cross or an "X" scratched into their bases. While the function of these intriguing marks remains open to speculation, these are signs that have mystical associations in Central Africa, where they are used in acts of prayer, particularly in summoning the protective power of ancestral spirits. As scholars have puzzled through the significance of these marks, they have surmised that the first slaves must have looked to their own inventory of cultural forms when they had to find an adequate way to feed themselves, and they simply turned to a familiar African craft tradition. When slaves next discovered that their owners would not interfere in their efforts, some of these Africans may have gone even further and used their African pots to regenerate their interrupted religious traditions.

By the middle of the nineteenth century, the production of earthenware on plantations had ended. By then there were relatively few Africans in the slave population left to carry on the practice. More important, slave owners were now providing more food preparation items, such as cast-iron cooking pots. The first quarter of the nineteenth century also witnessed an upsurge in the production of stoneware pottery, a durable type of ware shaped on a potter's wheel and fired to very high temperatures in a kiln. This type of pottery was produced mainly at small, family-run shops. Occasionally, slaves were employed in these shops, but chiefly as the laborers who cut the firewood or dug and mixed the clay; the more prestigious role of potter or turner was reserved for a white artisan. There was, however, one site where blacks were allowed more extensive participation, and it is there that one can identify a nineteenth-century tradition for African-American pottery.

About 1810, Abner Landrum, a prosperous white man living in the Edgefield District of west-central South Carolina, opened a pottery shop and was soon producing high-quality wares recognized as superior to any in the region. His shop would quickly grow into a booming industrial village, and before long Landrum was selling stock in his operation. His financial success, however, did not go unchallenged. Other entrepreneurs also set up potteries in the area, luring away many of Landrum's skilled artisans. When he solved this crisis by training slaves to make pottery, other pottery shop owners soon followed his example.

Most of these African-American artisans remain unnamed, but various records suggest that about fifty slaves were employed at various shops throughout the Edgefield District. The best known of this group was a man named Dave, who had once belonged to Abner Landrum. Trained first as a typesetter at Landrum's newspaper, Dave continued to display the fact that he was literate on his pots by signing and dating them, and occasionally inscribing them with rhymed couplets. These vessels, unlike most, carry terse captions describing the time of manufacture and their maker's identity. More important, that they publicly carry words at a time when it was illegal for slaves to be literate makes these pots statements of overt resistance. Other slaves, upon seeing Dave's works, were likely to know that one of their own was mocking the white man's law, and they may have derived some measure of inspiration from his audacious example.

Certainly many would have noticed Dave's pots, for he made some of the largest vessels known in Edgefield. The largest one, inscribed "Great and Noble Jar," has a capacity of almost forty-five gallons and stands thirty inches in height. Many of his other pots are in this same size range and are distinctively shaped, with walls that flare boldly from a relatively narrow base to a wide shoulder close to the top of the vessel. While white potters also made large storage jars, none of their works seem as daring. With their widest sections nearer their middles, they appear to squat safely on the floor, while Dave's pots seemingly leap up and threaten to teeter back and forth. The form of Dave's pots thus emphasize the rebelliousness signaled by his inscriptions.

Even though Dave's work is a reflection of commonplace African-American experiences of chattel slavery in the South, his pieces, as objects, are basically expressions of European ceramic traditions. The pot forms for which he is now so famous appear to take their lines ultimately from the bread pots of northeastern England, and his use of pottery wheels, kilns, and glazes are all manifestations of standardized Anglo-American ceramic technology. Yet within the community of black potters in Edgefield, there were opportunities for artisans to revisit ancestral aesthetic forms. In series of small vessels, averaging about five inches in height, slave potters were apparently able to rekindle memories of African sculpture.

Pots decorated with faces are known in every ceramic tradition on the globe, but those attributed to black people in Edgefield have several attributes not seen elsewhere. Their most distinctive feature is the use of a different clay body to mark the eyes and teeth: white porcelain clay contrasts sharply with the dark glaze covering the rest of the stoneware vessel. The riveting gaze and seeming snarl that results from this mode of decoration recalls the mixed-media approach to sculpture found in West and Central Africa, where all sorts of contrasting materials are applied to a wooden form for dramatic effect, particularly in the rendering of eyes and teeth on statues and masks. That a white substance is used in Edgefield is very significant, for the same visual effect might have been achieved by simply coloring the eyes and teeth with a light-colored slip, or liquid clay. That the look of an Edgefield face jug was created by the rather difficult technique of embedding an entirely different clay body into the walls of the pot suggests that both the material and the behavior are charged with important symbolic meanings. In Central Africa, homeland to seventy-five percent of all slaves imported into South

Carolina, white clay has sacred associations with ancestral authority.

Among the Central-African Kongo people, for example, white is the color of the dead, so that white objects are offered to them and effigies of the dead are marked with white eyes. The strong stylistic affinities between Kongo sculpture and Edgefield vessels suggest that the enslaved artisans took advantage of their access to ceramic technology and used it to enhance African-inspired religious ceremonies held on the plantations in the region. These rituals could be carried on without detection because during the antebellum period blacks outnumbered whites in the Edgefield District by more than four to one. The African-ness of slave life in this area was sustained as well by constant illegal smuggling of new African captives into the area; in fact, one of the last known cargoes of slaves to the United States was a group of Kongo captives landed on the Georgia coast, carried up the Savannah River, and sold into Edgefield County in 1858. The face vessels of Edgefield are evidence, then, of how African-American artisans could, when circumstances allowed, counter the assimilationist trajectory of their experiences and use new foreign means to re-establish ties to their African roots.

WOODCARVING

The prodigious woodcarving skills of African artisans are widely recognized, and their masks and statues are granted honored places in first-rank museums along with noteworthy masterpieces of Western art. Since these works, so abundant in Africa, seem to be noticeably absent in the United States, assessments of African-American culture often begin by lamenting the loss of these skills. However, this carving tradition, while diminished in scale, is not altogether absent.

African slaves seem to have remembered their traditions for woodcarving. According to an old African-American man from Georgia who was interviewed in the late 1930s for the Georgia Writer's Project: "I remember the African men used to all the time make little clay images. Sometimes they like men, sometimes they like animals. Once they put a spear in his hand and walk around him and he was the chief. . . . Sometimes they try to make the image out of wood." Specific examples also exist. In 1819, in Congo Square in New Orleans, the architect Benjamin Latrobe saw a banjo that had an unmistakable African figure carved at the top of the instrument's neck just above the tuning pegs. A remarkable table was built sometime in the 1850s on a plantation in north-central North Carolina with each of its legs carved into figures highly reminiscent of African figures. A drum now in the collections of the British Museum, but which was collected in 1753 in Virginia, is in every respect an excellent example of an Akan-Ashanti *apentemma* drum. However, since it was carved from a piece of American cedar, it is American rather than African in origin. From this smattering of examples, one can conclude that African proclivities for working creatively in wood did not simply end upon Africans' arrival in the Americas. These skills were carried on when and wherever possible.

Most often, African woodcarving skills were turned in other directions—generally to the production of useful household objects such as bowls, trays, mortars and pestles, and handles for various metal tools. The severely functional nature of these items did not provide much of an opportunity for creative expression, even if the artisan did his work with diligence and commitment. Yet in the carving of wooden canes some degree of African inspiration was seemingly able to re-emerge. Numerous walking sticks carved by African Americans, from the nineteenth century to the present, sometimes bear distinctive marks that may relate to African traditions kept alive mainly among country people. These canes are often decorated with a wide range of media, including brass tacks, colored beads and marbles, aluminum foil, and other shiny materials. In one case from Mississippi, the carver attached a silver thermometer to the handle of a cane that was already elaborately carved with figures of humans and serpents. Yet it was not judged to be complete without the bit of flash that a seemingly incongruous temperature gauge could provide. While this decorative gesture could be nothing more than a whimsical act of personal innovation, the fact that such acts are so commonplace among African-American cane makers in the South implies the presence of a shared style. Certainly one senses in the construct of these decorated canes a parallel to the African use of mixed-media assembly in sculpture.

Closer African affinities are seen in the selection of certain motifs. Reptiles dominate the shafts of most of the walking sticks that have clear attributions to African-American carvers. In addition to snakes (which are common to decorators of canes everywhere), black carvers also render alligators, turtles, and lizards, and as they are often combined with figures of human beings, the contrast may be read as symbolic of supernatural communication. According to widely held African beliefs, reptiles are appropriate symbols of messages between the spirit and human domains because they are creatures able to travel in two realms (e.g., in the water and on the land, or underground and above ground). Just like spiritual messages, they move back and forth between the human environment and another, unseen place. The chief linkage between this symbolism and African-American traditions in woodcarving

Harriet Powers Quilts

Harriet Powers is one of the most well-known quilt makers of the nineteenth century. Powers's quilts are relevant mainly for their bold use of appliqué, for storytelling, and for the extensive care and detail that go into making them. The technique and design indicate an African and African-American influence and sensibility. Telling stories using appliqué designs for visual narratives, for instance, was an artistic practice common in Benin, West Africa.

Typical scenes depicted on the cotton quilts contain celestial phenomena for the most part, as well as biblical imagery. Due to financial difficulty, Powers decided to sell her beloved quilts. In one instance, a person who purchased one of the quilts tells of Powers making repeated visits back to her home just to get another look at her creation almost as if it were one of her children. Only two of the quilts, which Powers stitched, remain well-preserved. One is located at the Museum of Fine Arts in Boston, while the other is a part of the National Museum of History collection at the Smithsonian Institution in Washington, D.C.

may lie in the fact that throughout the nineteenth century, traditional healers, or "root doctors," are said to have carried carved walking sticks decorated with reptiles as a sign of their authority. Since their cures are likely to have been based on African practices, it follows that the rest of their paraphernalia (which was often as instrumental in affecting a cure as the medicines administered) was also African-derived. Consequently, when an African American carved a snake or an alligator on a walking stick, it may have carried a different meaning and function than a similar animal carved by a white artisan.

QUILTING

Quilted bedcovers are objects that are unknown and unnecessary in tropical Africa. However, some West African ceremonial textiles are decorated with colorful appliqué figures, and large pieces of cloth for everyday use are assembled by sewing narrow strips together. Thus, enslaved

African women may have been somewhat prepared to make quilts, since they already had the requisite skills needed to piece quilt tops from scraps and remnants. While the actual quilting process was, for the most part, new and different—that is, the binding of two large pieces of cloth together with a layer of batting in between by means of thousands of geometrically patterned stitches—extant quilts alleged to be slave-made show that these women were certainly capable of mastering the task.

Very little about the oldest surviving African-American quilts seems to demonstrate any affinity for African textile traditions. What one mainly sees is the strict guidance of the plantation mistress. However, during the last decades of the nineteenth century, Harriet Powers of Athens, Georgia, produced two quilts filled with images that seem to come straight out of Dahomey, a prominent kingdom on the West African coast. While her links to Africa are less than certain—and would have been, at best, indirect—the figures on her two "bible" quilts compare closely with appliqué figures found on sewn narrative textiles of the Fon people. More commonplace and perhaps even more profoundly associated with African textiles are the "strip quilts," which appear with great regularity wherever African Americans make quilts. In this type of bedcover, long, thin strip units are sewn edge-to-edge to form the large square or rectangular quilt top. The "strips" may be single pieces; or they may be assembled from blocks, from thin remnants called "strings," or from assorted remnants. Regardless of the technique, the overall linear composition of the top cannot be missed. Since most contemporary African-American quilters claim that quilts of this type are the oldest pattern they know, there is a good possibility that such quilts were made during slavery. Certainly they resemble in form and technique the strip cloths of West and Central Africa. These textiles are assembled from narrow pieces about five inches wide and eight feet long that are sewn edge-to-edge to create a large rectangular panel. This tradition is seemingly perpetuated in a modified form in the African-American strip quilt.

Even if this mode of quilt assembly proves not to be African in origin, it is certainly a marker of African-American style. While white quilters also make such quilts, they will usually protest that they were a simple type made when they were "just learning" or that they were quilts merely "thrown together" and thus were nothing to be proud of. Black quilters, on the other hand, celebrate strip patterns as among the most significant in their repertories and produce them from childhood to old age. They constantly work at refining the form as they explore the nuances of the genre. These quilters are fully aware of the geometric patterns common in Euro-American quilting, patterns usually generated from block units, but they prefer to use strips. The strip format is by nature innovative and open-ended, and thus, unlike Euro-American quilt genres, is considerably less bound by formal conventions. There is, then, a sense of design permission about strip quilts, even a sense of liberation. With this mode of quilting, and with other forms of art and craft, African-American folk traditions make vital and enduring contributions to the aesthetic mosaic of the United States.

See also Art; Gardens and Yard Art; Maroon Arts

■ ■ *Bibliography*

Beardsley, John, William Arnett, Paul Arnett, and Jane Livingston. *Gee's Bend: The Women and Their Quilts.* Atlanta: Tinwood, 2002.

Benberry, Cuesta. *Always There: The African-American Presence in American Quilts.* Louisville: Kentucky Quilt Project, 1992.

Bolster, W. Jeffrey. *Black Jacks: African American Seamen in the Age of Sail.* Cambridge, Mass.: Harvard University Press, 1998.

Cecelski, David S. *The Waterman's Song: Slavery and Freedom in Maritime North Carolina.* Chapel Hill: University of North Carolina Press, 2001.

Deetz, James. *Flowerdew Hundred: The Archaeology of a Virginia Plantation, 1617–1864.* Charlottesville: University Press of Virginia, 1993.

Ferguson, Leland. *Uncommon Ground: Archaeology and Early African America, 16501800.* Washington, D.C.: Smithsonian Institution Press, 1992.

Ferris, William H., ed. *Afro-American Folk Art and Crafts.* Jackson: University Press of Mississippi, 1983.

Freeman, Roland L., *A Communion of the Spirits: African-American Quilters, Preservers, and Their Stories.* Nashville, Tenn.: Rutledge Hill Press, 1996.

Fry, Gladys-Marie. *Stitched from the Soul: Slave Quilts from the Ante-Bellum South.* New York: Dutton, 1990. Reprint, Chapel Hill: University of North Carolina Press, 2002

Georgia Council for the Arts and Humanities. *Missing Pieces: Georgia Folk Art 1770-1976.* Atlanta: Georgia Council for the Arts and Humanities, 1977.

Georgia Writer's Project. *Drums and Shadows: Survival Studies among Georgia Coastal Negroes.* Athens: University of Georgia Press, 1940.

Greenville County Museum of Art. *Early Decorated Stoneware of the Edgefield District, South Carolina.* Greenville, S.C.: Greenville County Museum of Art, 1976.

Gura, Philip F. and James F. Bollman, *America's Instrument: The Banjo in the Nineteenth Century.* Chapel Hill: University of North Carolina Press, 1999.

Kouverman, Jill Beute. *"I made this jar" . . . The Life and Work of the Enslaved African-American Potter, Dave.* Columbia: McKissick Museum, University of South Carolina, 1998.

Henry, Susan L. *Physical, Spatial, and Temporal Dimensions of Colono Ware in the Chesapeake, 1600–1800.* Columbia: South Carolina Institute of Archaeology and Anthropology, 1992.

Horne, Catherine Wilson, ed. *Crossroads of Clay: The Southern Alkaline-Glazed Stoneware Tradition.* Columbia, S.C.: McKissick Museum, University of South Carolina, 1990.

Leon, Eli. *Who'd A Thought It: Improvisation in African-American Quiltmaking.* San Francisco: San Francisco Craft and Folk Art Museum, 1987.

Myers, Lynn Robertson, and George D. Terry. *Carolina Folk: The Cradle of a Southern Tradition.* Columbia, S.C.: McKissick Museum, University of South Carolina, 1985.

Myers, Lynn Robertson, and George D. Terry. *Southern Make: The Southern Folk Heritage.* Columbia, S.C.: McKissick Museum, University of South Carolina, 1977.

Newton, James E., and Ronald Lewis, eds. *The Other Slaves: Mechanics, Artisans, and Craftsmen.* Boston: G. K. Hall, 1978.

Rosengarten, Dale. *Row upon Row: Sea Grass Baskets of the South Carolina Low Country.* Columbia, S.C.: McKissick Museum, University of South Carolina, 1986.

Thompson, Robert F. "African Influences on the Art of the United States." In *Black Studies in the University,* edited by Armistead L. Robinson, et al. New Haven, Conn.: Yale University Press, 1969.

Thompson, Robert F. *Flash of the Spirit: African and Afro-American Art.* New York: Random House, 1983.

Vlach, John Michael. *The Afro-American Tradition in the Decorative Arts.* Cleveland: Cleveland Museum of Art, 1978. Reprint. Athens: University of Georgia Press, 1990.

Vlach, John Michael. *By the Work of Their Hands: Studies in Afro-American Folk Life.* Charlottesville: University Press of Virginia, 1991. Reprint, Athens: University of Georgia Press, 1999.

Webb, Robert Lloyd. *Ring the Banjar!: The Banjo from Folklore to Factory.* Cambridge, Mass.: MIT Museum, 1984.

Wood, Peter H. *Black Majority: Negroes in Colonial South Carolina from 1670 through the Stono Rebellion.* New York: Knopf, 1974.

JOHN MICHAEL VLACH (1996)
Updated by author 2005

FOLKLORE

┣┿┫

This entry consists of three distinct articles examining folklore, folk heroes, and folk culture in the Americas.

OVERVIEW
John W. Roberts

LATIN AMERICAN AND CARIBBEAN CULTURE HEROES AND CHARACTERS
Dellita Martin-Ogunsola

U.S. FOLK HEROES AND CHARACTERS
LaRose T. Parris

OVERVIEW

African-American folklore is a mode of creative cultural production that manifests itself in expressive forms such as tales, songs, proverbs, greetings, gestures, rhymes, material artifacts, and other created products and performances. Although African-American folklore is most often thought of in terms of these expressive forms, it is in reality a dynamic process of creativity that arises in performative contexts characterized by face-to-face interaction. The performative aspects of this folklore is what distinguishes it from other modes of creative cultural production within an African-American context. In other words, unlike other modes of African-American creative cultural production, such as literary and popular culture, folklore gains its meaning and value as a form of expression within unmediated performances on an ongoing basis in African-American communities.

Although African-American folklore should be conceptualized as a performed medium, it has an important historical dimension as well. That is, its performance even in contemporary settings entails the creative manipulation of historical forms of indefinite temporal origin. As such, it is intricately linked to processes of black culture building in that it has historically served as an important means of communicating shared cultural attitudes, beliefs, and values of and within an ever-changing African community in the United States. As interrelated phenomena, African American folklore creation and culture building are both dynamic creative processes with roots in the diverse African cultures from which contemporary African Americans originated.

Among scholars of African-American folklore, however, the existence of a dynamic relationship between African and African-American processes of folklore creation has historically been controversial. The controversy arose in large part from the intricate link that folklorists envisioned between folklore creation and culture building. Early in the study of African-American culture and folklore, scholars postulated that African people were so traumatized by the process of enslavement that they arrived in the New World culturally bankrupt and, therefore, dependent on Europeans for new cultural capital. In early studies, this view of a lack of African cultural retention contributed to a conception of the products of African-American folklore as mere imitations of European expressive forms. Although this view has been challenged over the years by the discovery of decidedly African cultural forms in the United States, these cultural expressions have been disparaged further by being identified as "Africanisms," isolated cases that somehow survived in the New World despite the trauma of enslavement. "Africanisms," however, represent the most obvious evidence that African culture and cultural forms have had a profound influence on black culture building and folklore creation in the United States (Roberts, 1989, p. 9).

FOLKLORE AND SLAVERY

Historically, the difficulty of appreciating and recognizing the influence of African culture and cultural forms on African-American folklore has been exacerbated by the fact that Africans brought to the United States as slaves did not themselves share a coherent culture. Only recently have scholars begun to realize the irrelevance of this perspective to an understanding of black culture building in African communities throughout the New World. For example, Sidney Mintz and Richard Price have suggested that although Africans enslaved in the New World did not share a common culture or folk tradition upon arrival, they did share "certain common orientations to reality which tended to focus the attention of individuals from West African cultures upon similar kinds of events, even though the ways of handling these events may seem quite diverse in formal terms." While these "common orientations to reality" may not have been sufficient to support the re-creation of African cultural institutions in their pristine form, they could and did serve as a foundation for culture building in a new environment (1972, p.5).

African people who were forcibly unrooted from their homelands and transplanted in America as slaves brought with them cherished memories of their traditional lifestyles and cultural forms that served as the foundations of African-American folk tradition. To understand the dynamic processes that characterized the development over time of an African-American folk tradition, we must recognize that both black culture building and folklore creation have proceeded as recursive rather than linear processes of endlessly devising solutions to both old and new problems of living under ever-changing social, political, and economic conditions. While both culture building and folklore creation are dynamic and creative in that they adapt to social needs and goals, they are also enduring in that they change by building upon previous manifestations of themselves. Cultural transformation is a normative process experienced and carried out by all groups. In the process, the institutional and expressive forms by which a group communicates and upholds the ideals by which it lives are equally subject to transformation.

As James Snead (1984, p. 61) has argued, however, the failure to recognize the dynamic and transformational properties of African cultures in the New World has been influenced historically by the view that African cultures are static. Only by recognizing that such cultures are and always have been dynamic (i.e., capable of transforming themselves in response to the social needs and goals of African people) is it possible to envision African-American folklore as a continuous process of creativity intricately linked to a historical tradition of black culture building with roots in Africa. During the period of black slavery in the United States, enslaved Africans began the process of building a culture based on their "common orientations to reality." Despite their lack of a sense of shared identity and values upon arrival, the similarity of the conditions and treatment that they faced in the slave system facilitated their ability to envision themselves as a community. To communicate their shared identity and value system, they transformed many of their African cultural forms by focusing on the common elements within them. In the process, their creative efforts as well as the final expressive products they created were greatly influenced by the differences in their situations in the United States from those they had known in Africa. In other words, the transformation of African cultural forms involved a process of creating new forms based on common elements from diverse African cultures and their infusion with insights and meanings relevant to contemporary situations in the United States. That these new forms did not always resemble some African original did not negate the debt they owed to African cultural roots.

The beginnings of an African-American folk tradition can be traced to the slavery period and to the efforts of African people from diverse cultural backgrounds to maintain a sense of continuity with their past. Throughout the period of slavery, scattered references to African-American folklore appeared in written records. Systematic efforts to collect and study such folklore, however, did not begin until the late nineteenth century. The earliest efforts to collect it were carried out primarily by white missionaries who flocked into the South following Emancipation to assist black freedpeople. Although these early efforts were motivated in large part by a desire to use African Americans' creative cultural production to demonstrate their humanity and fitness for freedom, such activities nevertheless preserved for posterity a vast body of African-American oral tradition.

An equally important motive for early collectors of black folklore was the prevalent belief in the late nineteenth century that folklore as a mode of creative cultural production was rapidly disappearing. In the case of African Americans, many envisioned the growing rate of literacy among freedpeople as a sure sign that the African-American folk tradition would soon disappear. Although contemporary folklorists realize the falsity of this perspective, it nevertheless provided a primary impetus for the collection of African-American folklore in the late nineteenth century and influenced a concentration on those forms that had obvious roots in slavery. During this productive period of African-American folklore gathering, collectors focused most of their attention on three forms: spirituals, animal-trickster tales, and folk beliefs.

SPIRITUALS. Spirituals received a great deal of attention, especially from northern missionaries, in the late nineteenth century. The first book-length collection of African-American folklore published was *Slave Songs of the United States*, which primarily contained spirituals. The spiritual song tradition of African Americans developed during the late eighteenth and early nineteenth centuries with the conversion of large numbers of enslaved African Americans to Christianity. Spirituals as a body of songs were developed primarily around the actions of Old Testament figures whose faith in God allowed them to be delivered from bondage and persecution in dramatic ways. The songs followed a pronounced leader/chorus pattern known as call and response, which in performance created a kind of communal dialogue about the power of faith and belief in an omnipotent God. While the songs often portrayed heaven as the ultimate reward of faith in God, their primary focus was on earthly deliverance from bondage and persecution. Through analogy to Old Testament stories of persecution and divine deliverance, the songs constantly reiterated the power of God to deliver the faithful.

Spirituals provided enslaved Africans with an alternative expressive form for communicating their vision of the power of God and the rewards of faith in Christianity to that offered by the slave masters. As enslaved Africans freely and often testified, masters frequently attempted to use slaves' Christian conversion and participation in white religious services to reinforce the masters' view of enslavement. The dominant message that enslaved Africans received from white preachers was, "Servants, obey your masters." In the spirituals, enslaved Africans were able to convey to members of their community a more empowering and liberating vision of God and the Christian religion. Of equal importance, the creation and performance of spirituals allowed them to incorporate more of their African cultural heritage into Christian worship. Despite general prohibitions against unsupervised worship, enslaved Africans created opportunities for separate worship in slave cabins, "hush harbors," and even their own churches, where they created and performed spirituals in a style and manner that incorporated African performance practices. These practices included the development of the "shout," a religious ritual characterized by a counterclockwise shuffling movement reminiscent of African ritual dancing. The primary purpose of the "shout" was to induce spirit possession, a form of communion with the supernatural valued by many people of African descent.

ANIMAL-TRICKSTER TALES. In the late nineteenth century, the collection of spirituals was rivaled only by the collection of animal-trickster tales. With the publication of Joel Chandler Harris's *Uncle Remus: His Songs and Sayings* in 1881, the collection of animal-trickster tales by various individuals escalated. By the end of the nineteenth century, literally hundreds of these tales had been collected and published. Early collectors of black folktales often expressed amazement over the variety of animal-trickster tales created by enslaved Africans. That tales of the animal trickster would become central in the narrative performances of enslaved Africans is not surprising, however. In the cultures from which enslaved Africans originated, folktales in which clever animals acted as humans to impart important lessons about survival were ubiquitous. Although various animals acted as tricksters in different African traditions, the tales of their exploits showed important similarities throughout sub-Saharan Africa. In fact, even the same plots could be found in the trickster-tale traditions of diverse African groups (Feldmann, 1973, p. 15).

In the United States, the animal trickster was most often represented by Brer Rabbit, although other animals acted as tricksters in some tales. Although a number of trickster tales found in the repertory of enslaved Africans retained plots from African tradition, many transformed the African trickster in ways that reflected the situation of enslavement. The impetus for transforming the African trickster was not only the need to create a single tradition out of many but also the differences in the situations faced by Africans in the New World from those in Africa that had given the exploits of tricksters there meaning and value. In the trickster tales of enslaved Africans, the trickster was an actor particularly adept at obtaining the material means of survival within an atmosphere similar to that in which enslaved Africans lived. Unlike African tricksters, whose behavior was often conceptualized as a response to famine or other conditions in which material shortage existed, the trickster of enslaved African Americans acted in a situation of material plenty.

The primary obstacle to the acquisition of the material means of survival for the trickster of enslaved Africans was the physical power and control wielded by the dupe. This situation reflected the conditions under which enslaved Africans lived, in which the material means of survival were readily available but were denied by the control of the slave masters. In these tales, the trickster was por-

trayed as developing clever strategies for obtaining material goods, especially food, despite the efforts of his dupes to deny access. As historians of the slave experience have noted, the concern with the acquisition of food was a common one during slavery (Blassingame, 1972, p. 158; Genovese, 1976, pp. 638–639). In tale after tale, Brer Rabbit proved to be a masterful manipulator of his dupes, who appeared most often in the guise of the wolf or the fox. The tales often portrayed situations in which cleverness, verbal dexterity, and native intelligence or wit allowed the trickster to triumph over the dupes. For enslaved Africans, this provided a model of behavior for dealing with the power and control of the slave masters over the material means of survival.

CONJURING. Often reported as case studies, the folk beliefs of enslaved Africans also seemed widespread to collectors in the late nineteenth century. In many ways, the concerns of collectors reflected a stereotypical view of many white Americans that African Americans were inordinately superstitious. The collection of folk beliefs centered primarily around the practice of conjuration. At the core of this practice was the conjurer, a figure transformed by enslaved Africans but based on African religious leaders such as medicine men. While the conjurer in different parts of the South was known by different names, including root doctor, hoodooer, and two-heads, the practice of conjuration was remarkably similar wherever it was found (Bacon and Herron, 1973, pp. 360–361). In most instances, conjurers were believed to be individuals possessed of a special gift to both cause and cure illness. Although the source of the conjurer's powers was usually believed to be mysterious, some believed it came from an evil source, others believed it came from God, and still others believed it could be taught by those possessed of it.

During the period of slavery, conjurers played a prominent role among enslaved Africans, especially as healers. Although most slave masters attempted to provide for the health needs of enslaved Africans, their efforts often fell short. In general, the state of scientific medicine during the period of slavery was so poorly developed that, even under ideal conditions, doctors were ineffective in treating many diseases. The importance of conjurers for enslaved Africans also had to do with beliefs about the causes of illness, beliefs deeply influenced by their African cultural heritage. Like their ancestors, many enslaved Africans continued to believe that illness was caused by the ill will of one individual against another through an act of conjuration. Individuals could induce illness either through their own action or by consulting a conjurer, who could be persuaded to "lay a spell." In these cases, only the power of a conjurer could alleviate the illness.

In their practices, conjurers used both material objects, such as charms and amulets, and verbal incantations in the form of curses and spells. However, theirs was primarily an herbal practice; hence, the common name of root doctor for these practitioners. The frequent use of verbal incantations derived from African beliefs about the power of the spoken word to influence forces in nature for good or ill. Although conjurers have often been associated with unrelieved evil, their role was a culturally sanctioned one. Within the belief and social system that supported the practice of conjuration, social strife, believed to be the dominant cause of illness, was seen as disruptive to the equilibrium and harmony of the community. The conjurer's role was to discover the identity of the individual responsible for the disruption and to restore harmony. For both the social and physical well being of enslaved Africans, the conjurer's abilities in this regard proved beneficial. Not only did the presence of conjurers provide them with a means of tending to their own health needs, it also provided a mechanism for addressing issues of social strife within the group without the intervention of slave masters.

Although spirituals, trickster tales, and folk beliefs were the focus of most early collecting, the folklore of enslaved Africans included more than these genres. Collectors seldom noted other vibrant genres that developed during slavery, including proverbs, courtship rituals, prayers, sermons, and forms of folktale other than trickster narratives. But while there was no concerted effort to collect these genres, examples sometimes found their way into collections. In addition, folklorists and other scholars have begun to utilize various kinds of records, including plantation journals, slave narratives, and diaries of various sorts in an effort to better understand the nature of black vernacular creativity during the slave period (Joyner, 1984; Ferris, 1983). These types of resources have proven particularly useful in the study of black material culture. Because slave masters were generally responsible for the material needs of enslaved Africans, the importance of knowledge possessed by Africans and applied to the production of various material objects has generally been overlooked. However, African skill and knowledge were responsible for the production of many material objects used in everyday life on farms and plantations. It has become evident, for example, that African knowledge and skill in rice cultivation were responsible for the profitable rice industry that thrived along the coast of Georgia and South Carolina. In addition, African knowledge of basketry and textiles was responsible for the development of a unique tradition of basketry and quilting that continues to be practiced today (Ferris, 1983, pp. 63–110 and 235–274). Of equal importance, many enslaved Africans who served as black-smiths, carpenters, cooks, and seamstresses on farms and plantations used African techniques in the production of the material products for which they were responsible.

POST-EMANCIPATION FOLKLORE

Despite early predictions of the demise of an African-American folk tradition with the advent of freedom and literacy, African Americans have continued to create and perform various genres of folklore. In many ways, the success of early collectors was a testament to the vibrancy and importance of vernacular creativity among African Americans. Although Emancipation brought about important changes in lifestyle, it did not alter many of the conditions that had made the forms of folklore created by enslaved Africans meaningful. In the post-Emancipation era, the development of the sharecropping system and the imposition of Jim Crow laws created patterns of economic and social oppression similar to those that had existed during slavery. In fact, the similarities in the conditions of freedpeople in the late nineteenth and early twentieth centuries to those endured by enslaved Africans allowed them to simply alter many of the forms they had created during slavery to reflect new realities.

As the conditions that would influence black culture building in the post-Emancipation era became clear, African Americans began the process of both transforming existing forms and creating new ones to communicate their perceptions of the economic, social, and political realties that informed their lives as freedpeople. With the failure of Reconstruction and growing patterns of segregation following Emancipation, African Americans came to realize that conditions imposed on them that inhibited their progress in society had to be addressed differently. In a general sense, the powerful role that the law played in the lives of freedpeople made many of the expressive strategies developed during slavery for dealing with white power and control no longer effective or in the best interest of African Americans. For example, the tales of the animal trickster, which had provided an important model of behavior for dealing with white economic exploitation and social oppression during slavery, gradually lost their effectiveness as the expressive embodiment of a strategy for freedpeople. In some animal-trickster tales collected in the late nineteenth century, contests between the animal trickster and dupe were settled in the courts.

BADMEN. Despite the decline of animal-trickster-tale narration, African Americans retained the trickster as a focus for folklore creation. In the late nineteenth and early twentieth centuries, the trickster was transformed into the badman, a character whose primary adversary was the law, personified by the white policeman or sheriff (Roberts, 1989, pp. 171–220). The emergence of white lawmen as powerful and often brutal defenders of white privilege made it extremely problematic for African Americans to retaliate directly against whites for their exploitation. At the same time, the proliferation of patterns of segregation and economic exploitation and the rise of Jim Crow laws made the black community an arena for the actions of badmen. Therefore, although badmen spent much of their energy attempting to elude the law, they found their dupes in members of the black community. As tricksters, they attempted to dupe members of the black community into participating in illegal activities such as gambling, bootlegging, prostitution, numbers running, and drug dealing. That is, badmen as tricksters sought material gain by outwitting both African Americans and the law. In this sense, the black badmen of the post-Emancipation era faced a double bind not unknown to many African Americans.

Folklore creation surrounding black badmen in the late nineteenth and early twentieth centuries reflected changed conditions faced by African Americans in society. As the law in both its abstract and personified forms became a powerful force in maintaining white privilege, African Americans were forced to turn increasingly to their own communities for solutions to their economic and social oppression. Because the law was often brutal in its treatment of African Americans, they made avoidance of the law a virtue and attempted to keep the law out of their communities. In so doing, they assumed a great deal of responsibility for maintaining harmony and peace among themselves. In economically deprived black communities, however, the means of enhancing one's economic status were extremely limited. The rise of secular entertainment establishments such as jukes and bars served as a focus for many of the activities associated with black badmen. In these establishments, many African Americans found activities by which they had the potential to enhance their economic well being, such as gambling and numbers playing, as well as offering psychological escape in whiskey and drugs from the oppressive conditions of their lives. Despite their illegal nature, these activities posed little danger to the black community as long as individuals who participated in them played by the unwritten rules. However, the consumption of alcohol and the existence of games of chance created an environment in which violence often erupted and the law intervened.

The exploits of black badmen typically unfolded in jukes and bars. The badman emerged in folklore as an individual who, in defense of his trade, committed an act of murder. The badman's exploits were celebrated in legends and ballads, narrative songs that told of their deeds. For example, the notorious gambling badman Stackolee purportedly shot Billy Lyons, who was cheating him in a card game. Duncan shot the white policeman, Brady, to end his bullying of patrons at Duncan's bar. Invariably caught and punished, the badman was treated sympathetically in folklore. The sympathy engendered by the badman derives from the importance to some members of the black community of the activities with which he became associated, as well as the individuals he killed. The badman's victims were usually cheaters or bullies whose actions threatened to bring the power and force of the law down on the community. In the late nineteenth and early twentieth centuries, many African Americans endured economic conditions that made the activities identified with black badmen important to their material well being. At the same time, they recognized the potential and real consequences of participating in these activities.

In many ways, the focus of folklore creation surrounding black badmen reflects the nature of black folklore since Emancipation. In a profound sense, expressive celebration of the black badman reflected a general pattern of forms that focused on conditions faced by African Americans on a recurrent basis yet suggested that the solutions lie within the black community. The most common types of folktale performed by African Americans since Emancipation attempt to identify the origins of conditions that inhibit black progress in society. These often humorous narratives attempt through suggestion and persuasion to address intragroup attitudes and behaviors perceived as responsible for the conditions faced by African Americans. At the same time, they suggest that when African Americans recognize their own role in maintaining behaviors not in their best interest, they gain the ability and power to change them.

ORIGIN TALES. In many narratives the focus of the tales is on the origins of certain animal characteristics. These tales were developed during slavery and usually involved animals from the trickster cycle. In some instances, the animal trickster is made the dupe. The best known of these tales purport to explain why the rabbit has a short tail or the buzzard a bald head. While these tales often seem to be naive explanations for the physical characteristics of different animals, in reality they impart useful lessons about African-American moral and social values. In most instances, the tales reveal that the acquisition of the physical characteristics came about as a result of obsessive pride and vanity, or a failure to evaluate the motives of one known to be an adversary.

The didactic intent of African-American origin tales is even more evident in those that involve human actors.

Many of these tales, which also originated in slavery, continue to be performed in African-American communities today (Dance, 1978, pp. 7–11). The focus is on the development of certain physical features associated with African Americans as a race. For example, the performer purports to explain why African Americans have big feet or hands, nappy hair, black skin, and so forth. The stories are invariably set at the beginning of time when God, a principal actor in the tales, gave out human traits. African Americans are envisioned as always getting the "worse" characteristics because they arrived late, were playing cards and did not hear God calling them, or were too impatient to wait for God. Despite the humor often evoked in these tales, they speak to African Americans about certain negative patterns of behavior stereotypically associated with the race—laziness, tardiness, impatience, and the like. Rather than being self-deprecating, as some scholars have suggested, these tales attempt in a humorous way to call attention to certain behavioral patterns perceived by some members of the black community as inhibitive to the advancement of African Americans. In addition, they reveal one of the ways in which African Americans have historically attempted to communicate in intragroup contexts the nature and consequences of negative stereotypes of them.

COLORED MAN TALES. Closely associated with tales of origin is a large group of tales that revolves around the character of "Colored Man" (Dorson, 1956, pp. 171–186). These tales often purport to explain the origins of conditions experienced by African Americans in society. From all internal evidence, Colored Man tales are a post-Emancipation invention that thrived in the early and mid-twentieth century. In this group of tales, Colored Man is pitted in a contest with White Man and a member of another racial or cultural group, either Jew or Mexican. In some instances, the three actors are given a task by God, usually involving the selection of packages of different sizes; in others, they are involved in a scheme of their own making. In the former case, Colored Man makes the wrong decision, whether he selects the largest or the smallest package. His choices are most often conceptualized as a result of his greed, his ability to be deceived by appearances of easy gain, his laziness, or even his efforts not to be outsmarted. The tales almost invariably revolve around some stereotype associated with African Americans. By portraying situations in which a generic African American acts out a stereotype, the performers of these tales implicitly call for critical self-examination. On the other hand, by setting these tales at the beginning of time, performers suggest that conditions experienced by African Americans in the present result from systemic sources.

Throughout the twentieth century, African Americans have created and performed folktales that deal realistically with their situation in society. Many function as jokes that revolve around stereotypes. However, these tales function to constantly remind African Americans that one of the most problematic aspects of their existence in American society derives from negative images of them held by other groups. In many of these tales, the African American appears as the dupe of the nonblacks, who use stereotypes to manipulate him into making bad choices. In other tales, African-American performers celebrate certain stereotypical images that seem to allow them to gain an advantage over other groups. This type of narrative usually revolves around sexual stereotypes; blacks triumph over members of other groups because they demonstrate superior sexual prowess or larger sexual organs. In their celebration of an image of self generally evaluated negatively in society, African Americans reveal an interesting ambivalence about such images and possibly a different value orientation.

THE BLUES. Besides narrative, other forms of African-American folklore created since Emancipation reveal an intimate concern with intragroup problems and solutions. Of the genres created and performed by African Americans, the blues is concerned directly with conditions and situations within the black community. As a body of song, the blues touches on various problematic areas of black life like unemployment, homelessness, sharecropping, police brutality, and economic exploitation (Titon, 1977; Keil, 1966; Oliver, 1963). However, it concentrates primarily on the problems of black male/female relationships. Although the blues celebrates the joys of being in a successful relationship, it most often focuses on the problems involved in sustaining one. These problems often revolve around economic issues, especially the inability of black males to provide for the material well being of lover, wife, or family.

In the late nineteenth century and the early decades of the twentieth, the blues served as an ongoing commentary on conditions faced by many African Americans. As an expressive form, the blues did not often propose solutions to the problems it identified but rather focused on defining the contours of situations shared by large numbers of African Americans. When the blues did offer a solution, it most often proposed mobility: either moving out of a troubled relationship or moving out of town. It might be suggested that the idea of mobility as a solution to problematic situations often found in the blues simply reflected a solution embraced by thousands of African Americans in the early twentieth century. During the heyday of the blues, African Americans witnessed the migration of thousands from the rural South into urban centers in search of better economic and social conditions.

For many African Americans, the blues reflected much about the nature of black culture building in the early twentieth century. It emerged as the first solo form of musical expression created by African Americans and signaled the growing diversity of the black population. In the midst of the Great Migration and other changes in black life, the blues revealed the difficulty of speaking about a common African-American experience in post-Emancipation America. It envisioned a community beset by various problems of identity, values, and even beliefs arising from mobility as well as economic and social upheaval. Although blues performers spoke from a first-person point of view, their popularity derived from their ability to use personal experience as a metaphor for shared realities. Despite its popularity with a large segment of the black population, however, the blues was not valued by all members of the community. Because of its association with secular entertainment establishments in which drinking alcohol, dancing, gambling, and often violent crimes occurred, as well as to its often sexually explicit lyrics, it was sometimes strongly disparaged by religious and socially conscious members of the black community.

GOSPEL. In the early twentieth century, however, the blues had its expressive and religious counterpart in the emergence of gospel music (Heilbut, 1975; Allen, 1991). The development of modern gospel can be attributed to two interrelated influences, which can be conceptualized as, on the one hand, musical and, on the other, social and religious. Although spirituals continued to be performed well after Emancipation, the message of deliverance from bondage and persecution through analogy to Old Testament figures and events lost much of its meaning for freedpeople. In addition, performance of spirituals in the post-Emancipation era was greatly influenced by efforts of some African-American religious leaders to make black religious practices more closely resemble those of white Americans. As a result, many black churches banned the "shout," an important context for spiritual song performance, and began to encourage the singing of European hymns to the neglect of spirituals. At the same time, the emergence of Europeanized arrangements and performances of spirituals proliferated, especially with touring college choirs such as those organized at Fisk University and Hampton Institute. The success of these choirs, as well as the barbershop-quartet craze of the nineteenth century, influenced the organization of hundreds of black harmonizing quartets that sang primarily arranged spirituals.

While these changes in the religious and musical life of African Americans in the South greatly influenced the attitude toward and performance of spirituals, the Great Migration confronted many African Americans with a new lifestyle and environment that threatened their ability to maintain the spiritual values that many had traditionally associated with black religion. In urban areas, many African Americans embraced not only new social and economic patterns but also modes of worship in churches that did not fulfill social and spiritual needs as southern churches had. In both South and North, many African Americans in the late nineteenth and early twentieth centuries turned to the newly developing Spiritual Church movement and Holiness movement and the storefront churches that arose to house them. In these churches, many African Americans found patterns of worship more conducive to their religious sensibilities, and an emerging musical style that came to be known as gospel. Unlike the spirituals of enslaved Africans, gospel songs tended to emphasize the New Testament message of love and faith in God as the solutions to human problems. As such, gospel relies less on analogy to Old Testament personalities and events and more on the abstract New Testament promise of rest and reward for the faithful.

In an important sense, gospel, like the blues, envisions a diverse black community, whereas spirituals relied on the existence of a coherent community sharing a single condition: slavery. As such, gospel songs tend to abstract the nature of the problems for which Christian faith provides a solution. In essence, the lyrics of gospel songs seldom identify specific conditions but, instead, speak of burdens, trials, and tribulations and offer faith in God as a solution. In this regard, gospel is a genre that gains its meaning in performance. Through performance, its apparent abstract message is concretized in messages delivered as sermons, prayers, and testimonies, which provide numerous illustrations of the situations of which gospel music speaks. Although gospel songs are usually written by individuals and recorded by commercial companies, a development that goes back to the 1920s and 1930s, gospel remains a vernacular form performed in African-American communities in churches and concert halls throughout the United States on a regular basis.

TOASTS. The study of African-American folklore in the twentieth century remains vital. The focus of collection in recent years has turned from the rural South to urban communities in both North and South where viable traditions of African-American oral expressive culture continue to thrive. In the process, folklorists continue to produce important collections of African-American folklore reflective of both historical and contemporary concerns. For example, the toast tradition, which involves the recitation of long narrative poems revolving around the actions of black badmen, has been collected extensively (Jackson, 1974; Wepman, Newman, and Binderman, 1976). These poems, which have been collected in prisons and on the streets, chronicle the lives of individuals involved in criminal activities and warn of the consequences of their behavior. Although a large number of toast texts have been published, the toast as a genre is not widely known among African Americans. In fact, it seems to be known and performed primarily by individuals who participate in a criminal lifestyle or individuals who have connections with it. While toasts seem to celebrate criminality and the peculiar brand of "badness" associated with it, these poems tend to be highly moralistic and realistic in terms of the consequences of criminal activity. In addition—despite their often offensive language, violent imagery, and seeming disregard for legal and moral authority in the black community and society—toasts give expressive embodiment to behavioral and economic strategies and reflect attitudes embraced by some individuals in African-American communities with regard to drug dealing, prostitution, gambling, and other so-called victimless crimes.

THE DOZENS. Although not primarily or exclusively an urban genre, the dozens became the focus of much study in the latter half of the twentieth century (Abrahams, 1970). The dozens is a generic name for a form of verbal artistry known variously in African-American communities as joning, wolfing, busting, breaking, cracking and snapping, and by a host of other names. Although the art of playing the dozens is generally associated with adolescent males, the practice in different ways is one that knows no age limit or gender. Generally speaking, younger males tend to play more often and to rely more on formulaic rhymes and phrases in their performances. Often discussed as verbal exchanges that disparage the mother through implications of sexual impropriety, playing the dozens just as often involves apparent insults to one's opponent. While playing the dozens has been associated with the acquisition of verbal skill, especially among young African-American males, it also serves as an intragroup mechanism for communicating information with negative import for individuals. Regardless of who plays the dozens or how it is played, the content of the exchanges focuses on behaviors that violate certain norms generally accepted by African Americans, whether they relate to sexual activity, personal habits, physical characteristics, modes of dress, and so forth.

A concern with playing the dozens in recent years has been accompanied by a general focus on other forms of African-American folklore that reveal a rich tradition of verbal play. Forms such as signifying, marking, and loud-talking have been discussed as a reflection of the art of ev-

eryday life in African-American communities (Mitchell-Kernan, 1972). The artistry of these forms derives from the ability of individuals to encode messages with serious import in humorous and witty forms. In addition, the rise of rap music, which transforms many African-American expressive forms into a flourishing narrative tradition, reflects the continuing verbal artistry in black communities. Rap, which exists as both a narrative and a musical tradition, reflects a continuing concern in African-American expressive culture with identifying conditions and situations that impact negatively on the black community. Though a diverse group, rap songs frequently point to the need for self-evaluation, criticism, and change in the black community itself without denying the impact of systemic causes for many of the conditions it identifies. The most recent genre of African American folklore to be identified is the urban legend, an amorphous expressive form that is often communicated as a rumor (Turner, 1993). One of the earliest examples of this genre concerns the fast-food franchise known as Churches Fried Chicken. According to the legend/rumor, Churches Fried Chicken, a once highly visible restaurant in African American neighborhoods in the United States, is owned by the Ku Klux Klan. The owners are reported to have injected into its chicken a substance that renders African-American males impotent. While no longer as popular as it once was, the Churches Fried Chicken legend has been found throughout the United States among African Americans. Over time other rumors emerged concerning high profile businesses that cater to or have become popular with African Americans, such as British Knight sports wear, Reebok Sneakers, and several soft drinks. In each case, the businesses have been associated with the Ku Klux Klan which inserts surreptitious messages in their products that identify this organization as owners. Other legend/rumors found among African Americans include an accusation that the CIA is responsible for introducing crack cocaine and other addictive substances into the African American community. In almost all cases, the performers of these narratives cite an authoritative source such as a newspaper or the popular television show *Sixty Minutes* as the source of their information. Although scholars have attempted to verify the accuracy of these accounts, the value of the stories to those who circulate and/or believe them has little to do with their factuality.

These narratives reveal a continuing concern in the African American community with its physical well being and survival. In the most general sense, they exist to remind the community of hidden dangers for African Americans that exist in the society. By associating the danger with the Ku Klux Klan, a racist organization with a history of ill-will and violent intentions toward African Americans, performers of such narratives single out an organization with a history of racist actions against the black community. In the minds of many, the Klan continues to be a secret source of evil in the society which it directs toward African Americans. The authority of claims of clandestine activities by this organization is enhanced by naming the media as the source of the story.

African-American folklore reflects many of the ways in which African Americans have historically communicated their attitudes, beliefs, and values in artistic forms in everyday life. Although the roots of the study of this folklore lie in beliefs about its ultimate demise, the African-American tradition of vernacular creativity and performance remains vital. While the genres that constitute the African-American folk tradition are too numerous to be examined in a short discussion, the basic categories of narrative, song, verbal artistry, and material culture suggest the tradition's contours. With African culture and cultural forms providing the tradition-rich source of African-American folklore, it has been endlessly transformed to both aid and reflect black culture building in the United States. On an everyday basis, African-American folklore continues to provide individuals with a rich creative outlet for expression and performance.

See also Africanisms; Blues, The; Dozens, The; Folk Arts and Crafts; Folklore: U.S. Folk Heroes and Characters; Folklore: Latin American and Caribbean Culture Heroes and Characters; Folk Medicine; Folk Music; Folk Religion; Gospel Music; Rap; Spirituals

■ ■ *Bibliography*

Abrahams, Roger. *Deep Down in the Jungle: Negro Narrative Folklore from the Streets of Philadelphia*. Chicago: Aldine, 1970.

Allen, Ray. *Singing in the Spirit: African-American Sacred Quartets in New York City*. Philadelphia: University of Pennsylvania Press, 1991.

Allen, William F., Charles P. Ware, and Lucy McKim Garrison. *Slave Songs of the United States*. 1867. Reprint. New York: Peter Smith, 1951.

Bacon, Alice M., and Leonora Herron. "Conjuring and Conjure-Doctors." In *Mother Wit from the Laughing Barrel: Readings in the Interpretation of Afro-American Folklore*, edited by Alan Dundes. Englewood Cliffs, N.J.: Prentice-Hall, 1973.

Blassingame, John W. *The Slave Community: Plantation Life in the Antebellum South*. New York: Oxford University Press, 1972.

Brown, Cecil. *Stagolee Shot Billy*. Cambridge, Mass.: Harvard University Press, 2003.

Bryant, Jerry H. *Born in a Mighty Bad Land: The Violent Man in African American Folklore and Fiction*. Bloomington: Indiana University Press, 2003.

Dance, Daryl C. *Shuckin' and Jivin': Folklore from Contemporary Black America*. Bloomington: Indiana University Press, 1978.

Dance, Daryl Cumber, ed. *From My People: 400 Years of African American Folklore*. New York: Norton, 2002.

Dorson, Richard M. *American Negro Folktales*. Greenwich, Conn.: Fawcett, 1956.

Feldmann, Susan. *African Myths and Tales*. New York: Dell, 1973.

Ferris, William. *Afro-American Art and Crafts*. Boston: G. K. Hall, 1983.

Fry, Gladys-Marie. *Night Riders in Black Folk History*. Chapel Hill: University of North Carolina Press, 2001.

Genovese, Eugene. *Roll, Jordan, Roll: The World the Slaves Made*. New York: Pantheon, 1976.

Harris, Joel Chandler. *Uncle Remus: His Songs and His Sayings*. 1881. Reprint. New York: Penguin, 1986.

Heilbut, Tony. *The Gospel Sound: Good News and Bad Times*. Garden City, N.Y.: Doubleday, 1975.

Jackson, Bruce. *Get Your Ass in the Water and Swim like Me: Narrative Poetry from Black Oral Tradition*. Cambridge, Mass.: Harvard University Press, 1974.

Jarmon, Laura C. *Wishbone: Reference and Interpretation in Black Folk Narrative*. Knoxville: University of Tennessee Press, 2003.

Joyner, Charles. *Down by the Riverside: A South Carolina Slave Community*. Urbana: University of Illinois Press, 1984.

Keil, Charles. *Urban Blues*. Chicago: University of Chicago Press, 1966.

Lovell, John, Jr. *Black Song: The Forge and the Flame*. New York: Macmillan, 1972.

Mintz, Sidney W., and Richard Price. *An Anthropological Approach to the Afro-American Past: A Caribbean Perspective*. Philadelphia, Pa.: Institute for the Study of Human Issues, 1972.

Mitchell-Kernan, Claudia. "Signifying, Loud-Talking, and Marking." In *Rappin' and Stylin' Out*, edited by Thomas Kochman. Urbana: University of Illinois Press, 1972.

Nicholls, David G. *Conjuring the Folk: Forms of Modernity in African America*. Ann Arbor: University of Michigan Press, 2000.

Oliver, Paul. *The Meaning of the Blues*. New York: Collier, 1963.

Roberts, John W. *From Trickster to Badman: The Black Folk Hero in Slavery and Freedom*. Philadelphia: University of Pennsylvania Press, 1989.

Sanders, Lynn Moss. *Howard W. Odum's Folklore Odyssey: Transformation to Tolerance through African American Folk Studies*. Athens: University of Georgia Press, 2003.

Snead, James. "Repetition as a Figure in Black Culture," In *Black Literature and Literary Theory*, edited by Henry Louis Gates Jr., pp. 59–80. New York: Methuen, 1984.

Titon, Jeff Todd. *Early Downhome Blues: A Musical and Cultural Analysis*. Urbana: University of Illinois Press, 1977.

Wepman, Dennis, Ronald B. Newman, and Murray B. Binderman. *The Life: The Lore and Folk Poetry of the Black Hustler*. Philadelphia: University of Pennsylvania Press, 1976.

JOHN W. ROBERTS (1996)
Updated by author 2005

LATIN AMERICAN AND CARIBBEAN CULTURE HEROES AND CHARACTERS

In order to make sense out of a senseless experience, people of African descent who were forcibly transported from the continent to the New World relied very heavily on their memory of various homelands, of their original roots in times and places that, for all practical purposes, ceased to exist except in their collective imagination. As many intellectuals and artists have illustrated, the enslaved Africans clung tenaciously to their ancestral mores both as a political statement, or act of rebellion, and as a psychological necessity. Moreover, they devised ways of camouflaging their expressions of Africanity, often with a thin veneer of European icons, when their captors tried to eradicate their history. In spite of a five-hundred-year transculturation process, African peoples in the New World struggled to maintain their psycho-emotional ties to cultures that were physically beyond their grasp but that were consistently and repeatedly evoked in their oral traditions. Thus, Isidore Okpewho (1999) observes that "in their folklore and their folklife, especially in tales they had learned from parents and other relatives, African-descended Americans found an outlet for reassuring themselves of indigenous values they found lacking in the culture of those who ruled their lives even in freedom" (Okpewho et. al., p. xv). On the other hand, one might very well argue that African-based cultural beliefs and practices were embedded as forms of resistance *because of* the imposition of Western cultures. Thus, Jesús García (2001) cautions against the trivialization of African-derived modes of being by labeling them as "folklore." He comments: "We need to develop a pedagogy of self-perception. . . . To fail to do so is to continue to view ourselves through borrowed eyes. African cultures in the Americas, rather than quaint but superficial folklore, are cultures of resistance based on African philosophical principles that we must rediscover, that persist and reshape themselves as time passes and as changes occur in our communities" (p. 288).

By "cultures of resistance" García means that African-American societies are engaged in "a dynamic process in which their original cultural elements are set in opposition to the pressure of colonial and postcolonial religious and governmental authorities' attempts to 'disappear' them. We deliberately imagine the possibility of cultural exchange in the Americas on an equal plane of mutual respect and tolerance, insisting upon the possibility of a reciprocal process of cultural transformation that guarantees

the peaceful coexistence of both colonial European and African cultural traditions in contemporary social contexts." García does not deny the impact of other groups on African-American cultures, for they are often the result of syncretism, or the blending of African and European ways of life with additional influences from a multitude of Native-American/indigenous and Asian ethnicities. In short, African-oriented traditions are replete with imaginary characters, historical personages, and legendary figures that became the culture heroes that have sustained people within the confines of race, class, and gender. Since the number of protagonists in the oral traditions is so large, time and space will permit examination of selected examples of black fictional characters and culture heroes in Latin America and the Caribbean. The discussion will begin with Anancy the Spider as the fictional prototype of the Maroon, or the historical and legendary figure who is elevated to the status of culture hero by virtue of his resistance to dominance and oppression. Then the focus will be on a few renowned leaders such as Zumbi as well as some lesser known figures such as Zeferina.

One of the most absurd consequences of the European encounter with peoples from Africa, Asia, and the Americas was the emphasis on skin color and its accompanying physical features as a sign of culture. The issue of black and white, brown and white, red and white, or yellow and white—in that order—is still current in the twenty-first century, and it does not seem inclined to vanish anytime soon. As far as Latin America and the Caribbean are concerned, the vast majority of the people are of mixed origin in various degrees, which comes from Amerindian, African, Asian, and European components. This phenomenon is called *mestizaje*. However, race is a volatile subject because there is a vehement denial that race counts or that racism exists, even in the face of racial and ethnic awareness movements in communities throughout the Southern Hemisphere. Darien Davis (2000) comments on race in that region:

> Blackness, like any ethnic or racial categorization, is an arbitrary social construct nuanced by geography, language and history. What North Americans call *black* may in Latin America and the Caribbean be translated in a variety of ways, including *negro, mulato, cafuso, moreno, trigueño, antillano, prieto,* Afro–Latin American, creole, light-skinned and so on. Furthermore, social and personal relations, education, economic opportunities and other variables make it possible to change one's racial classification. These distinctions notwithstanding, blackness in Latin America is inextricably connected to the trans-Atlantic

Soucouyant

The figure known as the *Soucouyant* (or *soucougnan/ soukounyan*) in much of the Eastern Caribbean and referred to by a variety of other names across the Caribbean as a whole—Fire Hag, Old Heg, Old Hige, Gagé, Volant, Azeman—is usually represented as a woman who sheds her skin at night, stores it in a jar, transforms herself into a ball of fire, and roams around sucking the blood from her sleeping victims, particularly babies. To defeat her, members of the community can throw salt or pepper on themselves and on any expected victims, or on the skin she has abandoned, or they can scatter rice grains or salt on the windows and doors through which she will pass. Her torment from itching or her failure to count every single rice grain will make her vulnerable to capture, at which point she might be beaten, exiled, killed, or boiled alive in a vat of tar.

Like the part-human, part-horse *bête a man ibé* who wanders around screaming at night dragging an iron chain around her waist, and the *Rolling Calf* (also known as *Steel Donkey* or *May Cow*) whose bloodshot eyes and nighttime wanderings indicate the restlessness of an evil person who cannot find peace after death, the *Soucouyant* reflects the richness of the imaginative resources and cultural origins of the Caribbean's oral traditions. The *loup garou*—literally werewolf—of some Francophone-Creole-speaking territories, often depicted as old women who need blood every night in exchange for the devil's powers, seem to be more closely related, for example, to vampires. Besides Europe's vampires, the *obayfo* of the Akan of West Africa, which sheds its skin after turning into a ball of fire, and the *sukunya* and her male counterpart, *sukunyadyo*, of the Fula/Soninke people—witches who eat humans—provide sources that help to explain the *origin* of these figures, but not necessarily their meanings, since the significance of such figures changes over time in every society, in transference from one space to another.

Witches who are gender-neutral, or typical of both genders in West Africa in the eighteenth and nineteenth centuries, are gendered female in many Caribbean tales, according to Giselle Anatol, just as the significance of vampires has altered according to fears about women's sexuality and independence. The moral ambivalence generated by slavery and the slave trade, the ways in which colonial authorities in the region made their own interpretations of the oral narratives they heard and then transcribed into court records or anthropological documents, the impact of Protestantism and Catholicism on the worldview of storytellers: all necessarily produced changes in the moral implications of these figures over time. Just as the connections between the Caribbean water goddess *Mama Dlo* (*Mama Glo*, *River Mumma*, *Water-Mama*, *Fairmaid*) and the West African water deity *Mammywata* might tell us more about the specific

slave trade which brought the majority of blacks to the Americas.

Blackness is not a monolithic entity, for each nation espouses unique values and patterns of classification that determine its own definition of black culture. However, it must be pointed out that changing one's racial category, originally known as "*gracias al sacar,*" or "thanks for taking me out of my blackness," constitutes by its very nature an identity crisis because the movement is always "up and away from blackness." No one wishes to change from white, however that is defined, to black. The process of "improving" one's self and/or family by "marrying up" is called *blanqueamiento* (Spanish) or *branqueamento* (Por-tuguese), and it is embedded in the concept of *Hispanidad* or *Lusofonidad*. While this might bring a degree of tolerance, it does not guarantee unconditional acceptance. The specter of the black ancestor (grandmother) is always lurking in the shadows, and those who would define or redefine themselves as "white" live in constant dread of that skeleton. One must understand these contradictory discourses in Latin America and the Caribbean in order to appreciate fully their oral and written literature. To facilitate the discussion of the fictional characters and culture heroes, this article will proceed in a somewhat chronological order according to the unfolding of historical events in the Caribbean, Mexico, the Andes, Brazil, the Guyanas, Haiti, the Southern Cone, and Central America. Haiti

Soucouyant (continued)

economic and psychological impact of the slave trade on Africa's west coast than her general identification with the Ibo *Uhamiri/Idemili* and Yoruba *Osun* deities, critics caution against romanticizing these figures and the supposedly simple and cohesive oral communities which they are often held to reflect, and against giving them a one-to-one correspondence with "Old World" African, European, or Asian sources.

They point out that the fiction of recent Caribbean women is critical of the ways in which repressive political regimes draw on the moral authority of the folktale by using the *soucouyant* and other figures to terrorize the society or to demonize women who have passed the age of childbearing, and whose autonomy is thus potentially threatening.

The characters who inhabit the oral tales of the region certainly indicate a longstanding tradition of storytelling characterized by interaction between storyteller and audience—"Krik?" "Krak! Monkey break he back on a rotten pomerac!"—as well as by the ironic disavowal of the storyteller: "So me get it, so me gi' it, Jack Mandora, me no choose none." But they also suggest that the interpretive possibilities of these figures remain as rich as the variety of social contexts—theater, art, dance, popular music, religion, politics, fiction, and poetry—that continue to make use of them.

Bibliography

Allsopp, Richard. *Dictionary of Caribbean English Usage.* New York: Oxford University Press, 1996.

Anatol, Giselle. "Transforming the Skin-Shedding Soucouyant: Using Folklore to Reclaim Female Agency in Caribbean Literature." *Small Axe* 7 (March 2000): 44–59.

Cobham, Rhonda. "Mwen na rien, Msieu: Jamaica Kincaid and the Problem of Creole Gnosis." *Callaloo* 25, 3 (Summer 2002): 868–884.

Danticat, Edwidge. "Nineteen Thirty-Seven." *Krik? Krak!* 33–49. New York: Soho Press, 1995.

Davies, Carole Boyce. "'Woman Is a Nation...' Women in Caribbean Oral Literature." *Out of the Kumbla: Caribbean Women and Literature.* 165–193. Trenton, N.J.: Africa World Press, 1990.

Francis, Donette. "Uncovered Stories: Politicizing Sexual histories in Third Wave Caribbean Women's Writings." *Black Renaissance Noire* 6 (Fall 2004): 61–81.

Mulrain, George. *Theology in Folk Culture: The Theological Significance of Haitian Folk Religion.* New York: Verlag Peter Lang, 1984.

Parsons, Elsie Clews. *Folklore of the Antilles, French and English.* 3 vols. New York: American Folk-Lore Society: 1933, 1936, 1943.

Szwed, John and Roger Abrahams. *Afro-American Folk Culture: An Annotated Bibliography from North, Central and South America and the West Indies.* 2 vols. New York: Publications of the American Folklore Society, 1978.

Warner-Lewis, Maureen. *Guinea's Other Suns: The African Dynamic in Trinidad Culture.* Dover, Mass.: The Majority Press, 1991.

FAITH SMITH (2005)

merits separate treatment because it stands in a class by itself in terms of its cultural resistance to European hegemony.

THE CARIBBEAN BASIN

Anancy the Spider (also written as Ananci, Ananse, Anansy, Ananncy, or Nancy) is a protagonist of African origin who is very popular in Jamaica and other areas of the Caribbean. Moreover, Mariela Gutiérrez (1999) informs readers that the name "Anancy" is derived from the Ashanti word for "spider" because many Africans transported to Jamaica were of Ashanti origin. According to Benjamín Núñez (1980), the most recurrent Jamaican version of Anancy is a humanized character, a "little-bald-headed man with a falsetto voice and cringing manner ... who ... lives by his wits and treats outrageously anyone on whom he can impose his superior cunning" (p. 26). Anancy can also assume other human forms: a famous fiddler, a magician, or a quick-witted son who outsmarts his father. In Haiti Anancy is a spider trickster-hero and a buffoon. Henry Louis Gates (1988) identifies Anancy as one of the many animal characters like B'rer Rabbit in the United States whose African archetype was Eleggua, a capricious deity of the crossroads and guardian of the household. The body of oral tales centered around Anancy's exploits are called Anancy (Nancy) stories, and they have spread all over the Caribbean as highly eclectic tales loved by adults and children alike. When Anancy is presented as an animal in a fable, the story is connected to its African origins. However, when he is a character in a fairy tale, there is some modifying European influence in play. Nevertheless, in some Anancy tales both traditions are operative. The Anancy stories frequently maintain the traditional device, almost universal in African societies, of interjecting a short song at crucial moments in the narrative.

Dorothy Mosby (2003) informs readers that in the migration of the Ashanti people from Africa (present-day Ghana) to Jamaica, and the relocation of the Jamaican people from that island to the Atlantic Coast of Central America (Costa Rica), Anancy was transformed from a demigod into a symbol of cultural *marronage*. Moreover, this transformation is signified by a change in language. That is, Anancy, or Brother Spider in English, becomes Hermano Araña in Spanish or Bredda Spider in Creole. Like his counterpart B'rer Rabbit in the United States, Anancy is perceived as a small, weak animal that survives by outwitting others—Hermano Tigre (Bredda Tiger), Hermano Tacuma (Bredda Tacuma), Hermano Conejo (Bredda Rabbit), Hermano Mono (Bredda Monkey), Hermano Perro (Bredda Dog), and Hermano Cabra (Bredda Goat). On the other hand, behind Anancy's affable mask and whimsical nature lies a formidable personage who can devastate his enemy. Consequently, the Anancy stories throughout the Caribbean have served multiple functions: as forms of entertainment to revive the human spirit, as learning tools to teach survival skills, as antidotes for feelings of alienation and displacement, as consolation for depression and despair, and as liberating sites of cultural resistance to oppression. The enslaved Africans were steeped in traditions like the Anancy stories and used them as models for real-life encounters.

Ronald Segal observes that the harsh conditions of slavery led to revolts from the moment the Africans set foot on the shores of the Americas. In Hispaniola (Dominican Republic and Haiti) one of the first uprisings occurred on December 27, 1522, when twenty slaves belonging to Diego Columbus (son of the admiral himself) joined with twenty other captives from a neighboring plantation to attack the Spaniards. The Africans took refuge in none other than the mountain retreat of Enrique, an indigenous *cacique* (chief) who had already rebelled against the *encomienda* by conducting his own kind of guerrilla warfare against the Spanish authorities. Although the defiant Africans were hunted down and captured, their message was clear—they would risk everything for freedom. As Spain advanced its empire, there were similar uprisings on other islands and the mainland of South America—in Puerto Rico (1527); in Panama, led by King Bayano (1550s); in Venezuela, led by Andresoto (1730s) and Miguel Luango (1749); and in Cuba, led by José Antonio Aponte (1812). However, one of the most successful instances of cultural resistance in the Americas took place in Mexico at the beginning of the seventeenth century.

MEXICO

Yanga (Nyanga) is the most famous black leader in Mexican history, but most official history books do not acknowledge him. Perhaps a native of Angola, Yanga maintained that he was a Congolese prince. Michael C. Meyer and William L. Sherman report that "around the beginning of the seventeenth century the threat of black resistance centered in the eastern region, especially near Veracruz. There an elderly slave named Yanga had held out in the mountains for thirty years" (Meyer and Sherman, p. 216). From that site Yanga and his warriors regularly assaulted travelers on the Mexico City–Veracruz highway, and they raided *haciendas* in the vicinity. The Spaniards undertook a military campaign against Yanga's maroon colony in 1609, and they were met with fierce resistance. However, they finally defeated Yanga's troops in 1611. Yet like Anancy, Yanga managed to persuade Viceroy Luis De Velazco to concede his freedom and that of his people on the condition that the Maroons kept the peace, took no more fugitives, and obeyed Spanish laws. By 1612 Yanga's settlement was relocated to a place called San Lorenzo de los Negros de Córdoba. Today the descendants of the *cimarrones* (Maroons) still live there, albeit in deplorable conditions. In fact, they are Mexico's "forgotten people." Furthermore, there is a museum in the city and state of Jalapa with a statue honoring Yanga along with archival information and illustrations documenting his courageous deeds. Perhaps the modern observer might view Yanga as a "sellout," but considering his options at the time, his negotiations with the Spaniards are to be commended. Besides, many *cimarrones* often ignored the stipulation to turn away other Maroons, so their settlements were often replenished with newcomers. In the course of time, blacks were erased from Mexican history. Thus, the unacknowledged African presence in Mexico, or *la tercera raíz* (the third root), is documented by Marco Polo Hernández-Cuevas in *African Mexicans and the Discourse on Modern Nation* (2004).

THE ANDES

As early as 1544 *cimarrones* were attacking and robbing farms on the outskirts of Lima and Trujillo, Peru. However, many were subdued and executed but at great cost to the Spanish officials. Peru was also the site of two significant revolts that involved an alliance of Africans and indigenous people. Near Cuzco in the highland province of Vilcabamba, the Spaniards had enslaved a large workforce to mine the gold deposits. In response to this particularly harsh form of exploitation, the fugitives from Vilcabamba united in 1609 with Aymara-speaking forces under the leadership of the Amerindian Francisco Chichima. This coalition was so formidable that the Spaniards had to rely on the help of "loyal" (pacified) Native-American groups to stamp out the rebellion. A second wave consisting of galley slaves fled from the port city of Callao to the hills above Lima. Moreover, the maroon community they established successfully evaded the authorities until a free mulatto soldier located its hideout and led a detachment of Spanish troops there to capture them. The same kinds of resistance occurred in parts of Bolivia and Ecuador, although historians are still documenting them. In every instance one sees that enslaved peoples realized that they could not engage in open combat with the European colonials because the latter had the advantage of an endless supply of weapons and horses. Consequently, like Anancy the Trickster, the maroon leader had to rely on flight, subterfuge, attack, withdrawal, and, above all, strategy, to engage in guerrilla warfare in territory that was unfamiliar to him. This put the Spanish officials on notice that the cost of empire was much greater than they had anticipated. Even more important, word of successful rebellions, revolts, and uprisings inevitably spread through the oral traditions of the enslaved Africans, thus boosting their morale. Anancy kept hope alive.

BRAZIL

In his study of the maroon communities known as *quilombos* in Brazil, Gilberto Leal (2001) distinguishes between passive and active forms of resistance. A kind of passive resistance called *banzo* was a lingering melancholia that was tantamount to work slowdown or stoppage, catatonia, playing dumb, or other kinds of physical and psychophysical inactivity. On the other hand, the establishment of a *quilombo* was an act of open rebellion. The most triumphant maroon community in the seventeenth century was the Palmares Republic, a confederation of several *mocambos* (settlements) in the district of Alagoas, in the captaincy of Pernambuco (northeastern Brazil), which lasted from 1605 to 1695. Two of its most renowned leaders came to be known as Ganza Zumba (uncle) and Zumbi (nephew), although it is not clear whether these were proper names or titles. (Segal [1995] asserts that *ganga-zumba* means "supreme chief," like pharaoh, while *zumbi* means "war

chief.") The Maroons who lived in the *quilombos* were called *quilombolas*. João Reis (2001) observes that:

> the population of the quilombo initially consisted of formerly enslaved Africans from several ethnic groups from the present-day Angolo-Congo areas. Some of its military and political organizations have been linked to an Imbangala military society called *kilombo*. This institution was probably reinvented, although not entirely reproduced, by the Palmarinos to respond to the military circumstances that they faced in Brazil. It was only after Palmares was established that the word quilombo became synonymous with mocambo, the term most often used until then to describe maroon settlements, as if Palmares had become symbolic of future maroon communities. (p. 302)

One military expedition after another was sent by the Dutch and Portuguese to capture the Palmarinos, but the *quilombolas* successfully resisted the hegemonic forces until internal differences began to divide them.

In 1678 Ganga Zumba signed a treaty with the colonial government in which the Maroons would be guaranteed land and freedom for those born in the *quilombos* in exchange for loyalty to the Portuguese crown and a pledge to turn in all runaways from slavery. Naturally the Portuguese did not honor the treaty and the Maroons quarreled over what should be the proper response to them. It appears that the faction supporting the nephew poisoned his uncle, and Zumbi became the supreme ruler. Under his leadership, Palmares survived assaults from combined European forces for nearly twenty years, and when it was finally subjugated, it was due to betrayal by one of its own. On November 20, 1695, the remaining guerrillas in Zumbi's battalion were captured and killed. It is believed that Zumbi himself committed suicide rather than submit to enslavement.

In the spirit of Zumbi and the Palmarinos, a courageous Yoruba woman by the name of Zeferina headed a maroon settlement formed by other Yoruba people outside the city of Bahia, Brazil. In 1826 Zeferina organized and led an uprising against the plantation masters, but it was quelled by government troops. The insurgents were incarcerated and subsequently executed. Thus, cultural resistance was not the exclusive patrimony of males, and today these figures are heroes who inspire Afro-Brazilians with black awareness to continue the liberation struggle. November 20, 1695, the date of the death of Zumbi/Palmares, has been designated as the National Day of Black Consciousness by Afro-Brazilian civil rights and cultural organizations. Furthermore, in 1995 three significant events occurred in Brazil: "the commemoration of Three Hundred Years of Immortality for Zumbi of Palmares; the Zumbi of Palmares March Against Racism and for Equality and Life; and the selection of 'Zumbi, 300 years of Courage' as the theme of the Bahian carnival" (Leal, p. 299). Anancy the Spider lives on.

THE GUYANAS

The northern area of *Tierra Firme*, or continental South American, presents an interesting parallel in black cultural resistance to oppression. For one thing, it was the scene of rivalry among various European powers. Sir Walter Raleigh initiated England's interest in the Guyanas in his pursuit of El Dorado, or the legend of the "Gilded One." When he published *The Discoverie of Guiana* (1595), other nations took note and soon began sending expeditions to that region. By 1665 the British, Dutch, and French had founded settlements in Guyana territory, all three claiming the entire area between the Orinoco and Amazon rivers. After skirmishes in Europe and the Americas, the Dutch and English finally came to terms with each other, trading New Amsterdam (New York) and Surinam, respectively. No sooner had the smoke cleared than a slave revolt broke out in 1730, and although the Dutch attempted to crush it, the settlers and Maroons continued to fight each other up to 1749. Circumstances were so bad for the Dutch colonists that they sued the rebels for peace. In 1762 the Dutch recognized two large black communities, the Saramaca and the Ouca, by granting them their freedom. Just as the case of Yanga, the Maroons were given arms and ammunition in exchange for their promise to be loyal allies to the Dutch, to deliver up future runaways, and to keep their "proper distance" from the capital and plantations. By the 1770s the maroon communities had organized themselves into a dozen villages each under a local leader, among whom were Chief Baron, Chief Kofi (Coffi, Cuffee), Chief Atta, and Chief Akkara. As expected, the Maroons of Surinam did not keep their promise to turn away other rebels, so their forces grew and the Dutch went on the offensive. John Stedman, captain of the Scots Brigade in mercenary recruitment, documents the strategies of the Saramaka warriors, as reported by Ronald Segal (1995): "Against the well-armed military forces, they employed their developing skills as guerrilla fighters. They would shoot from behind trees and use spies to track the troops until these were so weakened by disease or vulnerably positioned as to invite attack" (p. 98). In addition, the Maroons would often lure Dutch battalions into the swamps and when the latter were stuck in the mud, take leisurely pot shots at them from the surrounding bushes.

Inevitably, human factors such as rivalry, jealousy, and greed divided the rebels, who were finally defeated by 1780. Nevertheless, the Dutch soldiers and colonists suffered great loss of life and property, and many fled the Guyanas for the Netherlands or other parts of the Americas. It was indeed a Pyrrhic victory.

HAITI

Although Haiti is part of the Caribbean Basin, the events that transpired there a century ago merit a distinct treatment. Of all the sites of cultural resistance, Haiti provided the perfect setting for the ultimate experiment—unconditional freedom for enslaved Africans. For one thing, the mistreatment of enslaved Africans in France's prized possession of Saint Domingue was among the worst in the Americas. For another, the mortality rate was astronomical, and slaves had to be replaced so quickly that the process of creolization (acculturation) could not take effect on the replacements. This tragic irony made possible the growth of an active resistance movement on the island.

There is no doubt that men like Toussaint-Louverture, Henri Christophe, and Jean-Jacques Dessalines stand out in their roles as leaders of the Haitian Revolution. However, their contributions are well documented in many sources, especially in C. L. R. James's classic, *The Black Jacobins* (1938). Less prominent is the role of the common people, those who lived and moved along the fringes and in the shadows but who, nevertheless, played significant parts in the liberation of Haiti. One such historical figure is Mackandal (Macandal), who worked in a sugar mill of the Lenormand plantation near the northern city of Le Cap. One day Mackandal's arm got crushed in the sugar press and the overseer had to amputate it. The astute, one-armed worker was then placed in the pasturelands to guard the cattle, but he escaped sometime around 1751 and joined a community of Maroons in the mountains. Mackandal soon became their leader, organized raids on plantations in the vicinity, and gained a reputation for bravery as well as immortality. Like Anancy, Mackandal uses his intelligence to plot his enemy's downfall.

Skilled in herbal medicine, the priest/seer/chieftain arranged for the distribution of poison to his followers on a certain day in 1757. All whites were targets. However, Mackandal's scheme was uncovered and the French authorities were able to ambush him. The official version of Mackandal's destiny is that he was captured in March 1758 and burned at the stake. Conversely, his disciples believed that just as the flames were about to engulf him, their hero broke the chains that bound him and, in a final act of defiance, changed into a mosquito that flew away, but that would return in human form one day. Cuban Alejo Carpentier captures the drama of Mackandal's death in *The Kingdom of This World* (1949), a novel about the Haitian Revolution. More germane to this study, the tale of aerial flight evokes the popular belief of enslaved Africans throughout the Americas that upon death their souls would fly back to Guinea (Africa). The flight motif is succinctly projected in *The People Could Fly* (1985), a collection of tales by U.S. writer Virginia Hamilton.

Mackandal's death was only a temporary setback. Bouckman (Boukman) was a second religious figure and political leader who took up the baton of freedom. A fugitive from Jamaica and a priest of Vodun, Bouckman resorted to the strategies of that cult to forge a system of communication for organizing the next phase of the Haitian Revolution, which began on August 14, 1791. Although Bouckman, too, was killed early in the battle, other equally committed individuals and groups continued to fight until they were united under Toussaint-Louverture. The rest is history as Saint Domingue was the first American colony to successfully throw off the yoke of colonialism and slavery from the most powerful European power in the eighteenth and nineteenth centuries—France under the dictatorship of Napoleon Bonaparte. It is fitting that the black rebels chose the indigenous name Haiti, which means "mountain," to designate their new nation and new identity. Not only did the Haitian Revolution shake the foundations of European hegemony, it also set the tone of rebellion for the entire hemisphere. The irony is that the white Creole colonials feared the emancipated slaves more than they yearned for freedom from the metropolises, and this ambivalence delayed their own independence movements, especially in the Caribbean. Haiti was the anathema of the entire hemisphere, for the European settlers could not conceive of sharing freedom, equality, and brotherhood with the enslaved Africans in their respective enclaves. All the strategies of resistance available to the trickster—concoction, dissimulation, stealth, attack, retreat, confrontation, and negotiation—came into play during the Haitian Revolution. Anancy was truly a disturber of the peace.

THE SOUTHERN CONE

At the southern end of South America lies a conical-shaped area called the Southern Cone, which includes the countries of Argentina, Chile, Paraguay, and Uruguay (and sometimes southern Brazil). Moreover, these nations boast of uniqueness based on their "whiteness" in contrast to the rest of the continent. It is appropriate that the "disappearance" of black peoples and cultures in the Southern Cone be addressed just as the "disappeared ones" during the repressive governments of the 1970s and 1980s has

been the focus of intense publicity in recent times. While academic opinion varies on Chile, recent studies have brought to light information of the African presence in Argentina. Romero Jorge Rodríguez (2001) informs readers that:

> Beginning in 1538, Buenos Aires was one of the principal ports of entrance for Africans to South America. Buenos Aires also served as a stopover for thousands of Africans en route to the mines and the Casa de la Moneda (the Mint) in Potosí, Bolivia. Many enslaved Africans remained in Argentinean villages and towns along the way. Census figures from the colonial period demonstrate a significant African presence. As early as 1778, one-third of the population of Buenos Aires was of African origin, and according to the 1810 census, in some cities Blacks comprised 60 percent of the population. Thus, the Black population was demographically, hence socially and culturally, significant in Argentina's early history. (p. 316)

What happened to the descendants of all these people? Scholars debate the issue, but the most common reasons given include the end of the legal slave trade in 1813 (although contraband activity continued for a long time); the drafting of enslaved Africans with the promise of freedom, or the forced recruitment of freed Africans to serve in the colonial and national armies; the high mortality rate caused by disease and poverty; and the wave of European immigration that came about as a result of certain practices under the presidencies of Domingo Faustino Sarmiento and Juan Bautista Alberdi. The last reason is of great concern because Sarmiento and Alberdi engineered a state policy of deliberate extermination of the indigenous and African populations during the 1880s. European immigration was seen by some as a way to erase blackness from Argentina and Latin America, and considered, by these same individuals, as a necessary step on the road to progress and modernization.

A case in point is the story of Falucho, the nickname for a black soldier of the Regiment of the Río de la Plata who was a native of Buenos Aires. Falucho was stationed in the port of Callao, near Lima, Peru, along with other soldiers in combined forces against the Spanish government. After a mutiny on February 7, 1824, royalist troops stormed the rebel barracks and raised the Spanish banner. The Argentine regiment was ordered to mount guard and salute the enemy flag. Instead, the black freedman broke his musket against the flagstaff and was shot to death as he yelled out, "Viva Buenos Aires!" (Núñez, p. 186). More often than not, soldiers like Falucho were sent to the front lines without the benefit of weapons to defend themselves. Lucía Dominga Molina and Mario Luis López (2001) provide ample statistics on Afro-Argentine soldiers. Rodríguez supplies information on Afro-Bolivians of the Yungas provinces in Bolivia and the Afro-Paraguayans called *Cambá Cuá*, of mixed African and Guaraní heritages. In the face of overwhelming odds, these groups forged viable identities by maintaining elements of African cultures, resisting those aspects of Western cultures they considered harmful and embracing those that were beneficial. Anancy is famous for his adaptability.

CENTRAL AMERICA

To represent the Afro-Caribbean experience in Central America, it is fitting to end this discussion with a focus on Anancy in Costa Rica, who emerges in the historical and legendary figure of Joe Gordon during the 1930s. There are no official documents attesting to the reality of Joe Gordon, a banana worker who revolted against the exploitation of the United Fruit Enterprise, but that is often the case in African-American history. According to popular legend, Joe Gordon was fired from his job when he let a carload of bananas plunge into a ravine to save a fellow worker. Gordon placed a higher value on human life than on a wagonful of fruit, but the management of the company was incensed over the material loss. After his dismissal, Gordon had plenty of time to think about the implications of his mistreatment and that of people like him. He soon realized that systemic, rather than individual, oppression was the real issue that had to be addressed. Thus, Gordon carefully planned attacks on the banana plantation, raided the company store, and surprised the manager in his residence to take back from the exploiters, redistribute the wealth to the most indigent in their community, and inspire fear in the authorities. In true Robin Hood fashion, this Anancy figure draws a following. Joe Gordon's exploits are extracted from the oral tradition in a poem called "The Outlaw," by Alderman Roden Johnson, a first-generation writer of Jamaican descent in Costa Rica who wrote in English:

He had a grievance that he nursed
Against the bad white man.
He nurtured it until it worsened
And grew clear out of hand.

Thence Joe went on to plunder
The Fruit Company's store,
With skill and without blunder
He would "even the score."
And very many were the poor
Who at morn did arise
To find a fortune at their door

And scarce could believe their eyes.
It was a present from their "Joe"
Left there during the night.
Thus Joe stole from the hated foe
To relieve the oppressed poor's plight. (Cited in Mosby, p. 51)

Eventually Joe Gordon is hunted down, captured, and executed, but in the popular imagination he resurrects himself. He becomes a community legend, a culture hero, and a symbol of resistance to an oppressed people, just as Yanga, Zumbi, Mackandal, Zeferina, and all the others who resisted, struggled, sacrificed, and triumphed, if not in body then certainly in spirit. Fiction writer Quince Duncan metaphorically captures the absurdity/ tragicomedy of the African experience in the West in "The Legend of Joe Gordon," which is part of the *Best Short Stories* collection (1995). In concrete historical terms, Anancy's story unfolds in Limón Province, Costa Rica, where the Trickster always manages to overcome or defeat all rivals/enemies except Brother Tacuma (Tucuma). Gutiérrez (1999) proposes that since Anancy represents intelligence and Tucuma justice, the two culture heroes of oral tradition might collaborate in the continuing struggle for liberation. Joe Gordon is the literary manifestation of that union.

In response to García's call for a pedagogy of self-perception, Duncan proffers a model he refers to as *afrorealismo* (Afro-realism) in his approach to the creation and study of Afro–Costa Rican literature and all African-inspired writing in the Americas. Simply stated, Afro-realism functions according to six principles: the restitution of the African and African-American voices based on an Afrocentric terminology; the vindication of the symbolic African memory; the reconstruction of an informed historical memory based on diaspora experiences; the reaffirmation of the concept of ancestral community; the adoption of an intracentric narrative perspective; and the quest and proclamation of a black identity. Paradoxically, Afro-realism can be explored through the use of languages originating in Europe—Spanish, Portuguese, French, English, and Dutch—because it is informed by an African-derived worldview. The fictional characters and culture heroes of the American diaspora are the seeds and fragments of a reality that must be reconstructed to achieve spiritual and psycho-emotional wholeness. That task is left to the writer.

See also African Diaspora; Christophe, Henri; Dessalines, Jean-Jacques; Folklore: Overview; Folklore: U.S. Folk Heroes and Characters; Haitian Revolution; Maroon Wars; Toussaint-Louverture

■ ■ *Bibliography*

Collier, Simon, Harold Blakemore, and Thomas E. Skidmore, eds. *Cambridge Encyclopedia of Latin America and the Caribbean.* Cambridge, U.K.: Cambridge University Press, 1992.

Davis, Darien. "Black Cultures." In *Encyclopedia of Contemporary Latin American and Caribbean Cultures*, edited by Daniel Balderston, Mike González, and Ana M. López, vol. 1, pp. 182–185. London and New York: Routledge, 2000.

Duncan, Quince. "El afrorealismo: Una dimensión nueva de la literatura latinoamericana." *Revista Virtual ISTMO* (July 2004): 1–8.

García, Jesús. "Desmystifying Africa's Absence in Venezuelan History and Culture." In *African Roots/American Cultures: Africa in the Creation of the Americas,* edited by Sheila S. Walker, pp. 284–289. Lanham, N.J.: Rowman & Littlefield, 2001.

Gates, Henry Louis, Jr. *The Signifying Monkey: A Theory of Afro-American Literary Criticism.* Oxford, U.K.: Oxford University Press, 1988.

Gutiérrez, Mariela. "La herencia afrocaribeña de Anansi, el hermano araña, en Costa Rica." *Revista Iberoamericana* 65/188 (1999): 519–535.

Hamilton, Virginia. *The People Could Fly: American Black Folktales.* New York: Knopf Books for Young Readers, 1985.

Hernández-Cuevas, Marco Polo. *African Mexicans and the Discourse on Modern Nation.* Dallas: University Press of America, 2004.

Leal, Gilberto R. N. "Fárígá/Ìfaradà: Black Renaissance and Achievement in Brazil." In *African Roots/American Cultures: Africa in the Creation of the Americas,* edited by Sheila S. Walker, pp. 291–300. Lanham, N.J.: Rowman & Littlefield, 2001.

Martin-Ogunsola, Dellita, ed. and trans. *The Best Short Stories of Quince Duncan/Las mejores historias de Quince Duncan.* San José: Editorial Costa Rica, 1995.

Meyer, Michael C., and William L. Sherman. *The Course of Mexican History*, 4th ed. Oxford, U.K.: Oxford University Press, 1991.

Molina Lucía Dominga, and Mario Luis López. "Afro-Argentineans: 'Forgotten' and 'Disappeared'—Yet Still Present." In *African Roots/American Cultures: Africa in the Creation of the Americas,* edited by Sheila S. Walker, pp. 332–347. Lanham, N.J.: Rowman & Littlefield, 2001.

Mosby, Dorothy E. *Place, Language, and Identity in Afro-Costa Rican Literature.* Columbia: University of Missouri Press, 2003.

Núñez, Benjamin. *Dictionary of Afro-Latin American Civilization.* Westport, Conn.: Greenwood Press, 1980.

Okpewho, Isidore, Carole Boyce Davies, and Ali A. Mazrui, eds. *The African Diaspora: African Origins and New World Identities,* pp. xi–xxviii. Bloomington and Indianapolis: Indiana University Press, 1999.

Reis, Jõao José. "*Quilombos* and Rebellions in Brazil." In *African Roots/American Cultures: Africa in the Creation of the Americas,* edited by Sheila S. Walker, pp. 301–313. Lanham, N.J.: Rowman & Littlefield, 2001.

Rodríguez, Romero Jorge. "The Afro Populations of America's Southern Cone: Organization, Development, and Culture in Argentina, Bolivia, Paraguay, and Uruguay." In *African Roots/American Cultures: Africa in the Creation of the Americas,* edited by Sheila S. Walker, pp. 314–331. Lanham, N.J.: Rowman & Littlefield, 2001.

Segal, Ronald. *The Black Diaspora.* New York: Farrar, Strauss and Giroux, 1995.

Walker, Sheila S., ed. *African Roots/American Cultures: Africa in the Creation of the Americas.* Lanham, N.J.: Rowman & Littlefield, 2001.

DELLITA MARTIN-OGUNSOLA (2005)

U.S. FOLK HEROES AND CHARACTERS

Throughout U.S. history, the African-American folk hero has appeared in related incarnations that reflect both the enslaved Africans' cultural heritage and the shifting American sociopolitical landscape that produced them. The cunning animal and slave tricksters, represented by Brer Rabbit and John the slave, the defiant slave ancestors who risked death to flee North, the indomitable Moses figure of Harriet Tubman, the moral hard man John Henry, and the badman Stagolee represent African-American folk heroes whose tales have been passed on through the oral tradition for over six centuries. These folk heroes represent, according to the folklorist John Roberts, historical figures who stand as cornerstones in the foundation of African-American culture: "In this regard, heroic creation is a process very much like culture building—the means by which a group creates and maintains an image of itself to proclaim difference from others by objectifying in its institutions the ideals it claims for itself" (Roberts, 1989, p. 1).

SUBVERSIVE HEROES

Personified within African-American folk heroes are the cultural ideals that led to their creation. Subversion, confrontation, and resistance against racist oppression are thematically embedded within these tales. These ideals emboldened enslaved Africans in the antebellum South to survive and eventually free themselves from bondage; moreover, the sense of sociocultural distinction provided by folk heroes instilled pride and perseverance among African Americans during the Reconstruction era, when a combination of legislative, economic, and social controls were established to perpetuate a de facto state of slavery following Emancipation. Thus the African-American folk hero emerges as a cultural hero who consistently challenges the forces of racist domination to emerge victorious and who simultaneously recontextualizes American history in a manner that highlights the ingenuity, fortitude, and resilience of the African-American people.

Brer Rabbit pours scalding water on Brer Wolf, in an illustration from the 1899 edition of **Uncle Remus and his Friends.** *Enslaved Africans in the Americas delighted in the oral tales of the exploits of Brer Rabbit, and the popularity of the rabbit hero in subsequent folktales is a testament to the trickster's African cultural roots and to the enslaved peoples' need for an unlikely hero with which to identify.*
THE LIBRARY OF CONGRESS

During slavery, animal and slave trickster tales were prevalent. Enslaved Africans embraced the diminutive Brer Rabbit because he continually outsmarted his fiercer animal rivals through his innate intelligence and guile. According to several folklorists, Brer Rabbit should be viewed as an African diasporic folk hero since rabbit and other animal trickster tales may be found on the African continent, in the Caribbean, and in South America. On Brer Rabbit's African roots and subsequent New World incarnations, Jacqueline Shachter Weiss notes:

> In the African folktales, small animals, such as the turtle or praying mantis, were praised for what they did well. Among the Ashanti of West Africa, the hero was the spider, Anansi. . . .

Though Anansi is a well-known folk character in Guyana, Jamaica and the Virgin Islands, the rabbit is appreciated more in the Americas. Brer Rabbit is his name in most English-speaking lands. In Venezuela, where he is especially popular today, as well as Colombia and Panama, he is called *Tio Conejo* ("Uncle Rabbit"). In Cuba, he is *Hermano Rabito* ("Brother Rabbit") and in Brazil, *o coelho* ("the rabbit"). (Weiss, 1985, p. 3)

Most folklorists consider Brer Rabbit's trickster-hero ethos of survival integral to the enslaved Africans' self-conceptualization. Robert Hemenway notes, "The point cannot be overemphasized that black people identified with Brer Rabbit. When Brer Rabbit triumphed over a physically superior foe, black people fantasized themselves in an identical situation" (1982, p. 19). Furthermore, through the oral performance of Brer Rabbit tales, enslaved Africans found diversion from the backbreaking labor of slavery and simultaneously created a distinctly African-American cultural tradition that celebrated their identity. As Roger Abrahams comments in the introduction to *Afro-American Folktales*, "Told at night, for entertainment as well as instruction, in the traditional African style. . .these stories. . .provided entertainment by which the community could celebrate its identity as a group" (1985, p. 18).

Enslaved Africans in the United States reveled in the exploits of Brer Rabbit, but it is important to note that these trickster tales diverge greatly from the Indo-European and Euro-American folktale tradition. In considering Brer Rabbit's place within the Western canon of fairytales, Abrahams further advises readers:

> Contrast this with the intent of the usual Indo-European fairytale, where action is initiated by an individual seeking to better herself or himself and advance to the point of happily-ever-aftering. We also fail to find the style of story, so common in Euro-American traditions, that conveys the message that moral violations be punished. The African and Afro-American stories more commonly chronicle how a trickster or a hero uses his wits to get something he wants. (Abrahams, 1985, p. 18)

Brer Rabbit's predominance in the folktales of the Americas is a testament to the trickster's African cultural roots and the enslaved Africans' need for an unlikely hero; this animal trickster's implausible victories seem to have enabled slaves to insert themselves into the trickster tale. From this root, the slave trickster in the person of John was born.

In many of the John-Master tales, John is cast in the role of ego-affirming sidekick. He is forced to reaffirm his owner's precarious sense of superiority while the plot reveals John's innate intelligence. To bolster his owner's insecure sense of self, John must wear the dual mask of ignorance and stupidity to ensure his survival.

ANCESTORS, LIBERATORS, AND INSURRECTIONISTS

Unlike the implicitly subversive Brer Rabbit and John-Master tales, histories of slave ancestors, liberators, and insurrectionists were explicit, and they were prevalent in antebellum and postbellum American society. The descendants of slaves kept tales of defiant runaway ancestors alive through the oral tradition and wore their ancestors' rebellion as a badge of pride. In *Black Culture and Black Consciousness,* Lawrence Levine relates the experience of folklorist Richard Dorson, who collected tales of runaway slaves from their descendants in Michigan in the twentieth century:

> On my first meeting with E. L. Smith. . .he recited the superhuman adventures of his maternal grandfather, Romey Howard, in escaping from the patterollers and bloodhounds that pursued runaway slaves. . . .Mr. Smith told them for truth, having heard them firsthand from his grandfather, a self-made folk hero, who thwarted and rendered ridiculous the white oppressor. (quoted in Levine, 1977, p. 387)

The descendants of slaves embraced their ancestors as heroes because they risked torture and death to obtain their freedom. Outstanding among the enslaved Africans who cast their lot with flight and rebellion was Harriet Tubman. Known as the Moses of her people, Tubman led enslaved Africans from bondage in the American South to freedom in the North. According to historian Vincent Harding, biblical stories recounting the trials and tribulations of the Israelites were a source of great encouragement, for Tubman, who "grew up on stories of the Hebrew children, sang the songs of impossible hope. . . .She prayed and talked with God and became fully convinced that her God willed her freedom" (quoted in Roberts, 1989, p. 162). In accepting her role as the liberator of her people, Tubman came to see her mission as identical to that of Moses. Her life was significant to the extent that she used it to exercise the will of God, a will that included freedom for her people: "Like Moses, Harriet Tubman risked her own freedom to answer the call of God to lead her people out of slavery" (Roberts, 1989, p. 161). Harriet Tubman's proto-emancipatory legacy has become an integral part of most secondary-school and college curricula, but her contribution also lives on in the African-American oral tradition, in the Negro spiritual of the nineteenth century, and in the rap song of the twentieth century.

According to Eric Sundquist, "Steal Away" is one of the most evocative sorrow songs in the catalogue of Negro spirituals due to its use in the surreptitious planning of slave meetings, resistance, and flight: "'Steal Away,' as countless former slaves recalled the phrase, was a thinly coded song used to announce secret religious service or secular celebration; it could also act as a profession of rebellion, a call used by Nat Turner and Harriet Tubman. . .to organize slave resistance and plans of escape" (1993, p. 511). That this spiritual is still sung today recalls the power and continuity of the African-American oral tradition. It is a tradition that recalls the dualistic nature of the American slave past: a highly oppressive socioeconomic system that simultaneously engendered an irrepressible spirit of resistance within Tubman and other insurrectionists like her.

In the twentieth century, Tubman's historical role has not been lost on younger generations of African-Americans; the socially conscious rappers Nas and Rah Digga keep her memory alive. In the introduction to his 1996 platinum-selling compact disc *It Was Written,* Nas honors Tubman: "Man, damn dis place, damn dese chains. Harriet done gone de night befo', it's time we go. Dis ain't no place for black people; de promised lan' callin'." And in 2000 the rapper Rah Digga explained that she titled her album *Dirty Harriet* to honor Tubman's commitment to freedom and to warn female rappers against exploiting their sexuality in order to be marketable.

The defiance of Tubman and other slave ancestors stands in stark opposition to the white stereotype of the Sambo figure: "The docile, infantile, lazy, irresponsible personality. . .the product of a system of slavery that required absolute conformity" (White, 1985, p. 17).

THE HARD MAN AND THE BADMAN

The survival of enslaved Africans required a degree of conformity that was tested by countless runaways and rebels, but the years following Emancipation provided no relief. On the contrary, Reconstruction perpetuated chattel slavery's theoretical underpinnings of African-American disenfranchisement, oppression, and exploitation. As Jerry Bryant writes, "De facto slavery replaced the 'peculiar institution' in the form of Jim Crow, sharecropping, and a carefully controlled labor market that forced black men and women into the worst and lowest paying jobs" (2003, p. 9).

During the years following Reconstruction, African Americans were not only prevented from exercising the basic rights of citizenship, they were terrorized by the Ku Klux Klan and other bands of marauding whites who in some cases pillaged entire African-American communities. Levine writes, "What were referred to as race riots in the last half of the nineteenth century and the early years of the twentieth would be more accurately described as pogroms. Whites attacked, murdered, and pillaged blacks" (1977, p. 439). It was during these tumultuous decades that the African-American folk ballad emerged; this lyrical narrative extolled the virtues of the moral hard man John Henry and the legendary badman Stagolee.

John Henry, the steel-driving man who died proving that his natural might could surpass the manufactured power of the machine (the steam engine), is one of the greatest folk heroes in American history. In *John Henry: Tracking Down a Negro Legend,* Guy Johnson writes, "There is a vivid, fascinating, tragic legend about him which Negro folk have kept alive and have cherished. . .and in doing so they have enriched the cultural life of America" (1969, p. 151). The John Henry legend has indeed deepened the breadth of the American folk tradition, for in the many variants of John Henry lore Americans have, knowingly or unknowingly, embraced a folk hero whose initial declaration of humanity was formed by rejecting the white societal expectation of African-American subservience, even upon pain of death.

> John Henry's first assertion of his manhood and his equality—his single most dominant characteristic. . .comes when he refused to continue picking the white man's cotton. . . .The point made in this episode is that blacks must not allow white intimidation to prevent them from asserting themselves, even when they know there is the risk that they might be killed. (Thomas, 1988, p. 58)

Thus began the career of John Henry, a career built on the consistent expression of both moral and physical intractability in the face of white domination. In several different versions, his famed battle against the steam drill at Big Bend Tunnel spread to every region of the land. According to Daryl Cumber Dance, the numerous variants of the John Henry ballad, work song, and tale provide unique insight into the collective ethos of African Americans.

> A tale's growth and continued existence is contingent upon its acceptance by a larger group. The modifications it undergoes will reflect the soul of the group within which it circulates, so

that when a tale can be properly called a folktale—when it exists in variant forms—we should be aware that it is thereby an item of some significance in understanding something about that group. (Dance, 2002, p. xxvii)

Although the widespread circulation of John Henry lore throughout the country seems to attest to the African-American community's admiration for those who openly challenged white intimidation, John Henry's victory over the steam engine also reflects the actual and symbolic triumph of man over machine. His was an impossible feat that held even greater implications for the African-American workingman's place in an increasingly industrialized society. As Nigel Thomas writes, "John Henry's conquest of the white machine could be interpreted as his triumphing over white intelligence and capitalist indifference, a feat all oppressed blacks would want to perform" (Thomas, 1988, p. 57).

Although this analysis of John Henry's import for African Americans seems accurate, Thomas fails to acknowledge that the ubiquity of John Henry lore in America is indicative of the folk hero's legendary status beyond the African-American community. To this day, Henry remains one of the best-known American folk heroes; he is a universal symbol of the intrepid American laborer who strove to maintain his dignity in the face of obsolescence brought on by the industrial age.

From within the same ballad tradition that spawned the lore of John Henry, the steel-driving man, sprang narratives about a different type of intractable African-American man—the *badman.* Perhaps the most famous of these is Stagolee, whose multiple eponyms (comparable to Brer Rabbit's) testify to how deeply his legend has become embedded within the collective African-American consciousness. "Stagolee—a.k.a. Stacker Lee, Staggerlee, Stackalee, Stackolee, Stack-O-Lee, Staggalee, Stack-O, and Stack-Lee is the star of the badmen. The several forms his name takes suggest the numerousness of the versions of his story" (Bryant, 2003, p. 13). In several versions of the Stagolee tale, the hero shoots Billy Lyons, a suspected professional gambler on the grift, after a gambling match in which Lyons wins Stagolee's magic Stetson hat. While Stagolee has clearly committed murder, John Roberts advises readers to note that "in the badman folk heroic tradition, those individuals who served as a focus for folk heroic creation were not the professional criminals, but rather their victims who responded to victimization with violence" (1989, p. 207). Seen in this manner, Roberts argues, Stagolee's act of murder is an act of retaliation against a conman who attempted to dupe him. Viewed in a broader historical context, Stagolee and others in the badman tradition should be considered outlaw rebels who disregarded the law specifically because it was representative of—and was in most cases equivalent to—the existing white power structure that brutalized and oppressed African Americans in the decades following Emancipation.

Throughout the nineteenth and twentieth centuries, African-American folk heroes have embodied the ideals of resistance that enabled African Americans to rebel against slavery and following Emancipation to overcome the slave system's legacy of racist oppression and disenfranchisement. The guile of Brer Rabbit and John, the death-defying bravery of slave ancestors and liberators, the intractability of John Henry, and the iconoclasm of the badman all reflect a collective African-American will to resist racist domination. This collective will is an aspect of the African-American cultural tradition that reflects the indomitable nature of the human spirit. These heroes, both actual and fictitious, personify the struggle for self-definition, self-determination, and self-actualization that lies at the heart of the human condition.

See also Black Arts Movement; Comic Books; Comic Strips; Drama; Folklore: Latin American and Caribbean Culture Heroes and Characters; Folklore: Overview; Literary Magazines; Literature of the United States

■ ■ *Bibliography*

Abrahams, Roger D., ed. *Afro-American Folktales: Stories from the Black Tradition in the New World.* New York: Pantheon, 1985.

Bryant, Jerry H. *Born in a Mighty Bad Land: The Violent Man in African-American Folklore and Fiction.* Bloomington: University of Indiana Press, 2003.

Dance, Daryl Cumber, ed. *From My People: Four Hundred Years of African American Folklore.* New York: Norton, 2002.

Hemenway, Robert. "Introduction." In *Uncle Remus: His Songs and His Sayings,* by Joel Chandler Harris. New York: Penguin, 1982.

Johnson, Guy B. *John Henry: Tracking Down a Negro Legend* (1929). New York: AMS Press, 1969.

Levine, Lawrence W. *Black Culture and Black Consciousness: Afro American Folk Thought from Slavery to Freedom.* New York: Oxford University Press, 1977.

Nas (Nasir Jones). "Introduction." *It Was Written* (audio CD). New York: Columbia, 1996.

"Rah Digga: Biography." *Hiponline.com.* Available from <http://www.hiponline.com/artist/music/r/rah_digga>.

Roberts, John W. *From Trickster to Badman: The Black Folk Hero in Slavery and Freedom.* Philadelphia: University of Pennsylvania Press, 1989.

Sundquist, Eric J. *To Wake the Nations: Race in the Making of American Literature.* Cambridge, Mass.: Belknap Press of Harvard University Press, 1993.

Thomas, H. Nigel. *From Folklore to Fiction: A Study of Folk Heroes and Rituals in the Black American Novel.* New York: Greenwood, 1988.

Weiss, Jacqueline Shachter, comp. *Young Brer Rabbit, and Other Trickster Tales from the Americas.* Owing Mills, Md.: Stemmer House, 1985.

White, Deborah Gray. *Ar'n't I a Woman?: Female Slaves in the Plantation South.* New York: Norton, 1985.

LAROSE T. PARRIS (2005)

FOLK MEDICINE

Folk medicine has been a significant feature of the cultural and social heritage of African Americans since colonial times. Its origins trace back to traditions brought to the New World by slaves. African-based religious and medical customs were often closely intertwined, reflecting an effort to understand relationships between metaphysical and physical phenomena and to apply this knowledge in promoting the health and well-being of an individual or community. "Root doctor" is perhaps the best-known type of folk practitioner. Other types include "witch doctor," "hoodoo doctor," and "voodoo doctor." While the practice of folk medicine involves a complex, eclectic array of belief systems and therapies, the most common ingredient is a combination of incantations (the spiritual element) and herbal concoctions (the physical element).

Prior to Emancipation, planters tolerated and sometimes encouraged folk practice in order to save the expense of hiring white practitioners to treat slaves. Thus, a special class of folk practitioner evolved within the slave community. A number of these practitioners were women, the so-called Negro doctoresses, entrusted with health-care responsibilities ranging from midwifery to minor surgery and the preparation and dispensing of medicines.

After Emancipation, folk practitioners were confronted by two major obstacles. The first concerned developments in modern medicine, particularly the evolving notion of disease as a largely physical process involving specific tissues and organs and distinct from religious or spiritual traditions. Second, mainstream practitioners erected legal, educational, and other hurdles as part of the effort to increase professionalization of the field and to reduce competition from those using alternative approaches. The mainstream medical press highlighted instances of alleged malpractice by "unqualified" folk practitioners. In 1899, for example, the *Journal of the American Medical Association* noted: "A colored 'voodoo doctor' . . . was put on trial for manslaughter during the past week. In a raid of the man's house by the police, there was found a weird collection of things, including animal remains, herbs, charms, and medicines" (p. 1559).

Despite such pressures, folk practices continued to play a significant role in health care in the twentieth century. Deeply rooted in cultural experience, they provided options for those whose access to health care was otherwise limited. Tensions between folk practitioners and advocates of "community standards" in religious and health practice persist, as in legal actions in Florida, for example, against the Santería cult for violation of animal-sacrifice statutes during the late 1980s and early 1990s. A common thread that links these worlds—the promotion and preservation of health—is often buried under disputes over philosophy and methodology. Nevertheless, connections occur in unexpected ways, especially within the African-American community, where folk traditions run deep. Numa Pompilius Garfield Adams, a graduate of Rush Medical College (1924) and the first African-American dean of the Howard Medical School, always acknowledged the influence of his grandmother, Mrs. Amanda Adams, in his choice of a career. Mrs. Adams, a folk practitioner and midwife in rural Virginia, had introduced him as a child to the therapeutic properties of herbs.

See also Healing and the Arts in Afro-Caribbean Cultures; Voodoo

■ ■ *Bibliography*

Hurston, Zora Neale. *Mules and Men* (1935). Bloomington: Indiana University Press, 1978.

Journal of the American Medical Association 33 (December 16, 1899): 1559.

Puckett, Newbell Niles. *Folk Beliefs of the Southern Negro* (1926). Reprint. Montclair, N.J.: Patterson Smith, 1968.

Watson, Wilbur H. *Black Folk Medicine: The Therapeutic Significance of Faith and Trust.* New Brunswick, N.J.: Transaction Books, 1984.

KENNETH R. MANNING (1996)

FOLK MUSIC

African-American folk music embraces sacred songs known as spirituals and many kinds of secular music, both vocal and instrumental. These include work songs that regulated the rate of work, street cries, field "hollers" that enabled workers to communicate over long distances, lullabies, and various kinds of dance music—all known before the Civil War. The musical elements that character-

ized African music described by European traders in the early seventeenth century were common in African-American folk music.

Africans did not arrive in the New World culturally naked, despite many statements to that effect. Historians and anthropologists now agree that many elements of African culture converged with surrounding European influences to form a new African-American culture. In their free time, blacks continued to perform the songs and dances they had in Africa. Early contemporary descriptions depicted the same musical elements previously described in Africa: polyrhythms; a strained, rasping vocal quality; variable pitches; singing accompanied by bodily movement in which everyone participated; and the extremely common call-and-response form of singing, in which leader and chorus overlapped. African instruments also came to the New World: drums, banjo, a kind of flute, and the *balafo,* a kind of xylophone. Improvised satiric or derisive singing was used to regulate the rate of work in rowing, grinding grain, and harvesting, in both Africa and the Americas. Strong rhythms were accentuated by stamping, hand-clapping, and other percussive devices. Although European music shared some of these elements, contemporary observers emphasized the exotic qualities, not the similarities that were later cited erroneously as evidence of European origin. Until the invention of sound recording, the only means of preserving music was transcription into a notational system designed for European forms. In the process, many distinctive elements were lost, and what was transcribed looked like European music. Performance style and sound could not be captured, but until the mid-twentieth century, musicians tended to regard transcription as the equivalent of the music as it was performed.

African instruments reached the New World through the practice, common in the slave trade, of providing instruments aboard slave ships to encourage singing and dancing, a recognized means of combating depression, suicide, and revolt. As early as 1693, a slaving captain reported that music and dance provided exercise in a limited space, raising the captives' spirits. Some captains collected African instruments before sailing, thus transmitting African instruments to the New World.

When the Africans landed, concern for the continued health of their new possessions led some plantation owners to make efforts to acclimate them gradually to their new circumstances. Contemporary accounts describe the welcome of the new arrivals by older slaves, who sang and danced with them in a style characterized by Europeans as "exotic" or "barbaric." African instruments were described in the West Indies from the mid-seventeenth century, but reports from the mainland came later because of the relatively small number of blacks there until the mid-eighteenth century. As early as February 18, 1755, the *Virginia Gazette* printed an advertisement for a runaway slave who played well on the "Banjar," while Thomas Jefferson in his *Notes on the State of Virginia* (1781) described the "banjar, which they [blacks] brought hither from Africa."

The official report of the Stono, South Carolina, slave revolt of 1739 described "dancing, Singing and beating Drums" as the means used by the rebels to attract more blacks to their ranks. An African drum from Virginia was purchased in 1753 by the British Museum, where it remains today. In many mainland colonies the playing of drums or other loud instruments, being forbidden by law, was surreptitious, but drum-making continued; as late as the 1930s, it was observed in Georgia by Federal Writers' Project interviewers. In place of drums, other percussive devices were used to provide rhythmic support for singing and dancing—stamping, hand-clapping, and the less threatening sound of the banjo.

An African xylophone, the balafo (or barrafou), was reported in Virginia in 1775 by a schoolmaster, John Harrower, in his *Journal*, and in a news item in Purdie's Williamsburg *Virginia Gazette* in 1776. Blacks also learned to play European instruments such as the fiddle, the French horn, and the flute. As early as the 1690s, Accomack County records in Virginia reported a court case involving a slave fiddler. During the eighteenth century, reports of blacks fiddling for white dances were common, an indication of the progress of acculturation.

Most of the music blacks played for the dancing of whites consisted of conventional European country dances and minuets, but reports from the eighteenth century also described whites dancing "Negro jigs" as a change from the more formal dances. Published versions of these "jigs" show few African characteristics; how the music sounded in performance is conjectural.

With the beginning of evangelical efforts to convert blacks to Christianity in the mid-eighteenth century, reports of African dancing became less frequent except in New Orleans, where such activities continued into the nineteenth century in a specially designated area called Place Congo.

From a musical point of view, the characteristics of sacred and secular music were similar. In many instances, songs regulating work in the fields or on the water that originally had secular words were adapted to sacred texts when the singers joined churches that proscribed secular songs.

Learning to play European instruments and to sing Protestant hymns was part of a process of acculturation,

along with learning the English language and the ways of the white captors. But African ways were not forgotten. Even though new arrivals from Africa virtually stopped in 1808, many old customs persisted in secret, rarely witnessed by the whites who were the primary source of contemporary reports. Political and social pressures also influenced these nineteenth-century accounts, tending to divide them into two patterns: either to describe the singing and dancing as proof that the slaves were happy, or to deny that the slaves had any secular music, depicting them as singing only hymns. Pro-slavery arguments and the minstrel-theater tradition fit into the first pattern, while the abolitionists tended to the latter. Neither pattern conformed fully to reality. Contemporary accounts of slaves singing and dancing demonstrate beyond dispute that increasingly acculturated secular music and dance continued without interruption, despite the undeniable suffering of the slaves.

Songs to regulate the rate of work in Africa were easily adapted to the fields of the New World for planting, cultivating, and harvesting crops, whether they were sugar, rice, indigo, corn, tobacco, or cotton. These songs frequently were a dialogue between a leader and a chorus, although the chorus could play a relatively minor role in providing a rhythmic background. Later, such songs were adapted to the pace of railroad gangs for laying track. This kind of singing was observed in southern prison camps, where isolation and long association led to a higher development of the relation between leader and chorus.

Incredible as it seems, a belief that blacks had no secular music coexisted with the immense popularity of the white minstrel theater, which, initially at least, purported to show plantation life. The early shows were relatively simple, and it is not known how much the early minstrels knew of slavery. Dan Emmett, the reputed composer of "Dixie," had toured the southern states in a circus, but the extent of his contact with blacks is unknown. Little has been written about black secular folk music in the post–Civil War era, but it must have thrived to have produced a generation of talented black performers who themselves played in minstrel shows and popular theater.

Another form of improvised folk music was the Blues. Its origins are obscure, but the blues probably developed among rural blacks during Reconstruction. In contrast to the spiritual, which was usually a group performance with solo and chorus alternating, the blues was a solitary expression of loneliness and misery. It incorporated some elements of the so-called field holler and the gapped scales, blue notes, and syncopation of African music. As improvised utterances, the earliest blues songs were never written down and were lost. By the time blues achieved publication and recording, it had become to some extent professional.

Collections of black folk songs, as distinct from spirituals, began to be published after World War I. Natalie Curtis Burlin edited the *Hampton Series of Negro Folk Songs* (1918-1919), based on the singing of students at the Hampton Institute. Camille Nickerson of New Orleans specialized in Creole French folk songs. John Wesley Work III produced an important collection, *American Negro Songs and Spirituals,* in 1940. A very different collection was Lawrence Gellert's *Negro Songs of Protest* (1936), described as "the living voice of the otherwise inarticulate resentment against injustice." Initially, such songs were received with suspicion as reflecting an outside political motivation, but the civil rights struggle of the 1960s testified to their legitimacy.

The civil rights movement, beginning with the Montgomery, Alabama, bus boycott in December 1955, produced a group of songs that played a more important role in a political and social movement than any since the antislavery songs of a century earlier. "We Shall Overcome," based at least in part on a spiritual, "No More Auction Block for Me," was only the most famous of the freedom songs that inspired and inspirited a great movement.

In southern Louisiana, French-speaking blacks had made their own music for many years, unnoticed by the world outside. Only in the post–World War II period did the whole country become aware of it, largely through sound recordings. Zydeco, as it is called, has not been published much, for little has been written down, but it has become known through recordings.

No form of popular music in the United States, commercial or noncommercial, has remained uninfluenced by black folk music—its rhythmic drive, syncopated beat, gapped scales, and blue notes. The potency of this influence is now worldwide.

In the era after the Civil War, spirituals became the dominant form of black music in the thinking of the general public, both in Europe and in North America, since many writers denied the existence of black secular folk music. This misconception was due in part to the influence among many blacks of religious sects that denounced secular music and dancing as sinful. The many reports of blacks who refused to participate in dancing or to sing anything but sacred songs persuaded many whites outside the South that blacks had no secular music.

The origins of the spiritual are still uncertain. Conversion of the slaves to Christianity proceeded very slowly in the eighteenth century because of the opposition of some slave owners who worried that baptism might interfere with work or even lead to freedom. Moreover, missiona-

ries were few and plantations far apart. Gradually, ministers took an interest in converting slaves, who learned European psalms and hymns with alacrity. At the beginning of the nineteenth century, the camp-meeting movement brought whites and blacks together in large, emotional crowds where mutual influence in styles of singing was unavoidable. It is likely that a blending of African performance style with Protestant hymnody grew out of these encounters. The public in the North first became aware of spirituals through the concert tours in the 1870s of the Fisk Jubilee Singers and other groups, such as the Hampton Singers.

Among very pious slaves, the only form of dancing permitted was the "shout," or holy dance, performed after a church service. Witnesses described it as a circle dance in which the legs were not crossed, while the feet edged backward and forward or right and left, without being lifted from the floor. Music was provided by a separate group of singers who "based" the dancing with "shout" songs or "running" spirituals (Epstein 1977, pp. 278-287).

See also Africanisms; Fisk Jubilee Singers; Folk Arts and Crafts; Folklore; Gospel Music; Music in the United States; Spirituals

■ ■ *Bibliography*

Allen, William Francis, Charles Pickard Ware, and Lucy McKim Garrison. *Slave Songs of the United States.* New York: A. Simpson & Co., 1867. Reprint, Bedford, Mass.: Applewood Books, 1995.

Courlander, Harold. *Negro Folk Music, U.S.A.* New York: Columbia University Press, 1963.

Epstein, Dena J. *Sinful Tunes and Spirituals: Black Folk Music to the Civil War.* Urbana: University of Illinois Press, 2003.

Krehbiel, Henry Edward. *Afro-American Folksongs: A Study in Racial and National Music.* New York: G. Schirmer, 1914.

Small, Christopher. *Music of the Common Tongue: Survival and Celebration in African American Music.* Hanover, N.H.: University Press of New England / Wesleyan University Press, 1998.

Southern, Eileen. *The Music of Black Americans: A History*, 3rd ed. New York: W. W. North, 1997.

Walker, Wyatt Tee. *Spirits That Dwell in Deep Woods: The Prayer and Praise Hymns of the Black Religious Experience.* Chicago, IL: GIA Publications, 2004.

DENA J. EPSTEIN (1996)
Updated bibliography

FOLK RELIGION

The folk religious traditions of blacks in the United States have roots in a number of sources, but it is their African origins that have left the most indelible and distinctive cultural imprint. Of the 400,000 Africans who were held in bondage on the North American mainland during the slave trade, most if not all were influenced by some indigenous philosophical or sacred system for understanding and interpreting the world. Religion for Africans, however, was more a way of life than a system of creeds and doctrines. The African religious experience allowed for meaningful relations between members of the human community and personal interaction with the world of ancestors, spirits, and divinities, who closely guided mortal existence and provided their adherents with explanations and protections within the realm of earthly affairs. African religions, although differing according to their national origins, provided an overall theological perspective in which spirituality was infused into every aspect of life.

In the colonies, Africans came into contact for the first time with the customs and cultures of white Europeans and Native Americans. Although strange and unfamiliar, the perspectives of these groups did share certain aspects, particularly in the realm of beliefs surrounding the supernatural. Both whites and Indians had worldviews that encompassed mythical perceptions of the universe and powers that pervaded human life and nature. Spiritual beings, holy objects, and the workings of the enchanted world were thought to be powerful and efficacious. Evil and misfortune were perceived as personalized agents of affliction.

Such beliefs were expressed, for the most part, in folklore and legend. Africans themselves had corresponding ideas concerning the supernatural that included sacred entities, charms, and places, although it is difficult to disentangle these beliefs from their primary religious framework. We can speculate that from their initial periods of contact, blacks, whites, and Indians exchanged and adopted compatible ideas and visions of the world, each group drawing from the cultures of the others.

It was during the colonial era that enslaved Africans were first exposed to Christian missionary activity, although up to the mid-eighteenth century few blacks were actually converted. Evangelical revivalism, exploding among white Americans in the early national period, had a significant impact on blacks. Adopting their own interpretations and understandings of the message of the Christian faith, black preachers and laypersons developed unique and creative styles of religious devotion. It is here

that one of the prominent strands of African-American folk religion developed.

African-American religion, however, was characterized by diversity from the start. Scattered references to the activity of "sorcerers," "doctors," and "conjurers" from the 1700s and early 1800s indicate that black religious beliefs were multifaceted. Traditional African spirituality recognized the roles of individuals who were sacred practitioners, diviners, and healers, dynamic intermediaries between the unseen realm of spirits and the world of the living. Although they had been separated from the structures and institutions of their national homelands, African specialists recreated aspects of their religious identities within New World environments. Adapting their native beliefs and practices to the American context, these early black practitioners formed yet another thread in the evolving tapestry of African-American religion.

By the antebellum era, the second generation of blacks born in the United States had developed an indigenous culture. Although the overseas slave trade was declared illegal by 1808, most black Americans in the mid-nineteenth century had some knowledge of or acquaintance with recently arrived or native-born Africans who recalled the traditions and ways of their homeland. To the American-born slaves, these Africans represented the presence and mystery of a powerful sacred past. While some blacks converted to Christianity and a few adhered to Islam, others maintained the beliefs of their forebears through their observance of modified African ceremonies. Accordingly, the religion of slaves consisted of widely differing innovations of traditions and beliefs.

African-American folk religion thus emerged as a composite creation, drawn from scattered elements of older cultural memories and grafted New World traditions that were later passed on from generation to generation. An "invisible institution," the folk Christianity of the slave quarters developed as a religion of the vernacular. As a community, slaves prayed, sang, "shouted," and preached to one another in the manner and styles reminiscent of their African heritage. The emphasis on the verbal medium in performance generated the distinctive vocal traditions that became characteristic of African-American liturgy, including the inventive oral repertory of chanted sermon and song.

Other traditions made real the power and presence of the supernatural in human life. Belief in a variety of mysterious beings, including hags, witches, and ghosts, suggests that for many African Americans the spiritual world was alive and immediate, active with forces ominous and threatening. Sacred folk beliefs were derived from Old and New World sources: local variations of Haitian-derived vodun (see Voodoo), the interpretation of signs, the usage of charms, and the mystical knowledge of conjurers, root workers, and *hoodoo* practitioners, who tapped supernatural forces for prediction and protection. Although many of these traditions were deeply embedded in black folklore, they reflected viable perspectives on spirituality, the need for control and explanation that leads to religious thought.

Healing, another prominent dimension of African-American folk religion, was practiced by specialists who combined knowledge of traditional remedies with holistic therapy. As in Africa, the onset of sickness was understood by many blacks to have both physical and spiritual implications. Folk religion undergirded African-American faith in skilled practitioners who were able to counteract ailments with herbal and natural medicines, as well as techniques such as prayer. Folk beliefs also offered a theory or explanation for why such afflictions might occur. For example, illness was often thought to be caused by negative spiritual forces. In the early twentieth century, some of these latter impulses would find their way into sectarian Christianity, within groups such as the Holiness Movement, and Pentecostalism, churches that emphasized faith healing and physical wholeness through spiritual power.

With the drastic demographic shifts and movements in black life during the late nineteenth and early twentieth centuries, from South to North and from countryside to city, African-American folk religion took on a broader significance. The "old-time" revivalist traditions of worship in the rural churches would no longer be restricted to the South, as thousands of migrants made their way to northern urban areas. Relocating in search of new prospects and new lives, they brought their local traditions and beliefs with them, establishing new religious institutions within storefronts and homes. Many of these transplanted folk churches recalled features of African religion, especially the emphasis on emotional styles of worship, call and response, spirituals, and Holy Ghost spirit possession.

The folk religion of blacks also lived on in noninstitutionalized forms within urban centers. African-American conjurers, healers, and other specialists underwent a metamorphosis, some reemerging as leaders within the so-called cults and sects of the cities, and others setting up within occult shops and botanicas as spiritual advisers. This vast network of urban practitioners attracted devotees from diverse religious backgrounds, including members of the mainstream Christian denominations, who found in these traditions resolution and assistance for day-to-day concerns.

Although black folk religion continues to be varied and eclectic in its manifestations, it demonstrates a com-mon orientation toward spirituality that is dynamic, experimental, and intensely pragmatic. Characterized by pluralism, folk beliefs fulfill diverse needs and functions that cut across doctrinal barriers and creedal differences. They constitute a way of life that is at the heart of the African-American religious experience.

See also Africanisms; Candomblé; Religion; Santería; Voodoo; Yoruba Religion and Culture in the Americas

■ ■ *Bibliography*

Andrews, Dale P. *Practical Theology for Black Churches: Bridging Black Theology and African American Folk Religion.* Louisville, Ky.: Westminster John Knox Press, 2002.

Fauset, Arthur Huff. *Black Gods of the Metropolis: Negro Cults in the Urban North.* Philadelphia: University of Pennsylvania Press, 1944.

Hurston, Zora Neale. *The Sanctified Church.* Berkeley, Calif.: Turtle Island Foundation, 1981.

Levine, Lawrence. *Black Culture and Black Consciousness: Afro-American Folk Thought from Slavery to Freedom.* New York: Oxford University Press, 1977.

Puckett, Newbell Niles. *Folk Beliefs of the Southern Negro.* Chapel Hill: University of North Carolina Press, 1926.

Raboteau, Albert J. *Slave Religion: The Invisible Institution in the Antebellum South.* New York: Oxford University Press, 1978.

YVONNE P. CHIREAU (1996)
Updated by publisher 2005

FOOD AND CUISINE
▬ ▬ ▬ ━━━━━━

This entry consists of two distinct articles with differing geographic domains.

> FOOD AND CUISINE, LATIN AMERICAN AND CARIBBEAN
> *Diane M. Spivey*
>
> FOOD AND CUISINE, U.S.
> *Quandra Prettyman*

LATIN AMERICAN AND CARIBBEAN FOOD AND CUISINE

The forced migration of Africans to the Americas by way of the slave trade brought culinary artists, expert agriculturalists, and metallurgists, as well as African-derived beliefs regarding the omnipotence of blacksmiths. Trinidad and Tobago, for example, have yearly feasts to honor the Yoruba deity Ogun, the god of iron and of revolution. Bondsmen and women perceived iron as both the enslaving shackles of Europeans and the African's tool of liberation.

Self-liberation and cultural retention were synonymous with the formation of Maroon societies—known as *quilombos* in Brazil, *palenques* in Colombia and Cuba, and *cumbes* in Venezuela—created by Africans who escaped into forests, hills, and bush areas of the Caribbean and South America. Once isolated, they formed their own communities, where many African culinary and other cultural patterns could be preserved. Maroon communities, however, were not the only societies dominated by African traditions. The continual influx and steady increase of Africans into the Caribbean and South America constantly rejuvenated African cultures, a persistent African cultural input, and a culinary revolution under the influence of Africans that would permeate every aspect of cooking and cuisine in rural and urban areas of every country in the Americas.

THE CUISINE OF THE CARIBBEAN

One region that became home to African cuisine and culture was the Caribbean, including economically and culturally the South American countries of Guyana, Suriname, and French Guiana. Although geographically located in Central America, Belize and Mexico's Cancún and Cozumel are also part of the Caribbean. Mexicans of identifiable African descent are estimated at 120,000 to 300,000 persons, many of whom are farmers clinging to their ancestral roots and who live in Mexican towns such as Cuajiniculapa (formerly called "Little Africa"), located in the southwest corner of the state of Guerrero. Popular African-Mexican foods include *mondongo* (pig intestines), or chitlins in English. Many of these farm communities grow sesame seeds, beans, corn, and hot peppers, and they stew chicken with bananas, prunes, tomatoes, and *chicha* (corn liquor).

Mexico's neighbor, Belize, is home to the Garifuna, the descendants of the Black Caribs, a Maroon society on the island of St. Vincent. Before the Black Caribs' conquest by the British and their subsequent exile in 1797 from St. Vincent to Trujillo, Belize, and Roatan Island, off the coast of Honduras, their fishing and agricultural techniques produced an array of traditional dishes. Still served by the Garifuna are *boiline*, a stew combining fruits and vegetables with fish and dumplings; *hudut* (also known as *fufu* in Africa and Jamaica), small cakes formed from boiled and mashed plantains, then wrapped in banana leaves and steamed or roasted; *tapau*, consisting of fish and green ba-

nanas in coconut milk; and various chicken dishes and *bimekakule*, or puddings. The achiote seed is not only the source of red *gusewe* dye, produced by the Garifuna, but is also ground to make achiote paste for *recado*, an ingredient still added to stewed pork dishes. Breads include *areba*, or cassava bread, an important food symbol and indispensable item for the ritual *dugu*; and *bachati*, a fried bread consumed at the morning meal. The Caribbean also provides the Garifuna with lobster and conch, which is turned into ceviche and conch fritters. Seafood is steamed and barbecued, and when stewed with okra, pigeon peas, tomatoes, and hot peppers, it takes on the characteristics of gumbo. When seafood is not on the menu, pickled pig's tail and baking powder "biscuits" are the favorites. Coconut bread made with refined wheat flour and yeast is prominent in everyday meals. Beans and rice are also stewed together with the key flavor ingredient, coconut milk. These dishes are part of the standard repertoire at mealtime and consumed during religions celebrations and feasts for the deceased. The Black Caribs gradually migrated from Roatan along the coastal regions of Central America. As of the late 1990s, nearly 350,000 descendants lived in towns and villages in Belize, Honduras, Nicaragua, and Guatemala along a narrow coastal strip facing the Caribbean Sea.

Residents along this strip know that there is no shortage of libations, alcoholic and spirit-free, in the Caribbean's collection. One is ginger beer, made with fresh ginger boiled with cinnamon and cloves, then sweetened. A similar recipe produces mauby, which makes use of mauby bark, or tree bark, and is consumed as part of numerous social rituals. In addition, the tamarind fruit, indigenous to East Africa and grown in many areas of the Caribbean, is offered on many celebratory occasions in the form of the tamarind drink. Puerto Rico's *coquito*, a complex combination of eggs, rum, sweetened condensed milk, coconut, and spices, and Trinidad's peanut punch, which blends peanut butter with vanilla extract, eggs, milk, and rum, are tropical cocktails. For those who claim to drink strictly for medicinal purposes there is ti-punch, Martinique's lime juice and white rum cooler, as well as *muzik di zumbi* (which translates in Curaçao, Bonaire, and Aruba as "spirit music," a combination of reggae, African rhythms, and South American music), a mango, grenadine, rum, and lime juice concoction served in a sugar-rimmed glass.

These and many other creations accompany Curaçaoan soups containing *kadushi* cactus stem, crushed and ground into pulp. Curaçao's *giambo*, an okra soup, is sometimes presented with *funchi*, or *funche*, a moist cornmeal bread. In Nevis corn is also turned into mealtime staples along with pigeon peas, yams, sweet potatoes, cassava, bananas, and fruits from citrus trees. Highland garden farming and agriculture in St. Kitts is said to be a throwback to plantation days, when mountain plots were allocated for slave farming. As these plots are still estate owned, many villagers view highland farming with disdain. Private gardens in St. Kitts, however, typically produce pumpkins, potatoes, eggplant, beans, peppers, mangos, bananas, pineapples, coconut, citrus fruit, and breadfruit. Chickens and pigs are commonly kept and turned into such dishes as chicken cooked with pineapple, the sauce thickened with arrowroot, a popular cooking starch known to have medicinal properties and a high-volume export from St. Vincent; and pigs' feet with lime juice and onions. As late as the 1970s, Dieppe Bay, Sandy Point, Old Road Town, and Basseterre were bountiful fishing areas in St. Kitts, as was the Charlestown areas of Nevis.

Seafood dishes, including mussel pie, conch stew, and shark hash, as well as cassava pie, black-eyed peas and rice, and a chicken- and pork-filled baked pastry made from shredded cassava, to name just a few dishes, share the bill of fare during festival cricket in Bermuda. Like Carnival, celebrated in major cities in the Americas, and for which long periods of preparation are the tradition, festival cricket is said to be the time of "eating and drinking everything in Bermuda." High on surrounding hillsides, Rastafarians consume their vegetarian and health food dishes and philosophize about the ostentation and extravagance of the festival while "translat[ing] the festival ambiance into poetry" (Manning, 1998, p. 467).

A poetic culinary metaphor has been used to describe Cuban and Puerto Rican nationalist identity, just as the African dishes gumbo and jambalaya have been used to define many aspects of culture in Louisiana. *Ajiaco,* or *sancocho,* is a stew made up of spices, meats, and tubers from Africa and the Caribbean. Prepared in the Dominican Republic and on all the Spanish-speaking islands, *sancocho* is sometimes prepared with goat's head and salt pork in place of beef and/or chicken with pork. Hot peppers, yams, calalu—a type of spinach used in cooking and a staple West Indian soup throughout the Caribbean—cassava, rum, plantains, and pumpkin are some of the ingredients blended into this savory stew. Throughout Cuba's history the descendants of Africans have maintained distinct culinary traditions by way of soups, stews, and other meat dishes. *Sopa de pollo* (chicken soup) and *picadillo,* or beef simmered with orange annatto oil—a substitute for Africa's orange palm oil—are two such dishes still eaten today. During the era of slavery African domestics enriched the diets of planters in Cuba and became indispensable culi-

nary artisans. Many African cooks in bondage in the French colonized islands were reported to be male; however, in 1859 Cuba, black male cooks were famous as well. Although black Cubans were excluded from baking and pastry-making trades in the 1940s, they nevertheless continued their African tradition of bean cakes, meal dumplings, yam fritters, and tea buns, all of which were side dishes, as well as breads and desserts, baked or fried in hot oil. *Bunuelos de viento* are deep-fried dumplings drizzled with a sweet syrup and served as dessert in Cuba, the Dominican Republic, and Puerto Rico.

Tembleque, made with coconut milk, sugar, and arrowroot or cornstarch for thickening, is a popular coconut custard for African Antilleans in the Puerto Rican coastal towns of Maunabo, Patillas, Arroyo, and Guayama in the southeast. *Tembleque* and *flan de pina,* made with pineapple juice, eggs, rum, and liqueur or sherry, are both custard desserts seen on holiday and party tables in Puerto Rico, along with *lechon asado* (roast pig); *mofongo,* a spicy, garlic-flavored ground plantain side dish; and *chicharrones* (pork cracklings) and *tostones de plantano verde* (deep-fried plantains) for appetizers and snacks.

The Bahamas and Barbados are famous for their breadfruit, *christophene,* and salt fish hors d'oeuvres, as is Jamaica for one of its most famous appetizers/snacks, stamp and go, which is fried codfish fritters. Follow-up courses include mannish water, a traditional Jamaican soup consisting of goat's head and feet, pumpkin and plantain, potatoes, hot peppers, and spinners— which are small dumplings cooked in the hot broth; and fish tea, a seafood stew with a savory broth made from fish heads. Main meals include curried goat and jerk pork and chicken—the jerk process requires marinating meats in spices and hot peppers, then grilling or roasting over a fire made of aromatic leaves and branches. All of these dishes are part of a contemporary repertoire of African creations brought to Jamaican towns and rural areas and to iron-manufacturing communities in the eighteenth century, such as that of John Reeder's Foundry in Morant Bay.

Culinary creations produced in Guadeloupe, Martinique, and Haiti were also expressions of African cultural retentions. Haiti, the premier French-colonized island and the jewel of the Caribbean in the eighteenth century, catapulted French culinary society and economy to unparalleled heights by way of its slave labor in the kitchen. However, slave laborers in Saint Domingue (Haiti) and elsewhere were often underfed, and as with a number of slave societies in the Americas, bondsmen and -women had to cultivate a small piece of land for their own dietary upkeep. Although their rations were meager, African cooks in Saint Domingue prepared sumptuous meals for the planter/owners that remain permanent fixtures in Haiti and France. *Giraumon* soup and *griot* are samples of the fare prepared by Haitian cooks. Pumpkin is referred to as *giraumon* in the former French-colonized islands. In *giraumon* soup, pumpkin is seasoned with nutmeg, spices, and salt beef. *Griot* is a popular fried-pork appetizer/main dish. Other favorites include okra rice and fish (or chicken) braised in coconut milk and peanut sauce.

THE CUISINE OF SOUTH AMERICA

A popular Peruvian saying states that *"El que no tiene de inca, tiene de mandinga"* ("whoever does not have Incan ancestry has African ancestry"). The same statement, regarding African ancestry, is true for many of South America's thirteen countries. Black communities emerged in all South American countries as a result of the slave trade, marronage, and immigration. Black populations are said to range from less than 1 percent to as high as 30 percent in Colombia and between 50 and 75 percent in Brazil. Present throughout the societies is the African contribution to cuisine.

One of Africa's culinary legacies in the Santiago, Rancagua, Maule, and Aconcagua regions of Chile is bean soups—and there are numerous versions throughout South America—made with hot peppers, one to three kinds of peas or beans, and tomatoes and onions; *sopa de pescado* (fish soup), made with a hearty fish stock, shellfish, and vegetables; and a version of *humitas* (Chilean tamales), which are fresh corn husks stuffed with grated corn and chopped onions. *Bori-bori,* a seasoned broth with meat and dumplings, became a Paraguayan favorite after the establishment of the settlement of Laurelty, formed in 1820 by fifty African and mulatto followers of Uruguayan patriot José Artigas.

Uruguay's city of Montevideo was the port of entry for Africans in slavery bound for other parts of the region. At the same time, many Brazilian slaves sought freedom through escape to northern and eastern Uruguay and settled into areas such as Salto, Rivera, Artigas, Tacuarembó, and Cerro Largo, regions where the majority of black Uruguayans are found today. A favorite dish is *puchero,* a heavily seasoned poultry and sausage dish, braised with a variety of vegetables and sometimes referred to as *olla podrida,* or "rotten pot," although there is nothing rotten about it. *Yerba mate,* a drink served hot and cold, is made from dried yerba leaves, a shrub of the holly family that grows wild on the upper Paraguay River. *Yerba mate* is caffeine rich and is sometimes consumed in Uruguay, Paraguay, and other countries instead of coffee and tea.

Uruguay's Montevideo and Argentina's Buenos Aires are part of the Rio de la Plata region that received African bondspeople by way of Brazil. Memoirs of life in early nineteenth-century Buenos Aires never failed to mention black street vendors who monopolized the business, hawking all sorts of produce and dairy products, pastries and meat pies (*empanadas*), and a very famous *mazamorra* (corn chowder). One item sold by African street vendors emerged as a pattern of consumption forced on the African-Argentine community because of its poverty. Africans worked at slaughterhouses, salvaging cast-off (tripe, lung, and other organs) and diseased meat from slaughtered animals. *Achuradoras,* as they were called, sold this cast-off meat to blacks and poor whites. African Argentines thus gave Argentina one of its most famous dishes—*chinchulines,* which are braided and grilled intestines, or as southern U.S. blacks call them, chitlins. Such dishes are still served in black Argentine neighborhoods in outlying areas of Barracas, Flores, Floresta, and Boca.

Africans in Peru were frequently seen in the city of Lima and the port of Callao, as both depended largely on black labor for provisions. As in Buenos Aires, Africans worked in Lima's meat market and slaughterhouse, where they processed the meat used aboard navy ships. Male and female, slave and free, were extensively employed in the preparation and sale of preserves and candied fruit, pastries, bread, and hardtack (a saltless, hard biscuit or bread made of flour and water) for sailors. Black female food vendors (*vivenderas*) sold food to the masses, including donuts and confections, cheese, milk, whipped cream, various main dishes, and desserts of African origin, such as *anticucho bereber, sanguito naju del Congo* (a wheat-based dessert), *choncholi* (tripe brochettes), and, seasonally, the drinks *chicha de terranova* (corn liquor) and mead, all of which are still consumed today. Black male traveling street sellers (*pregoneros*) also produced and sold food products, especially sweets.

Today the communities and towns of African descendants include Callejón and the *callejones* (barrios), where urban popular culture took root and flourished, Yapatera (Piura), Zaña (Chiclayo) in the northern zone, Aucallama and Cañete on the central coast, and Chincha in the southern zone. These descendants still transmit their values, beliefs, and culture through the variety and flavors imparted to soups and other dishes handed down by African-Peruvian women and men who introduced them into Peru's popular cuisine and helped spread African culinary traditions throughout the country.

An extra helping of African culinary traditions would spread throughout Ecuador in the nineteenth century by way of Jamaicans who migrated into the country as laborers to help build the railway. Today, in Carchi and Imbabura at least 40 percent of the population has full or part

African blood. African Ecuadorians are also concentrated in the southern province of Loja and have been in Esmeraldas, the preeminent center of black settlement, since the sixteenth century. The lush vegetation in Esmeraldas has helped their cultural and culinary survival, allowing them to grow for northern markets and for their own consumption bananas, grapes, watermelon, plantains and citrus fruits, papaya, onions, tomatoes, sweet potatoes, avocados, anise, beans, manioc (cassava), and other crops. Game such as wild peccary (or *tatabro*), paca (or *guagua*), agouti (or *guatin*), wild pig, wild fowl, squirrels, rabbit, iguanas, and tortoises are all made into stews. Shellfish and seafood are obtained by traditional African hunting and fishing methods, and typical meals include fish and potato soup; the national dish, *ceviche de concha*, prepared with raw or cooked mussels, onions, *aji* (hot peppers), and lemon; and fried fish and potato cakes. Dishes with crab and shrimp are considered delicacies. Fruits and cooked root crops are pounded and fried and served with meat or fish; *culada*, a pounded and fried fish and plantain mixture, is served in the morning. Other dishes include *seco de pescado*, or fish with coconut; *sancocho*, a combination of meat, plantains, sweet manioc, and a tuber resembling taro called *rascadera; seco*, or concha with coconut; *locro de yucca*, meat with sweet manioc; and green boiled plantains, known as *pean piado*, which are eaten with most meals in place of bread.

Guarapo, a sugarcane beer; *aguardiente*, a potent liquor served by the shot with green mango or orange slices as a chaser; and *champus*, a cold *chirimoya* fruit drink, are all consumed with and without meals by indigenous and African-descendant populations in Ecuador and Colombia. Colombia has one of the largest black populations in the Spanish-speaking Americas, forming 80 to 90 percent of the population in the Pacific coastal region. The city of Cartagena is still home to the former *palenque* (Maroon) settlement of el Palenque de San Basilio, a village founded by runaway slaves *(palenqueros)* in the seventeenth century, who have developed a so-called Creole language yet managed to preserve many aspects of Angolan (Southwest African) culture. African-Colombian populations can also be found in the areas of Cauca, Valle, Bolívar, Caldas and Chocó. Sophisticated farming systems of forest farming communities, such as the Afro-Baudoseno, grow rice, corn, plantains, and fruit trees on one of the riverbanks while managing pigs on the other. One of their favorite foods is leafcup. Known as *arboloco* in Colombia, it is a sweet root eaten raw after exposure in the sun for several days. Easy to digest, it is used in the diets of invalids. Other favorites include the meat soup *sancocho*, vegetable tamales, corn *empanadas, chuzos* (kebabs), fried fish, *chorizos*

(sausages), *arepas de chocolo* (sweet corn cakes), rice and coconut dishes, and *patacones* (sliced plantains).

Preparations such as *quineo k'asurata,* a type of banana, peeled while green, then sun-dried for a few days before eaten boiled; beef, rice, and avocado dishes; and salt fish from Lake Titicaca are favorite meal items of the Yungas populations in Bolivia. The largest concentrations of African Bolivians are in the city of La Paz, the capital of Bolivia, and in the nearby agricultural provinces of Nor and Sud Yungas, on the eastern slopes of the Andes mountain range. The village of Mururata is home to a black population, as is the smaller village of Tocana, in La Paz's Nor Yungas Province. Tocanans cultivate bananas and citrus fruits, coffee beans, and coca, and speak a vocabulary that is a mix of African words, Aymara (the language of the mountain indigenous people), and Spanish. The location of the Yungas, with its semitropical valleys, has made the region an oasis of crop production. The greatest concentration of crops is grown in the Yungas provinces of La Paz and Cochabamba. Bolivians produce a wide range of vegetables, fruits, and other food crops, mostly for local consumption. Principal vegetable crops include kidney beans, green beans, chickpeas, green peas, lettuce, cabbage, tomatoes, carrots, onions, garlic, and chili peppers. One of the oldest cultivated Andean plants, *arracacha* (white carrot), known as *lakachu* in Aymara, is eaten boiled or as an ingredient in soups and stews; it is also roasted and fried in slices, and used as a puree.

Hervido (meat stew), as it is called in Venezuela, is a nourishing meat and vegetable dish enjoyed in many communities and during many religious and secular festivals, such as Los Tambores de Barlovento (Drums of Barlovento), celebrated at the beginning of the rainy season in March near Corpus Christi, in Barlovento, Miranda state. This is the region comprising the towns of Curiepe, Higuerote, Caucagua, Tacarigua, and others with large black populations. The Drums of Barlovento is an African-Caribbean tradition in which drums are the main theme complemented by various other wooden instruments of African origin. As in Ecuador, in addition to African importation for slave labor in agriculture, Venezuela imported blacks from the Caribbean (Trinidad, Aruba, Puerto Rico, and St. Thomas) to work the gold mines of El Callao in the state of Bolívar, in the south of the country, and by 1810 the majority of Venezuelans were of African blood. The descendants of Antillean immigrants still eat their traditional versions of calalu with salted codfish; *tarquery*, a meat and curry recipe from India that is very popular in Trinidad; and gateau, dumplings and *bolos.* They drink *yinya bie* and *mabi,* drinks that originated in Trinidad. African cultural survival can also be seen in Aripao, a community formed by descendants of runaway slaves living on the east bank of Lower Caura River in the northwestern region of Bolívar State. As in Bolivia, *arracacha* is consumed; the leaves are used in the same way as celery in raw or cooked salads. Venezuelans refer to it as "Creole celery."

"Creolization" was evident in the way African linguistic structure and expression influenced the Portuguese language in Brazil, the largest country in South America. However, every segment and enclave of Brazilian society, including its *quilombos* (Maroon communities), were influenced by, or had as its base, African cuisine and culture. "Negroes of the Palm Forests," or Palmares, was one of the most famous *quilombos*. Its residents were settled cultivators, producing maize, fruits, and all sorts of cereal and vegetables crops, which they stored in granaries against harsh weather and attack. They also supplemented their food supply with domesticated animals, fishing, and hunting. But those same customs and practices of African culinary culture that fed and gave security and continuity to the inhabitants of the ten major *quilombos* in Brazil permeated Brazilian cuisine in general. *Feijoada*, a rich combination of beans, blood sausages, and different cuts of pork or beef; *caruru*, prepared with leafy greens and smoked fish and dried shrimp, hot peppers, okra, and peanuts; *acaraje*, a bean flour and dried shrimp fritter; as well as coconut sauces and soups to complement a variety of seafood delicacies are only a few of the African dishes brought to Brazil.

THE CUISINE OF THE GUIANAS

In Brazil and throughout African America, as Richard Price points out, "[C]ooking and eating were core areas of cultural resistance and persistence, as well as foci of ongoing creativity and dynamism" (1991, p. 107). Much culinary and cultural resistance can still be observed in Suriname, formerly colonized by Holland; French Guiana, an "Overseas Department" of France, and thus considered an integral part of the French nation; and Guyana, formerly colonized by the British. All three countries sit side by side in the northeast corner of South America, bordering northern Brazil. People of African descent residing in Guyana prepare a multitude of fish dishes from bounty available all along the seacoast, such as double-belly basham, eyewater, red snapper, kingfish, patwa rock fish, and many others; as well as from rivers and canals providing shrimp, crab, clam, and mussels. Rice, yams, various tubers, mangos, coconuts, the oil palm, and other fruits are used in such dishes as pumpkin stewed with rice. All kinds of vegetables are sautéed and stewed, or baked with tomatoes, onions, and cinnamon, and remain a part of the vast variety of West African foods and spices imported into Guyana along with the traditions of meat and fish stews and *fufu*. "Bush meats," pork, chicken, mutton, beef, and goat are casseroled, roasted, barbecued, fried, and ground to produce a number of savory dishes, including garlic pork and beef baked with leafy greens and carrots, and various meat loaves.

Wedged between Guyana and Guiana is Suriname, the location of what are believed to be the best preserved African cultural patterns in the Western Hemisphere. Suriname is home to the descendants of the Saramaka (Saramacca, or Saramaccaners), who live along the banks of the Suriname River, and the Djuka Maroons (they prefer the term Aucans or Aucanners), communities formed in the early eighteenth century. Referring to themselves as "river" and "bush" people—there are other "bush" groups, such as the Matuari (or Matawai), Paramacca, and Boni—these Maroon descendants can be found in villages from a few miles south of the Atlantic Ocean down to the Brazilian border.

The ancestors of the Saramaka were agricultural specialists who already had a unique horticultural calendar set up by the mid-eighteenth century. Early Saramakans cultivated the same enormous array of crops their descendants produce today. One such crop is rice. Known as *alesi*, the seventy cultivated varieties comprise much of their current diet, although wild rice is grown today only for use in rituals to honor their eighteenth-century ancestors. Rice processing is carried out using African utensils and methods and the process is nearly identical to that of South Carolina plantation blacks during slavery. A mere sample of the game meat, fish, and birds, preserved primarily by smoking and salting, includes *akusuwe*, a kind of rabbit; *mbata*, a small deer; *malole*, which is armadillo; and *awali*, or opossum, eaten only when nothing else is available to accompany rice. Rounding out their larder is the tree porcupine, known as *adjindja*, in addition to *logoso* (turtle), *akomu* (eel), *peenya* (piranha), and *nyumaa*, or *pataka*, spoken of as "the best fish in the country." *Anamu* (bush hen), *maai* (bush turkey), *gbanini* (eagle), *patupatu* (wild duck), *soosoo* (large parakeet), and *pumba* (blue and red parrot) are also consumed in abundance. Large quantities of meat and fish are shared through family networks, lessening the need for preservation. Preparation of foods includes roasting, frying, boiling, or browning meats first in one or more of five varieties of palm oil, then simmering with vegetables and/or root crops and one or more of ten cultivated varieties of hot peppers. Fifteen varieties of okra are cultivated, along with *mboa* and *bokolele* (*mboa* is amaranth, but both are called wild spinach). *Tonka* (beans), seven varieties of yams, tania, cashews and peanuts, and wild limes, watermelon, lemons, oranges, and pineapples, and other fruits of African origin are also grown.

SUMMARY

From the fifteenth through the nineteenth centuries, Africans, as slaves, contributed their labor skills, religion, music, and culinary expertise to create societies and cultures in every country in the Americas. The reinvention of culinary traditions and social patterns based on African heritage demonstrated strong cultural persistence and resistance within plantation, and especially Maroon, communities, which were established wherever slavery existed.

Similarities in African culinary heritage, shared throughout Latin America and the Caribbean, have left enduring legacies. Those legacies are filled with cooking and cuisine strongly reminiscent of, or identical to, those of their African forebears and therefore continue to transmit the values and enrich the culinary experiences of not only Africans in the Americas but most other cultures in the Americas as well. Although these nations have adopted African culinary traditions as their own, in most cases there is little or no recognition of their roots. Too often seen as backward and lacking in value, the African contribution is regularly subjected to racism and societal repression. For Africans and their descendants in the Americas, food and its preparation are deeply infused with social and cultural meaning rooted in African traditions and have always held an intrinsic role in creating, preserving, and transmitting expressions of ethnic cohesion and continuity. It is hoped that there will be an eventual appreciation of African culinary heritage not just in Latin America and the Caribbean but throughout the world.

See also Africanisms; Food and Cuisine, U.S.

■ ■ *Bibliography*

Bastide, Roger. *African Civilisations in the New World.* New York: Harper, 1971.

Cools-Lartigue, Yolande. *The Art of Caribbean Cooking.* Richmond, B.C., Canada: KoolArt, 1983.

Counter, S. Allen, and David L. Evans. *I Sought My Brother: An Afro-American Reunion.* Cambridge, Mass.: MIT Press, 1981.

Gonzalez, Nancie L. *Sojourners of the Caribbean.* Urbana and Chicago: University of Illinois Press, 1988.

HISPA. *Buen Provecho: 500 Years of Hispanic Cuisine.* Basking Ridge, N.J.: Hispanic Association of AT&T Employees, New Jersey Chapter, 1995.

Irwin, Graham W. *Africans Abroad: A Documentary of the Black Diaspora in Asia, Latin America, and the Caribbean During the Age of Slavery.* New York: Columbia University Press, 1977.

John, Yvonne. *Guyanese Seed of Soul.* Holly Hill, S.C.: R&M, 1980.

Kloos, Peter. *The Maroni River Caribs of Surinam.* Assen, Netherlands: Van Gorcum, 1971.

Lalbachan, Pamela. *The Complete Caribbean Cookbook.* Vancouver: Raincoast Books, 1994.

Manning, Frank E. "Celebrating Cricket: The Symbolic Construction of Caribbean Politics (Bermuda)." In *Blackness in Latin America and the Caribbean: Social Dynamics and Cultural Transformations,* Vol. 2: *Eastern South America and the Caribbean,* edited by Norman E. Whitten Jr. and Arlene Torres. Bloomington: Indiana University Press, 1998.

Moore, Carlos, Tanya R. Saunders, and Shawna Moore, eds. *African Presence in the Americas.* Trenton, N.J.: Africa World Press, 1995.

Mutunhu, Tendai. "Africa: The Birthplace of Iron Mining." *Negro History Bulletin* 44, no. 1 (1981): 5–20.

Price, Richard. "Subsistence on the Plantation Periphery: Crops, Cooking, and Labour Among Eighteenth-Century Suriname Maroons." In *The Slaves Economy: Independent Production by Slaves in the Americas,* edited by I. Berlin and P. D. Morgan. London: Frank Cass, 1991.

Rahier, Jean. "Blackness as a Process of Creolization: The Afro-Esmeraldian Decimas (Ecuador)." In *The African Diaspora: African Origins and New World Identities,* edited by I. Okpewho, C. B. Davies, and A. A. Mazrui. Bloomington and Indianapolis: Indiana University Press, 1999.

Rama, Carlos M. "The Passing of the Afro-Uruguayans From Caste Society into Class Society." In *Race and Class in Latin America,* edited by M. Mörner. New York and London: Columbia University Press, 1970.

Rojas-Lombardi, Felipe. *The Art of South American Cooking.* New York: HarperCollins, 1991.

Rout, Leslie B., Jr. *The African Experience in Spanish America, 1502 to the Present Day.* Cambridge: Cambridge University Press, 1976.

Spivey, Diane M. *The Peppers, Cracklings, and Knots of Wool Cookbook: The Global Migration of African Cuisine.* Albany: State University of New York Press, 1999.

Torres, Arlene, and Norman E. Whitten Jr., eds. *Blackness in Latin America and the Caribbean: Social Dynamics and Cultural Transformations,* Vol. 2: *Eastern South America and the Caribbean.* Bloomington and Indianapolis: Indiana University Press, 1998.

Wiseman, Winston C. *Cuisine from the Island of St. Vincent.* New York: Carlton, 1991.

DIANE M. SPIVEY (2005)

U.S. FOOD AND CUISINE

The African-American culinary tradition derives from the foods and methods of preparation of the African continent, the diasporic sojourn of the enslaved peoples in South America and the Caribbean, and the dominance of blacks in the preparation of food in the South for themselves as well as for the planter class. The tradition was sustained and enriched as blacks traveled northward during the Great Migrations. Although corn and corn products, pork and pork products, and greens are dominant, it is a diverse cuisine as reflected in the heavy use of seasonal fruits and vegetables. Notable among cooking techniques were frying in deep fat, stewing diverse chopped ingredients in a single pot, and seasoning with hot peppers. By way of the Caribbean, it included the barbecue. Characteristic dishes include greens boiled with salt pork, deep-fried chicken and beef, and one-pot dishes (e.g., gumbos). During the 1960s and 1970s this traditional cuisine was popularly called "soul food"; as the sine qua non of southern cooking, it is the most universally identified American cuisine.

THE FIRST SOURCE: THE OLD HOMELAND

The transmigration of plants makes points of origin arguable, but it is generally acknowledged that Africans were responsible for the presence of certain foods (some of which, for example the peanut, had traveled from the New World to the Old World to Africa and back to the New World) in eighteenth- and nineteenth-century America. Before their arrival in the United States, West Africans, for example, had become familiar with corn, and Africans, particularly from Sierra Leone, were major rice cultivators. Although food historians differ, most include cowpeas (black-eyed peas), okra, peanuts, sesame, watermelon, and yams among the products that came to the United States directly with African slaves through the provisioning of slave ships, through items the slaves transported, or through trade with the West Indies. For some foods, the African origins of American use are evidenced linguistically (e.g., *gumbo* from the Tshiluba *kingombo* and Umbundo *tchingombo*); Americans used the word *pinder* (Congo *mpindo*) in the eighteenth century and the Bantu *goober* in the nineteenth, both as alternatives to the term *peanut*. Some sobriquets point to African sources as well (e.g., *guinea hen, guinea corn, guinea pepper*).

In addition to certain foods, Africans brought their familiar methods of preparation. To six practices (boiling in water, steaming in leaves, frying in deep oil, toasting beside the fire, roasting in the fire, baking in ashes) identified by anthropologist William Bascom, Jessica Harris adds seven as "emblematic of African-inspired cooking" (1995, p. 21): preparing composed rice dishes, creating various types of fritters, flavoring with smoked ingredients, thickening with okra, thickening with nuts and seeds, seasoning with hot sauces, and using leafy vegetables, such as collards.

THE SECOND SOURCE: COOKING IN THE AMERICAN SOUTH

The diverse origins of the slave population, the changing historical eras as the South moved from a pioneer society to a plantation one, and variations in the size, location, and tasks of the workforce as well as in the practices of slaveholders make most generalizations arguable. The African-American culinary tradition would develop from what the slaves wrought with their limited resources and from the preparation of food for their owners.

Those resources consisted of such rations (commonly corn and pork products) as were issued by the owners, supplemented by undesirable cast-offs, such as pigs' feet, pigs' tails, hog maw (the stomach), hog jowl, ham hocks, chitterlings, and neck and back bones, and bottom-feeding fish such as catfish. These were augmented, where possible, with food slaves gathered themselves through gardening, fishing, and hunting, particularly such nocturnal animals as the raccoon and the opossum. Some slaves were able to raise chickens, but usually for trade or barter rather than the common table.

Typically the ration resembled that described by former slave Allen Parker (1895): "The common allowance of a slave was four quarts of Indian meal and five pounds of salt pork. Sometimes one quart of molasses, per week, and all the sweet potatoes that they wanted. Whatever else they had, had to be earned by over work, or by selling a part of their allowance." Cooking was done on open fireplaces, as described by Parker: "The cooking utensils were few and all of the simplist [sic] kind. A long handled shallow iron skillet with long legs did duty as a spider in which to fry our salt pork, bacon and other meat, whenever we could get it. It was also sometimes used to bake 'hoe cake' in. These hoe cakes, which formed a large part of the slave's bill of fare, were made of Indian meal, and water with a little salt and sometimes a quantity of pork fat was added."

Neither the deficient food supplies nor the inadequate cooking apparatus limited the repertory of African-American traditional cuisine. As Parker observes, "On some plantations each slave had to do his or her own cooking, but on the others there was a cookhouse called the kitchen where not only food for the master's family was cooked, but also the food of such slaves as did not live in families." A significant part of the African-American culinary tradition would develop from the food slaves prepared for "the master's family"—choice cuts of meat, dairy products, and rich desserts. Out of such kitchens would come the feasts remembered by travelers. Hilliard (1988) reports an 1832 meal at Alston plantation that included turtle soup, a leg of boiled mutton, turtle steaks and fins, macaroni pie, oysters, boiled ham, venison haunch, roast turkey, bread pudding, jelly ice cream, a pie, bananas, oranges, and apples.

African-American cuisine is enriched by two distinct regional foodways—Gullah, from coastal Georgia and South Carolina, and from Louisiana, Creole. The insularity and concentration of the Gullah/Geechee people in the Sea Islands and Low Country led to the most directly African-influenced foodways in North America; at the other extremity, the more cosmopolitan settlement of Louisiana led to a cuisine that, while abundantly indebted to the African presence, absorbed elements of Spanish and French cooking as well. Significant retentions of African foodways are found among the Gullah, even today, in dishes of indisputable African origins such as Jollof rice, red rice, peanut soup, benne wafers, and the variety of perlou (one-pot rice stews). It differs from inland cooking in the central place of rice, the staple crop nurtured by the slaves, and the availability of various fish and shellfish.

Creole cuisine, with its amalgamation of Native American, French, Spanish, and African foodways, is an integral part of African-American traditional cuisine. As in other parts of the South, Africans brought indigenous foundation foods and methods to Louisiana from both the continent and the Caribbean islands, and African Americans managed the preparation of meals. Out of the one-pot came the signature Creole dishes, jambalaya and gumbo; out of the deep fat came beignets.

From the cauldron of slavery, African Americans merged a survival cuisine and a celebratory one. For the former slaves, freedom did not mean a full table. In the South, it meant sharecropping and peonage, conditions that sustained their poverty and traditional foodways. An 1895–1896 Tuskegee study reveals meals closely resembling Allen Parker's: salt pork cooked in the fireplace, bacon grease mixed with molasses for "sap," and bread made from cornmeal and water cooked on a hoe. North and South, it often meant work as cooks and caterers culminating, ironically, in the iconic image of the black cook (Aunt Jemima, Uncle Ben) used by the food industry.

THE THIRD SOURCE: THE TRADITION TRAVELS TO THE CITY

As African Americans moved north, particularly during the second Great Migration, they carried their foodways. Confronted by the absence of places to eat on the road and by northern discrimination, and longing for the food of home, the migrants went into the food business in significant numbers; eating places (simple as chicken shacks and barbecue wagons, fancier as restaurants) and grocery stores in the 1930s were the businesses with the largest

group of black entrepreneurs. Upwardly mobile blacks adopted new foodways consistent with higher incomes (more meat, less offal), but everywhere the church supper kept the traditional communal meal alive. At picnics and revivals, one found, and finds, the fried chicken, fried fish, pigs' feet, corn bread, cornmeal dumplings, hominy grits, beans and rice, sweet potatoes, chitterlings, souse, greens with "pot likker," black-eyed peas, fritters, gumbos, macaroni and cheese, rice pudding, and peach cobbler that enslaved African Americans made to the United States' contribution to world cuisine.

Cookbooks reveal three major trends emerging in the 1990s. The first was a deepening awareness of the African sources of African-American foodways explored by Jessica Harris and Joseph Holloway and of the traditional aspects of African-American foodways in the work of Edna Lewis and the Darden sisters. The second focused on nutrition, reducing both the fat and salt content of traditional dishes with, for example, the substitution of smoked turkey for ham hocks and vegetable oils for lard; the rise of the Nation of Islam devalued pork as well. Third, after the long history of slavery where the indispensable black chef was a "cook" and of segregation where the distinguished black caterer and restaurateur was a "cook" came the emergence of African-American celebrity chefs such as Patrick Clark and Joe Randall.

See also Africanisms; Folk Arts and Crafts; Food and Cuisine, Latin American and Caribbean; Gullah

■ *Bibliography*

Cusick, Heidi Haughy. *Soul and Spice: African Cooking in the Americas.* San Francisco: Chronicle Books, 1995.

Harris, Jessica B. *Iron Pots and Wooden Spoons: Africa's Gifts to New World Cooking.* New York: Atheneum, 1989.

Harris, Jessica B. *The Welcome Table: African-American Heritage Cooking.* New York: Simon and Schuster, 1995.

Hilliard, Sam B. "Hog Meat and Cornpone: Foodways in the Antebellum South." In *Material Life in America, 1600–1860,* edited by Robert Blair St. George. Boston: Northeastern University Press, 1988.

Paige, Howard. *Aspects of African Foodways.* Southfield, Mich.: Aspects Publishing Company, 1999.

Parker, Allen. *Recollections of Slavery Times.* Worcester, Mass.: Chas. W. Burbank & Co., 1895.

Spivey, Diane M. *The Peppers, Cracklings, and Knots of Wool Cookbook: The Global Migration of African Cuisine.* Albany: State University of New York Press, 1999.

White, Joyce. *Soul Food: Recipes and Reflections from African-American Churches.* New York: HarperCollins, 1998.

QUANDRA PRETTYMAN (2005)

FOOTBALL

▗▖▗

American-style intercollegiate football emerged from the English sport of rugby during the 1870s and 1880s. Almost immediately, African Americans distinguished themselves on college gridirons.

BLACK PIONEERS AT PREDOMINANTLY WHITE COLLEGES, 1889–1919

William Henry Lewis and William Tecumseh Sherman Jackson were two of the first blacks to play football at a predominantly white college. Both of these Virginians played for Amherst College from 1889 through 1891. Jackson was a running back, while Lewis was a blocker. In 1891 Lewis served as captain of the Amherst squad. After graduation, he attended Harvard Law School, and because of the lax eligibility rules of the time, played two years for Harvard. In 1892 and 1893 Yale coach Walter Camp named Lewis to the Collier's All-American team at the position of center. After his playing days, Lewis became an offensive line coach at Harvard, the first black coach at a predominantly white college. He left football when President William Howard Taft appointed him as U.S. assistant attorney general in 1903.

William Arthur Johnson, George Jewett, and George Flippin were other early black players. Johnson appeared as a running back for MIT in 1890. That same year, Jewett was a running back, punter, and field-goal kicker for the University of Michigan. Flippin, who played running back for the University of Nebraska from 1892 to 1893, was an intense athlete who would not tolerate foul play. The press reported that in one game he "was kicked, slugged, and jumped on, but never knocked out, and gave as good as he received" (Ashe, vol. 1, p. 91). Flippin went on to become a physician. Other African Americans who played in the 1890s included Charles Cook (Cornell), Howard J. Lee (Harvard), George Chadwell (Williams), William Washington (Oberlin), and Alton Washington (Northwestern).

After the turn of the century, numerous blacks played football for northern and midwestern schools. Two of the most talented stars were Edward B. Gray of Amherst and Robert Marshall of the University of Minnesota. A halfback and defensive end, Gray earned selection to Camp's All-American third team in 1906. Marshall was another skillful end and field-goal kicker who played from 1903 to 1906. In 1904 Minnesota defeated Grinnell College 146–0. Marshall scored 72 points in that contest, a record that still stands. He was named to the second All-American team in 1905 and 1906.

As intercollegiate football gained in popularity during World War I, two black players won national acclaim. Frederick Douglass "Fritz" Pollard entered Brown University in 1915. By mid-season, the 5'6" freshman had excelled as a kicker, runner, and defensive back. He helped take his team to the second Rose Bowl game in 1916, a 14–0 loss to Washington State. The following year also proved successful. Pollard starred in games against Rutgers, Harvard, and Yale, scoring two touchdowns in each contest. In naming Pollard to the All-American team in 1916, Walter Camp described him as "the most elusive back of the year, or any year. He is a good sprinter and once loose is a veritable will-o'-the-wisp that no one can lay hands on" (Ashe, 1988, vol. 1, pp. 102–103).

The son of a Presbyterian minister, Paul Robeson of Princeton, New Jersey, enrolled at Rutgers University in 1915 on an academic scholarship. Tall and rugged (6'3", 225 pounds), he played tackle and guard as a freshman and sophomore. In his final two seasons he was switched to end, where he gained All-American honors. Walter Camp described him in 1918 as "the greatest defensive end who ever trod a gridiron" (Chalk, 1975, p. 219). Besides football, Robeson lettered in track, baseball, and basketball. He also excelled academically, earning election to Phi Beta Kappa. Although he was excluded from the college glee club for racial reasons, he was named to Cap and Skull, a senior society composed of four men "who most truly and fully represent the finest ideals and traditions of Rutgers." After graduation, he played professional football to finance his way through Columbia Law School. He also began an acting and singing career that brought him international recognition.

Almost all of the pioneer African-American players experienced both subtle and overt forms of discrimination. Pollard was forced to enroll at several universities before he found one willing to let him play football. Often black players were left off their squads at the request of segregated opponents. And football, a violent game at best, provided ample opportunities for players to vent racial animosities at black players. Paul Robeson, for example, suffered a broken nose and a dislocated shoulder as a result of deliberately brutal tactics by opposing players. Despite the drawbacks, there probably was no venue of major sporting competition of the era that had as few impediments to black participation as major collegiate football.

PIONEERS AT BLACK COLLEGES, 1889–1919

The first football game between black colleges occurred in North Carolina in 1892 when Biddle defeated Livingstone, 4–0. Owing to inadequate funding, it took nearly two decades for most black colleges to establish football programs.

On New Year's Day in 1897, as a forerunner of the bowl games, Atlanta University and Tuskegee Institute met in what was billed as a "championship game." But major rivalries eventually developed between Fisk and Meharry in Tennessee, Livingstone and Biddle in North Carolina, Tuskegee and Talladega in Alabama, Atlanta University and Atlanta Baptist (Morehouse), and Virginia Union and Virginia State. By 1912 Howard and Lincoln in Pennsylvania, Hampton in Virginia, and Shaw in North Carolina had organized the Colored (later Central) Intercollegiate Athletic Association (CIAA).

The black press began to select All-American teams in 1911. Two of the players on that first team were Edward B. Gray, a running back from Howard who had played the same position from 1906 to 1908 at Amherst, and Leslie Pollard, older brother of Fritz, who had played halfback for one year at Dartmouth before resuming his career at Lincoln University. Two other standout athletes who played for black colleges were Floyd Wellman "Terrible" Terry of Talladega and Henry E. Barco of Virginia Union.

PIONEERS: BLACK PROFESSIONALS, 1889–1919

Charles Follis of Wooster, Ohio, is credited with being the first African-American professional football player. He was recruited by the Shelby, Ohio, Athletic Club, where he played professionally from 1902 to 1906. One of his teammates during the first two years was Branch Rickey, who would, as general manager and president of the Brooklyn Dodgers in 1947, desegregate major league baseball by signing Jackie Robinson. A darting halfback, Follis often experienced insults and dirty play. In one game in 1905 the Toledo captain urged fans to refrain from calling Follis a "nigger." By 1906 the abuse had become unendurable and Follis quit the game. He died of pneumonia in 1910, at the age of thirty-one. Three other blacks appeared on professional club rosters prior to 1919. Charles "Doc" Baker ran halfback for the Akron Indians from 1906 to 1908, and again in 1911. Gideon "Charlie" Smith of Hampton Institute appeared as a tackle in one game in 1915 for the Canton Bulldogs. And Henry McDonald, probably the most talented black professional during the early years, played halfback for the Rochester Jeffersons from 1911 to 1917. In one game against Canton in 1917, Earle "Greasy" Neale hurled McDonald out of bounds and snarled, "Black is black and white is white . . . and the two don't mix" (Rathert and Smith, 1984, p. 217). Racial incidents and segregation would become even more severe in the interwar years.

BLACK STARS AT PREDOMINANTLY WHITE COLLEGES, 1919–1945

Following World War I a number of blacks gained national celebrity for their football skills. John Shelburne played fullback at Dartmouth from 1919 through 1921. During those same years, Fred "Duke" Slater was a dominant tackle at the University of Iowa. In the early 1920s Charles West and Charles Drew played halfback for Washington and Jefferson (in Washington, Pennsylvania) and Amherst, respectively. West became the second African American to appear in a Rose Bowl game. After their football careers, both men became medical doctors. Drew achieved international acclaim for perfecting the method of preserving blood plasma. Toward the end of the decade, David Myers appeared as a tackle and end for New York University and Ray Kemp played tackle for Duquesne.

Although scores of blacks played football for major colleges, they constantly faced racial prejudice. Some colleges denied blacks dormitory space, thus forcing them to live off campus. Others practiced a quota system by limiting the number of black players on a squad to one or two. Others benched minority athletes when they played segregated southern schools. In 1937 Boston College surrendered to southern custom when it asked Louis Montgomery to sit out the Cotton Bowl game against Clemson. One sportswriter complained that "even Hitler, to give the bum his due, didn't treat Jesse Owens the way the Cotton Bowl folk are treating Lou Montgomery—with the consent of the young Negro's alma mater" (Smith, 1988, p. 270). African Americans also encountered excessive roughness from white players. Jack Trice of Iowa State was deliberately maimed by Minnesota players in 1923 and died of internal bleeding. Finally, minority players were snubbed by white sportswriters. No blacks were named first-team All Americans from 1918 to 1937, including Duke Slater, probably the best tackle of that era.

In the 1930s dozens of black players had outstanding careers. The Big Ten Conference featured a number of gifted running backs, especially Oze Simmons of Iowa and Bernard Jefferson of Northwestern. Talented linemen included William Bell, a guard at Ohio State, and Homer Harris, a tackle at the University of Iowa. Two of the best black athletes at eastern colleges were Wilmeth Sidat-Singh, a rifle-armed quarterback at Syracuse, and Jerome "Brud" Holland, an exceptional end at Cornell. Named first-team All American in 1937 and 1938, Holland was the first black to be so honored since Robeson two decades earlier. In the West Joe Lillard was a punishing running back at Oregon State in 1930 and 1931, and Woodrow "Woody" Strode and Kenny Washington starred for UCLA from 1937 to 1940. Strode was a 220-pound end

Kenny Washington, a teammate of Jackie Robinson on UCLA's football teams of the late 1930s. Washington preceded Robinson in breaking the color barrier in major professional sports when he played with the NFL's Los Angeles Rams in 1946. PHOTOGRAPHS AND PRINTS DIVISION, SCHOMBURG CENTER FOR RESEARCH IN BLACK CULTURE, THE NEW YORK PUBLIC LIBRARY, ASTOR, LENOX AND TILDEN FOUNDATIONS.

with sure hands and quickness. Washington, a 195-pound halfback, was one of the nation's premier players. In 1939 he led all college players in total yardage with 1,370 but failed to win first-team All-American honors.

During the war years, there were five exceptional African-American college players. Marion Motley was a bruising 220-pound fullback at the University of Nevada. Two guards, Julius Franks of the University of Michigan and Bill Willis of Ohio State, were named to several All-American teams. And Claude "Buddy" Young was a brilliant running back at the University of Illinois. As a freshman in 1944, the diminutive, speedy halfback tied Harold "Red" Grange's single-season scoring record with thirteen touchdowns. He spent the next year in the armed services but continued his career after the war. Finally, Joe Perry was a standout running back at Compton Junior College in Southern California.

BLACK COLLEGE PLAY, 1919–1945

Although black colleges lacked sufficient funds for equipment and stadiums, football grew in popularity after

World War I. Black conferences sprang up throughout the South, but the CIAA, created in 1912, fielded the most talented teams. In the immediate postwar period, Franz Alfred "Jazz" Bird of Lincoln was the dominant player. A small but powerful running back, Bird was nicknamed "the black Red Grange."

Morgan State University was the dominant black college team of the 1930s and early 1940s. Coached by Edward Hurt, Morgan State won seven CIAA titles between 1930 and 1941. Running backs Otis Troupe and Thomas "Tank" Conrad were the star athletes for the Morgan State teams. In the Deep South, Tuskegee Institute overwhelmed its opponents, winning nine Southern Intercollegiate Athletic Conference (SIAC) titles in ten years from 1924 through 1933. Tuskegee's team was led by Benjamin Franklin Stevenson, a skilled running back who played eight seasons from 1924 through 1931. (Eligibility rules were not enforced at the time.) In the more competitive Southwest Athletic Conference (SWAC), Wiley University boasted fullback Elza Odell and halfback Andrew Patterson. Langston College in Oklahoma, which won four championships in the 1930s, featured running back Tim Crisp. The Midwestern Athletic Conference (MWAC), started in 1932, was dominated by Kentucky State, which topped the conference four times in the 1930s. Its key players were ends William Reed and Robert Hardin, running back George "Big Bertha" Edwards, and quarterback Joseph "Tarzan" Kendall. During World War II, fullback John "Big Train" Moody of Morris Brown College and guard Herbert "Lord" Trawik of Kentucky State were consensus picks for the Black All-American team.

BLACK PROFESSIONALS, 1919–1945

In 1919 several midwestern clubs organized the American Professional Football Association, the forerunner of the National Football League (NFL) created two years later. The first African Americans to play in the NFL were Robert "Rube" Marshall and Fritz Pollard. Over forty years old, Marshall performed as an end with the Rock Island Independents from 1919 through 1921. Pollard appeared as a running back with the Akron Pros during those same years. Racial incidents were commonplace. Pollard recalled fans at away games taunting him with the song "Bye, Bye, Blackbird." Occasionally, they hurled stones at him. Even at home games, fans sometimes booed him. Besides playing, Pollard served as the first black NFL coach, directing Akron in 1920, Milwaukee in 1922, Hammond in 1923 and 1924, and Akron again in 1925 and 1926. A pioneer, Pollard was elected to the Pro Football Hall of Fame in 2005. Other blacks who performed in the NFL during the 1920s were Paul Robeson, Jay "Inky" Williams, John Shelbourne, James Turner, Edward "Sol" Butler, Dick Hudson, Harold Bradley, and David Myers. Those athletes did not compete without incident. In 1926 the New York Giants refused to take the field until the Canton Bulldogs removed their quarterback, Sol Butler, from the game. Canton obliged. The last three minority athletes to play in the desegregated NFL were Duke Slater, Joe Lillard, and Ray Kemp. An exceptional tackle who often played without a helmet, Slater performed for Milwaukee (1922), Rock Island (1922–1925), and the Chicago Cardinals (1926–1931). Joe Lillard also starred for the Cardinals from 1932 to 1933. He was a skillful punt returner, kicker, and runner, but his contract was not renewed after the 1933 season. Ray Kemp, a tackle with the Pittsburgh Pirates (later renamed the Steelers), met a similar fate.

In 1933 NFL owners established an informal racial ban that lasted until 1946. The reasons for the exclusionary policy are not entirely clear. Probably NFL moguls were attempting to please bigoted fans, players, and owners. In addition, professional football hoped to compete with baseball for fans and adopted that sport's winning formula on racial segregation. Southern-born George Preston Marshall, who owned the Boston franchise, was especially influential in the shaping of NFL policy. A powerful personality with a knack for innovation and organization, Marshall in 1933 spearheaded the reorganization of the NFL into two five-team divisions with a season-ending championship game. Four years later, he moved his Boston team to Washington, D.C., a segregated city. Marshall once vowed that he would never employ minority athletes. Indeed, the Redskins were in fact the last NFL team to desegregate, resisting until 1962.

Other owners implausibly attributed the absence of African-American athletes to the shortage of quality college players. The NFL draft was established in 1935, but owners overlooked such talented stars as Oze Simmons, Brud Holland, Wilmeth Sidat-Singh, Woody Strode, and Kenny Washington. Owners also lamely argued that they purposely did not hire blacks in order to protect them from physical abuse by bigoted white players.

Denied an opportunity in the NFL, blacks formed their own professional teams. The New York Brown Bombers, organized in 1935 by Harlem sports promoter Hershel "Rip" Day, was one of the most talented squads. Taking their nickname from the popular heavyweight fighter Joe Louis, the Brown Bombers recruited Fritz Pollard as coach. Pollard agreed to coach, in part, to showcase minority athletes. He signed Tank Conrad, Joe Lillard, Dave Myers, Otis Troupe, Hallie Harding, and Howard "Dixie" Matthews. The Bombers competed mainly against semipro white teams such as the New Rochelle Bulldogs.

Pollard coached the Bombers to three winning seasons, but he resigned in 1937 when the team was denied use of Dyckman Oval Field in the Bronx. The Brown Bombers continued for several more years as a road team and then disappeared.

During the war years blacks played professionally on the West Coast. In 1944 both the American Professional League and the Pacific Coast Professional Football League fielded integrated teams. Kenny Washington starred for the San Francisco Clippers and Ezzrett Anderson for the Los Angeles Mustangs. In the Pacific Coast League Jackie Robinson, who would integrate major league baseball, represented the Los Angeles Bulldogs, and Mel Reid performed for the Oakland Giants. The following year the two leagues merged into the Pacific Coast League. The Hollywood Bears, with Washington, Anderson, and Woody Strode, won the title.

THE POSTWAR YEARS: BLACKS AT PREDOMINANTLY WHITE COLLEGES

World War II and the cold war proved instrumental in breaking down racial barriers. After all, how could Americans criticize Nazi Germany and then the Soviet Union for racism and totalitarianism when blacks were denied first-class citizenship in the United States? During the 1940s and 1950s blacks worked diligently to topple segregation in all areas, including athletics. In football their efforts met with considerable success.

During the postwar years several minority athletes performed admirably at big-time schools. Buddy Young returned to the University of Illinois and helped lead his team to a Rose Bowl victory over UCLA. Levi Jackson, a fleet running back, became the first African American to play for Yale and was elected team captain for 1949. Wally Triplett and Denny Hoggard became the first blacks to play in the Cotton Bowl when Penn State met Southern Methodist in 1948. And Bob Mann, Len Ford, and Gene Derricotte helped the University of Michigan trounce the University of Southern California in the 1949 Rose Bowl, 49–0.

Blacks continued to make their mark in intercollegiate football in the 1950s. Ollie Matson excelled as a running back at the University of San Francisco from 1949 through 1951. The following year he won two medals in track at the Olympics in Helsinki. Jim Parker was a dominant guard at Ohio State. In 1956 he became the first African American to win the Outland Trophy, awarded to the nation's foremost collegiate lineman. Bobby Mitchell and Lenny Moore starred at halfback for the University of Illinois and Penn State, respectively. Prentiss Gautt took to the gridiron for the University of Oklahoma in 1958, the first black to perform for a major, predominantly white southern school. And Jim Brown, perhaps the greatest running back in the history of the game, debuted at Syracuse University in 1954. There, Brown lettered in basketball, track, lacrosse, and football and was named All American in the latter two sports. As a senior he rushed for 986 yards, third highest in the nation. In the final regular season game he scored forty-three points on six touchdowns and seven conversions. In the 1957 Cotton Bowl game against Texas Christian University, he scored twenty-one points in a losing cause and was named MVP. Brown would go on to have a spectacular career in the NFL.

Literally and figuratively, African Americans made great strides on the gridiron in the 1950s. Yet barriers continued to exist. Dormitories at many colleges remained off limits. Blacks were denied access to most major colleges in the South. They were virtually excluded from some football positions, especially quarterback. And they were not seriously considered for the Heisman Trophy, an award presented to the best collegiate player.

In the 1960s, a landmark decade in the advancement of civil rights, black gridiron stars abounded. Ernie Davis, Brown's successor at fullback for Syracuse, was an exciting and powerful runner who shattered most of Brown's records. As a sophomore in 1959, Davis averaged seven yards per carry and helped lead Syracuse to its first undefeated season. Ranked first in the nation, Syracuse defeated Texas in the Cotton Bowl and Davis was named MVP. The following year Davis gained 877 yards on 112 carries and scored ten touchdowns. As a senior, he had another outstanding season and became the first African American to win the Heisman Trophy. Tragically, he was diagnosed with leukemia in 1962 and never played professional football. He died at the age of twenty-three.

The 1960s produced a number of sensational black running backs. Leroy Keyes of Purdue and Gale Sayers of Kansas twice earned All-American recognition. Floyd Little and Jim Nance proved worthy successors to Brown and Davis at Syracuse. And Mike Garrett and O. J. Simpson, both of USC, won Heisman awards. The decade's greatest breakaway runner, Simpson rushed for 3,295 yards and twenty-two touchdowns in only twenty-two games. Blacks also excelled as linemen, receivers, and defensive backs. Bobby Bell and Carl Eller both won All-American acclaim as tackles with the University of Minnesota. Bell also captured the Outland Trophy in 1962. Bob Brown of Nebraska and Joe Greene of North Texas State also were All-American tackles. Paul Warfield was a crafty wide receiver for Ohio State. And George Webster of Michigan State twice earned All-American distinction as a defensive back. Also from Michigan State was the feared defensive end

Charles "Bubba" Smith, who joined the Baltimore Colts in 1967.

In the 1960s bastions of bigotry collapsed. The last three lily-white college conferences—the Southwest, Southeast, and Atlantic Coast—all desegregated. Blacks, too, put the lie to the stereotype that they lacked the intellectual necessities to perform as quarterbacks. Sandy Stephens was voted an All American at Minnesota, and Marlin Briscoe and Gene Washington called signals at the University of Omaha and Stanford, respectively. Yet the NFL showed little or no interest in Stephens, and the other two were converted to wide receivers.

During the 1970s, 1980s, and 1990s, major colleges actively recruited African-American athletes. Considered essential to the success of the football program, blacks at some schools were illegally offered monetary and material inducements. Meager grade-point averages and low graduation rates also brought accusations that universities were exploiting minority athletes. After all, the vast majority of varsity players do not go on to enjoy lucrative professional athletic careers. To blunt the criticism, the NCAA instituted Proposition 48 in 1983. That directive required entering freshman varsity athletes to achieve a combined score of 700 on the Scholastic Aptitude Test (SAT) and to maintain at least a C average.

Blacks have only slowly been hired as collegiate coaches. The first African-American head coach at a major college football program was Dennis Green, who was head coach at Northwestern (1981–1985) and at Stanford (1989–1991) before being named head coach of the Minnesota Vikings in the NFL. By the early 1990s the only African-American coaches at Division 1-A colleges were Ron Cooper at Eastern Michigan University, Ron Dickerson at Temple University, and Jim Caldwell at Wake Forest University. In 1998, Division 1-A schools listed a total of eight black head coaches, an all-time high. Six years later, at the start of the 2004 collegiate season, five black Americans were head coaches at level 1-A, including two (Tyrone Willingham of Notre Dame and Tony Samuel of New Mexico State) who were fired later that year.

BLACK COLLEGE PLAY IN THE POSTWAR ERA

Although football programs at black colleges continued to be strapped financially, they still produced some superb players and coaches. Eddie Robinson of Grambling, Ed Hurt and Earl Banks of Morgan State, and Jake Gaither of Florida A & M were four of the most successful black college coaches. Each won several conference titles and sent numerous players to the NFL. Morgan State produced three premier NFL players—Roosevelt Brown, a guard with the New York Giants in the mid-1950s; Leroy Kelly, a running back with the Cleveland Browns in the mid-1960s; and Willie Lanier, a linebacker with the Kansas City Chiefs from 1967 to 1977—among numerous other stars. Florida A & M yielded Willie Gallimore, a running back with the Chicago Bears (1957–1963), and Bob Hayes, a sprinter who played wide receiver for the Dallas Cowboys (1965–1974). Grambling has sent scores of players to the NFL, including quarterback James Harris, running backs Paul Younger and Sammy White, wide receiver Charlie Joiner, defensive tackles Ernest Ladd and Junious "Buck" Buchanan, defensive backs Everson Walls, Roosevelt Taylor, and Willie Brown, and defensive end Willie Davis.

Two of the greatest offensive players in NFL history graduated from black colleges in Mississippi. Former NFL career rushing leader Walter Payton, whose record for total yards rushing was later eclipsed by Emmitt Smith, attended Jackson State before joining the Chicago Bears in 1975, and wide receiver Jerry Rice, the holder of career records for receptions, receiving yards, and touchdown receptions, among many others, graduated from Mississippi Valley State in 1985. Other notable products of black colleges include defensive specialists David "Deacon" Jones and Donnie Schell from South Carolina State, defensive end Elvin Bethea from North Carolina A & T, wide receivers John Stallworth and Harold Jackson of Alabama A & M and Jackson State, respectively, and guard Larry Little of Bethune-Cookman. Prairie View A & M produced safety Ken Houston and wide receiver Otis Taylor. Maryland State delivered defensive back Johnny Sample and two dominant linemen, Roger Brown and Art Shell. Savannah State yielded tight end Shannon Sharpe.

THE NFL IN THE POSTWAR YEARS

The democratic idealism of World War II and the emergence of a rival professional league, the All-America Football Conference (AAFC), proved instrumental in the toppling of the racial barrier in 1946. That year the Los Angeles Rams of the NFL hired Kenny Washington and Woody Strode, and the Cleveland Browns of the AAFC signed Marion Motley and Bill Willis. Washington and Strode were beyond their prime, but Motley and Willis were at their peak. They helped lead the Browns to the first of four consecutive league championships. Both athletes were named first-team All-Pros, an honor that became perennial. Both would also be inducted into the Pro Football Hall of Fame.

The success of the Browns prompted desegregation among other teams, especially in the AAFC, which lasted until 1949. The football New York Yankees signed Buddy Young and the gridiron Brooklyn Dodgers took Elmore

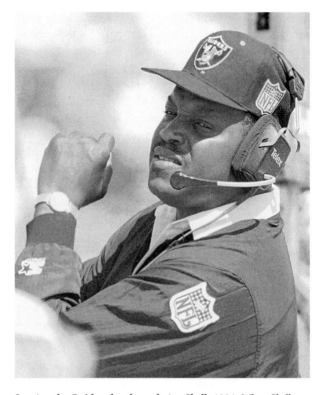

Los Angeles Raiders head coach Art Shell, 1994. When Shell was named head coach of the Raiders in 1989, he became the first African-American head coach in the National Football League since Fritz Pollard in the 1920s. AP/WIDE WORLD PHOTOS. REPRODUCED BY PERMISSION.

Harris of Morgan State. The Los Angeles Dons recruited Len Ford, Ezzrett Anderson, and Bert Piggott. Ford would go on to star as a defensive end for the Cleveland Browns. The San Francisco 49ers, originally an AAFC team, in 1948 signed Joe Perry, who would, in his second season, lead the league in rushing. After the 49ers joined the NFL, he became the first back to amass back-to-back thousand-yard rushing seasons, in 1953 and 1954.

Among NFL teams, only the Rams, the New York Giants, and the Detroit Lions took a chance on African-American athletes in the 1940s. The Lions signed Melvin Grooms and Bob Mann, and the Giants acquired Emlen Tunnell, one of the sport's greatest safeties. In the early 1950s the Giants also obtained Roosevelt Brown, a superior tackle. The Baltimore Colts acquired Buddy Young from the Yankees, and the Chicago Cardinals signed Wally Triplett, Ollie Matson, and Dick "Night Train" Lane. Matson was a crafty runner and dangerous receiver who rushed for 5,173 yards and caught 222 passes in fourteen NFL seasons. He was inducted into the Pro Football Hall of Fame in 1972. Dick Lane, another Hall of Fame inductee, excelled as a cornerback for the Cardinals and Lions. The Washington Redskins, the last NFL team to desegregate in 1962, acquired Bobby Mitchell from the Cleveland Browns for the draft rights to Ernie Davis. Mitchell was a gifted wide receiver and an explosive kick returner. He, too, was elected to the Pro Football Hall of Fame in 1983.

Jim Brown, Lenny Moore, and John Henry Johnson were all premier running backs in the 1950s and early 1960s. In nine seasons with Cleveland, Brown led the NFL in rushing eight times, amassing 12,312 yards and 126 touchdowns, a career record. He was selected Rookie of the Year in 1957 and MVP in 1958 and 1965. He was also voted to nine All-Pro teams. At 6'2" and 230 pounds, Brown ideally combined power, speed, and endurance. Lenny Moore was the epitome of a runner-receiver. He gained 5,174 yards as a halfback and another 6,039 yards as a receiver. He was named Rookie of the Year in 1956 and helped propel the Baltimore Colts to NFL championships in 1958 and 1959. He was elected to the Pro Football Hall of Fame in 1975. John Henry Johnson, a powerful running back and ferocious blocker, played for San Francisco, Detroit, and Pittsburgh (1954–1966). In thirteen seasons, he totaled 6,803 yards on 1,571 carries.

The formation of the American Football League (AFL) in 1959 presented opportunities on the new teams for scores of African Americans. Prior to its merger with the NFL, the AFL produced many exciting black players. Carlton "Cookie" Gilchrist of the Buffalo Bills became the league's first thousand-yard rusher in 1962. Other excellent running backs included Abner Haynes of the Dallas Texans, Paul Lowe of Oakland, Jim Nance of Boston, and Mike Garrett of Kansas City. Lionel Taylor of Denver, Art Powell of Oakland, and Otis Taylor of Kansas City were all gifted receivers. Willie Brown and Dave Grayson were prominent defensive backs for Oakland. And three future Hall of Famers all played for Kansas City: Buck Buchanan, Bobby Bell, and Willie Lanier.

Minority athletes also excelled in the NFL during the 1960s. Roosevelt Brown of New York and Jim Parker of Baltimore were frequent All-Pros on the offensive line. The successful Green Bay teams were anchored on defense by Willie Davis at end, Herb Adderly at cornerback, and Willie Wood at safety. Other defensive standouts were Roger Brown and Dick Lane of Detroit, Abe Woodson of San Francisco, Roosevelt "Rosey" Grier of New York and Los Angeles, and Carl Eller and Alan Page of Minnesota.

Gale Sayers of the Chicago Bears was probably the most electrifying offensive star of the 1960s. A graceful back with breakaway speed, he won Rookie of the Year honors in 1965, scoring twenty-two touchdowns. The following year he led the NFL in rushing with 1,231 yards. After leading the league in rushing for a second time in 1969, injuries ended his career. The decade also yielded

two superior pass receivers: Paul Warfield and Charlie Taylor. Playing thirteen seasons for Cleveland and Miami, Warfield caught 427 passes for 8,565 yards. Another Hall of Famer, Taylor played his entire thirteen-year career for Washington, totaling 649 passes for 9,140 yards.

The 1970 merger of the AFL and NFL set the stage for the emergence of professional football as America's most popular spectator sport. Since the merger the NFL has been split into two divisions, the National Football Conference (NFC) and the American Football Conference (AFC). During the era of the unified league, African Americans have managed to topple virtually every existing sports barrier. In football they have continued to dominate the skill positions of running back, receiver, and defensive back. In the 1970s Orenthal James "O. J." Simpson became the dominant back. A slashing and darting runner for the Buffalo Bills, Simpson led the AFC in rushing in 1972, 1973, 1975, and 1976. In 1973 he shattered Jim Brown's single-season record by rushing for 2,003 yards. In eleven seasons he rushed for 11,236 yards and caught 232 passes for 2,142 yards. Walter "Sweetness" Payton became the game's most statistically accomplished running back, establishing an NFL record of 16,726 yards during his thirteen seasons with the Chicago Bears. A durable player who missed only four of 194 games, he also established new records for most thousand-yard seasons (10), most hundred-yard games (77), most yards rushing in a single game (275), and finished his career second to Jim Brown for most touchdowns (125).

A number of blacks have gained recognition as receivers. Possessing both blocking and pass-catching ability, Kellen Winslow, Ozzie Newsome, Shannon Sharpe, and John Mackey have served as model tight ends. Mackey was elected to the Pro Football Hall of Fame in 1991—an honor long overdue and probably denied him earlier because of his union fights against management and the NFL office. Notable wide receivers have included Otis Taylor, Paul Warfield, Harold Jackson, Cliff Branch, Drew Pearson, Mel Gray, Lynn Swann, John Stallworth, Isaac Curtis, James Lofton, Charlie Joiner, Mike Quick, Art Monk, Al Toon, Andre Rison, Andre Reed, John Taylor, Ahmad Rashad, Mark Duper, Mark Clayton, Michael Irvin, Sterling Sharpe, Jerry Rice, and Randy Moss.

Blacks have also distinguished themselves as defensive backs, interior linemen, and linebackers. Art Shell, Gene Upshaw, Bob Brown, Leon Gray, Reggie McKenzie, Anthony Munoz, and Larry Little all have excelled on the offensive line. Little was selected to the Pro Football Hall of Fame in 1993. A frequent All-Pro selection, Dwight Stephenson of the Miami Dolphins became the first outstanding black center in the mid-1980s. Claude Humphrey, Leroy Selmon, Joe Greene, Bruce Smith, Reggie White, and Charlie Johnson have all been standout defensive linemen. Defensive backs include Ronnie Lott, Mel Blount, Lem Barney, Jimmy Johnson, Emmitt Thomas, Donnie Schell, Louis Wright, Mike Haynes, Albert Lewis, Ron Woodson, Deion Sanders, and Charles Woodson. And some of the best linebackers in the game have been minority athletes such as George Webster, David Robinson, Willie Lanier, Robert Brazille, Lawrence Taylor, Mike Singletary, Cornelius Bennett, Seth Joyner, Hugh Green, Andre Tippett, Derrik Thomas, Vincent Brown, Junior Seau, and Rickey Jackson.

Blacks, too, have dispelled the myth that they lack the intellectual gifts to play certain positions, especially quarterback. In 1953 the Chicago Bears signed a black Michigan State signal caller appropriately named Willie Thrower. He appeared in several games but did not distinguish himself and was released at the end of the year. George Taliaferro of Indiana University appeared as a quarterback for Baltimore in 1953, but he also failed to make an impression. Two years later, the Green Bay Packers signed Charlie Brackins from Prairie View A & M, but he was used sparingly. Marlin Briscoe of the University of Omaha quarterbacked several games for the Denver Broncos in 1968 but was released the following year and became a wide receiver for Buffalo. James Harris of Grambling took snaps for Buffalo in 1969 and led the Los Angeles Rams to a division title in 1974. Joe Gilliam played adequately for Pittsburgh in 1974 but lost the job to Terry Bradshaw, who became the offensive leader of the Super Bowl champions.

The performance of Doug Williams for the Washington Redskins in the 1988 Super Bowl against Denver demonstrated that a black possessed the athletic and intellectual necessities to direct an NFL football team. In Super Bowl XXII Williams captured the MVP award by completing 18 of 29 passes for a record 340 yards and four touchdowns.

In 1988 Randall Cunningham demonstrated dazzling running and passing ability and directed the Philadelphia Eagles to their first division title since 1980. Warren Moon, leader of the high-powered "run and shoot" Houston Oiler offense, was one of the most accomplished passers in football. In 1990 his receiving corps of Haywood Jeffries, Drew Hill, Ernest Givens, and Curtis Duncan each caught more than sixty-five passes, an unparalleled gridiron feat. The later successes of quarterbacks Steve McNair, Daunte Culpepper, Michael Vick, and Donovan McNabb has continued to demonstrate the competence and skill of many African Americans in leading their team's offense on the field.

While distinguishing themselves at every playing position and earning salaries commensurate with their performances, blacks remained a novelty in terms of football management positions. For much of the twentieth century, there were no black owners and few African Americans in NFL front office jobs. Minority head coaches were rare, even though by the 1990s 60 percent of the players were black. Art Shell was named head coach of the Los Angeles Raiders in 1989, becoming the first black NFL coach since Fritz Pollard. After the 2003 Super Bowl, the Black Coaches Association was formed to work with the NFL to promote the hiring of minorities in professional football. At that time, the league's only black head coaches were Tony Dungy of the Indianapolis Colts, Herman Edwards of the New York Jets, and Marvin Lewis of the Cincinnati Bengals.

The status of African Americans in football in recent decades has been impressive, though many problems remain. Their entrance into leadership roles has been slow. In the past, high-salaried minority players have been criticized for being aloof. In part, blacks have been reluctant to speak out for fear of alienating the white majority. But highly visible minority athletes are increasingly speaking out on social issues in order to improve the human condition for athletes and nonathletes alike.

See also Robinson, Jackie; Simpson, O. J.; Sports

■ ■ *Bibliography*

Ashe, Arthur R., Jr. *A Hard Road to Glory: A History of the African-American Athlete, 1619–1987*. 3 vols. New York: Warner, 1988.

Carroll, John M. "Fritz Pollard and the Brown Bombers." *The Coffin Corner* 12 (1990): 14–17.

Chalk, Ocania. *Pioneers of Black Sport*. New York: Dodd, Mead, 1975.

Chalk, Ocania. *Black College Sport*. New York: Dodd, Mead, 1976.

Edwards, Harry. "Black Athletes and Sports in America." *The Western Journal of Black Studies* 6 (1982): 138–144.

Henderson, Edwin B. *The Negro In Sports*. Washington, D.C.: Associated Publishers, 1949.

Henderson, Edwin B. *The Black Athlete: Emergence and Arrival*. New York: Publishers Co., 1968.

Johnson, William Oscar. "How Far Have We Come?" *Sports Illustrated* 75 (August 5, 1991): 39–46.

Pennington, Richard. *Breaking the Ice: The Racial Integration of Southwest Conference Football*. Jefferson, N.C.: McFarland, 1987.

Rathert, Mike, and Don R. Smith. *The Pro Football Hall of Fame Presents: Their Deeds and Dogged Faith*. New York: Balsam Press, 1984.

Roberts, Milton. "Black College All-Time, All-Star Football Team." *Black Sports* (June 1976): 47–50.

Smith, Thomas G. "Civil Rights on the Gridiron: The Kennedy Administration and the Desegregation of the Washington Redskins." *Journal of Sport History* 14 (1987): 189–208.

Smith, Thomas G. "Outside the Pale: The Exclusion of Blacks from the National Football League." *Journal of Sport History* 15 (1988): 255–281.

Spivey, Donald. "The Black Athlete in Big-Time Intercollegiate Sports, 1941–1968." *Phylon* 44 (1983): 116–125.

THOMAS G. SMITH (1996)
Updated by publisher 2005

FORD, JAMES W.

DECEMBER 22, 1893
JUNE 21, 1957

James Ford, a Communist Party official, was born in Pratt City, Alabama. He worked on railroads and in steel mills while in high school. In 1913 he entered Fisk University in Nashville, Tennessee, but before receiving his degree he enlisted in the army and served in France during World War I. Following the war he returned to Fisk and completed his degree in 1920.

Ford then moved to Chicago, where he went to work with the postal service. He joined the Chicago Postal Workers Union and the American Negro Labor Congress, both affiliated with the Communist Party, U.S.A. (CPUSA), and through these organizations was recruited into the party in 1926. Ford demonstrated considerable bureaucratic skill and political savvy, and he rose rapidly in the party hierarchy. In 1928 he was selected as a delegate to the Congress of the Communist Trade International, or Profintern, held in Moscow. Ford stayed in the Soviet Union for nine months and was elected to the executive committee of the Profintern. In 1930 he moved to Hamburg, Germany, where he cofounded the International Conference of Negro Workers and became the first editor of its *Negro Worker*.

Ford returned to the United States in 1931 and was selected to be the party's leading spokesperson on "the Negro question." Shortly after his return from Europe, Ford was made vice president of the party's League of Struggle for Negro Rights, and in 1932 he became the first black member of the American Politburo. Ford received national attention in 1932 when he was selected as the party's vice presidential candidate, becoming the first African American to appear on the ballot for national executive office. He and his running mate, party chair William Z. Foster, received 102,991 votes.

In 1933 Ford was installed as leader of the party's section in Harlem. Through the 1930s he transformed the Harlem party from a relatively decentralized, iconoclastic communist organization into a model of Stalinist orthodoxy. He quickly undercut the power of several black leaders in Harlem, including such leading black communists of the period as Cyril Briggs, Richard Moore, and Harry Haywood. In particular, Ford set out to rid the Harlem section of black nationalism, which had gained considerable currency among the membership. In his first year in Harlem Ford terminated communist participation in campaigns to boycott those Harlem stores that did not hire African Americans, arguing that such a strategy of local black empowerment would exacerbate divisions between black and white workers. Ford redirected Harlem communists to boycott only institutions with unionized workers whose unions supported the campaign, a strategy that proved successful in desegregating several private businesses and government agencies located in Harlem. Ford was also successful in expanding the Harlem party, which in the first two years of his leadership increased its black membership from 87 to more than 300 and its general membership from 560 to 1,000.

In 1936 Ford helped found the National Negro Congress, a civil rights organization closely aligned with the Communist Party. In that year he was again selected to be the CPUSA's vice presidential candidate, this time as a running mate with new party chair Earl Browder. Ford and Browder ran again in 1940 but received fewer than fifty thousand votes.

During World War II Ford's power within the national party diminished as he was eclipsed by the more dynamic Benjamin J. Davis as the party's leading black spokesperson. Ford was deposed from the National Committee (the renamed Politburo) at the party's congress in 1945 and was selected as chairperson of a newly formed internal security committee, though he remained the leader of the Harlem party.

After World War II Ford languished as an obscure party bureaucrat, escaping the federal prosecution that sent many of the Communist Party's leadership to prison. In the 1950s he served as executive director of the National Committee to Defend Negro Leadership, a party group set up to support black members convicted under federal antisubversion laws. Ford died in New York in 1957.

See also Briggs, Cyril; Communist Party of the United States; Haywood, Harry; Moore, Richard Benjamin

■ ■ *Bibliography*

Klehr, Harvey. *The Heyday of American Communism: The Depression Decade*. New York: Basic Books, 1984.

Klehr, Harvey. *Biographical Dictionary of the American Left.* Westport, Conn.: Greenwood Press, 1986.

THADDEUS RUSSELL (1996)

FOREMAN, GEORGE

JANUARY 22, 1948

▌▌▌

Born in Marshall, Texas, boxer, minister, and actor George Edward Foreman grew up in a poor Houston neighborhood, where he dropped out of school in the tenth grade, drifted into petty crime and heavy drinking, and gained a reputation as a mean street fighter. In August 1965 he joined the Job Corps, where Charles "Doc" Broadus introduced him to boxing. At the 1968 Olympic Games in Mexico City, Foreman won the gold medal as a heavyweight. After his victory he waved an American flag in the ring, an action that contrasted dramatically with the behavior of two other black athletes at the games, sprinters John Carlos and Tommie Smith, who had protested racial injustice by raising black-gloved fists during the playing of the national anthem.

Foreman turned professional in 1969. He won his first thirty-seven professional fights, and in Kingston, Jamaica, on January 22, 1973, he knocked out the reigning champion, Joe Frazier, in two rounds to take the title. Foreman successfully defended his championship against Jose "King" Roman and Ken Norton, but on October 30, 1974, he lost it to Muhammad Ali in Kinshasa, Zaire. In that fight, billed as the "Rumble in the Jungle," Ali used an unorthodox "rope-a-dope" strategy, allowing Foreman to tire himself out by throwing most of the punches as Ali leaned back against the ropes and protected his head. By the eighth round, Foreman had tired significantly, and Ali was able to knock him out. Foreman won a number of fights in succeeding years, including a second match with Frazier. But he dropped a twelve-round decision to Jimmy Young in San Juan, Puerto Rico, on March 17, 1977, and retired, disheartened.

After his retirement from boxing, Foreman experienced a religious conversion and became a self-ordained evangelical preacher and pastor of the Church of the Lord Jesus Christ in Houston. He also straightened out his personal life, which he described as a "total mess," including four failed marriages and a flamboyant lifestyle. In 1984 he established the George Foreman Youth and Community Center in Aldine, Texas.

In 1987, at the age of thirty-nine and badly overweight (267 pounds, compared to 217½ when he beat Fra-

zier), Foreman returned to the ring in what was originally described as an effort to raise funds for his youth center. Many observers found it difficult to take his comeback seriously, but, after beating twenty-four lesser-known opponents, he gained credibility by making a good showing in a close twelve-round loss to Evander Holyfield on April 19, 1991, in Atlantic City, New Jersey. After winning several more fights, Foreman faced Tommy Morrison in a match for the World Boxing Organization title in Las Vegas, Nevada, on June 7, 1993, but lost in a unanimous twelve-round decision. After that fight Foreman's career record stood at seventy-three wins (including sixty-seven knockouts) and four losses. In a stunning reversal Foreman regained the heavyweight crown in 1994, fully twenty-one years after he first won it.

By that time Foreman had become something of a media celebrity. His easygoing and cheerful attitude, his unique appearance (besides his girth, Foreman's shaved head made him easily recognizable), and his unlikely status as a boxer in his forties made Foreman a favorite with many fans. He appeared on television in advertisements for a number of products, and in the fall of 1993 he briefly had his own television program on ABC, a situation comedy called *George*, in which he played a retired boxer who ran a youth center.

Foreman was stripped of his WBA crown in March 1995 for failing to fight contender Tony Tucker, and he retained his title as IBC champion until June 1995. Following his defeat by Shannon Briggs on November 22, 1997, Foreman dropped out of competition for the heavyweight championship.

In 2003, Foreman was inducted into the International Boxing Hall of Fame. That same year, he published a book, *George Foreman's Guide to Life*, with coauthor Linda Kulman.

See also Ali, Muhammad; Boxing; Frazier, Joe

■ ■ *Bibliography*

Ashe, Arthur R., Jr. *A Hard Road to Glory: A History of the African-American Athlete Since 1946.* New York: Warner, 1988.

Berger, Phil. "Body and Soul." *New York Times Magazine*, March 24, 1991, pp. 41–42, 62–64.

Foreman, George, and Joel Engel. *By George: The Autobiography of George Foreman.* New York: Simon and Schuster, 2000.

Foreman, George, and Linda Kulman. *George Foreman's Guide to Life.* New York: Simon and Schuster, 2003.

DANIEL SOYE (1996)
Updated by publisher 2005

FORTEN, JAMES

SEPTEMBER 2, 1766
MARCH 15, 1842

The businessman and abolitionist James Forten was born free in Philadelphia in 1766. He attended a Quaker school headed by abolitionist Anthony Benezet. At the age of fourteen he went to sea and became a powder boy on the *Royal Louis,* a colonial privateer under the command of Captain Stephen Decatur, father of the nineteenth-century naval hero of the same name. After one successful sortie against the British, the *Royal Louis* was captured by a group of British ships, and Forten and the rest of the crew were taken prisoner. Had he not befriended the son of the British captain, Forten, like many African Americans in his situation, might have been sent into slavery in the West Indies. Instead the British captain ensured that Forten would be transferred to the *Jersey,* a prison hulk in New York harbor, where many prisoners succumbed to rampant disease; Forten avoided serious illness and after seven months was released.

Shortly after his release, Forten began to work under the tutelage of Robert Bridges, a Philadelphia sail maker. Forten's skill and aptitude guaranteed his success in the industry, and by the age of twenty he was the foreman of Bridges's shop. Upon Bridges's retirement in 1798, Forten became the undisputed master of the shop and developed a reputation for excellent service and innovative sail handling techniques. His business grew; some estimates suggest that he had a fortune of over $100,000 by the early 1830s.

Forten used both his fortune and his fame to forward his agenda for the destruction of slavery. One of the most prominent and vocal Philadelphians on the issue, Forten was a lifelong advocate of immediate abolition. In 1800 he was a petitioner to the U.S. Congress to change the terms of the 1793 Fugitive Slave Law, which permitted suspected runaways to be seized and arrested without a warrant or access to due process. Forten refused to rig sails for ships that had participated in or were suspected of participating in the slave trade. In 1812, along with well-known Philadelphians Richard Allen and Absalom Jones, he helped raise a volunteer regiment of African Americans to help defend Philadelphia were the city to be threatened by the British.

In September 1830 Forten was a participant in the first National Negro Convention in Philadelphia. Its goal was to "consider the plight of the free Negro" and to "plan his social redemption." At the next annual convention, Forten used his influence to oppose funding for the Amer-ican Colonization Society, which supported black emigration to Liberia; at other times, however, Philadelphia's black elite, including Forten, had advocated emigration to Haiti and Canada.

In 1832 Forten and several other African Americans forwarded another petition to the Pennsylvania legislature asking it not to restrict the immigration of free blacks into the state, nor to begin more rigorous enforcement of the 1793 federal Fugitive Slave Law. Much of their argument was based on two main principles: a moral argument based on the evils of slavery and an economic argument—that free blacks were extremely productive members of the Philadelphia and Pennsylvania communities. As one of the organizers of the American Anti-Slavery Society in 1833, Forten provided support, especially economic, to abolitionist activities. Forten's generous support greatly aided the continuing publication of William Lloyd Garrison's abolitionist *Liberator.* Around 1838 he also went to court in a vain attempt to secure the right to vote.

Forten was a founder and presiding officer of the American Moral Reform Society. The society stressed temperance, peace, and other Garrisonian ideals, which included the full and equal participation of women in antislavery activism and society in general. Forten's reputation for good works was well known: He received an award from the city of Philadelphia for saving at least four, and perhaps as many as twelve, people from drowning in the river near his shop. When he died in 1842, thousands of people, many of whom were white, reportedly attended his funeral.

Even before his death in 1842, the legacy of Forten's deep belief in abolition was carried on by his family. Forten's children, and later his grandchildren, would figure as prominent abolitionists and civil rights activists throughout the nineteenth century. Forten's son James Jr. and his son-in-law Robert Purvis were active in the abolitionist movement from the 1830s onward and often collaborated with the elder Forten in his various activities. All of Forten's daughters were involved in antislavery affairs, and Charlotte Forten Grimké, Forten's granddaughter, became a well-known author, educator, and civil rights activist.

See also Abolition; Grimké, Charlotte L. Forten; *Liberator, The*; Purvis, Robert

■ ■ *Bibliography*

Aptheker, Herbert, ed. *A Documentary History of the Negro People in the United States.* New York: Citadel, 1951, pp. 126–133.

"The Forten Family." *Negro History Bulletin* 10, no. 4 (January 1947): 75–79.

Purvis, Robert. *Remarks on the Life and Character of James Forten, Delivered at Bethel Church,* March 30, 1842. Philadelphia, 1842.

Winch, Julie. *Philadelphia's Black Elite: Activism, Accommodation, and the Struggle for Autonomy, 1787–1848.* Philadelphia: Temple University Press, 1988.

Winch, Julie. *A Gentleman of Color: The Life of James Forten.* New York: Oxford University Press, 2002.

EVAN A. SHORE (1996)
Updated bibliography

FORTUNE, T. THOMAS

OCTOBER 3, 1856
JUNE 2, 1928

Timothy Thomas Fortune, a journalist and civil rights activist, was born a slave in Marianna, Florida, to Emanuel and Sarah Jane Fortune. After Emancipation his father, active in Republican politics, was forced by white violence to flee to Jacksonville, where young Fortune became a compositor at a local newspaper. In the winter of 1874, Fortune enrolled at Howard University with less than three years of formal education behind him. However, financial troubles compelled him to drop out, and he began working for a black weekly paper. Fortune married Carrie C. Smiley in the late 1870s and returned to Florida, where he worked on several newspapers. Chafing under southern racism, Fortune gladly moved to New York City in 1881 to accept a position with a white-owned weekly publication.

In New York, Fortune joined with other African Americans who had founded a tabloid called *Rumor* (soon known as the *New York Globe*), and he became managing editor. Fortune set the *Globe*'s militant tone in his editorial advocacy of black civil rights and self-defense; he also shared Henry George's critique of monopoly and endorsed his land distribution program. Moreover, at a time when most black newspapers backed the Republican Party, Fortune favored political independence. He expanded on these radical themes in his book, *Black and White: Land, Labor, and Politics in the South,* published in 1884.

The *Globe* folded in early November 1884. Just two weeks later, however, Fortune was producing the *Freeman* (soon called the *New York Freeman*), a four-page weekly whose circulation stood at five thousand by the end of its first year. In October 1887 Fortune left the *Freeman,* which

Wood engraving of T. Thomas Fortune, c. 1891. The editor and publisher of the New York Freeman *(later the* New York Age*), which he founded in 1884, Fortune was the best known and most outspoken black editor of his era, and a key figure in the Afro-American League (AAL), an early and important vehicle for the cause of civil rights.* MANUSCRIPTS, ARCHIVES AND RARE BOOKS DIVISION, SCHOMBURG CENTER FOR RESEARCH IN BLACK CULTURE, THE NEW YORK PUBLIC LIBRARY, ASTOR, LENOX AND TILDEN FOUNDATIONS.

became the *New York Age,* and began to court Republican support. (Fortune supported Democratic presidential candidate Grover Cleveland in 1888.) He returned as editor in February 1889, renouncing his past alliance with the Democrats but continuing to criticize the Republicans' inaction on racial issues. He supplemented his income by writing for the *New York Sun,* a leading newspaper.

Fortune was also a key figure in the Afro-American League (AAL), an early and important vehicle for civil rights agitation. In May 1887, Fortune proposed the formation of a nonpartisan organization to challenge lynch law in the South and to demand equal opportunities in voting, education, and public accommodations. He also issued the call for the AAL's first national convention; at the January 1890 meeting, he was elected secretary. The AAL planned to fight Jim Crow through legal means; after

Fortune himself was refused service at a New York hotel bar, the AAL sued the proprietor and won. But without adequate resources to mount regular legal challenges, and lacking support from prominent black Republicans, by 1893 the organization had sunk into decline.

Fortune continued to expose racist abuses, particularly in the South. After Ida B. Wells's Memphis newspaper office was destroyed by a mob, he offered her work on the *Age* and published her stunning exposé of lynching. In 1894 to 1895, Fortune himself toured the South and reported on worsening conditions there. Despite the revival in 1898 of the old AAL as the Afro-American Council (AAC), Fortune had by then grown deeply pessimistic about the possibilities for securing racial justice.

During this period of disaffection, Fortune solidified his relationship with Booker T. Washington. The two had first come into contact in the early 1880s and, despite their differences, Fortune helped launch the accommodationist Washington as a national figure. Fortune not only publicized the Tuskegee Institute in the *Age*, but also employed his literary talents to polish and promote Washington's views; he wrote a long introduction to *Black-Belt Diamonds* (1898), a collection of Washington's speeches, and he edited and revised Washington's *The Future of the American Negro* (1898). Because Fortune's only income came from journalism, the remuneration he received for these efforts, as well as emergency loans from Washington, helped tide him over through hard times.

As Washington rose in national stature, he relied increasingly on Fortune—his closest ally in the North—to advance his political agenda. Fortune, aware that Washington occasionally backed legal challenges to Jim Crow behind the scenes, tried to make Washington's views more palatable to a northern black audience. Fortune served as chair of the executive committee of the National Negro Business League (NNBL), formed by Washington in 1900. As AAC president in the early 1900s, Fortune helped squelch anti-Washington sentiment spearheaded by William Monroe Trotter of the *Boston Guardian*.

One reason for Fortune's efforts on Washington's behalf was that he hoped for a political appointment to resolve his financial difficulties. He did manage, in late 1902, to secure a six-month post as special immigrant agent of the U.S. Treasury Department, investigating racial conditions in Hawaii and the Philippine Islands. Evidence suggests, however, that Washington thwarted Fortune's future aspirations, possibly because he realized a government position would increase Fortune's economic independence.

Fortune's greatest usefulness to Washington had been as an "independent" journalist, and observers had grown

> ## T. Thomas Fortune
>
> "We know our rights ... and have the power to defend them."
>
> JOHN BRACEY, AUGUST MEIER AND ELLIOTT RUDWICK, EDS., *BLACK NATIONALISM IN AMERICA (INDIANAPOLIS: BOBS-MERRILL, 1970)*, P. 212.

skeptical of his independence; as early as 1902 the *Guardian* had written scathingly that "much of the fat that now greases the way for the *Age*, comes out of the Tuskegee larder." Moreover, Fortune continued to take militant political stances that were not in line with Washington's own positions.

In February 1907 Washington secretly acquired direct control of the *Age*, and his heavy-handed management contributed to Fortune's nervous breakdown later that year. Believing he had been called by God to preach to the race, Fortune sold his shares in the *Age* to Fred R. Moore (1857–1943), a Washington loyalist, who claimed a "white friend" had backed the transaction. Unknown to Fortune, it was Washington's money that had clinched the deal.

Fortune left for Chicago and sought unsuccessfully to reestablish himself. With little to lose, he disclosed Washington's financial interest in the *Age* and was lauded by Washington's rivals. But this did nothing to resolve his deepening financial crisis. His marriage had collapsed by 1906; now he lost his home. Suffering from alcoholism and unable to obtain steady work, he scraped by for years on whatever intermittent journalistic employment he could find.

The *Age*, meanwhile, deteriorated dramatically in quality, and Washington lured Fortune back in the fall of 1914. While the compensation was poor and Fortune's editorial independence limited, he remained with the *Age* for three years. Thereafter he worked for papers in Philadelphia, Indianapolis, Washington, D.C., and elsewhere.

The early 1920s ushered in new political possibilities for African Americans and brought Fortune back from the edge of destitution and despair. In 1923 he became editor of the *Negro World*, the organ of Marcus Garvey's Universal Negro Improvement Association. While Fortune never embraced the Garvey movement, he had become deeply disillusioned by black people's failure to attain equality and justice by means of the political process. Through his work for the *Negro World*, he was able to regain his self-respect. In the late 1920s Fortune's colleagues in the National Negro Press Association (over which he himself had presided some thirty years before) lauded him as the "dean" of Negro journalists. He edited the *World* until his death on June 2, 1928, at the home of his son Fred in the Philadelphia area.

Fortune's erratic career has somewhat obscured his own historical importance. Before Booker T. Washington's ascent as a national figure began in 1895, Fortune himself was acknowledged as the major spokesperson for black America. His leadership role in the late nineteenth-century civil rights movement was instrumental in shaping the debate over how African Americans would respond to their legal and social oppression in the decades to come.

See also *Guardian, The*; Emancipation in the United States; Garvey, Marcus; Journalism; *Negro World*; Trotter, William Monroe; Tuskegee University; Universal Negro Improvement Association; Washington, Booker T.; Wells-Barnett, Ida B.

■ ■ *Bibliography*

Harlan, Louis R. *Booker T. Washington: The Wizard of Tuskegee, 1901–1915*. New York: Oxford University Press, 1983.

Penn, I. Garland. *The Afro-American Press and its Editors* (1891). Reprint, New York: Arno, 1969.

Thornbrough, Emma Lou. *T. Thomas Fortune, Militant Journalist*. Chicago: University of Chicago Press, 1972.

Wolseley, Roland E. *The Black Press, U.S.A.*, 2d ed. Ames: Iowa State University Press, 1990.

TAMI J. FRIEDMAN (1996)

FOURTEENTH AMENDMENT

▪▪▪

Coming approximately ten years after the *Dred Scott* decision had ruled that all slaves and their descendants were not citizens of the United States, the Fourteenth Amendment, ratified on July 28, 1868, granted both state and federal citizenship to "all persons born or naturalized in the United States" (with the notable exception of Native Americans living on reservations). It also pledged that no state shall "abridge the privileges or immunities" of citizens nor "deny to any person within its jurisdiction the equal protection of the laws." Along with the Fifteenth Amendment, which sought to extend the franchise to all

blacks, the Fourteenth Amendment was drafted by Radical Republican members of Congress, who were uneasy with President Andrew Johnson's lenient policies toward the South in the wake of the Civil War. These Republicans aimed at giving meaning to the freedom that had been legally granted to slaves by the Thirteenth Amendment. In particular, they hoped to invalidate the discriminatory black codes that had been passed by various state legislatures.

Radical Republicans were also concerned that, with the emancipation of slaves, southern representation in Congress would dramatically increase when the former Confederate states reentered the Union—according to Article I, Section 2 of the Constitution, only three-fifths of the slave population had previously been counted for purposes of representation. To ensure that newly freed blacks would have a voice in choosing their political leaders, Section 2 of the amendment promised to reduce congressional representation proportionately for each male citizen denied suffrage. (Despite severe restrictions placed on black suffrage, however, this section was never applied.)

Section 3 of the Fourteenth Amendment excluded former Confederates from holding political office even if they had previously taken an oath to support the U.S. Constitution. This section aimed at keeping former Confederate officers from regaining political office. It had only a temporary effect. Section 4 declared the government of the United States not liable for the Confederate debt.

The intentions of the Radical Republicans were undermined by a series of conservative Supreme Court decisions. In the *Slaughterhouse Cases* (1873), the Court held that state law, rather than federal law, controlled the basic civil liberties of citizens. Further, it interpreted the "privileges and immunities" of citizens in a narrow way, covering such matters as protection on the high seas. The Court also declared that states were not required to enforce the liberties guaranteed in the Bill of Rights. In the 1883 *Civil Rights* cases, the Court ruled that the Fourteenth Amendment did not ensure citizens equal access to public accommodations, and in *Plessy v. Ferguson* (1896), that racial segregation of railways was not a violation of the amendment's "equal protection" clause.

After World War II, a different interpretation of the Fourteenth Amendment evolved from a less conservative Supreme Court. The "equal protection" clause began to be used to fight racial discrimination in such cases as *Brown v. the Board of Education of Topeka, Kansas* (1954), against school segregation, and the *Reapportionment Cases* (1964), against unfairly drawn state legislative districts. Additionally, the Court came to hold a broader interpretation of the civil rights protected under the Fourteenth Amendment. *Shelley v. Kraemer* (1948) outlawed racially restrictive covenants in housing. *U.S. v. Guest* (1966) applied the Fourteenth Amendment to cover private violence that was racially motivated. Under Chief Justice Earl Warren, the Court ruled, in a series of cases, that most of the Bill of Rights had to be respected by the states. The liberal Court of the late 1960s and early 1970s found other rights guaranteed by the amendment, such as the right to use birth control devices (*Griswold v. Connecticut,* 1965) and the right to an abortion (*Roe v. Wade,* 1973). The appointees of several conservative Republican presidents from the 1970s and 1980s, however, have interpreted the rights protected under the amendment more narrowly.

It took approximately a century before the federal government was willing to enforce the provisions of the Fourteenth Amendment as its authors had envisioned. The amendment will no doubt continue to be interpreted in ways that will either broaden or narrow federal protection of civil rights, according to the political climate of the nation and the makeup of the Court.

See also *Brown v. Board of Education of Topeka, Kansas*; *Dred Scott v. Sandford*; Fifteenth Amendment; *Plessy v. Ferguson*; Thirteenth Amendment

■ ■ *Bibliography*

Berger, Raoul. *The Fourteenth Amendment and the Bill of Rights.* Norman: University of Oklahoma Press, 1989.

Nelson, William E. *The Fourteenth Amendment: From Political Principle to Judicial Doctrine.* Cambridge, Mass.: Harvard University Press, 1988.

WALTER FRIEDMAN (1996)

FOXX, REDD

DECEMBER 9, 1922
OCTOBER 11, 1991

Comedian Redd Foxx was born John Elroy Sanford in St. Louis, Missouri, the second son of Fred Sanford, an electrician, and Mary Alma Hughes Sanford, a minister. Foxx's father deserted the family when Foxx was four, and Foxx was raised first by his grandmother, and then in Chicago by his mother, who at that time was employed as a domestic.

Foxx quit high school after one year to play in a washtub band with two friends, Lamont Ousley and Steve Trimel. In 1939 they ran away to New York City, called themselves the Bon-Bons, and earned money performing on street corners and in subways. World War II broke up the band, and Foxx, rejected by the military, began to play in a tramp band act at the Apollo Theater with Jimmie Lunceford.

About this time, Foxx adopted his professional name. Called "Red" because of his red hair and light complexion, he added an extra *d* to "Red" and took the name "Foxx" with the term "foxy" (and the baseball player Jimmy Foxx) in mind. He began landing nightclub jobs, where he developed his stand-up routine. After four years of teaming with comedian Slappy White (1947–1951), Foxx worked on the West Coast. In 1956 he recorded the first of what would become more than fifty "party records"—comedy albums specializing in raunchy humor.

Although Foxx had never done any straight acting, he accepted the small role of Uncle Bud in the 1969 film *Cotton Comes to Harlem.* Executives at NBC developed the character into the situation comedy *Sanford and Son* and cast Foxx in the title role of a cantankerous junk dealer who spent more time malingering and badgering his son than working. The program, which premiered in 1972 and ran through 1977, brought Foxx considerable acclaim and popularity. He attempted to recreate his role as Fred Sanford in a series that ran in 1980, but was unable to revive the original program's appeal.

While *Sanford and Son* made Foxx wealthy, in 1983 he filed for bankruptcy protection, citing mounting debts. In 1985 the Internal Revenue Service claimed Foxx owed almost $3 million in taxes, interest, and penalties, and seized many of his possessions, including his home in Las Vegas.

Foxx was working on the set of a new NBC series, *The Royal Family,* when he suffered a heart attack and died in 1991.

See also Apollo Theater; Comedians; Television

■ ■ *Bibliography*

Bogle, Donald. *Blacks in American Films and Television: An Illustrated Encyclopedia.* New York: Simon and Schuster, 1988.

Mapp, Edward. *Directory of Blacks in the Performing Arts.* Metuchen, N.J.: Scarecrow Press, 1990.

Travis, Dempsey J. *The Life and Times of Redd Foxx.* Chicago: Urban Research Press, 1999.

SUSAN MCINTOSH (1996)
MICHAEL PALLER (1996)
Updated bibliography

FRANCISCO, SLINGER "THE MIGHTY SPARROW"

JULY 9, 1935

◼◼◼

Slinger Francisco, called "The Mighty Sparrow," is an internationally recognized calypsonian, one of the very few known by both his real name and his sobriquet. He has repeatedly filled some of the largest world venues, including New York City's Madison Square Garden. He is an eleven-time Trinidad and Tobago Calypso Monarch and an eight-time Trinidad and Tobago Carnival Road March Competition winner.

Sparrow was born in the small fishing village of Gran Roi, Grenada, in 1935 and migrated with his family to Trinidad when he was one. At the Newtown Boys' School in Port-of-Spain, Sparrow was head choirboy, singing baritone and tenor in Gregorian chants and classic hymns in Latin. At the age of twenty, he ventured into calypso, drawing inspiration from Lord Melody, Lord Invader (the original singer of the famed "Rum and Coca-Cola"), Lord Kitchener, and others. Sparrow taught himself to play the guitar and studied the composition styles of the reigning calypsonians of the 1950s to work out where he wanted the art form to go. Although he has admitted to working with writers and arrangers at times, he has composed a great deal of his own music. In 1954 he first performed his own work at a calypso tent on South Quay, Port-of-Spain, performing "The Parrot and the Monkey" under the sobriquet Little Sparrow. The release of "Jean and Dinah," a song protesting the behavior of the Americans stationed at Trinidad's military bases during World War II, earned him the title Calypso King at the 1956 Dimanche Gras show, the annual exhibition show for calypsonians on the night before the opening of carnival. With this, Sparrow became a star.

Sparrow's contributions to the development of the carnival festivities in Trinidad and Tobago are unprecedented. His 1957 song "Carnival Boycott" protested the Trinidad and Tobago government's failed attempts at promoting calypso and carnival. As a result of the developments set in motion by the song, the Carnival Development Committee was created in 1958, and it has gone on to support Calypsonians, steel bands, *mas* (the actual carnival parade itself, shortened from the word "masquerade"), and other crucial elements of the Trinidad and Tobago carnival. In 1958, for the first time, a calypsonian had a triple win in the Road March Competition: The three

most popular songs played in the streets of Trinidad and Tobago during carnival Monday and Tuesday were The Mighty Sparrow's.

In the tradition of calypso, many of The Mighty Sparrow's songs are social commentary, including his 1962 "Federation," which lamented the break-up of the proposed Caribbean Federation. His musical aims have been to amuse, uplift, and poke fun at the people of the Caribbean, and his long career is a testament to his ability to keep his calypsos fresh and relevant.

See also Calypso

◼◼ *Bibliography*

Hill, Donald R. *Calypso Calaloo: Early Carnival Music in Trinidad.* Gainesville: University Press of Florida, 1993.

Warner, Keith Q. *Kaiso! The Trinidad Calypso: A Study of the Calypso as Oral Literature.* Washington, D.C.: Three Continents, 1982.

TOMIKO C. BALLANTYNE-NISBETT (2005)

FRANÇOIS, ELMA

OCTOBER 14, 1897
APRIL 17, 1944

◼◼◼

Elma François was born in Overland, St. Vincent, to Stanley and Estina François. Her early years were shaped by her primary school education and her remarkable awareness of the straitened conditions of life in Kingstown, the capital city, an awareness that François acquired after her family moved there when she was five years old to escape the ravages of volcanic eruptions. Her genuine appreciation and concern for the plight of fellow workers on the cotton estates gave rise to her labor activism and association with labor organizer George McIntosh.

In 1919 at the age of twenty-two, leaving behind a son who would later join her, François was lured to Trinidad by the promise of greater economic opportunities. In the prevailing depression conditions she worked as a domestic and soon joined the Trinidad Workingmen's Association (TWA), known as the Trinidad Labour Party (TLP) after 1934. For François, political activity meant working among people, so her "rap sessions," political speeches, and hunger marches in and around Port of Spain often went beyond the parameters set by the TWA/TLP.

In 1934 François was one of the founders of the National Unemployed Movement (NUM), which transformed itself into the more structured Negro Welfare Cultural and Social Association (NWCSA) at the end of 1935. This association embraced political, trade union, cooperative, research, educational, and social work activities and was responsible for the formation of three major trade unions in Trinidad and Tobago: the Seamen and Waterfront Workers' Trade Union (SWWTU), the National Union of Government Workers (NUGW), and the Federated Workers Union, which later joined with the NUGW to form the NUGFW. One member, Dudley Mahon, aptly described François's role in the organization: "We looked up to her for leadership and she was always right. We had a lot of confidence in her." (Reddock, 1988, p.17)

The communist-inspired NWCSA concentrated on the country's poor and working class, organizing domestic servants and women transporting coal on the Port of Spain docks, and by the end of 1936 it was challenging the more mainstream TWA/TLP leader, A. A. Cipriani. The NWCSA highlighted the high cost of living, petitioned against the destruction of small black businesses by the Shop Hours (Opening and Closing) Ordinance, which favored larger enterprises, and led the campaign against the Italian invasion of Ethiopia in 1935. With T. U. B. Butler, a catalyst of the labor movement, the NWCSA was part of the historic labor disturbances starting June 19, 1937. These led to the arrest of François, Butler, and other NWCSA members, and the Sedition Trials of 1937–1938. François, who undertook her own successful defense, earned the distinction of being the first woman in Trinidad and Tobago's history to be tried for sedition.

François identified June 19, 1937, as the date of the new emancipation of labor, and in 1939 the NWCSA reactivated the celebration of August 1, the first Emancipation Day, at a time when others preferred to forget the slave experience. In 1939, unlike most organizations, François and the NWCSA campaigned against Caribbean workers' participation in World War II, an extremely radical action at that time.

With her untimely death, the NWCSA lost much of its momentum, but her historical significance in the cause of labor and socialism is undisputed. On September 26, 1987 (Republic Day), she was made a National Heroine of Trinidad and Tobago, and she remains the source of much pride in her native St. Vincent and the Grenadines.

See also McIntosh, George; Politics: Women and Politics in Latin America and the Caribbean

■ ■ *Bibliography*

Reddock, Rhoda. *Elma François, the NWCSA, and the Worker's Struggle for Change in the Caribbean.* London: New Beacon Books, 1988.

Reddock, Rhoda. *Women, Labour, and Politics in Trinidad and Tobago: A History.* London: Zed Books, 1994.

Rennie, Bukka. *The History of the Working Class in the 20th Century (1919–1950).* Trinidad and Tobago: New Beacon Movement, 1973.

Yelvington, Kevin. "The War in Ethiopia and Trinidad: 1935–1936." In *The Colonial Caribbean in Transition,* edited by Bridget Brereton and Kevin Yelvington, pp. 189–225. Mona, Jamaica: University of the West Indies Press, 1999.

RHODA E. REDDOCK (2005)

FRANKLIN, ARETHA

MARCH 25, 1942

Known as "Lady Soul" and "The Queen of Soul," singer Aretha Franklin brought the undiluted power of black gospel singing to American popular music beginning in the late 1960s. Born March 25, 1942, in Memphis, Tennessee, and raised in Detroit, Michigan, she was the fourth of five children of Barbara Siggers Franklin and the well-known gospel preacher and singer, the Rev. C. L. Franklin of Detroit's New Bethel Baptist Church. Her mother, also a gospel singer, left her husband and children in 1948 when Aretha was six, and died shortly thereafter.

Aretha's formative years were spent singing in her father's church choir and traveling with him on the gospel circuit. Numerous jazz and gospel figures visited the Franklin's home, and James Cleveland boarded with the family and worked with Aretha as she practiced playing the piano and singing. Clara Ward sang at an aunt's funeral, and Franklin was so moved she decided to become a professional singer herself. At fourteen she recorded a selection of gospel songs including Thomas A. Dorsey's "Precious Lord, Take My Hand." She became pregnant at fifteen and dropped out of school.

At eighteen Franklin was brought to the attention of John Hammond, the producer at Columbia Records who had "discovered" Bessie Smith, Billie Holiday, and other African-American musicians. Hammond praised Franklin's voice as the best he had heard in twenty years. Franklin signed with Columbia and moved to New York but achieved only marginal success as a pop singer because of Columbia's material and arrangements, a confused hodgepodge of jazz, pop, and standards.

Her breakthrough came in 1966 when her Columbia contract expired and she signed with Atlantic Records, where she was teamed with veteran producer Jerry Wexler. He constructed simple, gospel-influenced arrangements for her, often based on her own piano playing. In these comfortable musical settings her true voice emerged with intensity and emotion. Wexler said, "I took her to church, sat her down at the piano, and let her be herself." Franklin's first record with Wexler was "I Never Loved a Man (The Way I Love You)" in February 1967. It was an immediate success and topped *Billboard*'s charts. Her second hit, "Respect," was sung with such conviction it became a call for black and feminist pride and empowerment.

Often compared to Ray Charles for her fusion of sacred and secular styles, Franklin came to personify African-American "soul" music. She produced a series of top records including "Chain of Fools," "Think," and "Don't Play That Song." She has won fifteen Grammy Awards, three American Music Awards, and a Grammy Living Legend Award. With thirty-five albums, she has had seventeen number one rhythm-and-blues singles, and more million-selling singles than any other woman singer. In 1980 she switched to the Arista label.

Franklin experienced further triumphs in the 1980s. In 1987 she was the first woman inducted into the Rock and Roll Hall of Fame. In 1988 she won a Grammy for best soul gospel performance. In the 1990s she sang at the 1993 and 1997 inaugurations of President Bill Clinton, and in the mid-1990s she launched her own record label, World Class Records. Two more albums followed—*A Rose Is Still a Rose* in 1998 and *So Damn Happy* in 2003.

Throughout her career, her dominant public voice has been contrasted with her private, even reclusive, personality, although she carefully monitors her career and the music industry. Her personal life has at times been difficult, with her mother's abandonment, her own pregnancy at age fifteen, several unsuccessful marriages and, particularly, the fact that her father, to whom she was very close, spent five years in a coma from a gunshot wound in 1979 until his death in 1984.

See also Franklin, C. L.; Gospel Music; Music in the United States; Rhythm and Blues

■ ■ *Bibliography*

Bego, Mark. *Aretha Franklin: The Queen of Soul*. New York: St. Martin's Press, 1989.

Werner, Craig Hansen. *Higher Ground: Stevie Wonder, Aretha Franklin, Curtis Mayfield, and the Rise and Fall of American Soul*. New York: Crown, 2004.

BUD KLIMENT (1996)
Updated by publisher 2005

FRANKLIN, C. L.

JANUARY 22, 1915
JULY 27, 1984

Clarence LaVaughn Franklin, father of the singer Aretha Franklin, was the most popular African-American preacher of his generation. Born in Sunflower County, Mississippi, near Indianola, he was raised by his mother, Rachel, and stepfather, Henry Franklin, a sharecropper, near Cleveland, Mississippi. The segregation, discrimination, and material poverty of that time and place made an enduring impression on him, but so did his mother's constant love and support. At about the age of nine, he was converted, joined St. Peter's Rock Baptist Church in Cleveland, and sang in the church choir, eventually becoming a soloist. Inspired by the preaching of Dr. Benjamin J. Perkins, then president of the State Baptist Convention, he felt that God had called him to preach. A dream or vision in which he saw a burning plank confirmed the call; he preached his first sermon at age fifteen or sixteen, was ordained by St. Peter's Rock Church two years later, and began preaching regularly. He left his parents' farm and moved to Cleveland, then to Clarksdale, where he pastored several rural churches and married. He and his wife, Barbara, moved to Greenville, where he attended Greenville Industrial College, a combined seminary and trade school, supporting his new family by preaching. In his early twenties the Franklins moved to Memphis, Tennessee, and for three years he pastored two churches while attending LeMoyne College as a special student, taking courses in literature and social science. His next pastorate was Friendship Baptist Church in Buffalo, New York. Although he liked the congregation, he regretted that Buffalo was outside the mainstream of African-American culture and resolved to look elsewhere. In 1946 he became pastor of New Bethel Baptist Church in Detroit, a position he held until his death.

A handsome man of uncommon intelligence and theological insight, and a brilliant orator with a rich, forceful delivery and masterful powers of organization and concentration, Franklin became a national celebrity as a result of sermon recordings and groundbreaking preaching tours. Joe von Battle, an entrepreneur in the Detroit black community, recorded Franklin's Sunday sermons at New Bethel beginning in the early 1950s, and for the next twenty-five years these were issued on long-playing records, played on black radio programs, and distributed throughout the nation. From about 1953 through the mid-1960s, until his health could no longer stand the strain, he combined time at New Bethel with preaching tours that took him to almost every city in the United States. The programs began with gospel singing and concluded after he delivered a sermon. Millions of people bought his records and heard him preach at churches, city auditoriums, and stadiums. His sermon recordings were (and still are) used in seminaries, and his influence on other African-American preachers was enormous. It is said that every preacher either tried to imitate him or tried to avoid doing so. New Bethel's membership grew to more than ten thousand, and visitors to Detroit made it a point to hear him preach, swelling the congregation until his sermons had to be broadcast to crowds gathered in the city blocks near the church.

Franklin's sermons were well informed historically and theologically, and he sought to instruct as well as inspire his listeners. He thought about his subjects and planned his sermons in advance, but he delivered them extemporaneously. Always based on a passage from the Bible, each sermon brought biblical characters and theological insights to life in historical and contemporary contexts, with special relevance to African-American experience. A consummate orator, Franklin began his sermons as interactive rhetorical demonstrations, making theological concepts plain and incorporating traditional African-American biblical storytelling and dramatic monologues while members of the congregation responded aloud, punctuating his phrases with encouraging cries. After these expositions, Franklin changed his delivery to "whooping" (intonational or chanted preaching), often carrying on to the climax of a story with shouts and moans amid a poetic eloquence that brought congregations to their feet, shouting, moaning, and dancing in response. His sermons thus combined traditional African-American subjects and techniques with modern theological insight (he left fundamentalism behind in Mississippi) and appealed to people over a broad spectrum of age and experience.

Although best known as a gospel preacher, Franklin participated in the civil rights movement and helped African Americans obtain political office. Many black political figures, including Detroit mayor Coleman Young and Michigan congressman John Conyers, were close to Franklin and campaigned in New Bethel. Against much opposition from the white power structure, Franklin organized the 1963 civil rights march in Detroit, which drew a quarter million people and where the Rev. Dr. Martin Luther King, Jr., first presented his "I Have a Dream" speech. King invited Franklin to preach at the 1968 Poor People's Campaign in Washington, where he electrified the assembled crowd.

In the 1970s Franklin ceased his preaching tours and concentrated on his New Bethel ministry. He was shot by robbers in 1979 and remained in a coma until he died in 1984. His most popular recorded sermons were "The Eagle Stirreth Her Nest," "Give Me This Mountain," "Dry Bones in the Valley," and "The Prodigal Son." They rank among the most outstanding documented sermons in the English language.

See also Civil Rights Movement, U.S.; Franklin, Aretha

■ ■ *Bibliography*

Titon, Jeff Todd, ed. *C. L. Franklin, Give Me This Mountain: Life History and Selected Sermons.* Urbana: University of Illinois Press, 1989.

Salvatore, Nick. *Singing in a Strange Land: C. L. Franklin and the Rise of the Black Church in America.* New York: Little Brown, 2005.

JEFF TODD TITON (1996)
Updated bibliography

FRANKLIN, JOHN HOPE

JANUARY 2, 1915

Historian and educator John Hope Franklin was born in Rentiesville, Oklahoma, an exclusively African-American town. At an early age he came to be introduced to white custom, law, and justice in the South. His father, a lawyer, was expelled from court by a white judge who told him that no black person could ever practice law in his court. Young Franklin was himself ejected, along with his mother (an elementary school teacher) and sister, from a train because his mother refused to move from the coach designated for whites. After moving to Tulsa in 1926, Franklin attended Booker T. Washington High School and learned the meaning of a "separate but equal" education—inferior facilities and a sharply limited curriculum. His avid interest in music introduced him to the Jim Crow seats in the local concert hall. He went on to receive his B.A. at Fisk University in 1935 and his Ph.D. in history at Harvard University in 1941.

Throughout his career, Franklin combined scholarship with social activism. As student body president at Fisk University, he protested the lynching of a local black man to the mayor, the governor, and President Franklin D. Roosevelt. Having once been barred from entering the University of Oklahoma to pursue graduate studies, he readily agreed to the request of the National Association for the Advancement of Colored People (NAACP) that he be an expert witness for a black student seeking admission to the graduate program in history at the University of Kentucky. At the request of Thurgood Marshall, he served on the research team whose work led to the Supreme Court's *Brown v. Board of Education* decision outlawing school segregation. In 1965 he joined more than thirty other historians on the civil rights march into Montgomery, Alabama.

Like Carter Woodson and W. E. B. Du Bois, Franklin demonstrated to a skeptical or indifferent profession that the history of black Americans was a legitimate field for scholarly research. His first book, *The Free Negro in North Carolina, 1790–1860* (1943), explored the anomalous position of free blacks in the slave South. *Reconstruction After the Civil War* (1961) was a revisionist treatment of the unique experiment in biracial democratic government in the postwar South, particularly in its depiction of blacks as active participants and leaders, not simply as victims or passive tools of white politicians. In *The Militant South* (1956) and *A Southern Odyssey* (1976), Franklin explored different facets of the southern experience and varieties of southern white expression. His Jefferson Lecture in the Humanities for 1976, "Racial Equality in America," probed that troubled and elusive search. In a turn to biography, his *George Washington Williams* (1985) traced the life of a historian who wrote in the 1880s the first substantial and scholarly history of black Americans. For hundreds of thousands of students, Franklin's *From Slavery to Freedom* (first published in 1947) introduced them to African-American history. In *Race and History* (1989) he brought together his most important essays and lectures, including his autobiographical sketch and reflections, "A Life of Learning."

In his books, as in his teaching, Franklin transcends the distinction between African-American and American history. He has underscored the unique quality of the history of African Americans even as he has viewed that history as an intimate part of American history, inseparable from and a central theme in the national experience. Rejecting the need to replace old distortions with new myths and eulogistic sketches of heroes and heroines, he has demonstrated his full appreciation of the complexity and integrity of the American and African-American past.

Franklin's early teaching career included stints at Fisk University, St. Augustine's College, North Carolina Central College, and Howard University. In 1956 he went to Brooklyn College as chairman of the department of history—a department of fifty-two white historians. (The appointment made the front page of the *New York Times*; Franklin's troubled search for housing did not.) In 1964 he joined the history faculty of the University of Chicago,

serving as chair from 1967 to 1970 and as the John Matthews Manly Distinguished Service Professor from 1969 to 1982. Moving to Durham, North Carolina, he chose to diversify rather than retire, becoming the James B. Duke Professor of History and professor of legal history in the law school at Duke University.

Franklin has been elected to the presidencies of the American Studies Association, the Southern Historical Association, the United Chapters of Phi Beta Kappa, the Organization of American Historians, and the American Historical Association. More than seventy colleges and universities have awarded him an honorary degree. He has served on numerous national commissions, and in 1980 was a United States delegate to the 21st General Conference of UNESCO. In 1978 the state that initially forced John Hope Franklin to undergo the humiliating rites of racial passage elected him to the Oklahoma Hall of Fame. Franklin retired in 1992. In 1995, he was awarded the Presidential Medal of Freedom and also received the Spingarn Medal from the NAACP. In 1997 he was called out of retirement to chair President Bill Clinton's Initiative on Race. Conservative critics accused the panel of problack bias on racial issues, and Franklin was criticized for his statement that the period after Emancipation was in many ways worse for black Americans than slavery. Despite the controversy, the commission's final report, issued in September 1998, was almost completely ignored by Congress.

In Franklin's honor, the John Hope Franklin Center for Interdisciplinary and International Studies opened at Duke University in 2000. In 2004 the John Hope Franklin Award was established to point the spotlight on scholars and education activists.

See also *Brown v. Board of Education of Topeka, Kansas*; Du Bois, W.E.B.; Fisk University; Howard University; Woodson, Carter G.

■ ■ *Bibliography*

Franklin, John Hope. *Race and History: Selected Essays, 1938–1988.* Baton Rouge: Louisiana University Press, 1989. See especially "John Hope Franklin: A Life of Learning," pp. 277–291.

LEON F. LITWACK (1996)
Updated by publisher 2005

FRANKS, GARY

1954?

Politician and entrepreneur Gary Franks was the first African-American congressman elected from Connecticut. His father, who had not completed the sixth grade, was determined that his six children would become college graduates, and all did. A Connecticut native, Franks graduated from Yale University in 1975. In the late 1970s, after working as an industrial and labor relations executive in Fairfield County, Connecticut, he opened his own real estate business and became highly successful.

Franks entered local politics as alderman in Waterbury, where he served three terms. He ran unsuccessfully for state alderman in 1986. His earlier success, however, led him to run on the Republican ticket for the U.S. House of Representatives. He won the seat in November 1990, at a time when African-American representation in highly visible positions, such as mayors of major cities or in the U.S. Senate, was slight. Franks platform included advocacy of abortion rights, the death penalty for top drug dealers, and a constitutional amendment to prohibit burning the U.S. flag. Franks also favored cuts in the capital gains tax and opposed increases in federal income taxes.

His victory made him the nation's top-ranking elected black Republican, and he was highly touted by Republicans, who saw him as attractive enough to encourage more minorities to join the Republican Party.

After serving three terms in Congress, Franks was unsuccessful in his bid for reelection in 1996. He was a candidate for election to the U.S. Senate in 1998, but was defeated.

See also Congressional Black Caucus; Politics in the United States

■ ■ *Bibliography*

Bigelow, Barbara Carlisle, ed. *Contemporary Black Biography,* vol. 2. Detroit, Mich.: Gale, 1992.

"Connecticut Salon a Favorite among 3 Blacks Seeking GOP Seats in U.S. House." *Jet.* September 24, 1990, 16.

Franks, Gary. *Searching for the Promised Land.* New York: ReganBooks, 1996.

McCoy, Frank. "Freshmen on the Hill." *Black Enterprise.* April 1991, 25.

RAYMOND WINBUSH (2001)

FRATERNAL ORDERS

At the height of their popularity between 1870 and 1930, fraternal societies in the United States defined community roles for many middle-class men and women from coast to coast. The groups arose as local chapters of national organizations, forming essential relationships between citizens and their neighbors. While their economic and political power derived mainly from the distribution of membership dues for various charities, such as local lobbying, community insurance, mutual aid, scholarships, or nonalcoholic leisure, the most significant fraternal societies met with pomp and decoration to cement individual identities to the rituals of status associated with male Masonic orders originating in Europe, such as the Freemasons. African-Americans were early and important agents of fraternal orders, though their organized practices were both symbolically similar and socially distinct from the white fraternal orders operating in nearby locations. In any event, American fraternal orders performed ornate ceremonies to embed member identities in mythological narratives about past connections to great leaders, and used racial and gender divisions to maintain the illusion of the group's selectiveness for its members, who desired more social status from their middle-class lives.

Since fraternal orders originated in Europe, the development of the American orders was always rebounding over the Atlantic, especially to England and its colonies. The first black member of any fraternal order was reputedly John Pine (1690–1756), a member the English Freemasons in the Globe Tavern Lodge in Morgate, England. He may have served as a critical precedent for Prince Hall, probably the primary early figure in African-American fraternal history. In 1787 Hall led a group to seek a Masonic charter from England, which was then and remains now the most important fraternal order. The charter issued to him for African Lodge 459 was legitimate and remains a controversial point of origin for a schism within American Masonry. White Massachusetts elites rejected Hall's leadership based on his skin color and applied for a separate charter, and fraternal orders thus developed segregated, with the Prince Hall faction becoming the eponymous Prince Hall Masonry. While contemporary Freemasons now claim to be legally integrated, the separation of fraternal orders explicitly by race was unique to the United States.

The Boston Prince Hall lodge dispersed and mutated for a few decades. By the time its remaining leader, John T. Hilton, organized his own fraternal order in 1847, other Prince Hall lodges had already spread west and south. The Grand Lodge of Ohio alone disseminated the order into

Kentucky, Indiana, Louisiana, Tennessee, Alabama, and Missouri. As the order traveled, its influence grew in new communities. Soon the antebellum period saw the rise of several new African-American fraternal orders. The Grand United Order of Odd Fellows established itself in New York in March 1843, and like the Prince Hall Masons sought its legitimacy abroad from an Odd Fellows lodge in England. By the late 1850s, it had over sixty-one different lodges, and such growth was typical. Other orders grew from charismatic and original leadership: when Moses Dickinson founded the Twelve Knights of Tabor in 1872, he had already operated a secret Knights of Liberty group on the Mississippi River composed of men who aided runaway slaves.

The Civil War and Reconstruction period saw an even more explosive rise in African-American fraternal orders, with African-Americans creating new local organizations or observing white formations and fusing elements of different local cultures. The Colored Knights of Pythias, for instance, began in Washington, D.C., in 1863, and like Prince Hall and Odd Fellows followed the same traditions as similarly named white institutions in the same cities and towns. Some groups, like the Independent Order of Good Templars or Grand United Order of True Reformers, grew from temperance or insurance societies that actually included white members, and then splintered during the onset of Jim Crow. The ex-slave Mary Prout founded another important society from Baltimore, the Independent Order of Saint Luke, in 1867. The Prince Hall lodges and Odd Fellows began their own interdependent female orders during that era, and many others followed.

Throughout the decades leading to the close of the nineteenth century, the fraternal societies recruited members, collected dues, performed rituals and rites, administered regalia, and provided money for burial services. By 1900, membership continued to expand and fraternal treasuries funded independent savings banks and mortgage lending. These orders flourished through the 1920s, and membership in more than one order was common in certain places. The orders built temples, which served as spaces for multiple purposes, whether political, economic, or leisure. Many orders grew politically active. The Order of the Eastern Star, the female component of the Prince Hall Masons, lobbied for antilynching bills in Congress. Despite racist suffrage laws, they exerted pressure on local economies through middle-class purchasing power, and influenced decisions about spending in the regular fraternal publications, where friendly businesses advertised. Regionally, their competition for legitimacy and power in local communities often became protracted legal battles in the public courts.

The Great Depression and World War II sent most orders into bankruptcy, and those that survived grew slowly in the twentieth century. Although academic scholarship largely ignored or forgot fraternal orders until the late twentieth century, Prince Hall Masonry and its sister component, Order of the Eastern Star, boast hundreds of thousands of members in the United States, the Caribbean, the Bahamas, Liberia, and Ontario.

The Schomburg Center for Research in Black Culture in Harlem, New York, houses countless African-American fraternal publications, as does the Livingston Masonic Library of Grand Lodge in Manhattan.

See also Hall, Prince; Jim Crow

■ ■ *Bibliography*

Carnes, Mark C. *Secret Ritual and Manhood in Victorian America.* New Haven, Conn.: Yale University Press, 1989.

Mjagkij, Nina, ed. *Organizing Black America: An Encyclopedia of African American Associations.* New York: Garland, 2001.

Muraskin, William A. *Middle-Class Blacks in a White Society: Prince Hall Freemasonry in America.* Berkeley: University of California Press, 1975.

Trotter, Joe. "African American Fraternal Associations in American History: An Introduction." *Social Science History* 28, no. 3 (2004): 355–366.

JUSTIN ROGERS-COOPER (2005)

FRATERNITIES, U.S.
▪ ▪ ▪

Black fraternities are Greek-lettered organizations that cater to black populations in colleges across the nation. Alpha Phi Alpha, Kappa Alpha Psi, Phi Beta Sigma, Iota Phi Theta, and Omega Psi Phi are all black Greek fraternities with their own distinct social practices, histories, and goals. Although there are many differences between fraternities, they can be thought of collectively as organizations that have historically provided African-American undergraduate and graduate students with a unique social experience. Whether at historically black colleges or universities or predominantly white college campuses, black fraternities can create an environment that nurtures lifelong relationships and a commitment to the black Greek experience.

The founding of Alpha Phi Alpha fraternity at Cornell University in 1906 is commonly considered the beginning of black Greek college organizations. However, there is evidence of black Greek-lettered organizations prior to the

Alphas. These other groups have not existed continuously since their founding, nor have they been as successful as the abovementioned fraternities in sustaining their membership. For these reasons, it is acceptable to recognize the beginning of the black Greek experience with Alpha Phi Alpha.

From the beginning, black fraternities have cultivated a certain mystique. Like other social organizations, black fraternities are selective in terms of membership. Once accepted into a fraternity, initiates are treated as members, learning the symbolic meanings behind the fraternity's distinct hand signs, calls, and apparel. Members of Kappa Alpha Psi, for example, are known to carry and perform with canes, and they display the colors red and white. Members of Omega Psi Phi, in contrast, flaunt purple and gold clothing, identify themselves with a distinctive *Que-dog* bark, and recognize Delta Sigma Theta as a sister organization. Members of Phi Beta Sigma present themselves in blue and white and are formally allied with Zeta Phi Beta Sorority. For college-age youth in particular, membership in a fraternity is appealing for primarily social reasons. Along with participation in exclusive social events, membership also means access to extensive alumni contacts and associations with black sororities, often enabling romantic relationships.

The social privileges of membership in a black fraternity continue after graduation. Alumni and graduate chapters are also active and, through the use of alumni membership dues and other contributions, provide services to the community as a whole. For example, the U.S. federal government commissioned Alpha Phi Alpha to oversee the construction of the Martin Luther King Jr. National Memorial in Washington, D.C. After concluding a design competition in September 2000, Alpha Phi Alpha proceeded to spearhead a funding campaign to memorialize the civil rights leader.

Television and films have brought black fraternities national attention. Spike Lee's *School Daze* (1988) and the television programs *A Different World*, *Moesha*, and *The Parkers* have all presented aspects of the black fraternal experience. These fictional accounts also dramatized the procedures surrounding entrance into black Greek organizations. Such practices, commonly known as *pledging*, are one of the predominant characteristics of the black Greek experience.

Historically, pledging is the means by which a fraternity chapter determines who, among a number of interested individuals, will be admitted. Essentially, prospective members must prove their worth over a period of time (from two weeks to a few months) through a series of difficult tasks and rituals. These trials can be mentally challenging, such as researching and reciting obscure historical details about the fraternity. They can also be revolting, such as drinking toilet water, and even physically traumatizing. Physical violence, such as paddle beatings, is a documented aspect of pledging practices.

Following the death of a pledging student at Morehouse College, the leadership of the National Pan-Hellenic Council (comprised of the five abovementioned fraternities as well as the four major black sororities) convened in February 1990 to discuss the ramifications of pledging. They decided to officially adopt the process of *membership intake* to replace pledging as the method of initiating members into a fraternity or sorority. Membership intake sought to eliminate the potential physically abusive nature of pledging, which, in its extreme forms, is also known as *hazing*. However, membership intake did not replace pledging and hazing in any significant way. Interpreted as less demanding than, not equivalent to, pledging, membership intake is frequently understood as a less meaningful rite of passage. Interestingly, prospective initiates protested the official end of pledging, often citing a need for respect as a reason for enduring these hardships.

As fraternities attempted to implement membership-intake guidelines, the practice of pledging went underground, unrecognized officially but still very much a part of the black Greek experience. In 1994 another student died, this time at Missouri State University. In 1999 a student at the University of Louisville successfully sued Omega Psi Phi after voluntarily enduring a beating by some members of the fraternity.

Black fraternities and sororities, nonblack Greek organizations, and college sports teams all confront the issue of hazing with difficulty. Because of this persistent problem, college officials have previously initiated temporary moratoriums on all Greek activity, and considered full-scale bans of black fraternities.

The issue of hazing remains unresolved as black fraternities adapt to an American social terrain drastically different from the social world of 1906. Openly homosexual members, as well as increasing numbers of nonblack members, indicate different directions for black fraternities. As more people identify themselves as members, either as alumni or collegiate Greeks, black fraternities continue to negotiate how to preserve their traditions and prepare for the future.

See also Christian Denominations, Independent; Education in the United States; Fraternal Orders; Mutual Aid Societies; Sororities, U.S.

■ ■ *Bibliography*

Brown, Patricia Lee. "For a King Memorial, Metaphors in Stone" *The New York Times* (September 21, 2000).

Jones, Ricky L. *Black Haze: Violence, Sacrifice, and Manhood in Black Greek-letter Fraternities.* Albany: State University of New York Press, 2004.

Kimbrough, Walter M. *Black Greek 101: The Culture, Customs, and Challenges of Black Fraternities and Sororities.* Madison, N.J.: Fairleigh Dickinson University Press, 2003.

DEREK LEE MCPHATTER (2005)

FRAZIER, EDWARD FRANKLIN

SEPTEMBER 24, 1894
MAY 17, 1962

Born in Baltimore in 1894, the year in which W. E. B. Du Bois was working on his doctoral degree at Harvard and 135 blacks were lynched in the South, essayist and activist E. Franklin Frazier was encouraged in his formative years by his parents, especially his working-class father, to seek upward mobility and social justice through education. With a scholarship from Colored High School he went on to Howard University, where he graduated cum laude in 1916 after four years of rigorous education and political activism at the "capstone of Negro education." For the rest of his academic career, he taught primarily in segregated, African-American schools and colleges, first in the South in the 1920s and early 1930s, then for most of his career in Howard's sociology department. Between teaching jobs he received scholarships that enabled him to get a master's degree at Clark University (1920) and a Ph.D. in sociology from the University of Chicago (1931). Despite his election as the first African-American president of the American Sociological Association (1948) and his recognition by UNESCO in the 1950s as a leading international authority on race relations, Frazier was never offered a regular faculty appointment by a predominantly white university.

With minimal institutional and foundation support, Frazier managed to produce eight books and over one hundred articles. He is best known for his pioneering studies of African-American families, especially *The Negro Family in the United States* (1939/2001), which demonstrated that the internal problems of black families were socially created within and by Western civilization, not by the failure of Africans to live up to American standards. Building upon Du Bois's 1908 essay, "The Negro American Family," Frazier refuted the prevailing social scientific

wisdom that, in his words, "most often dealt with the pathological side of [black] family life." In contrast, Frazier's family is a broad spectrum of households, constantly in a process of change and reorganization, sometimes disorganized and demoralized, sometimes tenacious and resourceful. To Frazier the serious problems within African-American families—"the waste of human life . . . delinquency, desertions, and broken homes"—was the result not of cultural backwardness but rather of economic exploitation and the social damage inflicted by racism.

Frazier also made a variety of other important intellectual contributions: as an ethnographer and historian of everyday life in black communities; as a trenchant and subtle critic of the dynamics and etiquette of racism; as an influential consultant to Gunnar Myrdal's *An American Dilemma* (1944); as the author of the first systematic textbook on *The Negro in the United States* (1949); and as a critic of overly specialized, narrowly conceived studies in the social sciences. Frazier's popular reputation was made by *Black Bourgeoisie* (first published in the United States in 1957), but he explored the controversial relationship between class, politics, and culture all his life, beginning with a polemical essay on "La Bourgeoisie Noire" in 1928 and ending with his scholarly assessment of *Race and Culture Contacts in the Modern World* (1957). In this body of work he challenged monolithic portraits of African-American communities and documented their socioeconomic diversity; in particular, he exposed the collaborative and opportunistic role played by the black middle class in holding back the struggle for social equality and ensuring that "bourgeois ideals are implanted in the Negro's mind." Instead of being "seduced by dreams of final assimilation," Frazier called upon black leaders to envision "a common humanity and a feeling of human solidarity" in which "racial and cultural differentiation without implications of superiority and inferiority will become the basic pattern of a world order."

Frazier was part of a cadre of activists, intellectuals, and artists who after World War I formed the cutting edge of the New Negro movement that irrevocably changed conceptions of race and the politics of race relations. Though a loner who distrusted organizations, Frazier had close and respectful relationships with civil rights leaders such as W. E. B. Du Bois, Paul Robeson, and A. Philip Randolph, as well as with scholars such as Ralph Bunche and Abram Harris who tried to bridge the gap between university and community, theory and practice. From his undergraduate days at Howard, when he was a vigorous opponent of U.S. entry into World War I, until his last years, when he welcomed a revitalized civil rights movement, Frazier was a politicized intellectual who believed that "a moral life is a life of activity in society."

See also Black Middle Class; Bunche, Ralph; Du Bois, W.E.B.; Harris, Abram; New Negro; Randolph, A. Philip; Robeson, Paul; Sociology

■ ■ *Bibliography*

Edwards, G. Franklin, ed. *E. Franklin Frazier on Race Relations.* Chicago: University of Chicago Press, 1968.

Frazier, E. Franklin. *The Negro in the United States.* New York: Macmillan, 1949.

Frazier, E. Franklin. *The Negro Family in the United States.* Chicago: University of Chicago Press, 1939; South Bend, Ind.: University of Notre Dame Press, 2001.

Holloway, Jonathan Scott. *Confronting the Veil: Abram Harris Jr., E. Franklin Frazier, and Ralph Bunche, 1919–1941.* Chapel Hill: University of North Carolina Press, 2002.

Platt, Anthony M. *E. Franklin Frazier Reconsidered.* New Brunswick, N.J.: Rutgers University Press, 1991.

ANTHONY M. PLATT (1996)
Updated bibliography

FRAZIER, JOE

JANUARY 12, 1944

Joe Frazier. Winner of an Olympic Gold Medal in 1964, boxer Frazier gained a fifteen-round unanimous decision victory over Muhammad Ali in the "Fight of the Century" at New York City's Madison Square Garden, 1971. © BETTMANN/CORBIS. REPRODUCED BY PERMISSION.

"Smokin'" Joe Frazier was the World Heavyweight Boxing champion from 1970 to 1973. Born in Beaufort, South Carolina, Frazier grew up in Philadelphia and began boxing at a Police Athletic League gym. After he won Golden Gloves titles in 1962, 1963, and 1964, as well as a gold medal in the 1964 Olympics in Tokyo, Japan, a consortium of investors, incorporated as Cloverlay, Inc., sponsored Frazier's professional career.

Frazier was only 5'11½" tall and 205 pounds, small for a heavyweight. Managed by Yancey Durham, Frazier adopted a crowded and hard-hitting style that compensated for his relative slow-footedness. Beginning with a one-round knockout of Woody Goss in August 1965, Frazier won his first eleven professional bouts by knockout, none of which went beyond six rounds, and he won thirty-one straight fights before George Foreman defeated him in 1973.

After Muhammad Ali gave up his title in 1970, Frazier won the World Heavyweight Championship, defeating Jimmy Ellis in a five-round knockout. Ali, who had been stripped of his title after the U.S. government convicted him of draft evasion (later overturned), also claimed to be the heavyweight champion because he had never retired or been defeated.

On March 8, 1971, in New York City's Madison Square Garden, Frazier defeated Ali after fifteen rounds of such ferocious boxing that both men entered hospitals after its conclusion; they would later fight twice more, both times with great intensity. After the first fight with Ali, Frazier did not fight a title bout again for ten months. He then defended his championship twice, winning both bouts, but on January 22, 1973, George Foreman knocked him out in the second round of a heavyweight title bout.

Having lost his title to Foreman, Frazier again fought Ali in a nontitle bout in New York City on January 28, 1974, and lost in twelve rounds. Frazier had fights with two lesser boxers, both of whom he knocked out, then faced Ali for the heavyweight title on October 1, 1975, in the Philippines. The fight, dubbed by Ali "The Thrilla in Manila," was a hard-fought contest. Ali knocked Frazier out in the fourteenth round.

On June 15, 1976, Frazier followed the Manila bout with a second fight against Foreman, who knocked him out early in the fight. Frazier then retired from the ring. He made a brief appearance playing himself in the movie *Rocky* (1976) and tried unsuccessfully to build a singing career with a group called the Knockouts. In 1981 he attempted a comeback but was defeated by Floyd Cummings. Of his thirty-seven career bouts, Frazier won thirty-two, twenty-seven by knockout. He then managed his son Marvis's short boxing career. In 1980 Frazier was elected to the Boxing Hall of Fame.

Frazier published *Smokin' Joe: The Autobiography of a Heavyweight Champion of the World, Smokin' Joe Frazier,* in 1996.

See also Ali, Muhammad; Boxing; Foreman, George; Robinson, Sugar Ray

■ ■ *Bibliography*

Ashe, Arthur R., Jr. *A Hard Road to Glory: A History of the African-American Athlete Since 1946.* New York: Warner, 1988.

Frazier, Joe, and Phil Berger. *Smokin' Joe: The Autobiography of a Heavyweight Champion of the World, Smokin' Joe Frazier.* New York: Macmillan, 1996.

GREG ROBINSON (1996)
Updated by publisher 2005

dience. Despite financial difficulties and criticism from white reformers and black leaders, Douglass succeeded in making his weekly publication the most influential black newspaper of the antebellum period.

See also Abolition; Delany, Martin R.; Douglass, Frederick; Nell, William Cooper; *North Star*; Smith, James McCune

■ ■ *Bibliography*

Ripley, C. Peter, et al., eds. *The Black Abolitionist Papers, Volume 3: The United States, 1830–1846.* Chapel Hill: University of North Carolina Press, 1991.

Ripley, C. Peter, et al., eds. *The Black Abolitionist Papers, Volume 4: The United States, 1847–1859.* Chapel Hill: University of North Carolina Press, 1991.

MICHAEL F. HEMBREE (1996)
Updated by publisher 2005

FREDERICK DOUGLASS' PAPER

━ ┃ ┃ ┃ ━━━━━━━━

The abolitionist newspaper *Frederick Douglass' Paper* was founded in December 1847 in Rochester, New York by Frederick Douglass as the *North Star*. Douglass renamed the paper when it merged with the *Liberty Party Paper* of Syracuse, New York, in June 1851. During its thirteen-year history, several black intellectuals collaborated on it with Douglass, including Martin R. Delany, William C. Nell, William J. Watkins, and James McCune Smith. Douglass also received assistance from a British abolitionist, Julia Griffiths, who helped him hone his writing skills and, as the paper's business manager, organized fund-raising fairs and lecture tours in England and the United States. The success of Douglass's newspaper can be attributed in large part to an elaborate network of support. Contributions from British abolitionists encouraged Douglass to start the paper in 1847. Later, women's auxiliaries in several cities organized antislavery fairs and bazaars on his behalf.

Douglass recognized the symbolic as well as practical value of a viable black press in the struggle against slavery. He gave the paper his own name to emphasize to a skeptical public that a former slave could master the editor's craft. His paper followed the eclectic approach of the antebellum reform press, but it was first and foremost an antislavery organ, and it carried the bold imprint of one man's thought. Douglass directed his message beyond the black community to the broader Anglo-American reformist au-

FREE BLACKS, 1619–1860

━ ┃ ┃ ┃ ━━━━━━━━

In 1860 some half a million free people of African descent resided in the United States. Known alternately as free Negroes, free blacks, free people of color, or simply freepeople (to distinguish them from post–Civil War freedpeople), they composed less than 2 percent of the nation's population and about 9 percent of all black people. Although the free black population grew in the centuries before the universal emancipation that accompanied the Civil War, it generally increased far more slowly than either the white or the slave population, so that it was a shrinking proportion of American society.

But free blacks were important far beyond their numbers. They played a pivotal role in American society during slave times and set precedents for both race relations and relations among black people when slavery ended. Their status and treatment were harbingers of the postemancipation world. Often the laws, attitudes, and institutions that victimized free blacks during the slave years—political proscription, segregation, and various forms of debt peonage—became the dominant modes of racial oppression once slavery ended. Similarly, their years of liberty profoundly influenced the pattern of postemancipation black life. Free people of African descent moved in disproportionate numbers into positions of leadership in black society after emancipation. For example, nearly half of the twenty-two black men who served in Congress between 1869 and 1900 had been free before the Civil War.

Scene depicting the daily activity of free blacks in Brazil. From Debret, Jean Baptiste. Voyage Pittoresque et Historique au Bresil, ou Sejour d'un artiste francais au Bresil, depuis 1816 jusqu'en 1831 inclusivement, epoques de l'avenement et de l'abdication de S. M. D. Pedro 1er, fondateur de l'Empire bresilien. Dedie a l'Academie des Beaux-Arts de l'Institut de France. Published 1834–1839. ART AND ARTIFACTS DIVISION, SCHOMBURG CENTER FOR RESEARCH IN BLACK CULTURE, THE NEW YORK PUBLIC LIBRARY, ASTOR, LENOX AND TILDEN FOUNDATIONS.

Although free blacks have been described as more black than free, they were not a monolithic group. Their numbers, status, and circumstances changed from time to time and differed from place to place, in some measure based on their origins, their social role, and relations with the dominant Euro-American population, on the one hand, and the enslaved African-American population, on the other.

THE COLONIAL ERA

Before the American Revolution, few free blacks could be found in colonial North America. The overwhelming majority of these were light-skinned children of mixed racial unions, freed by birth if their mother was white, as colonial law generally provided that a child's status followed that of its mother. Others were manumitted (i.e., freed) by conscience-stricken white fathers. A 1775 Maryland census, the fullest colonial enumeration of free blacks, counted slightly more than 1,800 free people of African descent, 80 percent of whom were people of mixed racial

origins. Like Maryland whites, about half of these free black people were under sixteen years old, and, of these, almost nine in ten were of mixed racial origins. Few black people of unmixed racial parentage enjoyed freedom in colonial Maryland; the free black population was not only light skinned but also getting lighter. Unlike slaveholders in the Caribbean and South America, Maryland slave owners emancipated their sons as well as their daughters with equal—if not greater—facility. The sex ratio, following that of slaves, generally favored males. In addition, about one-sixth of adult free blacks were crippled or elderly persons deemed "past labor," whom heartless slaveholders had discarded when they could no longer wring a profit from them. In all, free black people composed 4 percent of the colony's black population and less than 2 percent of its free population. Almost a century after slavery had been written into law, the vast majority of Maryland black people remained locked in bonded servitude. The routes to freedom were narrow and dismal.

Fragmentary evidence from elsewhere on the North American continent suggests that free black people were rarely a larger proportion of the population than in Maryland. In most places they made up a considerably smaller share of the whole, and in some places they were almost nonexistent.

Although their numbers were universally small, the status of free people of African descent differed from place to place in colonial North America. In Spanish Florida and in French and (after 1763) Spanish Louisiana, black people generally gained their freedom as soldiers and slave catchers in defense of colonies vulnerable to foreign invasion and domestic insurrection. Playing off the weakness of European colonists, free African and Afro-American men gained special standing by taming interlopers, disciplining plantation slaves, and capturing runaways. However grossly discriminated against they were, service in the white man's cause enabled some free black men to inch up the social ladder, taking their families with them.

Spanish authorities first employed black men, many of them runaways from English colonies, in defense of St. Augustine in the late seventeenth century. Eager to keep the English enemy at bay, Spanish officials instructed the fugitives in the Catholic faith, allowed them to be baptized and married within the Church, and then sent them against their former enslavers in raids on the English settlements at Port Royal and Edisto. Black militiamen later fought against the English in the Yamassee War and protected Spanish Florida against retaliatory raids. During the eighteenth century, Spanish officials stationed black militiamen and their families at Gracia Reál de Santa Terésa de Mosé, a fortified settlement north of St. Augustine.

Mosé became the center of free black life in colonial Florida until its destruction in 1740. Thereafter, free blacks were more fully integrated into Spanish life in St. Augustine. They married among themselves, with Native Americans, and with African and Afro-American slaves; worked as craftsmen, sailors, and laborers; purchased property; and enjoyed a degree of prosperity and respectability. The free black settlement at Mosé was rebuilt in the 1750s, and it once again became a center of free black life in colonial Florida until the Spanish evacuated the colony in 1763.

French authorities in Louisiana first enlisted black soldiers in quelling an Afro-Indian revolt in 1730. Thereafter, officials incorporated black men into Louisiana's defense force and called upon them whenever Indian confederations, European colonial rivals, or slave insurrectionists jeopardized the safety of the colony. On each such occasion—whether the Chickasaw war of the 1730s, the Choctaw war of the 1740s, or the threatened English invasion of the 1750s—French officials mobilized black men, free and slave, with slaves offered freedom in exchange for military service. By 1739 at least 270 black men were under arms in Louisiana, of whom some 50 were free.

The black militia played an even larger role in Spanish Louisiana than it had under the French. Spain gained control of the colony in 1763 as part of the settlement of the Seven Years' War. Finding themselves surrounded by hostile French planters, Spanish authorities embraced free people of African descent as an ally against internal as well as external foes. They recommissioned the Louisiana free black militia, adopting the division between *pardo* (light-skinned) and *moreno* (dark-skinned) units present elsewhere in Spanish America. Officials clad the free black militiamen in striking uniforms and granted them *fuero militar* rights, thereby exempting the black militiamen from civil prosecution, certain taxes, and licensing fees—no mean privileges for free black men in a slave society.

The free black militia thrived under the Spanish rule, becoming an integral part of the colony's defense force. When not fighting foreign enemies, free black militiamen were employed to maintain the levees that protected New Orleans and the great riverfront plantations, to fight fires in the city limits, and to hunt fugitive slaves. As the value of the free black militia to Spain increased, so did the size and status of the class from which the militia sprang. In 1803, when the Americans took control over Louisiana, the free black militia numbered over five hundred men.

The central role of free black men in defense of colonial Florida and Louisiana allowed them to enlarge their numbers and improve their place within those colonies. Black militiamen employed their pay and bounties to secure the freedom of their families and a modest place in societies that were otherwise hostile to free people of African descent. From their strategic position they entered the artisan trades, frequently controlling many of the interstitial positions as shopkeepers, tradesmen, and market women—occasionally even as plantation overseers and midwives.

In English seaboard colonies white nonslaveholders served as soldiers and slave catchers and monopolized the middling occupations as artisans, tradesmen, and overseers. Free blacks, as a result, were confined to the most marginal social roles. They had few opportunities to advance themselves, accumulate property, gain respectability, and buy their loved ones out of bondage. Their status fell far below that enjoyed by free blacks in the Gulf region.

THE ANTEBELLUM PERIOD

The American Revolution transformed the free black population. But because the Revolution took a different course in different places and because of differences within the extant slave and free black populations, the reformation of black life moved in different directions in different parts of the new republic. Post-Revolutionary free black life can best be understood from a regional perspective. During the antebellum years, there were three distinctive groups of free blacks in the United States: one in the northern or free states, a second in the upper South, and a third in the lower South. Each had its own demographic, economic, social, and somatic characteristics. These differences, in turn, bred different relations with whites and slaves and, most important, distinctive modes of social action.

First, the Revolution transformed the North from a slave to a free society, greatly enlarging its free black population. But slavery died hard in the northern states, and the gradualist process by which northern courts and legislatures abolished slavery left some black people in bondage until the eve of the Civil War. Still, post-Revolutionary emancipation ensured that eventually all northern blacks would be free, and by the first decade of the nineteenth century the vast majority had emerged from slavery. To their number were added immigrants from the South, most of them fugitive slaves. In 1860 about a quarter of a million blacks, slightly less than half of the nation's free blacks, lived in the free states.

But universal emancipation in the North did not transform the economic status or social standing of black people—except perhaps for the worse. Before the Revolution, northern slaves had been disproportionately urban in residence, black in color, and unskilled in occupation. Free blacks followed that pattern, becoming in fact more

MINUTES

AND

PROCEEDINGS

OF THE

FIRST ANNUAL CONVENTION

OF THE

PEOPLE OF COLOUR.

HELD BY ADJOURNMENTS

IN THE CITY OF PHILADELPHIA,

FROM THE SIXTH TO THE ELEVENTH OF JUNE, INCLUSIVE, 1831.

Philadelphia:

PUBLISHED BY ORDER OF THE COMMITTEE
OF ARRANGEMENTS.

1831.

Cover page of the summary report for the "First Annual Convention of the People of Colour," 1831. Convened in Philadelphia at the Wesleyan Church on Lombard Street, the convention was held to organize African-American opposition to slavery, discrimination in the free states, and the colonization movement. MANUSCRIPTS, ARCHIVES AND RARE BOOKS DIVISION, SCHOMBURG CENTER FOR RESEARCH IN BLACK CULTURE, THE NEW YORK PUBLIC LIBRARY, ASTOR, LENOX AND TILDEN FOUNDATIONS.

urban and unskilled during the antebellum years, as they increasingly migrated to cities and found themselves pushed out of artisan trades by European immigrants.

Nevertheless, post-Revolutionary emancipation allowed black people certain rights. Because the abolition of slavery freed northern whites from the fear of slave revolts, they did not look upon every gathering of black people as the beginning of a revolution. They limited the political rights of free blacks, but they allowed them to travel freely, organize their own institutions, publish newspapers, and petition and protest. Black men and women transformed these liberties into a powerful associational and political tradition. African churches, schools, fraternal organizations, and literary societies flourished in the northern states. The African Methodist Episcopal and African

Methodist Episcopal Zion denominations and the Prince Hall Masons, the Grand United Order of Odd Fellows, and the Knights of Pythias were among the largest of these, extending their reach to all portions of the North. Every black community also supported a host of locally based institutions and organizations. Members of these institutions, national and local, joined together to hold regional and national conventions that protested discrimination and worked for group improvement. From Richard Allen to Frederick Douglass, the black leaders forged a tradition of protests that demanded full equality.

As in the North, the free black population in the upper South was largely a product of the American Revolution. But in this region, the ideas and events—along with the economic changes—of the Revolutionary era merely loosened the fabric of slavery by increasing manumission, self-purchase, and successful suits for freedom. Slavery survived the challenge of the Revolutionary years, and indeed flourished. Nevertheless, the free black population grew rapidly, so that by 1810 the upper South contained nearly 100,000 free blacks, who composed about 8 percent of the black population in the region and almost 60 percent of all free people of African descent. Thereafter, the tightening noose of slavery slowed the growth of the free black population, and the proportion of free black people residing in the region declined.

The free black population in the upper South was the product of two patterns of manumission. The first and most important occurred on a large scale; it was indiscriminate and rooted in ideological and economic changes of the Revolutionary era. The second, smaller and more selective, originated in personal relations between master and slave. The first wave of manumissions produced a population that, like the slave population, was largely rural and black in color. To the extent, however, that post-Revolutionary emancipation was selective—with masters choosing whom they would free—it produced a free black population that was more skilled and lighter in color than that of the North. In the course of the nineteenth century, manumission became even more selective, so that freepeople of the upper South became increasingly skilled in occupation, urban in residence, and light in skin color. The absence of large-scale European immigration to the slave states and a long-standing reliance on black labor allowed upper South free blacks to enjoy a higher economic standing than those in the free states. In 1860, a quarter to a third of free black men practiced skilled trades in Nashville, Richmond, and other upper South cities.

But if the presence of slavery helped elevate their economic status, it severely limited the freepeople's opportunities for political or communal activism, for southern whites looked upon free black people as the chief inspiration and instigators of slave unrest. White southerners not only prevented free black people from voting, sitting on juries, and testifying in court but also barred them from traveling without permission and meeting without the supervision of some white notable. These constraints circumscribed political and organizational opportunities. No black newspapers were published and no black conventions met in the South. There were no southern counterparts of Allen or Douglass. Black churches, schools, and fraternal societies were fragile organizations, often forced to meet clandestinely. With limited opportunities for political outlets, free black men and women poured their energies into economic opportunities, and, as tradesmen and artisans, made considerable gains.

This tendency toward economic advancement at the expense of political activism was present in an even more exaggerated form in the lower South, particularly the port cities of Charleston, Mobile, and New Orleans. These places were largely untouched by the egalitarian thrust of the Revolutionary era. Moreover, when the United States gained control of Louisiana and Florida, American officials decommissioned and dispersed the free black militias, and slaveholder-dominated legislatures subjected the existing free black population to considerable restrictions. The free black population increased slowly in the nineteenth century, its growth the product of natural increase and sexual relations between masters and slaves. Almost all free blacks were drawn from the small group of privileged slaves who had lived in close contact with their owners, connections that often bespoke family ties. As a result, former slaves were overwhelmingly urban and light skinned, a quality that earned them the title "free people of color," or in New Orleans *gens de couleur*. Although comparatively few in number, most were far more skilled than free blacks in the upper South. In some places, such as Charleston and New Orleans, over three-quarters of the free men of color practiced skilled crafts, and they monopolized some trades on the eve of the Civil War. A handful of wealthy free people of color even purchased slaves and moved into the planter class.

As in the upper South, the presence of slavery in the lower South prevented free people of color from translating their higher economic standing into social and political gains. Denied suffrage and proscribed from office, they found a political voice only by acting through white patrons—their manumittors, their customers, and occasionally their fathers. Their own organizations remained private, exclusive, and often shadowy, especially in comparison to the robust public institutions created by free black people in the North. Although some were well

traveled and highly educated, as much at home in Paris and Glasgow as in New Orleans and Charleston, they dared not attack slavery or racial inequality publicly. Many feared to identify with slaves in any fashion. Rather, they saw themselves—and increasingly came to be seen by whites—as a third caste, distinct from both free whites and enslaved blacks.

With the general emancipation of 1863, free people of African descent carried their diverse histories into freedom. Although Civil War emancipation liquidated their special status, their collective experience continued to shape American race relations and Afro-American life.

See also Antebellum Convention Movement; Coartación; Emancipation; Fraternal Orders; Freeman, Elizabeth (Mum Bett, Mumbet); Manumission Societies; Migration; Mutual Aid Societies

■ ■ *Bibliography*

Berlin, Ira. *Slaves Without Masters: The Free Negro in the Antebellum South.* New York: Pantheon Books, 1974.

Breen, T. H., and Stephen Innes. *"Myne Owne Ground": Race and Freedom on Virginia's Eastern Shore, 1640–1676.* New York: Oxford University Press, 1980.

Curry, Leonard P. *The Free Black in Urban America, 1800–1865: The Shadow of the Dream.* Chicago: University of Chicago Press, 1987.

Deal, Douglas. "A Constricted World: Free Blacks on Virginia's Eastern Shore, 1680–1750." In *Colonial Chesapeake Society*, edited by Lois Green Carr, Philip D. Morgan, and Jean B. Russo, pp. 275–305. Chapel Hill, N.C.: University of North Carolina Press, 1988.

Foner, Laura. "The Free People of Color in Louisiana and St. Dominque: A Comparative Portrait of Two Three-Caste Societies." *Journal of Social History* 3 (1970): 406–430.

Gaspar, David Barry, and Darlene Clark Hine, eds. *Beyond Bondage: Free Women of Color in the Americas.* Urbana: University of Illinois Press, 2004.

Johnson, Michael P., and James L. Roark. *Blacks Masters: A Free Family of Color in the Old South.* New York: Norton, 1984.

Litwack, Leon F. *North of Slavery: The Negro in the Free States, 1790–1860.* Chicago: University of Chicago Press, 1961.

Sterkx, Herbert. *The Free Negro in Ante-Bellum Louisiana, 1724–1860.* Rutherford, N.J.: Fairleigh Dickinson University Press, 1972.

IRA BERLIN (1996)
Updated bibliography

FREEDMAN'S BANK

The short history of the Freedman's Bank, officially titled the Freedman's Savings and Trust Company, exemplifies both the promise and the frustrations of African-American economic development immediately after the Civil War. The Freedman's Bank was incorporated by Congress on March 3, 1865, absorbing the military banks that had been established by the Union army during the Civil War in Norfolk, Virginia, Beaufort, South Carolina, and New Orleans to provide depository services for African-American troops. John W. Alvord, superintendent of schools and finances for the federal Freedmen's Bureau, spearheaded the drive to establish the bank and organized the bank's original founders, a group of white businessmen, philanthropists, and humanitarians.

Created as a missionary endeavor to promote thrift among the freed slaves, the Freedman's Bank was to serve as a mutual savings bank for the benefit of the black community. The first interstate bank established after the charter of the Bank of the United States expired in 1836, the Freedman's Savings and Trust Company was a nonprofit organization. Its original charter made no provisions for loans but stated that it would receive deposits from freedmen and -women, invest them in government securities, and return the profits to the depositors in the form of interest.

Although the bank remained legally a private corporation, its concurrent establishment with the Freedmen's Bureau and the appointment of many Freedmen's Bureau officers as bank trustees misled many African Americans into believing that the federal government had assumed responsibility for the institution's financial solvency. Hoping to attract black support for the bank, the trustees used the bank's advertisements to reinforce the public's belief that the bank had government backing. Principal control of the bank was held by the bank's all-white trustees operating at the national headquarters, located first in New York City and then in Washington, D.C. However, the bank gradually hired local black leaders, usually politicians, ministers, and businessmen, as cashiers and as members of the advisory boards in a further attempt to win the trust of the black community.

Encouraged by the bank's government charter and endorsement by the commissioner of the Freedmen's Bureau, many African Americans deposited funds in the bank. Thirty-four branch offices eventually were established, covering every southern state, as well as Washington, D.C., Philadelphia, and New York City. By 1874, 72,000 depositors had entrusted over $3,000,000 to the bank.

Buoyed by its success and seeking to increase interest payments, the bank's predominantly white board of trustees amended the bank's charter in 1870, allowing the trustees to invest half of its deposits allotted for government securities in speculative stocks and bonds and in real estate. Led by the chairman of the finance committee, Henry Cooke, the bank invested heavily in Washington real estate in the 1870s and made several large, unsecured loans. Among these loans was one for $50,000 to Jay Cooke and Company, run by Henry Cooke's brother and business partner, Jay Cooke, to finance the Northern Pacific Railroad. This loan, along with a number of other unsecured investments, left the bank severely overextended and vulnerable when the banking firm of Jay Cooke and Company failed in 1873. The ensuing national financial panic crippled the bank, forcing it to sacrifice its best securities and borrow at ruinous rates in order to remain solvent.

The 1870 amendment to the bank's charter was intended to increase the profits of the depositors and was restricted principally to the Washington office. This policy ensured that the majority of the bank's investments would go to white business ventures. In addition, the collateral requirements for blacks requesting loans were far more stringent than those for whites. As a result, few blacks were able to borrow from the bank, and very little of its money was invested in the black community. Many blacks were vocal about their dissatisfaction with the bank's limited lending policies and its failure to stimulate black business and economic development, but the trustees did not persuade Congress to amend the charter until June 1874. This amendment would have allowed money to be returned to the branch offices for investment, but its late passage prevented its implementation.

With the onset of the Panic of 1873, most of the bank's white trustees resigned, leaving the bank's black trustees, whose numbers had increased steadily since the original appointments made in 1867, in control of the institution. Among the active black trustees in 1874 were Charles B. Purvis, John Mercer Langston, and A. T. Augusta. Along with the other remaining trustees, they made a desperate effort to save the bank and to restore the confidence of depositors by electing Frederick Douglass as president in 1874. Even his efforts to reorganize the bank, however, could not make up for years of mismanagement and the devastating effects of the national economic crisis. Careless lending, the incompetence of certain bank officials, and poor management proved an insurmountable legacy. The failure of the bank struck a deep blow to African-American economic development after the Civil War.

Despite a good deal of support for a bill introduced into Congress that would have reimbursed the depositors in full with federal funds, the legislation never passed. Only by selling off its assets was the bank able to begin reimbursing its depositors in 1875, offering each 20 percent of their total deposits. Many of the small depositors, however, could not be located and thus lost everything. By 1883 less than one-quarter of the depositors had received complete reimbursements, which amounted to only 62 percent of their original deposits. The bank's collapse and the government's unwillingness to shoulder responsibility for the depositors' investments left a legacy of suspicion and distrust among the black community. The bank's monetary losses were especially tragic because they represented one of the first attempts of the newly freed slaves to grasp economic security and equal citizenship.

See also Bureau of Refugees, Freedmen, and Abandoned Lands; Douglass, Frederick; Economic Condition, U.S.; Langston, John Mercer

■ ■ *Bibliography*

Fleming, Walter. *The Freedman's Savings Bank: A Chapter in the Economic History of the Negro Race.* Chapel Hill: University of North Carolina Press, 1927.

Osthaus, Carl. *The Freedman's Savings Bank: Philanthropy and Fraud.* Urbana: University of Illinois Press, 1976.

LOUISE P. MAXWELL (1996)

FREEDMEN'S HOSPITAL

Originally established in 1862 at Camp Barker, a Washington, D.C., army barracks, to serve displaced former slaves and other Civil War refugees, this medical facility was named Freedmen's Hospital in 1863. Alexander T. Augusta, a black army physician, served as its surgeon-in-chief for a short time, succeeding Dr. Daniel Breed. Augusta was the first of many staff physicians to complain about the substandard physical conditions of the hospital. Freedmen's would continue to struggle to serve its indigent clients in the face of economic hardship and outdated equipment.

In January 1865, Dr. Robert Reyburn assumed the leadership of Freedmen's Hospital. The following year Reyburn was appointed to the medical faculty of the proposed Howard University, establishing the longstanding connection between the two institutions. In 1869 the hospital moved to buildings newly built by the Freedmen's Bureau on the university campus. This relationship kept the hospital alive past 1872, when the Freedmen's Bureau was officially dismantled. However, the staff of the hospital fought to retain their autonomy as the university sought to gain control of the facilities, which served the

important function of a teaching hospital for black nursing and medical students.

After the demise of the Freedmen's Bureau, the hospital was placed under the Department of the Interior. In 1873 a black doctor, Dr. Charles B. Purvis, was named surgeon-in-chief. In 1894, Dr. Daniel Hale Williams, the black physician credited with performing the first open-heart surgery, replaced Purvis. In 1897 he was replaced by Dr. Austin M. Curtis, who was succeeded four years later by Dr. William A. Warfield.

In 1892, Congress passed a law requiring the District of Columbia commissioners to contribute half of the hospital's funding and to control financing while the Department of the Interior continued to manage the hospital. This complicated arrangement proved inefficient, and the condition of the hospital worsened under it. In 1903 Congress authorized $350,000 for the construction of a new hospital. Two years later it put the hospital completely under the Department of the Interior, with a new arrangement whereby the hospital would contract in advance for an estimated allotment of patients. The number of patients admitted, however, always exceeded the number allowed for in the contract, and the hospital administrators were forced to run the facility under a financial deficit. On February 26, 1908, the new facilities were occupied. On June 26, 1912, a law was passed allowing the hospital, which until this time had been restricted to treating indigents, to admit paying patients.

In 1936, Dr. T. Edward Jones was named Freedmen's surgeon-in-chief. His successor, in 1944, was Charles Richard Drew. These two leaders had to negotiate the hospital's conflicting purposes of providing medical care to its indigent clients, one third of whom were white, and providing medical training to black students who continued to be denied access to white hospitals. In 1955 a government study deploring the substandard physical conditions recommended that a new hospital be built and turned over to Howard. On September 15, 1961, President John F. Kennedy signed a bill officially placing Freedmen's Hospital under Howard University's control and authorizing the construction of a new facility. On March 2, 1975, Howard University Hospital was opened, replacing Freedmen's Hospital.

See also Bureau of Refugees, Freedmen, and Abandoned Lands; Drew, Charles Richard; Howard University

■ ■ *Bibliography*

Holt, Thomas, Cassandra Smith-Parker, and Rosalyn Terborg-Penn. *A Special Mission: The Story of Freedmen's Hospital,*

1862–1962. Washington, D.C.: Academic Affairs Division, Howard University, 1975.

Logan, Rayford W. *Howard University: The First Hundred Years, 1867–1967.* New York: New York University Press, 1969.

Robinson, Harry G., III, and Hazel Ruth Edwards. *The Long Walk: The Placemaking Legacy of Howard University.* Washington, D.C.: Moorland-Spingarn Research Center, Howard University, 1996.

LYDIA MCNEILL (1996)

FREEDOM RIDES

Initially organized by the Congress of Racial Equality (CORE) in 1961, the Freedom Rides were trips made by interracial groups riding throughout the South on buses. Freedom Rides attempted to galvanize the U.S. Justice Department into enforcing federal desegregation laws in interstate travel, especially in bus and train terminals. White riders sat on the back of the bus, and black riders on the front, challenging long-standing southern racist transportation practices. Once at the terminal, white Freedom Riders proceeded to the "black" waiting room, while blacks attempted to use the facilities in the "white" waiting room.

Freedom Rides were a continuation of the student-led sit-in movement that was sparked in February 1, 1960, by four African-American college freshmen in Greensboro, North Carolina. When these students remained at a Woolworth's lunch counter after being refused service, they inspired hundreds of similar nonviolent student demonstrations. Essentially, Freedom Rides took the tradition of sit-ins on the road.

The idea for the 1961 Freedom Rides was conceived by Tom Gaither, a black man, and Gordon Carvey, a white man, who were field secretaries of CORE. In light of the 1960 *Boynton v. Virginia Supreme Court* judgment that banned segregation in bus and train terminals, Gaither and Carvey decided that compliance with the law should be gauged. The two activists were also inspired by the 1947 Journey of Reconciliation. Motivated by another Supreme Court ruling, the Journey of Reconciliation was made by an interracial group of sixteen activists that traveled through the South to test *Morgan v. Virginia,* the 1946 federal case that resulted in the legal ban of segregation on interstate buses and trains. In the spirit of the Journey of Reconciliation, CORE began organizing and planning for the first Freedom Rides.

In early 1961, CORE, headed by its director and co-founder, James Farmer (1920–1999), began carefully selecting the thirteen original Freedom Riders. The chosen group comprised seven blacks and six whites, from college students to civil rights veterans, including a Journey of Reconciliation participant, the white activist James Peck. The journey for the riders began on May 4 from Washington D.C. to Atlanta, Georgia, on two buses. The plan was to continue through Alabama, Mississippi, and finally to New Orleans, Louisiana, on May 17 for a desegregation rally.

The first episode of violence occurred in Rock Hill, South Carolina, where twenty-one-year old John Lewis (b. 1940), the future Student Nonviolent Coordinating Committee (SNCC) national chairman and U.S. congressman, and Albert Bigelow, an elderly white pacifist, were knocked unconscious by young white men. On May 14, 1961, the Freedom Riders boarded a Greyhound bus and a Trailways bus in Atlanta and headed for Birmingham, Alabama. The Trailways bus met six Ku Klux Klansmen in Anniston, Alabama, who threw the African Americans into seats in the back of the bus and hit two white riders on the head. In Birmingham, the bus encountered about twenty men with pipes who beat the riders when they disembarked.

In Anniston, the Greyhound bus faced two hundred angry whites. The bus retreated, but its tires were slashed. Once the tires blew out, a firebomb was tossed into the bus. The riders managed to escape before the bus went up in flames. The following day, another mob prevented the Freedom Riders from boarding a bus in Birmingham. With the help of John Seigenthaler, Attorney General Robert Kennedy's administrative assistant, the riders took a plane to New Orleans instead. The bus journey was continued under the leadership of SNCC, with the coordination efforts of SNCC members Diane Nash and John Lewis.

The Birmingham police commissioner, "Bull" Connor, used many tactics, including incarceration, to try to stop the students, but to no avail. Finally, the governor of Alabama, John Patterson, very reluctantly promised Robert Kennedy to protect the riders. As the new Freedom Riders left for Montgomery on May 20, 1961, it appeared that Governor Patterson had kept his word. However, by the time the bus arrived in Montgomery, all forms of police protection had disappeared. A mob of over one thousand whites viciously attacked the riders and Seigenthaler.

On May 24, twenty-seven determined Freedom Riders, with the protection of National Guardsmen, headed for Jackson, Mississippi. In Mississippi, they were arrested and jailed for sixty days. A new group of riders came to Jackson, and they were also arrested. Eventually, 328 Freedom Riders were incarcerated in Jackson. As per their philosophy, the riders chose jail over bail.

The Freedom Rides brought international attention to the southern struggle for desegregation, which put pressure on the authorities. Finally, on November 1, 1961, a huge victory for the Freedom Riders and all integrationists was won when the Interstate Commerce Commission (ICC) made segregated travel facilities illegal.

See also Civil Rights Movement, U.S.; Congress of Racial Equality (CORE); Farmer, James; Lewis, John; Student Nonviolent Coordinating Committee (SNCC)

■ ■ *Bibliography*

Farmer, James. *Lay Bare the Heart: An Autobiography of the Civil Rights Movement.* New York: Arbor House, 1985.

Hampton, Henry, and Steve Fayer. *Voices of Freedom: An Oral History of the Civil Rights Movement from the 1950s through the 1980s.* New York: Bantam Books, 1990.

Meier August, and Elliot Rudwick. *CORE: A Study in the Civil Rights Movement, 1942–1968.* New York: Oxford University Press, 1973.

Peck, James. *Freedom Ride.* New York: Simon & Schuster, 1962.

Zinn, Howard. *SNCC: The New Abolitionists.* Boston: Beacon Press, 1965.

JESSICA L. GRAHAM (2001)

FREEDOM'S JOURNAL

Freedom's Journal, founded in March 1827, was the first African-American weekly newspaper. The idea of a black press arose among New York City blacks who sought a public voice to respond to racist commentary in local white newspapers. Samuel E. Cornish (1795–1858), a Presbyterian minister, and John B. Russwurm (1799–1851), a graduate of Bowdoin College, took charge of the enterprise. *Freedom's Journal* followed a format common to antebellum reform newspapers by using current events, anecdotes, and editorials to convey the message of moral reform. The editors also focused on issues of interest to northern free blacks: racial prejudice, slavery, and particularly the threat of colonization (the efforts by the American Colonization Society to expatriate free blacks to Africa).

The newspaper received widespread support from blacks outside New York City. Over two dozen authorized agents, including David Walker in Boston, collected subscriptions and distributed the paper. Within a year, Freedom's Journal reached an audience in eleven northern and southern states, Upper Canada, England, and Haiti.

When Russwurm assumed total control of *Freedom's Journal* in September 1827, he gradually shifted the paper's editorial position on colonization. Few readers knew that he had actually developed an interest in colonization during his college days, and his announced "conversion" to colonization in 1828 severely damaged the paper's credibility and eroded its base of support. In March 1829 the paper ceased publication, and Russwurm departed for the American Colonization Society's settlement in Liberia. Cornish attempted to revive the newspaper in May 1829 as *The Rights of All,* but he succeeded in publishing only six monthly issues.

See also Cornish, Samuel E.; Journalism; Russwurm, John Brown

■ ■ *Bibliography*

Gross, Bella. "Freedom's Journal and the Rights of All." *Journal of Negro History* 17 (1932): 241–286.

Jacobs, Donald M., ed. *Antebellum Black Newspapers.* Westport, Conn.: Greenwood Press, 1976.

MICHAEL F. HEMBREE (1996)

FREEDOM SUMMER

In the summer of 1964 the Council of Federated Organizations (COFO), a Mississippi coalition of the Congress of Racial Equality (CORE), the Student Nonviolent Coordinating Committee (SNCC), and the National Association for the Advancement of Colored People (NAACP), invited northern white college students to spearhead a massive black voter-registration and education campaign aimed at challenging white supremacy in the Deep South. This campaign, which became known as Freedom Summer, was the culmination of COFO's efforts to attack black disfranchisement in Mississippi. COFO had been formed in 1962 in response to the Kennedy administration's offer of tax-exempt status and funding from liberal philanthropies to civil rights organizations that focused their activities on increasing black voter registration. The considerable success of COFO activists in sparking the interest of black Mississippians in voter registration during the summer of 1963 prompted them to propose an entire summer of civil rights activities in 1964 to focus national attention on the disfranchisement of blacks in Mississippi, and to force the federal government to protect the civil rights of African Americans in the South.

The SNCC played the largest role in the project and provided most of its funding. Robert Moses of the SNCC was the guiding force behind the summer project, and the overwhelming majority of COFO staff workers were SNCC members who were veterans of the long fight for racial equality in Mississippi.

Approximately a thousand northern white college students, committed to social change and imbued with liberal ideals, volunteered to participate in the Freedom Summer campaign. Under the direction of SNCC veterans, these volunteers created community centers that provided basic services such as health care to the black community and initiated voter education activities and literacy classes aimed at encouraging black Mississippians to register to vote. SNCC activists also directly challenged the segregated policies of the all-white Mississippi Democratic Party by supporting the efforts of local black leaders to run their own candidates under the party name Mississippi Freedom Democratic Party (MFDP). The MFDP efforts encouraged over seventeen thousand African Americans to vote for the sixty-eight delegates who attended the Democratic National Convention in Atlantic City in the summer of 1964 and demanded to be seated in replacement of the regular Democratic organization. The MFDP challenge, though unsuccessful, focused national attention on Mississippi and propelled Fanny Lou Hamer, a local activist, into the national spotlight.

Another focus of the Freedom Summer was institutionalized educational inequities in Mississippi. Thirty COFO project sites created "Freedom Schools," administered under the direction of Staughton Lynd, a white Spelman College history professor, to provide an alternative education to empower black children to challenge their oppression. These schools provided students with academic training in remedial topics, as well as in more specialized subjects such as art and French. A key goal of the schools was to develop student leadership and foster activism through discussions about current events, black history, the philosophy behind the civil rights movement, and other cultural activities. Despite the overcrowding and the perennial lack of facilities, over three thousand African-American students attended the Freedom Schools.

Violence framed the context of all COFO activities and created a climate of tension and fear within the organization. White supremacists bombed or burned sixty-seven homes, churches, and black businesses over the course of the summer, and by the end of the project, at least three civil rights workers—James Chaney, Michael Schwerner, and Andrew Goodman—had been killed by southern whites, four had been critically wounded, eight hundred had been beaten, and over a thousand had been arrested. The reluctance of the state government to prosecute the perpetrators of these acts of violence and the failure of the federal government to intervene to provide pro-

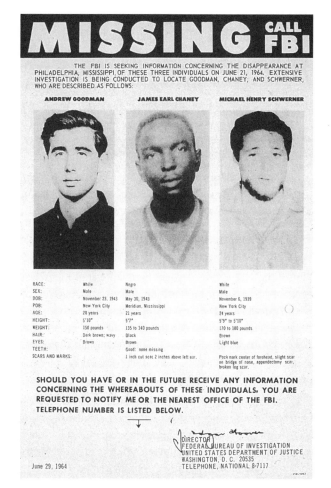

An FBI poster seeking information on Andrew Goodman, James Earl Chaney, and Michael Henry Schwerner, civil rights workers who went missing near the town of Philadephia, Mississippi, in 1964. GETTY IMAGES

tection for civil rights workers left many activists disillusioned about the federal government's ability or desire to ensure racial justice.

The impact and legacy of the Freedom Summer stretched far beyond the borders of Mississippi. Many Freedom Summer programs lived on when the project ended and COFO disbanded. Freedom Summer community centers provided a model for federally funded clinics, Head Start programs, and other War on Poverty programs. Freedom Schools served as models for nationwide projects in alternative schooling. The barriers to black voting uncovered and publicized during the summer project provided stark evidence of the need for the Voting Rights Act of 1965, which made literacy tests and poll taxes illegal.

The Freedom Summer facilitated the development of a radical new political consciousness among many white volunteers, who found the summer to be a powerful experience of political education and personal discovery. At least one-third of the volunteers stayed on in Mississippi to continue the struggle for black equality. Many volunteers who returned to the North were disillusioned with the promises of the federal government and became activists in the New Left and the antiwar movement. Mario Savio, a Freedom Summer veteran, emerged in the fall of 1964 as the principal spokesperson of the free speech movement at the University of California at Berkeley, a key event in the emergence of the New Left.

The Freedom Summer experience was also an important catalyst for the women's liberation movement. Group consciousness of gender oppression among white women grew markedly during the summer as male volunteers were assigned more visible organizing tasks. In November 1964, at a SNCC staff meeting in Waveland, Mississippi, Mary King and Casey Hayden, two white staff members, presented an anonymous position paper criticizing the enforced inferiority of women in the Freedom Summer project and their exclusion from the decision-making process. This memo was one of the first discussions of the issues that would form the basis of the emerging women's movement within the New Left.

The experience of the Freedom Summer also radicalized black civil rights workers—though in quite different ways from white radicals. The summer helped steer black radicals in the SNCC away from interracial movements and toward a suspicion of white participation that came to characterize the Black Power movement. Subsequent debates in the civil rights movement about the doctrine of interracialism were fueled by what the Freedom Summer revealed about the successes, and inherent limitations, of interracial civil rights activity. From the inception of the project, some black SNCC activists contested the Freedom Summer's premise that national attention could only be garnered by exposing white people to the violence and brutality that black people faced daily. These blacks were veterans of the long battle with white racists that the SNCC had waged in Mississippi since 1961, were increasingly skeptical of liberal politics, and believed that the presence of white volunteers—who often tended to appropriate leadership roles and interact with black people in a paternalistic manner—would undermine their goal of empowering Mississippi blacks and hamper their efforts to foster and support black-controlled institutions in Mississippi. Tensions and hostility between black and white COFO activists were further inflamed by interracial liaisons that were often premised on the very racial stereotypes and misconceptions that they sought to surmount.

However, the Freedom Summer's most enduring legacy was the change of consciousness it engendered among black Mississippians. The Freedom Summer succeeded in initiating thousands of African Americans into political action, providing thousands of black children with an antiracist education, and creating such black-led institutions as the Mississippi Freedom Democratic Party. Fannie Lou Hamer provided a fitting testament to the impact of the Freedom Summer when she stated in 1966, "Before the 1964 summer project there were people that wanted change, but they hadn't dared to come out. After 1964 people began moving. To me it's one of the greatest things that ever happened in Mississippi."

See also Chaney, James Earl; Civil Rights Movement, U.S.; Congress of Racial Equality (CORE); Mississippi Freedom Democratic Party; Moses, Robert Parris; National Association for the Advancement of Colored People (NAACP); Student Nonviolent Coordinating Committee (SNCC)

■ ■ *Bibliography*

Cagin, Seth, and Philip Dray. *We Are Not Afraid: The Story of Goodman, Schwerner, and Chaney and the Civil Rights Campaign for Mississippi.* New York: Bantam Books, 1988.

Martinez, Elizabeth Sutherland, ed. *Letters from Mississippi.* Brookline, Mass.: Zephyr Press, 2002.

McAdam, Doug. *Freedom Summer.* New York: Oxford University Press, 1988.

Weisbrot, Robert. *Freedom Bound: A History of America's Civil Rights Movement.* New York: Norton, 1990.

ROBYN SPENCER (1996)
Updated bibliography

FREEMAN, ELIZABETH (MUM BETT, MUMBET)

C. 1744
DECEMBER 28, 1829

As plaintiff in a law suit, Mum Bett, a slave, joined a black laborer named Bront in suing for their freedom in 1781. After winning that case, she adopted the name Elizabeth Freeman. The victory was a significant step in the abolition of slavery in Massachusetts, although the final decision by the Massachusetts Supreme Court that the new state constitution prohibited slavery came in another case.

Freeman was born a slave in New York State and in 1758 seems to have passed into the possession of John Ashley of Sheffield, Massachusetts, a judge in the Court of Common Pleas from 1761 to 1781. Freeman never learned to read or write, but she heard discussions of the Bill of Rights and the Massachusetts constitution, which was adopted in 1780. She considered that the language about all people being created free and equal might well apply to her.

In 1780 Mrs. Ashley became angry and struck at Freeman's sister with a heated shovel; Freeman was burned on the arm when she intervened. Leaving the house, she sued for her freedom in a case heard on August 21, 1781. She won. Her lawyer was Theodore Sedgwick, father of Theodore Sedgwick Jr., a noted abolitionist. Freeman became a servant in the Sedgwick family and followed them to Stockbridge in 1785. When Freeman retired, she had accumulated enough money to buy a small house. She mentions great-grandchildren in the will she signed with a cross on October 18, 1829. She was buried in the Sedgwick family plot in Stockbridge Cemetery.

See also Free Blacks, 1619–1860; Slavery and the Constitution

■ ■ *Bibliography*

Dermus, Betty. "Some of Us Are Brave." *Essence* 28, no. 10 (1998): 84.

Johns, Robert L. "Elizabeth Freeman, 'Mum Bett,' 'Mumbet.'" In *Notable Black American Women,* edited by Jessie Carney Smith. Detroit: Gale, 1992.

Logan, Rayford W. "Elizabeth [Mumbet, Mum Bett] Freeman." In *Dictionary of American Negro Biography,* edited by Rayford W. Logan and Michael R. Winston. New York: Norton, 1982.

ROBERT L. JOHNS (2001)
Updated bibliography

FREEMAN, MORGAN

JUNE 1, 1937

Actor Morgan Freeman was born and raised in rural Greenwood, Mississippi. He first acted in an elementary school production of Little Boy Blue and won a statewide acting competition in junior high school. Upon graduating from high school, Freeman worked as a radar technician in the U.S. Air Force. He moved to California, where he took acting lessons at the Pasadena Playhouse and dancing lessons in San Francisco. In 1964 Freeman moved to New York and danced at the World's Fair. Three years later he made his Off-Broadway debut in *The Nigger Lovers.* His first Broadway appearance was in an all-black pro-

duction of *Hello, Dolly!* in 1967, and from 1971 until 1976 he portrayed the character Easy Reader on Public Television's *The Electric Company.* He continued to do theater work on and off Broadway and received Obie Awards in 1980 for the title role in *Coriolanus,* and in 1984 for his role as the preacher in *The Gospel at Colonus* (1983). Freeman also won a Drama Desk Award and a Clarence Derwent Award (as a promising newcomer) for his role as a wino in *The Mighty Gents* (1978). He received a third Obie Award for his role as a soft-spoken southern chauffeur for a Mississippi Jewish widow in *Driving Miss Daisy* (1987), which was adapted for the screen in 1989.

Freeman made his film debut in 1980, playing minor roles in *Harry and Son* and *Brubaker.* He also appeared in *Eyewitness* (1981), *Death of a Prophet* (1983), *Teachers* (1984), *Marie* (1985), and *That Was Then, This Is Now* (1985). He gained recognition with his motion picture appearance in *Street Smart* (1987) with Christopher Reeve, for which Freeman received an Oscar nomination. In 1988 he played a reformed drug addict who counsels Michael Keaton in *Clean and Sober.* The following year was a turning point in Freeman's career. In 1989 he had starring roles as the school principal Joe Clark in *Lean on Me,* as the chauffeur in the movie adaptation of *Driving Miss Daisy,* for which he received an Oscar nomination, and as the first black sergeant of a northern black regiment during the Civil War in *Glory.* In 1991, he appeared in *Robin Hood,* and the following year he fulfilled a lifelong ambition to play a cowboy by starring in the Oscar-winning western *Unforgiven* opposite Clint Eastwood. Freeman was also hailed for his performances in *The Shawshank Redemption* (1994), *Outbreak* (1997), *Seven* (1997), *Amistad* (1997), *Kiss the Girls* (1997), *Moll Flanders* (1997), *Deep Impact* (1998), and *Hard Rain* (1998). In the fall of 1993, Freeman made his directorial debut with *Bopha!,* a film set in South Africa and filmed in Zimbabwe, about the 1976 Soweto uprisings.

Into the new century, Freeman has been one of Hollywood's busiest actors, with credits including *Nurse Betty* (2000), *Along Came a Spider* (2001), *The Sum of All Fears* (2002), *Runaway Jury, Antwone Fisher,* and *Dreamcatcher* (all 2003), *The Big Bounce* (2004), and *Million Dollar Baby* (2004), among many others. For his performance in *Million Dollar Baby,* Freeman was honored with an Academy Award for best supporting actor in 2005.

See also Film in the United States, Contemporary

■ ■ *Bibliography*

Mapp, Edward. *Dictionary of the Performing Arts,* 2nd ed. Metuchen, N.J.: Scarecrow Press, 1990.

"Morgan Freeman." *International Dictionary of Films and Film-makers, Volume 3: Actors and Actresses*, 4th ed. Detroit: St. James Press, 2000.

Wetzsteon, Ross. "Morgan Freeman Takes Off." *New York* (March 14, 1988): 54–56.

Whitaker, Charles. "Is Morgan Freeman America's Greatest Actor?" *Ebony* (April 1990): 32–34.

SABRINA FUCHS (1996)
Updated by publisher 2005

FREE VILLAGES

In the early postslavery period after 1838, freedpeople in the Caribbean viewed the acquisition of land as one of the most important badges of freedom. As was the case elsewhere in the Americas, the Caribbean freedpeople's vision of freedom incorporated much more than the mere absence of slavery, for emancipation provided them with an opportunity to exercise control over the rhythms of their own lives. Crucial to this control was establishing residences outside of the plantations, even when economic survival made it necessary to seek employment there. Land availability was a critical determinant to this process, and it was mainly in the eastern province of Santiago de Cuba, where plantations had not yet monopolized the landscape in the 1880s, that the freedpeople of Cuba had the greatest opportunity to access land. Similarly, freedpeople in Guadeloupe had more access to land than in Martinique, where sugar production dominated cultivable land. In the Anglophone (English-speaking) Caribbean, the freedpeople's hunger for land was manifested in the rapid emergence of free villages, particularly in Jamaica and Guyana, but also in Trinidad and the Windward Islands. In these areas they established settlements on their own initiative or with the assistance of various missionary intermediaries, despite various strategies that restricted access to land, such as legislation, the planters' refusal to sell, and prohibitive prices.

In the first decade after 1838, the Jamaican freedpeople constructed a society beyond the boundaries of the plantations in partnership with several groups of white evangelical missionaries, particularly the Baptists, though the Methodists, Moravians, and Presbyterians were also active in assisting freedpeople settlements. The freedpeople contributed their labor and invested their material resources in the establishment of "Christian villages" that revolved around the chapel and the school. Generally, the missionaries viewed the free villages as an immediate refuge from the planters' coercive labor recruitment policies as well as an opportunity to transform the freedpeople's characters and cultures. Reflecting the accepted gender order, the missionaries anticipated that the male villagers would look to the estates for regular employment, albeit on agreed terms, and that the freedwomen would devote their energies mainly to the family and the growth of provisions. The children would attend school. As Catherine Hall has noted, these villages were to be utopias where the missionaries could create "a new moral and material world in which Christianity and freedom reigned" (Catherine Hall, 1992, p. 254) in a new society constructed on the ruins of slavery.

In the early euphoria of the immediate postslavery period after 1838, the freedpeople in Jamaica embraced the missionaries' vision, and through family networks and church linkages freedpeople pooled their financial resources and invested in their own piece of ground. For instance, by 1842 freedmen and freedwomen in the parish of Trelawny spent about twenty thousand pounds sterling (the equivalent of about $100,000 US dollars at that time) in purchasing land and in erecting homes. In the neighboring parish of St. Ann, freedpeople connected with the Baptist church had, by 1841, spent ten thousand pounds on purchasing land, much of which formed new free villages bearing the name of abolitionists, such as Buxton, Clarksonville, Sturge Town, and Wilberforce. Generally, whether with the missionary as intermediary or on their own initiative, freedpeople in Jamaica rapidly bought up small freeholds. Consequently, whereas in 1840 there were 883 freeholds of less than ten acres, by 1845 there were 20,724, and about a third of the former enslaved population had relocated to new settlements. Clearly, the freedpeople's actions based on self-help and community effort reconfigured the Jamaican countryside. Utilizing their skills as agriculturists and artisans, freedpeople expanded internal trading networks and provided the foundation for new interior market towns that flourished around the new settlements. In addition, some of the new villagers gained the political freehold franchise and assisted free blacks, free coloreds (blacks and coloreds who were never enslaved), and Jewish elites in altering the racial and ethnic composition of the island's political institutions by the 1850s.

After 1838, Guyana witnessed the unique development of communal villages as whole plantations were bought by large groups of freedpeople who became joint stockholders of the purchased estate. By 1850, twenty-five plantations, with a total of 9,050 acres, were under new collective ownership in Guyana. Significantly, despite the vast amount of land available in the hinterland at lower prices, the freedpeople generally preferred to remain within the cleared, settled, better-drained, cultivated parts of the country, where they benefited from the proximity to markets, churches, schools, and the plantations where they supplemented their income. These Guyanese communal free villages breached an aspect of the white power structure, as elements of "cooperative self-government" characterized the villages' administrative arrangements in their infancy. However, the planter legislature reasserted itself after the 1850s by way of legal restrictions of group purchases, and a series of Village Ordinances curbed the early experiments in local government. Further, the communal villager settlements became problematic because of drainage problems and uncertain land tenure arrangements.

Wherever possible, freedpeople constructed new communities and settlements beyond the plantation, knowing that independent landownership underscored their struggle for autonomy of the estates and increased their bargaining power. Additionally, growing and marketing of provisions were well established during slavery and were crucial to the freedpeople's strategies of combining wage labor with family-based independent farming. This enabled women to withdraw from regular estate labor while contributing significantly to family income. Indeed, in the construction of the new communities beyond the plantations, freedpeople drew on their own material, spiritual, and intellectual resources, placing the goals of family and community above the assertion of simple individual autonomy. Finally, the rapid establishment of free villages represented one of the most enduring lessons from the postslavery experience in the Caribbean, for they exhibited the earliest examples of the dynamic possibilities of sustained, self-help projects founded on community action.

See also Emancipation in Latin America and the Caribbean; Nationalism and Race in the Caribbean

■ ■ *Bibliography*

Brereton, Bridget. "Family Strategies, Gender, and the Shift to Wage Labour in the British Caribbean." In *The Colonial Caribbean in Transition: Essays on Postemancipation Social and Cultural History,* edited by Bridget Brereton and Kevin A. Yelvington. Kingston, Jamaica: University of the West Indies Press, 1999, pp. 77-107.

Hall, Catherine. "Missionary Stories: Gender and Ethnicity in England in the 1830s and 1840s." In *Cultural Studies,* edited by Lawrence Grossberg, Cary Nelson, and Paula Treichler, London: Routledge, 1992, pp. 205–255.

Hall, Douglas. *Free Jamaica, 1838–1865: An Economic History.* New Haven, Ct.: Yale University Press, 1959. Reprint, Barbados: Caribbean Universities Press, 1970.

Moore, Brian L. *Race, Power, and Social Segmentation in Colonial Society: Guyana after Slavery, 1838–1891.* New York: Gordon and Breach, 1987.

Rodney, Walter. *A History of the Guyanese Working People, 1881–1905.* Baltimore, Md.: Johns Hopkins University Press, 1981.

Underhill, Edward B. *The West Indies: Their Social and Religious Condition.* London: Jackson, Walford, and Hodder, 1862. Reprint, Westport, Ct.: Negro Universities Press, 1970.

Wilmot, Swithin. "'A Stake in the Soil': Land and Creole Politics in Free Jamaica, the 1849 Elections." In *In the Shadow of the Plantation: Caribbean History and Legacy,* edited by Alvin O. Thompson. Kingston, Jamaica: Ian Randle, 2002, pp. 314-333.

SWITHIN WILMOT (2005)

FRENTE NEGRA BRASILEIRA

━ ■ ■ ■ ━

The Frente Negra Brasileira, or Brazilian Black Front, was founded in the city of São Paulo on September 28, 1931. Open to "all productive Black people," its aims were to "foster the political and social unification of the Black People of this Nation . . . and to demand their social and political rights in the Brazilian Community" (*Diario Oficial de São Paulo,* p. 12). To achieve this goal, the Frente Negra outlined three strategies: promoting education and training, providing assistance and legal defense, and operating as a formal political party. Under the leadership of its president and founder Arlindo Veiga dos Santos, the Frente Negra eventually grew to include chapters throughout Brazil, with concentrations in the states of São Paulo, Rio de Janeiro, Minas Gerais, and Rio Grande do Sul. Membership estimates range as high as several thousand, but the Frente Negra's impact radiated far beyond its card-bearing members. In the six years between its creation and its forced closure in 1937, the Frente Negra Brasileira became the most influential voice of Afro-Brazilian identity and civic aspiration.

The Frente Negra evolved from the experiences of the numerous Afro-Brazilian organizations active in the city of São Paulo since the turn of the twentieth century. The twin engines of coffee exports and industrialization fueled a rapid urban expansion that attracted unprecedented numbers of European immigrants. Also drawn to the city were the descendants of Afro-Brazilian slaves from the surrounding countryside, displaced by European contract laborers as slavery ended. Living alongside the ethnic enclaves of Italians, Germans, Portuguese, Spaniards, and other Europeans, Afro-Brazilians came to constitute a community of their own, with social clubs sponsoring activities such as dances, athletics, excursions, and newsletters. Opportunities nonetheless remained limited for

Afro-Brazilians. The newsletters became a political forum voicing their shared frustrations, and in 1926 a group of young men founded the Centro Cívico Palmares, the community's first advocacy group. Central to their concerns was the social ideology of race and its material and political concomitants. Veiga and the other founding members were active in all these efforts and brought lessons from their experience into the formation and operations of the Frente Negra.

From the start, the Frente Negra set itself apart from earlier organizations with its emphasis on activism. One of its first actions was to encourage members to integrate public places such as city parks and skating rinks, and the success of these actions garnered both attention and support. It also made the city fulfill its promise to hire black police officers by training candidates in advance to pass the test. It continued to attack the societal constraints of de facto segregation and discrimination by assisting members with housing and employment disputes. At the same time, the Frente dealt with other needs of the black community, such as financial management, job training, and literacy, that were obstacles to their full participation in the economic and political life of the nation. One of the greatest obstacles, however, was an Afro-Brazilian self-identity distorted by internalized racism. By adopting the word *Negra,* the Frente embraced an emerging identity of resistance as *black* people, as opposed to a host of what were considered more polite terms for African descendants. As the Frente Negra cultivated a sense of dignity and entitlement, it simultaneously sought to redefine what was considered a derogatory term associated closely with slavery. It also challenged the contemporary notion that Brazil was a racial democracy, free of racism, an ideology developed in explicit contrast to the blatant anti-black violence in the United States and colonial Africa. The masthead of the Frente Negra's official newspaper carried the reminder in each edition: "Color Prejudice in Brazil, Only We, the Blacks, Can Feel."

The leadership of the Frente Negra consisted of the president and a Grand Council with twenty members. The administration also included a council of branch leaders and departments for public relations and voter registration. The organization simultaneously put great effort into providing services and activities for its members, sponsoring music classes and groups, a theater company, elementary education and literacy training, employment advocacy and training, sewing classes, and numerous committees to organize festivities. Some of its services, like the hair salon and dental clinic, provided much needed on-the-job training. A credit union helped members manage their finances. Among the Frente Negra's most fondly remem-

bered activities were the *domingueiras,* the Sunday meetings that began with stirring speeches about black history and current conditions by some of the city's best orators, segued into classes, lectures, and demonstrations, and continued on for hours with dance parties and performances featuring music, poetry, and theater.

In 1932, the Frente Negra began publishing its newspaper, *A Voz da Raça* (voice of the race). In addition to notices from the organization, the paper published hard news and commentary at the local, national, and even international level. It was widely circulated in the Frente Negra's areas of strongest influence, but copies made their way throughout Brazil. Many writers from earlier black newspapers joined the staff.

Despite its ambitions, the Frente's operations as a formal political entity were limited. It was founded shortly after the overthrow of the republic in 1930, which had brought to power Geúlio Vargas, an ambitious politician who cultivated direct relationships with interest groups. In mobilizing Afro-Brazilians as a political force, the Frente Negra attempted to position itself to win direct concessions from Vargas, a strategy other groups were also developing at the time, including the Catholic Church and new organizations such as the Brazilian Federation for the Advancement of Women.

Its first foray into electoral politics came in 1933. The Frente Negra had not yet registered as a political party, so its president, Arlindo Veiga dos Santos, ran as an independent candidate for delegate to the upcoming constitutional convention. Although unsuccessful, his campaign generated considerable visibility for the organization. Veiga articulated a political ideology which became associated with the Frente Negra, although it was in many ways highly controversial within the membership and the Afro-Brazilian community as a whole. Veiga endorsed the ethnonationalism espoused by Nazi and Fascist factions within São Paulo's German and Italian immigrant communities. He adapted their motto, "God, Homeland, and Family," for the *Voz da Raça*'s slogan, "God, Homeland, Race, and Family." Yet Veiga called for black rights in the face of perceived preferences given to immigrants and a suspension of immigration in his platform of "Brazil for the Brazilians." In this, Veiga reflected the Frente's strong focus on patriotism and integration, which Veiga articulated as a mandate to "assimilate nationally and racially" (Veiga, *Voz da Raça*). The Frente Negra registered as a political party in 1936 in preparation for elections cancelled by Geúlio Vargas' political coup in 1937. On December 2, 1937, Vargas dissolved all political parties, including the Frente Negra (which had, ironically, supported Vargas). The group renamed itself the Brazilian

Black Union under the leadership of board member Raul Joviano de Amaral, but only continued just long enough to commemorate the fiftieth anniversary of the abolition of slavery on May 13, 1938.

The Frente Negra was not the only political organization of Afro-Brazilians but it was the most influential voice of its day. Its members went on to participate in Afro-Brazilian advocacy groups throughout the twentieth century and left an enduring legacy that placed Afro-Brazilian rights and self-determination on the national political, economic, social, and moral agenda from that point forward.

See also Politics and Politicians in Latin America

■ ■ *Bibliography*

Andrews, George Reid. *Blacks and Whites in São Paulo, Brazil, 1888–1988.* Madison: University of Wisconsin Press, 1991.

Butler, Kim D. *Freedoms Given, Freedoms Won: Afro-Brazilians in Post-Abolition São Paulo and Salvador.* New Brunswick, N.J.: Rutgers University Press, 1998.

Diario Oficial de São Paulo (November 4, 1931): 12.

Leite, Jose Correia. *E Disse o Velho Militante Jose Correia Leite.* São Paulo: Secretaria Municipal de Cultura, 1992.

Mitchell, Michael. "Racial Consciousness and the Political Attitudes and Behavior of Blacks in São Paulo, Brazil." Ph.D. diss., Indiana University, 1977.

Veiga dos Santos, Arlindo. In *Voz da Raça* (April 29, 1933).

KIM D. BUTLER (2005)

FULLER, CHARLES

MARCH 5, 1939

The playwright and short-story writer Charles Henry Fuller Jr. was born in Philadelphia to Charles H. Fuller Sr., a printer, and Lillian Anderson Fuller. He attended Villanova College from 1956 to 1958, and he served for four years as an Army petroleum laboratory technician in Japan and Korea. He then returned to Philadelphia, attended La Salle College from 1965 to 1968, and completed his degree.

Although he had been writing since he was a teenager, Fuller began writing in earnest in the 1960s, usually at night while attending school or holding a number of jobs, from bank loan collector to counselor at Temple University to housing inspector for the city of Philadelphia. His early writing was mostly poetry, essays, and stories. Realizing that his stories were composed mostly of dialogue, Ful-

ler turned to playwriting. His first short plays were written for the Afro-American Arts Theatre of Philadelphia, which he cofounded and codirected from 1967 through 1971. In 1970 he moved to New York City and devoted himself to writing full-time.

His first full-length play, *The Village: A Party,* was produced at the McCarter Theater in Princeton, New Jersey, in 1968. The play illustrates the conflicts inherent in a racially integrated community. When the black head of the community, who is married to a white woman, falls in love with a black woman, the other racially mixed couples in the community feel threatened and destroy him.

Other Fuller plays include *In the Deepest Part of Sleep,* which was produced at St. Marks Playhouse in New York in 1974, and *The Brownsville Raid,* also produced in New York, at the Negro Ensemble Company, in 1976. It was based on a 1906 incident involving a black United States Army regiment that was dishonorably discharged for allegedly inciting a riot in Brownsville, Texas.

In 1981 Fuller won an Obie Award and an Audelco Award for *Zooman and the Sign,* a play about inner-city violence in Philadelphia. The play dramatizes the accidental death of a young girl and its effects. In 1982 Fuller became the second black playwright to win a Pulitzer Prize for drama for *A Soldier's Play,* for which he also received a New York Drama Critics Award, an Audelco Award, a Theatre Club Award, and an Outer Circle Award for best off-Broadway play. In *A Soldier's Play,* which centers on the investigation of the murder of a black sergeant at an army base in Louisiana during World War II, Fuller explores racial prejudice by a white southern community as well as self-hatred by black soldiers. The play was adapted for the screen and released as *A Soldier's Story* by Columbia Pictures in 1984.

In 1987, CBS televised Fuller's adaptation of Ernest J. Gaines's novel *A Gathering of Old Men;* in 1988, two related one-act plays, *Sally* and *Prince,* were produced first in Atlanta by the First National Black Arts Festival, and then in New York by the Negro Ensemble Company. The first parts of the *We* series, a projected five- or six-part cycle chronicling the experience of African Americans from the Civil War through the end of the nineteenth century, the plays relate the life of Prince Logan, an educated former slave. In *Sally,* he participates in the rebellion of the country's first all-black Army regiment during the Civil War, when they learn they are to be paid three dollars less per month than white Union soldiers. In *Prince,* former slaves working a plantation discover there is little difference between their condition as free men and women under northern sponsorship and their condition as slaves before the war. They remain victims of economic, political, and social exploitation, and realize the promise of freedom had been an illusion. The third and fourth plays in the *We* series, *Jonquil* and *Burner's Frolic,* were produced in 1989–1990 by the Negro Ensemble Company in New York.

Fuller has been a Rockefeller Foundation Fellow (1975), a National Endowment for the Arts Fellow (1976), and a Guggenheim Fellow (1977–1978). In addition to writing plays, Fuller wrote and directed a radio talk show about the black experience for WIP-Radio in Philadelphia (1970–1971). He has also contributed both fiction and nonfiction to such magazines as *Black Dialogue, Liberator,* and *Negro Digest.*

See also Drama; Gaines, Ernest J.; Literature of the United States

■ ■ *Bibliography*

Anadolu-Okur, Nilgun *Contemporary African American Theater: Afrocentricity in the Works of Larry Neal, Amiri Baraka and Charles Fuller* New York: Garland, 1997.

Üsekes, Çiôdem. "Charles Fuller." *Dictionary of Literary Biography, Volume 266: Twentieth-Century American Dramatists, Fourth Series.* A Bruccoli Clark Layman Book. Edited by Christopher J. Wheatley. Detroit: Gale, 2002, pp. 110-116.

SABRINA FUCHS (1996)
MICHAEL PALLER (1996)
Updated bibliography

FULLER, META VAUX WARRICK

JUNE 9, 1877
MARCH 18, 1968

Named for one of her mother's clients (Meta, daughter of Pennsylvania senator Richard Vaux), sculptor Meta Vaux Warrick Fuller was born in Philadelphia, the youngest of three children of William and Emma (Jones) Warrick, prosperous hairstylists. She enjoyed a privileged childhood, with dancing and horseback-riding lessons. While attending Philadelphia public schools, Fuller took weekly courses at J. Liberty Tadd, an industrial arts school. At eighteen she won a three-year scholarship to the Pennsylvania Museum and School for Industrial Art. In 1898 she graduated with honors, a prize in metalwork for her *Crucifix of Christ in Anguish,* and a one-year graduate scholarship. The following year she was awarded the Crozer (first) Prize in sculpture for *Procession of the Arts and Crafts,* a terra-cotta bas-relief of thirty-seven medieval costumed figures.

From 1899 to 1903 Fuller studied in Paris, at first privately with Raphael Collin, and then at the Colarossi Academy. Among her supporters in France were expatriate painter Henry O. Tanner and philosopher W. E. B. Du Bois, who encouraged her to depict her racial heritage. Fuller produced clay, painted-plaster, and bronze figurative works based on Egyptian history, Greek myths, French literature, and the Bible.

In 1901, sculptor Auguste Rodin praised Fuller's clay piece *Secret Sorrow* (or *Man Eating His Heart*). With his sponsorship, Fuller began to receive wider notice. Art dealer Samuel Bing exhibited twenty-two of her sculptures at his L'Art Nouveau Gallery in June 1902. *The Wretched,* a bronze group of seven figures suffering physical and mental disabilities (as well as other macabre pieces, such as *Carrying the Dead Body* and *Oedipus,* in the latter of which the figure is blinding himself), earned Fuller the title "delicate sculptor of horrors" from the French press. She later enlarged a plaster model of *The Impenitent Thief,* which she had shown at Bing's gallery. Although she never finished the piece, Rodin saw that it was exhibited at the prestigious Société National des Beaux Arts Salon in April 1903.

Upon her return to Philadelphia, Fuller established a studio on South Camac Street in a flourishing artistic neighborhood. Her sculptures were exhibited at the Pennsylvania Academy of Fine Arts in 1906, 1908, 1920, and 1928. In 1907 the Jamestown Tercentennial Exposition commissioned Fuller to create fifteen tableaux of twenty-four-inch-high plaster figures depicting African-American progress since the Jamestown settlement in 1607. She received a gold medal for *The Warrick Tableaux,* a ten-foot-by-ten-foot diorama.

The artist's career slowed considerably after her marriage in 1909 to the Liberian neurologist Solomon C. Fuller and a fire in 1910 that destroyed the bulk of her work in storage. By 1911 Fuller was the devoted mother of two sons (the last was born in 1916), an active member of Saint Andrew's Episcopal Church, and host to prominent guests who frequently visited the family in the quiet town of Framingham, Massachusetts.

Fuller began to sculpt again in 1913 when Du Bois commissioned a piece for New York State's celebration of the fiftieth anniversary of the Emancipation Proclamation. *The Spirit of Emancipation* represented Humanity weeping for her freed children (a man and woman) as Fate tried to hold them back. Positive public response promoted Fuller to continue working. In 1914 the Boston Public Li-

The Awakening of Ethiopia, c. 1914. *Considered a powerful symbol of the spirit of the Harlem Renaissance, Fuller's sculpture represents a partially wrapped mummy bound from the waist down but revealing the headdress of an ancient Egyptian queen. As the title reveals, Fuller used the Egyptian motifs to symbolize the African American's awakening and gradual unwrapping of the bandages of an oppressive past.* SCHOMBURG CENTER FOR RESEARCH IN BLACK CULTURE, THE NEW YORK PUBLIC LIBRARY/ART RESOURCE, NY. REPRODUCED BY PERMISSION.

brary exhibited twenty-two of her recent works. Among the numerous requests and awards that followed from African-American and women's groups were a plaster medallion commissioned by the Framingham Equal Suffrage

League (1915); a plaster group, *Peace Halting the Ruthlessness of War* (for which she received second prize from the Massachusetts branch of the Women's Peace Party in 1917); and a portrait relief of the NAACP's first president, Moorfield Storey, commissioned by Du Bois in 1922. The same year, the New York Making of America Exposition displayed Fuller's *Ethiopia Awakening,* a one-foot-high bronze sculpture of a woman shedding mummy cloths. This Pan-Africanist work symbolized the strength of womanhood, the emergence of nationhood, and the birth of what Alain Locke would call three years later the "New Negro." One of Fuller's most poignant works, *Mary Turner: A Silent Protest Against Mob Violence* (1919), commemorates both the silent parade of ten thousand black New Yorkers against lynching in 1917 and the lynching of a Georgian woman and her unborn child in 1918. Fuller never finished the piece because she believed northerners would find it too inflammatory and southerners would not accept it. She created numerous other works that depicted symbolic and actual African and African-American culture, including her celebrated *Talking Skull* (1937), based on an African fable. She also produced portrait busts of friends, family members, and African-American abolitionists and other black leaders, such as educator Charlotte Hawkins Brown, composer Samuel Coleridge Taylor, and Menelik II of Abyssinia. The Harmon Foundation exhibited Fuller's work in 1931 and 1933. She later served as a Harmon juror.

Fuller participated in numerous local organizations; she was a member of the Boston Art Club, an honorary member of the Business and Professional Women's Club, chair of the Framingham Women's Club art committee, and the only African-American president of Zonta, a women's service club. Additionally, she designed costumes for theatrical groups and produced "living pictures": recreations of artistic masterpieces with actors, costumes, sets, and lighting.

In the 1940s Fuller's husband went blind and became increasingly ill. She nursed him until his death in 1953, then contracted tuberculosis herself and stayed at the Middlesex County Sanatorium for two years. She wrote poetry there, too frail to create more than a few small sculptures.

By 1957 Fuller was strong enough to continue her work. She produced models of ten notable African-American women for the Afro-American Women's Council in Washington, D.C. She also created a number of sculptures for her community, including several religious pieces for Saint Andrew's Church, a plaque for the Framingham Union Hospital, and the bronze *Storytime* for the Framingham Public Library. For her achievements, Livingstone College (her husband's alma mater) awarded her an honorary doctorate of letters in 1962, and Framingham posthumously dedicated a public park in the honor of Meta and Solomon Fuller in 1973. Since then, Fuller's sculptures have been included in numerous exhibitions.

See also Du Bois, W. E. B.; Painting and Sculpture; Tanner, Henry Ossawa

■ ■ *Bibliography*

Gordon, Joy L., and Harriet Forte Kennedy. *An Independent Woman: The Life and Art of Meta Warrick Fuller.* Framingham, Mass.: Danforth Museum, 1985.

Kerr, Judith Nina. "God-Given Work: The Life and Times of Sculptor Meta Vaux Warrick Fuller, 1877–1968." Ph.D. diss., University of Massachusetts, Amherst, 1986.

THERESA LEININGER-MILLER (1996)